SATELLITE COMMUNICATIONS

[Covering Latest Digital Satellite Technologies and Systems]

Dr. D.C. Agarwal

M.Sc. Tech., Ph.D.F. Inst. T.P., FIETE

Fifth Edition Revised by :

A.K. Maini

Scientist, DRDO, New Delhi

Sixth Edition Revised by :

Ashok Raj

B.Tech (I.I.T., Delhi), M. Phil. (JNU)

Engineering Consultant

KHANNA PUBLISHERS®

Investing in Learning®

Operational Office :

4575/15, Onkar House, Opp. Happy School,

Ground Floor, Daryaganj, New Delhi 110 002

Phones : 011-45033819 • *Mob.* 09811541460

email : contactus@khannapublishers.in

Published by :

Romesh Chander Khanna & Vineet Khanna
for **KHANNA PUBLISHERS**
2-B, Nath Market, Nai Sarak
Delhi- 110 006 (India)

Website : www.khannapublishers.in

Hologram & Description

To all readers of our books, from yourself if being defrauded by pirates to prevent, please make sure that there is an Hologram on the cover of our books with the below specifications. If you find any book without Hologram and Description, please mail us at **contactus@khannapublishers.in**

Thanking you

ISBN No. 978-81-7409-213-7

First Edition : 1989
Seventh Edition :
Thirteenth ***Reprint : 2024***

Price Rs. 639.00

Preface to the Seventh Edition

It is indeed a matter of great satisfaction that an over whelming response recieved to the Sixth Edition from both the teachers and the students from all over India which was a completely revised and updated edition covering the latest on **"Digital Satellite Technologies and Systems".**

In the present edition chapter on Global Positioning Satellite Systems and Satellite Program of India has been completely revised and new development in the field has been incorporated. The book in its present form contains large number of solved problems and multichoice questions. The Illustrated Glossary too contains over 120 new terms and definitions. Also, the new chapter on Amateur Radio Satellites will interest the hobbists and ambitious students aiming for some projcct work.

It is hoped that the book in its revised form will enjoy its ever increasing popularity.

Again, we will welcome suggestions for improvement of the text and will be greatful if any misprint or error is pointed out.

—Khanna Publishers

Preface

Satellite communication is of much importance for both the national and international communications which may be in the form of telephone transmission, television and radio program distribution, computer communications, ISDNs, martime navigation and military command and control. Satellite communication is a very vast topic and involves several aspects of communication technology including both the analog and digital techniques. Communication engineers are therefore supposed to have appropriate knowledge in satellite technology, link design and operations. Knowledge in the additional topics such as those or radio wave propagation, antennas, orbital mechanics, modulation, detection, coding, radio electronics, microwave techniques, lasers and fibre optic communication etc. is also required. Intercooperation between the mechanical engineers, electrical engineers, communication engineers and aeronautical engineers is extensively needed for rocket technology for lauching and manning the satellite.

India is having an ambitious program for communication as well as remote sensing satellites, the INSAT and IRS series of satellites. Several organizations including the Government laboratories and academic institutions are actively engaged in developing and implementing the Indian satellite communication program. And therefore it is now essential for all engineers to have knowledge in the techniques of communication through satellite communication in comprehensive manner. The book deals with the requisite communications technologies such as those of analog and digital satellite communication, multiple access technique, demand assignment, spread spectrum, random access techniques etc ; earth station technology and laser satellite communication. Discussions about satellite orbits and inclination, important subsystems of the communication satellites and various international as well as national communication satellites have been extensively made.

A separate chapter is given for Indian activities in satellite communication. At the end of each chapter, appropriate reference are also given alongwith the review questions.

The present book has come up by way of my teaching for several years the satellite communication to both the undergraduate and postgraduate students of electronic and communication engineering of the Allahabad University. The book infact covers far from the syllabi of satellite communication prescribed by various engineering colleges, IITs and IISc, Bangalore. In the preparation of manuscript I was greatly benefitted by discussions with several of my colleagues at Allahabad and also especially with Prof. V.N. Sinha of IIT, Kanpur, Prof. H.M. Gupta of IIT Delhi and Prof. R.K. Jha of IT, BHU. I would like to thank the library incharges of ITI, Naini and M.N.R. Engg. College, Allahabad for providing their excellent library facilities. Prof M.S. Bisht was kind to provide moral support. Finally I owe my special thanks to my wife Abha for always encouraging me to complete the writing work

—Dr. D.C. Agarwal

Contents

1

Principles of Satellite Communication

1.1. Evolution and Growth of Communication Satellites

The idea of communication through a satellite, in particular with a synchronous satellite was conceived by Arthur C. Clarke, a famous British science fiction writer in 1945[1]. Clarke had already pointed out that a satellite in a circular equatorial orbit with a radius of about 42,242 km would have an angular velocity that matched the earth's. Thus, it would always remain above the same spot on ground and it could receive and relay signals from most of a hemisphere. Three satellites spaced 120 degrees apart could cover the whole world with some overlap provided that messages could be relayed between satellites and thus reliable communication between any two points in the world was possible. Clarke had also stated that the electrical power for the satellite would be obtained by conversion of the sun's radiation by means of solar cells. Clarke's paper went almost totally unnoticed until man-made satellites became a reality with Sputnik (October 4, 1957). However, it may be noted that the synchronous orbit was not achieved until 1963.

The Russian launch of Sputnik I started 'space race between super powers (USA and USSR). USA launched SCORE on Dec 18, 1958[2]. It was a kind of Explorer satellite. On Aug. 12, 1960 ECHO I was launched by AT and T, USA. It was an orbiting balloon 100 ft in diameter which served as passive reflector. A similar ECHO II was launched by AT & T again on Jan 25, 1964. These provided communications between Bell Lab in New Jersey and JPL in California. However, the power and antenna requirements were severe and so it could not be used for communications between East and West Coast of USA. The TELSTAR I and II satellites of AT and T launched on July 10, 1962 and May 7, 1963 established the basis of modem technique of communication satellite. The TELSTAR I demonstrated for the first time a television link between the United States and Europe. The *Communications Satellite Corporation* (Comsat) was established in 1963 in USA and then SYNCOM series of communication satellites were launched. SYNCOM I was launched in the beginning of 1963. SYNCOM II was launched on July 26, 1963 and SYNCOM III was launched on July 19, 1964. The International Telecommunications Satellite Organisation (INTELSAT) was established in 1964. The INTELSAT I also called the *Early Bird* was launched on April 6, 1965. The same year Russian Communication satellite MOLNYA was also launched. Since these launches the INTELSAT organisation has grown to over 100 member nations and over 33 INTELSAT satellites have been launched(3) ranging from instruments with a small capacity (240 voice circuits or one television channel) to those with a huge capacity (12500 voice circuits and two television channels) and covering three regions-the Atlantic, Pacific and Indian Oceans. Thus a new era of Communication via satellite (satellite Communication) had begun and now over hundreds of geostationary satellites of different countries of the world are in the service. This is expected to grow in a very large number in near future(4,5).

1.2. Synchronous Satellites

As already mentioned the synchronous satellites also called the geostationary satellites go round the globe in 24 hours so they seem to us on earth to keep station some 36000 km vertically above the same point on the earth's surface. In fact a stationary satellite is a synchronous satellite that has sufficiently small values of orbital eccentricity and inclination to the Equator that the changes in its apparent direction relative to the rotating earth are negligible for practical purposes. The other advantages of synchronous altitude is that it is well above the high intensity inner radiation belt and above the most intense region of the considerably milder outer belt. Thus, adequate protection can be obtained with negligible weight. The stationary orbit is sunlit over 99% of the time (the infrequent eclipses can occur only at midnight at the meridian of the satellite, and then only at certain times of the year), simplifying the generation and storage of power and reducing the number of temperature cycles. The strength of the earth's magnetic field is only a hundredth of its value at lower altitudes, and spin-damping time constants are consequently 10,000 times as long-long enough to be neglected(6). The high altitude of the synchronous orbit makes such a satellite visible from 40% of the earth's surface. A single satellite may provide continuous coverage for the major portion of the world's communication market. The ground stations may be of sufficiently low cost that each country served by the system can readily afford to its own terminal, and the rf spectrum required for the system can be readily shared with other services. There are a few problems with these synchronous communication satellites, namely the time delay, in connection with telephony and the establishment of the synchronous orbit.

The synchronous satellites used for communication are widely called the *communication satellites*. These satellites are classified in terms of their territorial coverages-*e.g.* global, regional, or national (domestic)-or in terms of the type of services offered -*e.g.* fixed, mobile, maritime, aeronautical, etc or point to point, broadcasting, commercial, military, amateur, experimental etc. The global or international satellite communications is served primarily through the INTELSAT satellite system which serves over 100 nations interconnected through 200 Earth Stations. Another system, the Inter Sputnik satellite system primarily serves Eastern Block Communist Countries and Cuba. There are over 2 dozen countries including India which have their domestic satellite systems either operational or in advanced planning stages. These satellites have special shaped antenna beams to provide domestic overage and are employed for telephony, data and television distribution. Some regional satellites have also been developed such as those to serve Europe, the Arab states, portions of Africa, South America and Nordic regions. Such regional satellites have users and characteristics similar to domestic systems.

Military satellites are principally those of super powers. A Typical example is that of US's *Defence Satellite Communications System (DSCS)* which constitutes a series of satellites to provide worldwide military communications. The circuit capacities of military satellites are modest compared to international and domestic satellites. The broadcast satellites are used for domestic or regional coverage. These radiate a high powered TV signal down to a large number of small receiving antennas (one meter diameter of less). Special purpose satellites are those such as maritime satellite (MARISAT), remote sensing satellite and tracking and data relay satellite system etc. The experimental satellites are also a kind of special purpose satellites. Typical examples are NASA's application technology satellite (ATS), communication technology satellites (CTS), Lincoln Laboratories (LES), the European Space Agency Orbital test satellite (OTS) and the Japanese (ECS) etc. A variety of experiments concerning with communication technology and space propagation/communication at various frequency bands have been carried out by these experimental satellites.

1.3. International Regulation and Frequency Coordination

The International Telecommunication Union (ITU), a specialised agency of United Nations has developed a series of radio regulations for frequency allocations international wise for different purposes[7]. ITU carries out such activities through its tour permanent organs, namely the General Secretariat, International Frequency Registration Board (IFRB), International Radio Consultative Committee (CCIR) and the International Telegraph and Telephone Consultative Committee (CCITT). The General Secretariat is located in Geneva. It is responsible for the executive management and technical cooperation. The IFRB is responsible for recording frequencies and orbital positions and for advising member countries on operation of the maximum practical number of radio channels in portions of the spectrum where harmful interference may occur. The CCIR is responsible for studying technical and operational questions relating to radio communications which results in reports, recommendations, resolutions, and decisions published as a group in Green Books every 4 year following CCIR Planery Assemblies. The CCITT is responsible for studying technical, operational, and tariff questions relating to telegraphy and telephony and for adopting reports and recommendations.

The international radio conferences held under the auspices of ITU from time to time issue guidelines for frequencies etc. Such a conference widely known as World Administrative Radio Conference (WARC) was held in 1979 that allocated frequency bands for satellite communications. WARC described the various satellite services under 17 categories, namely the fixed, intersatellite, mobile, land mobile, maritime mobile, aeronautical mobile, broadcasting, earth exploration, space research, meteorological, space operation, amateur, radio determination, radio navigation, aeronautical radio navigation, maritime radio navigation and standard frequency and time signal. WARC also divided the globe into three geographic regions for the purposes of frequency allocations. These regions are: *Region 1*, including Europe, Africa, the USSR and Mongolia; *Region 2* including North and South America and Greenland ; and *Region 3* including Asia (except the USSR and Mongolia), Australia and the Southwest Pacific.

1.4. Satellite Frequency Allocations and Band Spectrum

There are six frequency bands that have been allocated for the use with satellite communications. Table 1.1 gives these bands. It may be noted that in addition to these bands given in Table 1.1, millimetre waves in the frequency ranges 40-300 GHz are also allocated for satellite communication purposes. Table 1.2 lists frequency allocations for fixed satellite service and broadcasting satellites. The frequency allocations for mobile satellite services are listed in Table 1.3. In addition to frequencies listed above there are allocations for meteorological satellites and for experimental and amateur use. Frequency ranges allocated for meteorological aids/meteorological satellites are in the band 1668.4-1670 MHz, 1670-1690 MHz, 1690-1700 MHz, 1700-1710 MHz, 7450-7550 MHz.

Table 1.1. Frequency Bands for Satellite Communication

Band	*Downward bands MHz*	*Uplink Bands MHz*
Uhf–Military	250–270 (Approx)	292–312 (Approx)
C Band–Commercial	3700–4200	5925–6425
X Band–Military	7250–7750	7900–8400
Ku Band–Commercial	11700–12200	14000–14500
Ka Band–Commercial	17,700–21200	27500–30,000
Ka Band–Military	20200–21200	43500–45500

Table 1.2. Frequency Allocations for Fixed Satellite Service and Broadcasting Satellites

Frequency	*Fixed Satellite Service*	*Broadcasting Satellites*
2500–2535 MHz	Down Region II and III	Down
2535–2655	Down Region II	Down
2655–2690	Up region II and III	Down
3400–3700	Down	
3700–4200	Down	
4500–4800	Down	
5725–5850	Up Region I	
5850–5925	Up	
5925–7075	Up	
7250–7450	Down	
7450–7550	Down	
7900–8025	Up	
8025–8400	Up	
10.7–11.7 GHz	Down	Up Region I
11.7–12.1	Down Region II	Down Region I and III
12.1–12.2	Down Region II	Down

(Table contd...)

Frequency	*Fixed Satellite Service*	*Broadcasting Satellites*
12.2–12.3	Down Region II	Down Region I & II
12.3–12.5		Down Region I & II
12.5–12.75	UP/Down	Down Region II
12.75–13.25	Up	
14.0–14.5	Up	
14.5–14.8		Up
17.3–17.7		Up
17.7–18.1		Up
18.1–18.6	Down	
18.6–18.8	Down	
18.8–20.2	Down	
20.2–21.2	Down	
22.5–23.0		Down Region II & III
27.0–27.5	Up Region II & III	
27.5–29.5		
29.5–31.0	Up	
37.5–39.5	Down	
39.5–40.5	Down	
40.5–42.5		Down
42.5–43.5	Up	Down
47.2–49.2		Up
49.2–50.2	Up	
50.4–51.4	Up	
71.0–75.5	Up	
81–84	Down	
84–86		Down
92–95	Up	
102–105	Down	
149–164	Down	
202–217	Up	
231–241	Down	
265–275	Up	

Table 1.3. Frequency Allocations for Mobile Satellite Service

Frequency	*Aeronautical Mobile*	*Maritime Mobile*	*General Mobile*
806–890 Mhz			Region II & III (limited use)
1530–1535		Down, Shared	
1535–1544		Down, Exclusive	
1544–1545			Down
1545–1559	Down, Exclusive		Down
1626.5–1645.5		Up, Exclusive	
1645.5–1646.5			Up

(*Table contd...*)

Frequency	*Aeronautical Mobile*	*Maritime Mobile*	*General Mobile*
1446.5–1660.5	Up, Exclusive		
1660–1660.5	Up, Shared		
19.7–21.2 GHz			Down
29.5–31.0			Up
39.5–40.5			Down
43.5–47			Up
66–71			Up/Down
71–74			Up/Down
81–84			Up/Down
95–100			Up/Down
134–142			Up/Down
190–200			Up/Down
252–265			Up/Down

1.5. General and Technical Characteristics of A Satellite Communication System

Fig. 1.1 indicates the general structure of a satellite communication system. This consists of a satellite in space that links many earth stations on the ground. The user is connected to the earth station through terrestrial network. This terrestrial network may be a telephone switch or a dedicated link to the earth station. The user generates the baseband signal that is processed and transmitted to the satellite at the earth station. Thus the satellite may be thought of a large repeater in space that receives the modulated rf carriers in its uplink (earth-to-space) frequency spectrum from all the earth stations in the network, amplifies these carriers and retransmits them back to the earth in the downlink (space-to-earth) frequency spectrum which is different from the uplink frequency spectrum in order to avoid the interference. The signal at the receiving earth station is processed to get back the baseband signal which is then sent to the user through a terrestrial network. Had there been no difference in the uplink and downlink frequencies, the satellite's transmitted signals would have blocked up the uplink received signals and so there would have been no isolation between the transmitter output and the receiver input.

On the guidelines of WARC - 1979 commercial communication satellites use a frequency band of 500 MHz bandwidth near 6 GHz for up-link transmissions and another 500 MHz bandwidth near 4 GHz for downlink transmission. Infact an uplink of 5.725 to 7.075 GHz and a downlink of 3.4 to 4.8 GHz is used. It may be noted that this 6/4 GHz band is also used in many countries for terrestrial communications (microwave links) and so the problem of mutual interference is seriously to be looked into. The 500 MHz allocation is usually divided into 12 channels of approximately 40 MHz each and the level of transmit power per 40 MHz channel is typically of the order of 5 to 10 W. This allows each of up to the 12 transponders to carry one TV channel or about 1500 analog FM voice circuits. If digital modulation is used, transponder data rates from 50 to 100 Mb are achieveable. With the use of single side band (SSB) modulation technique about 10,000 voice circuits could be carried over a single satellite transponder. Modern communication satellites also employ frequency reuse to increase the number of transponders in the 500 MHz allocated to them.

It should be of importance to note that 6/4 bands have been the most popular because they offer the fewest propagation problems and historically RF components for these bands have been readily available. Rain attenuation is also not much serious at these bands. Sky noise is also low at 4 GHz and so it is possible to build receiving systems with lower noise temperatures at 4 GHz. With the overcrowding of geostationary satellites at 6/4 GHz band, 14/12 GHz band is also being used in commercial communication satellites. Here uplink is of 12.75 to 14.8 GHz and downlink of either 10.7 to 12.3 GHz or 12.5 to 12.7 GHz. This frequency band is not yet congested and is hoped to be used extensively in future. Rain attenuation is a problem at this frequency band. A third band where extremely high capacities are potentially available is the 20/30 GHz band where 2.5 GHz bandwidth has been allocated. Here the uplink is of 27.5 to 31 GHz and downlink is of 18.1 to 21.2 GHz. The future advanced technology of satellite communication has been focussed on these bands. Equipments on these frequency bands are in progress and experimental stage.

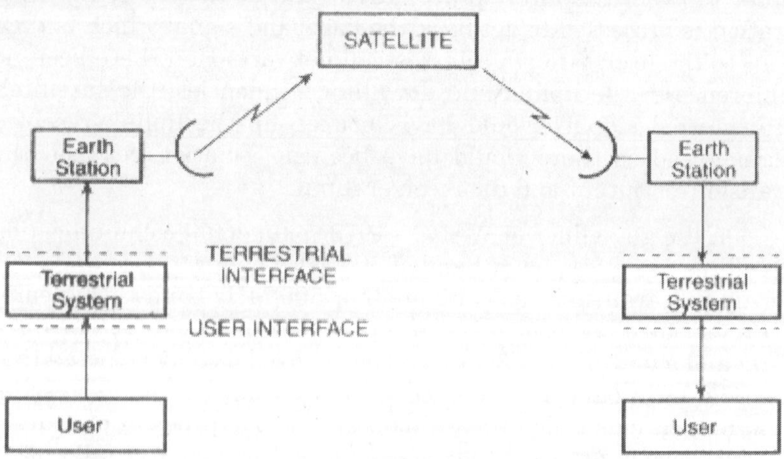

Fig. 1.1. General Structure of A Satellite Communication System.

The basic block diagram of an earth station that transmits to and receives information from a satellite is shown in Fig. 1.2. The baseband signal from the terrestrial network enters the earth station at the transmitter after having processed (buffered, multiplexed, formatted, etc.) by the baseband equipment. After the encoder and modulator have acted upon the baseband signal, it is converted to the uplink frequency. Then it is amplified and directed to the appropriate polarization port of the antenna feed. The signal received from the satellite is amplified in an LNA first and is then downconverted from the downlink frequency. It is then demodulated and decoded and then the original baseband signal is obtained. Critical components will often be installed redundantly with automatic switch over in the event of failure so that uninterrupted operation is maintained. The isolation of low noise receiver from the high power transmitter is of much concern in the design considerations of earth station. There may also be satellite/earth terminal mutual interference effects. These effects include the interference caused by sidelobes if antenna interferes with an adjacent satellite or earth terminal equipment. Other sources of interference include ground microwave relay links, sun transit effects and intermodulation products generated in the transponder or earth terminal. It would be of importance to mention here that before 1983 the spacing between two geostationary satellites was established at 4° of the equatorial arc and the smallest earth station antenna for the simultaneous transmit-receive operation was 5m in diameter. Now a days the spacing allowed between two adjacent satellites in sapce is 2° along the equatorial arc instead of 4°. The closer spacing has allowed twice as many satellites to occupy the same orbital arc and therefore now all the earth station antennas are designed to accommodate this spacing of 2°.

1.6. Advantages of Satellite Communication

Communication through satellite has several advantages and disadvantages. Until the advent of communication satellites, the long distance communication through space could be done by using cascaded radio relays, very low frequency radio (below 30 kHz) and high frequency or short wave radio (3-30 MHz). The latter two are inherently low capacity media suitable only for specialized applications and the cascaded radio relays were limited to overland spans. Thus the satellite has filled a huge void in the sense that has been capable of transmitting high capacities over long distances, either overland or water. Also, because of its unique geometry, it is inherently a broadcast medium with a natural ability to transmit simultaneously from one pint to an arbitrary number of other points within its coverage area.

Some of the typical advantages of satellite communication are automatically derived when compared it with other kind of signal relay systems. Firstly the satellite relays are inherently wide-area broadcast, *i.e.* the *point-to-multipoint* whereas all the terrestrial

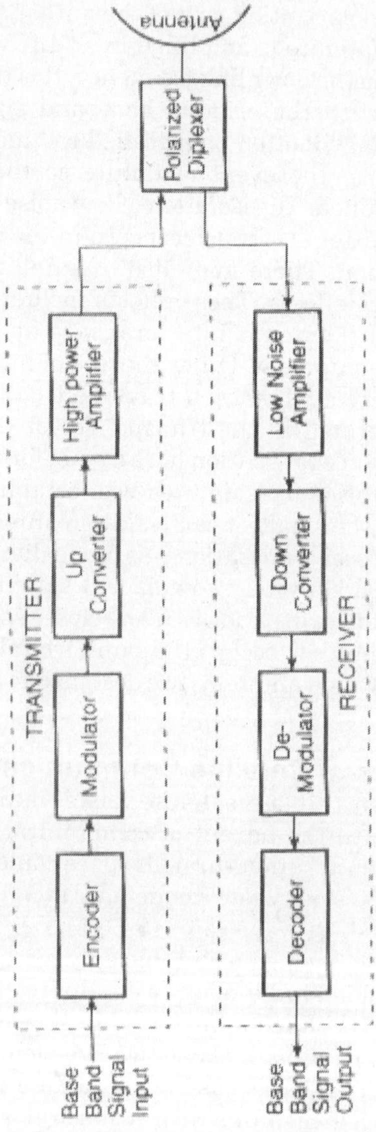

Fig. 1.2. Basic Block Diagram of an Earth Station.

relays are point-to-point. Secondly the satellite circuits can be installed rapidly. Once the satellite is in position, the earth stations can be installed and communication may be established in days or even hours. Thus a station may be removed relatively quickly from one location and reinstalled elsewhere. The terrestrial circuits of any kind would require a time consuming installations. The third advantage is that the mobile communication can be easily achieved by satellite communications as it has a unique degree of flexibility in interconnecting mobile vehicles. Thus the satellite has become an alternative to short wave radio in this specialised area and has significant reliability advantages (terrestrial networks may interconnect mobile vehicles by cellular radios).

The satellite communications has certain disadvantages as well. With the satellite in position the communication path between the terrestrial transmitter and the receiver is approximately 75000 km long. Since the velocity of em waves is 3×10^5 km/s, there is a delay of 1/4 second between the transmission and reception of a signal. Thus between talks there is an elapse of 1/2 second and one may feel it annoying. The delay exacerbates *echo* which actually is caused by an imperfect impedance matching. Thus there is an audible reflection with 1/2 second delay. Though a variety of echo suppressors have been deployed in satellite communications, one may still feel the echo. The above time delay of 1/2 second also reduces the efficiency of satellite in data transmission and long file transfers when carried out over the satellites.

Satellite communication, however, has the economical advantages. The satellite costs are independent of distance whereas the terrestrial network costs are proportional to the distance. The cross over distance at which the costs are equal is relatively much better with the satellite. However, if needed repair is nearly impossible after launching the satellite and also the equipments are subject to extreme environmental stresses. As compared to the fibre optic cable, the satellite communication has the advantage that the quality of transmitted signal and the locations of stations sending and receiving information are independent of distance. So long as two stations fall within the geographic coverage area of the satellite antenna pattern, those two stations maintain the same quality of information transfer whether they are 60 km or 2000 km apart.

It would be of importance to note that undersea copper cables have relatively limited capacities and when the undersea optical cable makes its first appearance it will provide for the first time an alternative way of transmitting wide-bandwidth signals across the ocean. For thin route remote area communications in the plains as well as hilly terrains like India's N-E region, Himachal Pradesh, Ladakh, Sikkim and communications between the Islands and the mainland satellite communication is the only cost-effective option. Similarly for search, rescue and navigation efforts satellites offer the advantages which no other systems can offer.

1.7. Active and Passive Satellites

The difference between a passive and an active communication satellite arises from the fact whether the communication relay (here satellite) involves passive reflection or an active electronics system. As mentioned in Section 1.1, the early project ECHO was a passive reflector (satellite) that consisted of a large reflector such as a spherical balloon. In the passive satellite system the ground transmitting system beams power at the reflector. The receiving ground system receives a fraction of the power that has been intercepted by the reflector and reradiated. In active satellite, the satellite receives a fraction of the energy beamed toward it by the ground transmitting system and the received power is amplified by active electronic means, usually in conjuction with frequency shifting. The power received by the ground receiving system is determined by the power level of the space craft transmitter.

The most important comparison of the communication capability of active and passive satellites is the amount of power radiated toward the receiving ground stations by the satellite. Actually the communication capability of active systems with directional antennas rapidly becomes much greater than that of the passive systems as the altitude is increased. Passive systems are incapable of competing with active systems with respect to communication capability except at low altitudes. Passive systems may have significant advantages for military systems because of the relative invulnerability of the satellites. However, the principal interest in the society is on systems that are capable of providing appreciable communication capability and hence the modern communication satellites are active satellite systems. Now a days space qualified reliable, long life electronic equipment are available and these have enhanced the capability of active satellite system.

1.8. From Analog to Digital Satellite Communication

For the first 20 years of satellite communications, analog signals were widely used, with most links employing frequency modulation (FM). Wideband FM can operate at low carrier-to-noise ratios (C/N) in the 5 to 15 dB range, but adds a signal-to-noise improvement so that video and telephone signals can be delivered with signal-to-noise ratios (S/N) of 50 dB. The penalty for the improvement is that the radio frequency (RF) signal occupies a much larger bandwidth than the baseband signal. In satellite links, this penalty is because signals are always weak and the improvement in signal-to-noise ratio is essential.

However, the rapid change in technology over the past fifteen years has been the transition from analog to digital transmission techniques. The move towards digital communications in terrestrial telephone and data transmission has been seen in a similar move towards digital transmission over satellite links. Thus, digital modulation is the obvious choice for satellite transmission of signals that originate in digital form and that are used by digital devices. In digital transmission, analog signals that are transmitted digitally can share channels with digital data, since all digital signals are handled in the same way, and their content is immaterial. Thus a digital satellite link can carry a mix of telephone and data signals that varies with traffic demand.

Today, virtually all signals sent via satellites are now digital. Familiar examples are data transmissions to and from the Internet, communication between remote terminals and computers, digital telephone, and TV signals in digital form, such as HDTV and DBS-TV. More importantly, dual standards permitting the transmission of not only digital TV but also high definition TV (HDTV), is eventually making analog TV obsolete. Even cable TV stations are switching over to digital receivers that allow many TV signals to be sent though use of single Ku-band. In addition, all LEO (low-earth orbit) and MEO (medium-earth orbit) mobile communication systems are digital, taking advantage of voice compression techniques that allow digital voice signal to be compressed into a bit stream at 4.8 kbits/sec (kbps). Similarly, MPEG-2 (Moving Picture Coding Expert Group) and other video compression techniques allow video signals to be transmitted in full fidelity at rates less than 6.2 kbps.

The advent of personal communication via LEO satellites and of direct broadcasting from satellites using digital transmission has resulted in the development of very small aperature terminal (VSAT) systems. The Global Positioning System (GPS) has become the dominate radio navigation aid and digital and mobile telephony. Domestic satellites now carry video signals for distribution to cable TV companies or direct to homes and serve networks of VSAT stations linked to central hubs in major cities. The development of direct to home satellite broadcast television (DBS-TV) has had a major impact on the market place. It is estimated that the worldwide revenue from all satellite communication services will increase from about 100 billion US dollars in 1990 to 200 billion US dollars in 2010.

The high capacity of digital satellites results from the use of high-power terrestrial transmitters and relatively high gain earth station antennas. Satellite communication systems are dominated by the need to receive very weak signals. In the early days, very large receiving antennas, with diameters up to 30m, were needed to collect sufficient signal power to drive video signals or multiplexed telephone channels. As satellites have become larger, heavier, and more powerful, smaller earth antennas have become feasible, and Direct Broadcast Satellite TV (DBS-TV) receiving systems can use dish antennas as small as 0.5 m in diameter. High earth station antenna gain now translates directly into communication capacity, and therefore into revenue. Increased capacity lowers the delivery cost per bit for a customer. Systems with fixed directional antennas can deliver bits at a significantly lower cost than system using low gain antennas, such as those designed for use by mobile users.

Satellite communication systems started in C band, with an allocation of 500 MHz, shared with terrestrial microwave links. As the GEO orbit filled up with satellites operating at C band, satellites were built for the next available frequency band, Ku band. There is a continuing demand for ever more spectrum to allow satellites to provide new services, with high speed access to the Internet forcing a move to Ka-band and even higher frequencies. Access to the Internet from small transmitting Ka-band earth stations located at the home offers a way to bypass the terrestrial telephone network with the Astra-K satellite, and the next generation of Ka-band satellites in the United States will offer similar services.

The World Radio Conferences of the International Telecommunication Union (ITU) have allocated new frequency bands for commercial satellite services that now include, L, S, C, Ku, K, Ka, V, and Q bands. Mobile satellite systems use VHF, UHF, L, and S band with carrier frequencies from 137 to 2500 MHz, and GEO satellites use frequency bands extending from 3.2 to 50 GHz.

Despite the growth of fiber-optic links with very high capacity, the demand for satellite systems continues to increase. Satellites have also become integrated into complex communications architectures that use each element of the network to its best advantage. Examples are VSAT/WLL (very small aperture/terminals local loop) in countries where the communications infrastructure is not yet mature and GEO/LMDS (local multipoint distribution systems) for the urban fringes of development nations where the build-out of fiber has yet to be an economic proposition.

With the fast development in digital electronics technology, access techniques and possibility of expanded communication network, digital signalling techniques have been introduced in communication by satellites. The advantages of digital signal transmission are now very well established and can be easily numbered as[8] (*i*) the ease and efficiency of multiplexing multiple signals or handling digital messages in 'packets' for convenient switching ; (*ii*) the relative insensitivity of digital circuits to retransmission noise, commonly a problem with analog systems, (*iii*) potential for extremely low error rates and high fidelity through error detection and correction, (*iv*) communications privacy and (*v*) the flexibility of digital hardware implementation, which permits the use of microprocessors and miniprocessors, digital switching and the use of large scale integrated circuits (LSI). Thus the digital transmission techniques have gained increased usage for satellite communication, microwave relay, and cable or waveguide transmission. In laser satellite communication too digital techniques have been successfully utilised.

Though the various digital modulation techniques will be discussed in later chapter, it may be mentioned here that in analog communication systems, frequency division multiplexing-frequency modulation-frequency division multiple access (FDM-FM-FDMA) has been widely used and it provided good quality satellite links. But here the number of earth stations is limited. A digital satellite system such as that using quaternary phase shift keying-time division multiple access (QPSK-TDMA) can accommodate a large number of earth stations with a small loss in transponder capacity. Further the system can quickly respond to traffic variations. A further increase in efficiency can be easily obtained by using the techniques known as demand assignment and digital speech interpolation. The advanced satellite systems that use onboard switching and processing, multiple spot beams and beam hopping use the digital communication techniques and such digital systems are capable of serving a mixture of large, medium and small earth stations with high efficiency. The recent technique of code division multiple access has allowed to employ micro earth stations (0.5 m antenna) at an extremely low cost ($ 3000) with a good quality service. ISDN systems will further enhance the importance of digital communication networking with satellites.

1.9. Modem and Codec

The equipment that carries out modulation (MOD) and demodulation (DEMOD) is called *modem*. Similarly the equipment responsible for carrying out coding and decoding is termed *codec*. These two devices are widely used in digital satellite communication. Modem is used as an interface between analog and digital systems. These play an important role in computer communication networks and ISDN systems. Codecs are used in digital television systems and normally consists of a pair of A/D converter and D/A converter. It is a kind of black box digital device as shown in Fig 1.3.

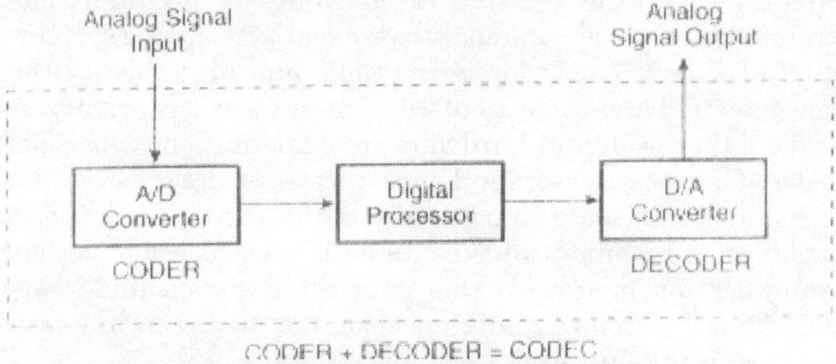

Fig. 1.3. Basic Block Diagram of Codec.

1.10. Review Questions

1. What is a satellite and how does a communication satellite differ from a communication relay ?
2. Explain the basic differences between an active and passive satellite systems. Discuss their merits and demerits.
3. Prove that for covering the globe three communication satellites would be sufficient.
4. What is the difference between a geostationary satellite and a low altitude satellite ? Can a low altitude satellite be also used for communication purposes ? If not why?
5. List various frequency bands being used in satellite communication. Compare the advantages and disadvantages of different bands considering the effects of propagation media.
6. Give the reasons as to why the uplink frequency is different than the down link frequency. Also mention the reasons for keeping uplink frequency higher than the downlink frequency.
7. What are the elements of satellite communication system ? Explain each with a suitable block diagram.
8. List various advantages and disadvantages of satellite communication. Give the reasons that optical fibres inspite of being high bandwidth channel, satellite communication has an edge over it.
9. What are the advantages of a communication system that uses digital signal transmission ? Explain as to how the digital satellite communication has reduced the size of earth station?

10. What are Modem and Codec ? Both are A/D and D/A converters but what makes the difference between the two? Mention the areas of their applications.

1.11. References

1. Clarke, A.C., Extraterrestrial Relays, Wireless World, 51 (1945), 305-308.
2. Pratt, T. and Bostian, C.W., Satellite Communication, John Wiley and Sons, NY, 1986.
3. Ha, T.T., Digital Satellite Communication, H.W. Sams & Co., NY, 1986.
4. Feher, K., Advanced Digital Communications, Prentice- Hall Inc., 1987.
5. Morgan, W.L., Satellite Locations-1984, Proc IEEE, Vol 72, No 11, Nov 1984, pp 1434-1444.
6. Williams, D.D., Synchronous Satellite Communication Systems, in Advances in Communication Systems, Theory and Applications, Ed. A.V. Balkrishnan, Vol 2, p. 151-171, Academic Press, NY, 1966.
7. Jordan, E.C. (Ed). Reference Data for Engineers, Radio, Electronics, Computers and Communication, H.W. Sams and Co., Indianapolis,USA, 1986.
8. Spilker, J.J., Digital Communication by Satellites, Prentice Hall Inc., NJ, 1977.

Other Suggested References

1. Bharagava, V.K., Haccoun, D., Matyas, R. and Nuspe, P.P., Digital Communications by Satellite, Wiley Interscience Publication, NY, 1981.
2. Lebow, I.L., Satellite Communications, in Digital Communications (Ed Bartree, T.C.). H.W. Sams & Co., 1986.
3. Maral, G. and Bousquet, M., Satellite Communications Systems, John Wiley & Sons, 1986.
4. Yuen, J.H. (Ed). Deep Space Telecommunications Systems Engineering, Plenum Press, NY, 1983.
5. Jefferis, D. Watts, Satellites, USA, 1987.
6. Elbert, V.B.R. Introduction to Satellite Communication, Artech House, 1987.
7. Lewis, G.E. Communications *via* Satellites, Blackwell Scientific, 1988.
8. Jansky, D.M. and Jeruchim, M.C., Communication Satellites in the Geostationary Orbit, Artech House, Inc., 1987.
9. Wu, W.M., Elements of Digital Satellite Communications, Computer Science Press, NY, 1984.
10. Gagliardi, R.M. Satellite Communication, Van Nostrand Reinhold, 1987.

2

Satellite Orbits and Inclination

2.1. Introduction

The orbit of satellite in use for communication purposes has special significance. It is geostationary and has to be maintained geostationary at all costs. Thus there are two main problems involved with the communication satellites regarding the orbit, namely the (*i*) launching and putting the satellite into geostationary orbit and (*ii*) maintaining it (station keeping). The importance of geostationary orbit has already been discussed in chapter 1. Once the satellite is placed in geostationary orbit, it has to be parked in the desired slot till its whole life. Various kinds of manoeuvre are needed to do that. There are standard techniques to achieve them and all these are specified and recommended by the International Telecommunication Union (ITU) and International Consulative Committee (CCIR) which also prescribe the parking slots for individual countries. This helps in avoiding unnecessary overlapping of the satellite coverage area and thus avoiding the unnecessary losses of information or traffic capacity. The communication satellite is a very large investment and its life is limited. It is therefore very essential that its full and proper utilization be made. In this chapter therefore the orbital aspects of the communication satellite are discussed.

Communication satellites move around the earth as planets do around the sun and therefore the three Keplers' laws apply to them also. These Kepler's laws are : (*i*) the orbit of satellites is an ellipse with the center of the earth at one focus, (*ii*) the line joining the center of earth and the satellite sweeps over equal areas in equal time intervals and (*iii*) the squares of the orbital periods of two satellite have the same ratio as the cubes of their mean distances from the center of the earth. The satellite orbit may be either elliptical or circular and its characteristics are governed by these laws. Infact these are the laws that initially developed the techniques for launching and putting the communication satellite in geostationary or any orbit (*e.g.* low altitude satellites for special research purposes). The tracking of the satellite, its station keeping etc all depend on these Kepler's laws. The Newton's gravitational law of force also controls the satellite's orbits and infact a very simple calculation regarding the geostationary satellite distance etc may be carried out from Newton's law of force.

The orbital aspects which are of importance are the determination of the orbit of the satellite, the distance between the satellite and earth stations, coverage angle, earth station pointing angles, eclipses and solar interference. The orbits may be far, near, equatorial, polar or inclined. The earth station antenna that communicates with the geostationary satellite requires a knowledge of azimuth angle and the elevation angle with respect to latitude and longitude of the location of the earth station. A knowledge of the polarization angle is also necessary. The study of coverage areas requires the knowledge of the coverage angle and slant range. The duration of eclipse is essential to be calculated because during these periods the satellite has to depend on its own stored power as solar batteries remain idle then. The eclipse may be caused by the earth and the moon. The solar interference appears in a variety of ways. It increases the antenna noise temperature when the sun is within the earth station beam. There is also a continuous drift in the satellite orbit both in longitude and latitude due to various disturbances. This drift is to be constantly nullified so that the orbit be stationary but perfect stationarity is not possible and so a satellite is constrained to remain within a 'window' whose limits are defined by an angular shift as seen from the center of the earth around the required nominal position, Usually this window is about 75 km on the sphere containing the geostationary satellite orbit.

2.2. Synchronous Orbit

A *geostationary satellite* is synchronous and has an equatorial, circular and direct orbit. It should be noted that synchronous is often confused with stationary. Polar and inclined orbits may be synchronous but never stationary. At the geosynchronous altitude and orbital velocity of the satellite equals the velocity of a point on the earth's equator. The geosynchronous altitude can be easily calculated. The movement of the satellite with respect to the earth can be considered as that shown in Fig. 2.1. Let M and m be the mass of the earth and the satellite respectively. Similarly let R_E be the radius of synchronous circular orbit of the satellite. If ω is the angular velocity of the circular motion of the satellite in radians per second then the centripetal force acting on the satellite would be

$mR\omega^2$. This centripetal force equal to the gravitational force (Newtons gravitational law) between the satellite and the earth expressed by GmM/R^2 where G is the gravitational constant. Thus

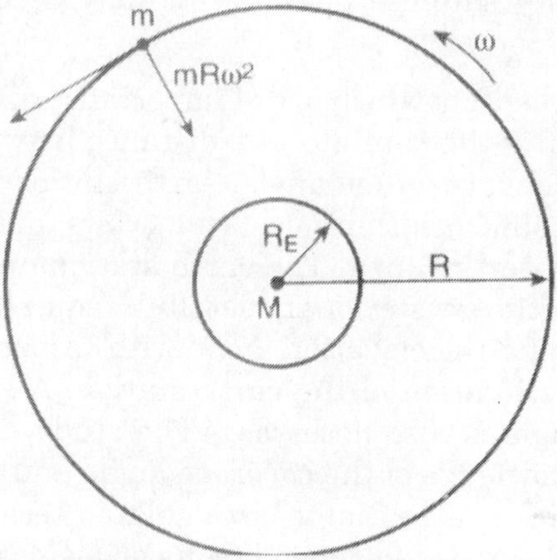

Fig. 2.1. Geostationary Orbit.

$$mR\omega^2 = \frac{GmM}{R^2} \qquad \text{...(2.1)}$$

At the earth's surface the gravitational force in mg where g is the acceleration due to gravity. Then

$$\frac{GmM}{R_E^2} = mg \qquad \text{...(2.2)}$$

From Eqs. (2.1) and (2.2) one can have

$$R = \left(\frac{gR_E^2}{\omega^2}\right)^{1/3} = \left(\frac{gR_E^2}{4\pi^2 f^2}\right)^{1/3} \qquad \text{...(2.3)}$$

where $f = \omega/2\pi$ is the rotation rate in revolutions per second. Putting $f = 1$ revolution per day and $R_E = 6370$ km, $g = 9.9$ m/s, one obtains $R = 42{,}208$ km. Subtracting R_E form R one gets 35,838 km as the orbital height above the equator which is quite close to the precise value of 35,860 km. The maximum illumination of earth by a geosynchronous satellite is as that shown in Fig. 2.2. It is evident that polar regions are not illuminated by the geosynchronous satellite. The angle subtended by the earth is 17.3° and the highest latitude at which satellite is visible is 81.3°. Further for all practical purposes an earth station requires a minimum elevation angle of atleast 5° above the horizon. This reduces the highest latitude to about 76° at the longitude of the satellite. Corresponding to this 76° latitude of illumination the maximum distance illuminated by the geostationary satellite is about 16,900 km which is around 42%

of the equatorial distance. To cover the polar regions therefore a satellite with an elliptical and inclined orbit is needed. A typical example is Molniya series of satellite of USSR. Molniya orbit is elliptical, inclined 65° with respect to the earth with a 40,000 km apogee in the northern hemisphere and a 500 km perigee in the southern hemisphere. 3 Moliniya satellites are required to provide 24 hour coverage of the polar regions.

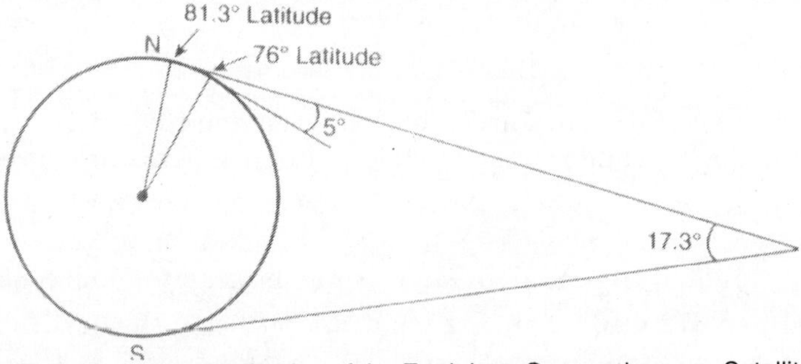

Fig. 2.2. Maximum Illumination of the Earth by a Geosynchronous Satellite.

2.3. Orbital Parameters

The satellite's movement in an orbit follows the three Kepler's laws. The first Kepler's law gives that the satellite moves along a conic (orbit) on the orbit plane, the equation for which is

$$r = p/(1 + e \cos \upsilon) \quad ...(2.4)$$

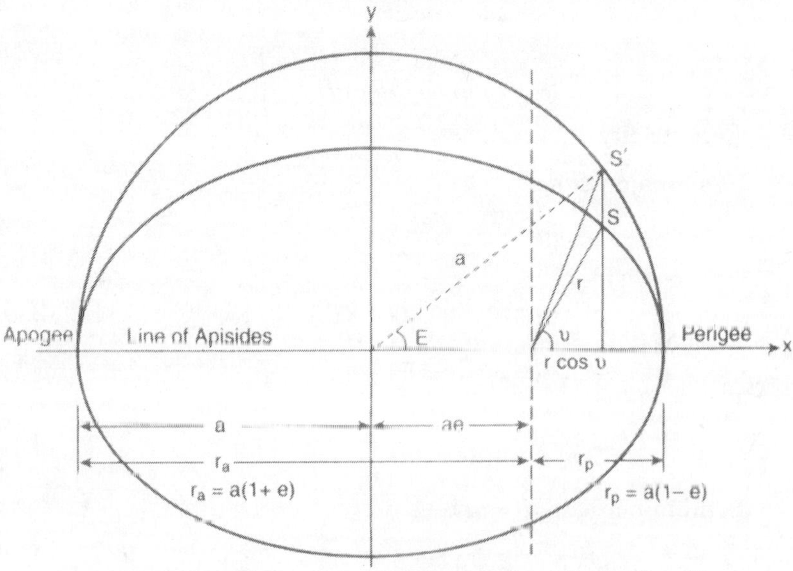

Fig. 2.3. Geometry of an Elliptical Orbit of Communication Satellite.

where p is a parameter, e is the eccentricity and v is the central angle (also called the true anomaly). Fig. 2.3 represents the above orbit of satellite. In fact the value of the eccentricity e determines the type of the conic (orbit).

$$e = \left\{ \begin{array}{c} 0 \rightarrow circle \\ < 1 \rightarrow ellipse \\ 1 \rightarrow parabola \\ > 1 \rightarrow hyperbola \end{array} \right\} \quad ...(2.5)$$

In Fig. 9.3 the elliptical orbit has been depicted. Here a is the semi-major axis and is linked to the orbital period by the expression

$$T = 2\pi \sqrt{\frac{a^3}{\mu}} \quad ...(2.6)$$

where μ is quantity equal to GM, G being the gravitational constant, equal to 6.672×10^{-11} m^3 kg^{-1}s^{-2} and M being the earth's mass equal to 5974×10^{24} kg. Thus $\mu = GM = 3.986 \times 10^{14}$ m^3/s^2.

Satellite velocity for a circular orbit is $\sqrt{\mu/a}$ where a is the orbit radius. In fact the satellite velocity at an orbital point s (distance to the centre of the earth r) is given by

$$V_s^2 = \frac{2\mu}{r} - \frac{\mu}{a} \quad ...(2.7)$$

It should be remembered that in Fig. 2.3 following definitions are made

$$x = r \cos v = a (\cos E - e) \quad ...(2.8)$$

$$y = r \sin v = a \sin E(1 - e^2)^{1/2} \quad ...(2.9)$$

Eccentricity : $e = c/a = \dfrac{(r_a - r_p)}{(r_a + r_p)}$ ...(2.10)

Semi major axis :

$$a = \frac{(r_a + r_p)}{2} \quad ...(2.11)$$

Apogee distance :

$$r_a = a + c = a(1 + e) \quad ...(2.12)$$

Perigee distance :

$$r_p = a - c = a(1 - e) \quad ...(2.13)$$

Locus parameter :

$$p = a(1 - e^2) = \frac{2r_a r_p}{(r_a + r_p)} \quad ...(2.14)$$

Semi minor axis $b = a(1 - e^2)^{1/2}$

$$= (r_a\, r_p)^{1/2} \quad ...(2.15)$$

A synchronous satellite has T as the *sideral period* of rotation of its primary body, T_P (*i.e.* the period in any fixed reference coordinate system). It should be noted that for the earth T_P is not 24 hours (the so called *synodal period*) because in one day the earth both rotates once around its polar axis and also completes 1/36524 of the annual earth orbit around the sun. Consequently a geosynchronous satellite must have a period

$$T = T_P = \left(1 - \frac{1}{36524}\right) \times 24\ h$$

$$= 86163{,}44\ s$$

$$= 23\ h\ 56\ m\ 4\ s \qquad ...(2.16)$$

in any fixed coordinate system. If

$$T = nT_P,\ n = 2, 3, 4, \qquad ...(2.17)$$

the satellite is called *super-synchronous* whereas a *sub-synchronous* satellite has T and T_P interchanged in Eq. (2.17). In Eqs. (2.12) and (2.13), *perigee is* defined as a point in the orbit where the satellite is closest to the earth and similarly the point where the satellite is farthest from the earth is called the *apogee.*

As already mentioned before v is termed the *true anomaly* and is the positive angle oriented according to the velocity vector of the spacecraft, between the earth center to the satellite axis and the earth center to the perigee axis. Thus v specifies the position of the satellite on the orbit. Angle E is called the *eccentric anomaly* and is the central angle measured from the x axis to the vertical projection of the satellite point over the circle of radius a. The true anomaly v and the ecentric anomaly E are related by any of the expressions

$$\cos E = \frac{(e + \cos v)}{(1 + e \cos v)} \qquad ...(2.18)$$

$$\cos v = \frac{(e - \cos E)}{(e \cos E - 1)} \qquad ...(2.19)$$

$$\tan (v/2) = [(1 + e)/(1 - e)]^{1/2} \tan (E/2) \qquad ...(2.20)$$

Another kind of anomaly usually defined is M which is also called the *mean anomaly*. It may be considered as a true anomaly the satellite would have if it proceeded along a circular orbit of the same period T. This hypothetical circle may be considered as circumscribing the ellipse as shown in Fig. 2.3. Thus

$$m = \frac{2\pi t}{T} \qquad ...(2.21)$$

where $2\pi/T$ is the satellite mean motion. Angles M and E are related by the equation

$$M = E - e \sin E \qquad ...(2.22)$$

2.4. Satellite Location with Respect to the Earth

For an earth satellite, the reference frame is taken as rectangular coordinate system (OXYZ) with origin O in the earth's center of gravity. The z axis coincides with the polar axis and is oriented towards the north. The X-Y plane is thus the equatorial plane of the earth. Its angle i with the satellite orbit plane (or the conic section) is called the *inclination* and is defined in the interval $(0° < i < 180°)$. A satellite orbit is *equatorial* if the orbit plane coincides with the reference plane of the primary body ($i = 0°$). An orbit is *polar* if the orbit plane contains the polar axis of the primary body ($i = 90°$). An orbit is inclined if it is neither equatorial nor polar. Fig. 2.4 indicates these equatorial and inclined orbits of the satellite. Inclined or equatorial orbits in which the satellite's projection on the equatorial plane of the primary body revolves in the same direction as the primary body itself are known as *direct orbits*. They have inclinations less than 90°. Earth rotation is seen to assist the launching of satellites into direct orbits. Orbits for which $i > 90°$ are called *retrograde orbits*.

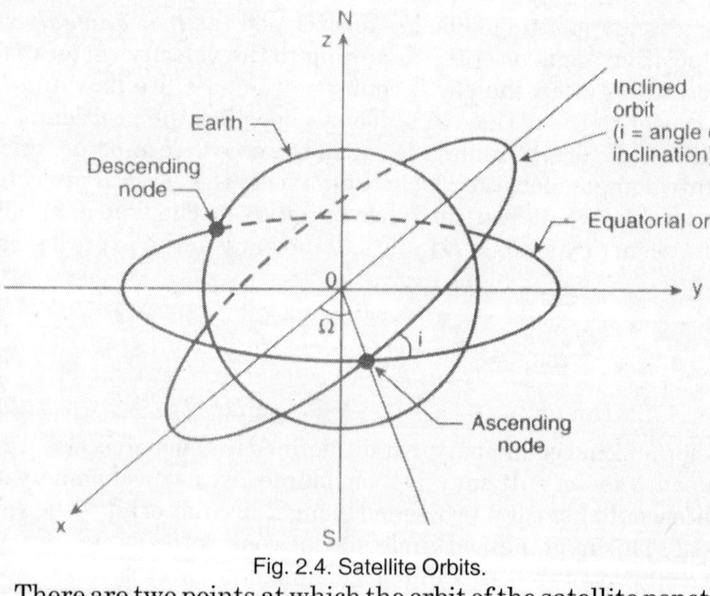

Fig. 2.4. Satellite Orbits.

There are two points at which the orbit of the satellite penetrates the equatorial plane. These points are called nodes. There are two such nodes, namely the *ascending node* and the *descending node* as shown in Fig. 2.4. The satellite moves upward through the equatorial plane at the ascending node and downward through the equatorial plane at the descending node. It should be noted that in the reference frame OXYZ mentioned above the x axis (Fig. 2.4) points towards a fixed location in the free space called the *first point of Aries*. This is the direction of a line from the center of the earth through the center of the sun at the vernal equinox (about March 21), the instant when the subsolar point crosses the equator north to south. Angular distance measured eastward in the equatorial plane from the x axis is called the *right ascension* and is represented by the symbol RA. The right ascension of the ascending node is called Ω. Thus Ω is the longitude of the ascending node. Infact the variables Ω and i together locate the orbital plane with respect to the equatorial plane.

Another parameter of interest for the satellite orbit location with respect to earth is ω the *argument of perigee*. This is the angle measured along the orbit from the ascending node to the perigee. Thus the five parameters (i, a, e, Ω, ω) completely define the satellite orbit in the space. Inclusion of sixth parameter which may be either the true anomaly v or the mean anomaly or the eccentric anomaly will define the motion of the satellite on its orbit.

It would be of importance to mention here that the nonspherety of the earth, the nonuniform distribution of masses of its surface and the effects of lunar and solar gravitation all make the actual motion of satellites depart from that described above. These variation in the satellite orbit are called *secular variations* and are of two type known as the *nodal regression* and the *rotation of the lines of the apsides*. The nodal regression is a rotation of the orbit plane in the direction opposite to the satellite motion around the axis of rotation of the earth. The rate of this motion in degrees per day is given as

$$\Omega^0 = -\,[10/(1-e^2)^2]\,(R/a)^{7/2} \cos i \qquad \ldots(2.24)$$

The rotation of the line of the apsides is the rotation of the ellipse major axis around the center of the earth on a fixed orbit plane. Apogee and perigee move then with respect to the earth, and the rate of motion of the argument of perigee is also a function of orbit inclination angle i, or

$$\omega^0 = [5/(1-e^2)^2]\,(R/a)^{7/2}\,(5\cos^2 i - 1)°/\text{day} \ldots(2.25)$$

The critical value $i = \cos^{-1}(1/\sqrt{5}) = 63°24'$ stops this motion. Smaller values of i make the ellipse rotate in the same sense as the satellite motion along it. Higher values of i make the ellipse rotate in the opposite sense. The effect becomes smaller for higher orbits. For lower altitude orbits the earth's gravitational field affects the satellite orbit but for higher orbits the solar and lunar gravitational fields are of much concern. For geostationary orbit these effects cause a change in satellite inclination by 1° per year. It may be noted that the inclination causes the satellite to move in the form of figure of eight (Fig. 2.5) which gives the corresponding amount of drift in distance (km) both in longitude and latitude of satellite. An inclination of 1° causes drift of satellite around 735.9 km in latitude side and 3.23 km in longitude side.

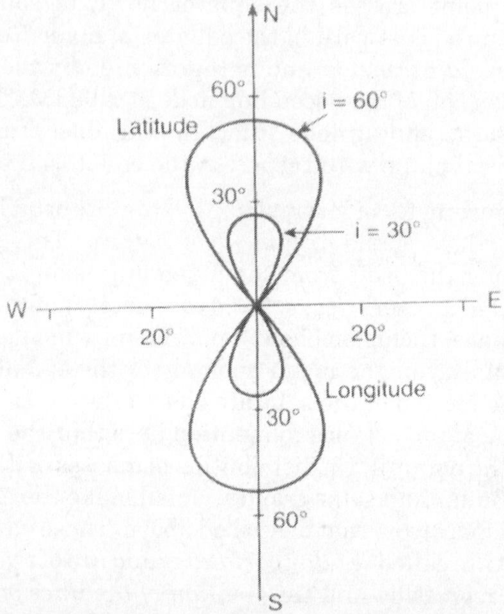

Fig. 2.5. Satellite's Apparent Movement in an Inclined and Synchronous Orbit with respect to the Ascending Node.

2.5. Look Angles

The look angles are the angles (coordinates) to which an earth station antenna must be pointed to communicate with the geosynchronous satellite. These angles are the azimuth (A) and elevation angle (E). These are calculated on the basis of a knowledge of latitude (ϕ) and relative longitude (θ) both in degrees of the earth station. Infact θ is the absolute value of the difference between the geostationary satellite longitude and that of the earth station. Azimuth angle is usually defined as the angle by which the antenna, pointing at the horizon must be rotated clockwise around its vertical axis, from the geographical north, to bring the antenna boresight into the vertical plane containing the satellite direction. Value of the azimuth angle is between 0° and 360°. Its value is calculated from Fig. 2.6 by determining the value of angle γ from the chart and then deriving A from angle γ using the insert table. Angle γ may also be calculated from the geometry, of satellite orbit in the reference system shown in Fig. 2.7. Angle γ can be calculated from the formula

$$\gamma = \text{arc } tg\ (tg\ \theta / \sin \phi) \quad ...(2.26)$$

True Azimuth	Earth station Quadrant
A = 180−γ	NW
A = 180+γ	NW
A = γ	SW
A = 360−γ	SE

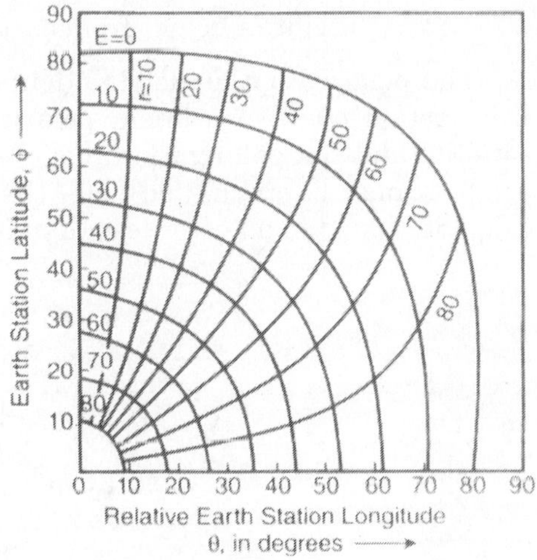

Fig. 2.6. Azimuth Angle γ and Elevation Angle E for Earth's Station Antennas.

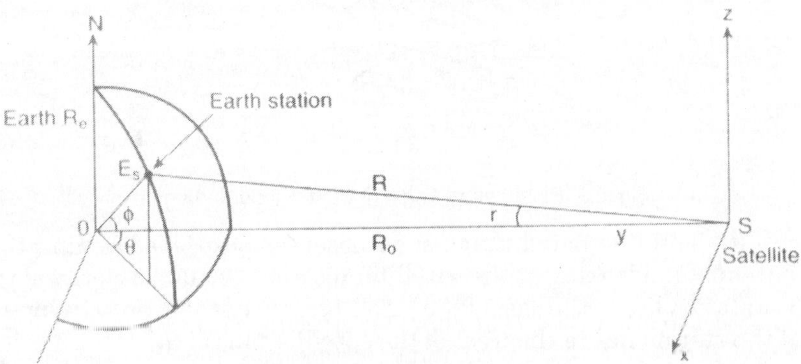

Fig. 2.7. Calculation of Angle γ from the Geometry of Satellite Orbit in the Reference System.

The *elevation angle* is defined as the angle by which the antenna boresight should be rotated in the vertical plane that contains the satellite direction from the horizontal to the satellite direction. Elevation angle E is also calculated from the chart given in Fig. 2.6. It is also calculated from the formula given below :

$$E = \frac{Arc\ tg\left(\cos\theta\cos\phi - \dfrac{R_e}{R_e + R_o}\right)}{[1 - (\cos\theta\cos\phi)^2)]^{1/2}} \qquad \text{...(2.27)}$$

where R_e is the earth radius = 6378 km and

R_o = satellite's height from earth's centre = 35786 km.

The polarization angle ψ is defined as the angle between the polarization plane of a linear polarized wave transmitted by the satellite and the polarization plane of the earth station antenna. Angle ψ may be calculated from the chart of Fig. 2.8. It is also calculated (within an error less than 0.1° by the formula

$$tg\ \psi = \frac{\sin\theta}{tg\ \phi} \qquad \text{...(2.28)}$$

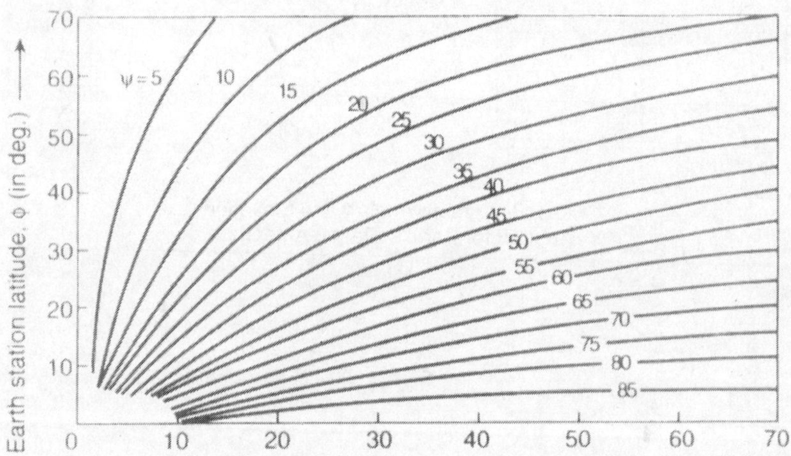

Fig. 2.8. Polarization Angle of Earth Station Antenna.

It should be noted that for an observer positioned behind the antenna and looking at the satellite, rotation should be clockwise if the station lies to the east of the satellite meridian and anticlockwise if the station lies to the west of the satellite meridian.

2.6. Earth Coverage and Slant Range

In Fig. 2.7 the coordinates of the earth station may be written as

$$x = R_e \cos\phi \sin\theta$$

$$y = R_0 + R_e (1 - \cos\phi \cos\theta)$$

$$z = R_e \sin\phi$$

The range R (also called *slant range*) from satellite to earth station then would be given as

$$R^2 = R_0^2 + 2R_e\,(R_0 + R_e)\,(1 - \cos\phi\cos\theta) \quad ...(2.30)$$

For $R_e/R_o \approx 0.178$,

$$(R/R_0)^2 \approx 1 + 0.42\,(1 - \cos\phi\cos\theta) \quad ...(2.31)$$

It can be seen from Eq. (2.31) that the maximum value of $(R/R_0)^2$ is 1.356 and if R^2 is approximated by R_0^2 it would lead to a maximum error of 1.3 dB in the power link budget.

Regarding the coverage of the earth by a single beam communication satellite there are two things to be considered. Firstly it is desired that it should atleast cover the country and then the coverage should be as maximum as possible. The maximum coverage (illumination) of the earth by a geostationary satellite is already shown in Fig. 2.2. In other words the maximum geometrical coverage is given by the portion of the earth within a cone with the satellite at its apex and tangent of the earth's surface. The apex angle (coverage angle) 2 α_{MAT} of this cone is

$$2 \text{ Arc sin} \frac{R_e}{R_o + R_e} = 17.4° \quad ...(2.32)$$

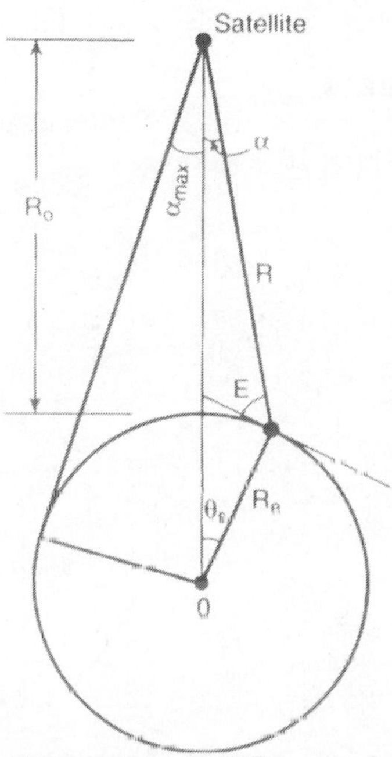

Fig. 2.9. Elevation Angle and Coverage Angle with Reference to Synchronous Satellite.

This angle is also shown in Fig. 2.2 and is redrawn in Fig. 2.9. In Fig. 2.9, θ_s is the central angle that represents the angular radius of the satellite footprint. It is given by

$$\theta_s = 180° - (90° + E + \alpha) = 90° - E - \alpha \quad ...(2.33)$$

For a geostationary orbit, corresponding to coverage angle α_{max}, the central angle θ_s, is obtained from Eq. (2.33) by substituting $E = 0$ and $\alpha = \alpha_{max}$, this gives $\theta_s = 81.3°$. But as mentioned in Section 2.2 a minimum elevation angle of 5° is required then $\theta_s = 76.3°$. Thus not more than 76.3° of northern or southern latitudes will be covered by the geosynchronous satellite.

The slant range R may also be calculated in terms of elevation angle E as shown in Fig. 2.9. Its value would be

$$R^2 = (R_e + R_o)^2 + R_e^2 - 2R_e\,(R_e - R_o) \times \sin\left[E + \sin^{-1}\left(\frac{R_e}{R_e + R_o}\cos E\right)\right] \quad ...(2.34)$$

which for $E_{min} = 5°$ would give the maximum slant range R = 41,127 km which gives a satellite round trip delay of $2d/c = 0.274$ s where c is the velocity of light. To this delay, delays caused by terrestrial extensions (which are of the order of 10-50 ms) are also added. However, because of the use of echo suppressor or echo cancellers the delay is not troublesome in telephone conversations.

2.7. Eclipse Effects

Solar eclipses caused by the earth and moon to the satellite are important as these affect the working of satellites and in particular

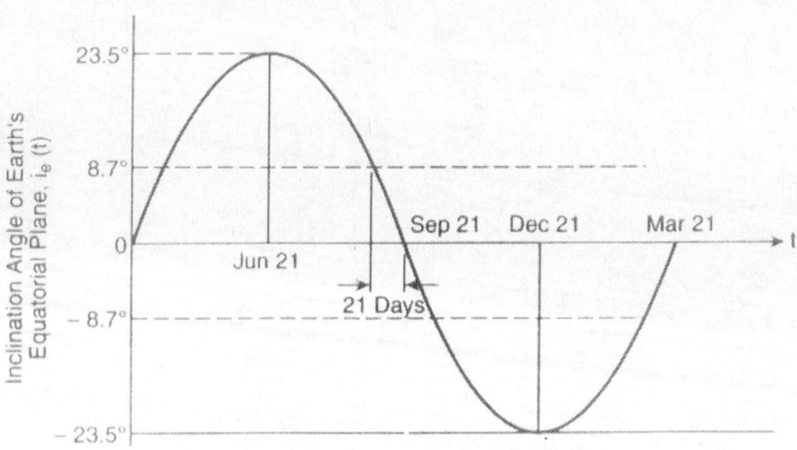

Fig. 2.10. (*a*) Variation of the Earth's Equatorial Plane Inclination Angle i_e (*t*).

the energy generated by solar cells is greatly affected then. Therefore the periodicity and duration of these solar eclipses are important. It should be noted that solar eclipse due to earth is of more importance than due to moon on the communication satellite as the former lasts for several days. In this section firstly the solar eclipse that due to earth would be discussed and then that due to moon would be discussed.

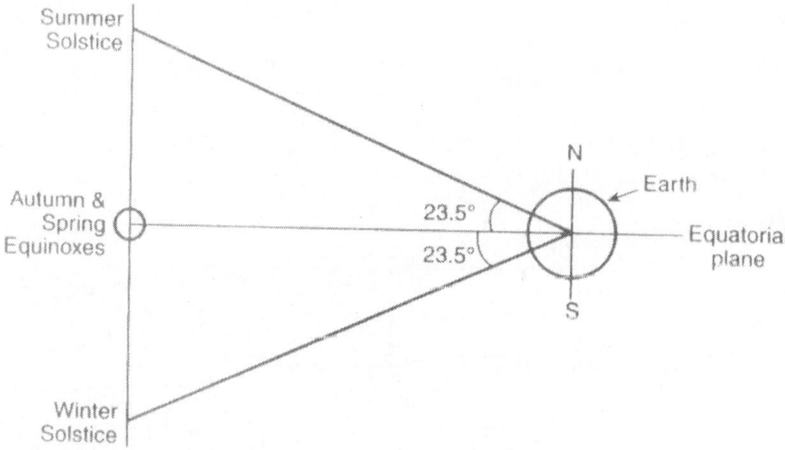

Fig. 2.10. (*b*) Apparent Movement of the Sun Relative to the Earth.

The inclination angle of the earth's equatorial plane i_e (t) with respect to the sun's direction is as that shown in Fig. 2.10. Here angle i_e (t) is in degrees. The annual variation i_e (t) is sinusoidal in nature. Fig. 2.10 (*b*) shows the apparent movement of the sun relative to the earth. It is apparent that summer solstice occurs on 21st June and winter solstice is on 21st Dec. Similarly Spring and Autumn equinoxes occur on 21st March and 21st September respectively. The variation of i_e (t) as that shown in Fig. 2.10 (*a*) can be written mathematically as

$$i_e\,(t) = 23.5 \sin \frac{2\pi t}{T} \qquad ...(2.35)$$

where T is the annual period equal to 365 days and the maximum inclination angle i_e (t) is 23.5°. At the spring and autumn equinoxes the inclination angle is zero whereas it is at its maximum on summer and winter solstices.

The satellite is always illuminated at the solstice. It goes the maximum duration of eclipse during equinoxes. The solar eclipse during equinox is as that shown in Fig. 2.11. Here the earth's shadow is considered to be a cylinder of constant diameter. The maximum shadow angle occurs at equinoxes and is given as

$$\phi_{max} = 180° - 2\cos^{-1}\frac{R_e}{R_o + R_e} \qquad ...(2.36)$$

which is same as that of coverage angle given in Eq. (2.32). Substituting value of $R_e = 6378$ km and $R_0 = 35786$ km (satellite altitude), $\phi_{max} = 17.4°$. Corresponding to this shadow angle, the duration of eclipse for the geostationary satellite whose period is 24 hours can be given as

$$t_{max} = \frac{17.4°}{360°} \times 24 \equiv 69.4 \text{ minutes} = 1.16 \text{ hrs} \qquad ...(2.37)$$

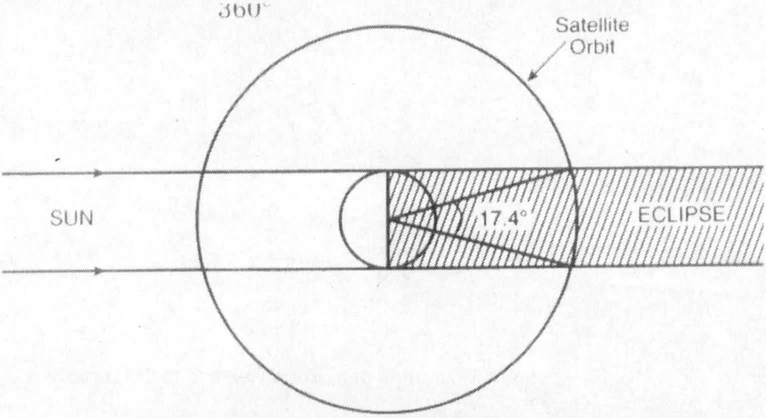

Fig. 2.11. Eclipse Due to Earth when Sun is at Equinox.

The first eclipse day before an equinox and the last day of eclipse after an equinox correspond to the relative position of the sun such that the sun rays tangent to the earth pass through the satellite orbit. Such a situation is shown in Fig. 2.12. In these cases the

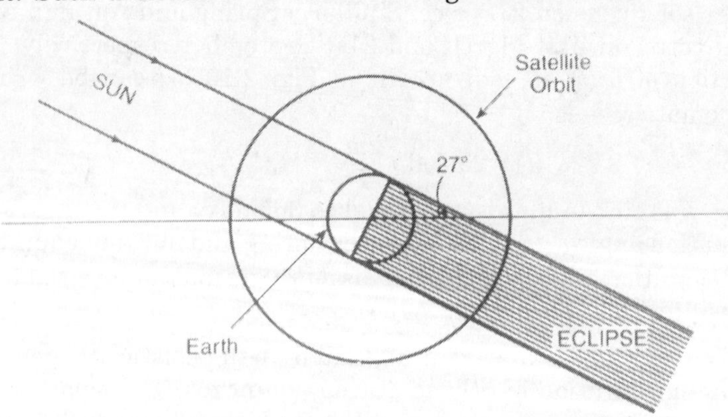

Fig. 2.12. Inclination of Earth at the First Day of Eclipse Before Equinox for a Geostationary Satellite.

inclination angle of the equatorial plane with respect to the direction of the sun is

$$i_e = \frac{1}{2}\,\phi_{\max} = 8.7° \qquad ...(2.38)$$

Corresponding to this inclination angle of the earth's equatorial plane, from Eq. (2.35), the time t from the first day of eclipse to the equinox and the time from equinox to the last day of eclipse may be derived as

$$t = \frac{365}{\pi}\sin^{-1}\left(\frac{87}{23.5}\right)$$

$$\approx 21 \text{ days} \qquad ...(2.39)$$

Thus from the first day of eclipse 21 days are needed to reach the equinox. This is shown in Fig. 2.10 (*b*) as well as in Fig. 2.13. Thus in total for 42 days the solar eclipse near equinox affects the satellite's working. It should be noted that at half of the daily duration period of eclipse the satellite crosses the plane formed by the sun and the earth's axis where the local time at the satellite's longitude is mid night. Thus the satellite services are interrupted at midnight and the satellite needs a battery backup.

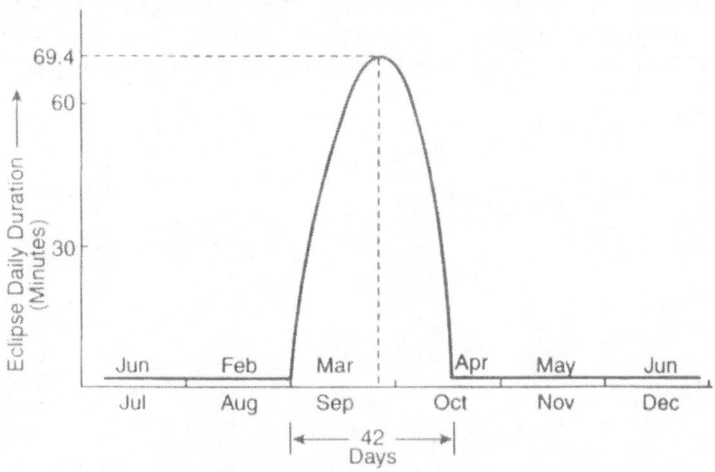

Fig. 2.13. Daily Duration of Solar Eclipse Caused by Earth.

The solar eclipse caused by moon to the geostationary satellite occurs when the moon passes in front of the sun. The eclipse occurs irregularly in time of duration and depth. Oftenly eclipses may occur twice within a 24 hour period. Eclipse duration may range from a few minutes to over two hours with an average duration of about 40 minutes. Compared to earth-solar eclipse, the number of moon solar eclipse range from zero to four with an average of two per year. It is worthwhile to note that if the moon solar eclipse of long duration occurs just before or just after the earth-solar eclipse, the satellite has to face special problems in connection with battery recharging and spacecraft thermal reliability. In order to cope up with the solar battery problems during eclipses an energy reserve is provided with the satellite.

2.8. Satellite Placement in Geostationary Orbit

The placement of satellite in the geostationary orbit is carried out on the principle of *Hohmann transfer* and is as that shown in Fig. 2.14. Here the satellite firstly has the lower circular earth orbit at an altitude of around 300 km or so. Then a velocity increment changes the satellite's lower circular earth orbit into an elliptical transfer orbit with the perigee at initial altitude (300 km) and with apogee at the altitude of final circular orbit (radius of the geosynchronous orbit is equal to 42,164.2 km). A second velocity increment then finally places the satellite into this desired orbit. The velocity increments are carried out by various auxiliary propulsion stages. There are three ways to carry out above procedure, of course depending upon the launch vehicle. The first technique is same as that mentioned above, *i.e.* placing the satellite in geosynchronous orbit from a circular low earth orbit. Space Transport System (STS)

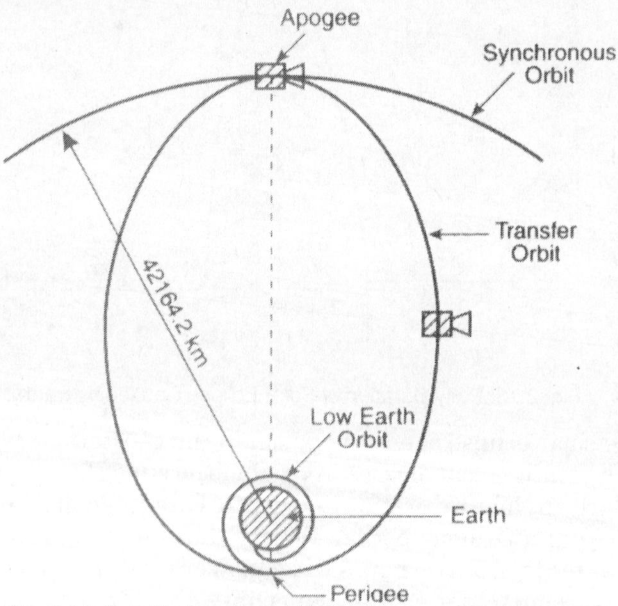

Fig. 2.14. Satellite Placement in Synchronous (Geostationary) Orbit from a low Earth Orbit.

follows this technique. In the second technique, there is no initial circular orbit and the vehicle provides the necessary velocity at the perigee of the elliptical transfer orbit. Thus here only one velocity increment is required from the satellite at the apogee. This technique has been used by expendable launch vehicles such as Ariane, Delta or Atlas-Centaur launchers. In the third technique, satellites are directly placed into geostationary (geosynchronous) orbit. This is achieved by special expendable launch vehicles such as US Titan III *C* and the USSR Proton launchers.

The velocity of satellite (V_S) at the perigee and apogee of the elliptical transfer orbit can be calculated from Eq. (2.7), namely

$$V_S^2 = \frac{2\mu}{r} - \frac{\mu}{a} \qquad ...(2.40)$$

where a is the semi-major axis of the ellipse, μ is gravitational constant of the earth ($\mu = 398600$ km^3/s^2). r is the distance from the center of the earth to the point at which the velocity V is required to maintain the ellipse.

Thus at perigee (of 300 km), $r = 6678.2$ km, $a = (6678.2 + 42164.2)/2 = 24421.2$ km. The velocity is then $V_{ps} = 10.15$ km/s. At the Apogee, $r = 42164.2$ km and there the velocity $V_{AS} = 1.61$ km/s. Since the velocity in a synchronous orbit ($r = a = 42164.2$ km) is $V_{cs} = 3.07$ km/s so the required velocity increment at apogee is $\Delta V_{cs} = V_{cs} - V_{as} = 3.07$ km/s $- 1.61$ km/s $= 1.46$ km/s. This velocity increment value corresponds to a minimum and applies to a circularization manoeuvre when transfer orbit and circular orbit lie in the same plane.

The above discussions about velocity increment at apogee of transfer orbit is true when the launch is carried out at the equator (0° latitude). In case the satellite is launched from other sites (launching station latitudes other than 0°) then the satellite's final

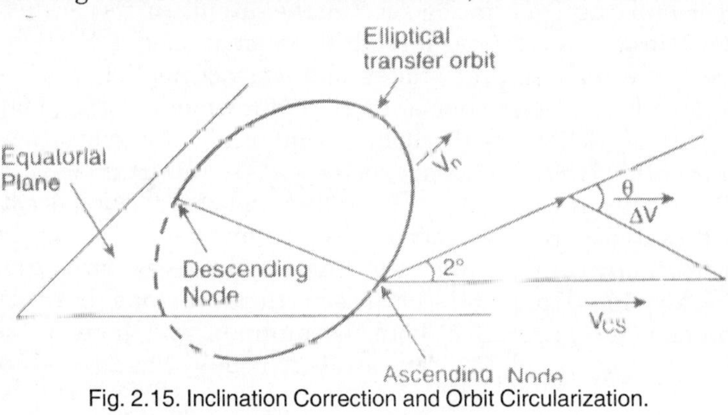

Fig. 2.15. Inclination Correction and Orbit Circularization.

orbit would be a synchronous orbit with an inclination i greater than or equal to the latitude of the launch point. It is therefore then essential to have an *orbit inclination correction manoeuvre.* Since the inclination of transfer orbit is the angle between the plane of the transfer orbit and the equatorial plane, correction of this inclination will help in converting the transfer orbit plane into the equatorial plane. Fig. 2.15 shows this orbit inclination correction. This orbit inclination correction is obtained by applying a velocity increment at one of nodes of the orbit which will cause a resultant velocity vector in the equatorial plane. Thus the magnitude of the incremental velocity vector ΔV required to correct the inclination is

$$\Delta V = \sqrt{V_n^2 + V_{cs}^2 - 2V_n V_{cs} \cos(i)} \qquad ...(2.41)$$

where V_n is the velocity magnitude at node and V_{cs} is the satellite velocity in geostationary orbit in the equatorial plane. If the line connecting the apogee and perigee is the node line and the inclination correction is made at the apogee in conjunction with orbit circularization, then

$$\Delta V = \sqrt{V_{as}^2 + V_{cs}^2 - 2V_{as} V_{cs} \cos(i)} \qquad ...(2.42)$$

Thus for $i = 28$, $V_{AS} = 1.61$ km/s and $V_{CS} = 3.07$ km/s, the incremental velocity required to correct the orbit inclination and to achieve orbit circularization obtained from Eq. (2.42) is $\Delta V = 1.81$ km/s. It is evident from Fig. 2.15 that the angle θ at which the main axis of satellite is correctly oriented relative to the satellite velocity in a plane perpendicular to the line of nodes is derived from expression given by

$$\theta = Arc \sin \left(\frac{V_{cs} \sin(i)}{\Delta V} \right) \qquad ...(2.43)$$

Since V_{cs} is nearly equal to V_{as} so θ is nearly equal to $2i$.

2.9. Station keeping

The importance of station keeping the satellite in its geostationary (synchronous) orbit has already been mentioned in Section 2.1 where the 'window' in which the satellite may be kept always is also explained. It is also mentioned there that a window corresponding to a drift of 75 km on the sphere containing the geostationary satellite orbit is allowed. This corresponds to an angular shift of $\pm 0.1°$ in longitude for the fixed satellite and also for broadcasting satellite services. This station keeping accuracy of $\pm 0.1°$ has been internationally standardized by CCIR. It is always essential that in station keeping whatever the orbit correction techniques be utilized, the propellent consumption should be minimum and therefore some kind of strategy is followed. The strategy usually has several steps as given below. Firstly the direction and speed of drift of the satellite is determined. Then by extrapolation prediction is made as to which day the satellite will escape the window and a few days before this date the true orbit is determined using a new series of measurement. After that calculations are carried out regarding the date, the amplitude and duration of the velocity increments required to modify the orbital parameters. Appropriate thrusters are then fired and then the effects of correction are monitored.

Compensation of the inclination increments correspond to *North-South (N-S) station keeping* and requires a thrust impulse perpendicular to the orbital plane. *East-West (E-W) station keeping* (as well as quick relocation to a different satellite position in the geostationary orbit) are obtained by applying thrusts in the orbital plane. The above mentioned station keeping accuracy of ± 0.1° actually corresponds to *E-W* accuracy. Internationally there is no such demand on *N-S* station keeping accuracy. However, it should be noted that *NS* corrections are considerably more costly in terms of fuel expenditure for the reaction equipment (thrusters) and therefore for moderate *NS* movements correction are not carried out at all. For this reason, the satellite is launched into a slightly inclined orbit such that inclination decreases from its maximum value (i_{max}) to zero and then again increases to i_{max}. Then if the planned lifetime of the satellite is T_L years, i_{max} would be approximately

$$i_{max} = \frac{1}{2} i_{av} T_L \qquad ...(2.44)$$

were i_{av} is the natural annual change of inclination averaged over the lifetime T_L. A typical value for long lived satellite is $i_{av} = 0.86°$ which corresponds to the velocity increment correction of $\Delta V = 460$ m/s. Compared to this, the required velocity increment correction for east-west station keeping of ± 0.1° is around 27 m/s which is much less than required for *NS* station keeping. Thus if the ground network could tolerate complete absence of *NS* corrections of the orbit of a nominally geostationary satellite, more than 90% of the thruster fuel for station keeping may be saved. This allows for an extra useful payload on board the satellite. Though this is an attractive tradeoff but involves careful consideration of the wider pointing or beamwidth margins of the antennas required in the absence of *N-S* station keeping.

2.10. Satellite Stabilization

Even if a perfect station keeping manoeuvre is carried out, the satellite may display motions about its center of mass. This will disturb the pointing of satellite antennas narrow beam towards the earth. It is therefore essential that the satellite be perfectly balanced. It may be noted that the disbalancing of satellite is caused by several reasons such as gravitational force from the sun, moon, and planets, solar pressure acting on the antennas, spacecraft body and solar cells, and earth's magnetic field etc. These forces vary cyclically through a 24th period and cause wobbling of the spacecraft which requires to be damped out mechanically. This is achieved by the techniques called *Satellite stabilization or attitude control*.

The disbalanced satellite may display its motion on either of the three axes as shown in Fig. 2.16. These axes are termed yaw, roll and pitch axes. If the satellite is stabilized about these axes, the stabilization is termed as *three axis body stabilization* and the corresponding satellite is calld *three axis body stabilized satellite*. Since a rotating body offers an inherent gyroscopic stiffness to torques tending to disturb the orientation of the rotational axis, so this technique may be used to stabilize the satellite. This kind of satellite stabilization is called *spin stabilization*. Fig. 2.17 shows the spin stabilized satellite. Here the spin stabilization is achieved by rotation of the geostationary satellite body between 30 and 120 rpm creating an inertial stiffness which maintains the satellite spin axis perpendicular to the equatorial plane. The satellite spin axis is thus North/South oriented. The spin stabilization has the disadvantage that it requires the use of a de-spun antenna. Thus here the satellite is cylindrical spinning about the axis of the cylinder. Solar cells cover the cylindrical surface and antennas are mounted on a de-spun plateform. The despun section is kept stationary by counter rotation so that the antennas mounted on it are constantly pointing toward the earth. In the three axis body stabilized satellite as shown in Fig. 2.18 a spinning momentum wheel within the satellite establishes

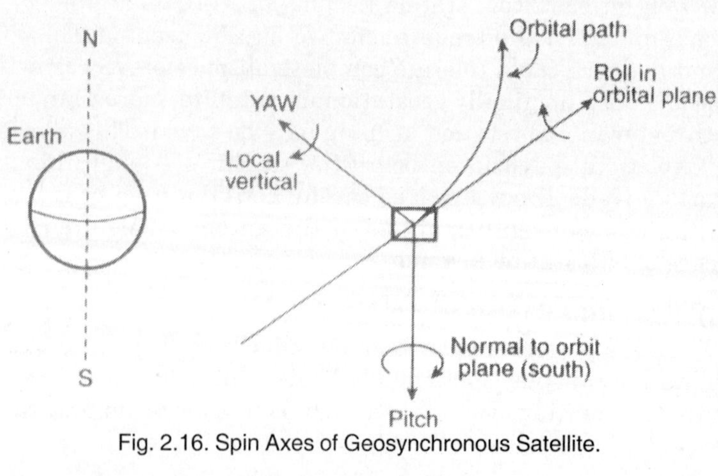

Fig. 2.16. Spin Axes of Geosynchronous Satellite.

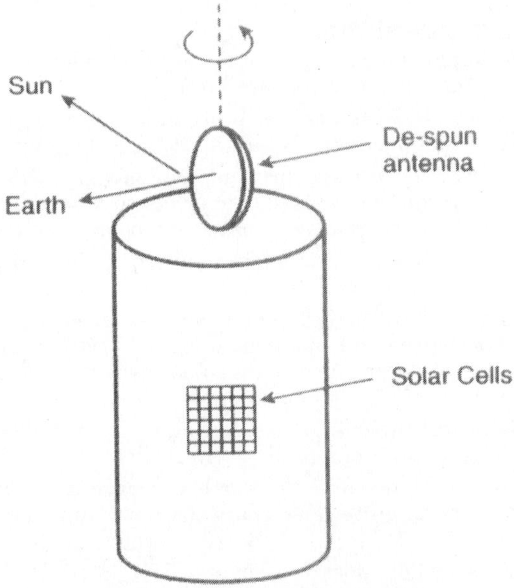

Fig. 2.17. Spin Stabilized Satellite.

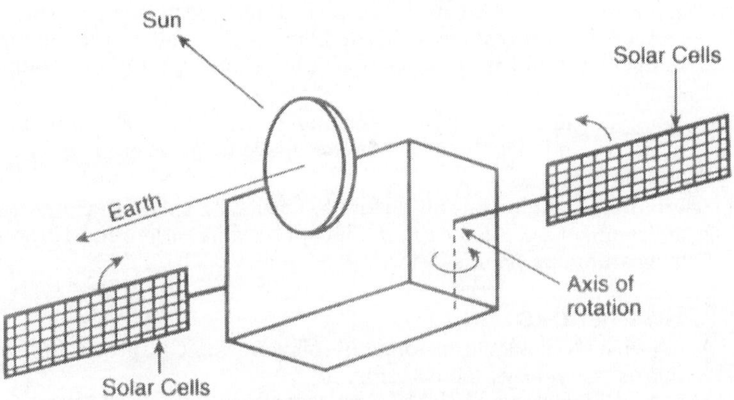

Fig. 2.18. Three Axis (body) Stabilized Satellite.

the same frame of reference as the spinning cylinder of the spin stabilized satellite. In this case, however the entire spacecraft is effectively the despun platcform which maintains its orientation in space relative to the momentum wheel axis. The solar cells in such kind of stabilized satellite are mounted on panels external to the spacecraft body, allowing them to be oriented toward the sun. The control system is therefore more complex for a three axis body stabilized satellite.

2.11. Review Questions

1. Explain Kepler's laws of planetary rotation. How are these applied to the case of geostationary satellite ?
2. Name the orbital aspects which are of importance in synchronous satellite communication. Explain these aspects in brief.
3. Explain as to how the synchronous orbit of a geostationary satellite is being determined ? Also explain as to why the geostationary satellite are not capable of illuminating polar regions ?
4. What are the orbital parameters required to determine a satellite's orbit ? Name and explain them.
5. Explain as to how the location of satellite in an orbit is carried out with respect to earth ? What are direct and retrograde orbits ? Also explain the ascending, descending nodes, right ascension and nodal regression.
6. What is meant by look angles ? Explain them with reference to a geostationary satellite and the earth station.
7. How can one determine the earth coverage and slant range for geostationary satellite ? What are the maximum values of the two parameters ?
8. Explain as to how does the solar eclipse affect the working of a communication satellite ? Mention the duration and the month when the eclipse effects are maximum ?
9. Explain as to how a satellite is placed into geostationary orbit from earth ? What is transfer orbit and how is the orbit correction for the launch of satellite at latitutde other than equator is obtained ? Explain.
10. What is meant by station keeping of satellite ? Explain its significance and also the methods to achieve it. What are N-S and E-W station keeping ?
11. What is meant by the satellite stabilization ? Explain the importance of stabilization. Also explain the spin stabilization and three axis body stabilization of satellite.

2.12. References

Alongwith the books mentioned in references of Chapter 1, following books and articles may also be referred.

1. Ash, M.E., Determination of Earth satellite orbits, Tech Note 1972-5, Lincoln Laboratory, MIT, April, 1972.
2. Ash, M.E., Communications Terminal Orbit Calculations, Tech Note 1973-74, Lincoln Lab, MIT, May 24, 1973.
3. Kaplan, M.H., Modern Spacecraft Dynamics and Control, New York, Wiley, 1976.
4. Miya, K., Satellite Communications Engineering, Tokyo, Lattice, 1975.
5. Martin, J., Communications Satellite Systems, Englewood Cliffs, NJ, Prentice Hall, 1979.
6. Fithenakis, E., 1984, Manuals of Satellite Communications, NY, McGraw Hill.

7. Van Trees, H.L., Ed, 1979, Satellite Communications, NY, IEEE Press.
8. Mittra, R., Imbriade, W.A., and Maariders, E.J., Satellite Communication Antenna Technology, North Holland, Amsterdam, 1983.
9. Avdnyevsky, V.S., Uspensky, G.R., Scientific and Economy Oriented Space Systems, MIR Publishers, 1988, Moscow.
10. Smith, F.L., 1972, A Nomogram for look to geostationary satellites, IEEE Trans Aerospace and Electtron Sys., Vol AES No. 5 (May), p. 394.
11. CCIR, 1982, Report 843, Station Keeping Techniques for Geostationary Satellites, Vol II, Geneva.

3

Communication Satellite Link Design

3.1. Introduction

The development of satellite-communication systems is constrained by various external factor[1,2]. The most important of these are the demand for the services that satellites can economically provide, the geometry of suitable orbits, the available radio frequency allocations and the cost of launching satellite of the necessary mass into the desired orbit. The design of satellite link is quite important as it gives the estimate of power that the satellite would be able to receive from the transmitting earth satellite and the power received from satellite repeater by the receiving earth station. This link budget calculation takes into account several factors such as absorption by the space media through which the satellite signals propagate, various kind of noise sources and the various design considerations of the earth station. In fact the main controlling factor in the design of links is the frequency of the uplink and downlink (6/4 GHz). It may be noted that the satellite links may be point to point (uplink and downlink) or point to multipoint (Direct Broadcasting links). In this chapter link design considerations are given for the uplink and downlink.

The frequency allocations and band spectrum to be used in communication satellite are discussed already in Section 1.4. The optimum radio frequency range of satellite communications is determined technically by (*a*) absorption, scattering and refraction phenomena rising in the atmosphere, (*b*) galactic noise and thermal nose emitted by the atmosphere, (*c*) the feasibility of constructing satellite antennas with gains appropriate to the service area required. The best frequency range for systems serving fixed earth stations is about 1-10 GHz. The lower limit is set mainly by galactic noise and the size and mass of satellite antennas. A lower minimum is appropriate for wide coverage systems using a relatively high earth station-noise temperature. A higher minimum is preferable where relatively small area of earth's surface is to be served. The upper limit is usually set by attenuation due to heavy rain. A higher limit is acceptable where rain is seldom very heavy. Molecular absorption by gasses is also important at higher frequencies such as absorption lines of oxygen and water vapour at 22 GHz, 60 GHz and 180 GHz. However, in the present calculations attenuation is limited to 6/4 GHz only.

The cost of launching a satellite is extremely high and is now over $ 100,000 cast. per kg per launch with final positioning. This limits the size and weight of the satellite. This causes deployment of limited number of solar cells, and limited size of satellite antennas. These size limitations combine to produce a situation in which the spacecraft has a limited RF output power which can not be concentrated onto a very small areas of the earth. The resulting flux density at the earth's surface for a typical communications satellite is – 127 dB W/m^2 [(3)]. A direct broadcast satellite using a 200 W transmitter and directional beam can achieve – 100 db W/m^2. This is very weak signal compared to that found in terrestrial microwave links and all satellite systems are constrained by this problem. This limited satellite transmitter power and antenna size (gain) are compensated by large earth receive antennas and low noise amplifiers, In the present day communication satellites narrow beam antennas are used in satellite. This has increased the requirement for precise satellite positioning, station keeping and antenna pointing with a consequent increase in the amount of onboard fuel required for the above mention functions.

It may be noted that now larger satellites can be launched by space shuttle which in fact carries the satellite first into low earth orbit and then injects it into geostationary orbit. Space shuttle is capable of lifting nearly 30,000 kg into low earth orbit. Payloads as large as 2,000 kg in geostationary orbit are readily achievable and it is projected that payloads as large as 6,000 kg will be available when high energy upper stages are developed to transport satellites from low earth orbit to geostationary orbit. This increased size in satellite will allow the use of larger diameter antennas with their narrow antenna beams which will create the potential for generating several independent beams on board the satellite. When a particular region or a country is to be served, the antenna beam may be shaped to follow the contour of the region requiring coverage. The technique was firstly used in INTELSAT III and is now quite popular in domestic satellite systems.

3.2. General Link Design Equations

In satellite communications links design the important calculation is the power received by the receiving station (satellite receiver and the earth station). This calculation is similar to that of the simple radio link as shown in Fig. 3.1. The transmitting source is considered to be located in free space and may be supposed to radiate the power P_T watts uniformly in all directions (isotropic radiation). Of course an isotropic radiation is physically not possible as it is not possible to create transverse polarised electromagnetic wave. Normally a directive antenna is used in satellite communication link and the directivity, as shown in Fig. 3.1 is represented by a finite beam of

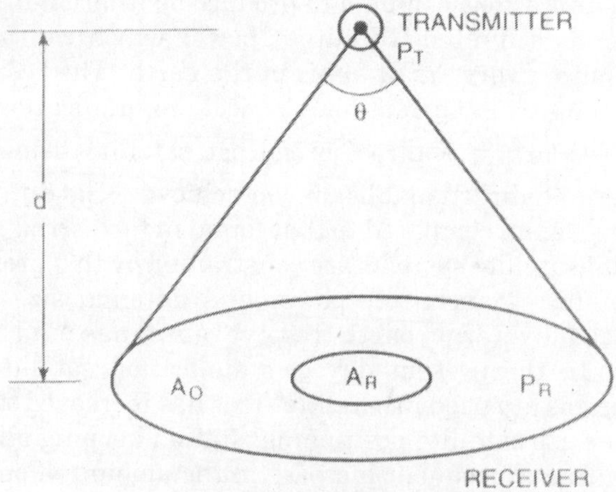

Fig. 3.1. Geometry of a Simple Radio Link.

width θ. The receiver is characterized by the effective area A_R of its antenna and by the noise temperature T of its low noise amplifier (LNA). For the moment, the temperature T is not considered. In Fig. 3.1 the transmitting antenna beam illuminates an area A_0 at the receiver. The distance between transmitter and receiver is d. Thus the receiving antenna intercepts the fraction A_R/A_0 of the transmitted power. Therefore the power received by the receiving antenna is given by

$$P_R = P_T A_R/A_0 \qquad ...(3.1)$$

The directivity of antenna is described by its gain as

$$G_T = \frac{4\pi d^2}{A_0} \qquad ...(3.2)$$

which is actually the ratio of the area illuminated by an isotropic antenna to that illuminated by the antenna in question. From Eqs. (3.2) and (3.1), one gets

$$P_R = P_T G_T A_R / (4\pi d^2) \qquad ...(3.3)$$

The product $P_T G_T$ is called *effective isotropic radiated power* (EIRP of the transmitter and is a figure of merit for a transmitter. The receiving antenna gain G_R is related to its effective area A_R by the relationship

$$G_R = \frac{4\pi A_R}{\lambda^2} \qquad ...(3.4)$$

Substituting Eq. (3.4) into Eq. (3.3) one gets

$$P_R = P_T G_T G_R \left(\frac{\lambda}{4\pi d}\right)^2 \qquad ...(3.5)$$

The power attenuation expressed in decibels is

$$\alpha_{dB} = 10 \text{ Log}_{10} \frac{P_T}{P_R}.$$

Thus $$\alpha_{dB} = 22 + 20 \text{ Log}_{10}\left(\frac{d}{\lambda}\right) - G_T - G_R \qquad ...(3.6)$$

where G_T and G_R represent the antenna gains in decibels. In Eq. (3.6) the first two factors, namely $22 + 20 \log_{10} (d/\lambda)$ constitute what is called as path Loss or free space loss (L_{FS}). Thus

$$L_{FS} = 22 + 20 \text{ Log}_{10} (d/\lambda) \ dB \qquad ...(3.7)$$

This free space loss L_{FS} is expressed in dB and actually expresses the signal power attenuation between two isotropic antennas in free space. Eq. (3.7) indicates that this free space loss varies with frequency, the higher the frequency, the higher the free loss. However, this increased loss is compensated by the increase in the antenna gain with increased frequency, for a given antenna aperture area. Thus the path Loss between a satellite in geostationary orbit and the earth station (sub satellite point) is 195.6 dB and 199.1 dB at 4 GHz and 6 GHz respectively.

Eq. (3.5) represents the caso for an idealized situation. In real sense there would be a variety of losses and so instead of L_{FS} it may be L, where $L = L_{FS} * L_A$ (L_A being the additional losses). Thus Eq. (3.5) gives

$$\frac{P_R}{P_T} = \frac{G_T G_R}{L} \qquad ...(3.8)$$

Here the additional losses L_A be written as[4]

$$L_A = L_{FTX} {}^* A_{AG} {}^* A_{rain} {}^* L_{POL} {}^* L_{Point} {}^* L_{FRX} \quad ...(3.9)$$

where

L_{FTX} = losses between the transmitter output and the transmitting antenna (wiring, duplexers, filters etc),

A_{AG} = attenuation by the atmosphere and ionosphere,

A_{rain} = attenuation due to precipitations and clouds,

L_{POL} = losses caused by polarization mismatch between the transmitting and receiving antenna

L_{point} = losses caused by a antenna depointing,

L_{FRX} = losses between the receiving antenna and the receiver input (wiring, duplexer etc).

Thus Eq. (3.8) can be written as

$$P_R = EIRP + G_R - L_{FS} - L_{FTX} - A_{AG} - A_{rain} - L_{POL} - L_{Point} - L_{FRX} \quad ...(3.10)$$

It may be noted that the gain of an antenna is expressed in terms of the actual surface area A by the equation

$$G = \frac{4\pi\,\eta\,A}{\lambda^2} \quad ...(3.11)$$

where η is the efficiency of the antenna. The product ηA corresponds to the effective surface area A_R in formula (3.4). Normally the efficiency of 60% is taken as good though some antennas may achieve efficiency upto 70%. It would be of importance to mention that the received power P_R in Eq. (3.5) is also commonly referred to as *carrier power* (C) in satellite communication.

3.3. System Noise Temperature, C/N and G/T Ratio

The *noise temperature* is an important parameter that governs the performance of receiver and therefore the design of satellite links. Infact the most important source of noise in the receiver is the thermal noise in its preamplifier. The noise power P_N in the receiver is given by

$$P_N = KTB \quad ...(3.12)$$

where T is the receiver noise temperature, B is the bandwidth and K is the Boltzman constant.

Actually P_N is the available noise power and is delivered only to a device that is impedance matched to the source. The system noise temperature T_s is also called the *effective input noise temperature* of the receiver and is defined as the noise temperature of a noise source located at the input of a noiseless receiver which would produce the same contribution to the receive output noise as the internal noise of the actual system itself. The equivalent noise source T_s is usually located at the input to the receiver replacing the antenna. The receiver has a *RF* amplifier and *IF* amplifier prior to its demodulator. So, if the overall *RF* and *IF* gain of the receiver is *G* (*G* is ratio, not *dB*) and its narrowest bandwidth is *B*, the noise power at the demodulator input is

$$P_n = KT_s BG \qquad ...(3.13)$$

If P_r is the signal power at the input to the *RF* section of the receiver, the signal power at the demodulator input would be P_rG. Hence the carrier to noise ratio (*C/N*) at the demodulator input is given by

$$\frac{C}{N} = \frac{P_r G}{KT_s BG} = \frac{P_r}{KT_s B} \qquad ...(3.14)$$

In Eq. (3.14) T_s represents the several sources of noise in the receiver in the form of system noise temperature. In case the individual noise temperatures and the gain of corresponding individual units are available, an expression for T_s may be derived. Thus, let the *RF* amplifier, down converter (mixer) and *IF* amplifier by noiseless units with their respective equivalent noise temperatures as T_{rf}, T_m and T_{if}. Similarly let their respective gains be G_r, G_m and G_{if}. If T_{in} is input noise temperature at the *RF* section then the total noise power at the output of the *IF* amplifier would be given by

$$P_n = G_{If} K\, T_{If} B + G_{If}\, G_m\, K\, I_m\, B + G_{If}\, G_m\, G_{RF}\, KB\, (T_{RF} + T_{in}) \qquad ...(3.15)$$

T_{in} is actually the noise temperature of the antenna measured at the receiver input. Rewriting Eq. (3.15) in the following form as

$$P_n = G_{If}\, G_m\, G_{Rf}\left[\frac{KT_{If} B}{G_m\, G_{If}} + \frac{KT_m B}{G_{RF}} + kB\,\{T_{Rf} + T_{in}\}\right]$$

$$= G_{If}\, G_m\, G_{Rf}\, KB\left[T_{Rf} + T_{in} + \frac{T_m}{G_{RF}} + \frac{T_{If}}{G_m\, G_{Rf}}\right] \qquad ...(3.16)$$

In terms of T_s, the same noise power P_s at the output of *IF* amplifier would be given by

$$P_n = G_{If}\, G_m\, G_{Rf}\, KT_s\, B \qquad ...(3.17)$$

From Eqs. (3.16) and (3.17) one gets

$$KT_s B = KB\left[T_{Rf} + T_{in} + \frac{T_m}{G_{RF}} + \frac{T_{if}}{G_m G_{Rf}}\right]$$

or

$$T_s = \left[T_{Rf} + T_{in} + \frac{T_m}{G_{RF}} + \frac{T_{if}}{G_m G_{Rf}}\right] \quad ...(3.18)$$

It would be of importance to note that beyond *IF* stages, the noise contributed by other units are negligible. From Eqs. (3.5) and (3.8), Eq. (3.14) can be rewritten as

$$\frac{C}{N} = \frac{P_T G_T G_R \left(\frac{\lambda}{4\pi d}\right)^2}{KT_s BL_A} \quad ...(3.19)$$

If $N_0 = N/B$ which is also called the noise power spectral density (W/Hz) the carrier power to noise power spectral density ratio is given by

$$\left(\frac{C}{N_0}\right)_{dBHz} = \underset{\text{EIRP (dBW)}}{10\text{Log}\, P_T G_T} - \underset{\text{free Space Loss } (dB)}{20\text{Log}\, \frac{4\pi d}{\lambda}} + 10\text{Log}\frac{G_R}{T_s} - \underset{\text{Additional Loss}}{10\text{Log}\, L_A} - 10\text{Log}\, K \quad ...(3.20)$$

In above equations G_R/T_s represents a ratio (dBK^{-1}) that can be used to specify the 'quality of an earth station Eq. (3.19) shows that (C/N) and G_R/T_s and so increasing G_r/T_s, C/N increases. This G_r/T_s ratio is widely known as G/T ratio and is the *figure of merit*.

For standard A earth station (*e.g.* used in Intelsat network) G/T ratio is 40.7 dB K^{-1} at 4.0 GHZ and 5° elevation angle. It should be noted that while describing the G/T ratio especially at 4 GHz, it is essential to specify the frequency and elevation angle because G_r varies as f^2 across the frequency band and T_s depends on sky noise temperature, which increases as the elevation angle is reduced below 10°. At higher frequencies, say 11 GHz, the noise contribution of low noise *rf* amplifier is higher and since the narrow functional bandwidth are used, the variations in G_r and T_s are quite small. Satellite antennas have negative G/T, *i.e* it is below 0 dB K^{-1}. Here the numerical value of G_r is smaller than the numerical value of T_s.

It would be of importance to note that any increase in the earth station system noise temperature may be made offset by an increased antenna diameter or satellite power, if the system capacity is to remain unchanged. At 4 GHz, the earth-station designs normally exhibit the system noise temperatures of 65-75 K at a 5° elevation angle. Such a system noise temperature comes from four main components : 25 K being due primarily to atmospheric attenuation in the main beam, the remainder being due to sidelobe pickup, the low noise amplifier and miscellaneous ohmic losses in the feed and waveguide system. These latter components usually contribute approximately 15 K each.

3.4. Atmospheric and Ionospheric Effects on Link Design

The free space loss and other losses (such as those of atmospheric and ionospheric) encountered when the satellite signals traverse the propagating medium are explained in Eq. (3.8). Rain attenuation problems were also explained in Section 3.1 while deciding the frequencies for upper link and lower links. In this section the atmospheric and ionospheric attenuation will be discussed in some details. It is widely known that the atmospheric and ionospheric propagation are subject to absorption, diffusion (or diffraction), refraction, rotation of the polarization plane of the electromagnetic wave. These effects are dependent on the path length and so are more

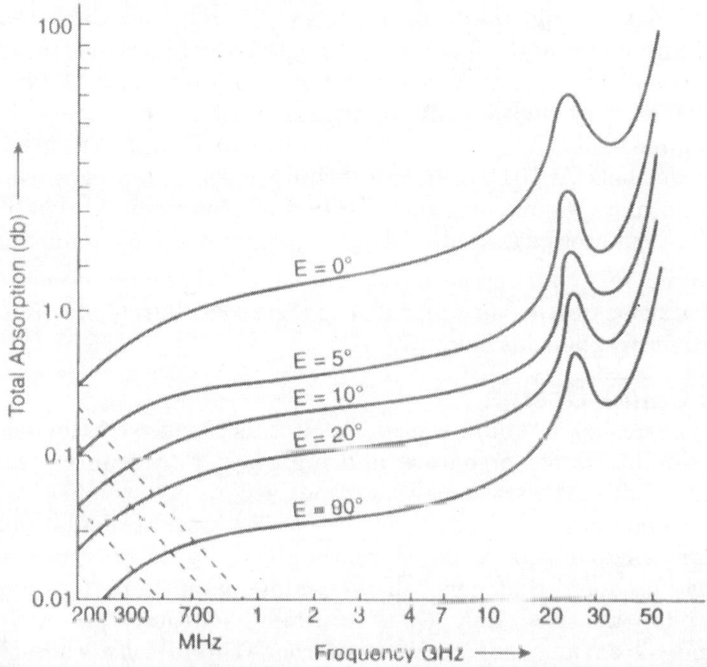

Fig. 3.2. Total Atmospheric Attenuation as a Function of Frequency for Different Elevation Angles E. Solid Lines (———) Represent Tropospheric Attenuation and Dash Lines(----) Represent Ionospheric Attenuation.

pronounced at small elevation angles. The lower layers of atmosphere cause absorption and diffusion. These cause some kind of emission and so an increase in the noise power at the receiving antenna is created. The upper layer of the atmosphere (the troposphere) causes refraction and the depolarization is produced when the radio waves traverse the ionosphere.

Atmospheric attenuation is of no importance at frequencies below 10 GHz but as mentioned in Section 3.1 there are a few molecular resonance absorption lines at which the signal attenuation is extreme. Oxygen and water vapour have such absorption bands but these are of no significance at 6/4 GHz. Fig. 3.2 represents a set of typical total atmospheric attenuation curves as a function of frequency for different elevation angles. It is evident that the atmosphere has a small effect on the link quality at frequencies between 2 GHz and 10 GHz and for high elevation angles.

The rain attenuation depends on frequency, rainfall rate, diameter and distribution of raindrops. It is estimated by the formula.

$$A_{rain} = \gamma_r L_e \quad ...(3.21)$$

where γ_r is the specific rain attenuation in db/km and L_e is the effective path length. Various reports of CCIR are available regarding rainfall rate and effective path lengths as a function of elevation angle for different zones of the world. At the frequencies 4 and 6 GHz except at very heavy rain conditions, rain attenuation effect is negligible. Under very heavy rain conditions, the rain attenuation is a few decibels. At 10 GHz and above the atmospheric and rain effects become more significant and margins of approximately 20-30 dB would be necessary at 30 GHz to give protection against fades occurring for small percentages of the time[2]. Actually the contribution of noise due to rains and ionospheric scintillation etc are quite small for frequencies below 30 GHz.

3.5. Uplink Design

The design of uplink is easier as in this case firstly the noise at the satellite is of no concern and high power transmitter can be designed at earth station so as to put accurately specified carrier power density at the satellite transponder input. Calculations for uplink design may be easily carried out by using Eq. (3.8) and (3.14). It may be noted that generally speaking, satellite performance is limited by the down link because far more additional power can be provided from an earth station than from a satellite. This additional power is large enough to allow us to neglect (in a simple analysis) the noise contributions caused in the satellite receiver[5]. In above uplink power budget calculations the nonlinear effects of the travelling wave tube amplifier in satellite transponder are not included. Here it is assumed that the TWTA is working near its linear region and so the above equations are valid for small power gains. The nonlinear effects are included by including back off terms. In that case equation of C/N_0 for uplink is given by

$$\left(\frac{C}{N_o}\right)_{uplink\ in\ dBHz} = 10 \log P_T G_T - 20 \log \frac{4\pi d}{\lambda} + 10 \log \frac{G}{T} - 10 \log L_A - 10 \log K - BO_i \quad ...(3.22)$$

where BO_i is the input back off in dB[7]. This backoff is of the order of 3 to 7 dB.

3.6. Complete Link Design

A single complete link consists of two earth stations and a satellite. Here radio relay is done by the satellite. Thus the complete link is made up of *uplink* and *downlink*. Therefore the ultimate information quality received on earth depends on the uplink, the satellite transponder and the downlink. The uplink is characterized by the carrier power (signal power) to noise power spectral density ratio $(C/N_0)_U$ at the transponder input. The downlink is similarly characterized by the ratio $(C/N_0)_D$. The carrier to noise power spectral density ratio $(C/N_0)_T$ at the receiving earth station taking into account the uplink and downlink can be derived in the following way. The useful carrier (signal) at the receiving earth station receiver input is given as

$$C = \frac{C_u G_B G_T G_R}{L} \quad ...(3.23)$$

where C_u is the signal power at the satellite transponder input (uplink power), G_S, G_T and G_R are the satellite transponder gain, the satellite transmitting antenna gain and the receiving station antenna gain respectively, L is the loss on downlink. The noise power spectral density at the input to receiving earth station receiver would be given by

$$N_0 = N_{0D} + N_{0u} (G_s G_T G_R) / L \quad ...(3.24)$$

where N_{0u} is the noise power density at the transponder input and N_{0D} is the noise power density at the input to receiving earth station receiver. Thus

$$\left(\frac{C}{N_0}\right)_T = \frac{C}{N_0} = \frac{C_u G_s G_T G_R / L}{N_{0D} + N_{0u} (G_s G_T G_R) / L}$$

$$= \frac{C_u}{N_{Ou} + \dfrac{N_{OD} \cdot L}{G_s\, G_T\, G_R}} \qquad \text{...(3.25)}$$

Now, if the transponder has bandwidth B and radiates a constant power P_T, its gain G_s would be expressed by

$$G_s = \frac{P_T}{C_u + N_{Ou} {}^* B} \qquad \text{...(3.26)}$$

For downlink only the signal power C_D is

$$C_D = \frac{P_T\, G_T\, G_R}{L} \qquad \text{...(3.27)}$$

Thus
$$\frac{C}{N_O} = \frac{C_u}{N_{Ou} + \dfrac{N_{OD} \cdot L\, (C_u + N_{Ou} {}^* B)}{P_T \cdot G_T\, G_R}}$$

or
$$\frac{C}{N_O} = \frac{C_u}{N_{Ou} + \dfrac{N_{OD} \cdot (C_u + N_{Ou} {}^* B)}{C_D}}$$

$$= \frac{(C/N_O)_u \cdot (C/N_O)_D}{(C/N_O)_D + (C/N_O)_u + B} \qquad \text{...(3.28)}$$

In most of the cases, B is much smaller than $(C/N_O)_D$ and $(C/N_O)_u$. So neglecting B, Eq. (3.28) gives

$$(C/N_O)_T^{-1} = (C/N_O)_u^{-1} + (C/N_O)_D^{-1} \qquad \text{...(3.29)}$$

Normally $(C/N_O)_u$ is much greater than $(C/N_O)_D$. Though N_{OD} is much higher (around 10 times) than N_{Ou}, C_u is around 100 times higher than C_D. Therefore, $(C/N_O)_u$ is 10 times $(C/N_O)_D$. In such a case

$$(C/N_O)_T \cong (C/N_O)_D \qquad \text{...(3.30)}$$

Thus the overall (complete) link design depends on the quality of downlink and especially on $(C/N_O)_D$. Since with a geostationary satellite the value of $(C/N_O)_D$ depends only on EIRP of the satellite plus the figure of merit of the earth station, Eq. (3.30) indicates that in the complete design link the capabilities of satellite transmitter and earth station receiver are dominant factors.

Eq. (3.29) may be extended to include the effects of interfering signals too. If I represents the noise power involved with the interfering signals under the bandwidth of the desired carrier than, the net (C/N) ratio is given by (for uplink)

$$(C/N)_{Net\ uplink} = [(C/N)_u^{-1} + (C/I)_u^{-1}]^{-1} \qquad \text{...(3.31)}$$

where $(C/N)_u$ is the carrier to noise ratio for uplink in the absence of interference signals and $(C/I)_u$ is the carrier to noise ratio of the interference signals for uplink. A similar expression for downlink net carrier to noise ratio is given by

$$(C/N)_{Net\ downlink} = [(C/N)_D^{-1} + (C/I)_D^{-1}]^{-1} \quad ...(3.32)$$

Thus from Eq. (3.29) the net carrier to noise ratio is given by

$$(C/N)_{Net} = [(C/N)_{Net\ uplink}^{-1} + (C/N)_{Net\ downlink}^{-1}]^{-1}$$

$$= [(C/N)_u^{-1} + (C/I)_u^{-1} + (C/N)_D^{-1} + (C/I)_D^{-1}]^{-1}$$

$$= [(C/N)^{-1} + (C/I)^{-1}]^{-1} \quad ...(3.33)$$

where $$(C/I)^{-1} = (C/I)_u^{-1} + (C/I)_D^{-1} \quad ...(3.34)$$

Here C/N represents the carrier to noise ratio of overall link and C/I the carrier to interference ratio of the overall link. In case $C/I > C/N$ where (C/I) is considered to be of the order of 20 dB or more and is at least 3 dB larger than (C/N), the satellite link is called *noise-dominant*. For $C/I < C/N$, the link is called *interference dominant*. Thus for a given C/N a complete satellite link between two earth stations may be designed to achieve a specified performance. It would be worthwhile to mention here that then limiting factor for (C/N) in almost all satellite systems is the threshold effect in the receiver demodulator. There exists a linear relationship between the signal to noise ratio (S/N) of the demodulator output and the (C/N) at the demodulator input provided that (C/N) is above a specified threshold. For a typical *FM* demodulator the output S/N after the demodulator is given by

$$(S/N)_{out} = (C/N)_{in} + FM\ \ improvement \quad ...(3.35)$$

It is evident from Eq. (3.35) that one can obtain adequate (S/N) with low (C/N) at the receiving system. This is because of *FM* improvement term and therefore it is the main reason for using *FM* in satellite communication, particularly with the analog signals. In terms of power ratios rather than db, Eq. (3.35) can be written as

$$\left(\frac{S}{N}\right)_{out} = \frac{C * FM \text{ improvement}}{N_{in}} \quad ...(3.36)$$

3.7. Interference Effects On Complete Link Design

The interference effects on the satellite complete link design has been taken into Eq. (3.31) by way of including the noise power of interfering signals (power I) and carrier to I ratio. These interfering signals contributing to noise power are usually uplink thermal noise and satellite intermodulation contributions. In practice, in addition to these extra noise signals some other kind of interference may be experienced at the receiving earth station. One such important interference arises from terrestrial microwave links. As mentioned previously the 6/4 GHz frequency bands allocated to the satellite communications are also allocated to the terrestrial microwave links. Thus the receiving earth station working at 4 GHz band is susceptible to interference from terrestrial microwave transmissions at 4 GHz. Similarly the transmitting earth station working at 6 GHz may generate interference into terrestrial microwave reception at 6 GHz. Thus there may be mutual interference between an earth station and a terrestrial microwave system. It has been established that this mutual interference (*M*) is a function of the carrier power, the carrier spectral density and the frequency offset between the two carriers [(8)]. This interfering signal, may be reduced by using carrier frequency offset. The details of such technique will be discussed in later chapter while discussing analog signal propagation over the satellite link. The standard specification for such interference power has been 25 dB below the satellite carrier power. In other words the carrier to terrestrial interference ratio is 25 dB.

Another kind of interference that comes into effect in satellite link is the *cross-polarization interference and depolarization* caused by rain. The cross-polarization interference arises with satellite links which employ orthogonal polarization to transmit two different channels on a common or overlapping frequency band. Actually this arises in satellite communications systems that use frequency reuse techniques where either the orthogonal linear polarization (vertical and horizontal linear polarizations) or orthogonal circular polarizations (left-hand and right-hand circular polarization) are being used for transmission purposes. In such cases there may exist a conversion/coupling of some of the energy in a transmitted signal from one polarization to another. This arises from the finite cross-polarization discrimination of the earth station and satellite antennas and by the depolarization caused by the rain. Since rain has little effect in 6/4 GHz band, so it is mainly the discrimination provided by the earth station and satellite antennas that determines the cross-polarization interference.

The *cross-polarization discrimination* is defined as the ratio of the power received in the principal polarization to the power received in the orthogonal polarization from the same incident signal and thus it represents the carrier to cross polarization interference ratio when the two polarized signals have the same power. 30 to 40 dB cross polarization discrimination has been achieved for high quality antennas along the antenna axis. It should be noted that in the complete satellite link this cross-polarization discrimination is to be considered for both the uplink and downlink. Thus if X_1 and X_2 represent the cross polarization discrimination of earth station and satellite antennas respectively the minimum net link cross polarization discrimination is given by

$$X_{\min} = \frac{1}{2}(X_1^{-1} + X_2^{-1})^{-1} \qquad ...(3.37)$$

$X_{\min}$ is actually the worst case carrier to cross polarization interference ratio $(C/I)_x$ and can be used in Eqs. (3.33) and (3.34) as an additional interference source to obtain the total carrier-to-noise ratio plus the interference ratio.

The third kind of interference that might take place in a satellite link is the adjacent channel interference (or adjacent transponder interference). This arises mainly in band limited channels. The situation is severe where the High Power Amplifier (HPA) and or the satellite TWTA operate near or at saturation point. (Detailed studies on adjacent channel interference would be carried out in chapter dealing with digital modulation techniques). Actually, working at or near saturation point the TWTA may also create *inter symbol interference* which also degrades the link performance. In linear channels the intersymbol interference may be removed by using the *Nyquist pulse shaping criterion*. For nonlinear channels it can not be removed and so the degradation in C/N ratio occurs. This degradation represented in terms of dB should be taken into account in Eqs. (3.33) and (3.34).

3.8. Earth Station Parameters

From Eq. (3.19), the C/N ratio is given by

$$\frac{C}{N_0} = \frac{P_T G_T G_R}{N_0}\left(\frac{\lambda}{4\pi d}\right)^2 \frac{1}{L_A} \qquad ...(3.38)$$

Here d is the range between transmitting and receiving antennas. The antenna parameters such as its diameter D and antenna beam width θ_{3dB} affect the C/N_0 as these are linked to the gain by the expressions given by

$$G = \eta\left(\frac{4\pi D}{\lambda}\right)^2 \qquad ...(3.39)$$

and

$$G = \frac{\eta 4\pi^2 70^2}{\theta_{3dB}^2} \qquad ...(3.40)$$

where η is the antenna efficiency. The satellite antenna beamwidth $(\theta_{3dB})_{sat}$ is determined by the required earth coverage. For a given earth station antenna diameter D_{ES}, Eq. (3.38) gives C/N_0 as

$$\frac{C}{N_0} = \frac{P_T}{L_A N_0} \eta_T \eta_R - \frac{\pi^2 70^2}{d^2} \frac{D_{ES}^2}{(\theta_{3dB})_{sat}^2} \qquad ...(3.41)$$

where η_T and η_P are the efficiencies of transmitting and receiving antennas respectively. It is evident from Eq. (3.41) that frequency does not come into the C/N_0. However, if the earth station antenna beamwidth (θ_{3dB}) is fixed, then C/N_0 is given by

$$\frac{C}{N_0} = \frac{P_T}{L_A N_0} \eta_T \eta_R \frac{\pi^2 C^2 70^4}{(4d)^2 (\theta_{3dB})_{sat}^2 (\theta_{3dB})_{ES}^2 \cdot f^2} \qquad ...(3.42)$$

Eq. (3.42) shows that C/N_0 increases with low frequencies. In case antenna diameter D_{SAT} and D_{ES} are given (which may be due to restricted dimension of the launcher fairing and from the need to avoid a deployable antenna), the expression for C/N_0 reduces to

$$\frac{C}{N_0} = \frac{P_R}{L_A N_0} \eta_T \eta_R \left(\frac{\pi D_{sat} D_{ES}}{4dC} \right)^2 f^2 \qquad ...(3.43)$$

In such cases C/N_0 increases with frequency. It may be recalled that it is the G/T ratio that characterizes the earth stations. This is due to the fact that (C/N) is directly related to G/T. The minimum to maximum value of G/T varies between $-10\ dBK^{-1}$ upto 46 dBK^{-1}. Actually most satellite communication systems are designed around a specified earth station G/T and there may be minimum earth station G/T that can be used in the system. For example INTELSAT standard A earth stations are required by Intelsat to have a G/T of 40.7 db or greater at 4 GHz and 5° elevation angle. Before an earth station is permitted to join the network it has to prove INTELSAT that this G/T ratio is achieved. Thus an optimum, value of G/T ratio is to be achieved by having a compromise between the cost of a large antenna, to increase G and the cost of lower system noise to decrease T. A large antenna earth station therefore uses cryogenically cooled low noise amplifier in an attempt to obtain the lowest possible system noise temperature. With the small earth station antenna, it has been found that increasing the antenna aperature area is more cost effective than to lower the system noise temperature.

3.9. Review Questions

1. What are the factors that affect the uplink design and the downlink design in geostationary satellite communications ? Discuss in detail.
2. Derive general link equations. Find out expressions for *C/N* and *G/T* ratios. Explain the importance of these ratios on satellite link design.
3. What is the system noise temperature ? How does it affect the *C/N* and *G/T* ratios ?
4. A satellite at a distance of 40,000 km from a point on the earth's surface radiates a power of 2 W from an antenna with a gain of 17 dB in the direction of observer. Find the flux density at the receiving point, and the power received by an antenna with an effective area of 10 m^2. If the operating frequency of satellite is 11 GHz and the receiving antenna has a gain of 52.3 dB, find the received power.

   [**Ans.** Flux density $= 4.97 \times 10^{-15} W \cdot m^2$,
   Power received = – 133 dBW for both the cases]
5. For a satellite earth station receiver working on 4 GHz, the typical various gains and noise temperatures are $T_{in} = 50\,K$, $T_{RF} = 50\,K$, $T_m = 500\,K$, $T_{IF} = 1000\,K$, $G_{RF} = 23\,dB$, $G_m = 0dB$, $G_{IF} = 30\,dB$. Calculate the system noise temperature.

   [**Ans.** $T_s = 107.5\,K$]
6. For an earth station having an antenna of diameter 30m and overall efficiency of 68%, the working signal frequency is 4150MHz. At this frequency the system noise temperature is 79 K when the antenna points at the satellite at an elevation angle of 28° K. Calculate *G/T* ratio of the earth station. In case the sky noise temperature rises to 88 K, what would be the new G/T ratio ?

   [**Ans.** 41.6 dBK^{-1}, 41.2 dBK^{-1}]
7. Consider a single channel per carrier (SCPC) link between two earth stations via a geostationary satellite. Voice is transmitted using 8 bits and QPSK modulation. The satellite ensures total coverage of the earth. Antenna gain is 20 dB, and the noise temperature as its receiver input is 1000 K. The two earth stations have 2 m diameter antennas, and the receiver noise temperature is 125 K. The same antenna is used for both transmission and reception. Calculate the power transmitted by the satellite and the earth station, knowing that the uplink is at 6 GHz and the down link at 4.6 GHz.
8. How is the uplink design different than the downlink design ? In what conditions a complete satellite link become down link limited ?
9. What are the various interferences that may effect the satellite link performance ? Explain as to how these interference effects are taken into account in the satellite link design ?
10. Explain the parameters that control the design of earth station. What is the optimum *G/T* ratio for a standard *A* earth station ?

3.10. References

1. Rechtin, E., Basic Constraints of Space Communications, in Space Communications (Ed : Balkrishnan, A.V.) pp 4-30, McGraw Hill Book Co., 1963.

2. Back, R.E., Wilkinson, D. and Withers, D.J., Commercial Satellite Communication, Proc IEE, IEE Review, Vol 119, No 8 R, Aug., 1972, pp. 929-955.
3. Pratt, T. and Bostian, C.W., Satellite Communication, John Wiley & Sons, NY, p. 1986.
4. Maral, G and Bousquet, M., Satellite Communications Systems, John Wiley & Sons, 1986.
5. Reudink, D., Advanced Concepts and Technologies for Communications Satellites, in Advanced Digital Communications (Ed K. Feher), Prentice-Hall Inc, 1987, p. 573.
6. Bhargava, V.K., Haccoun, D., Matyas, R., and Naspal, p.p., Digital Communication by satellite, John Wiley & Sons, NY, 1981.
7. Ha, T.T., Digital Satellite Communications, MacMillan Co., NY, 1986.

4

Satellite Analog Communication

4.1. Introduction

During 1960's analog communication was predominant in terrestrial communication systems and therefore such analog voice and video transmission systems were also adopted in commercial communication satellites with the use of FDM/FM/FDMA techniques. Since in such modulation techniques the signal had no amplitude fluctuation, the transmitter could be operated in its most efficient manner, that is with full power. A user may not need full bandwidth of the satellite transponder and so several signals may be transmitted simultaneously and independently (FDM) provided they are amplified undisturbed. However, when several carriers occupy a transponder there is a loss of communications capacity resulting from the nonlinear channel characteristics. Infact with fdm satellite systems intermodulation products are also present and a common TWTA that amplifies the multiple carriers may exhibit amplitude as well as phase nonlinearities particularly while operating at its saturation point. This causes an increase in the level of intermodulation products affecting the overall performance.

In the modern communication satellites, however, digital modulation methods are used as it helps to transmit the signals in time division multiplexing mode (TDM). This has also been assisted by the expansion of digital systems, particularly accelerated by the advances in solid state devices that have made possible rugged, reliable and cost effective signal processing equipments. The various other advantages of digital satellite communications are already mentioned in Section 1.8. It may be noted that in several satellite communication systems like those of INTELSAT huge investment has already been made of FDM/FM telephone systems and are still widely used. And therefore in this chapter the satellite analog communication techniques are discussed.

4.2. Baseband Analog (Voice) Signal

The baseband signal may be analog or digital. The analog baseband signal is the voice signal (in the form of voltage) generated by a telephone set. The digital baseband signal is the output from a computer terminal or so. The digital baseband signal would be discussed in next chapter. Normally the characteristics of a baseband voice signal would depend on the speaker but the Bell system treats it as having a flat spectrum extending from 300 to 3100 GHz. CCITT has recommended 3000 to 3400 Hz for it and this is being followed now internationally *e.g.* Intelsat system follows the same. The spectrum of such a baseband voice signal is represented in the form of a triangle[(1)]. Fig. 4.1 indicates the spectrum of baseband voice signal. The normal spectrum represents a triangular with the peak in the reader's right (Fig. 4.1 *a*) and the inverted spectrum is the triangle with the peak in the reader's left. It may be noted that the spectrum is really not triangular but conventionally it is taken as triangular[(1)].

As usual the amplitude of baseband voice signal of telephone output is expressed in terms of signal powers *i.e.* in terms of *transmission level* with respect to a reference point. The signal power at the reference point is indicated by the unit dbmo where o represents zero transmission level point or the test point. Thus a –2 dbmo signal means a signal producing an average power of –2 dbm at the reference point. The CCIR assumes that the long term average power carried by a single voice channel in a telephone system is taken to be – 15 dbmo. However, in most of the cases, it is taken as – 18 dbmo. The peak instantaneous power in the channel is about 18 db higher or 0 dbmo. Thus telephone equipment is often adjusted by applying a 1 kHz tone at 0 dbmo to the system to simulate peak power on one channel. This is termed the *test tone.* RCA bases its designs on –22 dbmo but the Bell System uses –19.8 dbmo for terrestrial FDM/FM links and –22 dbmo for some satellite links.

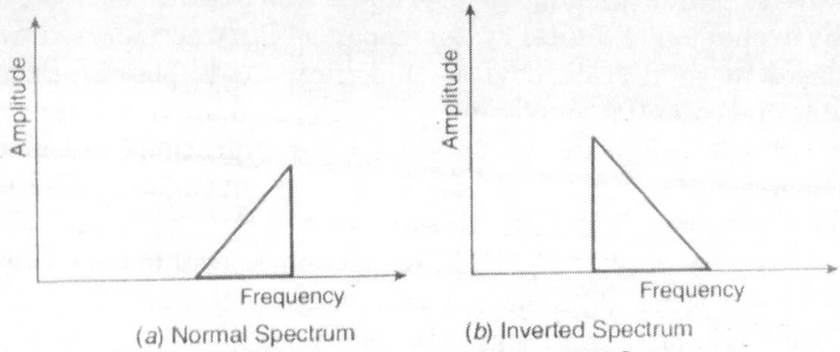

(*a*) Normal Spectrum, (*b*) Inverted Spectrum.

Fig. 4.1. Spectrum of Baseband Voice Signal from a Telephone Set

4.3. Frequency Division Multiplexing Techniques

As previously mentioned in satellite communications (analog) frequency modulation is being used. From economic point of view several users can share a satellite and so the satellite link will normally relay many signal from a single earth station. The transmission of these different signals in a form that these do not interfere with each other is termed multiplexing. For analog communications it is *frequency division multiplexing (FDM)* and for digital communications it is *time division multiplexing (TDM)*. Here we shall discuss only *FDM*. In a simplified approach, the *FDM* allows transmission of signals on different frequencies whereas in the *TDM* the signals enter the transponder at different times.

The FDM scheme for the satellite communications is shown in Fig. 4.2. Actually each satellite has a certain number of transponders which work as receiver-transmitter pair. The satellite receiver is a wide-band receiver and it covers the entire range of uplink frequencies. Though the uplink frequency is said to be around 6 GHz, it has a bandwidth of 500 MHz to accommodate various channels. In Fig. 4.2 (*a*) this uplink frequency range is from 5.925 to 6.425 GHz (a bandwidth of 500 MHz) that incorporates 12 channels. The wideband receiver of the satellite will receive all these 12 different channels. In order that these 12 different channels may not interfere with each order, each channel is assigned a bandwidth of 36 MHz with a 4 MHz spacing between channels. Above 12th channel there is a 20 MHz command and control of telemetry channel. After having these different frequencies received by the satellite wide band receiver, the transponder converts the uplink frequency ranges in the form as shown in Fig. 4.2 (*b*). This range of downlink frequencies varies between 3.72 to 4.20 GHz.

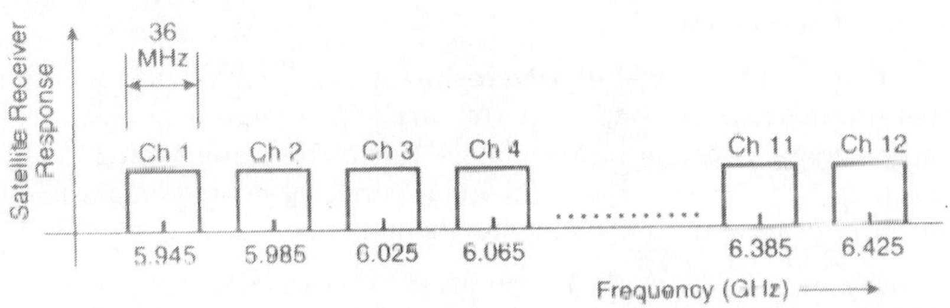

(a) SATELLITE RECEIVER CHANNELS.

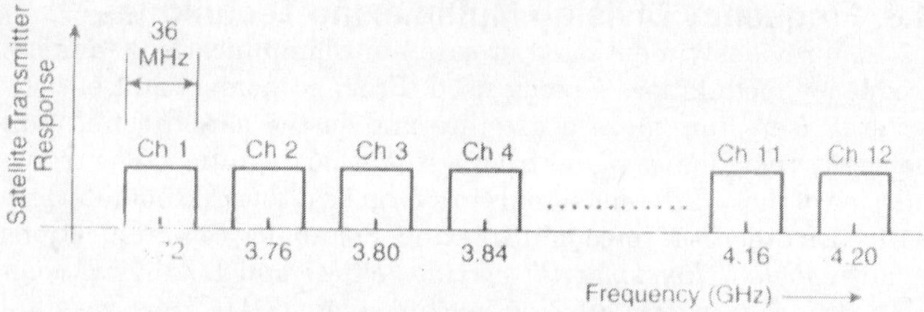

(b) SATELLITE TRANSMITTER CHANNELS

Fig. 4.2. Frequency Division Multiplexing in a Communication Satellite

4.4. Signal to Noise (S/N) Ratio and (C/N) Ratio in Frequency Modulation in Satellite Link

Frequency modulation has poor spectral efficiency but it offers wider bandwidth and considerable *S/N* (signal to noise ratio) improvement. This *S/N* ratio at the output of FM detector is much larger than the carrier to noise ratio (C/N) at the detector input provided that the input (C/N) is above a threshold value that is characteristics of that detector. This larger value of S/N in FM has actually allowed for the use of frequency modulation in satellite analog communication links. In subsequent discussions we shall see as to how this improvement in S/N ratio of the FM detector occurs.

A frequency modulated signal is expressed by

$$E(t) = A \cos(\omega_c t + m \sin \omega_{mt}) \quad ...(4.1)$$

where ω_c is the carrier frequency, ω_m is the modulating signal and m is the *FM* modulation index given by

$$m = \frac{\Delta\omega}{\omega_m} \quad ...(4.2)$$

where $\Delta\omega$ is the frequency deviation. It is related to the instantaneous amplitude of the modulating signal (A_m) by the expression

$$\Delta f = KA_m \quad ...(4.3)$$

where K is constant.

Thus frequency modulation results when the deviation Δf of the instantaneous frequency f from the carrier f_c is directly proportional to the instantaneous amplitude of the modulating voltage. The frequency spectrum of the fm modulated signal consists of an infinite series of discrete components and may be expressed as

$$E(t) = A \{J_0(m) \cos \omega_c t + \sum_{n=1} J_n(m) [\cos(\omega_c + n\omega_m) t + \{(-1)^n \cos(\omega_c - n\omega_m) t]\} \quad ...(4.4)$$

where the $J_0, J_1, ... J_n$ are Bessel functions of the first kind and order 0, 1, 2, ...n. From Eq. (4.4) it is evident that the FM signal has infinite number of side frequencies and so has infinite bandwidth. However, for most of the transmission purposes a finite bandwidth is needed and so some of the side frequencies need to be filtered out by means of a band limiting filter. This finite bandwidth of FM signal is represented by Carson's rule

$$B = 2 f_m (m + 1)$$
$$= 2 (\Delta f + f_m) \qquad ...(4.5)$$

Here Δf is the peak frequency deviation of the system, and f_m is the modulating frequency. It may be noted that the spectrum of an fm waveform modulated by a real signal is much more complicated than that for a single-frequency sinusoid. In such a case f_m is replaced by f_{max}, the maximum modulating frequency and then

$$B = 2 (\Delta f + f_{max}) \qquad ...(4.6)$$

The energy associated with the sidebands outside the bandwidth B is very small and so when the fm, signal is passed through a filter of bandwidth B, very little distortion occurs in the resulting FM signal. Now, the output of a FM detector is the original modulating waveform (signal) whereas the input to the FM detector is the FM signal. Thus the bandwidth of the detected output signal is much smaller than that of the input signal. The means that a bandwidth compression has been achieved by the FM detector. There is an improvement in the signal-to-noise ratio $(S/N)_o$ accociated with this bandwidth compression.

In practice, the performance of a conventional FM receiver in the presence of random fluctuation noise is commonly judged on the basis of the variation of the output signal to noise $(S/N)_0$ power ratio as function of the carrier to noise power ratio $(C/N)_i$ measured at the input to the limiter. Since there is an improvement in $(S/N)_0$ so this $(S/N)_0$ may be considerably larger than $(C/N)_i$ (even upto 20 dB or so). The relationship between the $(S/N)_0$ and $(C/N)_i$ at FM detector is given by[2]

$$(S/N)_0 - (C/N)_i \left(\frac{3}{2} m^2\right) \qquad ...(4.7)$$

$$(S/N)_{0dB} = (C/N)_{idB} + 10 \log \frac{3}{2} m^2 \qquad ...(4.8)$$

The factor 10 kg (3/2) m^2 expresses in decibels precisely the improvement afforded by the FM system is return for a sacrifice for bandwidth. The relationship Eq. (4.8) is plotted as that shown in Fig. 4.3. It is evident that as $(C/N)_i$ decreases, a point is reached where

$(S/N)_0$ falls off much more sharply than $(C/N)_i$. This point represents a *threshold* value of $(C/N)_i$. However, the threshold value of $(C/N)_i$ is arbitrarily taken to be the value at which $(S/N)_0$ falls 1 db below the dashed extension. It may be noted that for higher m, the threshold $(C/N)_i$ is also higher. It has been observed that the threshold of a full improvement with FM $(S/N)_0$ occurs when $(C/N)_i$ is about 12 decibels. For all values of the carrier greater than the threshold, the output $(S/N)_0$ is proportional to the input $(C/N)_i$. The above mentioned fm improvement has been discussed for a single channel FM system. The case of a multiplex system will be discussed in the next section. With a phase detector, Eq. (4.7) of signal-to-noise improvement ratio is given by

$$(S/N)_0 \,/\, (C/N)_i = (\Delta\phi)^2 \qquad ...(4.9)$$

where $\Delta\phi$ = peak phase deviation. The above discussion about the $(S/N)_0$ improvement was limited to the case of a single frequency sinusoidally modulated FM signal. For the case of a non sinusoidal modulating signal *e.g.* for the case where spectrum of the modulating waveform extends from 0 to f_{max} Hz, the $(S/N)_0$ is given as

$$(S/N)_0 = (C/N)_i \cdot \frac{3}{2}\frac{B}{f_{max}}\left(\frac{\Delta f_{peak}}{f_{max}}\right)^2 \qquad ...(4.10)$$

where B is the bandwidth expressed in terms of Carson's rule as

$$B = 2\,f_{max}\,(1 + m) \qquad ...(4.11)$$

Here f_{max} is the highest modulating frequency and Δf_{peak} is the peak frequency deviation. Since

$$m = \Delta f_{peak} / f_{max} \qquad ...(4.12)$$

Eq. (4.10) gives

$$(S/N)_0 = (C/N)_i \; 3(1 + m)\, m^2 \qquad ...(4.13)$$

For large m, $3(1 + m)\, m^2 \approx 3m^3$

Similarly, for $m \ll 1$, $3(1 + m)\, m^2 \approx 3m^2$

Thus Eq. (4.13) shown that better $(S/N)_0$ can be improved by increasing the carrier power (or in other words) by increasing the level of modulating baseband signal) to the maximum extent possible until the distortion exceeds a specified value. The distortion occurs because eventually the frequency deviation exceeds the specified IF bandwidth.

Now, an audio baseband signal the power spectral density is relatively high in the low frequency range and falls off rapidly at higher frequencies. For example, speech has little spectral density above about 3 kHz. And while music, of course extends farther into the high frequency range, the feature still persists that most of its

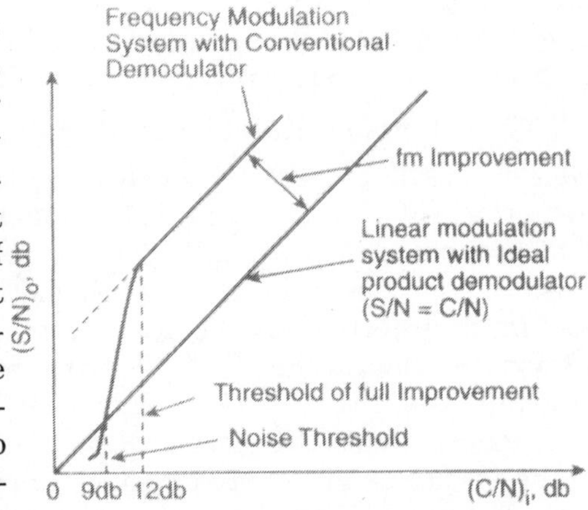

Fig. 4.3. Threshold in FM Detector.

power is in the low frequency region. Thus if the spectrum of the sidebands associated with a carrier frequency modulated by an audio signal is examined, it is noticed that power spectral density of the sidebands is greatest near the carrier and relatively small near the limits of the allowable frequency band allocated to the transmission. The signal-to-noise ratio is also improved for transmitting fm audio signals by using preemphasis networks in the transmitting systems and deemphasis networks in the demodulating networks. An improvement of 6.7 dB occurs when pre-emphasis is being used. Actually the spectral density of high frequency components of audio signal is rated to a high level by pre-emphasis and so the improvement in SNR occurs.

4.5. S/N Ratio in Frequency Modulation with Multiplexed Telephone Signals in Satellite Link : (Noise Performance in Telephone Channel)

The above calculation of $(S/N)_0$ is for the multiplexed signal. In the present section, the signal to noise power ratio in the worst (top) voice channel at the output of the demodulator will be discussed. The worst (top) voice channel means that this particular channel is located at the high frequency end of the multiplex signal. The signal to noise ratio for this kind of worst channel case is given by[1]

$$(S/N)_{\omega c} = (C/N)_i \, (B/b) \left(\frac{\Delta f_{rms}}{f_{\max}} \right)^2 \qquad \text{...(4.14)}$$

where the subscript ωc represent worst channel, b is the voice channel bandwidth (usually 3100 Hz), B is the rf bandwidth, Δf_{ms} is the rms frequency deviation and $(C/N)_i$ is the overall carrier to noise ratio of the link. Since the frequency response of either the human ear or telephone receiver is not flat, so the telephone listener will respond differently to noise in different parts of the audio spectrum And therefore some of the noise that is present in bandwidth b will be unnoticed and the effective signal to noise ratio will be higher than that given by Eq. (4.14) by a certain factor that is widely termed as *weighting factor* whose values actually depends on the frequency response of the telephone receiver and of the user's ear.

The Bell System calls this weighting factor as *C-message weighting*. The CCITT calls it *psophometric weighting factor*$^{(p)}$ whose numerical value is 1.78 (2.5 db). It would be worthwhile to mention that 'psophometrically weighted power' means that the noise power has been measured using a psophometric filter that takes into account the filtering effect of the human ear on noise. In the previous section the improvement of S/N ratio resulting from the use of pre-emphasis circuit has already been discussed. In FDM/FM telephone systems therefore such pre-emphasis/de-emphasis networks are used and so a pre-emphasis improvement factor q is to be included in S/N ratio. Thus, taking into account both the psophometric weighting factor p and pre-emphasis improvement factor q, the expression (4.14) of $(S/N)_{\omega c}$ becomes

$$(S/N)_{\omega c} = (C/N)_i\ (B/b) \left(\frac{\Delta f_{\text{rms}}}{f_{\max}}\right)^2 pq \qquad \text{...(4.15)}$$

which may be rewritten in the decibel form as

$$(S/N)_{\omega c} = (C/N)_i + 10 \log_{10} (B/b) + 20 \log_{10} \left(\frac{\Delta f_{\text{rms}}}{f_{\max}}\right) + p + q \text{ dB} \qquad \text{...(4.16)}$$

where p is 2.5 dB and q is 4 dB. The above quantities Δf_{rms} and B are also used to calculate the number of channels N carried by a multiplex telephone signal and to the available transponder bandwidth. For such a calculation the concept of *rms test-tone deviation* (also abbreviated at Δf_{rms}) is used. Actually this is a rms carrier deviation that a single 1-kHz-0 dBm sine wave called the test tone would produce when supplied to the modulator input and it represents a standardized test signal in one telephone channel. This rms test-tone deviation is related to the rms deviation caused by a multiplexed signal by a factor called *loading factor*(l) For N voice channels this loading factor is given by[1]

$$\begin{aligned} 20 \log(l) &= -1 + 4 \log_{10} (N),\ 12 \le N \le 240 \\ &= 15 + 10 \log_{10} (N),\ N > 240 \end{aligned} \qquad \text{...(4.17)}$$

The product $l\Delta f_{rms}$ is termed the *rms multicarrier deviation.* Another factor g is defined as the ratio of the peak frequency deviation Δf_p to the rms multicarrier deviation $l\ \Delta f_{rms}$, *i.e.*

$$g = \frac{\Delta f_p}{l \Delta f_{\text{rms}}} \qquad \text{...(4.18)}$$

For $N > 24$, g is taken as 3.16 (corresponding to 10 dB) and for small number of channels ($N < 24$), g has value of 6.5 (18.8 dB). Now the Carson's rule defines the channel bandwidth as

$$B = 2\,(\Delta f_p + f_{max}) \qquad ...(4.19)$$

where Δf_p is peak frequency deviation and f_{max} is the maximum frequency component of the baseband modulating signal. Eq. (4.19) combined with Eq. (4.18) gives

$$B = 2\,(gl\Delta f_{rms} + f_{max}) \qquad ...(4.20)$$

which gives the expression for Δf_{rms}, the rms test deviation as

$$\Delta f_{rms} = \left(\frac{B}{2} - f_{max}\right)/gl \qquad ...(4.21)$$

The value of B being fixed for a given transponder design, the number of voice channels per transponder is computed by an iterative procedure. Starting with an estimate for N, computed values of f_{max} and Δf_{rms} are introduced in Eq. (4.16) together with the rf channel C/N power ratio. If the resulting S/N turns out to be greater (or smaller) than the prescribed S/N (normally 51.25 dB), the estimate for N was too low (or too high) and needs to be changed until the correct value of S/N is found.

Note that the above mentioned prescribed value of weighted S/N of 51.25 dB for 1 mW test tone may be obtained as per CCIR recommendations. According to CCIR, the average noise power should not exceed 10000 pw psophometrically weighted (abbreviated as pwp). Allowing 1000 pwp for the earth station equipment noise, 1000 pwp for interference noise an 500 pwp for the earth station put-of-band noise, the balance of 7500 pwp is the noise allowed for the combination of the up and down links. Hence

$$\frac{S}{N} = 10^{-3}/(7500 \times 10^{-12}) = 1.33 \times 10^{5}$$

or

$$\frac{S}{N}\ \text{dB} = 51.25\ \text{dB} \qquad ...(4.22)$$

4.6. Single Channel Pre Carrier (SCPC) Systems

The FM-FDM is used with large earth stations which serve large capacity links. The single channel per carrier system or (SCPC technique) is suitable for small earth stations with relatively few channels. Here each channel independently modulates its own carrier and is transmitted to transponder. Earth stations using SCPC systems thus do not need expensive multiplexing and demultiplexing equipment and so the cost of such earth stations is considerably reduced. Further in such earth stations the carrier would be transmitted only when the link is active or needed. In large earth stations the carrier is always present as there are permanently assigned channels for the various other stations. This causes a continuous consumption of satellite transponder power. In SCPC the link is active for less than half the time under fully loaded conditions. This permits a considerable saving in the transponder power. The SCPC lends itself to efficient use of the spectrum in that the various carrier frequencies may be assigned to which ever station requests circuits at a given time. To accomplish this sharing requires a central control station, or equivalent means, to do the assigning on demand using manual, semiautomatic, or fully automatic methods. Also, each station must have equipment to permit a given voice channel to be switched to any of the assignable frequencies for both transmission and reception. It would be worthwhile to mention here that SCPC requires more bandwidth than FM/FDM for the same number of channels and so it is not an economical way to move large amounts of traffic over a fixed route between two earth terminals.

The signal to noise (S/N) behaviour of an SCPC link is described by Eq. (4.13) alongwith the modification for appropriate preemphasis and weighting. Using 6.3 dB for preemphasis improvement and 2.5 db for psophometric noise weighting, the $(S/N)_0$ for an analog FMSCPC system is given as

$$(S/N)_0 = (C/N_0)_i - 95.4 + 20 \log_{10} (\Delta f_p) \; dB \qquad ...(4.23)$$

where N_0 is the noise power density in Watts per hertz and Δf_p is the peak test tone deviation in hertz. It should be noted that (C/N_0) is related to (C/N) by the expression given by

$$(C/N) = (C/N_0) - 10 \log_{10} (B) \; dB$$

where B is the bandwidth given by Eq. (4.19). By using a technique called *companding* where the dynamic range of speech is compressed before transmission and is expanded after detection, an improvement in S/N is obtained. Actually companding distorts a voice waveform in a way that increases the average power by bringing the level of the soft portions close to that of the loud. By having such companding, an improvement of the order of 17 dB in S/N ratio is obtained. This modifies the relation (4.32) to the form given as

$$(S/N)_0 = (C/N_0)_i - 78.4 + 20 \log_{10} (\Delta f_p) \qquad ...(4.24)$$

A typical improvement of the order of 16 dB in S/N ratio has been obtained by such companding technique in Satellite Communication systems.

4.7. Companded Single Sideband (CSSB) Systems

The advantages of companding in FM-FDM are explained above and it is clear that an improvement of the order of 16-17 dB in overall signal to noise ratio is obtained. This is due to compression of signals at the transmit side and expansion at the receive side. The compression is obtained by a variable gain amplifier that gives more gain to weak signals than to strong signals. The expander at the receive side restores the signal's level by attenuating the low-level speech signals. During pauses in the speech signal, channel noise is further reduced by expander. Thus whereas an uncompanded FM/FDM 36 MHz could accommodate 1100 voice channels, the companding increases the capacity to about 2100 channels and with over deviation beyond its allocated bandwidth (with no loss in the quality of the channels), about 2900 channels could be carried by such a transponder.

In the single side band suppressed carrier system the individual voice channels are 'stacked' in frequency and then added to form a multiplexed telephone signal. Thus including the guardbands if each voice channel has bandwidth of 4 kHz, the same exact replica of 4 kHz would be received in the downlink and therefore the occupied bandwidth of uplink and downlink signals would be exactly 4 kHz times the number of channels. Hence, theoretically for 36 MHz, 9000 channels could be accommodated but due to certain practical considerations, only 6000 channels are allowed. Companding to this will provide improvement in overall S/N ratio.

4.8. Analog FM/FDM TV Satellite Link

For satellite TV transmission the base-band video signal (luminance and chrominance) frequency modulates a video carrier and the two audio signals frequency modulate two audio carriers. The details of the video modulation depend on the transponder bandwidth available. Typical values for network TV are a peak deviation Δf_p of 10.75 MHz and a maximum video modulating frequency f_v of 4.2 MHz.

The performance of FM-FDM television channel is expressed in terms of the peak to peak luminance signal-to-noise ratio. For a sinusoidal wave, the peak-to-peak power is $(2\sqrt{2})^2$ times the rms power. Also, the peak-to-peak value of the luminance signal is $1/\sqrt{2}$ times the peak-to-peak value of the composite television channel. Thus, from Eq. (4.10) and taking into account the preemphasis factor and weighting factor as discussed in Eq. (4.15), the peak-to-peak luminance signal-to-noise ratio for a FM-FDM TV signal is

$$(S/N)_{pp} = (2\sqrt{2})^2 \left(\frac{1}{\sqrt{2}}\right)^2 . (C/N)_i . \frac{3}{2}\frac{B}{f_{\max}}\left(\frac{\Delta f_{peak}}{f_{\max}}\right)^2 pq$$

$$= 6\left(\frac{C}{N}\right)_i \left(\frac{B}{f_{\max}}\right)\left(\frac{\Delta f_{peak}}{f_{\max}}\right)^2 pq \qquad ...(4.25)$$

where p is the preemphasis factor, q is the weighting, factor, $f_{\max}$ is the maximum video modulating frequency (4.2 MHz by US standards) and the modulation index m is the ratio of $\Delta f_{peak}/f_{\max}$. Eq. (4.25) can also be written in the form similar to Eq. (4.13) as

$$(S/N)_{pp} = 6\ (C/N)_i\ 3\ (1+m)_m^2\ pq \qquad ...(4.26)$$

In some cases, the peak frequency deviation is different than 10.75 MHz and the various parameters are as follows :

For fixed satellite service (FSS), direct broadcast satellites (DBS), these parameters are $B = 24$ MHz, $f_m = 4.2$ MHz, Δf_p $B/2 - f_{\max} = 7.8$ MHz and $pq = 12.8$ db. Then $(S/N)_{pp}$ reduces to

$$(S/N)_{pp} = 40.24 + (C/N)_i\ (dB) \rightarrow (FSS) \qquad ...(4.27)$$

$$(S/N)_{pp} = 33.53 + (C/N)_i\ (dB) \rightarrow (DBS) \qquad ...(4.28)$$

Thus, for a clear sky C/N ratio of 14 dB, the receiver (S/N) ratio for a DBS TV channel is 47.5 dB.

4.9. Intermodulation Products and their Effects in FM/FDM Systems

It has been already mentioned that TWTA while operating at its saturation point introduces amplitude as well as phase non-linearities in FM/FDM signals. This generates the intermodulation products. A typical operational characteristics of TWTA is shown in Fig. 4.4. The back off is therefore introduced in the TWTA amplifier design so that TWTA may not work near its saturation region and this will reduce the intermodulation effects. The multicarrier amplitude transfer characteristics of TWTA is represented by an odd polynomial such as[4]

$$V_0 = a_1 V_i + a_3 V_i^3 + a_5 V_i^5 + ... \qquad ...(4.29)$$

where V_0 = output voltage of TWTA

V_i = input voltage

a_i = constants having positive and negative values alternatively. Then carrier input signal is considered to be of equal amplitude and may be expressed as

$$V_i = \sum_{i=1}^{n} A \cos(\omega_i t + \theta_i(t)) \qquad ...(4.30)$$

Therefore the total input power P_{ti} is

$$P_{ti} = \frac{nA^2}{2} \qquad ...(4.31)$$

or

$$A = \sqrt{\frac{2P_{ti}}{n}} \qquad ...(4.32)$$

On substituting Eq. (4.30) for V_i into Eq. (4.29) one gets

$$V_0 = \sum_{i=1}^{n} B_n \cos[\omega_i t + \phi_i(t)] + IM + H \qquad ...(4.33)$$

where H represents harmonics kw_i that can be filtered out. IM represents intermodulation products which fail into the bandwidth of the carriers. These intermodulation products are located at frequencies $2\omega_i - \omega_{i+1}$, $\omega_i + \omega_{i+1} - \omega_{i+2}$, and so on. These fall within the transponder bandwidth and interfere with each other. Westcott[5] has calculated the amplitude B_n of the individual output carrier and the expression is given as

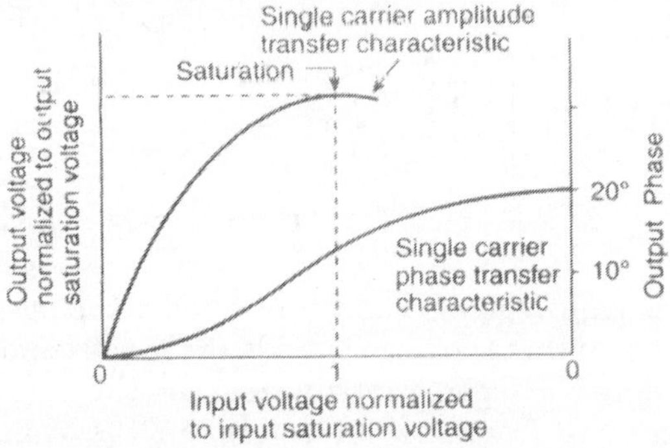

Fig. 4.4. Operational Characteristics of TWTA Near at its Saturation Point.

$$B_n = a_1\sqrt{\frac{2P_{ti}}{n}}\left\{1 + \frac{3a_3}{a_1}\left(\frac{P_{ti}}{n}\right)\left(n - \frac{1}{2}\right)\right.$$

$$+ 15\frac{a_5}{a_1}\left(\frac{P_{ti}}{n}\right)^2\left[\frac{1}{6} + (n-1)(n-2) + \frac{3}{2}(n-1)\right]$$

$$+ 105\frac{a_7}{a_1}\left(\frac{P_{ti}}{n}\right)^3 [(n-1)(n-2)(n-3)]$$

$$\left. + 3(n-1)(n-2) + \frac{34}{24}(n-1) + \frac{1}{24}] + \ldots\ldots\right\} \qquad ...(4.34)$$

Here the term $a_1\sqrt{\frac{2P_{ti}}{n}}$ gives the output amplitude due to the first term of the amplitude transfer characteristic and the term inside the brackets is the amplitude compression factor due to amplitude non-linearity. It should be noted that the third order type of intermodulation products located at frequency $2\,\omega_i - \omega_{i+1}$ and $\omega_i + \omega_{i+1} - \omega_{i+2}$ are the most dominant. Among others the fifth order types at frequency $3\,\omega_i - 2\,\omega_{i+1}$ is less important. Westcott[5] has also calculated the amplitudes $V_{2,1}$, $V_{1,1,1}$ and $V_{3,2}$ of the intermodulation products $2\,\omega_i - \omega_{i+1}$, $\omega_i + \omega_{i+1} - \omega_{i+2}$ and $3\,\omega_{i-2}\,\omega_{i+1}$ for n carrier input and his expression are given as

$$V_{2,1} = \frac{3}{4}a_3\left(\frac{2\,P_{ti}}{n}\right)^{\frac{3}{2}}\left\{1 + \frac{2a_5}{3a_3}\left(\frac{P_{ti}}{n}\right)[12.5 + 15\,(n-2)]\right.$$

$$\left.+ 105\,\frac{a_7}{a_3}\left(\frac{P_{ti}}{n}\right)^2\left[(n-2)\,(n-3) + \frac{13}{6}\,(n-2) + \frac{7}{12}\right] + ...\right\} \quad ...(4.35)$$

$$V_{1,1} = \frac{3}{2}a_3\left(\frac{2\,P_{ti}}{n}\right)^{\frac{3}{2}}\left\{1 + 10\frac{a_5}{a_3}\left(\frac{P_{ti}}{n}\right)\left[\frac{3}{2} + (n-3)\right]\right.$$

$$\left.+ 210\,\frac{a_7}{a_3}\left(\frac{P_{ti}}{n}\right)^2\left[1 + \frac{7}{4}\,(n-3) + \frac{1}{2}\,(n-3)\,(n-4)\right] + ...\right\} \quad ...(4.36)$$

$$V_{3,2} = \frac{5}{8}a_5\left(\frac{2\,P_{ti}}{n}\right)^{\frac{5}{2}}\left\{1 + \frac{49a_7}{4a_5}\left(\frac{P_{ti}}{n}\right)\left[1 + \frac{12}{7}\,(n-2)\right] + ...\right\} \quad ...(4.37)$$

Here each expression is valid only when n-x is positive or zero. It should be noted that the term outside the brackets in above three equations represents the contributions of the intermodulation products resulting from the cubic term in the transfer characteristics. The term inside the brackets which is actually the intermodulation compression factor represents the intermodulation resulting from higher order nonlinearities. It may be seen that the amplitude of the third order intermodulation product $\omega_i + \omega_{i+1} - \omega_{i+2}$ is 3 db higher than that of the type $2\,\omega_i - \omega_{i+1}$. Further since $|a_5| << |a_3|$ and also the compression factor for the fifth order intermodulation product decreases rapidly with increasing n, so the fifth and higher order intermodulation products are neglected in comparison with the third order types. The amplitude of these third-order intermodulation products may be evaluated from the single-carrier amplitude transfer characteristics. Thus, once the number of third order intermodulation products which fall in bandwidth of the respective carriers is known, the carrier to third order intermodulation ratio C/I for n carrier input can be calculated. This C/I can be used in conjunction with the carrier to noise ratio on the uplink and the downlink to determine the overall carrier-to-intermodulation plus noise ratio. The expression for carrier to (third order) intermodulation ratio $(C/I)_r$ of any output carrier r is given by

$$(C/I)_r = \frac{B_n^2}{D_{2,1}(r, n) V_{2,1}^2 + D_{1,1,1}(r, n) V_{1,1,1}^2} \quad ...(4.38)$$

where $D_{2,1}$ represents the number of third order intermodulation products that fall right on the rth carrier and is for the $2\omega_i - \omega_{i+1}$ third order type. It is expressed as

$$D_{2,1}(r\ n) = \frac{1}{2}\left\{n - 2 - \frac{1}{2}[1 - (-1)^n](-1)^r\right\} \quad ...(4.39)$$

Similarly $D_{1,1,1}(r,n)$ is for the $\omega_i + \omega_{i+1} - \omega_{i+2}$ third order type and is expressed as

$$D_{1,1,1}(r\ n) = \frac{r}{2}(n - r + 1) + \frac{1}{4}[(n-3)^2 - 5] - \frac{1}{2}[1 - (-1)^n](-1)^{n+r} \quad ...(4.40)$$

It would be worthwhile to mention here that the total n carrier output power $nB_n^2/2$ is always smaller than the total single carrier output $B_1^2/2$ because power is lost in intermodulation products. This is shown in Fig. 4.5. The *output backoff* (BO_0) of TWTA is the indicator of its power drive level and is defined as the ratio of the peak single carrier output power ($n = 1$) to the total desired n-carrier output power.

$$\text{Thus } BO_0 = \frac{B_{1,\text{sat}}^2}{nB_n^2} \quad ...(4.41)$$

In case the normalized amplitude transfer characteristics (Fig. 4.4) is used, $B_{1,\,sat} = 1$ and then

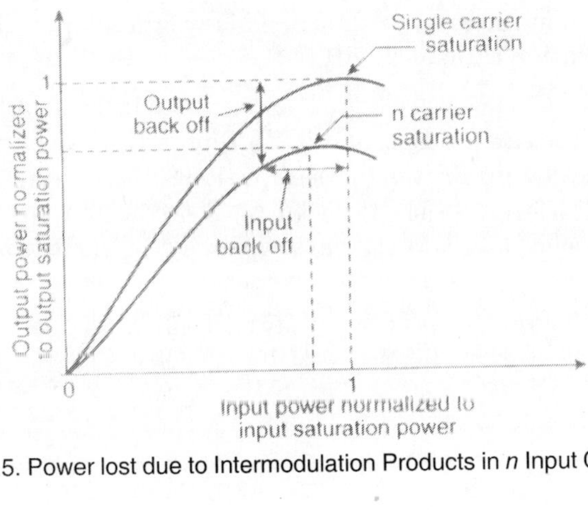

Fig. 4.5. Power lost due to Intermodulation Products in n Input Carrier.

$$BO_0 = \frac{1}{nB_n^2} \qquad ...(4.42)$$

The *input backoff* is defined as the ratio of the single carrier input power which yields the saturated output power $B_{1,\,sat}^2/2$ to the total input power of then carrier input at its operating point. Thus,

$$BO_i = 10 \log \frac{B_{1,\,sat}^2/2}{P_{ti}}$$

$$= 10 \log \frac{0.5}{P_{ti}} \qquad ...(4.43)$$

Normally, $B_{1,\,sat}^2/2$ is given. For example, a 15W TWTA means $B_{1,\,sat}^2/2 = 15W$. Thus BO_0 may be easily calculated.

Westcott[5] has also analysed the effects of intermodulation products taking into account the phase nonlinearities of TWTA. He has shown that to a first order approximation the amplitude of the dominant third order intermodulation products relative to the amplitude of the desired output signal is given by 0.1516 $K_0/_{2n}$ for $2\,\omega_1 - \omega_2$ products and 0.1516 $K_0/_n$ for the $\omega_1 + \omega_2 - \omega_3$ products. Here K_0 is the amplifier amplitude modulation-phase modulation (AM/PM) conversion coefficient (deg/dB) and is calculated from the phase nonlinearity. Typical values of K_0 range from 1.5 to 3 dB at and input backoff of 11 to 7 dB.

Thus, additional carrier to intermodulation ratio resulting from phase nonlinearity can be calculated. Typically, $K_o = 2^0$ dB at $BO_i = 11$ dB, the carrier-to-intermodulation resulting from phase nonlinearity is 26.4 dB whereas the same ratio resulting from amplitude non-linearity is 24 dB. This would give total carrier to intermodulation ratio as 22 dB.

Thus, if $(C/I)_{100}$ represents the carrier to intermodulation ratio for the center carrier 100, and $(C/I)_t$ represents the carrier to terrestrial interference ratio, $(C/I)_a$ represents the carrier to adjacent satellite interference ratio then the total carrier to noise plus interference ratio of the FDM system is given as (in line with Eq. 4.33).

$$\frac{C}{N} = \left[\left(\frac{C}{N}\right)^{-1} + \left(\frac{C}{I}\right)_{100}^{-1} + \left(\frac{C}{I}\right)_t^{-1} + \left(\frac{C}{I}\right)_a^{-1}\right]^{-1} \qquad ...(4.44)$$

Similarly if $(C/N)_u$ is the carrier to noise plus interference ratio in the uplink, $(C/N)_d$ is the carrier to noise plus interference ratio in the down link (C/I) is the carrier to intermodulation, ratio, then

$$\frac{C}{N}=\left[\left(\frac{C}{N}\right)_u^{-1}+\left(\frac{C}{N}\right)_d^{-1}+\left(\frac{C}{I}\right)^{-1}\right]^{-1} \qquad \text{...(4.45)}$$

Here $(C/N)_u$ is a function of the satellite TWTA input backoff and (C/N) is the function of TWTA output backoff. Since the TWTA input backoff BO relative to single carrier saturation is a function of the corresponding output backoff BO_0, therefore the carrier to noise plus interference ratio in the uplink is also a function of BO_0. Hence the total carrier to noise plus interference ratio of the satellite link is a function of the TWTA backoff BO_0 and by Eq. (4.45) it possesses a maximum value with respect to an optimum BO_0. Fig. 4.6 shows the graphical representation of $(C/N)_u$, $(C/N)_d$, (C/I) and (C/N) as functions of BO_0. The optimum BO_0 is the point where C/N reaches its maximum value.

4.10. Energy Dispersal in FM/FDM Signal

In a fm transmitter when the input modulating signal is absent, the transmitter radiates all of its power at the carrier frequency. With the modulation the average carrier power is spread over a large bandwidth and the larger is the amplitude of the modulating signal, the smaller is the average transmitted spectral power density in watts per hertz of bandwidth and the minimum spectral power density occurs with the maximum modulation amplitude. This condition is called *full loading*. Since terrestrial microwave systems use the same frequencies so the maximum spectral power density that a satellite may radiate towards the earth is restricted. For example in an Intelsat satellite, the radiated power per 4 kHz of bandwidth

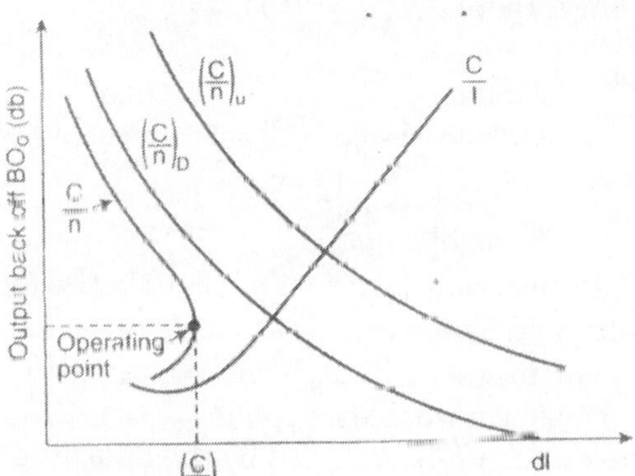

Fig. 4.6. Plot of (C/N) Ratios as a Function of BO_0.

must not rise more than 2 dB above its value for full loading. Controlling of the radiated spectral density is called *energy-dispersal*. In the uplink earth station it is done by adding a symmetric triangular waveform to the modulating waveform before modulation. This additional symmetric voltage waveform is called the *dispersal signal* and it is removed at the downlink earth station. It should be noted that type of dispersal signal (both amplitude and frequency) varies with the specific users/satellites. For example in TV transmission the dispersal signal has a constant amplitude and frequency of 30 Hz. In general the amplitude of the dispersal signal for multichannel telephone transmission is determined by finding the frequency shift (peak deviation) Δf that dispersal waveform must cause.

Miya[6] has discussed the calculations of Δf for a dispersal signal. Consider a FDM/FM analog telephone signal modulated onto a carrier whose power is c Watts and whose loading produces rms multichannel deviation dHz. Assume that the resulting spectrum is Gaussian and that its power density is W(f), then

$$W(f) = \left(\frac{c}{d\sqrt{2\pi}}\right) \exp\left[-(\Delta F)^2/(2d^2)\right] \qquad \text{...(4.46)}$$

where ΔF is the difference between the unmodulated carrier frequency f_c and f. At full loading the density W_{min} (f) and is given by

$$W_{min}(f) = \left[\frac{c}{d\sqrt{2\pi}}\right] \exp\left[-(\Delta F)^2/(2d_m^2)\right] \qquad \text{...(4.47)}$$

where d_m is the fully loaded rms multichannel deviation. At no loading the density W_{max} is determined by the deviation ΔF_{max}, which the maximum dispersal waveform causes. Assuming that the triangular dispersal signal simply spreads the carrier power c uniformly over a band that extends ΔF *Hz* on either side of the carrier frequency, then

$$W_{max} = \frac{c}{2\Delta F_{max}} \qquad \text{...(4.48)}$$

The usual practice is to choose $W_{max} = W_{min}$ (0), which gives

$$\Delta F_{max} = \frac{c}{2W_{min}(0)} = d_m\left(\frac{\pi}{2}\right)^2 \qquad \text{...(4.49)}$$

The rms multicarrier deviation d_m equals the loading factor of Eq. (4.16) multiplied by the rms test tone deviation Δf_{rms} of the link. Thus from d_m one may calculate the maximum deviation F_{max} that the dispersal waveform would be capable of producing. For less than full loading ($d < d_m$), ΔF is obtained by the following relation

$$\frac{1}{\sqrt{2\pi}} \frac{\Delta F}{d_m} = \frac{1}{\sqrt{2\pi}} \int_0^{\frac{\Delta F}{d_m} \cdot \frac{d_m}{d}} e^{-x^2/2} dX \qquad ...(4.50)$$

where the integrals may be evaluated from readily available tables.

4.11. Review Questions

1. (*a*) Compare the advantages / disadvantages of analog and digital communication through satellites.

   (*b*) What is analog baseband voice signal ? Explain its frequency spectrum. How does it compare with the digital baseband signal ?

2. What is meant by multiplexing the signals ? In analog means of satellite communication which multiplexing technique is used and why ? What are the main reasons for using multiplexing techniques in satellite communication ?

3. What is meant by 'threshold' in FM detector ? Explain FM improvement and derive the S/N ratio for SCPC signals.

4. What is loading factor and how does it affect the FM/FDM signal transmission ?

5. Compare the performance of FM/FDM SCPC and CSSB systems.

6. How does the non-linear behaviour of a TWTA affect the opera--tional characteristics (C/N) of a satellite link ? What are the inter-modulation products and how are these generated with TWTAs ? Discuss the carrier to intermodulation for amplitude nonlinearities of TWTA?

7. What is 'energy dispersal' ? Discuss its applications for satellite communication. Also, explain the dispersal signal.

8. For a SCPC-FM-FDMA system having $S/N = 33$ dB and a test tone deviation $\Delta f = 9.1$ kHz calculate the bandwidth. (For a speech signal the lowest frequency is 300 Hz and the highest frequency is $f_m = 3.4$ kHz). Also, calculate the C/N ratio of this SCPC system.

   [**Ans.** B = 25 kHz, $C/N = 14$ dB]

9. For a 60 channel FDM system with a maximum baseband frequency of $f_m = 252$ kHz and a specified top-channel signal-to-noise ratio $S/N = 52$ dB find out the bandwidth. The FDM multi-channel rms frequency deviation is 546 kHz. Also, find out the FDM multichannel loading factor, test tone rms frequency deviation and C/N ratio. The improvement in emphasis and psophometric weighting is around 6.5 dB.

   [**Ans.** B = 3.955 MHz, $l = 2$, $f_r = 273$ kHz, $C/N = 13.75$ dB].

10. Explain analog television transmission through satellite. Write down the expressions for S/N ratio calculation for satellite TV links.

4.12. References

1. Pratt, T. and Bostan, C.W., Satellite communications, John Wiley & Sons, 1986.
2. Taub, H. and Schilling, D.L., Principles of communication Systems, McGraw Hill Book Co., 1987.
3. Jordan, E.C., Reference data for Engineers, Howard W.Sams & Co., MacMillan Publishing Co., 1986.
4. Ha, T.T., Digital Satellite Communications, MacMillan Publishing Co., 1986.
5. WestCott, R.J., Investigation of Multiple FM/FDM carriers through a satellite TWTA operating near to saturation, Proc IEE (London), Vol 114, No 4, June, 1967, pp. 726-740.
6. Miya, K., Ed. Satellite Communications Engg, Lattice Publishing Co., Tokyo, 1975.

5

Digital Signal Transmission

5.1. Digital Communication

The advantages of digital communication have already been mentioned in Chapters 1 and 3. It may also be noted that the present day electronics is all digital whether it is circuitry, computer or communication. The main factors involved are compatibility, flexibility and economy available with the digital systems. As such the availability of high degrees of reliability, operating speed, miniaturization, precision in data handling and approaching the theoretical limits of communication efficiency have made the digital systems widely useful. Also, the operations and maintenance of digital systems are simplified and there are improved monitor, alarm and control mechanisms. The integrated circuit technology in particular, microprocessors, memory, MSI (medium scale integration) and VISI (very large scale integration) all have made the digital techniques quite successful.

The telegraph was the first modern form of digital communication but because of its much smaller bandwidth, voice telephone communication predominated. The voice telephone communication is basically the analog communication. With the advent of digital computers in the 1950's the communication technology entered into a new phase and it formed the genesis of today's data communication. In order to access the computers from a distance, mechanisms were developed worldwide for transmitting data over the analog voice communication systems. But due to better reliability and higher quality, digital voice telecommunication has become widespread over the last ten years and now it is in global use. The cost of transmitting the signal has also reduced considerably and this reduction has been in the exponential form. The development of monomode optical fibre has added a continuing decline in the transmitting cost. The use of digital networks has reduced the cost of private voice networks by significant factors, ranging from 10% to 30% for many large organisation.

5.2. Byte

A bit is an abbreviation for binary digit. Byte represents the storage position in the main memory. It represents one alphanumeric character in the storage and is hence six, seven, or eight bits long. Thus *byte* is a set of bits which together represent one character. Normally one byte represents 8 bits. It is also popularly known as *8 bit byte character*. In this way a 32 bit word may be portioned into four 8 bit byte or four 8 bit characters. The bytes may be grouped together to store a large integer or real number but for communications the value stored in each byte represents a character. Though the values chosen to represent a character may be arbitrary, it is essential that they are used consistently. Also, all the peripheral devices used in communications such as line printers, terminals, tape readers must conform to the same standard. The software used to interpret data has also to follow suit. The minimize the transmission errors various codes are used.

5.3. Baud

A *baud* is the unit of signalling speed and represents the speed of a communication channel. Historically it is a contraction of the surname of the Frenchman JME Baudot whose five bit code was adopted by the French telegraph system in 1877. Formally, a baud was defined as the number of codes element per second. If each signal element represents one bit of information, the baud is equal to the bit rate or bits per second. In order to remove any confusion, now a days in digital communication instead of Bauds, bits per second (bps) is used as the unit of signalling or data speed.

5.4. Elements of Digital Communication System

In any communication system one needs the sender, receiver, transmission medium, addressing and cooperation (a form of protocol between sender and receiver). The digital communication system essentially consists of the components as shown in Fig. 5.1. As compared to its analog counterpart, it has additional units of encoder and decoder and so here a knowledge of transmission codes, transmission rate, transmission synchronization, error detection and correction and transmission efficiency is needed. It would be worthwhile to note that the communication systems may be simplex or half duplex or full duplex ones. In the simplex systems communication is one way. In half duplex system communication is allowed in either direction at a time. In full duplex case communications may be done in both directions simultaneously.

In the present day standard digital voice communication, the amplitude of the voice signal is sampled at a rate of 8000 sample per second. An 8 bit value for the amplitude of the frequency is transmitted digitally. The requirement for 8000 samples per second, to faithfully reproduced voice, has become the standard on which the bulk of digital voice communication is based today. The encoding scheme is known as pulse code modulation (PCM) and requires a bandwidth of 64 kbps (8000 samples per second at bits per sample). As a result 64 kbps digital transmission has become widespread for voice communication on wide area networks and 64 kbps channels are switched in digital telephone exchange. In United States and most of the European countries, digital transmission is widely utilised and much of the world uses digital transmission links operating at 2.048 megabits per second.

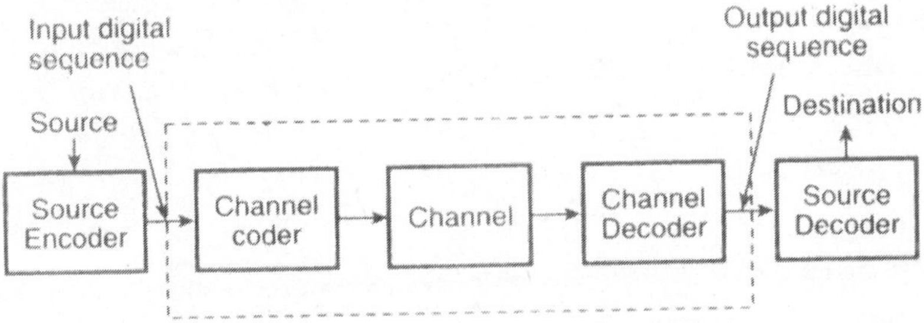

Fig. 5.1. Elements of a Digital Communication System.

In a digital communication system, a symbol is defined *by the rate at which information is sent over the link, in the form of pulses at baseband, or changes in phase angle of a carrier*, as in a PSK system. The digital transmission systems use transmission of symbols, rather than bits, because often more than one bit per symbol in an RF system is sent in order to conserve bandwidth. Digital links are designed for a specific symbol rate, but one symbol can carry more than one bit. It is important to distinguish between symbols and bits. They are easily confused because with binary modulations, such as BPSK, the symbol rate and bit rate are the same. Symbol rates are given in *band* or in *symbols per second*.

If the transmission is binary, the symbol is a bit, and the symbol has two states. When two bits are sent per symbol, the symbols have four possible states and the systems is denoted as quaternary, hence the Q in QPSK. If a symbol represents more than one bit, the system is known generically as m-ary, with one symbol having in states.

5.5. Digital Baseband Signals

The digital baseband signals are logically transmitted (serially transmitted) logical ones and zeroes. They have only two different levels of voltage or current. When the signal is at the first level (usually the most positive voltages) it is said to be ON or TRUE or a 1. Similarly when the signal is at the second level, it is said to be OFF or FALSE or a 0. This signal is very commonly used in communication because it is so simple to generate, detect and use. Since the two levels are fixed by the system that generates them, no information can be implied by the voltage level. The information has to be contained or encoded in the pattern of the levels with time. Typical example is as that of *Morse code.*

Fig. 5.2 shows some kind of digital baseband signals. Thus if S_k $(k = 0, 1, ... m_{-1})$ represents M baseband signals each of duration

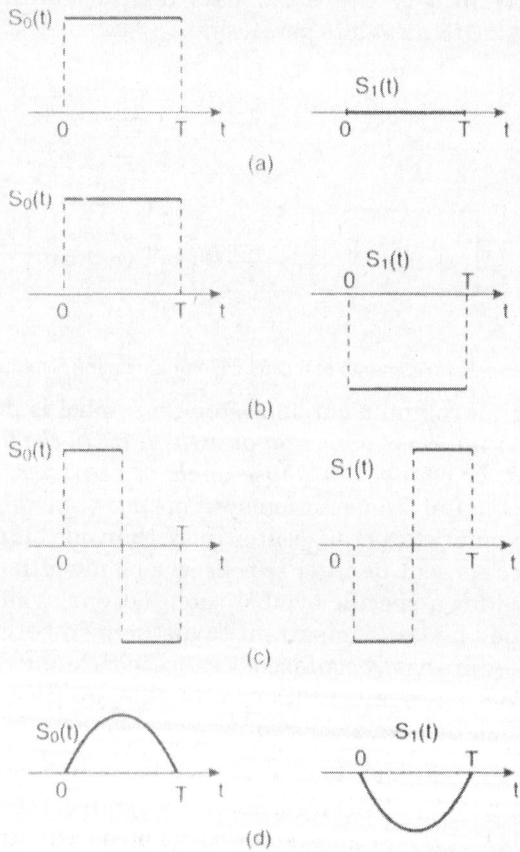

Fig. 5.2. Typical Examples of Digital Baseband Signals (*a*) and (*b*) Rectangular Pulse Waveforms, (*c*) Split Phase Pulse Waveform (*d*) Sine Pulse Waveform.

T, then their collection is called the *baseband signal set.* The energy in the kth signal in denoted by E_k. If all of the signals in the set have same energy, the common value is denoted by E. For two signals $S_k(t)$ and $s_j(t)$, their inner product (S_k, S_j) is defined as

$$(S_k, S_j) = \int_{-\infty}^{\infty} s_k(t)\, s_j(t)\, dt \qquad \text{...(5.1)}$$

The signal sets are of two kinds namely the *orthogonal signal sets* and *binary antipodal signal sets.* In general, a signal set is said to be an *orthogonal* set if $(s_k, s_j) = 0$ for all $k \neq j$. A binary signal set is antipodal if $s_o(t) = -s_i(t)$ for all t in the interval $[0, T]$. Antipodal signals have equal energy E and their inner product is $(s_o, s_1) = -E$.

The baseband signal sets can be represented in terms of a signal waveform $v(t)$. The examples of Fig. 5.2 represent binary baseband signal sets and those constitute a waveform. For the signal sets of Figs. 5.2 (a) and (b) the waveform is a rectangular pulse of duration T. Fig. 5.2 (c) is the split phase or Manchester coded pulse. Fig. 5.2 (d) is the basic waveform of sine pulse which is one half of a full period of a sine wave. It may be noted that there are several binary and M ary baseband signal sets which can not be described in terms of a single waveform of duration T.

The mathematical representation of digital baseband signal is carried out in the following way. Let m_n denote the message produced by the source during the nth interval $[nT, (n+1)T]$, then the sequences of the messages to be sent to the receiver is

$$(m_n) = ..., m_{-1}, m_o, m_1, m_2, ... \qquad \text{...(5.2)}$$

If the source output in the nth interval is k, $m_n = k$ and the transmitted signal is equal to $s_k(t - nT)$ for $nT \leq t\ (n+1)T$. The signal $s(t)$ is actually a sequence of replica of basic waveform and so one may have

$$s(t) = \sum_{n=\infty}^{\infty} s_{mn}(t - nT) \qquad \text{...(5.3)}$$

Actually the signals available for use in other intervals are simply replicas of those for $[0, T]$, most of the key features of the digital baseband signal modulation can be studied by considering the signal set $[s_k : k = 0, 1, \ldots M_{-1}]$ which is defined on the interval $[0, T]$. For a single waveform $v(t)$ of different sets on $[0, T]$.

$$s_k(t) = Ad_k\, v(t) \qquad \text{...(5.4)}$$

where A is a constant and represents the signal amplitude, d represents set of data variables, $(d_k : k = 0, 1, \ldots M_{-1})$, the subscript k represents the kth signal in the set of d_k. In order to define the transmitted signal, the message sequence (m_n) is represented by the corresponding sequence (b_n) of data variables and then the latter sequence is defined by $b_n = d_k$ if $m_n = k$. Then the transmitted signal is defined as

$$s(t) = \sum_{n=-\infty}^{\infty} A b_n \; v(t - nT) \quad ...(5.5)$$

In the analysis of various digital modulation techniques, the above form of digital baseband transmitted signal is normally used.

5.6. Digital Signal Processing and Satellite Link

5.6.1 Sampling Principle

An analog signal can be exactly specified, even if it is continuously varying with time, by its sample pulses. Only condition is that it has to be bandlimited. From the sampled pulses, the analog signal can be completely constructed at the receiving end if noise and other distortion do not pollute the samples during transmission.

For a band-limited time function transmission, it is *not* necessary to transmit the signal continuously so as to receive it comfortably. As would be seen later, most of pulse modulation based systems employ sampling principle to achieve the same objective. The signal is sampled at discrete times in such a way that sampled signal specifies the signal completely and transmitted over the channel. At the receiver, the signal is 'reassembled' again.

We therefore now discuss the basic guiding principles of the sampling procedure which can be stated in the form of four sampling theorems.

Sampling Theorem 1: The Sampling Principle. If a time function $x(t)$, which is continuous and has no frequency components $> W$, then the time function can be completely determined by specifying its ordinates at a series of points spaced 1/2 W sec or less.

Since $x(t)$ is band-limited, its frequency spectrum $X(f)$ exists only in the interval $(-W, W)$. Therefore, $x(t)$ is expressed as

$$x(t) = \frac{1}{2\pi} \int_{-2\pi W}^{2\pi W} X(f)\, e^{j\omega t}\, d\omega \quad ...(5.6)$$

We take the sampling points at intervals of $-n/2W$. Then Eq. 5.6 can be written as

$$x\left(\frac{-n}{2W}\right) = \frac{1}{2\pi} \int_{-2\pi W}^{2\pi W} X(f)\, e^{-jn\omega/2W}\, d\omega \quad ...(5.7)$$

This result clearly shows that the left-hand side is the value of $x(t)$ at the sampling points. The right-hand side is the same as Eq. 5.6. Therefore, the sampling values adequately and uniquely define the coefficient x_n and hence $X(f)$.

Sampling Theorem 2 : The Sampling Rate. If a time function $x(t)$ consists of a band of frequencies displaced from zero with a bandwidth of W, with highest frequency of f_s, then the minimum sampling rate is given by $2f_s/m$, where m is the largest integer not to exceed f_s/W.

Sampling Theorem 3 : The Frequency Domain Specification. If the frequency spectrum of a time function $x(t)$ is represented by $X(\omega)$ which is zero except in the range of $T_1 \le t \le T_2$, then $X(\omega)$ can be uniquely determined by specifying its values at a series of points spaced every $1/(T_2 - T_1)$.

Sampling Theorem 4: The Signal Reconstruction. If a signal with highest frequency W has been sampled at a rate of $2W$ *samples / sec,* and the samples are in the form of impulses whose area is proportional to the magnitude of the sample at that instant, then the sampled signal may be reconstructed by passing the impulse train through an ideal low-pass filter with cut-off frequency of W.

The implications of this result are as follows :

1. The function $x(t)$ can be reconstructed at the receiver by (a) taking each sampled value corresponding to each interval $(-n/2W)$, and (b) passing it through a network whose response is of the form sin x/x.
2. An ideal low-pass filter with bandwidth W has a response of $\frac{\sin x}{x}$ form, and therefore can be used for reconstruction of this signal.

Fig. 5.3 shows how the sampling theory can be applied to a message $x(t)$ to obtain expressions of sampled $x(t)$. Here the switch makes to and fro contacts between the two points at a rate of $f_s = 1/T_s$ Hz so that it makes the input signal to pass for τ *sec* and gets connected to ground for the remaining of each period.

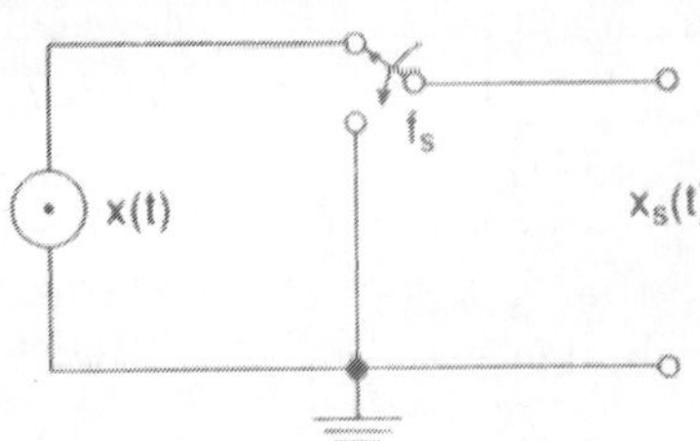

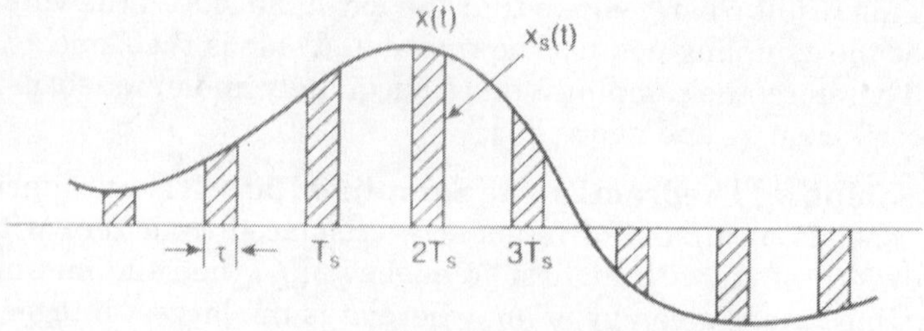

Fig. 5.3. Sampling Principles.

5.7. Pulse-Code Modulation

Pulse-code modulation embodies all of the principles of information theory, and one can fully realize the possibilities of this method only after much consideration of the study of information. The pulse-code system is quantized, which implies that the information signal is separated into discrete packets. This idea is not new, since some information by its very nature is quantized–that is, letters form words, sentences, and so on. Discrete packets of information are called *quanta*.

For pulse-code modulation, we must define a code in order to determine how the information packets are coded. The choice of a proper code is an important consideration in establishing a *PCM* system.

In most modulation systems, either the information signal continuously modulated a sinusoidal carrier, or the information signal was sampled and the sample periodically modulated a pulse. In all cases the actual information signal was used to obtain the modulated output directly. A pulse-code modulation scheme involves the replacement of the original information signal with another signal. As before, the information signal is sampled, but now the sampled signal is replaced by one of a previously determined set of signals, whichever will best represent it. If the original signal was continuous, the process of replacing the continuous signal by discrete signals is known as *quantizing.* If the original signal is already discrete, as are the letters and spaces of this page, the replacement of these symbols for another set of symbols is called *encoding*.

In general, many possible codes can be transmitted in digital binary form. In this code there are two levels of transmittal, which could be the presence or absence of a pulse, or a normal or inverted pulse, representing the **1** and **0** of the binary code. Each signal constitutes a binary digit or bit of information. The complexity of the information signal and the complexity of the coding process both determine the number of bits required to define the sampled signal.

The number of bits required to specify a code group is determined from the complexity of the information signal. This code group forms a message. There are as many code groups as there are messages, each one formed by a unique series of binary digits. A collection of all possible code groups, forming all possible messages, is a *set*.

Codes have been designed to use code groups that are longer than the minimum necessary to establish the message, so that the receiver is able to detect whether an error has been made and even ask the transmitter to repeat. The result is a system with error-free capabilities in the presence of severe noise – a distinct advantage offered by pulse-code modulation systems over other communication systems.

5.7.1 Generation of PCM

The *PCM* generation process is shown in Fig. 5.4 which constitutes the following steps :

The continuous signal $x(t)$ is first converted into sampled signal $x_s(t)$ as in conventional pulse systems. The sampled values are now quantized, *i.e.*, they are approximated to pre-determined discrete values called *quantum levels* giving the quantized signal $x_{sq}(t)$. Note that $x_{sq}(t)$ is discrete both in time due to sampling, and in amplitude due to quantization process.

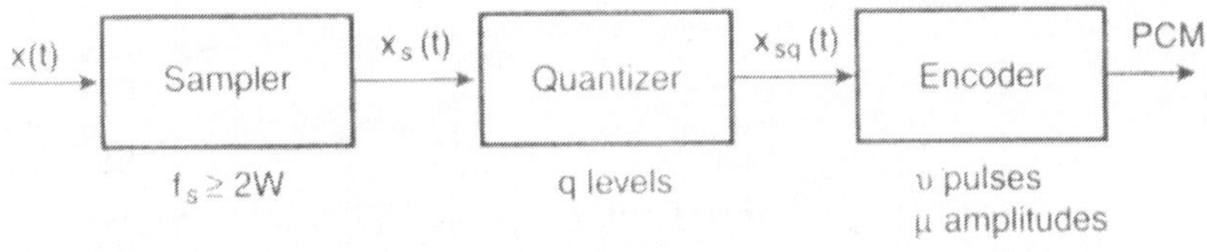

Fig. 5.4. Generation of PCM.

The signal $x_{sq}(t)$ is now digitised and coded, *i.e.*, the quantized samples are converted into appropriate code groups–with one code group for each sample. This gives the final baseband *PCM* signal in the form of digital pulsed wave.

Now let the number of quantum levels = q; the number of pulses (or digits) in each code group = υ; and number of discrete values in each code group = μ

Clearly, there will be $\mu\upsilon$ different combinations of ν pulses with μ possible amplitudes. Therefore, the unique coding requires

$$\mu^{\nu} \geq q$$

or $\nu \geq \log_{\mu} q$

When $\mu = q$, $\nu = 1$, which means the quantized signal requires no code translation. In general, $\mu < q$ and $\nu > 1$.

When $\mu = 2$, $q = 2^{\nu}$ or $\nu = \log_2 q$. That is the number of quantum levels is taken as some power of 2. This is the case of most common form of *PCM*, called *binary PCM*.

5.7.2. Binary PCM

Let us examine a simple pulse-code modulation technique. We shall assume the information signal to be an audio signal that varies between 0 and *V volts* upon application of the appropriate bias. It is desired to encode this information into binary-digit form. For this, the signal must be sampled at a rate equal to the Nyquist sampling rate, or twice the highest harmonic in the information signal. This will allow us to sample other signals and transmit them in a time-sequential manner.

The messages with their associated code group are shown in Table 5.1.

Table 5.1 : Pulse Coding: An Example

Message	*Code*	*Message*	*Code*
0	00000	9	01001
1	00001	10	01010
2	00010	11	01011
3	00011	12	01100
4	00100	13	01101
5	00101	14	01110
6	00110	15	01111
7	00111	16	10000
8	01000		

Fig. 5.5 show a portion of the sampled information signal in case of binary *PCM*. Here eight quantum levels are used corresponding to 1, 0,....7*V*. The encoder translates quantised voltage to its binary equivalent according to the above table. Clearly we need three binary digits since $\nu = \log_2 8 = 3$.

Detection of the pulse-code modulation requires a knowledge of the code and the synchronization. This information can be transmitted by appropriate pulse-code information.

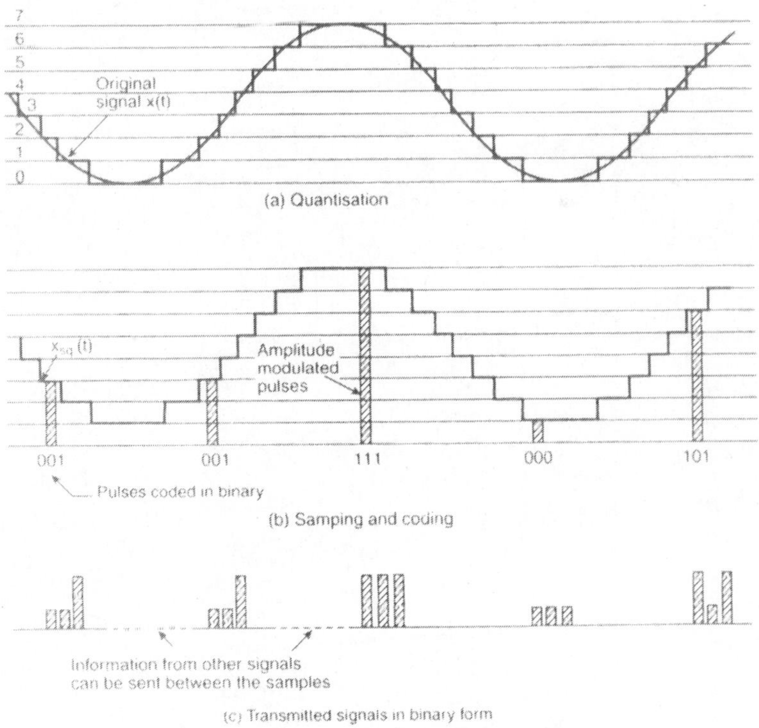

Fig. 5.5. Waveforms in Binary *PCM* Signals.

Regeneration with very little side effects can now be done as shown in Fig. 5.5. Although the signal is subject to noise, distortion, and bandwidth limitation, if these effects are small enough, the regenerated signal will correspond to the original one. Thus, with suitable spacing, a series of regenerative repeaters will pall along a discrete signal without any accumulation of error along the route.

The regenerator compares the signal with the threshold decision level or the level midway between the two expected signal levels at each sampling instant. If positive, a positive pulse is generated ; if negative, a negative pulse is generated. As can be seen from Fig 5.5 fairly large impairments can be encountered before the signal is lost. Clearly, the possibility of regeneration makes digital transmission more reliable than analog transmission.

The immunity of *PCM* to interference and noise is very high. However, this noise immunity is not gained without compromise, but at the expense of increased bandwidth. To transmit the pulse stream of 8 bits/sample shown in Fig. 5.6, $8 \times 2 \times 4000 = 64$ Kbits/sec must be transmitted for a 4 kHz bandwidth limited signal which repre-

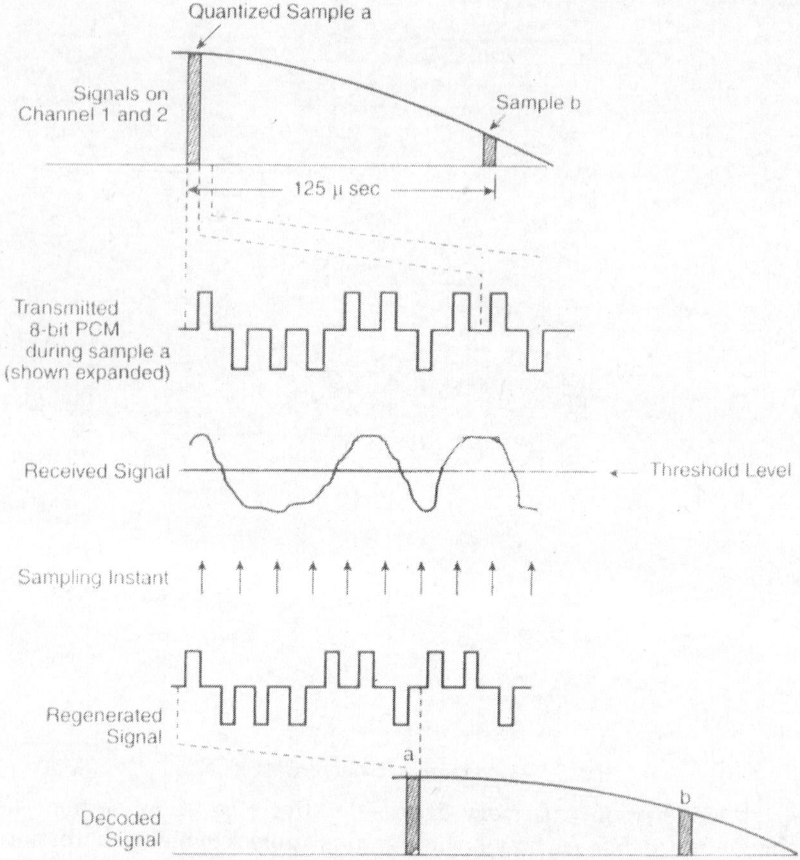

Fig. 5.6. Regeneration Process of PCM Signals.

sents a minimum baseband bandwidth of 32 kHz. Thus, practical *PCM* systems require 32/4, or 8 times the bandwidth of their analog counterparts.

On a *PCM* channel, in addition to speech signal information, signaling information such as *ON* and *OFF* hook and dialing must also be transmitted. Moreover, synchronizing information (framing code) must be generated so that the receiver can sort out the code words and signaling bits into the proper channels. Alarm code can also be added to inform the user of local trouble.

5.7.3. PCM Bandwidth

The PCM bandwidth is determined by the minimum pulse width. This, in turn, is controlled by the number of pulses needed to establish a message and the rate at which the information is transmitted. Since the information is not in the rise or fall-time that establishes the position of the pulse from some reference, the bandwidth requirement is less stricted. Spill-over of one pulse into the next is tolerable, provided that the presence of a pulse is detectable.

The rate at which quantized samples occur is $f_S \geq 2W$ *samples/sec*. It means that there must be νf_S coded pulses per second. Assuming there are no spaces in the coded signal, the maximum permitted duration of any one pulse will be

$$\tau = 1/\nu f_S.$$

Therefore, to ensure pulse resolution, the required bandwidth should at least correspond to $1/2\tau$. That is

$$B_T \geq \frac{1}{2\tau} = \frac{1}{2}\nu f_S$$

or

$$B_T \geq \frac{1}{2}\nu f_S \geq \nu W$$

Since $\nu = \log_{\mu} q$, the *PCM* bandwidth is

or

$$B_T \geq (\log_{\mu} q)\, W \qquad \ldots (5.8)$$

For binary *PCM,*

$$B_T \geq (\log_2 q) W.$$

5.7.4. PCM Reception and Noise

The functions of the *PCM* receiver are :

1. To decode the signal to get $x_{sq}(t)$, and
2. To reconstruct the signal $x(t)$ from the samples by lowpass filtering.

A typical *PCM* receiver is shown in Fig. 5.7. The decoder first recognises the binary digits with the help of a decision circuit whose threshold is set at zero *volts*. When the received wave is positive, the digit is taken as a 1 and vice versa. For maximum reliability, the decision at the threshold must be made at the centre of each pulse. To ensure this, synchronising signals are often included so that the decoder is triggered at the appropriate moments.

Upon reception of a pulse-coded sequence in the binary form, the only decision the receiver must make from the information of the received noisy signal is whether a pulse was transmitted or not. No information is contained in the amplitude, the position, or the duration of the pulse, and any distortion occurring to any of these parameters will not affect the quality of the signal. A wrong decision by the receiver may cause an error. If, however, long code groups are used to form these messages, and there are only a limited number

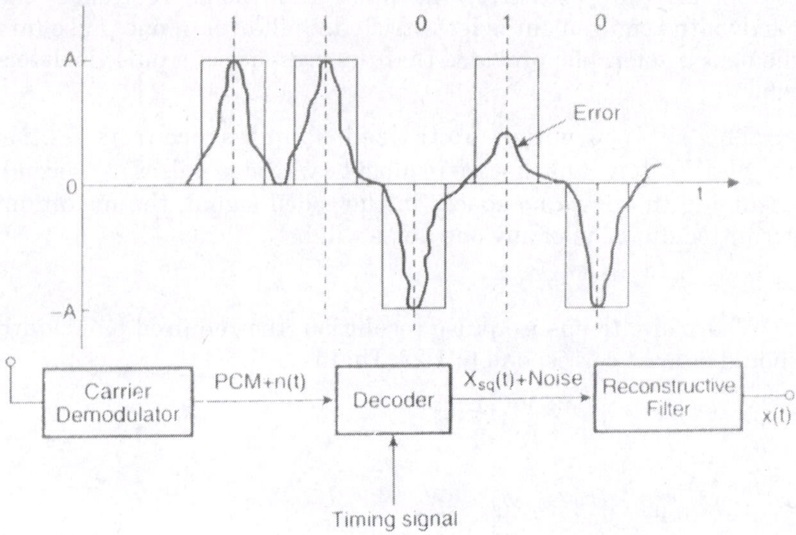

Fig. 5.7. PCM receiver.

of valid message groups. Then, if the received code group is not considered a valid message, it is disregarded or a repeat transmission is called for. An addition advantage is that the signal can be directly processed by a computer, which means it can be amplified, recorded, played back, stored, recovered, and reamplified many times without any loss of the signal information.

When random noise variations present cause the encoder to make wrong decision, an error occurs in the output of the receiver. That is, if a 1 is sent and the received signal $A + n\ (t)$ becomes less than zero at the decision time, a 0 is received. Similarly $A + n(t) > 0$ at the receiver for a 0 sent would cause an error. Clearly, errors depend on the relative strength $n(t)$ of the noise and its statistical behaviour.

5.7.5. Companding

If the signal being transmitted were of low amplitude, then the procedure illustrated in Fig. 5.7 would not, by itself, be so satisfactory. The quantizing noise, still the same absolute magnitude, would now be larger relative to the signal magnitude. The quantizing error is a function of interval between levels and not of the signal amplitude ; therefore the signal-to-quantizing noise ratio is lower for smaller signals. For this reason a compandor is normally used.

The function of a compandor to compress the higher amplitude parts of a signal before modulation, and expand them back to normal again after demodulation. It means preferential treatment is given to the weaker parts of a signal. The weaker signals traverse more quantum steps than they would otherwise, and so the quantizing error is less. This is done at the expense of the higher amplitude parts of the signal for these cover less quantum steps.

As the signal is instantaneously compressed at the transmitter, it is expanded at the receiver after decoding is completed. Companding can improve the S/N ratio in voice circuit by up to 25 dB. It is not used in data communications where each level (0 and 1) is equally probable, and thus there is no advantage to using companders. The compander, because of its nonlinear characteristics, however, adds *intermodulation distortion*.

5.7.6. Pulse Rate

Let us now see what are the pulse rates possible with *PCM*. If pulse code modulation is used to transmit the human voice frequencies below 3000 Hz, then, as previously stated, a theoretical minimum of 6000 samples per second are needed.

If each sample codes of 128 permitted signal levels needs seven bits for each sample, then not less than $6000 \times 7 = 42{,}000$ bits/sec will be needed to convey this telephone voice. If the systems transmit the voice channel with frequencies up to 4000 Hz, then at least $8000 \times 7 = 56{,}000$ bits/sec are needed.

For transmission of 42,000 pulses per second, a bandwidth of not less than 21 kHz is required. 56,000 bits per second needs at least 28 kilohertz.

In practice, the bandwidth needed for the pulses to be recognizable and reconstructable is somewhat more than half the pulse rate. The bandwidth needed for this type of modulation is thus a minimum of seven times the sum of bandwidth of the individual signals, and practical systems commonly need as much as twice this bandwidth. This could be reduced by having a smaller number of quantizing levels, but the reduction in bandwidth would give a corresponding increase in quantizing noise. Compared for example, with single-sideband amplitude modulation in which a bandwidth only very slightly higher than the signal bandwidth is needed, it is much worst performance of *PCM*.

In typical voice systems, seven bits per sample are used and so it will be normal for *PCM* to use a bandwidth seven or more times that of the voice signal transmitted. In practice, the *Bell T1* system transmits 24 voice channels each of 4 KHz ; and for this system bandwidth of 1.5 MHz is used, which is over 15 times the sum of the signal bandwidths.

In a *PCM*-based telephone link, the 56,000 bits per second that are needed to carry a telephone conversation could equally well be used for data. With synchronous transmission of 7-bit characters, this gives about 8000 characters per second over a single telephone channel.

5.7.7. Advantages of PCM

1. *PCM* near threshold gives most superior performance as compared to all other forms of pulse modulation, therefore most suitable in time-division multiplexing (*TDM*).
2. As compared to *FM, PCM* has a small but definite margin as the lower values of *S* / *N* ratios.
3. Since *PCM* designed for analog message transmission can easily be adaptable to other input signals like digital data, it is highly flexible and leads to high system utilization.
4. It has regeneration capabilities and therefore advantages for systems having many repeater stations, particularly in long-distance telephony.

5.8. Codecs

The Codecs (Coder–Decoder) are monolithic integrated circuit chips which convert voice signals. These are now being produced on a massive scale and are becoming so inexpensive that they are being installed in the individual channel units rather than as a single encoder/decoder unit that is time shared by all the channels. In the system shown in Fig. 5.8 each channel contains a coder for sampling, quantizing, and encoding. The digital outputs are then passed to a digital multiplexer where they are combined to form a single serial bit stream for transmission. The inverse process occurs in the receiving section of the codec.

Codecs employ digital multiplexing which tends to be simpler and easier to implement than analog multiplexing. By the proper combining of digital pulse streams, analog baseband signals of various bandwidths can be digitized and carried over the digital system.

Intel 2910A PCM Codec. This chip provides full-duplex *PCM* operation and consists of :

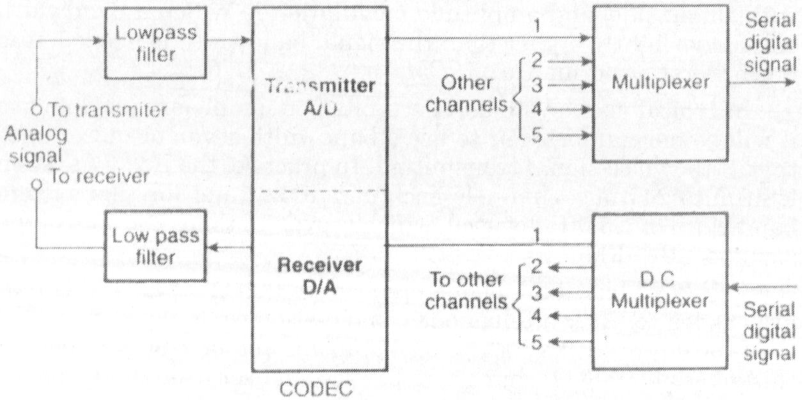

Fig. 5.8. *PCM* system employing One Codec-per-Channel.

(*i*) Sample-and-hold circuits,
(*ii*) *A*/*D* converter of successive approximate type,
(*iii*) *D*/*A* converter, and
(*iv*) Logic and interface circuitry.

Major functions provided by this chip are : Analog signal encoding and decoding for voice, dial tone, busy tone, ring-back tone. Signaling and supervision information encoding and decoding such as OFF or ON Hook, rotatory dial pulse, etc.

5.7.8. The PCM Channel Bank

Fig. 5.9 shows the block diagram of a typical channel bank. It performs all the functions inherent in a *PCM* system, namely, sampling and multiplexing, quantizing, encodering on transmitter side, and demultiplexing and decoding on receiver side.

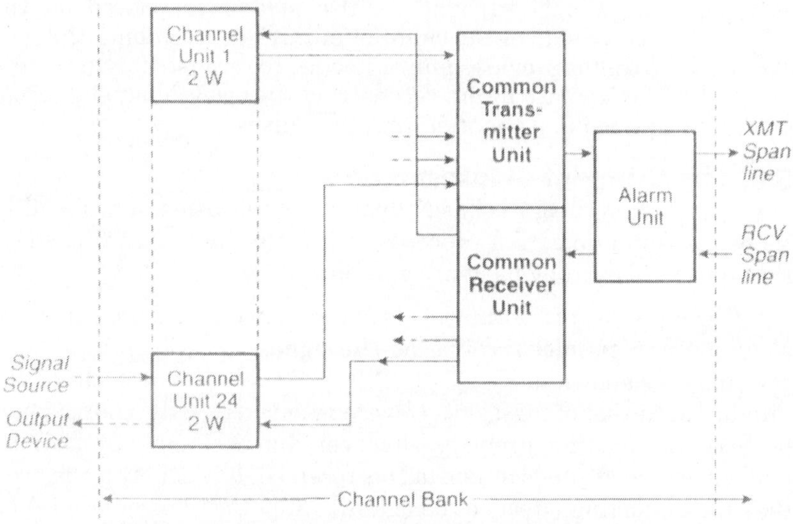

Fig. 5.9. A Typical 24-Channel Bank.

The channel bank consists of 24 plug-in channel units, a common transmit unit, a common receive unit, and a common alarm unit. The 24 analog signals are time-division multiplexed. Note that the handsets and signal source become the analog input signals into the system. The usual range of voice frequencies used is 200 to 3400 *Hz*. Its various elements are:

1. Channel unit (*CU*)–It performs the following functions :
   (*a*) Bandlimiting the input signal through the use of bandpass filters, and
   (*b*) Sampling at a rate of 8 *kHz* which corresponds to multiplexing.
2. Common Transmit Unit (*CTU*)–It performs quantizing and encoding functions.

3. Common Alarm Unit (*CAU*) and Office Repeater–It set up standard pulse levels and detects basic system failures.

The signal coming out of *CAU* is transmitted on span line.

The receiver constituent of the channel bank works as follows :

1. The office repeater, if used, regenerates the generally low amplitude pulses to make them acceptable to the decoder.
2. The alarm unit works as a signal monitor for obvious system failures such as loss of pulses.
3. Common Receive Unit–It examines the pulse stream fed to it to determine timing information regarding the location of each bit (bit timing) and the start of the frame, *i.e.,* first channel out of 24 channel set. The information is then applied to the decoder which provides the quantized analog pulse stream.
4. The quantized analog pulse stream is passed on the receive side of the channel unit. Here it is demultiplexed so that it provides pulses needed to reconstruct the signal.
5. The lowpass filters reconstruct the original analog signal applied to a channel from the pulses.

5.8. The Concept of Information

Information theory is based upon the application of probability theory to communication concepts, especially the results based on the concept of entropy measure of information.

Transmission of information is in the form data originating from some source *S* to some receiver *R*. The signals are transmitted via a channel *C* as shown in Fig. 5.10. If the channel were such that each number of the set of messages *U* were received exactly, there would be no communication problem. However, due to channel limitations and noise, a corrupted version of *U* is received. It is generally desired that the distorting effects of be channel imperfections and noise be minimised and the number of messages sent over the channel in a given time is maximised. However, these two requirements are

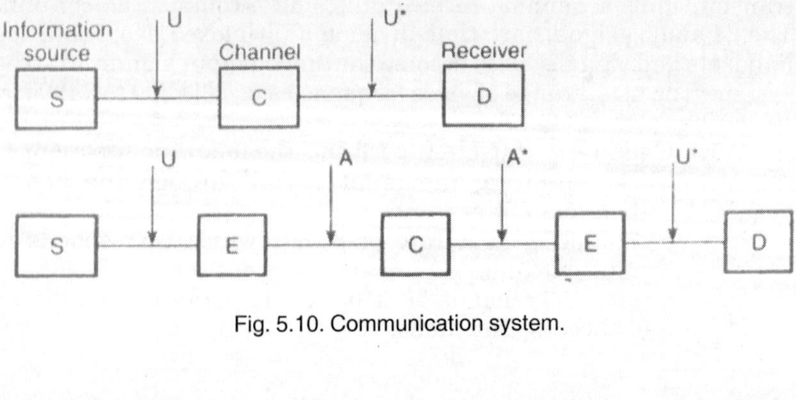

Fig. 5.10. Communication system.

interacting and require to modify the message-set U by a suitable encoder E to produce a new set A, more suitable for the given channel capacity. Therefore, a decoder D, is required at the receiver to extract the desired information.

The basic goal of a communication system is to transmit and subsequently receive the desired information as efficiently as possible. Therefore, it is necessary to understand the concept of information and the ways it can be measured. The definition of information is based on the idea of lack of information. That is, the less information one has, the greater is the information to be gained. What already is known cannot be gained. Thus *information is a measure of uncertainty, i.e., the less is the possibility of occurence of a certain message, the higher is its information content.* However, in contrast to knowledge, information is independent of the background of the destination. It has an element of spontaneity.

5.9 Channel Capacity of a Discrete Channel

Channel capacity specifies the ability of a system to transmit information. Since the information contained in a message is a fixed quantity, the rate at which the symbols can be transmitted is a measure of system capability. The rate at which the symbols can be generated by the source is an important consideration in determining channel capacity ; ideally the two should be matched.

Since the system we are considering has no memory, we must use maximum entropy conditions in establishing a code. That is, the transmitter must be able to send any signal which the message source is capable of producing with the symbols or letter available to it, even if the destination can only interpret them as noise. The message rate is directly proportional to the speed of symbol generator, and consequently the channel capacity is ideally directly proportional to the rate of information generation. Note that the channel capacity can *never* be less than information rate if the message is to be preserved. Increasing the information rate requires that the channel capacity also be increased. The rate of information transmission is a function of the time response of the physical device producing the symbol.

It has been observed that the system efficiency can be improved by removal of redundancy from the message, in effect lowering the number of symbols necessary to carry the information generated by the source. However, once the symbol is established, the channel capacity is determined by the physical device generating the symbol. If the symbols are produced by the vocal cords, the system channel capacity is determined from the microphone time response and the faithfulness the transmitted signal is to retain. If the symbols are to carry information used to form a picture, the response of the vidicon tube to the changes of light controls the system time response. If the symbols are pulses representing "on" and "off" states of bistable circuits, the switching time of the system will control the channel capacity.

5.9.1. Discrete Noiseless Channel

Consider a discrete channel having μ states or channel symbols and uniform signalling speed $s = 1/\tau$ where τ is the duration of each state or symbol being transmitted. If the signal-to-noise ratio is large, the error probability at the receiver would be small so that the channel is virtually noiseless.

5.9.2. Discrete Noisy Channel

When the channel has noise, it becomes difficult to reconstruct the transmitted signal faithfully. The received signal becomes a function of two processes–the source and the noise.

The noisy channel can be represented by an equivalent noise-less channel as shown in Fig. 5.11. The role of the error-correcting system is to correct the received digit if it is incorrect. If the received digit is correct, no correction is made and a 0 is sent. On the other hand, if the received digit is incorrect, the system transmits a 1. It means that additional information is supplied to the receiver to compensate for the loss of information owing to the noise on the channel. Therefore, the actual rate at which the information is received is equal to the transmitted information less the information supplied by the compensator.

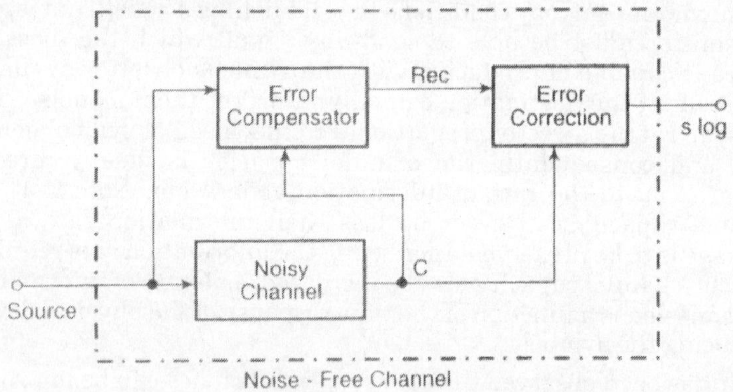

Fig. 5.11. Equivalent Noise-less Discrete Channel.

5.9.3. The Entropy Rate

The entropy rate R (bits/sec) introduced in the above analysis, brings the time element in the description of the information system. Suppose two sources have equal entropies but one is 'faster' than the other, producing more symbols for unit time. In a given period, more information must be transferred from the faster source than from the slower, which obviously places greater demands on the communication system. Thus, the description of a source is not its entropy alone, in bits-per-symbol, but also its entropy rate or information rate in bits/sec.

In regard to information transmission, the **Shanon theorem** states : *Given a source having entropy rate R and a channel of capacity C, then if* $R \leq C$, *there exists a coding technique such that the output of the source can be transmitted over the channel with an arbitrary small frequency of error, despite the presence of noise. If* $R > C$, *it is not possible to transmit without errors.*

5.9.4. Signalling speed

In a discrete channel, the capacity depends on signaling speed, which in turn in related to channel bandwidth B. If the signal is sent at $s > 2B$, overlapping of waveforms takes place resulting in *intersymbol interference.* This result is formally stated as **Nyquist Law** : *With an ideal lowpass channel of bandwidth B, it is possible to send independent symbols at a rate* $s \leq 2B$ *without intersymbol interference. It is not possible to send independent symbols at* $s > 2B$.

The rate $s = 2B$ is called *Nyquist sampling rate.*

5.9.5. Calculation of Channel Capacity : Hartley Shannon Law

The Hartley Shannon Law states :

It is possible to transmit over a channel of bandwidth B pertubed by white noise, at a rate of C bits/sec with an arbtirarily small frequency of error if the signal is encoded in such a manner that its probability density function is gaussian. That is

$$B \log \left(1 + \frac{S}{N}\right) \text{ bits/sec.} \qquad ...(5.9)$$

The results of Eq. 5.9 are highly specialised, but they are often used as a basis of interchangeability of bandwidth and signal-to-noise rates in a communication system.

Some of the implications of Eq. 5.9 can be understood with the example where a bandlimited time function is sampled every $1/2\,B$ sec. The samples are quantized into n discrete levels and transmitted over a channel of minimum bandwidth B. The bandwidth requirement may be deduced by encoding every pair of samples into one sample having n^2 discrete levels. The encoded signal needs only a channel bandwidth of $B/2$, but the signal power and, hence the S/N ratio has been greatly increased, a result predictable by Eq. 5.9. The converse effect can be achieved by encoding each sample into two samples each with $\sqrt{n}$ discrete levels.

6

Digital Carrier Systems and Satellite Links

6.1. Principle of Data Communication

Data communication is primarily concerned with the movement of data from one location to another. The term data refers to alphabetical, numerical, or special purpose characters which, when appropriately grouped, constitute some word or message. Data communication is the basis of computer-based communication systems. By using communication facilities that can handle digital data, interconnected digital computers can directly process the data.

The design of a practical data system is based on two fundamental criteria :

1. The gross source rate (*binary digits per sec.*), as distinguished from the entry rate (*bits per sec*). It, therefore, dictates signaling speed.
2. The described transmission reliability, *i.e.*, the tolerated error rate. It, therefore, dictates error-probability requirements.

Thus, *signaling speed* and *error probability* are the defining parameters of digital systems. Analogous to analog systems, signaling speed is equivalent to bandwidth and error probability is equivalent to signal-to-noise ratio.

Similar to analog signals, the digital signals have a wide range of bit rates depending on the source and application. Typical bit rates may range from 100 bits/sec for manual keyboard devices such as tele-typewriter to 10^9 bits/sec for a computer. Most digital transmission, however, is via standard telephone voice circuits with top speeds of 1,000 to 5,000 bits/sec.

In contrast to signaling speed, the issue of acceptable error rates is rather cumbersome. For systems like defence surveillance, error is of great concern; an error probability of 10^{-5} may even be intolerable. For telemetering data from measuring instruments having 10 per cent accuracy, the error rate may not be that stringent; a probability of 10^{-3} may be unnecessary. However, error probabilities of order of 10^{-4} are typical and suitable for many applications.

One fundamental difference between digital and analog transmission must be properly noticed here : In analog transmission, the aim is to reproduce the actual *message waveform* as closely as possible. In digital transmission, the goal is to transmit the *message information* as accurately as possible. Therefore, the design of digitals system is not bound to any particular waveform and can be evolved by variety of ways in which digital message can be represented.

In addition, since a digital signal is discrete in nature, system refinements such as regeneration and error-control coding can be employed. It is also possible to provide the receiver with a reference list before hand what the massage elements should look like in the absence of noise and other contamination. Then, given the contaminated signal at the receiver, transmission reliability can be further improved by a matching procedure wherein the received waveform is compared with the possible transmitted waveforms. Referred as coherent detection, it provides system optimization through the use of statistical decision theory.

6.2. Representation of Data Signal

6.2.1. Unipolar and Polar Signals

Generally digital signal is visualised as a train of discrete-amplitude rectangular pulses. In fact, this is often the way it comes from the data source. Fig. 6.1 (*a*) shows the binary message 10110100 as it might appear at the output of a digital computer. The waveform, a simple on-off sequence, is said to be unipolar, because it has only one polarity. It is also synchronous because all pulses have equal duration and there is no separation between them.

The *disadvantages* of unipolar signals are :

1. They contain a nonzero dc component that is difficult to transmit, carries no information, and is a waste of power.

2. Synchronous signals require timing co-ordination at transmitter and receiver (like synchronous demodulation), which means design complications.

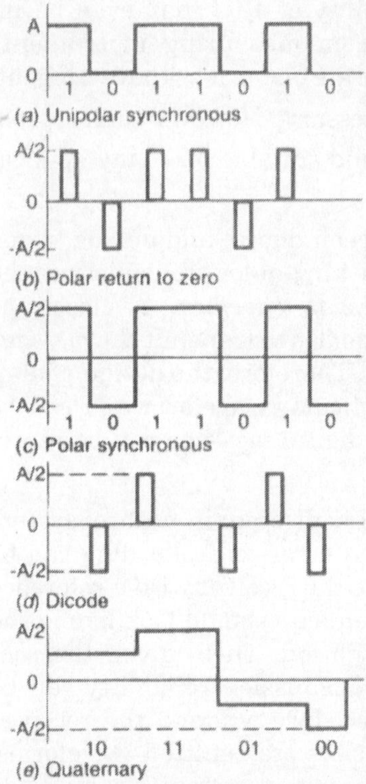

Fig. 6.1.

3. It has the limitation of speed due to above factors and also because pulse-width margin is necessary in order to accommodate distortions and timing error.

The polar (two-polarity) return-to-zero signal of Fig. 6.1 (*b*) overcomes both of these problems. However, the "spaces" making the signal self-clocking are a waste of transmission time. If efficiency is a dominant consideration the polar synchronous signal of Fig. 6.1 (*c*) would be preferable. As in case of analog systems, there is a trade-off between efficient transmission and simpler design.

Binary messages can also be represented as shown in Fig. 6.1 (*d*) and (*e*). The dicode wave consists of polar pulses denoting only the symbol transitions. The quaternary (fourlevel) signal is derived by grouping the binary digits in blocks of two as will be seen later.

Synchronous transmission. This system does not employ start-and-stop pulses, but instead a common clock pulse at the transmitting and receiving end (and a few framing pulses) to achieve synchronization and character pulse identification. As the receiver recognizes a unique code in the received bit stream, it locks it is on an incoming bit stream and help in identifying the characters. Its features are :

1. Synchronous transmission tends to have a larger net data throughput than synchronous transmission since it does not require the special start-and-stop bits. For example, while a 5-bit code in asynchronous transmission requires from 6 to 7 bits per character, it requires slightly more than 5 in synchronous operation. In other words, asynchronous transmitters requires characters 33 per cent less than synchronous transmitters for the same bit speed.

2. In synchronous transmission, data is transmitted in the form of an entire block, which can consist of many signal elements with no separations.

3. A unique code is used to frame the entire block. This code indicates to the receiver the beginning, end, and other information on the blocks.

4. Every bit in the receiver and transmitter is synchronized to common clock.

5. Timing signals included in the data bits govern the timing of sampling of data by the receiver.

Advantages : 1. It has high efficiency with on synchronizing bits required although block framing is required.

2. It is less sensitive to distortion because timing is included along with data.

Disadvantages : 1. In this system, bit loss can make whole message erroneous.

2. Special codes must be detected for timing and logic control.

3. Its equipment is costly because of the more complex circuit required.

6.2. Data Signal : Signal Shaping and Signaling Speed

Ignoring the specific details, the input signal to a data system can generally be described as a pulse train of the form

$$x(t) = \Sigma_k\, a_k p\left(t - \frac{k}{s}\right) \qquad \text{...(6.1)}$$

where a_K = the amplitude level representing the kth message digit,

$p(t)$ = the basic pulse shape with peak value $p(0)$=1,

$1/s$ = pulse-to-pulse spacing, and

s = the signaling speed.

For example, for the polar synchronous signal of Fig. 6.1 (c),

$$a_k = \pm\frac{a}{2},\quad p(t) = \Pi\left(\frac{t}{\tau}\right),\quad \text{where } \tau = \frac{1}{s}.$$

In an ideal system, which is linear and distortionless over all frequencies, *i.e.*, has infinite bandwidth, then $p(t)$ suffers no degradation in transmission, and an arbitrarily large signaling speed can be achieved by using very short pulses.

However, a practical system has finite bandwidth and less than ideal frequency response, causing the pulses to spread out and overlap. Therefore, the output signal should be shaped so as to minimize intersymbol interference due to overlapping and, at the same time, maximize signaling rate. However, these two goals undermine each other.

Assuming a linear system and superposition, the output waveform resulting from the input $x(t)$ can be written as

$$y(t) = \sum_k A_k\, x\left(t - \frac{k}{s} - t_d\right) \qquad \text{...(6.2)}$$

where $A_k/a_k = K_0 =$ system voltage gain,

$t_d =$ time delay, and

$x(t) =$ output pulse shape normalized to the peak value $x(0) = 1$.

Let us concentrate on the single pulse shape $x(t)$ and its spectrum $X(f)$, rather than complete messages.

Expressed in terms of the system transfer function $H(f)$ and the input pulse spectrum $P(f) = F[p(t)]$, we have

$$Y(f) = H(f)\, P(f)$$

or $$K_0\, x(t - t_d) = F^{-1}[H(f)\, P(f)]$$

or $$K_0\, e^{-j\omega t_d} X(f) = H(f)\, P(f).$$

But the problems at hand, namely, intersymbol interference and signaling rate, are time-domain problems. We, therefore, write,

$$x(t) = \frac{1}{K_0} \int_{-\infty}^{\infty} H(f)\, P(f)\, e^{j\omega(t + t_d)}\, df. \qquad \text{...(6.3)}$$

Here, $x(t)$ is essentially the impulse response of a filter having transfer function $H(f)\, P(f)$. This viewpoint has important practical implications on the selection of $x(t)$, since $H(f)$ must be physically realizable.

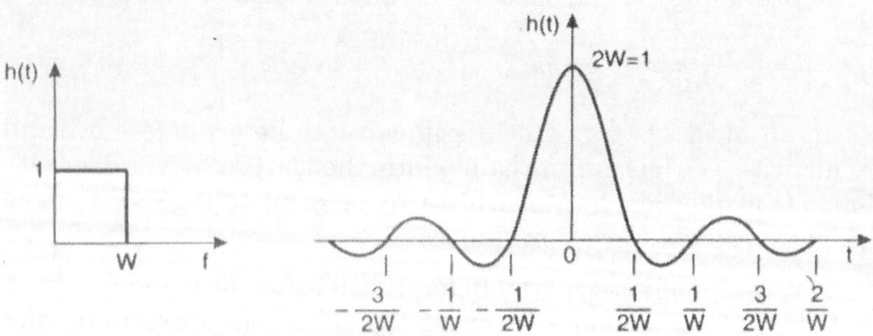

(*a*) Ideal or Brickwall Filter (*b*) Output Signal or Time Response

Fig. 6.2. Impulse Response of Ideal Filter.

6.2.1. Frequency Response of an Ideal Filter : The Nyquist First Criterion.

Now consider the system shown in Fig. 6.2. In this system, an impulse input of $\delta(t)$ is applied to a transmission channel which has a frequency response corresponding to that of an ideal, or brickwall, low-pass filter of bandwidth W. Although such a filter, and therefore such a response, is unrealizable due to the *infinite roll-off* of the filter skirts, the ideal gives the approximate response that would be realistically observed when a short pulse is applied to a bandlimited system.

It is observed from Fig. 6.2 that the result of bandlimiting an impulse signal is ringing, or time spreading, of the pulse in the time domain. These ringing tails decay at a rate of $1/t$ and that the amplitude passes through zero at points, where $t = n/2W$, when n is an integer.

Now, if we apply a wavetrain of pulses to such a bandlimited system, the tails of several pulses can overlap, thus interfering with the major pulse of interest at the detector. For the case illustrated in Fig. 6.3 and ignoring any time delays through the system, we find that spurious responses from the third and fourth impulses also appear at the sampling moment $t = 0$. The interference is commonly termed as *inter-symbol interference* (*ISI*). If by some method the rate of decay of the tail could be increased from the $1/t$ rate, the *ISI* would be reduced.

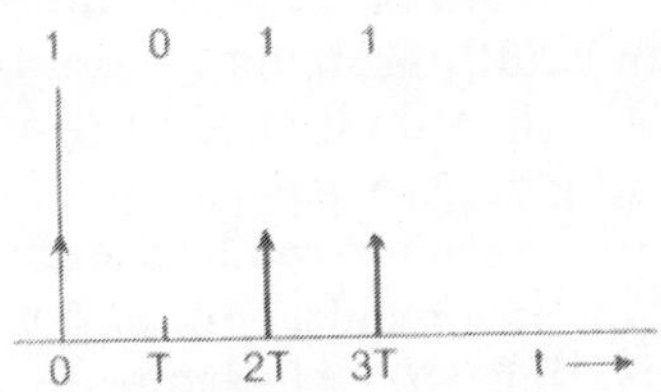

(*a*) Input Impulse Wavetrain

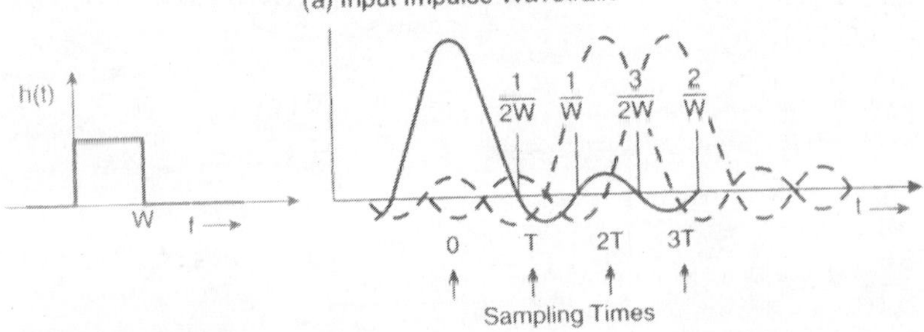

(*b*) Ideal or Brickwall Filter (*c*) Output Signal

Fig. 6.3. Response of ideal filter for 1011 input signal after bandlimiting.

At sampling time $t = T$, the tails of the several pulses appear within the sampling slot, which results in an observed voltage instead of none at all. This inter-symbol interference can seriously degrade the noise immunity of the system since the background *ISI* makes the system tolerant to a smaller amount of noise.

In order to minimise the effects of inter-symbol interference, the following methods are used :

1. By properly timing the pulse train and sampling intervals as they relate to the system bandwidth.
2. By pulse and channel shaping.

If the pulse train is timed so that pulses occur or do not occur at intervals of $T = 1/2\,W$, and are detected at the same rate, the tails of the neighbouring pulses are all at *zero volts* and interference does not occur. At the appropriate sampling instants, only the desired pulse or no pulse will be present.

The sampling times occur at multiples of $T = 1/f_s = 1/2\,W$, or a rate of f_s which is twice the transmission bandwidth. This is known as the *Nyquist rate.*

Consider the train of output pulses

$$\ldots + A_{-1}\,x\left(t + \frac{1}{s}\right) + A_0\,x\,(t) + A_1\,x\left(t - \frac{1}{s}\right) + \ldots \qquad \ldots(6.4)$$

Since $x(t)$ has its peak at $t = 0$ and all other pulses peak at $t_k = \pm\,1/s \pm 2/s, \ldots \pm k/s$, a sure remedy for intersymbol interference is to require that $x(t) = 0$ for $|\,t\,| \geq 1/2s$. However, practical pulse shapes in finite-bandwidth systems generally have decaying tails and cannot be strictly time-limited. On the other hand, asymptotically time-limited functions, such as the gaussian pulse, require excessive spacing, and therefore reduced signaling speed to suitably minimize the overlap. As a result, elimination of intersymbol interference. necessitates that $x(t_k) = 0$. It means that $x(t)$ should have periodic zero values spaced by $1/s$. This condition is called *Nyquist First Criterion.*

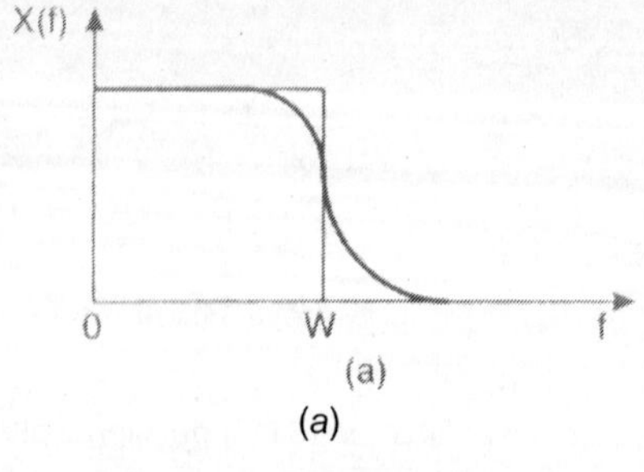

(*a*)

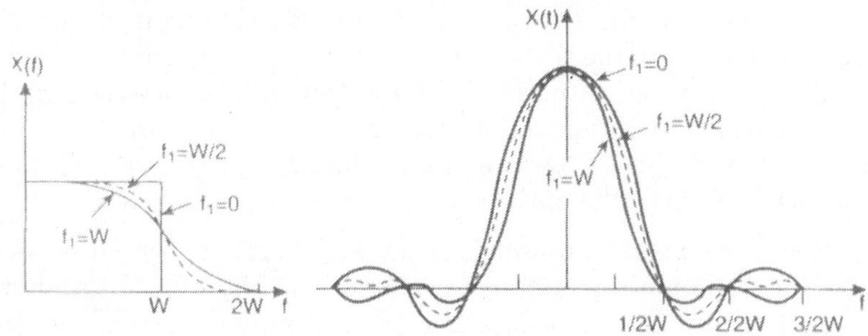

(b)

(b)

Fig. 6.4. Gradual Roll-off Filter Characteristics.

The pulse $x(t)$ = sinc $2Bt$ with $B = s/2$ satisfies the above condition. We have already seen that this pulse demonstrates signaling at the maximum rate $s = 2B$. But sinc pulses are not the most suitable because of the following reasons:

(1) The leading and trailing oscillations die off rather slowly; synchronization then becomes quite critical, and small variations of signaling speed result in substantial intersymbol interference.

(2) The pulse spectrum $X(f) = (1/2B)\ \Pi\ (f/2B)$ requires that $H(f)$ have sharp cutoff at $|f| = B$, which cannot be realized.

In the light of above remarks, let us restrict $X(f)$ to resemble filter functions with a more gradual roll-off characteristic, as in Fig. 6.4 (*a*). We then state the following important theorem :

Nyquist's Vestigial-Symmetry Theorem. *If X (f) is purely real (no imaginary part) and has odd symmetry about the nominal cutoff frequency W, then x (t) is an even time function with a peak at t=0 and periodic zero values spaced by 1 / 2W. Therefore, it is possible to sample the signal at s=2W without intersymbol interference.*

In the context of above theorem, we observe :

1. If the sampling at the receiver is performed at the correct instants, or at every T where $T = 1/f_s = 1/2W$, then no *ISI* occurs. Stating this somewhat differently, the bandwidth must be equal to one-half the pulse rate, or $W = f_s/2$.

2. This puts very severe restrictions on the sampling times at the receiver, A small time displacement would result in substantial spurious amplitude at the sampling times. Extremely accurate and stable oscillators, which deviate no more than about 50° in phase from the incoming signal, must be used. Thus, rather expensive equipment is required. Drift due to temperature variations also constitutes a real problem.

To overcome the above difficulty, pilot tones can be used to generate the sampling frequency, but noise in the system can cause timing jitter in the actual pilot. In addition, pilot tones require the use of a separate, but parallel, transmission path in order to avoid cross-talk, and phase jitter can be introduced as a result of variations in gains of the parallel path.

Because substantial undershoots and overshoots can appear at the adjacent sampling instants as a result of time shift in the signal and non zero pulse durations, other system frequency characteristics have been developed to reduce these problems. Furthermore, the ideal filter is unattainable in practice. Two solution in present use that have been found acceptable are the *raised cosine response* and *partial response encoding.*

6.2.2. The Sinusoidal Roll-Off

As impulses are unattainable in practice and the ideal, or brick-wall filter cannot be built, for designing a digital communication channel, we look for appropriate adjustments to be made to the impulse type signals and filters.

The desired end result is a filter response which is realizable and which produces minimum overshoots and undershoots in its ringing and which passes through zero at adjacent sampling times. When the combination of pulse shape, channel, and equalizer have an overall add symmetric transfer function about $W/2$, as illustrated by dotted wave in Fig. 6.4 (*b*), the response to an impulse results in small overshoots and undershoots and passes through zero at the sampling instances of $nT = n/W$. By selecting a suitable response, the filter becomes realizable since there are no abrupt changes and the slopes are finite. In such a model, the tails of neighbouring pulses do not interferes with the main pulse. The transmission channel can compensate for any deviation of the pulse from the impulse function.

As infinite number of functions have the vestigial symmetry ; some are practical, but most are not. Of particular interest is the *sinusoidal roll-off* defined by

$$X(f) = \left\{ \begin{array}{ll} \dfrac{1}{2W} & |f| < W - f_1 \\ \dfrac{1}{4W}\left[1 - \sin \dfrac{\pi\,(|f| - W)}{2f_1}\right] & W - f_1 \le |f| \le W + f_1 \\ 0 & |f| > W + f_1 \end{array} \right\} \quad \ldots(6.5)$$

where $f_1 \le W$ and the total bandwidth is $B = W + f_1$. The resultant pulse shape can be found by transforming $X(f)$ as

$$x(t) = \text{sinc } 2Wt \frac{\cos 2\pi f_1 t}{1 - (4f_1 t)^2} \qquad ...(6.6)$$

For $f_1 = 0$, this equation reduces to a sinc pulse.

In Fig. 6.4 (*b*), we have shown $X(f)$ and $x(t)$ for $f_1 = 0, W/2$, and W. We observe the following advantages :

1. In all cases of $x(t)$, the desired zeros occur at $t_k = k/2W$. It means that one can signal synchronously at $s = 2W$.

2. If $f_1 \neq 0$, the leading and trailing oscillations decay more rapidly. It means that synchronisation is less critical than with sinc pulses.

3. If $f_1 = W$, (*a*) the half-amplitude pulse width is exactly $1/2W$. This is equivalent to the pulse-to-pulse spacing if $s = 2W$; and (*b*) there are additional zero crossings at $t = \pm 3/4W, \pm 5/4W, ...$ Therefore, a digital waveform constructed from such pulses will have negligible inter-symbol interference for any signalling speed $s \leq 2W$. In addition, it is possible to closely approximate the corresponding system response.

In sinc pulse spectrum, energy exists at all frequencies, to retain the rectangular pulse shape would require an infinite transmission bandwidth. Practical communication systems are always bandwidth limited. Not only is infinite bandwidth not available, interference considerations in radio links dictate that a communication system should use the smallest possible bandwidth, and this is usually one of the design criteria of a communication system.

6.2.3. The Raised Cosine Channel Response

Another acceptable solution to the problem of designing a communication channel is the raised-cosine response. Although such a response is not strictly realizable, it can be more closely approximately than the brick-wall response. It has a gradual roll-off of up to about 1.5 times the Nyquist rate, but cuts-off rapidly at twice the Nyquist rate. It is given by :

$$X(f) = \frac{1}{2W} \cos^2 \frac{\pi |f|}{4W} \Pi \left(\frac{f}{2W} \right) \qquad ...(6.7)$$

The corresponding pulse shape would be given by the inverse transform of $X(f)$, *i.e.*,

$$x(t) = \frac{\text{sinc } 4Wt}{1 - (4Wt)^2} \qquad ...(6.8)$$

We now make the following observations:

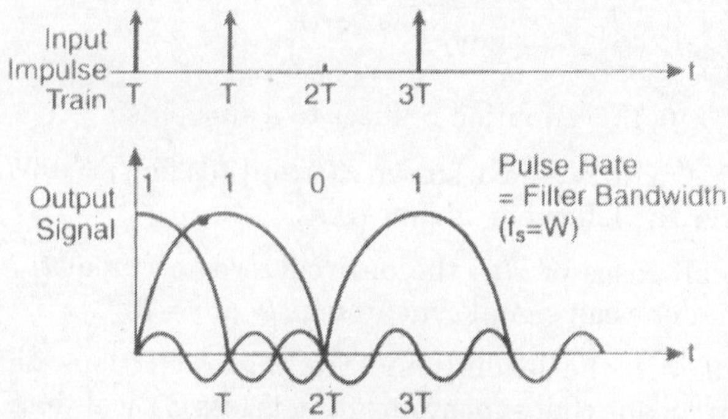

Fig. 6.5. Response of Raised-Cosine Filter for 1101 Input Signal Input after Bandlimiting.

1. Intersymbol interference will not occur if the pulse train is timed such that at every time interval $T = 1/W$, the tails of all neighbouring pulses are zero volts. Only the desired pulse or no pulse will be present at the appropriate sampling instants, as shown in Fig. 6.5.

2. The undershoot and overshoot errors are drastically reduced. The slope of the ringing curve is also much gentler near the sampling times, which permits more jitter, or room for time displacement, then the sin x/x type of ringing present in the case of the brickwall filter.

3. The total bandwidth required for a raised cosine spectrum is $B = W + f_1 = 2W$. It means that the maximum (synch- ronons) signaling speed is $s = B$. This is equal to half of the maximum signaling speed $s = 2B$ obtainable from an ideal rectangular response.

4. When $f_1 = W/2$, the sinusoidal roll-off is 50 per cent. Then the signaling speed becomes $s = 1.5B$. However, two problems may occur:

(*i*) It is difficult to obtain the necessary system response, and

(*ii*) Inter-symbol interference becomes a problem if synchronisation is lost.

In general, we conclude that the maximum signaling speed for a given bandwidth B is

$$S_{\max} = kB$$

$$1 \le k \le 2$$

Note that for larger values of k, the system's design becomes more complex.

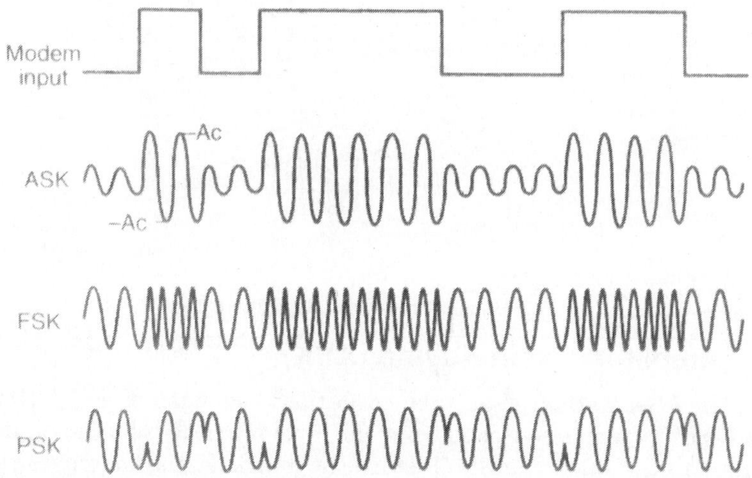

Fig. 6.6. Different Types of Digital Modulation.

6.3. Digital Carrier Systems

As there are many modulation methods for analog signals, the digital information can also be introduced to a carrier wave in many ways. Four basic forms of digital modulation schemes used to convert digital data into suitable analog signals for telephone lines are:

I. Amplitude Shift Keying (ASK).

II. Frequency Shift Keying (FSK).

III. Phase Shift Keying (PSK).

IV. Quadrature Amplitude Modulation (QAM).

For digital data transmitted at low bit rates, the modulated signal usually carries the information in two-level ASK, two-level FSK or two-level PSK. Each of these one-bit-per-state schemes is illustrated in Fig. 6.6.

Because FSK is relatively simple in its operation and thus inexpensive to implement, it is used extensively in low-speed modems for data rates below 1200 bits/sec. FSK is not efficient, however, in its use of spectrum space.

For the higher data rates, multi-phase PSK synchronous data transmission is generally used. Typically, four-phase PSK is used at 2400 bits/sec, and eight-phase PSK is used at 4800 bits/sec.

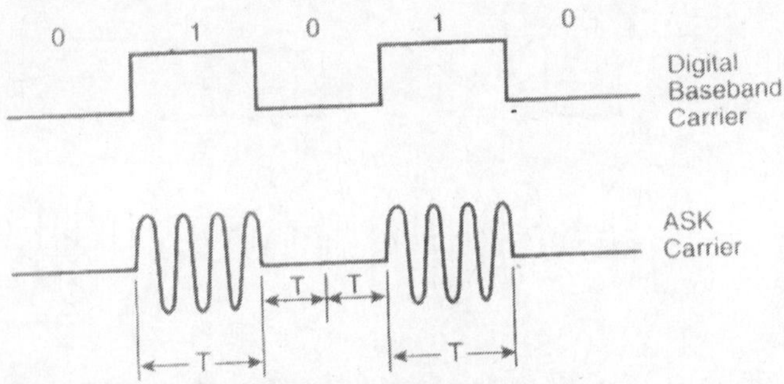

Fig. 6.7. Principle of Amplitude Shift Keying.

6.4. Amplitude-Shift Keying (ASK)

The ASK method of digital modulation is shown in Fig. 6.7. Here the carrier wave is switched from one level to another by the digital (binary) signal. During the '1' state the 'mark' signal increases the carrier level while during the '0' state of 'space' signal the carrier level is reduced. This method is also widely termed as *'ON-OFF' Keying* (OOK) when the carrier is made off during space periods. In fact, this method was originally used in wireless circuits. Thus if the carrier is represented by $e = E_c \sin(\omega_c t + \phi)$ then the modulated signal using on-off keying (ASK) may be expressed as

$$s(t) = a(t) \,.\, E_c \sin(\omega_c t + \phi) \qquad ...(6.9)$$

where $a(t)$ is the baseband signal represented as

$$a(t) = \sum_{n=-\infty}^{\infty} b_n \, v(t - nT)$$

In fact, for mark signal $a(t) = 1$ and $a(t) = 0$ for space signal.

On taking the fourier transform of Eq. (6.9) it will be noticed that the effect of *on-off* keying is to produce a pair of upper and lower sidebands. The bandwidth of such a system is therefore twice the highest frequency present in the signal.

A modification of ASK is the *quadrature* ASK (QASK) which is also known as quadrature AM (QAM). The QASK signal is of the form

$$s(t) = a_1(t)\, E_c \sin(\omega_c t + \phi) + a_2(t)\, E_c \cos(\omega_c t + \phi) \qquad ...(6.10)$$

where $a_1(t)\, E_c \sin(\omega_c t + \phi)$ represents inphase component and $a_2(t) E_c \cos(\omega_c t + \phi)$ represents quadrature component. Each of these two components of the QASK signal is an ASK signal with pulse duration T_s (where $T_s = 2T$ if the source produces binary digits at the rate of one bit every T seconds). Thus for binary ($m = 2$), $a_1(t)$ and

$a_2(t)$ signals are in-phase and quadrature signals are binary ASK signals of $(1/T_s)$ bits per second. In that case, the total data rate for QASK signal would be $2/T_s = 1/T$ bits per sec.

The *ASK* can be generated by either of these methods:

1. *AM* modulator having a polar input.

2. A balanced modulator with a unipolar input. In both cases, double-sideband linear modulation is achieved. The transmission bandwidth is, therefore, twice that of the baseband bandwidth. The necessary bandwidth is given by

$$B_T = 2B = 2\frac{s}{K} \qquad \text{...(6.11)}$$

where s = sigalling speed (digits/sec)

B = baseband bandwidth, and

K = pulse-shape factor.

In practice, larger values of B_T are used to facilitate minimization of noise with the help of pulse-shaping filters after detection.

6.4.1. VSB-ASK

One technique to reduce B_T or increase the signaling speed is to pass the modulated signal through a *VSB* filter. It makes the bandwidth equal to nearly half *i.e.* $B_T \cong B = s/K$. This is because one sideband has been removed except the vestigial portion. However, complete sideband suppression is not possible.

6.4.2. ASK Detection

The *ASK* wave can be detected by two methods :

1. Coherent or synchronous detection.
2. Non-coherent or envelope detection.

The *advantage* of coherent detection is its less vulnerability to noise and that of envelope detection is its simplicity of circuitry.

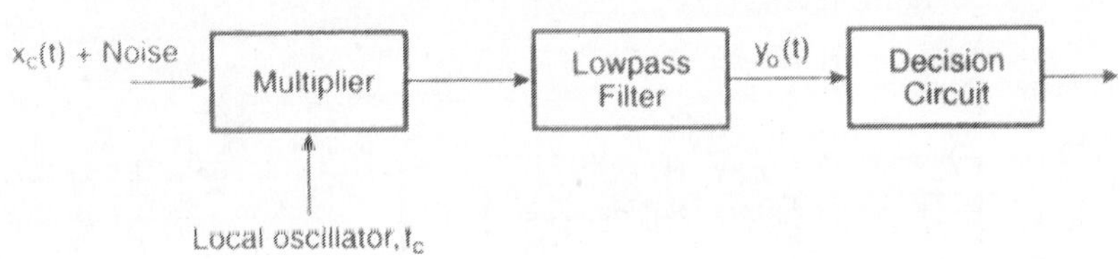

Fig. 6.8. *ASK* Coherent Detection.

As shown in Fig. 6.8, the *ASK* signal is multiplied by the output of a local oscillator which is synchronized to the carrier. The product is then passed through a lowpass filter

6.5. Frequency-Shift Keying (FSK)

In *FSK*, each of the possible message symbols varies frequency of an *RF* wave. Therefore, it is constant *RF* pulses having different frequencies as shown in Fig. 6.9. In other words, *FSK* wave is two (or more) interleaved on-off *ASK* signals of differing carrier frequencies.

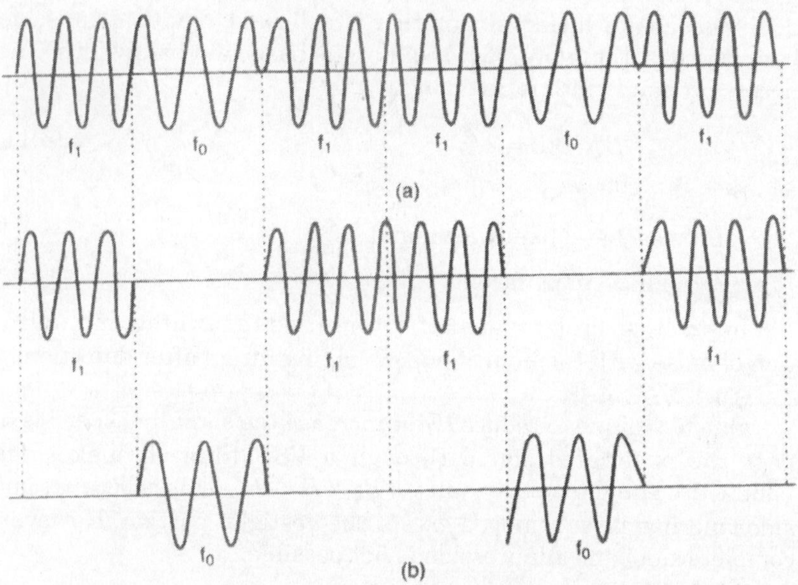

Fig. 6.9. (*a*) *FSK* Waveform ; (*b*) *FSK* as Two *ASK* Waves.

The principle of *FSK* detection is based on *ASK* technique and has following features :

(*i*) One synchronous or envelope detector is used for each frequency.

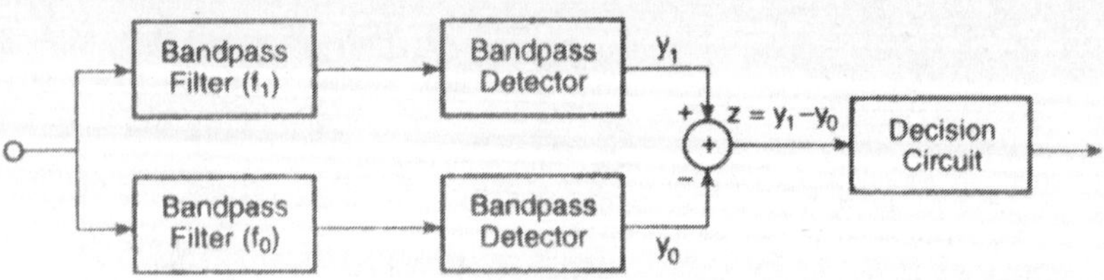

Fig. 6.10. Non-coherent *FSK* Detection.

(*ii*) The detector with the largest output indicates the transmitted frequency.

Fig. 6.10 shows the envelope detection system for binary *FSK*. The input to the decision circuit is the difference in the outputs of the two detectors, *i.e.*, $z = y_1 - y_o$.

When input frequency is f_1, $y_1 = k_D A_c$, and $y_o = 0$.

When input frequency is f_v, $y_1 = 0$, and $y_o = k_D A_c$.

Thus, the decision circuit choses **1** if $z > 0$, and choses **0** if $z < 0$. It means the threshold level is chosen to be zero.

6.5.1 Binary Frequency Shift Keying (BFSK)

The binary frequency shift keying employs two different carrier frequencies which are switched ON and OFF alternatively by the mark and space signals. A mark signal switches ON one carrier while the other carrier remains OFF. Under the space conditions the first carricr is switched off and the second carrier is switched ON. Thus mathematically

$$s_{UB}(t) = \sqrt{2P_s} \cos(\omega_c \pm \Omega) t \qquad \text{...(6.12)}$$

showing the two angular frequencies of $\omega_c + \Omega$ and $\omega_c - \Omega$ with Ω a constant offset from the normal carrier frequency ω. The quantity Ω is called the *frequency deviation* (f_d) and the parameter $h = 2f_dT$ is called the *deviation ratio* or *modulation index* for the FSK signal set. Conventionally the signal at $(f_c + f_d)$ is called the *space* signal (binary digit) and at $(f_c - f_d)$ is called the *mark signal* (binary digit). The bandwidth of BFSK signal is $4f_b \left(f_b = \dfrac{1}{T}\right)$ and is twice the bandwidth of BPSK.

A generalization of binary FSK can be carried out to *M*-ary FSK. The bandwidth in *M*-ary FSK would be

$$BW = 2Mf_s \qquad \text{... (6.13)}$$

where $f_s = f_b/N$ and $M = 2^N$.

Thus $BW = 2^{N+1} f_b/N$ ...(6.14)

Thus *M*-ary FSK requires a considerably increased bandwidth in comparison with *M* ary PSK. However, it has been established that the probability of error for *M*-ary FSK decreases as *M* increases while for *M*-ray FSK, the probability of error increases with *M*. Another modification of FSK is the *continuous phase frequency shift keying* (CPFSK) when alongwith the frequency shifts there is a phase shift too.

6.5.2. Comparison of FSK and ASK

1. Like *FM*, *FSK* has constant amplitude and, therefore, on this account provides the same advantages as the *FM*.

2. The error probability of *ASK* is less than that of *ASK* for smaller *S* / *N* ratios.

3. For *ASK*, The threshold level is a function of amplitude A_c, which, in turn, requires continuous readjustment as the signal strength varies with time. In case of *FSK*, on the other hand, the threshold level is zero *volts, i.e.*, independent of carrier amplitude. This makes *FSK* preferred to *ASK* in applications where fading of radio signal is prevalent and synchronous detection is not feasible.

6.5.3. FSK and FM Comparison

The binary *FSK*, as compared with *FM*, does not give the wideband noise reduction. The reason is that essentially *FSK* is *AM* rather than *FM*. In case of *FM*, detection by a limiter-discriminator makes the required transmission bandwidth to control intersymbol interference so large that the increased pre-detection noise is cancelled by the noise reduction effect. Only for multi-level signals (μ>2), some amount of bandwidth-power exchange is possible.

6.6. Phase-Shift Keying (PSK)

In the phase shift keying, the mark and space signal are represented by 180° phase shift and zero phase shift respectively. The amplitude of the *RF* carrier is kept fixed. The most important kind of phase shift keying technique is *binary phase shift keying* (BPSK). Here the transmitted *rf* signal is a sinusoid of fixed amplitude but its phase has been shifted by $+\pi/2$ radians or $-\pi/2$ radians depending upon the data bit 0 or 1 is being transmitted. Thus the total phase difference for the two levels (0 and 1) is 180°. Fig. 6.11 represents the principle of binary phase shift keying. In this figure the data bits

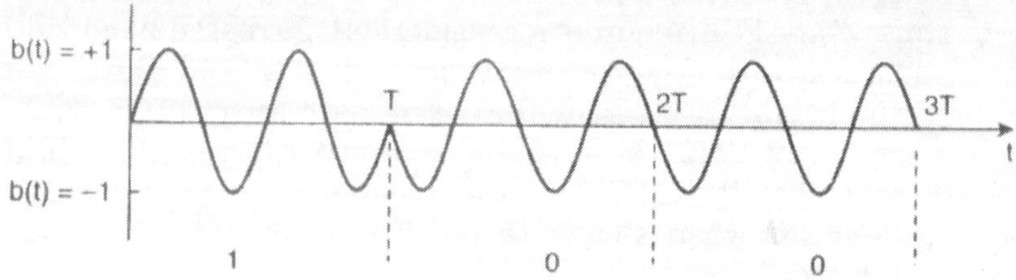

Fig. 6.11. Binary Phase Shift Keying Data Rate 1/T Bits/sec.

1, 0, 0 are being transmitted at the channel rate of $f_b = \frac{1}{T}$ bits per second (or the bandwidth = $2f_b$). Thus if the transmitted sinusoid is of amplitude A, it has a power $P_s = \frac{1}{2}A^2$ so that $A = \sqrt{2P_s}$. Thus the transmitted signal is either

$$S_{\text{bpsk}}(t) = \sqrt{2P_s}\cos(\omega_c t) \qquad \text{...(6.15)}$$

or

$$= \sqrt{2P_s}\cos(\omega_c t + \pi)$$

$$= -\sqrt{2P_s}\cos(\omega_c t) \qquad \text{... (6.16)}$$

$$S_{\text{bpsk}}(t) = b(t)\cos(\omega_c t) \qquad \text{...(6.17)}$$

where $b(t) = +1V$ represents the logical level 1 and $b(t) = -1V$ represents the logical level 0. It may be noted that the binary PSK may be considered as amplitude modulation by a sequence of rectangular pulses of duration T with amplitude + 1 and – 1.

We will now discuss a two-phase or binary phase-shift keying system and then briefly discuss the implementation of a four-phase *PSK* system.

Binary Phase Shift Keying (*BPSK*) is obtained through the system shown in Fig. 6.12. The data signal is translated into a non-return-to-zero (*NRZ*) code having no *dc* component. The resulting pulses of amplitude $+A_c$ or $-A_c$ represent the binary 1's and 0's.

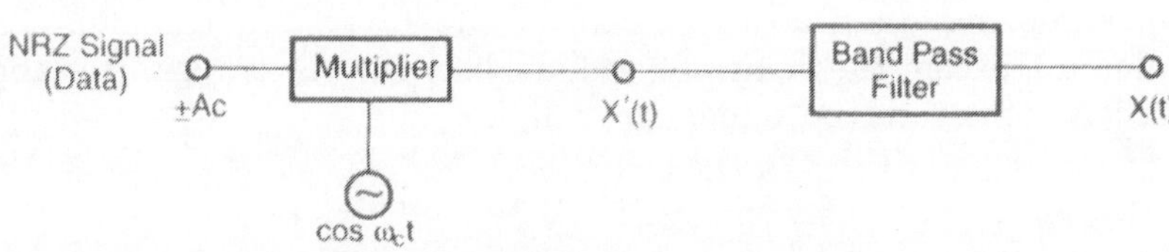

Fig. 6.12. *BPSK* Modulation.

A general expression of the $x'(t)$ spectrum can be obtained by considering the modulating *NRZ* signal to consist of a train of square wave pulses without a *dc* bias. If the pulse rate is f_m, the spectrum of this pulse train would have the typical $\sin x/x$ or sinc amplitude response for the odd harmonics of f_m.

When the square wave, which contains only odd harmonics of f_m, is multiplied by the sinusoid of frequency the harmonics of f_m are obtained as sidebands around the frequency f_c, where $f_c \geq f_m$. Since no *dc* is present in the *NRZ* signal, the carrier at f_c is suppressed.

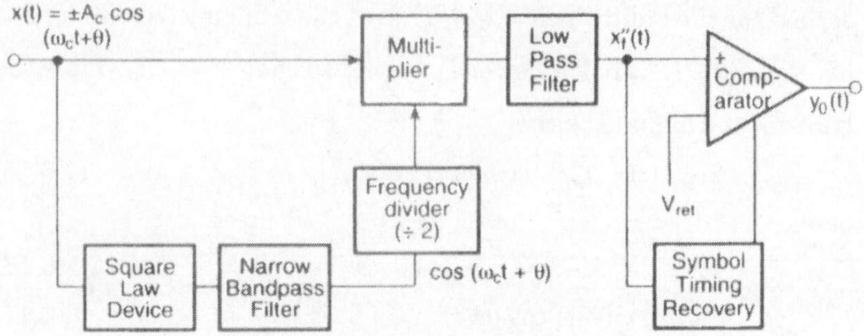

Fig. 6.13. *BPSK* Demodulator.

The spectrum bandwidth taken up by the modulated signal is twice the baseband or modulation bandwidth. The bandpass filter is inserted to limit the transmitted spectrum. A possible negative effect of adding such a filter might be a non-uniform time delay of the various frequency components in the signal, particularly for those lying near the filter skirts if the filter is not correctly designed. This makes the system more susceptible to noise.

Fig. 6.13. shows the corresponding *BPSK* demodulator or detector.

Ignoring all filtering effects of the filter and transmission medium except the delay of θ radians between the transmitter and receiver the received signal, $x(t)$ will be

$$x(t) = \pm A_c \cos(\omega_c t + \theta) \qquad \ldots (6.18)$$

Now in order to demodulate this signal, the carrier at the correct phase must be extracted. This is done in the carrier recovery section by squaring the received signal and then filtering out the desired second harmonic with a bandpass filter. The squared signal can be expressed as

$$x^2(t) = A_c^2 \cos^2(\omega_c t + \theta) = \frac{A_c^2}{2} + \frac{A_c^2}{2} \cos 2(\omega_c t + \theta) \ldots (6.19)$$

The divide-by-two circuit yields the desired *cos* $(\omega_c t + 0)$ carrier from the second term.

When the received modulated signal is mixed or multiplied by the extracted carrier, we get

$$y_D(t) = \pm A_c \cos(\omega_c t + \theta)\cos(\omega_c t + \theta) = \pm\frac{A_c}{2} \pm \frac{A_c}{2}\cos 2(\omega_c t + \theta) \quad \text{... (6.20)}$$

The desired signal $\pm A/2$ is extracted by the low-pass filter. The comparator circuit, which is clocked at the symbol rate, finally determines whether a 1 or a 0 logic state is detected.

6.7. Four-phase Or Quarternary PSK (QPSK)

In the BPSK the channel bandwidth is $2f_b$ where $f_b = \frac{1}{T}$ (T is the bit duration). In the quadrature phase shift keying QPSK, the data bits are allowed to be transmitted using half the bandwidth. Thus whereas the BPSK is a two state or biphase PSK, the QPSK is a four state or quadriphase PSK. Thus as M-phase PSK modulator would put the phase of the carrier into one of the M states according to the value of the modulating voltage. The transmitted signal QPSK or the interval $[nT, (n + 1) 1]$ can be written as

$$s(t) = A\cos(\omega_c t + \theta_k) \quad \text{...(6.21)}$$

where k denotes the message to be sent in the nth interval ($k = 0, 1, 2$ or 3). The four different values of θ_k must be separated by $\frac{\pi}{2}$ radians. For example one may have $\{\theta_k$: $k = 0, 1, 2, 3$ as the set $\left\{0, \frac{\pi}{2}, \pi, \frac{3\pi}{2}\right\}$ or the set $\left\{\frac{\pi}{4}, \frac{3\pi}{4}, \frac{5\pi}{4}, \frac{7\pi}{4}\right\}$. It is essential that the phase difference of $\frac{\pi}{2}$ is maintained. Eq. (6.21) may also be written as

$$s(t) = A\cos[\omega_c t + \theta(t)] \quad \text{...(6.22)}$$

where $\theta(t)$ represents phase modulation and is a sequence of rectangular pulses of duration T and amplitude $\left(\frac{\pi}{2}\right) b_n$ with $b_n = 0, 1, 2$ or 3.

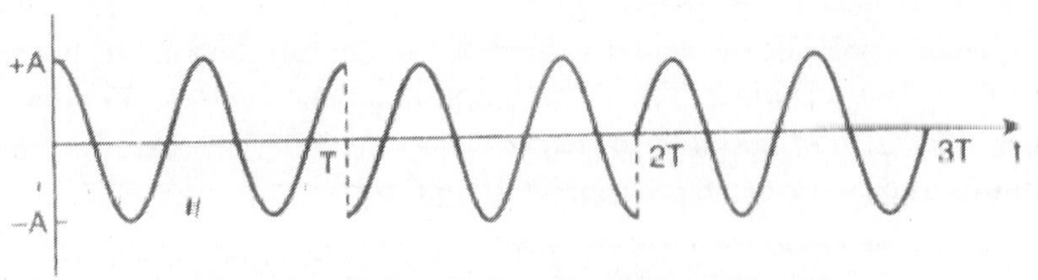

Fig. 6.14. Example of QPSK with Data Rate 2/T Bits/sec.

Fig. 6.14 indicates the QPSK signal for the data sequence in $b_0 = 0$, $b_1 = 2$ and $b_2 = 3$. Here the data rate is $2/T$ bits per second.

The power in QPSK signal is $A^2/2$, just as for BPSK and so the energy per pulse is $E = A^2 T/2$. The QPSK gives 2 bits of data per pulse and therefore the energy per bit for QPSK is $E_b = \frac{A^2T}{4}$ which is one half of the energy per bit for BPSK for the same pulse duration T. Thus when QPSK compared with BPSK for the same data rates, BPSK requires twice the bandwidth of QPSK. However, if the two signals have the same data rate and equal power, they also have the same energy per data bit.

It would be worthwhile to mention here that there are also some other modifications of BPSK such as differential phase-shift keying (DPSK), differentially-encoded PSK (DEPSK), offset QPSK (OQPSK), Non offset QPSK, Minimum shift keying (MSK). Infact all these kinds of PSK can be grouped under *direct* or *differential*, depending on whether it is the state of modulating voltage or the *change* in the state of the modulating voltage that determines the transmitted phase. A generalization of BPSK has also been carried out that is widely termed as *M-ary PSK* and-now-a days hardware to accomplish such M-ary communication is available. The principle of M-ary PSK is explained below :

We have seen above that in BPSK, each bit is transmitted individually. Depending on whether $b(t)$ is logic 0 or logic 1, one transmits one or another of a sinusoid for the bit time T_b, the sinusoids differing in phase by $\frac{2\pi}{2} = 180°$.

In QPSK, the two bits are lumped together and depending upon which of the four two-bit words develops, one transmits one or another of four sinusoids of duration $2T$, the sinusoids differing in phase by amount $\frac{2\pi}{4} = 90°$.

In M-ary PSK, the scheme is extended. On lumping together the N bits so that in this N-bit *symbol* extending over the time NT, there would be $2^N = M$ possible symbols. Thus, $N = 1$ or $M = 2$ represents binary and $N = 2$ or $M = 4$ represents quaternary.

Now let these N bit symbols be represented by sinusoids of duration $NT = T_s$ which differ from one another by the phase $2\pi/M$. Then the M-ary PSK waveforms could be represented as

$$S_m(t) = \sqrt{2P_s} \cos(\omega_c t + \phi_m), \; m = 0, 1, ... (M-1) \quad ...(6.23)$$

With the symbol phase angle given by

$$\phi_m = (2m + 1)\,\pi/M \qquad ...(6.24)$$

The bandwidth is therefore

$$B = \frac{2}{T_s} = 2f_s = \frac{2}{NT} = \frac{2f_b}{N} \qquad ...(6.25)$$

It is thus evident that as one increases the number of bits N per symbol the bandwidth becomes progressively smaller. It should be noted that the QPSK is the most popular choice of modulation techniques for use in satellite communication links carrying digital data. The main reason is the high values of (C/N) required for acceptable bit error rates, typically > 26 dB.

QPSK is used for higher bit rates typically 2400 bits/sec. For the four-phase PSK system, the data stream is divided into blocks of two bits each, called *dibits*, with each dibit related to one of the four phases. A 1200 *baud* system operates at an information rate of 2400 *bits / sec*.

QPSK is widely used on satellite links, including direct broadcast satellite television. High-speed modems designed for telephone lines use QAM to send a high bit rate in a small bandwidth (*e.g.* 28.8 Kbits/sec in 4 kHz bandwidth).

A typical waveform of a four-phase system is shown in Fig. 6.15. Here, the Gray code is used in which adjacent phases undergo only a one bit change in the two bits. This reduces the effects of noise on a data signal. In the straight binary code, going from a 1(01) to a 2(10) represents a two-bit error whereas for the Gray code only a single bit error is produced.

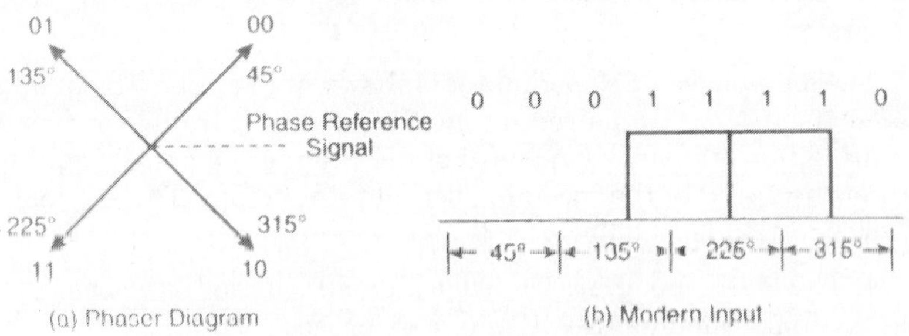

(*a*) Phaser Diagram (*b*) Modem Input

Fig. 6.15.

For bit rate of 1,800 bits/sec, *eight-phase PSK* is used, in which each phase is represented three bits, called a *tribit*. Here also as we move from phase to phase, only one bit undergoes a change because of use of Gray code.

6.7.1. Quadrature AM

For data transmission rates of 9600 bits/sec, a technique employing a combination of phase and amplitude modulation is used. Fig. 6.16 shows the phase diagram.

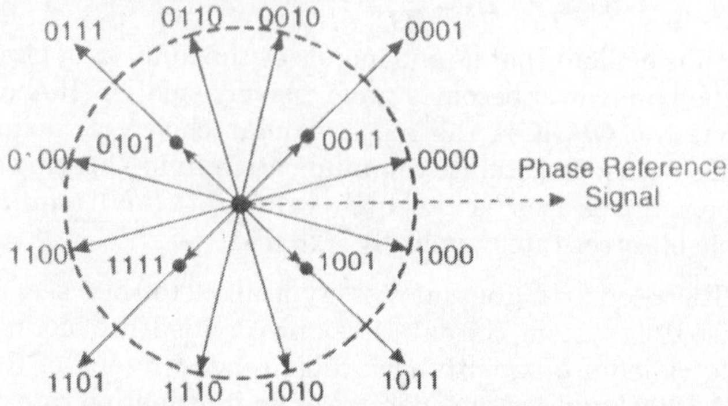

Fig. 6.16. Phase Diagram Of Quadrature Amplitude Modulation (*QAM*).

QAM is a modulation that combines the four phase states of QPSK with multiple pulse amplitudes as in m-ASK. For example, 256-QAM is a modulation in which each symbol represents 8 bits and bas 256 possible states. There are four phase states and pulses can have $2^6 = 64$ possible amplitude levels.

6.7.2. Generation of QPSK

For highest bit rates, each interval or symbol of the signal is made to carry two or three bit of information. The signal generation is based on a serial-to-parallel conversion performed at the transmitter to group the incoming data stream into groups of two or three bits, depending upon whether four or eight-phase modulation is used. The receiver performs the complementary parallel-to-serial conversion.

The four-phase PSK modulator is shown in Fig. 6.17. The binary digits, the *dibits*, are paired up by the serial-to-parallel converter resulting in a transmission speed of the channels X and Y equal to half of the speed of the incoming serial data stream. The sequence of its operation is as follows :

1. The lower modulator is fed with a 90° carrier ($\cos \omega_c t + \pi/2$), and the upper modulator with a 0° carrier ($\cos \omega_c t$).

2. When the lower modulator obtains an input X of digit 0, the output consists of a 90° carrier. When the input X digit is a 1, the output consists of a $-90°$ carrier.

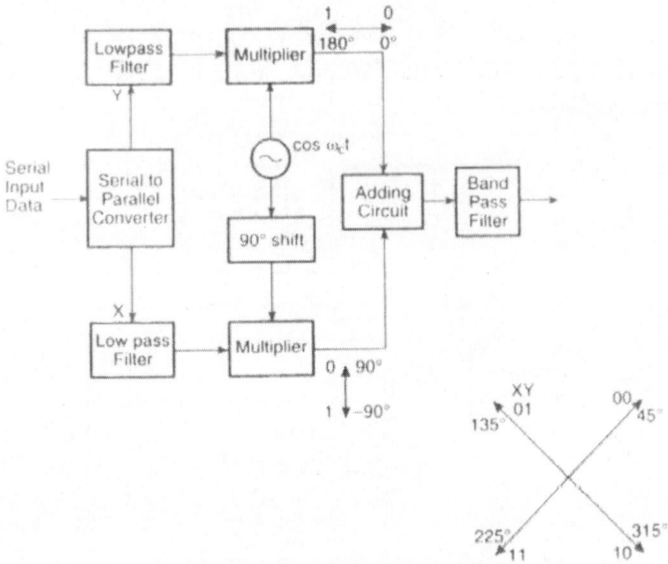

Fig. 6.17. Four-phase *PSK* Modulator.

3. Similarly, the output from the upper modulator is at 0° or 180° corresponding to input *Y* being equal to an 0 or a 1.

Table 6.1 presents the voltage signals for binary values of *X* and *Y*. The corresponding output voltage from the modulator can be represented by the phasors also shown in Fig. 6.17. By summing the two output signals from the modulators, the output phasor diagram is obtained.

Table 6.1. Four-Phase PSK Modulator Signal

Channel	*Binary Level*	*Voltages*	*Output*
	0	V	$A_c \cos \omega_c t$
Y	1	$-V$	$-A_c \cos \omega_c t = A_c \cos(\omega_c t + \pi)$
	0	V	$A_c \cos (\omega_c t + \pi/2)$
X	1	$-V$	$-A_c \cos(\omega_c t + \pi/2) = A_c \cos (\omega_c t + \pi/2)$

6.7.3. Detection of QPSK

For the detection of the four-phase signal, a fixed reference phase signal is made available at the receiver. Fig. 6.18 shows such a receiver. With a received signal of cos $(\omega_c t + \theta)$, the output from the multipliers can be written as

$$\cos(\omega_c t + \theta)\cos(\omega_c t + \phi) = \frac{1}{2}\cos(\theta - \phi) + \frac{1}{2}\cos(2\,\omega_c t + \theta + \phi) \quad ...(6.23)$$

where ϕ takes a value of 0 or 90°, depending upon which modulator is being considered.

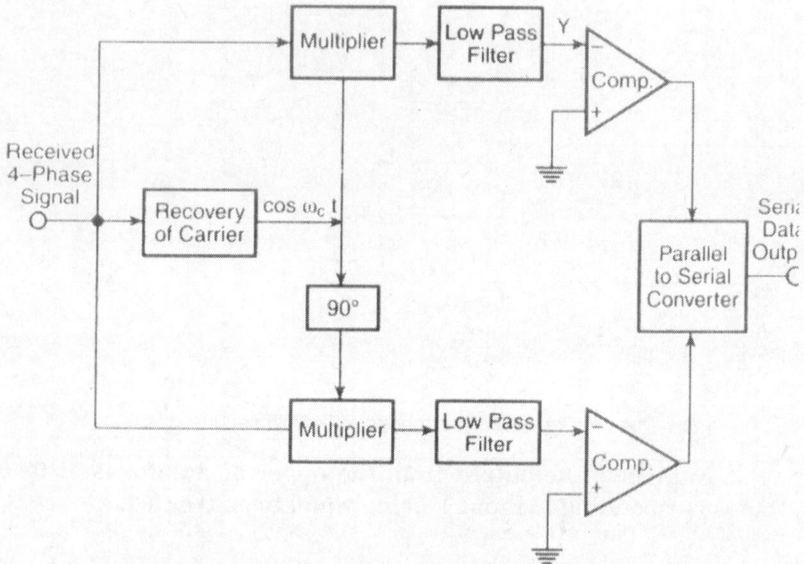

Fig. 6.18. Four-phase *PSK* Demodulator.

Table 6.2. Four-phase PSK Demodulator Output

Received Signal Phase	*Output X*	*Output Y*	*Data Output*	
			X	*Y*
45°	$\frac{1}{2}\cos 45° = 0.35$	$\frac{1}{2}\cos 45° = 0.35$	0	0
135°	$\frac{1}{2}\cos 45° = 0.35$	$\frac{1}{2}\cos 135° = -0.35$	0	1
225°	$\frac{1}{2}\cos 135° = -0.35$	$\frac{1}{2}\cos 225° = -0.35$	1	1
315°	$\frac{1}{2}\cos 225° = -0.35$	$\frac{1}{2}\cos 315° = 0.35$	1	0

The function of low-pass filter (LPF) is to remove the second harmonic components of $2\omega_c$. Note that the incoming signal phase must take on one of the values of ± 45° or ± 135°. When this signal is multiplied by the reference oscillator of phase $\phi = 0°$ or 90°, the signal obtained at the LPF output is as given in Table 6.2. The oscillator circuits detect the *dc* signal level from the LP filters to note the digital value. With the comparators shown, the comparator output goes low when the input exceeds *zero volts*, indicating a 0. With the help of parallel-to-serial converter the two-bit symbol is converted back to two bits of serial data.

6.7.4. Differential PSK (DPSK)

In a PSK system, although it is quite feasible to obtain a fixed phase recovered carrier, it is difficult to obtain the required absolute phase. The receiver must be given some indication of the proper phase reference since it is relatively easy for the carrier recovery phase to rest at 90° or 180° from the desired phase difference.

Morever, the advantages of coherent PSK have been obtained at the cost of synchronous detection. Non-coherent detection cannot be used because the information resides in phase reversals.

This difficulty is overcome in differential phase modulation and detection. In this modulation scheme, the information is encoded in terms of phase changes between adjacent symbols, rather than as an absolute phase for each symbol.

In the two-phase, coherent *PSK* system, we have seen that a 1 corresponds to a 0 phase signal and a 0 corresponds to a 180° phase signal. In the modified differential phase modulation system, a 1 may correspond to a 0° change between successive signals and a 0 correspond to a 180° change between successive signals. At the receiver, each succeeding signal is compared with the phase of the previously received signal. Note that since noise interfers with both the current signal and the reference signal, the signal-to-noise ratio must be slightly greater in order to achieve similar error rates.

Fig. 6.19 shows the block diagram of a differential phase shift keyed (*DPSK*) modulator.

Example below presents the encoding of a data bit stream. To begin the encoding, a reference binary digit of 1 is chosen. Because of the delay in the feedback path, the present message bit (data

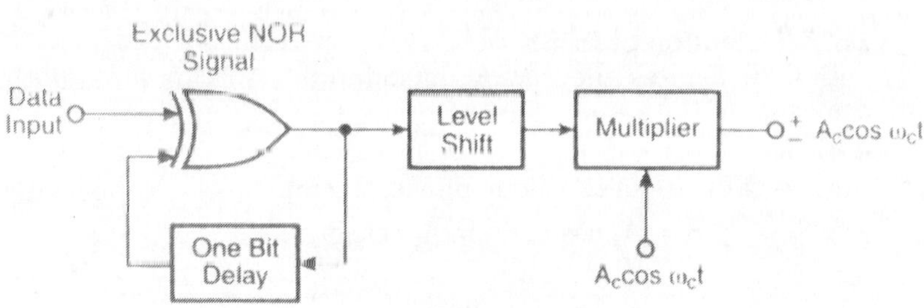

Fig. 6.19. *DPSK* Modulator.

input) is compared with the previously encoded signal bit to arrive at the following digit for the encoded signal.

Example – DPSK Encoding and Detection

Encoding

Data input		**0**	**1**	**0**	**1**	**1**	**1**	**0**	0	**1**	**1**	**0**
Encoded signal (reference digit)	1	0	0	1	1	1	1	0	1	1	1	0
Transmitted phase	0	π	π	0	0	0	0	π	0	0	0	π

Detection

Received message	0	π	π	0	0	0	0	π	0	0	0	π
Comparator input		$-\frac{A_c^2}{2}$	$\frac{A_c^2}{2}$	$-\frac{A_c^2}{2}$	$\frac{A_c^2}{2}$	$\frac{A_c^2}{2}$	$\frac{A_c^2}{2}$	$-\frac{A_c^2}{2}$	$-\frac{A_c^2}{2}$	$\frac{A_c^2}{2}$	$\frac{A_c^2}{2}$	$-\frac{A_c^2}{2}$
Output bit stream		0	1	0	1	1	1	0	0	1	1	0

Let us study the above example in detail:

1. The first digit in the message, namely a 0, is compared with the initialisation bit of 1, resulting in a 0 appearing as the next encoded bit.
2. The latter 0 bit is the reference for the next digit to be encoded.
3. Comparing this 0 with the next message digit of 1 results in another 0 as the next encoded digit.
4. The resulting encoded message is then level-shifted to a +1 or –1 to be multiplied by the unmodulated carrier $A \cos \omega_c t$, which results in a phase-shifted carrier of 0 or π radian.

6.7.5. Detection of DPSK

Fig. 6.20 depicts the *DPSK* demodulator. In this circuit, the adjacent bits of the received are compared bit by bit. There are two possibilities :

(*a*) If they are of the same phase, the multiplier output will be

$$y'_D = (A_c \cos \omega_c t)^2 = [A_c \cos (\omega_c t + \pi)]^2$$

$$= \frac{A_c^2}{2} + \ldots\ \frac{A_c^2}{2} \cos 2\omega_c t \qquad \ldots (6.24)$$

The desired component is $A_c^2/2$ and is positive.

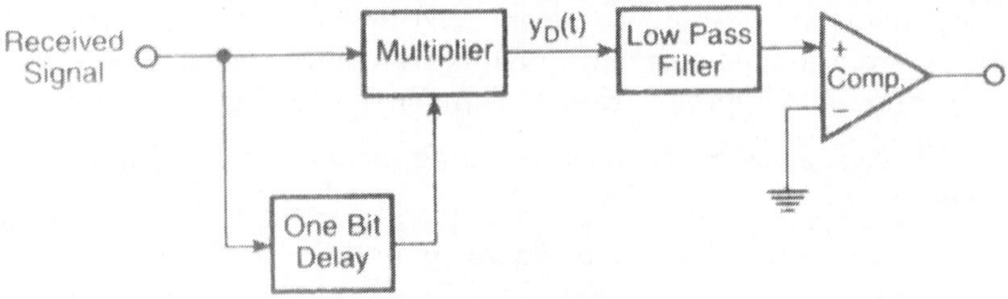

Fig. 6.20. *DPSK* Demodulator.

(*b*) If they are of different phases, the multiplier output will be

$$y_{D'} = A_c \cos \omega_c t . A_c \cos (\omega_c t + \pi)$$

$$= \frac{A_c^2}{2} \cos \pi + \frac{A_c^2}{2} \cos(2\omega_c t + \pi)$$

$$= -\frac{A_c^2}{2} + \frac{A_c^2}{2} \cos (2\omega_c t + \pi) \quad \text{... (6.25)}$$

The desired component is $-A_c^2/2$.

The dc term is fed to the low-pass filter so that it can be applied to a comparator. The comparator translates the *dc* levels of $+A_c^2/2$ and $-A_c^2/2$ to 1's and 0's.

When the threshold voltage of 0 *volts* is exceeded, a 1 results. If the input voltage below the zero threshold voltage, a 0 results. The detected message is also shown in the example above.

6.8. MODEMS

Modem is an abbreviation of the terms *modulator demodulator*. It permits digital signals to be sent over the telephone analog communication facilities (Fig. 6.21). Modems are frequently referred to as *data sets* by telephone companies. The interface between the modem and the computer/terminal facility is internationally standardized.

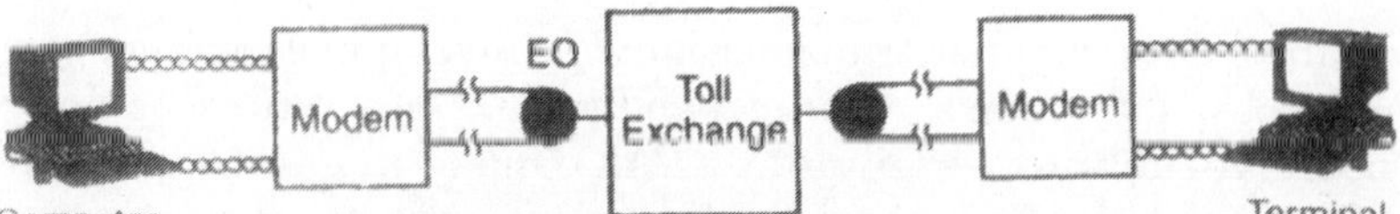

Fig. 6.21. Modems in Data Links.

The data signal spectrum connot be directly transmitted over an analog telephone line because it contains significant low-frequency components that would be attenuated by the telephone channel. Therefore, the modem's main task is translating the digital signal spectrum to an appropriate spectrum for the analog system.

There are two methods of coupling modem to the communications line :

1. **Indirect,** or **Acoustic coupling.** In this case the data signals are converted into audible sounds which are readily picked up by the telephone handset microphone, or transmitter. The audible signals are then converted back to electrical signals and transmitted over the telephone system.

Its disadvantage is that because of the extra conversion involved, it tends to introduce more noise and distortion than direct coupling and hence is limited to information rates of less than 1200 *bits/sec.*

2. **Direct hook-up.** It is used in permanent installations. When a non-standardised modem is used, a *Data Access Arrangement* (*DAA*) device or some other suitable protective device must be inserted to make a connection to the standardised-switched network. *DAA* is not required on leased lines.

6.8.1. Turn-Around and Message Acknowledgement

In a typical modem, two different frequencies can be used to represent the *MARK* or *SPACE* input data. The modem can operate in either the half duplex or full-duplex mode.

Half-duplex operation. It is a bi-directional operation but only in one direction at any given time. When modems switch from transmit to receive and vice versa, some data transmission time is lost in the line turnaround process.

In many systems, the receiver sends an acknowledgement back to the transmitter whenever a block of data is detected. This transmission reversal significantly reduces net data throughput since time is wasted in the establishing appropriate signal levels and synchronization. In order to overcome this problem, a narrow reverse channel bandwidth is often used simultaneously with the main, or data-channel, transmission. The reverse or secondary channel does not require a large bandwidth since return of only a **positive acknowledgement** (*PAK*) or a **negative acknowledgement** (*NAK*) is required. However, such a system remains a half-duplex system.

Fig. 6.22 shows data channel bandwidth of a typical modem, which employs a main data channel which denotes a *MARK* with a 1200 Hz tone and a *SPACE* with a 2200 Hz tone. Note that such FSK causes the data channel to extend over a bandwidth. The secondary channel is narrowly centred around 387 Hz. It can be used to inform the transmitting station that the previous message block contained errors and should be retransmitted.

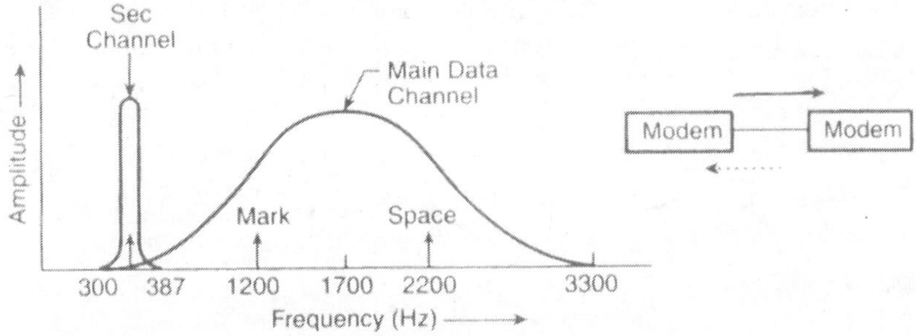

Fig. 6.22. Frequency Spectrum in a Half-Duplex Modem.

Full-duplex operation. It is characterized by simultaneous bidirectional data transmission. Typical modems used on a two-wire line divide the channel bandwidth into two transmit and receive subchannels. Fig. 6.23 shows the spectrum of a full-duplex modem using two-wire line.

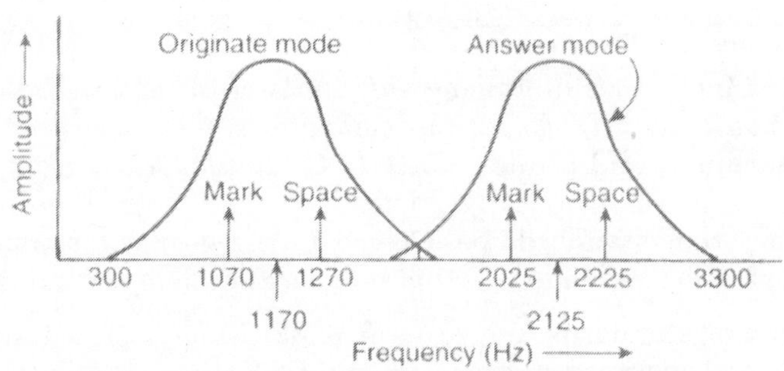

Fig 6.23 Frequency Spectrum in a Full-duplex Modom.

When the modem is in the originate mode, it transmits on 1070/1270 Hz. In the answer mode, it transmits on the 2025/2225 Hz frequencies. The modem goes into the originate mode when a call is originated through a modem. It goes into the answer mode, if it initially answers a call.

For the higher bit rates, 4-wire line is used in which a separate pair of wires is used for each direction. Often the electrical characteristics of the line for bit rates exceeding 2400 bits/sec is equalized or flattened out in order to achieve satisfactory performance. Since the attenuation characteristics and the propagation velocities experienced by the various frequency components in a signal are not constant, they result in distortion in the received signal. These variations in frequency are compensated out by employing *line equalizers.*

Fig. 6.24 shows the power spectrum of a 1200 baud, four-phase *PSK* voice band data signal. The power spectral density of most data signals is designed to have a *raised cosine spectrum* centered at about 1800 Hz.

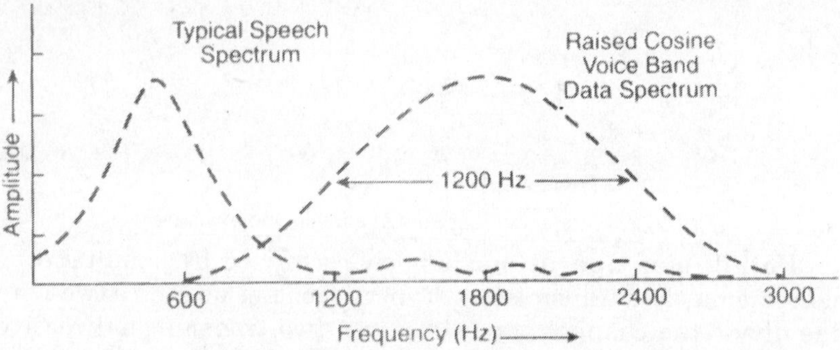

Fig. 6.24. Spectrum of Speech and Voice Band Data in four-phase *PSK*.

6.9. Interface Standards

The function of interfacing standards is to connect *Data Terminal Equipment* (*DTE*) such as computers, teletypewriters, business machines, and printers to *Data Communications Equipment* (*DCE*), or, more specifically, Modem or Data Sets. It is utmost necessary that standards be evolved in the design terminal and communication equipment so that interface problems are minimum.

A set of standards known as *RS-232-C* has been a universal practice and ensures between *DTE* and *DCE* three necessary conditions :

(*i*) Compatibility of voltage and signal levels,
(*ii*) Common pin wiring configurations, and
(*iii*) Minimum control information.

These standards conform to the internationally recognized CCITT V.24 standard.

The main characteristics of this interface standard are as follows :

(*a*) The RS-232-C standard not only conform to the *V*-24 standard, but it also specifies the mechanical connector type and pin assignments for each signal.

(*b*) Apart from the protective and signal grounds, all circuits carry bi-polar voltage signals. Voltages at the connector pins with respect to the signal ground may not exceed ± 25 *V*. Voltage between + 3*V* lie in the transition region and are not defined.

(*c*) A *MARK* is indicated by a voltage in the –3 to – 25 *V* range, while a *SPACE* is indicated by a voltage between 3 to 25 *V*.

(*d*) The interchange circuit can be used for control, data or timing, and its driver can be located in the *DTE* or *DCE*.

(*e*) For the control circuit, the time in the transition region must be less than 1 msec. For data circuits, the time in the transition region must be less than 1 msec or 4 per cent of the nominal signal element duration, whichever is the lesser. The generator circuit must be able to withstand an open circuit, or a shorting condition, to any other circuit at the interface.

6.10. Universal Synchronous Asynchronous Receiver Transmitter (USART)

The function of this system is to connect a digital computer with a parallel *n*-bit output to a single communications line. It performs both functions of transforming the parallel *n*-bits into a serial bit stream and converting the serial bit stream into *n*-parallel bits. In fact, the *USART* is an integral part of a computer system as shown in Fig. 6.25.

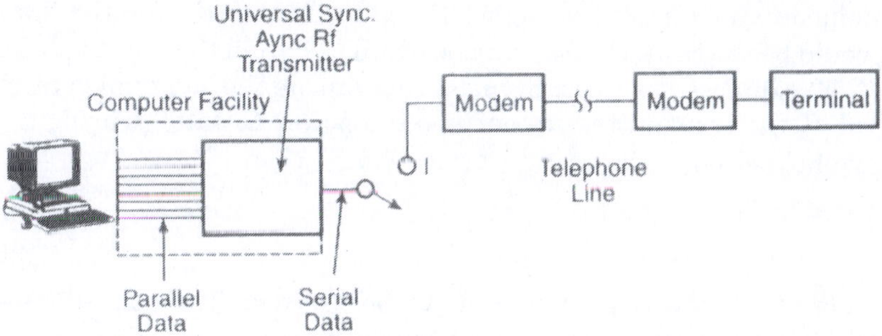

Fig. 6.25. Data Transmission to and from a Computer connected to a Telephone Line.

6.11. Satellite Digital Link Design

In the satellite analog communication, the important parameters are the ratios of carrier power-to-noise power (C/N) and carrier-to-noise density (C/N_0) which are used to design the uplink and downlinks. Similarly in the digital satellite communication the ratio of energy per bit to noise density (E_b/N_o) is important in the design of up and downlinks.

In fact, the ratio E_b/N_0 is the basis of comparison among modems, codecs and other processors of digital information, E_b/N_0 is dimensionless, since E_b has the unit joules and N_0 has the units of power per hertz which is (joules/second) × second. E_b is a fundamental quantity in digital communication because here a binary information digit (bit) is a measure of information and the energy required to convey that bit is E_b.

The *figure of merit* for a digital radio link is its *bit error rate* (BER) also called the *bit error probability*. It is defined as the probability that a bit sent over the link will be received incorrectly (*i.e.* that all 1s will be read as 0 or vice versa), or alternatively the fraction of a large number of bits that will be received incorrectively. Like a probability it is usually stated as a single number—for example, 1×10^{-4} or 0.0001. BER is analogous to SNR of the analog link.

The bit error arises due to symbol errors which arise mainly due to thermal noise, external interference and intersymbol interference. In case if only thermal noise is considered then the symbol error rate (SER) or symbol error probability may be calculated unambiguously from (E_s/N_0), the energy per symbol in joules divided by the noise density in W/Hz measured in the *IF* bandwidth at the demodulator input. The higher the value of the (E_s/N_0), the lower would be the SER, (E_s/N_0) may be evaluated from the input value of (C/N) expressed as ratio. Suppose that during the one symbol interval T_s the transmitted carrier has the power C watts. During this symbol period, if the energy received is E_s, then

$$E_s = CT_s = \frac{C}{R_s} \qquad \text{...(6.26)}$$

where R_s is the symbol rate in symbols/second. The noise-density (noise power per hertz) N_0 is the received noise power N divided by the *IF* bandwidth at the demodulator input

$$N_0 = \frac{N}{B} \qquad \text{...(6.27)}$$

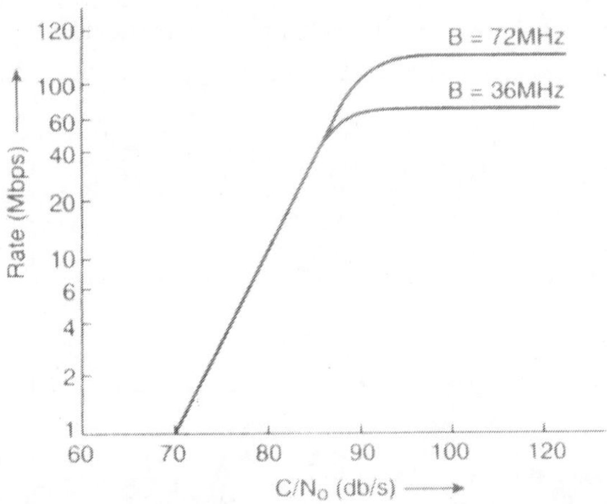

Fig. 6.26. Variation of Rate *R* as a Function of *C*/*N*0.

From these two equations

$$\frac{C}{N} = \left(\frac{E_s}{N_0}\right)\left(\frac{R_s}{B}\right) \quad ...(6.28)$$

Similarly, if E_b represents the bit energy and R_b represents the bit rate then

$$\frac{C}{N} = (E_b/N_0)\ (R_b/B) \quad ...(6.29)$$

In satellite communications, the quantity (*C*/*N*) is directly evaluated (Chapter 2). Once the *C*/*N* is known and the bandwidth of the receiver is selected, E_s/N_0 or E_b/N_0 can be calculated. From Eqs. (6.28) and (6.29) it is evident that the lower is required E_b/N_0 for a given rate, the less C/N_0 is required. In Fig. 6.26 a plot of R_s against C/N_0 is made (from Eq. 6.29) for two values of bandwidth, namely 36 MHz and 72 MHz for $E_b/N_0 = 10$. It is seen that when rate R_s reached its maximum value, the curve saturates. The left region is referred to as the *power limited region* ; the saturated region at the right is called the *bandwidth-limited region*. It may be noted that in order to recover the symbol stream with zero ISI (Intersymbol interference) it is desirable that the noise bandwidth *B* is equal to the symbol rate R_0 *i.e.* $BT_0 = 1$ or $E_s/N_0 = C/N$. Various filters such as square root Nyquist cosine filters, Butterworth and Chebyschev filters achieve this.

A knowledge of E_s/N_o helps to understand the ideal error rate performance of various digital modulation schemes which may be used for digital satellite communication. Table 6.2 indicates the expressions for ideal bit error rate performance of various digital modulation schemes. Similarly Fig. 6.27 indicates a plot of these expressions.

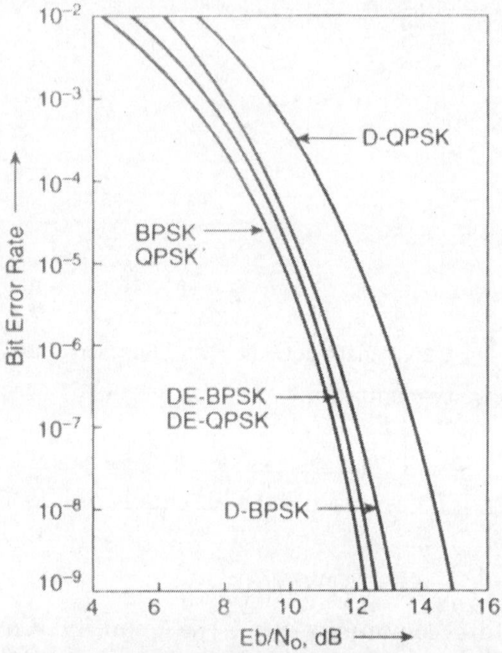

Fig. 6.27. Ideal Bit Error Rate Performance of Various Digital Modulation Schemes.

For M-ary modulation schemes the error rate performance is specified in terms of symbol error tate P_s but for BPSK bit and symbol errors are the same thing. For the symbol error probability (p_s) less than 1, the error rate performance is given as

$$P \cong \frac{P_s}{\log_2 M} \quad \text{...(6.30)}$$

Table 6.2. Ideal Error Rate Performance of Various Digital Modulation Schemes

Modulation Technique	*Ideal bit error rate performance*
MSK, BPSK/QPSK	$P = \frac{1}{2}\, erfc\, \sqrt{E_b/N_0}$
Orthogonal FSK with coherent detection	$P = \frac{1}{2}\, erfc\, \sqrt{E_b/N_0}$
Orthogonal FSK with noncoherent detection	$P = \frac{1}{2} \exp\,(-E_b/2N_0)$
D-PSK	$P = \frac{1}{2} \exp\,(-E_b/2N_0)$

For QPSK, $M = 4$ and then $P_S = 2P$. Thus the bit error rate for QPSK is smaller than the symbol error rate. It may be seen from Fig. 6.27 that QPSK has higher BER than BPSK but since QPSK carries twice as much data as BPSK for the same RF bandwidth and using QPSK can double the communication capacity (and renew earning power) of a transponder.

It would be worthwhile to mention here that CCIR recommendations also exist regarding telephony services. Thus according to CCIR recommendations. 522-1, 1982 the BER should not exceed:

(*i*) $\sqrt{10^{-6}}$ for more than 20 per cent of any month (10 minute mean value);

(*ii*) $\sqrt{10^{-4}}$ for more than 0.3 per cent of any month (1 minute each value); and

(*iii*) $\sqrt{10^{-3}}$ for more than 0.01 percent of any year (1 sec mean value).

For data transfers, error rates of 10^{-10} or better are needed.

6.12. Time Division Multiplexing

As mentioned in previous chapter, time division multiplexing of channels is used in digital signal transmission techniques. Here different channels are assigned different time slots in the specified time intervals for transmission. Here the intermodulation effects (cross talk) is not present though, as will be shown further, it requires perfect synchronism between the multiplexing and demultiplexing commutators. Time division multiplexing may also be said to have M information channels to be interleaved onto a single transmission channel in time. This process is *commutation*. Upon arrival at the receiver the interleaving channels are decommutated or distributed.

Fig. 6.28 indicates the principle of TDM as stated above. Here each channel is assigned a time slot of duration $T - T_s/M$ where T_s is $1/f_S$ (baseband signal frequency of transmission). Actually this time slot T for individual channel consists of the channel pulse time slot T_p and a guard time Δt to prevent excessive intersymbol interference or overlap of pulses from adjacent channels. This is shown in Fig. 6.29. Here each channel signal is band limited to frequency f_m Hz and the M channels are sampled at rate f_S.

Thus $$T_p \leq \frac{T_s}{M} - \Delta t = \frac{1}{2Mf_m} - \Delta t \qquad ...(6.31)$$

The TDM wave after interleaving of the M PAM waves is therefore expressed by

$$v_M(t) = \sum_{i=1}^{M} v_i(t) \qquad ...(6.32)$$

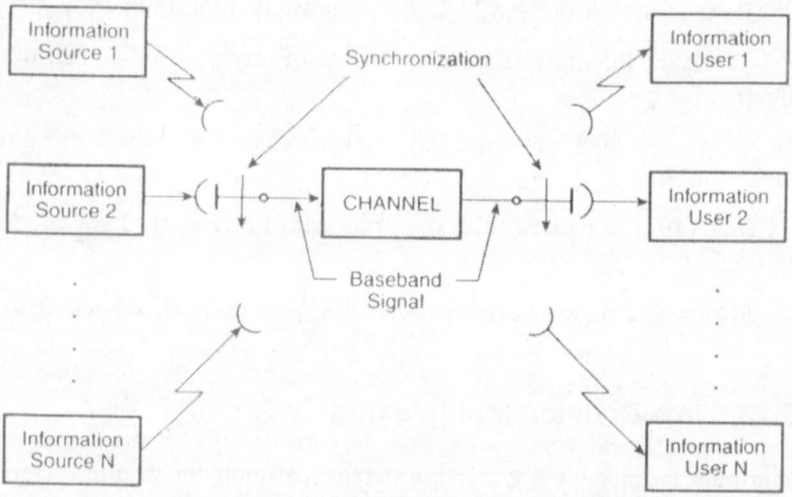

Fig. 6.28. Principle of TDM.

It may be noted that as shown in Fig. 6.30 the baseband TDM signal also includes the synchronization signal

$$C_s(t) = \cos \omega_s t \qquad ...(6.33)$$

Thus the baseband signal $v(t)$ is

$$v(t) = v_M(t) + C_s(t) \qquad ...(6.34)$$

The sync signal is used to synchronise the commutation (sampling), pulse time reference, and frame time, as well as to provide a receiver sync reference. This sync reference is derived from a frequency standard. At the receiver the sync tone is extracted by a pilot tone filter or phase locked loop and is employed to synchronise the distributor.

The PAM/TDM wave is then demultiplexed in time (distributed) to M individual channels. It should be noted that each channel in TDM transmits digital word in the form of a group of bits which are arranged in the prescribed time slot. These M time slots in time T_s constitute a *frame* where each channel is identified by its position in

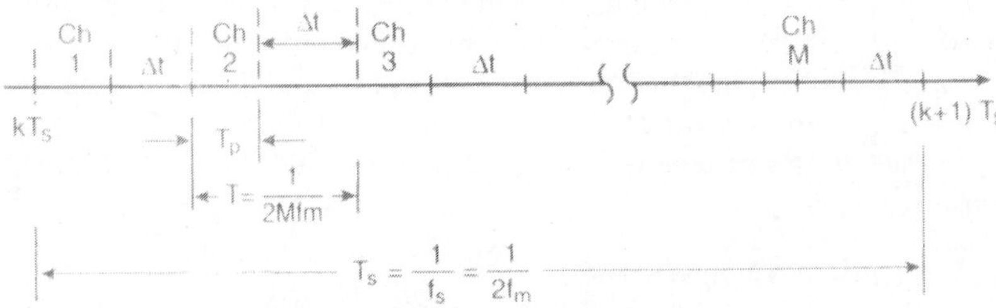

Fig. 6.29. Interleaving of *M* Channels Pulses on One Sampling Time Frame (Ts).

the frame and in the digital transmission, individual trams are identified by the presence of synchronization bits that repeat a known pattern.

6.13. US T_1 24-Channel System

The T_1 channel system was developed by Bell System USA for TDM operation in terrestrial microwave links. This is the best example to understand the principle of TDM explained above. The Bell T_1 system is shown in Fig. 6.30. It has 25 slots numbered 0 through 24. Slot 0 consists of 1 bit and carries synchronization information. Slots 1 through 24 each contain 8 bits and carry telephone channels 1 through 24. Thus there are $1 + (8 \times 24)$ or 193 bits in a T_1 frame. Since the sampling rate in standard telephone PCM systems is 8 kHz which means transmission of one sample every 125 μsec, therefore 193 bits are being transmitted in the 125 μs frame interval. Thus, the bit rate in T_1 24 channel system is 193 bits divided by 125 μsec or 1.5440 megabits.

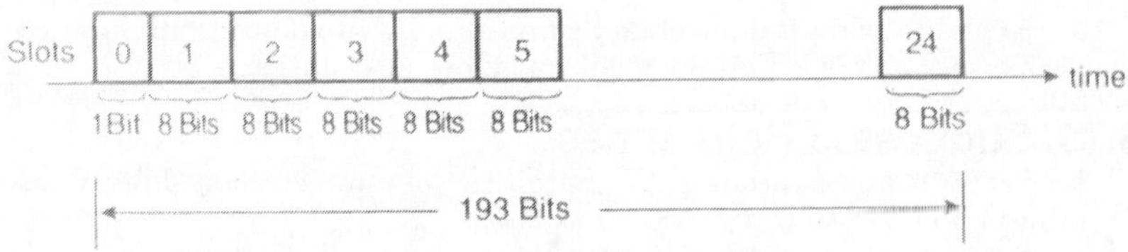

Fig. 6.30. Slots in Bell T_1 Frame.

As mentioned the slot 0 is the responsible for synchronisation information. This is done by a known bit pattern in slot 0. This bit pattern constitutes what is called the *frame alignment word* (FAW). The T_1 FAW is 100011011100 which contains 12 bits and requires 12 frames for transmission. The group of frames that transmit the

FAW make up a *superframe*. Thus in the first frame of a superframe, slot 0 contains *a* 1. In the second frame slot 0 contains a 0 and so on. It would be of importance to mention here that CCITT has recommended a standard 1.544 Mb system for satellite TDM systems (which is slightly different from the T_1) and a 2.048 Mbs 30 channel system.

6.14. Review Questions

1. How is the digital satellite communication different from analog satellite communication ? Explain the relative merits and demerits of these two methods.
2. What are the various methods of digital modulation techniques and which one is mostly used in digital satellite communications ? Explain with reasons.
3. What is meant by bit error rate ? Tell its optimum acceptable value for digital satellite communication ? What is its counterpart in an analog link ?
4. Derive an expression for a digital satellite link and explain as to how is it dependent on the system bandwidth ?
5. What is symbol error rate ? How is it different from bit error rate? For which ary modulation symbol error is similar to bit error rate and why ? What happens to the case of M-ary modulation ?
6. What is meant by error rate performance of a system ? How do you calculate the error rate performance for MSK, BPSK, QPSK, orthogonal FSK and DPSK system ?
7. What is time division multiplexing ? How does it differ from frequency division multiplexing ? Explain its merits.
8. Explain as to why time division multiplexing is the only option for digital satellite link and also as to why the intermodulation effects are not prevalent in TDM.
9. What is $T_1$24 channel frame ? Explain its operation with reference to terrestrial microwave links and digital satellite links. What is its equivalent CCITT standard ?
10. Explain the digital baseband signals and write down mathematical expression for a digital waveform before modulation.

6.15. Suggested References

1. Pratt, T. and Bostian, C.W., Satellite Communications, John Wiley and Sons, 1986.
2. Ziemer, R.E. and Tranter, W.H., Principles of Communications, Systems, Modulation and Noise, Houghton Mifflin Company, London, 1976.
3. Gregg, W.D., Analog and Digital Communication, John Wiley, 1977.
4. Jordan, E. C., Reference data for Engineers, Howard W Sams & Co., 1986, USA.

5. Ha, T. T., Digital Satellite Communications, MacMillan Publishing Co., 1986.
6. Kailatsh, T., Digital Communications by Satellite, Prentice-Hall, USA, 1977.
7. Feher, K., Advanced Digital Communications, Prentice Hall, 1987.
8. Maral, G and Bousquet, M., Satellite Communications Systems, John Wiley & Sons, 1986.
9. Bharagava, V.K., Haccum, D., Matyas, R. and Nuspl, P., Digital Satellite Communications, Wiley Interscience, 1981.
10. Bartree, T.C., Digital Communications, Howard W Sams & Co., 1986.

7

Multiple Access Techniques

7.1. Introduction

Multiple Access Techniques allow interconnection among large number of earth station terminals simultaneously via satellite. Alternately, with multiple access techniques any one earth station can communicate with all other earth stations using the same satellite. Infact the capacity of satellite transponder is quite high, say 120 Mbps and it can handle about 3562 voice channels at 32 Kbps. This much traffic is unlikely to be provided by a single earth station and therefore to have the best use of transponder's capacity, it must be allocated to other earth stations. This allocation must be wisely done in an orderly fashion so that there may not be any chaos. This scheme is called *multiple access* which allows the earth stations to give access to the transponder capacity allocated to them in orderly fashion. Thus the multiple access provides wide geography coverage capability and the best utilization or broadcast nature of satellite channel.

In the multiple access technique, the concepts of multiplexing techniques used in various communication systems are used. The frequency division multiplexing (FDM) of analog communication systems, or time division multiplexing (TDM) of digital communication systems may be used for the multiple access techniques. The corresponding access schemes will therefore be *frequency division multiple access* (FDMA) technique and *time division multiple access* (tdma) techniques. There has also been a *random access multiple* scheme which was used in ALOHA systems. With the development of spread spectrum techniques in communication systems, a new technique namely the code division multiple access (CDMA) is also getting very popular is satellite communication. In addition to these three multiple access techniques, the access of earth stations to the satellite may be based on the fixed or demand basis. In the fixed case, the proportion allocated to each earth station is fixed in advance and therefore it is termed as *fixed access* (FA) or preassigned access (PA). In the demand access the resource is allocated as needed in response to changing traffic conditions. It would be worthwhile to mention that in FDMA, the FDM of Fig. 4.2 is blended and as a matter of fact the discussions on FDM in Chapter 4 are the same as FDMA and therefore in the following sections fdma will not be discussed any more. Further the demand access techniques are quite efficient techniques and these will be explained in the next chapter.

7.2. Time Division Multiple Access (TDMA)

Conceptually TDMA is just a step beyond time division multiplexing but in practice it is a great deal more complex. Fig. 7.1 indicates the principle of TDMA. Here many earth stations in the satellite communication network use a single carrier for transmission via the satellite transponder on a time division basis. These earth stations transmit traffic bursts in a periodic time frame which is termed *TDMA frame*. It is normally of the order of 125 μs. The earth stations during their traffic transmission have access to the entire bandwidth of the transponder. There is also a guard time between the transmitting times of individual bursts so that the bursts may not overlap. The satellite transponder receives one burst at a time, amplifies it and retransmits back to the earth. In this way every receiving earth station that is served by the transponder may receive the entire burst stream and can extract the burst meant for it. TDMA would be called *fixed assignment TDMA (F-TDMA)* if the frame time is divided into slots of fixed duration with the slots equally divided among the stations. In case the transmission time allocations are based in instantaneous loads, the TDMA would be

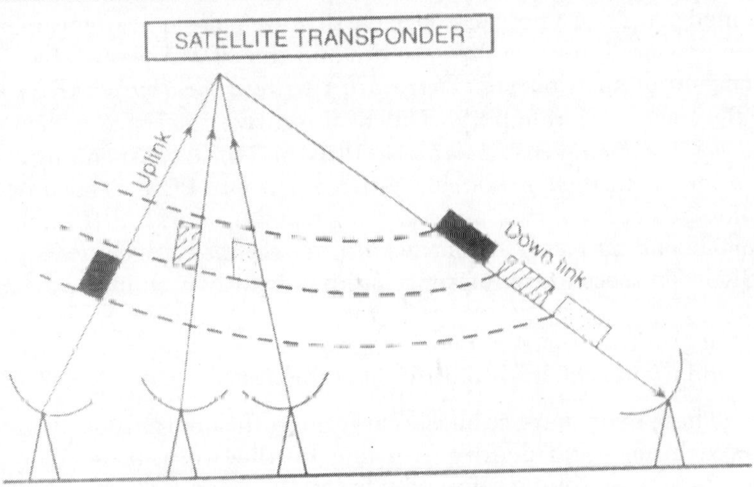

Fig. 7.1. Principle of Time Division Multiple Access.

called demand assignment TDMA (D-TDMA). Discussions on DTDMA would be carried out in the next chapter. It is the most sophisticated form of TDMA and has a very high transmission efficiency.

The number of voice channels in a TDMA system is given by

$$n = (1/r)\,(R - NP/T) \qquad \ldots(7.1)$$

where

r = voice channel bit rate

R = satellite channel bit rate (power or band limited)

N = number of bursts in a frame

P = number of digits in the preamble

T = frame period.

Some of the terms in Eq. (7.1) would be made clear in next section where TDMA frame structure would be discussed. TDMA has advantages over FDMA. The requirements of uplink power control which are very stringent in FDMA systems are greatly reduced in TDMA systems. Infact when TDMA is used, since only one carrier passes through the transponder at any one time, the output *twt* tube may be operated at saturation with a consequent increase in satellite *eirp* and no intermodulation will be produced. Also, for highly busy/density traffic TDMA is most efficient. Some of the other advantages of TDMA over FDMA are further discussed in Section 7.8.

7.3. TDMA Frame Structure

Fig. 7.2 indicates a typical frame structure. As already mentioned in a TDMA network each earth station periodically transmits one or more bursts to the satellite and the TDMA frame structure consists of such bursts. There are two *reference bursts* (RB_1 and RB_2) meant for reliability. Out of these two reference bursts one serves as *primary reference burst* (PRB) and the corresponding earth station is termed *primary reference station* (PRS). The another reference burst serves as *secondary reference burst* (SRB) and the corresponding earth station would be *secondary reference station* (SRS). The secondary reference burst is mainly used in the event of failure of primary reference burst so as to provide undistrupted service for the TDMA network. This *switchover* from the primary to secondary in such eventualities is automatic.

These two reference bursts carry no traffic information but serve to synchronise and identify the frame. In other words these reference bursts provide timing references for all the earth stations accessing a particular satellite transponder. It should be noted that in each TDMA frame only one reference burst (either PRB_1 or PRB_2 in case of failure of PRB_1) is transmitted and it allows a satisfactory interleaving of bursts within TDMA frame.

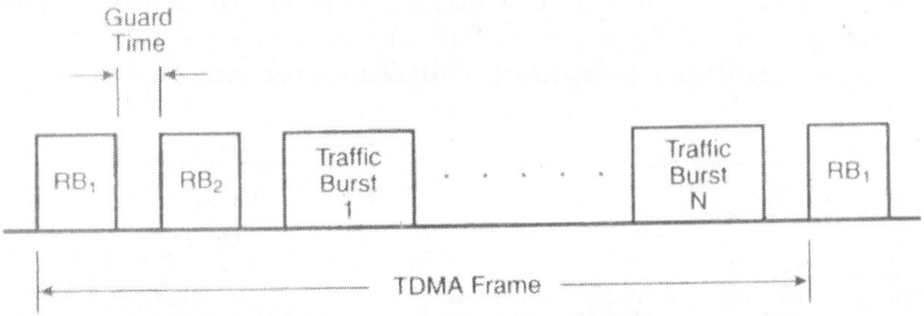

Fig. 7.2. The TDMA Frame Structure.

Alongwith the above reference bursts, there are *traffic bursts* which form the main parts of TDMA. The corresponding earth stations are termed *traffic stations.* These bursts carry the digital information and may be one or more in numbers in one TDMA frame as per requirement. The different traffic bursts occupy their positions in the TDMA frame according to a *burst time plan.* Traffic bursts may be long or short depending upon the amount of information to be transmitted. Thus by referencing the timing of the occurrence of primary reference, the traffic bursts are located in the TDMA frame. The traffic stations detect the primary reference burst and then locate and extract the traffic burst or portion of traffic bursts meant for them. They derive the transmit timings of their bursts precisely so that the corresponding bursts arrive at the satellite transponder within their allocated position in TDMA frame and no overlapping among the bursts may occur there.

In order to ensure that there may never be any overlapping between different traffic bursts from different traffic stations at the satellite transponder a short *guard time* is provided between the bursts (shown in Fig. 7.2) in TDMA frame. During this guard time there is no transmission of information. This guard time is long enough to allow differences in transmit timing accuracy and the range rate variation of the satellite. The required guard time is estimated by calculating the maximum uncertainty that could be observed between bursts and then doubling it. The results are represented in symbols. For example in INTELSAT TDMA guard time is specified as 60 symbols corresponding to 993 nsec or around 1 *μsec.*

It should be noted that the minimum frame time in TDMA is 125 μs, required by a voice channel sampled at the standard 8 KHz rate. The maximum frame time is arbitrary, provided that each frame contains one sample from each voice channel for each 125 μs, of frame duration. Thus the frame time affects the structure of the bursts from the individual stations. Typical frame time/frame periods of some of the communication satellites are as follows :

Table 7.1 Length of time frame for various satellite systems

Satellite	*Frame time*
Telesat Canada	250 μs
SBS	15 ms
Intelsat V	2 ms
Advanced West Star	125 – 750 μs
Telecom 1	20 ms
Intelsat VI	2 ms

7.4. TDMA Burst Structure

In the present section, it is seen that TDMA burst structure consists of a reference burst and traffic bursts. The structures of these reference burst and traffic bursts are shown in Fig. 7.3. The reference burst is composed of a groups of bits called *Preamble or header*. This consists of three contiguous parts, namely the *clock recovery sequence* (CCR), the *unique word* (UW) and the *signalling channel* or *control bits*. The clock recovery sequence is also sometimes called as *carrier and bit timing recovery* (CBR). The traffic burst has the preamble as well as the traffic data or Data message. The traffic data includes various information subbursts and supports the traffic from one station to the other.

The carrier and clock recovery sequence are the bits or symbols with which each burst begins. These enable the earth station demodulator to recover the carrier phase and regenerate the bit or symbol timing clock for data demodulation. These depend on the C/N ratio at the input of the demodulator and the acquisition range (carrier frequency uncertainty). Short CCR sequence is needed in the case of high C/N ratio and small acquisition range. Similarly for high bit rate TDMA system, a long CCR sequence is needed. For example for 120 Mbps TDMA, CCR sequence has 300 to 400 bits (150-200 symbols).

The unique word (UW) which is also called the *burst code word* (BCW) serves to mark each frame. UW follows the CCR sequence in the reference burst and it provides the receive frame timing that allows a station to locate the position of traffic burst in the frame.

The unique word in the traffic burst marks the time of occurrence of the traffic burst and provides the receive burst timing that allows the station to extract only the wanted subbursts within the traffic burst. The unique word is a sequence of ones and zeros and typical lengths range from 20 to 48 bits. For example, the *Inmersat* system uses 0111 1010 1100 1101 0000 for unique word. The *Intersat* uses 48 bit unique words in each of its three reference bursts (called UW_0, UW_1 and UW_2). Even the traffic burst of Intelsat uses a Unique word of 48 bits. At the receiving end of a link, the *UW*, are derived through a UW correlator which may tell about the errors in received *UW*, if there is any. These error in the received UW_s are called *miss* or *false alarm*. It has been seen that the larger unique words reduce the probabilities of such errors though there already exist various techniques to reduce the probabilities of such errors.

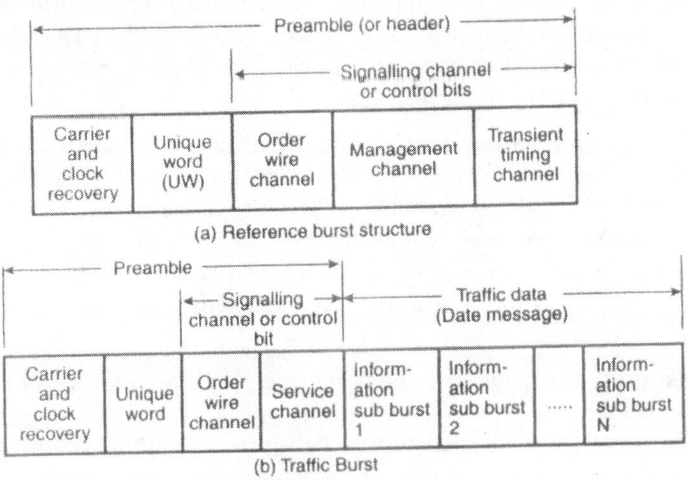

(*b*) Traffic Burst
Fig. 7.3. TDMA Burst Structure.

The signalling channel is present in both the reference and traffic bursts. The reference burst signalling channel consists of an order wire channel, a management channel and a transmit timing channel. The traffic burst, however, consists of only an order wire channel and a service channel. The order wire channels of both the reference and traffic bursts carry the voice (telephone) and data (Teletype) traffic via which instructions are passed to and from earth stations. It may be noted that the order wire is a term used in manual telephone switching to describe a circuit on which operators and maintenance personnel can talk to one another. In fact, the operators use the order wire for placing calls. The management channel of the reference burst is sent by the reference stations to all the traffic stations and carry instructions regarding frame management such as burst time plan changes, etc.

The burst time plan describes the coordination of traffic between stations and it identifies the boundaries of the time slots of the frame allocated to the stations *i.e.* the burst positions. It also identifies the position, length and source or destination stations corresponding to subbursts in the bursts. Whenever, the reference station wants to obtain a status report (monitoring) the management channel would also carry monitoring and control messages to the traffic stations.

The transmit timing channel carries the acquisition and synchronization information to the traffic stations and enables them to adjust their transmit burst timing so that transmitted bursts arrive at the satellite transponder within the correct time slots in the TDMA frame. The status codes are also carried by this channel so that the traffic stations may identify the primary reference burst transmitted from RB_1 and RB_2.

The service channel carries the traffic stations status to the reference station. It also carries the information such as the high bit error rate and unique word loss alarms to other traffic stations. It may be noted that both the reference and traffic bursts may carry the additional subbursts of frame identification number, station identification number and type of transmitting bursts.

The traffic data carries the traffic information and it follows immediately the preamble. The length of the information subbursts is decided by the type of service required and the total number of channels required for each service being supported in the burst. The information subbursts have the information such as voice, data, video or facsimile signals.

7.5. TDMA Frame Efficiency

The TDMA frame efficiency (η) depends on the ratio of the time devoted to transmission of information bits in the frame to the total frame length and is thus defined as

$$\eta = 1 - \frac{\Sigma t}{T_F} \qquad ...(7.2)$$

where Σt represents the sum of all the guard times and preambles including the reference burst and is also expressed as

$$\Sigma t = \frac{(n+2)\,P}{R} \qquad ...(7.3)$$

where R is the satellite transmission link bit rate, n is the number of traffic burst in a frame considering two reference bursts per frame,

p is the number of bits in the preamble plus guard time, and T_F is the frame period. From Eq. (7.2) it is evident that to have better frame efficiency, should be small and T_F should be large. In other words the overheads which represent guard times and preambles should be lowered but since the guard times are governed by synchronisation accuracy and preambles are governed by the demodulation and signalling requirements therefore these can not be lowered beyond certain limits.

The frame length has limitations. It cannot be increased beyond certain limit. The main constraint on the frame length is that the size of the buffers used for compression and expansion of the data to form the TDMA burst increases with the frame length and so increases the costs of the earth station equipment. Moreover, transmission delay increases with the frame length. It should be noted that the current frame efficiency in various digital communication satellites is of the order of 0.9.

Once the frame efficiency is known the number of telephone channels that may be supported by a TDMA system is

$$v = \frac{R}{r\eta} \qquad \text{...(7.4)}$$

where r is the bit rate of a voice channel.

Thus if $n = 12$ transmitting stations, $P = 680$, $T_F = 2$ ms, $r = 64$ K bit/s, $R = 120.832$ m bit/s and $\eta = 96\%$, the number of voice channels $v = 1813$.

7.6. TDMA Superframe

It has been found that if the sequential frames are combined in an orderly manner, the resulting combination reduces the overheads considerably, thus increasing the TDMA frame efficiency. This orderly arrangement of TDMA frame is called *TDMA Superframe.* It is also oftenly termed as *master frame* or *cycle*. Since the transmit timing channel of the reference burst controls the position of the bursts and the management channel helps in coordination of traffic, so to address N stations for control and coordination of traffic bursts, one needs N messages in both the above channels of the reference

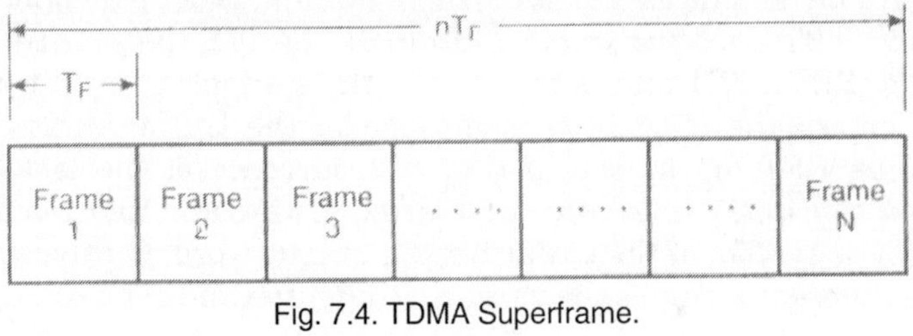

Fig. 7.4. TDMA Superframe.

burst in each frame. This would therefore increase the length of preamble in both the reference as well as traffic bursts.

However, if the frames are arranged in an orderly manner as shown in Fig. 7.4, the *N* stations would be addressed individually by a single message. In other words station 1 would be addressed by the reference station in frame 1, station 2 by the one in frame 2, so on and finally station *N* by the one in frame *N*. The procedure would be repeated in the same fashion by the next *N* frames until completion. This kind of structure increases the TDMA frame efficiency.

To identify the frames in a superframe a frame identification number is carried in the management channel or in a separate channel in the reference burst for each frame. Normally the identification number of frame 1 serves as the superframe marker. In some cases different unique words are also being used by the reference bursts to distinguish the superframe marker from the frame markers. It may be noted that when the number of stations *N* is variable, *i.e.* demand assignment is used, then a superframe short burst (SSB) is transmitted at the superframe rate. This will be made clear in the next chapter while dealing with DA-TDMA.

7.7. TDMA Frame Acquisition and Synchronization

In TDMA it is essential that the traffic stations while transmitting their bursts must transmit in the assigned time slot in every frame and similarly while receiving they must be capable of receiving traffic bursts meant for them in every frame. In other words the bursts should not overlap with each other in any case. This accuracy in the transmission and the reception of time bursts may only be achieved by the processes called *frame acquisition* and *frame synchronization*. These two processes help in the locating and controlling the traffic stations transmit burst time phase at the transmit side and carry out the similar processes at the receive side.

The various timing involved at the *transmit and receive* sides in TDMA may be put as *transmit frame timing* (TFT), transmit burst timing (TBT), *receive frame timing* (RFT) and the *receive burst timing* (RBT). TFT marks the start of the station's transmit frame, TBT marks the start of transmission of the traffic burst to the satellite, RFT marks the instant of occurrence of the last bit or symbol of primary reference burst's unique word and RBT marks the last bit or symbol of the traffic burst's unique word. On the basis of these different timings, the various acquisition and synchronization processes may be grouped as *receive frame acquisition* (*RFA*), transmit *frame acquisition (TFA), receive frame synchronization, transmit frame synchronization*.

The acquisition process is required when the traffic station enters or reenters operation. The synchronization process is needed due to satellite's movement in the orbit. The geostationary satellite is subject to small perturbations caused by the moon and sun. Also, there are other variations in the satellite movement such as peak to peak altitude variation, east-west drift and north-south peak to peak variations. These cause a range variation and a variation in the time delay between satellite and earth. Thus a Doppler shift is introduced in various timings which may introduce errors in the burst positions as they arrive at the transponder. Therefore a correct synchronization in necessary in every roundtrip delay to avoid errors. It may be noted that the Dopplershift is of the order of 40 ns/s.

The synchronization is achieved by introducing a transmit frame delay D_N to mark the transmit frame timing of station N such as

$$D_N = MT_f - \frac{2d_N}{C} \qquad ...(7.5)$$

where T_f is the frame period, d_N is the distance between the satellite N, C is the velocity of light and M is the smallest integer chosen such that $D_N \geq O$ for all d_N.

Thus, if station N transmits a burst at its transmit frame timing, this burst will arrive at the satellite at the same time as the reference burst. On the basis of the techniques for determining D_N, there may be two kinds of synchronization processes. In one of them, D_N is determined by the earth station directly from monitoring its own transmission and the method is called the *closed loop control* (or some times *loop back* method. In other technique transmitted bursts are not received by the transmitting stations themselves and some other methods are used to determine. This technique is called *open loop control* method (*e.g.* co-operative synchronization technique). In the closed loop synchronization method, the station observes the position of its own burst relative to the reference burst by measuring time interval between the reference burst unique word and the traffic burst unique word, computes the error and determines a new value for the delay D_N. Thus if E_N (i) is the observed error then the corrected delay D_N $(i + 1)$ would be

$$D_N (i + 1) = D_N (i) - E_N (i) \qquad ...(7.6)$$

This method of synchronization is not possible for a little complex TDMA systems such as those of multibeam or satellite switched TDMA systems. It also does not provide for the sort of synchronised network control that can monitor the synchronization of all the stations and automatically shut down any network members who are out of sync and unaware of the problems they are causing.

In the open loop synchronization such as that of co-operative synchronization used in Intelsat TDMA systems, a control station listens to the bursts and sends timing instructions back to each transmitting station. The main thing in the instructions is the time delay D_N. In the Intelsat TDMA system, the control station transmits D_N values to all the network members once every 32 multiframes. When entering the network the station uses the D_N supplied to it and in case it transmits abruptly, the error will be monitored by the control station which will then send the code for 'Don't transmit' (DNTX) for no more transmission from that particular station.

As in the synchronization technique the frame acquisition techniques may be either *closed loop acquisition* or *open loop acquisition*. Closed loop acquisition is obtained by transmitting either a low power burst, or a pseudo noise sequence modulated burst, observing its position, correcting it to an assigned position and then transmitting the traffic burst at full power. The open loop acquisition is initiated by informing the station entering the network of the time shift D_N relative to the reference burst at which the station should transmit a short burst consisting of a preamble and a unique word. It should be mentioned again that acquisition is performed prior to synchronization so as to bring the station into synchronism with an operating TDMA network.

7.8. TDMA as Compared to FDMA

FDMA is not suitable for the increased system traffic because of the impairments due to intermodulation products. In TDMA since only one burst resides in the transponder at any given instant, degradation caused by intermodulation distortion is avoided. The traffic capacities achieved in a typical transponder for FDMA and TDMA as a function of the number of accesses are compared in Fig. 7.5. It is evident from this figure that as the number of accesses increases, the FDMA capacity decreases significantly (due to intermodulation) whereas the TDMA capacity decreases only little (due to guard times and preamble). TDMA also provides a flexible means of adjusting traffic between various nodes in the system. It is

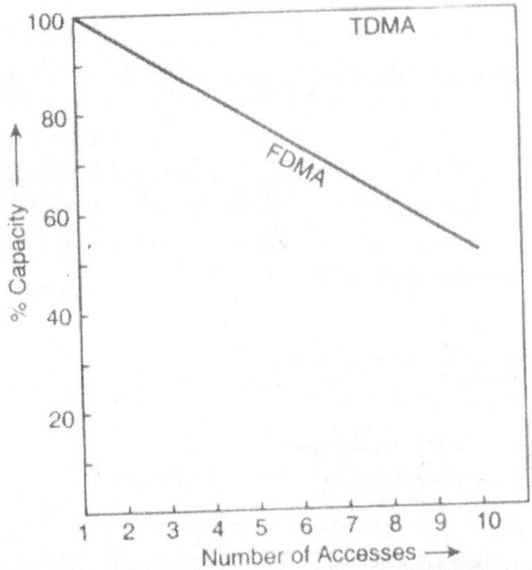

Fig. 7.5. Transponder Capacity for FDMA and TDMA Versus Number of Accesses.

cumbersome to modify the capacity in an FDMA system as it requires the change of many carrier center frequencies and carrier bandwidths. In a TDMA system the capacity is modified between nodes simply by changing the duration and position of each burst in the TDMA frame. This is quite easier especially if the computer control is used for the purpose.

The above advantages of TDMA were recognized early by INTELSAT. COSMAT laboratories had built their experimental systems in the late 1960s and had developed the technology necessary for the introduction of TDMA in early 1970s. Actually a 60 Mbit/s TDMA system was tested in Atlantic Ocean Region in 1978 which provided the valuable pre-operational experience. INTELSAT revised its TDMA specification on the basis of these experiments and it increased the transmission bit rate to 120 Mbit/s for compatibility with the 80 MHZ bandwidth transponder of INTELSAT V and VI. A network control system was needed to operate in the multibeam antenna environment of INTELSAT V. For INTELSAT VI the satellite switched multiple beams (SS-TDMA) was developed. Now-a-days all the communication satellites use TDMA systems designed as per their requirement.

7.9. TDMA Burst Time Plan

It is very essential that the transmission as well as reception of bursts in TDMA must be according to a time plan or *burst time plan* so that there may not be any overlapping of bursts at the satellite transponder. Thus for transmission purposes it is the *transmit burst time plan* and for the reception it is the *receive burst time plan*. The burst time plan is therefore a map that indicates the position and length of bursts in the frame and also the position and length of the information subbursts within a burst. In other words, the burst time plan is simply the traffic assignment within a frame. Following is the usual format for burst time plan :

Message Data
Burst time plan identification
Traffic station identification
Number of Transmit Bursts
Number of receive bursts

Burst Data
Burst identification
Transmit-receive Flag
Transponder identification
Burst Position
Number of transmit-receive subbursts

Subburst Data
Transmit receive subburst identification
Subburst position
Subburst length

It may be noted that when the network grows or when the network traffic changes, the burst-time plan has to be modified accordingly. Further transmission and reception of bursts are carried out according to this new burst time plan. The new burst time plan is sent by the reference station to individual traffic stations in the network which then store it in the background memory.

The adjustment of burst time plan according to the traffic changes is also called the *traffic planning process* which is usually assisted by computer analysis. It organises bursts in various beams and transponders to minimize burst overlaps from different transponders at participating stations while simultaneously achieving a maximum packing density in all TDMA frames. This process results in burst time plans that designate the position and duration of all traffic bursts in the TDMA frame for all stations in the network.

Once an overall burst time plan is determined for an entire network, it is transmitted to the participating stations in a background memory. It is essential that the changes in the burst time plane should be implemented in such a way that it does not affect the continuity of traffic. To ensure this, a *coordinated burst time plan change method* has been adopted that causes all traffic burst position and duration changes involved in the burst time plan change throughout the network to be synchronised to the same TDMA frame at the satellite. The delay compensation needed to synchronise is assured by the use of D_N whose value may range from 10 to 50 ms.

7.10. Multiple Beam (Satellite Switched) TDMA Satellite Systems

In the previous sections, discussions were on TDMA for satellite communication in concern with the fixed beams/antennas (radiations) and the beam interconnection was considered to *static*. There may be a *zone beam* or a *spot beam* antenna at the satellite. Zone beams can receive from transmitters anywhere within the coverage zone whereas the spotbeams have limited coverage. In the INTELSAT V there are four beams at C band interconnected by 80 MHz bandwidth transponders in which the beam interconnections are static and switched only occasionally to accommodate major adjustments in the traffic patterns.

Thus narrowing the satellite antenna beamwidth increases communications capacity. It provides a high gain for the coverage area and hence permits power savings in both the uplink and downlinks. The use of spot beam has the further advantage that the same frequency can be spatially reused many times. Thus if India is covered by N non-overlapping spot beam, the satellite capacity will increase N-fold over that achieved using one beam. INTELSAT VI utilised this multiple spot beam concepts. It has six upbeams (UBs) and six downbeams (DBs).

The main problem in the interconnection of UBS and DBs in the satellite communication system such as that of intelsat VI is their interconnectivity. This is achieved by introducing an onboard switching technique also called as *satellite switch*. The corresponding TDMA system would therefore be called *satellite switched TDMA (SS-TDMA)* system. This satellite switch is actually the dynamic satellite switching that uses a microwave switch matrix on board the satellite. The satellite switch can interconnect the six up beams to the six down beams in accordance with any desired single point connectivity matrix pattern (called a 'switch state') for a dwell interval of programmable location and duration. It should be noted that the satellite switching on board can be done at rf or at baseband. For the *rf* case microwave switching matrix mentioned above is utilized. The output signals from the matrix are amplified and enventually fed to the antennas. The switching matrix is steered by an inboard distribution control unit (dcu) (or the satellite switch control station) and an acquisition and synchronization unit provides the time references necessary for tdma operation. Cross bar configurations have been designed to provide bandwidth upto 500 MHz at 4 GHz as already being used in INTELSAT VI.

Fig. 7.6 indicates the concept of SS-TDMA used in INTELSAT VI. There are three upbeams and three downbeams. The onboard satellite switch control station (or the distribution control unit dcu) programmes the switch matrix to execute a cyclic set of switch states, each consisting of a set of connections between the uplink and downlink beams so that the traffic from various regions is routed to designated regions without conflict.

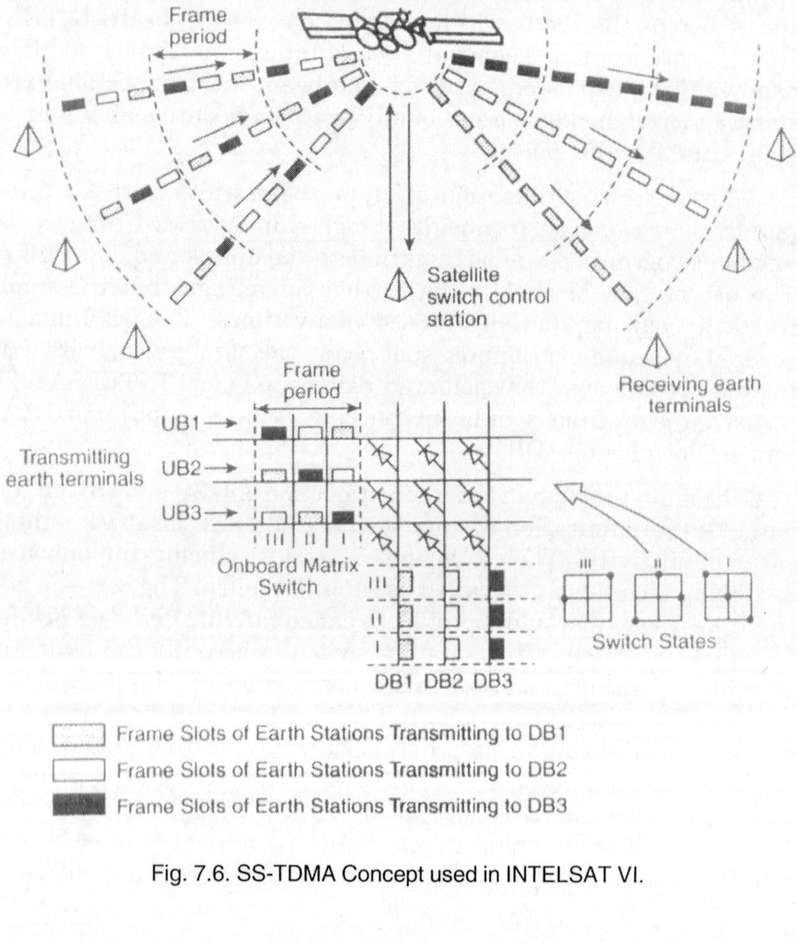

Fig. 7.6. SS-TDMA Concept used in INTELSAT VI.

The succession of switch states during a frame period is called the *switch state sequence.* Actually the direction of a given switch is selected to accommodate segment of the total traffic between earth stations but the sum of the segment provided by the switch sequence is equal to the total traffic of the network. Thus in Fig. 7.6, the SS-TDMA operates as a set or parallel TDMA frames on the uplink which are then switched by a sequence of switch states into a set of parallel TDMA frames on the down link. The time duration for the switch state is of concern for an optimal operation. An optimum set of switch states is one which fulfills the total traffic needs of the network with minimum duration.

It has been found that the maximum number of switch states required to accomplish the minimum duration switch pattern is $n^2 - 2n + 2$. Thus in the SSTDMSA of Fig. 7.6 where 6 beams are utilized the maximum number of switch states needed to optimally accommodate the traffic flow would be 26. In the Intelsat VI, facilities have been provided to accommodate 56 switch states. It would be worthwhile to mention here that the efficiency of SS-TDMA is defined as the ratio of the actually used capacity to the total capacity available from all the transponders.

7.11. Beam Hopping (Transponder Hopping) TDMA

In beam hopping TDMA the switching is achieved by each station hopping from one frequency to another according to the destination of the transmitted burst. Each earth station selects its transmission time on the corresponding frequency so as to transmit its burst within the correct time slot. It should be noted that the beam hopping is also carried out alongwith the on-board signal regeneration. This helps in avoiding the interburst interferences associated with conventional TDMA. Some other features of such satellite communication systems would be discussed in Chapter 8 where some more efficient and new TDMA systems (such as TDMA, etc.) used in recent communication satellites are discussed.

7.12. Code Division Multiple Access (CDMA) and Hybrid Access Techniques

In code division multiple access the whole bandwidth of the transponder is used all the time and signals from the users are encoded so that the information from an individual transmitter can be detected and recovered only by a properly synchronised receiving station that knows the code being used. Thus while the capacity of communication is increased by the multiple access, the secrecy of transmission is maintained. This has potential applications in military satellite communication. It should be noted that CDMA is quite similar to spread spectrum technique of satellite communication and therefore the further details of CDMA would be given in Chapter 7 where the details of the technique of satellite spread spectrum communications are given. Hybrid multiple access involves CDMA and it will also be studied in Chapter 9.

7.12. Suggested References

The references are same as those of previous chapter.

7.13. Review Questions

1. What is the difference between multiplexing and multiple access techniques? Are FDM and TDM similar to corresponding FDMA/TDMA respectively? If not why ? Explain the relative advantages and disadvantages of FDMA and TDMA.
2. What is burst? Explain the difference between the reference burst and traffic burst. Explain their positions in a TDMA frame. Explain their structures too.
3. What is guard time? Mention its value in a typical TDMA system. Explain its importance in TDMA frame efficiency.
4. What are the overheads in TDMA frame? Explain their structures. How the TDMA frame efficiency is affected by such overheads?
5. What is TDMA superframe? Explain its structures. How is it different from a simple TDMA frame?
6. What is meant by TDMA frame acquisition and frame synchronization? What is frame delay? How does it help in carrying out TDMA frame acquisition and frame synchronization techniques?
7. What is meant by burst time plan? Explain its structure and importance. What are the methods to control the burst time plan?
8. What is 'spot beam'? Explain the use of multiple spot beams in satellite communication. How does it increase the capacity of satellite transponder?
9. What is satellite switching? Explain the difference between static and dynamic switching. Discuss the operation of a typical SS-TDMA system. How is SS-TDMA different from a beam hopping TDMA?
10. What is CDMA? In what way is it superior to TDMA ? Mention the potential applications of CDMA.

8

Demand Assignment Multiple Access Techniques

8.1. Introduction

Multiple access techniques as discussed in the previous chapter were based on the division of frequency or the time domain. The channels may be assigned to the users as per requirement. In practice two methods have been suggested for the channel assignment, namely the *fixed assignment* and the *demand assignment* (*dynamic assignment*). However, care is taken regarding the needs of high capacity links between a few international transit centers and the low capacity links between a large number of small, low traffic stations, sometimes only necessitating a single channel.

In the fixed assignment, a station has periodic access to the channel independent of its actual need. By comparison demand assignment (dynamic assignment) gives the station access to the channel only when it requests access. Logically when most of the users in the communication system do not communicate continuously, the channels need not be allocated permanently (fixed assignment) and therefore it would be very advantageous to dynamically assign the different channels according to the traffic requirements imposed on the system. Thus the fixed assignment is best applied to high capacity commercial system. But if the traffic from a station tends to be burst like or intermittent, the dynamic assignment can be more efficient than the fixed assignment. This is because of the fact that in such cases as well as that of low traffic case, some of the circuits of the fixed assignment may not be used at all. This may be clearly understood with the help of Fig. 8.1 which represents a case of Time Division Multiplexing. In this example there are four slots per frame where each slot is preassigned to users A, B, C and D respectively. Fig. 8.1 (*a*) gives the typical activity profile of the four users. It is clear that during the first frame time, user C has no data to transmit. Similarly, during second frame time, user B has none and during the third frame time, user A has none. Since these slots are preassigned ones and if they have no data to send during the frame these are wasted. Fig. 8.1 (*b*) shows such wasted slots. Fig. 8.1 (*c*) indicates the availability of 3 such extra vacant slots which could be utilized well in the dynamic assignment schemes. Thus the dynamic assignment schemes (DAMA) are more efficient than the preassigned ones.

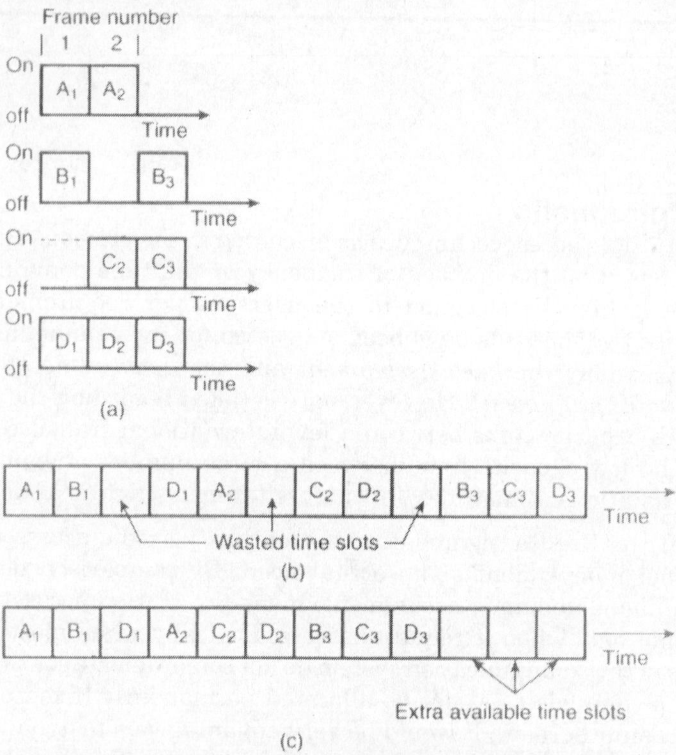

Fig. 8.1. Time Division Multiplexing
(*A*) Data Source Activity Profile, (*B*) Fixed Assignment TDM,
(*C*) Possible Utilization With Dynamic Assignment.

It may be noted that in any communication system the actual demand rarely equals the peak demand and so if the system's capacity is equal to the total peak demand, then for a burst or intermittent traffic, the system's capacity will be under utilized for most of the time. But by using buffers and DAMA, the system with reduced average capacity can handle bursty traffic at the cost of some queueing delay. Thus, in a fixed assignment case, the bandwidth (capacity) of the system would be $\sum_{n=1} W_N$, where W_1, W_2, ... W_N are the bandwidths of individuals users. For the dynamic assignment case it may be even $\frac{1}{N} \sum_{n=1}^{N} W_N$. All these indicate the versality and efficiency use of the available frequency spectrum (system capacity) with DAMA.

DAMA increases the cost of system because it requires a control mechanism that is common to all the earth stations to keep track of channel routing and the availability of each voice channel. Nevertheless, the advantages are high as no wastage of the system's capacity is allowed. Thus with the frequency division multiple access *the dynamic assignment is termed as demand assignment-frequency division multiplex* (*DA-FDMA*) and for TDMA it is *DA-TDMA*. There is another method of increasing the capacity of communication system and this is called *Digital Speech Interpolation (DSI)*. It doubles the number of terrestrial channels carried by a satellite transponder. Some of the other advantages of DAMA would be further cleared in the next section.

8.2. Erlang Call Congestion (Blocking or B) Formula

The demand assignment multiple access technique is based on a particular case of queueing theory which was discovered by a Danish mathematician A.K. Erlang (1878-1929) who was working for Copenhagen Telephone company. This is based on the fact that when all the channels (say, n) in a communication system are busy, a new arriving call will find a busy signal and will be blocked. This is also called the *call congestion problem*. The Erlang B formula tells the probability that an arriving call will be *blocked* on finding all the channels busy. In other words it helps to measure the traffic on the said communication system. This call congestion (blocking) probability is given as

$$p_n = B(n, a) = \frac{a^n/n!}{\sum_{k=0}^{n} a^k/k!} \quad \text{...(8.1)}$$

Here $B(n, a)$ is termed the Erlang B formula for an n channel group with a *traffic intensity* $a = \lambda/\mu$. λ is the call arrival rate and the calls arrive in a poisson scheme (process). μ is the mean hang up rate. In other words $\frac{1}{\mu}$ represents the average call service time or *holding time*. Thus a is the product of the number of calls per second and the mean service time per call in seconds. The unit of a is *erlang*. Eq. (8.1) is the cornerstone for evaluating the *grade of service* of a voice traffic network. It may be noted that the probability of k arrivals in time interval t is expressed by

$$p_k(t) = \frac{(\lambda t)^k}{k!} \exp(-\lambda t) \quad ...(8.2)$$

where λ is the call arrival rate.

Eq. (8.1) has been used to study the required number of channels in a fixed assignment as well as in the dynamic assignment schemes. For this purpose, use is made of a table (Table 8.1) called *Erlang B*

Table 8.1. Erlang B Table : Traffic Intensity Versus Number of Channels and Blocking Probability

	One lost call in					*One lost call in*			
n	50^a	100^b	200^c	1000^d	n	50^a	100^b	200^c	1000^d
1	0.020	0.010	0.005	0.001	31	22.9	21.2	19.8	17.4
2	0.22	0.15	0.105	0.046	32	23.8	22.1	20.6	18.2
3	0.60	0.45	0.35	0.19	33	24.7	23.0	21.4	18.9
4	1.1	0.9	0.7	0.44	34	25.6	23.8	22.3	19.7
5	1.7	1.4	1.1	0.8	35	26.5	24.6	23.1	20.5
6	2.3	1.9	1.6	1.1	36	27.4	25.5	23.9	21.3
7	2.9	2.5	2.2	1.6	37	28.3	26.4	24.8	22.1
8	3.6	3.2	2.7	2.1	38	29.3	27.3	25.6	22.9
9	4.3	3.8	3.3	2.6	39	30.1	28.2	26.5	23.7
10	5.1	4.5	4.0	3.1	40	31.0	29.0	27.3	24.5
11	5.8	5.2	4.6	3.6	41	32.0	29.9	28.2	25.3
12	6.6	5.9	5.3	4.2	42	32.9	30.8	29.0	26.1
13	7.4	6.6	6.0	4.8	43	33.8	31.7	29.9	26.9
14	8.2	7.4	6.6	5.4	44	34.7	32.6	30.8	27.7
15	9.0	8.1	7.4	6.1	45	35.6	33.4	31.6	28.5
16	9.8	8.9	8.1	6.7	46	36.6	34.3	32.5	29.3
17	10.7	9.6	8.8	7.4	47	37.5	35.2	33.3	30.1
18	11.5	10.4	9.6	8.0	48	38.4	36.1	34.2	30.9
19	12.3	11.2	10.3	8.7	49	39.4	37.0	35.1	31.7
20	13.2	12.0	11.1	9.4	50	40.3	37.9	35.9	32.5
21	14.0	12.8	11.9	10.1	51	41.2	38.8	36.8	33.4
22	14.9	13.7	12.6	10.8	52	42.1	39.7	37.6	34.2
23	15.7	14.5	13.4	11.5	53	43.1	40.6	38.5	35.0
24	16.6	15.3	14.2	12.2	54	44.0	41.5	39.4	35.8
25	17.3	16.1	15.0	13.0	55	45.0	42.4	40.3	36.7
26	18.4	16.9	15.8	13.7	56	45.9	43.3	41.2	37.5
27	19.3	17.7	16.6	14.4	57	46.9	44.2	42.1	38.3

n	50[a]	100[b]	200[c]	1000[d]	n	50[a]	100[b]	200[c]	1000[d]
28	20.2	18.6	17.4	15.2	58	47.8	45.1	43.0	39.1
29	21.1	19.5	18.2	15.9	59	48.7	46.0	43.9	40.0
30	22.0	20.4	19.0	16.7	60	49.7	46.9	44.7	40.8
61	50.6	47.9	45.6	41.6	81	69.6	66.3	63.6	60.3
62	51.6	48.8	46.5	42.5	82	70.5	67.2	64.5	59.5
63	52.5	49.7	47.4	43.4	83	71.5	68.1	65.4	60.4
64	53.4	50.6	48.3	44.1	84	72.4	69.1	66.3	61.3
65	54.4	51.5	49.2	45.0	85	73.4	70.1	67.2	62.1
66	55.3	52.4	50.1	45.8	86	74.4	71.0	68.1	63.0
67	56.3	53.3	51.0	46.6	87	75.4	71.9	69.0	63.9
68	57.2	54.2	51.9	47.5	88	76.3	72.8	69.9	64.8
69	58.2	55.1	52.8	48.3	89	77.2	73.7	70.8	65.6
70	59.1	56.0	53.7	49.2	90	78.2	74.7	71.8	66.6
71	60.1	57.0	54.6	50.1	91	79.2	75.6	72.7	67.4
72	61.0	58.0	55.5	50.9	92	80.1	76.6	73.6	68.3
73	62.0	58.9	56.4	51.8	93	81.0	77.5	74.3	69.1
74	62.9	59.8	57.3	52.6	94	81.9	78.4	75.4	70.0
75	63.9	60.7	58.2	53.5	95	82.9	79.3	76.3	70.9
76	64.8	61.7	59.1	54.3	96	83.8	80.3	77.2	71.8
77	65.8	62.6	60.0	55.2	97	84.8	81.2	78.2	72.6
78	66.7	63.6	60.9	56.1	98	85.7	82.2	79.1	73.5
79	67.7	64.5	61.8	56.9	99	86.7	83.2	80.0	74.4
80	68.6	65.4	62.7	57.8	100	87.6	84.0	80.9	75.3

[a]Probability of 0.02. [b]Probability of 0.01. [c]Probability of 0.005. [d]Probability of 0.001.

table that gives traffic intensity versus number of channels and blocking probability. Infact Table 8.1 has been prepared from Eq. (8.1) itself. It serves like a ready reckoner for the calculation of number of channels for both the fixed assignment and the demand assignment cases.

For example, consider a case of communications with a traffic intensity of 20 erlangs. Then if the blocking probability is 0.001 (*i.e.* one call lost in 1000 calls), then the number of channels n from Table 8.1 would be 35. This number of channels n represents the available channels to be assigned on demand. Now, if the same 20 erlang is to be divided equally between 5 destinations then with such a fixed assignment, each destination would carry 4 erlangs of traffic. For such 4 erlangs of traffic intensity and the locking probability of 0.001, Table 8.1 gives the number of channels as 12. Thus is such a fixed assignment arrangement, the total number of channels would be (for total 5 destinations) $= 12 \times 5 = 60$. This shows that the demand assignment in this particular example requires only about 58 per cent as many channels as fixed assignment to move the same amount of traffic between the same numbers of destinations.

Table 8.2 gives such an improvement for a typical blocking

Table 8.2. Comparison of Satellite Channel Requirements for Pre-Assignment and Demand Assignments Schemes for Blocking Probabilities of 0.01

Number of Destination per Station N	*Channel Requirement*								
	α = 0.1 Erlang			*α = 0.5 Erlang*			*α = 1.0 Erlang*		
	Pre assignment	*Demand assignment*	*Improvement*	*Pre assignment*	*Demand assignment*	*Improvement*	*Pre assignment*	*Demand assignment*	*Improvement*
1	2	2	–	4	4	–	5	5	–
2	4	3	1.3	8	5	1.6	10	7	1.4
4	8	3	2.7	16	7	2.9	20	10	2.0
8	16	4	4.0	32	10	3.2	40	15	2.7
10	20	5	4.0	40	11	3.6	50	18	2.7
20	40	7	5.7	80	18	4.4	100	30	3.0
40	80	10	8.0	160	30	5.3	200	53	3.8

probability of 0.01 and three traffic intensities a = 0.1, 0.5 and 1.0 erlangs. This clearly indicates the economy and efficiency involved with the number of channels used in demand assignment (dynamic assignment) multiple access scheme.

Keeping this in view, a variety of demand assignment multiple access schemes have been developed. These schemes are, namely:

(*a*) *variable capacity demand assignment* which is used for TDMA networks where each station has a large range of slowly varying traffic intensity and relatively few destinations,

(*b*) *per call variable capacity demand assignment* which is also used for TDMA networks where each station serves many destinations with low, rapidly varying traffic intensity,

(*c*) *per call demand assignment* which is used for TDMA networks where each station serves many destinations with low traffic intensity,

(*d*) *fully variable demand assignment* which is used for both the FDMA and TDMA networks where each station serves many destinations with rapidly varying traffic intensity and total traffic at each station is low.

With FDMA it is called *single channel per carrier demand assignment multiple access* and with TDMA it is called *single-channel per burst demand assignment multiple access*. It would be worthwhile to mention here that the demand assignment as mentioned above is *ordered* one because the assigned signals are kept separated and do not interfere with each other. There is another kind of demand assignment called *random* where interferences and collisions are possible. Random access techniques are mostly used in packet communication systems and these will be discussed in Chapter 10.

8.3. Demand Assignment Control

In the demand assignment system the most important function is the *control mechanism* by which calls are assigned to the channels. There are two such assignment control mechanism, namely the *centralized control* and the *distributed control*. In the centralized control system there is a master control station (central controller) that has the responsibility of assigning the available duplex circuit (two channels) required to establish a call between two traffic station. Fig. 8.2 indicates this centralized control DAMA system. Here requests for channels are sent over a control channel to the central controller which arbitrates requests and returns order wire information to the requesting terminals. Actually the master control unit first senses the initiating call from the traffic station. Then it locates the destination station to which call is directed. It then determines the availability of channels at the satellite or at the two stations.

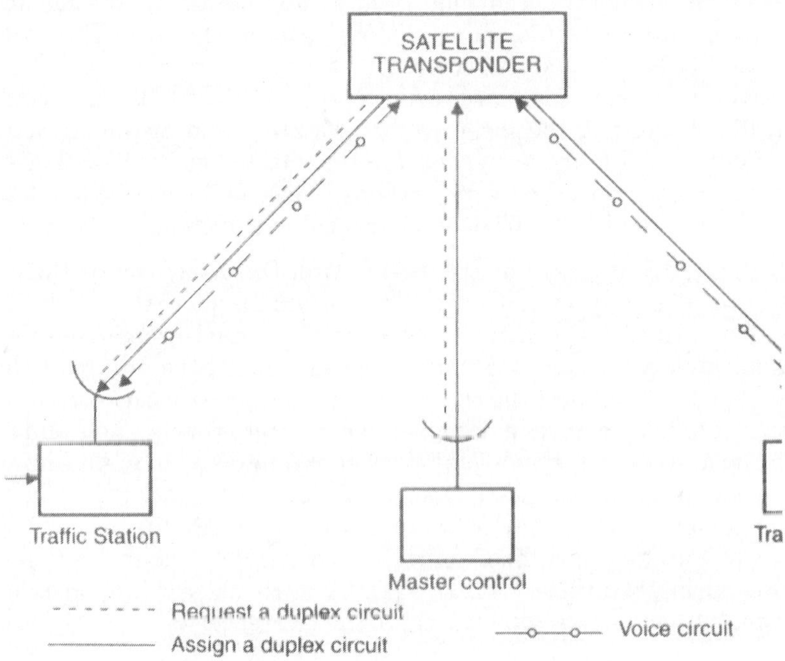

Fig. 8.2. Centralized Control Demand Assignment.

Then it assigns a pair of channels and allows the two stations to access each other through the satellite. When the call is completed, the master control station releases the duplex circuit and returns the pair of channels to the satellite pool or station pool so that these may be utilized to a new caller on demand. Thus the master control station keeps track of actual satellite channel occupancy or channel availability at all the stations in the network. The distributed control demand assignment does not use any master control station. Each traffic station has a data base of the status of the channels and selects the available channel according to its need.

Both the centralized and distributed mechanisms in the demand assignments have certain advantages as well as disadvantages. The advantages of centralized control system are that here individual terminals do not need to perform the function of channel assignment and so the terminal's cost is low. Since it maintains the status of the overall system so it can easily vary the capacity of each station according to traffic intensity and collect statistical data for traffic analysis and call logging data for off-line billing. Further, it requires less overheads as control data can be compact and status data for the whole network need not be transmitted. The disadvantages of centralized assignment is that the whole communication network relies on the central controller and so any outage at the master control station would cause a total system failure. Thus the reliability is poor and there is a need for spare, standby controller. Furthermore, it needs a large *capacity request channel* to connect all traffic stations to the master control station and also a *capacity assignment channel* is needed for the master control station to communicate with the traffic stations. These make the system less efficient for a high traffic demand assignment system.

The advantages of distributed control DAMA system is that it does not need any unique controller or so and therefore the reliability is good. Since the traffic stations make channel assignments by themselves via a *common signalling channel*, so, the failure of one station does not affect the other station. The disadvantages are that each terminal requires a data base for the status of channels and so the terminal's cost is high. Moreover, the equipment for maintaining the network data base itself is complex. Further the lack of coordination among stations may result in a poor use of satellite capacity. A mix of both the centralized control and distributed control is therefore normally utilized for DA-TDMA such as *per call variable capacity demand assignment* where the reference station varies the capacity allocated to each station based on its requests and the stations make channel assignments by themselves.

8.4. DA-FDMA (SPADE) System

SPADE system is a typical example of DA-FDMA which was used in Intelsat IV and Intelsat V. The name SPADE is loosely derived from *single channel per carrier access on demand equipment*. It is also reported to come from SCPC/PSK/FDMA/DA/EQUIPMENT. It is also considered an acronym representing *Single Channel per carrier PCM multiple access demand assignment equipment*. SPADE was originally developed by COMSAT for use in Intelsats. SPADE carries traffic using demand assignment SCPC FDMA with QPSK modulation of the individual carriers. Infact SPADE is a SCPC-DAMA satellite network using *distributed control.* There is no central controller or master control station. It uses a computer controlled demand assignment signalling and switching (DASS) system at each station for self assignment of circuits (each circuit consists of two channels) via a common signalling channel (CSC). DASS is a kind of data base that keeps the record status of all the channels. Thus SPADE is a fully variable system that allows all the circuits to be selected by any terminal on demand.

Fig. 8.3 shows the spade frequency plan at IF. With spade 800 PCM-encoded voice band channels separately QPSK modulate an IF carrier frequency (hence the name signal carrier per channel, SCPC). Each 4 kHz voice band channel is sampled at an 8 kHz rate

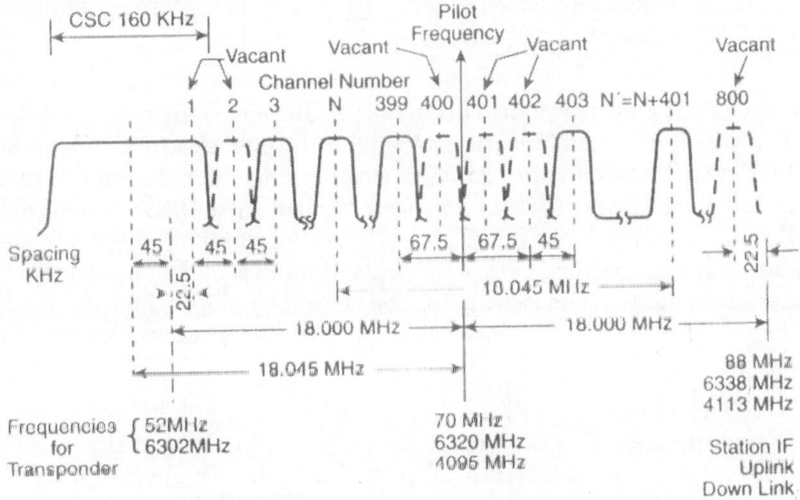

Fig. 8.3. Spade Frequency Plan.

and converted to an 8 bit PCM code. This produces a 64 Kbps PCM code for each voice band channel. The PCM code from each voice band channel QPSK modulates a different IF carrier frequency. With QPSK, the minimum required bandwidth is equal to one half the input rate. Therefore the output of each QPSK modulator requires a minimum bandwidth 32 kHz. There is a 45 kHz bandwidth allocated to each channel. This allows for a 13 kHz guard band between each frequency-division-multiplexed channel. The IF carrier frequencies begin at 52.0225 MHz (low band channel 1) and increase in 45 kHz steps to 87.9775 MHz (high band channel 400). The entire 36 MHz band (52 to 88 MHz) is divided in half, producing two 400 channels bands (a low band and a high band). For full duplex operation, four hundred 45 kHz channels are used for one direction of transmission and 400 are used for the opposite direction. The center frequency is 70 MHz. The center frequency of channel 400 is 22.5 kHz below the 70 MHz IF center frequency, and the frequency of channel 401 is 22.5 kHz above the IF center frequency. Thus channel 400 is centered at 69.9775 MHz and channel 401 is centered at 70.0225 MHz. Thus the IF center frequency of channel N may be expressed by

$$f_N = 0.045N + 51.9775 \text{ MHz} \qquad ...(8.3)$$

The center of the transponder band (70 MHz) is marked by a pilot carrier (pilot frequency) provided by the network's reference station. To avoid interference with the pilot, the channels immediately above and below it (401 and 400) are not used and these portions of the spectrum are unoccupied. In addition channels 1 and 2 are left vacant to accommodate the common signalling channel (CSC) that provides network control information.

The telephone conversation are carried by a pair of channels above and below the pilot. Thus a total of 397 such pairs are available and this is the number of simultaneous duplex channels that a 36 MHz transponder using SPADE can provide. The channel pair is automatically allocated to an incoming call by a DASS unit. Each SPADE terminal maintains a complete assignment map for the entire system. Before a station selects a channel, it first analyses the assignment map, chooses an unused channel and indicates its choice on the DASS network. The associated return channel completes the circuit.

The common signalling channel (CSC) is of 160 kHz that each IF channel has. The CSC is a time division multiplex transmission that is frequency division multiplexed onto the IF spectrum below the QPSK-encoded voice band channels. The TDM frame structure for the CSC consists of total frame time of 50 ms which is subdivided into fifty 1 ms epochs. Each earth stations transmits on the CSC channel only during its preassigned 1 ms time slot. The CSC signal is a 128 bit binary code. To transmit a 128 bit code in 1 ms, a transmission rate of 128 kbps is required. The CSC code is used for establishing and disconnecting voice band links between two earth stations users when demand-assignment channel allocation is used. Fig. 8.4 indicates the basic block diagram of the SPADE operation that includes all the operations discussed above. It is evident that SPADE has considerable capacity advantages over a 36 MHz bandwidth transponder using preassignment of carriers because there are 800 total voice channels available per transponder but the cost of ground equipment needed for signal processing is high.

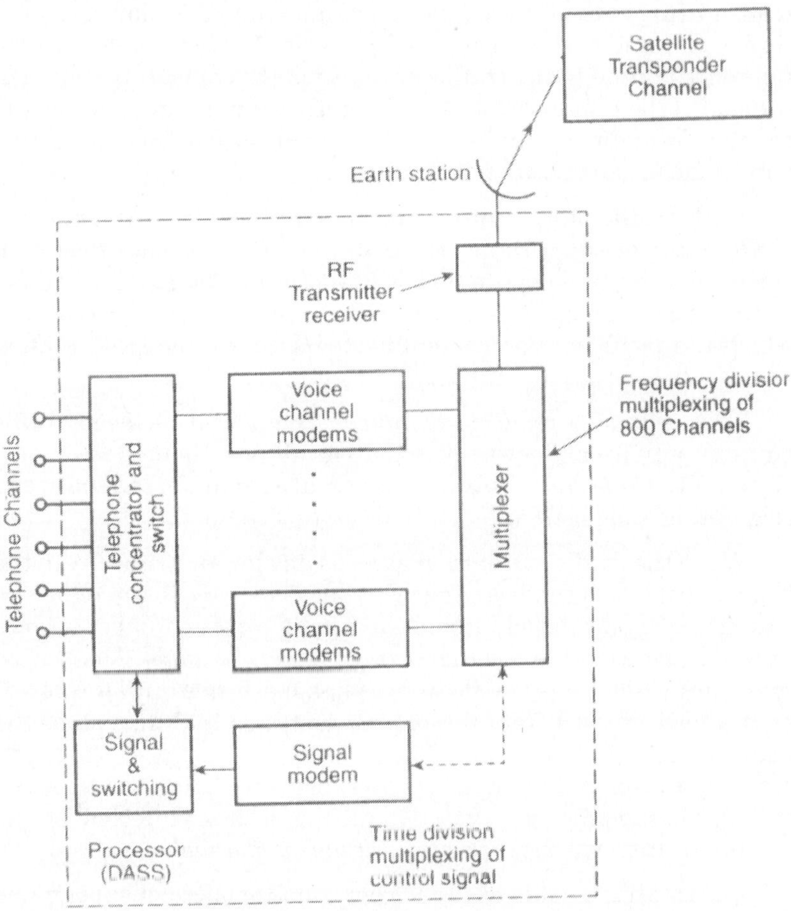

Fig. 8.4. Basic Block Diagram of SPADE Operation at an Earth Station.

8.5. Demand Assignment TDMA (DA-TDMA)

In the fixed assignment TDMA discussed in sections 7.2 and 7.3, the time frame has slots of fixed duration and the slots are permanently allocated to each of the stations. As already shown in Fig. 8.1 there is always a chance of slots getting wasted during lightly loaded earth stations. The demand assignment uses these empty slots and therefore DA-TDMA allows stations to be allocated variable duration slots or more slots per frame than others. Thus DA-TDMA frame structure would be different from TDMA frame structure (of Fig. 7.3) because of some additional channels for demand assignment.

Fig. 8.5 indicates a typical DA-TDMA frame structure. A superframe consists of frames where *N* represents the number of stations transmitting in the frame. The superframe timing is marked by the timing of frame 1. The *capacity assignment messages* are sent by the reference station to the traffic stations via the *capacity assignment channel* of the reference burst. Each traffic station can be addressed once per frame, for example, station 1 is addressed in frame 1, station 2 in frame 2..., and station *N* in frame N.

Each traffic station also transmits a *Superframe short burst (SSB)* once per superframe. The SSB in frame 1 belongs to station 1, that in frame 2 belongs to station 2, and so on. The SSB is normally at the end of the frame and carries the *capacity request channel* by which the traffic station communicates with the reference station and requests additional capacity to meet its traffic load.

The *common signalling channel* is employed between traffic stations only to implement distributed call processing and call assignment. *Call signalling messages* are transferred between originating and destination stations on this channel.

When the traffic at a station exceeds its allocated capacity in the frame, the station sends a *capacity request message* to the reference station asking for the additional capacity (a certain number of voice channels, for example) via the *capacity request channel*. The station continues to send this message once per superframe until it receives an acknowledgment from the reference station and then stops the transmission of the message. The reference station does the frame reconfiguration and after completing this reconfiguration, it sends *capacity assignment messages* to all the stations affected by the reconfiguration via the *capacity assignment channel*.

Each station is addressed once per frame or once per superframe sequentially depending on the channel rate. The capacity assignment message contains information on the burst length (in voice channels, for example), burst position (in symbols, relative to the last symbol of the unique word of the primary reference burst), and possibly the transponder.

It should be noted that the frame reconfiguration is not implemented until the reference station verifies that all the *capacity assignment messages* have been correctly received by the affected stations. Thus the most important function in DA-TDMA is the ability of the reference station to quickly search the frame to find available capacity and then assign it to the traffic stations that request it. Note also that the traffic station before transmitting the acknowledgment of the capacity assignment message to the reference station, repacks on going calls in its burst if the burst length is reduced by the frame reconfiguration as indicated in the *capacity assignment message*. DA-TDMA has also been achieved successfully and economically by using multidestination Terrestrial Interface Modules (TIM) at the traffic stations. Various satellites like TELECOM, INTELSAT etc use TIMs for DA-TDMA purposes.

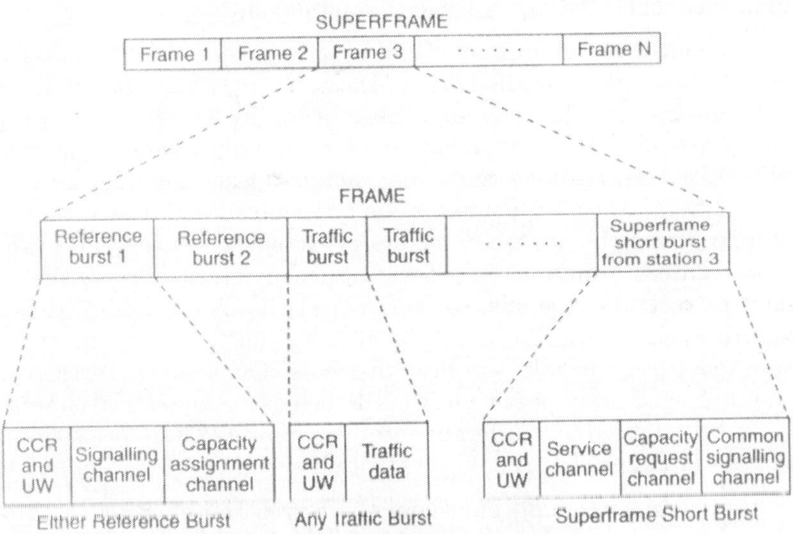

Fig. 8.5. DA-TDMA Frame Structure

8.6. Digital Speech Interpolation

Digital Speech Interpolation (DSI) is another efficient technique for increasing the satellite capacity. It does it by assigning the transmission capacity only to those circuits whose users are speaking. DSI's basic principle may be understood as below. In a normal conversation one person speaks and the other listens and so the active speech signals are present only for less than 50% of the time on a one way circuit. Further there are pauses between sentences, words and even syllables alongwith the availability of times during which the circuit is idle for thinking and so forth. Taking all these into account, it is clear that speech signals rarely exceed 40% of a typical two way telephone conversation time. Thus each channel is free 60% of the time on the average. DSI uses this available time for assigning to other active talkers. Thus in DSI, N conversations are carried out on M transmission channels where $M < N$. The ratio N/M is called *speech interpolation gain*. It may be noted that a similar technique with analog speech known as *time assignment speech interpolation* (TASI) is being used in long-distance submarine cables systems to double the capacity of analog FDM voice circuits there. In digital satellite communication DSI is usually combined with time division multiple access (TDMA) transmission. It has several advantages over analog TASI and is being used in INTELSAT satellites. There are two types of DSI, namely the Digital TASI and SPEC (speech predictive encoded communications). However, the DSI process is, because of its nature a complex one requiring a great deal of costly hardware for its implementation.

The basic block diagram of DSI system is shown in Fig. 8.6. The whole system is also called *digital speech interpolation interface*. In the transmit side the voice or speak detector detects whether speech signal are present or not on each of N incoming terrestrial channels and then the channels containing active speech signals are connected to M satellite channels for transmission to the receiving station. Thus the speech detectors sense speech energy and then seize a satellite channel. Whenever a speech detector senses energy on a terrestrial channels, the terrestrial channel is assigned to a satellite channel. The satellite channel assigned is randomly selected from the idle satellite channels. On a given terrestrial channel, each time speech energy is detected, the terrestrial channel could be assigned to a different satellite channel. Therefore a single terrestrial channel can use several satellite channels for a single call.

For demultiplexing purposes, the terrestrial channel/satellite channel assignment information is conveyed to the receive terminal. This is done through an assignment channel (a common signalling channel) similar to the one used on the SPADE system. Infact satellite channel assignments are transmitted by means of assignment messages (AMs) which consist of terrestrial channel number and an associated satellite channel number. In Fig. 8.6 the satellite channel assignment is carried out through the assignment control, assignment status buffer register and speech memory. Similar units are used in the receiving side for demultiplexing the signals. Thus it is now evident that Digital Speech Interpolation is a form of demand assignment because the satellite channels are randomly assigned on an as needed basis.

From above discussions on DSI, it is clear that the DSI has *channel compression.* In other words there can be more terrestrial channels than the satellite channels. Generally a terrestrial channel/satellite channel ratio of 2 : 1 is used. For a full duplex (2 way simultaneous) communication circuit, there is a speech in each

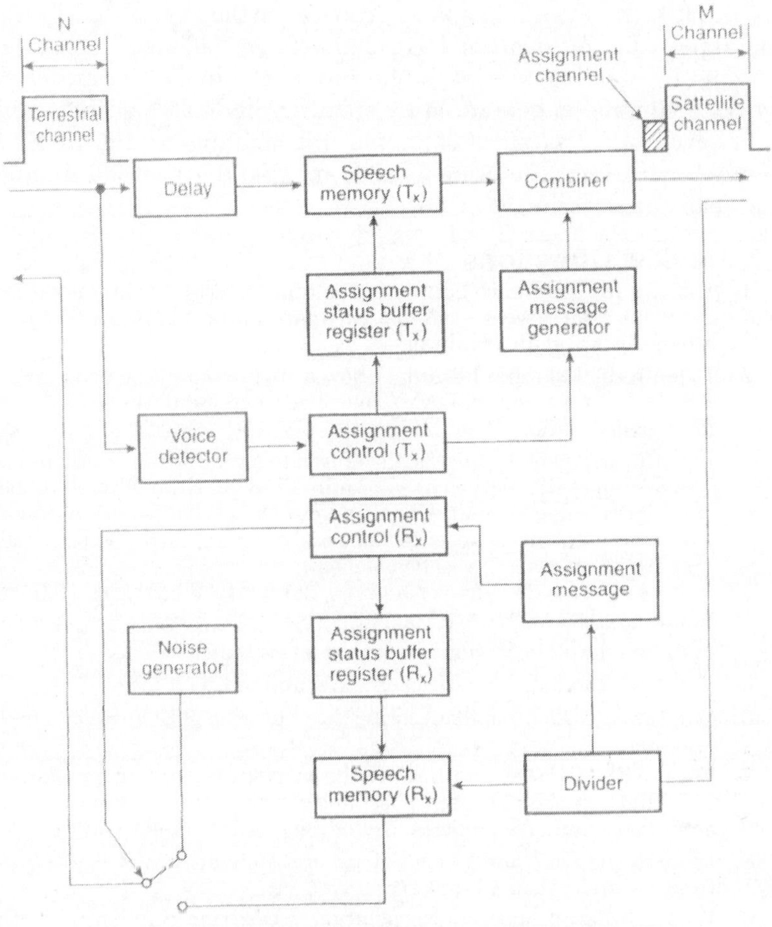

Fig. 8.6. Basic Block Diagram of DSI System.

direction 40% of the time and for 20% of the time the circuit is idle in both the directions. Therefore, a DSI gain slightly more than 2 is realized. In Intelsat 127 satellite channels support 240 terrestrial channels. It may be noted that the DSI gain is affected by a phenomenon called *competitive clipping*. The competitive clipping occurs when speech energy is detected on a terrestrial channel but there is no satellite channel to assign it to and during the wait time, speech information is lost. Competitive clipping is also oftenly termed as *freeze out phenomena* because in such a situation the incoming speech channel could not be assigned a satellite channel or is *frozen out*. Competitive clipping is not noticed by a subscriber if its duration is less than 50 ms.

In DSI, the channel capacity can be further enhanced by the technique called *bit stealing*. Here channels are added to fully loaded systems by stealing bits from the in-use channels. Generally an overload channel is generated by stealing the least significant bit from seven other satellite channels. Bit stealing results in eight channels with 7 bit resolution for the time that the overload channel is in use.

8.7. Review Questions

1. Explain the difference between preassignment and demand assignment multiple access systems. Compare and contrast the relative advantages and disadvantages.
2. Explain the Erlang B formula. Show as to how can it be used to find out the improvement of DAMA over Preassignment Multiple Access for a given traffic.
3. A Traffic intensity of 1 erlang is offered to a group of three channels. The average call holding time is 2 min. Find out the average number of calls arrivals per hour. Then find out the probability that no call will arrive during a specified period of 2 min. Also evaluate the probability that a call will be blocked.

   (**Ans** : λ = 30 calls per hour, p_o (2 min) 0.368, B (3,1) = 0.0625)
4. What is the function of Demand Assignment Control in DAMA systems ? Explain Various such control systems.
5. What is a common signalling channel and how is it used ?
6. What is SPADE ? Briefly describe the operation of COMSAT's spade system.
7. For the SPADE system what are the carrier frequencies for channel 7 ? What are the allocated passband for channel 7 ? What are the actual passband frequencies (excluding guard bands) required ?
8. Explain the DA-TDMA burst structure. In what way it is different from a simple TDMA burst structure ?
9. What is digital speech interpolation ? Describe the working of a digital speech interpolated iterfaces ?

10. What is channel compression and how is it accomplished with a DSI system ?
11. Describe competitive clipping and bit stealing in DSI systems. In what way do these affect the DSI working ?

8.8. References

1. Van Trees, H.L.(ed)., Satellite Communication, IEEE Press Book, New York, 1979.
2. Dill, G.D., Comparison of Circuit Call capacity of Demand Assignment and Preassignment operation, COSMAT Tech Rev., Vol 2, Spring, 1972, pp 243-256.
3. Miya, K., Ed., Satellite Communication Technology, Tokyo, KDD Engineering and Consulting Inc, 1982.
4. SPILKER J.J., Digital Communications by Satellite, Englewood Cliffs, NJ, Prentice-Hall, Inc, 1977.
5. Proceedings of the IEEE, Special Issue on Satellite Communications, Vol 65, No 3, March 1977.
6. Bargelini, P.L. Satellite and Space Communications in Reference Data for Engineers, Radio, Electronics, Computer and Communications, (Ed) E.C. Jordan, Howard W Sams & Co., Indianapolis, 1985.
7. Maral, G. and Bousquet, M., Satellite Communications Systems, John Wiley & Sons, NY, 1986.
8. Bharagava, V.K., Haccoun, D., Matyas, R. and Nuspul, P., Digital Communications by Satellite, John Wiley, NY, 1981.
9. Companella, S.J. 1976, Digital Speech Interpolation, COMSAT Tech Rev, 6, pp 127-158.
10. Edelson, B.I. and Werthy, A.M., 1972, Spade System Progress and Application, COMSAT Tech Rev, 2(1) pp 221-242.
11. Sklar, B., Digital Communications, Fundamentals and Applications, Prentice Hall, Englewood Cleffs, NJ, 1988.
12. Campanella, S. and Schaefer, D., Time Division Multiple Access Systems (TDMA) in K Feher, Digital Communications, Satellite/Earth Station Engineering, Prentice Hall Inc, Englewood Cliffs, NJ, 1983.
13. Keely, J.M., DSI Architectures for Present and Further Domestic and International Digital Satellite Communications, Proceedings on Satellite Communications Conference, Ottawa, Canada, June 14-17, 1983, pp 12.3.1.
14. Ha, T.T., Digital Satellite Communications, MacMillan Publishing Co. 1986, New York.
15. Tomasi, W., Advanced Electronic Communications Systems, Prentice-Hall Inc Englewood Cliffs, NJ, 1987.
16. Pratt, T. and Bostian, C.W., Satellite Communications, John Wiley and Sons, 1986.
17. Martin, J., Communications Satellite Systems, Prentice Hall Englewood Cliffs, NJ, 1978.
18. Gagliardi, R.M., Satellite Communications, Lifetime Learning Publications, Belmont, CA, 1984.

9

Spread Spectrum Technique and Code Division Multiple Access

9.1. Introduction

The spread spectrum system is one in which the transmitted signal is *spread* over a wide frequency band, much wider, infact, than the minimum bandwidth required to transmit the information being sent. In other words a spread spectrum system takes a baseband signal (say a voice channel) with a bandwidth of only a few kHz and distributes it over a band that may be many megahertz wide. This spreading is accomplished by means of a *spreading* signal, oftenly called as a *code signal* which is independent of the data. Thus the spread spectrum technique is simply the *code division multiple access* technique. A typical example of a spread spectrum modulation is that of conventional frequency modulation in which deviation ratios greater than one are used. The rf spectrum product is much wider than the transmitted information. At the receiving side of the spread spectrum systems, despreading is (recovering the original data) accomplished by the correlation of the received spread signal with a synchronised replica of the spreading signal used to spread the information.

Spread spectrum modulation techniques or spread spectrum multiple access techniques have several advantages as compared to conventional communication systems. A properly designed spread spectrum communication system can operate reliably in the presence of various types of radio-frequency interference (RFI) including multipath interference, multiple access interference and hostile jamming. In addition, when the signal power is spread over a large bandwidth, the signal has very small average power in any marrow band slot. At any rate the density of spread spectrum signal is far less than that of more conventional signals. This means that the spread spectrum systems can share a frequency band with several narrow band system. This clearly indicates that it is quite difficult to detect the presence of spread spectrum signal by the use of narrow band equipments. It requires special techniques to decode the transmitted messages. With these advantages, spread spectrum techniques are widely used in defense communication systems.

There are 3 kinds of modulation techniques normally being used in spread spectrum techniques. The first one is the *direct sequence modulation* (DS) technique in which modulation of a carrier is being done by a digital code sequence whose bit rate is much higher than the information signal bandwidth. The second technique is *frequency* hopping (FH) in which the carrier frequency shifting is done in discrete increments in a pattern dictated by a code sequence. Here the transmitter jumps from frequency to frequency within same predetermined set; the order of frequency usage is determined by a code sequence. In the third technique known as *chirp modulation* or *pulsed FM modulation* carrier is swept over a wide band during a given pulse interval. It may be noted that similar to frequency hopping there are *time hopping* and *time frequency hopping* where time of transmission (usually of low duty cycle and short duration) is governed by a code sequence. Also, sometimes *hybrid techniques* may also be used for spread spectrum systems. It would be worthwhile to mention here that in mid 1950s the Sylvania Engineers had developed a system named the *Buffalo Laboratories Application of Digital Exact Spectra* (BLADES) to defeat the repeat back jamming. However, the system, was not robust at all and so it did not become popular.

9.2. Process Gain and Jam Margin

The properties of spread spectrum communication systems are characterized by two important parameters, namely the *process gain* and *jamming margin*. The process gain is defined as the difference between the output and input signal to noise ratios. For example in the frequency modulation case it is called fm improvement and is equal to 10 log (3/2) m^2 (Discussed in Section 4.4) where m is the FM modulation index given by $m = \Delta\omega/\omega_m$, $\Delta\omega$ being the frequency deviation. Thus for a given processor with an input S/N ratio of 10 dB and output S/N ratio of 16 dB would have a *process gain* of 6 dB. In practice the process gain is estimated by the following formula as a rule of thumb, namely

$$\text{process gain, } G_p = \frac{BW_{rf}}{R_{inf}} \qquad ...(9.1)$$

where BW_{rf} is the rf bandwidth of the transmitted spread spectrum signal and the information rate (R_{inf}) is the data rate in the information baseband channel. BW_{rf} is also sometimes expressed as W_{ss}.

The importance of process gain can be further understood in the following way. It is well known that a digital communication system operates with a given required probability of error if the ratio of the energy per bit to the spectral density of the noise (or interference) exceeds some threshold value (typically around 10 db). The received signal power is the product of the energy per bit and the bit rate. Thus

$$P_r = E_b \text{ (Joules/bit)} \cdot R \text{ (bit/second)} \qquad ...(9.2)$$

Interference power from the other spread spectrum users is the product of their combined interference spectral density N_0, and the receiver input bandwidth B (or W_{ss})

$$P_i \text{ (watts)} = N_0 \text{ (watts/Hz)} \cdot W_{ss} \text{ (Hz)} \qquad ...(9.3)$$

Thus at the input of the receiver, the signal to interference power ratio is

$$\text{SIR} = \frac{P_r}{P_i} = \frac{E_b}{N_0} \cdot \frac{R}{W_{ss}} \qquad ...(9.4)$$

But in a spread spectrum signal, W_{ss} is much greater than R and so E_b/N_0 could be in the acceptable range (around 10) even when SIR is very small. For example, if $E_b/N_0 = 10$ and $W_{ss}/R = 1000$, SIR = 0.01 or -20 dB. For this reason W_{ss}/R is called processing gain of the system. It is thus possible for a spread spectrum receiver to operate even when its input signal is literally 'buried' in noise or interference. In the above example, it is clear that if all the signals were received with equal power there could be $(W_{ss}/R)/(E_b/N_0) = 100$ interferences present, in the same band at the same time, and the receiver could still operate with the required performance level.

Jamming margin expresses the capability of a system to perform in interfering (hostile) environments. Jamming margin takes into account the requirement for a useful system output signal to noise ratio (minimum $(S/N)_{out}$ of the system) and allows for internal losses. Thus the jamming margin is evaluated by the formula

$$M_j = \text{jamming margin} = G_p - [L_{sys} + (S/N)_{\min\, out}] \qquad ...(9.5)$$

where L_{sys} = system implementation losses. For example, a system with 30 dB process gain, minimum $(S/N)_{out}$ of 10 dB and L_{sys} of 2 dB would have an 18 dB jamming margin (M_j). Therefore it could not be expected to operate with interference more than 18 dB above the desired signal.

It should be remembered that jamming is not always the result of an intentional act. Sometimes, the jamming signal is caused by natural phenomena, and sometimes it is the result of self-interference caused by the multipath, in which delayed versions of the signal, arriving via alternative paths, interfere with the direct path transmission. It may, however, also be noted that though the spread spectrum technique offers good process gain (or undesired signal rejection) it does not provide highest process gain for every situation and therefore to obtain optimum results, the spread spectrum techniques should be combined with other signal to noise ratio improving techniques.

9.3. J/S Ratio and Antijam Margin

In Chapter 7 we had seen that the digital satellite communication requires a knowledge of E_b/N_0 for meeting a specified error performance. In the presence of jamming it becomes essential to know the link error performance as a function of interference. Thus, if J_0 is the noise power spectral density due to the jammer, than SNR of interest for digital satellite link would be $E_b/(N_0 + J_0)$. J_0 may also be expressed as

$$J_0 = J/W_{ss} \qquad \text{...(9.6)}$$

where J is the average received jammer power (jammer power referred to the receiver front end) and W_{ss} is the spread spectrum bandwidth. Since the jammer power is generally much greater than the thermal noise power, the SNR of interest in a jammed environment is usually taken to be E_b/J_0. Thus, similar to thermal noise case, the ratio $(E_b/J_0)_{reqd}$ may be defined as the bit energy per jammer noise power spectral density required for maintaining the link at a specified error probability. Now the parameter E_b may be written as

$$E_b = ST_b = S/R \qquad \text{...(9.7)}$$

where S is the received signal power, T_b is the bit duration, and R is the data rate expressed in bit/s.

Then $(E_b/J_0)_{reqd}$ may be expressed as

$$(E_b/J_0)\ reqd = \left(\frac{S/R}{J/W_{ss}}\right)_{reqd} = \frac{W_{ss}/R}{(J/S)_{reqd}} = \frac{G_p}{(J/S)_{reqd}} \qquad \text{...(9.8)}$$

where G_p is the process gain defined in Eq. (9.1)

Eq. (9.8) now gives

$$(J/S)_{reqd} = \frac{G_p}{(E_b/J_0)_{reqd}} \qquad \text{...(9.9)}$$

The ratio $(J/S)_{reqd}$ is a *figure of merit* that provides a measure of how *invulnerable* a system is to interference. The larger (J/S), the greater is the system's noise rejection capability but it forces the communications to employ a greater processing gain.

Antijam margin means the safety margin against a particular threat (jamming). It is represented by M_{AJ} and is given by

$$M_{AJ}\,(dB) = \left(\frac{E_b}{J_0}\right)_r dB - \left(\frac{E_b}{J_0}\right)_{\text{reqd}} dB \qquad ...(9.10)$$

where $(E_b/J_0)_r$, is the E_b/J_0 *actually received.* Now, $(E_b/j_0)_r$ may be expressed as

$$\left(\frac{E_b}{J_0}\right)_r = \frac{G_p}{(J/S)_r} \qquad ...(9.11)$$

where $(J/S)_r$ is the ratio of the actually received jammer power to signal power. Thus from Eqs. (9.8) to (9.11) one gets

$$M_{AJ}\,(dB) = \frac{G_p}{(J/S)_r}\,dB - \frac{G_p}{(J/S)_{\text{reqd}}}\,dB$$
$$= (J/S)_{\text{reqd}}\,dB - (J/S)_r\,dB \qquad ...(9.12)$$

It may be noted that quite often the ratio $(J/S)_{reqd}$ itself is called the anti-jam margin since it characterizes the system jammer-rejection capability. However, Eq. (9.12) represents the true *antijam margin* because it is based on the very definition of antijam margin as discussed above.

9.4. Direct Sequence Spread Spectrum Techniques

In the direct sequence modulation the amplitude of an already modulated signal is amplitude modulated by a very high rate NRZ binary stream of digits. In other words in the direct sequence modulation the carrier wave is first modulated with a data signal $d(t)$, then the data modulated signal is again modulated with a high

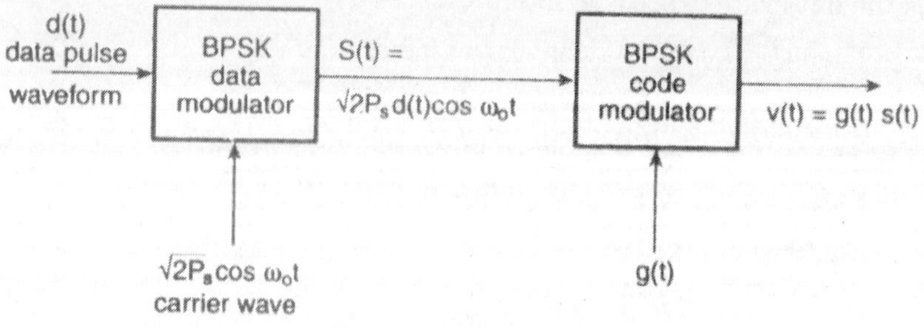

Fig. 9.1. Basic Block Diagram of a Simple DS Spread Spectrum Modulation.

speed (wide band) spreading signal $g(t)$. Thus for a constant envelope data modulated carrier with power P_s and radian frequency ω_0 which may be expressed as

$$s(t) = \sqrt{2p_s}\; d(t) \cos \omega_o t \qquad \text{...(9.13)}$$

(which is actually a binary PSK signal), the DS spread spectrum signal obtained by constant envelope modulation of wave (9.13) by the spreading signal $g(t)$, is expressed as

$$\begin{aligned} v(t) &= g(t)\, s(t) \\ &= \sqrt{2\rho s}\; g(t)\, d(t) \cos \omega_o t \qquad \text{...(9.14)} \end{aligned}$$

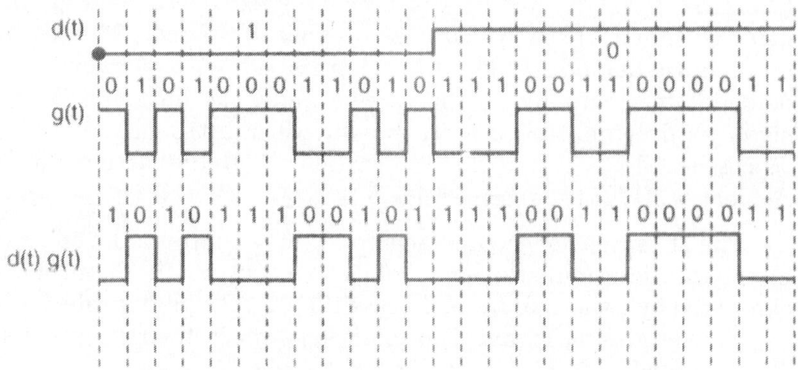

Fig. 9.2. Spread Spectrum Example Using Direct Sequencing (*a*) Binary Data Waveform d(t) (*b*) PN (code) Sequence g(t) (*c*) The Transmitted Waveform Product of d(t) g(t).

The spreading signal $g(t)$ is actually a pseudo-random noise $P(N)$ binary sequence having the values ± 1. The basic block diagram of DS spread spectrum modulator is shown in Fig. 9.1. Fig. 9.2 indicates the wave forms achieved by DS SS example. It shows a data sequence $d(t)$, a pseudo random noise sequence of $g(t)$ and the product sequence $g(t)\, d(t)$. It should be noted that $g(t)$ is a binary sequence as is the data $d(t)$. The sequence of $g(t)$ is generated in a deterministic manner and is repetitive. But without serious error it can be assumed as truly random *i.e.* there is no correlation between the value of a particular bit and the value of any other bits. The details of *PN* sequence are given in the next section.

The bit rate f_c of $g(t)$ is usually much greater than the bit rate f_b of $d(t)$. Actually the bit rate f_c is so high than f_b that one could easily say '$g(t)$ chops the bits of data (f_b) into chips' and therefore f_c is oftenly called *chip rate*. Thus whereas f_c is called chip rate, f_b would be simply the bit rate. The product sequence $d(t)\, g(t)$ in Fig. 9.2.(*c*) is similar to $g(t)$ and if $g(t)$ is truly random, the product sequence would be another sequence $g(t)$ having same chip rate f_c as $g(t)$. Now, the bandwidth of the BPSK signal $s(t)$ is nominally $2f_b$ and similarly the bandwidth of PBPSK spread spectrum signal $v(t)$ is $2f_c$. It can be easily said that the spectrum has been spread by the ratio f_c/f_b. Since the power transmitted by $s(t)$ and $v(t)$ is the same, *i.e.*, P_s, the power spectral density $G_s(f)$ is reduced by the factor f_b/f_c. The ratio f_c/f_b is the process gain G_p *i.e.*,

$$G_p = f_c/f_b \qquad ...(9.15)$$

In order to demodulate DS SS signal two step process is involved. The first step, despreading is accomplished by correlating the received signal with a synchronized replica of the code. The second step, data demodulation is accomplished with conventional demodulator. Actually, in the receiver side, the incoming DS SS signal is first multiplied with the waveform g(t) and the carrier $\sqrt{2}\cos \omega_o t$. This requires the regeneration of both the carrier and *PN* sequences g(t) at the receiver side.

The DS spread spectrum techniques may suppress the effect of interfering deterministic signal but it can not reduce the disturbance generated by a thermal noise. In case the DS SS signal is interfered with by a sinusoidal signal of normalized power P_J then the quantity P_{Jeff} given by

$$P_{Jeff} = \frac{P_J}{2(f_c/f_b)} \qquad ...(9.16)$$

represents the effective jamming power.

9.5. PN Sequences

As already mentioned the spreading signals used in the spread spectrum technique are the pseudo-random or pseudo-noise sequences. These are noise like but deterministic periodic sequences. These are also called code sequences which have much greater length than those considered in the usual areas of coding for information transfer, the reason being that they are intended for bandwidth spreading and not for the direct transfer of information. The *PN* sequence has a very important role to play in the spread spectrum system because it directly affects the capability of the system. In particular the type of *PN* code sequence, its length and its bits rate bounds are important to be considered seriously as the spread spectrum system's capability is directly dependent on them. It may be noted that though the type of *PN* sequences used in the spread spectrum system are deterministic but they have the statistical properties of a sampled white noise and to an unauthorised listener these appear to be a truly random signal. The randomness properties like those of *balance, run* and *correlation* are very well satisfied by these *PN* sequences.

The bandspreading codes (*PN* sequences) used are the maximal length codes. These are therefore oftenly called *m*-sequences. Infact these are the longest codes that can be generated by a given shift register or a delay element of a given length. The maximum length sequence is $2^n - 1$ bits where n is the number of stages in the shift register. The shift register sequence generator consists of a shift register working in conjuction with appropriate logic, which feeds back a logical combination of the state of two or more of its stages to its input. The output of a sequence generator and the contents of its n states at any sample (clock) time is a function of the outputs of the states fed back at the preceding sample time. Feedback connections have been tabulated for maximal code generators from 3 to 100 stages, so that some sequences of any length from 7 through $2^{36} - 1$ bits are readily available. The *PN* sequences may be represented by the polar waveform with a chip rate that is much larger than the information rate R_b. Infact the bit generated from the conventional digital modulator is being divided into pieces called *chips*. Each chip corresponds to a member of a *PN* sequence and a chip is transmitted as $a + 1$ or $a - 1$ depending on whether its corresponding element in the sequence is $a + 1$ or $a - 1$.

The *PN* sequences have certain other properties as described below. The number of ones in a sequence equals the number of zeros within one bit. For a 1023 bit code there are 512 ones and 511 zeros. The statistical distribution of ones and zero is well defined and always the same. The autocorrelation of a maximal linear code is such that for all values of phase shift the correlation value is –1, except for the 0 ± 1 bit phase shift area in which correlation varies linearly from the –1 value to $2^n - 1$ (the sequence length). A 1023 bit maximal code ($2^{10} - 1$) therefore has a peak to average autocorrela-

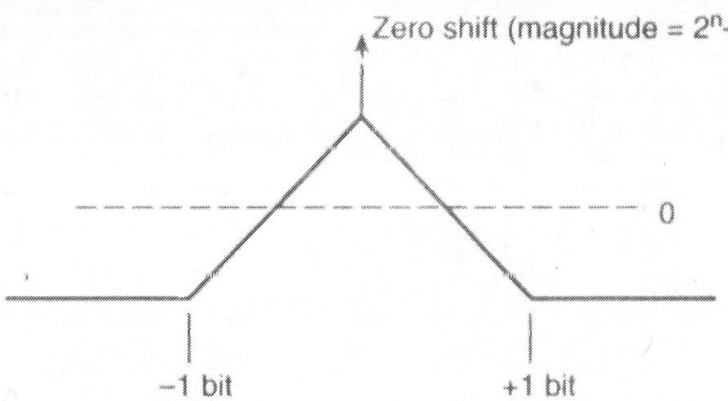

Fig. 9.3. *m* Sequence Auto Correlation Function.

tion value of 1024, a range of 30.1 dB. The *m* sequence autocorrelation function is as that shown in Fig. 9.3.

PN sequences follow the modulo 2 addition principle. A modulo-2 addition of a maximal linear code with a phase shifted replica of itself results in another replica with a phase different from either of the originals. The rules for modulo-2 addition are

$$\begin{Bmatrix} 0 \oplus 1 = 1 \\ 0 \oplus 0 = 0 \\ 1 \oplus 1 = 0 \end{Bmatrix} \qquad ...(9.17)$$

It would be worthwhile to mention here that various maximal length codes may be combined to give the so called composite codes which have also been used in spread spectrum communication systems. These composite codes are of several types such as JPL ranging codes, the Gold codes etc. These codes have better correlation properties.

9.6. DS CDMA

The spread spectrum technique has direct application in satellite communication system through code division multiple access where multiple signals occupying the same rf bandwidth are to be transmitted simultaneously without interfering with one another. The CDMA was already introduced in Section 7.12. If a single DS spread spectrum is used, it may provide protection against interference but the bandwidth is greatly wasted. To improve the bits-per-hertz throughout the advantage is taken of the low peak cross-correlation value in a set of DS addressed codes such as Gold sequences. Thus in a direct sequence CDMA satellite system, each uplink earth station has its own addressed *PN* sequence and unlike the situation in TDMA and FDMA where the carriers are separated by time or frequency, all active stations transmit their carriers on

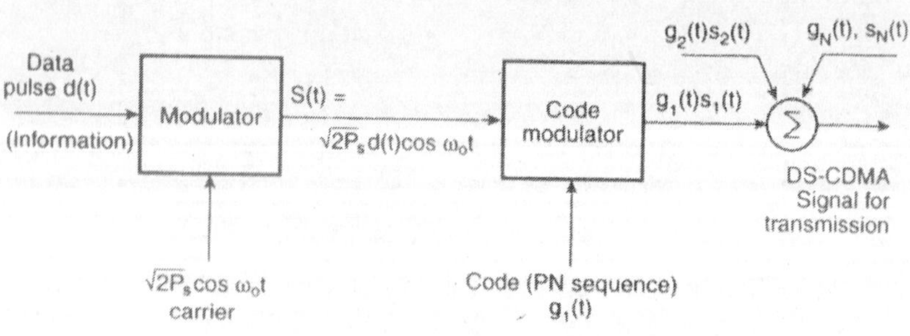

Fig. 9.4. Principle of DS-CDMA Technique.

the same allocated bandwidth and overlap in time Fig. 9.4. Indicates the Principle of DS-CDMA System transmission. Here the output of several DS-spread spectrum modulators, say N are using their own codes $g_1(t)$ where $i = 1, 2 \ldots N$. After combining these together these are transmitted. The user codes are approximately orthogonal so that the cross-correlation of two different codes is near zero. It should be noted that each of the users is transmitting data at the same carrier frequency and each pseudo-random frequency $g_i(t)$ has the same chip rate f_c. The data rate for each user is also the same f_b. Thus the signal after transmitted back by the satellite to the receiver would be a combination of

$$g_1(t)\, s_1(t) + g_2(t)\, s_2(t) + \ldots\ldots g_N(t)\, s_N(t) \qquad \ldots(9.18)$$

It is clear that multiplication of $s_1(t)$ by $g_1(t)$ produces a signal whose spectrum is the convolution of the spectrum of $s_1(t)$ with the spectrum of $g_1(t)$. Thus, assuming that the signal $s_1(t)$ is relatively narrowband compared with the code or spreading signal $g_1(t)$, the product signal $g_1(t)\, s_1(t)$ will have approximately the bandwidth of $g_1(t)$.

At the receiver side arrangements are being made to receive the message from desired user group. Here the corresponding $g_i(t)$ is generated at the receiver and is perfectly synchronized with the received signal from the corresponding wiht user. The first step in the receiving process is to multiply the incoming signal of Eq. (9.18) by $g_1(t)$. Suppose that the singal of $g_1(t)$ is to be received. Then at the receiver side the incoming signal would be multiplied by $g_1(t)$. The output of the multiplier will yield the following terms :

$$\text{Desired signal} : g_1^2(t)\, s_1(t) + \text{ a composite of undeshed signals}$$

$$g_1(t)\, g_2(t)\, s_2(t) + g_1(t)\, g_3(t)\, s_3(t) + \ldots\ldots + g_1(t)\, g_N(t)\, s_N(t) \qquad \ldots(9.19)$$

If the code functions $\{g_i(t)\}$ are chosen with orthogonal properties, the desired signal can be extracted perfectly in the absence of noise since $\int_0^T g_i^2(t) = 1$ and the undesired signals are easily rejected since $\int_0^T g_i(t)\, g_j(t)\, dt = 0$ for $i \neq j$. The basic block diagram of a typical DS spread spectrum receiver (decodor) is shown in Fig. 9.5.

As shown in Fig. 9.5 the incoming RF signal is first down converted to IF and then the $g_1(t)$ is multiplied to this IF signal and then the product is compared with the received IF signal in the

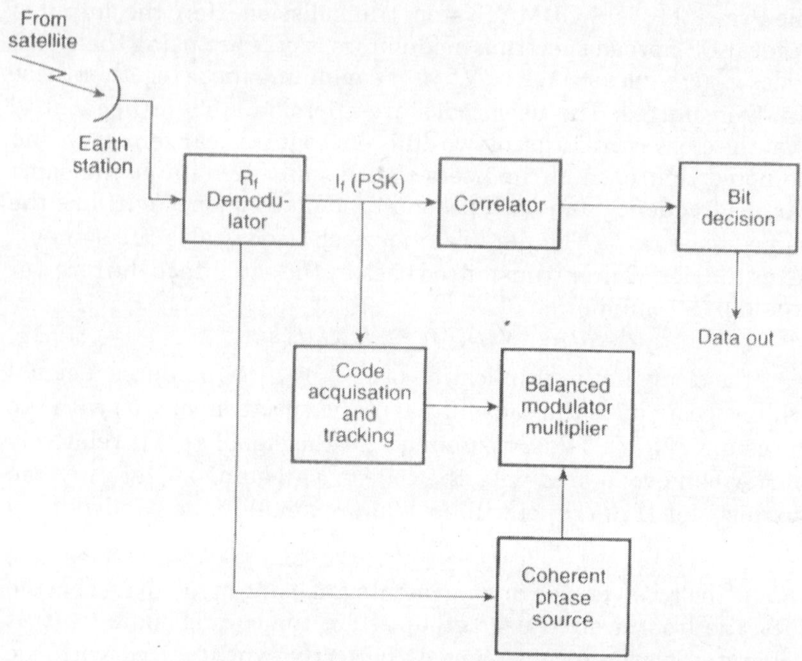

Fig. 9.5. Basic Block Diagram of a Typical DS-SS Receiver.

correlator. The function of the correlator is to compare the two signals and recover the original data. Essentially the correlator subtracts the recovered PSK carrier + chip code from the received PSK carrier + chip code + data. The resultant is data. In fact the output of correlator which is the desired signal occupies the information bandwidth centered at an intermediate frequency (IF). It is applied to a conventional demodulator with bandwidth just wide enough to accommodate the desperado signal. In the Fig. 9.5 the conventional demodulator has been represented by the unit *bit decision*. It must be remembered that the above process is completely *time synchronous transmission*. It requires the type of network synchronization as used in TDMA systems although at a much simpler level. Such a synchronization must be on the order of one fifth of a chip duration T_C. Thus though the CDMA has the advantage of immunity to interference (jamming) it has the disadvantage of requiring time synchronization of TDMA systems. It shows that CDMA is not all that it is cracked up to be. Conclusively CDMA has applications in military communications. It has no advantages over the cost due to hardware associated with CDMA code generators, correlators and matched filters etc.

9.7. Frequency-Hopping Spread Spectrum Communication System (FH-SS)

The main difference between frequency hopping SS system and a DS SS system is that in frequency hopping the total available bandwidth is partioned into smaller frequency bands and the total transmission time is subdivided into smaller time slots. Thus transmission takes place within a limited frequency band for only a short

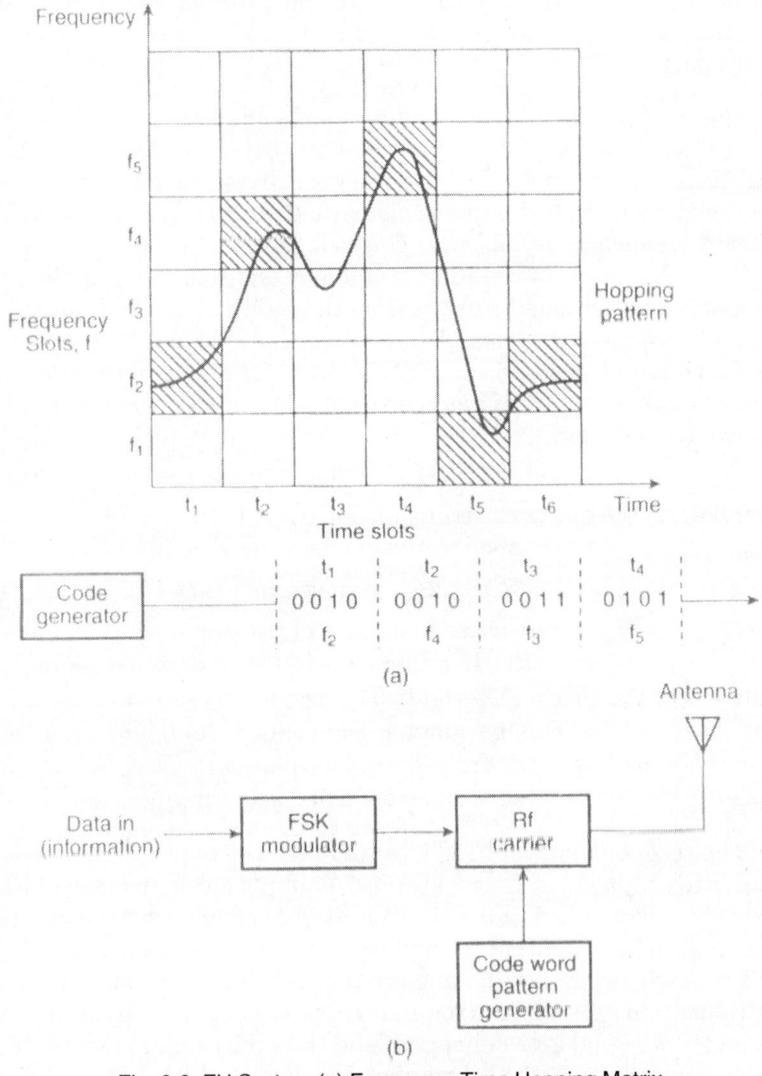

Fig. 9.6. FH System (*a*) Frequency Time Hopping Matrix (*b*) Frequency Hopping Transmitter.

period of time, then switches to another frequency band and so on. The process continues indefinitely. Fig. 9.6(a) first part indicates the way in which transmission takes place in frequency hopping (FH) system. Here, in first sequence, frequency band f_2 transmits in time slots t_1, f_4 in time slot t_2, f_3 in time slot t_3, f_5 in time slot t_4, f_1 in t_5 and f_2 in f_6. The resultant pattern is called *frequency hopping pattern*. Actually this FH pattern is determined by a binary code and each station uses a different code sequence. The hopping pattern is a kind of *frequency-time matrix*. Lower part in Fig. 9.6(a) indicates this frequency-time matrix alongwith the code for the example of upper part.

Fig. 9.6(b) indicates the way in which this FH pattern may be generated. It uses a FSK modulator. Thus FH SS system is a FM or FSK technique while DSSS is an AM (or PSK) technique. Therefore frequency hopping technique is also called *multiple frequency, code-selected, frequency shift keying*. The code pattern generator consists of *PN* code generator and a frequency synthesizer capable of responding to the coded outputs from the code generator. It must be remembered that the signal to be frequency hopped is usually a BFSK signal although M-ary FSK, MSK or TFM may be employed. Supposing that the BFSK has been used then the signal before FHSS is used, can be expressed as

$$s(t) = \sqrt{2P_s}\cos(\omega_c t + d(t)\,\Omega(t) + \theta) \quad ...(9.20)$$

where $d(t)$ is the data to be transmitted. After FHSS modulation the resulting frequency hopped signal can be expressed as

$$s(t) = \sqrt{2P_s}\cos(\omega_i t + d(t)\,\Omega(t) + \theta) \quad ...(9.21)$$

where $f_i = \omega_i/2\pi$, is the carrier frequency of FH signal which changes at the hopping rate R_h. In other words the carrier frequency f_i changes at each $1/R_h = T_h$ seconds. The frequency is constant on such time intervals T_h. This parameter T_h is called the *frequency dwell time* or *hop interval*. The frequency chosen at each T_h is selected in a pseudo-random manner from a specified set of frequencies.

The receiving side of FHSS system uses the correlation process similar to that used in DS SS system. A simple block diagram of FH receiver is shown in Fig 9.7. Here a local frequency synthesizer is switched with a synchronized replica of the transmitted PN code and the resultant signal is multiplied to the received FHSS signal. This multiplication removes the frequency hops on the received signal (*i.e.* the received signal gets dehopped) and thus the original modulated signal remains untouched. This signal is then applied to the conventional demodulator to get the orthogonal data/information. The process gain for the frequency hopping system (in which channels are contiguous) is the same as that for the direct sequence system which is very well expressed by Eq. (9.1), *i.e.* the ratio of the hopped bandwidth to the baseband information bandwidth. In case the channels are not contiguous, a better measure of process gain is

$$G_p = \text{the number of available frequency choices}$$
$$= N \quad \text{...(9.22)}$$

which also holds good for contiguous channels. Thus for a frequency hopping system containing 1000 frequency choices could have 30 dB available process gain. It may be mentioned that in above calculations for process gain the interchannel interference (cross-talk) is neglected. Therefore in practical systems an allowance is made for this source of error that of course, reduces the process gain.

FHSS system may be a fast FH SS system or a slow FHSS system. In fast FHSS system the hopping rates are larger than the data rate and so the duration of a data pulse is larger than the hop interval. In slow FHSS system hopping rates are smaller than the data rate and thus the hop interval is greater than the data symbol duration. If there are q numbers of frequency slots then the total RF bandwidth of a slow FHSS signal is approximately q times the bandwidth of the digital communication signal. It is usually independent of the hopping rate. The total bandwidth of a fast FH spread spectrum signal depends on the number of frequency slots and the hopping rate, but it does not depend very much on the data rate.

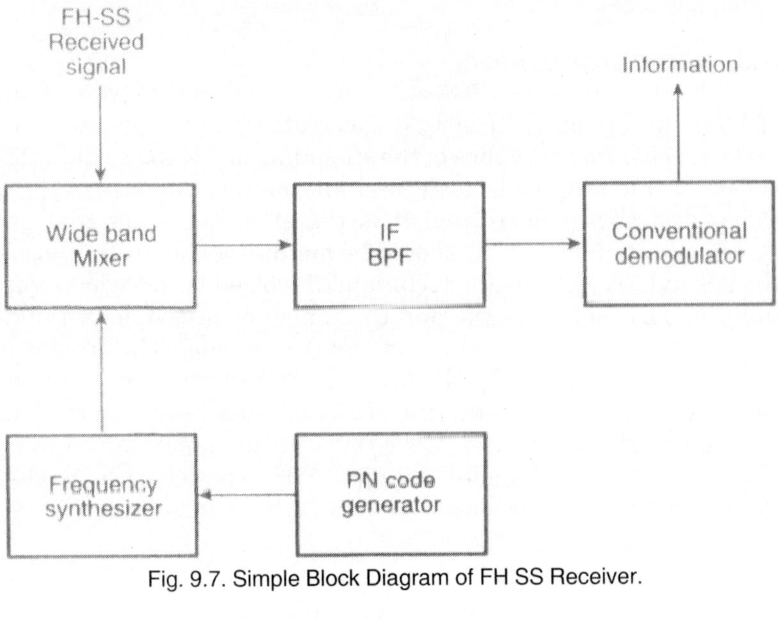

Fig. 9.7. Simple Block Diagram of FH SS Receiver.

9.8. Frequency Hop Spread Spectrum Code Division Multiple Access (FH-SS CDMA)

FHSS technique is also used in multiple access system in the way similar to that of DSSS-CDMA. With frequency hopping, each earth station within a CDMA network is assigned a different frequency hopping pattern. Each transmitter switches (hops) from one frequency band to the next according to their assigned pattern. With frequency hopping each station uses the entire RF spectrum but never occupies more than a small portion of that spectrum at any onetime. In FHCDMA the bit error probability is determined by the number of users, the spread bandwidth and the bit rate. Since it is easier to increase the spread bandwidth with the present technology, FHCDMA can accommodate many users with a low bit rate and may be favoured over DS-CDMA in many military applications. On the other hand DS-CDMA may be more suitable for commercial users.

It would be of interest to compare CDMA with FDMA or TDMA irrespective of the fact that CDMA is suitable for security reasons or interference rejection. Theoretically all the multiple access systems may support the same numbers of users in a given bandwidth. Differences in capacity between them arise from practical considerations like intermodulation distortion, synchronization and the like. The application of CDMA requires large processing gain (G_p) and the number of uncoordinated users that a CDMA system can support is $G_p/10$. This puts severe bandwidth or *PN* sequence length constraints on SS system and severely limits their attractiveness for multiple access.

9.9. Synchronization

It has been observed in Sections 9.5 to 9.8 that the receiving unit of both the DS and FH spread spectrum/CDMA systems need a *perfect synchronized* replica of the spreading or PN code signal. This is essential to despread the desired information and also to spread the undesired signal, if any. It is therefore necessary that once synchronization is done, it should be maintained for ever. For both the DS and FH systems the techniques involved in the synchronization are basically the same and these may be accomplished under two steps, namely the *acquisition* and the *tracking*. The acquisition brings two spreading signals into *coarse* or *initial alignment* with one another. After the initial alignment has been achieved the system enters into *tracking mode*. This tracking maintains the fine alignment of the PN signals by means of some feedback tracking loops such as delay lock or dither etc which consist of correlators.

The acquisition or initial synchronization process may be either as coherent or noncoherent. However, since the despreading process typically takes place before carrier synchronization and the carrier phase is not known at the point so most of the acquisition schemes utilize noncoherent detection. The simplest method of obtaining initial synchronization is through a *sliding correlator*. Fig. 9.8 indicates the principle of sliding correlator synchronization. Here the rate of the generation of the locally generated PN sequence is adjusted and correlated with the incoming code. This adjustment in rate of generation of PN signal allows a change in phase (or sometimes the frequency) of the locally generated PN signals such that when compared with the incoming received SS signal in the correlator, the desired satisfactory result is obtained. This method of searching the best correlation between the two signals is called *search technique* and direct sequence SS system may employ both the *parallel* or *serial* search acquisition technique for the purpose. The above discussed method is a typical example of serial search method. Sometimes special codes like those of JPL codes are used for initial synchronization.

The principle of parallel DS search technique is shown in Fig. 9.9. Here the locally generated code g(t) is available with the delays that are spaced one half chip ($T_c/2$) apart. Thus if the time uncertainty between the local code and the received code is N_c chips and

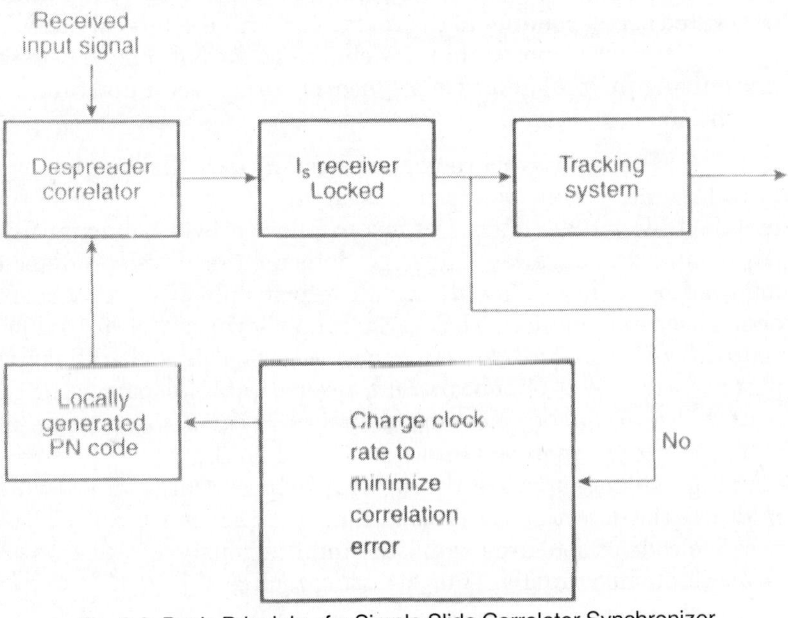

Fig. 9.8. Basic Principle of a Simple Slide Correlator Synchronizer.

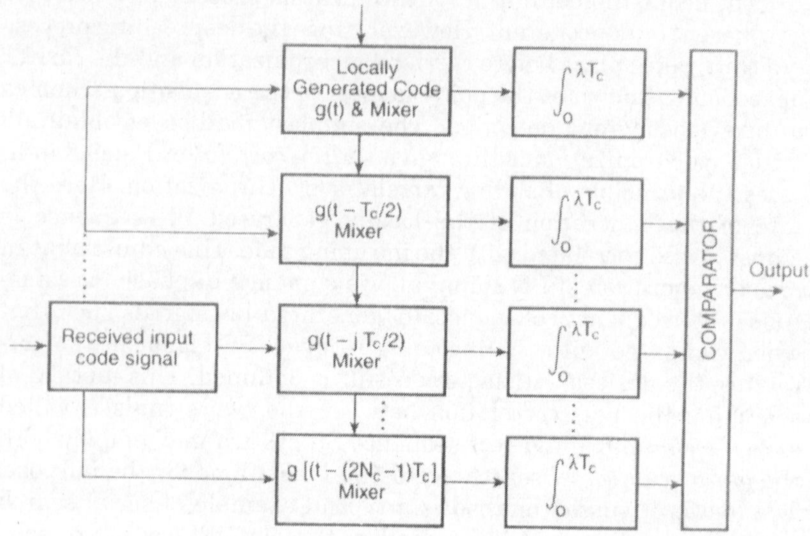

Fig. 9.9. Principle of Parallel DS-SS Search System.

a complete parallel search of the entire time uncertainty region is to be accomplished in a single search time, $2N_c$ correlators are used. Each correlator simultaneously examines a sequence of λ chips after which the $2N_c$ correlator outputs are compared. The locally generated corresponding to the correlator with the largest output is chosen. It must be noted that λ is chosen as a compromise between minimizing the probability of a synchronization error and minimizing the time to acquire.

The FH initial synchronization system may also employ both parallel and serial acquisition system. It uses a noncoherent matched filter that consists of mixer followed by a bandpass filter (BPF) and a square law envelope detector (an envelope detector followed by a square law device). The principle of parallel search acquisition scheme for FH SS system is shown in Fig. 9.10. For a sequence of N consecutive frequencies to be used for synchronization pattern, one needs N noncoherent method filters as shown in Fig. 9.10. If the frequency hopping sequence is $f_1, f_2, \ldots\ldots f_N$, delays are inserted into the matched filters so that when the correct frequency hopping sequence appears, the system produces a large output which indicates the detection of the synchronization sequence. Since all the possible code offsets are examined simultaneously, acquisition can be accomplished rapidly. Thus, if during each correlation, λ chips are examined the maximum time required $(T_{acq})_{\max}$ for a fully parallel search is

$$(T_{acq})_{\max} = \lambda T_c \qquad ...(9.23)$$

If P_D is the probability of detection for such correlated outputs, then in case some incorrect outputs appear, the further acquisition time to examine additional λ chips is

$$T_{acq} = \lambda T_c P_D + 2\lambda T_c P_D (1 - P_D) + 3\lambda T_c P_D (1 - P_D)^2 + ...$$
$$= \frac{\lambda T_c}{P_D} \qquad ...(9.24)$$

It must be remembered that parallel acquisition system requires several correlators or matched filters and so serial acquisition system is more economical and simple. In Fig. 9.8 which is essentially a serial acquisition system for DS-SS, a frequency hopper will be needed alongwith the PN code generator for FH systems. It would be of importance to mention here that recently another search technique called *Rapid Acquisition By Sequential Estimation* (RASE) has also been proposed for the initial synchronization which works in sequences and has a rapid acquisition capability. The RASE

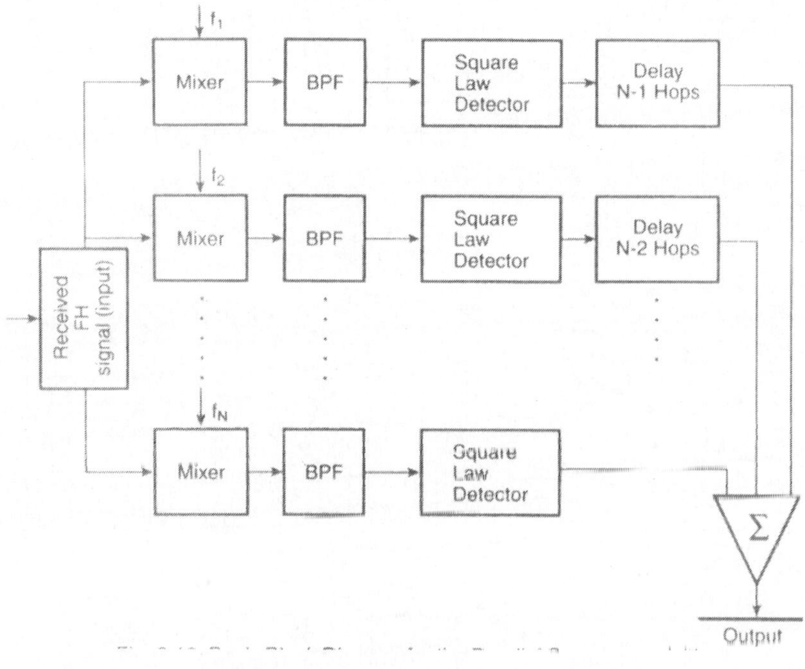

Fig. 9.10. Basic Block Diagram for the Parallel Search Acquisition for FH SS System.

system has the disadvantages of being highly vulnerable to noise and interference signals.

After initial acquisition has been achieved, the system takes to tracking or fine synchronization. As already mentioned the tracking systems are basically the loops which may be a *delay locked loop* (DLL) or *Tau-dither loop* (TDL). The DLL is a full-time early-late tracking loop and TDL is a time shared early-late tracking loop. Since in DS-SS and FH-SS, the carrier frequency and phase of the received signal are not known exactly so noncoherent tracking loops are used. Fig. 9.11 indicates the principle of the working of Delay locked loop for tracking the direct sequence spread spectrum signals. It is assumed that DS-SS signal is BPSK modulated and at the receiver input has the form (similar to that in Eq. 9.14)

$$v(t) = A\sqrt{2P_s}\, s(t) g(t) \cos(\omega_0 t + \phi) \qquad \text{...(9.25)}$$

where A is a constant and represents system gain parameter, ϕ is a random phase angle in the range $(0, 2\pi)$. The local PN code generator is adjusted such that the locally generated PN code is offset in phase from the incoming $g(t)$ by a time τ where $\tau < T_c/2$. The loop provides fine synchronization by first generating two PN sequences $g(t + T_c/2 + \tau)$ and $g(t - T_c/2 + \tau)$ delayed from each other by one

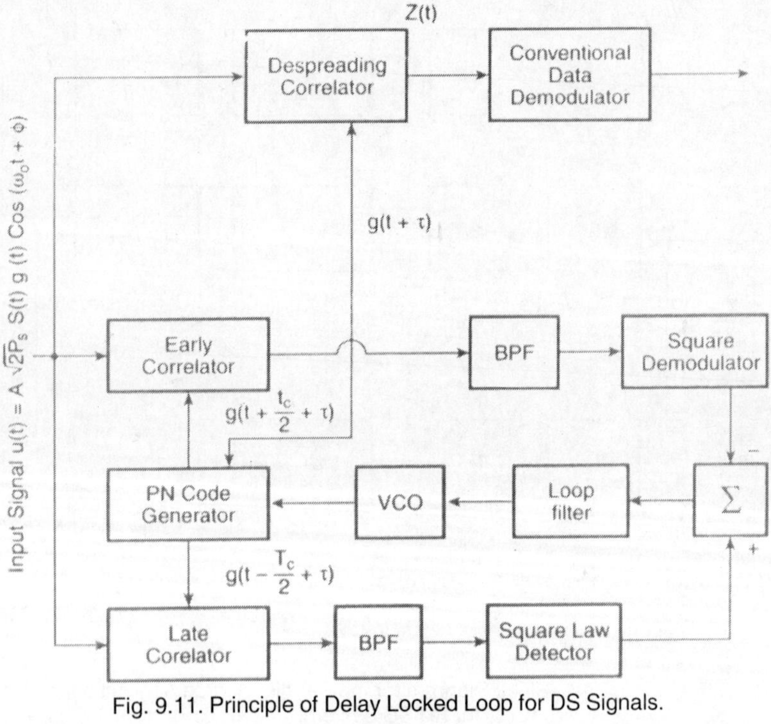

Fig. 9.11. Principle of Delay Locked Loop for DS Signals.

chip. DLL has also two band pass filters (BPF) which pass the data and help in averaging the product of $g(t)$ and two PN sequences $g(t \pm T_c/2 + \tau)$. Since $|s(t)| = 1$, so the two square law envelope detectors eliminate the date. The output of each envelope detector can be approximated as

$$E_D = E\left\{\left|g(t)\, g\left(t \pm \frac{T_c}{2} + \tau\right)\right|\right\}$$

$$= \left|R_s\left(\tau \pm \frac{T_c}{2}\right)\right| \qquad ...(9.26)$$

Here E $\{.\}$ means the *expected value* and $R_g(s)$ is the autocorrelation function of the PN waveform. Thus a resultant feedback signal $Y(z)$ is generated as shown in Fig. 9.11. When τ is positive the feedback signal $Y(\tau)$ instructs the voltage controlled oscillator (VCO) to increase its frequency. This would cause a decrease in τ. Similarly when τ is negative, $Y(\tau)$ instructs VCO to decrease its frequency. Then τ will be increased. Ultimately for very small values of τ, relation $g(t)\, g(t + \tau) = 1$ will be satisfied and the despreading signal $\tau(t)$ will be derived from the despreading correlator. This $z(t)$ is then applied to the input of conventional data demodulator. The main problem with DLL is that it requires the early and late arms to be precisely gain balanced otherwise the offset signal $Y(\tau)$ will be offset and will not produce a zero signal when the error is zero.

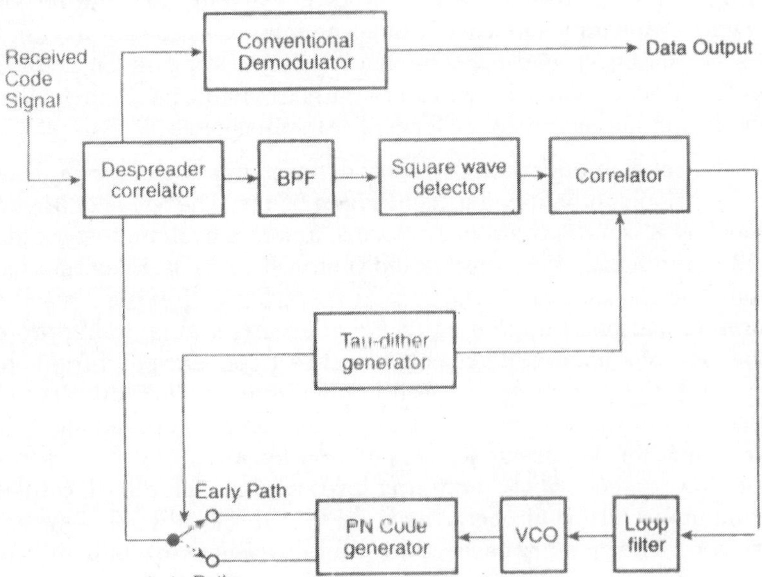

Fig. 9.12. Principle of TDL.

The above problem of DLL is solved by using a time shared tracking loop such as tau-dither loop (TDL) which shares the use of the early-late correlators. Infact TDL uses a single correlator and also it reduces the problems of dc offset. Fig. 9.12 explains the principle of TDL. Here PN code generator is driven by a clock signal whose phase is *dithered back* and forth with square wave switching function. This thus eliminates the necessity of ensuring the identical transfer functions of the early and late paths. There is only one correlator needed to provide code tracking function and the despreading function. Similar to that in DLL, here the received signal is correlated with an early and late version of the locally generated PN code. It may be noted that the signal to noise performance of the TDL is only about 1.1 dB worse than that of the DLL if the arm filters are designed properly.

9.10. Applications of Spread Spectrum Techniques

Spread spectrum techniques and CDMA systems can not compete with the potential capacity of FDMA and TDMA systems but there are applications in which practical operating constraints render the latter two systems highly inefficient and CDMA gains an edge because of its ability to handle low rate, bursty data more efficiently. Further if a satellite system is required to combat fading, multipath interference, jamming and noise, its multiple access capability will have to be sacrificed at least in part and for that CDMA is the only solution. It must be remembered that a satellite system using spread spectrum system operating at or near full multiple-access capacity will be roughly as visible and vulnerable to hostile action, as any other form of transmission.

Various applications of spread spectrum technique in communication can be listed as that given below. The areas of applications are normally the space systems, avionics system, test systems and equipment, signal protection (non military) and position location. For space systems the spread spectrum technique is used for communications, ranging, multiple accessing and jamming protection. The systems used are both the direct sequence and frequency hopping. Primary user of these applications are for military purposes. Similarly the avionics system may employ spread spectrum technique for communications, position location, discrete addressing, low detectability, jamming protection, radar and collision avoidance. Here again both the DS, FH and hybrid DS/FH systems are used. The primary users of these applications are again military.

The test systems and equipment area have the primary user commercial personnels. These are used for bit error detection, non-interfering-in service testing, signal correlation, privacy (pseudo) random selection and number generation. Here mainly the direct sequence SS techniques are used. Similarly the signal protection (non military) has commercial users and it also uses the direct sequence technique. Interference rejection, voice and data scrambling are the main applications for such area. The position location carried out by the spread spectrum technique has many users and these also employ SS techniques. It has the application in such as collision avoidance, direction finding and ranging. Thus it is evident that the spread spectrum techniques are considerably useful in the areas where conventional old communication techniques have undesirable problems.

9.11. Hybrid Systems

In hybrid Spread spectrum systems a combination of spread spectrum multiple access (or CDMA) and TDMA is used. The messages are sent through a SSMA modulator where messages are coded, encrypted, added or correlated to another signal such that messages acquire a larger bandwidth. The codes which generate the encrypted messages are of equal length, energy and distinct. The encrypted messages are sent to the satellite using TDMA. The satellite retransmits the signal back to the earth. The received signal is processed through a band of spread spectrum demodulators where the exact replica of the code is stored to make the inverse operation to extract the message. The encrypted message is processed through the TDMA demodulator. The hybrid system may use either of direct sequence and frequency hopping systems. Whereas the direct sequence hybrid system may provide the message privacy, the frequency hopping hybrid system would ensure the antijamming capability. Thus a combination of these two methods would provide secure, reliable and efficient system. In particular it provides the data security to the commercial satellite and antijamming capability to the military satellites.

9.12. Review Questions

1. What is meant by spread spectrum ? How can it be used for communication purpose ?
2. Explain the advantages and disadvantages of spread spectrum techniques.
3. What is meant by process gain, jam margin, J/S ratio and antijam margin ? Explain the importance of these parameters in spread spectrum communication systems ?

4. Explain the direct sequence and frequency hopping techniques of spread spectrum communication system. Compare the relative advantages and disadvantages.
5. In a spread spectrum satellite communication system the transmitted $EIRP_T$, is 20 dBW. The data rate is R = 100 bit/s. A jammer is transmitting wideband guassian noise continually with an $EIRP_T = 60$ dBW. Assume $(E_b/J_0)_{reqd} = 10$ dB. If the antijam margin is of 20 dB what should be the value of spread spectrum bandwidth WSS. (**Ans :** $W_{ss} = 1$ GHz)
6. What is PN sequence ? Discuss its characteristics. What is chip ?
7. What is CDMA ? How does it employ spread spectrum technique during the multiple access of the signals. Also explain the relative merits and demerits of CDMA, FDMA and TDMA.
8. Why is synchronization necessary for spread spectrum communication systems ? Explain the various steps involved to achieve this synchronization. Can both the DS and FH SS systems use the same synchronization techniques ? If not why ?
9. What is a hybrid CDMA system ? Compare its performance with that of pure CDMA, FDMA and TDMA system.
10. Explain various applications of spread spectrum systems.

9.13. References

1. Pursley, M.B., Spread Spectrum Multiple Access Communications in Multi-user Communication systems, G.Longo, Ed, Springer Verlag, Vienna and New York, 1981, PP 139-199.
2. Pickholtz, R.L., Schilling, D.L. and Milstein, L.B., Theory of Spread Spectrum Communications-A Tutotial, IEEE Transactions on Communications, Vol COM-30, May 1982, pp 855-884.
3. Holmes, J.K., Coherent Spread Spectrum Systems, John Wiley & Sons, NY, 1982.
4. MacWilliams, F.J. and Sloane, N.J.A., Pseudo-Random Sequences and Arrays, Proc IEEE, Vol 64, Dec 1976, pp 1715-29.
5. Sarwate, D.V. and Pursley, M.B., Cross Correlation Properties of Pseudorandom and Related Sequences, Proceedings of IEEE, Vol 68, May 1980, pp 593-619.
6. Geramotis, E.A. and Pursley, M.B., Error Probabilities for slow frequency hopped spread spectrum multiple access Communications Over Fading Channels, IEEE Transactions on Communications, Vol COM-30, May 1982, pp 996-1009.
7. Special Issue on Spread Spectrum Communications, IEEE Transactions on Communications, VOL COM-25, Aug. 1977.
8. Special issue on Mobile Spread Spectrum Communications, IEEE Transactions on vehicular Technology, Vol VT-30, Feb. 1981.
9. Special Issue on Spread Spectrum Communications, IEEE Transactions on Communications, Vol COM-30, May 1982.
10. Pursley, M.B., Digital Communications in Reference Data for Engineers, ED(EC Jordan) H.W. Sams and Co., 1985.

11. Dixon, R.C., Spread Spectrum Systems, John Wiley and Sons, NY, 1976.
12. Tomasi, W., Advanced Electronic Communications Systems, Prentice Hall Englewoods, NJ, 1987.
13. Sklar, B., Digital Communications, Fundamentals and Applications, Prentice Hall, Englewood Cliffs, NJ, 1988.
14. Ha, T.T., Digital Satellite Communications, MacMillan Publishing Co., 1986.
15. Taub, H. and Schilling, D.L., Principles of Communication Systems, McGraw Hill Book Co., 1987.
16. Nettleton, R.W., Spread Spectrum Principles for Multiple Access Systems in Proceedings of Satellite Communications, Conference SCC-1983 Canada, Ed K.Feher, North Holland Publishing Co., Amsterdam, p 9.21-9.24.
17. Simon, M.K., Omura, J.K. Scholtz, R.A. and Levit, B.K., Spread Spectrum Communications, Vols 1,2,3, Computer Science Press, Inc., Rockville, Md., 1985.
18. Ziemer, R.E. and Peterson, R.L., Digital Communications and Spread Spectrum Systems, MacMillan Publishing Co., NY., 1985.

10

Random Access Technique and Packet Satellite Communication

10.1. Introduction

The satellite demand assignments discussed in Chapter 6 are the *ordered* one because the assigned signals were kept separated and did not interfere with each other. A typical example was SPADE or DA-TDMA. These systems are *circuit oriented systems*. These systems are efficient for the voice calls they were designed to service because these calls are typically long compared to the time required to make new circuit allocations. If each circuit were used for bursty data traffic, however, then these systems would not appreciably improve channel efficiency over the case of fixed assignment. Packet communication systems utilizing random multiple access techniques were designed to provide satellite capacity demand assignment for bursty traffics.

In packet satellite communication packets of data are involved and the corresponding systems may be also packet radio or packet broadcasting systems too. The satellite system using packet communication is usually in the form of networks and the most common name of such networks is *packet satellite networks* (PSN). These networks use packet switching for accessing the satellite channel which is closely related to TDMA. Such packet satellite communication networks have existed since 1965. Though the first kind of such packet network, popularly known was ARPANET but the first use of satellite for packet communication started with the development of ALOHA systems at the University of Hawaii. ARPANET employed packet switching in the form of point-to-point store-and-forward type and packet switches were interconnected by point to data channels to form a mesh topology. These kinds of networks did not use satellite channel. Other such data networks are like Cigale Network, Telenet, Tymnet, Datapac, Transpac and Euronet etc.

Satellite channel used with packet switching (*e.g.* ALOHA) employs random access. In other words each station tries to access the satellite through *random access* in time domain and thus it is *multiaccess broadcast type*. Actually in the basic form of random access no network timing is present and each station transmits bursts of packets as necessary at random and some bursts overlap. Random access is notably inefficient because retransmission must occur when packets collide. Some modifications in ALOHA systems have also been developed. These employ *implicit reservation* or *explicit reservation access*. It must be remembered that broadcast data systems use satellites as a channel working in 3-10 GHz range where the packet radios operate in hf region (1-30 MHz).

A third type of packet communication network, the hybrid type also exists. It is the store and forward multiaccess broadcast type which combines the features exhibited in the two types mentioned above. The best such example is that of DARPA Communication network.

10.2. Packet Switching

Packet switching involves dividing the data messages into small bursts or information and transmitting them through communication networks to their intended destinations using computer-controlled switches. The overall concept of packet switching is not complicated since the whole system is acting like an electronic postal system. It is an extremely useful technique since it allows a source data station to send data only to a selected terminal in a network linked by radio or satellite or telephone links. It must be remembered that the term 'switching' involves connection of the data source to the destination and there are 3 kinds of such switching techniques. Packet switching is one of these. The other two switching techniques are *circuit switching* and the *message switching. Hybrid switching* may also be employed.

Circuit switching (CS) is analogous to the telephone (voice) network. Here a physical (copper wire or so) path or apparently physical path is set up and maintained for the duration of message transmission. The entire physical path remains allocated to the single set of users until released and during this time, no other potential user can use any part of the path, not even during intervals when the path happens to be idle. Circuit switching is also sometimes called 'space division multiplexing'. Circuit switching may be done manually or automatically.

Message switching (MS) is also called a 'store and forward' switching as it involves the store and forward action. Essentially the message switching system accepts data from a large number of terminals, stores it and then forwards it to other terminals as required. Thus whereas a circuit switch is a transparent switch, the message switch is a transactional switch. Message switching is subject to buffering or queueing delay and thus delay time or response time plays a critical role in their design. This is the main disadvantage of message switching compared to circuit switching particularly when the messages size are varying. The advantage of message switching over circuit switching is the increased circuit utilization.

In *packet switching* (PS) the message is divided into packets and thus the problem of variable length message in message switching (MS) is solved in PS. The 'packet' is a subdivision of message that has been prefaced with an identifier which contains suitable addresses information and the information that allows the message to be reconstructed. Thus the message is transmitted packet by packet and like the message in message switching, each packet must be stored or held and then forwarded. Packet switching is therefore a *store* or *hold and forward system*. Thus, compared to circuit switching, the packet switching allows to multiply the use of communication circuits among all the attached subscribers. It must be noted that in packet switching each packet can take a different path through the network and consequently all packets do not necessarily arrive at the receive end at the same time or in the same order in which they were transmitted. These give the packet switching additional advantages that the packet switched subnetworks implement a circuit path from source to destination with the properties of high availability, low error rate, fluctuating delay, fluctuating bandwidth and per packet overhead. However, packet switching networks require complex and expensive switching arrangements and complicated protocols. While selecting circuit switching or packet switching in use a number of factors are to be considered. These include mean message size, intermessage arrival and conversion length. For longer messages such as file transfers CS is better. For shorter messages such as database query or response or interactive traffic, PS is better suited. For a combination of both the short and long messages PS appears to be better than CS.

In *hybrid switching* a combination of both the CS and PS is carried out. This is achieved within a single data network. Here dynamic time division multiplexing is utilized to allocate a portion of channel bandwidth to circuit switching applications and the remaining channel bandwidth is utilized in packet switching service. Thus the hybrid architecture provides flexibility in a transport scheme selection. Here the positive features of both the packet and circuit switching are combined eliminating the disadvantages of each. The main advantages of hybrid switching are such as low overhead in short packet transmission (using the composite packet feature), low transmission delay of long messages (using the on-the-fly transmission feature), guaranteed delay and bandwidth for real time applications (using the circuit switched service) and networking partioning for security-or performance-sensitive environments (using the time-division switched structure). The disadvantages are the bandwidth fragmentation that causes a reduction in bandwidth sharing benefits. It needs sophisticated control schemes. The switch processor architectures are more complex than for simple packet or circuit systems. However, recent technological development like VLSI has reduced this problem to a great extent.

10.3. Packet Communication

In this section the definitions of various terminologies being used in packet switching, random access techniques and packet satellite networks would be explained.

Packet. A *packet* of information is a finite sequence of bits, divided into a control portion and a data portion. The common structure of a packet is shown in Fig. 10.1. It usually consists of around 128 bytes (or 128 × 8 = 1024 bits) with the first part of the packet providing routing and distribution information and the last part of the packet containing the data being transmitted. The control part of the packet consists of the source and destination codes, the packet number or termination code and the message priority information.

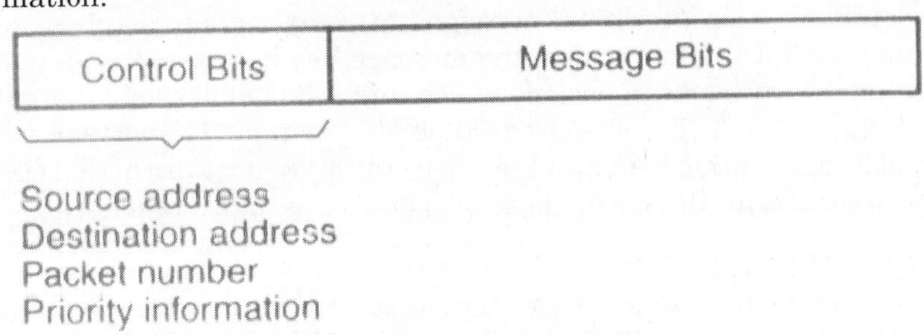

Fig. 10.1. Structure of Data Packet.

Packet Throughput. The throughput of the satellite channel is defined as the rate at which packets are successfully transmitted. It is also defined as the ratio of the useful traffic to the total number of bits. In other words, it is the ratio of successful packets to the total that were sent.

Packet Delay. The delay of a packet is simply the time between start and successful completion of transmission and delivery of the user. However, there are many detailed definitions of the delay and so comparisons may be difficult for different users.

Host. Host is the generic name in computer communications for the collection of hardware and software that uses the packet switching services to support user services.

Packet Switch. A packet switch at a node or station is the collection of hardware and software resources which implement all procedures within the network such as routing, resource allocation and error control, and which provides network services through a host.

Routing. It defines a set of rules to determine the path over which message should flow from one side to anothers. There are several categories of routing strategies in computer communication networks.

Protocols. A protocol is a set of communication conventions, including formats and procedures, which allow two or more end points to communicate. In general, the end point may be packet switches, hosts, terminals, data bases, people and so on.

Datagram. A datagram is a packet which is a set of self contained message. It is routed individually through the packet network rather like a telegram going through a message switching systems.

Virtual Circuit Call. Datagram and virtual circuit call are the two basic modes of operation of packet switched communication network. In the virtual call, the two users have a direct private circuit from one terminal through to the other for all practical purpose but the fact is that the message has been divided up into hundreds of separate packets which might have followed different routes through the network to their destination. The virtual call mode of operation is preferable when traffic volumes are high. With sporadic traffic datagram mode of operation is more economical.

10.4. Random Access Technique

As already mentioned the random multiple access technique for satellite communication was developed in 1970 at the University of Hawaii and the system was designated ALOHA systems. Here the packets are not being sent in FDMA or TDMA *i.e.* the user does not wait his 'turn' as in TDMA nor is he assigned a narrow bandwidth as in FDMA. Each station transmits a packet whenever its buffer has one and the stations do not need synchronization.

The random multiple access scheme works on four different steps, namely the transmission, listening, retransmission and time out. In the transmission step which is the first step, users transmit at anytime they desire encoding their transmission with an error detection code. In the next step known as listening, the user listens an acknowledgement (ACK) from the receiver. There is a possibility that the packets sent from the different terminals may overlap and result in transmission error. For such a situation of overlapping packets are said to have *collided* and the users receive a negative acknowledgement (NAK). After having received NAK, the third step of random access technique is followed which is actually the retransmission of collided packets. In order that these retransmitted packets may not collide again, the interval of packet retransmission is randomized in each terminal. In other words now the users retransmit after a *random delay*. In case if after a transmission the user does not receive either an ACK or NAK within a specified time, the user retransmits the message. This is the final step of random multiple access and is termed time out.

The analysis of ALOHA system involves message arrival statistics. Suppose that in the satellite system the rate of successful arrival of packets is λ per second. Since there would be some packets lost due to collision so if λ_r is the rate of such lost packets per second, then the total traffic arrival rate λ_t would be

$$\lambda_t = \lambda + \lambda_r \qquad \text{...(10.1)}$$

Let the length of each message or packet be b bits. Then the throughput of the system which is actually the average amount of successful traffic would be expressed as

$$\rho' = b\lambda \text{ bits per second} \qquad \text{...(10.2)}$$

Similarly the total traffic G' on the satellite channel would be

$$G' = b\lambda_t \text{ bits per second} \qquad \text{...(10.3)}$$

If R bits per second represents the channel capacity (maximum bit rate) then the *normalized throughput P* and the *normalized total traffic G* could be expressed as

$$\rho = \frac{b\lambda}{R} \qquad \text{...(10.4)}$$

$$G = \frac{b\lambda_t}{R} \qquad \text{...(10.5)}$$

Let the transmission time of each packet be τ given as

$$\tau = b/R \text{ seconds/packet} \qquad \text{...(10.6)}$$

Thus Eqs. (10.4) and (10.5) may be rewritten as

$$\rho = \lambda \tau \qquad ...(10.7)$$

$$G = \lambda_t \tau \qquad ...(10.8)$$

In order that there may not be any collision between individual packets, a space of 2τ seconds is needed between each packet. This is because of the fact that if another user began a message within the previous τ seconds, its tail will collide with the current message and similarly if another user begins a message within the next τ seconds, it will collide with the tail end of the current message. The traffic arrival to the satellite repeater may be considered as a Poisson process because in most of the communication systems modelled as Queueing systems the arrival of traffic is best explained by a Poisson process. Thus the probability of having K new messages arrive during a time interval of τ seconds is represented by the Poisson distribution as

$$P(K) = \frac{(\lambda\tau)^K e^{-\lambda\tau}}{K!}, K \geq 0 \qquad ...(10.9)$$

where λ is the average message arrival rate. Since within time interval of 2τ seconds no message is transmitted, *i.e.* $K = 0$ and then

$$P(K = 0) = P_s = \frac{(2\tau\lambda_t)^0 e^{-2\lambda_t}}{0!}$$

$$= e^{-2\tau\lambda_t} \qquad ...(10.10)$$

This is the case of a successful packet transmission because then there would be no collisions among packets. Here again λ_t represents the total traffic arrival rate. The probability of successful transmission, P_s can also be represented in a simple way as

$$P_s = \frac{\lambda}{\lambda_t} \qquad ...(10.11)$$

where λ is the successful portion of the total traffic rate λ_t. Thus from Eqs. (10.10) and (10.11) one gets

$$\lambda = \lambda_{te}^{-2\tau\lambda_t} \qquad ...(10.12)$$

Eqs. (10.12), (10.7) and (10.8) combined together would give

$$\rho = G_e^{-2G} \qquad ...(10.13)$$

Eq. (10.13) gives the relationship between the normalized throughput ρ and the normalized total traffic G for the ALOHA system. A plot of this relationship labelled as 'Pure Aloha' is shown in Fig. 10.2. This may be considered as a graph showing the successful transmission versus total transmission. It is evident that as G increases ρ increases but beyond $G = 0.5$, ρ starts decreasing. The maximum value of ρ corresponding to this $G = 0.5$ is equal to $1/2e = 0.18$. Thus in the above pure ALOHA system only 18% of the channel capacity would be utilized. In other words though in such random access technique control mechanism is simple, the channel capacity gets wasted (or not fully utilized).

To improve the usage of channel capacity of Pure ALOHA system, discussed above, a technique termed *slotted ALOHA* (S-ALOHA) is being utilized. Here a sequence of synchronization pulses is broadcast to all stations and the messages are required to be sent in the slot time between synchronization pulses. It must be remembered that the messages can be started only at the *beginning* of a time slot and as with the pure ALOHA, packet lengths are constant. This technique reduces the collision rates of packets by half since only messages transmitted in the same slot can interfere with one another. Thus with the reduction of collision window from 2 τ to τ,

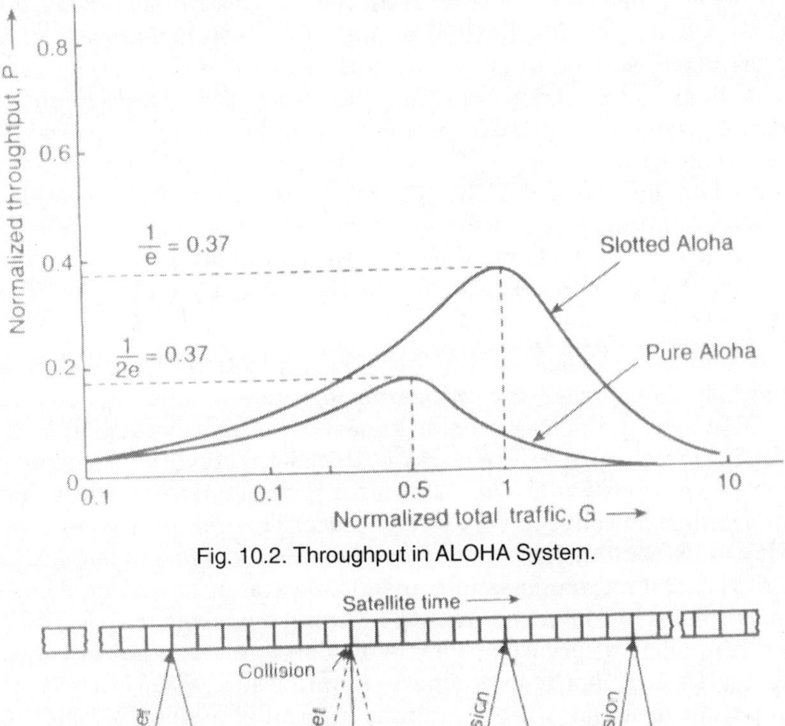

Fig. 10.2. Throughput in ALOHA System.

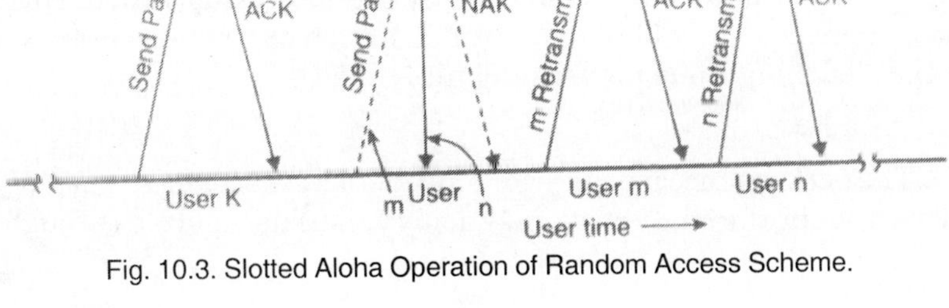

Fig. 10.3. Slotted Aloha Operation of Random Access Scheme.

the relationship between the normalized throughput ρ to the normalized total traffic G Eq. (10.13) now becomes

$$\rho = Ge^{-G} \qquad ...(10.14)$$

The plot of Eq. (10.14) labelled as Slotted Aloha is also shown in Fig. 10.2. Here the maximum value of ρ is $1/e = 0.37$ which shows an improvement of two times over pure Aloha system. Thus in slotted Aloha if a negative Acknowledgement (NAK) occurs, the user retransmits after a random delay of an integer number of slot times. Fig. 10.3 shows an example of slotted Aloha packet transmission of the random access scheme. Here user K transmits its packet and the successfull transmission is indicated by the return of ACK. When the users m and n simultaneously transmit their packets they collide with each other and a NAK is returned. After a random delay the users m and n retransmit their packets. Successful transmission, if takes place, will be informed by the return of ACK. In case the packets m and n again collide, another retransmission of m and n packets would take place after another random delay. The process may repeat till the successful transmission takes place and is informed by the return of ACKs. Thus here each using station employ a random-number generator to select its retransmission time. It would be worthwhile to mention here that the above Pure Aloha and Slotted Aloha schemes are also called ALOHA and S-ALOHA *protocols*.

The slotted Aloha shows only 36% utilization of the satellite channel. To increase the utilization of this channel capacity in ALOHA system another scheme known as reservation-ALOHA (R-ALOHA) was utilized. The object of this slot reservation scheme is to reserve a particular time slot for a given station which would ensure that no collision would take place. This reservation of time slot would result in some overhead cost and/or increased complexity of the control mechanisms in transmitting stations. These reservation schemes in Aloha system may be *implicit* or *explicit*. Actually it is the implicit reservation scheme of Aloha protocol that is called R-ALOHA. In this scheme whenever a station successfully transmits its packet in a slot, all the stations internally assign that slot in subsequent frames for exclusive use by the successful station. However, there is no way here to prevent a station capturing most or all of the slots in a frame for an indefinite time.

The performance measure for multiple access schemes is usually carried out by the study of average delay versus normalized throughput. Fig. 10.4 indicates the delay-throughput curve for random access multiple access techniques. For an ideal delay-throughput curve, the delay equals zero until the normalized throughput value $\rho = 1$ and then the delay increases without bound. Thus, it is apparent that R-Aloha is showing better performance than S-ALOHA. However, for values of ρ less than 0.2 the S-ALOHA manifests less average delay than R-ALOHA. But for values of ρ between 0.2 and a, R-ALOHA is superior since the average delay is less. Value a lies typically between 0.7 to 0.9. Thus at low traffic intensity S-ALOHA performs better. This is also due to the fact that S-ALOHA does not require the overhead slots as does the S-ALOHA. Therefore, at low values of ρ, R-ALOHA pays the price of greater delay due to the greater overhead. For $\rho > 0.2$, the collisions and retransmissions inherent in the S-ALOHA system cause it to incur greater delay (unbounded at $\rho = 0.37$), more quickly than the R-ALOHA system. At higher throughput ($0.2 < \rho < a$) the overhead structure of R-ALOHA ensures that its delay degradation grows in a more orderly manner than S-ALOHA. For R-ALOHA the unbounded delay reaches at $\rho = a$.

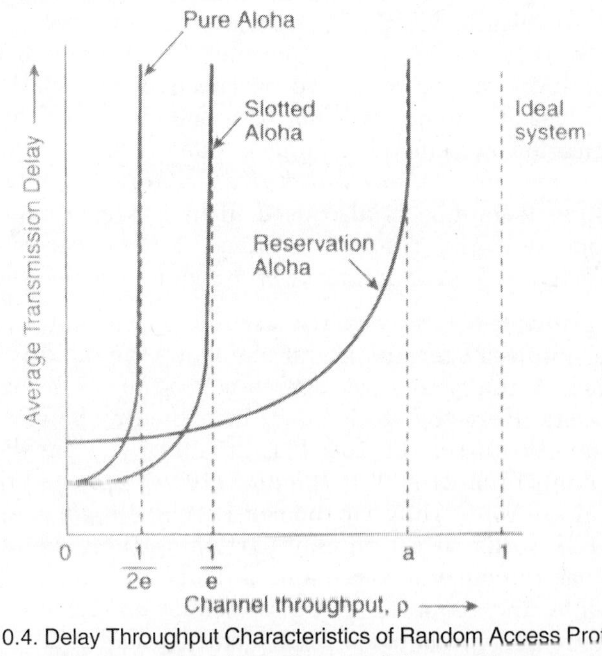

Fig. 10.4. Delay Throughput Characteristics of Random Access Protocols

In the explicit reservation scheme of the random access technique a network scheduler carries out a distinct and unique assignment of slots to a user. There are two such explicit reservation techniques, namely the R-TDMA and C-PODA (contention based.

Priority Oriented Demand Assignment). The R-TDMA protocol establishes a permanent association between slots and stations. The slots not claimed by the original owner may be reassigned on a round ribbon basis to the stations that have traffic to send (round ribbon means that each station gets access in an ordered, sequential but not necessarily predetermined manner). Thus it is a dynamic reservation scheme. The C-PODA is a satellite channel access scheme which allocates slots to users based on prior reservation. The performance characteristics of the explicit reservation is similar to that of R-ALOHA shown in Fig. 10.4. However, R-TDMA shows lower delays than C-PODA.

10.5. Polling Techniques

Polling technique allows order (discipline) on multiple users of the packet oriented systems in random access technique. There is a central controller that periodically polls the user population to determine their service requests. Polling technique is efficient only if ;

(*i*) round trip propagation delay is small,
(*ii*) the overhead due to polling messages is low ; and
(*iii*) the user population is not a large bursty one.

In case these conditions are not met, the time required to poll the population can be excessive overhead burden and then the random access technique will not be economical. For the satellite communication system the polling is done best by following the technique known as *binary search tree technique*. It may be noted that polling technique is also used in local area computer communication networks. There in addition to binary search tree, techniques such as *adaptive polling* or *probing* are also used.

The principle of binary search tree is shown as that in Fig. 10.5. It is an example of 8 terminals and this shows the rapidity of polling techniques. Actually this tree search is good to resolve contention among users. Here the stations are identified by binary numbers such as 000, 001, 010, 011, 100, 101, 110 and 111. Considering that the terminals numbered 001, 100 and 110 wish to send their messages and are contending for the service on a single channel. The tree search works on continually partioning the population until there is just a single branch remaining. Thus in the present example the satellite first requests for the transmission of contending terminals first (left most) bit of their identification numbers (in Fig. 10.5 indicated by (*b*). Then the satellite on the basis of received signal strength selects one or zero. In the present example satellite select '1') and notifies the contenders accordingly. The satellite then requests the transmission of the second identifying bit from the receiving contending terminals and again selects only one according to its hearing. In the example given above satellite selects zero and notifies the contenders accordingly. Thus here the terminal 100 is selected and other terminals are informed accordingly. The process continues until it is clear that terminal 100 is free to access the satellite. After the terminal 100 finishes transmission of its message, *i.e.* when the channel becomes available, steps 1-5 are repeated.

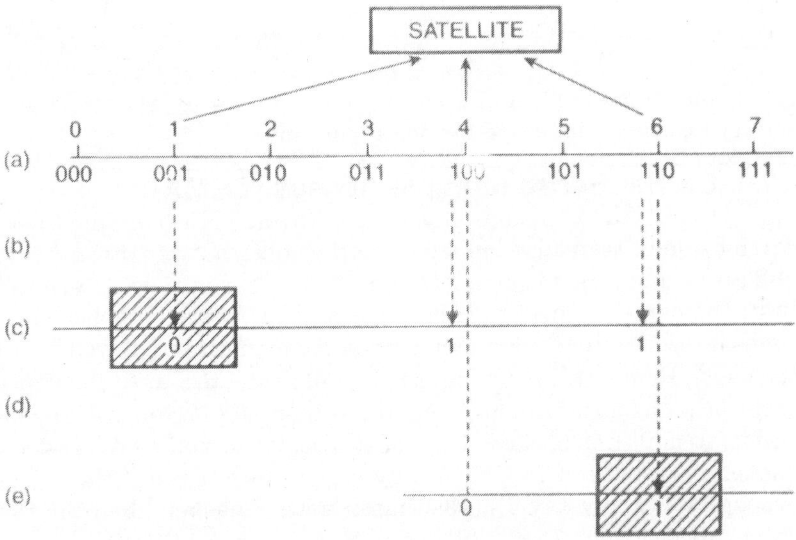

Fig. 10.5. A Typical Example of Tree Search Technique
(*a*) Terminals 1, 4 and 6 are contending (*b*) Satellite Requests Transmission of First Bit of ID (*c*) Satellite on the Basis of Maximum SNR Selects '1' and notifies contenders (*d*) Satellite Requests Transmission of Second Bit of ID, (*e*) Satellite Selects 'O' and Notifies Contender.

The binary tree search technique described above requires $n = \log_2 Q$ decisions for each pass through a population of Q terminals. Infact a savings in time is possible by this technique only if population is large and the average demand for the service is small. This advantage may be best understood by considering the following example.

Suppose that there is a population of 4096 terminals and the time required to poll one terminal is 1s. Then for straight polling of the population of 4096 terminals, it requires $4096 \times 1s = 4096s$. In case the channel availability is to be provided to 100 terminals (requesting service) by the binary search tree technique and the time required for one decision of binary tree search is again 1s then the time required by binary tree search technique may also be calculated easily. Here the binary tree search for 100 terminals requires 100 passes through the binary tree and thus time required would be $(100 \times \log_2 4096) \times 1 \text{ s} = 1200$ s. The maximum number of terminals being polled by the binary tree search technique in the time period equal to that required in straight polling is

$$Q' = \frac{Q}{\log_2 Q} \quad ...(10.15)$$

For the example above

$$Q' = \frac{4096}{\log_2 4096} = 341 \text{ terminals.}$$

Thus the maximum of terminals contending for service that a binary tree search may poll is 341 terminals.

10.6. Carrier Sense Multiple Access (CSMA)

In the CSMA, collisions of packet are avoided by listening to the carrier due to transmission from another user before transmitting and inhibiting transmission if the channel is sensed busy. Alternately in the carrier sense multiple access (CSMA) scheme each user tunes a receiver to the common carrier frequency f_c employed by all the users. Before transmitting, a user will listen, to determine if any of the other users is transmitting. If no other user is transmitting he will transmit his packet. In case there is no collision between packets, throughput in CSMA may reach unity. Even if there is a propagation delay say T_d, associated with a packet, then for the values of $T_d < 2T_p$ (T_p = received packet duration) CSMA is found to have significantly higher throughput than ALOHA and as a result CSMA has found numerous applications in computer communication field. The propagation delay of a packet arises due to the fact that when user transmits a packet it takes another user (d/c) seconds to receive the packet, where d is the distance between users and c is the velocity of light. Thus for a longer distance T_d will be very high and then CSMA will not be useful. Even if $T_d = 2T_p$, the maximum distance could be used with CSMA technique is fairly low and moreover for such a situation the throughput of ALOHA would be much higher than with CSMA. This may be understood by considering simple example of a packet consisting of 1000 bits, being transmitted at a bit rate of 10 Mb/s. Then $T_p = 100\ \mu s$ and therefore $T_d = 2T_p = 200\ \mu s$ and the distance travelled $d = cT_d = 3 \times 10^8$ m/s $\times 2 \times 10^{-4}$ s = 60 km. It is only due to this reason that CSMA is being used in computer communication only. It may be noted that CSMA can not prevent exactly simultaneously transmission from clashing, nor it can cope if stations are hidden from each other, either by distance or by terrain.

CSMA being used in Computer Communication can be *nonpersistent* or *persistent* type. Nonpersistent type is the simplest one and the transmission of packets is done by the user only when the channel is found to be idle. Persistent CSMA is of several types such as 1-persistent of p-persistent etc. p is the probability that a ready packet persists. But in these techniques too there is some chance of packet collisions. Further improvement has been obtained by the detection of collisions too. This is known as *Carrier Sense Multiple Access With Collision* Detection (CSMA-CD). In this technique when transmitting users detect interference among several transmissions (including their own), they abort the transmission of colliding packets. This technique is now-a-days being widely used in *Local Area Computer Communication Networks*.

10.7. Queueing Systems

In packet communication, series of packets are being transmitted and individual packets move independently in the packet communication network. Hence there are queues formed by packets waiting for processing and transmission. Therefore queueing theory plays a major role in the analysis and design of packet networks. Queueing theory has vast applications in several areas ranging from day-to-day department store, airport and hospital queues to industrial queues such as inventories, assembly (or production) lines and computer time-sharing systems. In queueing systems messages arrive, wait in a buffer for services, are serviced by servers and then leave. Fig. 10.6 indicates a simple basic block diagram of a queueing system. Here arriving messages or the input traffic are customers which wait at buffers for getting served. Servers serve the customers and satisfy their needs. After getting served the customers depart out. Thus queueing systems are characterized by the arrival process (interarrival time probability density function, message length probability density function), service discipline (priority scheme), number of servers and buffer size (finite or infinite).

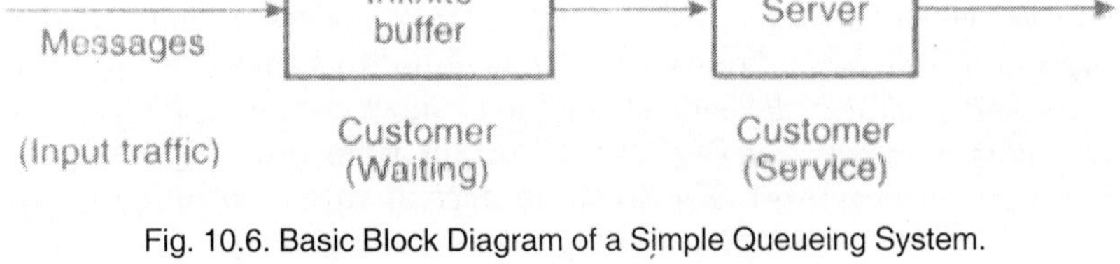

Fig. 10.6. Basic Block Diagram of a Simple Queueing System.

There are a variety of queueing systems and their general classification scheme is given as

$$(x \mid y \mid z) : (u \mid v \mid \omega) \qquad ...(10.16)$$

where various symbols are as follows :

x – arrival (or interarrival) distribution

y – departure (or service-time) distribution

z – number of parallel service channels in the system

u – service discipline

v – maximum number allowed in the system (in service plus waiting)

w – size of population

Symbols x and y are commonly replaced by the following codes :

M – Poisson arrival or departure distributions (or equivalently exponential interarrival of service time distributions ; M refers to the Markov property of the exponential distribution)

GI – general independent distribution of arrival (or interarrival times)

G – general distribution of departures (or service times)

D – deterministic interarrival or service times

The symbols Z, v and w are replaced by the appropriate numerical designations. The symbol u is replaced by a code similar to the following :

FCFS – first come first served

LCFS – last come first served

SIRO – service in random order

SPT – shortest processing (service) time

GD – general service discipline

In this section we will be concerned with the study of a queueing system with an infinite buffer and a single server using a first come first served discipline. Infact an M/G/1 queue would be considered which has a Poisson arrival, a general service distribution and one server. Also, with the help of this kind of M/G/1 queue analysis the throughput performance of fixed assignment FDMA will be carried out.

Here the general service distribution means that the message length or service time has a randomly varying length and the single server works on one message at a time until completion. It is assumed that message arrival rate is equal to λ messages per unit time and the message consists of one or more packets, the length of message being an average length of $1/\mu$ time units. (μ being the average service rate). The average arrival rate multiplied by the

$1/\mu$ service time is called the *traffic intensity* and represents the average load to the system

$$\rho = \frac{\lambda}{\mu} \qquad ...(10.17)$$

The probability of the arrival of exactly K messages during an interval of length t is given by the Poisson law

$$P(K, t) = \frac{(\lambda t)^K e^{-\lambda t}}{K!}, \quad \{t \geq 0, K = 0, 1, 2,....\} \qquad ...(10.18)$$

The expected value of K for a given interval t is

$$E\{K | t\} = \lambda t \qquad ...(10.19)$$

The average number of messages waiting in the buffer including the one being served is given by the Pollaczek-Khinchine equation and is expressed as

$$E\{n\} = \rho + \frac{\rho^2 + \lambda^2\sigma^2}{2(1-\rho)} \qquad ...(10.20)$$

where σ^2 represents variance.

Eq. (10.20) is also called the *average M/G/1 queue length* or the *average buffer occupancy*. The average message delay which actually is the time elapsing between the arrival of a message at the buffer and the departure of the complete message is found by the *Little Equation*, given by

$$T = \frac{E\{n\}}{\lambda} = \frac{1}{\mu} + \frac{\lambda(1/\mu^2 + \sigma^2)}{2(1-\rho)} \qquad ...(10.21)$$

The average time spent in a queue waiting to be served or the waiting or message is simply the average message delay less the average service time. This would be

$$W = T - \frac{1}{\mu} = \frac{\rho^2 + \lambda^2\sigma^2}{2\lambda(1-\rho)}$$

$$= \frac{\lambda(1/\mu^2 + \sigma^2)}{2(1-\rho)} \qquad ...(10.22)$$

In case the service time is exponentially distributed, *i.e.* when $\sigma^2 = 1/\mu^2$,

$$T = \frac{1}{\mu(1-\rho)} = \frac{1}{\mu - \lambda} \qquad ...(10.23)$$

Similarly when the service time is constant, *i.e.* when $\sigma^2 = 0$,

$$T = \frac{2-\rho}{2\mu(1-\rho)} = \frac{2-\lambda/\mu}{2(\mu-\lambda)} \qquad ...(10.24)$$

From Eqs. (10.23) and (10.24) it is seen that the message delay increases quickly as ρ approaches 1. The above relations now may be easily applied to a fixed assignment FDMA system. Suppose that the capacity of satellite channel is R bits per second and there are N users under the FA-FDMA system. Then each user would be assigned a channel of capacity R/N bits per second. If the average message length is b bits per channel then the average service rate of the FDMA channel would be

$$\mu = \frac{R}{N b} \qquad ...(10.25)$$

Now suppose μ be the average message arrival rate for each user. Then the traffic intensity for each channel would be

$$\rho = \frac{\lambda}{\mu} \qquad ...(10.26)$$

Thus if the satellite roundtrip delay is T_R then the total message delay (T_{FDMA}) for the FDMA channel would be

(*i*) for the case of an exponentially distributed message length :

$$T_{FDMA} = \frac{1}{(R/Nb)(1-\rho)} + T_R \qquad ...(10.27)$$

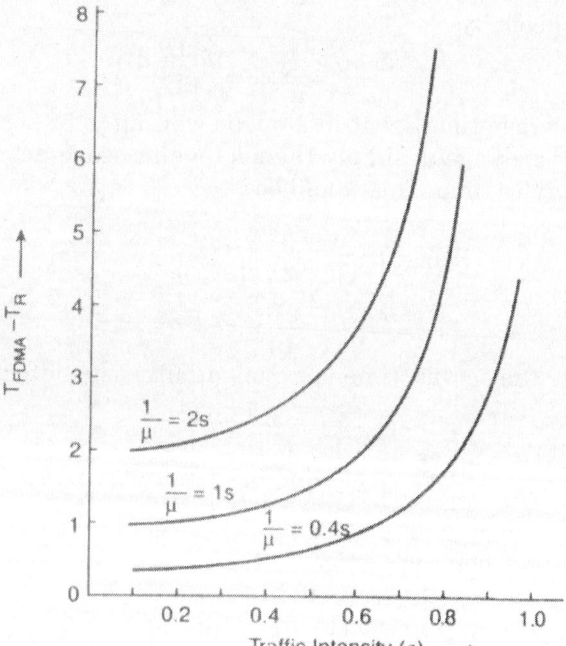

Fig. 10.7. Plot of $T_{FDMA} - T_R$ as a Function of ρ.

(*ii*) for the case of a constant message length

$$T_{FDMA} = \frac{2 - \rho}{2\,(R/Nb)\,(1 - \rho)} + T_R$$

$$= \frac{2 - \lambda/(R/Nb)}{2\,(R/Nb - \lambda)} + T_R \qquad ...(10.28)$$

Fig. 10.7 plots the average message delay $T_{FDMA} - T_R$ versus traffic intensity ρ for a constant message length as functions of $N/bR = 1/\mu$. Here three values of $1/\mu$ namely 0.4s, 1s and 2s have been considered. The case of fixed assignment TDMA may also be considered in a similar queueing M/G/1 system and there the average message delay would be

$$T_{\text{TDMA}} = T_{FDMA} - \frac{T_f}{2} + \frac{T_f}{N} \qquad ...(10.29)$$

where T_f is the TDMA frame length and N is the number of the time slots in which the frame length T_f has been divided.

Fig. 10.8 shows the plot of $T_{FDMA} - T_R$ versus ρ. Once again here T_R is the satellite round trip delay. The plots of Fig. 10.8 are for three different values of frame length T_f, namely 2s, 1s and 0.4s. It is thus evident that is regards to message delay TDMA performs $\frac{T_f}{2} - \frac{T_f}{N}$ seconds better than FDMA. However, as mentioned earlier, both the fixed assigned FDMA and TDMA are not suitable for bursty traffics and there one uses the random multiple access system described in previous sections.

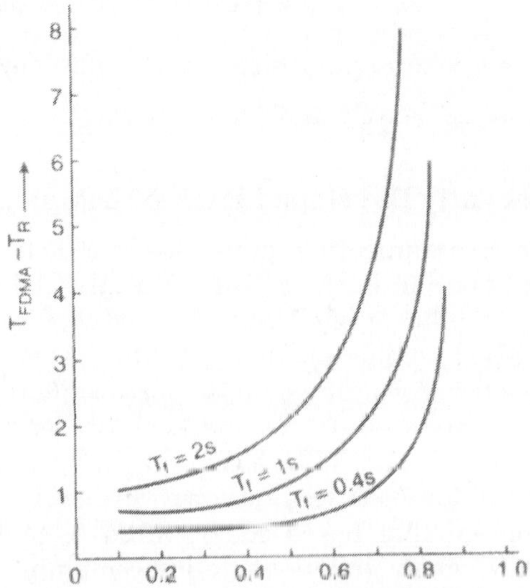

Fig. 10.8. Plot of $T_{FDMA} - T_R$ Versus ρ.

10.8. Packet Satellite Networks

A variety of data formats and services may be provided by satellite networks. These may be such as telephony signals, TV (visual and audio) signals, computer generated signals (computer communication), broadcast data for computer communications, teleprinter, larger screen teleconferencing, interactive education, medical data, emergency services, electronic mail, newspaper broadcast, control data for power systems and utilities, traffic information, weather and land surveillance, navigational data for ships and airplanes and military strategic data. In the coming years the above given list will increase as new requirements are created and accommodated. In the present section, however, some of the satellite networks using packet switching will be discussed.

ALOHA. As mentioned earlier it is a satellite based network developed in 1970 at the University of Hawaii. Its experiments were widely known as PACSAT experiments and utilized packet switching for the first time in satellite communication systems.

SATNET. It is Atlantic packet satellite network. Infact it was the most expensive field trial as of 1979 of packet satellite concepts, designs, developments and international cooperation.

WDPSN. It is wideband domestic packet satellite network. It uses SATNET technology in US Domestic *PSN*.

Data Retransmission. Here random access protocol is used and the satellite systems such as LANDSAT, NOAA/GOES etc use it.

GPSN. It is a general purpose packet satellite network.

SARSAT. It is Search and Rescue Satellite Aided Tracking System.

SOME Recently Developed Packet Networks

Computer communication networks like Telenet, Tymenet, Autonet, Graphnet and Pacnet, ISACOMM, ACCUNET, SKYNET etc are some of the latest ones that are used internationally. Now most of the modern communication satellites use packet switching in some or the other form. It would be worthwhile to mention here something about the satellite based packet switched networks being developed in India. PSTN VIKRAM is the foremost example. It is covering over 450 larger cities and towns in India. Another public network is the satellite based remote area telematic (message) network (RAMN) which provides satellite communication links between factories located in remote/backward areas and the offices in remote/backward areas and the offices in urban areas. Other such

Indian computer communication networks are NICNET, Business Subscriber network, Indonet, ERNET etc. which have found wide application in our country.

10.9. Review Questions

1. What are the various switching techniques and how packet switching is different from them ? Discuss various applications of packet switching.
2. What is meant by Random Multiple Access ? Compare its characteristics with those of FDMA and TDMA. Why is packet switching being used in random multiple access technique ?
3. What is queueing system ? How has it found applications in satellite communication system ? Discuss M/G/1 Queue system with regards to FDMA and TDMA satellite communication system.
4. In a satellite communication system using FDMA with 200 users and the channel capacity of R = 12.8 Mbps, each user generates a constant length message of 10^4 bits according to a Poisson process at a rate of three messages per second. Calculate the satellite capacity assigned to each user, average service rate of each FDMA channel and the average message delay for each user including a 270 ms satellite roundtrip delay.

   (**Ans** : 64 kbps, 6.4 messages per second, 495 ms)
5. What is ALOHA system ? Describe throughput and discuss the characteristics of Pure Aloha and Slotted Aloha in terms of throughput. What are the various techniques for improving throughputs ? Discuss a Reservation Aloha system.
6. What are Polling techniques ? Explain the polling technique used in binary tree search technique.
7. What is Carrier Sense Multiple Access Technique ? How is it different from ALOHA system ? Also discuss as to why CSMA is useful mainly to shorter distance communications in such as those of computer communication networks and not in satellite networks.
8. Assuming that Poisson process may be used for describing the packet transmission and retransmission, calculate the probability that a data packet transmission in an S-Aloha system will experience a collision with one other user. Assume that the total traffic rate λ_t = 10 packets/s and the packet duration τ = 10 ms. (**Ans** : 0.09)

10.10. References

Alongwith the references given in Chapter 7, following other references have also been used in preparing this section :

1. Agarwal, D.C., Computer Communication and ISDN systems, Khanna Publishers, Delhi, 1989.
2. White, J.A., Schmidt, J.W. and Bennett, G.K., Analysis of Queueing Systems, Academic Press, 1975.
3. Housley, T., Data Communications and Teleprocessing Systems, Prentice Hall, Inc, 1979.
4. Block, U., Computer, Networks, Protocols, Standards & Interfaces, Prentice Hall, Inc., 1987.

11

Satellite Earth Station

11.1. Introduction

Satellite communication is not complete without earth station which in fact transmits to and receives from satellite. The basic considerations of earth station are already discussed in Chapter 1 and the elementary block diagram is given in Fig. 1.2. Earth station may be located also on a ship at sea or on an aircraft but even then it is called earth station as it maintains communication link between earth and space or it forms the earth based end of the earth-space link. Fig. 1.2 indicates that in an earth station there are four major sub-systems namely the receiver, antenna, transmitter and tracking equipment alongwith terrestrial interface equipments and power supply (not shown in Fig. 1.2). It is, however, the antenna that is the most visible part of an earth station which may be as large as 30-m diameter in the INTELSAT network or as small as 0.7 m for reception of direct broadcast satellite television (DBS-TV). For deep space communication, the antenna size may still be larger.

Though every earth station would consist of above four major sub-systems but they can be classified according to the variety of equipments needed depending upon (*a*) function of the station, (*b*) type of service, (*c*) frequency bands used, (*d*) transmitter, (*e*) receiver and (*f*) antenna characteristics. Thus there are three categories of earth station namely (*a*) transmit and receive, (*b*) receive only and (*c*) transmit only earth stations. The first is encountered in two way communication systems. Receive only stations are mostly used in CATV systems and in direct TV broadcast satellite systems. Transmit only earth stations are used in data collection systems. Types of service for various earth stations include fixed, mobile (maritime, aeronautical and terrestrial), broadcasting and others. It would be of importance to mention here that one feature that is common to all the earth stations is the need to achieve a low system noise temperature in the receiving channel.

11.2. Earth Station Design Requirement

There are at least 8 important requirements that most of the earth stations have to meet. These are :

(*a*) high gain in the direction of wanted signals,
(*b*) low gain in the direction of unwanted signals,
(*c*) low effective noise temperature for the entire receiving system.
(*d*) high antenna efficiency,
(*e*) continuous satellite pointing with a specified accuracy,
(*f*) minimum performance variations caused by local wind and weather,
(*g*) minimal variation in the illumination of the satellite by the earth station and
(*h*) high discrimination between orthogonally polarized signals.

Most of the above design requirements are governed by the earth station. *G*/*T* ratio (figure of merit) which was discussed in Eq. (3.19) of chapter 3 and is re-written as

$$\frac{C}{N} = \frac{P_T\, G_T\, G_R\, (\lambda/4\pi d)^2}{K\, T_s\, B} \qquad ...(11.1)$$

where for simplicity the additional losses L_A have not been taken into account. Here G_R/T_S represents the *G*/*T* ratio of the earth station. It is evident that *C*/*N* ratio is directly proportional to *G*/*T* and so most of the above eight important design considerations of earth stations are met with the optimum value of *G*/*T* ratio. Depending upon the values of this *G*/*T* ratio earth stations have been classified as Type A, B or C given by INTELSAT standards. Table 11.1 gives the summary of characteristics of these three kinds of international earth stations.

Table 11.1. Characteristics of INTELSAT standard A, B and C earth Stations

Standard	*A*	*B*	*C*
Frequency (GHz)	6/4	6/4	14/11
Polarization	Circular	Circular	Linear
G/T dB K^4	40.7	31.7	39 + 20 log (f/11.2)
Typical dish diameter (m)	30	11-13	19
Antenna midband receive gain (dB)	61	51.5	65
Antenna midband transmit gain (dB)	64	54.1	66.4
Main reflector rms surface tolerance (mm)	1.0	0.8	0.6
Typical LNA noise temperature (K)	40	40	120

Over the years some more variety of INTELSAT earth stations have been designed. These are Standards *D, E, F* and *Z*.

Standard *D* has following characteristics : (6/4 GHz, *EIRP*=53-57 *dBW*, antenna diameter = 5 m (D_1) or 11 m (D_2), *G*/*T*=22.7 dBK^{-1} (D_1) or 31.7 dBk^{-1}(D_2).

Standard *E* earth station has characteristics such as frequencies 14/11 GHz, antenna diameter (E_1 3.5 m, E_2 5.5 m, E_3 8 to 10 m. *EIRP* 57 - 86 *dBW* (E_1), 55 - 83 *dBW* (E_2), 49 - 77*dBW* (E_3), *G/T* – 25 dBK^{-1} (E_1), 29 dBK^{-1} (E_2), 34 dBK^{-1}(E_3).

Standard *F* has characteristics such as (6/4 GHz, antenna diameter = 4.5-5 m (F_1), 7.5-8 m (F_2), 9-10 m (F_3), *EIRP* 63 – 91 *dBW* (F_1), 60–87 *dBW* (F_2), 59 – 86 *dBW* (F_3), *G/T* = 22.7 dBK^{-1} (F_1), 27 dBK^{-1} (F_2), 29 dBK^{-1}, (F_3),

Standard *Z* has characteristics (6/4 GHz, 14/11 GHz, *G/T* at 10° = 31.7 – 33.0 dBK^{-1} (for large). 24.5 – 26.9 dBK^{-1} (for small), 22.0 dBK^{-1} for TV/radio receive only.

It would be worthwhile to mention here that the diameter of the receiving antenna may be calculated either through Eq. (11.1) or by the following expression

$$D = 4R\left[\frac{LKTBFS/N}{P_T.\,G_T.\alpha}\right]^{1/2} \quad ...(11.2)$$

where *D* is the diameter of the receiving antenna in meters, *KT* = product of Boltzmann constant and absolute temperature, and the unit is joules, *R* = range to satellite in meters, *F* = noise figures of receiver, *S*/*N*=signal to noise ratio, P_T = total power transmitted from satellite, G_T = gain of satellite antenna, *B* = signal bandwidth in Hz, *L* = polarisation, cable etc. losses, α = antenna efficiency.

Similarly, the earth station transmitter power may be calculated from

$$P = \frac{16\,R^2\,LKTBFS/N}{D^2\,G_T\,\alpha} \quad ...(11.3)$$

This transmitter power ranges from a few tens of Watts to ten or twelve Kilowatts generated by vacuum tubes (klystrons or travelling wave tubes). Transmitters upto 400 KW are used in the deep-space network.

11.3. Earth Station Sub-Systems

(*a*) *Transmitter :* Here the signal to be transmitted is converted to the uplink frequency, with proper encoding and modulation. It is then amplified and directed to the appropriate polarization port of the antenna feed. In Fig. 1.2 the simple blocks of an earth station transmitters are given. In a large earth station there will be many transmitters as well as receivers multiplexed together onto one antenna to provide channelized communication through satellite transponders. Transmitters are very much expensive part of the earth station because of the tight specifications on out-of band emission, frequency stability and power control that are necessary to avoid interference with other channels and satellites. Further as transmitters are not manufactured in large scale so their cost is high. The cost increases with the increase in transmitted power which may vary from tens to thousands of watts.

Since earth stations require the transmission of microwave power, they use high power amplifiers (HPAs) such as travelling tubes and multi cavity klystrons. In fact compared to klystrons, TWTAs allow high powers over a wide bandwidth. These tubes require quite a good amount of cooling that is provided by water circulation using a closed refrigeration system. Table 11.2 gives a brief summary of the characteristics of HPAs used in earth station transmitters.

Table 11.2. Brief Summary of HPAs' Characteristics

Amplifier Type	*Output Power*	*Bandwidth*	*Cost*
Klystron	500-5000 W	Small 40 MHz	Medium
Travelling Wave Tube (TWT)	100-2500 W	Large (500 MHz)	High
FET (6 GHz, 14 GHz)	5-50 W, 1-6 W	Large	High
Bipolar Transistor	Upto 50 W	Wide	High

Note : (1.6 GHz) to be used in maritime satellite communication system.

When there are several HPAs working their output may be combined through bandpass filters and circulators or by means of hybrids. Thus a modified version of earth's station transmitter may be as that given in Fig. 11.1. Here modulation is performed at 70 MHz IF which is then upconverted. The configuration (arrangements) for HPAs to be employed depend on the number of carriers to be transmitted and whether these are FDM or TDM signals. The most common configuration employs one HPA for each transponder to be used. It must be remembered that reliability is of utmost importance in satellite communication and therefore the equipments in transmitters always employ some sort of redundancy configuration with automatic switch over in the event of some failure.

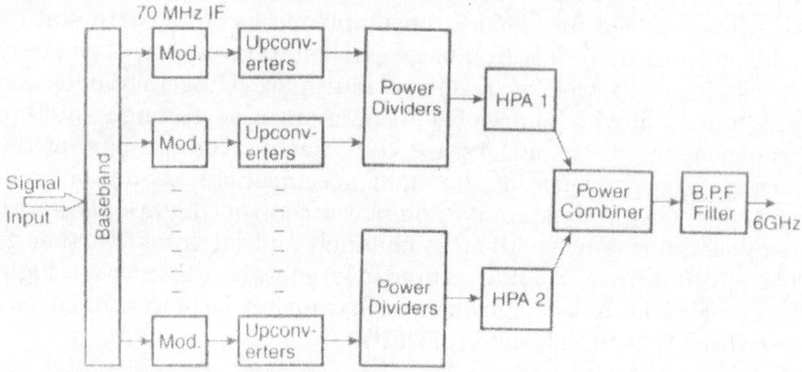

Fig. 11.1. Block Diagram of Transmitter.

(*b*) *Receiver* : Receiver of an earth station employs mainly low noise amplifier (LNA), down converter, demodulator, decoder and baseband signal treatment equipments. The basic block diagram of receiver is given in Fig. 11.2. Infact in the receive chain of the earth station the weak signals from the satellite are accepted by the same feed that carries the transmitter output. These two signals which differ in power by several orders of magnitude are kept separate in the frequency domain as they are assigned to the uplink and downlink bands, and in addition by means of orthogonal polarization. As shown in Fig. 1.1 (Chapter 1), diplexers are used to enhance the separation in the frequency domain.

In Chapter 3, the noise consideration has already been discussed while considering the design requirement of downlink. It is very essential that the receiver should have first stages with very low noise and sufficiently high gain. In particular the large earth stations require such very low noise amplifiers. And therefore there cryogenically cooled parametric amplifiers are widely used, with liquid helium cooling at 4° K above absolute zero to achieve noise temperatures of 20 to 40K at 4 GHz. Medium and small earth stations use GaAs FET amplifiers with no cooling or electron thermal (Peltier) cooling. These achieve noise temperatures in the range 50 to 120 K at 4 GHz and 120 to 300 K at 11 GHz. Table 11.3 gives a brief summary of the characteristics of various LNAs used in the receive part of earth station.

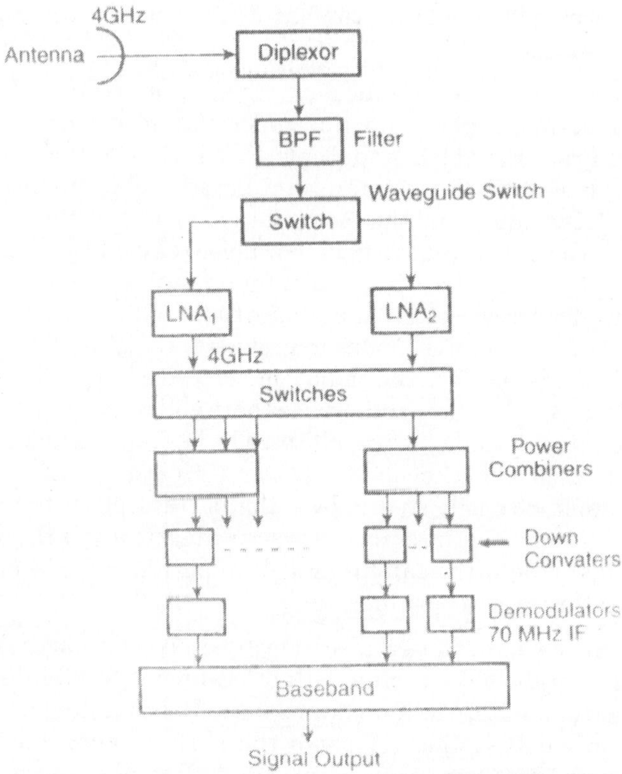

Fig. 11.2. Basic Block Diagram of Earth Station Receiver.

Table 11.3. Brief Summary of LNAs used in the Earth Station Receiver

Types of Amplifiers	*Frequency*	*Noise Temp.*	*Cost*	*Use*
Cryogenic parametric	4 GHz	15 K	High	Large station
Cooled parametric	4, 12 GHz	35,100 K	Medium	Standard A & B, Standard C,
Uncooled	4 GHz	50 K	Medium	Large domestic
Parametric	12 GHz	120 K	Medium	Eutelsat stations
Cooled FET	4 GHz	50 K	Low	Domestic
GaAs	12 GHz	130 K	Low	Domestic
Ambient	4 GHz	75 K	Low	Small domestic
FET GaAs	12 GHz	250 K	Low	Small domestic

With respect to Fig. 11.1 of the block diagram of transmitter, the receiver block diagram may be represented as that in Fig. 11.2. It may be noted that LNAs used in earth stations usually cover the 500 MHz fixed service band at 4 GHz and 750 MHz at 11 GHz. In receiver too some sort of redundancy configuration is used particularly for LNA.

(*c*) *Antenna :* Antenna is the most visible part of the earth station and it is normally placed in the upper side of the earth station building. From Eq. (11.1) and Table 11.1 it is seen that the earth station's characteristics are mainly governed by its antenna characteristics. It is evident that the earth station must meet three requirements such as high directive gain, low noise temperature and easily steerable. It is essential that the antenna must focus its radiated energy into a narrow beam to illuminate the satellite antenna in both the transmit and receive modes to provide the required uplink and downlink carrier power. The radiation pattern of antenna must not exhibit large sidelobe level otherwise there will be interference from unwanted signals and other satellites. The low noise temperature of antenna would allow to have a better C/N ratio. Similarly, the antenna must be easily steerable so that a tracking system may be employed to point the antenna beam accurately towards the satellite taking into account the satellite's drift in position. This would also allow pointing loss to be minimum.

Two basic kinds of antenna are mostly used in the earth stations. These are paraboloid antenna with a focal point feed and the cassagrain antenna. Horn antennas and phased array antenna may also be used in earth stations. Though the horn antenna has a good performance, it is expensive and very bulky when high gain is needed. Hence they are not used for earth stations.

The phased array antenna is of much use so long as it has small dimensions that is a low gain value. If the dimension is increased, it will require several mechanical performance so that there may not be any deformation. When antenna beam requires steering as in the case of stations on board mobiles, phased array antennas are quite suitable. The reflector or dish antennas have the advantages that they offer a wide range of gain values with affordable mechanical complexity. These reflector antennas are the paraboloid antenna (single parabolic reflector) with a focal point feed and the cassegrain antenna (Dual reflector) as already mentioned. There may be single offset reflector antenna also.

Fig. 11.3 illustrates a paraboloid antenna with a focal point feed. Here the feed's phase centre is located at the focal point of the paraboloid reflector. The feed is connected to HPA and LNA through an orthogonal mode transducer (OMT) which is usually a three port network. Thus when the antenna is transmitting the signal energy from the output of HPA is radiated at the focal point by the feed and illuminates the reflector that reflects and focusses the signal energy into a narrow beam. When the paraboloid is in the receive mode, it captures the signal energy and converges it on the focal point which is then received by the feed and routed to the input of LNA. This kind of paraboloid is easily steered and offers gain efficiency in the range of 50 to 60%. In case the antenna points to the satellite at a high elevation angle its focal point feed would face the ground. In such a situation the feed radiation will also spill over the edge of the reflector and illuminates the ground which may be as high as 290° K. This contributes a high antenna noise. This spill over may be reduced by tapering the aperture edge. The main problem with such antenna is that if a low noise temperature is needed it will require a highly directional feed that would mean a large focal length. This makes the antenna more cumbersome. There would be a possibility of increased feeder losses and partial blocking of aperture plane. Nevertheless the above paraboloid antenna with a focal point feed are mostly used in receive only applications. A slight modification such as offset reflector antenna has also been suggested to get rid of aperture blocking effect but here the supporting frame becomes costly. In any case it does not solve the spill over problem completely.

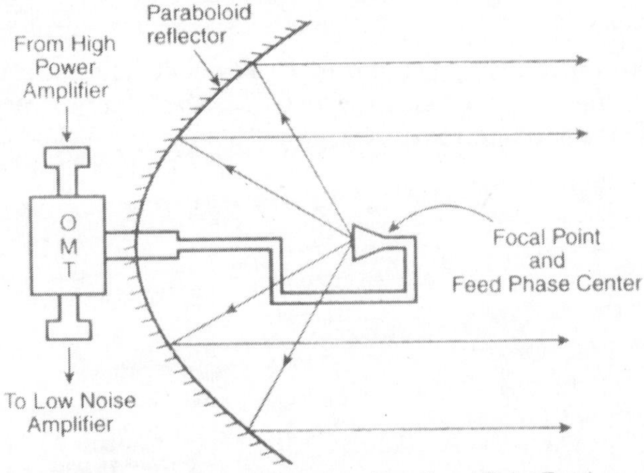

Fig. 11.3. Paraboloid Antenna with a Focal Point Feed.

It would be worthwhile to mention here that the size of earth station antenna affects allowable satellite spacing to avoid interfering with adjacent satellites. It is shown in Fig. 11.4. Considering the minimum allowable spacing, Fig. 11.4 shows that the earth station antenna would have to be at least 100 wavelengths in diameter. Thus holding the same beam width, the higher the carrier frequency the shorter the wavelength and the smaller the permissible antenna

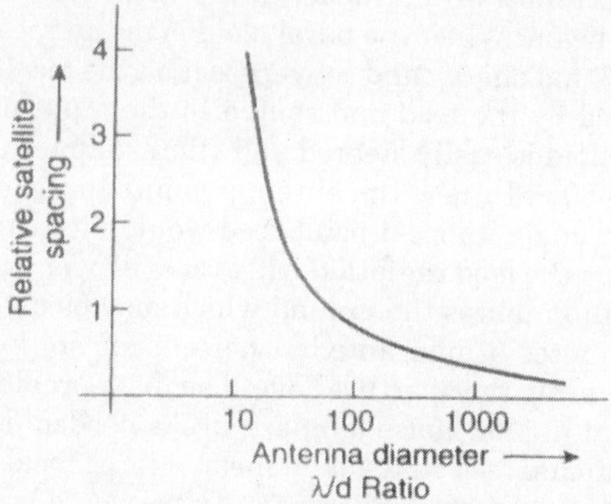

Fig. 11.4. Relationship between Antenna Diameter and Satellite Orbit Spacing.

diameter. For example a 6 GHz uplink carrier has a wavelength of 5 cm and in such a case the antenna would have to be above 5 meters (or about 15 feet) in diameter. Similarly, for carrier frequency of 15 GHz (wavelength of 2 cms), antenna diameter would be 2 meter (or about 6½ ft). For 30 GHz carrier frequency diameter reduces to 1 meter or about 3.3 ft which is quite suitable for mobile or home applications.

A better modification on the above parabolic reflector is to make it a dual reflector arrangement called *Cassegrain* antenna arrangement as shown in Fig. 11.5. It consists of a main paraboloid reflector

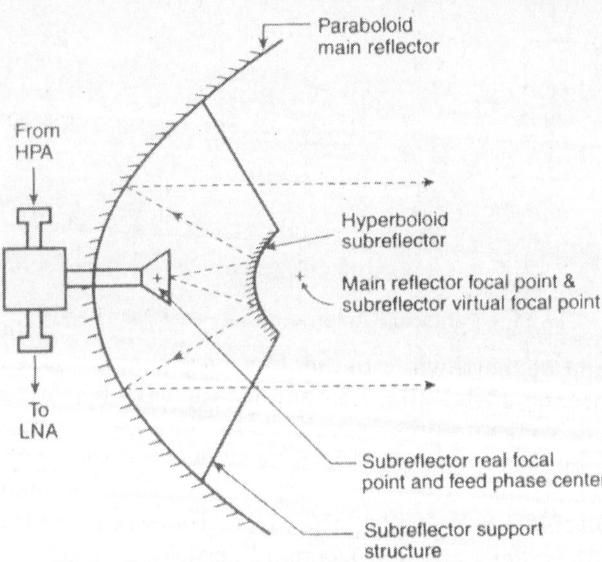

Fig. 11.5. Dual Reflector (Cassegrain) Arrangement.

whose focal point is coincident with the virtual focal point of a hyperboloid sub-reflector and a feed, whose phase centre is at the real focal point of the sub-reflector. When the antenna is in the transmit mode, firstly the signal energy from the output of HPA is being radiated at the real focal point of sub-reflector by the feed that illuminates the convex surface of the sub-reflector. The sub-reflector reflects the signal energy back as if it were incident from a feed whose center was located at the common focal point of the main reflector and sub-reflector. The reflected energy is then reflected by the main reflector and it forms the antenna beam. In case the antenna is in the receive mode the signal energy captured by the main reflector is directed towards its focal point and then the subreflector reflects the signal energy back to its real focal point where the phase center of the feed is located. Now the feed receives this incoming energy which is then routed to the input of LNA through OMT.

Though the cassegrain antenna is more expensive than the simple reflector because of the addition of more elements such as subreflector and its support but is has several advantages such as low noise temperature, pointing accuracy and flexibility in feed design. Further here the spillover energy from the feed is directed toward the sky whose noise temperature is typically less than 30°K and thus the contribution to the antenna noise temperature is small as compared to paraboloid antenna. The feed is located near the vertex of the main reflector and so greater mechanical stability is achieved. This allows very accurate pointing of the antenna narrow beam. Oftenly alongwith the cassegrain antenna, beam waveguide feed system is used. This arrangement minimizes losses in the transmission lines connecting the HPA and LNA to the feed. When frequency reuse is to be done, a wideband OMT diplexer type of frequency reuse feed for the cassegrain antenna is used. This feed provides horizontal and vertical polarization for a Ku band operation. It would be worthwhile to mention here that a kind of reflector antenna termed as multibeam Torus antenna has also been developed particularly by COMSAT laboratories which is capable of receiving simultaneously several satellites located in one section of the geostationary arc. This antenna is of small dimension such as a paraboloid antenna with diameter of 9.8 m with a gain of the order of 50 dB at 6/4 GHz and noise temperature of 30 K for an elevation angle of 20°.

(*d*) *Tracking and Pointing*. The efficiency of earth station depends as to how efficiently it points the antenna beam to the satellite both in the transmit and receive mode. In order to do this correctly round the clock it is essential for the earth station to continuously track the satellite and this requires a very accurate program-track facility or a kind of autotrack system. A typical example of pointing accuracy is that if the antennas' 3 dB bandwidth is typically of 10 min. arc., it must be pointed with an accuracy of ± 1 min of arc in order to avoid any pointing loss. For this purpose a careful mounting of antenna is required. There are 4 kinds of antenna mounting such as azimuth-elevation mounting, X-Y mounting, equatorial mounting and the tripod mounting. Out of these azimuth-elevation mounting is most popularly used by almost every earth station. Fig. 11.6 indicates a typical azimuth-elevation mounted antenna system for an earth station.

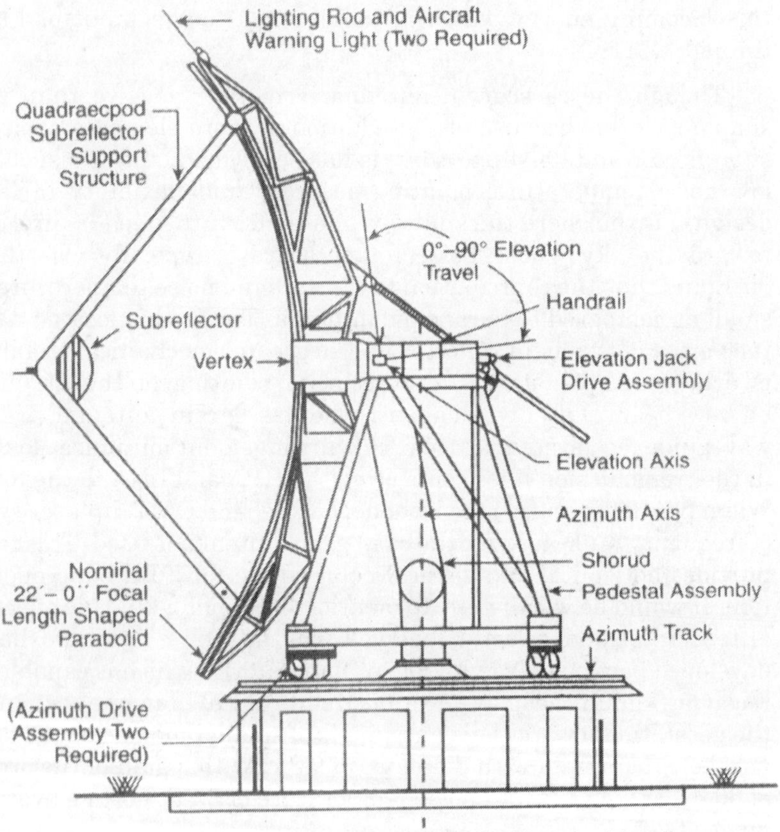

Fig. 11.6. Cassegrain Antenna with Azimuth-Elevation Mounting.

Tracking may be achieved by either of three methods, namely monopulse or multi-horn tracking, conical scanning, step by step (also called step-track or hill climb) techniques. In the monopulse technique the antenna generates difference patterns with nulls on the axis, in azimuth and elevation planes. Though the monopulse antenna presents a low systematic pointing error of the order of 0.1 θ_{3db}, it is complex and expensive and so it is not used. The most popular technique is step by step technique where a search for the maximum reception of the received signal is done. This requires a continuous moving and checking of the beam. From the knowledge of main beam shape the true direction of the satellite is estimated and then the antenna is pointed in that direction. Such kind of tracking gives the systematic pointing error of the order of $0.2\theta_{3db}$. Here the antenna is resetted by moving the sub-reflector. Sometimes the scintillations in the received signal may cause trouble in tracking and so continuous checking of scintillation amplitude is also needed.

11.4. Monitoring and Control

The importance of redundancy of some equipment in earth station such as HPA and LNA etc. has already been mentioned in the previous section. With this redundancy arrangement it is expected that when the on line equipment in the redundancy configuration fails, the standby (redundant) equipment has to automatically switch over and become the on line equipment. Infact this process of detecting critical failure modes and resolving all these failure modes by automatic switch over from the failed to the redundant system is termed *monitoring and control*. In a communication network using the communication satellite several earth stations alongwith a network control centre (NCC) are involved. Here this monitoring and control is quite important. This involves many levels such as rf terminal monitoring and control, remote monitoring and control of the earth station from the network control center *via* the satellite link with a backup terrestrial telephone line.

It is essential for monitoring and control system to have the capability to collect status data for classification, to convey status data to network operators, to interpret status data, to initiate fault isolations, to switch over redundant equipment on command, to convey control data to the baseband equipment for traffic assignment, antenna pointing and finally to maintain surveillance of equipment shelter facilities.

11.5. Frequency Coordination

Terrestrial microwave links and satellite communication systems share common frequency allocations in a number of bands. It is therefore essential that whenever a new earth station or terrestrial link is established it should not interfere with the existing systems. This is achieved by the technique called *frequency coordination* which has been specified by CCIR. This is of much significance for frequency bands of 4 and 6 GHz. Thus the area surrounding the earth station that comes under interference from other station is called *coordination area*. The curve binding this area is called coordination contour and the distance along any given azimuth from the earth station to the coordination contour is called the *coordination distance*.

CCIR vide its reports 724-1 and 382 has given the process to determine this coordination distance. The first step in the process is to determine the basic transmission loss L_b in decibels by the formula:

$$L_b = P_T + G_T + G_R - A_S - P_R \text{ dB} \quad \text{...(11.4)}$$

where P_T is the transmitter power in dBW, G_T and G_R are the transmitter and receiver gains in the appropriate directions and P_R is the maximum allowed received power from the interferer. A_s is called the site shielding factor. The second step in the process involves the determination of distance corresponding to this L_b. Again the curves and equations to calculate this distance have been provided by CCIR. For this two modes of propagation have been considered by CCIR. These modes are mode A and mode B where

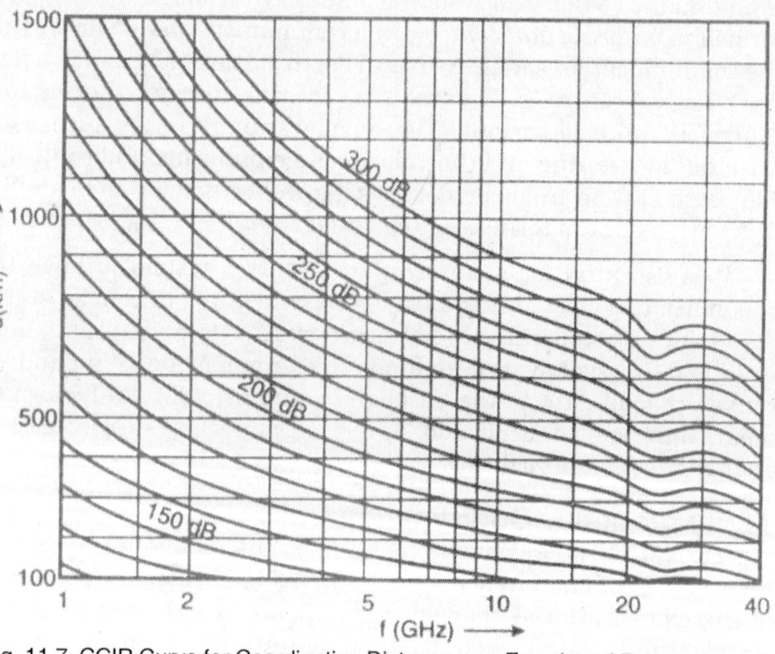

Fig. 11.7. CCIR Curve for Coordination Distance as a Function of Frequency and ($L_b - A_S$) for Mode *A* Propagation.

mode A corresponds to great circle path mechanisms and mode B corresponds to scattering by rain. It must be remembered that rain may cause interference by scattering energy from the beam of a transmitting antenna into the aperture of receiving antenna. For mode A CCIR has given a curve (shown in Fig. 11.7) that displays coordination distance as a function of frequency and $(L_b - A_s)$. Infact A_s is calculated by the formula :

$$A_s = 20 \, Log_{10} \, (1 + 4.5\theta \, f^{0.5}) + \theta f^{0.33} \quad \text{for } \theta \geq 0^0$$
$$= 0 \text{ for } \theta < 0° \qquad ...(11.5)$$

where θ is in degrees.

For mode B propagation the CCIR curve is shown in Fig. 11.8. Here the site shielding is not considered (in rain scatter interference) and the CCIR curves for rain scatter coordination distance involve rainfall rate and frequency directly.

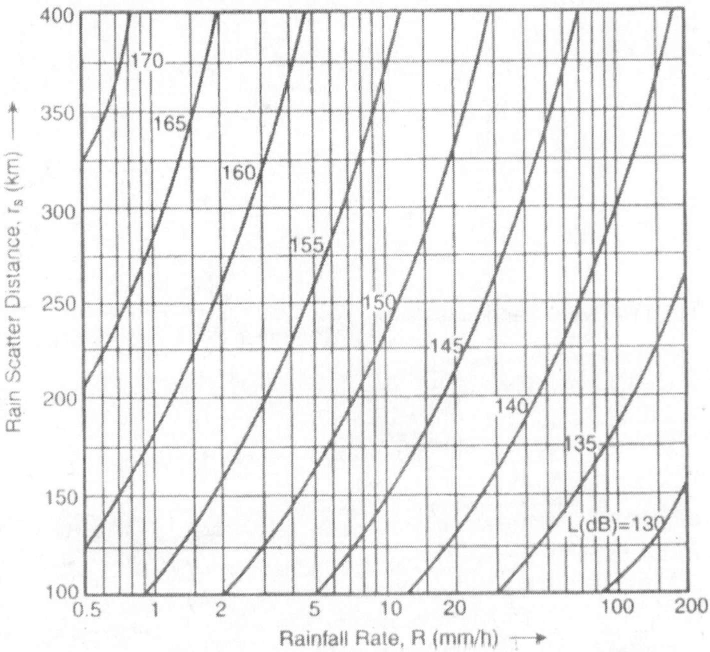

Fig. 11.8. Rain Scatter Distance as a Function of Basic Transmission loss and Rainfall rate at 4 GHz.

11.6. Small Earth Station

Basically small earth stations are defined as those which use antennas less than 60 wavelengths in diameter, corresponding to 5 m dishes at 4 GHz and 1.6 m dishes at 11 GHz, with gains below, about 44 dB. For such a case front feed paraboloid reflector is being used. Cassegrain or dual reflector is not used as blockage losses are then very high. Though the symmetrical front end paraboloids are widely used for small earth station antennas, offset-fed antennas employing single and dual reflector configurations may also be used. The torus is also used to multibeam service purpose. Small earth station do not need the expensive autotrack equipment, dual axis drivers and servo systems etc. for their antenna systems. Fixed

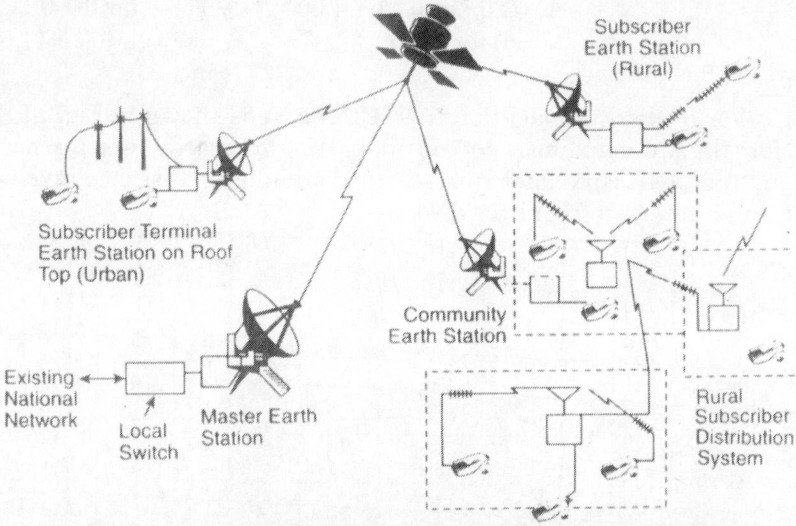

Fig. 11.9. Small Earth Stations in Telecommunication network Systems Operating in C/Ku Bands.

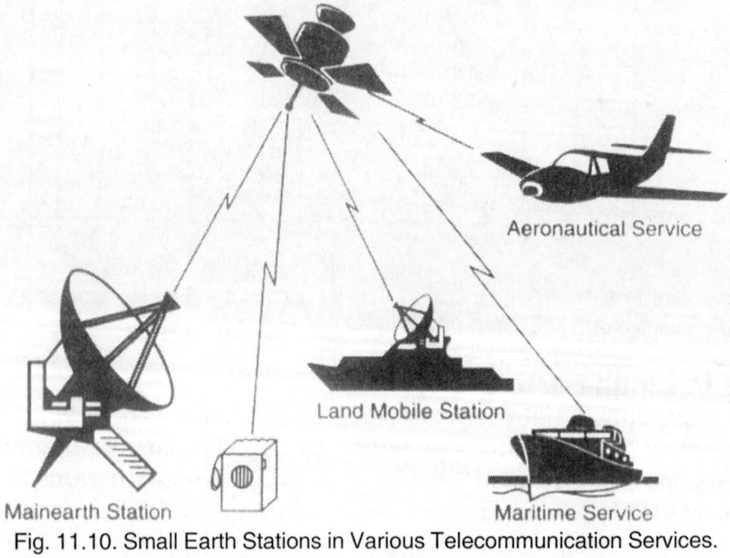

Fig. 11.10. Small Earth Stations in Various Telecommunication Services.

pointing and small aperture antennas serve the purpose. Thus the small earth stations escape many of the problems encountered with large antennas and cost a small fraction of their large counterparts.

Small earth stations were developed basically for TVRO (television receive only) systems but these find use also in Telecommunication networking systems as shown in Fig. 11.9 or in other kind of services such as land mobile services or maritime services etc. as shown in Fig. 11.10. With the introduction of direct broadcast satellites (DBS) where satellite power is increased, the cost of small earth station would be further reduced as in such case the antenna size could be further reduced to an extent of 2 to 6 ft. In such cases it would be proper to term the small earth station as *micro earth station* The cost of such small earth stations are a few thousand US dollars.

11.7. Mobile and Transportable Earth Station

In mobile and transport services small earth stations are used which are particularly of portable or transportable kind. For such services, it is essential that the earth stations should be able to move freely within a coverage area and the antenna be able to be pointed in all directions above the horizontal plane. For mobile stations azimuth-elevation mountings are not preferred and instead tripod mounting is preferred.

One of the applications of the mobile and transport services is the shipping and for that the satellite INMARSAT (International Maritime Satellite Organisation) is used in communications for global shipping. It involves two kinds of earth stations, namely the coast earth station (CES) and the ship earth station. In fact, CES is basically an earth station cum telephone exchange and the amount of software here is very high. It must be remembered that Intelsat ES has no software. There are two kinds of ship earth stations (SES) namely the standard A and standard C. Though the cost of SES is quite small compared to the cost of ship, the standard C type earth station is 10 times cheaper to standard A station and can be afforded even by fishing trawlers, road trucks and rail carriages

Standard A ship earth station consists of two main parts, namely the above deck equipment (ADE) and the below deck equipment (BDE). The ADE consists of a parabolic antenna mounted on a stabilized platform, a diplexer to separate the transmitting and receiving signals, a solid state HPA for transmission, a LNA for reception, and a power supply for the amplifiers. The system is housed in a fibre glass radome for protection against weather. The diameter of the parabolic antenna depends on the SES standard type. The antenna mounting unit comprises a four axis stabilizing system with appropriate sensors and servo control. Other characteristics of ADE are given in Table 11.4. The BDE is housed either in a rack or in desk-top console. It comprises units to control the antenna, modulate the baseband frequency signals (voice, telex, facsimile etc., into higher frequency signals, feed the antenna and viceversa. It also has controls, indicators and interface for telephone, teletype and other equipment.

Standard *C* earth stations have $G/T = -19\ dBK^{1}$. Standard *C* communications are message based. There was also a standard *B* type ship earth station with receive $G/T = -12\ dBK^{-1}$. Since standard *B* and standard *A* earth stations give similar operational characteristics and standard *C* is much cheaper than standard *B* so the standard *C* has been widely adopted. In such standard *C* type earth stations, communications are transmitted in bursts, at an information rate of 600 bps *via* satellite to CES. At the CES, the messages are stored and forwarded to their destinations is a form nominated by the sender, *i.e.* the telex, teletext, voice band data, electronic mail etc. *via* the national and international network. The procedure is reversed when a message is received by the terminal onboard. The standard *C* terminal is designed to operate at lower power through a non-stabilized omnidirectional antenna, anywhere within the INMARSAT satellite coverage.

Table 11.4. INMARSAT-Standard A Earth Station Characteristics

Antenna System	*Communication Systems*
Diameter : typically 12 m	Transmit band : 1636.5-1645.0 MHz
Gain : typically around 23 dB	Receive band : 1535-1543.5 MHz
Beamwidth : typically around 10°	Receive $G/T : \geq -4\ dBK^{-1}$
Polarization : right hand circular transmit and receive	Transmit EIRP : 37 dBW ± 1 dBW
	Capacity : single duplex telephony or telegraphy call at any time.

In addition to the ship services, aeronautical communication services through the satellite system are also being provided. Here the aeronautical ground earth station (GES) provides the link between the terrestrial system and the satellite network. They operate in C-band. The major components of a GES are the 12 meter diameter antenna, RF and IF equipment, and an Access control and signalling equipment (ACSE). The aircraft earth station (AES) falls into four categories depending on the equipment configuration and service capability. Class *I* AESS are fitted with low gain antennas and carry only medium rate data (300-600 bps). They support basic safety services. Class *II* AESS provide voice services only, and have high gain aircraft antennas. Class *III* AESS have high gain antenna and provide voice and data services. Class *IV* AESS combine classes *I* and *III*. They have low gain and high gain antennas, providing voice and data services. Besides the antenna, other important AESS units are : (*a*) the satellite data unit (SDU), performing most of the data handling, protocols, modulation and coding functions of the AES, (*b*) the radio frequency unit (RFU) performing frequency synthesis and up-and down conversions, and matching with SDU ; and (*c*) the Beam Steering Unit (BSU) or alternatively antenna control unit (ACU) for mechanical antennas, to control Carborne antenna pointing.

11.8. New Class of Earth Stations

The emerging earth stations are more complex because of their numerous applications in different frequency bands. Glass fibre reinforced plastic (CFRP) are poised to be used for reflector antennas particularly for transportable/mobile systems. This will also reduce the cost of antenna. The same reflector with composite feed for CLS band working will be common. Array antennas and printed circuit antennas are being developed for various applications. High efficiency feeds with improved side lobe levels for closer spacing of satellite is also predicted.

Solid State Power Amplifiers (HPA) are now increasingly used (*e.g.* upto 100 W at *C* band and 40 W at Ku band). For remote control and measurements IEEE bus compatible control units are being used in major earth stations. Similarly considerable improvement in the working of LNA with the decrease in its cost has taken place. A better noise temperature will be available with them. The developments in MMIC (monolithic microwave integrated circuits) and VLSI's (very large scale integrated) at lower cost has reduced size and cost of up and down converters. Also the number of microwave circuits and IF amplifiers, filters etc. are now smaller packaged units with the frequency synthesized local oscillator working at extended C-band, Ku and Ka bands. The frequency converters are compact and are of one third of the present size. Reliability also has improved as there is less inter unit wiring and connection.

Major earth stations now use micro computer controlled sub-systems, monitored and operated remotely with advanced data logging facilities. This avoids human errors in operation and data logging.

DAMA (demand assignment multiple access) is used by most of the small earth stations. Mobile satellite communication in L/S band are commonly used by small ships, trains, trucks and aeroplanes using INMARSAT or other satellites.

11.9. TVRO Systems (Television Receive Only Systems)

TVRO system have already been mentioned in the early part of this chapter. These are only the downlink side of satellite communications and consist of five major types of equipment, namely the dish (reflector), feed-horn/polarizer (antenna), low noise amplifier (LNA), receiver/downconverter and TV/video monitor. TVRO dishes are of two types, namely the spherical dishes and parabolic dishes. The spherical dishes are good when one wants to watch mainly one satellite. Parabolic dishes are more popular because these are cheaper than spherical ones and also allow the viewer to move from one satellite to another by using a polar mounting. Mesh dish is always preferable.

Signals from satellite are focussed by reflector onto the feed horn antenna which is situated at the focal point of the reflector dish. Some technique for polarity selection is also given. The LNA is a broadband mountable amplifier with the gain varying between 35 to 50 dB. LNAs are of GaAsFET and bipolar transistors. Sometimes LNA and downconverter are integrated into a single unit called low noise converter (LNC). The receiver part of TVRO consists of downconverter, IF amplifier/filter, demodulator and video/audio processor. Once the audio and video are properly processed, they may be viewed on a monitor.

11.11. Review Questions

1. What are the equipments that an earth station requires ? Discuss their design requirements.
2. What are the INTELSAT standards for earth stations ? Compare their relative major characteristics.
3. Explain with the block diagram the working of transmitter part of earth station. What are the HPA's being used here ? Compare their main characteristics.
4. Discuss the receiver's working in earth station with suitable block diagram. Also explain various LNAs used there.
5. Explain with suitable diagram the working of various antenna systems to be used in earth stations ? Give antenna requirements for large and small earth stations.

6. What is meant by tracking and pointing ? Explain its significance and the technique as to how these are achieved ?
7. Explain the monitoring and control requirements for earth station equipments. Why is it necessary to have these ? Discuss.
8. Explain as to why is it necessary to have frequency coordination among earth stations themselves and earth station-terrestrial microwave links ? Discuss the techniques to achieve them.
9. Explain the operational characteristics and performance requirements of very small aperture terminals (VSATs), mobile and transportable earth stations.
10. What is a TVRO system ? Explain the units that a TVRO terminal should have. Discuss their operations.

11.12. Reference

In addition to the books mentioned in reference of Chapter I, reference is also made to the following as well :

1. Mohanty, Earth station Technology, Tracking Satellites, Telematics India, Nov.-Dec. 1987, pp. 54-56.
2. Rao, Y.S. and Ghose, A.K., Voice Transmission Via Packets, Telematics India, June, 1988, pp. 46-48.
3. Rao, Y.S., Small Satcom. Terminals, ibid, pp. 49-50.
4. Verma, K., INMARSAT, Telematics India, July, 1988, pp. 49-57.
5. Chowdry, T.H., CES coming up, Telematics India, July, 1988, pp. 54-55.
6. Sinnema, W., Electronic Transmission Technology, Prentice Hall India, N.J., 1988.
7. Computer and Communications, May, 1988, issue.
8. Rao, Y.S. and Ghose, A.K., Voice Transmission in Satellite Based Packet Networks, Proc. Conf. Computer Communications for Developing Countries, 1987, Delhi, pp. 115-122.
9. Proceedings of IEE Vol. 72 No. 11, Nov. 1984, Special Issue on Satellite Communications Networks.

12

Communication Satellite Subsystems

12.1. Introduction

Geostationary communication satellite is a very complex system that comprises of several subsystems which have their own significance. These subsystems may be divided into two groups, namely

Table 12.1 Communication Satellite Subsystems, their Functions and Parameters of Importance

Subsystem	*Functions*	*Parameters of Importance*
Repeaters	Amplify signals and transmit back	Noise figure, linearity and output *rf* power
Antennas	Receive and transmit signals	Coverage, gain
Electric power supply	Provides electric energy at various voltage levels	Power, voltage regulation
Electric power supply	Provides electric energy at various voltage levels	Power, voltage regulation
Structure	Supports equipment	Stiffness
Altitude & Orbit control	Altitude stabilization, Orbit determination	Accuracy
Thermal Control	Temperature Regulation	Heat dissipation capability
Propulsion	Provides velocity increments and torques	Specific impulse, Mass of propellent
Telemetry, tracking & command	Exchange of house-keeping data with control centre	Number of channels, security of communications

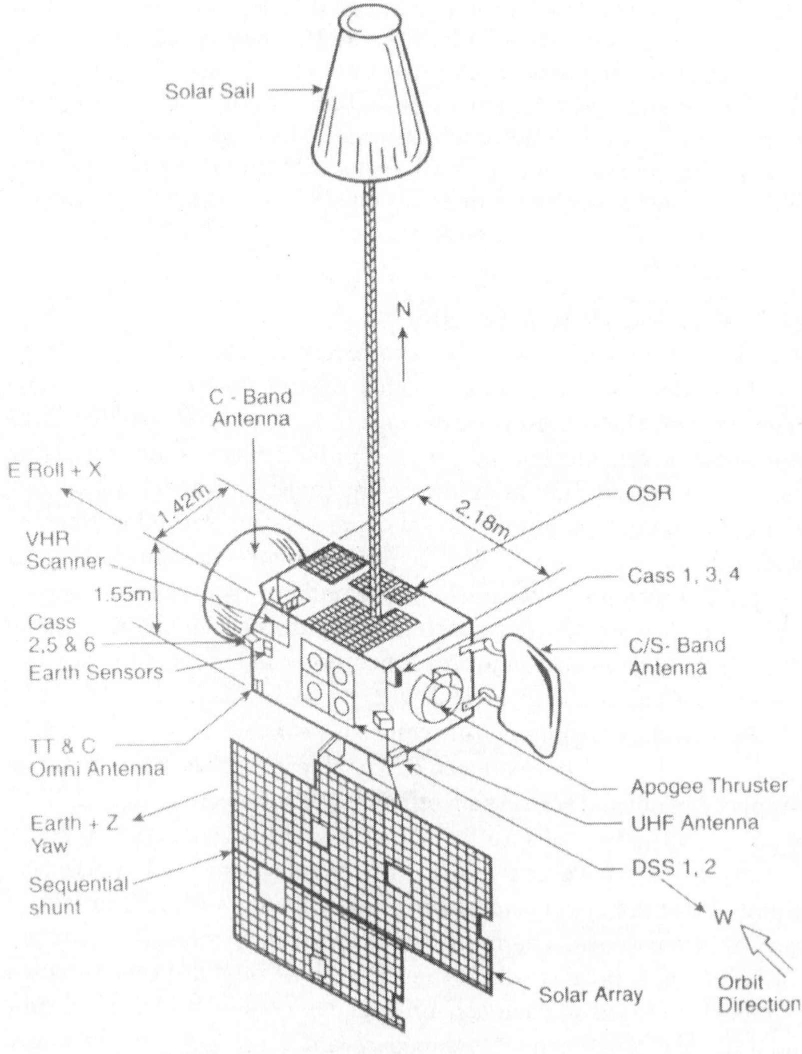

Fig. 12.1. INSAT on-Orbit Satellite Configuration.

the communication subsystems and the other subsystems (also called common subsystems all taken together) which support the communication subsystems. The communication subsystem is also oftenly termed payload that is mainly comprised of repeaters and antennas and it performs the primary mission. The other subsystems (common subsystems) have a common bus or platform. These other subsystems are power, stabilization, propulsion, station keeping, attitude control, and telemetry, tracking and command. Fig. 12.1 shows a typical INSAT -on-orbit satellite configuration in which these subsystems are well evident. Table 12.1 lists these subsystems indicating their important functions and parameters of importance. However, it should be remembered that all the subsystem work with high reliability and all the satellite projects be of minimal mass with least power consumption. It is also essential that these subsystems follow the electromagnetic interference (EMI) and electromagnetic compatibility (EMC) requirements.

12.2. Electric Power Supply

In communication satellite the electric power supply system provides the electrical energy needed to run the spacecraft (house keeping) and the communications system. When the satellite is in stationary orbit, electric power is obtained from solar cells. But during the first few hours following the injection into transfer orbit and prior to deployment of the solar panels, the electromechanical accumulators provide the electric power supply. In some satellites especially those of USSR, thermonuclear energy source are also used but due to dangers involved with nuclear fuels especially with their shielding etc, nuclear generators are not used in communication satellite for supplying electric power.

Solar cells are photovoltaic cells that convert solar radiation to electricity which is then converted to usable voltage levels in a power supply. The normal conversion efficiency of solar cells is around 12% to 15% and the typical satellite solar cell arrays generate 1 to 2 KW of power. The above conversion efficiency of solar cells decreases under the effect of the *radiations* and drops by about 30 to 35 per cent in seven years. The main radiations come from protons especially during solar flares and therefore solar cells are covered with shields from fused silica or cerium doped microsheets. The ultrathin (50 μ m) low mass cells developed recently are not very strongly affected by radiation. To have more conversion efficiency, solar cells with aluminium or gallium arsenide are also recommended. These give conversion efficiency of around 18%.

Since the satellite goes under solar eclipses which is of concern during Equinox (as discussed in Section 2.7) provision is made for the storage of power that can be used during the solar eclipse. For this purpose electro-chemical accumulators like those of nickel-cadmium accumulators are used. These are hermetically sealed ones and are designed to supply power required during eclipses and during those times when the solar cells are not aligned to intercept sufficient solar radiation, which could occur during launch. Thus in the communication satellite, solar cell-storage battery system is being used. It must be remembered that in the storage battery system, it is desired that the depth of discharge should be as maximum as possible. The *depth of discharge (DOD)* represents the percentage of the maximum stored energy which is actually used. But since the depth of discharge governs the lifetime of battery so the nickel cadmium batteries are not allowed to discharge beyond 50%. In some recent communication satellites nickel-hydrogen batteries are used which can be safely discharged to 60% of capacity. This higher energy-to-weight ratio of nickel- hydrogen batteries may allow sufficient extra station keeping fuel to be carried which might provide some additional life of satellite in the orbit. ADVANCED SATCOM spacecraft has claimed that its life time has increased by 1 year by the use of such storage battery system. All these batteries are regularly and continuously being charged by solar cells. Here the battery voltage are between 20 to 50 V with capacities between 20 to 50 ampere hours.

The solar cells panels for spin stabilized satellite and that for three-axis body stabilized satellite are shown in Figs. 2.17 and 2.18 respectively. It should be kept in mind that when the solar cells get heated their efficiency goes down. In the spin stabilized satellite the solar cells array is shaped as a cylinder and therefore as the satellite rotates, solar cells successively face the sun and the cold space (shadow). Hence the average temperature is relatively low (between 20 to 30° C, say around 25° C). At this temperature the solar cell efficiency is 14% which is reduced by 22% at the end of the satellite life due to various degradations. Therefore about 15% extra area of solar cells is usually provided as an allowance for aging. In the three axis body stabilized satellite, wings of solar panels are used which are folded in transfer orbit and then full power becomes available. These are required to have atleast one revolution per day so as to keep the face of the array pointing toward the sun. These kind of solar arrays are capable of providing more power as compared to that of spin stabilization satellite. But they have the disadvantages of higher weight and complexity of a deployed solar array drive motor and therefore for low power satellites spin type of stabilization is preferred.

12.3. Altitude and Orbit Control

The necessity of altitude and orbit control of the communication satellite was discussed in Sections 2.9 and 2.10. Corrections to achieve these are obtained by certain manoeuvres. These are carried out by control loops based on error detection and decision systems. These also involve the use of telemetry, telecommand (TTC) subsystem for information exchange between satellite and earth. The altitude control may be *passive* or *active*. In the former case the required altitude corresponds to a position of stable equilibrium of the satellite. In the latter, the satellite is unstable, or insufficiently stable within the desired altitude configuration. For active attitude control four operations are needed, namely :

(*i*) detection of the satellite altitude,
(*ii*) comparison with the reference axis,
(*iii*) determination of the corrective torques and
(*iv*) correction of the altitude by actuators mounted on the satellite.

To carry out above mentioned operations various kinds of sensors are used which infact detect the satellite altitude. For this purpose a variety of sensors such as sun sensors, earth horizon sensors, stellor sensors, inertial sensors, radio frequency sensors and laser sensors are being used. However, in most of the communication satellite systems the earth and sun sensors are used for altitude control. From these sensors the altitude is determined. The position of earth sensor is evident typically in INSAT of Fig. 12.1 Actually the earth sensor is a passive infrared device that has a pencil beam field of view and operates in the 14-to-16 μm wavelength carbon dioxide absorption band. It senses the infrared rays radiating from the earth's surface by scanning the boundary of the horizon between the earth and space. Normally two such earth sensors are used. They are about 5° north and 5° south of the spin plane respectively and provide the output radiance pulse as they scan the earth. In case these pulses are in-phase the attitude of the satellite is considered to be correctly maintained otherwise the spin axis would be inclined at an angle. In such a case the phase difference of the output pulses of North earth sensor and south earth sensors is utilized to control the altitude of the satellite. These are capable of allowing the altitude determination to an accuracy of ± 0.02°. It may be noted that earth sensors are sometimes also called horizon sensors.

The sun sensors provide data which are used primarily during transfer orbit. It has a fan shaped field of view and operates in visual spectral range. It is a photovoltaic device in which a current flows when it is illuminated by sunlight. The sun sensors can measure the angle between the direction of the sun and an axis related to the satellite within a tolerance of about 0.005°.

It might be recalled that in Sections 2.9 and 2.10 it has been mentioned that manouvering of altitude control involves firing of thrusters mounted on the satellite. Firing thrusters provides the required correcting torque to the satellite. The usual torque required for correcting torque is of the order of 10^{-4} to 10^{-1} Nm. In addition to these thrusters the other actuators for providing the correction torques are momentum devices such as those of reaction wheels and control moment gyroscopes ; magnetic coils and solar sails. Solar sails use the effect of solar radiation pressure to create a torque. The mounting of solar sail is also evident in INSAT of Fig. 12.1. Actually at a geostationary altitude the solar radiation pressure creates a significant disturbance torque and this disturbance torque is minimized by solar sail. It should be remembered that the altitude control that holds the spin axis within a $\pm 0.2°$) range is performed at intervals of approximately 6 days. Similarly the station keeping (accuracy of $\pm 0.05°$) manoeuvres (of the order of $\pm 0.05°$) are carried out at intervals of about of 21 days for east west manoeuvres and 28 days for north south manoeuvres.

It would be worthwhile to mention here that the above altitude control techniques are useful mainly for the spin stabilized satellites. For three axis body stabilized satellite, however, stabilization is achieved with a bias momentum system. Here a high speed wheel is used that provides the gyroscopic stability of the satellite. Magnetic torquing, wheel speed control and wheel axis trim automatically correct attitude errors after initial acquisition. Actually pitch axis is controlled by wheel speed changes and roll and yaw axis are controlled by magnetic torquing. In fact, these torques are converted into bias modulation on the ground observation that is programmed into the on-board control logic.

12.4. Propulsion Sub-system

The propulsion subsystem is the reaction control subsystem carried by the satellite in the geostationary orbit so as to generate forces on it whenever needed. The reaction control system has a supply of fuel and it helps the satellite to move to its assigned position in orbit, to maintain it in that position (station keeping) and to maintain the direction of spin axis attitude control in the face of forces that perturb it. Usually the propulsion subsystem is considered to comprise of 3 units namely

(*i*) low thrust (10^{-3} to 20N) actuators (Reaction Control System: RCS) devoted to attitude and orbit corrections that provide an annual velocity increment of the order of 50m/s ; and (*ii*) a high thrust (400 to 50,000 N) motor (Apogee Kick motor : AKM or Apogee Boost Motor : ABM) which provides the velocity increment required for the geostationary orbit injection at the transfer orbit apogee (about 1500 m/s) and (*iii*) with space shuttle launched satellites, eventually a perigee kick motor (PKM) which provides the velocity increment required to inject the satellite into the transfer orbit (about 2430 m/s).

Out of the above three units of propulsion subsystem the low thrust actuators are of much importance for geostationary orbit as these are responsible for keeping the satellite in orbit with its perfect attitude till its life end. The low thrust actuators or simply the thrusters can be either chemical ones or the electrical ones. The chemical thrusters have a thrust level of between 0.5 N and few 10000 N. On the other hand the electrical thrusters produce thrust only in between 2 and 10 mN and therefore chemical thrusters are being used in communication satellites. It is essential for a thruster that it should provide the specific impulse with smaller mass because weight on board satellites is limited.

In chemical thrusters, the gases are generated at high temperatures by chemical reaction of propellents which may be either solid or liquid. The gases are then accelerated by a nozzle. Solid propellent motors are used to provide the required velocity increment for orbital injection. The most popular liquid propellent is hydrazine (N_2H_4) which vaporizes and decomposes when in contact with a catalyst and thus produces a hot gas. This hot gas is a mixture of nitrogen, hydrogen and ammonia at temperatures of 900°C. A satellite typically would need 200-300 pounds of hydrazine on board to carry out all of its functions over its life time. Some satellites use electrothermal hydrazine thrusters (EHT) that provides the large specific impulse of the order of 300s. Here the temperature of the gas before existing through the nozzle may reach upto 1900°C. These provide a considerable savings in the mass of fuel to be carried with the satellite.

A further savings over the conventional combination of a solid apogee kick motor and a hydrazine reaction control system is being obtained by the use of bipropellent spacecraft propulsion systems for both the geostationary satellite orbit injection and on-orbit control. The bipropellent systems are based on spontaneous combustions resulting from the contact of two propellents for instance monomethyl hydrazine (combustible) and nitrogen tetroxide (oxident).

The electric thrusters provide thrust by accelerating ionized mass in an electromagnetic or electrostatic field. Though it gives low thrust (less than 0.1 N) but the specific impulse is very high (1000 to 10000s). However it needs a high voltage power supply that means an increase in the size of solar arrays. Electric thrusters are mainly of two types, the plasma thrusters and the ion thrusters. Plasma thrusters employ a solid fuel rod (Teflon) that is spring fed to the thruster. In ion thrusters changed particles are accelerated to high velocities by means of a high voltage grid system. Thus, it is evident that these electric thrusters are capable of providing specific impulses as high as 8000 to 10000s and so in principle the on board propellent mass of a electric thrusters should be lower compared with chemical thrusters. But as mentioned already, these demand an additional solar energy and so require an increase in the size of the solar arrays. These are therefore much useful only for extended satellite life time (more than seven years).

12.5. Repeaters/Transponders

Repeaters and antenna together make the communication subsystems of communication satellite. These provide the receive and transmit coverage for the satellite. Repeaters are also termed transponders. It performs two basic functions, namely (*i*) the amplification of signals from an input power of the range of -100 db W to an output power of about 10 db W (around 110 db gain) and (*ii*) the frequency down conversion (frequency translation) that avoids interference between transmitted signal and the weak incoming signal. The repeaters which perform the above functions are conventional repeaters. Sometimes there is also a provision of detection and demodulation process in the satellite transponders. Such transponders are called *regenerative transponders.*

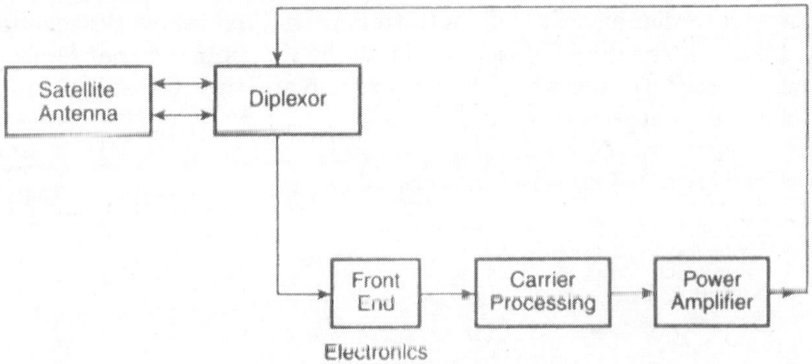

Fig. 12.2. Block Diagram of a Conventional Satellite Repeater/Transponders.

Fig. 12.2 indicates the block diagram of a conventional satellite repeater. Here the front end electronics is responsible for receiving the up link carrier, carrier processing for frequency translation and the power amplifier for bringing the signal to the desired power level. In the regenerative repeater the front end electronics would perform the receiving and detecting the uplink carrier. Carrier processing for demodulation of the detected uplink at lower carrier frequency and the power amplifier for bringing the demodulated carrier to the desired power level. There are certain advantages in regenerative repeaters over conventional repeaters such as advantages in decoding, generation of spot beams (power concentration) and interference rejection.

As it is evident, in Fig. 12.2, the same antenna is being used by the satellite for receiving the uplink and transmitting the downlink. Such antenna working is possible through the use of an electronic device called diplexor which is actually a two way microwave gate. This diplexor permits received carrier signals from the antenna and the transmitted carrier signals to the antenna to be independently coupled into and out of the antenna cabling. Since both the receive and transmit carriers are at different frequency so there would be no interference among them during their propagation through same cabling and antenna feeds.

The front end electronics system has usually the units as that shown in block diagram of Fig. 12.3. It consists of RF filtering, equalization and amplification. RF filters are typically constructed as microwave filters (waveguide filters) which are actually the integrated circuits and allow better packaging, lower weight and require less power. These filters are designed to achieve desired mask, noise rejection and equalization. Further, they should not have any significant contribution to circuit noise. Depending upon the requirements, either of the Butterworth, Chebyshev, Bessel and Legends filters may be used. It should be remembered that almost every filter introduces the delay distortion and then the equalizer is needed to cancel (correct) it.

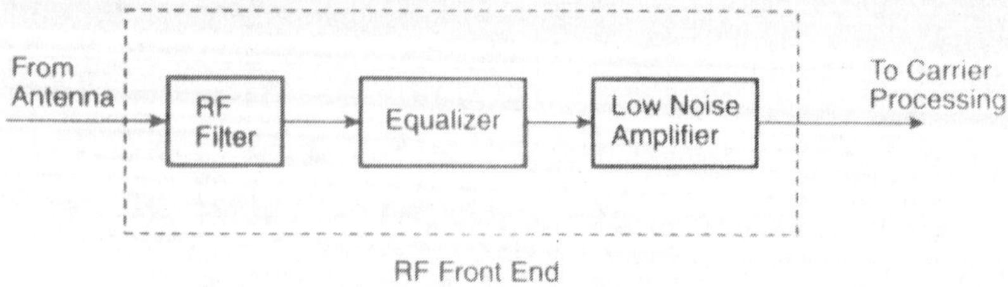

Fig. 12.3. Block Diagram of Front end Electronic System.

The equalizers are designed to behave in such a way that while they cancel delay distortion. In most of the present day communication satellite repeaters dual mode filters using cavity coupling are being used. These have centre frequency to band width ratios of about 10^4 at *C* band and about 10^3 at *K* bands. Thus at *C* band carrier filters have RF bandwidth of about 36 MHz.

The low noise amplifiers have high gain characteristics. These are basically solid state microwave amplifiers such as tunnel diode amplifiers (TDA) having their inherent low noise contributions and moderately high power gains. Such LNAs are being universally used for *C* band satellites. TDAs have the disadvantages of decreasing gain values at the higher microwave frequencies (> 10 GHz) and so now are being replaced by Field Effect Transistor amplifiers for *K* band satellite.

The carrier processing equipment determines whether the repeater is conventional one or the regenerative one. Its main work is frequency translation, *i.e.* to bring the uplink signal to a lower frequency for down link. Thus, there may be 4 different kinds of frequency translation in the satellite repeater as shown in Fig. 12.4. These may be RF-RF translation, RF-IF translation, IF remodulation and demodulation-remodulation. In Fig. 12.4 (*a*) a direct RF-to-RF conversion is carried out using a single mixer system. In the second method [Fig. 12.4 (*b*)] double conversion namely the RF to IF and IF to RF is carried out using a single local oscillator. This RF-IF-RF conversion has the advantages of operations such as those of carrier filtering and amplification going on mainly at IF band rather than at RF band. Further these allow uplink command carriers to be more easily removed (or newly telemetry carriers inserted) at the satellite before return retransmission.

In Figs. 12.4 (*c*) and (*d*) the regenerative frequency translators are shown. Actually these regenerative frequency translators or the remodulating processors involve a stage of modulation that generates the return carrier. In Fig. 12.4. (*c*) it is carried out by first translating the uplink RF spectrum down to a low IF band and then modulating the entire IF onto the return RF. In Fig. 12.4 (*d*) firstly the uplink carrier is demodulated to baseband and then this baseband is remodulated onto the return carrier. This last method of demodulation-remodulation have the advantages that the remodulation removes the uplink noise and interference from the return modulation. Also, these allow for the uplink commands transmitted with the carrier modulation to be recovered during the demodulation and the satellite telemetry to be inserted into the

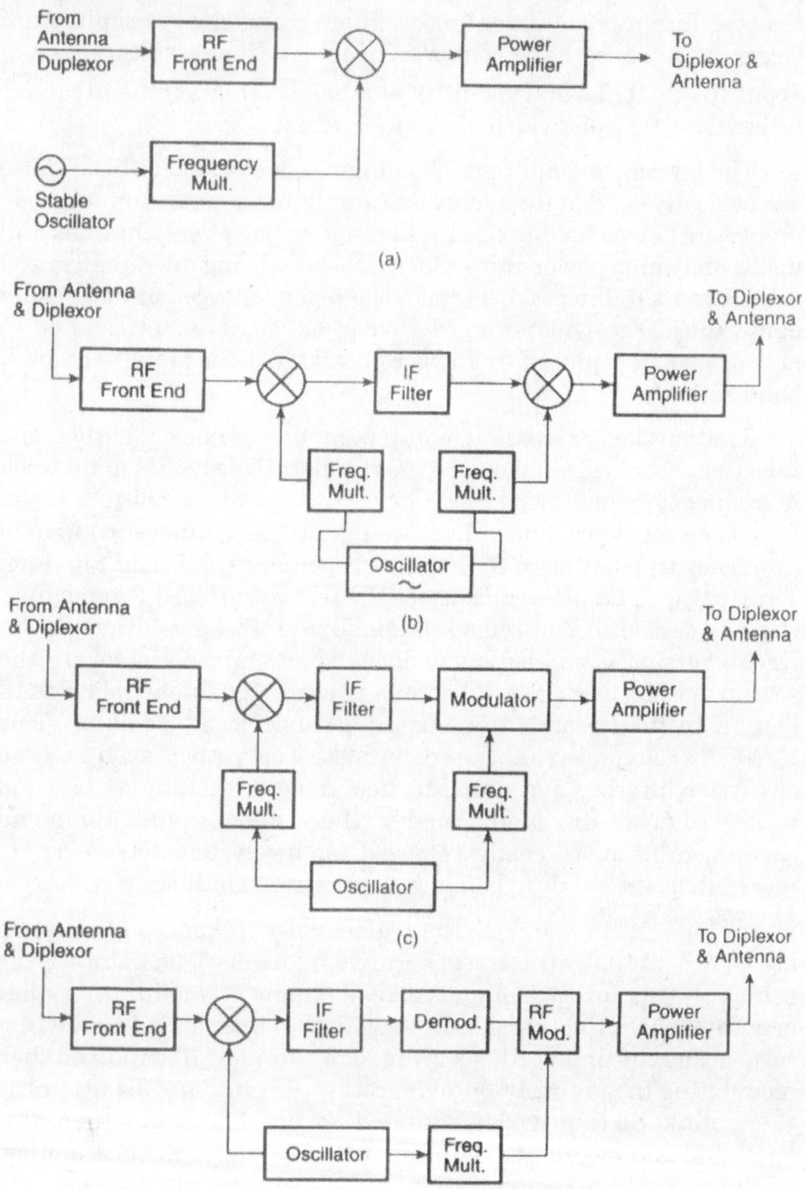

Fig. 12.4. Various Frequency Translation Systems
(*a*) RF-RF Translation (*b*) RF-IF-RF Translation (*c*) IF Remodulation
(*d*) Demodulation-Remodulation.

baseband for downlink modulation. It may be noted that often transponder signal processing includes hard limiting following frequency translation. Such hard limiters are non-linear device and are usually followed by bandpass filters tuned to the input carrier frequency. Such combined limiter-filter is also referred to as a *bandpass limiter (BPL)*.

After frequency translation, the next unit of transponder is the power amplifier. Travelling Wave Tube Amplifiers (TWTA) are commonly used as power amplifiers for satellites. The size of TWTA depends on the mission and their typical values are such as output saturated power : from 8.5 to 20 W (150 to 250 W for direct broadcasting applications), saturated gain: about 55 dB, carrier to intermodulation noise power ratio at saturation: 10 to 12 dB and AM/PM conversion coefficient: about 4.5°/db. Since the TWTA establishes the transponder output power so it is normally operated near saturation to achieve the desired output. Further since TWTAs amplify primarily the constant amplitude carriers so variations in input carrier amplitudes during amplification may produce an undesired phase interference on the amplified carrier.

Thus TWTA is the dominant non-linear device in the transponder that may affect the link signal performance significantly. Its effect on FDMA has already been discussed in Section 4.9. It is therefore necessary to have proper input control of the operating drive power of TWTA. This is being achieved by using a BPL-amplifier combination in front of high power TWTAs. It would be worthwhile to mention here that with the emerging solid state technology, solid state power amplifier (SSPA) are also recommended in place of TWTAs. These SSPAs make use of GaAs FET devices and are lighter in weight, more linear and offer a significant improvement in reliability which eventually would provide increased transponder capacity.

The above has been the discussion for the satellite repeater which has got single channel only. In case it is channelized one then the return *transponder* will refer to *one channel* of the channelized satellite repeater. Thus whereas the past satellite repeaters were of single channel the modern satellite repeater have several channels because of the availability of present day technology of reduction of weight, volume and power loss of the channel elements, *e.g.* filters, driver, attenuator, TWT etc. Moreover, the technology of launching satellites with heavier payloads has also considerably improved and thus allowing for more channels in satellite repeater. The Indian National Satellite INSAT-1 has 12 channel satellite repeater.

In such channelized satellite repeaters the two additional units are used, namely the input multiplexers (IMUX) and the output multiplexers (OMUX). The input multiplexer separates the 500 MHz bandwidth into individual transponder channels whose bandwidth depends on the satellite's mission. For example, a 500 MHz bandwidth can be divided into 8 transponder channels with a centre-to-centre frequency separation of 61 MHz. With the frequency reuse, in such a case there would be altogether 16 transponder channels in the satellite. The input multiplexers usually consist of input circulators, input filters, group delay equalizers, amplitude equalizers and output circulators. Fig. 12.5 indicates the basic block diagram of such an input multiplexer system.

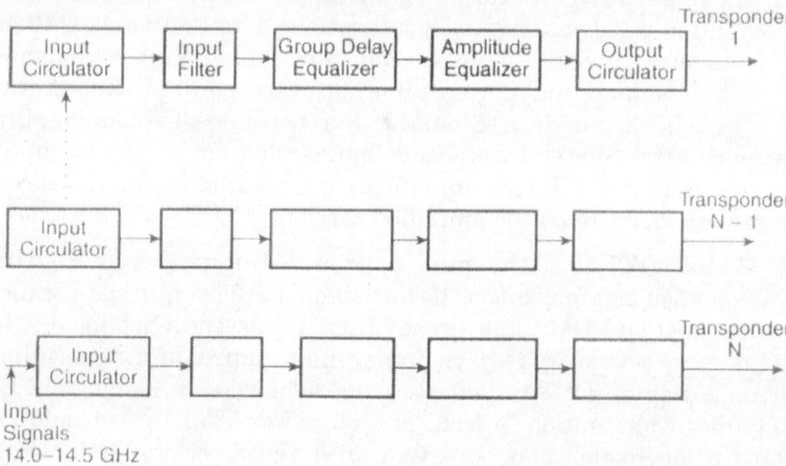

Fig. 12.5. Basic Block Diagram of Input Multiplexer System.

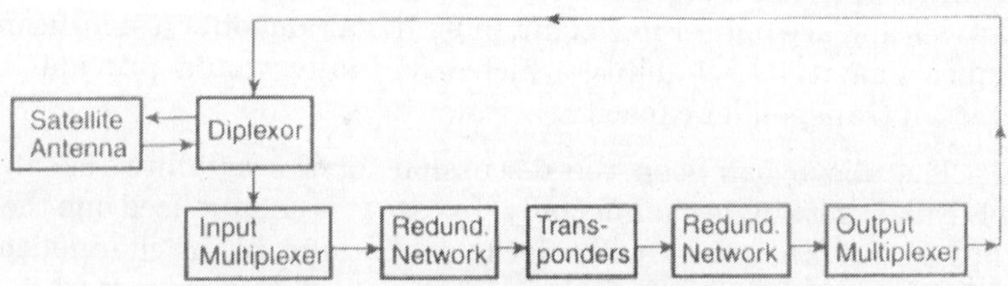

Fig. 12.6 Basic Block Diagram of a Channelized Satellite Repeater.

Similarly the output down link signals from TWTAs of different channel transponders are combined by the output multiplexer for retransmission to earth. The output multiplexer provides the required output out of band attenuation as well as the attenuation necessary to suppress signal harmonics and spurious noise generated by the TWTAs. Further for achieving the required reliability some kind of redundancy is to be incorporated both at the input and the output sides. Thus with all these modifications and additions the revised form of satellite repeater which was shown in Fig. 12.2 may be redrawn for channelized satellite repeater as per Fig. 12.6.

12.6. Antenna Systems

Antennas are another part of satellite communication subsystem. In fact the antennas on board the satellite serve as an interface between the earth stations on the ground and various satellite sub-systems during operations. Antennas receive the uplink signals and transmit the downlink signals. In addition they provide a signal link for the satellite telemetry, command and ranging systems which in conjunction with the attitude control subsystem provides beacon tracking signals for precise pointing of the antenna toward the earth coverage areas. The design of a satellite antenna is conditioned by the required coverage. It should be remembered that antennas are one of the key elements in a satellite communication system since their gain values directly determine the amount of received power.

However, it is the antenna pattern that describes the antenna characteristics required in the satellite communication. These are the gain (maximum value of the gain pattern), the beamwidth (a measure of the angle over which most of the gain occurs). In satellite communication it is essential that the desirable antenna patterns should be highly directional with high maximum gain concentrated over a narrow bandwidth with negligibly small sidelobe transmission.

Satellite communication system uses a variety of antenna system. These may be linear dipole, helix, horn, antenna array and the parabolic reflector. However, the parabolic reflector is the most commonly used one as it gives a highly directional symmetric pattern. The dipole produces a radiation pattern that is hemispherical. Helix and horn antennas are of small sizes and also produce reasonable directivity. But these antennas have several sidelobes much higher than parabolic reflectors. An array consisting of group of small antennas such as dipoles, horns or helics produce a combined beam with directivity.

Array have the advantages that by properly selecting the phase shifts between array elements the directivity of the beam may be oriented in a given direction. Moreover, the gain of arrays increases with the number of array elements and hence high gain is achieved with large arrays. Also, here the beamwidth changes with the beam direction, being narrowest for broadside beams and larger for axis beams. It is due to this reason that in most of the present day communication satellites phased array antennas are being used.

Among the antennas mentioned above, satellite communication utilizes reflector antennas both in communication sub-system as well as in the earth station. This reflector is the parabolic reflector or dish either with a front feed or rear (cassagrainian) feed. In reflector antennas there is oftenly the problem of aperture blocking effect which causes loss in the antenna gain and increase in sidelobes in the radiation pattern. This problem of aperture blocking is reduced by using an offset reflector configuration where an offset portion of the parabolic reflecting surface is used instead of an on axis portion. Moreover, an offset configuration can more easily be accommodated in satellite design especially when it is necessary to deploy the reflector after launching.

Inspite of these advantages, offset reflector, however, generates cross polarized component in the antenna radiation field when it is illuminated by a linearly polarized field and similarly when circular polarization is employed, the antenna beam is squinted from the electrical boresight. These problems create trouble when frequency reuse technique is used by orthogonal polarization. In frequency reuse two reflectors are needed for generating orthogonally polarized beam one for earth polarization. In actual practice these two reflectors are incorporated into a single physical structure. In such cases the single structure consists of two polarization-selective grided offset parabolic reflectors stacked one behind the other to facilitate aperture sharing. These two reflectors are fed by two independent multihorn arrays which do not interfere with each other either physically or electrically.

To provide high gain for the coverage areas, multiple beams or shaped beams may be required by the communications antenna. These may be designed by using a primary feed composed of an array or a set of feeds located in the vicinity of the focal point. Thus if the primary feed would consist of an array of feeds driven at same frequency by a beam forming network, the combination of the electric fields radiated by the individual feeds would result in shaped beam. Separate offset feeds generate distinct beams at a specific frequency and in a given direction, resulting in a multi-spot beam coverage. This technique is thus capable of providing a beam lattice coverage when the number of beams (and hence of feeds) is not too large.

In large communication satellites which operate at several frequency bands with different coverage zones, the primary feeds are designed in such a way that several primary feed arrays share one reflector. The problem of putting all such feed arrays at a focal point is overcome by the use of polarization and/or frequency sensitive surfaces which allow orthogonally polarized waves or waves at different frequencies to be focussed at distinct locations. It would be of importance to mention here that in multiple beam techniques it is essential that the antenna beams must be accurately pointed to avoid deviation of the beam boresight from its nominal direction. Typical antenna pointing accuracies are $\pm 0.05°$ for east-west (pitch) and north-south (roll) beam pointing errors and $\pm 0.2°$ for beam radiation (yaw) errors. Lens antennas are also used in multiple beam antenna technique and these have the advantages over offset reflector antennas to be axisymmetric and hence offering large cross polarization isolation.

Conclusively, in the satellite antenna it is essential that the antenna mainlobe should be such that the energy is concentrated towards the earth station and hence maximizing the EIRP. However, it is found that if the mainlobe consideration is given prime importance, the orbit utilization of the satellite will not be efficient. Therefore CCIR has recommended sidelobe radiation patterns which have a compromising effect on the orbit utilization and interference reduction. Further, the idea of scanning spot beams has also been introduced in some satellites for efficient coverage of the desired area. Deployable antennas (large reflectors) are also being used which give high directivity. The deployable antennas are made of fine mesh so that they may not be affected by the solar radiation pressure.

12.7. Telemetry, Tracking & Command (TTC) Sub-System

TTC sub-system is the most essential sub-system of the satellite because it keeps the satellite in working order and all sorts of manoeuvre are carried out through them. TTC sub-system involves the earth station and infact is a part of satellite management task. The main functions of TTC sub system are, namely ; (*i*) the transmission of house-keeping information and status of the satellite to the ground control station, (*ii*) carrying out angular and range measurement to permit localization of the satellite and (*iii*) receiving command signals from the ground control station to initiate attitude and station keeping manoeuvres and operations of the onboard equipments. For these functions frequencies used are at vhf or in (S band) during launch phase and in the frequency band allocated for main satellite telecommunications (6/4 GHz) during on station. It should be noted that in TTC sub-system, tracking is primarily done by the earth station.

The telemetry system provides a data stream to the ground that reports on each of the satellite sub-systems independent of any other communications link. This is achieved by the signals obtained from a variety of large number of sensors mounted on the satellite. Typical example of information collected by sensors are about the pressure in fuel tanks, voltage and current in the power conditioning unit, current drawn by each sub-system, critical voltages and currents in the communication electronics, temperature of other sub-systems, position of switches, altitude etc. Thus there are over 100 different kinds of sensors mounted on the satellite for the purpose.

There is a separate telemeter transmitter in the satellite which transmits the telemetry data *via* the communication antenna when the satellite is in orbit and in normal on station. When the satellite is in transfer orbit, the telemeter transmitter is connected to a TWTA in a satellite repeater. This then transmits telemetry data *via* an omni antenna mounted on the satellite. The telemetry data are digitized and transmitted as frequency of phase shift keying (FSK or PSK) of a low power telemetry carrier using time division techniques. The TTC earth station contains the necessary equipment to insert commands, receive and interpret the telemetry and compute orbital parameter.

For command operation, the satellite contains a receiver which works only for command signals transmitted from TTC earth station. Through this receiver the command sub-system controls the satellite operations through all phases of the mission by receiving and decoding command from the TTC earth station. The command sub-system also generates a verification signal and upon receipt of an execute signal carries out the commands. When the satellite is in synchronous orbit (on-station), communications antenna is used for command and ranging. During the satellite's position in transfer orbit the omni antenna is used for command and ranging. Actually during the launch phase and injection into geostationary orbit a back-up system is used which provides control of the apogee boost motor, the attitude control system and orbit control thrusters, the solar sail deployment machanism (if fitted), and the power conditioning unit. This back-up system works with the omni antenna mentioned above. Once the satellite is in geostationary orbit, the main TTC sub-system works.

Tracking consists of determination of the current orbit of the satellite. This is done by determining the range which in turn determines the orbital elements. The TTC earth station can observe the Doppler Shift of the telemetry carrier or beacon transmitter carrier to determine the rate at which range is changing. Another way of determining the change in orbit is by using the velocity and accelerator sensors on the spacecraft that establish a change in orbit from its last known position.

Some other methods such as triangulation method of transmission and reception of sequences of pulses (ranging tones) etc. may be used to determine range. The telemeter transmitter serves also as the downlink for the ranging tones. With such techniques and precision equipments at TTC earth station it has been possible now a days to determine the position of satellite within 100 m.

12.8. Thermal Control Sub-System

Thermal control of various satellite sub-systems are essential so that the satellite may work successfully till its whole life. The thermal control sub-system therefore maintains equipments and structure of the satellite within specified temperature ranges both during operation and idle time. Since the satellite is in synchronous orbit where extremes of solar radiations are present so special care regarding extreme heat and extreme cool (when the satellite parts are in shadow), temperature variations is needed. Similarly, during operational and transfer orbit phases the temperature variation requirements are different.

This situation has made necessary for the complete thermal control of the satellite so that as the sun moves around the satellite once every 24 hours the temperature range variations around various satellite sub-systems remain in the prescribed range. The typical temperature ranges for various satellite equipment as allowed are : batteries 0°C to + 20°C, solar cells − 100°C to + 50°C, electronic equipment − 10°C to 60°C, propellent tanks + 10°C to 50°C and infrared sensors − 20°C to + 45°C. Thus the mean temperature of the satellite is the result of the thermal balance between the energy received by radiation from external sources plus the energy dissipated inside the satellite mainly due to electrical losses and the energy radiated from the satellite to the outer space. The convection heat exchange due to vacuum is not there.

As a matter of fact all the electronic packages and other components that must be maintained at the correct temperature are tested for the proper temperature control under the simulated conditions of outer space in the laboratory. The temperature variation is considered 10° beyond extreme so that there may not be any failure in weak components when they are put inside the satellites.

Further the absorptance α and emittance ξ of the surface finish with respect to solar radiation conditions for various materials are also studied. In the satellite payloads it is essential to dissipate heat and therefore radiators with a very low α/ξ finishes (α about 0.08, ξ about 0.75) are employed. These consist of fused silica mirrors width silver backing, called optical solar reflectors (OSR) or second surface mirrors (SSM) made from plastic (Teflon, Kapton or Mylar) sheets with silver or aluminium backing. These reflectors are located on the north and south panels so that they may efficiently radiate their heat towards outer space since the north and south panels are least affected by daily variations in solar incidence. Such types of thermal control systems are passive ones and are based on multilayer-superinsulation blankets which are composed of alternate layers of thin Mylar and Kapton films coated with vacuum deposited aluminium. Such passive thermal control systems are capable of providing high isolation between the satellite inside parts and outer space.

In addition to these passive thermal control systems there are also various active thermal control systems which maintain the temperature of equipments inside the satellite. These active thermal control systems are such as heat pipes, hinged flaps, multiple blade louvres and electrical heaters. The heat pipes allow adiabatic transfer of heat from heat sources to radiators by successive vaporization and condensation of a fluid at the two extremities of the pipe. The fluid used have high latent heat and therefore the heat pipes provide a high capacity for heat transfer with small temperature differences. The hinged flaps and multiple blade louvers carry out arrangements for covering the radiator areas or exposing them as per requirement. The electrical heaters provide the thermal controlling either through telecommand signals or thermostat.

Thus it is seen that the satellite thermal control systems are quite complex and essential ones. Their requirement and design vary from satellites to satellite. For example, the spin stabilized satellites will need a different thermal control system as compared to a body fixed satellite.

12.9. Structure Sub-System

This sub-system supports the equipment carried by the satellite for communication and other purposes. Therefore stiffness is of major concern here. During launch phase where mechanical stresses may be highest the structure sub-system plays a major role. Similarly the structure sub-system ensures correct positioning of onboard equipment such as alignment of sensors, thrust axes of the thrusters, axes of antenna etc. The structure sub-system allows the various separations and deployments depending upon the satellite launch vehicles. Finally it avoids electrical charge accumulation. Though the structure sub-system carries out so many essential duties, it is necessary that its mass should be only 6% of the total satellite weight. Therefore, structural materials which are light weight and have resistance to deformation such as aluminium and magnesium alloys, honeycomb panels, bonded assemblies and carbon fibre reinforced plastic materials are used for structure purpose.

12.10. Reliability of Satellite Sub-System

It is expected that the satellite should work satisfactorily over its specified life. The reliability is the parameter through which such characteristics of the satellite operation is expressed. In fact reliability is the probability that the system will perform satisfactorily over its specified life. Since the satellite involves mostly electronic equipment and components so the reliability of satellite sub-systems will depend on the probability of failure of these electronic components. The probability of failure of electronic components is like a bath tube curve as shown in Fig. 12.7. In other words, for electronic components the probability of failure is higher at the beginning of life-the burn in period-than at some later time. Also as the component ages, failures become more likely.

Thus once the satellite is in synchronous orbit, it cannot be repaired and so several steps are already taken before the launch itself so that components remain useful for most of the satellite life time. For this purpose the components are rigorously tested under stimulated space and environmental conditions and then these are fitted with the satellite payloads.

Mathematically the reliability of a device or sub-system is defined as

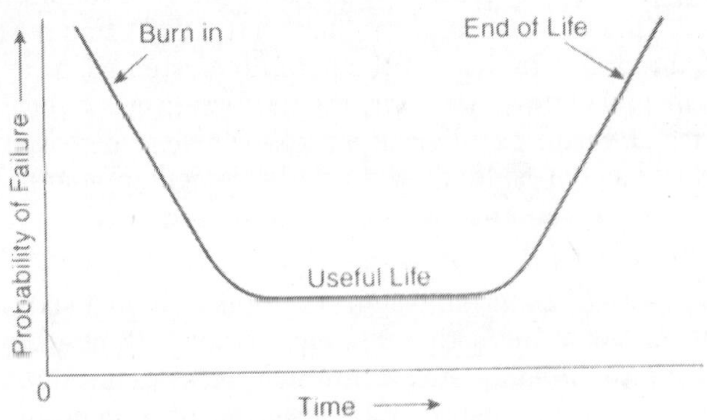

Fig. 12.7. Probability of Failure (Bath Tub) Curve.

$$R(t) = \frac{N_s(t)}{N_o}$$

$$= \frac{\text{Number of surviving components at time } t}{\text{Number of components at start of test period}} \quad ...(12.1)$$

Another important parameter in reliability studies is the *mean time before failure* (MTBF) defined as

$$MTBF = m = \frac{1}{N_o} \sum_{i=1}^{N_0} t_i \quad ...(12.2)$$

where t_i represents the time after which the *ith* device fails. MTBF is related to average failure rate λ by the formula

$$\lambda = \frac{1}{MTBF} \quad ...(12.3)$$

Failure rate (λ) is often given as the average failure rate per 10^9 hours. In terms of λ the reliability of the sub-system or device of Eq. (12.1) is given by

$$R = e^{-\lambda t} \quad ...(12.4)$$

which indicates that the reliability of a device decreases exponentially with t. In other words, after infinite time there will be zero reliability indicating a certain failure. However, in practice the end of useful life is usually taken to be the time t_e at which R fails to 0.37 or $(1/e)$ which is when

$$t_e = \frac{1}{\lambda} = m \quad ...(12.5)$$

Eqs. (12.4) and (12.5) indicate that the probability of a device failing has an exponential relationship to the MTBF. This is represented by the right hand end of the bathtub curve.

It is important to note here that if proper redundancy is maintained in the satellite, its reliability would be improved. Actually it is mainly with the TWTA in repeater for which redundancy is mostly provided. This is because of the fact that TWTA has a limited life time. Redundancy in most of the satellite systems is provided by a series, parallel or switched connections. Sometimes hybrid arrangement such as series/parallel connection is also provided. In practice the series/parallel connection is widely used in communications satellite transponders to provide redundancy of the high power amplifier.

Oftenly a combination of parallel and switched redundancy is used to combat failures that are catastrophic to one transponder channel and to the complete communication system. Another way of improving the relationship that has been also sometimes widely discussed is by derating, *i.e.* by reducing maximum power consumption, voltage, current, temperature or some combination of all. Actually derating reduces the wear out by a geometric relationship to the amount of derating applied.

12.11. Review Questions

1. Explain various satellite sub-systems telling their important functions and characteristics.
2. What kind of electric power supply is used in a satellite? Explain as to how precautions are taken for hostile environment regarding the smooth electric supply to various electronic components.
3. What are the altitude and orbit control sub-systems? Explain as to how these perform their functions.
4. What is the propulsion sub-system? Explain its constituent and their functions. Which is the most popular propellent being used?
5. What is the communication sub-system? Of which units it is composed of? Explain the construction of a repeater telling the difference between a simple repeater and a regenerative repeater. What is the difference between a repeater and a transponder ?
6. What kinds of antenna systems are being used in satellite communication sub-system ? What is the multiple beam technique ? What precautions are taken in mounting the antennas on spin stabilized and body fixed satellites?
7. What is the telemetry, tracking and command (TTC) sub-system ? Explain its functioning. What kind of antennas are used for TTC signal transmission during transfer orbit and on orbit?
8. Explain the working of Thermal Control sub-system ? What kind of thermal control sub-systems are being used in satellite?
9. What is structure sub-system ? What kind of operation does it perform ? Which materials are preferred for the design of this sub-system?
10. What do you mean by the reliability, mean-time before failure, effective failure rate as applied to satellite sub-system and components ? How are these related to each other ? Explain the 'bath tub' curve.
11. What is the redundancy and why is it necessary for the satellite sub-system particularly in repeaters? How can the redundancy be achieved by series, parallel and switched connections ?

12.12. References

Alongwith the references mentioned in previous chapter, reference is also made to

1. Indian National Satellite System, bulletin issued by ISRO, June, 1988.
2. Gagliardi, R.M., Satellite Communication, CBS Publishers and Distributors, New Delhi, 1987.
3. Avduyevsky, V.S. and Ushensky, G.R., Scientific and Economic Oriented Space Systems, Mir Publishers, Moscow, 1988.

13

Digital Speech Coding Techniques

13.1. Introduction

Speech coding technology or digital speech technology is needed in all the present day digital voice communication systems say, it is microwave, satellite or fibre optic. Digital telephony needs telephone speech coding. These have application areas such as cellular radio systems, mobile communication (GSH), Personal Communication Networks (PCNs), ISDNs, PSTNs, and other modem digital communication systems. In the early speech coding systems, coding was used to be done at 46 kb/s PCM. The recent emphasis is on low bit rate speech coding mainly because of two reasons namely (*i*) to increase revenue and/or (*ii*) to provide a service which could not otherwise be provided.[1] In fact low bit rate codecs allow multiplexing several conversations onto a channel which would normally carry a single conversation (*e.g.* to replace one 64 k bit/s PCM channel with 8 speech channels carrying speech coded at 8 kbit/s).

Speech coding allows to compress the speech, store it and use it whenever needed. This has opened technology not only in communication but in man-machine interaction. Low bit rate coding allows speech storage at lower costs because then the amount of random access memory (RAM) or disc memory needed can be greatly reduced in voice mailbox or telephone answering machines. Low bit rate codec utilize the radio spectrum efficiently. Personal cordless and mobile communication use the low bit rate codecs. Inmarsat is currently selecting a 9.6 kbit/s codec for use in a digital aeronautical telephone service. Their robustness to digital transmission error in the services using digital radio links is added quality. High secure telephone communication systems such as digital encryption devices and modems also use low bit rate codecs. Codecs working on variable bit rates have also been designed that allow for the flexibility to mix speech and data services over the same connection.

13.2. Some Facts About Speech

The simplified electronic representation of human speech production system is shown in Fig. 13.1 (ref. 2). According to this model, speech is generated by a sound source excitation that is either pulse like during voiced regions of speech, when the vocal cords are vibrating or noise like during unvoiced regions of speech because of turbulence at points of constriction in the vocal tract[3]. This excitation is then spectrally shaped by the vocal tract which acts as a

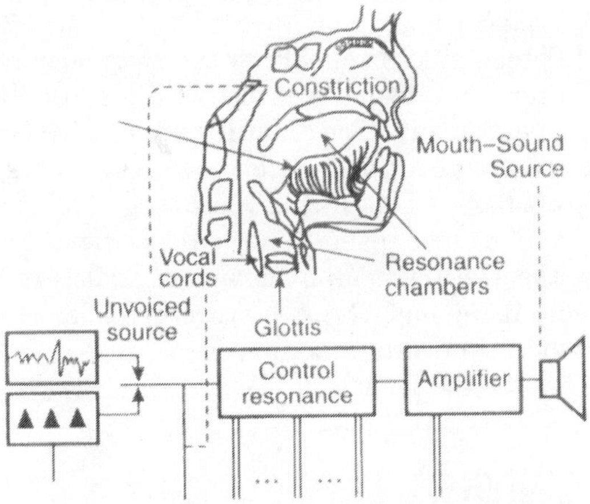

Fig. 13.1. Electronic Model of Speech Production.

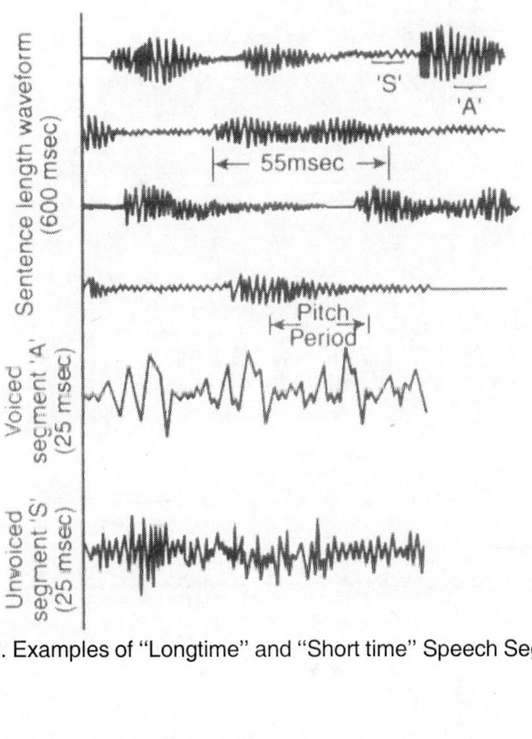

Fig. 13.2. Examples of "Longtime" and "Short time" Speech Segments.

time-varying acoustic filter. The speech waveform that is a result of this production process is shown in Fig. 13.2. When viewed over a "long" period of time (1/2 sec) speech is seen to be a highly nonstationary process due to the variation of amplitude, voiced/unvoiced/silence behaviour and the time varying vocal tract. However, over 'short' periods of time (20-40 ms), speech is locally stationary and has a well defined short-time spectrum.

The short time spectral models for the voiced and unvoiced segments of speech are given in Fig. 13.3. The envelope of the spectrum is determined primarily by the frequency response of the vocal tract filter. The resonances of this filter are observed as the peaks in the spectral envelope and they are referred to as *formants*. Typically there are about four observable resonances in the speech spectrums from 0 to 4 kHz. During voiced segments, one observes in the time waveforms a pseudo-periodic structure. This is also reflected in the spectrum as a harmonic structure in frequency. During unvoiced regions, the five structure has a noise liked appearance both in time and frequency.

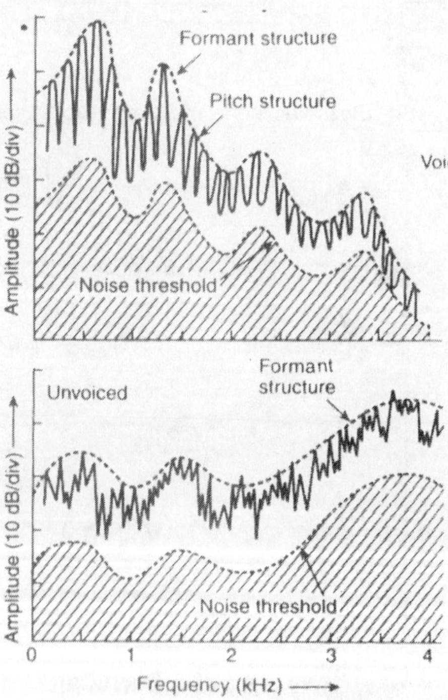

Fig. 13.3. Special Models for Voiced and Unvoiced Speech.

In the perception of human speech, the ear acts as like a Fourier spectrum analyzer or filler bank. Each channel of this and auditory filter bank appears to have its own automatic gain control and dynamic range limitations. Also, because of the construction of the ear, the presence of strong energy signals at low frequencies can interfere with and reduce the sensitivity of filter bands centered at high frequencies. This gives rise to the phenomenon called *auditory masking,* as illustrated by the shaded areas in Fig. 13.3. Essentially, any noise or distortion that is added to the signal is not perceived if it falls below this threshold.

Speech is a fascinating human attribute that can be analyzed, synthesised and recognised, it can also be compressed, stored and enchanced by digital signal processing techniques. The possible interactive speech systems and their strategic research areas are given in Fig. 13.4.

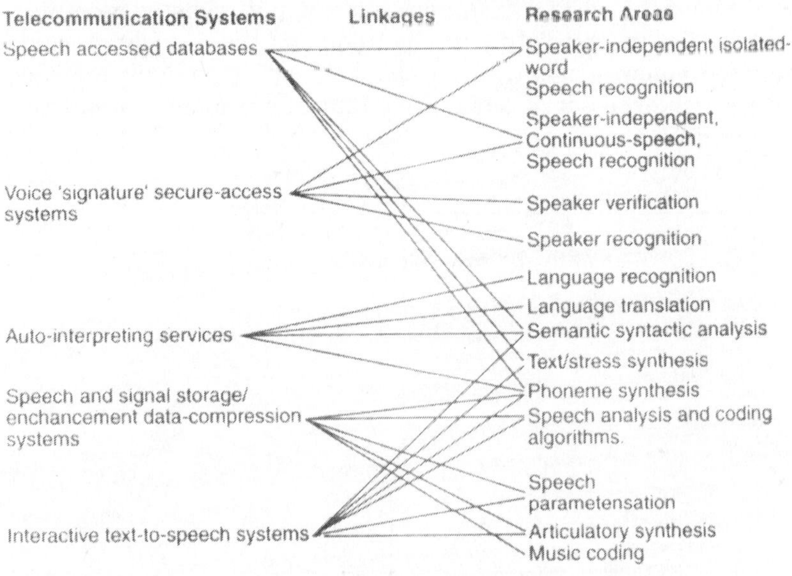

Fig. 13.4. Interactive Speech Systems and their Strategic Research Areas.

13.3. Digital Speech Quality and International Digital Telephony Standards

The bandwidth of input speech may vary from about 3 kHz to nearly 20 kHz. Measurement of speech quality is a difficult and long standing problem. A commonly used subjective rating scale of 1 to 5 is used wherever possible to quantify the level of digital speech quality. This is the so called *mean opinion score* (MOS) scale. A score of 4.0 on this scale is used to signify *high quality* or *near transparent coding*. The Term *network quality* implies high quality coding as a necessary but not sufficient condition. Sufficient requires further capabilities of the speech coder as demanded by the communication network environment. A score of 3.5 on the MOS scale denotes *communications quality*. This level of quality is characterized by a level of speech degradation that is easily detectable but not bad enough to impede natural telephone communications. The term *'Synthetic-quality' speech* implies a signal characterized by high intelligibility.

A description of current state of telephone speech coding in terms of international standards activity, bit rate, typical application and decoded speech quality is given in Fig. 13.5. The bandwidth of speech is 3.2 kHz and the quality is measured on the MOS scale of 1 to 5. It may be noted that MOS values of 4.0 and 3.5 is regarded as minimum requirement for near-transparent quality and robust communications quality respectively. Present trends in speech coding include the achievement of near transparent or transparent quality of 8 kb/s, and the achievement of robust communications quality at 4.8 kb/s and lower.

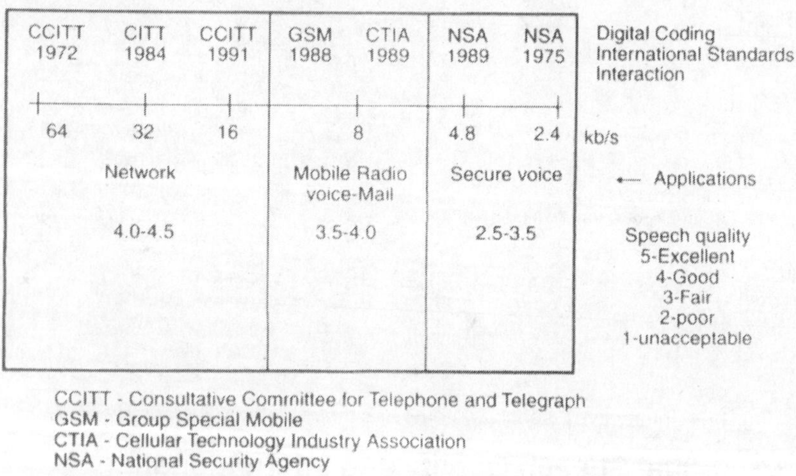

Fig. 13.5. Digital Telephony International Standards.

From Fig. 13.5 it is evident there are three major parameter in the design of a digital speech coding technique namely (*i*) the (average) binary rate, (*ii*) the overall transmission quality and (*iii*) the hardware complexity. Other considerations such as robustness to channel error and tandem behaviour are important in some applications, yet these remain secondary with respect to three basic requirements.[5]

13.4. Basic Speech Coding Methods

Basically all the existing speech coding methods may be grouped into three broad categories, namely (*i*) waveform coding where the speech signals are digitised directly from samples, (*ii*) parametric, where only certain parts of the signals are extracted and processed or hybrid using algorithms employing features of waveform and parametric coding techiques, (*iii*) vocoder (or source encoding). Fig. 13.6 indicates a quantitative description of these coding methods in terms of speech quality as a function of bit rate against the relative quality of 64 kbit/s PCM. Quality obtained by other than PCM such as ADPCM (adaptive differential pulse code modulation) SBC (Sub-band coding), MPLPC (multi pulse linear predictive coding) and LPC (linear predictive coding) are shown in Fig. 13.6.

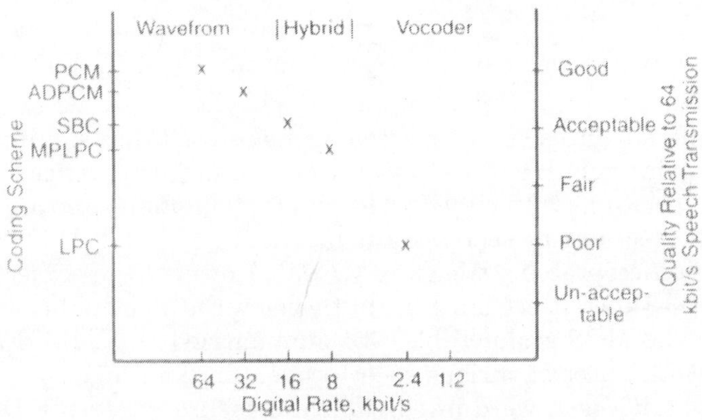

PCM = pulse code modulation
ADPCM = adaptive differential pulse code modulation
SBC = sub-band coding
MPLPC = multi-pulse linear predictive coding
LPC = linear predictive coding

Fig. 13.6. Relative Quality of Speech Coding Methods.

Generally speaking, waveform coding requires a high bit rate (>16 kbit/s) but can give speech quality suitable for use on the PSTN; vocoding requires a very lone bit rate (<4.8 kbit/s) but gives only synthetic quality speech and hybrid coding requires a low bit rate (4.8-16 Kbit/s) and gives speech quality that is not quite as good as that of waveform coders.

13.5. Low Bit Rate Speech Coding

Applications of low bit rate speech coding are already discussed in Section 13.1. The international CCITT standards for 64 kb/s PCM is G 711, for 32 kb/s ADPCM is G 721 and 16 kb/s CODER is G7 XY. In the range of 4 kb/s to 10 kb/s coding techiques are based on combined (hybrid) methods of waveform coding and vocoding. These are also known as parametric codes. They attempt to combine advantages of both methods to ahieve an intermediate performance, that is a good "Communication quality" in this bit range. Coding algorithms include PCM, ADPCM, Linear Predictive Coding (LPC) (also referred to as Vocoding), Code Excited Linear Predictive Coding (CELP) and Low-Delay CELP (LD-CELP). The CELP algorithms typify the hybrid coders.

Table 13.1 DRT, DAM and MOS Scores for Stand Speech Coders

Coder	*DRT*	*DAM*	*MOS*
64 kb/s PCM	95	73	4.3
32 kb/s ADPCM	94	68	4.1
16 kb/s LD-CELP	94	70	4.0
8 kb/s CELP	93	68	3.7
4.8 kb/s CELP	93	67	3.0
2.4 kb/s LPC	90	54	2.5

Recent advances in hybrid coding have produced significant improvements relative to 2.4 kb/s vocoding and this is reflected in 4.8 kb/s algorithms with very high levels of intelligibility and acceptability as described by scores of Diagnostic Rhyme Test (DRT) and Diagnostic Acceptability Measure (DAM). However the subjective quality of 4-8 kb/s speech is significantly below the high quality score of 4.0 on the MOS scale. Table 13.1 summarized DRT, DAM and MOS performances of various speech coders in the range 64 to 2.4 kb/s. The DRT is a word-intelligibility measure while the DAM reflects acceptability for speech communication in a broader multi-dimensional sense.

It would be worthwhile to mention here that telephone systems such as cellular telephony based on a hybrid coding algorithm at 8 kb/s has the speech quality that falls below the high quality threshold (MOS=4.0) but it provides a communication quality that is adequate to provide improvements over along FM telephony especially at low levels of radio channel quality (say, channel, signal-to-noise ratio or SNR below 15 to 18 dB). The communication delay to the speech codec is expected to be on the order of 40 ms.

13.6. Audio Coding

The audio bandwidth required for various audio systems such as in telephone, AM radio, FM radio and compact is as per given in Fig. 13.7. It is apparent that as the audio bandwidth increases the perceived gain in terms of intelligibility, naturalness and speaker recognition also increases. Low frequency enhancement contributes to increased naturalness and presence, and high frequency enhancement provides greater intelligibility and fricative differentiation. Thus, the naturalness of wideband speech is a significant feature for extended telecommunication processes such as audio conferencing and program broadcasting. Basic rate ISDN provides a natural framework for a 64 kb/s algorithm to encode wideband audio for such applications. The digital connectivity afforded by ISDN has promoted a worldwide revisiting of audio transmission quality. End to end digital connectivity in particular has made possible the inclusion of low frequencies, down to 50 Hz, in the transmitted audioband. The CCITT standard for 7 kHz audio (G. 722) is a 64 kbit/s algorithm developed primarily for ISDN teleconferencing and loud speaker telephony.

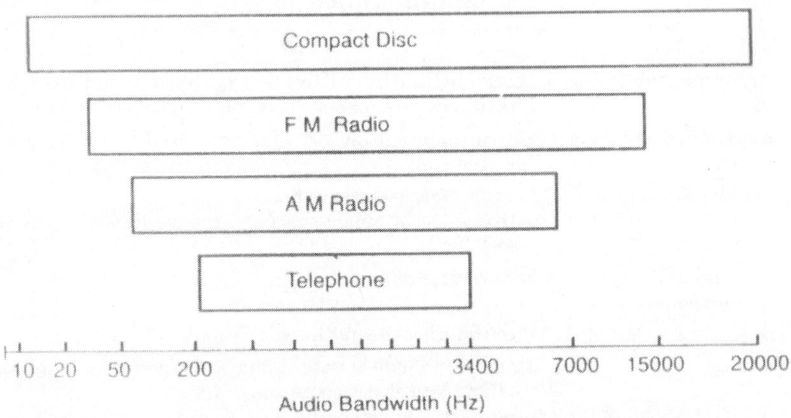

Fig. 13.7. Audio Bandwidth Requirement in Different Audio Systems

Present trends are there for coding of wideband speech at 20 kHz audio. Several applications have been listed by International Standards Organizations for 20 kHz audio coding Table 13.2 lists these. HDTV is another major application of 20 kHz digital audio.

13.7. Hardware Technology in Speech Coding

Custom chips and devices, high speed microprocessors and programmable ICs, array processors and specialized hardware have already been developed for speech coding. In the area of Waveform

Coding, Chips for complete μ law PCM A/D and D/A conversions (including anti aliasing functions) have been developed and are of interest in applications of digital telephony. Chips for ADM, ADPCM have also been available. In the vocoder area synthesizer chips or chip sets have become available. A typical example that has generated considerable attention is that of the Texas instruments 'speak and spell' chip which has been used for voice response in educational toys.

VLSI technology has helped in developing high speed microprocessors and programmable ICs. A typical example is that of Bell Lab Digital Signal processing integrated circuit which infact is a self contained processor with provision for program memory storage, data storage, address calculation, serial data input and output, and a main arithmetic unit for multiplication, accumulation and numerical roundoff and logic operations. With this device algorithms such as AD PCM and subband coding have been realized using one DSP for an encoder, a second DSP for a decode and a μ law PCM coder chip for A/D conversion.

Table 13.2. Applications of 20 kHz digital Audio recommended by ISO

Applications	*Usage*
Electronic Publishing (End user)	Integrated and interactive text, graphics, sound and video, Electronics Newspaper including text, sound, video
Electronic publishing (Production)	Digital audio editing of resource materials, for inclusion in Electronic texts
Travel guidance	Preview of city news, flight and driving simulation, interactive video in public spaces, active guidance, surrogate travel.
Educational Applications	Electronic books Remote Classroom instruction
Business Applications	Electronic books, multimedia E-mail
Games	Stand alone games with audio and video from a storage medium, Multilocation games
Entertainment Applications	MTV audio on CD, TV program and movie storage and distribution, broadband stereo distribution, Previewing Systems
Data base Applications	Audio database applications, Audio & video either with onside or off side databases
Multimedia Memo and Bulletin Board	Bulletin board, computer conferencing with multi-media memos including audio, face to face teleconferencing
Broadcast Sound	Production, transmission of 'Contribution quality' audio transmission for distribution, digital audio broadcasting
Multimedia Art & Medical Applications	Education

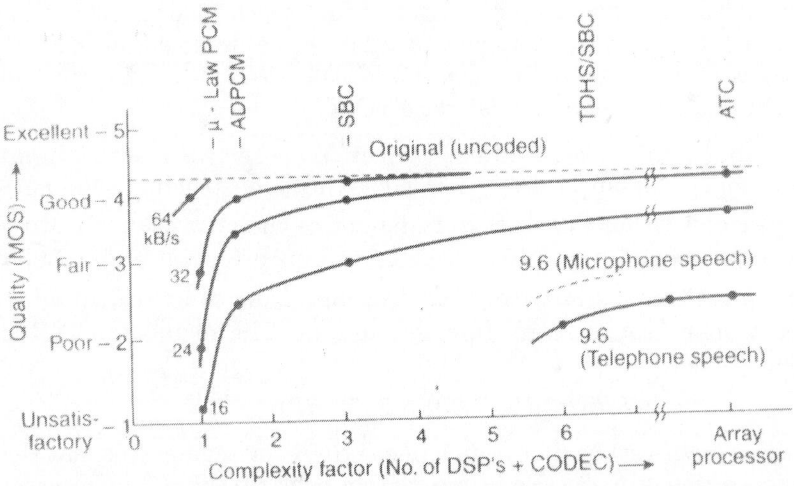

Fig. 13.8. Performance Versus bit rate and complexity for some speech codecs.

For algorithms of high complexity such as adoptive predictive coding, adaptive transform coding and vocoder analyzers, this microprocessor approach is not sufficient. However, these algorithms have been realized in real time using array processing computers or special purpose hardware. As VLSI technology advances it is believed to have a chip of the above approach which will be infact single-chip DSP type processor.

Note that there are three key tradeoffs that are of interest in the design of a speech codec, namely (*i*) overall quality, (*ii*) Cost or complexity and (*iii*) required bit rate. Fig. 13.8 illustrates these tradeoffs for some of the hardware realizations of speech coding. The vertical scale corresponds to measure of speech quality based on 1 to 5 MOS scale. The horizontal scale reflects a rough a measure of hardware complexity based on a total count of DSP chips plus the μ law codecs. The curves represent different bit rates, and points on the curves correspond to actual hardware realizations. It is evident that as the coding at low bit rate is done the complexity factor in the codec realization tremendously increases.

13.8. Speech Coder Performance

Speech Coder's performance in terms of speech quality measured on MOS scale of 1 to 5 is infact subjective one. For example, MOS values are very difficult to duplicate in repetitions of an experiment and several factors may contribute to its variability. In digital communications systems, toll quality speech and broad-cast-quality images cannot be always defined by means of an MOS requirement alone. An objective test for speech coder performance can be done by means of measuring its signal to noise ratio, *SNR*, Segmental Signal to noise ratio, *SNRSEG*, *SNR MAX*; *SNRMIN* and Signal to uncorrelated noise ratio, SNR_u.

In digital speech coding, the difference between coder input $x(n)$ and coder output (n) is defined as the reconstruction error $r(n)$. The signal to noise ratio *SNR* is defined as the ratio σ_x^2/σ_r^2, the ratio of input signal variance to reconstruction error variance. Coder designs that maximize the *SNR* by minimizing σ_r^2 are called minimum mean square error (mm se) designs. The segmental SNR is defined as,

$$SNSREG\ (dB) = E\ [SNR\ (m)\ dB]$$

where *SNR* (m) is that connectional *SNR* for segment m and the expectation is in practice a time average over all segments of interest in an input sequence. An appropriate segment length in speech work is in the order of 16 ms.

SNRMAX and *SNRMIN* give maximum and minimum values of SNR useful for the design of coders. SNRMAX indicates SNR values giving an enhanced quality of coding that is perceptually irrelevant typical *SNRMAX* value for speech and image signals may be in the order of 35 and 50 dB, respectively. Information about *SNRMAX* can prevent overdesigns of coders. *SNRMIN* values lie in the range of 0 to –20 dB. SNR_u in defined as signal to uncorrelated noise ratio given by

$$E[x^2\ (n)]/E\ [R_u^2(n)]$$

where $E\ [R_u^2\ (n)]$ is the residual uncorrelated noise power that is due to mainly input dependent components present in the reconstruction error. An example of such problems occurs during slope overload distortion in differential coding of speech and image signals SNR_u is found to be more meaningful than conventional total error variance.

References

1. Southcott, C.B. *et al,* low bit rate speech coding for practical applications Br Telecomm ; J., 6 (1988), 22-40.
2. Wheddon, C., Speech Communication, *ibid*, pp. 7-21.
3. Crochiere, R.E. and Flanagan, J-L., Current perspectives in Digital speech , IEEE Communications Magazine, January 1983. pp. 32-40.
4. Jayant, N.S., High quality coding of Telephone speech and Wideband Audio, IEEE Communications Magazine, January 1990. pp. 10-20.
5. Feher, K., Advanced Digital Communications Systems and Signal Processing Techniques, Prentice-Hall, Inc., 1987.

14

Echo-Cancellation

14.1. Introduction

In long distance telephone communication systems such as those through satellite link delayed echo is a great source of irritation and a variety of echo suppressors and cancellers, therefore, have been developed in practice. Fig. 14.1 is an illustration of a typical long distance telephone circuit indicating the echo travel emanating from an impedance mismatch such as that from a hybrid coupler. These hybrid couplers are located at the two wire/four wire interfaces in the telephone circuit. These devices, made up of inductive elements in a balanced bridge configuration are passive four port directional couples as shown in Fig. 14.2.

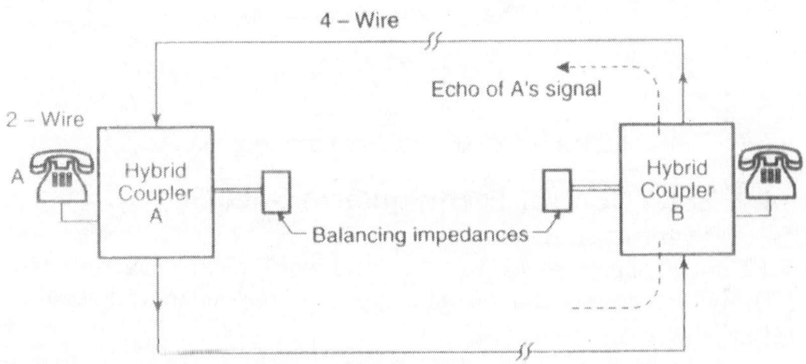

Fig. 14.1. Model for long distance telephone circuit. The four carrier section may possibly include a satellite link.

The ideal hybrid Coupler shall pass an incoming signal from "in" port to its "two-wire" port attenuating it by 3dB and does not pass any thing to the "out port". Conversely, it passes (again with 3 db - attenuation) signals from the two-wire port to the "out" port without reflecting any energy back into the two-wire line. However, this ideal performance is obtained only if the balancing impedance (Z_{BAL}) is equal to the impedance presented by the two wire line. Since many different local loops have access to a given hybrid coupler, it is very likely that a fixed balancing impedance will always be unsatisfactory. Considerable leakage and reflection signal may be generated by the hybrid computer. Thus, the echoes are generated at the hybrid and at all the other impedance mismatches in the telephone circuit including those at the telephone set or other terminating device. No echos will return from within the four wire part of the circuit since the channels are unidirectional. It can be seen from Fig. 14.1 that a long-delayed echo will result from speaker A's signal "leaking" through hybrid coupler B and returning to A's location. The echo also causes a serious trouble in digital data transmission.

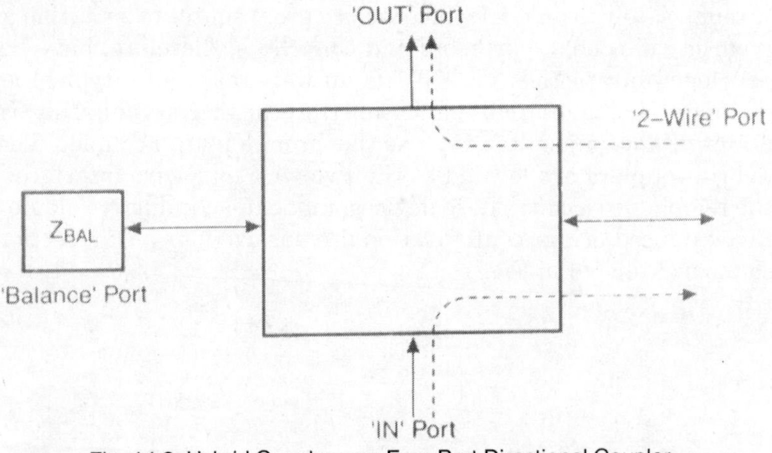

Fig. 14.2. Hybrid Coupler as a Four Port Directional Coupler.

14.2. Echo Control Techniques in Speech Transmission

Control of echo in the telephone network may be controlled by 3 techniques, namely the loss plans, echo suppression and echo cancellation.

Loss Plans. The technique is also known as **VNL plans** (Via net loss plan). Here a loss is introduced in the network in such a way that echo is lost. Infact the loss added to the trunk defends on its length. The expression governing the added loss is

$$DB = 4.0 + 0.4\,N + 1.102\,D$$

Where DB is the overall loss in decibels of the talker speech path, exclusive of the loss of the two subscriber loops at the two ends of the connection. N is the number of trunks in connection and D is the echo path round trip delay in milliseconds. The method is not suitable for very long distance trunks say over 1900 km where very long delays are involved.

Echo Suppressors. These are devices that introduce in connection a large loss in one direction or the other and the echo signal experiencing this large loss gets heavily attenuated. The principle of echo suppressor is as that shown in Fig. 14.3. A large attenuation pad is inserted in one direction or the other. A speech detector is used to determine the direction of the active speech controlling the direction to which pad is to be inserted. In Fig. 14.3, the echo suppressor passes speaker A's signal and blocks echo of speaker A's signal. A signal originating from speaker B will also be blocked.

The echo suppressor when operating properly has been a quite satisfactory solution to the echo problem on circuits with moderate (perhaps less than 100 ms) round trip delay. On circuits with long (more than 200 ms) round trip delay *e.g.* satellite routed circuits, the disorting effects are much more pronounced. The performance of echo supporessor has been improved by restricting the satellite to so called *half hop mode*, in which one direction of the four wire connection was on the satellite and the other direction on a terrestrial circuit. (Thus limiting the round trip delay). It may be noted that two or more echo suppressors may not be used in tandem because the two suppressors may lock out during double talk which shall make the conversation impossible.

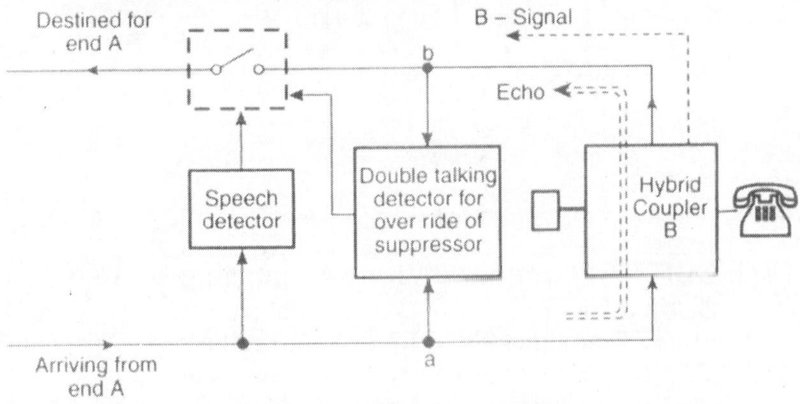

Fig. 14.3. Principle of Echo Suppressor.

Echo Canceller: Satellite communication which has round trip delay of about 550 ms needs devices better than echo suppressors known as echo canceller. Thus the echo canceller is a sophisticated form of echo control which can effectively eliminate echo as an impairment even on very long delay channels and without regard to the double talk situation. The echo canceller involves a filter that is used in the place of echo suppressor and simulates the replica of echo signal. On subtraction of this echo replica with echo signal, the resultant echo signal gets zero.

The schematic diagram of an echo canceller using a filter is as that shown in Fig. 14.4. Here the filter simulates the echo channel from point *a* to point *b*. In order that the filter may work automatically, adaptive filter has been used which can automatically learn the echo channel characteristic, take on this characteristic and adapt to changes in the characteristic. The echo canceller built around such an adaptive filter aligns itself automatically without human intervention to produce the minimum residual uncancelled echo possible within its structural limitations. Echo cancellers built on above idea are too large and expensive for commercial service. It may be noted that adaptive filter such as transversal filter, lattice filter and continuous time realization techniques have been used for echo cancellation.[2]

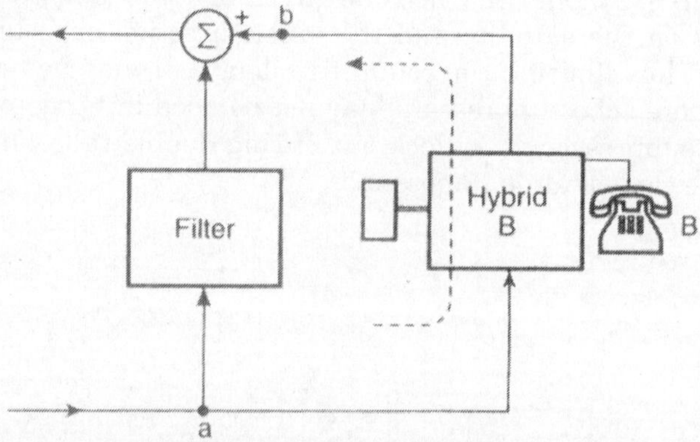

Fig. 14.4. Echo Canceller.

14.3. CCITT Recommendations Regarding Echo Control

The CCITT recommends (CCITT recommendation G-131, yellow Book, Vol III-I, Seventh Plenary Assembly, Geneva, 1980) that overall loss of a connection may be adjusted so that echo signals are sufficiently attenuated or alternately, an echo suppressor may be fitted if the loss adjustment results in an excessive insertion loss[3]. Table 14.1 gives the CCITT Rec G131 net loss.

Table 14.1. CCITT G131 Recommendations

Circuit Kilometer	*Length Status Miles*	*Net Loss dB*
0	0	0.5
250	155.3	0.5
500	310.7	0.5
750	466.0	1.0
1000	621.4	1.0
1250	776.7	1.5
1500	932.1	1.5
1750	1087.4	2.0
2000	1242.8	2.0
2250	1398.1	2.5
2500	1553.5	2.5

14.4. Echo Canceller for Digital/Data Communication

In digital networks the delays produced as a result of voice processing are significantly more problematic. The total end-path delay is comprised of three separate types : propagation delay over transmission lines, delays *via* the switching equipment and finally dispersion through channel banks and loaded VF Cable[4]. Typically a digital switch introduces upto 1.2 ms delay in one direction, together with between 1.8 and 6 ms for each transmux conversion and upto 0.5 ms plus dispersion *via* the PCM channel bank, and the transmission line causes even greater delays. In calculating true end-path delay, of course the full two way delays are taken into consideration. The result of these delays building up obviously creates havoc with transmission intelligibility.

For digital/data communication systems to get rid of echo problem, digital echo cancellers are used. The first digital VLSI echo canceller chip was introduced in 1979. Its operation is illustrated in Fig. 14.5[5].

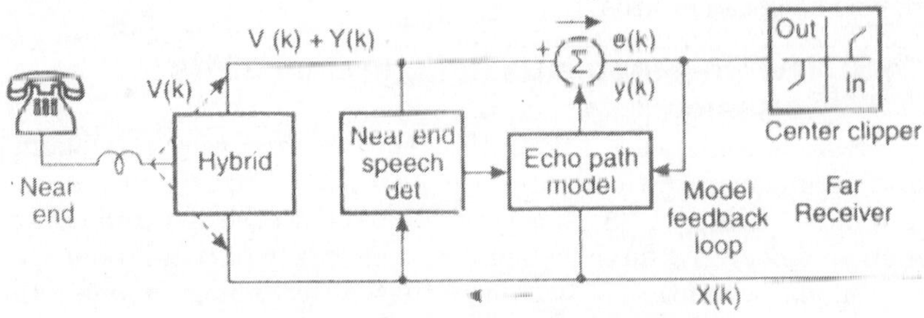

Fig. 14.5. Block diagram of digital echo canceller.

The echo $y(k)$ is formed by the discrete convolution of the far-end speech $x(k)$ and the echo path impulse response $h(k)$. When $x(k)$ is present but the near end speech $v(k)$ is not, the estimated echo path impulse response $h(k)$ is adaptively undated and stored in an internal delay line of the VLSI chip, called the *H-register*. The adaptive estimation algorithm tries to reduce the absolute magnitude of the error signal $e(k)$, which is difference between $y(k)$ and $\overline{y}$ (k). When $e(k)$ is small, the echo canceller chip is said to have converged.

The near end speech detector of the VLSI echo canceller prevents the canceller chip from attempting to cancel the near end speech signal. Normally the canceller chip updates its echo estimate once per sample period. When near end speech is detected in the presence of far end speech (double talk) the speech detector inhibits further updating. The H register still retains its echo path estimate, however, and is thus able to continue to cancel echoes during double talk.

The center chipper is an energy detector which in the presence of far end speech sets signals below a certain threshold to zero. The threshold can be either fixed at a low land or variable according to the level of the received far-end speech. If received speech is not present or if near end speech is present, the center clipper is bypassed. It has been tested that having the center clipper in the echo canceller chip indeed helps.

The echo canceller is needed at each end of the circuit. The near end canceller cancels echo for the far end speaker and vice-versa. Normally, the location of the echo canceller is at the intertoll side of the switch, where one can be sure whether or not a canceller is required. For each call connection, the canceller will have to estimate the new echo path impulse response. An echo canceller consists of the chip and its facility of interface circuitry. In an analog environment A/D and D/A conversions are required to interface with the chip. In digital environment, PCM digital streams will have to be demultiplexed to per-channel level for echo cancellation and multiplexed back afterwards.

14.5. New Developments in Echo Cancellers Design

Echo cancellers are differentiated by their accuracy, intelligence and significantly by their speed of convergence. The advent of ASICs and more recently VLSI, has transformed both the size and performance of modern echo cancelled. Two concepts in particular have led to a major revolution in each cancellation technology, namely the integration and specialization. The ability to customise microchips, which was helped by digital signal processing principles went a long way towards overcoming the early problems of space efficiency and slow convergence tunes within echo cancellers. It is primarily due to the fact that DSP chip allowed for the integration of other functions in addition to echo cancellation.

New developments in ASICs technology, such as sub-micron gate lengths have also enabled further significant improvements in performance. The utilization of ASICs has enabled components to be custom designed, consolidating functionality and leading to fewer external devices being required one example of this integration can be seen in the tone disabler to identify modem/facsimile transmission. Usually an external component, the tone disabler can now be fully integrated within the core ASIC chip in state of the art echo cancellers.

As mentioned, the advent of VLSI brought with it the ability to condense functionality and scale down size, with the outcome that 12 echo cancellers, each supporting 24 channels (TI Standard), or 30/31 channels (CEPT standard), take up little more than the space of a looseleaf file. VLSI will undoubtedly continue to have a profound impact on component design in future. Experts believe that it will be possible to quadruple the number of echo cancellers which can be placed on one match box-sized microchip. The tally currently stands at a total of two cancellers per chip. ASICs have already advanced echo cancellation from generic microprocessing to customised processing for network and acoustic application highlighting the move toward increased specialization.

14.6. Acoustic Echo and its Cancellation

Acoustic echo relates to reflected speech that might occur due to direct or multipath loudspeaker to microphone coupling. It is generally encountered in video/audio conferencing or in mobile hands-free applications. Acoustic echo in a conference room includes reflected coupling between the speaker and microphone as well as direct coupling. Contributing factors include the size and acoustic treatment of a room, the quality and compatibility of audio equipment, how much furniture is present and its construction and in the case of mobile use, the external noise factor. It is therefore quite essential to remove both multipath and direct coupled echo at source so that natural speech is experienced and howling is avoided. It must be remembered that acoustic echo has nothing to do with any impedance mismatching. As multipoint video conferencing becomes more common place, involving more than two different sites in the same meeting, the necessity for acoustic cancellation to be applied at each site is paramount in the system is to function successfully. It also puts additional emphasis on the performance of the acoustic echo canceller.

In the above multipoint videoconferencing context, the *echo return loss enhancement* (ERLE) becomes paramount because even a slight reflection in speech can create additive echo. Any or all of the multipath locations may cause, magnify and hear the echo and each connecting point contributes to the overall noise in the line. The aim, therefore is to isolate and eliminate echo at the individual sites so that the summed locations are not a cycle of interference.

Microphone gating techniques have been used in the past as one possibility to overcome acoustic echo. However their performance is limited as the acoustic echo suppressor because of half-duplex operation and clipped speech. The development of high performance acoustic echo cancellers has had a major impact in this field, providing the means to achieve completely natural speech. This has proved particularly important for video conferencing applications, where developments to improve picture quality have tended to leave audio a long way behind. With the use of echo cancellers video and audio performance are far more evenly matched.

14.7. Echo Cancellation Requirement in Other Communication Systems

Global mobile communication systems (GSM), digital cellular networks, personal communication networks (PCN), and VSATs all need echo cancellers. The requirement is for improved convergence times, ERLE and tail length flexibility especially with regard to GSM. Within the mobile cellular environment, compression techniques contribute significant delays as do transmission relays between the mobile vehicle, the cellular station and finally the telephone network. All of this necessitates longer tail length in echo cancellers in order to compensate. Convergence time is equally important for this application, with the mobile call undergoing inherently unstable network conditions. As a result the echo canceller must be able to converge readily on the changing telephone environment.

Echo cancellation is clearly a prerequisite for the rapidly growing digital network sector. The commercial realization of GSM in July 1991 has shown the need for echo cancellers whenever a call is made outside of the digital cellular network, as the call is patched through the analogue network. PCN, though working on different frequencies is a sister system and needs echo canceller. Based on recent projections, regarding the expansion of the cellular market, one can confidently predict that this sector alone will support the main bulk of future echo canceller requirement. In the mobile telephone systems there is need for a miniaturized echo canceller which can be integrated within the mobile equipment. With the use of ASIC and VLSI technologies it is now becoming possible to achieve this. It has also now been possible to use such components for more than one function or in various applications.

VSATs and compressed voice systems also require the use of echo cancellation due to the creation of processing delays from the voice/data integration process for digital transmission and the continued interface with analogue circuitry. For example, the codecs installed in videoconferencing systems process and compress the pricture for hundreds of milliseconds. Audio transmission, which is inherently faster, is deliberately delayed in order to achieve lip synchronization with video. If the teleconference occurs via a private satellite network, echo complexities are magnified, with tail length increasing.

14.8. Future of Echo Cancellers

The arrival of ISDN and digital networking has removed both the cause and effect of echo. However, less than 40% of the current global structures are digital and these has been a noticeable decrease in the ISDN conversion rate. This together with the longer life cycle for analogue within third word and soviet break countries indicates that a full conversion is unlikely for at least 30 years. The outcome of these predictions is that the echo cencellation is here to stay and within the next five years we are more likely to see new requirements emerging.

Algorithm development and integration will represent the most significant development thrusts. In the case of algorithm development, echo cancellation performance advances in line with the evolution of a proprietary algorithm. As new mathematical constants are researched tested and implemented, the formula becomes increasingly more accurate. Integration is another key development area, with echo cancellation in the future likely to be incorporated into PC compatible slip-in circuitry rather than external components.

Note that even the telephony requirement, predicted to decrease with the introduction of ISDN, will not infact diminish until we have a fully door to door ISDN structure–a situation which may never materialise in the fullest sense. All the time the new digital networks still have to patch into the old analogue circuitry and so echo will continue to make its presence felt. It can therefore be concluded that echo cancellers shall stay through the 21st century atleast.

14.9. References

1. Weinstein, S.B., Echo Cancellation in the Telephone Network, IEEE Communication Magazine, January, 1977, p. 9-15.
2. Feher, K., Advanced digital Communication Systems and signal processing Techniques. Prentice-Hall, Inc, 1987, p. 196.
3. Jordan, E.C. CED. Reference data for Engineers, Radio, Electronics, Computer and Communication, Howard W. Sams & Co. N.Y. 1986, p. 38-7.
4. Echo Canellation, Communications International Magazine, 1991, pp. 163-165.
5. Fang, G.S, Voice channel Echo Cancellation, IEEE Communication Magazine, December 1983 pp. 11-14.

15

Error Control Coding for Digital Satellite Links

15.1 The Need for Coding

When data is transmitted over a satellite communication link, there is a possibilities of some errors occurring in the received data because of noise added by the transmission system.

Most commercial links offer a guarantee only 10^{-6} bit error rate and but during periods of rain or other propagation disturbances, this accuracy is badly affected. Thus occurring bit error contribute to the baseband (S/N) ratio when digital speech is sent. However, in the case of speech, it is rarely necessary to correct bit errors. This is because the listener can make such corrections as there is a lot of redundancy in speech and for error rates up to 10^{-4} and so speech remains intelligible. When data are sent over a link, the received terminal does not know in advance what form the data will take and can only detect or correct errors if extra, redundant bits are added to the transmitted data.

Coding of data is a means of detecting errors at the receiving terminal. Error detecting codes allow the presence of one or more errors in a block of data bits to be detected. They also make the receiving terminal equipment to locate and correct a limited number of errors in a block of data.

Interference also causes burst errors in which many sequential bits are corrupted. Special burst-error correction codes are available with the capability of correcting errors in a number of adjacent bits.

Scrambling and interleaving of data bits are other ways in which the effect of burst errors can be reduced.

15.2 Encoding and Decoding

This refers to the process of adding coding bits to the uncoded bit stream, and decoding refers to the process of recovering the original (uncoded) bit stream from the coded bit stream. Both processes are usually combined in one unit termed a *codec*.

15.3 Principle of Error Control Coding

The principle of error detection coding is based on adding redundant bits to a data stream in such a way that one or more errors in the data stream can be detected. One redundant bit is added for every N data bits which allows a single error within that block of N bits to be detected, whatever the number of bits in the block.

To explain this principle, we take the simple example of an error detecting code system which uses the single bit parity as applied to the 7-bit ASCII code. The ASCII code is widely used for transmission of data over telephone lines and radio links. It consists of 128 characters representing the alphabet in uppercase and lowercase letters, numerals 0 to 9, and a set of useful commands, symbols, and punctuation marks. The eight bit, the *parity bit,* is used for detection of error in the 7 data bits of the character. There are now two possibilities as shown in Fig. 15.1:

(*i*) In a system using even parity, the parity bit is 0 when the sum of the data bits is even, and 1 when the sum is odd. Thus the sum of the data bits plus the parity bit is always made even, or 0 in modulo-2 arithmetic.

(*ii*) In odd parity, the sum of the data bits plus the parity bit is always odd, or 1 in modulo-2. Errors in the 7 data bits, or the parity bit, are detected at the receiving end of the link by checking the 8 received bits of each character for conformity with the parity rule. In modulo-2 arithmetic, $0 \oplus 0 = 0$, $0 \oplus 1 = 1$, $1 \oplus 0 = 1$, and $1 \oplus 1 = 0$. This is the exclusive OR function of digital logic. Similarly, $0 \otimes 0 = 0$, $0 \otimes 1 = 0$, $1 \otimes 0 = 0$, and $1 \otimes 1 = 1$.

Figure 15.2 shows an example of a system using even parity, which transmits the character A in ASCII code. At the receiving end of the link the 8 bits are checked by modulo-2 addition. If the sum is 0, we conclude that the character is correct. If the sum is 1, we detect an error. If 2 bits of the character are corrupted, the modulo-2 sum is 0 and therefore, we cannot detect this condition.

Data bits	Parity bit	Sum (Modulo-2)	
Even parity	0101101	0	0
Odd Parity	0101101	1	1

Fig. 15.1 Even and Odd Parity for a 7 Bit ASCII Word

Received codeword	Sum of bits	Error detected?	
One error	01010010	1	Yes
Two errors	01010110	0	No
Three errors	11010110	1	Yes

Fig. 15.2 Error Detection in a 7-bit ASCII Word with Even Parity (error bits are underlined).

Thus we achieve an improvement in rate of undetected errors for the ASCII words. However, the above benefit is for a price. When the single parity bit is added to a 7-bit ASCII character, the transmission bit rate goes up from 7 bits per character to 8 bit per character. This increase in bit rate will result in an increase in BER because the channel bandwidth must be increased and this increases the noise power in the receiver and reduces the *C/N* ratio. Therefore, complete expected decrease in character error rate can be achieved in practice.

15.4 Formation of Blocks of Data

In general, typically *n* bits are transmitted in a block, made up of k message bits plus r parity bits. There are two ways in which the blocks of data can be formed:

(*i*) In a packet transmission system, the block is usually long, typically 64 to 2048 bits, and checksum or cyclic redundancy check (CRC) bits are added to the block that generate an error condition at the receiver if there are errors in the block.

(*ii*) The blocks are made members of a set of *n*-bit codewords. Coding schemes in which the message bits appear at the beginning of the codeword, followed by the parity bits, are called *systematic block codes.*

15.5 Linear Block Codes

For a block code, it is necessary that the message stream be partitioned into blocks of bits. Considering only binary messages, suppose each block contains *k* bits, and let these *k* bits define a dataword. Therefore, the number of datawords is 2^k Clearly there is no redundancy in the system, which means that even a single bit error in transmission will convert one dataword into another, leading to an error.

We now encode the datawords into codewords which consist of n bits, where $n = k + r$. Here the additional r bits are derived from the message bit but are not part of the message. The number of possible codewords is 2^n, but only 2^k of these will contain dataword, and these are the ones that are transmitted. This means that the rest of the codewords are redundant, but only in the sense that they do not contribute to the message. The r additional bits are called *redundant* bits (also known as *parity check bits.*)

Now consider that errors have occured in transmission. Clearly there is high probability that they will convert the permissible codewords into one or another of the redundant words that the decoder at the receiver is designed to recognize as an error. Thus there is always the possibility that as enough errors occur, they transform a transmitted codeword into another legitimate codeword in error.

A code is termed linear when any linear combination of two codewords is also a codeword. For binary codewords in particular, the linear operation encountered is modulo-2 addition. All codes encountered in practice are linear.

A repetition code illustrates some of the general properties of block codes. In a repetition code, each bit is considered to be a dataword, in effect, $k = 1$. For n-redundancy encoding, the output of the encode is n bits, identical to the input bits.

Example: *Consider the situation when $n = 3$. A binary 1 at the input to the encoder results in a 111 codeword at the output, and a binary 0 at the input results in a 000 codeword at the output. At the receiver, the logic circuits in the decoder produce a 1 when 111 is present at the input and 0 when 000 is present. It is assumed that synchronisation is maintained between encoder and decoder. If a codeword other than 111 or 000 is received, the decoder detects an error and can request a retransmission (ARQ).*

15.6 Code Rate

The code rate r_c is defined as the ratio of dataword bits to codeword bits (note that although it is called a rate, it is not a rate in bits per second):

$$r_c = \frac{k}{n} \qquad \text{... (15.1)}$$

For a give level of performance (*i.e.*, number of errors detected or corrected), the greater the code rate, the more efficient is the code. In practice, codes that are more efficient than repetitive encoding are used.

15.7 Forward Error Correction (FEC)

This technique is employed for both detecting and correcting errors at the receiving terminal without retransmission of data. FEC codes add redundant parity check bits to the data bits in a way that allows errors to be located within a codeword. In general, twice as many errors can be detected by a FEC code as can be corrected.

FEC is carried out on the basis of a "majority vote." In this case, the logic circuits in the decoder are designed to produce a 1 at the output whenever two or three 1s occur in the received codeword (codewords 111, 101, 011, and 110) and a 0 whenever two or three 0s appear in the codeword 9 codewords 000, 001, 010, and 100). An odd number of "repeats" is used to avoid a tied vote.

Errors can still get through if the noise results in two or three successive errors in a codeword.

Example: *If the noise changes a 111 into a 000 or a 000 into a 111, the output will be in error whether error detection or forward error correction (FEC) is used. If two errors occur in a codeword, then the "majority vote" method for FEC will result in an error. However, the probability of two or three consecutive errors occurring is very much less than the probability of a single error.*

The advantage of FEC over error detection is that a single unit at each end of the link (a codec) can insert and remove the FEC code and make corrections as required. It also allows errors to be corrected without the need for retransmission, but this is more difficult and costly to implement than ARQ.

FEC is used on all satellite links where the *C/N* ratio at the receiver is likely to be low such as satellite telephones, VSAT terminals, and direct broadcast satellite television. These systems make use of the coding gain from rate one-half or rate three-quarters FEC to achieve low BER.

15.8 Cycle Codes

These are a subclass of linear block codes. They possess the property that a cycle shift of a codeword is also a codeword.

Example: *If a codeword consists of the elements* $c_1\, c_2\, c_3\, c_4\, c_5\, c_6\, c_7$, *then* $c_2\, c_3\, c_4\, c_5\, c_6\, c_7\, c_1$ *is also a codeword.*

The advantage of cycle codes is that they are easily implemented in practice through the use of shift registers and modulo-2 address. Cyclic codes are widely used in satellite transmission, and the properties of the most important of these are summarized in the following sections. Only certain combinations of k and n are permitted in these codes.

15.9 Hamming Codes

For an integer $m \geq 2$, the k and n values are related as

$$n = 2^m - 1 \text{ and } k = n - m.$$

Thus some of the permissible combinations are :

m	n	k
2	3	1
3	7	4
4	15	11
5	31	26
6	63	57
7	127	120

The code rate $r_c = \frac{k}{n}$ approaches unity as m increases, which leads to more efficient coding. Only a single error can be corrected with Hamming codes.

15.10 BCH Codes

These codes can correct upto t errors, and where m is any positive integer, the permissible values are $n = 2^m - 1$ and $k \geq n - mt$.

The integers m and t are arbitrary, which gives the code designer considerable flexibility in choice. listing of the parameters for BCH codes, from which the following values have been obtained :

n	k	t
7	4	1
15	11	1
15	7	2
15	5	3
31	26	1
31	21	2
31	16	3
31	11	5
31	6	7

The code rate is again $r_c = \frac{k}{n}$.

15.11 Reed-Solomon Codes

The codes described so far work well with errors that occur randomly rather than in bursts. However, there are situations where errors do occur in bursts; that is, a number of bits that are close together may experience errors as a result of impulse-type noise or impulse-type interference. Reed-Solomon codes are designed to correct errors under these conditions.

Instead of encoding directly in bits, the bits are grouped into symbols, and the dataword and codewords are encoded in these symbols. Errors affecting a group of bits are most likely to affect only one symbol that can be corrected by the Reed-Solomon code.

Let the number of bits per symbol be k.

Then the number of possible symbols is $q = 2^k$ (referred to as a q-ary alphabet).

Let K be the number of symbols in a dataword and N be the number of symbols in a codeword. As in the block code where k-bit datawords were mapped into n-bit codewords, with the R-S code, datawords of K symbols are mapped into codewords of N symbols. The additional N - K redundant symbols are derived from the message symbols but are not part of the message.

The number of possible codewords is 2^N, but only 2^k of these will contain datawords, and these are the ones that are transmitted. It follows that the rest of the codewords are redundant, but only in the sense that they do not contribute to the message.

If now errors occur in transmission, there is high probability that they will convert the permissible codewords into one or another of the redundant words that the decoder at the receiver is designed to recognize as an error. There is always the possibility, however remote, that enough errors occur to transform a transmitted codeword into another legitimate codeword even though this was not the one transmitted.

Some of the design rules for the R-S codes are

$$q = 2^k$$

$$N = q - 1$$

$$2t = N - K$$

Here, t is the number of symbol errors that can be corrected.

Let $k = 2$; then $q = 4$, and these four symbols may be labeled A, B, C, and D. In terms of the binary symbols (bits) for this simple case, we could have $A = 00$, $B = 01$, $C = 10$, and $D = 11$.

Now the number of symbols per codeword is $N = q - 1 = 3$.

Suppose that $t = 1$; then by rule $2t = N - K$, $K = 1$; that is, there will be one symbol per dataword.

Therefore, the number of datawords is $q^k = 4$ (i.e. A, B, C or D), and the number of codewords is $q^N = 4^3 = 64$. These will include permissible words of the form *AP1P2*, *BP3P4*, *CP5P6*, and *DP7P8*, where *P1P2*, etc. are the parity symbols selected by the encoding rules from the symbol alphabet A, B, C, and D (see Fig. 15.3). At the decoder, these are the only words that are recognized as being legitimate and can be decoded. The other possible codewords not formed by the rules but which may be formed by transmission errors will be detected as errors and corrected. Since a codeword consists of 6 bits, one or more of these in error will result in a symbol error. The R-S code is capable of correcting this symbol error, which means that a burst of up to 6 bit errors can be corrected.

Data bits	01	00	11	00	01	11	01	01	11	01	10	10
Data words	B	A	D	A	B	D	B	B	D	B	C	C
Codewords	BP_3P_4	AP_1P_2	DP_7P_8	AP_1P_2	DP_3P_4	DP_7P_8	BP_3P_4	DP_7P_8	DP_3P_4	BP_3P_4	CP_5P_6	CP_5P_6

Fig. 15.3: Representation of Reed-Solomon Coding.

R-S codes do not provide efficient error correction where the errors are randomly distributed as distinct from occurring in bursts. To deal with this situation, codes may be joined together or concatenated, one providing for random error correction and one for burst error correction.

Observe that although the encoder and decoder in R-S codes operate at the symbol level, the signal may be transmitted as a bit stream, it is also suitable for transmission with multilevel modulation, the levels being determined by the symbols.

The code rate is $r_c = \frac{K}{N}$, and the code is denoted by (N, K).

In practice, the symbols are bytes consisting of 8 bits. Therefore,

$q = 2^8 = 256$, and $N = q - 1 = 255$.

With $t = 8$, we get a NASA-standard (255, 239) R-S code.

15.12 Convolution Codes

These are another form of linear codes. A convolution encoder consists of a shift register which provides temporary storage and a shifting operation for the input bits and exclusive-OR logic circuits which generate the coded output from the bits currently held in the shift register.

In general, k data bits may be shifted into the register at once, and n code bits generated. In practice, it is often the case that $k = 1$ and $n = 2$, giving rise to a rate 1/2 code. Fig. 15.4 shows the encoding operation of a rate 1/2 encoder:

1. In the beginning, the shift register holds all binary 0s. The input data bits are fed in continuously at a bit rate R_b, and the shift register is clocked at this rate.

2. As the input moves through the register, the rightmost bit is shifted out so that there are always 3 bits held in the register. At the end of the message, three binary 0s are attached, to return the shift register to its initial condition.

3. The commutator at the output is switched at twice the input bit rate so that two output bits are generated for each input bit shifted in.

4. At any one time the register holds 3 bits, which form the inputs to the exclusive-OR circuits.

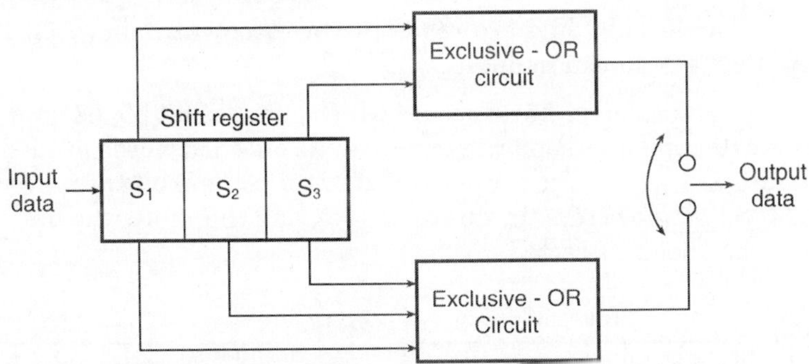

Fig. 15.4: Encoding Operation of a Rate 1/2 Encoder.

15.13 Trellis Codes

The trellis code is a combination of Convolutional or linear block coding and digital modulation Its features are:

1. It uses a high level modulation such as 8-PSK or 16-PSK and allows only certain sequences of modulation states to be transmitted.

2. The receiver detects errors in the received data strings if an invalid sequence of modulation states is received.

3. Coding gain can be achieved with a smaller increase in bit rate than with conventional convolution encoding.

However, trellis coding does not seem to have been adopted very widely.

Recently, turbo codes have been developed that allow links to operate down to *C/N* ratios of 2 dB at acceptable bit error rates. The decoding algorithms for turbo codes require powerful DSP integrated circuits, but these are now becoming available.

15.14 Interleaving

Interleaving is the process of changing the order in which the bits are encoded so that a burst of errors gets dispersed across a number of codewords rather than being concentrated in one codeword. Fig. 15.5 shows interleaving process used in block codes:

1. Part of the data bit stream (where the bits are labelled from b1 to b24) shown in Fig. 15.5 (*a*) is fed into shift registers.

2. Fig. 15.5 (*b*) shows seven rows and six columns as illustration. Here, the rows are not encoded but the columns are encoded so that the parity bits fill up the last three rows. As a result, the bits are not encoded in the order in which they appear in the data bit stream.

3. The encoded bits are read out row by row as shown in Fig. 14.6. Row 4 is shown in detail.

4. If now an error burst occurs which changes bit b5, b5, and b3, these will appear as separate errors in the encoded words formed by columns 2, 3, and 4. The words formed by the column bits are encoded to correct single errors (in this example), and therefore, the burst of errors has been corrected.

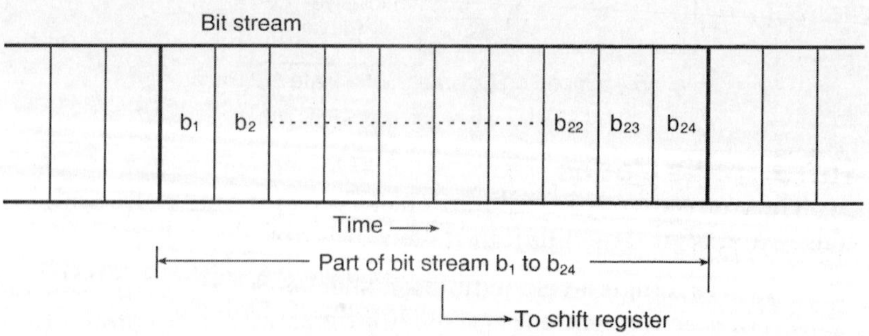

Fig. 15.5 (a) Part of Data Bit Stream

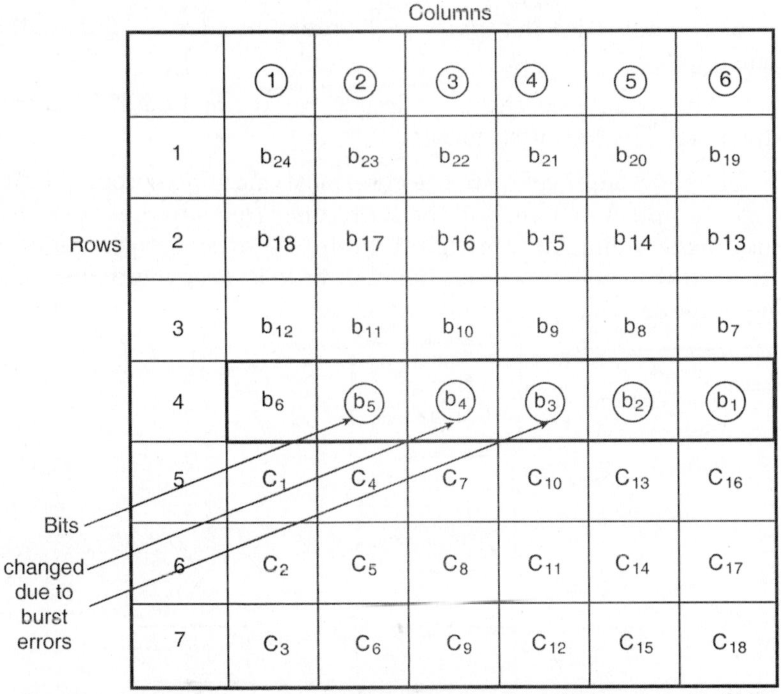

Fig. 15.5 (b) Seven Rows and Six Columns after Data Bit Stream fed to Shift Registers.

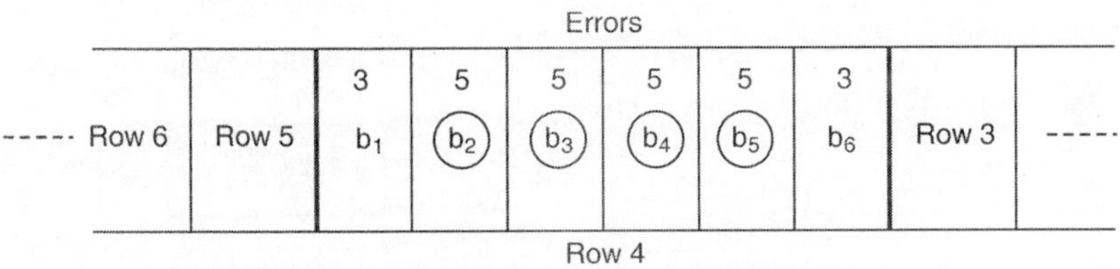

Fig. 15.6 Encoded Bits Row by Row and Details of Row 4.

15.15 Concatenated Codes

Concatenation is the process of combining codes designed to correct burst errors with codes designed to correct random errors. Fig. 15.7 shows the process of generating concatenated coding:

1. The input data are fed into the encoder designed for burst error correction. This is the outer encoder.

2. The output from the outer encoder is fed into the encoder designed for random error correction. This is the inner encoder.

3. The signal is then modulated and passed on for transmission.

4. At the receiver, the signal is demodulated.

5. The inner decoder matches the inner encoder and follows the demodulator.

6. The output from the inner decoder is fed into the outer decoder, which matches the outer encoder.

The term outer refers to the outermost encoding/decoding units in the equipment chain, and the term inner refers to the innermost encoding/decoding unit. In digital satellite television, the outer code is a Reed-Solomon code, and the inner code is a convolutional code. The inner decoder utilises Viterbi decoding.

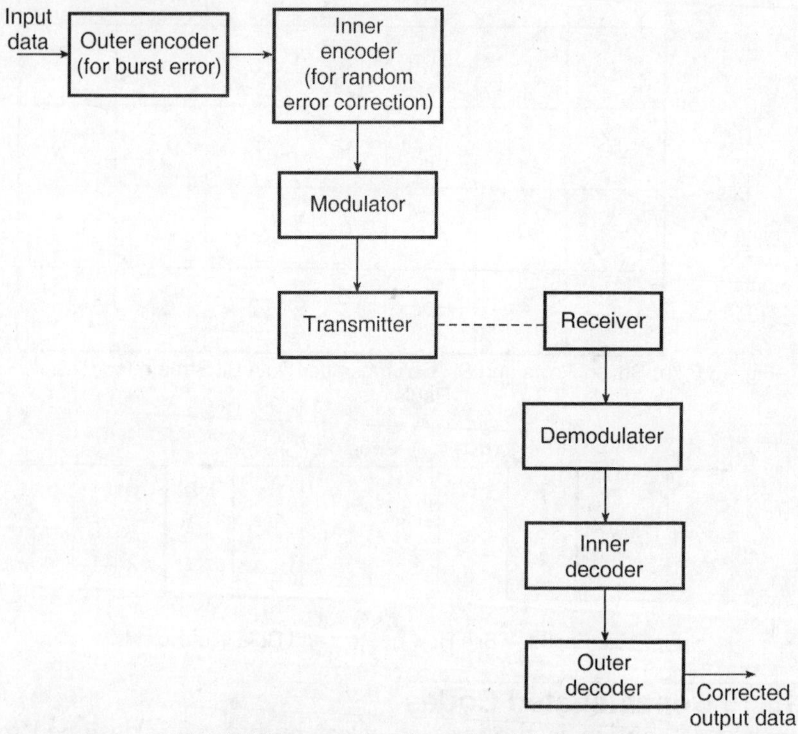

Fig. 15.7 Generation of Concatenated Codes.

15.16 Concatenated Coding and Interleaving

We have seen that with concatenated coding two coding operations can be applied in sequence to a data stream to decrease the probability of undetected errors occurring because of low C/N ratio on a satellite link. Concatenated coding can achieve coding gains up to 9 dB.

When concatenated coding is used, an interleaver is placed between the two stages of error control coding. This method is employed in audio compact disc recordings and also in direct broadcast TV satellite TV signals.

Interleaving is the process of spreading out the errors that occurred in a burst and thus to make it easier for an error correction system to recover the original data. A simple interleaver with 5 rows and 5 columns is shown in Fig. 15.8. Bits are read in to the rows and read out by columns, which spreads out the bits in the resulting bit stream. Interleaving can be illustrated more easily using letters of the alphabet rather than binary data as shown in the example below.

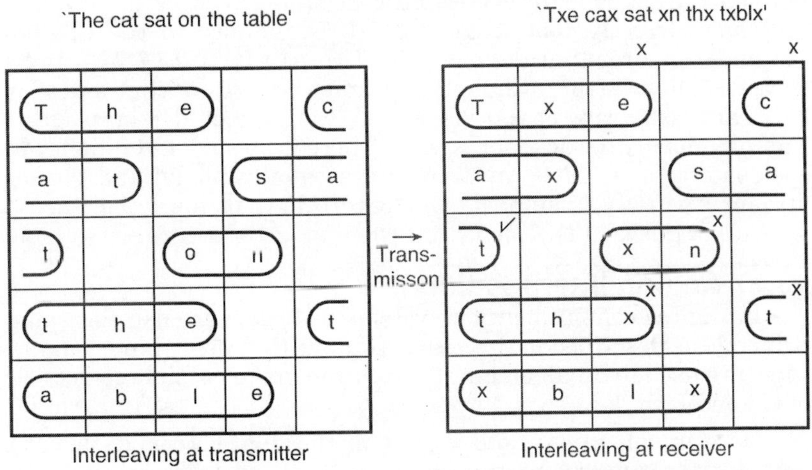

Fig. 15.8 5 × 5 Interleaver at Transmitter and Receiver.

Example: We consider the following message:

The cat sat on the table.

Let us first suppose that the message is transmitted with single bit error detection coding, and that two and three bit burst errors occur. This message, without interleaving, will be received as:

*The *** sat ** the * able*

where * indicates an error.

Since the English language is highly redundant, and only certain letter combination make valid English words, we can make a guess about the message based on what we received - we might guess dog or cup instead of cat, or cable instead of table.

When the 5 × 5 interleaver shown in Fig 15.8 is used at the transmitter, the message is read into the interleaver by row. The message is read out by column will be: *Tattaht hbe oel sn eca t.*

When this message is sent over the satellite link, it is received with bit errors in the same position as previously. We receive the following message : *Tatt*** hbe ** lsn *ca t.*

The message is now read into the de-interleaver at the receiver by column, and read out by row. The message at the receiver is then: *T*e ca* sat *n th* t*bl.*

This message could be corrected with a single-character error correction FEC code, or make an improved guess at the true message based on the received message. If there are no burst errors here, a single (character) error correction code would recover the original message correctly. The high level of redundancy in the English language ensures that the message *T*e ca* sat *n th* t*bl** can be read with little error, although we cannot be certain whether ca* is cat, cam, can, cap, or car. However, the rest of the message is unambiguous after de-interleaving. There is no such redundancy in a stream of bits. Ones and zeroes are equally likely; and the bit stream is usually scrambled to make certain that this is the case, so we cannot guess at the correct bit when an error occurs.

15.17 Analog Interpolation

In digital communication systems, interleavers use the same principle as described in the above example (but using binary data). They are used to break up burst errors and make possible correction of the received data.

Here important to note is that in the digital transmission of analog data, analog interpolation can be used to reconstruct an analog waveform containing single word errors. In the example above using letters, interpolation between the correctly received characters is much easier when the errors occurs singly. With interleaving, a much better guess at the message received can be made when there is no interleaving. The same principle holds true for binary transmission of analog data. As shown in Fig. 15.9, interpolation of an analog waveform is simple when only one point (a digital word) is missing.

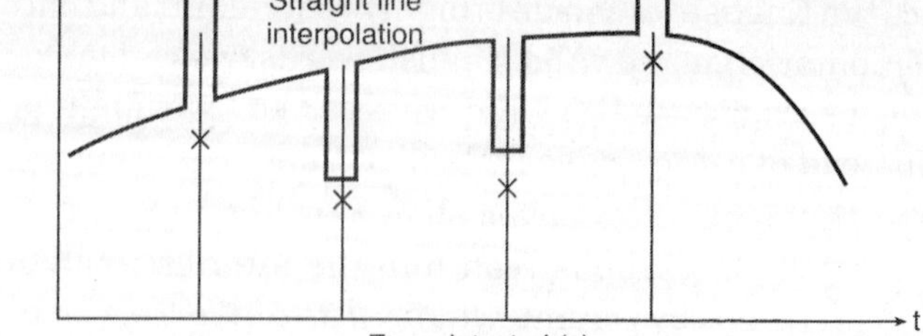

Fig. 15.9 Example of Analog Interpolation.

This method is used very successfully on audio compact discs and in digital video broadcast transmissions. Compact discs store audio data bits as changes in the reflectivity of the disc. Since the bits are about a micron long, a scratch or a speak of dust on the surface of the CD will cause a lengthy burst error. A long interleaver is used to spread out the burst error and this makes reconstruction of the analog waveform possible for burst errors as long as several thousand bits. The interleavers used in satellite transmission of digital video signals are generally shorter than those used on a CD, typically 12×7.

15.18 Error Detection on Satellite Links

In satellite links, error detection is a process of facilitating sending and reception of data with a greatly reduced probability of error with a very high probability that uncorrected errors are identified and located within a block of data, so that the existence of an error is known.

However, error detection leads to a reduced transmission rate, just as in FEC. But unlike FEC the transmission rate is reduced only when errors occur and not when the errors do not occur.

Error correction is applied in a communication system by use of error detection and retransmission which requires the use of protocols. A protocol is an agreed-upon set of actions that define how each end of the data link proceeds so that data are transmitted in an accurate and ordered fashion through the link.

Error detection in satellite links is implemented using the coding techniques described in the previous sections. Note here that it is not sufficient simply to detect an error; it must be corrected. Some systems such as speech and picture transmission may simply count errors to determine whether the link is above an operating threshold. Excessive error counts may cause the link to automatically shut down. For example, when a succession of pictures is transmitted, the previous value of a pixel can be used to know whether a new value is in error.

The terrestrial data communication systems use an acknowledge (ACK) signal sent by for the receiving terminal to the transmitting end whenever it receives an error-free block of data. Such protocols works well on terrestrial data links with relatively low data rates and short time delays. However, the long transmission delays in satellite communication systems make it highly undesirable to send ACK signals for every error free block that is received. This is reason why Internet access via satellites employ a different access protocol.

Spoofing: In this process, a satellite terminal receives data using a terrestrial protocol and generates the acknowledgements, then transmits the data over the satellite link using a different protocol.

Now consider a one-way, simplex link. Here, the ACK/NAK signals travel on the same path as that of the data, which means that the transmitter must stop after each block and wait for the receiver to send back an NAK or ACK before it retransmits the last data block or sends the next one. Since a one-way delay on a GEO satellite link is 240 msec, the data rate of such a system will be very low and is suitable only for links in which data are generated slowly.

Therefore, satellite links employ two-way communication (duplex channel) by the use of SCPC-FDM, or TDM. Here, the ACK/NAK signals is sent on the return channel while data are sent on the go channel, However, there is a problem in this case also - if the data rate is high, the acknowledgment will arrive long after the given block was transmitted.

15.18.1 Automatic Repeat Request (ARQ)

To overcome the above problem, an automatic repeat request (ARQ) system is used. It is an automatic procedure, by which the receiver requests a retransmission when an error has been detected. Its advantages are:

1. Error detection can be performed without correction which is more efficient than forward error correction in terms of code utilization.

2. It is less complicated to implement.

3. More errors can be detected.

Its disadvantages are:

1. The request for retransmission to be made over a low-bit-rate channel because here the probability of bit error can be kept negligible small.

2. Since the long round-trip delay time of the order of half a second or more is encountered with geostationary satellites, ARQ is only suitable for transmission that is not sensitive to long delays.

ARQ is mostly used with block encoding. We now make an estimate of the probability of an error remaining undeleted can be made. For an (n, k) block code, the number of datawords is $2k$, and the total number of codewords is $2n$.

Now when a given dataword is transmitted, an undetected error appears when the transmission errors convert the received codeword into one that contains a permissible dataword but not the one that was transmitted. The number of such datawords will be ($2k - 1$).

We can estimate an upper bound on the probability of an error getting through by assuming that all codewords are equiprobable. Therefore, the ratio of number of possible error words to total number of codewords gives the average probability of error as

$$BER \leq \frac{2^k - 1}{2^n} \leq 2^{-(n-k)}$$

$$\leq 2^{-r}$$

where r is the number of redundant bits in a codeword.

ARQ throughput: This is defined at the ratio of the average number of data bits accepted at the receiver in a given time to the number of data bits that could have been accepted if ARQ had not been used.

15.18.2 Types of ARQ

There are three types of ARQ as described below:

I. Stop-and-Wait ARQ: Here, as the data are sent in coded blocks, the receiver acknowledges receipt of each block by sending back a positive acknowledgement or ACK signal if no errors are detected in the block and a negative acknowledgement or NAK signal if errors are detected. Here the transmitter stores copy of the block just transmitted and waits for the acknowledgement signal. If a NAK signal is received, it retransmits the block, and if an ACK signals is received, it transmits the next block. In this ARQ, the delay between transmissions is about half a second, the round-trip time to and from

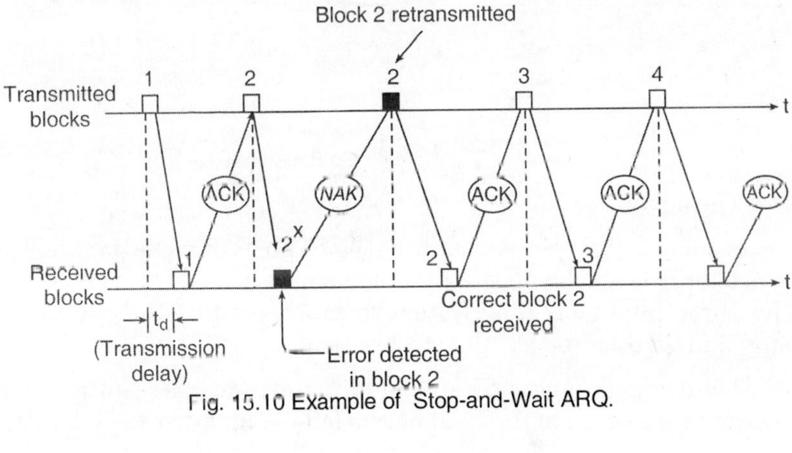

Fig. 15.10 Example of Stop-and-Wait ARQ.

a geostationary satellite, which are unacceptable in many applications. Fig. 15.10 shows as example of a stop-and-wait sequence.

II. Go back-N ARQ: This ARQ allows continuous transmission of blocks incorporating the retransmission of corrupted blocks when these are detected. It carries this out by having the blocks and the acknowledgement signals numbered. The procedure as shown in Fig. 15.11 (where *N* is three blocks) is as follows:

1. The transmitter stores the number of blocks *N* transmitted over the round-trip time and updating the storage as each ACK signal is received.

2. The data are sent in blocks continuously and held in a buffer at the receive end of the link.

3. If the receiver detects an error in block *i*, say, it transmits an NAKi signal and refuses to accept any further blocks until it has received the correct version of block *i*.

4. The transmitter now goes back to block *i* and once again begins retransmission from there. That is, this block and all subsequent blocks are retransmitted.

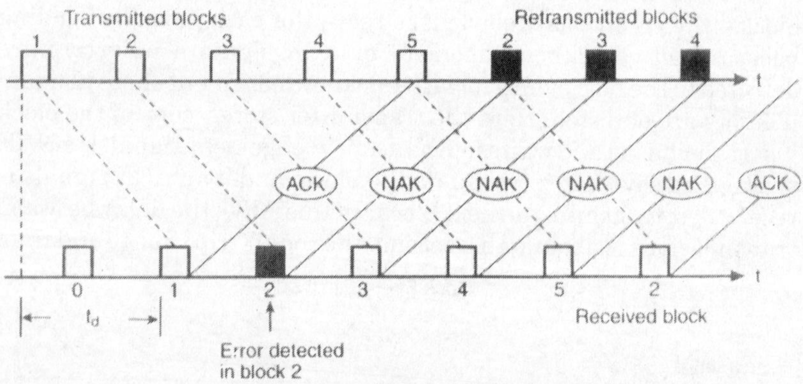

Fig. 15.11 Example of Go Back-N ARQ

The advantages are:

A delay will only be encountered when an NAK signal is received. Since there is a delay in transmission only when a NAK is received, the throutghput on this system is much greater than with the stop-and-wait method.

The disadvantage is: There is additional time loss resulting from the retransmission of the good blocks following the corrupted block.

If PA is the probability that a block is accepted, then throughput for Goback-N is given by

$$(Thp)_{\text{GobackN}} = \frac{K}{n} \frac{P_A}{P_A + N(1 - P_A)}$$

Typically, for a BCH (1023, 973) code and N = 4, the throughput (*Thp*) for Goback–N will be 0.915.

III. Selective repeat ARQ: This method is an improvement over the above method. Here, only a correct version of the corrupted block is retransmitted, and not the subsequent blocks. However, it is necessary in this case to have a storage arrangement in the receiver because it must be able to store the subsequent blocks as it waits for the corrected version of the corrupted block.

Fig. 15.11 can be used to explain this APQ:

1. Consider that block 2 is corrupted, and blocks 4, 5, 6 and 7 are transmitted before the NAK message is received.

2. At this point, we could transmit block 3 only if block 4, 5, 6 and 7 are stored at the receive end.

3. On receiving a correct version of block 3, the receive buffer substitutes it for the corrupted version and releases the data for retransmission.

4. If PA is the probability that a block is accepted, then throughput for Selective Repeat, throughput is given by

$$(Thp)_{\text{Selective repeat}} = \frac{K}{n} P_A$$

For a BCH (1023, 973) code and N = 4, the throughput for Selective Repeat, its value is 0.942.

In such systems, handling of data rates of megabits per second makes the buffer requirements for continuous transmission systems become quite large because of the delay on the link via a geostationary satellite.

Selective repeat ARQ is used in the Internet protocol TCP/IP (transmission control protocol/internet protocol) because of relatively short delays on terrestrial paths used for Internet traffic. However, the TCP/IP protocol cannot be used over a geostationary link without modification because it is designed for terrestrial links with short delays. The protocol times out before repeat retransmissions and relies are received when a GEO satellite link is used.

Apart from the ACK and NAK signals, the transmitter operates a timeout clock. If the ACK or NAK signal for a given block is not received within the timeout period, the transmitter puts the ARQ mechanism into operation.

15.18. References

1. Leon W. Couch, Modern Communications Systems : Principles ad Applications, Prentice Hall, Englewood Cliffs, NJ, 1995.
2. Dennis Roddy, Satellite Communication, McGraw Hill, Boston, 2001.
3. Timothy Pratt, Charles W. Bostian and J.E. Allnutt, Satellite Communication, John Wiley, NJ, 2003.

15.19. Review Questions

1. Explain the need for coding in data in transmission over a satellite communication link. Using the ASCII code, describe the use of parity bit in coding and detection of errors.
2. Explain how error detection and error correction differ. Why are forward error correction normally used on satellite circuits?
3. A transmission utilizes a code for which $k = 7$ and $n = 8$. How many codewords and how many datawords are possible?
4. An R-S code is byte oriented with $k = 8$. Given that there are eight redundant symbols, calculate the number of symbol errors that can be corrected.
5. Describe how convolution coding is achieved. State some of the main advantages and disadvantages of this type of code compared with block codes.
6. Explain what is meant by interleaving when applied to error control coding and why this might be used.
7. Explain what is meant by concatenated codes and why these might be used.
8. Explain what is meant by a forward error correcting (FEC) code. FEC coding at a code rate of 3/4 is used in a digital system. Given that the message bit rate is 1.544 Mb/s, calculate the transmission rate.

16

Satellite Applications

16.1. Introduction to Satellite Applications

In the last fifteen chapters so far, we have studied different aspects of satellites and satellite communication at length. The topics covered so far include the basic principles of satellite communication, different types of satellites, satellite link design, satellite transmission and reception, satellite communication's vital components such as antennas, recent trends in satellite communication technology, evolution and present status of different aspects of satellite technology in India and so on and so forth.

One vital area that still remains to be explored at length, though it was touched upon here and there depending upon the needs of the topic under discussion, is the area of satellite applications. The satellite technology and its use is no longer the prerogative of the chosen few. Its horizon of applications has extended far beyond providing intercontinental communication services such as Radio Telephone etc. It is a household name today. A satellite today is not being accessed by giant sized antennas located at the huge installations, the satellite signal today is also being tapped by roof top antennas. It not only provides long distance audio/video communications. It has started playing a significant role in the newer communication services such as Fax, Data communication, Cellular phones etc. Today, in addition to enabling you to talk to some one thousands of kilometers away within the comforts of your home in a matter of a few seconds, it also plays a pivotal role in the timely and accurate forecast of the weather. On one hand, satellites are being used as navigational aids by vehicles on land, in the air and on the sea, on the other hand, they are being used to unearth the hidden mineral resources which would otherwise have remained untapped particularly in countries having vast and not-so-friendly terrains. The list is endless. The application areas are multiplying and so are the quantum of applications in each one of these application areas.

It is surely going to be the most widely used and the most important communication medium of the twenty first century. And it is because of this reason that all developed countries and the major developing countries including India have full fledged space programmes. Indigenous development of satellites for communication and remote sensing applications and also the development of satellite launch vehicles of different classes are the major activities of the Indian Space Research Organisation (ISRO). An international directory of different classes of satellites and satellite launch vehicles highlighting their salient features follow this chapter.

In the section to follow in the present chapter, we shall take a closer look at different applications that the satellite systems in general and satellite communication in particular offer to us. The emphasis is on the underlying principle, the potential and the contemporary status of these application areas.

16.2. Satellite Applications—Different Areas

Satellite applications can be broadly classified into the following categories namely :

1. Satellite communication applications
2. Remote sensing and Earth observation application
3. Meteorological applications
4. Military applications
5. Scientific and Technological applications

In the field of satellite communication applications, Satellite television, Telephone and Data communication are the major application areas. In the category of Remote sensing/Earth observation applications, the typical ones are the discovery of hidden mineral resources, Terrain mapping etc. The meteorological applications include Weather forecasting. Flood forecast, Melting of glaciers etc. Military applications include providing strategic communication links between border forces and headquarters, spying, providing navigational aids to ships, aircrafts etc. In the category of satellites for science and technology, the applications include use of satellites for astronomical research, monitoring of different layers of atmosphere etc.

In the sections to follow, we shall discuss different applications belonging to each one of above the mentioned categories.

16.3. Satellite Television

Satellite television or satellite video communication belong to the same class of satellite applications. The two are one and the same. The two nomenclatures can be used interchangeably. Satellite television is infact one of the most widely used and talked about application areas of communication satellites as it involves masses at large. If the "satellite" has become a household name today, it is largely due to its television broadcast capability to bring live important events, sports or politically related, to our drawing rooms from places thousands of miles away. Who can ignore the small caption "Live via satellite" on the corner of TV screens when we are watching live telecast of a sports event.

Satellite television refers to the use of satellites for relaying TV programmes from a source point where these programmes originate to a large geographical area. There are various configurations used to implement what we call satellite TV depending upon the value of source end, role of satellite and the type of receive stations. But irrespective of the configuration used, the satellite basically receives a certain telecast that has been beamed up to the satellite by what is called the UP-LINK and then reflects the same without any change except carrier frequency translation towards earth for reception by all those who lie within its coverage area what we call as DOWN-LINK (remember uplink and downlink frequencies are different).

Direct Broadcast Satellite

One of the most common satellite TV configurations is based on simple point to multipoint connectivity feature of the satellite communication. It is diagrammatically shown in Fig. 16.1. It takes full advantage of the inside area coverage of the satellite's footprint. The TV broadcasting here is accomplished with one transmitting station and many receive only stations designated as TVRO stations. Fig. 16.2 shows a typical set up showing use of direct broadcast satellite. The programme to be telecast is beamed up to the DBS via up-link from the studio. In the figure shown, the TV-studio has its own earth station. In case the earth station with the up-link capability is remotely located, the programme is usually sent to the earth station over a microwave terrestrial link. The down link is received at each TV station by its own Receive only station, from there it is transmitted over the local TV channel stored on video tape.

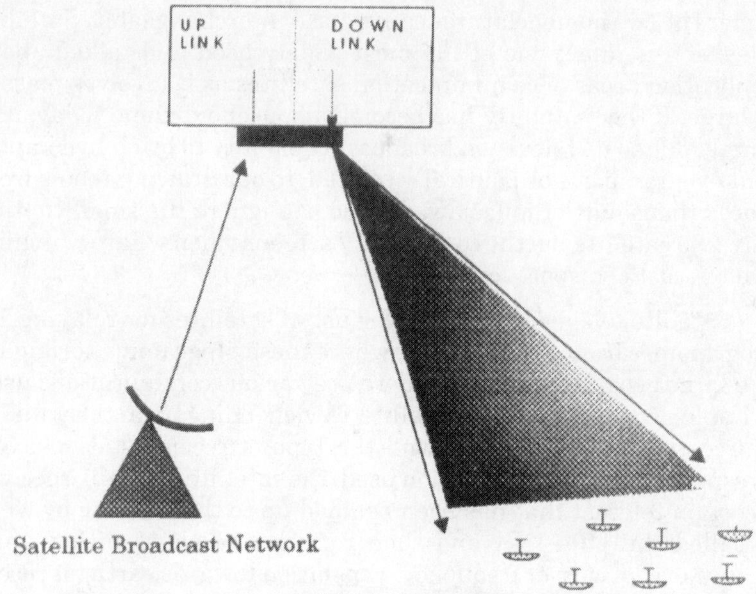

Fig. 16.1.

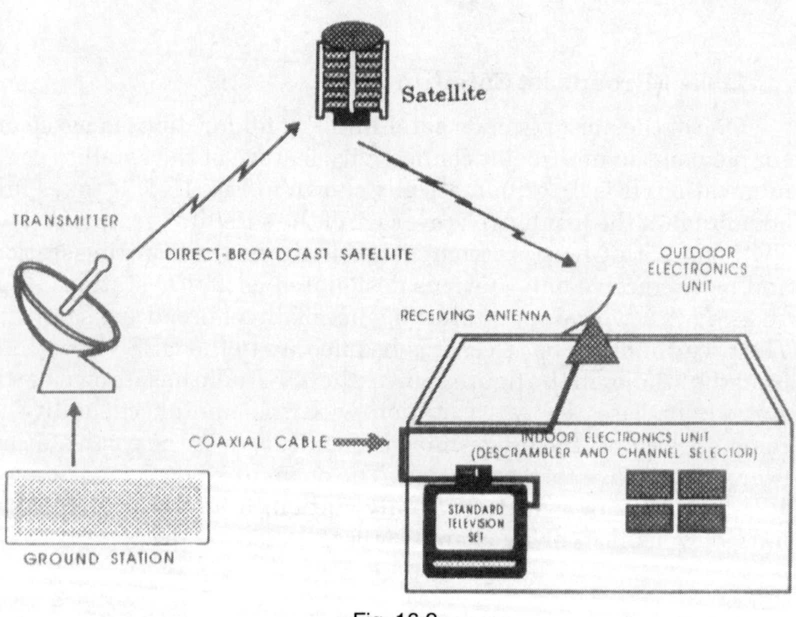

Fig. 16.2.

A small variation of the configuration is in the live telecast of certain events such as sports events. The place of action in such cases is remote. In such cases, the signal picked up by the cameras is transmitted to the TV station with up-link facility as a microwave link if the distance involved is not more than few tens of kms or a mobile earth station in the form of a van is posted at the site. The signal is then transmitted to the TV station over another satellite link on point to point connectivity basis (Fig. 16.3).

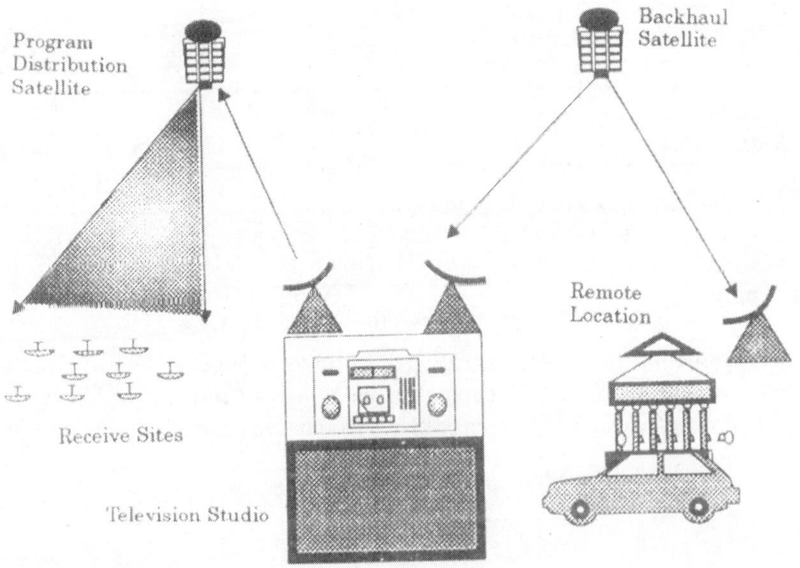

Fig. 16.3.

A large number of countries have their own domestic satellite systems to be used for direct broadcast purposes. INSAT series of satellites though multipurpose in nature, also have direct broadcasting capability and are in a fact being used for the purpose. Other popular DBS systems include AUSSAT (from Australia), TV SAT (West Germany), TDF 1 (France), STC (USA) etc.

Cable TV (CATV)

The abbreviation CATV originally stood for Community Antenna Television which meant a common receiving antenna for the community. The signal received by this common antenna was then distributed to large number of houses through network of coaxial cables. Such a concept is valid to huge buildings having hundreds of apartments thus eliminating the need for each house to have its own

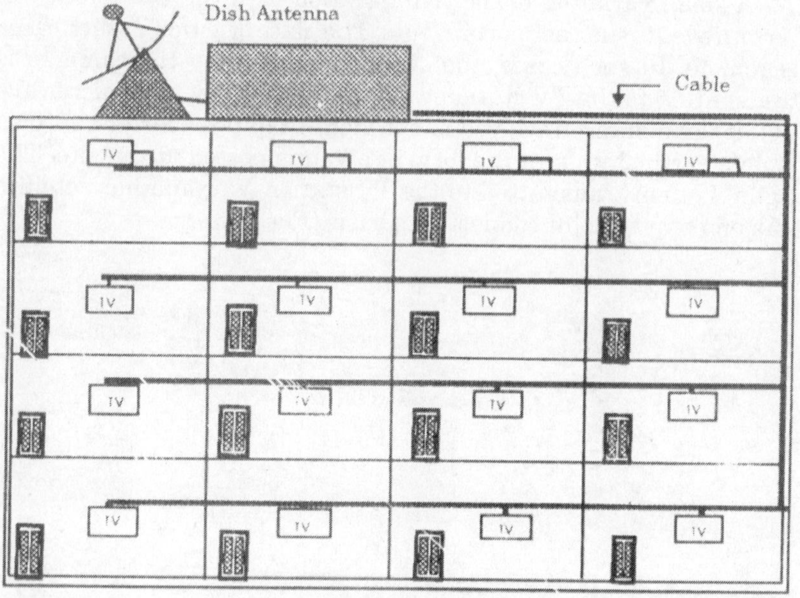

Fig. 16.4

antenna dish on roof top. Fig. 16.4 shows a typical set up. In the present day of cable TV, the cable TV operator has a root of receive only earth stations with a capability to receive telecast of one or even

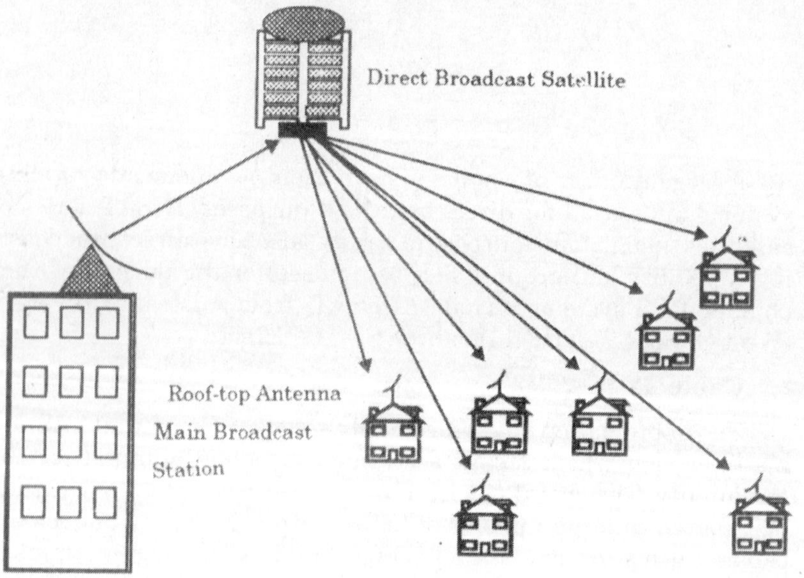

Fig. 16.5

more than one satellites. He can achieve this by either having more than one receiving dish antennas or even a single dish antenna with multiple feeds and each feed so aligned as to receive telecast from a different satellite. The received signal or signals are then simultaneously transmitted over a distribution network of coaxial cables on single point to multipoint connectivity basis to a large number of houses known as his subscribers who pay monthly fee for this service. The cable TV operator also transmit over the distribution network the video tape recorded programmes that they get from other sources in addition to showing programmes received from satellites.

Direct Home Reception

Gradually, we are entering an era where each house top will have its RO antenna capable of receiving TV programmes directly from satellite (Fig. 16.5). Infact some of the companies have already started marketing TV sets with a built-in decoder. These TV sets in conjunction with appropriate dish antenna are capable of direct satellite TV reception.

16.4. Telephone Services via Satellite

Satellites play a vital role in providing long distance trunk or point-to-point telephone services. Today infact about 80 per cent of international telephone traffic goes via satellite. Here too, the satel-

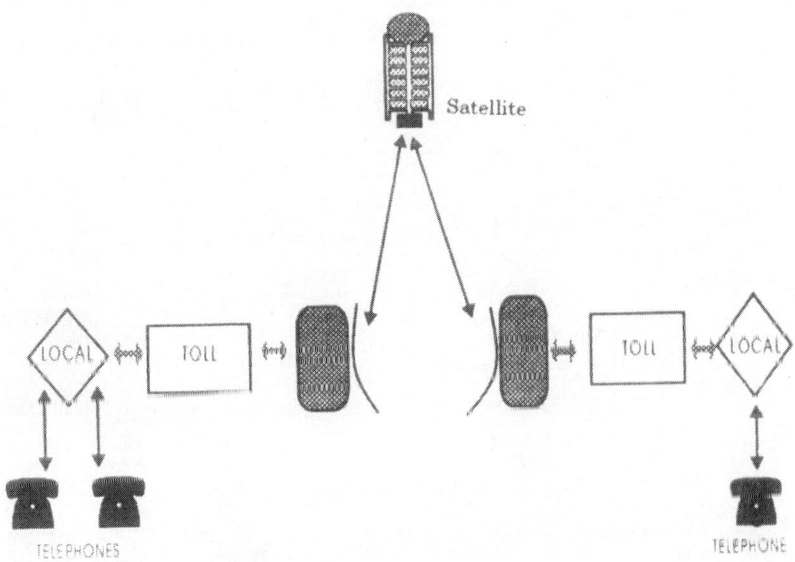

Fig. 16.6

lite like in any other telecom service serves the purpose of a repeater station. When compared to a terrestrial link, the satellite link is particularly advantageous when the distance involved exceeds 1000 kms or when the region to be covered is sparsely populated or has difficult geographical terrain. Fig. 16.6 shows a typical set up of international telephone service via satellite. Initially with communication via satellite suffered from echo problems leading to degradation in quality. With the development in device technology and digital techniques, this problem is overcome voice the introduction of echo cancellation measures.

16.5. Data Communication Services

Data communication services are the outcome of developments and advances made in the field of computers and telecommunications. The purpose of data communication is to link computers and other data processing facilities with other remotely located computers by a communication channel. The telecommunication channel could be terrestrial or satellite based. Terrestrial links for data communication have comparatively much lower data transfer speed, high cost, lesser reliability and throughput capability. Satellite links are attractive for data communication because of much higher data transfer rate capability, higher reliability and much higher performance to cost ratio particularly achieve able with VSAT networks (Very Small Aperture Terminal).

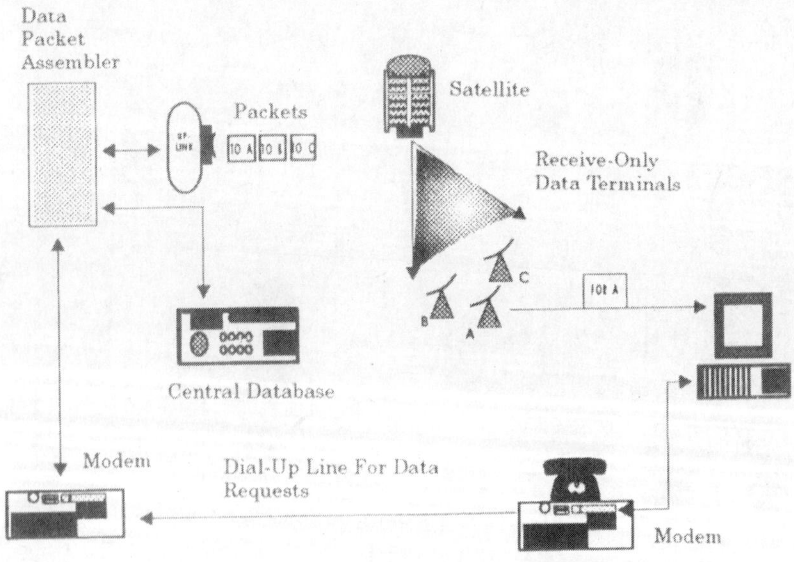

Fig. 16.7

Data Broadcasting Using Satellite

Data processing based on simple point to multipoint connectivity configuration is the most commonly used data communication application implemented using a satellite. Fig. 16.7 shows the set up. Data from a central facility (a database for instance) is routed to the earth station with the uplinking capability via another set up called data packet assembler. The data packet assmbler is a digital processing device that receives the data to be broadcast, organises it into packets and places appropriate address bits at the beginning of each packet. Each data packet is thus self contained with source and destination addresses and therefore can be routed in any way over satellite and finally through a terrestrial packet switched network. Each data packet is even coded so that only authorised users can have an access to the information. Full access to all data is also provided in case of a news service. The data beamed up at the satellite is retransmitted towards earth to be received by "Receive Only" terminals. The receive only terminals have digital processing capabilities to identify data packet addressed to them. The respective RO terminal receives the data meant for user terminals linked to them for subsequent delivery. As an illustration one of the user terminals at line A is a PC. The user terminals are usually linked to the central facility lines to enable them make request for broadcast of any additional data.

Interactive Data Communication

In an interactive data communication network, unlike data broadcasting, the remotely located user terminals are not only able to respond back to the central site, they can also exchange information between one another. Such a network is best implemented using VSATs, each VSAT supporting large number of user terminals. Fig. 16.8 shows the typical arrangement in such an interactive network when the remote stations can transmit information to the central facility of the same satellite that does the data broadcast and there is no need from terrestrial link. The data concentrator multiplexes the data flows from different user terminals and imports a single stream of bits to the VSAT indoor electronic unit. It also demultiplexes the data broadcast received from the satellite for delivery to prospective user terminals.

16.6. Satellites for Earth Observation

Use of satellites for a variety of earth observation applications has come of age beginning with use of TIROS weather satellite in early sixties, where TIROS sent map like outline of the world beneath the clouds, to the use of satellites for almost any conceivable application monitoring agriculture, forestry, detecting hidden

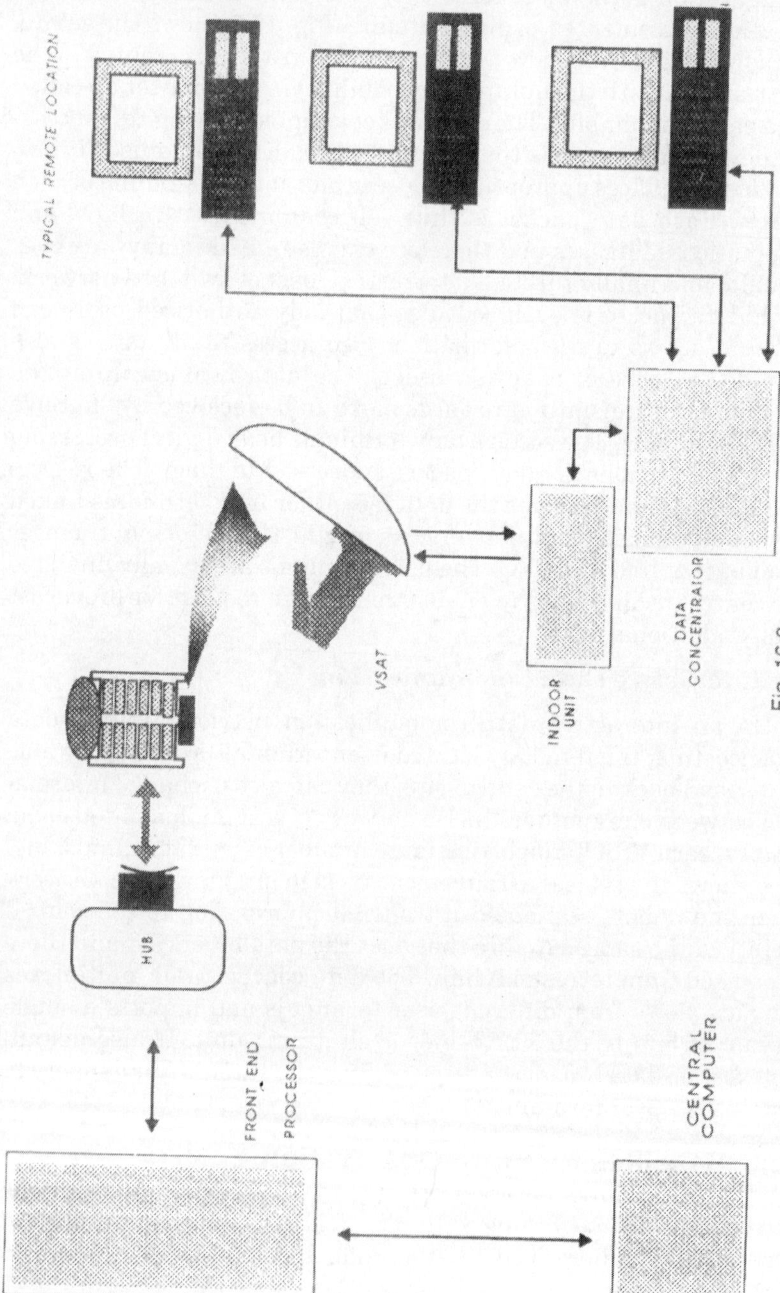

Fig. 16.8

mineral resources, forecasting weather and national calamities, oil exploration, cartography to mention some of the prominent ones. There has been a lot of work done on the development of satellites for earth observation not only in the developed world but also in the developing world. Some of the more popular and more recent satellite systems developed for this role internationally include LANDSAT, ERS-1, IRS etc. In the paragraphs to follow, we shall briefly discuss satellite based applications related to earth's observation. The applications being discussed include :

1. Cartography.
2. Monitoring agriculture and forestry.
3. Oceanography.
4. Ice Reconnaissance.
5. Monitoring oil pollution and air pollution.
6. Snow melt.
7. Mineral and oil exploration.

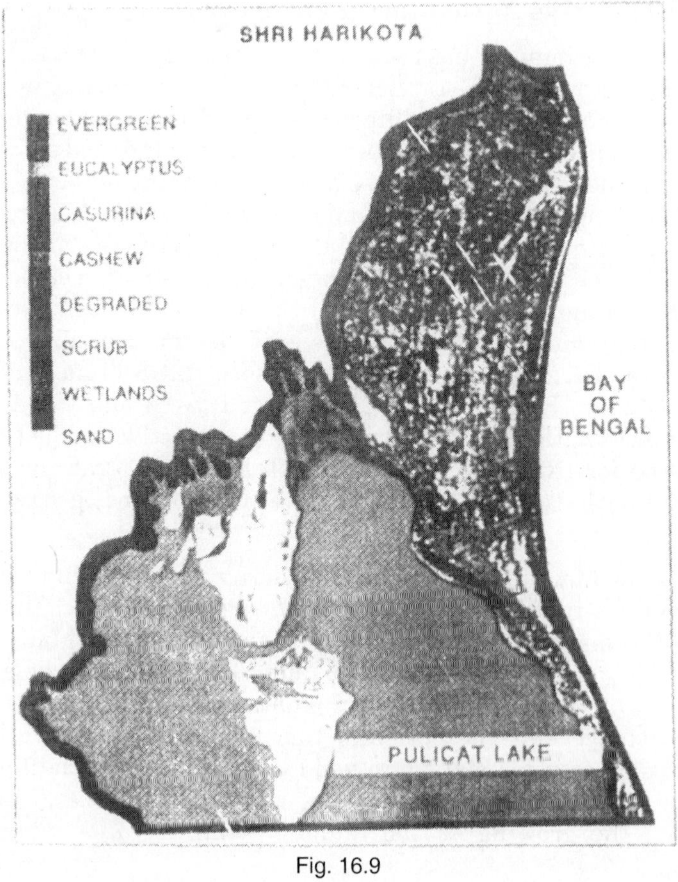

Fig. 16.9

Cartography

One of the early applications for earth resources' imagery has been in cartography *i.e.* map-making. Satellites equipped with high resolution cameras have been used to correct and update certain features of existing maps in countries like USA, Russia. Satellite imagery has also been used to produce related maps for the construction of roads, railways and irrigation channels. It has also been used to map underwater features such as coral reefs which are potentially dangerous to shipping. Infact LANDSAT has played a very vital role in mapping more than 50 per cent of unmapped areas of Asia, Africa and Latin America at scales larger than 1 : 1,000,000. Space imagery is more cost effective as compared to other alternative methods due to the speed with which space surveys can be made. Fig. 16.9 shows a photograph taken from remote sensing satellite IRS-1A showing land cover map of Sriharikota.

Monitoring Agriculture and Forestry

Satellite imagery has been quite successfully used for better and optimum crop and forestry management. Remote sensing data from the earth observation satellite is used for several applications such as crop identification, agricultural crop acreage and field estimation, drought monitoring and assessment, flood mapping, land use and land cover mapping, wasteland management, forest resources survey and management and so on. Present day remote sensing satellites equipped with the state-of-the-art high resolution cameras are capable of monitoring characteristics like crop identification, crop yield, optimum plantation and harvest times, land fertility etc. over much smaller areas. For instance, cameras LISS-I and LISS-II on board Indian Remote Sensing Satellites IRS-1A and IRS-1B have spatial resolution of 72.5 m and 36.25 m respectively. The cameras planned for IRS-1C and 1D have still better spectral and spatial resolution and other features like stereo viewing, on board recording etc.

Backed by the capabilities of modern remote sensing satellites emerges a situation where we can have a global food watch that could help the mankind avoid disasterous food shortages. Many of the difficulties accompanying over or under production can be avoided by accurate forecast of optimum plantations and harvest timings, crop acreage etc. The optimum time to plant and harvest for a particular crop for maximum yield can be found by checking soil condition and moisture content, by keeping an inventory of crops during the growing season and by giving advance warning of drought.

This type of agricultural watch could also allow an inventory to be made of tropical areas which could be potentially productive. It could also give data on fertile and arid regions which could be made more productive by irrigation.

Satellite data has shown clear advantages in estimating the volume of timber across a large area of forests. When forests are being cut, it has been possible to monitor this and if necessary to recommend changes in the cutting pattern in the best interest of observation. Proper management of forest resources is particularly attractive for developing countries. Developing countries are increasingly aware of the need to manage their forest resources not only to meet their timber requirements but also to preserve the ecological balance and to prevent erosion, silting of dams and pollution of coastal waters. In India, the IRS-series satellites have become the mainstay of National Natural Resources Management system with the department of space as the nodal agency. The remote sensing data from IRS satellites is used for several applications such as agricultural crop acreage and yield estimation, flood mapping, drought monitoring and assessment, forest resources survey and management, water resources management and so on.

In Brazil, LANDSAT imagery has been used to monitor a programme for controlled development of the Amazon forest for various purposes including cattle grazing. From satellite imagery, it has also been possible to make rapid assessment of places where forest fires have burnt the ground.

Fig. 16.10 shows IRS-1B imagery showing Bombay-Manmad pipeline corridor Fig.

Fig. 16.11 shows preliminary flood risk zone Kosi river interpreted from satellite images.

In India, satellite data was used to provide technical guidance and training to Gujrat forest department for making forest working plan. Soil moisture mapping capabilities were established by making use of data from ERS-1 satellite. Coral reef mapping on 1 : 50,000 scale was completed for the Gulf of Kachch, Lakshadeep, Gulf of Mannar and Andeman and Nicobar islands. Fishery prospect charts were generated for Gujrat estate using data from IRS series satellites. Data from IRS-1A was used in 1991 to study the environment impact of river valley project at Tehri. Satellite data is also been used to study the environmental impact of Sardar Sarovar project.

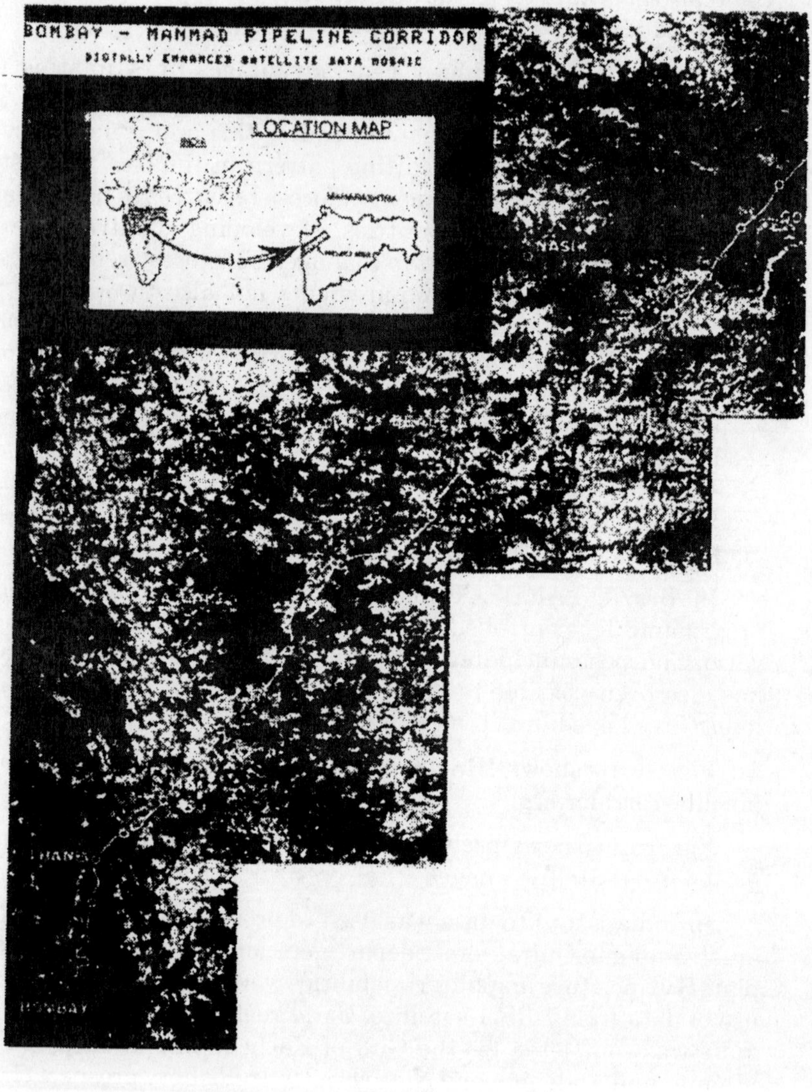
BOMBAY - MANMAD PIPELINE CORRIDOR
DIGITALLY ENHANCED SATELLITE DATA MOSAIC
LOCATION MAP
INDIA
MAHARASHTRA
NASIK
THANE
BOMBAY

Fig. 16.10

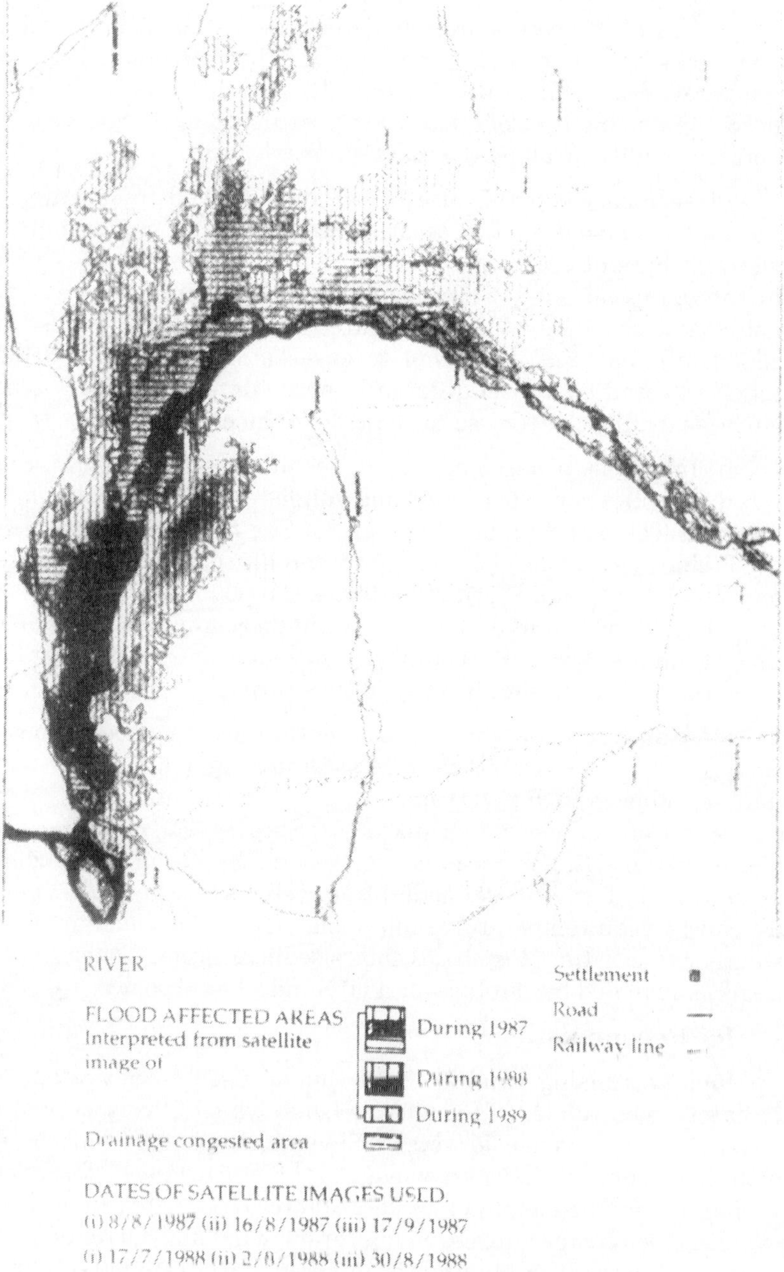
RIVER
Settlement
Road
Railway line
FLOOD AFFECTED AREAS
Interpreted from satellite image of
During 1987
During 1988
During 1989
Drainage congested area
DATES OF SATELLITE IMAGES USED.
(i) 8/8/1987 (ii) 16/8/1987 (iii) 17/9/1987
(i) 17/7/1988 (ii) 2/8/1988 (iii) 30/8/1988
(i) 20/7/1989 (ii) 5/8/1989 (iii) 22/9/1989

Fig. 16.11

Oceanography

Satellite data can be used to determine sea conditions such as Sea surface temperature, Wind speed, Wind direction, Local air temperature and Moisture content etc. Satellites have also been used to make pictures of ocean waves, ice fields, ice bergs, ice leads and sea conditions along the coastal lines.

Fishermen can make use of satellite derived information of thermal boundries in the ocean to get the additional catch advantage. Satellites are also being used by the countries, Russia for instance, to study oceans for measuring the sea surface electromagnetic radiation in the visible, infrared and microwave bands. Research of this kind is leading to observation systems in which different satellites collect different types of data from land and sea surfaces to allow better use to be made of the earth's resources.

In India too, a national remote sensing programme for ocean related application, sponsored and funded by the Department of Ocean Development is under progress. Sea Surface Temperature (SST) charts are being generated from satellite data analysis. Based on the SST data and thermal patterns, the potential fishing zones are being identified and maps are being disseminated to about 80 fishing land centres of the country. The feedback indicates that fish catch has increased significantly in these areas.

More and more different types of sensors getting placed on board the present day earth observation satellites, they are likely to get data on subjects such as (*i*) Coastal sedimentation and pollution (*ii*) Conservation and use of fish stocks (*iii*) Ship routing making use of ocean currents (*iv*) Wave forces for use in the design of off-shore structures and wave power generating systems (*v*) Mapping of polar ice caps, Ocean temperatures and winds for improved climate and weather forecasting. Fig. 16.12 shows sedimentation dispersal patterns as revealed by satellite data off Sunderbans coast.

Ice Reconnaissance

Remote sensing satellite data can be used to advantage in forecasting behaviour of ice and ice bergs which is very crucial to navigation of ships in cold waters. Navigation of ships in these cold waters depends upon the knowledge of the properties, distribution, variability and behaviour of ice bergs. Forecasts require knowledge of air and sea temperatures, precipitation, wind and currents. Data on ice thickness can be obtained by infrared sensors abroad satellites under cloud free conditions. Passive and microwave radiometry has

Fig. 16.12

shown promise for all weather conditions while high resolution photography monitors the coast and in-shore areas.

Monitoring Oil Pollution, Air Pollution

Satellites can be very effectively used for monitoring oil slicks in the sea. It is very difficult to see such leakage from aircrafts which in any case, are restricted in vision to narrow bands of ocean because of their low altitudes. On the contrary, the oil slicks can be spotted very effectively by satellites on global scale except in the places of persistent low clouds.

To do so, the space borne sensors measure the amount of sunlight reflected from the sea surface. Spilled oil stands out clearly from the ordinary sea water in the near ultraviolet region around 0.38 micron and in the near red around 0.6 micron. Polarisation measurements on the reflected light from the oil spills also shown sharp contrast. It is not only possible to detect just the oil spillage, light and heavy oils can also be distinguished. Light oils appears brighter. The volume of oil leakage can also be assessed by repeated observations. Knowledge of the type, quality and volume of oil is important in tracing their source of leakage.

Remote sensing satellites equipped with instruments like correlation interferometer are being used for mapping of those parts of atmosphere which have high, low and average concentration of carbon monoxide. By repetitive scanning over long periods it is possible to identify the so called REMOVAL SINKS. Unless the removal mechanism can be defined, it is very difficult to predict the futuristic behavioural pattern of carbon monoxide content in the atmosphere.

This study attains still more significance as there is also a growing concern that the amount of carbon dioxide in the atmosphere is increasing worldwide because 20th century man continues to burn so much fossil fuel. This will have the effect of putting on increasingly thick blanket over the earth which allows sunlight to reach the earth's surface as before but would reduce the escape of its heat by reflection back into space, thus trapping ever more heat near the surface. Use of remote sensing satellites for atmospheric studies is discussed again under the heading of Satellites for Scientific Applications.

Snow Melts

Routine photography of snow covered ground and mountains and monitoring of snow cover characteristics such as cover area, thickness, density etc. to make predictions of snow melt can be effectively, speedily and economically performed by satellites. Accurate predictions of snowmelt are important for optimum water management for power generation, irrigation, controlling flood water etc. In India, snow melt run-off predictions based on the satellite data have been made available to Bhakra-Beas Management Board.

Oil And Mineral Exploration

Satellite data can be used for oil and mineral exploration. The data can be used by geologists to see earth's interlocking features including large folds and ruptures which give clues to mineral deposits. Transcurrent faults as indicated by satellite data can be used to make searches from unknown deposits of oil. Minerals can be identified by rock colour and topographic form. Not only this, information about faults and fracture zones derived from LANDSAT imagery has been used in the past in selecting sites for nuclear power stations and routes for pipelines.

In India too, data from remote sensing satellites IRS has been effectively used for identifying favourable locates for gold mineralisation in the Schist belt near Garwal town in Mehboobnagar district of Andhra Pradesh. Structural continuity of the Garwal schist belt with that of the well known Kolar Schist belt was inferred from the IRS data.

16.7. Satellites For Weather Forecast

Satellite data is being used for forecasting weather for more than three decades now. The first weather satellite, TIROS-1, was launched by U.S.A. in 1960 and was used by a large number of countries to monitor the behaviour of atmosphere over a large area of the earth. The present day weather satellites equipped with highly sophisticated instrumentation provide information on cloud formation, cloud type and position, extent and intensity of frontal depression, thunderstorms, hurricanes, sea breeze circulation, typhoons and so on and so forth. Sequence of pictures covering the same area can be effectively used to determine the movement and development of different features. Details of snow cover, sea ice, sea surface temperatures, cloud top temperatures and wind at different heights in the atmosphere are also extracted regularly from satellite pictures. Measurements of temperature and humidity throughout the depth of the atmosphere are also sometimes carried out by weather satellites.

The accuracy of a weather forecast depends largely on the quantity and quality of observational data from the surface of the

Fig. 16.13

Fig. 16.14

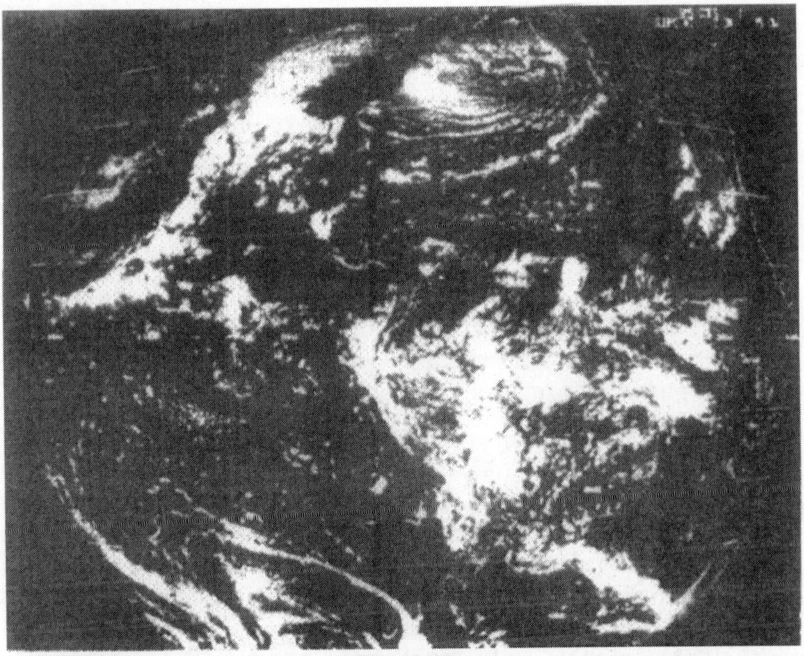

Fig. 16.15

Fig. 16.16

earth and surrounding atmosphere. The speed with which the data is made available to data computing and analysis facilities plays a major role. Satellites are particularly valuable for providing data where conventional observations are sparse or non-existent. Their ability to transmit data quickly to operational users is a very important asset.

There are two categories of operational weather satellite systems. The first operates in a polar orbit and the other operates in a geostationary orbit. The geostationary orbiting satellite can monitor weather determining atmosphere parameters over a very large area almost continuously whereas a polar orbiting satellite can provide complete global coverage every twelve hours.

The most important piece of equipment abroad a weather satellite is a RADIOMETER. The radiometer measures the amount of radiation. Measuring in the visible part of spectrum provides pictures about prominent features such as clouds, deserts etc. Infrared measurements provide information both during the day as well as during the night. Infrared pictures show the relative temperature of the different features. Pictures are usually obtained in black and white. Black areas indicate usually high temperatures while white areas indicate low temperatures. As a result high clouds appear in various shades of grey. Some weather satellite pictures are shown in (Figs. 16.13 to 16.16).

In India too, the multipurpose INSAT-series satellites have been providing meteorological data for years now. The Meteorological Data Utilization Centre (MDUC) of Indian Meteorological Department (IMD) processes and disseminates the INSAT meteorological images. Upper winds, Sea surface temperature and Precipitation index data are regularly generated by MDUC/IMD. The 0600 hours GMT VHRR image derived wind data are regularly put on the global telecommunication system (GTS) of the World Meteorological Organisation (WMO). The 0300 hours GMT full disk IR pictures are being transmitted as radio fascimile broadcast everyday for reception in the neighbouring countries. The INSAT VHRR (Very High Resolution Radiometer) data is now available in real time. With the commissioning of direct satellite retransmission service of processed VHRR data over a CXS link, it is now possible to provide SDUC (Secondary Data Utilisation Centre) type of data at any location in the country irrespective of its distance from MDUC/IMD and availability of point-to-point terrestrial transmission circuits.

The main weather satellite systems include the polar TIROSN/NOAA series from U.S.A., the geostationary orbiting GOES-Series (Geostationary Operational Environment Satellite) built by Hughs for Japan, Indian INSAT and Europe's METEOSAT-series.

16.8. Satellites For Scientific Studies

Satellites orbiting the planet earth at relatively lower altitudes (typically several hundreds of kilometers) have been and are being used to carry out a variety of scientific experimental studies including studying the characteristics of upper region of atmosphere, probing other planets and stars and so on. The significance of using satellites with significant payloads to carry out experiments of scientific and research nature arises from the fact that for many years, scientists were denied the insitu investigation of the upper reaches of the atmosphere except by observation from the earth and the instruments lifted by aeroplanes and sounding ballons. Earth observation had its own limitations. Only a few windows were open in the atmosphere for recording of data, generally those in the optical wavelengths. Also the atmosphere at low levels accessible to soil observations has become so polluted as to deny any useful observations. Satellites equipped with scientific payloads offer a very good and effective solution to carry out atmospheric and space studies.

One of the earlier studies was particularly designed to investigate aerosol concentration in the stratosphere. The experiment was known as Stratospheric Aerosol and Gas Experiment (abbreviated SAGE). The payload was launched in the satellite applications Explorer mission-B. The SAGE photometer looked at the sun through the stratosphere's gas and aerosols every time the satellite entered or left the earth's shadow. The instrument saw fifteen sun rises and an equal number of sunsets during each twenty four hour day. From repetitive observations, the concentrations of ozone and aerosols could be determined. Fig 16.17 shows the sketch of SAGE satellite. Studying space in another important mission of scientific satellites. Space studies include probing different planets, studying inter-planatory forces, solar wind and solar flare phenomenon etc. Fig. 16.18 shows a huge eruption on sun photographed by Skylab-3 and Fig. 16.19 shows solar flare prepared from data received from SMM.

In India too, Indian Space Research Organisation (ISRO) is pursuing the programme of using space borne vehicles for carrying out scientific experiments. Work on the development of Rohini series satellites stand testimany to that. The 106 kg SROSS-C satellite successfully launched on board the ASLV-D3 into a near earth orbit of 433 km apogee and 267 km perigee carried the scientific payloads namely (*i*) the Gamma ray burst experiment and (*ii*) Retarding potential analyser. Both the payloads functioned well and provided

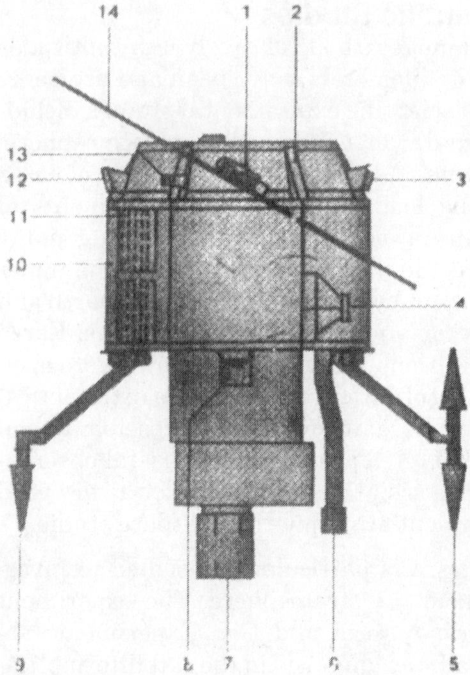

1. Solar array deployment mechanism.
2. Yo-Yo despin support (4).
3. Sun sensor No. 3
4. Scan wheel A
5. S-band telemetry antennas B
6. Magnetometer
7. SAGE instrument
8. Sun sensor No. 4 near side No. 5. far side
9. S-band data antenna A
10. Louvre panel (under)
11. Thermal control radiator
12. Sun sensor No 2
13. Electrical umbilical connector
14. Deployable solar arrays

Fig. 16.17

a lot of useful data for scientists till the satellite re-entered the atmosphere.

SROSS-C2 launched subsequently in May, 1994 from another ASLV flight has also started providing data. The Retarding Potential Analyser (RPA), one of the two payloads on board SROSS C-2 has started collecting data on thermal structure and electron densities of the ionosphere. SROSS-C3 is also planned for launch in 1995-1996.

IRAS (Infrared Astronomical Satellite) has been another revolutionary satellite launched in 1983. It was the first satellite to carry an all-sky survey to look for astronomical objects emitting infrared radiation. It was an international venture involving the U.S., the U.K. and Netherlands. Fig. 16.20 shows the IRAS image of a recently discovered new born star (arrowed) embedded in a cloud of dust and

Fig. 16.18

gas. The young protostar called B5-IRS1 is about 100,000 years old only. Another astronomical satellite of European origin was EXOSAT designed to measure position, structural aspects and spectral and temporal characteristics of X-ray sources. This satellite made detailed studies of known and new X-ray sources in our and other galaxies. It made more than 2000 observations mainly on the physics of Neutron stars and Black holes. EXOSAT also discovered quasi-periodic oscillations in the star GX5-1.

Hubble Telescope, Infrared Space Observatory (ISO), Granat, Gamma Rays Observatory (GRO), Advanced X-ray Astrophysics Facility (AXAF), Hipparcos, Extreme Ultraviolet Explorer (EUV) and Soho-Cluster missions are some of the newer craft for scientific studies.

Hubble telescope will allow observations of stars as faint as the 27th magnitude. In the ESA's Soho-cluster project, Soho will observe the sun, its corona and the solar wind while the four cluster craft will study the reactions of the magnetosphere to varying solar conditions (Fig. 18.21). Hipparcos was an astronomical satellite intended to make accurate measurements of the parallaxes, proper

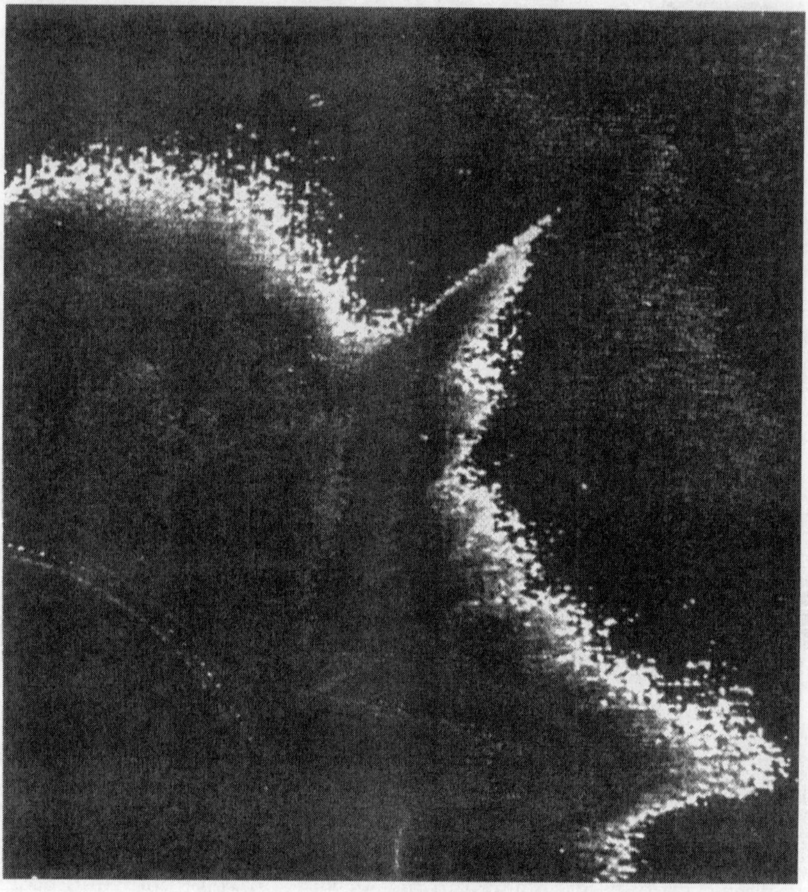

Fig. 16.19

motion and position of 115000 selected stars in our galaxy. It was launched in 1989 but it failed to attain geostationary orbit.

16.9. Satellites For Military Applications

Right from the beginning, satellites have had important military roles to play both during war time as well as peace time but in recent years, dependence on them has increased dramatically. The earlier methods of reconnaissance, communication, navigation, remote sensing etc. have always had some constraints or the other due to being land based or needing the services of specialised aircrafts or ships. The extent to which satellite technology has superseded these earlier methods of communication, remote sensing, reconnaissance etc. is largely responsible for ever increasing role of military satel-

Fig. 16.20

lites. Some of the more commonly heard military satellite applications include :

1. Reconnaissance and Intelligence gathering functions
2. Command and Communications
3. Navigation satellites
4. Early warning satellites
5. Meteorological functions
6. Nuclear detection

Reconnaissance and Intelligence gathering functions

The most widely known types of military satellites are those used to verify the extent and composition of military forces. One of the most important role of reconnaissance and intelligence gathering satellites is the verification of the agreed limitations of strategic arms and the monitoring of new military developments. This is achieved by a variety of electronic and photographic means.

One of the earlier satellite-series launched by U.S.A in early sixties was the Discoverer. The data from Discoverer, basically a

Fig. 16.21

photo reconnsaissance satellite was instrumental in ending US fears of a massive earstwhile Soviet ICBM build-up. Infact, Discoverer-29 was credited with photographing the ICBM base at Plesetsk. The Discoverer-series photo-reconnaissance satellites had re-entry capsule which could be used to carry the exposed photographic film (if the satellite carried a camera) back to earth. This capsule had a retro-rocket and could be recovered as it descended by a parachute. Fig. 16.22 shows labelled pictures of "Discoverer" and the "Re-entry capsule", "Search-and-find" satellites followed Discoverer series in U.S.A. And subsequently, different generation of reconnaissance satellites were evolved with the advances made in the instrumentation and satellite technology and also with ever increasing complexity of strategic military requirements. In addition to U.S.A., Russia and China are other countries pursuing active reconnaissance satellite programmes. Infact, Russian reconnaissance satellites account for largest percentage of Russian space launches. Both U.S.A. and Russia have tested manned orbital reconnaissance ; Russians have done it in the military adaptation of Salyut space station and conducted such experiments in Salyut-6 and 7 and Mir space stations, Americans have done it under MOL (Manned Orbital

Laboratory) project. Fig 16.23 shows the labelled sketch of Manned Orbital Laboratory.

Another space borne reconnaissance technique that has emerged in the late eighties is the use of radar. The radar signals from a reconnaissance satellite penetrate the cloud cover. The reflected echoes can be processed to produce images that resemble photographs. Photography using radar has the advantage that it is not hampered by bad weather's darkness.

The other surveillance and reconnaissance related military applications of satellites include (*i*) the electromagnetic reconnaissance (or ferret) dealing in the location and cataloging of military radio and radar stations and (*ii*) ocean surveillance.

Command and Communication

The reconnaissance and intelligence gathering functions though very important represent however a very small fraction of the true scope and diversity of the capabilities of the military satellites. Command and Communications is one such application. The satellites today meant for the purpose can provide instant communication between the operational forces and their national command authorities irrespective of the distance or time of the day. The idea of military communication satellites took shape with launching of Courier 1B in 1960 to be followed by the DSCS-series (Defence Satellite Communication System) Satellites beginning in 1966. DSCS-1, DSCS-2 and DSCS-3 series launching continuing till the mid eighties. The other popular military communications satellites (both past and present) include SEASAT for naval applications, SDS (Satellite Data System) used to communicate with US nuclear forces in polar regions, LES-series (Lincoln Experimental Satellite) for tactical communication and TACSAT used to link, by means of small transmitters, aircrafts, ships, land vehicles, FLEETSATCOM to provide global military coverage for USAF and Navy (Fig. 16.24), MILSTAR intended to be successor to FLEETSATCOM to provide strategic and tactical communications for USAF, Army and Navy, NATO-III series to provide rapid and secure communications among NATO members and SKYNET-IV (Britain's military communications satellite to replace SKYNET-II) to provide links among ships, mobile terminals on land and control centres.

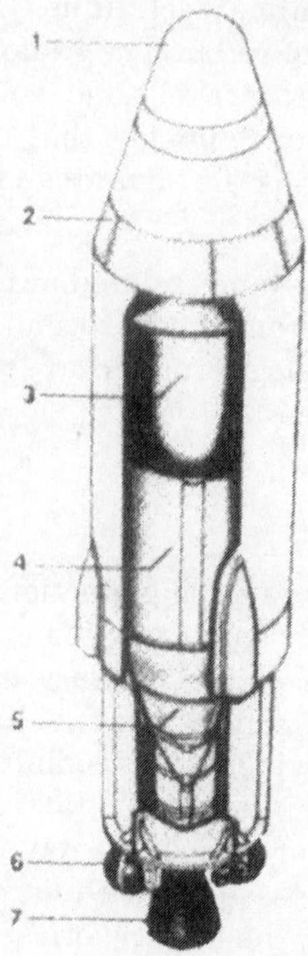

1 . Re-entry capsule
2. Equipment bay including computer inertial reference package, propellant pressurisation and horizon scanner
3. Fuel (UDMH)
4. Oxidant (IRFNA)
5. Destruct charge
6. Nitrogen and helium bottles.
7. Bell 8096 rocket engine. Agena B Length 25ft (7.6m)

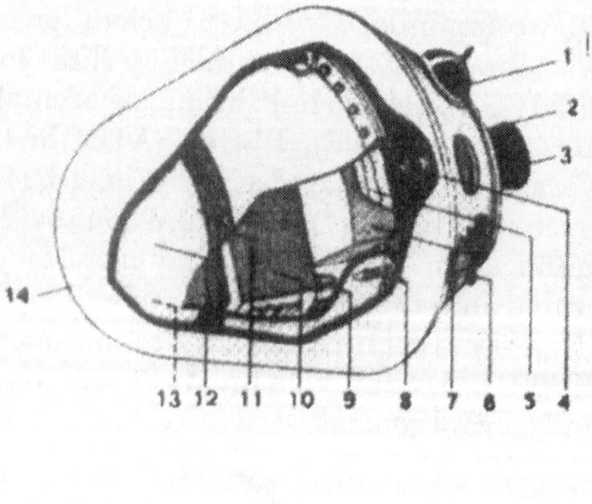

1. Cold gas storage tank
2. Thrust cone
3. Retro-rocket
4. Explosive bolt
5. Recovery parachute and chaff
6. Stabilization jets.
7. Parachute cover.
8. Explosive pistons
9. Flashing light
10. Instrumentation package
11. Dye markers
12. Recovery capsule
13. Radio beacon (inside).
14. Ablating re-entry sheild

Fig. 16.22.

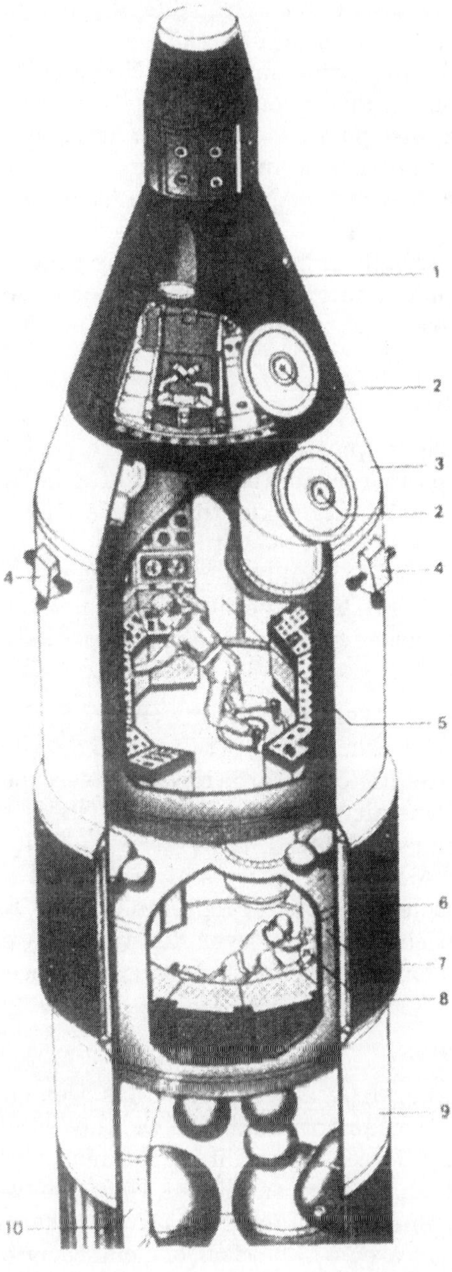

1. Gemini B spacecraft
2. Hatchness for external inflatable tunnel (one of four different crewtransfer methods considered)
3. Gemini adapter
4. Attitude control jets
5. Pressurised lab with control consoles air purification and circulation systems toilet (commode) and hygiene area main control consoles food storage and preparation bio-med sleeping couches spare spacesuit and other emergency equipment
6. Solar panels (stowed)
7. Pressurised lab with control and telemetry consoles attitude control TV extra emergency gear spare spacesuit food and water second commode etc.
8. Console for pointing and tracking telescope
9. Test module for experiments and/or equipment
10. Aft tunnel

Fig. 16.23.

Navigation Satellites

The navigational satellites are currently capable of providing data to enable position fixing with an accuracy of a few meters. NAVSTAR is one such satellite to provide navigation. NAVSTAR is designed to aid weapon aiming to enable users fix their position with much higher accuracy than was possible with other navigation systems. NAVSTAR provides a position accuracy of 15m. NAVSTAR is a replacement for the US Navy's TRANSIT-series. TRANSIT-series is a series of navigation satellites operated by the US Navy but also used by civilians, especially sailors. Receivers fix position through a combination of Doppler effect and accurate orbital details transmitted by satellites. Positional accuracy of about 100 m is possible in most parts of the world.

Early Warning Satellites

Early warning satellite development was basically aimed at providing an advance warning to the owners of a missile attack. The initial experiment in this direction began under the USAF's MIDAS (Missile Defence Alarm System) programme with the idea that the infrared sensor on board the satellite would detect the exhaust of a rising ICBM. The results of the MIDAS experiment were not very encouraging due to sunlight reflected from clouds and the operational system was abandoned.

The Integrated Missile Early Warning Satellite (IMEWS) first launched in 1970 has means of discriminating between real missiles and spurious effects. These satellites carry large infrared telescopes and television cameras to transmit photos of detected ICBMs to prevent false alarms that plagued MIDAS. IMEWS series satellites are capable of detecting ICBMs within seconds of ignition. This programme was renamed as Defence Support Programme (DSP). By mid 1980's, a network of four satellites, one over Russia, two over Pacific and Atlantic, and the fourth over South America had been established.

Meteorological Functions

Use of satellite data for accurate weather forecast has been one of the earlier benefits of the space programme. The weather satellites not only provide long range forecast for military planners, they also play a key role in reconnaissance satellites. They provide advance information to the mission planners of reconnaissance satellites on whether the target area will be clear of cloud cover or not when the reconnaissance satellite makes its pan. This eliminates wastage of limited reconnaissance film. DMSP/BLOCK-5D (DMSP

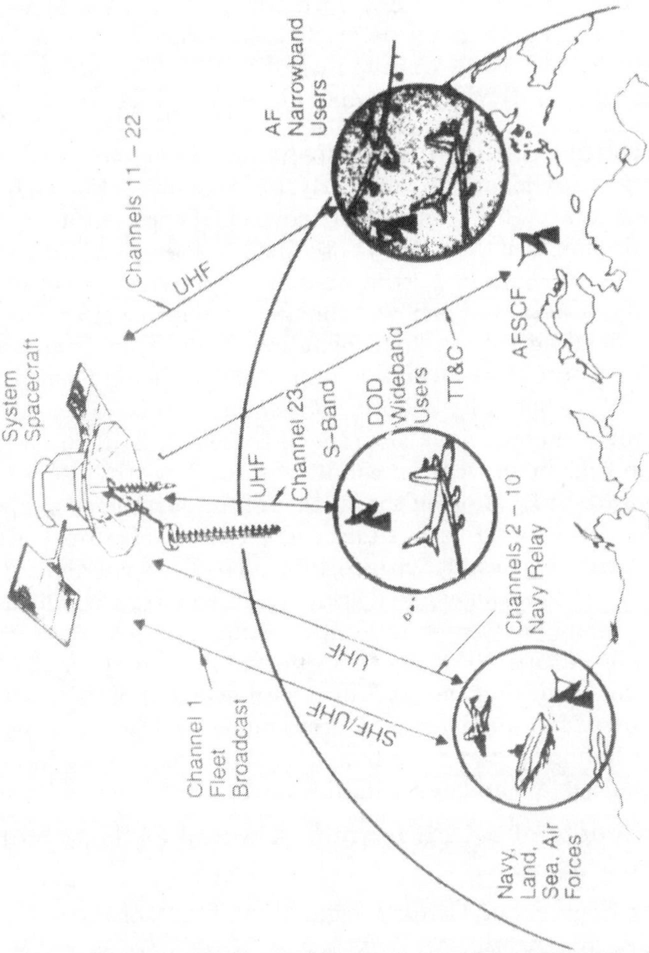

Fig. 16.24.

stands for Defence Meteorological Satellite Programme) series satellites provide weather information to both military and civilian users. Data is made available to the civilian users through NOAA (National Oceanographic and Atmospheric Administration). The payload includes line scanning radiometer operating in visual and infrared and precipitating electron spectrometer. These satellites provide infrared and visual imagery, temperature, moisture soundings, auroroal detection and upper atmosphere soundings.

Nuclear Detection

The idea of nuclear detection using satellites perhaps originated in U.S.A. while finding ways to police a nuclear test ban treaty. The solution came in the form of Vela Satellite which had the capability of detection a nuclear explosion at the distance of Venus or Mars and report its yield and other characteristics. Twelve satellites of Vela-series (Vela-1 and Vela-2) were launched during time period 1963-1970. Thereafter, IMEWS early warning satellite had taken over.

16.10. Global Positioning System

Although the Global Positioning System, popularly known by its abbreviated name, GPS, was initially developed to meet the navigational requirements of the Armed Forces, it has found a wide use and acceptance for navigational requirements of a large segment of the commercial market. That is how, I thought I would cover this under a separate heading rather than including it as a part of military applications of satellites covered in section 16.9. Global Positioning System (GPS) is basically a *Radio Based Navigation System* that gives you three dimensional coverage of the earth 24 hours a day, 365 days an year in all weather conditions. It allows the user of the system know their location on the surface of the earth or even above the surface of the earth with an accuracy of about 300 feet. Even greater accuracy is possible with certain corrections carried out by the GPS receiver at a known fixed location. GPS is today widely used for the purpose of navigation in aircraft, ships, cars etc. According to reported literature, GPS was very effectively used by US Armed Forces during Operation Desert Storm for movement of their troops in an unknown land amidst sand storm and other obstacles. Today, Global Positioning System is an indispensable component of almost every weapon system and every military operation.

Constituents of a GPS System. A typical GPS system has three components namely :

1. Space Segment, **2.** Control Segment and **3.** User Segment

Space Segment : The Space Segment of the Global Positioning System is a constellation of a total of 24 satellites operated by the US Department of Defence, out of which there are 21 Navigational satellites and 3 in-orbit active spares. The 24 satellites are arranged in a constellation orbiting at a height of about 11000 nautical miles (10900 Nautical Miles to be precise) above the surface of earth. These satellites are arranged in six orbiting planes having an inclination of 55 degree. Each orbital plane has six satellites spaced 60 degree apart. The orbital time period of each of these satellites is 11 hours and 58 minutes. This allows a receiver to receive signal from 5 to 8 of these satellites at any time. Fig. 16.25 shows the constellation of 24 satellites in different orbital planes as described above.

The first GPS satellite was launched in 1978. First ten satellites were in fact development satellites called Block-I satellites. During the period 1989-1993, 23 satellites, called Block-II satellites were launched. The 24th satellite was launched in 1994, which completed the constellation of satellites.

Each of these satellites has an internal atomic clock, accurate to within 3 nano-seconds. Each of the satellites emits synchronous time signals at regular intervals. These signals can be detected by anyone in possession of a GPS receiver. The receiver identifies the transmitting satellites by the received signals and thus determine the satellite's known position in space. If we know our exact distance from a given satellite in space, we can visualize that we are somewhere on the surface of an imaginary sphere with the radius of the sphere being equal to the satellite orbit radius. Going a step further, if we know our distance from two different satellites with known positions, we know that we are located somewhere on the line of intersection of the two imaginary spheres. And with the induction of a third satellite, we are left with only two possible locations. One of these locations is usually impossible. The GPS receivers are equipped with mathematical tools that can eliminate the impossible location.

Control Segment : The Control Segment is nothing but a system of monitoring stations located around the world. These are located Diego Garcia in the Indian Ocean, Hawaii and Kwajalein in

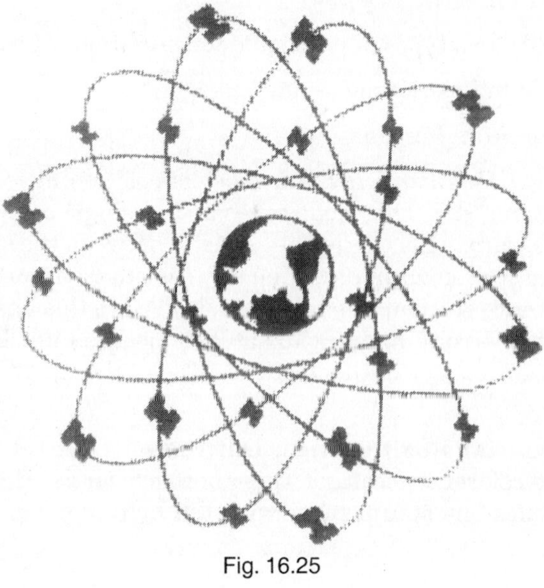

Fig. 16.25

the Pacific Ocean, Ascension Island in the Atlantic Ocean and Colorado springs in Colorado, a Master ground station at Falcon Air Base in Colorado Springs, Colorado and four large ground antenna stations that broadcast signals to the satellites. Three of these stations at Diego Garcia, Ascension and Kwajalein serve as up-link installations, capable of transmitting data to the satellites including new satellite positions as a function of time, clock corrections and other broadcast message data. The Colorado Springs station serves as the Master Control Station. The monitoring stations track all GPS signals for use in controlling the satellites. Satellite tracking data from the monitoring stations are transmitted to the master control station for processing. The Master Control Station processes the data and carries out required corrections.

User Segment : The User Segment consists of all earth-based GPS receivers including those for civilian and military use. A typical GPS receiver comprises of an antenna, a pre-amplifier, radio signal microprocessor, control and display device, a data recording unit and a power supply.

The GPS receiver decodes the timing signals from the satellites (usually four or more), it is able to access from his location at a given time. It computes their distances from the received signals. It computes its own latitude, longitude, elevation and time. The position computation is a continuous process and is generally up-dated on a second-by-second basis.

GPS Positioning Types

There are two types of position determination. These are :

1. Absolute Positioning

2. Differential Positioning

Absolute Positioning : This mode of positioning is also known as Stand-alone GPS. This mode relies upon a single receiver station. In this case, ranging is carried out strictly between the satellite and the receiver station without taking any assistance from any ground based reference station. The positions derived in this absolute mode are subject to errors inherent to satellite positioning. The position determining accuracy in this mode may be in the range of 50 to 100 meters.

Differential Positioning : Differential GPS relies upon an established reference location. This approach carries the triangulation principles one step further with the help of a second receiver placed at the known reference point. This approach takes care of the errors inherent to the satellite positioning process.

Precise and Standard Positioning Systems. The current series of GPS satellites broadcast data using two distinct signals, one for *Standard Positioning System* (SPS) at L1 frequency (1547.24 MHz) and the other for *Precise Positioning System* at L2 frequency (1227.60 MHz). The signal is shifted by 3 binary codes. Only the authorized users use the PPS. The signal here is the encrypted military signal, which is designed to be accurate within 15 to 30 meters. PPS could achieve resolution of 10 meters. The authorized users have the cryptographic equipment and the keys to decode the PPS signal. The Standard Positioning System has an accuracy of 100 meters. With assistance from a ground station, as described earlier in case Differential GPS, achievable accuracy may be even better than the original PPS.

17

Global, Regional and National Communication Satellites Systems

17.1. Global Communication Satellite Systems

17.1.1. INTELSAT

Intelsat Program: The International Telecommunications Satellite Organization (ITSO) is the world's largest commercial satellite communications services provider. It is an international consortium that owns and manages a constellation of communications satellites (Intelsats) to provide international broadcast services. Ownership and investment in ITSO (measured in shares) is distributed among ITSO members according to their respective use of services. Investment shares determine each member's percentage of the total contribution needed to finance capital expenditures. The organization's primary source of revenue comes from satellite usage fees which, after deduction of operating costs, are redistributed to ITSO members in proportion to their shares as repayment of capital and compensation for use of capital. Satellite services are available to any organization (both ITSO members and non-members), and all users pay the same rates.

The consortium began on August 20, 1964 as the International Telecommunications Satellite Consortium with 11 participating countires. In 1973, the name was changed and there were 80 signatories. ITSO currently has over 150 members and provides service to over 900 Earth stations in more than 149 countries, territories and dependancies. Intelsat maintains it headquarters in Washington, DC.

Spacecraft operations are controlled through ground stations in Fucino (Italy), Clarksburg (Maryland, USA), Beijing (PRC), Raisting (Germany), Perth (Australia), and Paumalu (Hawaii, USA).

Since its inception, ITSO has used several versions(blocks) of its dedicated Intelsat satellites. ITSO competes each block of spacecraft independently, leading to a variety of contractors over the years.

It is Washington, DC, USA based Internatinal Telecommunication Satellite Organisation that provides telecommunication services to its member countries throughout the world by means of satellite systems owned by it. Its first satellite was launched in April 1965 (also known as *Early Bird*). It could support either one TV channel or 240 voice circuits but not both, a limitation that made it costly to use. In the spring of 1967, Early Bird was joined by two larger companions-Intelsat 2 over the Pacific and Intelsat 3 over the Atlantic. With these three satellites, all the world's TV networks could be linked together, and the first global telecast was broadcast on Jun, 27, 1967. The telecommunications services included not only just telephone but also the TV, digital transmissions services, telex, computer to computer, video conferencing, video text etc.

It provides international links to 180 member and non-member countries, domestic links to 40 member countries and 900 separate ground stations through its network of satellites, teleports and fiber connections.

The INTELSAT traffic has been increasing day by day and idea to this can be had from Fig. 17.1. This has been accomplished by INTELSAT through an ensemble of satellites and earth stations operating with a wide variety of modulation techniques to provide diverse services globally.

The increase in worldwide satellite communication facilities has increased the world market for communication satellite equipment. A US report says that even the US market for communication satellite equipment is projected to increase 13.4% per year through 1995, to $ 9.8 billion.

There are nine INTELSAT satellite systems which have been launched from time to time. These are probably known as INTELSAT, I, II, III, IV, V, VI, VII, VIII and IX. Table 17.3 indicates in brief the characteristics and operational activities of these satellites. Note, that under one INTELSAT system several satellites are simultaneously in operation because of the global coverage requirement.

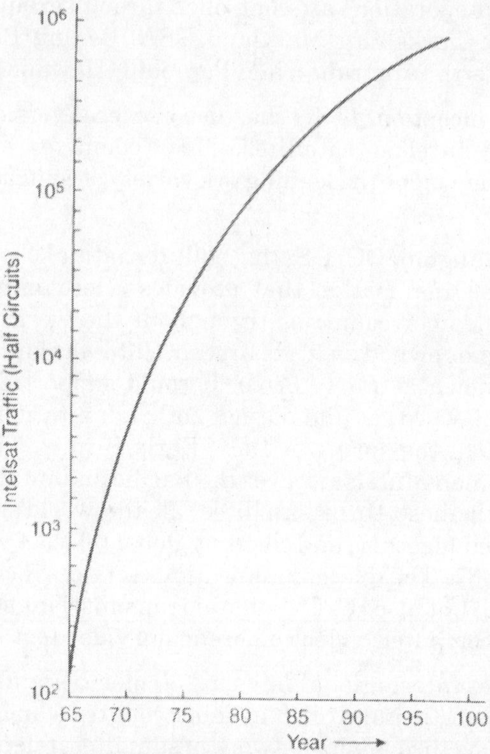

Fig. 17.1. Intelsat International Traffic Growth.

Intelsat-I and II used single isotropic antenna whereas Intelsat-III employed a de-spinning directional antenna. This helped in maintaining an intense beam on the surface of the earth. The Intelsat-IV satellites had reshaped beams so that it does not cover the ocean areas. There was also tremendous increase in the transponder capacity. Intelsat-V used Ku band antennas in addition to the C-band antennas. Intelsat - 10 has 45 C band and 16 Ku band transponders. While Intelsat 1 having the capability of handling 240 telephone calls or a single TV channel, Intelsat-VIII can handle more than 120,000 telephone calls or 500 TV channels.

There are around 20 Intelsat satellites positioned over the Atlantic, Pacific and the Indian Oceans in the GEO orbit to provide global communication services, covering 99% of the world's populated areas. These satellites cover four regions : (*i*) Atlantic Ocean Region (AOR) North America Central America, South America, India, Africa and western portions of Europe. (*ii*) Indian Ocean Region (IOR) which covers Eastern Europe, Africa, India, South East

Asia, Japan and Western Australia, (*iii*) Asia Pacific Region (APR) which includes Eastern Europe, the former USSR and all the regions from India to Japan and Australia. (*iv*) Pacific Ocean Region (POR) covering Southeast Asia to Australia, the Pacific and the western regions of America and Canada.

Fig. 17.2 indicates various INTELSAT satellite configurations. The INTELSAT networks are controlled from the INTELSAT Space Craft Technical Control Centre in Washington, D.C. Techincal details of INTELSAT spacecraft and member country earth station operation are adopted by a Board of Governors which follows general rules established by the Meeting of Signatories. The Meetings of Signatories takes place once a year and discusses general operational and financial matters. The constitution of Board of Governors has representatives from 20 largest investors and five regional representatives. The Board of Governors publishes mandatory technical

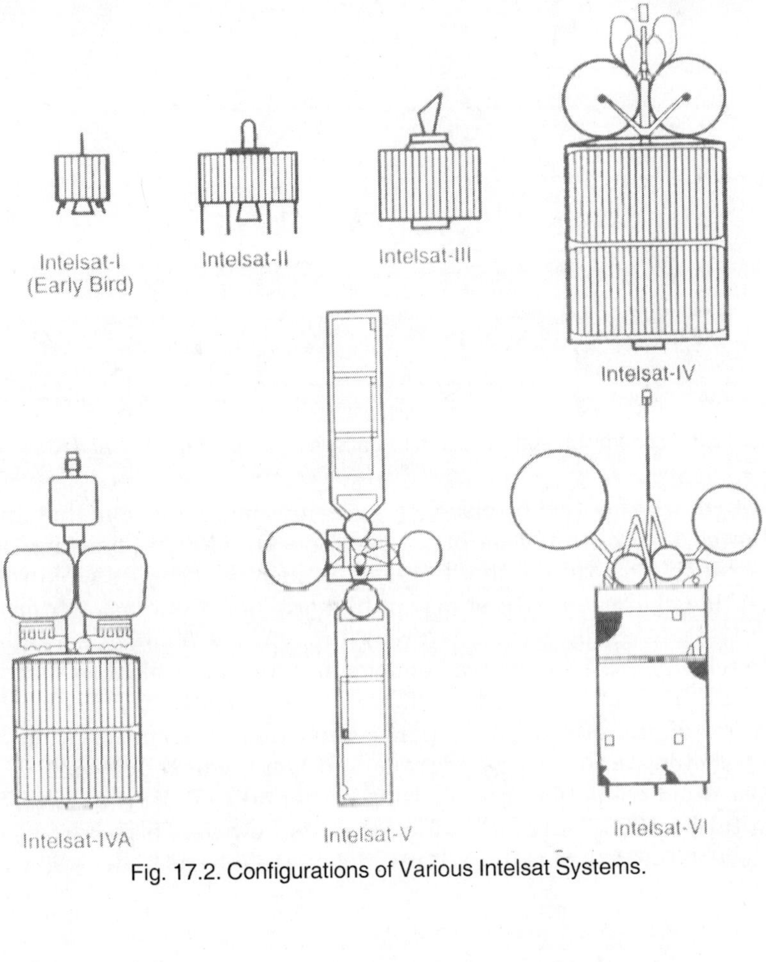

Fig. 17.2. Configurations of Various Intelsat Systems.

and performance characteristic that earth stations meet in order to participate in the Intelsat system.

From Table 17.1 it is evident that with the new generation Intelsat satellite systems the telecommunication capabilities have increased tremendously. It can be seen that the Intelsat I, the world's first commercial communication satellite was launched in 1965 which was designed to operate for 1.5 years and 480 half circuits. By contrast Intelsat VI is designed to operate for 10 years and provide upto 80,000 half circuits. It is worthwhile to mention here that as the technology developed there was economy in the space segment cost per transponder year. Fig. 17.3. shows it clearly. It shows a very strong and consistent downward trendline. In recent years and

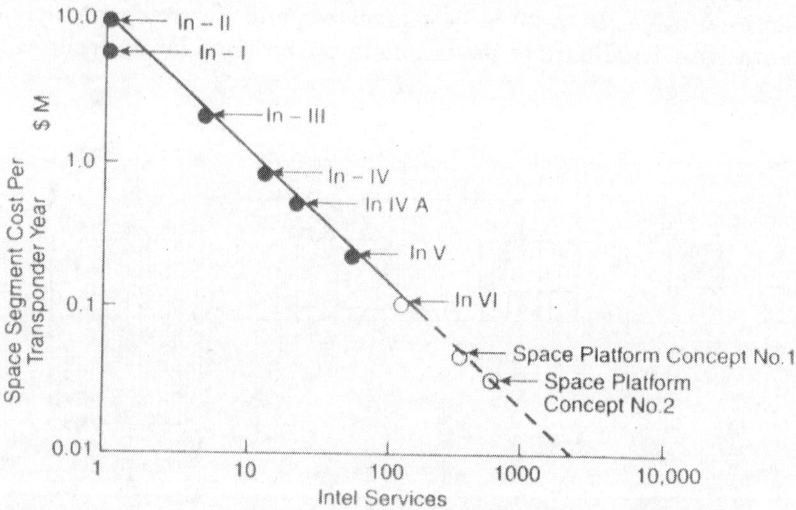

Fig. 17.3. Economy of Scale in Communications space craft of (Past and Present) Intelsat series.

particularly for the Intelsat VI, it is lifetime extension that has allowed the continuation of this positive trend. The main reason responsible for this is the decrease in micro electronics circuitory cost though the launch cost may be higher. The life extension to orbit for 15-18 years has been new 'breakthrough' developments in satellite technology. There is tremendous pressure in intelsat to shift to digital. Intelsat believes that its new digital tariff structure which reward digital effectiveness, particularly digital circuit multiplication should stimulate a rapid transition over the next ten years. The most rapid transition model assumes that 80% of all traffic will be digital by 1996. Current traffic forecasts however, place the level below 50%. A range of digital traffic that could be as high as 80% or as low as 45% wideband. Actual Intelsat planning will probably assume in between figure of 65%.

17.2. EUTELSAT System

The launch of ECS-1 satellite in 1983 announced the setting up of European Satellite Telecommunication Organisation (Eutelsat), with an aim to broadcast TV programmes and to provide communication services to various departments. The Eutelsat system provides television, telephony and data transmission services in the European region. The system consists of satellites in the Hot Bird series, eBird series, EuroBird series and Atlantic Gate satellites. At present, there are total 24 Eutelsat satellites operating from various departments.

17.2.1. Telstar

These satellites provide varied applications ranging from cable, DTH television, internet applications, to news gathering, distance learning, business learning and telephony.

Telstar 1 and *Telstar 2* became the first commercial satellites in low orbits with which it opened an era of transatlantic television transmission.

Telstar 1 was launched through Delta Rocket from Cape Canaveral on July 10, 1962 and it transmitted the first ever direct television pictures from the United States to Europe thereby becoming the first satellite to relay signals from the earth to a satellite and then back.

Telstar 2 was launched on May 7, 1963, and it replaced Telstar 1 to became the first satellite to transmit transatlantic television transmission.

Telstar 301, 302, 303, 401, 402 and currently operational Telstar 5, 6, 7, 10, 11, 12 are the stellites in this series. Telstar 8 and 9 hybrid C, Ka and Ku band satellites which were launched in the year 2003 and 2004 respectively.

Telstar II (Orion 1) It was developed by Matra Marconi company of France and launched on 29th November, 1994 from Kennedy Space Center in Cape Canaveral, USA, on Atlas 2A, in its Orbit GEO 37.5°E The payloads consists of 34 Ku band Transponders and it is, 3-axis stabilized.

17.2.2. New Skies Satellites

This is one of four fixed satellite communications companies with truly global satellite coverage. It provides video, voice, data and Internet communications services to a range of telecommunications carriers, broadcasters, large corporations and Internet service provides around the world. New Skies currently has six operational satellites in geosynchronous orbit.

Table 17.1. Features of INTELSAT System

	No. of Satellites	*Transmission Capability*	*Stabilization*
Intelsat 1	One satellite Intelsat 1 1	1 transponder (240 circuits/one TV channel)	Spin Stabilized
Intelsat 2	Four Satellites Intelsat 2 1, 2 2, 2 3 and 2 4	2 VHF transponders each (240 two-way telephone circuits or one two-way TV channel.)	Spin Stabilized
Intelsat 3 (Intelsat 31, 35 and 38 failed on launch)	Engine Intelsat 3 1, 3 2, 3 3, 3 4, 3 5, 3 6, 3 7, 3 8	1,500 voice or 4 TV channels	Spin Stabilized
Intelsat 4	Eight Satellites : Intelsat 4 1, 4 2, 4 3, 4 4, 4 5, 4 6, 4 7 and 4 8	12 C band transponders each (4000 voice circuits or 2 TV channels each)	Spin Stabilized
Intelsat 4A	Six Satellites: Intelsat 4A 1, 4A 2, 4A 3, 4A 4, 4A 5 and 4A 6	20 C band transponders each (7,250 voice or 2 TV channels each)	Spin Stabilized
Intelsat 5	Nine Satellites; Intelsat 501, 502, 503, 504, 505, 506, 507, 508 and 509	21 C band and 4 Ku band transponders (12,000 voice + 2 TV channels)	3-axis Stabilized
Intelsat 5A	Six Satellites: Intelsat 510, 511, 512, 513, 5A 14 and 515)	26 C band and 6 Ku band transponders each (15,000 voice + 2 TV channels)	3-axis Stabilized
Intelsat 6	Five Satellites: Intelsat 601, 602, 603, 604, 605 and 606)	38 C band and 10 Ku band transponders each (920,000 two way telephone calls, as well as three television channels each)	Spin Stabilized
Intelsat 7	Six Satellites: Intelsat 701, 702, 703, 704, 705 and 709)	28 C band and 10 Ku band transponders each (18,000 telephone calls and 3 colour TV broadcasts simultaneously or upto 90,000 telephone circuits using digital circuit multiplication equipment (DCME)	3-axis Stabilized
Intelsat 7A	Three Satellites: 706, 707 and 708)	26 C band transponders and 14 Ku band transponders each (22,500 telephone calls and 3 colour TV broadcasts simultaneously. Or upto 1,12,500 telephone circuits using DCME)	3-axis Stabilized
Intelsat 8	Four Satellites: Intelsat 801, 802, 803 and 804	38 C band transponders and 6 Ku band transponders each (22,000 telephone calls and 3 colour TV broadcasts simultaneously or upto 1,12,500 telephone circuits using DCME)	3-axis Stabilized

	No. of Satellites	*Transmission Capability*	*Stabilization*
Intelsat 8A	Two satellites: Intelsat 805 and 806	28 C band transponders and 3 Ku band transponders each	3-axis Stabilized
Intelsat 9	Seven Satellites: Intelsat 901, 902, 903, 904, 905, 906 and 907	44 C band transponders and 12 Ku band transponders each	3-axis Stabilized
Intelsat 10	One Satellite: Intelsat 10-02)	45 C band and 16 Ku band transponders	3-axis Stabilized

17.2.3. Apstar

Apstar satellites are the China's communication satellites and were developed by APT satellite company. Apstar 1 was the first satellite which was launched in this series followed by Apstar 1A, 2, 3, 4.

ApStar 2 was lost shortly after its liftoff in 1995, Apstar 2R (Apstar 4 or Telstar 10) was launched in the year 1997 and is one of the most powerful spacecraft in Asia-Pacific service which provides regional voice, video, and data services to link Europe, Russia, the Middle East, Africa, and the Asia-Pacific region into a broad telecommunications network.

Latest Apstar satellites include Apstar 5 and Apstar 6, which are hybrid C and Ku band satellites. Apstar 5 provides voice, video and data services to China, Hawaii, and East Asia, and C-band services in the Asia-Pacific region, including Australia and Hawaii. It also provides space-based Internet services to cities in Asia from the U.S. through Hawaii. Apstar 6 which is to be launched in 2006 will provide communication services in the Asia Pacific region which will be the first civil satellite in China to be equipped with anti jamming system.

Apstar 1 and 1A were developed Hughes Space and Communications company in California, USA. Apstar 1 was launched on 21st July 1994 and Apstar 1A was launched on 3rd July 1996. Both these satellites were launched from Xichang, China on Chinese CZ-3. The Orbit of Apstar 1 is GEO 138°E while of Apstar 1 A is GEO 134°E. The Payload consists of 24 (+6) C-band Transponders each, and are is spin stabilized.

The main aim of APSTAR I is to provide general communications services such as voice, fax, data, and television signals across China, Hong Kong, Indonesia, Japan, Singapore and Vietnam. Apstar 1A provides television and other telecommunication services as a back up satellite to Apstar 1 with an aim to expand the coverage in the South Asian region.

17.2.4. Galaxy

Galaxy satellite were developed by PanAmSat global satellite system in 1983 which provides satellite communicaiton services to America, Europe, Africa, the Middle East and Asia. It revolutionized the U.S. television industry by broad casting TV channels to cable service providers throughout the country. Since then Galaxy 1, 1R1, 1R2, 2, 3, 4, 5, 6, 7, 8i, 8iR, 9, 10, 10R, 11, 12 and 13 have been launched and Galaxy 14 and 15 are being planned to be launched in the near future.

17.2.5. Orbcomm

The main aim of this satellite is to provide messaging services globally. It was developed by Orbital Science Corporation of Canada. The programme began with launch of Orbcomm FM 1 FM 2 on 2nd April 1995. Later Orbcomm FM3- FM4, Orbcomm FM5-FM12, and Orbcomm FM13-FM20 were launched in this series. Orbcomm FM1-FM2 were placed in Polar orbit, mean radius 785km and other satellites are in inclined orbit in three planes with eight equidistantly spaced satellites in each plane, 780 km cirucular, 45° inclination. Its payloads are 17 data processors and seven antennas.

These satellites handles around 5 million messages from users having small, portable terminals to transmit and receive messages directly to the satellites. The satellites are *orbiting packet routers* which grabs small data packets from sensors in vehicles, vessels or from remote sites and then relays them through a tracking earth station.

17.2.6. Afristar Satellite

It was developed by Alcatel Space Industries of France and launched on 28th August, 1998 from Kourou in French Guiana, France,through Ariane 44L in its orbit- GEO 21°E, on broad with 3 L-band transponders and was 3-axis stabilized.

The main aim of this satellite is to provide direct satellite digital audio and multimedia communications services to Africa, Middle East, Asia, Latin America and the Caribbean.

Currently, Afristar and Asiastar are operational and both these satellites together broadcast audio, text and images to more than 4.6 billion people all over the world.

17.2.7. ICO

The ICO Global Communications, the satellites provide global mobile communications services using a constellation of 10 operational Medium Earth Orbit (MEO) satellites with 2 in-orbit spares in a 45° inclination orbit and a global ground telecommunications network.

It offers a wide range of satellite-based mobile telecommunications through handheld, speciality and fixed phones manufactured by Hughes, Mitsubishi, NEC, Nera Panasonic, and Samsung. The services include voice, data, and fax with voicemail, messaging, three way calling and call forwarding

17.3. Regional Communication Satellite Systems

These systems provide services to a group of countries belonging to the same region and therefore not only promote a sharing of communication facilities on regional basis but also long-term cooperation and goodwill among the member countries. This section presents an overview of the important regional systems currently in operation.

17.3.1. EUTELSAT System.

The launch of ECS-1 satellite in 1983 begun the period of the setting up of European Satellite Telecommunication Organisation (Eutelsat) with an aim to broadcast TV programmes and provide communication services to various departments. The Eutelsat system provides television, telephony and data transmission services in the European region. The system consists of satellites in the Hot Bird, eBird, Eurobird Series and Atlantic Gate satellites. At present, there are total 24 Eutelsat satellites operating from over various locations from 15° West and 70.5° East in the GEO Orbit. It serves to 90 percent of the population around Globe in over 150 countries with 24 satellites (20 of these satellites belongs to Eutelsat, one each includes Express A3, Express AM22, Telecom 2D and Telstar 12).

The Eutelsat system offers many services which includes television and radio broadcasting for the consumer public, professional video broadcasting, corporate networks, Internet services, mobile communications and broadband services. Using its HOT BIRD system transmits more than 1,400 television channels to an overall audience of 110 million homes connected to a cable network or equipped for direct-to-home reception.

Eutelsat series of satellites : These till date consist of Eutelsat 1F series, Eutelsat 2F and Eutelsat W series of satellites have been launched. Eutelsat 1 and 2 series comprises of 5 satellites each (Eutelsat 1 F1, F2, F3, F4, F5 and Eutelsat 2F1, F2, F3, F4 and F5). Eutelsat W series comprises of 5 satellites ; the latest Eutelsat W 1, 2, 3, 4, 5. All Eutelsat W satellites and some satellites of Eutelsat 2 series are currently operations. The W satellites provides many services *viz.*, Internet, public telephony, business networks, satellite news gathering, television and radio programme broadcasting.

e-Bird : This Eutelsat satellite provides high-speed broadband Internet services in all over Europe and Turkey with its proximity to EUROBIRD 1 at 28.5° East, e-BIRD is in good position for digital TV and broadband services that can be even received by small domestic antennas.

Eurobird satellites : These offer broadcasting and telecommunication services primarily to the Western and Central European region. EUROBIRD 1 is an extension of the telecommunication services previously provided by the EUTELSAT II-F4 satellite, including business services, satellite news gathering and television and radio programme distribution. It also broadcast programmes and multimedia services into very small and inexpensive satellites dishes.

HOT BIRD system : This system consists of five satellites, and provides nearly 700 analogue and digital television channels to satellite and cable homes in Europe, North Africa and large parts of the Middle East. It also provides over 560 radio and multimedia services.

SESAT satellite system : Thus system called Siberia - Europe Satellites offer telecommunications services over the Altantic Ocean to Eastern Russia, including a large part of Siberia. It also provides similar services within the Indian Sub-Continent by means of steerable spotbeams. SESAT - 1 provides international, regional and domestic services, such as thin route telephony, corporate and specialized data services and long distance trunk telephony. SESAT - 2 has a highly flexible configuration of fixed and steerable beams and provides high-power Ku-band capacity over Europe, Africa, the Middle East and central Asia.

Atlantic Bird Satellite System : This system three satellites - ATLANTIC BIRD1, ATLANTIC BIRD2, and ATLANTIC BIRD 3 all with Ku band transponders - and provides video, IP and data communication services to Europe, Middle East and North African regions. It provides American video professionals with seamless access to over 100 million homes via bundled turnarounds on Eutelsat's leading DTH orbital positions. It also provides the important Internet links.

Table 17.2. Features of Eutelsat, e-Bird, Eurobird, Hot Bird, SESAT and Atlantic Bird Satellite Systems.

Satellite	*Transmission Capability*	*Stabilization*
Eutelsat W (comprising of 5 satellites Eutelsat W1, 2, 3, 3A, 4, 5	1-28 Ku band transponders 2, 3, 5- 24 Ku band transponders each 4-31 Ku band transponders. 3A-38 Ku and 3 Ka band transponders.	3-axis
e-Bird 1	20 Ku band transponders	3-axis
Eurobird 1	24 (+6) Ku band transponders	3-axis
Eurobird 2		3-axis
Hotbird 1	16 (+8) Ku band transponders	3-axis
Hotbird 6	28 Ku band transponders and 4 Ka band transponders	3-axis
SESAT 1	18 Ku band transponders	3-axis
SESAT 2	24 Ku band transponders (12 are leased to Eutelsat)	3-axis
Atlantic Bird 1	24 Ku band transponders	3-axis
Atlantic Bird 2	26 Ku band transponders	3-axis
Atlantic Bird 3	35 Ku band and 10 C band transponders	3-axis

17.3.2. Eurasiasat

Eurasiasat 1. It was developed by Aerospatiale of France and was launched on 10th January, 2001 from Kourou in French Guiana, France. through Airane 44P, in its Orbit - GEO 42°E, with 32 Ku band Transponders on board and is 3-axis stabilized.

This satellite provides high-powered Ku and BSS coverage from Western Europe to Central Asia, including Middle East and Russia, with an overlapping of the coverage over Turkey.

17.3.3. Europestar

Europestar series of satellites comprises of Europestar 1 Europestar, B, and Europestar 2 launched in the year 2004. Europestar 1 provides broadband serivices to Europe, Southern Africa, the Middle East, the Indian subcontinent and South East Asia. Europestar B provides point-to-point connections such as internet backbone circuits, TV and telephony services with in Europe.

Europestar E1. It was developed by Alcatel Space company of France and launched on 29th October, 2000 from Kourou in French

Guiana, France through Ariane 44LP into its orbit - GEO 47.5°E stabilized at 3-axis with on board 30 Ku band Transponders.

17.3.4. Astra

Astra 2D, 3A It was developed by Hughes Space and Communication USA. Astra 2D was launched on 19 December 2000 and Astra 3A on 29 March 2002. Both the satellites were launched from Kourou in French Guiana, France. Astra 2D : is placed in its orbit GEO 28.2°E and Astra 3A in GEO 23.5°E. Payload on board Astra 2D consists of 18 Ku band transponders and Astra 3A of 30 Ku band transponders. Stabilization of both is spin stabilized.

This series of satellites, is operated by SES Astra, and it comprises of three series:

Astra 1 series has five operational satellites (Astra 1D, 1E, 1F, 1G and 1H).

Astra 2 has four operational satellites (Astra 2A, 2B, 2C and 2D).

Astra 3 has two operational satellites (Astra 3A and 3B).

Astra satellites provides broadband satellite communication services like TV, broadband data, radio and Internet services in Europe.

Astra 1 KR, is a Ku band satellite, and Astra 1L is hybrid Ku, and Ka band satellite, which provides improved DTH broadcast services across Europe.

17.3.5 AAP-1 (Americom Asia Pacific-1) or GE 1A

It was developed by Lockheed Martin Commercial Space Systems (LMCSS), USA. It was launched on 2nd October, 2000 from Baikonur, Cosmodrome in Kaakhstan by ILS through Proton K in its orbit GEO 108.2°E. The Payload consisted of 28 Ku band transponders and was 3-axis stabilized.

This satellite is a high-powered, Ku-band FSS providing coverage in China, Northeast Asia, the Philippines and India. The AAP is currently operating 15 spacecraft in orbital positions providing service throughout the Americas, across Europe, over the Atlantic and Pacific Oceans, and throughout Asia. The main aim of this satellite is to Broadcast program , DTH applications, broadband data networks and VSAT applications.

17.3.6 Americom (AMC) series

AMC series of satellites developed by Alcatel space company of France comprised of total 17 satellites.

Currently, AMC- 1, 2, 3, 4, 5, 6, 7, 8 and 9 are operational while AMC 10, 11, 12, 13, 14, 15, 16 and 18 are slated to be launched in coming years. The satient features of these satellites are:

1. AMC-1 provides high speed video and data services to United States, Alaska, Hawaii, Northern Mexico and Southern Canada.
2. AMC-2 provides dedicated Ku-band services for television broadcasting to Canada, Hawaii and the Caribbean.
3. AMC-3 provides C-band cable, radio and educational programming distribution services and Ku-band education, broadcast, business television and broadband Internet services to CONUC, Hawaii and southern Canada.
4. AMC-4 serves North and South America.
5. AMC-5 serves the SNG, occasional services, VSAT, business television and broadband Internet market in CONUS, Hawaii, Carribean and Southern Canada.
6. AMC-6 provides direct-to-home (DTH), media and entertainment distribution plus enterprise and internet protocol (IP) services in North America.
7. AMC-7 and 8 provides distribution of cable, broadcast television and radio telecommunciations services, business television and broadband data distribution throughtout North America, the Caribbean, Latin America, Europe and Asia.
8. AMC-9 provides communication services to USA, Mexico and the Caribbean.

17.3.7. Asiasat

The Asiasat 4 was developed by Hughes Space and Communications company, USA and launched on 11th April, 2003 from Kennedy Space Centre in Cape Canaveral, USA through Atlas IIIB,in its orbit GEO 122°E. The payload on board consists of 28 C band and 20 Ku band Transponders, and is 3-axis stabilized. This system provides extensive C band coverage across Asia and target Ku-band beams for Australasia, East Asia and DTH services in Hong Kong.

This is the regional satellite system operating in Asia, which provides broadcast and telecommunication services to two-thirds of the world population in Asia. The Asiasat series consists of Asiasat 1, Asiasat 2, Asiasat G, Asiasat 3S and Asiasat 4 satellites out of which Asiasat2, Asiasat 3A and Asiasat 4 are currently operational. The first satellite in the series, Asiasat 1 was launched in 1990.

17.3.8. Asiastar

It is developed Alcatel Space Industries of France and Matra Marconi Space company of France and launched on 21th March, 2000 from Kourou in French Guiana, France through Ariane 5G in, its Orbit in GEO 105°E. The payload consists of 96 L band transponders and stabilization is 3-axis.

This system provides direct satellite services of digital audio and multi-media communications services in Africa, Middle East, Asia, Latin America and the Caribbean. It consists of four satellites - Afristar, Ameristar, Asiastar and Worldstar. Currently, Afristar and Asiastar are operational and they broadcast audio, text and images to more than 1.6 billion people all over the world.

17.3.9. Arabsat

Arabsat 1 : The first generation of **ARABSAT** setellite was developed in 1981 when ARABSAT signed with Aerospatiale of France for the latter to manufacture three identical satellites to provide television, voice and data links to the Arab league countries.

ARABSAT 1A (were in Orbital 19° East) and ARABSAT 1 B (were in orbital 26° East) satellites of the first generation were launched in 1985 and completed their operational lifetime and were switched off completely in 1992 and 1993 respectively.

ARABSAT 1C satellite was launched in Febraury 1992 to the orbital 31° East with excess fuel, and it expected to be in operation until 2002.

On November 26, 1997, ARABSAT sold out 1C to the Indian Space Research Organization (ISRO) when the INSAT 2D satellite failed.

Arabsat 2 : The second generation of ARABSAT satellite was developed to meet the increasing demand of traditional and new telecommunications services and to ensure the continuity of services. It consisted of 4 satellites.

ARABSAT-2A was successfully launched on July 9, 1996 to 26° East as well as ARABSAT-2B was successfully launched on November 13, 1996 to 30.5° East. The satellites reflect improvements over the first generation of ARABSAT satellites in capacity, power, coverage and lifetime.

ARABSAT 2-C was deployed to the orbital location 26° East. It carried 18 operational transponders in C-Band, covering most of the Arab world. ARABSAT thereby transferred the C-Band traffic from ARABSAT 2-A to ARABSAT 2-C in June 2003.

ARABSAT is currently operating its new satellite, ARABSAT 2-D, carrying 22 Transponders in Ku-band dedicated for Direct TV broadcasting. Each transponder can carry up to 10 digital TV programs. ARABSAT 2-D Co-located with (2-A) and (3-A) satellites enhancing its Hot-Spot orbital location at 26° east, which enables viewers within the coverage areas to receive the TV programs from these 3 satellites with one receiving antenna.

ARABSAT 3: It is the first satellite of ARABSAT third generation, and was successfully launched on February 26, 1999. After the success of ARABSAT in manufacturing, launching and operating two generations of Satellites, ARABSAT stepped into manufacturing the first satellite of its third generation. ARABSAT-3A is unique in power and coverage and is co-located with ARABSAT-2A to further enhance the Arabsat satellite system's capability.

Features:

- 20 Transponders in Ku-band dedicated for Direct TV broadcasting, each transponder can carry up to 10 TV channels when digital compression technology is used.
- ARABSAT-3A has been co-located with ARABSAT-2A at the orbital location 26° East creating a hot-spot for Digital and Analog TV broadcasting. This enables viewers within the coverage area to receive the TV programms from both satellites with one receiving antenna.
- ARABSAT-3A covers the following countries: Saudi Arabia, Kuwait, Libya, Qatar, Emirates, Jordan, Lebanon, Bahrian, Syria, Iraq, Algeria, Yemen, Egypt, Oman, Tunisia, Morocco, Mauritania, Sudan, Palestine, Djibouti, and parts of Somalia, Senegal, Mali, Niger, and Chad. It also covers Portugal, Spain, France, UK, Ireland, Switzerland, Luxembourg, Belgium, Germany, Austria, Yugoslavia, Albania, Italy, Malta, Greece, Cyprus, Hungary, Czech Republic and Slovak, Bulgaria, Turkey, and parts of Romania, Poland, and Denmark.
- ARABSAT-3A is recognized by a unique coverage for all Arab states and western European countries, thus one transponder on one satellite covers it all.
- ARABSAT-3A tariff is also very competitive.

17.3.10. LMI-1

The Russian Communication Satellite LMI-1 provides high-quality and relaiable fixed service telephony and direct broadcast television services to satisfy the rapidly growing demand of Russian telecommunication and broadcasting needs. The spacecraft is the first of several planned state-of-the-art satellites meant to provide connectivity to business and residents. In addition to its Russian coverage, it delivers telecommuncations services in the Commonwealth of Independent States, Eastern and Central Europe, Asia and Africa.

17.3.11. Orion

Orion satellites, the USA's communication satellite system was launched in 1994, to cater to the needs of people across Europe, the United States and parts of Canada and Mexico, providing video for broadcast and business television, high-speed Internet access and multimedia services, broadband and data networking.

17.3.12. PAS

With the launch of PAS-1 in 1988, 13 satellites are in space. This global satellite system of America and provides communcation services to USA, Europe, Africa, the Middle East and Asia. They provide DTH, video, data communication services to South America, India, China, Middle East, South Africa, Europe etc.

17.3.13. Garuda

Garuda are the series of satellites of Indonesia's communication satellites. Garuda-1 provides geo-based mobile telephone communications across Asia. It is part of the ACeS satellites constellation that provides telephony and data service communication services that enables customers equipped with hand-held terminals to communicate via high-quality, low cost digital signals and gives access to voice, data, and fax services.

Garuda 1. It was launched on 12th February, 2000 from Baikonour Cosmodrome in Kaakhstan through Proton-K, in its Orbit of GEO 123°E with payload of 18 C and 16 Ku band transponders in 3-axis stabilized mode.

The Garuda-2, serves as a back-up to Garuda-1, and allows the ACeS system to expand coverage to western and central Asia, the Middle East, Europe and northern Africa operated by Asia Cellular Satellite (ACeS) of Indonesia.

17.4. National Communication Satellite Systems

These systems are dedicated to meet the domestic communication needs of countries and therefore are an expression of a nation's self-reliance in a frontier area of technology. While the developed countries like the USA, Russia and Canada were the first to install national systems, a large number of developing nations like China, India and Brazil also achieved national capabilities in this field. Below is given a short description of important national satellites presently operational. Note that India's INSAT system is not included here and has been described in chapter 25.

17.4.1. National Communication Satellite Systems:

I. Canada's and North America's Communication Satellites.

1. Anik and Anik F : This is Canada's Communication satellite system which is owned by Telesat. Launch of Anik-A satellite in 1972 made the country the first to have a domestic communications satellite system, besides this it provides services to both North and South America. There are till now twelve Anik satellites, including: three Anik A satellites, one Anik B satellite, three Anik C satellites, two Anik D satellites, two Anik E satellites and Anik F1 satellite. Currently, Anik F1, E1 and E2 are the operational satellites.

Anik F series is the sixth in the Anik series of satellites and has Anik F1, Anik F2 and Anik F3 with F2 and F3 launched in 2004. Anik F2 will have 24 C-band transponders, 32 Ku-band transponders and an advanced Ka-band payload, and provide interactive multimedia services such as high-speed Internet, telemedicine, tele-learning, tele-working and e-commerce. Anik F3 has expanded existing services and provide backup within Telesat fleet.

2. Direct TV : The DirecTV satellites launched in 1994 provides Direct Broadcast System (DBS) services in North America. It transmits more than 200 channels of high-fidelity to cable companies and home dishes. The series has DirecTV 1, 2, 3, 1R, 4S, 5, 6, 7S and 9S.

3. Echostar : The Echostar provides Direct Broadcast Satellite television services to American homes. Owned by Echostrar communications corporation, an American broadcasting satellite company, it has nine Echostar satellites. The latest in series, Echostar 10 has 32 Ku transponders which was launched in 2005. It provides DISH Network customers with hundreds of all-digital television channels including interactive TV services, sports programming, high definition television and international programming.

4. GStar : GStar satellites are operated by SES Americom Systems and are part of the USA's communication satellite system. Till date four satellites - GStar 1, 2, 3 and 4 - have been launched. Now only GStar 4 is operational.

5. Satcom : This USA's communication series was launched in 1975 with the launch of Satcom1, followed by Satcom 2, 3, 3R, 4, 5, 1R, 3R, 4R, K2, C1, C5, C3 and C4. Currently Satcom C4 and C5 are operational. The series is owned by Comsat General Corporation, a subsidiary of Communications Satellite Corporation.

6. Sirius Satellite Radio : Sirius Satellite Radio consists of four satellites - Sirius 1, Sirius 2, Sirius 3 and Sirius 4, providing digital radio to mobile receivers in North America through 24 C Band and 14 Ku Band Transponders.

7. Nimiq : Nimiq 1 and 2 are the Canada's communication Satellites which provides its services in Canada and North America. Nimiq 1 was launched on 25th May 1999, and Nimiq 2 on 30th Decembe,2002 with 32 Ku and a Ka band payload on board.

II. Russian Communication Satellite Systems :

1. Ekran and Ekran-M: Ekran consists of 17 satellites owned by Russia's Direct Broadcasting communication satellites. The Ekran-M series has six 6 satellites - Ekran-M 11L, Ekran-M 13L, Ekran-M 12L, Ekran-M 14L, Ekran-M 15L and Ekran-M 18L each having only a single TV-relay channel. Ekran M-18L is currently operational and provides TV and sound radio distribution services to communal antennas in all towns in Siberia and Far East Russia.

2. Gonets: Gonets are Russian communication satellites operated by SmolSat. Its series are:

1. Gonets D series: Gonets D#1 (Kosmos 2199) and Gonets D#2 (Kosmos 2201) but is now out of service.
2. Gonets D1 series: 12 satellites, Gonets D1 1 to Gonets D1 12 is currently operational.

3. Gorizont: Gorizont satellites, are Russian Communication Satellites and they provide telephone, telegraph, and fascimile communications services, TV and radio broadcasts and maritime and international communications. Till date 33 satellites have been launched out of which Gorizont 31, 32 and 33 are currently operational. This system is operated by Intersputnik.

4. Gals: Gals (1 and 2) also represent Russia's communication satellite system providing a variety of direct broadcasting communication services. They are operated by Informcosmos of Russia.

5. Molniya : Molniya of the erstwhile Soviet Union was launched in 1965 to provide telecommuniation and television services. Molniya satellites use a highly inclined elliptical orbit, as Russian cities are at high latitudes where it is impractical to use geostationary satellites. Molniya orbit is 12 hour period orbit with a perigee of 1470 km and apogee of 38900 km and inclined at an angle of 63.4. Hence, the satellite remains almost stationary over high northern latitudes for about 8 hours. There are 87 satellites in the series:

1. Molniya 1 series provided military and government communication services.
2. Molniya 2 series has 17 satellites and provides television and military communication services.
3. Molniya 3 series has 52 satellite and provides television, telephone and telegraph communication services.

III. Europe's Communication Satellite Systems :

1. Hispasat: These are Spain's communication satellites operated by Spanish satellite communication agency Hispasat. It comprises four satellites:

1. Hispasat 1a and 1b provides civil and military communication services, offering services to telecommunications operators and radio broadcasting both in Europe and North Africa and America.
2. Hispasat X-band governmental mission is intensively used by the Spanish Ministry of Defence for communicating with Spanish forces.
3. Hispasat 1c and 1d provide civil communication services.

2. Sirius : This is Sweden's communication satellite system having two currently operational satellites Sirius 2 and Sirius 3. Sirius 2 was the largest telecom satellite ever built in Europe at the time of its launch and provides analog and digital DTH transmissions as well as video and data communication services.

3. Thor : Thor satellites are dedicated to provide Direct Broadcasting Communication services in Norway. Thor 1, 2 and 3, deliver television and telephony/data services to Scandinavia and Northern Europe, with western offshore beams to the Iceland, and Greenland. It is operated by Telenor Satellite Services.

4. TV Sat: TV Sat satellites are Germany's communication satellites that provide Direct TV Broadcasting services to Europe. TV Sat 1 was launched in 1987 and TV Sat 2 in 1989. Now TV Sat 2 is operational.

IV Asia's Communication Satellite Systems

1. B-Sat (Broadcasting Satellite) : B-Sat is Japan's domestic stellite system which provides its broadcast services throughout

Japan. They provide direct-to-home digital high-definition television, in a wider-screen format than traditional analog systems. It is owned by Broadcasting Satellite System Corporation of Tokyo.

Till date two series of five satellites namely BSAT-1 and BSAT-2 have been launched. BSAT-2b was launched in 2001 to serve as in-orbit backup but could not be placed in its orbit, hence BSAT 2C was launched in 2003 to continue with their services.

2. BS (Broadcasting Satellites) : Telecom Advancement Organisation, of Japan operate these communication satellites. The series comprises BS 2 series (BS 2a, 2b and 2x satellites); and BS 3 series (BS 3h, 3a, 3b and 3n satellites).

3. CS series : CS satellites are Japan's communication satellites. CS satellites comprise of CS1 series having 1 satellite CS-1 (Sakura 1), CS-2 series having CS-2a (Sakura 2a), -2b (Sakura 2b) satellites and CS-3 series having CS-3a (Sakura 3a), -3b (Sakura 3b) satellites.

4. CSat : Operated by Japan Satellite Systems, Inc. (JSAT), JCS at satellites, are the Japan's first commercial communications satellite system. Both JCSAT 1 and JCSAT 2 were launched in 1989. These satellites provide voice, television, fassimile and high-speed data services for business use Japan and also transmitted high-quality broadcast video and data directly to customer sites.

JCSat 3 and 4 launched in 1995 and 1997 relay voice, data, and television signals via Ku-band to eastern Asia, Australia, New Zealand, and India; and via C-band to eastern and southern Asia and Hawaii. JCSat 5 and 6 launched in 1997 and 1999, meet increased customer demand for multimedia and Internet access and carry voice, data and television signals to Japan.

JCSAT-8 launched in 2002, provides coverage to Japan, East Asia, Australia and Hawaii. The JCSAT-110 (N-Sat 110, Superbird 5(D)) telecommunications satellite, launched in 2000, is used for various telecommunication applications including direct TV broadcasting to Japan and nearby regions. JCSAT-9, slated for launch in 2005, will provide satellite communications services throughout Asia and Japan.

5. Koreasat : Koreasat satellites, operated by Korea Telecom, are South Korea's communication satellites providing both fixed and direct broadcast services. Till date three satellites, Koresat 1, 2 and 3, have been launched in this series followed by Koresat 5 to provide military and civil communication services.

6. Measat series : Measat is Malaysia's regional satellite communication system. Owned by Binariang Sdn. Bhd. of Kuala Lumpur, it provides the first direct-to-user (DTU) services, including the television and educational communication services in Malaysia and the general regional communications services including telephony, television, data transmission, and business in an area reaching from India to Hawaii and from Japan to East Australia.

7. Palapa : Palaya satellite system is Indonesia's Domestic Satellite System which provides communication link to the Indonesian islands, and covers parts of Australia and New Zealand. It is operated by Satelindo company of Indonesia. Palapa A-1 was launched in 1976 followed by Palapa A-2 in 1977. Palapa B series consists of Palapa B-1, B2P, B2R and B4. The last satellite in the B series Palapa B4 was launched in 1990. Palapa C series has two satellites - Palapa C1, launched in 1996 and Palapa C2.

8. Superbird : This system of communication satellites is owned by Space Communication Corporation (SCC), a Japanese satellite communiation service company. Superbird A was launched in 1989 and Superbird B in 1990 and both have completed their operational life time. Till today, 7 Superbird satellites have been launched superbird A, A1, B, B1, C, 4 (B2), 5 (D). Superbird-6, launched in 2003, provides Ka and Ku band business telecommunication services to Japan.

9. Thaicom series : Thaicom series of satellites are Thailand's first communication satellites. The Thaicom series comprises of 3 satellites, Thaicom 1, 2 and 3.

10. Thuraya : Thuraya satellites United Arab Emirates's communication satellites and provide GSM-compatible mobile telephone services. They are operated by Thuraya Satellite Telecommuniations Co.

V. South America's, Australia's and Africa's Communication Satellite System:

1. Brazilsat : The EMBRATEL systems operates Brazils communication satellite which provides its services for telephone, television, data transmission and business networks. This comprises of Brazilsat A and Brazilsat B series of satellites.

2. Nilesat : It is the Eqypt's direct TV broadcast satellite system the first to be launched in the African continent. It provides data transmission services, internet and relays over 150 digital TV channels.

3. Optus Satellites : These are Australia's communication satellites comprising of Optus A, Optus B and Optus C series. It provides direct broadcasting services, digital data transmission, television relays, air traffic control services. It's services are being used in New Zealand and Asia-Pacific region. Its latest Optus C series provides commercial services in Ku-band and at UHF, while X and Ka-band provides important military communications to its Defense.

18

Digital Satellite (Direct-to-Home) TV Systems

18.1 Requirements for Digital Television

The main requirement of digital TV is the very high bit rate, hence bandwidth, required to provide 'virtually transparent' studio quality pictures, that is, there is little reduction in quality between the studio production and the reception. The techniques of digital video compression and digital modulation technology have made it possible to have fairly acceptable direct-to-home (DTH) TV reception via direct broadcast service (DBS) using the existing Ku-band allocations.

For transmission, a studio-quality digital signal would require about 1 Gbit/sec for interlaced pictures and 2 Gbit/sec for non-interlaced pictures. This is far too high for a practical satellite delivery system, because of demand for such services and a choice of programmes. Therefore, a certain amount of compression coding will be necessary in order to reduce the transmission bit rate to a practical level.

The bite-rate reduction systems have inherent errors which are divided between those received and those due to the coding process itself. It has been found that a 'virtually transparent' TV picture will need a transmission bit rate of about 110–120 Mbit/sec to be free of preceptible coding artefacts. Lower bit rates of 30–40 Mbit/sec may provide tolerable quality.

Another important area in overall bit-rate reduction is the channel coding and modulation scheme adopted. The modulation system adopted for digital TV is a compromise based on the following requirements and considerations:

1. Tolerant of high levels of noise to conserve transponder power requirements and allow acceptable sized dishes for reception.

2. Tolerant of high levels of interference to allow efficient use of the available spectrum.

3. Satellite transponders use travelling wave tubes (TWTs) driven close to saturation for efficient use of energy. Unfortunately, this is not a linear region of operation.

4. Simplicity of modulation system.

5. Complexity of error-correction system.

6. Conservation of bandwidth (maximize the number of bits coded per signlling state).

Commercial satellite transmissions, as well as terrestrial transmissions, must remain economically viable in order to make the most efficient use of available channels and storage capacity. The choice lies between: (i) a few high-quality transmissions, each occupying a wide bandwidth, or (ii) a greater number of transmissions of an acceptable quality, each occupying a narrow bandwidth by employing techniques based on the concept of redundancy.

A normal, uncompressed, PAL 1 video signal occupies a bandwidth of about 5.5 MHz. Now according to the Nyquist theorem, the signal must be digitally sampled at 11 MHz. For reasonable resolution, each sample requires at least eight binary bits so the transmission bit rate works out to 88 Mbit/sec for even a monochrome picture. A colour transmission has red, green and blue components, so the bit rate must be three times greater, resulting in a final transmission rate of 264 Mbit/sec.

Apart from the transmission problems, high bit rate would also create storage problems. For example, a typical feature film run for about 90 min (5400 sec). A typical 340 Mbyte hard disk fitted in a PC has a capacity of 2.7 Gbit so it would take 528 such hard disks to store one feature-length film!

To allow for this and future technological advances, such as improved picture quality and stereoscopic (three-dimensional) extensions, the World Administrative Radio Conference (WARC) 1992 has allocated new frequency bands. Satellites covering Region –2 were allocated the 17.3–17.8 GHz band and regions –1 and –3 the 21.4–22 GHz band. These proposals will come into effect by 2007.

18.2 Digital DBS-TV

Satellite broadcasting of television has become a major part of the satellite communications industry. In 1999, DBS-TV and video distribution earned more than half the revenues of the satellite communications industry, worldwide. Most DBS-TV and distribution of video signals is now digital. DBS-TV systems operate with small antennas and low cost receiving systems, and offer a very larger number of video and audio channels, making them attractive to customers.

Fig. 18.1 shows the components of a DBS-TV system. The television signal from the studio is relayed over a terrestrial link to the uplink station. This transmits a very narrowbeam signal to the satellite in the 14–GHz band. The satellite retransmits the television signal in a wide beam in the 12–GHz frequency band. Individual TV receivers within the beam coverage area are able to receive the satellite signal.

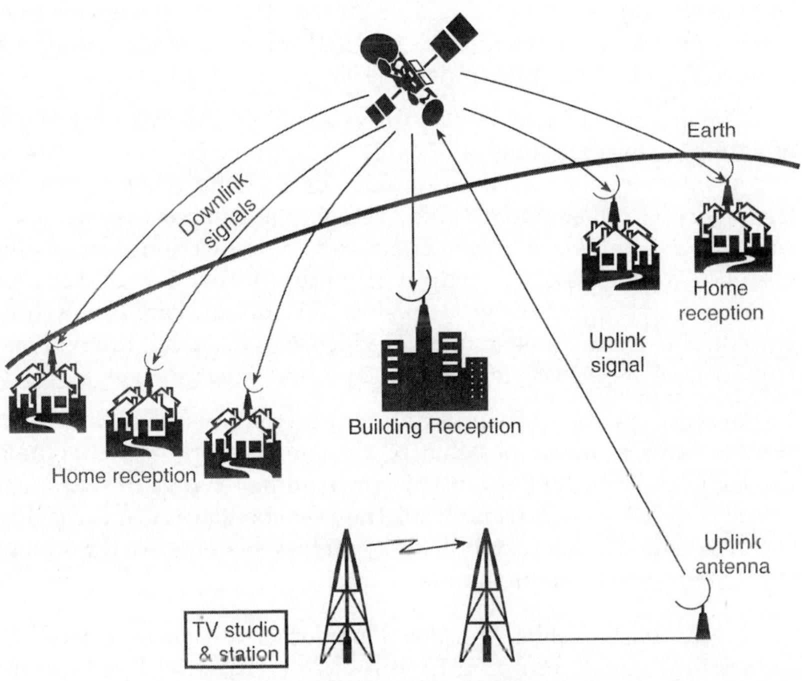

Fig, 18.1 Basic DBS-TV System.

Digital DBS-TV signals are transmitted as a 20–Msps QPSK signal occupying about 27 MHz of transponder bandwidth. The 40–Mbps signal has a data rate between 23 and 27 Mbps with the remaining bits used for error control and system operation. DBS-TV digital signals make extensive use of error correction and error detection techniques in the form of a double layer of error control coding with interleaving. The recovery of a good quality analog signal from a bit stream with bit errors relies on deinterleaving to spread out bursty errors, correction of some errors by the inner layer of convolutional coding, and detection of remaining, uncorrected, errors by the outer layer of Reed-Solomon linear block coding. Detected errors that remain after the decoding of the digital signal typically result in single word effors.

Delivery of a bit stream through a direct broadcast satellite can be adapted to serve Internet users who require the download of large block of data. The development of DBS-TV satellites with spot beams for local new broadcasts has provided the higher satellite antenna gain needed for uplinks from 0.5–m dishes. Both directv and Dish-network offer Internet access terminals with uplink capability, although the service is not available outside the spot beam coverage areas, where the connection to the ISP must be made through a terrestrial telephone link and a PSTN.

The growth of cable TV (CTV) systems laid the way for the use of satellites for distribution of cable TV signals. In such a system, one transponder on a GEO satellite can send a video signal to thousands of independent cable systems distributed throughout a country. Satellites are a very effective way to distribute wideband signals, and there was rapid growth in the use of C-band transponders for video signals, using FM and one rapid growth in the use of C-band transponders for video signals, using FM and one transponder for each video signal.

In recent years, Ku-band satellites and compressed digital video signals have made it possible to transmit several video signals through one transponder, with corresponding savings in transmission costs. A large fraction of all the transponders in most of the world's domestic and regional GEO satellite systems are devoted to the distribution of video signals.

In the early 1980s, the development of low noise GaAsFET amplifiers for C-band, and improved threshold extension demodulators for video signal receivers, allowed much smaller diameter antennas to be used to receive C-band FM video signals distributed through GEO satellites. For home satellite TV systems with 3–m and 3.6–m dish antennas (10–ft and 12–ft diameter) and set-top receivers that could receive the video signals from domestic GEO satellites.

In the 1990s, digital video transmission became feasible, and several systems were developed in the 12.2 to 12.7–GHz band allocated to DBS-TV services. The development of low cost Ku-band antennas and receivers, and high-speed digital integrated circuits specifically for DBS television that incorporate QPSK demodulation, error control, decryption, and MPEG decoding made DBS-TV practical.

18.3 EIRP Standards and Number of Transponders

DBS-satellites have a higher (EIRP) than for the other categories of satellites. Typically value of EIRP is in the range 51 to 60 dBW. According to the standards laid by the Regional Administrative Radio Conference (RARC), this value is 57 dBW. Transponders are rated by the power output of their high-power amplifiers. Typically, a satellite may carry 32 transponders. If all 32 are in use, each will operate at the lower power rating of 120 W. If the high-power amplifiers are doubled, the number of transponders will be 16. But each transponder now has to operate at the higher power rating of 240 W.

18.4 Transponder Capacity

The 24–MHz bandwidth of a transponder is capable of carrying one analog television channel. For its commercial viability, direct broadcast satellite television needs many more channels. This in turn requires a move from analog to digital television. When the audio and video components of a television program are digitized, signal compression can be applied, which greatly reduces the bandwidth requirements. The signal compression used in DBS can be described as follows:

First let us make an estimate of the bit rate that can be carried in a 24-MHz transponder. For QPSK modulation used in satellite digital television, the symbol rate that can be transmitted in a given bandwidth is given by

$$r_{sy} = \frac{B_{IF}}{1+\alpha} \qquad \text{...(18.1)}$$

where α is the roll-off factor.

Now for a bandwidth of 24 MHz and with $\alpha = 0.2$, the symbol rate will be

$$r_{sy} = \frac{24 \times 10^6}{1.2} = 20 \times 10^6 \text{ symbols/sec.}$$

For QPSK used in digital TV satellite systems, the number of levels in the waveform (M) is 4. Therefore, the number of bits in each symbol will be

$$m = \log_2 M = \log_2 4 = 2$$

The symbol rate in terms of bit rate will be

$$R_{bit} = 2\, r_{sy} = 2 \times 20 \times 10^6 = 40 \text{ Mb/sec}$$

Thus the bit rate required for the 24-MHz channel using QPSK is 40 Mb/sec.

18.5 Bit Rates for Digital Television

The bit rate for digital television depends very much on the picture format. It varies from 118 Mb/sec for standard television at the lowest pixel resolution to 995 Mb/sec for high-definition TV at the highest resolution. According to the international CCIR-601 television standard, for studio-quality television pictures when digitized, the required bit rate is 216 Mb/sec.

For commercial viability reasons, a single DBS transponder needs to carry somewhere between four and eight TV programmes. The programmes may originate from a variety of sources, film, analog TV, CDs and videocassette. Before transmission, these are all converted to digital, compressed, and then time-division multiplexed (TDM). This TDM baseband signal is applied as QPSK modulation to the uplink carrier reaching a given transponder.

The compressed bit rate, and hence the number of channels that are carried, depends on the type of programme material. For programmes like talk shows since there is little movement lowest bit rate is required. But sports channels with lots of movement require comparative large bit rates. Typical values for various programmes are: 4 Mb/sec for a movie channel, 5 Mb/sec for a variety channel, and 6 Mb/sec for a sports channel.

Compression of bit rate is carried out to MPEG (Moving Pictures Expert Group) standards. MPEG is a group within the International Standards Organization and the International Electrochemical Commission (ISO/IEC), which has defined standards for the transmission and storage of moving pictures and sound. Note that the standards are concerned only with the bit-stream syntax and the decoding process and not with the encoding and decoding processes.

Syntax covers such matters as bit rate, picture resolution, time frames for audio, and the packet details for transmission

The MPEG currently in use are: MPEG-1, MPEG-2, MPEG-4 and MPEG-7.

18.6 MPEG Compression

I. Video compression

For this, MPEG-2 is used. Fig. 18.2 shows the process. The analog outputs from the red (R), green (G), and blue (B) colour cameras are converted to a luminance component (Y) and two chrominance components (C_r) and (C_b). The matrix equation relating the three primary colours (R, G, B) to the Y, C_r, and C_b components in matrix

$$\begin{vmatrix} Y_r \\ C_r \\ C_b \end{vmatrix} = \begin{vmatrix} 0.299 & 0.587 & 0.114 \\ -0.169 & -0.331 & 0.500 \\ 0.500 & -0.419 & 0.081 \end{vmatrix} \begin{vmatrix} R \\ G \\ B \end{vmatrix}$$

The digitizer samples the Y, C_r, and C_b signals. It is has been found that the human eye is less sensitive to resolution in the colour components (C_r and C_b) than the luminance (Y) component. It means a lower sampling rate can be used for the colour components. This sampling is called *chroma subsampling,* and it is one step in the compression process.

The difference signals are now created and fed to the *discrete cosine transform* (DCT) block which converts these to a "spatial frequency" domain. Here, a time signal $g(t)$ gets transformed into a

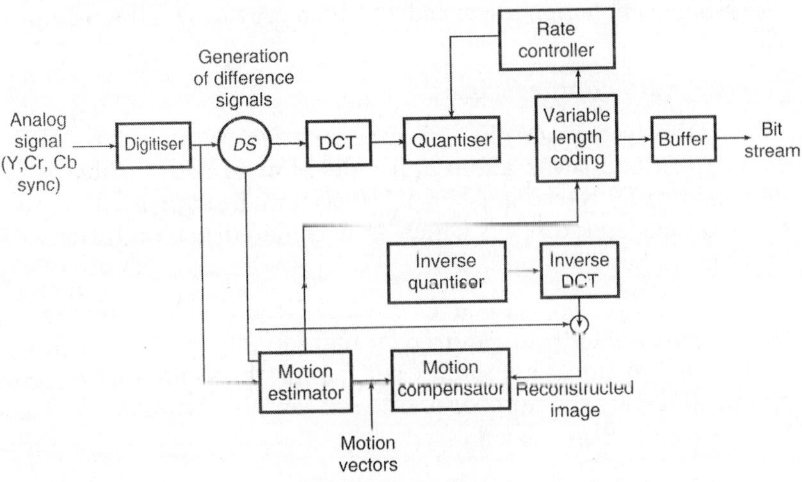

Fig, 18.2 Block Diagram of MPEG-2 Encoder.

frequency domain representation $G(f)$, allowing the signal to be filtered in the frequency domain. For the DCT, the input signals are functions of the x (horizontal) and y (vertical) space coordinates, $g(x, y)$, and it transforms these into a domain of new variables u and v, $G(u, v)$. The variables are called *spatial frequencies* in analogy with the time-frequency transform. Note that $g(x,y)$ and $G(u,v)$ are discrete functions.

(*a*) *Compression through quantisiation:* The discrete values of $G(u, v)$ are quantized to predetermined levels. This reduces the number of levels to be transmitted and therefore provides compression. The components of $G(u,v)$ at the higher spatial frequencies represent finer spatial resolution. The human eye is less sensitive to resolution at these high spatial frequencies and as a result, these can be quantised in much coarser steps, leading to further compression.

(*b*) *Compression through motion estimation*: Frames in MPEG-2 are designated *I, P, and B* frames, and motion prediction is achieved by comparing certain frames with other frames. An independent frame called I frame is used, which is reconstructed without reference to any other frames. The comparsion is as follows:

1. AP (for previous) frame is now compared with the previous *I* frame, and only those parts which differ as a result of movement need to be encoded. The comparison is carried out in sections called macroblocks for the frames.

2. AB (for bi-directional) frame is compared with the previous *I* or *P* frame and with the next *P* frame. Now only the changes resulting from motion are encoded, which provides further compression.

II. Audio compression

In DBS systems, MPEG-1 is used for audio compression. MPEG-1 and MPEG-2 cover audio and video, but MPEG-1 video is not designed for DBS transmissions. MPEG-1 audio supports mono and two-channel stereo only, which is considered adequate for DBS systems currently in use.

Why audio compression is needed? This can be explained by considering the bit rate required for high-quality audio. The bit rate is equal to the number of sample per second (the sampling frequency f_s) multiplied by the number of bits per sample n, that is

$$R_{bits} = f_s \times n \qquad ...(18.3)$$

Since for a stereo CD recording, the sampling frequency is 44.1 kHz, and the number of bits per sample is 16, the bit rate will be

$$R_{bits} = 2 \times 44.1 \times 16$$
$$= 1411.2 \text{ Kb/sec}$$

The factor 2 is due to the two channels in stereo. This bit rate is too high part of the total bit rate allowance per channel, and therefore, audio compression is needed.

The audio signal is a complex signal covering a wide spectrum of frequencies. Audio compression in MPEG uses perceptual phenomena in the human ears. For instance, we know that a loud sound at one particular frequency masks a less intense sound at a nearby frequency. This frequency becomes inaudible when it is below the level of the masking tone by what is referred as the *masking threshold.* Clearly, any noise below the masking threshold also will be masked. It has been found that if the number of bits per sample is increased by 1 bit, it increases signal-to-quantization noise ratio by 6 dB. Alternatively, it means that a 1-bit decrease in n increases the quantization noise by 6 dB. It means the level of quantisation can be reduced without much effect on the overall quality of reproduced sound.

In MPEG-1, audio compression is carried out by two processes taking place in parallel. This is shown in Fig. 18.3:

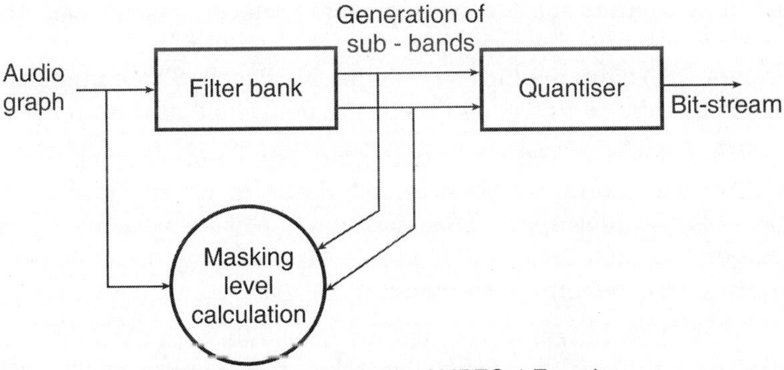

Fig. 18.3 Block Diagram of MPEG-1 Encoder

1. The filter bank divides the spectrum of the incoming signal into subbands. At the same time, the spectrum is analyzed for identification of the masking levels.

2. The masking information is passed to the quantizer, which then quantizes the subbands

18.7 Use of Circular Polarisation

The satellites at each orbit location transmit in opposite hands of circular polarization (CP). Signals with opposite hands of circular polarization are orthogonal, and a suitably designed earth station antenna can separate two signals with opposite hands of circular polarization. In the simplest DBS-TV receiving terminal, an electronically controlled polarizer is used immediately behind the antenna feed. The polarizer can be set to receive LHCP (left-hand circular polarization) of RHCP (right-hand circular polarization) by changing the voltage supplied to the low noise block converter (LNB) unit at the antenna.

Typically, a supply voltage of 7V will cause the antenna to receive one polarization and reject the other. Increasing the voltage above 14 V causes the antenna to switch polarizations. The polarizer converts the circularly received polarization signal to a lineraly polarized signa l in a section of waveguide, and a linear probe in the waveguide converts the signals to currents that drive the LNA input.

18.7.1 Orthogonal Mode Transducer

More complex receivers use an orthogonal mode transducer (OMT) with two LNBs so that both hands of circular polarization can be received at the same time by using two LNBs and two receivers. The dual-polarization receiving system is needed when more than one channel must be received at a time. A dual-channel DBS-TV receiver with a dual-polarized antenna allows two TV channels to be viewed by different people in the same household at the same time.

When it is required to receive signals from more than one orbital location, an antenna with two feeds is used. Reception from two satellites spaced 9° apart in geostationary orbit can be achieved with a larger antenna, 0.45 × 0.6 m (18" × 24") that produces two beams separated by the appropriate angle.

DBS-TV receiving antennas are typically an offset parabolic reflector design with the feed below the antenna aperture. The offset feed design eliminates blockage of the aperture by the feed which occurs in symmetrical reflector antenna designs, and improves the aperture efficiency of the antenna, and therefore increases its gain.

Offset fed parabolic reflectors have a beam squint effect in the plane of symmetry when operated in opposite hands of circular polarizations. For the 0.45 m diameter antenna widely used for DBS-TV reception, the LHCP and RHCP beams are squinted about

0.25° from the antenna's boresight. The 3-dB beamwidth of the antenna is around 4°, so the squint effect does not cause significant loss of gain.

18.8 Features and Specifications of A Typical DBS-TV Satellite System

These are as follows:

1. The 12.2 to 12.7 GHz band has been set aside for exclusive use by DBS-TV satellites in geostationary orbit so that high-power transponders could be used on specially designed DBS-TV satellites.

2. Typical transponder output levels are 100 to 240 W with flux density at the earth's surface up to – 105 dBW/m^2.

3. The satellites can carry up to 32 transponders, giving a total transmitted RF power up to 3.2 kW, higher than for any other commercial satellite.

4. DBS-TV satellites are typically large and heavy, generally use a three-axis stabilized design, and have large solar sails to generate the DC power required by the transponders.

5. The flux density at the earth surface produced by medium and high-power transponders used on DBS satellites is in the range – 105 to – 115 dBW/m^2, which allows small receiving antennas (dishes) to be used for DBS-TV reception, with diameters in the range 0.45—0.9 m.

6. The small dish required for DBS-TV reception played a critical part in the acceptance of DBS-TV. Previously, DBS-TV reception of cable television signals was possible at C band and Ku band with 2.5 to 3.5 m dishes.

7. The small receiving antenna has a wide beam, typically 40 for a 0.45-m dish, which forces wide spacing of DBS-TV satellites. A 90 spacing in the GEO has been adopted which restricts the number of DBS-TV satellites that can be placed in geostationary orbit.

8. Each DBS-TV satellite carries up to 32 high-power transponders covering part of the 12.2 to 12.7 GHz broadcast satellite band (BSS).

18.9 DBS-TV Receiver

The receiving segment of a BDS-TV system is of two types: the DTH home receiver; and common antenna reception for cable distribution.

18.9.1 The DTH Home Receiver

Fig. 18.4 is a block schematic of the DTH receiver. It consists of two units, an outdoor unit and an indoor unit togther called complete receiver as an *integrated receiver decoder* (IRD). Its operation is as follows:

1. The antenna works with an offset feed. The antenna must have an unobstructed view of the satellite cluster to which it is aligned.

2. The receive horn focusses the downlink signal (in the frequency range 12.2 to 12.7 GHz) into the antenna.

3. The horn feeds the signal into a polariser which is switched to pass either left-hand circular to right-hand circular polarized signals.

4. The low-noise block consists of a low-noise amplifier (LNA) and a downconverter. The amplifier amplies the signal and the downconverter converts the 12.2 to 12.7 GHz band to 950 to 1450 MHz, a frequency range used to transmit the signal through the connecting cable to the indoor unit.

The size of the antenna is typically is around 18 in (46 cm) in diameter. The advantages of small antennas are: They are less intrusive visually and are less effected by wind loading.

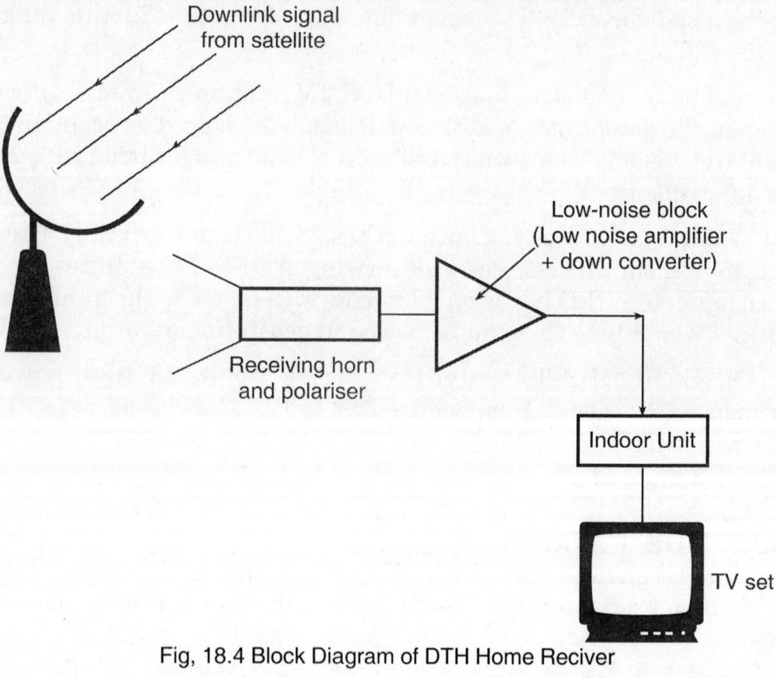

Fig, 18.4 Block Diagram of DTH Home Reciver

Fig. 18.5 shows the details the DTH-TV receiver:

1. The entire front end of the receiver is located at the antenna feed in the form of an LNB to minimize loss of signal and hence to maintain the lowest possible system noise temperature.

2. The electronic polariser is switched by changing the voltage supplied to the LNB via the cable that interconnects the antenna and set-top receiver.

3. The entire 12.2—12.7 GHz band is down-converted by the LNB to the 900-1400 MHz band can be used to boost the signal strength.

4. The set-top box accepts the entire 500 MHz band and separates out the individual transponder frequencies. Any one of these frequencies (and the corresponding polarization) can be selected on demand by the user.

5. The user enters a desired channel number into the set-top box using an IR remote control, for example, channel 362, which is converted via a stored look-up table in the receiver to an RF channel frequency and polarization.

6. The signal from the required transponder is then selected by the receiver by setting the correct polarization at the antenna and tuning the set-top local oscillator to the appropriate IF channel frequency.

7. The QPSK signals signal is then demodulated. The result is a multiplexed bit stream, typically at a bit rate up to 40 Mbps, which contains the bits for channel 362 and several other video signal. The bit stream is encrypted and contains error control coding bits and data bits. The bit stream is processed to correct and detect errors, de-interleaved, and decrypted.

8. A digital demultiplexer extracts the bits for the wanted channel, 362 in this example send them to a MPEG 2 decoder, and finally generates analog video and audio signals with D/D converters to drive the TV set.

9. The look-up table in the receiver that relates channel numbers to frequencies, polarizations, and instructions for the TDM demultiplexer is downloaded from the satellite on a regular schedule. This allows the service provider to change the transponder which carries a particular signal, and to alter the mix of signals on a given transponder as required, without the customer being aware of the changes.

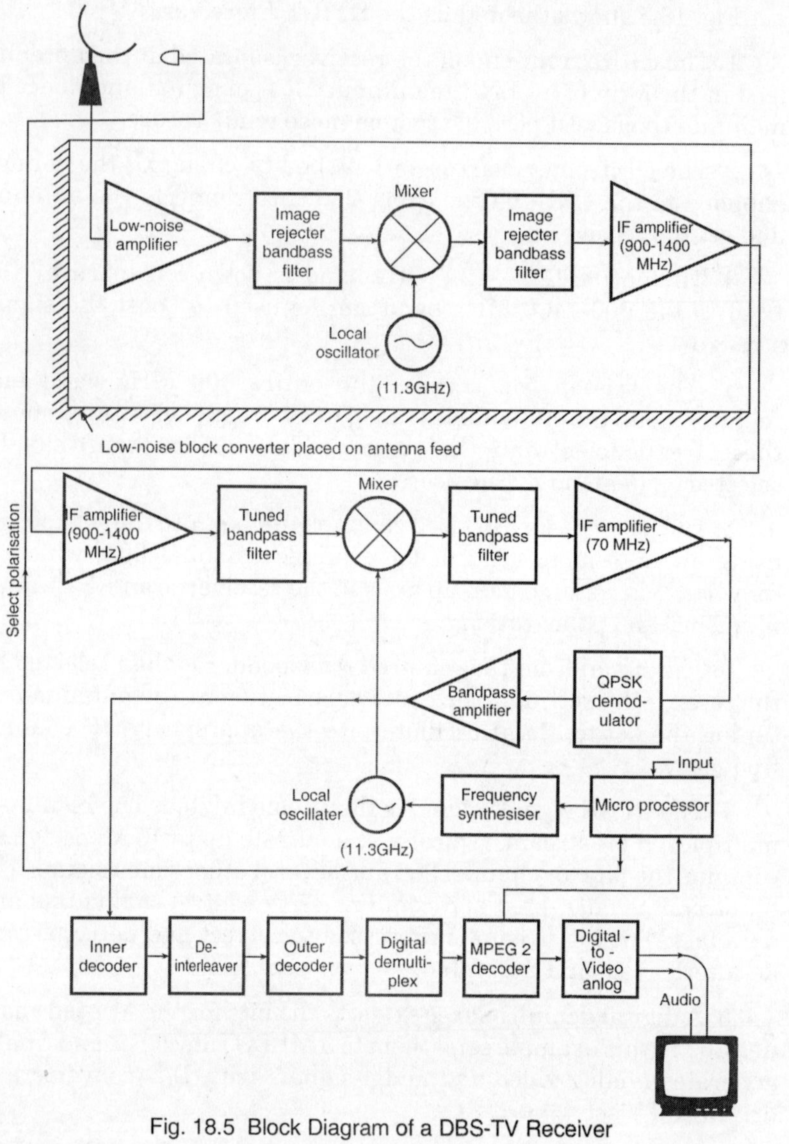

Fig. 18.5 Block Diagram of a DBS-TV Receiver

18.9.2 Common Antenna TV System

The common or community antenna TV system is used to receive the DBS signal from the satellite which after processing is sent to various TV units in the homes in a locality. There is no separate receiver for each user.

Fig. 18.6 shows the arrangement. This system employs a single outdoor unit, with separate feeds available for each sense of polarisation so that all channels are made available simultaneously at the indoor receiver. All the channel carriers are demodulated in a common receiver-filter system. The various channels are now combined into a standard multiplexed signal for transmision over cable to the subscribers. In remote areas which may not have a cable distribution system, a low-power VHF TV transmitter is often employed to the signal rebroadcast to the subscribers.

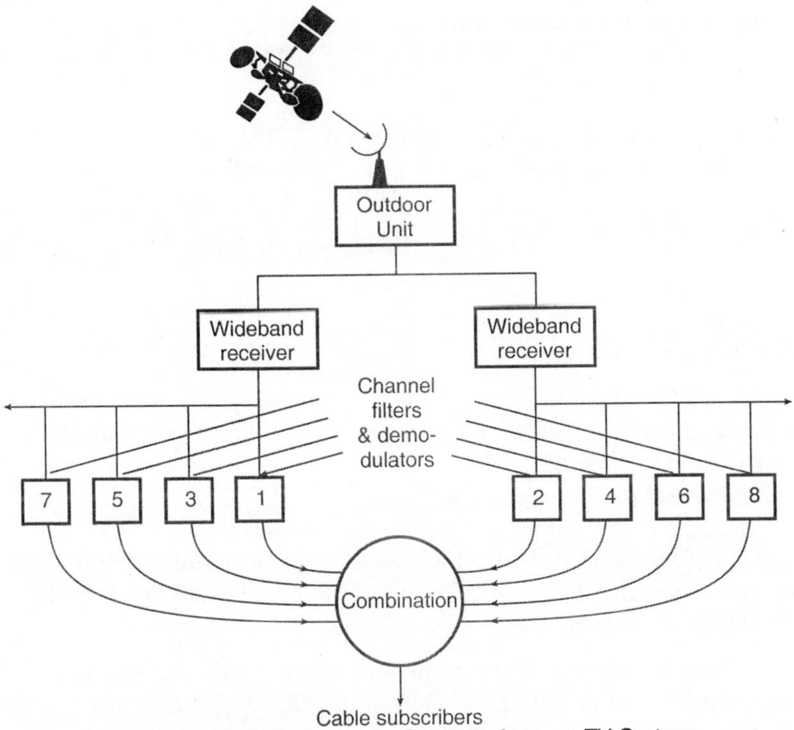

Fig. 18.6 Block Diagram of a Common Antenna TV System

18.9.1 Pay-up Services

The DBS-satellites are also used to address individual receivers and to load another lookup table that specifies which channels the user is authorized to receive. If the user fails to pay his or her bills to the service provider, the receiver will eventually be instructed to show only a message that it has been disconnected for failure to make timely payment for the service. This process involves a *smart card,* which identifies each receiving system, and enables decryption of the satellite signals.

Pay per view channels are handled differently from broadcast channels. A customer wishing to buy a movie or a sporting event selects the desired channel and authorizes the system to make a charge. The Directv-receive terminals have no uplink capacity, and must therefore use terrestrial telephone circuits to send charging information to the central office of the TV series provider. The cost of the pay per view event is then added to the customer's monthly bill. This requires a connection between the DBS-TV receiver and the PSTN at the customer's premises. The receiver dials a toll free number, and downloads a record of the charges for that customer, and any other information that the receiver is programmed to deliver to the service provider.

18.10 Error Control in Digital DBS-TV

The main features of digital DBS-TV transmissions are:

1. Digital DBS-TV transmissions typically use a transmitted symbol rate of 20 Msps using QPSK, which gives a bit rate of 40 Mbps.

2. Error correction coding and control bit occupy 13 to 17 Mbits of the bit stream, leaving 23 to 27 Mbits for digital TV data.

3. A 23 Mbps data stream can carry three live compressed digital video signals using MPEG 2 encoding, or up to 10 prerecorded and processed video signals.

18.10.1 Processing of Prerecorded material

Prerecorded material, which comprises the majority of programming on satellite TV channels, is heavily processed to reduce its bit rate as far as 1.6 Mb/sec.

When prerecorded material such as movies is digitized and processed through MPEG-2 compression, the data rate can be reduced to 1.6 Mbps, but results in digital artifacts appearing in the picture, especially when there is a lot of motion in the sense. A digital artifact appears as a freezing of the entire picture for a fraction of a second, caused by overloading of the MPEG-2 processing, or as a block or pixel of the wrong colour.

The artifacts can be removed one by one by a digital artist who works on the recorded material to paint out the effects. The final result is a movie or show that can be recorded in digital compressed form at an average rate of 1.6 Mbps for replay over the satellite. Live program material with a lot of motion in the picture can cause the bit rate of an MPEG-2 coded signal to increase above the average value of 6.2 Mbps. Mixing prerecorded and live material a in single transponder helps even out the bursty nature of live material.

18.10.2 Error Control by Coding, Decoding and Interleaving

Error control in the digital video standard is achieved in a similar way to compact disc recording. Figure 18.7 shows a block diagram of the coding and decoding operations performed on the bits stream:

1. The compressed digital video signal bit stream is first split into blocks of bits and encoded with a 188/204 rate Reed-Solomon code.

2. The coded bit stream is then interleaved with a 12×7 interleaver.

3. It is finally encoded with a rate three-quarters convolutional code with constraint length 7. As we already know, the double layer of error control coding is called a concatenated code.

4. At the receiver, the convolutional code is used to correct some errors, which improves the BER, but when the C/N ratio in the receiver is low not all the errors will be corrected.

5. The signal is de-interleaved, which spreads out any uncorrected errors so that the probability of a burst error longer than a couple of bits becomes small.

6. The Reed-Solomon code is then used to detect the location of the remaining errors and to flag video words which have errors.

7. The video decoder now looks at the digital words on each side of a word that has been flagged with an error and replaces the flagged word with a new word that is found by interpolation between the two neighboring words, as illustrated in Fig 18.8. The resulting error in the analog video waveform is small.

8. Thus the Reed-Solomon coding, which has a high code rate and uses only error detection properties allows errors in the video signal to be corrected.

Overall, the combined coding of the DVB signal increases the bit rate by 45% when rate three-quarter convolutional encoding and 188/204 Reed-Solomon coding is employed. The coding gain is typically 5.5 dB with BER = 10^{-6} at the output of the convolutional decoder, and very few errors are left in the analog waveform after Reed-Solomon decoding and analog interpolation.

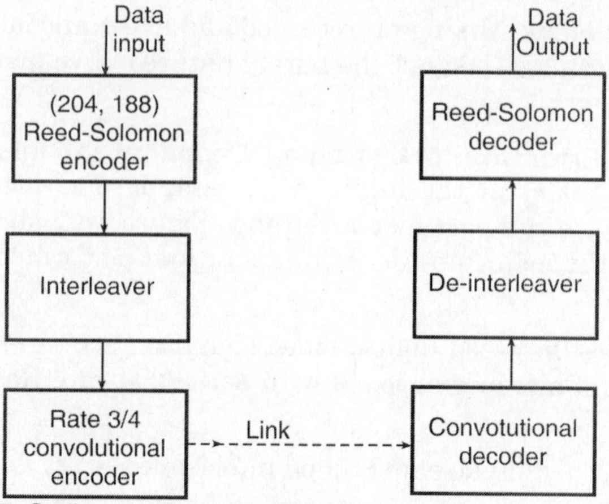

Figure 18.7: Coding and Decoding Operations performed on the Bit Stream.

The coding process used for digital video and audio bit streams relies for much of its error correction capability on the fact that the end signal delivered to the user is analog.

Bit errors in a digital video or audio signal result in the wrong voltage occurring when the errored word is converted to an voltage by the receiver's digital-to-analog converter (DAC).

If the system knows that a particular word is in error (*i.e.*, the coding scheme detected an error but was unable to correct it), that word can be flagged and the error can be removed by interpolation of the analog waveform. When a word is known to contain a bit error, it is replaced by a new word which is calculated to have a value midway between the two adjacent words in the bit stream, as illustrated in Fig 18.8.

The result is an interpolated value in the analog voltage waveform output by the DAC. The interleaving process ensures that most bit errors are single errors, increasing the probability that words contain only a single error and that the error can be detected.

All error correcting codes are able to detect at least twice as many errors as they can correct. The use of analog waveform interpolation allows the video (and CD) error correction process to take advantage of the error detection capabilities of the outer layer of Reed-Solomon (R-S) coding to correct errors in the analog waveform without using error correction coding.

If error correction coding were used instead of analog interpolation, at least twice as many parity bits would be needed in the bit stream, which would reduce the number of data bits drastically.

The outer layer of Reed-Solomon linear block coding has good error detection properties, and the decoding process can be implemented in real time in a high-speed microprocessor. This is an important consideration in a real time system, like TV broadcasting. Decoding of the error control codes must be possible in real time in a low-cost processor, and this is one of the driving factors in the selection of the concatenated code used for CDs and for the video broadcast standard. Bit errors that are not corrected or detected by the error control coding process result in individual words that are in error.

In an uncompressed digital television picture, a single word error would result in a pixel on the TV screen that is the wrong colour. In a digital compressed TV signal, each word influences many pixels on the screen, and a word error may result in a block of the wrong colour. MPEG-2 achieves a compression ratio of 8 to 10 with live video, so a single word error in an MPEG-2 encoded bit stream might be expected to cause errors in 8 or 10 pixels on the TV screen, or even more pixels if error propagation occurs.

However, all digital compression schemes are designed to minimize the effect of errors in incoming words, so the impact of single word errors is usually confined to a small square on the screen which has the wrong information. As the bit error rate of the recovered bit stream in the receiver increases, the impact of the word errors becomes more severe, and larger blocks of the TV picture are corrupted. The receiving system is able to recognize the high error rate and will blank the screen until an acceptable error rate is restored. That is why a rain fade on a DBS-TV link which goes below the receiver threshold is characterized by the initial appearance of small squares of incorrect colour on the TV screen, followed by larger block errors, and then a blank screen. When the rain intensity eases as the storm moves through the slant path, the signal will return above threshold and the picture will reappear on the TV screen.

18.11 Uplink Master Control Station

The large number of signals that are sent by the satellites are collected at a master control station and uplinked to the satellites by a group of large antennas with fade margins sufficient to overcome any expected rain fade. The video and audio signals that are uplinked to the satellites are available in prerecorded from on video tape or disc, or are collected from other satellites or fiber-optic lines. The uplink stations have hundreds of tape and video disc players, all under computer control, which supply the video and audio signals for each channel.

In the station, the signals are mainly stored in digital form, allowing direct multiplexing into bit streams for the individual transponders. Analog signals are digitized and compressed before being multiplexed with other signals into the bit stream that are sent to each transponder.

Fig. 18.8 shows a simplified block diagram of an uplink station:

1. One uplink antenna will typically transmit up to 16 RF channels to one DBS-TV satellite.

2. Each RF signal is a QPSK modulated Ku-band carrier with a symbol rate of up to 20 Msps, occupying a bandwidth up to 27 MHz.

3. The encoded, compressed, and multiplexed bit stream drives video exciter which generates QPSK modulation of an intermediate

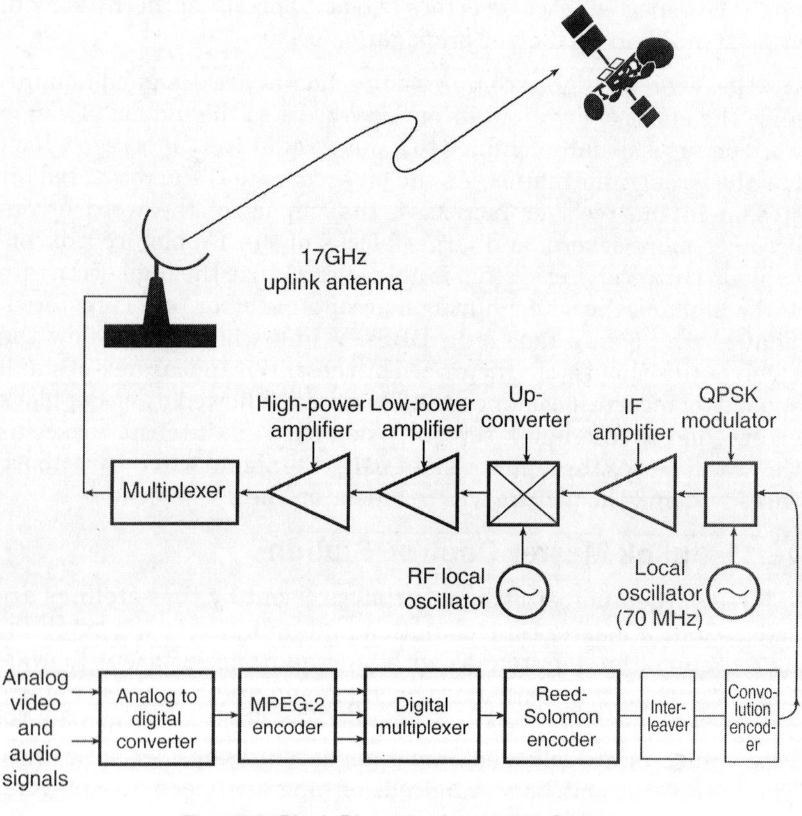

Fig. 18.8: Block Diagram of an Uplink Station.

frequency carrier, typically at 70 MHz. The 70 MHz signal is upconverted to the transponder input frequency in the transmitter, which contains a traveling wave tube high-power amplifier (HPA). The HPA is usually rated at a much higher power than its normal operating output power level, which provides sufficient output back-off of the HPA to ensure linear operation.

4. The signals from any number of HPAs are multiplexed together in microwave combiners and sent to the antenna feed for transmission to the satellite.

18.12 DBS-TV System Design Considerations

The most important requirement for a DBS-TV system is that it must provide a received signal power at the small receiving antenna that provides an adequate C/N margin in clear air. However, there are two difficulties. First is that the C/N margins used in DBS-TV systems are small, to avoid the need for a large receiving antenna. Second, heavy rain will cause attenuation that exceeds the link margin, so occasional outages will be experienced, especially during the summer months when thunderstorms and heavy rain more frequent.

The selection of a C/N margin for a DBS-TV system, therefore, is a design trade-off between:

1. outrage level that customers can be expected to tolerate,

2. maximum allowable diameter of the receiving dish antenna, and

3. power output from the satellite transponders.

Typical designs with receiving antennas in the 0.45 to 0.9 m range and 100 to 250 W satellite transponders yield rain attenuation margins of 3 to 8 dB and outage time totaling 5 to 40 hours per year depending on the receiver's location. However, since most customers do not watch TV for 24 hours per day, they will not be aware of all the outages.

The Ku band transmit beam from the satellite carrying the DBS TV signals is shaped to deliver more power to those areas that suffer the highest occurrence of heavy rain. This creates a larger link margin in those areas and helps to keep outages to an acceptable level

Some manufacturers of DBS-TV receiving systems offer larger dishes for customers living in high rainfall zones. Increasing the antenna diameter from 18 inches to 24 inches, for example, increases its gain by 2.5 dB. This increase in antenna gain adds directly to the rain fade margin of the receiver, and lowers the outage time in heavy rains.

18.13 Link Budget for Ku-Band DBS-TV Receiver

Table 18.1. gives a typical link budget for a GEO DBS-TV system. In this system, the path length of 38,500 km is the maximum expected path length for a receiver and a satellite at longitude 101° W.

The threshold C/N value is set at 8.6 dB, corresponding to a system using QPSK with an implementation margin of 0.8 dB, forward error correction coding that produces 6 dB of coding gain, and a maximum BER of 10^{-6}. This requires a clear air C/N ratio in the DBS-TV receiver of 8.6 + 5.7 = 14.3 dB in clear air.

Table 18.1 Link Budget for Ku-Band DBS-TV Receiver

Downlink power budget	
Transponder output power, 160 W	22.0 dBW
Antenna beam on-axis gain (Cone coverage)	36.5 dB
Path loss at 12.2 GHz, 38,550 km path	– 205.9 dB
Receiving antenna gain, on axis	33.5 dB
Beam contour loss	– 0.3 dB
Miscellaneous and gaseous attenuation losses	– 0.8 dB
Received power, *C*	– 117.7 dBW
Noise power budget	
Boltzmann's constant, *k*	– 228.6 dBW/K/Hz
System noise temperature, clear air, 143 *K*°	21.6 dBK
Receiver noise bandwidth, 20 MHz	73.0 dBHz
Noise power, *N*	– 134.0 dBW
C/N in clear air	16.3 dB
Link margin over 8.6 dB threshold	7.7 dB

I. Downlink power budget. A link margin of 7.7 dB is achieved for a receiver located on the –3 dB contour of the satellite antenna beam. Earth stations close to the –6 dB contour of the satellite beam have a link margin of 4.7 dB. A receiver located within the –2dB contour of the satellite beam, has a link margin of 8.7 dB.

The transponder output power is 160 W, corresponding to a transponder with a saturated output power of 200 W and 1 dB output backoff. A small amount of output backoff is normally used to avoid excessive AM-PM and PM-AM conversion in the transponder.

The receiving antenna is a high efficiency design with an offset parabolic reflector 0.45 m in diameter and a circularly polarized feed. The offset design ensures that the feed system does not block the aperture of the antenna, which increases its efficiency. The gain of this antenna is 33.5 dB at 12.2 GHz assuming an aperture efficiency of 66%.

II. Noise power budget. The noise power budget of the link is based on a receiver noise bandwidth of 20 MHz, an antenna noise temperature of 35 K in clear air, and a 12 GHz LNA with a noise temperature of 110 K. The result is a noise power of – 134.0 dBW in a noise bandwidth of 20 MHz, referred to the input of the LNA, and a clear air C/N ratio of 14.3 dB.

The noise bandwidth of a digital receiver is set by the bandpass filter is designed to match the symbol rate of the transmitted signal, and has a root raised cosine (RRC) transfer function. The noise bandwidth of all RCC filters is always equal to the symbol rate of the digital transmission. If a QPSK signal with a symbol rate of 20 Mbits/sec is assumed, a receiver noise bandwidth of 20 MHz is obtained. However, with MPEG-2 encoding of the video signals, the data rate is not constant. The DBS-TV digital video standard is designed to allow for variable bit rates, and the figure of 20 Msps is probably a maximum value. Complex coding schemes are used on DBS-TV digital transmissions, making use of Reed-Solomon block encoding, irreleaving, and an inner layer of convolutional encoding.

The error removal scheme allows 6 dB of coding gain to be achieved with a code rate greater than half rate FEC, which allows more of the bit in the 40 Mbps bit stream to be allocated to data and fewer to parity bits. Data rates of 23 to 27 Mbps are used for the data stream of some DBS-TV systems, with rate three-quarter inner convolutional coding. The overall code rate with 188/204 outer Reed-Solomon coding and rate three-quarter inner convolutional coding is 0.69, which provides a message data rate of 27 Mbps with a coded bit rate of 39.1 Mbps.

18.14 DBS Frequency Band in India

Frequency for DBS TV transmission allocated to India are given in Table 18.2 where the requisite orbit location. EIRP for each channel are also lifted. These have been assigned by WARC in consultation with ITU.

Table 18.2. DBS Frequency Allocated to India

Ch. No.	*Frequency*	*Orb. Lo*	*EIRP*	*Ch. No.*	*Frequency*	*ORB. Lo.*	*EIRP*
1.	11727.48	56° 68°	63.1 63.3	13.	11957.64	56° 68°	63.3 63.5
2.	11746.66	56° 68°	63.9 63.3	14.	11976.82	56° 68°	63.7 64.1
3.	11765.84	56° 68°	63.3 63.4	15.	11996.00	56° 68°	63.5 63.6,
4.	11785.02	56° 68°	63.6 63.7	16.	12015.18	56° 68°	63.8 65.5,
5.	11804.2	56° 68°	63.1 63.4	17.	12034.36	56° 68°	64.3 63.6,
6.	11823.38	56° 68°	63.6 64.0	18.	12053.54	56° 68°	63.8 63.8
7.	11842.56	56° 68° 68°	63.4 63.5	19.	12072.72	56° 68°	64.3 63.6
8.	11861.74	56° 68°	63.7 63.7	20.	12091.90	56° 68°	63.8 63.8
9.	11880.92	56° 68°	63.2 63.5	21.	12111.08	56° 68°	64.4 63.7
10.	11900.10	56° 68°	63.6 64.0	22.	12130.26	56° 68°	63.8 63.8
11.	11919.28	56° 68°	63.5 63.5	23.	12149.44	56° 68°	64.4 63.7
12.	11938.46	56° 68°	63.8 63.8	24.	12168.62	56° 68°	63.9 63.9

18.15 References

1. Leon W. Couch, *Modern Communications Systems : Principles ad Applications*, Prentice hall, Englewood Cliffs, NJ, 1995.
2. Dennis Roddy, *Satellite Communication,* McGraw Hill, Boston, 2001.

18.16 Review Questions

1. Describe the bandwidth and bit rate requirements for digital television in DBS-TV systems.
2. Describe briefly the video compression method employed in MPEG-2.
3. Explain what is meant by masking in the context of audio compression. Describe how MPEG-1 utilizes the phenomenon of masking to achieve compression.
4. Describe the working of a DTH-TV receiver. What is the function of polariser in its outdoor unit? Which type of receiving antenna is used?
5. Discuss error control by coding, decoding and interleaving in a DBS-TV satellite system.
6. Describe briefly the requirements to be met in the design of a DBS-TV system.

19

Satellites and Cable Transmission Systems

19.1. Introduction

Cable TV transmission systems have been in operation since as early as 1949 even when there was no satellite communication system. With the availability of communication satellites and optical fibre cables new vistas in cable transmission systems have come up. The Cable transmission systems now help the viewers to receive signals not only from different parts of the country but also from different parts of the world. Teleports are advanced versions of cable transmission systems which are meant for TV signals, data and a variety of information transmission to the viewers. The modern concept of a Cable TV transmission network is as that shown in Fig. 19.1.[2]. Hence along with the Satellite based TV signals, off air radio and TV signals, other kinds of information is also available to the subscriber. The uniqueness of the system is the two-way capabilities of the cable system which enables the subscriber to 'talk-back' to the programme provider.

19.2. Cable Channel Frequencies

Cable transmission systems are usually classified as MATV of CATV systems depending upon their configuration MATV, master aerial television generally refers to small distribution systems providing a service to blocks of flats and maisonettes, to office blocks and even to small housing estates. MATV systems initially used UHF but now a days these also employee VHF channels. CATV, community antenna television are fairly large systems which distribute television signals to large number of homes in towns and villages. Such systems usually contain special compensating equipment to ensure that the picture quality is not degraded as the signals travel along the length of the system which may cover many miles.

In India CATV is also oftenly confused with the term *communal television* which is a television system that uses a master antenna to feed one or more centrally located television receivers that are set up in public places so that villagers can gather together to watch the programmes. CATVs employ VHF. It would be worthwhile to mention here that sometimes the term SMATV (Satellite Master Antenna Television) is used to describe systems which have a satellite receiving antenna as well as the normal MATV receiving aerials.

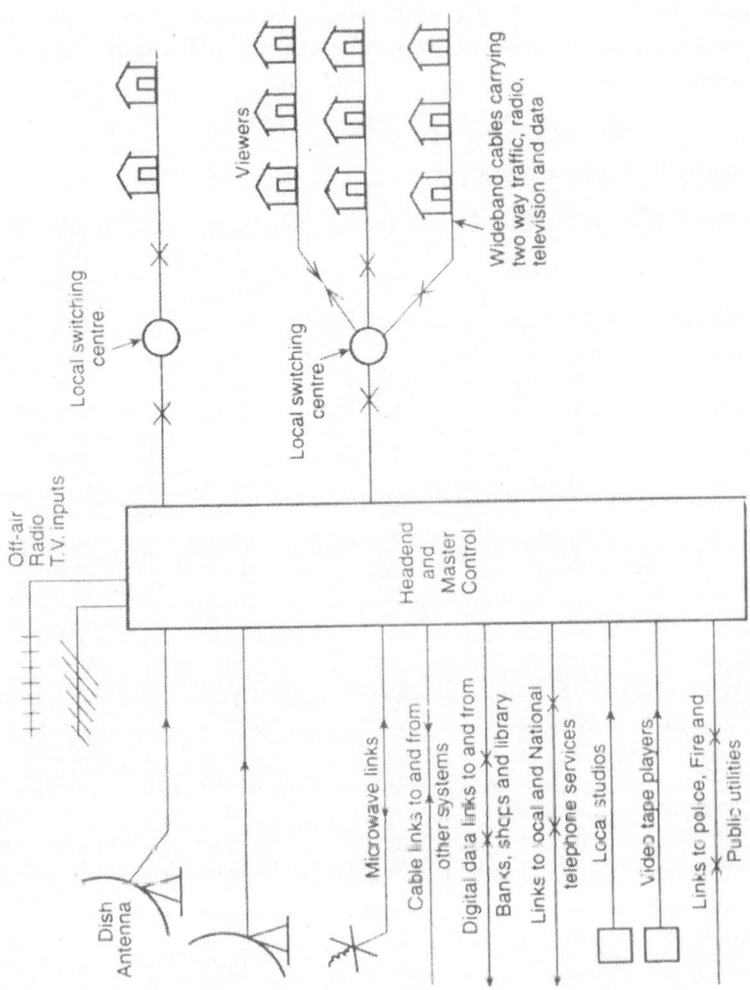

Fig. 19.1. Modern Concept of a Cable Transmission Network.

Fig. 19.1. Modern Concept of a Cable Transmission Network.

Since the Cable transmission systems receive different frequencies from different sources so converters are used to change nonstandard channel frequencies to standard VHF channel so that ordinary TV receivers can demodulate the signals. Newer receivers are being manufactured with tuners capable of turning more than one hundred channels. The cable channel frequency assignments generally used are given in Table 19.1[3]. Bidirectional cable systems normally employ a low band split (*i.e.* downstream channels above 50 MHz and upstream channels below 50 MHz) or a midband split with the division occurring at 150 MHz. As the upper limit of usnable cable-system frequencies increases, the frequency where the split occurs is also raised.

Table 19.1. Cable TV Channel Frequencies

Channel	*Frequency Range (MHz)*	*Carriers (MHz)*		
		Video	*Colour*	*Sound*
T-7	5.75-11.75	7	10.58	11.5
T-8	11.75-17.75	13	16.58	17.5
T-9	17.75-23.75	19	22.58	23.5
T-10	23.75-29.75	25	28.58	29.5
T-11	29.75-35.75	31	34.58	35.5
T-12	35.75-41.75	37	40.58	41.5
T-13	41.75-47.55	43	46.58	47.5
2	54-60	55.25	58.83	59.75
3	60-66	61.25	64.83	65.75
4	66-72	67.25	70.83	71.75
5	76-82	77.25	80.83	81.75
6	82-88	83.25	86.83	87.75
7	174-180	175.25	178.83	179.75
8	180-186	181.25	184.83	185.75
9	186-192	187.25	190.83	191.75
10	192-198	193.25	196.83	197.75
11	198-204	199.25	202.83	203.75
12	204-210	205.25	208.83	209.75
13	210-216	211.25	214.83	215.75
FM	88-108	—	—	—
14	120-126	121.25	124.83	125.75
15	126-132	127.25	130.83	131.75
16	132-138	133.25	136.83	137.75
17	138-144	139.25	142.83	143.75
18	144-150	145.25	148.83	149.75
19	150-156	151.25	154.83	155.75
20	156-162	157.25	160.83	161.75
21	162-168	163.25	166.83	167.75

(Contd...)

Channel	Frequency Range (MHz)	Carriers (MHz)		
		Video	Colour	Sound
22	168-174	169.25	172.83	173.75
23	216-222	217.25	220.83	221.75
24	222-228	223.25	226.83	227.75
25	228-234	229.25	232.83	233.75
26	234-240	235.25	238.83	239.75
27	240-246	241.25	244.83	245.75
28	246-252	247.25	250.83	251.75
29	252-258	253.25	256.83	257.75
30	258-264	259.25	262.83	263.75
31	264-270	265.25	268.83	269.75
32	270-276	271.25	274.83	275.75
33	276-282	277.25	280.83	281.75
34	282-288	283.25	286.83	287.75
35	288-294	289.25	292.83	293.75
36	294-300	295.25	298.83	299.75
37	300-306	301.25	304.83	305.75
38	306-312	307.25	310.83	311.75
39	312-318	313.25	316.83	317.75
40	318-324	319.25	322.83	323.75
41	324-330	325.25	328.83	329.75
42	330-336	331.25	334.83	335.75
43	336-342	337.25	340.83	341.75
44	342-348	343.25	346.83	347.75
45	348-354	349.25	352.83	353.75
46	354-360	355.25	358.83	359.75
47	360-366	361.25	364.83	365.75
48	366-372	367.25	370.83	371.75
49	372-378	373.25	376.83	377.75
50	378-384	379.25	382.83	383.75
51	384-390	385.25	388.83	389.75
52	390-396	391.25	394.83	395.75
53	396-402	397.25	400.83	401.75
54	72-78	73.25	76.83	77.75
55	78-84	79.25	82.83	83.75
56	84-90	85.25	88.83	89.75
57	90-96	91.25	94.83	95.75
58	96-102	97.25	100.83	101.75
59	102-108	103.25	106.83	107.75
60	108-114	109.25	112.83	113.75
61	114-120	115.25	118.83	119.75

19.3. Head-End Equipment

This consists of the antenna and amplifier to feed the signal into the main line for the splitter (local switches) to the trunk lines. When there are several antennas receiving signals for a cable transmission system then a balun is used with each antenna to convert the impedance to 75Ω which is that of coaxial line (cable). Output of these antennas is then fed into a 4 way hybrid (linear mixer). The output from the hybrid feeds into the distribution amplifier via a pre-amplifier. It may be noted that when some of the antennas receive UHF, then the single from UHF channel is first translated to VHF through a converter and then fed to the hybrid. In case the number of antennas exceeds 4, the hybrid is replaced by a combining network which provides necessary impedance match between coaxial cable and the antenna systems. The gain of both the VHF or UHF amplifiers is around 45 db, or more.

19.4. Distribution of the Signal

A splitter is also sometimes called local switch, it divides the signal from the main cable to the individual trunk lines. A multitap or single tapoff takes a small part of the signal from the trunk line for individual receivers. Splitters may be 2 way or 4 way. Since coaxial Cables suffer due to losses particularly at high frequency ends so equalizers are used alongwith the distribution amplifiers. It is necessary that the single level provided to a television receiver is of the order of 1.5 mV so as to provide a good quality reception. It may be noted that CATV test instruments also called as single analyzes are oftenly used for testing the system regarding interference, signal leakage and overall performance[4]. In the test equipment the counter measures the frequency of a single frequency signal. The oscilloscope provides an amplitude versus line display of the signal. The RF voltmeter, and power meter measure signal level over a wide bandwidth. The tuned voltmeter (wave analyzer and field strength meter) measure singal level at a specific frequency. The spectrum analyzer is an automatic tuned voltmeter capable of displaying a continuous spectrum and a noise meter is used to determine absolute noise power density measurements.

19.5. Important Cable Television Network Specifications

In order that CATV systems have good quality working even with large number of channels, certain standards (internationally accepted) have been formulated[5]. These are as under :

(*a*) **Television Carrier Levels :** The visual carrier level of every television signal at any subscriber terminal shall be not less than 0dBm V and not more than 14 dBmV. The visual carrier levels of the television signals on adjacent channels shall not differ from each other by more than 3 dB. The maximum difference between carrier lends within any 90 MHz range of frequencies shall be not greater than 8 dB. The aural carrier level of every television signal shall be not less than 10 dB and not more than 20 dB below its associated visual carrier level.

(*b*) **Carrier to Noise Ratio (CNR) :** The carrier to noise ratio for each television channel at any subscriber terminal shall be not less than 40 dB.

(*c*) **Carrier-to-Beat Ratio (CBR) :** The carrier to beat ratio for single frequency intermodulation products and other discrete frequency interfering signals in any television channels at any subscriber terminal shall be not less than that indicated by a given curve. This is not applicable to intermodulation products or other discrete signals which are zero beat with visual carrier.

Carrier to-composite-Beat Ratio : The carrier to composite beat ratio in any television channel at any subscriber terminal shall be not less than 53 dB.

Echo Rating : The echo rating in any television channel at any subscriber terminal shall not exceed 7 percent.

Radiation : Radiation from a cable television system shall not be exceed the limits set out in Table 19.12.

Table 19.2. Radiation Limit

Frequency Range MHz	*Radiation Limit*	*Test Distance*
Upto 54	20	10
54-108	20	3
108-174	10	3
174-216	20	3
216-444	20	10

19.6. Network Architecture

In the earlier CATV systems tree and branch distribution architecture was used. Infact tree and branch architecture is most efficient in terms of cable and distribution equipment usage when signals have to be distributed in one direction, from head-end to customer's home. It is why so many of this type are already in use. In the case of pay-television (where individual TV Programmes are being changed) and two way interactive services, tree and branch system is not suitable. Infact for the satisfactory operation of two way interactive services it is essential that the customer requesting the service can be identified and charged accordingly and that the resulting information be sent to his house and not to any other. For such systems, star network topology is found to be suitable where the head end is being kept at the hub of star and each house is being fed by its own individual cable or cables. Such a star network system allows easily the cable network operator to send each household the programmes that it wanted and was prepared to pay for, and it would be easy to charge each customer the appropriate amount for each programme or service that was provided.

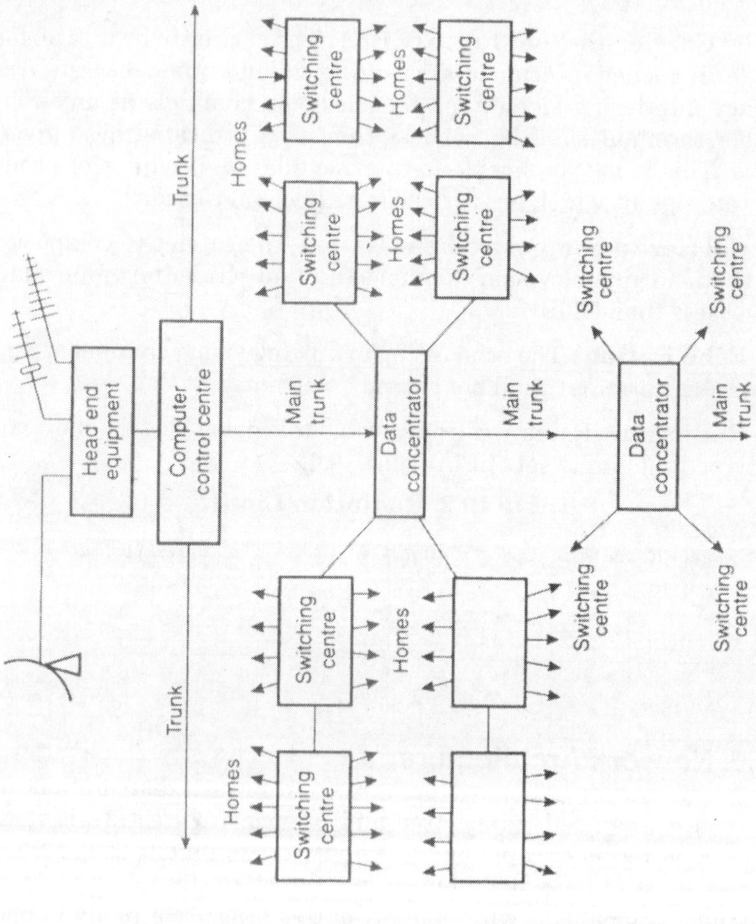

Fig. 19.2. Switched Star Topology in Cable TV System.

A better approach to serve a large community with two way interactive services is with the use of *switched star* network topology.

The system concept is as that shown in Fig 19.2 and is in wide use in both the European as well as American cities. Here each switching centre is capable of serving 40 homes. Data concentrators are substations and each concentrator feeds up to eight switching centres by means of a subtrunk cable. The central computer and equipment area is equipped with two mini computers which provide and store the data needed to keep control the switching and routing of programmes and control information. These central computers control the two way flow of information passing through the data concentrators but the customer's equipment receives its commands from the concentrator via the switching centre.

The design of main truck feeder consists of seven coaxial cables bound together into a multi-coaxial cable which is about an inch in diameter. Six of the seven inner cables carry up to five television programmes, each on VHF frequencies to give a maximum of 20 channels and the seventh is used for the VHF/FM B and II radio programmes. It would be worthwhile to mention here that a variety of switched star type systems such as those of 'mini star' and 'multi-star' etc. have also been developed and are in use.

19.7. Optical Fibre CATV Systems

The inherent advantages of optical fibres over copper wire and also of optical fibre cables over coaxial cables prompt the use of fibre optics in Cable TV transmission especially when large number of satellite TV signals are to be transmitted simultaneously to the subscribers[6]. However, fibre optic transmission systems are sophisticated ones involving optical transmitters/receivers which need expertise in high technology. Further the costs of laying out fibre optic cables, and associated equipment etc. are quite high as compared to that of established coaxial cable technology. Also the number of channels transmitted to the subscriber by Cable TV companies is still quite below which optical fibre cables can easily handle. All these increase the cost of subscriber at least 3 times which may not be tolerated by viewers at the moment. Thus, in future when the two way interactive services increase and cost of opto electronic equipments decrease, Fibre Optic Cable TV may be widely acceptable. At the moment these are used in Teleport systems only.

Optical fibre cable TV networks are proposed to have some sort of star topology, rather than tree and branch. Infact optical fibre does not lend itself to the latter, because of the difficulty of splitting and tapping signals. Two variations of topology have been oftenly proposed, namely (a) the pure star in which every subscriber location is directly connected to a central switch by a fibre pair to provide two way services and (*b*) the hybrid star, in which subscribers are connected by their own fibre or wire pair to a nearby local switch where all the signals are available. Whether fibre optics are used in the local loop or not, it seems apparent that fibres carrying multiplexed signals will be used in the future Fibre Optic Cable TV Systems for the long runs from a central switch to local switches close to the subscriber. Sometimes optical fibres are proposed to be in the primary links and coaxial cable in the secondary links. Such hybrid cable TV systems are underway or being planned in bigger way in North America, Europe and Japan. It is believed that costs for hybrid fibre systems are to be around $ 350 per service unit.

19.8. Indian Perspective

Satellite Cable TV Systems got momentum in India during gulf war when CNN of USA broadcasted live within India from the war zone. CNN (Cable News Network) offered free broadcasting rights to Doordarshan of CNN satellite broadcasts for a certain period. But free right to India automatically encouraged entrepreneurs to receive it directly from the CNN satellite broadcast through their own dish antennas. Since then Cable TV with the satellite dish antenna has been widely popularized in India. Several satellite antenna producing companies have come up. Shyam communications, which claims 10 million viewers and producing satellite antennas since 1978 see a better future for satellite communications. Other producers such as MC Engineering, Cable vision by Su-Kam and Pioneer Electronics also in satellite antennas are gearing up hoping for a major demand in the near future. Su-Kam Cable TV Systems are working to take a slice of the growing Cable TV market. With the *S* band satellite dish antenna any satellite which has footprint on India whether it is Asiasat, Intelsat, CNN or any other can be easily accessed and can be connected to the viewers through cable TV networks.

The concept of cable TV, however, is not a very new phenomena in India too. The concept was first launched in India in 1978 in hotels[8]. Dish antenna installation began in 1983 and gathered momentum by 1989, shortly after colour TV sets got into middle class households. The growth of Cable TV networks has been reportedly quite fast. According to a rough estimate over 50 million Cable TV subscribes are in India and in Delhi only growth rate of Cable TV views is around 250 per day. Popular system models are CATV - 43%, MATV –44%, Combination 13%. CATV Connotes satellite reception common dish antenna while MATV denotes feeding subscribers through common antenna. The distribution cost per connection is Rs 500-700 and the service charges are : deposits Rs 350-500 per channel and subscription Rs 100-175 per month. Usually the viewing time provided by the Cable TV operations is from 8 to 18 hours. While for Star Plus, BBC etc. separate for 24 hours. The programme menu is : Residential – Line 50% Indian 42% (Doordarshan), Foreign 8%, Recorded – 50% Indian 32%, Foreign 18%.

With the rapid development of Cable TV in India and fast infiltration of foreign signals like those CNN, Asiasat (STAR TV), BBC, etc. Govt. of India appointed a Cable TV committee in June 1989 headed by M. Damodaran, joint secretary in the Ministry of Information and Broadcasting[9]. The Committee comprised representatives from the Ministry of Information and Broadcasting, the Department of Electronics, the Department of space, the Communications Ministry, the Department of Culture, the Foreign Ministry, the Law Ministry, the VSNL and Doordarshan. The Committee submitted its report on February 21, 1991. It said that 'in the national interest' transborder TV signals should be restricted for which it suggested controls. The main recommendations are:

(*a*) CTV nets without a dish antenna may be permitted after devising a regulatory mechanism to cover their operation,

(*b*) Only those programmes may be distributed which are declared fit for public consumption by the Central Board of Film certification. Programmes distributed by CTV nets should not offend national sensitivity or violate accepted values.

(*c*) it should be compulsory for a CTV net to carry all signals which are available in that area and beamed by Doordarshan.

(*d*) CTV nets should distribute recorded programmes unless exempted in special cases.

(*e*) Fresh legislation is suggested to enable government to prescribe the necessary guidelines for regulating broadcasts,

(*f*) A national cable authority should be established for regulating CTV nets and to ensure some uniformity regarding standards but licences should be given on the condition that programmes received are not redistributed.

(*g*) There should not be a total ban on dish antennas but control must be exercised on reception of foreign signals,

(*h*) There should be no restriction on setting up master antennas for high rise buildings to receive Doordarshan signals if individual antennas are incapable of receiving programmes from satellites.

Government of India has installed a 90 tone, 55 foot antenna at Jalna, Maharashtra (project cost Rs 120 million) to strictly monitor the incoming foreign signals.

19.9. Future of Cable TV Systems

For developing countries like those of India, Cable TV has bright future and as happened with radio transistors, black and white/colour TVs, Cable TVs is becoming must for each and every house hold. It is now needed by every house in the same way as electricity or water is needed. CTV has become a sort of cottage industry and a cheaper means of information/entertainment. CTV has helped in developing the indigenous electronic technology related to satellite communication, VCR etc. C band antenna systems are being manufactured commercially (16 feet diameter to 20 feet diameter range) which receives the programmes from about 25 satellites. All the associated equipments like lone noise block converter, modulator, amplifier splitter and tap of junctions are indigenously manufactured. Antennas are fitted with a remote control that can be used for changing the elevation and azimuth of antenna for receiving various satellites like stationer (for CNN), Asiaset, Intelsat etc. Programmes originating from USA, Malaysia, China, Moscow, Hong Kong and other countries can be viewed with Razor Sharp picture clarity. Mainly with the arrival of High Definition TV, the importance of CTV is becoming more and it will need to have better quality transmission.

References

1. Yates, R.K., Mahe, N. and Masson, J, Fibre optics & CATV Business Strategy, Artech House, USA, 1990.
2. Slater, J.N., Cable Tele. Technology, Ellis Horwood Ltd. 1988, U.K.
3. Jordau, E.C. (Editor), Reference Data for Engineers, Radio, Electronics, Computer and Communications, Howard W SAMs & Co., 1986, Chapter 35.
4. Sundaram, P.S. & Sundareshan, B., Cable TV Technical Aspects, Telematics India March, 1992 pp. 50-53.
5. Coll, D.C. and Hancock, K.E., A Review of Cable TV : The Urban distribution of broad band visual signals, Proc IEEE 73 (1985), 773-788.
6. Agarwal, D.C., Fibre Optics Communication, A.H. Wheeler & Co., Allahabad, 1988.
7. Bhattacharya, A., Singh, R. and Colhando, K. Cable TV - Gulf War Fall Out in India, Telematics India, April 1991, pp. 46-56.
8. Khare, V.C. Cable TV what it's all about, *ibid*, April 1992, pp 72-73.
9. Colhando, K., India to shadow Foreign Signals, *ibid*, July 1991,

20

VSAT Satellite Systems

20.1 The VSAT Concept

In their early phase of development, the earth station antennas used in commercial satellite communications systems were very large and expensive with typical aperture diameters of 30 m. These large antennas operated in C band (6/4 GHz). However, as satellite telecommunications expanded over the years, there was a need to decrease in the size and cost of the earth station antenna. This need was met by two developments in satellite technology:

1. Increase in the transmit power capabilities of satellites; and
2. move to frequency bands above C band.

The above two developments lead to the development of VSAT (very small aperture terminal) satellite systems. The main characteristics of the VSAT systems are:

1. Most VSAT systems operate in Ku band, with earth station antenna diameters of 1 to 2 m and transmitter power of 1 or 2 W.

2. The earth stations are usually organized in a star network, in which the earth station connect to a central hub station via a GEO satellite.

3. Data rates on the links are from a few thousand bits per second up to 256 kbps, depending on the traffic requirements.

In large antennas, a symmetrical configuration is used because of ease of construction, with the feed on the boresight axis. The feed can either be in front of the antenna (a front-fed design) or behind the antenna, as in Cassegrain or Gregorian designs, axially symmetric or offset. However, it has been found that a common break point in the design of antennas occurs at a main reflector diameter of about 100 wavelengths. There are two possibilities:

(*a*) If the diameter is larger than 100 wavelengths, the additional cost of a Cassegrain or Gregorian design is more than outweighed by the superior off-axis and polarization performance achievable, and also the increased gain that can be achieved by shaping the reflectors. Cassegrain and Gregorian antennas also require a subreflector with a minimum diameter of about 10 wavelengths.

(*b*) If the main reflector is less than 100 wavelengths in diameter, the subreflector becomes an appreciable fraction of the main reflector diameter and causes significant blockage and scattering problems.

Earth station with antenna aperture diameters less than 100 wavelengths were called very small aperture terminals or VSAT.

VSAT systems are used to link businesses and stores to a central computer system so that sales transactions can be completed more rapidly than by using a telephone line and modem, and so that a central office can rapidly distribute and collect information from a large number of locations in a region or country.

20.2 VSAT/ Wireless Local Loop (WLL) Networks

In these systems, wireless local loop is coupled with VSAT distribution architectures. As shown in Fig. 20.1 the geostationary satellite links a large number of VSATs with the main switching center in a large city. Each VSAT acts as the link to the local switching center in the village or rural community, with the final mile of the telephony link being carried over a wireless local loop.

The characteristics of VSAT networks are:

1. They allow multimedia traffic to be brought directly to the end user, but generally handle only small traffic streams.

2. The traffic stream is usually intermittent in nature: the user accesses the satellite in a demand assigned multiple access (DAMA) mode whenever a message is to be sent and receives a short reply in due course. This is typical in a point of sale (POS) VSAT system that is used to transmit credit card information at a gas pump or a store register. Information about the sale and the customer's credit is sent to a central computer facility, and an authorization or denial is received in response.

3. The interaction between the VSAT and the main hub earth station in the POS transaction is completely automatic and transparent to the user, the customer in this case.

4. The VSAT/WLL system usually has an optimum range of user densities where the economics are most favourable. The information is only approximate and can be affected by local topography (e.g., a large mountain range, which would favour satellite delivery), the availability of optical fibres in the country's telecommunications network.

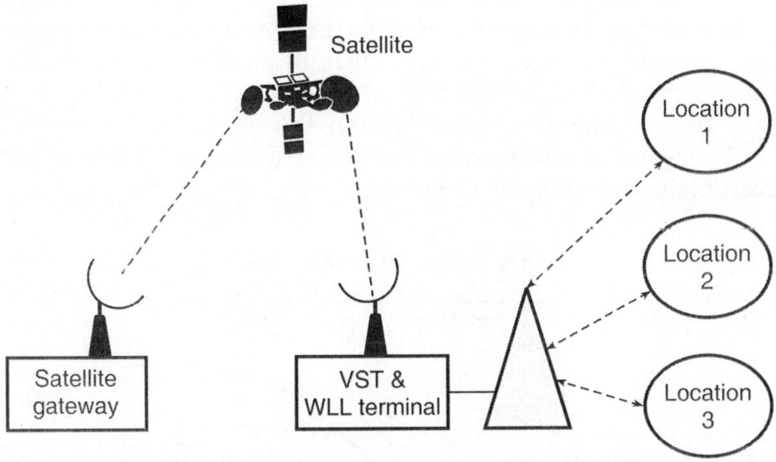

Fig. 20.1 VSAT/Wireless Local Loop (WLL) Network

VSAT networks often do not generate enough traffic to justify a dedicated satellite or one complete satellite transponder. Therefore, most VSAT networks are designed around the use of leased transponders in the case of a large network, or a fractional transponder lease for a medium to small network.

20.3 VSAT Network Architectures

The VSAT network architecture selected depend on a number of factors.

There are three basic implementations of any telecommunications service:

1. one-way implementation;

2. two-way implementation; and

3. split-two-way implementation (also called split-IP, when referring to Internet traffic, since the outbound and inbound channels are routed over different systems).

20.3.1 One-Way Implementation

This is the mode of a satellite used in the broadcast satellite service (BSS). The introduction of digital technology allows the provider and user much greater flexibility in the operation of a broadcast network. By means of proprietary software in the user terminals, different parts of the downlink can be accessed by different subscribers according to the programs ordered from the supplier (and paid for by the user). This type of channel selection is called *narrowcasting*. There can be many *narrowcasting* groups within a large broadcasting area.

The system is shown in Fig. 20.2. Here a broadcast satellite service coverage region is a number of smaller, narrowcasting groups exist within the broader coverage area. The master control station sends encoded signals within the broadcast stream that enables certain users to have access to particular channel groupings according to the subscriber's choice.

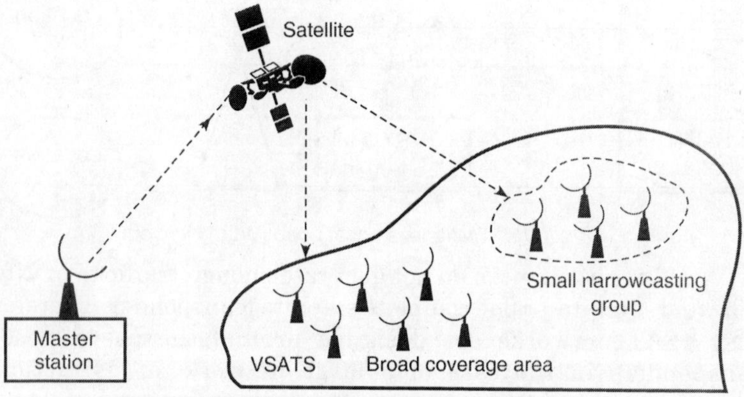

Fig. 20.2 One-Way Implementation for VSAT System

20.3.2 Split-Two-Way (Split IP) Implementation

This system is used when there is no normal return channel. For example, with Ku-band boradcast satellite service (BSS) systems that carry Internet traffic. The relatively high capacity downlink stream is not complemented by an uplink capability from the user terminal. If the BSS downlink is used as the download channel from an Internet service provider, the only option the user has for a return link is via another telecommunications channel, such as standard telephone line. The Internet protocol (IP) is therefore split between a satellite downlink (outbound) channel and a terrestrial telephone (inbound, or return) channel; hence the term split-IP for this implementation.

Its advantage is that the VSAT terminal does not require a transmit capability, which significantly reduces its cost and complexity.

Its disadvantage is that the telephone line connection must usually be through a modem, with a bit rate generally restricted to 56 kbps or less.

20.3.3 Two-Way Implementation

This system has a return link so that two-way communications can be set up over the same satellite, from the hub to the user and from the user back to the hub. Fig 20.3 shows a two-way service between the hub (in this case the satellite gateway) and any VSAT terminal. The architecture selected is the key to the economics of two-way connections. It is of two types: Mesh or Star netwoks.

(*a*) **Star VSAT network :** In this network architecture, all of the traffic is routed via the master control station, or hub. If a VSAT wishes to communicate with another VSAT, it has to go via the hub, thus necessitating a "double hop" link via the satellite. Since all of the traffic radiates at one time or another from the hub, this architecture is referred to as a Star network.

(*b*) **Mesh VSAT network :** In this architecture, each of the VSATs has the ability to communicate directly with any of the other VSATs. Since the traffic can go to or from any VSAT, this architecture is referred to as a Mesh network. It will still be necessary to have network control and the duties of the hub can either be handled by one of the VSATs or the master control station functions can be shared among the VSATs.

In contrast with earlier systems which had one large hub for all of the VSAT networks sharing the same satellite, the current networks allow each subnetwork to have its own hub. The host computer of each VSAT network is co-located with its own hub, thus eliminating the cost of the interconnection between the hub earth station and the computer controlling the service offered through the VSAT network. An access control protocol is established when the hub is shared or dedicated or when the VSAT is connected to a single user or a local area network (LAN) with multiple users sharing access through an Ethernet connection.

15.4 Multiple Access Methods

As already seen in Chapter 5, there are three main multiple access schemes, that is frequency division multiple access (FDMA),

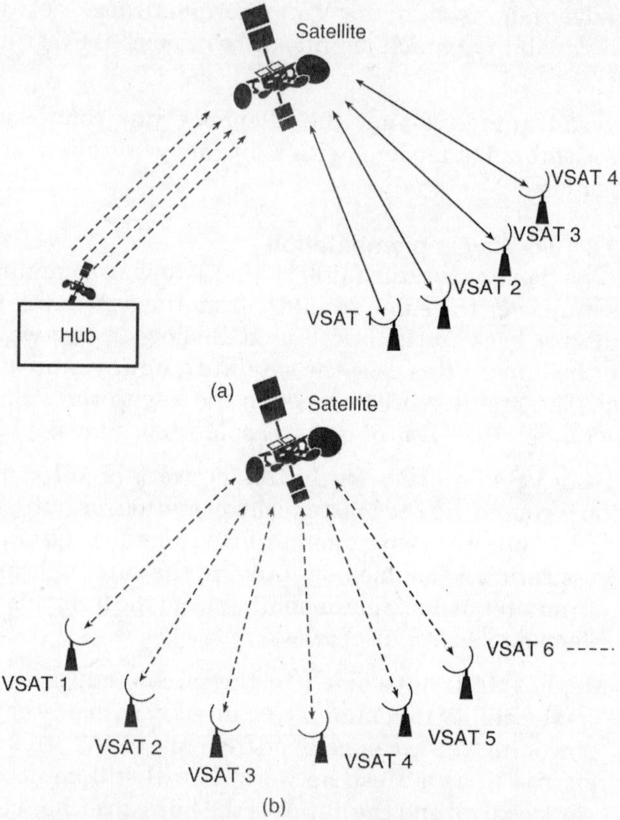

Fig. 20.3 (a) Star VSAT network (b) Mesh VSAT network

time division multiple access (TDMA), and code division multiple access (CDMA). TDMA is further divided into two broad subdivisions of access: (i) those closely controlled in time and access ability; and (ii) those which are loosely controlled in time and access ability (examples: ALOHA which is a random access scheme and other Ethernet-like connections).

The choice between FDMA, TDMA and CDMA for VSAT networks is determined by the intended application, the potential interference environment and economics.

20.4.1 FDMA-based access systems

These systems are used for thin route traffic, typically the equivalent of one digital voice channel at 64 kbits/sec. They offer the lowest cost for entry-level VSAT systems from the user's perspective because the receiver bandwidth and terminal transmit power required are the lowest.

The occupied bandwidth of an RF channel carrying a digital signal with a symbol rate r_{sy} and using error control coding with a code rate r_c is given by

$$B_{RF} = \frac{r_{sy}(1+\alpha)}{r_c} \text{ Hz} \qquad ...(20.1)$$

where α is roll-off factor of the root-raised cosine (RRC) filters in the link. α for satellite links lie between 0.25 and 0.5, with the higher value being easier, and thus cheaper to realize when conventional analog filters are used in the transmitter and receiver.

Example : *In a link using QPSK modulation where two bits of information are carried by each transmitted symbol, a message information rate of 64 kbits / sec results in a transmission symbol rate of* r_{sy} *= 32 ksps. If the message data bits are encoded with one-half rate FEC, code rate* r_c*= 1 / 2 and the roll-up factor of the filters is 0.25, the occupied bandwidth required for a 64 kbits / sec signal will be*

$$B_{RF} = \frac{32 \times 10^3 \,(1+0.25)}{1/2} \, Hz$$

$$= 2 \times 32 \times 1.25 = 96 \, KHz = 80 \, kHz$$

Clearly, a VSAT which has to transmit a 64 kbits/sec stream of data using QPSK modulation, using half rate FEC and a raised cosine filter with a roll-off factor of greater than 0.5 would require an RF channel bandwidth of 96 kHz and a receiver noise bandwidth of 64 kHz.

It is important to note that the roll-off of the RRC filter, while adding additional spectrum requirements, does not alter the noise bandwidth. Therefore, RF and IF RRC filters used in digital radio links have a noise bandwidth in hertz equal to the symbol rate in symbols per second.

There is also a need to add a guard band is added between FDMA channels. This is due to for three reasons:

1. To avoid overlap of adjacent signals in frequency at the satellite,

2. To allow the filters in the receiver that extract individuals channels to roll off between channels.

3. To avoid drift in the frequency of the fundamental oscillator due to weather conditions.

Therefore, fairly large guard bands are added which makes spectrum allocation at the satellite around 120 kHz for each 64-kbits/sec (voice) channel.

Fig. 20.4 shows the process of a 64-kbits/sec equivalent voice channel accessing a satellite using FDMA.

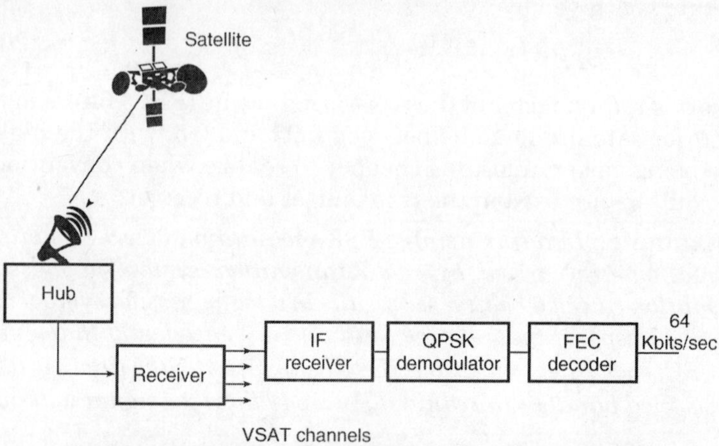

Fig. 20.4 A 64-kbits/sec Voice Channel Accessing a Satellite.

1. The 64 kbits/sec information rate is contained in a bandwidth of 96 kHz when transmitted to the satellite.

2. The bandwidth of the satellite transponder (from frequency f_1 to frequency f_2) is divided up, or channelized, into increments of 96 kHz so that a large number of VSATs can access the transponder at the same time.

3. Each of the 96-kHz channels requires a certain amount of spectrum on either side to guard against drift in frequency, poor VSAT filtering, etc. The 96 kHz channels plus the guard bands on either side add up to a channel allocation of about 120 kHz per VSAT.

4. From a spectrum allocation viewpoint, therefore, a typical 36-MHz satellite transponder would permit the simultaneous access of 300 VSATs, each of which is transmitting the equivalent of 64-kbits/sec voice channel.

Here each VSAT uses a single channel continuously on the uplink and therefore it is called SCPC (single channel per carrier)-FDMA.

The 64 kbits/sec equivalent voice channel shown in Fig. 20.5 is the output of the terrestrial-satellite interface equipment, after the required emulations and protocol conversions have taken place prior to transmission over a satellite network. This channel from the VSAT to the hub via the satellite is called the *inbound* or *inroute channel.*

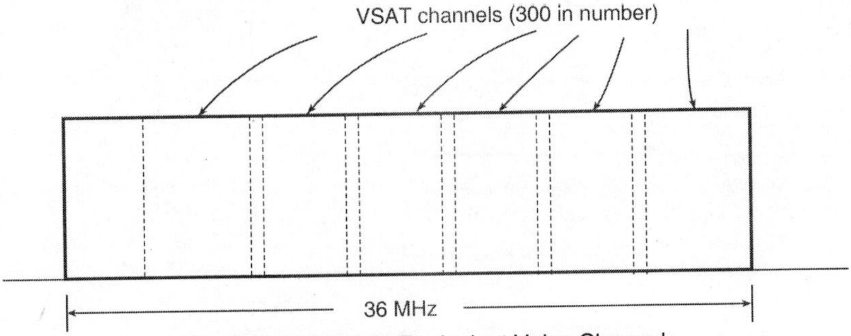

Fig. 20.5 64-kbit/sec Equivalent Voice Channel accessing a Satellite using FDMA.

This 64 kbits/sec data stream equivalent to a PCM digital voice channel, is often used as a sale device, say as a credit card reader, an Internet access request, digitized analog voice channel, and others, which require onward transmission over a VSAT network.

20.4.2 Channelisation by Transponder

The RF transmission to the satellite from the VSAT will have to be a frequency that falls within the bandwidth of a specific transponder on the satellite. Two cases arise:

(*a*) If the transponder operates in a bent pipe mode, with no onboard processing, the satellite will retransmit the multiple VSAT channels on the downlink with exactly the same channelization as on the uplink. Thus, in the example used in Fig. 20.6, a transponder with 36-MHz bandwidth would transmit 300 channels to the hub station or other VSATs in the network.

(*b*) If the VSAT network is being operated in a Mesh mode, each VSAT must have a frequency synthesizer that allow it to select any of the 300 possible downlink channels, and the network must have a control channel that tells each terminal at which frequencies it should receive and transmit.

20.4.3 TDM Downlink

The return link from the hub to the VSAT terminals, called the *outbound* or *outroute channel*. It is not normally employs a multitude of narrowband FDMA channels, but a single, wideband stream in a time division multiplexing (TDM) format. Figure 20.6 shows the schematic of a TDM downlink used in FDMA VSAT Star networks:

1. The 300 individual, narrowband, "inbound" channels received at the hub from the VSATs are sent back of the VSATs in a single, wideband, "outbound" TDM stream at a combined transmission rate of about 20 Mbits/sec.

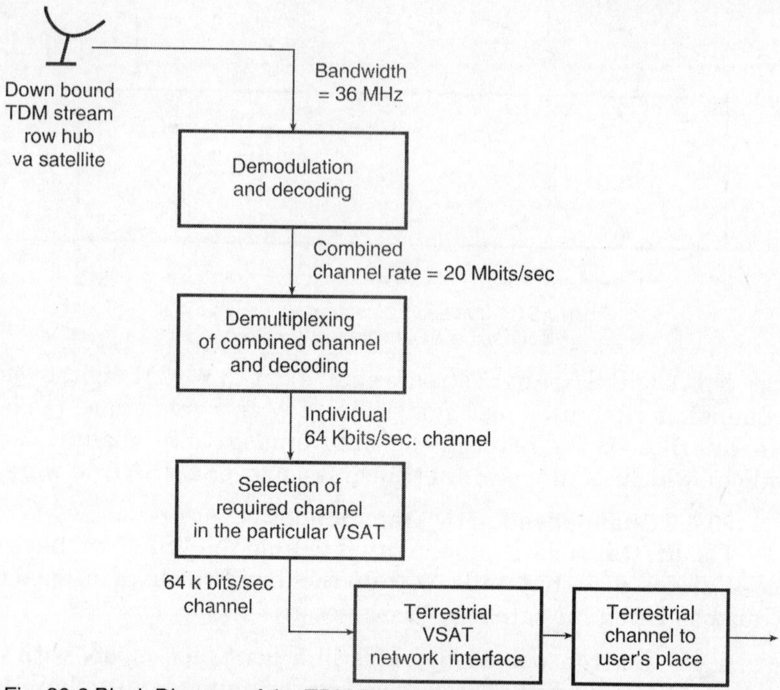

Fig. 20.6 Block Diagram of the TDM Downlink Outbound Channel from the Hub, via the Satellite to the Individual VSAT Terminals.

2. Each VSAT receives the downlink TDM stream and then demodulates and decodes it (that is, changes the modulated band-pass signal into a baseband line code and removed the FEC).

3. The line code is now passed through the demuliplexer which takes out the required part which contains the equivalent 64-kbits/sec voice channel to be sent to the VSAT terminal.

4. Carrier recovery and bit recovery circuits are used in the receiver in order to be able to identify the exact position of the required VSAT channel in time.

20.4.4 Use of Shared Transponder

In the FDMA Star VSAT network discussed above, separate transponders are used for the inbound and the outbound channels, which makes the VSAT network quite large. Also in many VSAT networks, the total instantaneous capacity required does not justify two separate transponders for the inbound and outbound signals. Therefore, a shared transponder is used as shown in Figure 15.7:

1. 18 MHz of spectrum is allocated for each side of the system connection.

2. On the uplink to the satellite, the collection of FDMA narrowband channels transmitted by the VSATs coexists in the same transponder with the wideband TDM stream transmitted up by the hub.

3. On the downlink from the satellite, the hub receives the collection of individual narrowband channels while the wideband TDM downlink stream is received by each VSAT. The precise frequency assignment can vary to suit the capacity of the VSAT network.

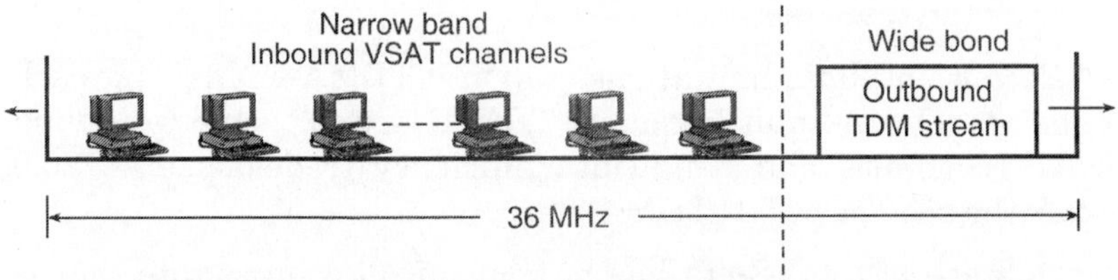

Fig. 20.7 A VSAT Network Frequency Assignment in which the Inbound and Outbound Channels share the Same Transponder in the Satellite.

There are two conditions for successful operation of FDMA links:

(*a*) It is necessary that correct transmit power per channel is allocated in calculating the link budget so that the power spectral density is the same for every channel.

(*b*) Operating a transponder in an FDMA mode also requires careful power balancing to ensure linear operation, which usually requires the output amplifier to be backed off.

Example: *If a 54-MHz transponder is operated at an output power of 54 W, the power spectral density at the transponder output is 1 W per MHz. A single inbound 120-kHz downlink channel transmitted by the satellite will therefore have a transmit power level of (120 kHz / 54 MHz) x 54 W = 120 mW. The effective isotropic radiated power or EIRP per 120-kHz channel is equal to the transmit power multiplied by the gain of the antenna in the direction of the hub (less feed and other losses).*

20.4.5 MF-TDMA (Multi-Frequency TDMA)

In certain systems such as advanced multimedia services that operate in Ka band (30/20 GHz), a TDM downlink format is often combined with a TDMA uplink plan. This is due to the following reasons:

1. Uplink FDMA formats are not as bandwidth efficient as TDMA.

2. A VSAT which employs TDMA on the uplink is required to transmit at the full burst rate of the TDMA scheme, and must therefore have a much more powerful transmitter than an SCPC-FDMA VSAT.

3. In cases where the average traffic for an individual VSAT is only one equivalent voice circuit (64 kbits/sec), having to transmit at 5 Mbits/sec, (instead of 64 kbits/sec), the VSAT transmit power must be increased by a factor of 5000/64 = 78 to maintain the same uplink C/N, since the earth station received must have a bandwidth that is wider by the same factor.

Because of these limitations, a hybrid TDMA-FDMA approach called MF-TDMA (multifrequency TDMA) is used to ensure a sound VSAT economics and bandwidth efficiency trade-offs. Fig. 20.8 shows the scheme of MF-TDMA:

1. Each of the VSATs has to transmit at a burst rate that is approximately five times the normal single VSAT single-channel rate.

2. If each VSAT transmits at a message data rate of 64 kbits/s and there are five VSATs sharing the same frequency, the minimum

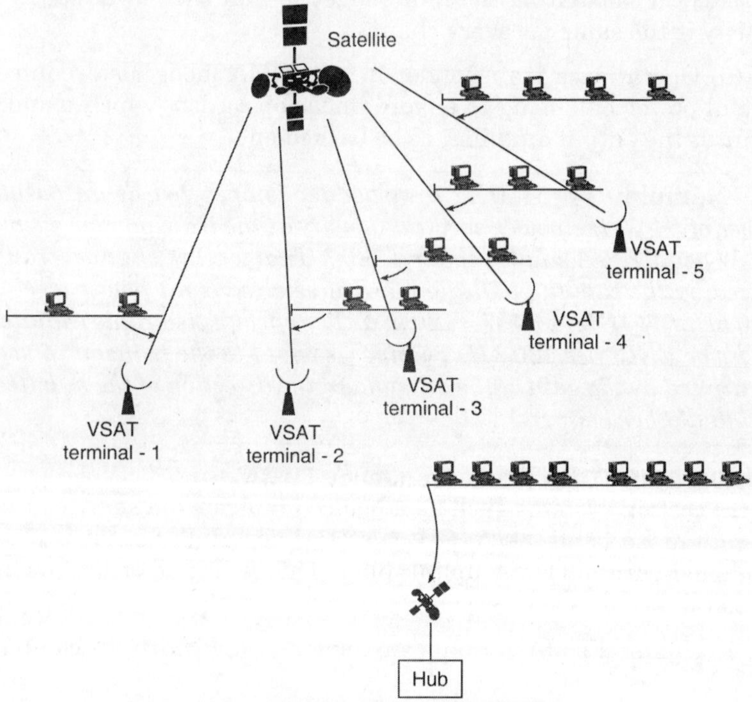

Fig. 20.8. Schematic of MF-TDMA

burst rate would be 5 × 64 kbits/sec = 320 kbits/sec. However time gaps (the equivalent of frequency guard band in an FDMA scheme) have to be left in between each of the individual payloads within the TDMA frame to avoid overlaps due to incorrect clock timing.

3. As in the FDMA scheme in which the hub detects all of the individual inbound VSAT frequencies and then bundles the outbound return traffic into one wideband TDM stream, the hub in the MF-TDMA scheme also detects each of the inbound MF-TDMA VSAT signals and bundles the outbound traffic into a wideband TDM stream.

20.5 Modulation, Channel Coding, and Interference Considerations

Modulation and channel coding are key considerations in determining the efficient and error-free transfer of information over a communications channels. They also have an impact on the potential for interference to one system and from another system.

The main considerations are:

1. Modulation with a large number of bits per symbol (e.g., 64 QAM) will occupy a relatively small bandwidth but it will require relatively high amplifier linearity and a high C/N ratio in the receiver. It is also more susceptible to interference than modulations with fewer bits per symbol.

2. High-index modulations require significantly more margins than low-index modulations.

3. The choice of the most appropriate modulation and channel coding for a VSAT system depends on ease of implementation because VSAT system have to be of afforadable cost.

To meet these limitations, trade-off is made in the design of the systems. The most common forms of modulation used in VSAT systems are QPSK. In cases where spectrum efficiency is less important, BPSK is used. In an ideal QPSK system with ideal RCC filters and no channel coding, a value of E_b/N_0 of 10.6 dB will provide a BER of 10^{-6}, corresponding to a receiver overall C/N ratio of 13.6 dB, ignoring any implementation margin.

20.5.1 Channel Coding and Decoding

The C/N requirement in VSATs can be significantly reduced if channel coding is applied. There are two types of channel coding:

(*a*) Block code or a convolutional coding in which the encoding and decoding process is applied to a group of bits in sequence rather than a bit at a time. The number of bits in the encoding sequence, k, is called the constraint length of the convolutional code. In the decoding process, k bits are used to evaluate the value of each bit transmitted. Since the encoding process is applied to the signal prior to transmission and is used to detect and correct for bit errors, it is called a *forward error correcting* (FEC) code as already discussed in Chapter 15.

(*b*) Block FEC code, which is applied to the channel prior to transmission.

Convolutional and block codes can be used together on a channel. Fig 20.9 shows the encoding and decoding scheme. Here, in the channel, first an inner convolution code is applied to the bit sequence. It is followed by an outer interleaved code such as a Reed-Solomon code. This code provides good error detection capability with high code rates. The reverse occurs on the decoding side. The FEC code is outside the Reed-Solomon code. It is the time they are applied that counts. As the FEC is applied first in the encoding process, it gets wrapped by the Reed-Solomon code. This then becomes the outer wrapping of the doubly-coded signal.

This form of concatenated coding is used extensively in many communications systems (for example in direct broadcast satellite television systems described in Chapter 18), since the interleaved coding will counter burst errors while the convolutional FEC coding

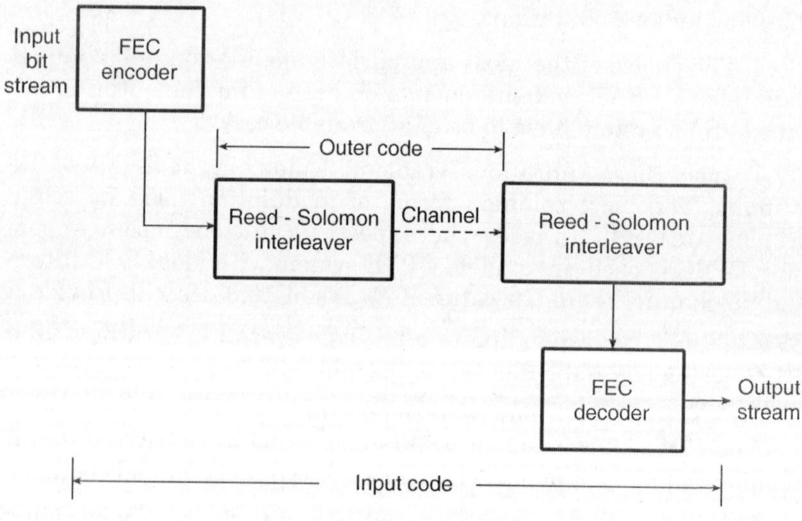

Fig. 20.9 Encoding and Decoding Process with Inner and Outer Codes.

will counter individual bit errors. It is also used in the recording of music on CDs.

20.6 VSAT Earth Station: The VSAT User Setup

The design of an earth station is typical of a hub station used in a VSAT network. Earlier discrete component were used in their construction, but introduction of digital receivers and the need to develop cheap, mass-produced VSAT terminals has totally changed the technology.

In its current design, the VSAT earth station can now be considered as two basic components - an outdoor unit (ODU) and an indoor unit (IDU). This is illustrated in Fig. 20.10.

1. The VSAT outdoor unit (ODU) is located where it will have a clear line of sight to the satellite and is free from casual blockage by people and/or equipment moving in front of it.

2. The inter-facility link (IFL) carries the electronic signal between the ODU and the indoor unit (IDU) as well as power cables for the ODU and control signals from the IDU.

3. The IDU is usually housed in a desktop computer at the user's workstation and consists of the baseband processor units and interface equipment (*e.g.*, computer screen and keyboard). It also has the modem and multiplexer/demultilexer (mux/demux) units if these are not already houses in the ODU.

Fig. 20.10 also shows details of the IDU and the modulator/demodulator (modem) equipment located in the IDU:

1. The low noise converter (LNC) receives RF signal and, after amplification, mixes it down to IF for passing over the inter-facility link (IFL) to the IDU.

2. The demodulator in the IDU extracts the information signal from the carrier and passes it at baseband to the baseband processor. The data terminal equipment then provides the application layer for the user to interact with the information input.

3. On the transmit side, the user inputs data via the terminal equipment to the baseband processor and from there to the modulator.

4. The modulator modulates the information on a carrier at IF and this is sent via the inter-facility link to the high-power converter (HPC) for upconversion to RF, amplification, and transmission via the antenna to the satellite.

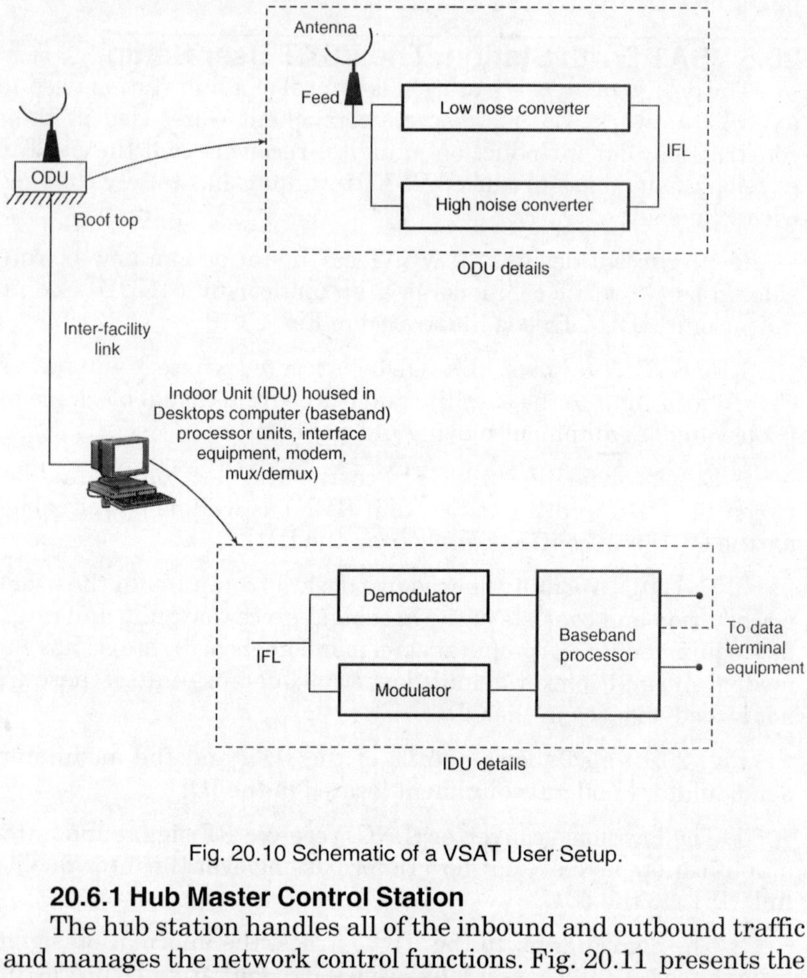

Fig. 20.10 Schematic of a VSAT User Setup.

20.6.1 Hub Master Control Station

The hub station handles all of the inbound and outbound traffic and manages the network control functions. Fig. 20.11 presents the block diagram of a typical hub earth station:

1. The hub line interface equipment handles the terrestrial ports to the host computer.

2. The control bus via the hub control interface permits the transmit, receive, and switching functions to be carried out.

3. The transmit processing and control equipment (PCE) creates the TDM stream for the outbound link to the VSATs.

4. This steam passes through the IF interface to the up-converter (UC).

5. The up-converter (UC) converts the IF to RF.

6. The high-power amplifier (HPA) amplifies the TDM stream which is transmitted by the antenna.

7. At the receive side, the antenna passes the individual inbound MF-TDMA signals to the low noise amplifier (LNA) which amplifies the signals before they are fed to the down-converter (DC), demodulator and finally to the user.

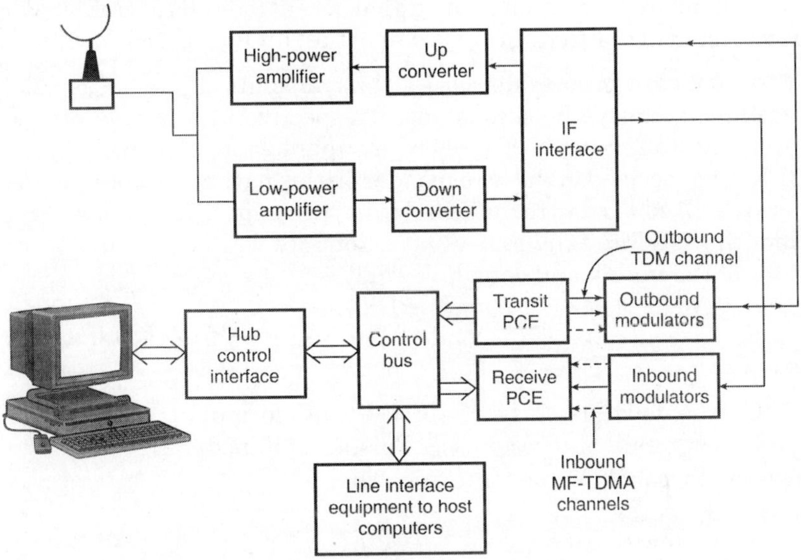

Fig 20.11 Hub Master Control Station.

20.7 Link Margins for a VSAT STAR DBS System

These margins are described below.

I. Threshold $(C/N)_0$ value: This value is the minimum allowed carrier to noise ratio $(C/N)_0$. For a typical inbound VSAT link its value is 6.0 dB, with BPSK modulation and half rate FEC encoding, giving a BER of 10^{-6}. This value varies depending on the modulation and FEC methods used on the link. Ignoring system errors, such as wrong pointing of the antennas or satellite problems, the clear sky C/N ratio on a given inbound link can be reduced to the threshold $(C/N)_0$ by either a rain fade on the uplink or a rain fade on the downlink.

II. Rain fade margins: There are two rain fade margins for the outbound link: (*i*) from the hub to the satellite (uplink); and (*ii*) from the satellite to the VSAT (downlink). The entire two-way system drops below the performance minimum when any one of the low margin links becomes below threshold.

The link fade margin can be estimated by using the reciprocal formula (C/N) ratio with the $(C/N)_0$ value set to its threshold value. Consider a VSAT system which has linear, bent pipe transponders and networks that are connected via a satellite and which uses onboard processing (OBP). Now since a bent pipe transponder simply translates the uplink frequency to the downlink frequency, without any regeneration of the signal, a rain fade on the uplink will be reflected in reduced output power of the satellite on the downlink.

In onboard processing (OBP), the transmitted power from the satellite is always held constant, irrespective of any fade on the incoming, uplink signal. Therefore, an uplink fade will cause a worse BER to be received in the transponder on this particular uplink. This in turn will add errors to the signal to be transmitted on the downlink from the satellite. The overall bit error rate will be the sum of bit rates of the uplink and downlink. That is

$$BER_{overall} = (BER)_{UL} + (BER)_{DL} \quad ...(20.2)$$

For a bent pipe transponder, link margins are calculated as follows :

On the downlinks, the reciprocal (C/N) formula is used to find the lowest value of $(C/N)_{DN\ min.}$ This is combined with $(C/N)_{UP}$ to give the threshold value for $(C/N)_0$. That is

$$\frac{1}{(C/N)_{Th}} = \frac{1}{(C/N)_{UP}} + \frac{1}{(C/N)_{DN\ \text{min}}} \quad ...(20.3)$$

or $$\frac{1}{(C/N)_{DN\ \text{min}}} = \frac{1}{(C/N)_{TN}} - \frac{1}{(C/N)_{UP}} \quad ...(20.4)$$

Because of rain attenuation on the uplink, the power received at the transponder will fall, causing reduced output power from the transponder.

On an inbound link with many VSAT stations operating in SCPC-FDMA, rain fading on the VSAT uplink will not significantly affect the total power received by the satellite, so the transponder operating point will not change and the transponder output power for that link will fall linearly with uplink attentuation. Therefore, $(C/N)_{DL}$ at the hub station receiver will fall as $(C/N)_{UL}$ fades as indicated in the equation below :

$$(C/N)_{0\ fade} = (C/N)_{0\ clear\ sky} - A_{dB\ UP\ fade} \quad ...(20.5)$$

For a nonlinear transponder, obviously the downlink (C/N) ratio will be higher because, when the transponder is operated at the beginning of its nonlinear region (as most are) to maximize transponder output power, a 1 dB reduction in input power will cause less than a 1 db change in output power.

Secondly, since the downlink attenuation margin in most VSAT networks is relatively small, and is usually the limiting factor in the network design, uplink power control (ULPC) at the hub station can maintain a relatively constant power level at the input to the transponder over the operating range of the ULPC system. As a result, the fade margin by the available range of the ULPC system increases.

20.8 A Typical VSAT System

The characteristics of a typical VSAT system are:

1. The satellite communications system consists of a single hub earth station, a geostationary satellite operating with a linear transponder, and a number of VSAT stations.

2. The system uses two Ku-band transponders on the GEO satellite.

3. Each VSAT station sends and receives a 64 kbits/sec data stream to and from the hub.

4. Digital data are sent to the hub from the VSATs by the inbound link via one transponder at a message bit rate of 64 kbit/sec using binary phase shift keying (BPSK) and half rate forward error correction (FEC) coding, giving a transmitted bit rate of 128 kbph.

5. The occupied RF bandwidth of each VSAT channel is 160 kHz, corresponding to ideal RRC filters with $\alpha = 0.25$.

6. Multiple access for the inbound link is by SCPC-FDMA with RF channels spaced 200 kHz apart to allow a 40-kHz guard band between channels.

7. Data form the hub station to the VSATs (the outbound link) are sent as a continuous TDM stream of packets using a second transponder and BPSK with half rate FEC.

8. The VSAT antenna has a diameter of 1m and 1 saturated out power of 2 W.

The design procedure is focused on developing the basic link calculations so that the operation of the system is understood and then to perform a trade-off analysis.

Now the four RF links in a two-way VSAT system are: (*i*) the inbound link from the VSAT to the hub station has an uplink to Transponder-1 on the satellite and a downlink to the hub station; and (*ii*) the outbound link from the hub station to the VSAT has an uplink to Transponder-2 on the satellite and a downlink to the VSAT.

The *C/N* ratios for each of the above links are calculated from a separate link budget. The uplink and downlink *C/N* values on the inbound link are combined to give an overall inbound $(C/N)_0$ in the hub station IF receiver. The uplink and downlink *C/N* values on the outbound link are combined to give an overall outbound $(C/N)_0$ in the VSAT receiver. The bit error ratios for the inbound and outbound links are then calculated from the inbound and outbound *C/N* values.

I. Free Space Path Loss. For calculation of the above link budgets, it is necessary to estimate the free space path loss between the early station and the satellite and the noise powers in the operating bandwidths. The free space path loss, *Lp*, for a range of 38,500 km is calculated as follows. The path loss, *Lp*, is given by

$$Lp = 20 \log (4\pi R/\lambda)\ dB \qquad ...(20.5)$$

where R is the range (38,500 km) and λ is the wavelength, in metres.

II. Noise Powers

(*a*) **Noise Power in Transponder-1, Inbound SCPC FDMA Channels:** This noise power, is given by

$$NT_1 = kT_{s_1} B_n \text{ Watts} \qquad ...(20.6)$$

where $k = -228.6$ dBW/KHz.

(*b*) **Noise Power in the Hub Station Receiver, Inbound SCPC FDMA Channel:** The inbound VSAT signals arrive at the hub station after being retransmitted by the satellite. If the system noise temperature of the hub station is $T_{s,\,hub}$, then

$$N_{hub} = kT_{s\,hub}B_n \quad \text{Watts} \qquad ...(20.7)$$

(*c*) **Noise Power in Transponder-2, Outbound TDM Channels:** The outbound TDM bit stream from the hub station to the VSATs passes through Transponder-2. Not all of the VSATs will be transmitting and receiving simultaneously and so the TDM stream should be sized for the likely average activity rate of the network. If the starting value noise bandwidth is B_{n2} MHz in the VSAT receiver, then

$$N_{sT2} = kT_{st2}B_{n2} \text{ Watts} \qquad ...(20.8)$$

(*c*) **Noise Power in the VSAT Receivers, Outbound TDM Channel:** Each of the VSATs receives the outbound TDM stream from the hub station in a noise bandwidth of B_{n2}. If the system noise temperature of the VSAT receiver is T_{st2}, then

$$N_{VSAT} = kT_{st2}\, B_{n2} \text{ Watts} \qquad \dots (20.9)$$

III. Inbound Links. Now link power budgets and the C/N ratios of the inbound and outbound links need to be estimated. A worst-case design is adopted, with the VSAT station on the –2 dB contour of the satellite beam, and losses included in the link budget to account for earth station antenna wrong-spointing, polarization mismatch, etc. The idea is that if the link works successfully under worst-case conditions, it will always work for any VSAT station under those conditions.

(*a*) **VSAT Uplink Power Budget:** Assume that the VSAT is located at the satellite beam's edge-of-coverage, the –3 dB contour of the satellite's uplink (receiving) antenna pattern. The power received at the satellite from a single VSAT, in dB, is given by

$$P_r = P_t + G_t + G_r - L_p - \text{Losses} \qquad \dots (20.10)$$

where P_t = transmit power;

G_t = gain of the VSAT antenna;

G_r = gain of the satellite receive antenna;

L_p = free space path loss; and

Losses = satellite antenna edge of beam loss, clear air uplink atmospheric loss due to gases, and miscellaneous losses of 0.5 dB to account for antenna wrong pointing, feed loss, etc.

(*b*) **Overall Inbound C/N at the Hub:** The overall C/N of the inbound VSAT channels is calculated by the reciprocal formula where the C/N values are power rations and not their dB values. That is

$$1/[(C/N)_{overall}] = 1/[(C/N)_{hub\ inbound}] + 1/[C/N)_{TR1}] \qquad \dots (20.11)$$

IV. Outbound links. The outbound, TDM link goes from the hub, via the satellite, to the VSAT stations. The TDM link is a continuous bit stream at a bit rate R_b bits per second using BPSK modulation and half rate FEC. The bit stream conveys data packets that are addressed to the relevant VSATs sequentially. The C/N ratio in the VSAT receiver must not be lower than the 6.1 dB threshold that gives $BER = 10^{-6}$ with this modulation. We will initially design the outbound link for an overall $(C/N)_0 = 10$ dB in clear air in the VSAT receiver, giving a link margin of 3.9 dB to overcome rain attenuation and noise temperature increase (during rain). In the same way as for the inbound links, a link power budget is tabulated and the C/N margins evaluated to provide the necessary insights into the performance of the overall system.

(*c*) **Hub Uplink Power Budget:** The received power at satellite transponder input will be given by

$$P_{rs} = P_{t,hub} + G_{t,hub} + G_{rs} - L_p - \text{Losses} \quad \text{... (15.12)}$$

where $P_{t,hub}$ = hub station transmit power;

$G_{t,hub}$ = is the hub transmit antenna gain at 14 GHz;

G_{rs} = satellite receive antenna gain at 14 GHz;

L_p = free space path loss at 14 GHz; and

Losses = L_{ec} (edge of coverage loss of satellite antenna), L_{atmos} (atmospheric gaseous loss) and L_{misc} (miscellaneous losses).

(*b*) **Uplink C/N in Transponder-2:** The received power of the TDM stream at this transponder is $P_{t,hub}$ as calculated above and the noise power in the satellite transponder for the TDM stream is N_{tr_2} so that the uplink C/N will be

$$(C/N)_{tr_2} = P_{t,hub} - N_{tr2} \quad \text{... (20.13)}$$

(*c*) **Outbound Downlink Power Budget at the VSAT Transponder-2**: It carries a single TDM-BPSK carrier. If output backoff is $G_{r\,VSAT}$, then the received power at the hub station receiver output will be

$$P_{rhub} = P_{ts} + G_{ts} + G_{rVSAT} - L_p - \text{Losses} \quad \text{... (20.14)}$$

where,

P_{rhub} = maximum satellite transmit power ;

G_{ts} = satellite transmit antenna gain;

G_{rVSAT} = VSAT receive antenna gain;

L_p = free space path loss; and

Losses = L_{eoc} (1-dB contour of satellite antenna; L_{atmos} (atmospheric gaseous loss) and L_{misc} (miscellaneous losses).

(*d*) **Downlink C/N Ratio at the VSATs from Transponder-2 on the Outbound Links:** The outbound TDM stream from the hub station, transmitted down by Transponder-2 in the satellite, is received at each VSAT. Therefore the outbound downlink *C/N* is therefore

$$(C/N)\ VSAT_{outbound} = P_{r,hub} - N_{VSAT} \quad \text{... (20.15)}$$

(*e*) **Overall Outbound C/N at the VSATs:** The overall *C/N* of the outbound TDM stream reeived by the VSAT receiver is calculated, using the reciprocal formula with the *C/N* values as power ratios, that is

$$1/[(C/N)overall] = 1/[C/N_{VSAT}\ outbound] + 1/[C/N)_{TR2}] \ldots (20.16)$$

20.9. System Design Considerations

The main guidelines for designing a VSAT system are:

(*a*) The VSAT system needs to be optimized carefully, balancing the transmission requirements of the inbound and outbound links so that the space segment capacity is used efficiently.

(*b*) Since Ku-band satellite transponders are to be used in a VSAT system, the steps are to be taken to develop a link budget, determine capacity information, and carry out trade-off calculations to optimize the links for a Star VSAT network.

(*c*) The design of a VSAT network is dominated by the low gain and small transmitter power of the VSAT station.

(*d*) The links must operate with low *C/N* ratios at the VSAT receivers and with low fade margins.

20.10 VSAT Antennas: Shaped Reflector Cassegrain antenna

From cost point of view, the earth station antenna used at the VSAT earth stations is the most important element in the system. As already observed, the small size and low transmit power of a VSAT station are the factors that keep the price of the earth station at a level that makes a VSAT network an economic alternative to a terrestrial data network using telephone lines and modems.

An offset reflector fed by a scalar horn is used as the preferred configuration for most DBS-TV receiving antennas. This is called a *shaped reflector Cassegrain antenna* (Fig. 20.12). The basic design features of this Cassegrain antenna are:

1. It has a paraboloidal main reflector and a hyperbooloidal subreflector. One focus of the subreflector is coincident with the focus of the main reflector; the feed is at the other focus of the subreflector.

2. The surface profile of both reflectors are be modified by redistributing energy across the aperture so as to increase the aperture efficiency and reduce blockage caused by the subreflector.

The main advantage of the Cassegrain is that the subreflector is closer to the main reflector and therefore easier to support. In situations, where there is a severe off-axis interference environment, an offset-fed Gregorian design is the best to use.

Though the use of a VSAT depends upon the secific application but in general a company for organisation definitely saves money both in terms of lower initial costs and more predictable costs in the future. Costs for terrestrial services are rising in an unpredictable manner and their installation often produces significant, random delays. A VSAT network solution will allow to eliminate these delays, stabilize costs and still be able to easily expand or reconfigure the network in future.

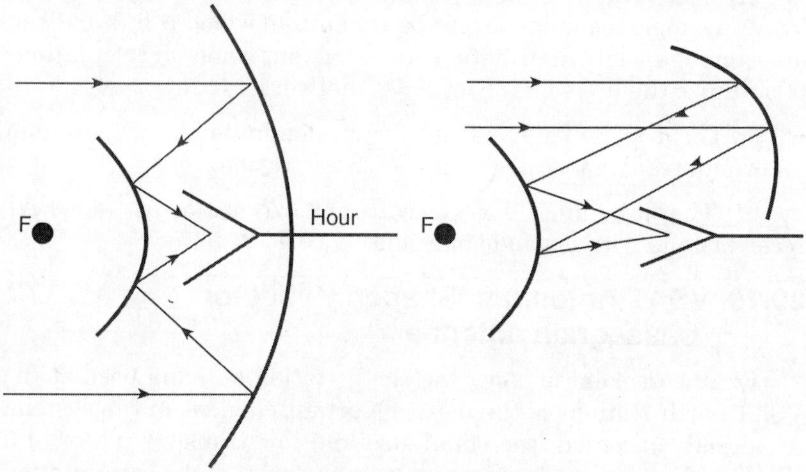

(*a*) Symmetric (*b*) Offset

Fig. 20.12. VSAT Casse Grain Antenna.

20.11. Applications of VSAT Networks

Fig. 20.13 indicates some of the typical application areas of VSAT and Data Broadcast Satellites. Fig. 20.13. (*a*) is an example of Intelligent service which has an application such as in a retail data network using interactive transaction processing for credit card verification, inventory control and broadcast video for branch store training, sales and product promotions. Fig. 20.13 (*b*) indicates an example of 56 kbps transmission between two customer locations. An application area is such as that of transfer and updates of data files between a company's corporate headquarters and one of its district offices.

Fig. 20.13 (*c*) indicates once again the example of an intelligent service. Typical application area is that of a corporate data network using interactive transaction processing for inventory, payroll and other administrative requirements, interspersed with large data file transfers. Finally in Fig. 20.13 (*d*) service of 56 kbps between customer premise and the company's national network is shown. Typical application is that of bulk data transfers between a company's MIS center and corporate headquarters. Since earth

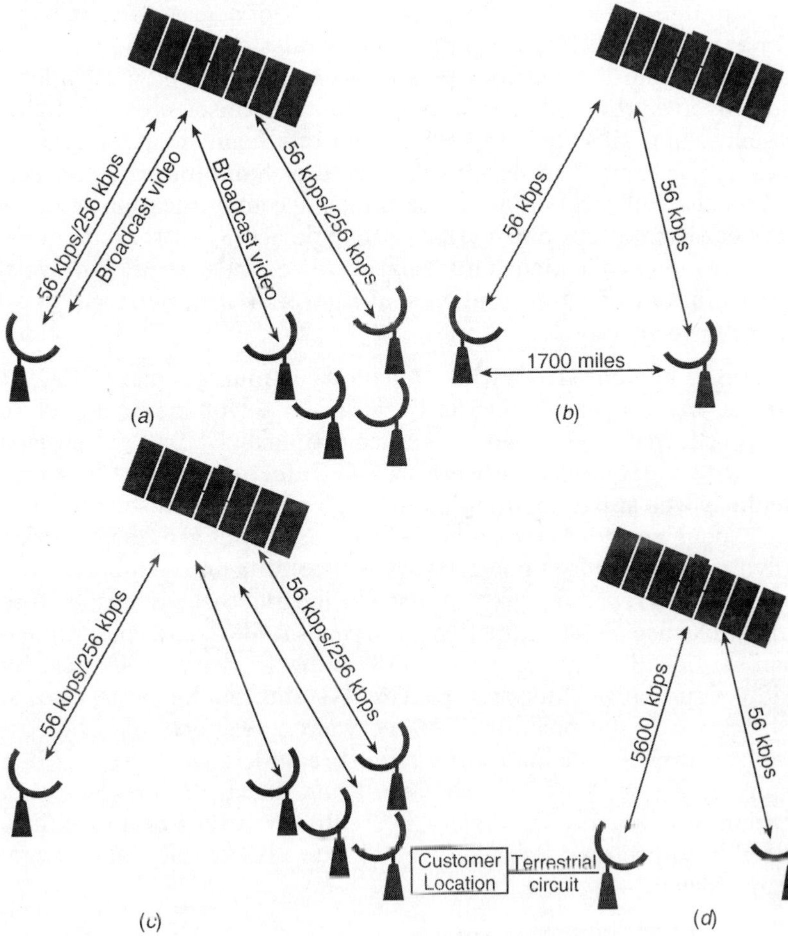

Fig. 20.13. Some Typical Application Services of Data Broadcast Satellite and VSATs :
(*a*) Intelligent Service
(*b*) 56 Kbps Transmission Between two Customer Locations
(*c*) Intelligent Service
(*d*) 56 kbps Between Customer premise and a National Network.

station could not be located on site, so costomer interfaces with the company's national network.

From above example it is clear that VSAT data networks create and manage transmission media. This is done by performing five basic functions, namely transmission, multiplexing, bandwidth allocations, protocol, handling and network management. Transmission refers to the ability to establish a physical channel using the VSAT microwave radio and satellite modem equipment alongwith the satellite itself. Multiplexing is the task of aggregating streams of data from multiple sources for transmission over the network. Normally time division multiplexing is employed. Bandwidth allocation involves the ability to manage the transmission channel as a resource and allocate it to VSAT in an intelligent manner so as to meet their instantaneous needs. Protocol handling refers to the ability to establish and maintain multiple communication sessions between computers and various other devices. Network management involves collection of information about the network, analysis, determination of action, and presentation of information to allow an operator to effectively control the network.

VSAT evaluated as a wide area data communication network fit almost any application currently served by telephone lines and an array of devices such as modems and multiplexers. VSAT can be used also with value added network (VAN). Infact a VSATVAN is particularly well suited to prividing network management services that are expensive or difficult to obtain from conventional data networks. Advantages include support, network flexibility and reliability, network control reporting, ease of installation and cost savings. VSATs and VANs are a cost competitive reliable satellite data communication service ideal for networks with as few as two to 100 sites. By adding specialized network control systems to the large central master earth station in a VSAT network its capacity can be customized, divided and made a available to small network users. When many small networks are combined and share the master earth station, a value added network is created. With a VSATVAN it is possible to broacast data and/or video to all locations in a single transmission.

VSAT have become popular because they were successfully used with Ku band (12—14 GHz) satellite systems. This is because of the fact that Ku band is less congested and the available EIRP is much stronger, though the radio path loss is greater compared to C band propagation. Nevertheless the enhanced receiving gain of VSATs is more than sufficient to counteract the weather related propagation loss and yet provide a high quality data communications service. This has resulted in a proliferation of VSATs. However, in two satellite systems such as Indian National Satellite (INSAT) and ARABSAT satellite there has been provided the unusual facility of special interest to developing countries. They have an arrangement by which transmissions sent in the C band will be amplified on broad and broadcast on the S band. The transmission in S band has two advantages, namely (*a*) more powerful transmission in S band than *C* band and (*b*) cheaper in cost for antennas and receivers required for S Band reception. In addition, direct broadcast receivers have been produced in large numbers at low cost for use in receiving S band TV transmissions. While they are designed for direct reception of TV transmissions, they can be used for data broadcast reception as well. The above technique of transmitting to the satellite in C band and broadcast carried in S band is often referred to CXS scheme. Though this will require a special transponder on the satellite but the scheme can be implemented using a single channel per carrier (SCPC) modem.

VSAT systems are, however, unbalanced and consist of a large central or hub and a large number of VSATs. For such a situation RA/TDMA protocols are found to be much successful. Table 20.10 gives a summary of various multiaccess protocols applicable to VSAT data networks.

Today's very small aperture terminals represent the first generation in a long line of future satellite communication products. Without the encumberance of geographical barriers, succeeding generation of VSATs will evolve into multi-featured systems with astounding capabilities at very cost effective prices. For example, the technology of 'switched board in the sky' will be utilized where instead of broadcasting over the whole country, broadcast over a multiplicity of sub-regions will be carried out. With this more power would be focussed into a particular area and thus the available bandwidth will be increased by having the same frequencies used again in spatially isolated regions or beams. NASA's Advanced Communications Technology Satellite (ACTS) incorporates the above and other advanced concepts. These and other useful trends and technologies are reducing equipment costs etc. of VSATs. The size of VSAT antennas is believed to be reduced in near future and there phased array antennas might be used instead of parabolic reflectors. Further as the technology develops in next 10 years it will be possible to locate VSATs in doors in many places. Also then more power with satellites would be available.

Table 20.10. Summary Comparison of Multiple Access Protocols Applicable to VSAT Data Networks

Multiple Access protocoal	*Capacity (max through-put)*	*Delay*	*Stability*	*Robustness*	*Vsat cost / complex*	*Remarks*
TDMA	0.7-0.8	med-high	good	medium	medium	Delay increases sharply with the number of Stations
FDMA-SCPC	0.7-0.8	med	good	high	very low	Applicable only to high traffic Stations
	FIXED	ASSIGNMENT		TECHNIQUES		
	RANDOM	ASSIGNMENT		TECHNIQUES		
ALOHA	0.13-0.18	low	poor	high	very low	Applicable to variable length messages, turning not required
Slotted ALOHA	0.25-0.368	low	moderate	high	low med	Simplest Slotted technique: Suitable for fixed length message traffic capacity competitive with slotted Aloha Without tuning
SREJ-ALOHA (selective reject)	0.2-0.3	low	maderate	high	low	Well suited to variable length messages
Tree CRA	0.43-0.49	med	good	poor	med-high	Suitable for fixed length messages, interleav-ing delay & deadlock problems
ARRA	0.5-0.6	low	moderate	med	med-high	Side information used to improve slotted Aloha type channel performance

Multiple Access protocol	*Capacity (max through-put)*	*Delay*	*Stability*	*Robustness*	*Vsat cost / complex*	*Remarks*
Random Access CDMA	0.1-0.4	V-low	moderate	high	med	Offers low delay with SSMA advantages, operated with or without tuning, comlex FEC required for good through put
Time of arrival CRA, FLAP etc	0.4-0.7	low	moderate	high	med	Exploits arrival time information in collisions to improve performance of ALOHA channels
Controlled Access Techniques						
DAMA/TDMA	0.6-0.8	med-high	good	pocr	high	generally attractive for long messages; high latency delay due to reservation

20.11. Review Questions

1. With the help of a sketch, describe the working of a VSAT/WLL network. Why such a system facilitates the use of very small antenna terminals?
2. Describe the operation of a typical VSAT user set-up giving details of the outdoor and indoor units.
3. With the help of a block diagram, describe how the sub stake in a VSAT system handles large inbound and outbound traffic.
4. Explain why FEC and Reed-solution interleavers are used coding and decoding of channels in a VSAT systems?
5. Describe how the TDM downlink outbound channels is linked to VSAT terminals how is the 64 kbts/sec equivalent voice channel is received?
6. What is the typical range, in metres, of the aperature diameter for a VSAT operating with a Ku-band satellite ?
7. Explain what Mesh and Star architectures are in a VSAT network. State two advantages and disadvantages of each.
8. Describe the three major types of multiple access schyemes that are used in satellite systems.
9. What are the advantages and disadvantages of an MF-TDMA access scheme in a VSAT system?
10. Why has a TDM approach been adopted for most downlink applications for digital VSAT and Internet applications to small terminals?
11. What do the symbols ACK and NAK mean when applied to a packet switched communications system?
12. What does the term spoofing mean when applied to the interface between dissimilar networks.

20.12. References

1. Timothy Pratt, Charles W. Bostian and J.E. Allnutt, *Satellite Communication*, John Wiley, NJ, 2003.
2. VSAT Systems and Earth Stations, *Handbook on Satellite Communications,* International Telecommunications Union, Geneva, 1994.

21

Global Positioning Satellite Systems

GPS Development

In the late 1950's, scientists as John Hopkins University developed a way to use radio signals originating from a satellite in space to provide accurate position updates to navigation equipment located on the US Navy's ships and submarines. By the mid-1960's, the Air Force initiated a program consisting of several satellites with very accurate clocks onboard that could give off timing signals of their location in space which would accurately determine the position of a vehicle moving on land or in the air. In 1973, the Navy and the Air Force programs combined to form the Navigation Technology Program, which later evolved into the Navstar Global Positioning System (GPS) in operation today.

Navstar GPS became the world's premier position, navigation and timing information service. Civilian users around the globe rely upon Navstar GPS as well. In fact, the system serves millions of civil users with over a 1.4 million handheld and vehicle-mounted GPS receivers having been produced each year since 1997. The rapidly growing GPS market, including equipment and applications, reached over $8.2 billion in 2005 and is expected to rise due to its wide applications.

21.1 The Technical Structure

The Global Positioning Satellite Systems are used as means of navigation for ships and aircrafts and in surveying and many other applications.

The main features Global Positioning Satellite Systems (GPSs) are:

1. The GPS space segment consists of 24 orbiting satellites in medium earth orbit (MEO) at a nominal altitude of 20,200 km with an orbital inclination of 55° that provides navigation and timing information to military and civilian users world wide. The system also consists of a worldwide satellite control network and GPS receiver units that acquire the satellite's signals and translates them into position information.

2. The satellites are clustered in groups of four, called constellations, with each constellation separated by 60° in longitude.

3. The orbital period is approximately one-half a sidereal day (11 hours 58 minutes) so the same satellites appear in the same position in the sky twice each day.

4. The satellites carry station-keeping fuel and are maintained in the required orbits by occasional station keeping maneuvers, just like GEO satellites.

5. The orbits of the 24 GPS satellites ensure that at any time, anywhere in the world, a GPS receiver can pick up signals from at least four satellites. Upto 10 satellites may be visible at some times, and more than four satellites are visible nearly all of the time. They provide a direct readout of the present position of a GPS receiver with a typical accuracy of 30 m.

6. A large number of GPS receivers can operate simultaneously because all that a GPS receiver has to do to locate itself is to receive signals from four GPS satellites.

Other position location systems, such as LORAN (long range navigation) that can also provide direct readout of position, but have far less accuracy and reliability.

GPS provides the following:

- 24-hour, worldwide services
- Extremely accurate, three-dimensional location information (providing latitude, longitude, and altitude readings)
- Extremely accurate velocity information
- Precise timing services
- A worldwide common grid that is easily converted to any local grid
- Continuous real-time information
- Accessibility to an unlimited number of worldwide users
- Civilian user support at a slightly less accurate level

The GPS worldwide satellite control system consists of five monitor stations and four ground antennas. The monitor stations use GPS receivers to passively track the navigation signals of all the satellites. Information from the monitor stations is then processed at the master control stations, operated by the Operations Squadron Base which sends updated navigation information to the GPS satellites through ground antennas using an S-band signal. The ground antennas are also used to transmit commands to satellite and to receive the satellites' state-of-the-art telemetry data.

The signals are so accurate that time can be figured to within 100 nanoseconds, velocity can be figured to within a fraction of a km per hour, and location can be figured to within meters.

GPS satellites orbit the earth every 12 hours emitting continuous navigation signals on two different L-band frequencies, L1 and L2.

The fundamental concept of GPS is to use simultaneous distance measurements from four satellites to compute the position and time of any receiver on or above the Earth's surface. The GPS satellites broadcast signals on two different frequencies so that sophisticated user receivers can correct for distortion effects due to the ionosphere, a layer of the atmosphere several hundred miles above the Earth. It takes between 65 and 85 milliseconds for a signal to travel from a GPS satellite to a receiver on the surface of the Earth. The signals are so accurate that time can be figured to much less than a millionth of a second, velocity can be figured to within a fraction of a km per hour, and location can be figured to within a few meters. Typical horizontal positioning accuracy for military users is 7 to 10 meters. Prior to the mid-1990's a purposely 'degraded signal' was provided for civilian users, limiting their accuracy to 70 to 100 meters. This was then eliminated as it became obvious that civilian and commercial users had many unimagined uses for precise location and timing information as well.

Each Block II or IIA satellite has two cesium atomic clocks and two rubidium atomic clocks, while each Block IIR has three rubidium atomic clocks. The stability of these clocks is estimated to be approximately 1 second per 300,000 years. Only one clock is in use on each satellite at a time. The others are backups.

The GPS worldwide satellite network consists of six monitor stations and four ground antenna stations. The monitor stations use specially-designed GPS receivers to passively track the navigation signals of all of the satellites. Data from the monitor stations is continually sent to the GPS Master Control Station (MCS), for processing. The MCS computes precise, updated information on the satellites' orbits and clock status every 15 minutes, 24 hours a day, seven days a week. Updated navigation information is sent from the MCS to the ground antenna stations and then to the satellites. These "uploads" are done once ar twice per day for each satellite. This is sufficient to maintain the high accuracy of the GPS constellation.

GPS satellites broadcast on two links to users: L1 and L2. L1 is transmitted at a frequency of 1575.42 MHz, and carries both a Coarse/Acquisition (C/A) ranging code and a Precise (P(Y)) ranging code. L2 is transmitted at a frequency of 1227.6 MHz and carries only the P(Y) code. Only the C/A code on L1 was originally available to all users. The military users have access to both the C/A code on L1 and the P(Y) code on L1 and L2. To access GPS for general use, a civilian user may purchase a hand-held or vehicle-mounted GPS receiver. The civil signal is free to all users worldwide. No subscription, license, fee or registration is required.

The future of plans for GPS included increased power and accuracy, as well as increased civil navigation safety with addition of a new civil signal on the L2 link and a new civil-only signal on a new link, L5, to be broadcast at 1176.45 MHz. A new military-only signal (M-code) on the L1 and L2 links will be fully operational in 2010. It will have increased power and reduced vulnerability to signal jamming.

21.2 Applications of GPS

1. TIMING

In addition to longitude, latitude, and altitude, the Global Positioning System (GPS) provides a critical fourth dimension time. Each GPS satellite contains multiple atomic clocks that contribute very precise time data to the GPS signals. GPS receivers decode these signals, effectively synchronizing each receiver to the atomic clocks. This enables users to determine the time to within 100 billionths of a second, without the cost of owning and operating atomic clocks.

Precise time is crucial to a variety of economic activities around the world. Communication systems, electrical power grids, and financial networks all rely on precision timing for synchronization and operational efficiency. The free availability of GPS time has enabled cost savings for companies that depend on precise time and has led to significant advances in capability.

For, example wireless telephone and data networks use GPS time to keep all of their base stations in perfect synchronization. This allows mobile handsets to share limited radio spectrum more efficiently. Similarly, digital broadcast radio services use GPS time to ensure that the bits from all radio stations arrive at receivers in lockstep. This allows listeners to tune between stations with a minimum of delay.

Companies worldwide use GPS to time-stamp business transactions, providing a consistent and accurate way to maintain records and ensure their traceability. Major investment banks use GPS to synchronize their network computers located around the world. Large and small businesses are turning to automated systems that can track, update, and manage multiple transactions made by a global network of customers, and these require accurate timing information available through GPS.

GPS can be used to synchronize reporting of hazardous weather from its Terminal Doppler Weather Radars.

Instrumentation is another application that requires precise timing. Distributed networks of instruments that must work together to precisely measure common events require timing sources that can guarantee accuracy at several points. GPS-based timing works exceptionally well for any application in which precise timing is required by devices that are dispersed over wide geographic areas. For example, integration of GPS time into seismic monitoring networks that enables researchers to quickly locate the epicenters of earthquakes and other seismic events.

Power companies and utilities have fundamental requirements for time and frequency to enable efficient power transmission and distribution. Repeated power blackouts have demonstrated to power companies the need for improved time synchronization throughout the power grid. Analyses of these blackouts have led many companies to place GPS-based time synchronization devices in power plants and substations. By analyzing the precise timing of an electrical anomaly as it propagates through a grid, engineers can trace back the exact location of a power line break.

Some users, such as national laboratories, require the time at a higher level of precision than GPS provides. These users routinely use GPS satellites not for direct time acquisition, but for communication of high-precision time over long distances. By simultaneously receiving the same GPS signal in two places and comparing the results, the atomic clock time at one location can be communicated to the other. National laboratories around the world use this "common view" technique to compare their time scales and establish Coordinated Universal Time (UTC). They use the same technique to disseminate their time scales to their own nations.

New applications of GPS timing technology appear every day. Hollywood studios are incorporating GPS in their movie slates, allowing for unparalleled control of audio and video data, as well as multi-camera sequencing. The ultimate applications for GPS, like the time it measures, are limitless.

As GPS becomes modernized, further benefits await users. The addition of the second and third civilian GPS signals will increase the accuracy and reliability of GPS time, which will remain free and available to the entire world.

BENEFITS

- Widespread availability of atomic clock time, without the atomic clocks.
- Precise synchronization of communications systems, power grids, financial networks, and other critical infrastructure.
- More efficient use of limited radio spectrum by wireless networks.
- Improved network management and optimization, making traceable time tags possible for financial transactions and billing.
- Communication of high-precision time among national laboratories using "common view" techniques.

2. ROADS & HIGHWAYS

It is estimated that delays from congestion on highways, streets, and transit systems throughout the world result in productivity losses in the hundreds of billions of money annually. Other negative effects of congestion include property damage, personal injuries, increased air pollution, and inefficient fuel consumption.

The availability and accuracy of the Global Positioning System (GPS) offers increased efficiencies and safety for vehicles using highways, streets, and mass transit systems. Many of the problems associated with the routing and dispatch of commercial vehicles is significantly reduced or eliminated with the help of GPS. This is also true for the management of mass transit systems, road maintenance crews, and emergency vehicles,

GPS enables automatic vehicles location and in-vehicle navigation systems that are widely used throughout the world today. By combining GPS position technology with systems that can display geographic information or with systems that can automatically transmit data to display screens or computers, a new dimension in surface transportation is realized.

A geographic information system (GIS) stores, analyzes, and displays geographically referenced information provided in large part by GPS. Today GIS is used to monitor vehicle location, making possible effective strategies that can keep transit vehicles on schedule and inform passengers of precise arrival times. Mass transit systems use this capability to track rail, bus, and other services to improve on-time performance.

Many new capabilities are made possible with the help of GPS. Instant car pools are feasible since people desiring a ride can be instantly matched with a vehicle in a nearby area.

Using GPS technology to help track and forecast the movement of freight has made a logistical revolution, including an application known as time-definite delivery. In time-definite delivery, trucking companies use GPS for tracking to guarantee delivery and pickup at the time promised, whether over short distances or across time zones. When an order comes in, a dispatcher punches a computer function, and a list of trucks appears on the screen, displaying a full array of detailed information on the status of each of them. If a truck is running late or strays off route, an alert is sent to the dispatcher.

Many nations use GPS to help survey their road and highway networks, by identifying the location of features on, near, or adjacent to the road networks. These include service stations, maintenance and emergency services and supplies, entry and exit ramps, damage to the road system, etc. The information serves as an input to the GIS data gathering process. This database of knowledge helps transportation agencies to reduce maintenance and service costs and enhances the safety of drives using the roads.

Research is underway to provide warnings to drivers of potential critical situations, such as traffic violations or crashes. Additional research is being conducted to examine the potential for minimal vehicle control when there is a clear need for action, such as the pre-deployment of air bags. The position information provided by GPS is an integral part of this research.

BENEFITS

- Higher levels of safety and mobility for all surface transportation system users.

- More accurate position determination to provide greater passenger information
- More effective monitoring to ensure schedule adherence, creating a transit system more responsive to transportation users needs.
- Better location information with electronic maps to provide in-vehicle navigation systems for both commercial and private users.
- Increased efficiencies and reduced costs in surveying roads.

3. SPACE

Earth Orbit: The Global Positioning System (GPS) is revolutionizing and revitalizing the way nations operate in space, from guidance systems for crewed vehicles to the management, tracking, and control of communication satellite constellations, to monitoring the Earth from space. Benefits of using GPS include:

- Navigation solutions-providing high precision orbit determination, and minimum ground control crews, with existing space-qualified GPS units.
- Attitude solutions--replacing high cost on-board attitude sensors with low-cost multiple GPS antenna and specialized algorithms.
- Timing solutions-replacing expensive spacecraft atomic clocks with low-cost, precise time GPS receivers.
- Constellation control--providing single point-of-contact to control for the orbit maintenance of large numbers of space vehicles such as telecommunications satellites.
- Formation flying--allowing precision satellite formations with minimal intervention from ground crews.
- Virtual platforms--providing automatic "station-keeping" and relative position services for advanced science tracking maneuvers such as interferometry.
- Launch vehicle tracking replacing or augmenting tracking radars with higher precision, lower-cost GPS units for range safety and autonomous flight termination.

The Moon, Mars and Beyond: The U.S. vision for space exploration, being implemented by the National Aeronautics and Space Administration (NASA), includes developing innovative technologies, knowledge, and infrastructures for returning to the Moon and preparing the way for future human missions to Mars and beyond. The vision will stimulate new research that will literally become the final frontier in navigation. Drawing on the experience with GPS, one could imagine creating a GPS-like network of satellites around the Moon and Mars. A Lunar or Martian network could provide an integrated communications and navigation infrastructure to support exploration and science missions both in lunar orbit and on the surface of the Moon and Mars.

NASA is also studying the utility of placing GPS-like beacons on satellites destined for the Sun-Earth Lagrangian points. Geodetic reference points could be established at these locations to support the future exploration of the Solar System.

The figure 21.0 depicts a Martian communication and navigation concept of two satellites in areostationary orbit (equivalent of geostationary orbit in Mars).

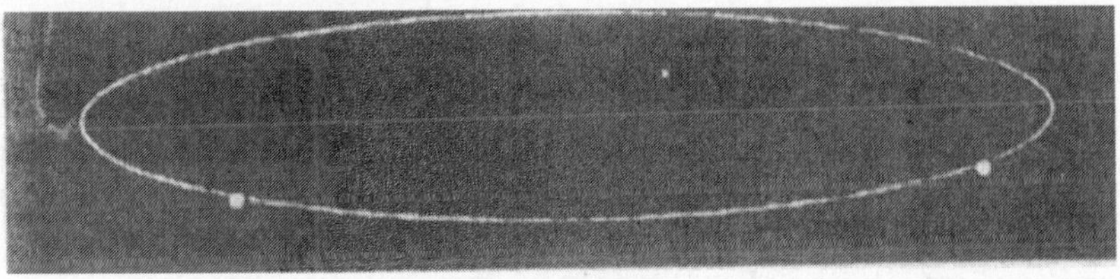

Fig. 21.0

BENEFITS

- Providing high precision positioning with minimum ground control.
- Replacing high cost, and high mass, on-board sensors.

4. AVIATION

Aviators throughout the world use the Global Positioning System (GPS) to increase the safety and efficiency of flight. With its accurate, continuous, and global capabilities, GPS offers seamless satellite navigation services that satisfy many of the requirements for aviation users. Space-based position and navigation enables three-dimensional position determination for all phases of flight from departure, enroute and arrival, to airport surface navigation.

The trend towards an Area Navigation concept means a greater role for GPS. Area Navigation allows aircraft to fly user-preferred routes from waypoint to waypoint, where waypoints do not depend on ground infrastructure. Procedures have been expanded to use GPS and augmented services for all phases of flight. This has been especially true in areas that lack suitable ground based navigation aids or surveillance equipment.

New and more efficient air routes made possible by GPS are continuing to expand. Vast savings in time and money are being realized. In many cases, aircraft flying over data-sparse areas such as oceans have been able to safely reduce their separation between one another, allowing more aircraft to fly more favorable and efficient routes, saving time, fuel and increasing cargo revenue.

Improved approaches to airports, which significantly increase operational benefits and safety, are now being implemented even at remote locations where traditional ground-based services are unavailable. In some regions of the world, satellite signals are augmented, or improved for special aviation applications, such as landing planes during poor visibility conditions. In those cases, even greater precision operations are possible.

The good news for the aviation community is that GPS is being constantly improved and modernized. A main component of the ongoing civilian modernization effort is the addition of two new signals. These signals complement the existing civilian service. The first of these new signals is for general use in non-safety critical applications. The second new signal will be internationally protected for aviation navigational purpose. This additional safety-of-life civilian signal will make GPS an even more robust navigation service for many aviation applications.

The second safety-of-life signal will enable significant benefits above and beyond the capabilities of the current GPS services. The availability of this signal offers increased instrument approach opportunity throughout the world by making the use of dual-frequency avionics possible. Dual frequency means that errors that occur in the signals due to disturbances in the ionosphere can be significantly reduced through the simultaneous use of two signals. This will improve the overall system robustness, to include accuracy, availability and integrity and will allow a precise approach capability with little or no ground infrastructure investment.

Reliance on GPS as the foundation for today and tomorrow's air traffic management system is a major part of many national plans. Those aviation authorities that are moving forward with GPS have observed and documented reductions in flight time, workload, and operating costs for both the airspace user and service provider. GPS also serves as an essential component for many other aviation systems, such as the Enhanced Ground Proximity Warning System (EGPWS) that has proven successful in reducing the risk of Controlled Flight into Terrain, a major cause of many aircraft accidents.

BENEFITS

- Continuous, reliable and accurate positioning information for all phases of flight on a global basis, freely available to all.
- Safe, flexible and fuel-efficient routes for airspace service providers and airspace users.
- Potential decommissioning and reduction of expensive ground based navigation facilities, system and services.
- Increased safety for surface movement operations made possible by situational awareness.
- Reduced aircraft delays due to increased capacity made possible through reduced separation minimums and more efficient air traffic management, particularly during inclement weather.
- Increased safety-of-life capabilities such as EGPWS.

5. AGRICULTURE

The development and implementation of precision agriculture or site-specific farming has been made possible by combining the Global Positioning System (GPS) and geographic information systems (GIS). These technologies enable the coupling of real-time data collection with accurate position information, leading to the efficient manipulation and analysis of large amounts of geospatial data. GPS-based applications in precision farming are being used for farm planning, field mapping, soil sampling, tractor guidance, crop scouting, variable rate applications, and yield mapping. GPS allows farmers to work during low visibility field conditions such as rain, dust, fog, and darkness.

In the past, it was difficult for farmers to correlate production techniques and crop yields with land variability. This limited their ability to develop the most effective soil/plant treatment strategies that could have enhanced their production. Today, more precise application of pesticides, herbicides, and fertilizers and better control of the dispersion of those chemicals are possible through precision agriculture, thus reducing expenses, producing a higher yield, and creating a more environmentally friendly farm.

Precision agriculture is now changing the way farmers and agribusinesses view the land from which they reap their profits. Precision agriculture is about collecting timely geospatial information on soil-plant-animal requirements and prescribing and applying site-specific treatments to increase agricultural production and protect the environment. Where farmers may have once treated their fields uniformly, they are now seeing benefits from micromanaging their fields. Precision agriculture is gaining in popularity largely due to the introduction of high technology tools into the agricultural community that are more accurate, cost effective, and user friendly. Many of the new innovations rely on the integration of on-board computers, data collection sensors, and GPS time and position reference systems.

Many believe that the benefits of precision agriculture can only be realized on large farms with huge capital investments and experience with information technologies. Such is not the case. There are inexpensive and easy-to-use methods and techniques that can be developed for use by all farmers. Through the use of GPS, GIS, and remote sensing, information needed for improving land and water use can be collected. Farmers can achieve additional benefits by combining better utilization of fertilizers and other soil amendments, determining the economic threshold for treating pest and weed infestations, and protecting the natural resources for future use.

GPS equipment manufacturers have developed several tools to help farmers and agribusinesses become more productive and efficient in their precision farming activities. Today, many farmers use GPS-derived products to enhance operations in their farming businesses. Location information is collected by GPS receivers for mapping field boundaries, roads, irrigation systems, and problem areas in crops such as weeds or disease. The accuracy of GPS allows farmers to create farm maps with precise acreage for field areas, road locations and distances between points of interest. GPS allows farmers to accurately navigate to specific locations in the field, year after year, to collect soil samples or monitor crop conditions.

Crop advisors use rugged data collection devices with GPS for accurate positioning to map pest, insect, and weed infestations in the field. Pest problem areas in crops can be pinpointed and mapped for future management decisions and input recommendations. The same field data can be also used by aircraft sprayers, enabling accurate swathing of fields without use of human "flaggers" to guide them. Crop dusters equipped with GPS are able to fly accurate swaths over the field, applying chemicals only where needed, minimizing chemical drift, reducing the amount of chemicals needed, thereby benefiting the environment. GPS also allows pilots to provide farmers with accurate maps.

Farmers and agriculture service providers can expect even further improvements as GPS continues to modernize.

BENEFITS

- Precision soil sampling, data collection and data analysis, enable localized variation of chemical applications and planting density to suit specific areas of the field.
- Accurate field navigation minimizes redundant applications and skipped areas, and enables maximum ground coverage in the shortest possible time.
- Ability to work through low visibility field conditions such as rain, dust, fog and darkness increases productivity.
- Accurately monitored yield data enables future site-specific field preparation.
- Elimination of the need for human "flaggers" increases spray efficiency and minimizes over-spray.

6. MARINE

The Global Positioning System (GPS) has changed the way the world operates. This is especially true for marine operations, including search and rescue. GPS provides the fastest and most accurate method for mariners to navigate, measure speed, and determine location. This enables increased levels of safety and efficiency for mariners worldwide.

It is important in marine navigation for the ship's officer to know the vessel's position while in open sea and also in congested harbors and waterways. While at sea, accurate position, speed, and heading are needed to ensure the vessel reaches its destination in the safest, most economical and timely fashion that conditions will permit. The need for accurate position information becomes even more critical as the vessel departs from or arrives in port. Vessel traffic and other waterway hazards make maneuvering more difficult, and the risk of accidents becomes greater.

Mariners and oceanographers are increasingly using GPS data for underwater surveying, buoy placement and navigational hazard location and mapping. Commercial fleets can use GPS to navigate to optimum fishing locations, track fish migrations, and ensure compliance with regulations.

An enhancement to the basic GPS signal known as Differential GPS (DGPS) provides much higher precision and increased safety in its coverage areas for maritime operations. Many nations use DGPS for operations such as buoy positioning, sweeping and dredging. This enhancement improves harbor navigation.

Governments and industrial organizations around the world are working together to develop performance standards for Electronic Chart Display and Information Systems, which use GPS and /or DGPS for positioning information. These systems are revolutionizing marine navigation and are leading to the replacement of paper nautical charts. With DGPS, position and radar information can be integrated and displayed on an electronic chart, forming the basis of the Integrated Bridge System which is being installed on commercial vessels of all types.

GPS is playing an increasingly important role in the management of maritime port facilities. GPS technology, coupled with geographic information system (GIS) software, is key to the efficient management and operation of automated container placement in the world's largest port facilities. GPS facilitates the automation of the pick-up, transfer, and placement process of containers by tracking them from port entry to exit. With millions of container shipments being placed in port terminals annually, GPS has greatly reduced the number of lost or misdirected containers and lowered associated operation costs.

GPS information is embedded within a system known as the Automatic Identification System (AIS) transmission. The AIS, which is endorsed by the International Maritime Organization, is used for vessel traffic control around busy seaways. This service is not only vital for navigation, but is increasingly used to bolster the security of ports and waterways by providing governments with greater situational awareness of commercial vessels and their cargo.

AIS uses a transponder system that operates in the VHF maritime band and is capable of communicating ship to ship as well as ship to shore, transmitting information relating to ship identification, geographic location, vessel type, and cargo information all on a real-time, wholly automated basis. Because the ship's GPS position is embedded in these transmissions, all essential information about vessel movements and contents can be uploaded automatically to electronic charts. The safety and security of vessels using this system is significantly enhanced.

BENEFITS

- Allows access to fast and accurate position, course, and speed information, saving navigators time and fuel through more efficient traffic routing.
- Provides precise navigation information to boaters.
- Improves precision and efficiency of buoy positioning, sweeping, and dredging operations.

- Enhances efficiency and economy for container management in port facilities.
- Increases safety and security for vessels using the AIS.

7. RAIL

Rail systems in many parts of the world use the Global Positioning System (GPS) in combination with various sensors, computers and communication systems to improve safety, security and operational effectiveness. These technologies help to reduce accidents, delays, operating costs and dangerous emissions, while increasing track capacity, customer satisfaction and cost effectiveness. Integral to the efficient operation of rail systems is the requirement for accurate, real-time position information of locomotives, rail cars, maintenance-of-way vehicles, and wayside equipment.

Ensuring high levels of safety, improving the efficiency of rail operations and expanding system capacity are all key objectives of today's railroad industry. Unlike most other modes of transportation, there is little flexibility in managing rail traffic. Most rail systems are comprised of long stretches of a single set of tracks. Trains bound for thousands of destinations must simultaneously share the use of these single line tracks.

Precise knowledge of where a train is located is essential to prevent collisions, maintain smooth flow of traffic, and minimize costly delays due to waiting for clearance for track use. Only the skill of the crews, accurate timing, a dynamic dispatching capability, and a critical array of "meet and passes" locations on short stretches of parallel tracks, allow rail dispatchers to guide their trains safely through. It is therefore critical for safety and efficiency reasons to know the position and performance of these trains both individually and system-wide.

GPS also contributes to dependable scheduling through train location awareness, enhancing connectivity with other modes of transportation, such as rail station to airport transfers.

An enhancement to the basic GPS signal known as Differential GPS (DGPS) improves accuracy and safety within its coverage areas. The enhanced position information enables the dispatcher to determine on which of two parallel tracks a train is located. When coupled with other location and navigation devices to account for time in tunnels, behind hills, and other obstructions, DGPS can provide a reliable and accurate position-locating capability for rail traffic management systems.

Differential GPS is an essential element of the Positive Train Control (PTC) concept being adopted in many parts of the world. This concept involves providing precise railroad position information to sophisticated command and control systems to produce the best operating plan to include varying train speed, re-routing traffic, and safely moving maintenance crews onto and off tracks.

A PTC system can track the location and speed of a train more accurately than was previously possible, providing train movement information to rail management personnel who can then enforce speeds and limits of authority, as necessary. By providing better tracking of train location and speed, PTC increases operational efficiency, allows higher track capacity, enhances crew, passenger and cargo safety and also results in a safer environment for personal working on the track.

Differential GPS can also aid in surveying and mapping track structure for maintenance and future system planning. By using DGPS, one can precisely locate mileposts, signal masts, switch points, bridges, road crossings, signal equipment, etc. GPS can satisfy the high level of accuracy needed for operation in terminal areas and rail yards, where dozens of tracks may run in parallel.

- Enhanced levels of safety.
- Increased capacity and efficiency for all rail users.
- Dependable schedule and equipment location awareness.
- Improved track, traffic, and train sensor information that flows together and produces a constantly updated plan to manage operations.
- Increased situational awareness for improved safety of trains and maintenance crews.

8. ENVIRONMENT

To sustain the Earth's environment while balancing human needs requires better decision making with more up-to-date information. Gathering accurate and timely information has been one of the greatest challenges facing both government and private organizations that must make these decisions. The Global Positioning System (GPS) helps to address that need.

Data collection systems provide decision makers with descriptive information and accurate positional data about items that are spread across many kilometers of terrain. By connecting position information with other types of data, it is possible to analyze many environmental problems from a new perspective. Position data collected through GPS can be imported into geographic information system (GIS) software, allowing spatial aspects to be analyzed with other information to create a far more complete understanding of a particular situation than might be possible through conventional means.

Aerial studies of some of the world's most impenetrable wilderness are conducted with the aid of GPS technology to evaluate an area's wildlife, terrain, and human infrastructure. By tagging imagery with GPS coordinates it is possible to evaluate conservation efforts and assist in strategy planning.

Some nations collect and use mapping information to manage their regulatory programs such as the control of royalties from mining operations, delineation of borders, and the management of logging in their forests.

GPS technology supports efforts to understand and forecast changes in the environment. By integrating GPS measurements into operational methods used by meteorlogists, the atmosphere's water content can be determined, improving the accuracy of weather forecasts. In addition, the proliferation of GPS tidal tracking sites, and improvement in estimating the vertical component of a site's position from GPS measurements, present a unique opportunity to directly observe the effects of ocean tides.

GPS receivers mounted on buoys track the movement and spread of oil spills. Helicopters use GPS to map the perimeter of forest fires and allow efficient use of fire fighting resources.

The migratory patterns of endangered species, such as the mountain gorillas of Rwanda, are tracked and mapped using GPS, helping to preserve and enhance declining populations.

In earthquake prone areas, GPS is playing an increasingly prominent role in helping scientists to anticipate earthquakes. Using the precise position information provided by GPS, scientists can study how strain builds up slowly over time in an attempt to characterize, and in the future perhaps anticipate, earthquakes.

Another benefit to using GPS is timeliness with which critical products can be generated. Because GPS data are in a digital form available at all times and in all parts of the world, they can be captured and analyzed very quickly. This means that it is possible for analysis to be completed in hours or days rather than weeks or months, thus ensuring that the final product is timelier. With the rapid pace of change in the world today, these savings in time can be critical.

The modernization of GPS will further enhance the support of GPS technology to the study and management of the world's environment. It can provide ecological and conservation applications with increased accuracy, availability, and reliability. Tropical rain forest ecology, for example, will benefit from the increased availability of GPS within heavy foliage areas and the reduction of spatial error in fine-scale vegetation mapping.

BENEFITS

- GPS data collection systems complemented with GIS packages provide a means for comprehensive analysis of environmental concerns.
- Environmental patterns and trends can be efficiently recognized with GPS/GIS data collection systems, and thematic maps can be easily created.
- GPS data can be quickly analyzed without the preliminary requirement for field data transcription into a digitized form.
- Accurate tracking of environmental disasters such as fires and oil spills can be conducted more efficiently.
- Precise positional data from GPS can assist scientists in seismic monitoring.
- Monitoring and preservation of endangered species can be facilitated through GPS tracking and mapping.

9. PUBLIC SAFETY & DISASTER RELIEF

A critical component of any successful rescue operation is time. Knowing the precise location of landmarks, streets, buildings, emerency service resources, and disaster relief sites reduces that time- and saves lives. This information is critical to disaster relief teams and public safety personnel in order to protect life and reduce property loss. The Global Positioning System (GPS) serves as a facilitating technology in addressing these needs.

GPS has played a vital role in relief efforts for global disasters such as the tsunami that struck in the India Ocean region in 2004, Hurricanes Katrina and Rita that wreaked havoc in the Gulf of Mexico in 2005, and the Pakistan- India earthquake in 2005. Search and rescue teams used GPS, geographic information system (GIS), and remote sensing technology to create maps of the disaster areas for rescue and aid operations, as well as to assess damage.

Another important area of disaster relief is in the management of wildfires. To contain and manage forest fires, aircraft combine GPS with infrared scanners to identify fire boundaries and "hot spots." Within minutes, fire maps are transmitted to a portable field computer at the firefighters' camp. Armed with this information, firefighters have a greater chance of winning the battle against the blaze.

In earthquake prone areas such as the Pacific Rim, GPS is playing an increasingly prominent role in helping scientists to anticipate earthquakes. Using the precise position information provided by GPS, scientists can study how strain builds up slowly over time in an attempt to characterize, and in the future perhaps anticipate, earthquakes.

Meteorologists responsible for storm tracking and flood prediction also rely on GPS. They can assess water vapor content by analyzing transmissions of GPS data through the atmosphere.

GPS has become an integral part of modern emergency response systems, whether helping stranded motorists find assistance or guiding emergency vehicles.

As the international industry positioning standard for use by emergency and other specialty vehicle fleets, GPS has given managers a quantum leap forward in efficient operation of their emergency response teams. The ability to effectively identify and view the location of police, fire, rescue, and individual vehicles or boats, and how their location relates to an entire network of transportation systems in a geographic area, has resulted in a whole new way of doing business. Location information provided by GPS, coupled with automation, reduces delay in the dispatch of emergency services.

Incorporation of GPS in mobile phones an emergency location capability in the hands of everyday users. Today's widespread placement of GPS location systems in passenger cars provides another leap in developing a comprehensive safety net. Today, many ground and maritime vehicles are equipped with autonomous crash sensors and GPS. This information, when coupled with automatic communication systems, enables a call for help even when occupants are unable to do so.

The modernization of GPS will further facilitate disaster relief and public safety services. The addition of new civil signals will increase accuracy and reliability all over the world. In short, GPS modernization translates to more lives saved and faster recovery for victims of global tragedies.

BENEFITS

- Deliver disaster relief to areas in a more timely and accurate manner, saving lives and restoring critical infrastructure.
- Provide position information for mapping of disaster regions where little or no mapping information is available.
- Enhance capability for flood prediction and monitoring of seismic precursors and events.
- Provide positional information about individuals with mobile phones and in vehicles in case of emergency.

10.SURVEYING & MAPPING

As technology evolves and expands throughout the world, the surveying and mapping community is steadily redefining the tools required to increase productivity and obtain highly accurate data.

Using the near pinpoint accuracy provided by the Global Positioning System (GPS) with ground augmentations, highly accurate surveying and mapping results can be rapidly obtained, thereby significantly reducing the amount of equipment and labor hours that are normally required of other conventional surveying and mapping techniques. Today it is possible for a single surveyor to accomplish in one day what used to take weeks with an entire team. GPS is unaffected by rain, wind, or reduced sunlight, and is rapidly being adopted by professional surveyors and mapping personnel throughout the world.

GPS provides accurate three dimensional positioning information for natural and artificial features that can be displayed on maps and models of everything in the world; mountains, rivers, forests, endangered animals, precious minerals and many other resources. GPS position information for these features serves as a prime input to geographic information systems (GIS), that assemble, store, manipulate, and display geographically referenced information.

GPS has played a vital role in relief efforts for global disasters such as the tsunami that struck in the India Ocean region in 2004, Hurricanes Katrina and Rita that wreaked havoc in the Gulf of Mexico in 2005, and the Pakistan- India earthquake in 2005. Search and rescue teams used GPS position information to create maps of the disaster areas for rescue and aid operations, as well as to help assess damage.

Throughout the world, government agencies, scientific organizations, and commercial operations are using the surveys and maps deriving from GPS and GIS for timely decision-making and wiser use of resources. Any organization or agency that requires accurate location information can benefit from the efficiency and productivity provided by the positioning capability of GPS.

Unlike traditional techniques, GPS surveying is not bound by constraints such as line-of-sight visibility between reference stations. Also, the spacing between stations can be increased. The increased flexibility of GPS also permits survey stations to be established at easily accessible sites rather than being confined to hilltops as previously required.

Remote GPS systems may be carried by one person in a backpack, mounted on the roof of an automobile, or fastened atop an all-terrain vehicle to permit rapid and accurate field data collection. With a GPS radio communication link, real-time, continuous centimeter-level accuracy makes possible a productivity level that is virtually unattainable using optical survey instruments.

With the modernization of GPS even further enhancements are in the works. In addition to the current GPS civilian service, the United States is committed to implementing two additional civilian signals. The extra signals will for example, provide a means for correcting errors caused by the ionosphere, thus improving positioning accuracy. The new signals will also improve the availability and over all integrity of the system for all users.

BENEFITS

- Provides significant productivity gains over traditional surveying by eliminating many of its inherent limitations, such as the requirement for a line of sight between surveying points.
- Provides accurate positioning of natural and artificial features that can be used to create maps and models that are used for a wide range of services such as disaster relief and public safety.
- Gives decision-makers timely and valuable information for wise use of resources.
- Yields highly accurate surveying results in real-time at the centimeter-level.
- Allows surveyors to work uninterrupted in periods of poor weather conditions or reduced sunlight.

11. RECREATION

The Global Positioning System (GPS) has eliminated many of the hazards associated with common recreational activities by providing a capability to determine a precise location. GPS receivers have also broadened the scope and enjoyment of outdoor activities by simplifying many of the traditional problems, such as staying on the "correct trail" or returning to the best fishing spot.

Outdoor exploration carries with it many intrinsic dangers, one of the most important of which is the potential for getting lost in unfamiliar or unsafe territory. Hikers, bicyclists, and outdoor adventurers are increasingly relying on GPS instead of traditional paper maps, compasses, or landmarks. Paper maps are often outdated, and compasses and landmarks may not provide the precise location information necessary to avoid venturing into unfamiliar areas. In addition, darkness and adverse weather conditions may also contribute to imprecise navigation results.

GPS technology coupled with electronic mapping has helped to overcome much of the traditional hardships associated with unbounded exploration. GPS handsets allow users to safely traverse trails with the confidence of knowing precisely where they are at all times, as well as how to return to their starting point. One of the benefits is the ability to record and return to waypoints. Similarly, fishermen typically use GPS signals as a means to continually stay apprised of location, heading bearing, speed, distance-to-go, time-to-go, chart plotting functions, and most importantly, returning to a location where the fish are plentiful.

An advantage in newer GPS receivers is the capability to transfer data to and from a computer. Outdoor enthusiasts can download waypoints from an exciting adventure and share them. An example of this is a web site based in Malaysia dedicated to GPS for mountain biking enthusiasts. Riders post waypoint files marking their favorite rides allowing other riders to try out the trails.

Golfers use GPS to measure precise distances within the course and improve their game. Other applications include skiing, as well as recreational aviation and boating.

GPS technology has generated entirely new sports and outdoor activities. An example of this is geocaching, a sport which rolls a pleasurable day's outing and a treasure hunt into one. Another new sport is geodashing, a cross-country race to a predefined GPS coordinate.

GPS modernization efforts, designed to enhance more serious applications than recreation have provided direct and indirect benefits to the user. Various GPS augmentation systems that were developed in several countries for commerce and transportation are also being widely used by outdoor enthusiasts for recreational purposes. Modernization plans for GPS will results in even greater reliability and availability for all users, such as under a denser forest cover, just the environment in which many adventurers most need this capability.

BENEFITS

- Highly accurate all-weather positioning information using GPS receivers helps outdoor adventurers with safer exploration anywhere in the world.
- Ability to return to favorite fishing spots, trails, campsites or other locations with precision year after year, despite changing terrain conditions.
- New and interesting activities (based solely on the capabilities of GPS) are developed every day by outdoor enthusiasts and shared with others.
- Relatively small, portable, and affordable handsets can be used for multiple types of recreation activities.

21.3 Finding the Position of GPS Receiver: The Trilateration Method

One of the simplest and most accurate methods of locating an unknown position is the *trilateration method.* In this method, the distance of the unknown point from three known points is measured. The intersection of the arcs corresponding to three distances defines the unknown point relative to the known points, since three measurements can be used to solve three equations to give the latitude, longitude, and elevation for the receiver.

In the GPS systems, the trilateration method is used to locate a GPS receiver. Here the distance between a transmitter and a receiver is estimated by measuring the time taken by a pulse of RF energy to travel between the two. This distance is calculated using the velocity of electromagnetic waves in free space (the velocity of light of 299,972,458 m/s). Time is measured electronically more accurately by the use of atomic clocks so that the GPS position location system is able to achieve a measurement accuracy of 1 metre in a distance of 20,000 km. However, this position location accuracy can be obtained if timing measurements have an accuracy better than 3 nano-seconds. This is achieved as follows:

1. Each satellite carries several high accuracy atomic clocks and radiates a sequence of bits that starts at a precisely known time.

2. A GPS receiver contains a clock that is synchronized in turn to the clock on each satellite that it is receiving.

3. The receiver measures the time delay of the arrival of the bit sequence, which is proportional to the distance between the satellite and the GPS receiver.

4. After the distance of a GPS receiver from three satellites has been measured, it is now required to know the position of each satellite. This is calculated in the GPS receiver using the *ephemperis* for the satellite orbits that are broadcast by each satellite in its navigation message.

5. As the time at which the transmitted bit sequence is started is known at the receiver, the position of the satellite at that time can be calculated from its orbital data.

6. Apart from the three satellites, a fourth satellite is also used because the clock in the receiver is not inherently accurate enough. The fourth distance measurement provides information from which clock errors in the receiver can be corrected and the receiver clock synchronised to GPS time with an accuracy better than 100 neno-seconds.

21.4 Frequencies Used by GPS satellites

GPS satellites transmit two signals at different frequencies, known at L1 and L2:

(*i*) The L2 signal is modulated with 10.23 Mbps pseudo-random (PN) bit sequence called the *P* code. This is used by military positioning systems. The *P* code is transmitted in an encrypted form known as the *Y* code, which restricts the use of is the *P* code to authorized users.

(*ii*) The L1 frequency carrier is modulated by a 1.023 Mbps PN sequence called the *Coarse Acquisition (C/A)* code that is available for public use, and also carries the *P* code as a quadrature modulation. The higher bit rate of the *P* code provides better measurement accuracy than the 1.023 Mbps *C/A* code.

21.5 Types of GPS Services

The GPS system provides two types of services:

I. Precise positioning service (PPS): Here the receivers track both *P* code and *C/A* code on L1 and L2 frequencies. The PPS is used mainly by military users, since the *P* code is encrypted into the *Y* code before transmission and requires decryption equipment in the receiver.

II. Standard positioning service (SPS): Here the receivers track the *C/A* code on L1. This is the service that is used by the general public. The *P(Y)* and *C/A* code transmitted by each satellite create direct sequence spread spectrum signals which occupy the same frequency bands. Both the *C/A* code and the *P* code are publicly available.

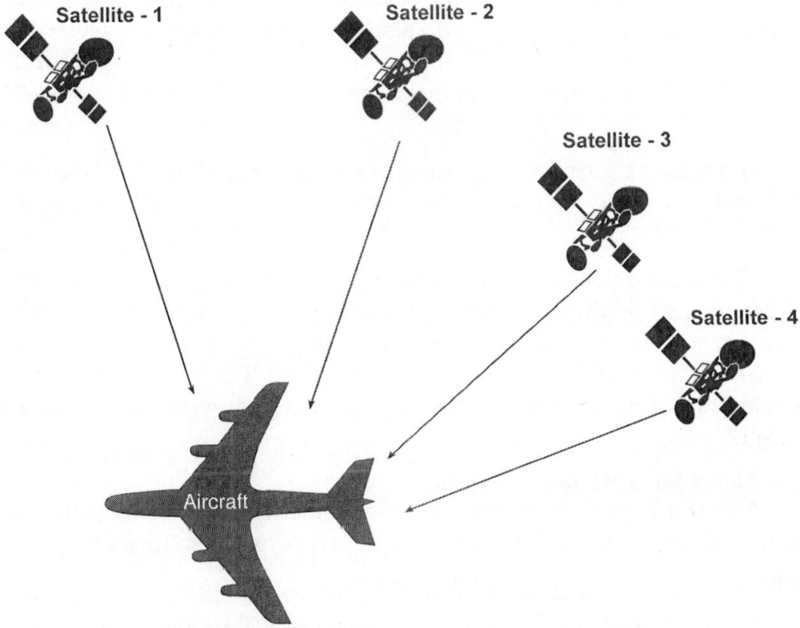

Fig. 21.1 GPS Position Location using Four Satellites.

21.6 GPS Position Location Layout

Fig. 21.1 shows the schematic of position location with GPS. The principle is as follows:

1. The three satellites provide distance information when the GPS receiver makes three measurements of range, R_i, from the receiver to three known points.

2. Each distance R_i can be thought of as the radius of a sphere with a GPS satellite at its center. The receiver lies at the intersection of three such spheres, with a satellite at the center of each sphere. Locally, at the receiver, the spheres will appear to be planes since the radii of the spheres are very large.

3. Since the intersection of three planes completely defines a point, three satellites, through measurement of their distances to the receiver, define the receiver location close to the earth's surface.

21.6.1 GPS Satellite Clocks

Each GPS satellite has an atomic clock, which is calibrated against time standards in the GPS control stations around the world. This is called GPS time, a time standard that is available in every GPS satellite. The accuracy of an atomic clock is typically 1 part in 10^{11}.

The time standard system in each GPS satellite consists of a set of four atomic clocks: two cesium clocks and two rubidium clocks. An atomic clock employs the fundamental resonance of the cesium or rubidium molecule as a frequency reference to lock a crystal oscillator.

In the GPS satellites, the master oscillator is at 10.23 MHz. All code rates, the L1, and L2 RF frequencies are multiples or sub-multiples of 10.23 MHz.

The atomic clocks are updated by the controlling ground stations to keep them within 1 μsec of Universal Time Coordinated (UTC). The navigation message sent by each satellite contains information about its current clock error relative to GPS time. UTC is a worldwide time standard, and equal to Greenwich Mean Time (GMT).

21.6.2 GPS Receiver Clock

An atomic clock is very expensive and therefore is not included in the GPS receivers. Instead, a standard crystal oscillator with an accuracy of 1 in 10^5 or 1 in 10^6 is used.

Since the receiver clock has an offset of 10 ms relative to GPS time, the distance measurements will have an error of 3000 km. Therefore, it is necessary to remove the time error from the receiver clock before taking position measurements. *C/A* code receivers synchronize their internal clocks to GPS time within 170 ns, corresponding to a distance measurement inaccuracy of 50 metres. A number of measurements and integration helps in improving the position location error to well below 50 metres.

As already discussed, a time measurement from a fourth satellite provides distance error corrections. Three time measurements are made to define the location of the receiver in the three unknown coordinates x, y, and z. When a fourth time measurement is added, we can solve the basic position location equations for a fourth unknown, the receiver clock offset error t_e. Thus the four unknowns in the calculation of the location of the receiver are x, y, z and t_e.

21.7 Calculation of Position Location in GPS Systems

In position location, first, the coordinates of the GPS receiver and the GPS satellites are defined in a rectangular coordinate system with its origin at the center of the earth. This is called the *earth centered earth fixed* (ECEF) coordinate system.

The ECEF coordinate system is part of the WGS-84 description of the earth. WGS-84 is an internationally agreed description of the earth's shape and parameters, derived from observations in many countries.

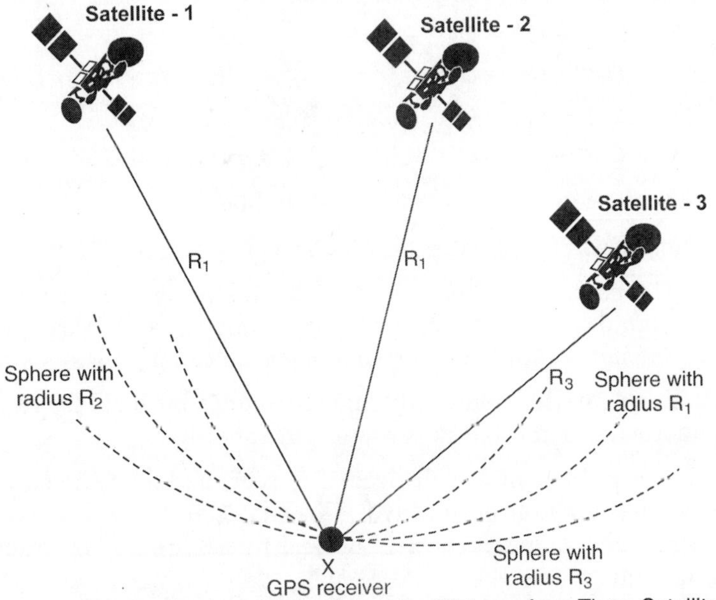

Fig. 21.2 GPS Position Location by Measuring Distance from Three Satellites.

GPS receivers use the WGS-84 parameters to calculate the orbits of the GPS satellites with the accuracy required for precise measurement of the range to the satellites. Fig. 21.2 shows the geometry of a GPS measurement system:

1. The Z-axis of the coordinate system is directed through the earth's North Pole and the X- and Y-axes are in the equatorial plane.

2. The X-axis passes through the Greenwich meridian - the line of zero ECEF coordinate system rotates with the earth.

3. The receiver coordinates are (U_x, U_y, U_z), and the four satellites have coordinates (X_x, Y_y, Z_z), where i = 1, 2, 3, 4.

4. The measured distance to satellite i is called a psuedo-range, R_{Pi}, because it uses the internal clock of the receiver to make a timing measurement that includes errors caused by receiver clock offset.

Psuedo-range R_{Pi} is measured from the propagation time delay T_i between the satellite i and the GPS receiver. That is

$$R_{Pi} = T_i \times c \quad \text{... (21.1)}$$

We know from geometry that the distance R between two points A and B is a rectangular coordinate system will be

$$R^2 = (x_A - x_B)^2 + (y_A - y_B)^2 + (z_A - z_B)^2$$

Using this above equation, the ranging equations which relate pseudo-range to time delay are

$$\left.\begin{bmatrix} (X_1 - U_x)^2 + (Y_1 - U_y)^2 + (Z_1 - U_z)^2 = (PR_1 - t_e^2) \\ (X_2 - U_x)^2 + (Y_2 - U_y)^2 + (Z_2 - U_z)^2 = (PR_2 - t_e^2) \\ (X_3 - U_x)^2 + (Y_3 - U_y)^2 + (Z_3 - U_z)^2 = (PR_3 - t_e^2) \\ (X_4 - U_x)^2 + (Y_4 - U_y)^2 + (Z_4 - U_z)^2 = (PR_4 - t_e^2) \end{bmatrix}\right\} \quad \text{... (21.2)}$$

where t_e is receiver clock error (offset, or bias).

The process for position location is as follows:

1. The position of the satellite at the instant when it sends the timing signal (that is, the start of a long sequence of bits) is obtained from ephemeris data transmitted along with the timing signals.

2. Each satellite sends out a data stream that includes its own ephemeris data and that of the adjacent satellites.

3. The receiver now calculates the coordinates of the satellite relative to the center of the earth, (X_i, Y_i, Z_i), and then its circuitry solves the four ranging equations of Eq. 21.2 using standard numerical techniques.

4. Solving of above equations leads to the values of the four unknowns - the location of the GPS receiver (U_x, U_y, U_z), relative to the center of the earth and the clock offset t - called *clock bias* in GPS terminology.

5. The receiver position is now referenced to the surface of the earth, and is displayed in latitude, longitude, and elevation.

21.7.2 2-DRMS error

The accuracy measurement for a low-cost GPS receiver using the GPS C/A code is called 2-DRMS error, where DRMS is the distance root mean square error of the measured position relative to the true position of the receiver. Its typical value is 30 metres.

It has been found that since often the measurement errors are Gaussian distributed, 68% of the measured position results will be within a distance of 1 DRMS from the true location and 95% of the results will be within 2DRMS of the true location.

21.7.3 Standardisation of GPS Time

The clock bias value in the ranging equations for position location calculations is also added to the GPS receiver clock time to yield a time measurement that is synchronised to the GPS standard.

The crystal oscillator used in the GPS receiver is highly stable only over a period of a few seconds. Its frequency changes for longer periods are caused by:

(*i*) Temperature changes results in changes in the quartz crystal of crystal oscillator to expand or contract, and this changes the oscillator frequency.

(*ii*) Aging of crystals leads to the frequency to change with time. The changes are very small, but sufficient to cause errors in the clock time at the receiver when the clock is not synchronized to a satellite.

Thus, when the clock bias is calculated by solving ranging equations, it allows the receiver clock time to be updated every second or two with the result that the GPS receiver time- readout is identical to GPS time.

Every GPS receiver is automatically synchronized to every other GPS receiver anywhere in the world through GPS time. This makes every GPS receiver a super clock, which knows time more accurately than any other time standard.

21.8 GPS Codes

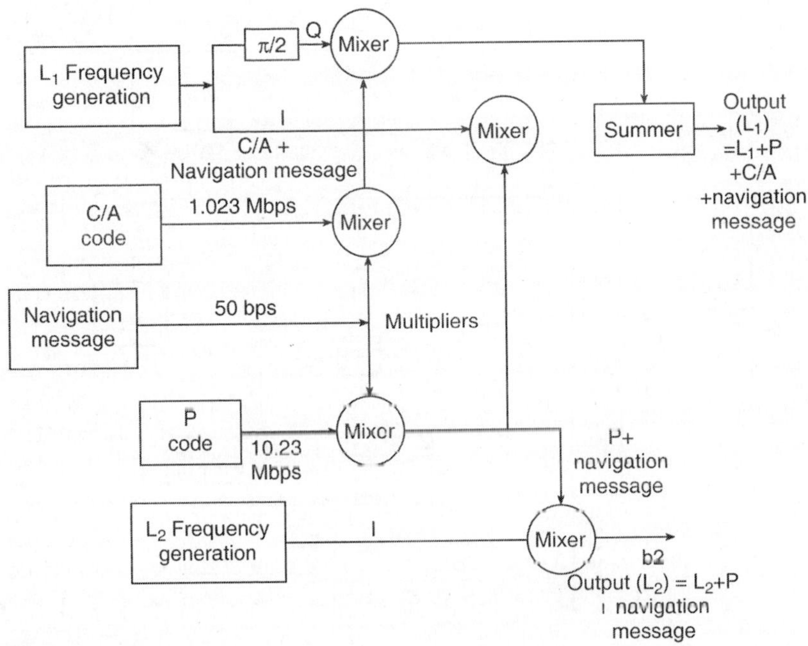

Fig. 21.3 Generation of L1 and L2 Signals in a GPS Satellite.

As already seen, the transmission by GPS satellites is based on pseudo-random sequence (PN) codes. Fig. 21.3 shows the generation of L1 and L2 signals in a GPS satellite:

1. All satellites in the GPS system transmit a *C/A* code at the same carrier frequency, 1575.42 MHz, called L1, using BPSK modulation. The L1 frequency is 154 times the master clock frequency of 10.23 MHz.

2. The clock rate of the *C/A* code is 1.023 MHz and the *C/A* code sequence has 1023 bits, so that the PN sequence lasts exactly 1.0 msec. The exact values of the frequencies are about 0.005 Hz lower than stated here to allow for relativistic effects caused by the high velocity of the satellites in their orbits (3.865 km/sec).

3. The transmission of the *P* code is by using BPSK modulation at the L2 carrier frequency of 1227.6 MHz (120 x 10.23 MHz), and it is also transmitted with BPSK modulation on the L1 carrier frequency, in phase quadrature with the *C/A* code BPSK modulation.

4. The *C/A* and *P* code transmissions from all GPS satellites are overlaid in the L1 and L2 frequency bands, making GPS a direct sequence spread spectrum (DSSS) system.

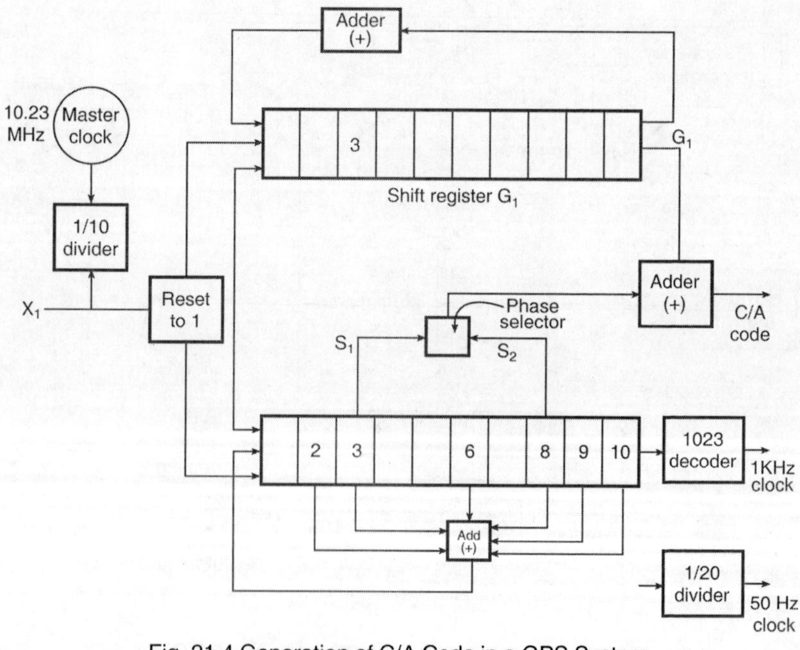

Fig. 21.4 Generation of C/A Code in a GPS System.

5. At the receiver, the signals from individual GPS satellites are separated using knowledge of the unique *C/A* code that is allocated to each satellite.

21.8.1 The C/A Code

Figure 21.4 shows the schematic of a *C/A* code generator :

1. The *C/A* codes transmitted by GPS satellites are all 1023 bit Gold codes. The GPS *C/A* Gold codes are created from two 1023 bit m-sequences, called G1 and G2, by multiplying together the G1 and G2 sequences with different time offsets.
2. An *m*-sequence is a maximum length pseudo-random (PN) sequence, which is easy to generate with a shift register and feedback taps.
3. As a shift register with *n* stages can generate a PN sequence of $2n - 1$ bits in length, the bit pattern is set by its feedback taps and combining logic. The PN sequences G1 and G2 are both generated by 10-bit shift registers and are therefore both 1023 bits long.
4. The clock rate for the *C/A* code is 1.023 MHz, so each sequence lasts 1.0 msec.

For a particular satellite in the GPS system, the *C/A* code is created with an algorithm that includes the identification number (ID) of the GPS satellite, thus creating a unique code for each satellite. For the satellite with ID number i, a *C/A* code sequence $C_i\,(t)$ is given by

$$C_i\,(t) = G_1(t) \times G_2\,(t + 10iT_c) \qquad ...(21.3)$$

where T_c is the clock period for the C/A code.

Since there are 64 Gold sequences available for satellites numbered 1 through 64, a total of 100 Gold sequences can be created using the algorithm of Eq. (21.3). However, not all the sequences have sufficient low cross-corelation properties, and it has been seen that only 37 are actually used in the GPS system. Low cross-corelation of the sequences is necessary because the GPS receiver can pick up signals from 12 satellites at the same time.

The corelator in the receiver searches one of the sequences and must reject all other that are present. Two *C/A* code sequences with zero cross-corelation would achieve a rejection ratio of 1023, but the 64 available *C/A* code sequences will not all have zero cross-corelation. The selected group of 37 are the sequences with the lowest levels of cross-corelation among the available set of 100 Gold code sequences.

21.9 GPS Receiver

Figure 21.5 shows a schematic of a C/A code GPS receiver:

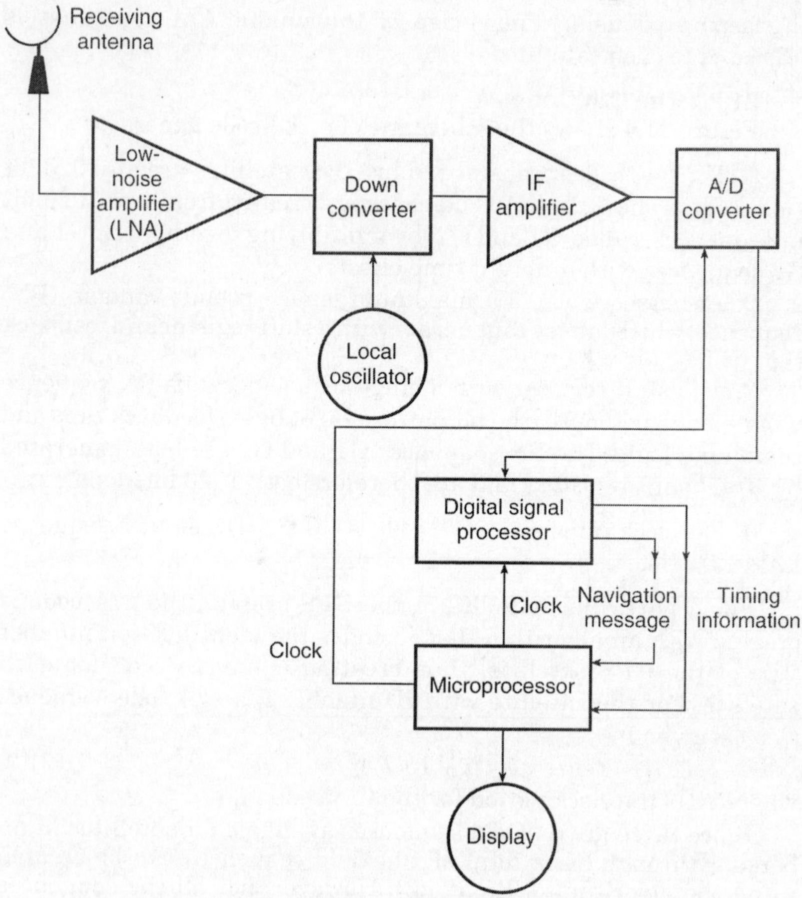

Fig. 21.5 Block Diagram of a GPS Receiver.

1. The antenna is a circularly polarized patch antenna with an LNA mounted on it.

2. The super-heterodyne receiver generates an IF signal in a bandwidth of about 2 MHz, which is sampled and processed using *I* and *Q* sampling techniques by A/D converter and digital signal processing (DSP) circuit.

3. The digital portion of the receiver includes a *C/A* code generator and a corelator which selects the necessary Gold sequences.

4. The microprocessor carries out the timing measurements and calculate the receiver's position.

21.10 Method of Satellite Signal Acquisition by GPS Receiver

This is carried out by the GPS receiver by two corelation processes: (*a*) code synchronisation with the satellites; and (*b*) Doppler frequency offset measurements.

21.10.1 Code Synchronisation

Step-1: The GPS receiver first determines the starting time of the unique *C/A* code for each of four satellites. This it does by corelating the received signal with stored *C/A* codes, as in any direct sequence spread spectrum system. In practice, the receiver automatically selects the four strongest signals and corelate to those. However, it faces two problems:

(*i*) In case the strongest satellites are quite close to each other, and have nealy equal pseudo-ranges, the receiver also uses several weaker signals.

(*ii*) If in a situation called *cold start*, the receiver makes with no information about the current position of GPS satellites, or its own location, it takes up search of all 37 possible *C/A* codes until it can correlate with one of the satellites.

Step-2: Once correlation is obtained, the data stream, called the *navigation message* from that satellite can be read by the receiver. This stream contains information about the adjacent satellites, so that once one signal is correlated, there is no need for the receiver to search through all the other 36 possible codes to find the next satellites and thus can go directly to the correct code.

Step-3: The receiver now locks to a given code by matching the locally generated code to the code received from the wanted satellite. Since the start time of the code transmitted by the satellite is not known when the receiver commences the locking process, it selects an arbitrary start point. The locally generated code is compared to the received code, bit by bit, through all 1023 bits of the sequence, untill the lock is traced. Otherwise the receiver realises that it is not receiving the correct code for the satellite in question.

Step-4: If the correct code for the satellite has not been found, the receiver moves the locally generated code forward one bit in time and attempts correlation again. The process is continued 1023 times untill all possible starting times for the locally generated code have been evaluated. It takes a minimum of 1 sec to search all 1023 bit positions of a 1023 bit *C/A* code, so in a typical case, it will take at least 15 sec to acquire the first satellite.

Step-5: Once one *C/A* code is found, the remaining satellites can then be acquired in a few seconds because their IDs are known from the data transmitted in the navigation message of each satellite.

21.10.2 Tracking Doppler frequency offset

Apart from locking to the *C/A* code of one satellite, the GPS receiver has to simutanously estimate the Doppler frequency offset for at least one satellite before final correlation can occur. To understand this process, we first carry out an estimate of the Doppler shift that must be accommodated by the receiver. The facts of the situation are:

1. The receiver bandwidth is matched to the bandwidth of the *C/A* code.

2. The theoretical noise bandwidth of the *C/A* code receiver = 1.023 MHz.

3. Velocity of the satellites = 3.865 km/sec.

Since the angle between the spacecraft velocity vector and a receiver on earth is 76.1° when a GPS satellite is at the horizon, the maximum velocity component toward a receiver is v_r = 928 m/s.

Therefore, the maximum Doppler shift in the L1 signal will be

Doppler shift (L1)= v_r/λ = 4.872 kHz

Therefore, allowing the satellite to reach an elevation angle of 5° before it is used for a position measurement, limits the value of Doppler shift which must be accommodated by the receiver upto ± 4 kHz.

The search for Doppler shift is now carried out as follows:

Step-1: From a cold start, the receiver attempts eight Doppler frequency shifts of up to ± 4 kHz in 1-kHz steps when searching for the signal from a satellite as shown in Fig. 21.6. Therefore, there are eight possible Doppler shifts for each signal, and 1023 possible code positions, giving 8184 possible signal states that must be searched.

Step-2: Once any of the GPS satellites has been acquired, the navigation message provides sufficient information about the ad-

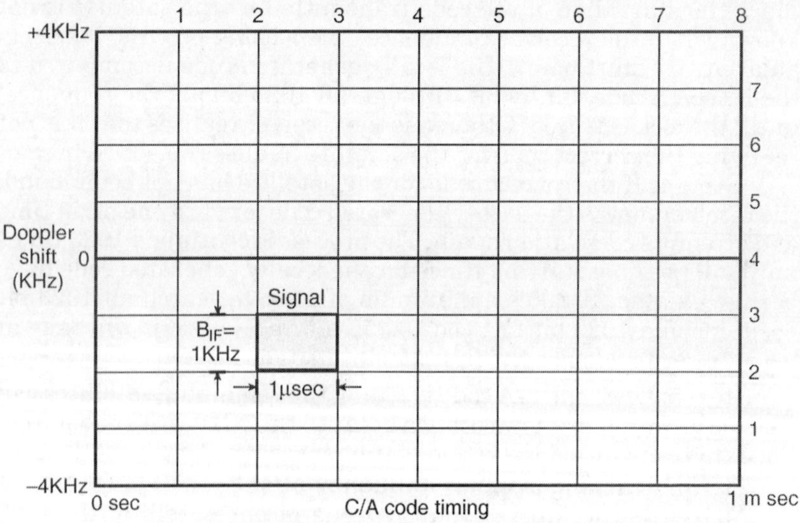

Fig. 21.6 Syncronisation between C/A Code Timing and Doppler Shift for a GPS Satellite Search.

jacent satellites for the remaining visible satellites to be acquired quickly. The receiver carries out the search in Doppler shift because the position of the receiver relative to the satellites is not known, but their C/A codes are.

Step-3 : The receiver stores the information from the navigation message when switched off, and starts running its internal clock. When it is switched on again, it assumes that its position is close to its last known position when it was switched off. It, therefore, calculates which satellite should be visible, and search for those first. This greatly speeds up the acquisition process.

In the correlation process described above, it is assumed that each satellite is acquired sequentially, one at a time, as in the case of lower cost GPS receivers. However, sophisticated receivers are designed to have parallel correlators which can search for and acquire satellites in parallel. It has been found that 12 parallel correlators allows acquiring of all visible GPS satellites. As a result, the start-up time is much shorter than with sequential acquisition. Parallel processing of the signals also leads to better accuracy.

The *P* code for GPS satellites is typically of long sequences because the long length of the *P* code sequene makes the distance measurements unambiguous. It repeats after 266.4 days, but is changed every 7 days for security reasons. Therefore, the *P* code sequences cannot be acquired easily because they do not repeat, and thus their unauthorized use is prevented.

21.11. References

1. B.H. Hofman-Wellwenhof, H. Lichtenegger and J. Collins, *GPS Theory and Practice*, Springer Verlag, New York, NY, 1992.
2. B. Clarke, *Aviation Application of GPS*, McGraw-Hill, New York, NY, 1996.
3. Timothy Pratt, Charles W. Bostian and J.E. Allnutt, *Satellite Communication*, John Wiley, NJ, 2003.

21.12. Review Questions

1. Describe The main features of the technical Structure of a Global Positioning Satellite System.
2. Explain the trilateration method used in GPS systems to locate a receiver.
3. Derive the four ranging equations used in locating the position of a receiver in a global positioning satellite system.
4. Describe the method of satellite signal acquisition by GPS Receiver by code synchronisation
5. Describe how the Doppler frequency offset is tracked in a GPS system and taking an example explain how it is synchronised with C/A coding timing.

22

Internet and the Satellite Links

22.1 Introduction to Internet

The Internet is a collection of computer networks connected to each other through telephone cables satellites and various other modes, which have a common way of passing material between them, in effect creating a single world-wide network. Thus, the Internet is the global network of networks, which use certain protocols to interact with other networks via gateway.

Access to the Internet follows well-defined rules. Users connect to Internet service providers (ISPs), who in turn connect to network service providers (NSPs), who complete the connections to other users and to servers.

Servers are computers dedicated to the purpose of providing information to the Internet. They run specialized software for each type of Internet applications. These include email, discussion groups, long-distance computing, and file transfers.

Routers are computers that form part of the communications net and which route or direct the data along the best available paths in the network.

Browser is a software used for viewing different sites on the Internet as well as sending and receiving e-mails. The most well-known browsers are Internet Explorer and Netscape.

There are three main types of Internet applications:

1. Those based on sending and receiving mail messages
2. Those based on logging in to a remote Internet host.
3. Those based on browsing.

22.2 Internet Protocols

Protocols are the rules which govern how the Internet works. It uses the following protocols in order to get logically linked together by a globally unique address space:

(*a*) The Internet Protocol (IP) takes care of addressing, or making sure that the routers know what to do with the data when it arrives. Some addressing information goes at the beginning of a message sent, giving enough information to the network to deliver the necessary packet of data.

(*b*) The Transmission Control Protocol (TCP) or its subsequent extensions/follow-ons, and/or other IP-compatible protocols to support the desired communication links.

The TCP and the IP are usually lumped together as TCP/IP and are embedded in the software for operating systems and browsers such as Windows and Netscape.

The File Transfer Protocol (FTP) allows transfer of files between computers on the Internet. It serves two purposes: providing to a user access to computing facilities at another institution; and access to a vast repository of publicly available files of very conceivable type: electronic scholarly journals, text files containing literary texts, bibliographies or episode guides to cult TV series, graphics files of great works of art, fonts for various operating systems and large amounts of free shareware software. All of these can be downloaded to a local system.

Using these protocols, the Internet provides, uses or makes accessible, either publicly or privately, high level services layered on the communications and related infrastructure.

22.3 Types of Internet Connections

There are mainly two ways to connect to the Internet: *PC dial-up access*, and *Dedicated Internet Access.*

I. PC Dial-up Access. This is the simplest type of connection to Internet. You need a computer modem (attached to a phone line) and any of the popular telecommunications packages. The user dials-in to an Internet Service Provider. Each user has an account on the Internet Services provider host computer. You ask the host computer to go out onto the Internet to do what you want to be done. Host providers will send and receive E mail, transfer files from a remote internet computer to the host from where you can then down load them to your own computer.

Communication software called *terminal emulation software* enables a computer to communicate with another computer. Communications software is used in combination with modem. The software is used to give commands to the modem, to dial the other computer's modem, and then to issue commands and receive responses from the remote computer. As already seen in Chapter 4, the purpose of the modem (modulator–demodulator) is to translate the digital signals that computers use to store and transmit information into the analog signals that telephone lines (or radio data systems) use to transmit information. A network that allows dial-in access provides one modem at its end, while a user who dials in provides the other, as shown in Fig. 30.1. These modems have to be compatible to be able to communicate.

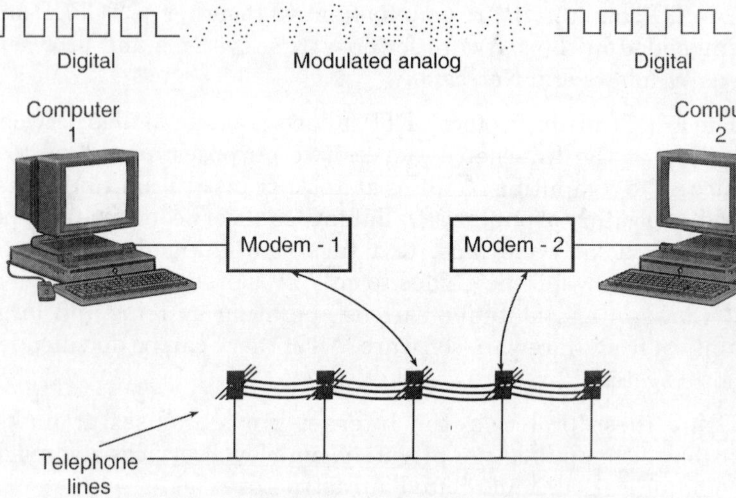

Fig. 22.1 Use of Modems in Computer Links.

Many different packages of communication software are available today. They are of three categories:

(*a*) Terminal packages used for accessing most host/shell account systems.

(*b*) TCP/IP-based packages, which let a computer become a host on the Internet. They establish a computer as a workstation on a network.

(*c*) Dumb terminal packages like ProComm Plus for DOS/Windows use a computer as a keyboard and display attached to the remote machine.

Based on these software, the dial-up connections are of two types:

***(i)* Host/Terminal Connection (Shell Accounts).** In a host/terminal connection, a given computer acts as if it were a terminal directly connected to some Internet host. The programme signals its modem to dial and handles the transfer of characters from user's terminal to the host computer and back. It means that the host computer is one that is "on the Internet", and therefore, when it transfers files, the files are transferred to the host. The user now can download the files to his/her computer using communications programmes.

***(ii)* Individual Computer TCP/IP Link.** An individual computer TCP/IP link allows a computer to function as an Internet host. It is the user as host running whatever software he elects to run, providing only the service he has chosen to provide. These links are called either SLIP (serial link Internet protocol) or PPP (point to point protocol) links. Both types of links can handle dialup. Both take advantage of new software techniques that condense or compress the data being transmitted so that transferring information takes less time.

II. Dedicated Internet Access. This access needs a dedicated phone line connecting a LAN or PC to the Internet 24 hours a day. A dedicated Internet access requires substantial initial investment in equipment and a high monthly fee for the user of the line. It varies with line capacity, and line capacity determines how many users can connect to the Internet simultaneously.

22.4 World Wide Web (WWW)

The World Wide Web (WWW) is the most widely used application on the Internet. The evolution and growth of the WWW has been rather similar to that of the Internet itself. It represents a convergence of computational concepts for presenting and linking information dispersed across the Internet in an easily accessible way.

In March 1989, Tim Berners-Lee of Geneva's European Particle Physics Laboratory (CERN) circulated a proposal to develop a 'hypertext system' for the purpose of enabling efficient and easy information sharing among geographically separated teams of researchers in the High Energy Physics community.

The three important components of the proposed system were the following:

- A consistent user interface.
- The ability to incorporate a wide range of technologies and document types.

- Its 'universal readership' 'that is' anyone sitting anywhere on the network, on a wide variety of different computers, could read the same document as anyone else, and could do so easily.

In 1990, the first line browser (called WWW) was launched. In 1991, the WWW line-mode browser began its first limited network use, followed by WWW being made available more extensively at CERN.

In 1992, the WWW browser was made available via FTP from CERN, and in January 1993, 50 Web servers were launched. At that time the Viola browser was made available for the X window system. Viola was the early leader in Web browsing technology, offering the first glimpse of the graphical, mouse-based hypertext system originally conceived in the Web proposal.

In 1993, CERN's Macintosh browser brought the Mac into the WWW system, The first alpha version of X Mosaic (Mosaic for X Window) was released by NCSA (the National Center for Supercomputing Applications in Champaign, Illinois USA). In 1994, the development of 'Secure' Web access took place to provide security needed by users.

In early 1995, the World Wide Web Consortium was constituted under the leadership of the Web Founder Tim Berners-Lee. In 1995, MIT was joined by the French National Institute for Research in Computer Science and Control (INRIA) as co-host of the Consortium. CERN remains an important collaborator.

22.4.1 Working of World Wide Web

Technically, the Web is a distributed hypermedia system. A hypertext document provides clearly visible links to other documents; and in a hypertext computer envorinment, selecting a link in one document makes the user to make a link directly to the other.

HTTP (Hyper Text Transport Protocol):

The Web document prepared by CERN (http:// info.cern.ch/hypertext/www/Protocols/HTTP/HTTP2.HTML) tells us, the transaction takes place in four basic HTTP phases:

I. Connection: In the connection phase, the Web client (for example, Mosaic, Netscape, Lynx) attempts to connect with the server. This appears on the status line of most browsers in the form connecting to HTTP server.

II. Request: Once the connection to the HTTP server is established, the client sends a request to the server. The request specifies which protocol is being used and it tells the server what object it is looking for and how it wants the server to respond. The protocol can be HTTP, but it can also be FTP, NNTP (Network News Transfer Protocol) Gopher method, which essentially is the client's command to the server. The most common method is GET, which is basically a request to retrieve the object in question.

III. Response: It indicates the protocol being used, and it also offers a reason line, which appears on the browser's status line, represented by a transferring message.

IV. Close: When the connection is closed, the browser loads and displays the requested data, saves the data to a file, or launches a viewer. If the object is a text file, the browser will display it as a non-hypertext ASCII document. If it is a graphic image (such as a GIF file), the browser will launch the graphics viewer specified in its configuration settings. If it is sound or video file (AU, WAV, MPEG, or other), the browser will launch a similarly configured player. Mostly, however, the browser displays an HTML (Hyper Text Markup Language) document described below. These documents show the graphics, links, icons, and formatting for which the web has become so famous.

HTML (Hyper Text Markup Language):

HTML is the native language for HTTP. It is the format used for writing the hypertext web documents. It is a code used to make documents readable across a variety of platform and software. It operates through a series of codes placed within an ASCII (that is, text) document. These codes are translated by a World Wide Web client, such as Netscape, Internet Explorer, NetCruiser, or Mac Web, into specific kinds of formats to be displayed on the screen. These items include links, lists, headings, titles, images,forms, and maps.

22.5 Internet Addressing Schemes

Using the Internet requires an understanding of different addressing schemes. People are identified with electronic mail addresses. Computers are identified with IP addresses and domain names. Resources and files available through the World Wide Web are identified using URLs.

I. IP Address. An IP address is a unique, numeric identifier used to specify a particular host on a particular network, and is part of a global, standardized scheme for identifying machines that are connected to the Internet.

IP addresses consist of four number between 0 and 255, separated by periods, which represent both the network and the host machines. IP addresses are also referred to as IP numbers and Internet addresses. The InterNIC, under the authority of the Internet Assigned Numbers Authority (IANA), allocates the network portions of IP addresses to Internet Service Providers (ISPs) : ISPs are responsible for assigning the host portion of the IP address to machines within their local networks.

If one wants to connect to another computer, transfer files to or from another computer, or send an e-mail message, he first needs to know where the other computer is - one first needs the computer's "address".

II. Domain. It is a sub-section of the Internet. It is a space anyone can purchase and book on the Internet under a specific name to display information of his/her particular choice. The main domains are COM,INT,NET, MIL, and ORG, which refer to Commercial, International, Network Military, and Organisation.

(*a*) *Domain Name System Structure:* It is a method of administering names by giving different groups responsibility for subsets of the names. Each level in this system is called a domain. The domains are separated by periods.

Example: *cedtm.stpm.soft.net*

Thus we see that every one on the Internet has both a domain name and an IP address, and when a user uses a domain name, the computers translate that name to the corresponding IP address. The names of the domain describe organizational or geographic realities. They indicate what country the network connection is in, what kind of organization owns it, and further details if any. These domain are given below:

(*b*) *Non-Geographic Domains:* There are six common top level domain types that are non-geographical:

.com: for commercial organizations, such as *Netcom.com, apple.com, sun.com*

.net: for network organizations, such as *internic.net*

.gov: for parts of governments within a country

.edu: for organizations of higher education, such as *sjsu.edu, ucsc.edu, mit.edu,* etc.

.mil: for non classified military networks, such as *army.mil,* etc.

.int: International Institutions (e.g. UNESCO).

.org: for organizations that do not otherwise fit the commercial or educational designation, such as *eff.org, farnet.org* etc.

(*c*) *Geographic Domains:* The geographically based top level domains use two-letter country designations. For example, .us is used for the United States, .ca for Canada, .uk for the United Kingdom and .in for India.

A domain name always contains two or more components separated by periods, called "dots":

internet.net

netsol.com

nasa.gov

utexas.edu

reston.va.uis

Therefore, the Domain Name System completes the task of matching domain names to IP (Internet Protocol) addresses. Domain names, and their corresponding IP addresses, must be unique. If more than one organization on the Internet had the same domain name, confusion would occur when the network tries to identify and communicate with the computer within those organizations.

III. Internet account. An Internet account is a user's gateway to the Internet. It is bought as an ISP such as VSNL , MTNL, Satyam Online, Dishnet, Mantra Online, and BPL Net. The ISP is a user sign-up which will give the local telephone number(s), which you will dial to access the Internet through a modem. Once connected, the user will have to type his name and password to gain access to the Internet.

IV. URL (Uniform Resources Locator). Some Internet applications use what is called a "Uniform Resource Location" (URL) to locate resources on the Internet. This is in a sense simply a more elaborate form of address, specifying not only the Internet site name, but also the directory and file in which a resource is located as well as which method to use to retrieve it. Currently, only the World-wide Web uses URLs.

Therefore, URL is a way to locate people, computers, and Internet resources and is used to identify specific sites and files available on the World Wide Web.

The structure of a URL is: Protocol://server.subdomain.top-level-domain/directory/filename

Not all URLs will have the directory and filename. For example: *http: / / www.lycos.com / welcome.html*

V. Sites and Hosts. All the information available on the Internet is located on specific computers (called "hosts") at particular sites. Each host has a unique number - the "IP number", - and a unique name, which functions as its address. That name (often called the domain name) is made up of a number of components (typically 4) separated by periods, as seen earlier. Example : *Cedtm.stpm.soft.net*

Here, cedtm is the name of the individual server, stpm the name of the site the server is located at, and soft.net refers to the Network resource provider domain in which that site is located. With the exception of the Internet sites in the USA, all Internet addresses end with a two letter country code. US addresses have as their final element not a country code, but a three letter abbreviation indication which network they are on. The IP number of cedtm is 12.3.72.137.

22.6 Accessing the Web

The World Wide Web can be accessed through both direct and indirect Internet connection, and through a variety of browsers. There are two main types of Internet connection: indirect and direct.

I. Direct connection. Here, a user's computer is an individual node on the Internet (or, in some cases, a simulated node). This computer has its own IP and can be established as a server for FTP, Gopher, News, or the World Wide Web. Direct access is often necessary if the programmes such as Internet Explorer for Windows are to be used.

II. Indirect connection. Here, the user's computer acts as a terminal on a computer or on a network that is itself an individual node on the Internet. The user is given disk space and access time on another computer. When he receives information, it stays on that server, and files are transferred, they are stored on that server as well.

22.6.1 Forms of Internet Connectivity

These are of three types:

I. Gateway connectivity: In this connection, when one of the computers on a small network or BBS gets the Internet access, all the remaining computers on the network get hooked up to it. Thus this intersection point computer provides a gateway to Internet access for the rest of the network (see Fig. 30.2).

Its advantages are:

1. The low cost of access as the cost is shared by the whole network

2. Even the existing non-IP based networks can be easily connected.

Examples of gateway connectivity: The AOL (America On-Line) Compuserve, Prodigy and VSNL GIAS.

Many of the gateways provide access to only e-mail service of the Internet. VSNL gateway is providing e-mail, FTP Telnet, Chat, Kermit, Zmodem Upload/ download and UNIX prompt facilities to its subscribers.

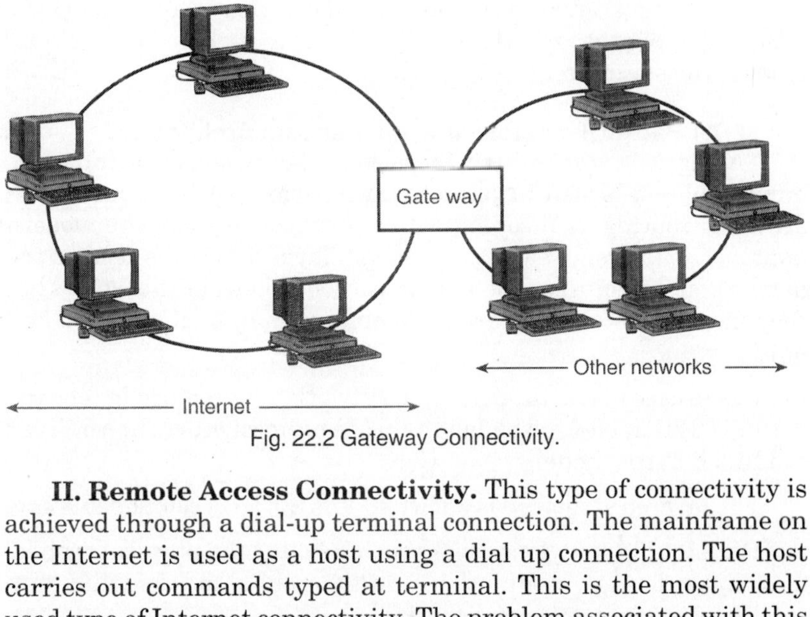

Fig. 22.2 Gateway Connectivity.

II. Remote Access Connectivity. This type of connectivity is achieved through a dial-up terminal connection. The mainframe on the Internet is used as a host using a dial up connection. The host carries out commands typed at terminal. This is the most widely used type of Internet connectivity. The problem associated with this level is that only the programs present at the host can be executed. Loading a new program or client does not provide the ability to execute it. Similarly downloading a file from any site becomes a two step process. Downloading from the site to host and then transferring from host to local terminal.

III. Direct Connectivity. This highest and most expensive type of connectivity is achieved by high speed lines to go on-line on the Internet. Internet is available round the clock. It is usually opted with heavy load and a number of users using a mainframe computer.

A new class of connectivity that is now coming into existence is the On-Demand Direct connectivity. The direct connection is provided on demand by the service providers based on Point to Point Protocol (PPP) or the Serial Line Internet Protocol (SLIP). It costs very less and still gives the power of direct connection.

22.7 Layered Structure for TCP/IP:The Network Layers

After reviewing the basic concepts of the Internet, we now describe its technology and the role of satellite links in the functioning of the Internet.

In the Internet system, the uplink and downlink between satellite and earth stations form what is known as the physical layer in a data communication system. By data communications is meant communications between computers and peripheral equipment. The signals are digital, and the satellite links must be able to accommodate the special requirements imposed by networks.

22.7.1 Packet Transmission and Network Architecture

The data is transmitted in packets. Many separate functions have to be performed in packet transmission, such as packet addressing, routing, and coping with packet congestion. The modern approach is to assign each function to a layer in what is termed the network architecture. The layers are conceptual in the sense that they may consist of software or some combination of software and hardware.

In the case of the Internet, the network architecture is referred to the TCP/IP model, although there are protocol other than TCP/IP contained in the model.

The layered structure is shown in Fig. 30.3. Its components are:

Physical layer : This covers such items as the physical connectors, signal format, modulation, and the uplink and downlink in a satellite communications system.

Data-link layer : The function of this layer is to organize the digital data into blocks as required by the physical layer. For example, if the physical layer uses Asynchronous Transfer Mode (ATM) technology, the data is organized into cells. Digital transmission by satellite frequently uses TDMA, and satellite systems are being developed which transmit Internet data over ATM. Thus the data-link layer has to organize the data into a suitable format to suite the physical layer technology. In the terrestrial Internet, the data link converts the data into frames. The data-link layer and the

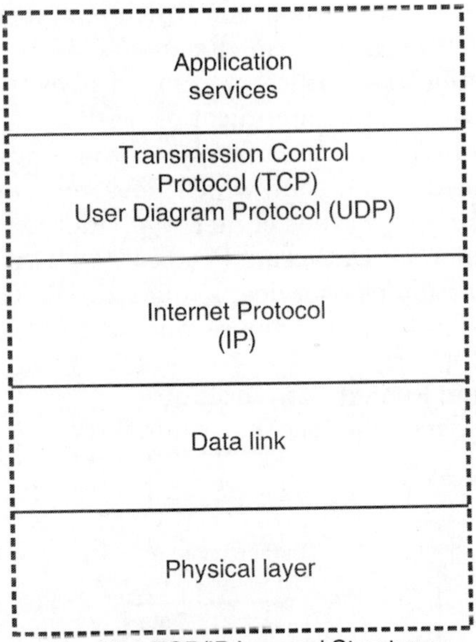

Fig. 22.3 TCP/IP Layered Structure.

physical layer are closely interrelated, and it can be difficult sometimes to identify the interface between these two layers

Network layer: This is strictly an Internet Protocol (IP) layer. The packets are passed along the Internet from router to router and to the host stations. No exact path is laid out beforehand, and the IP layers in the routers must provide the destination address for the next leg of the journey so to speak. This destination address is part of the IP header attached to the packet. The source address is also included as part of the IP header. The problems of lost packets or packets arriving out of sequence are not a concern of the IP layer, and for this reason, the IP layer is called connectionless (i.e., it does not require a connection to be established before sending a packet on). These problems are taken care of by the transport layer.

Transport layer : Two sets of protocol are provided in this layer. With the Transmission Control Protocol (TCP), information is passed back and forth between transport layers, which controls the information flow. This includes such functions as the correct sequencing of packets, replacement of lost packets, and adjusting the transmission rate of packets to prevent congestion.

In the early days of the Internet when traffic was comparatively light, these problems could be handled even where satellite transmissions were involved. With the enoromous increase in traffic on the present-day Internet, these problems require special solutions where satellite systems are used, which are discussed in later sections. The TCP layer is termed connection-oriented (compared with the connectionless service mentioned above) because sender and receiver must be in communication with each other to implement the protocol. There are situations where a simple stand-alone message may need to be sent which does not require the more complex TCP. For these types of message, another transport layer protocol called the User Datagram Protocol (UDP) is used. The UDP provides a connectionless service, similar to IP. The UDP header adds the port numbers for the source and destination applications.

22.7.2 Detailed Packet Terminology

Fig. 22.4 describes the packet terminology :

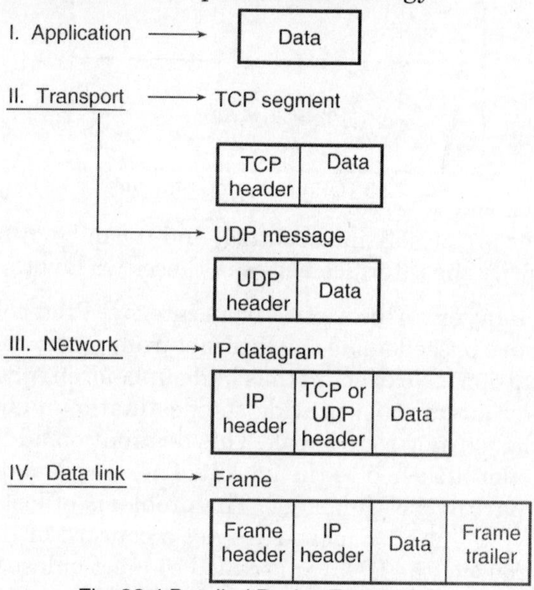

Fig. 22.4 Detailed Packet Terminology.

1. At the application level the packet is simply referred to as data. The packet comprising the TCP header, and the data are a TCP segment.

2. The packet comprising the UDP header and the data is a UDP message.

3. The packet comprising the IP header, the TCP or UDP header, and the data is an IP diagram.

4. The packet comprising the data-link frame header, the frame trailer (used for error control), and the IP datagram is a frame.

It should be noted here that the preceding definitions are those used in version 4 of the Internet Protocol (Ipv4). Internet Protocol version 6 (Ipv6) is a more recent version being brought on-stream in which the IP datagram is in fact called and IP packet.

22.8 The TCP Link

A virtual communication link exists between corresponding layers in a network.

The header in the TCP segment (see Fig. 30.4) carries instructions that enable communication between the send and receive TCP layers. Of course, the communication has to pass through the other layers and along the physical link, but only the TCP layers act on the Transmission Control Protocol (TCPs) contained in the segment header. There is no direct physical link between the TCP layers, and for this reason, it is called a virtual link.

22.8.1 The Send-and-Receive TCP Layers

The send and receive TCP layers have buffer memories (usually just called buffers). The receive buffer holds incoming data while they are being processed. The send buffer holds data until they are ready for transmission. It also holds copies of data already sent until it receives an acknowledgement that the original has been received correctly.

The receive window is the amount of receive buffer space available at any given time. This changes as the received data are processed and removed from the buffer. The receive TCP layer sends an acknowledgement (ACK) signal to the send TCP layer when it has cleared data from its buffer, and the ACK signal also provides an update on the current size of the receive window.

The send TCP layer keep track of the amount of data in transit and therefore it is unacknowledged. It can calculate the amount of receive buffer space remaining, allowing for the data in transit. This remaining buffer space represents the amount of data that can still be sent and is termed the send window.

The send TCP layer also sets a timeout period, and failure to receive an ACK signal within this period results in a duplicate packet being sent. On terrestrial networks, the probability of bit error is extremely low, and congestion is the most likely reason for loss of ACK signals. Because a network carries traffic from many sources, traffic congestion can occur.

22.8.2 Congestion Control

In such a situation, the IP layer of the TCP/IP discards packets when congestion occurs, and hence the corresponding ACK signals from the TCP layers do not get sent. Rather than continually resending packets, the send station reduces its rate of transmission, this being known as congestion control.

A congestion window is applied, which starts at a size of one segment for a new connection. The window is doubled in size for each ACK received until it reaches a maximum value determined by the number of failed ACKs experienced.

For normal operation, the congestion window grows in size to equal the receive window. The congestion window increases slowly at first, but as each doubling takes effect, the size increases exponentially. This controlling mechanism is known as slow start. If congestion sets in, this will be evident by an increase in the failure to receive ACKs, and the send TCP will revert to the slow start.

22.9 Satellite Links and TCP

Although satellite links have formed part of the Internet from its beginning, the rapid expansion of the Internet and the need to introduce congestion control have highlighted certain performance limitations imposed by the satellite links.

In the ideal case, the virtual link between TCP layers should not be affected by the physical link, and certainly the Transmission Control Protocol (TCP) is so well established that it would be undesirable to modify it to accommodate peculiarities of the physical link.

The factors that can adversely affect TCP performance over satellite links are as follows:

(*a*) Bit error rate (BER): Satellite links have a higher bit error rate (BER) than the terrestrial links forming the Internet. Typically, the satellite link BER without error control coding is around 10^{-6}, whereas a level of 10^{-8} or lower is needed for successful TCP transfer.

The comparatively low BER on terrestrial links means that most packet losses are the result of congestion, and the TCP send layer is programmed to act on this assumption. When packets are lost as a result of high BER, therefore, as they might on satellite links, the TCP layer assumes that congestion is at fault and automatically invokes the congestion control measures. This slows the throughput.

***(b)* Round-trip time (RTT):** The round-trip time (RTT) is the time interval that elapses between sending a TCP segment and receiving its ACK. With geostationary (GEO) satellites, the round-trip propagation path is ground station-to-satellite-to-ground station and back again.

The range from ground station to the satellite (see Chapter 3) is of the order of 40,000 km, and therefore, the propagation path for the round trip is $4 \times 40{,}000 = 160{,}000$ km. The propagation delay is therefore $160{,}000/3 \times 10^5 = 0.532$ sec. This is just the space propagation delay. The total round-trip time must take into account the propagation delays on the terrestrial circuits and the delays resulting from signal processing.

For order of magnitude calculations, an RTT value of 0.55 sec is considered appropriate. The send TCP layer must wait this length of time to receive the ACKs, and of course, it cannot send new segments until the ACKs are received, which is going to slow the throughput. The send TCP timeout period is also based on the RTT, and this will be unduly lengthened. Also, with interactive applications such as Telnet, this delay is highly undesirable.

***(c)* Bandwidth-delay product (BDP):** The RTT is also used in determining an important factor known as the bandwidth delay product (BDP). The delay part of this refers to the RTT, since a sender has to wait this amount of time for the ACK before sending more data. The bandwidth refers to the channel bandwidth.

Bandwidth and bit rate are directly related. In network terminology, the bandwidth is usually specified in bytes per second (or multiples of this), where it is understood that 1 byte is equal to 8 bits.

Example: *A satellite bandwidth of 36 MHz carrying a BPSK signal could handle a bit rate of 30Mbits/sec. This is equivalent to* 3.75×10^6 *bytes per second or about 3662 kilobytes per second. If the sender transmits at this rate, the largest packet it can send within the RTT of 0.55 sec is* $3662 \times 0.55 = 20.14$ *kilobytes approximately. This is the BDP for the two-way satellite channel.*

Such a channel is sometimes referred to as a *pipeline*, and one that has a high BDP, as a *long fat pipe*. Now the receiver TCP layer uses a 16-bit word to notify the send TCP layer of the size of the receive window it is going to use. Allowing 1 byte for certain overheads, the biggest segment size that can be declared for the receive window is $2^{16} - 1 = 65{,}535$ bytes, or approximately 64 kilobytes.

(Recall that 1 kilobyte is equal to 1024 bytes.) This falls well short of the 20.14 kilobytes set by the BDP for the channel as estimated in the example above. Thus the channel is very underutilized.

Variable Round-Trip Time: Where lower earth orbiting satellites are used such as those in low earth orbits (LEOs) and medium earth orbits (MEOs), the propagation delays will be much less than that for the GEO. The slant range to LEOs is typically of the order of a few thousand kilometers at most, and for MEOs, a few tens of thousand kilometers. The problems with these orbits is not so much the absolute value of delay as the variability. Because these satellites are not geo-stationary, the slant range varies, and for continuous communications there is the need for intersatellite links, which also adds to the delay and the variability. For example, for LEOs, the delay can vary from a few to about 80 msec.

Thus, the increasing demand for Internet services may well be met best with satellite direct-to-home links, and many companies are setting up such systems.

22.10 Modification of TCP Over Satellite Channels Using Standard Mechanisms

Since in general the TCP itself should not be modified to accommodate satellite links, the Request for Comments 2488 (RFC-2488) is used to improve the performance over satellite links. The methods used are discussed below.

The first two mechanisms listed do not require any changes to the TCP. The others do require extensions to the TCP with the condition that any extensions to the TCP must maintain compatibility with networks that do not employ the extensions.

Path MTU (Maximum Transmission Unit) Discovery: This method allows the sender to find the largest packet and hence largest TCP segment size that can be sent without fragmentation. The congestion window is incremented in segments; hence larger segments allow the congestion window to be incremented faster in terms of number of bytes carried. There is a delay involved in implementing Path MTU-Discovery.

Forward Error Correction (FEC): Lost packets, whether from transmission errors or congestion, are assumed by the TCP to happen as a result of congestion, which means that congestion control is implemented, with its resulting reduction in throughput. Application of FEC therefore should be used where possible.

Slow Start and Congestion Avoidance: Slow start and congestion avoidance control the number of segments transmitted, but not the size of the segments. Using Path MTU-Discovery can increase the size, and hence the data throughput is improved.

Fast Retransmit and Fast Recovery: From the nature of the ACKs received, the fast retransmit algorithm enables the sender to identify and resend a lost segment before its timeout expires. Since the data flow is not interrupted by timeouts, the sender can infer that congestion is not a problem, and the fast recovery algorithm prevents the congestion window from reverting to slow start. The fast retransmit algorithm can only respond to one lost segment per send window. If there is more than one, the others trigger the slow start mechanism.

TCP Large Windows: As already seen with the bandwidth delay product, the receive window size is limited by the address field to 64 kilobytes maximum. By introducing a window scale extension into the TCP header, the address field can be effectively increased to 32 bits. Allowing for certain overheads, the maximum window size that can be declared is 230 = 1 gigabyte (1 gigabyte = 10243 bytes). The window size and hence the scale factor can be set locally by the receive TCP layer. Note, however, that the TCP extension has to be implemented at both the sender and the receiver.

22.11 Split TCP Connections

As already seen, the Transmission Control Protocol (TCP) provides end-to-end connection, that is, the TCP layers at the sender and receiver are connected through a virtual link so that such matters as congestion control, regulation of data flow, etc. can be carried out without intervention of intermediate stages. The extensions to TCP described in the preceding section are used to preserve this end-to-end connection.

Now consider the case when the end-to-end connectivity is split. This offers new possibilities for the introduction of satellite links as part of the overall Internet. One arrangement called spoofing for breaking the network is shown in Fig. 23.5. Spoofing refers to the fact that the TCP source thinks it is connected to the TCP destination, whereas the interworking unit (IWU) performs a protocol conversion.

In this figure, TCP Reno refers to the TCP with extensions: slow start, congestion avoidance, fast retransmit, fast recovery, support for large windows and delayed ACKs. At the IWU, the data is transferred from the TCP Reno to the data-link protocol. As shown in the figure, any one of link layer protocols may be used. At the destination end, the IWU performs the conversion back to TCP Reno.

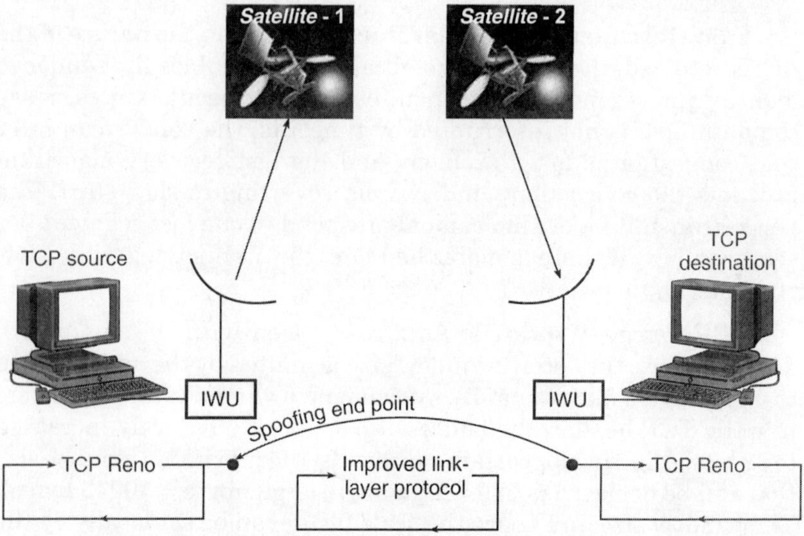

Fig. 22.5 Split TCP/IP Satellite Link.

22.12 Asymmetric Channels

For an Internet connection, the term asymmetry applies in two senses: firstly it refers the asymmetric nature of the data flow. For example, a short request is sent for a Web page but the returned Web page may be a much larger document. Moreover, the acknowledgment packets sent on the return or reverse link are generally shorter than the TCP segments sent on the forward link.

Secondly, astymmetry also exists with respect to the physical capacities of the links. For example, small earth stations (e.g. VSATs), transmit power and antenna size (in effect, the EIRP) that limit the uplink data rate and it may be much less than the downlink data rate. Such asymmetry can result in ACK congestion. Further, using some values given in RFC-2760, for a 1.5 Mb/sec data link a reverse link of less than 20 kb/sec can result in ACK congestion. The levels of asymmetry that lead to ACK congestion are encountered in VSAT networks that share the uplink through multiple access.

22.12.1 Asymmetric channel-based Satellite Internet Network

Fig. 30.6 shows DirecPC turbo Webcast developed by Hughes Network Systems, which employs asymmetric channels to provide

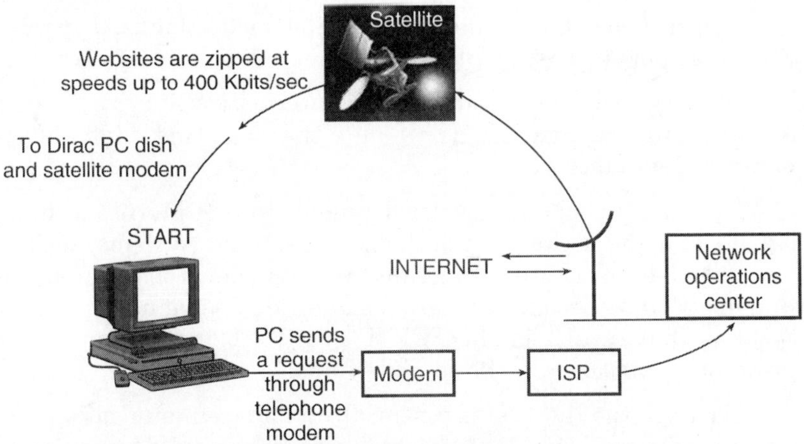

Fig. 22.6 An Example of the Use of Asymmetrical Channels for Satellite Transfer of Internet Data.

satellite transfer of Internet data to the individual consumers and homeowners. The system can be used for all TCP/IP-based software applications such as email, Telnet, and the World Wide Web (WWW).

1. A customer URL (uniform, or universal resource locator) request goes out through a modem to the Internet service provider (ISP) at normal modem speeds (typically in the range 28.6 to 56 kb/sec).

2. Before sending the URL, the DirecPC software installed in the customer's PC attaches what is termed a tunneling code to the URL. This instructs the ISP to forword this request to the DirecPC network operations centre (NOC) instead of to the Internet server.

3. At the NOC, the tunneling code is stripped away, and the request is forwarded to the Internet site through high-speed lines.

4. The requested content is now returned to the NOC, which then downloads it to the customer through the satellite link, at a bit rate of up to 400 kbits/sec.

Advantage: Large data files are returned over a high-speed link rather than back through the low-speed modem.

The system's downlink is in the Ku band (20 to 30 GHz). It can have variety of system configurations, ranging from Internet-only connections to a combined DirecPC and DirecTV system.

22.13 New Satellite Systems for Internet

Most of the currently employed satellitesa:

(*i*) operate in what is called a "bent pipe" mode; that is, they relay the data from one host to another without any onboard processing.

(*ii*) use geostationary satellites for Internet traffic arise because of the long propagation delay and the resulting high delay-bandwidth product.

There are two main new developments in the Internet technology: First is the use of some of the newer satellite systems, such as low and medium earth orbiting satellites to cut down on the propagation delay time. Second is onboard signal processing used in many systems that results in the TCP/IP protocol being exchanged for propriety protocols over the satellite links.

Although the Internet is essentially a data communication system, new deveopment also indicate incorporating voice communications along with data in what is known as Voice Over Internet Protocol (VolP).

Asynchronous Transfer Mode (ATM): In such systems, the satellite part of the network may carry the Internet Protocol (IP) over what is known as Asynchronous Transfer Mode (ATM). With ATM, the data are partitioned into fixed-length packets, called cells, of length 53 bytes. Five bytes form the header for the cell, and the remaining 48 bytes are the payload.

However, with ATM, the "payload" also carries additional overhead bytes, specifically bytes for what is called the ATM adaptation layer. The asynchronous part of the ATM refers to the fact that cells are transmitted asynchronously; that is, they do not need to be assigned regular time slots. The cell size of 53 bytes is a compromise between what is suitable for time-sensitive traffic such as voice and video and what is suitable for non-time-sensitive data.

For high-bit-rate traffic, many cells can be transmitted in sequence, and traffic bursts also can be handled in this way. This is sometimes referred to as bandwidth on demand. Note that synchronous digital signals may be carried in the cells, even though the system is referred to as asynchronous.

The Ka band, which covers from 27 to 40 GHz, is used in many (but not all) of these newer systems. Wider bandwidths are available for carriers in the Ka band compared with those in the Ku band.

22.14 Organisational Structure of Internet and World Wide Web

There is no central management or authority for the Internet, yet its extraordinarily rapid growth has meant that some control has to be exercised over what is permitted. A summary of the controlling groups is shown in Fig. 22.7.

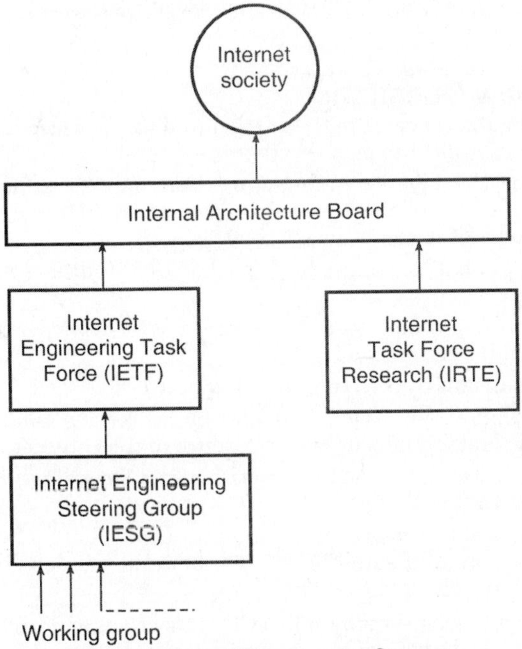

Fig. 22.7 Internet Management Structure.

The World Wide Web (WWW) has no central authority but still it has a structure that attempts to regulate what happens. The World Wide Web Consortium, referred to as W3C, was founded in October 1994. W3C oversees a number of special interest groups, as shown in Fig. 22.8, and coordinates its efforts with the IETF and with other standards bodies.

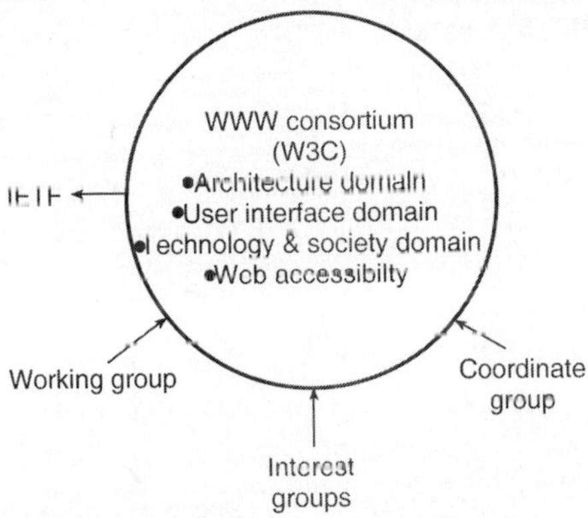

Fig. 22.8 WWW Management Structure.

22.15 References

1. Dennis Roddy, Satellite Communication, McGraw Hill, Boston, 2001.
2. Discover the World Wide Web with Your Sportster, Sam.net, 1996.

22.16 Review Questions

1. Describe the concepts of the Intrnet and the World Wide Web showing the relationship between them.
2. Describe the layered architecture that applies to networks, and indicate which of these layers contain (a) the IP and (b) the TCP. Explain what is meant by protocol.
3. Describe what is meant by a packet in the different layers of a network.
4. Binary transmission occurs at a rate of 5000 bytes per second. What is this in bit per second?
5. What is meant by a virtual link in a network?
6. Define and explain what is meant by (a) receive window, (b) send window, and (c) timeout with reference to the Internet.
7. Explain what is meant by congestion and slow start in relation to Internet traffic.
8. Explain what is meant by round-trip time (RTT). Given that the uplink range to a satellite is 3,000 km and the downlink range is 40,000 km, calculate the RTT.
9. Explain what is meant by split TCP connections and why these might be considered undesirable for Internet use.
10. Explain what is meant by asymmetric channels. Describe how asymmetric channels may be incorporated in Internet connections via satellites.
11. The overall bandwidth for a satellite link is 36 MHz, and the filtering is raised-cosine with a rolloff factor of 0.2 BPSK modulation is used. The range to the satellite is 39,000 km in both directions. Calculate the size of the largest packet that could be in transit if the bandwidth-delay product (BDP) was the limiting factor. Assume that the RTT is equal to the space propagation delay.

    (Ans. 1904 kilobytes)

23

Satellites, Digital Telephony, E-mail, FAX, Video Conferencing and Mobile Telephony and Wireless Internet

Both geostationey and low-earth orbit satellites are employed to provide digital and mobile telephone links. In this chapter, the principles of digital telephony and mobile telephony are discussed. Also provided are the concepts of wireless internet and the role of satellites.

23.1 Digital Exchange: Use of Stored Program Control (SPC)

The world's first experimental electronic exchange was put into operation by the Bell Telephone Laboratories in April 1961, with a capacity of 500 subscriber lines. Further development resulted in the first commercial electronic exchange commissioned in New Jersey, the USA, in 1965. Subsequently Canada, Japan, Belgium, Sweden, France, the Netherlands, Germany and the UK developed different SPC systems.

In electronic exchanges, common control features of the cross-bar exchange are provided by computer programmes, called *stored program control* (SPC). This system is similar to the manual exchange, except that just one unit performs the function of digit storage, path selection and translation for the entire exchange.

The SPC electronic exchange has fully centralised common control. This common control is basically a switching processor, which masterminds the call set-up. It is a digital computer specially designed for handling telephone-switching functions in real time. Its functions are:

1. It collects the dial pulses and transmits them correctly.
2. It controls the calls but also ensures automatic and continuous self-checking while processing the calls.
3. If a fault is detected, a replacement is switched on automatically.
4. It measures traffic, indicates the status of the systems, takes into account up-to-the-minute changes, monitors calls for assessing the quality of service and records details of overload, if need be.

Digital exchanges consist of the basic components shown in Fig. 23.1. Most of the control of the system is handled by microprocessor devices, singly or in clusters which are driven by software.

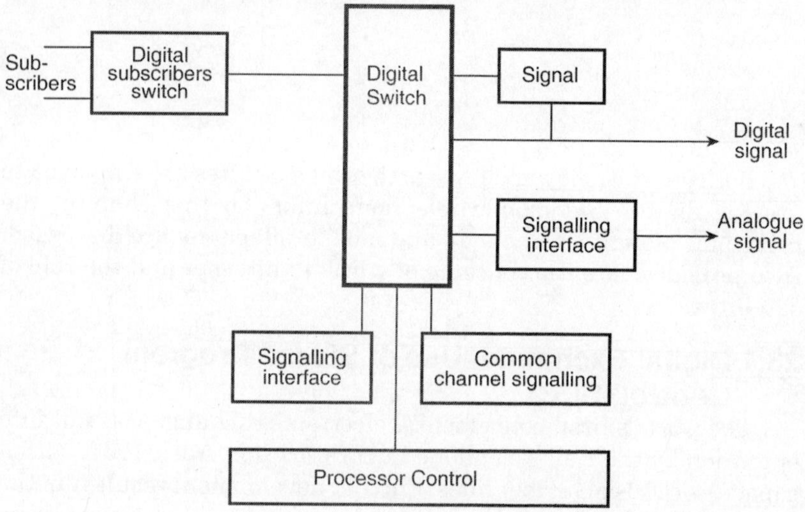

Fig. 23.1 Digital Exchange.

The line features include: STD, international STD, coin-box, abbreviated dialing, automatic call back, temporary transfer, call restriction and charge indication, 'switching features include alternate routing, random selection (in contrast to sequential selection) of trunk numbers, abbreviated dialing, malicious call tracing, data switching and centralized observation and maintenance. If a subscriber wants to block STD for others, he chooses a secret code number for his telephone. When he dials, the telephone is automatically tested without your asking for it.

In the international switching, the features available are: call transfer, automatic card check, indication of a waiting call or a route being busy and even installation of house meters to record the calls made.

23.1.1 Mass Memory

The SPC system has a 'mass memory' with very short access time. The memory relates to programme store, translation store and data on subscribers and route information. The translation store contains data like the charging information, status of the calling lines called and their calling codes. Purely transient data like busy or idle state of a line are also held in memory. It is arranged in words containing 16, 18 or 32 bits. Each word has a unique address for location: 1 mean 'busy' and 0 is for 'idle'. A word stores the address and the operation to be carried out.

Call processing involves lime scanning to see who wants to speak, digit analysis, search of a free path and setting up of the connection.

One important feature about the hardware of an SPC exchange is its flexibility to take on more traffic - a feature absent in crossbar exchanges. In an SPC electronic exchange (which physically occupies less space than its earlier counterparts), one more quota of printed cards will take care of the extra traffic need.

Example: *Two processors can handle 120,000 call attempts in a busy hour. Three processors can take this capacity upto 220,000 and four will handle 300,000 attempts. Assuming a high rate of 100 calls per line during the busy hour, four processors can handle 30,000 lines.*

23.1.2 Call Processing in an Electronic Exchange

The processor takes time off every 10 milliseconds to look for any dial pulse, disconnection or origin of a call. The scanning will last for 3 microseconds. In one second, it can scan 3,000,000 subscriber lines. One subscriber is scanned five times a second. The processing is carried out in following steps :

1. When the caller lifts the receiver, the line scanner detects the electrical change of state of the loop and informs the processor.

2. The main control finds from the memory the class of service and the type of signaling (dial or push-button) and assigns the call to a 'register' in its memory.

3. It then finds an idle dialing junctor, looks for a free path in the memory to the calling line, controls the markers to set up a path between the dialing junctor and the calling number. It immediately busies the line the dial tone sending device is activated.

4. Complete numbers of pulses are received by the dialing junctor. The processor turns them into appropriate digits.

5. Analysing the first two digits, it can be found if the call is a local call or not. If it is one, then the memory is searched to find out whether the called line is busy or not.

6. If it is busy, the processor releases the dialing junctor and orders the markers to release the path and connect the caller to a device to get the busy tone. The paths in the memory map are updated.

7. If the called line is free, the processor selects a free local-feed junctor, considered possible paths, selects one, connects it and releases the dialing junctor and its path.

8. The local junctor is ordered to transmit ringing tone to the called party, the ring-back tone to the caller, till the party answers. At the end of the conversation, the line status is noticed and the paths are released.

9. If it is an outside call, the register remains with the call unit, until it has transmitted all the dialed or translated information to the distant exchange.

23.1.3 Types of Signaling

Signalling is the means and the process by which the various elements of a telephone connection communicate to establish and maintain that connections.

There are three categories of signaling:

(*i*) between subscribers and exchanges

(*ii*) between exchanges and

(*iii*) between international exchanges.

Signalling on subscriber lines depends on whether a subscriber uses a dial or a push-button telephone. In the older strowger system, the subscriber signals to the exchange by raising the handset. This closes contact on the switch hook, allowing the current to flow in the loop. The dialing of digits interrupts the current. The central battery gives current to the telephone (that is why it works even when power fails). When the calling subscriber finishes the call and replaces the handset on the hook, the circuit is broken.

In the push-button telephone set, different frequencies rather than DC pulses are generated for different digits dialed. A combination of two frequencies, one from a group of low and the other from a group of high frequencies, is selected to signal each digit.

I. Out-to-band Signalling. In this widely used signaling method, the signaling frequency (3,825 Hz) is within the 4 KHz voice frequency channel, though it is outside the normal voice frequency range of 300-3400 Hz. This method is economical as voice transmission contains very little speech energy at the upper end of the voice band. Some filtering is also done by the telephone handset itself and the balance by the multiplex equipment. Higher signal levels can also be used. However, it needs coordination between voice and signaling channels.

The frequency of 3,825 Hz is added on to the telephone band of 4 KHz. With the help of filters, the signaling information conveyed through 3,825 Hz is identified. This will actuate a relay for ringing the particular telephone.

Depending on the system adopted, 3,825 Hz will be of two types: *Tone-on-idle* or a *tone-off-idle condition*. In the first one, the frequency of 3,825 Hz will be present when the circuit is not used. It will be interrupted at a constant speed of 10 impulses per second, while the wanted numbers are dialed. For example, the signaling tone is interrupted four times, if digit 4 is dialed, and once only, if 1 is dialed. The inter-digit pause and speed of the 10 impulses per second are fixed so as to facilitate the associated step in the exchanges, which are time-bound.

The out-of-band signal frequency is also used for point-to-point STD calls.

II. In-band Signalling. It is used between crossbar exchanges. It is a multi-frequency signaling in which instead of using 3,825 Hz, which is outside the speech band, two out of six frequencies inside the voice band are selected to establish the digits. The combination of one lower and one higher frequency identifies the digit dialed. For example, the digit 0 in a push button dial is a combination of 941 Hz and 1,336 Hz.

Multi-frequency signaling is used only for conveying the dialed digit information and its acknowledgement. Out-of-band signaling is used in addition, for supervision of calls during and after speech.

Supervisory signals are on the line only before and after a call. There are also guard circuits to distinguish between speech and signaling tones. Whether it is out-of-band or in-band, the signaling paths associated with each individual channel. In a 12-channel system, for example, each one of them will carry speech and signaling information.

III. Common Channel Signalling. In this signaling, a separate channel - a high-speed 64 Kbits/sec-link is provided to carry out for signaling functions. It is actually computer-to-computer communication, as all the switches used are under stored program control.

Networks are used more efficiently because no trunks are committed to a call until the path between stations and the destination become available. Signalling rates are also faster.

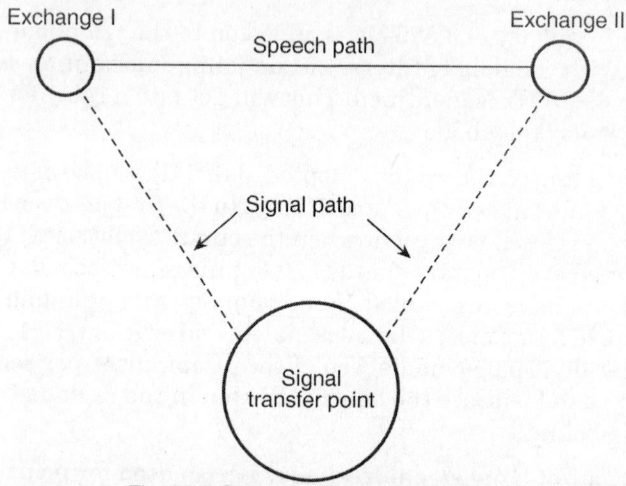

Fig. 23.2 Common Channel Signalling

23.1.4 National Subscriber Dialling

The hierarchical telephone plan provides the national subscriber trunk dialing (STD) facility as anyone connected to a trunk automatic exchange (TAX) is able to dial any other phone connected to a similar exchange in any part of the country.

The national numbering scheme enables a user to dial any city connected to subscriber trunk dialing, with the same city code wherever he dials it from. Without this plan, there are any number of codes to call a city from different places. The routing of the signals is done by the group switching exchange as follows:

1. As soon as we dial the first 0, we are connected to a group switching center (within the country) which has a register-translator.

2. The register will not the city wanted and ask the translator for the routing digits (which can be longer than the original code but different for different cities) to the city dialed and make the connection to the other city's exchange.

3. The pulses for the local telephone number dialed (and held temporarily by the group switching exchange) are released to set up the call.

4. Technical arrangements are also made to time the duration of the call and charge it, depending on the time and distance.

In our country, main TAXs are located in Chennai, New Delhi, Calcutta and Mumbai. Inter-dialling among the stations connected with them was possible during low traffic periods such as Sundays and night time. STD among all connected phones including international phones and fax machines is now a reliable routine. National subscriber dialing is provided through 18,000 stations served by 390 TAXs.

23.1.5 Basic Telecommunication Network

Fig. 23.3 shows the basic telecommunication network. It is a land-based network traditional telephone system in which all telephone subscribers are connected to a central switching network It consists of terminals, a public switching telephone network (PSTN), cables, and microwave links or optical fiber links. A terminal can be a simple telephone set, a computer, a modem, or several workstations.

The PSTN is a digitally controlled switching matrix that provides connectivity between two or more terminals. Depending on the population density, a PSTN may have well over 1,00,000 terminals connected to it. As a result, a major metropolitan area may have more than one PSTN switch connected to each other.

It provides the following basic functions:

1. Switching;

2. Billing;

3. 911 dialing;

4. 1-800 and 1-900 calling features;

5. Call waiting, call transfer conferencing calling, and voice mail;

6. Global connectivity;

7. Interfacing wish cellular networks.

Tens of thousands of simultaneous calls can be handled by means of a single PSTN.

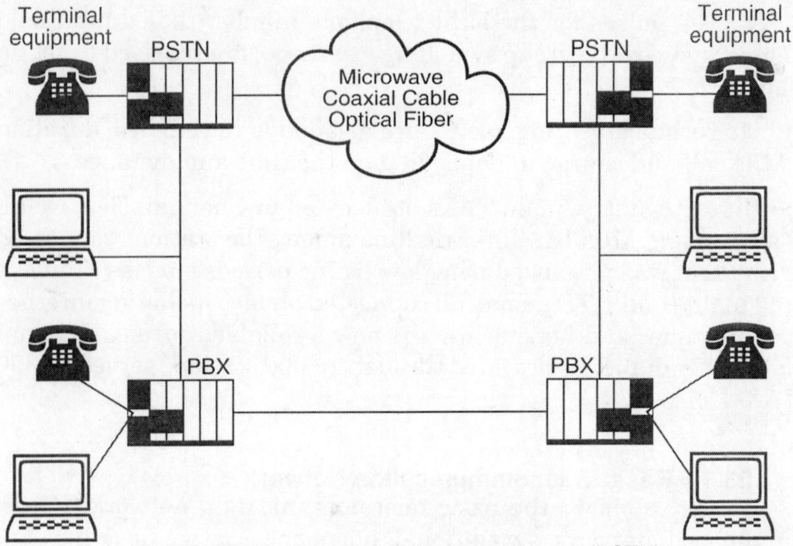

Fig. 23.3 Public Switching Telephone Network (PSTN).

Telephone services to small communities such as offices and business communities are provided by means of a small switch known as a private branch exchange (PBX), which enables an internal office call to bypass the PSTN. PBX switches are generally installed within the business subscriber's premises. Several PBXs can be installed in one or in different buildings and are connected to each other by cables.

Data transmission takes place over cables, microwave links, or optical fiber links, providing global coverage via satellites, underwater cables, and optical cables. Various transmission equipment and protocol converters are also used to establish global connectivity.

23.1.6 ISDN

The subscriber lines that could be used for both speech and data is called ISDN. It is provided on ordinary telephone lines of subscribers. ISDN is not a separate network, as it is based on PSTN with some changes. By using ISDN, it is possible to have two simultaneous calls on the existing pair to wires of the telephone. The two calls can be of any type: data, image, video or speech. Its features are:

1. The call set-up time is only one to two seconds. Upto eight ISDN terminals can be connected including a TV and a computer.

2. The speed of data on the ISDN line is 64 Kbits/sec and for downloading files or video conferencing, the speed could go upto 128

Kbits/sec. Using ISDN, a 1.44 Mb floppy can be transmitted in less than four minutes. And data, using both the channels, can be sent or received at 128 Kbits/sec.

3. It has display of calling number and call units charged, call forwarding, redialing and speaker phone, etc.

4. ISDN is useful for gaining access to the Internet.

The basis for ISDN is CCS-7, approved by ITU, and introduced in India in 1996. CCS-7 enables processors to exchange information needed for providing the desired services. It is essential for operating the so-called intelligent network which involves access to different databases (e.g., an 800 toll-free number for calling business firms) and working personal communication systems.

However, ISDN as well as broad-ISDN (deigned to provide a little more bandwidth) have a technology based on circuit-switching within digital telephone networks. It has therefore limited efficiency and flexibility in transporting data. In contrast, ATM, which is a form of the broadband ISDN, uses packet-switched data networks with improvements in the transport of delay-sensitive data such as voice or video.

23.1.7 Network Hierarchy

Because of widespread telecommunication services, it is necessary to group telephones around a central point (PSTN) and then group several points with higher interchange points. For long-distance dialing, each point associated with the call is classified and designated according to the highest rank of switching functions. The passage of a call through a national network can be represented by the multi-level diagram shown in Fig. 23.4. There are several levels of switching that combine to form the complete network. It is usual to think of the systems in two parts The first is the junction network, serving the subscriber and consisting of the link from subscriber to local exchange, from local exchange to primary switching entire, and back to the called subscriber via another local exchange. The second part of the system is the trunk network, which is concerned only with calls passing at primary centre level and above. Thus the primary centre is associated with both parts of the network.

The structure shown by the solid lines represents the basic hierarchical network of the system, and telephone calls routed along these links are said to be traveling on a backbone or final route. When there is much traffic between exchanges, either belonging to the same cluster, or at different levels, direct routes may be installed to save a stage of switching. Such routes are shown as dotted lines in Fig. 23.4. These direct routes are dimensioned to different grade of service from the final routes. Because a call finding all the direct-route circuits busy can be placed on the backbone route, the direct route can be designed to provide a higher grade of service than the final route, and thus works more efficiently.

The number of exchanges at the various levels depends on several factors – the physical extent of the network, the number of subscribers, the amount of traffic, the forecast growth and the transmission methods used. Beyond the top level of the actional system is a layer that gives access to international network. This layer may consist of one or more international (usually called gateway) exchanges.

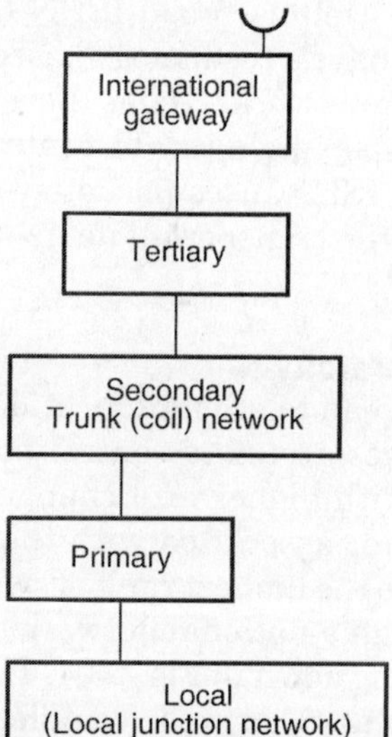

Fig. 23.4 Network Hierarchy.

End Office: It is the central switching office or the PSTN where telephone loops are terminated for switching to another telephone or a terminal. A PSTN may have well over 100,000 telephones connected to it.

Toll Office: The switching center that handles the first stage of long-distance traffic is called the toll office. Operator-assisted calls are also handled in this location if the caller intends to do so.

23.1.8 Formation of Digital Hierarchy

A telephone speech is sampled (at 8,000 times a second with 8 bits per sample) we need 64,000 bits/sec. If there are 24 telephone channels, there are as many time slots of eight digits with a total of 192 digits and a spare one for synchronization. The time slots are repeated 8,000 times a second making a total of 1,544,000 bits/sec.

As shown in Fig. 23.5, in TDM, 32 voice channels are sampled in sequence, 8,000 times a second, and the amplitude of each sample is represented in binary forms as a PCM, which are interleaved and transmitted as ones and zeros. Thirty-two time slots of eight digits (256) plus a spare (257) are repeated 8,000 times a second for a total of 2,056,000 digits per second.

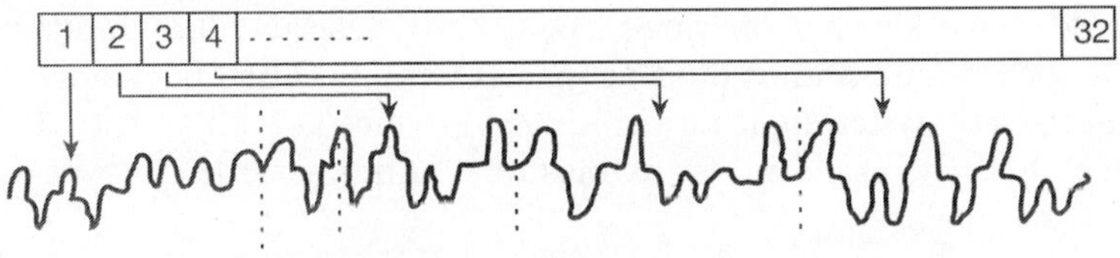

Fig. 23.5 Digital Telephone Signal using TDM.

1. The 2 Mbits/sec transmission forms the primary level of a digital hierarchy. Digital pulses from four of the channel multiplexes can be interleaved on a single cable, which will then carry 120 conversations as 8 million bits every second.

2. Subsequently, four sets of 8 million bit multiplexes can be interleaved on one cable to get a 480-channel link with a 34 million bit stream.

3. Also, four of these streams can be sent together on a single telephone cable.

4. All the series of pulses are 'reconstructed' again into speech at the receive-end.

23.1.9 Packet Switching

In a telephone network, the maximum speed of data possible is normally 1,200 bitsec/sec and it can go upto 2,400 bits/sec. Therefore, it has the following disadvantages:

1. Only low-speed traffic can go through the switched telephone network.

2. The call set-up time is rather long, ranging from 6-15 seconds on trunk lines. On the other hand, the time in which the message is actually transmitted for data calls is much shorter in general than

that for telephone or telex calls. The call set-up time becomes relatively longer than the actual call duration. Therefore, the computer is occupied in an inefficient manner.

3. The transmission of speech can tolerate a wide margin or noise, interruption and other defects but data transmission cannot.

4. The telephone network as it consist of various switching and transmission systems, uses one of the many alternative routes to establish a call.

In order to handle increased demand for data transmission, a dedicated digital network becomes a necessity. In such a network, there is no need for modems and the transmission path will be digital. Such a network can operate at very high data transmission speeds with lower error rates. As already described in Chapter 10, this technique handles data as packets and is called packet switching. Packet switching is now taking over voice as well as data. It has become as the essential transmission technique for the Internet.

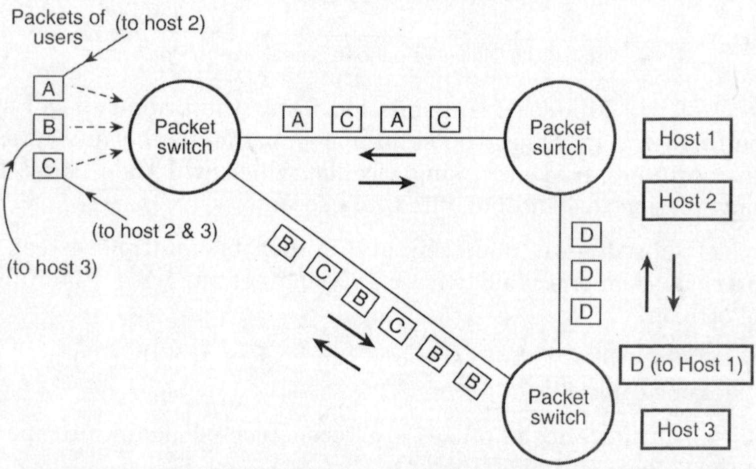

Fig. 23.6 Packet-switched Network.

The details of this technique are (Fig. 23.6):

1. Data were broken up into numerous packets and sent to the network with individual address to each packet. Since no single user needs the entire channel all the time, customers' messages are chopped up as packets of data (mixed with other users' data) and sent over a shared communications line and reassembled at the other end.

2. The packets may not take the same route. The packets are handled by shifting them from one router to another and reassembled at the destination.

3. A router en route stores the packets in memory and selects a suitable output link.

4. The silent periods of a link (voice or its data equivalent and other data) are used to transmit other data. Silent periods are detected by a device called voice activity detector (VAD).

Frame Relay: Frames of data are relayed by what is called frame relay. It involves the following functions (Fig. 23.7):

1. The grouping of data into packets of digital data and transferring them as discrete units of information. In frame relay (middle), frames of data are transmitted by means of addresses contained within the packets of data. The cells have a variable length of information (64 to over 1,500 bytes, besides a 2-byte header).

2. The Frame Relay Protocol allots bandwidth dynamically. Note that unlike time division multiplexing (TDM) where sound as well as silence are transmitted, frame relay does not allocate a path until data have to be sent.

3. The packets or frames can vary in length (e.g. 64 to over 1,500 bytes). It is a standard method of connecting data communication devices for bit rates ranging from 56 thousand bits to 2 million bits per second, although it can support lower or higher speeds.

4. Frame relay can also compress speech and multiplex upto 255 sub-channels. It can permanently interconnect local area networks in different buildings.

5. Frame relay guarantees data transmission only at the committed rate. Other frames that cause congestion are discarded.

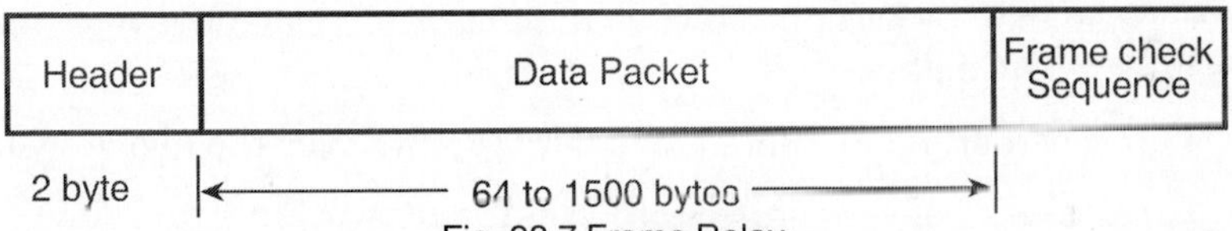

Fig. 23.7 Frame Relay

6. Frame relay network itself does not process data by detecting or correcting errors. The end stations handle the system for error-prone frames.

Advantage: Frame relay provided a useful technique to provide a variable bandwidth service. It can also allot priorities in transmitting data, fax or voice.

23.1.10 Asynchronous Transport Mode (ATM)

This digital packet-switching technique is used to handle bursts of high-speed data as well as the ebb and flow of the slower phone calls. It is now a popular high-speed switching technology, which integrates voice, data and video, besides connecting local and wide area networks and services into a seamless link. It is based on the so-called *statistical multiplexing technique*. It takes advantage of the statistical nature of the need to transfer information. Accordingly, it suppresses the silent periods and carries other voices or data in the gaps.

The basic unit of transmission is called a *cell*, a short, fixed length packet. Each cell is 53 bytes long (48 bytes of information and a 5-byte header for path and channel identifiers, cell loss priority and generic flow control, etc.). No speed rates are specified. It can move data at varying speeds (e.g. 100 Mbits/sec or 155 Mbits/sec or higher).

The *synchronous transfer mode* (STM) is a common carrier system which carries voice over dedicated physical path connected by a dialed call or on a leased line, and is not routed by address. The cells have no address and are identified by their time slots. No other user can access the path for the duration of the call.

The *Ethernet protocol* which uses 'connection-less' transmission techniques do not set up any path whatsoever for the various packets of data from their source to destination. Each packet takes a different route and gets reassembled at the end. There could be some delay in the arrival of the packets in this manner. While delayed data reception may be acceptable, it would not be tolerated if a voice link is affected by delays.

In contrast, ATM offers two basic benefits over the above two:

(*i*) stability of the connection-oriented networking; and

(*ii*) bandwidth on demand provided by the connection-less packet systems. It does not rely on the dedicated transmission path as well as connection-less links.

ATM is therefore a connection-oriented technique, which moves all the cells of data over the same route, earlier allotted to other users. The connections are based on virtual circuits. It can send as many or as few cells as demanded to transfer data.

Its features are:

1. It allocates bandwidth on demand instead a reserving capacity for each connection. It uses capacity according to a specific level of service with each virtual circuit. Current standards specify five service levels ranging from low-speed to constant-bit rate voice), high-speed, and bursty service (file transfer).

2. Unlike the connection-less packet network, which do not assign priority to critical data ATM can guarantee a high quality of service to critical data (voice or video), if demanded, in preference to other services such as e-mail. The user may be charged a higher rate for a guaranteed minimum bandwidth.

3. ATM is quite flexible, unlike the TDM technique, where each channel is given a fixed time-slot of the bandwidth. ATM is not tied down to any hierarchy of a digital network.

4. Access to bandwidth is dynamically provided as and when needed. Users need pay only for the cells of data they send and for the quality of service demanded.

5. ATM maximizes the use of communication channels, especially those which are idle most of the time. When we talk, only 40 per cent of the voice circuit is used. Even data often flow in one direction. Short, bursty transmissions are punctuated by lengthy silence. ATM is 'generous' in providing the entire communication channel when required, though it does not carry pauses.

By dividing long data messages (e.g. upto 64 Kilobytes) into short cells, ATM is capable of giving priority to voice or video traffic over data though the efficiency in data transfer is somewhat reduced.

Disadvantages: The 48-byte fixed length of an ATM cell is not fully occupied by voice channels (each sent at only 64 Kbits/sec, or less if compression techniques are used). ATM's utilization of the bandwidth is thus inefficient. ATM cannot alter the size of the bandwidth once allotted and the circuit is not fully used.

23.2 Global Telecommunications Links

The global trunk network links fixed points at national centers and provincial centers all over the world, carrying massive amounts of telephone, data and video channels and all the other kinds of telecommunication facilities that can be conveyed by such channels.

It is routed mainly by terrestrial and submarine cable (increasingly optical fibre) and terrestrial radio relay systems. As compared to satellite systems, these systems are very competitive in cost, for short distances. However, if the distance between link terminals is sometimes large, the satellite medium is used, the costs of which are little affected by distance, are lower than those of terrestrial media.

In the satellite systems, some of the transponders are leased for domestic networks but the larger part of the system provides facilities for an international network linking earth stations owned by national telecommunications operating organizations. The advantages of this global network are:

1. The total required capacity is very large and large numbers of national earth stations can access to it.

2. Most of the earth stations are able to communicate directly with many of the other earth stations having access.

3. The country to country links can be on big scale, some requiring only one circuit but others requiring thousands of circuits.

23.2.1 INTELSAT Global Telecommunication System

All current INTELSAT satellite series have transponders operating in both the 6GHz and 4GHz and the 14GHz and 111-12GHz bands. High gain spot beam dish antennas, steerable from the ground, are used for the transponders operating in the higher frequency band.

For the lower bands, some transponders used dual polar horn antennas covering the whole Earth visible from the satellite whilst other transponders use higher gain reconfigurable dual polar multifeed reflector antennas to cover smaller areas, the footprints being shaped to fit the geographical configuration of important service areas.

Both traveling wave tube and solid state power amplifiers are used with single carrier saturated output power rating up to 20 watts, and transponder bandwidths ranging between 36 MHz and 112 MHz.

Earth station antennas having access to INTELSAT satellite for the global network are required to have high performance, to ensure that bandwidth and satellite power can be used efficiently. Until recently the standard receiving Figure of Merit (G/T) was 40.7 dB/K at 4 GHz and 39 dB/K at 11 GHz, requiring antennas with primary reflectors about 32 metres and 17 metres in diameter respectively.

Most antennas now in service meet these requirements, but the minimum G/T requirements for new all purpose antenna has been reduced to 37 dB/K (1GHz) and 35 dB/K (11GHz).

Both time division and frequency division multiple methods are used in the INTELSAT global network for the transmission of narrow band channels which are designed priority telephony. The earth stations combine the telephone channels is transmits to many onto one or a few multiplexed carriers. A typical station, therefore, receives multiplex carriers from many other earth extracting.

The INTELSAT-TDMA systems operate at 120.832Mbits/sec, using 4-phase PSK modulation and colour modulation, with transponders of 72MHz bandwidth. Digital speech interpolation (DSI) is used to increase the capacity of the system for telephone traffic, Satellite switched TDMA is available with INTELSAT visual to enable up-beam or down-beam connectivity to be optimized.

However, most INTELSAT transponders are operated FDMA mode, with various modulation method. Multiplexed analogue systems use FM and FDM, arised basebands of various capacities, the structure baseband being related to the CCIR and CCITT standard analogue radio relay system basebands. The deviation level of the carriers are optimized to give channels which performance objectives with economical use of transponders and modulator allotments of bandwidth. Most digital system TDM and 4-phase PSK, with channels 8-bit encoded, single channel PSK systems are also used.

Another important function of the INTELSAT global to provide temporary, brief wideband links for the transmission news, in the form of television pictures, from the scene of all parts of the world, for re-broadcasting. A transponder for this purpose in each primary satellite deals with analogue video signals, which may contain a digilated signal, time division multiplexed.

The INTELSAT system is by far the biggest providered facilities for trunk telecommunications but the EUTELSAT provides digital international links with Europe.

23.2.2 Thin-route telecommunications

The terrestrial transmission media are costly when used to provide public telecommunications facilities over relatively short distance when the level of demand is low, especially where the intervening terrain is underdeveloped and rugged. Such facilities may be provided economically by satellites. They can also be used to build private telecommunication networks covering extensive geographical areas and requiring flexibility or non-standard facilities (such as high speed of application which is already important in some countries).

Number of large countries where high quality terrestrial facilities do not link all centers of population, networks have been set up to provide trunk connections provincial centers. Elsewhere, where the population is distributed over inaccessible terrain, amongst mountains, across archipelagos, satellites may provide reliable to isolated communities. The trunk network configuration will usually resemble the INTELSAT global network, although on a smaller scale, using FDMA and with analgue telephone channels in frequency division multiplexed basebands frequency modulating the radio carriers, or digital channels in time division multiplexes phase shift modulating the carriers. Networks serving isolated communities are likely to use voice switched carriers for single telephone channels, analogue or digital.

23.2.3 FAX

Fig. 23.8 shows a schematic of Fax system. A fax modem converts a documents into a low resolution digital bit mapped image by the

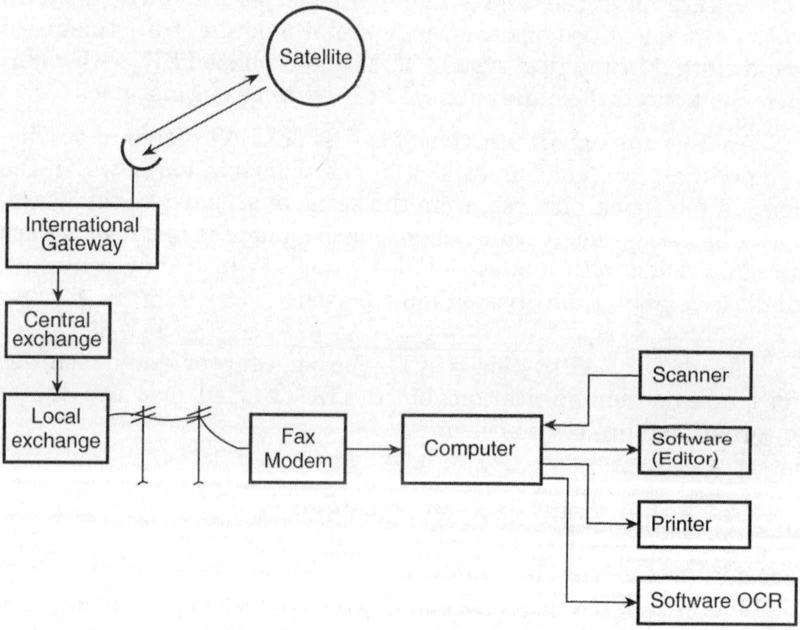

Fig. 23.8 Schematic of Fax System.

scanner and the edited by the computer using editor software. The digital stream is then transmitted over the phone line as an analog signal and sent to the exchanges from where it is sent to the destination. At the receiving end, the text is extracted from the fax image through processing by Optical Character Recognition (OCR) software. The OCR outputs either plain text or formatted text in a word processor format.

23.3 Mobile Telephony

Cellular technology has reached all walks of life, bringing communities and business closer than even before. Mobility is one of the major features of cellular communication systems. It implies that a cellular call, originating from anywhere, any time within the service area, would be able to maintain the same call without service interruption, while in motion.

Fig. 23.9 depicts today's wireless communication systems which are based on a composite wireless and wired system. Here the wireless segment of the communication system is shown as a cluster of seven hexagonal cells. This is a widely used cell plan, also known as the N=7 frequency plan in which all the available channels are evenly distributed among seven cells.

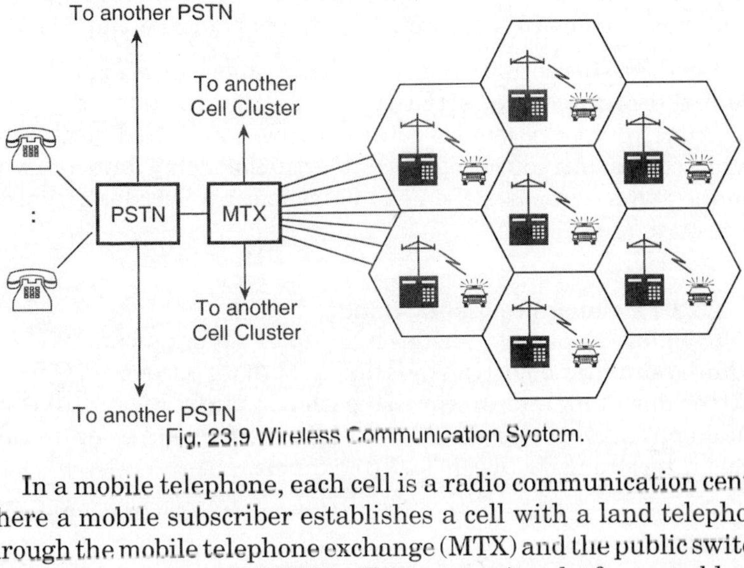

Fig. 23.9 Wireless Communication System.

In a mobile telephone, each cell is a radio communication centre where a mobile subscriber establishes a cell with a land telephone through the mobile telephone exchange (MTX) and the public switching telephone network (PSTN). This composite platform enables to communicate with anyone at any time from anywhere within the service area. Note that MTX and PSTN are essentially multiple access points serving as system intelligence.

A basic concept of a cellular system is to provide ever-increasing capacity by dividing cells into smaller and smaller sizes to increase frequency reuse. Unfortunately, the cell division concept has proven to be impractical in terms of finding suitable locations for base station antennas and for getting repeated construction authorisations from governing organizations. Two basic approaches have been pursued to accommodate the demand:

(*a*) expanding the channel capacity of existing systems; and

(*b*) allocating new frequency bands to cellular mobile phone service.

Currently, mobile systems utilise digital transmission in lieu of the analog FDM transmission used by analog cellular systems such as AMPS in North America, TACS in Great Britian, and NMT in Scandinavia.

Commercially viable digital cellular systems are enabled by the availability of low-cost digital signal processing technology to provide solutions to problems in several key areas: First, it is necessary to compress a digital speech signal into a low enough bit rate that digital voice transmission does not impose a spectrum penalty with respect to analog systems. Speech compression algorithms have advanced to the point that digitization can, in some cases, provide greater spectrum of dynamic multi-path transmission impairments.

Further, susceptibility of the speech compression algorithms to channel errors requires sophisticated error correction and control measures. Moreover, low-bit-rate voice coders and the digital system architectures introduce significant artificial delay into the voice channel, which imposes the need for echo cancellers for acceptable voice quality.

23.3.1 Cellular Frequency Bands

Cellular telephony provides full-duplex communications, which requires simultaneous transmission in both directions : (1) forward path or downlink and (2) reverse path or uplink. Fig. 23.10 shows cellular frequency allocation. A 45-MHz guardband is provided to avoid interference between Tx/Rx channels.

The frequency bands are further divided into several sub-bands. It is as follows:

1. Each band occupies 12.5 MHz, of which 10 MHz is Non-expanded Spectrum (NES) and 2.5 MHz is Expanded Spectrum (ES).

2. These bands are divided into several channels of 30 kHz each, and each channel is assigned to a subscriber. This arrangement

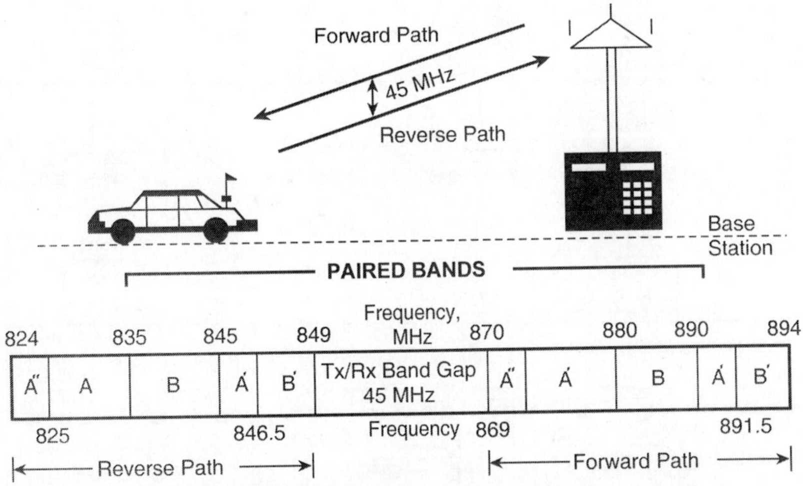

Fig. 23.10 Cellular Frequency Allocation.

provides 10 MHz/30 kHz - 333 channels per band in the NES and 2.5 MHz/30 kHz = 83 channels per band in the ES.

3. The total number of channels per band is therefore 333 + 83 = 416 in each band.

4. Among these, 21 channels are used as control channels, which are used for channel assignment, paging, messaging, etc.

5. The remaining 395 channels are used as voice channels for conversations.

The first-generation mobile system is AMPS, which is based on frequency-division multiple access (FDMA). In the 1990s, new communication standards came into effect, such as time-division multiple access (TDMA) and code-division multiple access (CDMA).

In the TDMA (IS-54) standard, each AMPS channel is time shared by six mobiles (see Fig. 23.11). When one mobile has access to the channel, the other two are idle. This is accomplished by a special frame structure. TDMA channel capacity is therefore 3x FDMA or 6 × FDMA.

23.3.2 CDMA Standard

It is based on the *spread-spectrum* (*SS*) *technique* in which multiple users have access to the same band. This is done by assigning a unique orthogonal code (Walsh code) to each user. The spreading is also accomplished by means of the same code. This code is generated from a pseudonise (PN) sequence whose chip rate

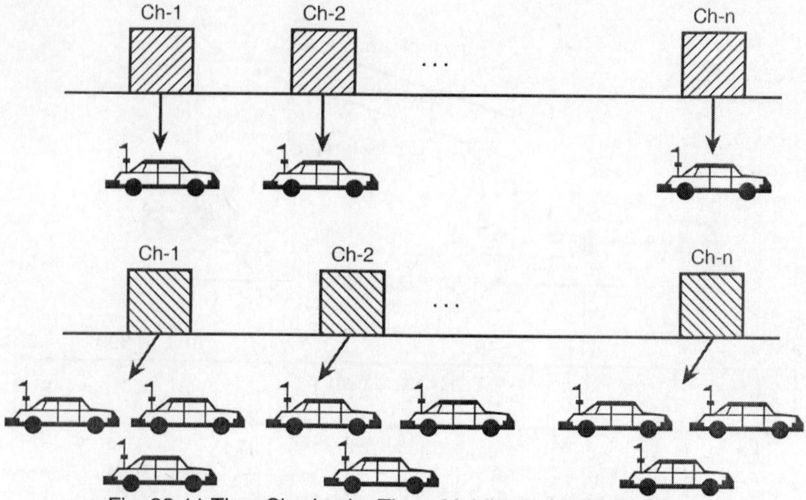

Fig. 23.11 Time Sharing by Three Mobiles in AMPS Channel.

(switching rate) is many times that of the input binary data. As shown in Fig. 24.12, the chip rate of the PN sequence is typically 1.25 MHz which derives 10 different frequency bands from the existing 12.5MHz cellular carrier (A or B). Each of these bands can support 64 Walsh codes.

23.3.3 CDMA Air-Link

It is based on a forward link and a reverse link, separated by 45 MHz (Fig. 23.13). The forward link consists of four different link protocols:

(*i*) pilot channel,
(*ii*) paging channel,
(*iii*) sync channel; and
(*iv*) traffic channel.

The reverse link consists of two different link protocols:

(*i*) an access channel; and
(*ii*) a traffic channel.

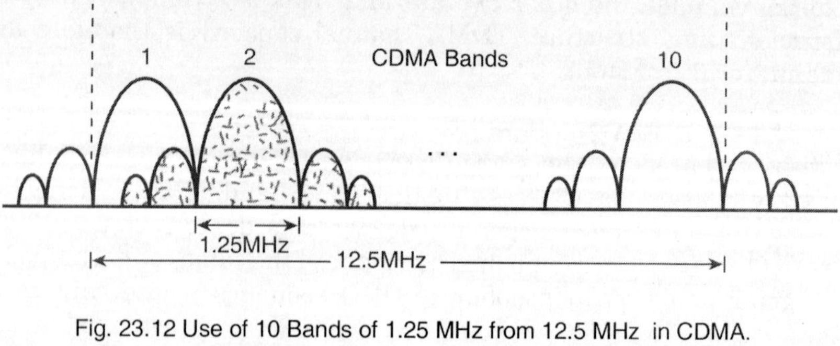

Fig. 23.12 Use of 10 Bands of 1.25 MHz from 12.5 MHz in CDMA.

In this link, six different bands are allocated for major trading areas (MTAs) and basic trading areas (BTAs). The MTAs are allocated a 15-MHz band and all BTAs are allocated 5-MHz bands for a total of 60-MHz bands. This is also a full-duplex system having a 20-MHz band gap. This band gap is allocated to unlicensed operators for voice and data at 10 MHz each.

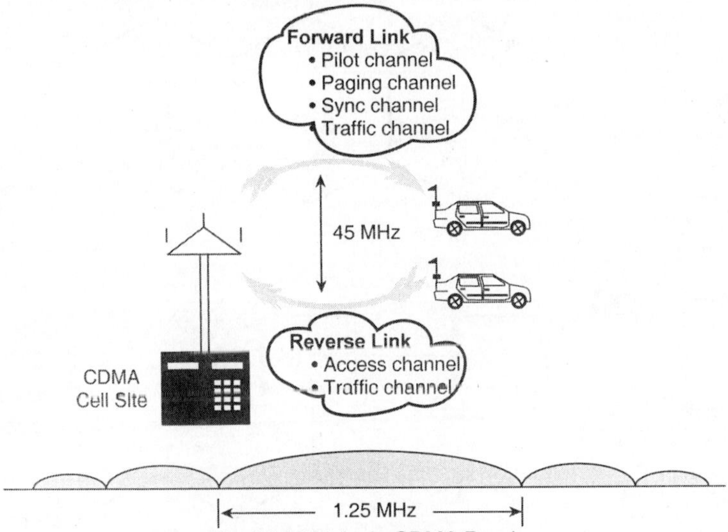

Fig. 23.13 Links in CDMA Band.

23.3.4 Features of Cellular Telephony

I. Mobility. This is achieved by the built-in hand-off mechanism, which is based on a process of changing the carrier frequency. As shown in Fig. 23.14, when a mobile moves into a new cell, a new frequency is assigned. This is done as follows:

A hand-off threshold is set in which if the received signal level is too low and it reaches a predefined threshold, the system controller called mobile switching centre (MTX), provides a stronger free channel (frequency) from an adjacent cell. This process continues from cell to cell as long as the mobile is in the coverage area, maintains the call, and is also in motion.

II. Capacity. Channel capacity in a mobile system expressed as the available voice channels per cell, translated into Erlangs. Assuming 10 square miles/cell in an area, a cluster of seven cells will be able to serve 7,350 subscribers/7,000 square miles in the NES and 9,660 subscribers/7,000 square miles in the ES.

III. Frequency Reuse. Since the number of channels is limited, these channel groups are reused at regular distance intervals. The

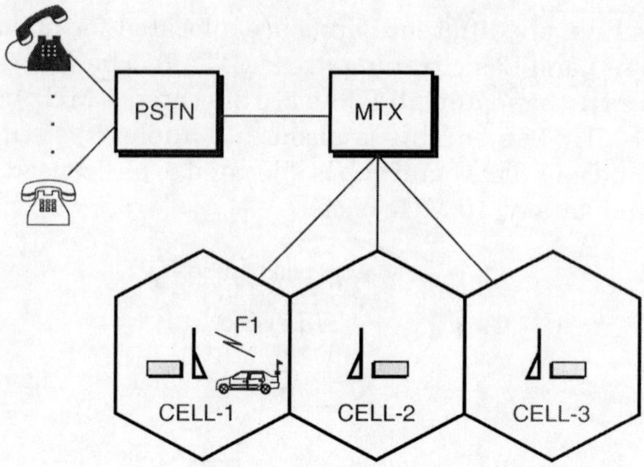

(a)

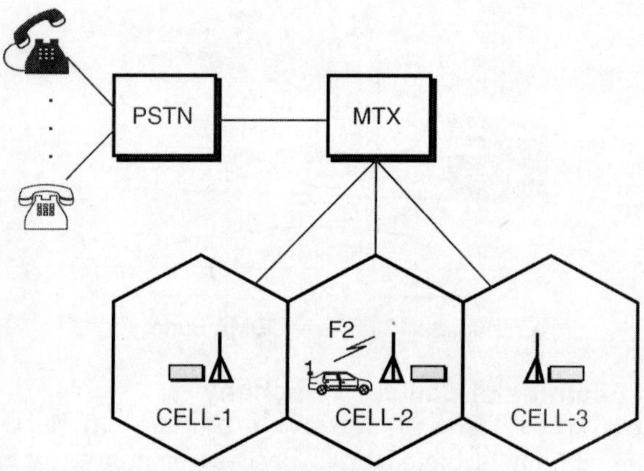

(b)

Fig. 23.14 Call Making.

mechanism that governs this process is called *frequency planning*. Several frequency planning techniques are available today.

***N* = 7 frequency plan :** This is the most widely used frequency planning technique. In this plan, all the available channels are divided into 21 frequency groups, numbered 1 to 21. These frequency groups are then evenly distributed among seven cells, three groups per cell. This group (cluster) of 7 cells is then reused along with the associated frequency groups A 7-cell cluster is further surrounded by 12 cluster (not shown). In this manner, a given service area can be covered by cluster of cells with frequency reuse, thus providing mobility and capacity.

Disadvantage: With subscriber growth, the existing frequency plans do not provide adequate service due to limitations which as cochannel interference and capacity.

Direction frequency reuse plan : This method enhances cellular performance and capacity. It provides an additional carrier-to-interference ratio (*C/I*), determined by the antenna front-to-back ratio. As shown in Fig. In this method, a group of channels is reused in the same direction in which the antenna is pointing, thus fully exploiting the antenna front-to-back ratio. Because a typical directional antenna has more than a 210 dB front-to-back ratio, a frequency can be reused more often as long as it repeats in the same direction, leading to enhanced AMPS-TDMA capacity.

IV. Roaming. A mobile moving out of its own territory and establishing a call from a foreign territory is known as a *roamer* and the process itself is known as *roaming*. Clearly, roaming enhances mobility.

There are many cellular operators within the same city, using different switches, radios, and cell site equipment. But a subscriber

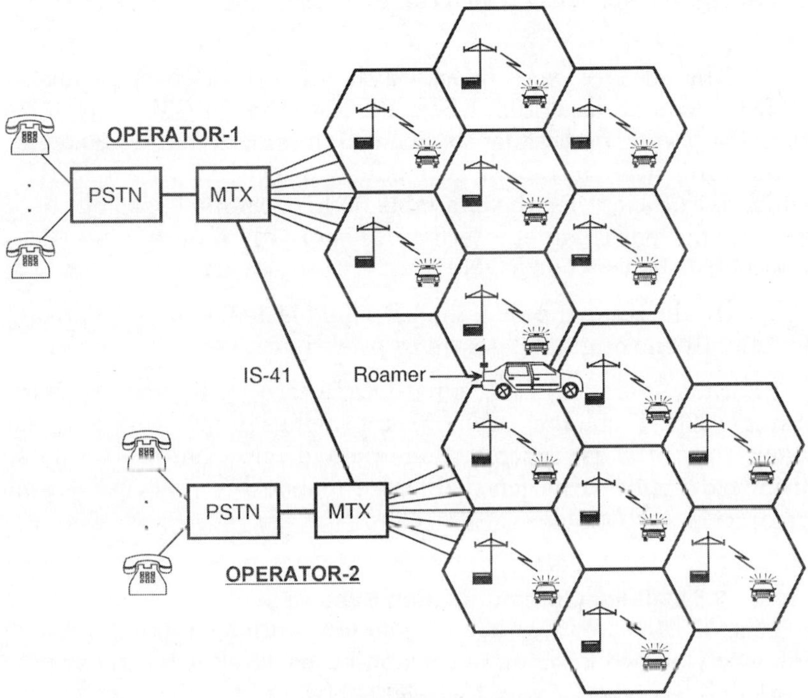

Fig. 23.15 Example of Roaming.

is registered to one operator only. As a result, an agreement between these operators is needed to provide services to any subscriber irrespective of a call's origin. This is accomplished by means of a separate link between various switches, which is established by the IS-41 link protocol (see Fig. 23.15).

V. Data Transmission: Cellular Digital Packet Data (CDPD). Data transmission over the analog cellular channel can be carried out by cellular digital packet data (CDPD). It is based on the existing cellular networks and uses an unused AMPS channel from a given frequency set in a cell site. Many services can be provided over the CDPD channel, including fax transmission, computer data transmission, stock exchange portfolio access, news wire service access, commodity price list access, travel information and many more services that current rely on e-mail.

The CDPD channel is composed of a forward CDPD (FOCDPD) channel and a reverse CDPD (RECDPD) channel over which data transmission takes place between the base station and the mobile. Its features are :

1. Data transmission is based on encoding 47 data bits into a (63, 47) Reed-Solomon code, which can correct as high as (63 - 47)/2 = 8 errors.

2. The encoded word (block) is then transmitted by means of GMSK modulation at 10.2 Kbits/sec. Note that in GMSK modulation, the power spectral density in such that more than 90% energy is retained within a transmission bandwidth of 19.2 x 1.2 = 23 kHz, which is sufficient for the available 30-kHz channel spacing. As a result, adjacent channel interference is greatly reduced and is expected to be lower than TDMA.

3. On the receiving side, the RF signal is demodulated, decoded and finally the original data are recovered.

Because it is a packet-oriented data service, multiple users share a single 30-kHz channel - a significant savings in spectrum usage as compared to the use of connection-oriented voice channels for data. Principal applications for CDPD are mobile Internet access and credit card verification.

23.3.5 Cellular Communication System

Fig. 23.16 shows a cellular communication system. It is an integrated network comprising a land-based wireline telephone network and a composite wired-wireless network.

The composite wires-wireless system is the basis of the cellular network. The heart of this system is also a *digital multiplex switch*, which has been derived from the PSTN used in line telephony by adding several functions required by the mobile phone system. It is called mobile switching center (MSC). The function of the MSC is to:

1. provide connectivity between PSTN and cellular base stations by means of trunks (T1 links);
2. facilitate communication between mobile to mobile, mobile to land, land to mobile, and MSC to PSTN networks;
3. manage, control, and monitor various call processing activities; and
4. keep detailed records of each call for billing.

Cellular base stations are located at different convenient locations within the service area. The coverage of a base station varies from less than a kilometer to then to kilometers, depending on the propagation environment and traffic density. For example, in a dense urban environment, typical cell radii would be less than a kilometer to a few kilometers (km), whereas in a flat rural environment, the cell radii would be tens of kilometers.

The mobile and portable units are generally known as *subscriber units*. The cell site (base station) includes the needed cell equipment, towers, and antennas, and the supporting base station's equipment.

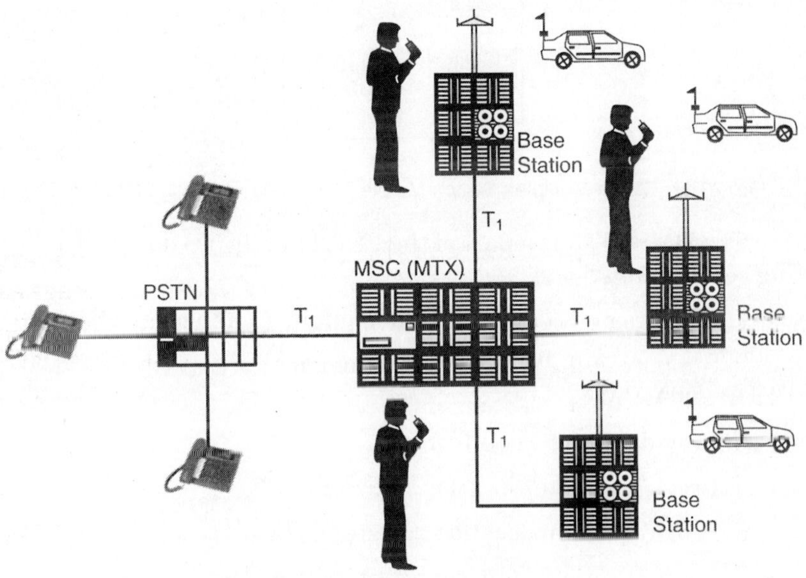

Fig. 23.16 Cellular Communication System.

23.3.6 Digital Multiplex Switch-Mobile Telephone Exchange (DMS-MTX)

Fig. 23.17 shows the digital multiplex switch-mobile telephone exchange (DMS-MTX), also called mobile telephone switching office (MTSO), mobile switching centre (MSC) (depending on the manufacturer) which supporting 800-MHz cellular communication systems.

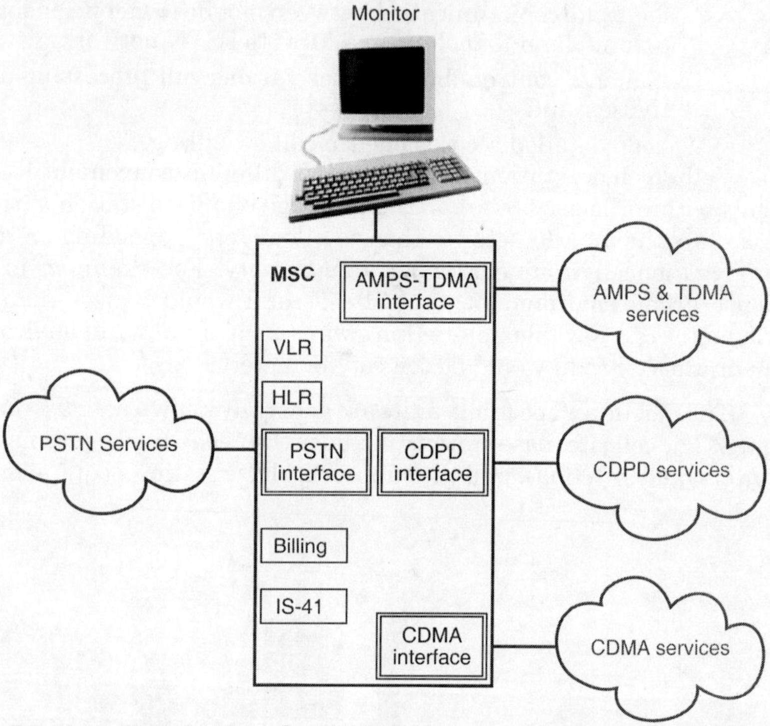

Fig. 23.17 Digital Multiplex Switch-Mobile Telephone Exchange (DMS-MTX).

The DMS-MTX is a part of the PSTN family provides the following cellular functions:

1. Manage and control cell site equipment and connections.

2. Support multiple-access technologies such as AMPS, TDMA, CPDP and CDMA.

3. Provide the PSTN interface.

4. Provide a visitor location register (VLR)

5. Provide a home location register (HLR).

6. Support intersystem connectivity (IS-41)

7. Support call processing functions.

8. Provide billing and operation and measurement (O&M).

9. Provide trunking facilities (T1 link) between the cell site and the DMS-MTX and between the DMS-MTX and the PSTN.

Each of these blocks is further divided into several unique functional elements, supporting the end-to-end communication protocol specified by several FCC and CCITT standards.

As mobiles call into MTSO,each message contains the mobile's ID, and the serving cell identification. Incorrect or incomplete message are rejected and recorded after the MTSO orders a designated voice channel setup. Where successful, the MTSO seizes a network trunk and outpulses the particular number. Cell site trunk and outgoing trunk are now switch-connected and a talking channel is established.

Messages on incoming trunk (a call to a mobile) are first collected as digits, analyzed and identified as being proper or improper for the called subscriber, then either processed as a ringing tone to the caller or routed as an invalid number to be intercepted. On valid numbers, the MTSO begins systemwide paging to the various paging cell sites to locate the mobile. If no response is forthcoming, even on the second try, the caller is automatically connected to a recording announcing failure.

23.3.7 Advanced Mobile Phone Service (AMPS)

This mobile system has been set up in the USA and has the following features:

1. There are two separate frequency bands, adjacent to each other. Each band provides 416 channel frequency pairs, having 30-kHz channel separation. Each frequency pair is isolated by 45 MHz, which permits duplex operation.

2. Out of 416 channels, 21 channels are designated control channels. Control channels are used for call setup. The remaining channels are used as voice channels. In a cellular base station, a single transceiver is used per channel.

3. Each voice channel pair supports a single conversation at a time. Four different types of signals are transmitted over the voice channel during the course of a cellular call: voice signals; supervisory audio tone; signaling tone; and data.

4. On the transmitting side, the voice signals are first compressed by a 2:1 syllabic compressor and then modulated by an FM modulator. On the receiving side, the incoming signal is demodulated and decompressed as 1:2 to recover the voice. This process improves the performance of FM transmission.

5. The supervisory audio tone (SAT) is transmitted over the forward voice channel (base to mobile) and retransmitted by the mobile back to the base. Its purpose is to indicate the continuity of the conversation. Loss of SAT indicates call completion and hand-off. Only three SAT frequencies are available (5970, 6000, and 6030 Hz). Each SAT is assigned to a cluster to cells in such a way that the same SAT is not used in a reused channel. SAT frequencies distinguish cochannel sites.

6. A 10-kHz signaling tone (ST) is transmitted by the mobile over the reverse voice channel to acknowledge certain commands received from the base station. This is similar to the supervisory signaling tone used in conventional telephone networks.

7. During hand-off, the voice channel momentarily becomes a digital channel and behaves like a control channel. A 10-Kbits/sec data transmission takes place between the base and the mobile for channel assignment and signaling. SAT and ST tones are muted during data transmission. Once the channel assignment is complete, regular conversation resumes. About 200 msec worth of voice is muted during this process, which is heard as a "clicking" noise during a conversation.

In this system, the control channel is composed of a forward control channel (FOCC) and a reverse control channel over which data transmission takes place between the base station and mobile at 10 Kbits/sec. Data transmission over the FOCC is based on encoding 28 control bits, (40 – 28) = 12 parity bits, and Hamming distance of 5, the number of errors that can be detected by means of this encoded word is (5 - 1)/2 = 2. The encoded word is then transmitted by means of FSK modulation with 1 8 kHz discrete level frequency deviations to represent 1 and 0. On the receiving side, the RF signal is demodulated and decoding; finally the original data are recovered.

RECC is the reverse control channel over which control data are transmitted from the mobile unit to the base station. This channel is also known as an *access channel* and is used by a mobile to access a land telephone or a mobile telephone.

Data transmission over the RECC is based on encoding 36 control bits into a (48, 36, 5) BCH code. This code has a word length of 48 bits, 36 control bits, (48 – 36) = 12 parity bits, and a Hamming distance of 5. The number of errors that can be detected by means of this encoded word is (5 – 1)/2 = 2. This means that if the decoded word encounters more than two errors due to noise, interference, and fading, an alarm will be generated and the word will be declared invalid, thus reducing the RECC capacity. Both FOCC and RECC channels are full duplex and operate in a coordinated manner.

Each cell also has located channel transceivers, as well as sectors that scan neighboring mobiles and measure the signal strengths. These signal strengths are reported to the MSC for hand-off, where hand-off is a process of changing the frequency. Its primary purpose is to assign a new frequency while a mobile moves into a new cells. This is accomplished by setting a hand-off threshold. That is, if the received signal level is too low and reaches a predefined threshold, the system controller, namely, the MSC, provides a stronger free channel (frequency) from an adjacent cell. Hand-off provides mobility, which means that a caller can move without interruption or call drop.

23.4 Global System for Mobile Communications

Global System for Mobile Communications (GSM) is a cellular mobile communications system that has been adopted worldwide as the international digital mobile standard. For this system, the International Telecommunication Union (ITU) allocated frequency spectrum at:

(*i*) 935-960 MHz for the downlink (base station to mobile); and

(*ii*) 890-915 MHz for the established analog systems.

GSM is a circuit-switched system, like most wireless networks. As already said, nowadays, packet-switching is favoured to provide high bandwidth and operate packet-based microcells instead of today's broad areas of wireless coverage, using high power. Microcells facilitate spectrum reuse and address the problem of spectrum shortage.

GSM Channel Structure: Its features are:

1. This uses 200-kHz-wide digital RF channels as opposed to the 30-kHz-wide D-AMPS RF channels.

2. Each GSM RF channel operates at 270-833 Mbps using GMSK modulation. GMSK modulation is fairly closely related to 4-PSK

modulation as used in D-AMPS. GMSK modulation does, however, require more bandwidth than tightly filtered 4-PSK.

3. The GMSK modulation format of GSM provides a constant-envelope RF signal that is more efficient for RF power generation than is tightly filtered 4-PSK modulation used by D-AMPS. This efficiency is most important for hand-held battery life.

4. GSM uses less speech compression than does D-AMPS, which leads to a higher rate digital channel for voice and in turn requires more transmit power).

Fig. 23.18 (a) shows TDMA format for GSM RF channel. It utilises digital TDMA with eight full-rate voice channels, in contrast to three full-rate voice channels supported by a single D-AMPS RF channel. The ability to terminate more TDMA channels on a single transceiver leads to more cost savings. The GSM system carries eight full-rate voice channel in 200 kHz of bandwidth, which amounts to 26 kHz per voice channel.

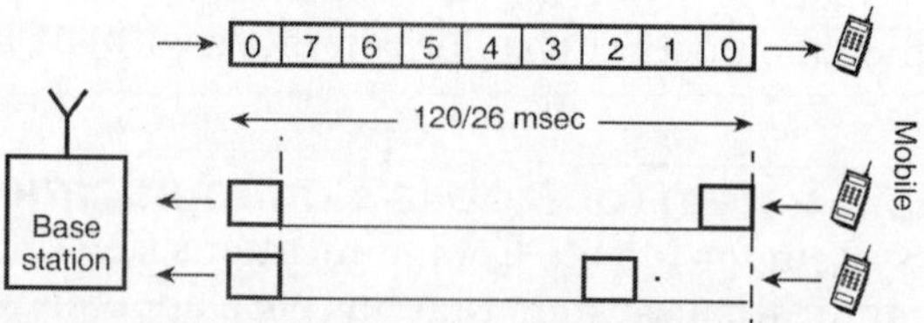

Fig. 23.18 TDMA Format for GSM RF Channel.

Advantages:

1. A GSM system provides cellular system efficiencies in that digital transmission, in general, and strong error correction, in particular, allow operation at lower signal-to-noise ratios.

2. Greater noise or interference tolerance leads to longer transmission distances and/or greater amounts of frequency reuse.

3. In GSM, in contrast with D-AMPS, a TDMA burst format is used in both directions of transmission, as opposed to only on the uplink from the mobile to the base station.

The burst period of a GSM system is 120/26/8 = 15/26 msec. This burst period is derived from 120-msec superframe consisting of 26 TDMA frames and 8 bursts per TDMA frame. Twenty-four frames of a 26-frame super frame are allocated to traffic (e.g., voice) transmission while one of the frames is allocated to a SACCH control channel for each traffic channel. The last TDMA frame of a superframe is reserved.

Fig. 23.18 (*b*) shows the format of these bursts. There are 148 bits of data and an idle guard time corresponding to the period of 8.25 bits. The burst transmission rate of a traffic channel can now be determined as 156.25/15/26 = 270.833 kbits/sec.

The use of multiple burst in the downlink direction, as opposed to continuous transmission, is advantageous in that it inherently allows turning off the base station transmitter during idle channels, which in turn reduces the total amount of interference between cells in a widespread and congested installation.

GSM Channel Coding and Modulation: GSM utilizes error control mechanisms as follows:

1. All 260 bits of a speech frame are divided into three classes: Class Ia, 50 bits - most sensitive to bit errors; Class Ib, 132 bits - moderately sensitive to bit errors; and Class II, 78 bits - least sensitive to bit errors

2. In Class Ia, a 3-bit CRC is added for error detection. If an error is detected, the frame is replaced by a slightly attenuated version of the previous correctly received frame.

3. The 50 Class Ia, 3 CRC, 132 Class Ib, and a 4-bit tail sequence (a total of 189 bits) are processed by a half-rate convolutional encoder for error correction.

4. The output of the convolutional encoder is added to the 78 Class II bits to produce an aggregate speech frame of 456 bits. Thus, the redundantly encoding speech rate is 456/0.020 = 22.8 kbits/sec.

5. To further protect against the burst errors, each sample is interleaved. The 456 bits of output by the convolutional encoder are divided into eight blocks of 57 bits, and these blocks are spread across eight consecutive time slot bursts. Since a time slot burst carries two 57-bit blocks, each burst contains traffic from two different speech samples.

GSM Mobile Station: The GSM mobile station (MS) consists of:

(*i*) Mobile equipment (the terminal); and

(*ii*) A smart card called the Subscriber Identity Module (SIM).

SIM: Its function is to provide personal mobility, so that the user can have access to subscribed services irrespective of a specific terminal. When a user inserts the SIM card into another GSM terminal, he is able to receive calls at the terminal, make calls from that terminal, and receive other subscribed services.

Mobile equipment: It is uniquely identified by the International Mobile Equipment Identity (IMEI). The SIM card contains the International Mobile Subscriber Identity (IMSI) used to identify the subscriber to the system, a secret key for authentication, and other information. The IMEI and the IMSI are independent, thereby allowing personal mobility. The SIM card may be protected against unauthorized use by a password or personal identity number.

GSM Network: A GSM network divides the service area into a number of cells, each of which is serviced by a base station. A switching center processes the calls (between GSM and the public-switched telephone network) and handles billing. Each cell is divided into several sectors, each of which is given radio frequency carriers. Each carrier has eight timeslots for voice/data, allowed on a TDMA basis. One carrier is reserved for paging mobile units. There is provision to track the location of the mobile units, check their identity and monitor and control the network.

GSM Frequency Hopping: The mobile station can move between a transmit, receive, and monitor time slot within one TDMA frame, all of which are normally on different frequencies. For this, it uses slow frequency hopping. In this, the mobile and BTS transmit each TDMA frame on a different carrier frequency. The frequency-hopping algorithm is broadcast on the broadcast control channel. Since multi-path fading is dependent on carrier frequency, slow frequency hopping helps alleviate the problem. Moreover, co-channel interference is more random than in fixed-frequency allocations.

GSM Short Message Service (SMS): This is a bi-directional messaging service that allows GSM cellular subscribers to send and receive data, Individual messages (with GSM) can be up to 160 bits in length. Because the SACCH is used for SMS data transmission, messages can be received or transmitted during a voice call. Initial applications of SMS focused on alphanumeric paging services with fundamental differences: SMS is bi-directional and message delivery is guaranteed. Subsequent applications served by SMS are voice mail notification, e-mail delivery, stock quotes, and downloading/updating of SIM cards.

23.4.1 Global Cellular System Using Code Division Multiple Access

GSM utilises a combinatory of frequency division multiplexing and time division multiplexing as a method of partitioning a block of allocated frequency spectrum into individual communication channels. Within a particular GSM cell, a single FDM channel supporting eight TDMA channels is sufficient for sufficiently low traffic situations. In this case, the particular cell utilizes only TDMA.

Code division multiple access (CDMA) allows sharing of time and frequency by the transmitters located near one another. This technique defines GSM channel in a different way. It is basically a spread spectrum communications system. In this, transmission bandwidth used by an individual channel is much wider than the inherent bandwidth required by the message being transmitted.

Two general categories of spread spectrum communications are:

(I) Frequency-hopping systems. In this system, transmission at any particular instant is confined to a relatively narrow band of frequencies commensurate with the inherent bandwidth of the message. Instead of staying within one particular band as a conventional communications system does, a frequency- hopping system jumps between narrow bands of frequencies within a large block of spectrum in some prescribed manner. As said earlier, a GSM cellular system has the ability to operate with frequency hopping (specifically, slow frequency hopping).

(II) Direct-sequence modulation systems: CDMA channel establishment. This method of implementing a direct-sequence spectrum spreading system is shown in Fig. 23.19. In this system:

1. The source data is first "exclusive ORed" with a relatively long digital codeword. The "exclusive OR" operation replaces a 1 of the source data with the given codeword while a 0 of the source data is replaced with the bit-wise complement of the codeword. If a codeword contains n bits, the occupied spectrum of the transmitted signal is n times as wide as if the source data were directly transmitted.

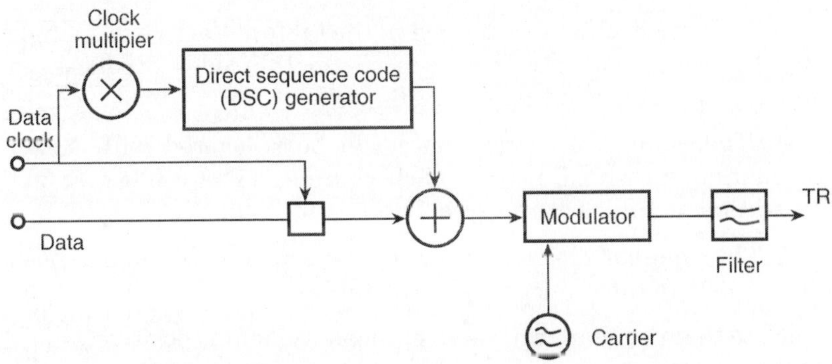

Fig. 23.19 Direct-sequence Spectrum Spreading System.

2. Signals of other CDMA channels occupy the same band of frequencies but do so with different spectrum-spreading codes, which allows separation of the signals in the signal processing circuitry of a receiver.

3. The separating of CDMA channels in a receiver is carried out by correlating a received signal with each of the various codewords (i.e., channels) assigned to the cell.

The correlation process results in a correlation measurement by subtracting the number of mismatches in a codeword from the number of matches. An example of set of codewords with net correlation is shown in Table 23.1.

Table 23.1 Example of Direct-Sequence Spectrum-Spreading Codes of desired channel : 1110010

Channel Number	*Channel Code*	*Number of Matches*	*Number of Mismatches*	*Net Correlation*
0	1110010	7	0	+7
1	0111001	3	4	–1
2	1011100	3	4	–1
3	0101110	3	4	–1
4	0010111	3	4	–1
5	1001011	3	4	–1
6	1100101	3	4	–1

1. A codeword has seven matches with itself and no mismatches for a net correlation of +7.

2. A source data value of 0 produces no matches and seven mismatches for a net correlation of –7. The measurement weights for all other codewords are either +1 or –1, depending on the values of the source data.

3. If all seven channels defined in the table are active in a single cell, the worst-case interference between the codes produces an interference value of either +6 or –6.

4. Therefore, the desired data can be recovered with a discrimination threshold of 0 for each channel. (The worst-case net measurement values are +1 or a 1 and –1 for a 0).

5. The same correlation properties also exist for all channel codes with respect to the other codes in the table.

Note that the channel 0 receiver measurement is positive, which implies a data value of 1. In this example interference from the adjacent channels actually enhanced the channel 0 measurement from an expected value of 7 to 9. Discriminating between nominal measurement values of +7 for a desired signal and +6 for worst-case interference is obviously very tenuous, particularly because the individual channels will be received with different power levels.

It is important to note that individual channels will be received with different power levels. However, that an interference value of +6 can arise only if the data values of all interfering channels destructively coincide. On average, the composite interference has an average value of 0. The length of a spectrum-spreading code in IS-95 is actually 64 bits long, which means that the example of worst-case interference would be 63 in relation to a desired channel value of 64. The chances of destructive interference from all 63 channels, or even a large number of channels, is astronomically small.

It has been found that an error rate is acceptable if the effective power level of all channels can be maintained to be equal. In fact, a CDMA deployment does not use all possible codes in a single cell, just as an FDM system does not use all frequencies in one cell. Thus, the amount of interference in a cell is limited by the number of codes assigned to the cell and a lesser amount of interference from adjacent cells (assuming the adjacent cells do not use identical, synchronous spectrum-spreading codes).

CDMA Multi-path Tolerance: A primary advantage of a CDMA transmission system is its robustness in the presence of multi-path conditions. The basic reason for multi-path tolerance can be appreciated by examining the example codes given in Table 23.1:

1. Each code is a cyclic shift of all other codes in the table.

2. Because the selected codes have low correlation with each other, a delayed version of an particular codes has the same low correlation with an undelayed version of itself.

3. Therefore, the effect of a multipath delay of more than one spread spectrum bit (referred to as a chip) is no more than the effect of the interference from another CDMA channel, even if the delayed version is at the same power level as the primary signal.

The slow frequency-hopping feature of GSM ameliorates the effect of a complete multi-path fade to a greater degree, but not as effectively as a CDMA system. In GSM there may be momentary dropouts, but they are not long enough to cause a dropped connection and do not require a handoff, even if a user dwells in a physical location where one particular frequency is totally lost. In essence, the frequency-hopping process of GSM is equivalent to repeated and automatic handoffs to different frequencies.

CDMA Power Control: Effective transmit power control of the mobile units in a CDMA system is an important requirement. This is because a mobile transmitter that is close to a base station receiver will dominate other mobiles in the same cell that are farther away. This is referred to as the near-far problem of CDMA. If the transmit power levels of all mobiles in a CDMA system are controlled to be no higher than absolutely necessary, the channels can be reused more often.

In FDM/TDMA systems, although power control is used, it is not possible to operate with bare minimum power levels because the system cannot respond fast enough to adjust the power levels for fast multi-path fades. A side benefit of using minimum power levels in a CDMA mobile is increased battery life.

The power levels of a mobile are controlled in two ways:

(*i*) **Open loop:** In the open-loop mode, a mobile can determine its transmit power level by measuring its received power level under the assumption that transmission losses are equal in both directions. This assumption is reasonable for a CDMA system but not for a FDM/TDMA system because the latter are much more susceptible to independent frequency-selective fading (multipath).

(*ii*) **Closed loop:** Closed-loop power control involves base station measures of mobile received power and adjustments to the mobile power levels with the control channel.

Table 23.2 lists the basic parameters of the IS-95 CDMA digital cellular system for the 800-MHz cellular band. The speech compression algorithm uses QCELP (Qualcomm code excited linear prediction).

Table 23.2: IS-95 CDMA Mobile Telephone System Parameters

Channel bandwidth	: 1.25 MHz
Voice-Coding Rate	: 9.6 kbits/sec (maximum)
Error control overhead	: 9.6 kbits/sec (downlink), 19.2 kbits/sec (uplink)
Aggregate channel rate	: 19.2 kbits/sec (downlink), 28.8 kbits/sec (uplink)
Code length	: 64 chips
Spread spectrum channel rate	: 1.2288 Mbits/sec
Modulation format	: QPSK (base to mobile), offset QPSK (mobile to base)

CDMA Soft Handoff: A unique feature of a CDMA system is the ability of a mobile to simultaneously receive from more than one source. Because each cell in a CDMA cellular network transmits in a common frequency, a common RF receiver inherently receives the spread spectrum signal from all adjacent base stations. Signals from multiple base stations can then be acquired with multiple baseband code correlators or by time sharing a single correlator with the separate codes.

In a soft handoff operation, the same voice signal is distributed to selected cells adjacent to a currently active cell. An active mobile can then compare the quality of the signals and switch to the best one before disconnecting from the established base station.

A "make-before-break" operation is not feasible in an FDM/TDMA system wherein adjacent cells utilize separate frequencies that require separate RF receivers. FDM/TDMA systems inherently use hard handoffs, which require disconnecting from one base station before connecting to a new one.

Disadvantage: A soft handoff operation in a CDMA system increases the background interference because of the multiple active signals for a single connection.

23.5 Use Of Leo And Meo Satellites in Telephony

While three satellites in the geosynchronous orbit are adequate for interlinking almost the entire world, failure of any one of them will degrade the system, unless spares are available readily. The geostationary earth orbit (GEO) satellites need a complex ground antenna system and their stability should be maintained very accurately. Furthermore, the GEO satellites suffer from low elevation angles of transmission in the high northern and southern latitudes (i.e. more than 60°).

The spectacular progress made in digital technology and satellite communication has made it possible to use narrow beams at well as light-weight hand-held terminals to establish a direct link with end users. A satellite-based communication system is emerging as a logical extension to the cellular telephones.

The low earth orbit (LEO) satellites, typically at 760-1,800 km (below 2,000 km) and the medium Earth orbit (MEO) generally at 10,000 km have been launched to provide mobile communication links, supplementing the services from GEO satellites (e.g. INTELSAT) at about 35,800 km above the equator. The signal power decreases with the square of the distance. If the orbit is down from

36,000—10,000 km, the strength of the signal goes up by 13 times for a hand-held phone.

If the orbit height of the satellite is lower than that of a GEO satellite, then the coverage is complete including the polar regions. The propagation delay of a signal is one hop, which is 250 msec (ms) for a GEO satellite, comes down to 70 msec and 10 msec for MEO and LEO satellites, respectively.

Technically, it is a LEO system but its satellites can go up to the higher MEO orbits at 7,846 km and descend to 520 km or stay at 8,040 km over the equator. The orbits allow coverage of densely populated areas.

The footprint of a satellite is divided into spot beams, which facilitate the reuse of frequencies. A geosynchronous satellite can serve upto 150 spot beams, while satellites in the middle Earth orbit (MEO) and low Earth orbit (LEO) serve typically 60 (maximum) and 20 spot beams, respectively. In lower orbits, several satellites and required to ensure continuity to service.

Table 23.3: LEO/MEO Satellites

Overview of Major Personal Mobile Satellite Systems

System name	*Iridium*	*Globalstar*	*ICO*	*Ellipso*	*Asian Cellular System*	*Thuraya*
Orbit type	LEO	MEO	MEO	LEO	GEO	GEO
Primary		(All provide voice, data, fax)				
		Worldwide		Asia-Pacific		Arab States Central Asia and East Europe
No. of satellites	66	48	10	14	1 + spare	1 plus spare
Orbit (km)	780	1,400	10,355	8,040 520-7,846 (ellipt.)	35,800	35,800

The lower orbits of LEO and MEO satellites demand a larger number of satellites to keep up the links. However, the number of spot beams needed for MEO (typically 60) and LEO (18 to 20) is less than that for GEO. The satellites can provide overlapping coverage and ensure a continuous service for an overview of major personal mobile satellite systems. However, sophisticated 'hand-off' techniques are involved as the calls are handed over from one cell to another, as the satellite moves on, unlike in a terrestrial cellular system where the mobile terminal moves from one cell to another.

23.5.1 Types of LEOs

Non-geostationary satellites are grouped into three main types:

(*a*) **Little LEOs:** These satellites provide low-speed text and data services and are comparable to paging systems. The word 'little' indicates both the small size of the satellite and the low cost of implementation. They are useful in a wide range of applications; limited Internet access, two-way paging, emergency services, tracking transportation, environmental monitoring, remote monitoring, weather monitoring, educational information, and medical advice to remote areas. Little LEOs do not replace existing services but enhance them.

(*b*) **Big LEOs:** These are equivalent of cellular telephone service and offer global voice, facsimile and possibly broadband services, and computer (Internet) networking which may be offered by optical fibres in many countries.

(*c*) **Broadband LEOs**: There are similar to fibre-optic networks.

The applications are grouped into three categories, based on bandwidth requirements.

1. Narrowband (upto 64 Kbits/sec) for voice transmission, e-mail, facsimile, etc.

2. Wideband (from 64 Kbits/sec to 1.544/2.048 Mbit/sec) for voice/data networking, e-mail, business, TV, etc.

3. Broadband (above 1.544/2.048 Mbits/sec) for voice/data turnking; high-definition TV, etc.

The Ka-band provides four to seven times the spectrum used by C-band satellite operators. Ka-band satellites contribute to the convergence of telecommunications, computing and broadcast technologies. Generally, Ka band satellites are associated with onboard processing and switching offering two-way services to and from small Earth stations like satellite TV dishes. The users can avail themselves of a wide variety of services ranging from narrowband to broadband applications.

The satellite system is expected to be a cheaper alternative to the world's telephone infrastructure, providing high-speed Internet access, tele-education and telemedicine, TV services to aircraft, rural telephony, etc.

A Ka-band satellite uses a large number of 'pencil' spot beams, each covering very small area with high radiated power, thereby allowing frequency reuse as in a cellular phone system. Each transmission path between different spot beams is processed and switched by the satellite's onboard processor. The terminals, each with a diameter of 66 cm, will be capable of tracking the satellites and handing over the links every few minutes because of the large number of small spot beams.

We now describe important LEO sytems.

Globalstar. Globalstar inaugurated its commercial satellite telephone service in October 1999. Its features are:

1. It is a low Earth orbit satellite system with 52 satellites, including four spares aimed at the populous regions of the earth. The Globalstar orbital planes are therefore inclined at 50° to the equator, thus ignoring the sparsely populated high-latitude regions.

2. The satellites are simpler in design than some others. The satellite functions as a 'bent pipe' transponder. The satellites go in circular orbits at 1,414 km altitude and concentrate on the areas between 70° North and South latitudes.

3. There is neither onboard processing nor inter-satellite links. All processing and switching are done by ground stations each with three or four antennas, track and work with the satellites. The signals received at the satellite are simply transponded down and the 78 gateway earth stations process the signals for the onward routing. Like Ellipso, service over water is restricted to coastal regions where the satellite is within radio range of a gateway earth station.

4. A call can be pushed through at least two of the satellites. Signals from three or four satellites are combined and the stronger signal can be selected for reception using CDMA. If the TDMA technique is used, them signals from more than one satellite cannot be combined.

Fig. 23.20 shows the operation of the system. Assume that User A is in a different instantaneous coverage region than that occupied by user B. The signal from User A is picked up by the gateway earth station and relayed to the gateway earth station of User B. The signal is then sent up to the satellite from the second gateway earth station and then down to User B. If User A or User B is using a fixed telephone (or computer) the signal would simply pass over the regular PSTN circuits and not via the space segment. Because the users must be in line-of-sight contact with a gateway earth station, no maritime traffic can be picked unless the ship is close to land (and a gateway earth stations).

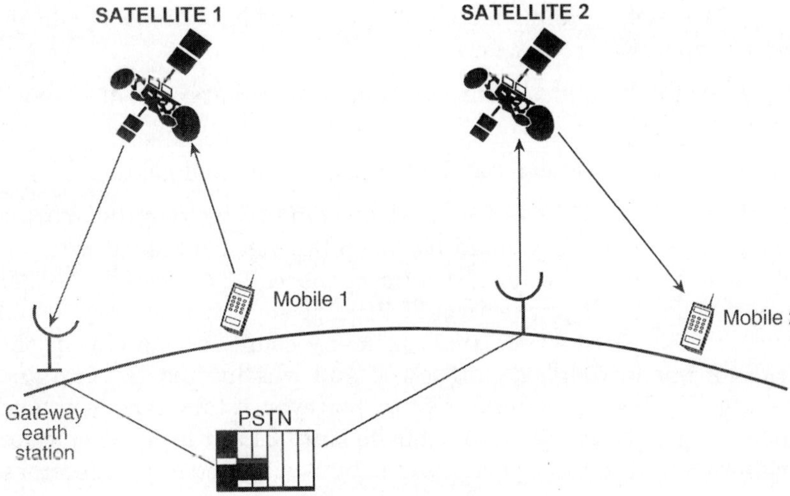

Fig. 23.20 Operation of Globalstar.

Iridium. This system, which became operational in 1998, facilitates communication from anywhere to anywhere in the world, even where there is no telecommunications infrastructure from low power handset. Its features are:

1. It consists of 72 polar orbitating LEO satellites at 780 km above the Earth and are linked via ISLs.

2. Each of the satellites in the constellation acts as a switching mode. Uplink signals are received and demodulated at the satellite using onboard processing to recover individual data packets at baseband so that the header information can be read.

3. This information and links to the network control stations are used to find out the next mode for each packet and the packet is reformatted with the next address.

4. The baseband data packet is now processed and up-converted for transmission either to the ground at L-band directly to another Iridium user or at 20 GHz to a gateway earth station, or over one of the four ISL links (at 23 GHz) to the next satellite in the chain.

5. Onboard processing carries out the entire message routing and formatting functions.

6. Each satellite can process 1,100 simultaneous calls and can directly link with hand-held, pocket-size satellite phones. The global coverage through 48 spot beams includes the higher latitudes and polar areas.

7. The solar panels have gallium arsenide (instead of silicon) which provide more power.

8. On the ground, the three antennas of the gateways are located about 48 km apart, so that they can avoid rain showers.

9. The satellites can handle voice, data, fax and paging.

Iridium has lost its commercial viability by reduced market demand. It eventually could not keep the venture afloat. When it planned the service in 1987, Iridium sponsors did not anticipate that ground-based cell phones would develop so well that they would cover the majority of locations in many countries. Moreover, the Iridium phone weighed half a kilo and was limited to voice and paging. The Iridium satellites were, however, retained in orbit, and their services have been re-established in 2001 by the newly founded Iridium Satellite LLC, partly owned by Boeing and other investors.

Table 23.3: Iridium System Parameters

Number of satellites	: 66
Satellite orbit	: 485 miles (780 km)
Orbit period	: 100 min
Transmission protocol	: QPSK
RF modulation	: 2.4 kbits/sec
Speech data rate	: 1.6 MHz handheld to satellite
Radio frequency	: 23 GHz satellite to satellite, 19 GHz uplink to satellite, 29 GHz downlink from satellite

Skybridge. Skybridge evolved a similar approach to coverage as Globalstar, by selecting an inclined orbit that covers the major population densities. Like Flobalstar, Skybridge satellites carry a nonprocessing payload and do not have intersatellite links; so all traffic is transponded down to the gateway earth stations for processing and onward routing. However, Skybridge satellites are intended to carry wideband traffic and therefore use frequencies above 10 GHz. They chose to employ the same Ku-band frequencies as the FSS service in GEO uses: 12.75 - 14.5 GHz on the uplink 10-7-12.75 GHz on the downlink. To allow successful coordination with existing GSS GEO systems, they elected to prevent any operations (up or down) whenever a satellite look angle is within 10° of the GEO orbital plane. This requirement led to a relatively large number of satellites (80 vs 48) for the constellation. The decision not to use ISLs also required a very large number of gateway earth stations (on the order of 200). Skybridge also uses the concept of a fixed earth cell (Fig. 23.21).

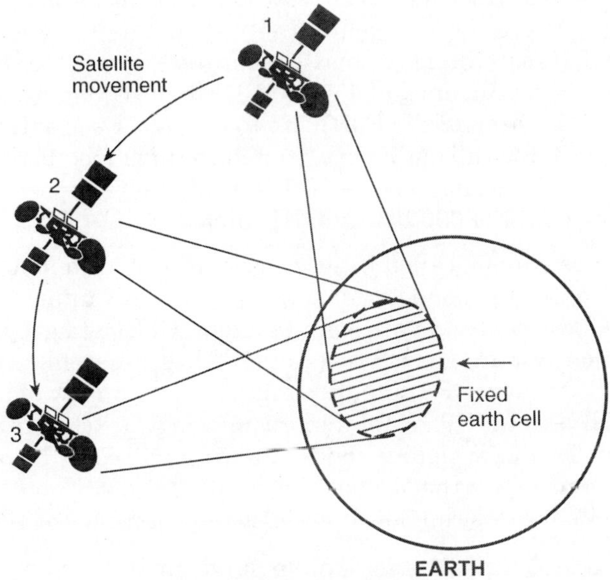

Fig. 23.21 Skybridge.

New ICO. ICO Global is the company that was spun off from the International Maritime Satellite Organization (Inmarsat). Inmarsat was initially set up solely for the purpose of providing reliable communications to maritime traffic. Later, Inmarsat also provided aeronautical services, in addition to priority links for safety communications, whether on land or sea. New ICO, although primarily aimed at the LMS market (Land Mobile Services), also needed to provide capacity for maritime links.

New ICO elected not to include ISLs in their system architecture nor any significant onboard processing. Since a LEO constellation would not provide maritime coverage without ISLs, a higher orbit was necessary. If little onboard processing is used, traffic routing from mobile to mobile would have to be carried out at the gateway earth stations (as it is for Ellipso and Globalstar) necessitating a double-hop link. A double-hop link involves two uplinks and two downlinks. A double-hop configuration is not feasible for a GEO constellation since the overall delay would be completely unacceptable at about 1 sec. New ICO therefore adopted a MEO constellation. An inclination of 45° is used, but since the orbit altitude is so high, full global coverage is possible. Since 2000, New ICO has modified the payload and service offered to provide two-way Internet-like connections in a joint venture with Teledesic.

The ICO service will also be restructured to focus on global data transmission and Internet connectivity so that it does not face lack of demand. Its satellites (10 plus two spare) are to be placed at 10,355 km in two planes inclined at 45° and 135° to the equator and twelve satellite nodes around the Earth are to be built. Each satellite now can handle 4,500 calls at a time, routed through mobiles or PSTN. The array on board has a state-of-the-art digital processor, with the computing power of 600 Pentium III chips.

Another system, called Ellipso, seeks to provide a mobile satellite service. Mobile phones will soon bring the advantages of satellite-based geographical positioning system (GPS) and geographical information system. The US Navstar GPS has 24 satellites in Earth orbit. As least four GPS satellites must be within view of a ground user. Each Navstar GPS satellite transmits in two exclusive frequency bands. Two new signals for civilian use will soon be added to improve accuracy in the located of non-military users - within 10 m or so. Civilian users can now have a location accuracy of 100 m.

23.5.2 GEO Satellites for Mobile Services

Hand-held phones can work with satellites in the geostationary orbit also. The Asia cellular satellite (ACS) system is designed to cover a large region from India to Indonesia and Australia. The satellite has onboard processor and unfurlable antenna. The satellite located at 118°E over Borneo, can form a maximum of 150 spot beams in its coverage area. The ACS will link not only with hand-held devices but also with mobile and fixed terminals.

Another regional GEO satellite proposed is Thuraya, which is designed to connect 58 countries from West Asia to the Indian subcontinent. Positioned at 44°E over the Indian Ocean, its target users are those not covered by cellular or fixed phone service. The satellite is designed to operate through a single primary gateway that controls and allocates power and bandwidth for the spot beams.

23.5.3 Satellite Telephone Network

Satellite telephony networks employ point-to-point duplex satellite links enabling simultaneous communication in both in directions. Single GEO satellites or a constellation of LEO, MEO and GEO satellite are used for providing telephony services. Telephone satellite links generally employ circuit-switched services offering constant bit rate service but only for the limited duration of the call. But sometimes dedicated or pre-assigned bandwidth services are used, in which the communication is maintained continuously for an extended period of time, for heavy telephone trucking applications.

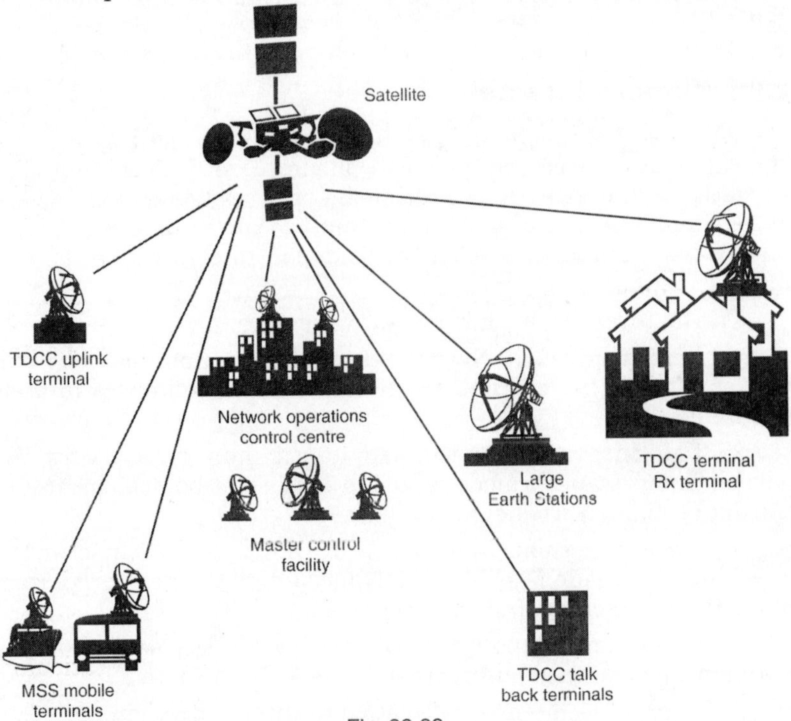

Fig. 23.22.

Fig. 23.22 shows a variety of satellite point-to-point telephone networks, in this the call is made as follows :

1. The user lifts the receiver when he wants to make to call. This sends a request to the local earth station, which in turn sends a service request to the master station.

2. If the master station is able to provide the satellite capacity it sends a confirmation signal to the local earth station resulting in a dial tone in the telephone instrument.

3. The user then dials the destination number, which are transferred to the control station, which determines the destination earth station and signals it that a connection is to be established.

4. The destination earth station then signals the called party of the incoming call by ringing of that telephone instrument.

5. Satellite capacity is allocated to the connection and the telephone link is established once the called party lifts the handset.

6. Once, the conversation is over, the calling party hangs up the receiver, hence indicating to the local earth station to terminate the call.

23.6 Wireless Internet

Web-enabled mobile devices have been introduced by which a Website can be accessed on a cell phone to get information. The wireless system delivering multimedia services (voice, data, video, etc.) to a global base of mobile terminals locate roaming terminals and transfer the call, if need be, from cell to cell (called handoff management).

The features of such a wireless system are:

1. Users are given a universal personal telecommunication number, as against the current practice of allotting numbers to their terminals.

2. The Internet service provider sends data using the asynchronous transfer mode switch to a base station, which encodes the data into high-frequency radio waves.

3. The use of same frequency with multiple antennas at the receive-end is made possible by advanced digital signal processors and gallium arsenide integrated circuits.

4. In another technology developed in the US 'self-adjusting' antennas look on to moving targets.

5. The network has a home location register and a visitor location register. As a mobile terminal enters an area outside its location, the information on the moving terminal is downloaded to the visitor location. In low-Earth orbit satellite systems, polling signals are broadcast to all cells within its area of coverage and the exact location of the terminals is recorded.

High-speed packet switching on wireless with speeds upto 2 Mbits/sec have now been introduced to function with the third generation (3G) wireless systems. The data traffic will flow direct to packet-switched networks (Internet/internet).

23.6.1 Wireless Application Protocol (WAP)

This is a set of communication protocols adopted to standardise the way hand-held wireless devices access e-mail or the Web. WAP supports most wireless technologies (GSM, TDMA and CDMA). It also works with operating systems designed for hand-held devices. WAP is designed for applications including wireless, e-commerce, on-line banking and information access.

The facilities include interactive news, data retrieval and online services. The mobile multimedia mode (WWW:MMM) initiative by three leading communications companies has simplified the identification of Internet sites and smart phones that can be connected by the mobile wireless terminal.

The concept of WAP is the equivalent of the hypertext mark-up language (HTML) used for writing Web pages. In this way, HTML serves as a common basic language that can be understood by any computer. WAP-enabled phones and other hand-held wireless devices permit interaction across different infrastructures.

The WAP is specified by the WAP-Forum. It was founded in December 1997 by Nokia, Ericsson, Motorola and Phone.com. Today, the WAP-Forum has more than 100 companies as members and associate members. Version 1.0 of WAP was published by the WAP-Forum in 1998. In 1999 Version 1.1 was presented and in November 1999 Version 1.2.

Fig. 23.22A shows a schematic of the WAP architecture. It is very similar to the WWW architecture. The WWW model specifies a client-server architecture. The client requests information from a server that answers with a response. Normally no other entity is involved in the communication path.

The WAP model also specifies also a client-server architecture but with an additional gateway in the communication path between client and server. Between the client and the gateway encoded communication by means of the WAP protocol stack is accomplished.

The gateway now translates requests from the WAP stack to the WWW protocol stack and sends it further on to the origin server. On the way back from the origin server to the client, the gateway also encodes the content into compact format suitable for communication over low-capacity (wireless) links. Gateway and origin server may reside physically in the same entity (that is computer).

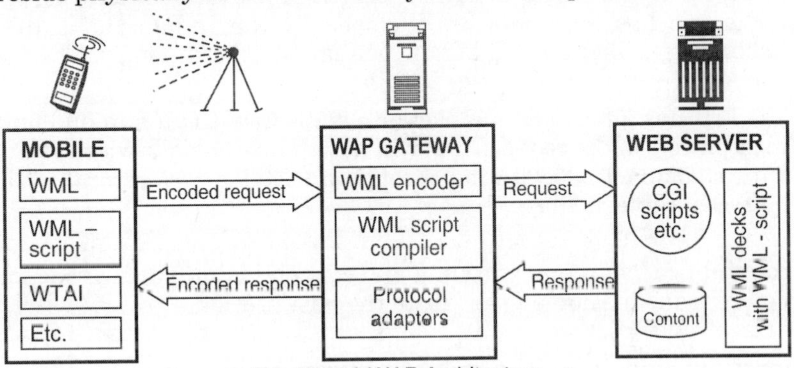

Fig. 23.22A WAP Architecture.

In WAP, a set of standard components are defined which include a naming model, content typing, standard content formats and standard communication protocols. A micro browser in the wireless terminal co-ordinates the user interface and is similar to a standard web browser.

23.6.2 Wireless Local Loop

Wireless local loop (WLL), refer to the use of wireless technologies in the local loop between a subscriber and a based station instead of copper wire to access the public switched network. Since a part of the link (between the exchange and a base station) is wired, the technology is better termed wireless in local loop (WILL) and not WLL.

In one technique, called micro-cellular approach, the area to be served is divided into cells. Different methods (e.g. FDMA, TDMA and CDMA) are used to increase the use of given bandwidths. It has been found that a reduction in the size of the cells would result in better reuse of the frequency. If the cell radius is reduced, then the bandwidth required would also be reduced. The base station of each cell has a wireless link with the subscriber's telephone or wall sets. The base station, placed on roof-tops or posts is typically located every 250 m. The base station and the public switch in the exchange may be linked by copper wire or by optical fibre.

Instead of increasing the number of exchanges, remote line units and remote switching units may also be set up. The units reduce the local loop's length and concentrate the traffic, thereby minimizing the channels required between them and the exchange. Moreover, frequencies are reused and allotted when required.

23.6.3 Wireless Access to the Internet and Phone

The digital enhanced cordless telecommunications (DECT) a standard proposed by the European Telecommunications Standards Institute, is a variation of the cellular system. It defines the wireless interface to the user. Known as CorDECT wireless in local loop, a technique has been jointly developed by the Indian Institute of Technology, Chennai, and five Chennai-based companies. The features of the system are (Fig. 23.23):

1. It has a portable handset or a wallset, with an antenna built in or placed on the roof-top and will have a line-of-sight wireless link with a compact base station through a DECT interface unit (DIU) by radio, cable or fibre.

2. The wallset can be linked to a fax or modem or computer. Voice communication requires coding and conversion into digital packets before transmission on the air to the base station.

3. Apart from the wireless link, the wallset is connected to the existing land line. The subscriber can simultaneously use the telephone and the Internet, though the speed of the phone link comes down to 35 Kbits/sec, when both channels are used. If only the Internet is used, the speed is 70 Kbits/sec.

4. One base station can serve 1,000 subscribers with 120 channels. The system can handle a million subscribers in a city using dynamic channel selection.

5. A handset can set up a call on any of the channels, choosing the best available. Each subscriber will have a dedicated channel. In the wireless link, data are compressed and set as codes. The base stations transmit a 'beacon' signal even if no calls are in progress.

In rural areas, the CorDECT system consists of a two-hop link, one from the wallset to a relay base station which is connected to a compact base station which is connected to a compact base station (both mounted on towers) some 25 km away.

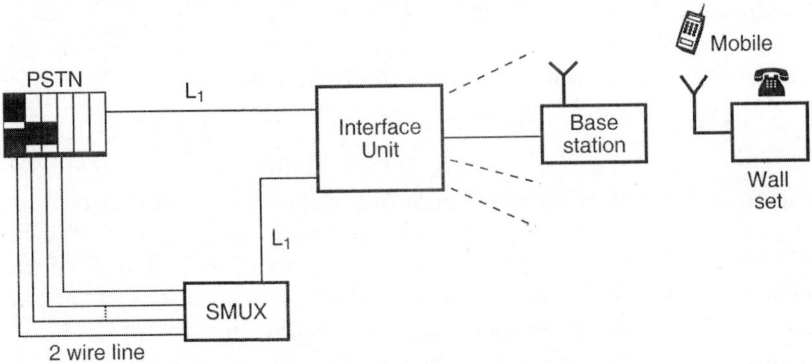

Fig. 23.23 Cordet WLL System.

Advantages:

1. The existing copper network can send data at a maximum speed of 9.6 Kbits/sec only. In WLL, the data speed can increase to 35 Kbits/sec or more to get the benefits of the Internet database.

2. No frequency planning is required.

3. It offers interference-free communication and good voice quality

4. It leads to efficient working with the country's cellular technology

5. It requires lower investment.

23.6.4 CDMA-based WLL

DECT has emerged from cordless telephones and is used in micro-cellular applications. Another technology called CDMA-based WLL, is based on cellular telephony with applications in macro-cells. In this technique, CDMA is used whereby multiple transmitters occupy the same frequency and time space. The features of the system are:

1. Transmitted data are spread over the space and each all is assigned a unique sequence code.

2. The data rate of 32 Kbits/sec claimed for the DECT technology is not really necessary for carrying voice because the actual information content of the human voice is very low and sophisticated coding techniques can support it at a lower data rate.

3. A mix of data rates is possible in a packet format in line with the varying requirements instead of a fixed data rate of 32 Kbits/sec.

4. CDMA-based WLL (IS-95 standard) achieves maximum efficiency in using frequencies through a common frequency (as in CDMA), signal processing and power control. Using CDMA, one can derive 80-90 per cent of the theoretical limit predicted by Shannon as against 5-10 per cent in other systems.

Several leading companies have made equipment based on CDMA technology and it is used in many countries.

23.6.5 GPS Links with Mobile Phones and Internet

Geographical maps, updated from satellite data are integrated and analysed in the light of other data such as traffic updates in what is known as the geographical information system (GIS). It is a computer-based, map-oriented data display combining physical data with social and economic data. The display of locations, maps of areas and related information can now possible because of the links of mobile phones with the Internet. And the information can be downloaded from the Internet by mobile cellular phones.

In CDMA-GPS networks, several base stations are in contact with a cell phone as it approaches its own base station's border, until the strongest signal is available. The base stations are distinguished and synchronized by very accurate timing (within 10 msec). GPS provides position coordinates as well as a time reference. Ideally every cell phone base station should have a GPS receiver. Soon, GPS is likely to be installed in every cell phone itself.

Satellite-based navigator assistance for vehicles on roads is already available in some cities in the US and Japan. The receiver signals a satellite in the GPS (geographical positioning system), covering the world to accurately download its location on the ground. A voice-assisted device can then guide the driver to the desired destination. Mobile phone-linked GIS and GPS are know exactly where they are and have a reliable and accurate guide to where they desire to go. This technology has numerous applications: from pizza-delivery to emergency medical attention. The Russians also operate a similar satellite system, called Glonass, while the Europeans are planning their own system, called Galileo. Several companies in India use satellite maps and develop value-added products based on GIS. Soon GPS will become as common as a wristwatch.

23.6.6 General packet-switching radio services (GPRS)

This technology offers a low-cost access to the Internet. It will be linked to the GSM, which has already been adopted in India. Existing GSM networks can be upgraded in a cost-effective manner. Mobile wireless phone operators around the world have decided to market GPRS phones. The technique will facilitate access to the Internet. Several applications of GPRS are: e-mail, e-commerce, file transfer and weather/sports/stocks/travel updates. GPRS is making the Internet mobile, just as GSM has made voice mobile.

The features of the GPRS are:

1. GPRS provides wireless packet-data communication. Unlike the current GSM technique which is based on circuit-switched mode, GPRS works on a packet-switched basis.

2. GPRS enables users to share circuits, unlike GSM. Though the mobile phone is always connected to the network, the channel is provided only when there are data to be transmitted.

3. Users need to pay for the amount of data and not for the connection time. The call set-up time is very much shorter than in GSM. GPRS can transmit at a higher speed (21.4 Kbit/s as against 9.6 Kbit/s in GSM). GPRS is well suited for random bursts of data.

4. GPRS can also be connected to telephone lines, intranet and local area networks.

5. A widely used data service is called the short message service. There is provision for increasing the data throughout with a decreasing level of protection.

6. It is possible to charge for the usage by volume rather than for the time used.

7. As it allows more users of the same frequencies, a ten-fold increase in the number of users is possible. Data transmission can also go up to 115 Kbits/sec (against 14.4 Kbits/sec currently offered) in view of the 'bursty' nature of the use punctuated by long periods of silence. Mobile devices can send large files in no time as it is always connected and always online, so that data are sent and received instantaneously.

23.6.7 Handy-21: Combination of Cellular, Wireless Internet, Digital Radio, TV and Pager

This system developed by M.I.T. Laboratory consists of a powerful hand-held computer that combines the functions of a cellular phone, a wireless link to the Internet, a radio, a TV and a pager. Various functions can be selected by changing the software. It has an antenna to transmit and receive signals, which are handled by a general-purpose microprocessor. A number of new features are being introduced, for instance, if a mobile unit experiences high data transmission, Handy-21 may transfer the link to a dedicated, more powerful link.

23.6.8 Internet Telephony

Although the Internet is based on the link with the telephone system, the telephone is now set to become an inexpensive add-on to the Internet. This technology is based on packet switching in which as we know, the analogue signal of the caller's voice is digitized, formed into digital packets, time-stamped and transmitted in a compressed format, to be decoded and converted back to analogue form at the other end.

Packet switching in the Internet employs out-of-band signaling which enables the separation and processing of signaling information. The service will have general-purpose computing facilities without the need of the switching system.

23.6.9 Universal Mobile Telephone System (UMTS)

While the second generation of mobile phones solved some of the problems encountered in the first, the third generation devices (abbreviated as 3G and 3Gt) are designed to offer a whole range of new services, such as Web browsing and multimedia access, personal location transfer of information and data, e-business, video conferencing and entertainment.

1. The US and Japan were developing their own standards for the third generation system (likely to be known as 363x).

2. The European Telecommunications Standards Institute was developing its standard known as the universal mobile telephone system (UMTS).

3. Since 1990, the International Telecommunications Union (ITU) had been reviewing several standards proposed for specifying a common but flexible standard (a family of systems) to be known as the International Mobile Telecommunications - 2000 (IMT-2000).

4. IMT-2000, approved in May 2000 by ITU, is interoperable throughout the world, for e-commerce, multimedia Web access and data transfer. The standard would serve both fixed and mobile users through public and private networks.

The key requirements for UMTS are:

1. small, low-cost pocket terminals
2. worldwide roaming
3. a single system for cellular and satellite as well as local calls
4. capacity to handle high-speed data.

The new system would use more spectrum and have advanced networking capabilities not only with the public-switched telephone networks but also with packet-based networks, including the Internet.

IMTS is designed on the basis of a different network architecture and radio access method. It uses wideband CDMA, instead of a narrowband TDMA as in the GSM. The GSM is switch-centric, as all calls would pass through a mobile switching center. UMTS would be data-centric in line with the expected increase in Internet growth. It will resemble the Internet, with no single central switch, but a collection of broadband networks interconnected by packet switches. This arrangement would result in greater flexibility in providing new services and in better use of the switching functions by service providers. Users will be able to access different channels depending on the data rate chosen by them.

The new standard provides for faster data transmission in the packed-switching mode:

(*i*) 144 Kbits/sec for fast-moving users in vehicles (as against 14.4 Kbit/sec now)

(*ii*) 384 Kbits/sec for slower pedestrian users

(*iii*) 2.05 Mbits/sec from fixed locations (as against 128 Kbits/sec) or low-speed terminals.

Devices that are hard-wired will soon be connected by wireless reliably. A technology initiative called 'Bluetooth' has been developed to link mobile PCs, cell phones and other devices. A single wireless link will replace multiple cable connections. It will enable mobile phones to get information from a home PC or stereo, a hand-free car phone and similar gadgets.

23.7 Convergence of Fixed and Mobile Communications

Convergence of fixed and mobile communication is a recent technological trend. The convergence would provide benefits to users.

The convergence can be at different levels. The services offered can be made equally available to both fixed and mobile users. For example, the user can have only on number and one bill. The networks can use the same physical infrastructure including transmission and switching systems. The users can also have the same number where they go.

Universal mobile telephone system (UMTS) provides a 'pipe' which subscribers can use to access a wide range of information and services. For example, a personalized daily newspaper can be delivered electronically to a user. Current systems (e.g. GSM) are voice-centric; UMTS changes the scenario to a data-centric system.

In UK, for example, the 'one phone' is designed with a dual-mode handset. The handset can function as a cordless phone within a certain range and as a mobile phone (using digital mobile technology or GSM) in other areas.

The fixed-mobile convergence is expected to be boosted by the universal mobile telecommunications systems (UMTS). The full potential of a seamless service integrating both fixed and mobile access needs further technology development. The concept of any service, anywhere, anytime is however not a different target, given the advances in computer, communication, consumer electronics and information technologies. But it is a real challenge to make such advanced technologies affordable to the message.

Ruggedised personal digital assistant (PDA) devices work in wireless local-area networks and enable their users to browse the Web and download scanned pages to PDAs by using an infrared link.

The interaction between information appliances and information infrastructure is done by the so-called IrDA technology (named after the standard specified by Infrared Data Association) formed in 1993 in the US. The lowcost, easy-to-use, interoperable wireless technology provides short-range connectivity between various devices such as mobile phones, PDAs and pagers without going through common control points.

Indeed, the boom in wireless links is leading to the emergence of the second generation of the Internet. New Web portals are being designed to function effectively within the constraints of wireless devices with small screens and slower Internet connections. Concurrently, a separate Internet standard for mobile phones is being considered.

23.8 Videophony and videoconferencing

Videophony and videoconferencing are companion audiovisual services which are, at the present time, generally distinguishable by the factors given in Table 23.4.

However, for some applications at least, the boundaries between the two services are becoming less distinct; for example, desktop videoconferencing terminals operating over switched 56kbits/sec and 64kbits/sec networks.

Table 23.4: Comparison between Videophony and Videoconferencing

Videophony	*Videoconferencing*
Primarily person-to-person	Primarily group-to-group
Office environment	Studio or specially equipped room environment
Compact desk top terminals	Large floor standing terminals
On demand service via customer switched digital networks	Bookable service via digital leased lines
Picture quality consistent with low bit rate transmission (e.g. 64kbits/sec or 128kbits/sec)	Picture quality consistent with high bit rate transmission (e.g. 384kbits/sec upto 2Mbits/sec
Telephony quality speech	Wideband speech quality

The CCITT, which is responsible for the video coding, audio coding and protocol standards for audiovisual services, has appreciated the future need for both types of service to interwork. As a result, the relevant standards ensure that any audiovisual terminal adhering to the standards will auditomacally interwork with any other standard terminal with the same or lesser capabilities.

23.8.1 Videoconferencing

A videoconference is a meeting between two or more groups of people in different locations any where in the world, which is organized via a two-way sound and vision link. The locations can be in very different parts of the world, in which case, satellites can play a vital role in the provision of the link. The effectiveness of these services lies in the reduction of travel for personnel and the speed with which international videoconferences can be organized. Typically, upto six persons can be comfortably catered for at each end terminal or studio.

The space links for videoconference services are provided by such organizations as Eutelsat and Intelsat, with the large earth stations and back-haul links being provided by the PTTs and other national telecommunication organizations over wideband land lines.

The essential elements of this system are based on closed circuit TV (CCTV). Its features are:

1. It consists of two face-to-face cameras and two colour TV receivers for the incoming signals. A local colour monitor is also provided and the terminal is often housed in a roll-away provided and the terminal is often housed in a roll-away cabinet.

2. A high resolution graphics camera is incorporated and an alphanumeric keyboard to insert text data as the need arises, together with a video printer and interface for a CD.

3. Local control over the system is via a conventional infra-red remote control, similar to that which is used on many TV receivers. This control also has focus and zoom functions on the graphics camera.

4. The central element in each terminal is an image compression codec. Its function is to code and decode the vision, sound and data signals that are transmitted over land lines.

Face-to-face vision sub-system: This is the main information channel for the system. Its operation is as follows:

1. Each camera often provides a full frame view of up to three persons, sitting side by side.

2. The middle strip of each frame from each camera output is selected and then electronically stacked, to provide a three-over-three, full frame view for transmission. This split screen approach avoids the corners of the camera images, where resolution and distortion is not of the best.

3. The decoder receives this stacked image and generates two half-size images. These are now centrally positioned in each video frame, with the top and bottom sections blanked to black level. These are then displayed on two adjacent monitors to give a wide screen image of the distant studio.

Codecs: The conventional codecs (which are still in use) have two modes of operation: (*i*) fast for high resolution graphics; and (*ii*) slow for moving picture face-to-face operation.

The graphics mode uses a systematic replenishment coding system, where only every 19th pixel is transmitted. The transmission time for one complete frame is then in the order of 2 sec. Initial sampling rates of 12.5 MHz and 4.166 MHz are used for luminance and chrominance respectively. Six-bit PCM coding provides adequate definition for the detailed display of a document.

In the fast mode, the luminance and chrominance signals are sampled at 5 MHz and 2.5 MHz, respectively, and then coded in 8-bit PCM. The moving areas are detected and coded using DPCM which generates a non-uniform bit rate. This data stream is buffered in a memory which was then read out a either 1.544 or 2.048 Mbits/sec as required. The transmitted code combines moving area addresses with line and field start data to ensure that the receiver maintained synchronism with the transmission.

CCITT H.261 algorithm image processing: Current videoconferencing systems use a codec based on the H.261 algorithm image processing to squeeze a video signal into the limited band space of a telephone line and They are basically designed to run at Integrated Services Digital Network (ISDN) data rates. CCIT Committee has laid an international standard for world-wide application which permits users to converse without having to concern themselves over the existence of the two different television scanning standards, namely 625/50 and 525/60.

The H.261 recommendation deals with the video codec for telecommunication audio-visual services to be at multiples of 64 kbits/sec up to 2 Mbits/sec (video bit rate in the range 46.4kbits/s to 1856kbits/sec). Its features are:

1. The coding kernel operates on a single format known as the Common Intermediate Format (CIF) or its simple related, downsized version called Quarter CIF (QCIF).

2. The luminance component of CIF has 288 lines of 352 coded pels, repeated 29.97 times per second. The two colour components each have half these numbers of pels and lines.

3. Either TV or standard signals are used to generate a common image format (CIF) signal for the transmission channel. This is based on 288 non-interlaced lines per picture and 30 pictures per second. 625 line systems use 576 active lines per frame, so that 288 lines form one field. Therefore, 625/25 codecs only have to perform a conversion to meet the 30 Hz picture rate and 525/30 codecs already operate at he correct frame rate so these only have to convert between 240 and 288 active lines.

4. QCIF has half the corresponding spatial sampling densities of CIF and is more suitable for the lower bit rates especially when the decoded images are for display on small screens.

5. CIF and QCIF are a technical compromise between 625/50 and 525/60, the number of lines being simply related to the visible portion of the 625 system and the picture repetition rate being exactly half the field rate of the 60Hz format.

6. At bit rates below about 1 Mbits/sec it is often preferable to reduce the coded picture rate and introduce motion jerkiness rather than accept the full amount of spatial quantisation noise.

7. The motion compensation range is 115 pels and 115 lines Weighting of transform coefficients is not incorporated.

Audio channel: This provides sound-in-vision (SIV) for stereo as well as mono signals, using companding and PCM coding. This employs a time multiplex to avoid the necessity for separate sound and control channels. The audio signal is sampled at a rate synchronised to the line frequency of the local camera and the derived data words were inserted, one in each line blanking period.

The sound sub-system also includes an echo canceling unit. Echoes can be caused by the outputs from the terminal loudspeakers which may be retransmitted by the terminals microphones. This unit samples the incoming audio signal, compared it with the studio sound and estimated the echo component, which was then subtracted from the out-going audio signal.

23.8.2 Videotelephony

The CIF is formed by sampling he video signal luminance at 6.75 MHz and chrominance at 3.375 MHz to produce 352, 8-bit samples per line. This is equivalent to an analogue bandwidth of about 3.4 MHz which is too wide for videotelephony. Therefore, a lower image quality is acceptable so that a further degree of compression can be made. This is achieved by using only the luminance component with 176 samples per line and 144 lines per frame. Since this represents half-resolution in each dimension, the standard is referred to as the quarter common image format (QCIF).

Integrated videophone terminals tend to use LCDs up to like videophone terminal implementation, particularly where the partial user already has such a unit on his desk. In this case, where bit rate coding is utilized, a reasonable implementation is to be dow' the small videophone picture into one of the top corner PC screen. For wideband videophone terminals, the screen can be used for the displayed picture if required.

23.8.3 Display systems

The optimum size of the display screen in a videophone terminal is a function of a number of factors including the picture scanning standard, picture resolution (signal bandwidth), viewing distance and, if a data compression scheme is implemented, the visibility of coding artifacts.

For videoconferencing terminals in a meeting room equipped with large (65cm diagonal) CRT displays, a viewing distance of at least 2.5m is recommended. Videophone or desk top videoconferencing terminals are usually positioned from 70cm to 1.5m from a single user; for easy reach of controls which are integral with the terminal. At the distance of 70cm, the display size should be about 20cm diagonal to preserve a viewing ratio of 6H. When low bit rate coding algorithms are used, usually accompanied by a deliberate reduction of the available picture resolution, a smaller size (10cm to 15cm) to mask tis used to mask the resulting loss of picture quality.

The development of colour liquid crystal display (LCD) has provided much more freedom to design an attractive, compact unit than would be the case with conventional cathode ray tube displays. Sizes upto 15cm diagonal (larger panels upto 35cm exist as development samples) and virtually all employ an active matrix of thin film transistors to control the transmittance of each cell. Colour is provided by having 3 cells per picture element and an overlay colour filter. A light source must be provided behind the LCD, usually by means of a colour matched cold cathode fluorescent tube.

For videoconferences involving groups of people at each a 4:3 aspect ratio display is non-optimum, resulting in the of say 6 participants in a central band occupying less than 125 the picture area. This situation can be significantly improved at the expense of a second camera, display and some processing, by the 'split-screen' technique. The best aspect ratio of the display is 16:3 which is close to the optimum value for 6 participants.

23.8.4 Multipoint Operation

Although telecommunication systems are designed to operate on a point to point basis between two end users, multipoint operation can also be provided when 3 or more users are required to be involved at the same time. This is usually provided as a network-based service via a multipoint control unit (MCU) embedded in the network.

In a 'switched' audiovisual MCU, the video signals are voice switched and forwarded from the MCU to each location according to the following rules :

1. The picture of the person currently speaking is forwarded to all the other locations.

2. The person currently speaking is sent the picture of the previous speaker.

Such a system has the advantages of relative simplicity, operates automatically and, apart from some additional control features, uses the same terminals and transmission capacity as point to point connections. The multipoint control data is transmitted in the message channel in the H.221 framing structure.

If all the other participants are required to be seen all of the time, so called 'continuous presence' multipoint operation, two methods are used. In the first, the number of receive channels and decoders at each location are increased, and all the incoming picture are displayed at smaller sizes on the existing display screen.

In another system, a single receive channel and decoder is used but with a more complex MCU which generates a composite picture of all the other incoming pictures. The picture of the current speaker is of higher resolution than the others and therefore allocated a greater proportion of the channel capacity.

23.9 Elements of the Indian Telecommunications System

The Indian telecommunications network consists of:

(*i*) 26,000 telephone exchanges with 21.6 million direct exchange lines, as well as 1.5 million trunk automatic exchange lines.

(*ii*) Open-wire carrier channels (90,900 route km), coaxial cable (31,0000 route km), microwave and UHF (150,000 route km) and optical fibre (1,10,000 route km), with another 250,000 route km now added.

(*iii*) Packed-switched public data network called INET covering more than 100 cities and based on X.25.

(*iv*) Satellite-based packet-switched data network with VSATs, known as the remote area business message network.

(*v*) Education research network (ERNET) providing high speed connectivity between computers and terminals.

(*vi*) Intelligent network (IN) service introduced in 16 cities (1999), which provides new services to businesses and industries (the services offered are: toll-free phone call for customers using designated business numbers, account card calling and virtual private network).

(*vii*) ISDN service in 80 cities and towns.

The tele-density has increased from 1 to 2.5 per cent during the last five years (preceding 1999), but still lags behind the world average of 14.3 per cent (China has 6 per cent and USA has 64 per cent). Rural India accounts for only one-fifth (about 4.5 million) lines of the total exchange lines.

In our country, the first experimental SPC electronic exchange was commissioned in Delhi in 1974. The country's first factory to make digital electronic switching equipment has been set up, at Mankapur in Gonda district of Uttar Pradesh, as a branch of the Indian Telephone Industries Limited (ITI). The factory was built in technical collaboration with a French firm, ALCATEL-Thomson. The Indian factory is based on the firm's fully digital E-10 B design and the software of the system is adapted to Indian conditions and traffic demands. The first E-10 exchange was commissioned in Worli, Mumbai, in April 1985.

The French-designed digital electronic exchange combines the flexibility of time division switching and power of the computer. The E-10 system has three basic components, viz. a computer for management purposes, switching and control and subscriber line terminals. Each of them can be independently developed.

23.9.1 C-DOT's Effort

The Centre for Development of Telematics (C-DoT) has designed and developed a family of digital electronic switching systems for a variety of telecommunication applications - local, trunk tandem and a combination of them for rural as well as urban areas. The systems focus on typical Indian conditions such as high traffic loads and low telephone density, busy hour attempts, high temperature, dusty environment and power supply problem.

The development of the main automatic exchange (MAX) was carried out in three stages, viz. MAX-M, capable of handling 1,500 lines, MAX-L with 10,00-20,000 lines and MAX-XL with 40,000 lines. The products include 128 port (lines) private branch exchanges and 512 port rural ex-changes.

C-DoT technology is particularly recommended for rural areas which do not have air-conditioning facilities. It is easy to install, use and maintain, thus avoiding the need for skilled manpower in places where small exchanges are located. The rural exchange has been upgraded to support 10-channel digital radio for point-to-point linking of exchanges. A point-to-multipoint system is under development for handling upto 64 remote stations, each with eight remote subscribers.

The digital switch for ISDN, being developed by C-DoT, provides for sophisticated technical features: voice/data channels and a message channel over the existing copper wire loops for small users; use of the same two-wire loops for access to different services; selective call diversion and similar facilities.

C-DoT's PABX technology has been made available to many manufactures. The Indian Telephone Industries Ltd. Makes the XL and other exchanges. C-DoT's switches handle over a third of the country's telecommunication network, including PABXs. C-DoT's rural automatic exchanges have been installed in Bangladesh, Vietnam, Russia, Yemen, Nigeria and Nepal.

23.9.2 Role of VSNL

All telecom services from India to other countries are provided by Videsh Sanchar Nigam Ltd. (VSNL).

It operates international telephone and telex circuits via seven satellite earth stations each at Mumbai, New Delhi, Chennai, Calcutta, Arvi (near Pune), Dehradun and Bangalore. It handles all TV programmes via satellites from India to other countries.

As a signatory to INTELSAT, VSNL provides access to its satellites in the Indian Ocean region. It also offers INMARSAT satellite services. Mumbai and Chennai are linked by submarine cables besides satellite links. The earth station at Bangalore provides for international business service (leased data services at bit rates ranging from 64 Kbits/sec to 2 Mbits/sec).

Packet switching was introduced in Mumbai in 1998 to provide computer connections, e-mail and data base access. Packet switching nodes have since been commissioned at New Delhi and Calcutta.

VSNL is also setting up gateway facilities at various centers to work with mobile satellite systems, the Afro-Asian Communications Satellite and the ICO Global Communications system. The capacity of the gateway digital switches is being increased to 56,000 international trunks. The gateways will include those in Ernakulam, Jalandhar, Kanpur and Gandhinagar. Advance facilities such as bandwidth on demand are being introduced in metro cities.

24

Laser Satellite Communication

24.1. Introduction

Laser satellite communication involves transmission at frequencies in the 10^{14} (optical) range which is around seven or eight orders of magnitude higher than the radio frequency (RF) systems. Transmission at such frequencies provides three main advantages, namely the greater bandwidth, smaller beam divergence angles and smaller antennas. In fact, communication with lasers is being used now a days in three modes of communications. These are aerial laser-beam communications fibre optic communication and optical computers.

In aerial laser beam communications, data and images are transmitted through the atmosphere using low power laser beams. It has the advantage that it is almost impossible to jam by known means. Moreover, because of the extremely widebandwidth of laser radiation, upto 10 discrete conversions can be executed simultaneously. Such as aerial laser beam communications is, however, completely weather dependent. On a clear day, a laser beam can be transmitted several miles but when atmospheric conditions involve fog, mist, rain or smog, the transmission is limited to shorter distances.

In fibre optic communications, laser transmission is carried out through guided media of optical fibres. This system is capable of transmitting 4 gigabits of information per second over a span of some 120 km.

Optical computer solves the problems of slowness and heat build up associated with electronic computers. This is because here light is used instead of electrical current. Further light being at the upper end of the electromagnetic spectrum can be encoded with much more information. Also an optical circuit has a zero resistance to flow and therefore is capable to carry much more information than the equivalent sized electronic circuit. There is no problem in using optical signals in parallel channels.

Being atmospheric dependent, laser communication therefore cannot be used for communication between earth station and a geosynchronous satellite However, it is quite suitable for communication between the satellites themselves or deep space communication.

A typical example for such a cross satellite laser communication is as that shown in Fig. 24.11 Here GSs are the geosynchronous satellites whereas ESS are some other satellites (*e.g.* earth observation or special purpose satellites). These ESs communicate to GSs with laser communication and eventually the GSs communicate with the earth station through RF microwave communication. The optical transmitters and receiver packages are smaller and lighter than the equivalent HF microwave subsystems. This helps in reducing the spacecraft cost and weight. For deep space communication where the planets desired to be communicated with the earth are quite far, the received signals are very weak and then this intersatellite laser communication solves problem. Here the deep space-craft will have deep space optical link with a geosynchronous satellite which provides microwave link to the earth station. Conclusively, therefore the laser satellite communication serves for intersatellite communications and here the analysis of cross optical-link is necessary.

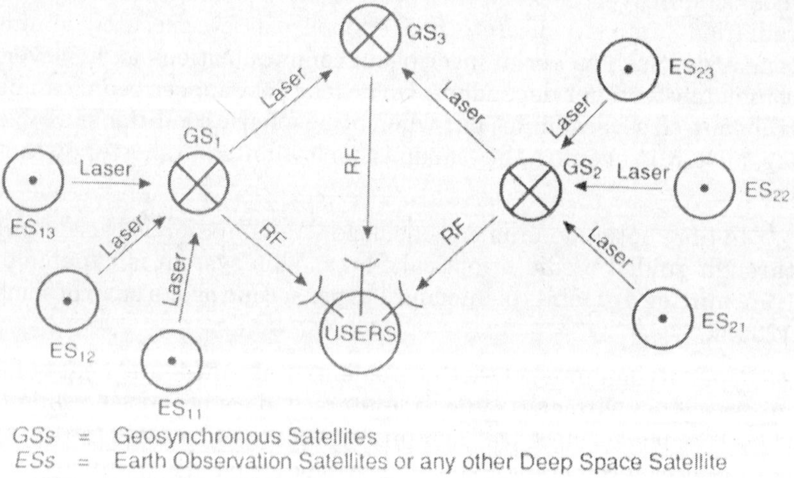

GSs = Geosynchronous Satellites
ESs = Earth Observation Satellites or any other Deep Space Satellite

GSs = Geosynchronous Satellites
ESs = Earth Observation Satellites or any other Deep Space Satellite

Fig. 24.1. Example of Laser Satellite Communication

24.2. Link Analysis

(*a*) *Atmospheric Effects :* While analyzing the satellite cross-link, the effects of earth's atmosphere on the laser signals should be carefully studied. The earth's atmosphere affects the optical signals in a variety of ways such as attenuation due to energy absorption, beam spreading due to scattering of light waves, beams bending due to refocussing of optical beams and beam breakup due to loss of field coherence over the beamfront.

The atmospheric attenuation is dependent on the wavelength as shown in Fig. 24.2 (*a*). It is also dependent on the elevation angle particularly for satellite optical downlink as shown in Fig. 24.2 (*b*). The beam spreading caused by atmospheric scattering results into weakening of power received at the optical receiver. Infact the received downlink beam appears to be about 10μ radians larger. In clear days the mixing of warm and cool atmospheric strata produce turbulence which may interact with impinging light waves causing

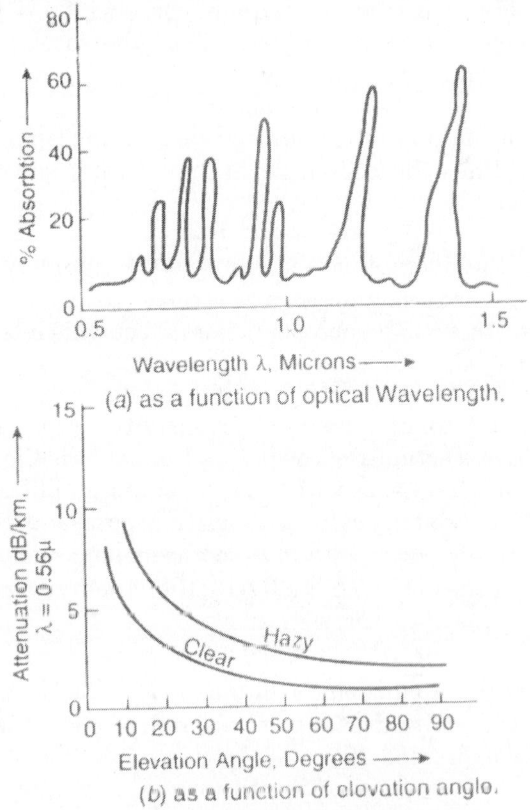

(*a*) as a function of optical Wavelength.

(*b*) as a function of elevation angle.

Fig. 24.2. Atomospheric Attenuation

the refocussing and reorienting the impinging beam. This causes the beam to move off-foresight (beam steering) and create optical pointing problems. Similarly the atmosphere also introduces loss in beam front coherence which means that two points on the beam front would be no longer in phase. This affects both the direct and hetrodyne optical detection systems.

(*b*) *Complete Link Analysis :* Satellite optical cross link analysis given below is suitable to the case when the effects of atmosphere are considered to be negligible in satellite cross links (*e.g.* the space between two satellites). Here it has been assumed that the RF link is used for uplink and downlink transmission to the satellite and the crosslink between two satellites is optical link that uses direct detection system. Thus when the satellite receives uplink, it directly intensity modulates the uplink carrier bandwidth onto the optical carrier for the crosslink. For this it is essential that the upper limit of the uplink frequency band is within the receiving photodetector bandwidth otherwise then the uplink bandwidth is firstly down connected before laser modulation. Thus the satellite RF uplink waveform may be represented as

$$s(t) = u(t) + n_u(t) \qquad ...(24.1)$$

where $u(t)$ is the uplink carrier and $n_u(t)$ is the uplink noise and interference. Since the laser power at the optical receiver is intensity modulated so

$$P(t) = P_r\,(1 + \beta s\,(t)) \qquad ...(24.2)$$

where P_r is the average power and β is the intensity modulation index ($\beta \le 1$). The receiving satellite receives the signal of Eq. (24.2) by photodetecting it. The photodetector detects this intensity modulated signal as

$$R\,[\beta\,P_r\,s\,(t)] = R\,\beta\,P_r\,[u\,(t) + n_u\,(t)] \qquad ...(24.3)$$

where R is the photodetector responsivity. The photodetected waveform that is actually of the uplink frequency is then translated to the downlink frequency which is then power amplified and transmitted to the receiving earth station. If P_r represents the available downlink satellite power, α_s and α_n as the signal and noise suppressions and L as the net downlink losses, then the recovered downlink carrier power may be expressed as

$$P_s = \alpha_s^2\,P_t\,[(R\,\beta\,P_r)^2\,P_{cu}]L \qquad ...(24.4)$$

where P_{cu} is the uplink power of $u(t)$ in Eq. (24.1). Also the total downlink retransmitted noise power (uplink plus total photodetector noise) can be expressed as

$$P_{ns} = \alpha_n^2\,P_t\,[(R\,P_r\,\beta)^2 P_{nu} + P_{PD})]L \qquad ...(24.5)$$

where P_{nu} is the uplink noise power and P_{pd} is the combined photodetector noise power (shot, dark current, and thermal) in the satellite bandwidth. In addition the downlink receiver adds its thermal noise P_{nd}. Hence the resulting downlink signal to noise ratio $(C/N)_d$, after uplink, crosslink and downlink transmission is finally

$$(C/N)_T = \frac{P_s}{P_{ns} + P_{nd}} \quad ...(24.6)$$

Defining

$$(C/N)_u \approx \frac{P_{cu}}{P_{nu}} \quad ...(24.7)$$

$$(C/N)_{op} \approx \frac{P_s}{P_{pd}} \quad ...(24.8)$$

$$(C/N)_r \approx \frac{L\, P_t\, \alpha_s^2}{P_{nd}} \quad ...(24.9)$$

and

$$\alpha_s^2 = \left[1 + \frac{1}{(C/N)_{op}}\right]^{-1} \quad ...(24.10)$$

one may write Eq. (24.6) in the form as

$$(C/N)_T = [(C/N)_u^{-1} + (C/N)_{op}^{-1} + (C/N)_r^{-1}] \quad ...(24.11)$$

where all (C/N) ratios refer to the uplink satellite carrier bandwidth. Eq. (24.11) when compared with the case of analog satellite link formula of Eq. (3.29) shows that here the term due to the presence of optical crosslink is simply added and also the usual downlink $(C/N)_r$ term is modified. This modification is due to the satellite amplifier carrier suppression effects that are now determined by the optical link.

In Eq. (24.11) it can be seen that the weaker of three link terms would control the overall performance. Thus if $(C/N)_{op}$ is maintained at a high value (higher than that of uplink and downlink values) the satellite communication system would remain *transparent* to the optics. For digital satellite communication one would need (E_b/N_0) as given in Eq. (6.29) in terms of (C/N_0). Here one needs two more information, the information bit rate and the system link margin (for degradation). This margin is usually taken for satellite cross links as one or two dB. The required error probability in digital satellite communication is of the order of 10^{-5}.

24.3. Optical Satellite Link Transmitter

Basically the transmitter part of an optical satellite link consists of a laser source, modulator and antenna alongwith some data handling electronics. Infact this optical transmitter is quite analogous to its RF counterpart.

Laser Source : A variety of laser sources may be used for optical satellite communication systems. These may be gas lasers, solid-state lasers and semi-conductor lasers. Selection of laser source is dependent upon a number of factors that include link range, propagation medium, data rate and platform limitations. Table 24.1 gives a brief summary of the various laser sources commonly used in optical satellite communication system. Lasers extend from high powered, low efficiency, bulky devices to the smaller light weight Ga As (gallium arsenide) solid state diodes. Semiconductor lasers are also being used such as AlGaAs and In GaAsP. The AlGaAs lasers emit reliably between 0.78 and 0.86 μm and In GaAsP lasers emit between 1.2 and 1.65 μm.

Table 24.1. Laser Sources Commonly Used in Satellite Optical Communication

Laser types	*Wavelength*	*Average power output*	*Efficiency*	*Characteristics*
Nd-YAG (neodynium Yittrium, aluminium garnet)	1.06 μ	0.5-1 W	0.5-1%	Requires elaborate modulation equipment, diode or solar pumping. Has 10,000 life hours. Frequency doubling loses efficiency.
crystal	0.532 μ	100 MW	0.5-1%	
GaAs (Gallium Arsenide, solid state)	0.8–0.9 μ	40 MW	5-10%	Life hours 50,000, reliable , small, rugged, compact, directly and easily modulated, easily combined into arrays, Nanosecond pulsing.
CO_2 (gas lasers) carbon dioxide	10.6 μ	1-2 W	10-15%	Life hours 20,000 used in IR range, Detector are poor, uses a discharge tube, modulation is difficult.
HeNe (Helium Neon)	0.63 μ	10 MW	1%	Life hours 50,000. Requires external modulation, Has gas tube, is power limited and is inefficient.

The satellite crosslink uses preferably the laser diodes because of their light weight. But since these are low powered devices (output power on the order of tens of milliwatts), the laser diodes are arranged in the satellite payloads to form arrays so that the laser source output power increases. It may, however, be mentioned that during 1977-1980 space communication with CO_2 lasers and Nd: YAG laser were also successfully tried. But with the development in the technology, it is now confirmed that the semiconductor lasers are the ideal light source for optical communication in space communication due to their small size and weight, high efficiency and reliability. In addition semiconductor lasers are easily modulated by direct current injection. The laser diode has long potential life (~10^5 hr).

The main disadvantage of the laser diode is the limited power per diode so that most applications require the use of diode arrays, leading to the beam-combining problems. The integrated optics technology has developed the coherent combining, thus increasing the power in the beam while decreasing the beam divergence. Monolithically fabricated laser array designs have further solved the above beam divergence problem.

Modulators : In laser space communication the most preferable modulation is direct intensity modulation. Various methods that can be used to modulate laser can be as that given in Table 24.2. These are the direct modulation methods. Here the driving current of the laser is varied in accordance with the type of modulation required. Modulation rates of about 1 Gbits/s with the laser diodes have also been achieved. Direct modulation of light *via* the sources drive current causes dynamic effects on the emitted spectrum like those of changes in the peak wavelength and in laser modes. The latter effect is particularly strong in monomode lasers.

Table 24.2. Various Optical (Laser) Modulation Methods

Modulation Type	*Analog*	*Pulse*	*Digital*
Information Signal	Time Continuous	Time continuous or sampled	Time Sampling
Carrier parameter (amplitude, intensity, frequency, phase or polarzation)	Continuous	Continuous or quantized	Quantized and coded
Example	Intensity modulation	Pulse Intensity modulation	Pulse Code modulation, Intensity Modulation

Other light sources *e.g.* gas lasers may not be capable of being modulated at all. This makes external modulators attractive. Solid state lasers such as Nd: YAG which are capable of achieving a modulation rate of more than 1 Gbit/s also require external modulators. The external modulators utilize miniature guiding structures (integrated optics) and operate with much less modulating power. A variety of effects such as electro-optic, acoustic optic, magneto-optic have been employed in a number of configurations (channel waveguides, planar wave guides, etc.) to realize modulation.

Antennas : As with the *RF* communication systems, the laser satellite communication systems also utilize antennas to direct the transmitted energy. Here the antennas are nothing more than the conventional design telescopes where the size and geometry are dictated by the wavelength and system requirements. Thus the optical satellite communication system requires narrow light beam-widths (fractions of a degree) instead of antenna gain patterns of several degrees needed by *RF* systems. They also have lensing system for beam transmission and focussing instead of *RF* antennas.

The concept and some elementary mathematics concerned with the laser optics can be studied with the help of Fig. 24.3. Here a laser source generates a light wave which is focussed into an optical beam and then propagates a distance z over a free space path to a collecting area A_r. It should be noted that the focussed beams are usually modelled as having circular symmetric beam patterns with beam-width.

$$\phi_b \approx \frac{\lambda}{d_t} \qquad ...(24.12)$$

where λ is the wavelength of the laser light and d_t is the diameter of the transmitting optics of the laser. In a typical example of visible optical range, $\lambda = 1$, $\mu = 10^{-6}$ meter and a transmitting lens of only 6 inches (0.5 meter), a beam of about 10 microradian will be produced 1° = 17.5) milli-radian.

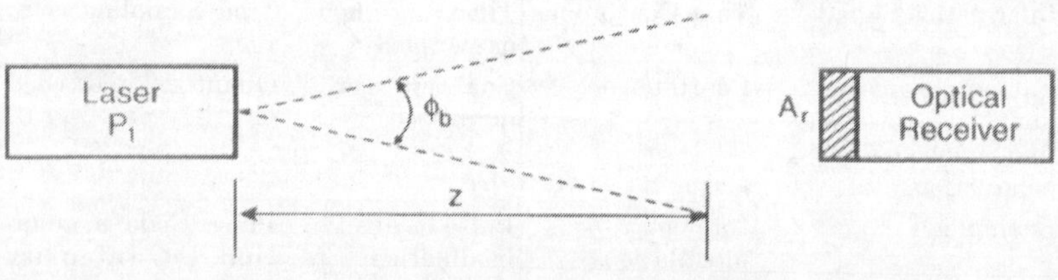

Fig. 24.3. Optic Antenna Transmission.

Therefore, compared to *RF* systems, a laser transmitter produces beams widths several orders of magnitude narrower which is measured in terms of microradians instead of degrees.

The basic calculations for beam power etc, however, may be easily carried out as per conventional *RF* communication system. Let the laser source power P_t be distributed over the beamfront at the distance z. The optical power collected over the collecting area A_r at the receiving side would be then

$$P_r = \frac{P_t A_r}{\phi_b^2 z^2} \quad \text{...(24.13)}$$

Eq. (24.13), may be rewritten in terms of antenna gain values and propagation losses as being done in *RF* link analysis by using

$$g_t = \frac{4\pi}{\phi_b^2} \quad \text{...(24.14)}$$

and $$L_p \approx (4\pi/\lambda z)^2 \quad \text{...(24.15)}$$

But since here the focussing parameters are also involved so the results given by Eqs. (24.14) and (24.15) for optical antennas would become misleading. Therefore these two equations are not used. Instead, Eq. (24.12) is substituted into Eq. (24.13) that gives

$$P_r = \frac{P_t (d_t d_r)^2}{\lambda^2 z^2} \quad \text{...(24.16)}$$

where d_r is the diameter of the receiving optics. From Eq. (24.16) it is seen that P_r depends on the squared product of transmit and receive diameters. Considering that both the transmit and receive optics (optical antennas) are of the same size, for $\lambda = 1$ micron, P_r can be calculated for $Z = 45000$ miles (twice synchronous range) and the results are shown in Fig. 24.4 for three values of P_t, namely, $P_t = 1\ W$, 100 mW and 10 mW.

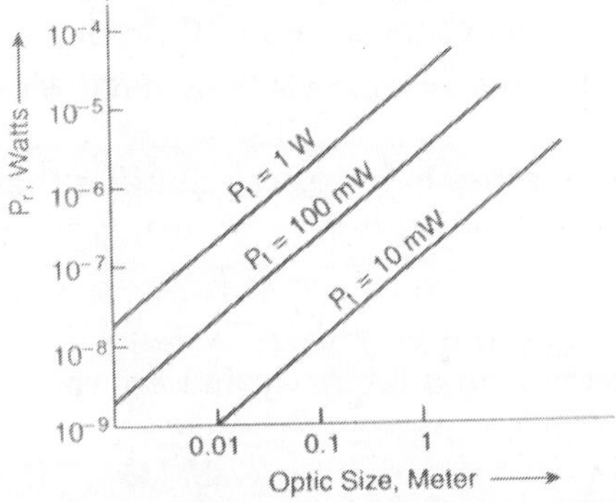

Fig. 24.4. Received Optical Power Versus Optical Size.

It is evident that power levels comparable to those received in rf links are obtainable with only milliwatts of source power and with optic (lens) diameters on the orders of a foot or less. This thus shows the significance of optical satellite communication. The received power P_r can also be converted to equivalent *photoelectron count rates* by the formula

$$n_r = \frac{P_r}{h f_0} \quad \text{...(24.17)}$$

where h is the planck's constant and f_0 is the optical frequency, n_r is represented in terms of photoelectrons per second. In actual practice the optical antenna system design is quite complex. The system combines the diode beams using a focal telescope with the cassegrainian structure. Mirrors also help in providing the perfect collimation.

24.4 Optical-Satellite Link Receiver

Analogous to its RF counterpart, the optical receiver consists of an antenna, filter, photodetector and then conventional receive electronic system. Receive antennas are also the telescopes whose main purpose is to focus the optical signal onto the photodetector and to reject as much as of the background radiation as is practical. The receive optical filters (also known as interference filters) are employed to eliminate background radiation that is not of the same wavelength as the optical signal. Infact the range of wavelengths around the laser wavelength allowed by the optical filter is called *optical bandwidth.* In terms of wavelength this optical bandwidth $\Delta\lambda$ around wavelength λ_0 is related to the optical bandwidth B_0 in Hz around the frequecny f_0 corresponding to λ_0 by

$$\frac{\Delta\lambda}{\lambda_0} \approx \frac{B_0}{f_0} \qquad ...(24.18)$$

Typical optical filter bandwidths at 1 micron generally range from 10–100 angstroms (1 angstrom = 10^{-4} microns) corresponding to an equivalent frequency bandwidth of about $B_0 \approx 10^{11} - 10^{12}$ Hz (100–1000 GHz). It may be noted that sometimes field stop iris are also used whose purpose is to reject radiation that is not emitted from the region surrounding the transmitting telescope.

Optical detection systems are of two types namely the direct detection system and the hetrodyne system. Direct detection systems respond to the signal intensity and are the most widely used

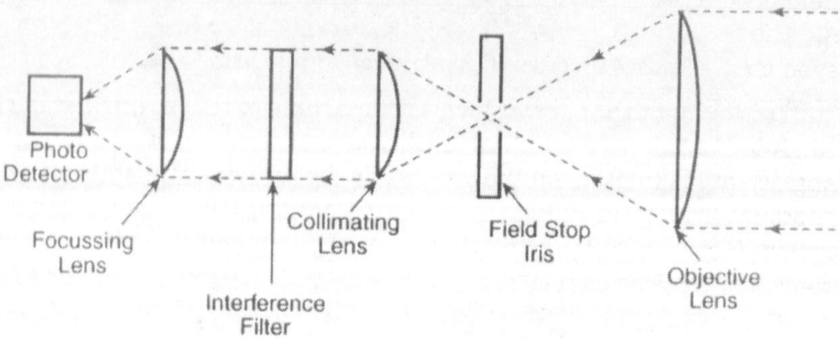

Fig. 24.5. Principle of Direct Detection System.

in optical communications systems. In the hetrodyne detection system the optical signal is combined with a local oscillator beam and then both the signals are focussed onto the same detector. Hetrodyne-detection systems are used primarily in the far-infrared region and they respond to signal amplitude. Figs. 24.5 and 24.6 indicate the basic principles involved with the direct detection and hetrodyne detection systems respectively.

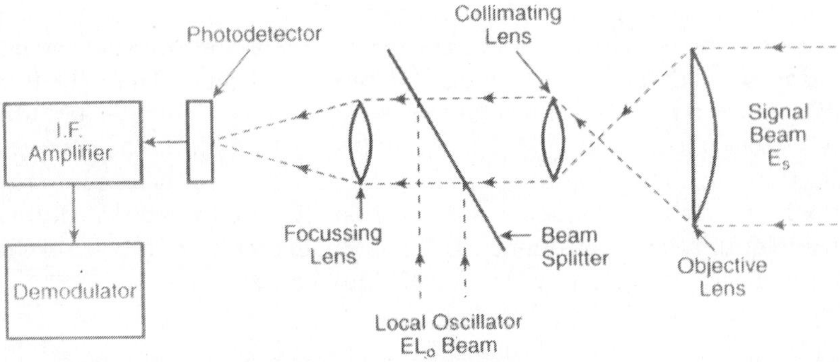

Fig. 24.6. Principle of Hetrodyne Detection.

From Figs. (24.5) and (24.6) it is evident that in the optical receiver the photodetector converts quantum mechanically the light radiated on it into photoelectron current flow. Various lenses focus the received light on the photodetector. Actually the photodetector detects the instantaneous field power of the focussed field on it. Since the amount ot field power focussed onto the detector is equal to the amount of field power incident on the focussing lens so the photodetected power can be equivalently computed by determining receiving field power over the lens area instead of by focussed field power over the detector area. Thus if the lens aperture area is A_r the Eq. (24.13) is still used for computing detector field power even though it does not explicitly involve the actual photodetecting area.

An optical receiver field of view is defined as the field arrival angles over which the lens will focus the impinging field onto the photodetector surface. This depends on the detector area A_d and the optical focal length f_c (note that $f_c = \sqrt{A_r}$). Thus the optical field of view is given as

$$\Omega_{fv} = \frac{A_d}{f_c^2} \approx \frac{A_d}{A_r} = \left(\frac{A_d}{\lambda^2}\right)\left(\frac{\lambda^2}{A_r}\right) \qquad ...(24.19)$$

In above Eq. (24.19) (λ^2/A_r) is termed *diffraction-limited field of view*. Since detector area is on the order of millimeters or centimeters and is on the order of microns, so it is evident that optical field of view is many times larger than the diffraction limited field of view of the same aperture area.

Photodetector normally used in optical detection may be PIN diode or Avalanche photodiode (APD). These photodetectors are governed by their characteristic properties such as detection efficiency, gain, responsivity and bandwidth. Infact these are the parameters which a communication engineer has to know while using photodetectors in the optical receiver design. The detection efficiency indicates the fraction of received power which is actually detected. It is wavelength dependent. It also depends on the material used in the photoemmissive surface. Its value lies in the range 0.15~ 0.90 for visible frequencies but falls off rapidly at the higher wavelength (lower frequencies). Thus the detected count rate of the optical receiver given by Eq. (24.17) may be written as

$$n_s \approx \left(\frac{\eta}{hf_0}\right) P_r \qquad ...(24.20)$$

The gain of photodetector is increased by cascading the photoemmissive surface but this increases noise. This excess noise is represented in terms of excess noise factor defined as

$$F \approx \frac{1 + \sigma_d^2}{(\overline{G})^2} \qquad ...(24.21)$$

where $\overline{G}$ is the mean gain and σ_d^2 is the gain variance. For an APD having gain of about 50—300, the excess noise factor is usually in the range of 2 to 5.

The responsivity of photodiode indicates as to how much current will be produced for a given power input. It is indicated by amps/watts. Mathematically it is expressed by

$$R = \frac{e\,\eta\,\overline{G}}{hf_0} \text{ amps/watt} \qquad ...(24.22)$$

where e is charge on electron ($e = 1.97 \times 10^{-19}$ coulombs.)

The bandwidth of photodetector is different than the optical bandwidth defined by (24.18). The photodetector bandwidth actually determines the rate of power variation that can be detected. It indicates the highest frequency at which the power can be varied and have the variation detected by the output current. Typical bandwidth are usually 1—10 GHz.

It would be worthwhile to mention here that while using photodetector noise considerations are also to be taken into account. Here shot noise, dark current and thermal noise current of the post detection circuitry are taken into account. In addition some background noise power is also taken into account. All these together make the photodetector noise model as that shown in Fig. 24.7. In above figure $P_r(t)$ is the average laser power intensity modulated incident on the photodetector. P_b is the background radiation power. The noise processes as indicated in Fig. 24.7 may be expressed as

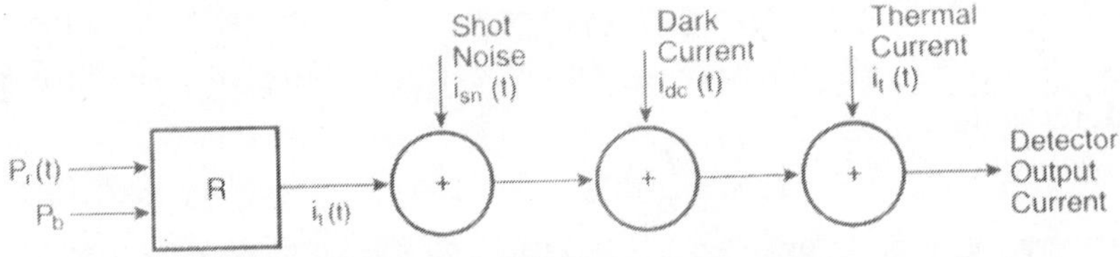

Fig. 24.7. Photodetector Noise Model.

$$N_0 \approx N_{sn} + N_{dc} + N_t \text{ amps}^2/\text{Hz} \quad ...(24.23)$$

Here N_0 represents the total receiver current process in terms of two sided spectral level. Similarly N_{sn}, N_{dc}, N_t are the two sided spectral levels for shot noise, dark current and thermal current respectively. These spectral levels are given as

$$N_{sn}(w) = \overline{G}^2 F e R \overline{P} \text{ amps}^2/\text{Hz} \quad ...(24.24)$$

$$N_{dc}(w) = eI_{dc} \frac{\text{amps}^2}{\text{Hz}} \quad ...(24.25)$$

$$N_t(w) = \frac{4kT_{eq}^0}{R_L} \text{ amps}^2/\text{Hz} \quad ...(24.26)$$

Here $\overline{G}$, F and R are the detector gain, noise factor and responsivity, e is the electron change $\overline{p}$ is the time averaged mean received power, I_{dc} is the detector mean dark current (of the order of 10^{-16} ~10^{-12} amperes), k is the Boltzmann constant, R_L is the impedance loading the photodetector and T_{eq}^0 is its equivalent noise temperature. Since the intensity modulation is used so if the information waveform $s(t)$ is modulated onto the laser field then

$$P_r(t) \approx P_r [1 + \beta s(t)] \quad ...(24.27)$$

where P_r is the average power given by Eq. (24.16) and β is the modulation index, $\beta << 1$. After detection (direct-detection) the output photodetected current would be given as

$$i(t) \approx R\,[P_r\,(t) + P_b] + i_{sn}\,(t) + i_{dc}\,(t) + i_t\,(t) \qquad ...(24.28)$$

where the first term in Eq. (24.28) is due to the impinging and background fields and the remaining terms are due to various noise sources as shown in Fig. 24.7. From Eqs. (24.27) and (24.28) it is evident that the first term of Eq. (24.28) can be expanded to give a constant term $[R\,(P_r + P_b)]$ plus a modulation term $[RP_r\,\beta\, s(t)]$. A filter for $s(t)$ with bandwidth B_m will produce a signal power

$$P_s = (RP_r\,\beta)^2 \qquad ...(24.29)$$

and a total noise power

$$P_n = N_o\,(2B_m) \qquad ...(24.30)$$

Therefore the photodetected S/N would be given as (direct detection)

$$S/N = \frac{P_s}{P_n} \qquad ...(24.31)$$

From Eqs. (24.29), (24.30) and Eqs. (24.23) to (24.26), Eq. (24.31) gives

$$S/N = \frac{(RP_r\,\beta)^2}{\left[eR\overline{G}^2\,F\,(P_r + P_b) + eI_{dc} + \dfrac{2KT_{eq}^0}{R_L}\right] 2B_m} \qquad ...(24.32)$$

S/N given in Eq. (24.32) is also called *electronic* or *photodetection* S/N as opposed to the optical S/R at the input P_r/P_b. Eq. (24.32) may be rewritten as

$$S/N \approx \beta^2 \left[\frac{(n\,P_r/h\,f_0)^2}{\left[(n/hf_0)\,F\,(P_r + P_b) + \dfrac{I_{dc}}{\overline{G}_e^2} + \dfrac{2KT_{eq}^0}{\overline{G}_e^2\,e^2\,R_L}\right] .\ 2B_m}\right] \qquad ...(24.33)$$

From Eq. (24.33) it is evident that the S/R is dependent on both P_r and P_b whereas both the dark current and thermal noise effects are reduced by the square or photodetector mean gain. Thus if high gain photomultipliers are used, it will aid in reducing the effect of post detection noise. In terms of count rate such as that described in Eq. (24.20), Eq. (24.33) may be written in the form as

$$S/R \approx \beta^2 \left[\frac{n_s^2}{\left[F\,\{(n_s + n_b) + n_d + n_t\}\ .\ 2B_m\right]}\right] \qquad ...(24.34)$$

where n_s is the detected current rate of optical receiver given in Eq. (24.20), n_b is the equivalent receiver back-ground count rate given by

$$n_b \approx \left(\frac{n}{hf_0}\right) P_b \qquad ...(24.35)$$

Similarly $$n_d \approx \frac{I_{dc}}{\overline{G}_e^2} \qquad ...(24.36)$$

which may be considered as average number of dark current photoelectrons per second.

$$n_r = \frac{2K\,T_{eq}^0}{\overline{G}^2\,e^2\,R_L} \qquad ...(24.37)$$

which is the average number of thermal photoelectrons per second. Eq. (24.34) may also be rewritten as

$$S/N \approx \beta^2 \left(\frac{n_s}{2B_m}\right)\left[\frac{n_s}{n_s + (n_b + n_d + n_t)}\right] \qquad ...(24.38)$$

Since n_s is a count rate, the term $[n_s/2B_m]$ can be interpreted as the number of signal counts in a time 1/2 B_m seconds and is often referred to as the *quantum limited* S/N for a bandwidth B_m.

In hetrodyne detection system as shown in Fig. 24.6, a strong local field relative to received powers P_r and P_b) is added to the received field prior to photodetection. Thus here the photodetector responds to the intensity of the combined field (laser plus background plus local field). Here the local laser power is much larger than the received power so the photodetected response current may be given as

$$i\,(t) = RP_L + 2Rf_s\,(t)\,f_L\,(t)\,A_r + 2R\,P_b\,(t)\,f_L\,(t)\,A_c \qquad ...(24.39)$$

Here P_L is the laser power over the detector area, $f_s(t)$ and $f_L(t)$ are the received loss and local laser fields repectively over the receiver area and $P_b(t)$ is the background power collected over the detector area common to both the local and focussed fields. It should be remebered that here A_r is the area corresponding to receive lens and A_c is the area on the photodetected. From Eq. (24.39) it is evident that in hetrodyne system the local laser power P_L plays quite an important role. It governs the average current and therefore the shot noise spectrum. The detection takes place for the product of incoming (modulated) laser field and the local laser field. This makes the modulation system for the laser satellite transmitter to use modulation techniques other than intensity modulation such as phase modulation, frequency modulation or amplitude modulation. Thus in hetrodyne system a difference frequency term (corresponding to the difference in frequency of transmitting laser and the local laser) is generated which is set to an RF frequency and further demodulation is carried out by conventional methods. It may be mentioned here that by focussing the local laser, the effective detector area can be reduced that will cause an equivalent reduction in the receiver field of view. Therefore the hetrodyne receivers receive less background noise and compared to that in direct detection receivers.

The post detection S/N in hetrodyne system may be calculated from Eq. (24.39). Assuming that the laser transmitter remains in the reduced field of view, the received power is

$$P_s = (2R)^2 P_L P_r \qquad ...(24.40)$$

where P_r is the received power over the area A_r. (A_r is the area of the receive lens). The detected noise is due to the mixed background, the shot noise and the detector output noises [$i_{dc}(t)$ and $i_t(t)$) in Fig. (24.7)]. Hence S/N post detection for hetrodyne system can be written as

$$S/N = \frac{4R^2 P_L P_r}{\left[eRP_L + \dfrac{4eRP_L N_b}{2} + eI_{dc} + \dfrac{2KT_{eq}}{R_L}\right]. 2B_c} \qquad ...(24.41)$$

where B_c is the modulated carrier bandwidth at RF

and $N_b = \eta N(f)\, \lambda^2/hf.$

Eq. (24.41) may be rewritten as

$$S/R = \frac{4\,(n/hf)\, P_r}{\left[1 + 2N_b + \dfrac{I_{dc}}{RP_L} + \dfrac{2KT^o_{eq}}{eRP_L R_L}\right]. 2B_c}$$

$$\approx \frac{4n_s/2B_c}{1 + 2N_b + \left(\dfrac{n_d}{n_L}\right) + \dfrac{n_t}{n_L}} \qquad ...(24.43)$$

Here $n_L = (nP_L/hf)$ is the effective local laser count rate. It is evident from Eq. (24.42) that in hetrodyne system the laser power P_L acts like detector gain in reducing the effect of post detection noise. Hence high-gain photomultipliers are not needed in hetrodyne receivers. Further the background noise is also reduced and all these make the hetrodyne system quite attractive. But the overall design is quite complex. Because of these reasons such a system is not preferred in use with optical satellite cross-link. It should be noted that it is very essential that the polarization, amplitude distribution and phase of the local oscillator beam are matched to the signal beam.

24.5. Satellite Beam Acquisition, Tracking and Pointing

In optical satellite communication the transmitting beam should be quite narrow because it would then have maximum power spectrum. But this extreme narrowness in the beam creates beam pointing problems. It is infact very essential that the beam should be correctly pointed always to the receiving satellite otherwise the communication link will be disturbed. However it is allowed that the beam may be pointing within an pointing error $\pm \theta_c$ radians (normally θ_c is in microradians). This problem is not faced with the rf systems because there beamwidth are much wider. It is therfore clear that to determine pointing error, the transmitting satellite must illuminate the receiving satellite as accurately as possible. It then requires that the transmitting satellite should know the location of receiving satellite as accurately as possible. Also, it has to know its own altitude as accurately as possible so that it may aim its beam at the known direction correctly.

For correct information regarding the receiving satellite's location, an optical beacon (unmodulated light source) transmitted by the receiving satellite back to the transmitting satellite is also being used. Here infact the transmitting satellite firstly receives the beacon from the receiving satellite and then transmits its modulated laser beam (data etc) back to the receiving satellite. Thus the receiving satellite's location can be obtained and the pointing error be minimized. However, there might be a situation in which though the transmitting satellite has received the beacon but before it could transmit the laser-modulated beam, the receiving satellite may move out of the transmitter's beamwidth (transmitted beamwidth is kept nearly equal to twice of pointing error). This situation would be as that shown in Fig. 24.8. In such a case it is necessary to know the angle by which the receiving satellite has moved ahead (or back) of the transmitting satellite. This angle of drifting of the receiving satellite is called the 'point ahead angle'.

Thus if the tangential velocity of the receiving satellite is V_T meters/sec, then the point-ahead angle in given as

$$\alpha = \frac{V_T}{150} \text{ micro radians} \qquad \ldots(24.44)$$

In case the above point ahead angle exceeds the one half of the laser modulated beam's beamwidth then the use of this point ahead angle is being made. It is clear from Eq. (24.44) that the point-ahead angle is independent of the distance of optical satellite cross-link. For Velocities at earth orbiting speeds ($V_T = 30$ km/sec), the point ahead angle is approximately equal to 200 micro radians. Thus whereas the laser modulated beam's beamwidth may be of the order 10 to 100μ radians, the point ahead angle is of the order of 200μ radians.

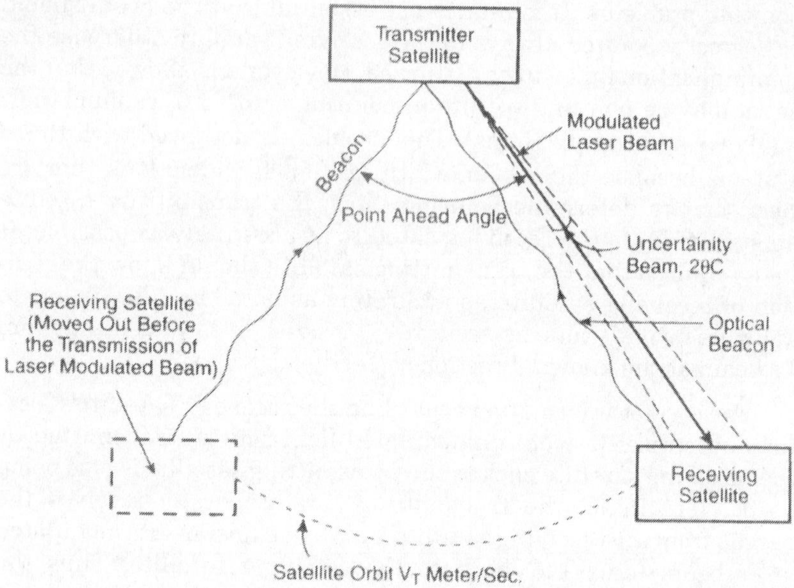

Fig. 24.8. Point ahead Angle and Pointing Error Representation for Optical Satellite Cross Link.

In case the optical beacon is to be used both the transmitting as well as the receiving satellites would have optical transmitters and receiver and in such a situation the basic block diagram of the optical-satellite cross link would be as that shown in Fig. 24.9. Here the receiving optics tracks the arrival beam direction and adjusts the transmitting beam direction. Normally separate wavelengths are used for the optical beams in each direction When there is no need of point-ahead angle the transmit and receive optics can be gimballed together and the laser transmits through the receive optics. But when the point ahead is needed then command control (either stored or received from earth station) must adjust transmitting direction relative to receive direction. This requires an accurate satellite attitude control.

With above discussions it is evident that before optical data transmissions, the transmitting antenna must acquire the beacon from the receiver. This beacon is transmitted from the receiving satellite with a beamwidth wide enough to cover the uncertainty angle of the beacon-receiving satellite. Once the beacon has been acquisitioned the satellite continuously tracks the LOS (line of sight vector) of the arriving beacon since the latter may vary due to the relative motion. In case the point ahead is needed, the satellite laser

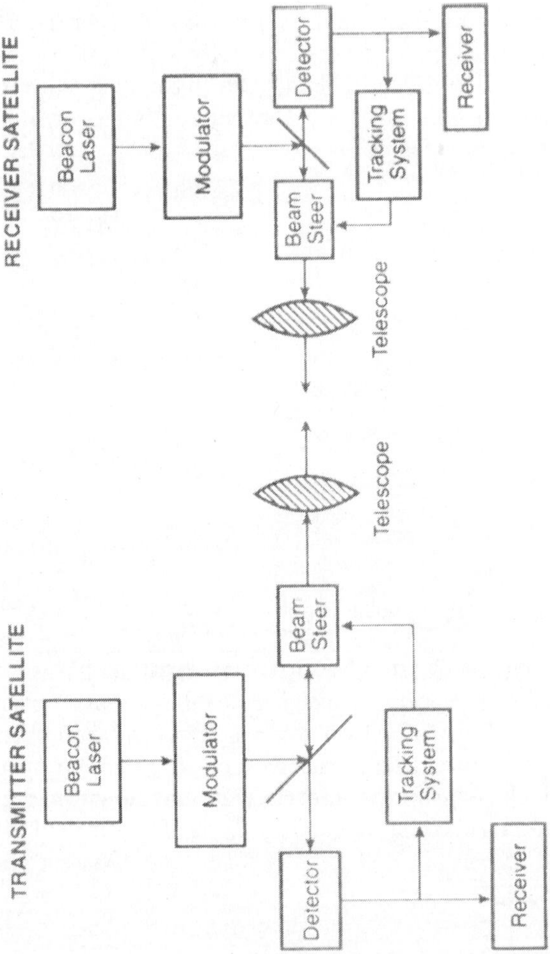

Fig. 24.9. Basic Block Diagram of Optical-Satellite Cross link (with the use of beacon).

transmitter must point ahead by the proper angle and direction. In some cases commands for the point ahead are given from the earth station through the RF or microwave links. For that it is essential that the earth station accurately knows the instantaneous V_T and also it is accurately transmitted to the satellite. After having LOS tracked and point-ahead angle determined the satellite optics points the return data beam to the proper position.

It would be of importance to mention here that though the above manouvers may be quite accurately carried out, even then some errors might be present there. These might be due to altitude reference errors in the satellite, mechanical and structural variations, boresight errors. However, the contributions of these errors are relatively quite small. But these errors can not be completely overcome as these errors are open loop errors. The contribution due to vibration and boresight errors is generally below microradians but the error due to altitude control may be high. It is therefore very essential to have proper altitude control so that overall pointing accuracy be as high as possible.

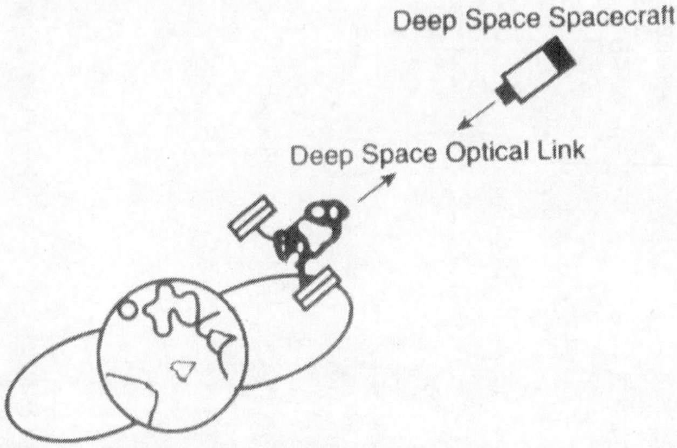

Fig. 24.10. Basic Overall Configuration of a Typical Deep Space Optical Communication link of NASA.

24.6. Deep Space Optical Communication Link

Fig. 24.10 shows a typical example of deep-space optical communication link of NASA. Here main space craft communication instrument is the optical transreceiver package called optranspac whose basic block diagram (isometric view) is shown in Fig. 24.11. The optranspac carries out various functions of the optical transmit-

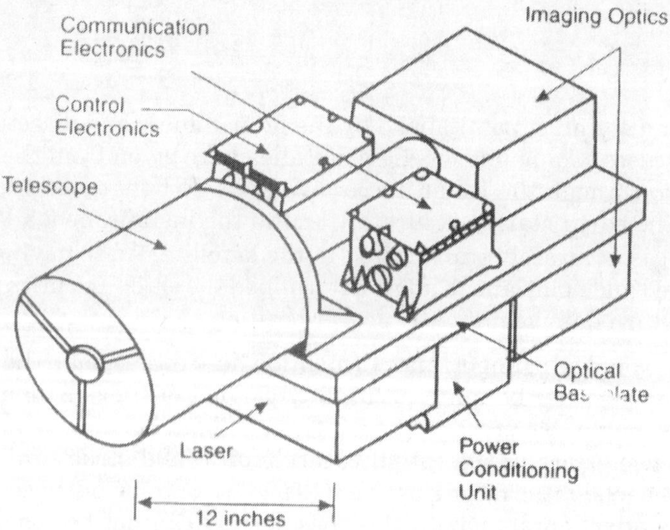

Fig. 24.11. An Isometric View of NASA's Optranspac.

ter and revceiver as discussed in previous sections. For example it receives beacon signal and performs beam acquisition, Tracking and pointing functions alongwith the uplink optical commands and ranging signals. It then returns coded data beam filled with telemetry data.

In the NASA's transpac of Fig. 24.11 there is a telescope of 10-30 cm diameter used both for receiving and transmitting. A typical telescope of 27 cm diameter and 400 mW laser enables a 100 Kbps data stream to be recovered from Saturn with a 10-metre orbiting photon bucket (receive optics). The optranspac ordinarily weights 50 kg and consumes 57 W of power. The imaging optics includes steering mirrors, beam splitters, alignment optics and detectors.

24.7. Review Questions

1. Explain the basic differences between the optical satellite communication link and RF satellite communication link. Mention their relative advantages and disadvantages.
2. Why is it not possible to have a direct optical communication link between earth station and communication satellite ? How does the atmospheric attenuation play its role?
3. Explain the basic blocks of an optical transmitter and compare it with the analogous RF transmitter.
4. Explain and compare various laser sources being used in laser communication systems.
5. Explain optical satellite cross-link. How do different noises affect the working of the link ? Derive the expression for resulting downlink signal after the uplink, cross-link and downlink transmission have taken place.
6. What types of modulation techniques may be used in optical satellite communication? Explain their working.
7. Explain the working of direct and hetrodyne optical satellite receivers. Which one is preferred and why?
8. What kind of photodetectors are being used in optical communications ? Explain their working principles.
9. What are point error, point ahead angle, acquisition, tracking and pointing in optical satellite communications?
10. Explain various noises that can affect photodetector's working? Find out the S/N formulas for the optical direct detection and hetrodyne detection cases.

25

Satellite Program of India: from INSAT to Chandrayaan

25.1. Introduction

India like any other developing country had long back realized the fact that better communication in the country is must for the national economic development.

Space science and technology has progressed by leaps and bounds in India, particularly in the last one decade or so. The space programme of India has had many a successes and international class achievements in almost all areas of Satellite technology, be it manufacturing of different types of satellites or be it the development and successful missions with the satellite launch vehicles. The level of achievement can be gauged from the fact that today. India is not only fully self-reliant technologically in manufacturing her own satellites for various missions, it has also made a beginning in the recent times to offer its launch vehicle services to other countries for launching their satellites. Also, the dgree once maturity of our space activities is amply evident from the fact that the largest organisation of the world in Satellite field, that is, INTELSAT is using the transponders on Indian Communication Satellites for providing certain services to their users.

India's commitment to space is part of her larger commitment to communicate to over three quarter of a billion of her population. Both research in space and in atomic energy started almost immediately after independence, and the space commitment increased with the growing responsibility of educating the illiterate masses whose number in numerical terms is almost five times to day than at the time of independence Dr. Vikram Sarabhai, the founder of Indian space Programme in the 1960's had already envisioned the importance of space to the real problems of man and society of Indian subcontinent. It was made clear then to the developed world that India's space programme was not to compete with the developed countries' space programmes such as the exploration of the planets or manned space flights but its purpose was solely for the development of Indian nation in economic and social terms.

25.2. Indian Space Research Organization

Overview. The national space programme was formally organized in 1972 with the formations of Space Commission, the Department of Space (DOS) and the Indian Space Research Organization (ISRO) to promote the development and application of space technology for the socio-economic benefit of the country. Space Commission is the policy making body and their policies are implemented by Department of Space. Research and Development activities are carried out through Indian Space Research Organization (ISRO). The overall co-ordination of the space programme is carried out programme offices of ISRO Headquarters in different areas like Satellite Communication, Earth Observation Systems, Space Science Launch Vehicles, International Co-operation, Industry Coordination and so on.

Figure showing various centres of ISRO.

Major establishments of Department of Space include National Remote Sensing Agency (NRSA), Physical Research Laboratory (PRL), National Mesosphere-Stratosphere-Troposphere Radar Facility (NMRF), Vikram Sarabhai Space Centre (VSSC), ISRO Satellite Centre (ISAC), SHAR Centre, Liquid Propulsion Systems Centre (LPSC), Space Applications Centre (SAC), ISRO Telemetry, Tracking and Command Network (ISTRAC), Development and Educational Communication Unit, INSAT Master Control Facility (MCF), ISRO Inertial Systems Unit (IISU) and Antrix Corporation Limited.

Activity Profile. A brief on the board activity profile of various major establishments of Department of Space is given in the following paragraphs to be followed by another brief on the major technological achievements of the Indian Space Research Organization.

Vikram Sarabhai Space Centre (VSSC). Vikram Sarabhai Space Centre (VSSC) is located at Thiruvanthapuram and is the main establishment for all Rocket and Launch Vehicle programmes. Major areas of R & D activity at VSSC include Aeronautics, Avionics, Materials, Composites, Solid Propulsion, Propellants, Polymers, Chemicals, Mechanical Engineering, Launch Vehicle, Computers and Information Technology and Systems Reliability. The Space Physics Laboratory located at Thumba does research in atmospheric and related space sciences.

ISRO Satellite Centre (ISAC). ISAC is the lead establishment engaged in Research and Development of Satellite Technology. The areas of R & D activity at this centre mainly include Power Systems, Digital Systems, Communications, Microwaves, Spacecraft Assembly and Testing, Structures, Thermal Systems, Spacecraft Mechanisms and Computers and Information. The centre also has a Laboratory for Electro-Optics Sensors (LEOS) that carries out Research and Development in the field of electro-optic sensors and systems relevant to satellites.

Space Applications Centre (SAC). Space Applications Centre (SAC), located at Ahmedabad is engaged in Research and Development related to space applications. The two major areas of activity include Satellite Communication and Remote Sensing, including Microwave Remote Sensing, for earth resource applications. The centre is also responsible for operating the Delhi Earth Station for satellite communication. The centre has facilities for Electronic, mechanical and spacecraft payload fabrication and also has facilities for their Environmental testing and Quality Assurance.

INSAT Master Control Facility (MCF). INSAT Master Control Facility located at Hassan (Karnataka) is responsible for all post launch operations on INSAT Satellites. The operations include Orbit Manoeuvres, Station Keeping and On-Orbit operation of the Spacecraft. ISAT MCF is an integrated facility consisting of satellite control earth stations with associated electronics and a spacecraft control centre for executing satellite control operations.

ISRO Telemetry, Tracking and Command Network (ISTRAC). This establishment provides mission support to near earth satellites and launch vehicle missions. ISTRAC has established an integrated network of ground stations at Bangalore, Lucknow, Port Blair, Sriharikota, Thiruvanthapuram, Bears Lake and Mauritius with a multimission spacecraft control centre located at Bangalore. ISTRAC is also responsible for operation of the Local User Terminal (LUT)/Mission Control Centre (MCC) under the international programme for satellite aided search and rescue.

ISRO Inertial Systems Unit (IISU). The main activity at the ISRO Inertial Systems Unit (IISU), as the name of the establishment suggests, is in the field of Inertial Sensors and related systems required by satellites and launch vehicles. IISU is located at Thiruvanthapuram and the areas of R & D thrust include Navigation Systems, Satellite Inertial Systems, Inertial Systems Intergration and Simulation, Bearing and Space Tribology.

Liquid Propulsion Systems Centre (LPSC). The activities of Liquid Propulsion Systems Centre (LPSC) are carried out at Bangalore, Thiruvanthapuram and Mahendragiri (Tamil Nadu). The activities related to liquid propulsion stages, cryogenic propulsion stages and control systems for launch vehicles and spacecraft are carried out a Thiruvanthapuram. The Bangalore unit is responsible for Integrations of Satellite Propulsion systems, Development of Transducers etc. and the Tamil Nadu unit is equipped with various test facilities.

SHAR Centre. SHAR Centre located in Sriharikota (Tamil Nadu) is the main launch centre of ISRO. It has all the required facilities needed for a launch mission including Range Instrumentation, Mission Analysis, Range Safety and Meteorology. The centre also has facilities for processing and ground testing solid propellant motors required for launch vehicles. SHAR also operates the launch ranges at Thumba (Kerala) for conducting sounding rocket flights for scientific studies.

National Remote Sensing Agency (NRSA). NRSA located at Hyderabad is an autonomous institution supported by Department of Space. The agency's main task is acquisition, processing and distribution of data from remote sensing satellites. The agency has an earth station that receives data from Indian Remote Sensing satellites, US LANDSAT and NOAA, French SPOT and also microwave data from European Remote Sensing Satellite (ERS). NRSA is also in-charge of Indian Institute of Remote Sensing at Dehradun. NRSA is also engaged various applications projects in collaboration with users.

Physical Research Laboratory (PRL). Physical Research Laboratory (PRL), located at Ahmedabad, is the premier centre for research in space and allied science. It is also an autonomous institution supported mainly by Department of Space. The research areas at PRL include Astronomy and Astrophysics, Planetary Atmosphere and Aeronomy, Earth Sciences and Solar System Studies and Theoretical Physics. It also manages Udaipur Solar Observatory.

Antrix Corporation Limited. It is the apex marketing agency under the Department of Space. It markets components and sub-systems for satellites, provides satellite fabrication (to user specifications), launch services and tracking facilities.

National Mesosphere-Stratosphere-Troposphere Radar Facility (NMRF). It is a national facility available for national and international scientists to conduct atmospheric research. It is an autonomous society.

Development and Educational Communication Unit (DECU). Located at Ahmedabad, DECU is involved in the conception, definition, planning, implementation and socio-economic evaluation of space applications. It works very closely with users to try out new and innovative system configurations to meet their specific requirements. Their primary functions include Organizing space application experiments and demonstrations, providing communications support for application projects, production of video programmes for education and training and so on.

Major Technological Programmes and Achievements. From a modest beginning in 1963 with the launch of small sounding rocket from Thumba near Thiruvanthapuram, Indian space programme has come a long way. Today, Indian National Satellite System (INSAT) and the Indian Remote Sensing Satellite System (IRS) which are the vital elements of national infrastructure for

Telecommunication, Television Broadcasting, Meteorology, Survey and Management of Resources are now designed and built indigenously.

INSAT Satellite System. INSAT System is one of the largest domestic satellite systems in the world today. This system provides Telecommunications, TV Broadcasting, Radio Networking, Meteorological Services and Disaster Management Services. INSAT transponder capacity is also being leased to other countries.

IRS Satellite System. Indian Remote Sensing. Satellite System comprises a constellation of four satellites. IRS satellite system provides remote sensing services. Data provided by these satellites is put to use for applications like Agricultural crop acreage and yield estimation, Ground water targetting, Identification of waste land for possible reclamation, Forest survey, Snow melt run-off estimates, Irrigation command area management, Mineral prospecting, Urban planning, Environment monitoring, Identification of potential fishing zones, Thematic mapping and so on.

Data from IRS satellites is also acquired and used by several other countries including those in North America, Europe, Thailand, Japan, Korea and Dubai under commercial agreements.

The follow-on satellites in the IRS series include IRS-P4 (named OCEANSAT and launched by indigenously developed Polar Satellite Launch Vehicle, PSLV), IRS-P5 (named CARTOSAT) and IRS-P6 (named RESOURCESAT). While IRS-P4 carries instruments like Ocean Colour Monitor and Multi Frequency Scanning Microwave Radiometer, IRS-P5 will provide high resolution stereo images for cartographic applications and Digital Terrain Modelling. IRS-P6 will continue further and enhance the services at present being provided by IRS-1C and IRS-1D satellites.

Satellite Launch Vehicles: ISRO has made substantial progress in the development of launch vehicles. The Polar Satellite Launch Vehicle (PSLV) has already become operational with the successful launch of IRS-1D in 1997. In fact, it is planned to launch all future satellites in the IRS-series by this vehicle. The launch vehicle PSLV is also being offered to other countries for launching of their satellites. A beginning was made by launching IRS-P4. PSLV-C2 will be used to launch two small satellites namely the Korean KISAT and the German TUBSAT as piggyback payloads. Another satellite named PROBA of Belgium is also booked for launch by PSLV. An agreement has been arrived at with ARIANSPACE to evolve a common interface so as to make possible launching of small satellites either by PSLV or Ariane.

ISRO has also developed a Geostationary Launch Vehicle (GSLV) needed for launching communication satellites in the geosynchronous orbit. First development test flight was tested in 2001 which launched an experimental satellite called GSAT-1. GSAT satellites are being used for conducting experiments/demonstrations of advanced communication technologies such as Digital Audio, Data and Video Broadcasting, INTERNET services, Wideband Multimedia and so on. GSAT-2, second satellite in the series, was launched by the second developmental flight of GSLV in 2003. The first operational figure of GSLV was conducted in 2004 cayying EDUSAT as its payload.

SROSS-series Satellites: The SROSS (Stretched Rohini Satellite Series) satellites are meant for carrying out scientific studies. SROSS-C2, the latest in SROSS series was launched by ASLV-D4 in 1994 and it carried two scientific payloads namely Gamma Ray Burst Experiment and a Retarding Potential Analyzer.

25.3. Indian Space Program

Table 25.1 presents the list of satellite developments and the launches undertaken by the country. Indian activities in space technology started in the early 1960's with the firing of sounding rockets from Thumba, located on the magnetic equator to study the earth's atmosphere. Ionospheric X-ray astronomical experiments were carried out with the help of such rockets.

Table 25.1

1962 :	Indian National Committee for Space Research (INCOSPAR) formed by the Department of Atomic Energy and work on establishing Thumba Equatorial Rocket Launching Station (TERLS) started.
1963 :	First sounding rocket launched from TERLS (November 21, 1963).
1965 :	Space Science & Technology Centre (SSTC) established in Thumba.
1967 :	Satellite Telecommunication Earth Station set up at Ahmedabad.
1968 :	TERLS dedicated to the United Nations (February 2, 1968),
1969 :	Indian Space Research Organisation (ISRO) formed under Department of Atomic Energy (August 15, 1969).
1972-1976 :	Space Commission and Department of Space set up (June 1, 1972). ISRO brought under DOS. Air-borne remote sensing experiments.
1975 :	ISRO's First Indian Satellite, Aryabhata, launched (April 19, 1975). Provided technological experience in building & operating a satellite system.
1975-1976 :	Satellite Instructional Television Experiment (SITE) conducted.
1977 :	Satellite Telecommunication Experiments Project (STEP) carried out.
1979 :	First Experimental launch of SLV-3, the first Indian launch vehicle with Rohini Technology Payload on board (August 10, 1979). Satellite could not be placed in orbit. Bhaskara-I, an experimental remote sensing satellite for earth observations carried TV and microwave cameras, launched (June 7, 1979).

1980 : Second Experimental launch of SLV-3, Rohini satellite successfully placed in orbit. (July 18, 1980

1981 : Bhaskara-II launched (November 20, 1981) Second experimental remote sensing satellite similar to Bhaskar-1. Provided experience in building and operating a remote sensing satellite system.
APPLE, an experimental geo-stationary communication satellite successfully launched (June 19, 1981). It provided experience in building and operating a 3-axis stabilized communication satellite.
Rohini (RS-D1) placed in orbit, used for conducting some remote sensing technology 1 studies using a land mark sensor payload. (May 31, 1981)
First developmental launch of SLV-3.

1982: INSAT-1A launched (April 10, 1982).
Deactivated on September 6, 1982.

1983 : INSAT-1B, launched (August 30, 1983). Second developmental launch of SLV-3, RS-D2 placed in orbit (April 17, 1983).

1984 : Indo-Soviet manned space mission (April 1984).

1987 : First developmental launch of ASLV with SROSS-1 satellite on board for Gamma Ray astronomy (March 24, 1987). Satellite could not be placed in orbit.

1988 : INSAT-1C launched (July 21, 1988). Abandoned in November 1989.
Second development launch of ASLV with SROSS-2 on board (July 13, 1988). Satellite could not be placed in orbit.
Launch of first operational Indian Remote Sensing Satellite, IRS-1A (March 17, 1988).

1990 : INSAT-1D launched (June 12, 1990).

1991 : Second operational Remote Sensing satellite, IRS-1B, launched (August 29, 1991).

1992 : INSAT-2A, the first satellite of the indigenously-built second-generation INSAT series, launched (July 10, 1992).
Third development launch of ASLV with SROSS-C on board (May 20, 1992). Satellite placed in orbit. It carried Gamma Ray astronomy and aeronomy payload.

1993 : First developmental launch of PSLV with IRS-1E on board (September 20, 1993). Satellite could not be placed in orbit.
INSAT-2B, the second satellite in the INSAT-2 series, launched (July 23, 1993).

1994 : Second developmental launch of PSLV with IRS-P2 on board (October 15, 1994). Satellite successfully placed in polar sunsynchronous orbit.
Fourth developmental launch of ASLV with SROSS-C2 on board (May 4, 1994). Satellite placed in orbit.

1995 : Launch of third operational Indian Remote Sensing Satellite, IRS-1C (December 28, 1995).
INSAT-2C, the third satellite in the INSAT-2 series, launched on December 7, 1995. Has additional capabilities such as mobile satellite service, business communication and television out reach beyond Indian boundaries.

1996 : Third development launch of PSLV with IRS-P3 on board (March 21, 1996). Satellite placed in polar sunsynchronous orbit.

1997 : INSAT-2D, fourth satellite in the INSAT series, launched (June 4, 1997). Becomes inoperable on October 4, 1997. (An in-orbit satellite, ARABSAT-1C, since renamed INSAT-2DT, was acquired in November 1997 to partly augment the INSAT system).
First operational launch of PSLV with IRS-1D on board (September 29, 1997). Satellite placed in orbit.

1998 : INSAT system capacity augmented with the readiness of INSAT-2DT acquired from ARABSAT (January 1998).

1999 : Indian Remote Sensing Satellite, IRS-P4 (OCEANSAT), launched by Polar Satellite Launch Vehicle (PSLV-C2) along with Korean KITSAT-3 and German DLR-TUBSAT from Sriharikota (May 26, 1999).
INSAT-2E, the last satellite in the multipurpose communication & meteorological INSAT-2 series, launched by Ariane from Kourou French Guyana, (April 3, 1999).

2000 : INSAT-3B, the first satellite in the third generation INSAT-3 series, launched by Ariane from Kourou French Guyana, (March 22, 2000).

2001 : ISRO's Polar Satellite Lauch Vehicle, PSLV-C3, successfully launched three satellites -- Technology Experiement Satellite (TES) of ISRO, BIRD of Germany and PROBA of Belgium - into their intended orbits (October 22, 2001).
The first developmental launch of GSLV-D1 with GSAT-1 on board from Sriharikota (April 18, 2001).

2002 : ISRO's Polar Satellite Launch Vehicle, PSLV-C4, successfully launched KALPANA-1 satellite from Sriharikota (September 12, 2002).
Successful launch of INSAT-3C by Ariane from Kourou French Guyana, (January 24, 2002).

2003 : ISRO's Polar Satellite Launch Vehicle, PSLV-C5, successfully launched RESOURCESAT-1 (IRS-P6) satellite from Sriharikota (October 17, 2003).
Successful launch of INSAT-3E by Ariane from Kourou French Guyana, (September 28, 2003).
The Second developmental launch of GSLV-D2 with GSAT-2 on board from Sriharikota (May 8, 2003).
Successful launch of INSAT-2A by Ariane from Kourou French Guyana, (April 10, 2003).

2004 : The first operational flight of GSLV (GSLV-D1) successfully launched EDUSAT from SDSC SHAR, Sriharikota (September 20, 2004).

2005 : ISRO's Polar Satellite Launch Vehicle, PSLV-C6, successfully launched CARTOSAT-1 and HAMSAT satellites from Sriharikota (May 5, 2005).

2006 : 2nd operational flight of GSLV (FO2) on July 10, carrying INSAT-4C.

2007 : Launch of CARTOSAT-2, SRE-1, LAPAN-TUBSAT and PEHUENSAT-1 on PSLV C7, Jan, 10.

2007 : INSAT-4B launched by Arian space on March 12.

2007 : SRE-1 splashed in Bay of Bengal on 22, Jan., 2007 and recovered by the Indian Coast Gaurd and Indian Navy, making India one of the few countries to have re-entry technology.

2007 : PSLV-08 places Italian Sattelite AGILE in its orbit on April 23. Weighing at 352 kgs sattelite is meant to gather information about the origins of the universe. It is country's first commercial space mission. The PSLV on its 11th flight since 1993, put the Agile satellite into its intended orbit about 550 kms above the earth, 20 min. after the blast off. ISRO has charged $11 million for this launch.

This Thumb Equatorial Rocket Launching Station (TERLS) was established with support from USSR, USA and France. TERLS is now an *International Range* under UN sponsorship and is available to the scientific community of the world. With this rocket technology know-how, Indian scientists started work on developing their own sounding rockets and payloads. At the same time an Experimental Earth Station (ESCES) was established in 1967 at Ahmedabad with the help from UN and ITU. It was used for training engineers from

Table 25.2 INSAT Series

Satellite	*Manufacturer*	*Stabilization*	*Payload*	*Design Life*	*Location*	*Launch*
INSAT-1B	Ford Aerospace	3-axis	2 S-band, 1 C-band transponders	7 yrs.	74° E	Aug, 83 STS
INSAT-2C	Ford Aerospace	3-axis	2 S-band, 1 C-band transponders	7 yrs.	94° E	July, 88 Ariane
INSAT-2D	Ford Aerospace	3-axis	2 S-band, 2 C-band transponders	7 yrs.	83° E	June, 90 Delta
INSAT-2A	ISRO	3-axis	2 S-band, 18 C-band	7 yrs.	74° E	July, 1992 Ariane
INSAT-2B	ISRO	3-axis	2 S-band, 18 C-band transponders	7 yrs.	93.5° E	July, 1993 Ariane
INSAT-2C	ISRO	3-axis	12 C-band, 6 extended C-band, 3 Ku-band transponders	—	93.5° E	December, 1995 Ariane
INSAT-2D	ISRO	3-axis	25 C-Band and IS band BSS Transponder	—	55° E	1996
INSAT-2E	ISRO	3-axis	12 C-band, 5 extended C-band transponders A VHRR, A CCD camera with 1 km resolution	—	83° E	April, 1999 Ariane
INSAT-3C	ISRO	3-axis	24 Normal C-band, 6 extended C-band, 2 S-band BSS Transponders and a Mobile Service Transponder operating in S-band for up-link and C-Band for downlink and mobile communication	—	74° E	Jan, 2002 Ariane
INSAT-3B	ISRO	3-axis	12 Extended C-band, 3 Ku band and IS band transponder Mobile Service Transponder and 1 Ku Beacon	—	83° E	March 2003
INSAT-3A	ISRO	3-axis	12 C-band, 6 ext. C-band 6 Ku-band transponders, 1 S-band transponder and Satellite Aided Search and Rescue (SAS&R) Transponder, Meteorological Payload of VHRR, CCD Camera and 1 Data Relay (DR) Transponder	—	93.5° E	April 2003
INSAT-3E	ISRO	3-axis	24 C Band and 12 Extended C-Band Transponders	—	55° E	Sept 2003

INSAT is a satellite project of Govt. of India and operated by Deptt. of space. It is a multi-purpose communication and meteorological satellite system providing TV traffic, telephony, meteorology, radio and private network services.

Table 25.3 Indian Remoting Sensing Satellite Program

Satellite	*Stabilization*	*Design Life (yrs.)*	*Payload*	*Orbit*	*Launch*
BHASKARA-I	Spin	—	—	535 km inclined at $50.7^\circ E$	June, 1979 Inter Cosmos Rocket
BHASKARA-II	Spin	—	A TV camera operating in visible and Infra-red and a microwave imaging system	—	November, 1981 Inter Cosmos Rocket
RS-IA	3-axis	3 yrs	Cameras LISS-I and LISS-II	Polar, Sun-synchronous 904 km high	March, 1988, VOSTOK
RS-IB	3-axis	3 yrs	Cameras LISS-I and LISS-II	Same as above	Vostok in August, 1991
RS-IC	3-axis	—	Cameras with resolution better than that of LISS-I and LISS-II	—	Vostok in December, 1995
IRS-ID	3-axis	—	—	—	September, 1997 PSLV-C1
IRS-P3	3-axis	—	Wide Field Sensor, X-ray Monitor, Modular optoelectronics Scanner	Polar Sun-synchronous 817 km	PSLV on March, 1996
IRS-P4	3-axis	—	Ocean Colour Monitor (OCM), Multispectral Scanning Microwave Radiometer (MSMR)	720 km, Polar Sun-synchronous Orbit	May, 1999, PSLV-C2
IRS-P5 (Cartosat-1)	3-axis	—	Panchromatic Cameras with resolution of 2.5 m and width of 30 km	617 km, Polar Sun-synchronous Orbit	PSLV-C6 May 2005
IRS-P6 (Resouresat)	3-axis	—	Multi-spectral Cameras, LISS-III, LISS-IV, Advanced Wide Field Sensor	817 km, Polar Sun Synchronous Orbit	PSLV-C5 in October 2003
Cartosat-2	3-axis	—	—	—	

India and other developing countries in handling advanced equipment. Since the establishment of ESCES, the development of satellite communications in India has been in constant advance. Technology development, studies, experiments and launchers etc. have been going on leading to the establishment of operational facilities, use of INTELSAT and INMARSAT systems and establishment of a unique multi-agency multipurpose domestic satellite system, the Indian National Satellite System (INSAT). Table 25.2 presents a summary of the INSAT system. Satellites for earth observation under the Remote Sensing program are given in the Table 25.4.

Table 25.4 Indian Remote Sensing Satellite (IRS) System

- Commissioned with the launch of IRS-1A in March 1988
- IRS system under National Natural Resources Management System (NNRMS) corordinated at national level by the Planning Committee of NNRMS (PC-NNRMS).
- At present has four satellites, IRS-1B launched in August 1991, IRS-1C launched in December 1995 and IRS-1D launched on September 29, 1997.
- **IRS-P3** and IRS-1D launched by India's Polar Satellite Launch Vehicle (PSLV).
- **OCEANSAT-1** with an Ocean Colour Monitor (OCM) and a Multi-frequency Scanning Microwave Radiometer (MSMR) launched by PSLV-C2.
- **RESOURCESAT-1** for agricultural applications launched by **PSLV-C5.**
- **CARTOSAT-1** with a Very High Resolution Panchromatic camera for cartographic applications launched by **PSLV-C6.**
- Data from IRS satellites received and processed by the **National Remote Sensing Agency, Hyderabad.**
- SI,a US Company also receives and markets IRS data worldwide under a commercial contract with **Antrix Corporation of the Department of Space.**

The satellites for scientific and technological experiments have also been developed on a large scale (Table 25.5). Weather forecast function is provided by the communication satellites of INSAT-series.

The country has now achieved capabilities in the development of launch vehicles for satellites after its first launch rocket SLV-3 in 1979. Dr. Abdul Kalaam, the President of India and a reverved space scientist was the leader of the team which developed SLV-3. The Polar Satellite Launch Vehicle (PSLV) represents India's capability of satellite in polar orbits for remote sensing satellites and Geosynchronous Satellite Launch Vehicle (GSLV).

Table 25.5 SROSS Series for Scientific Experiments

Satellite	*Payload*	*Launch*
SROSS-C1	Two Scientific Payloads : 1. Gamma Ray Burst (GRB) Experiment, 2. Retarding Potential Analyzer (RPA)	May, 1992 by ASLV-D3
SROSS-C2	Two Scientific Payloads : 1. Gamma-Ray Burst (GRB) Experiment, 2. Retarding Potential Analyzer (RPA)	May, 1994 by ASLV-D4

Features of Polar Satellite Launch Vehicle (PSLV)

- Developmental flights completed with successful third developmetal launch in March 1996.
- Now available for launching 1,000-1,200 kg class of remote sensing satellites into polar sun-synchronous orbit. IRS-1D launched on September 29, 1997.
- IRS-P4 (OCEANSAT) and two small satellites (KITSAT of Korea and TUBSAT of Germany) launched on May 26, 1999 by **PSLV-C2.**
- **PSLV-C3** launched three satellites — Technology Experiment Satellite (TES) of ISRO, BIRD of Germany and PROBA of Belgium - into their intended orbits on October 22, 2001.
- ISRO's Polar Satellite Launch Vehicle, **PSLV-C4** launched KALPANA-1 satellite on September 12, 2002.
- ISRO's Polar Satellite Launch Vehicle, **PSLV-C5** launched **RESOURCESAT-1 (IRS-P6)** satellite on October 17, 2003.
- ISRO's Polar Satellite Launch Vehicle, **PSLV-C6** launched **CARTOSAT-1** and **HAMSAT** satellites on May 5, 2005.

Features of Geosynchronous Satellite Launch Vehicle (GSLV)

- For launching 2,000 kg class of communication satellites into geosynchronous transfer orbit.
- A three stage vehicle; first stage is a 129 tonne solid propellant core motor with four liquid propellant strap-ons with 40 tonne propellant each, second stage is a liquid propulsion system with 37.5 tonne propellant and a cryogenic upper stage with 12 tonne of liquid oxygen and liquid hydrogen.
- First developmental flight **GSLV-D1** completed with successful launch on April 18, 2001.
- Second developmental flight **GSLV-D2** launched **GSAT-2** satellite on May 8, 2003. It carries a heavier satellite, to be placed in a GTO of 180 km perigee (nearest point to earth) and 36,000 km apogee (farthest point to earth). Its higher payload was achieved by incorporating enhanced propellant loading in

the core solid motor, a high pressure engine on the liquid propellant strap-on motors used in the 2nd stage of the vehicle and optimisation of structural elements. It also consists hundreds of sub-systems built by 150 Indian companies from both public and private sectors.

- First operational flight of **GSLV (GSLV-F01)** and the third in the GSLV series launched **EDUSAT** satellite on September 20, 2004.

Table 25.6 Indian Space Program — Calender for Space Events 2003 to 2008

Mission	*2003-2004*	*2004-2005*	*2005-2006*	*2006-2007*	*2007-2008*
IRS	RESOUR-CESAT-1	CARTOSAT-1	CARTOSAT-2	OCEAN-SAT T-2	RISAT-1
INSAT	3A 3E		4A 4B	4C 4D	4E
METSAT					INSAT-3D
Expt/Tech. Payloads	GSAT-2	EDUSAT HAMSAT	SRE-1	GSAT-4	GSAT (MK III)
Space Science					CHANDRAYAAN ASTROSAT
PSLV	C5	C6	C7	C8	C9 C10 C11
GSLV-MK I& II	D2	F1		F2 D3 F3	F4 F5
GSLV-MK III					D1

25.4 Satellite Launch Programme

25.4.1. Geosynchronous Satellite Launch Vehicle (GSLV)

The GSLV, has demonstrated the country's capability to place 2000 kg class of satellites into GTO. The 49 metre tall, 414 tonne GSLV is a three stage vehicle, which is a conglomerate of Indian, European and Russian components.

ISRO adapted stages from India's Polar Satellite Launch Vehicle (PSLV) for GSLV. The first stage solid propellant motor and the liquid propellant second stage of PSLV, itself powered by engines used by Europe's Ariane 1, serve as the core first stage motor and the second stage of GSLV. The PSLV second stage was also used as the basis for the GSLV first stage liquid strap-on stages.

First stage : It uses a 20.3 × 2.8 m 480 ton thrust solid motor, augmented by four 19.7 × 2.1 m L40 liquid strap-on motors. The non-separating L40s are powered by 70 ton thrust Viking 2 engines that burn UDMH/N204 for 160 seconds, 60 seconds longer than the core.

Second stage : GSLV's 11.6 × 2.8 m GS-2 second stage starts its Viking 470 ton thrust engine just before first stage cutoff, to ensure propellant settling, and burns for 160 seconds.

Third stage : The Glavkosmos 12KRB Cryogenic Stage (CS) then ignites its 73.5 kN KVD-1 LH2/LOX engine for a planned 710 second burn. CS is the first Russian-built liquid-hydrogen upper stage to fly, but ISRO plans to replace it with its own LH2 third stage in a few years.

The vehicle is controlled by a strap-down inertial navigation/guidance system housed in a vehicle equipment bay that is mounted on a truss structure atop the third stage. A 7.8 meter tall, 3.4 meter diameter payload fairing protects the payload during ascent until it is jettisoned at an attitude of about 10 km during the second stage burn.

During a typical flight, the four liquid propellant (L-40) strap-on stages are ignited first. The solid propellant core stage, S125, is ignited 4.6 seconds later and lift off occurs. The core stage burns for 100 seconds and the four L-40 strap-on stages continue to burn for an additional 60 seconds. Staging occurs at an altitude of about 73 km.

The GS2 liquid propellant second stage ignites 1.6 second before the separation of first stage, using a "fire in the hole" start sequence. The second stage burns for about 150 seconds. The payload fairing separates at about the 260 second point. Second stage separation occurs about 314 seconds after lift-off at an altitude of about 127 km.

The cryogenic third performs a single 710 second burn, boosting the payload to a velocity of 10.2 km per second, at an altitude of 195 km. This injects the payload into an elliptical transfer orbit (GTO) with a perigee of 180 km and an apogee of 35,975 km.

The original PSLV/GSLV launch complex was replaced in 2005 with a new, mobile launch facility. Whereas, the original pad featured fixed launch stand and a 75 meter tall mobile service tower, the new pad uses rail-mobile launch stands that allow vehicles to be stacked in a vertical integration building located some distance from the launch pad itself.

The three-axis attitude (orientation) stabilization : It is achieved by autonomous control systems provided in each stage. Single plane Engine Gimbal Control (EGC) of the four strap-ons of the first stage are used for pitch, yaw and roll control. The second stage has EGC for pitch and yaw and hot gas Reaction Control System (RCS) for roll control. Two swivellable vernier engines using LH2 and LOX provide pitch, yaw and roll control for the third stage; during thrust phase and cold gas system during coast phase. The Inertial Guidance System in the equipment bay housed above the third stage guides the vehicle till spacecraft injection. The closed loop guidance scheme located in the on-board computer ensures the required accuracy in the injection conditions.

Vehicle performance monitoring : GSLV employs S-band telemetry and C-band transponders for the vehicle performance monitoring, tracking, range safety/flight safety and preliminary orbit determination.

Separation systems : GSLV employs various separation systems such as Flexible Linear Shaped Charge for the first stage, pyro-actuated release mechanism for second stage and Merman band bolt cutter separation mechanism for the third stage. Spacecraft separation is by spring thrusters, mounted at the separation interface.

25.4.2. GSLV Series

GSLV D-01. ISRO launched its first GSLV from Satish Dhawan Space Centre, SHAR, Sriharikota on April 18, 2001. An early third stage cutoff denied the 49-meter tall rocket's total success in the inaugural D-1 mission. G-Sat 1, a 1,540 kg test payload, fell about 4,000 km short of its planned 36,000 km geosynchronous transfer orbit (GTO) apogee. G-Sat was unable to make up the difference with its apogee motor and it ended up stranded in a 23-hour drift orbit.

GSLV D2. Launched on May 8, 2003, this vehicle launched 1820 kg GSAT-2.

GSLV F-01. This was first operational GSLV flight launched on September 20, 2004 and placed 1950 kg EDUSAT into GTO with a perigee of 180 km and an apogee of 35,985 km with an orbital inclination of 19.2 deg with respect to the equator.

GSLV F-02. Launched on 10 July 2006, the 49-metre-tall, 414 tonne, three-stage GSLV F-02 failed to orbit INSAT 4C. The failure was caused by a malfunction of the thrust controller in the strap-on booster engine. Each booster is powered by a single 70-tonne thrust Vikas engine fed by 42 tonnes of hyperlogic liquid propellant. Vikas are derived form Viking 2 engines originally used by Europe's Ariane 1 launcher.

Table 25.1 GSLV-F02 Configurations

	LEO Payload (*metric tons*) 200 *km* × 45 *deg*	*GTO Payload* (*metric tons*)	*Configuration*	*Liftoff Height* (*meters*)	*Liftoff Mass* (*metric tons*)
GSLV	5 t	2 t	3 stage GSLV with Russian 3rd Stage Engine	49 m	401 t

Vehicle Components

	Stage 1 Core GS1 S125	*Stage 1 (GS1) L40 Strap-On Boosters (Each of 4) (Not Jettisoned)*	*Stage 2 GS2 L40*	*Stage 3 GS3 "CS"*	*Payload Fairing*
Diameter (m)	2.8 m	2.1 m	2.8 m	2.8 m	2.8 m
Length (m)	20.3 m	19.7 m	11.6 m	8.7 m	7.8 m
Propellant Mass (tons)	129 t	40 t	37.5 t	12.5 t	
Total Mass (tons)	156 t	46 t	42.8 t	15 t	
Engine	S125	Viking 2	Viking 4	12KRB	
Engine Mfgr		SEP	SEP	Glavkosmos	
Fuel	HTPB	UDMH	UDMH	LH2	
Oxidizer		N204	N204	LOX	
Thrust (SL tons)					
Thrust (Vac tons)	479.3 t	69.34 t	73.41 t	7.65 t	
ISP (SL sec)	237 s	240 s			
ISP (Vac sec)	266 s	281 s	295 s	460 s	
Burn Time (sec)	100 s	160 s	150 s	750 s	
No. Engines	1	4	1	1	1

Time	*Event*	*Altitude*	*Velocity*
T-4.6 s	L40 Strap-on Boosters Ignite	0 km	0
T+0 s	S 125 Core Stage Ignites - Liftoff	0 km	0
T+ 100 s	S 125 Core Stage Burn Out	km	
T+158.4 s	L40 Second Stage Ignites	km	
T+160 s	L40 First Stage Boosters Burn Out/Stage Separation	73 km	
T+260 s	Payload Fairing Separation	110 km	
T+310 s	Second Stage Shut Down	120 km	
T+314 s	Second/Third Stage Separation/Third Stage Ignition	127 km	
T+1024 s	Third Stage Shut Down	195 km	10.2 km/s

GSLV V-04, the launch vehicle injecting the communication satellite, INSAT-4CR, in its pre-determined orbit in September 2007. This was the heaviest satellite to the launched by the Indian Space Research Organisation (ISRO), with the INSAT-4CR tilting the scales at 2,130 kg.

GSLV F-05 more satellites towards a commercial capability

GSLV-D3, the Mark II, is a new design, capable of carrying heavy satellites and has one of the stages powered by an indigenous cryogenic engine. The GSLV flights, up to now, have employed Russian cryogenic engines.

During the first half, the indigenous Geosynchronous Satellite Launch Vehicle (GSLV) will put in space GSAT-3, which will have unique transponders dedicated for tele-education.

GSLV Mark III (GSLV-D4). This vehicle has a larger cryogenic stage with more fuel equipped to carry very heavy satellites, say 4000 kg. into orbit. The GSLV Mark-III is not derived from PSLV or GSLV Mark-I or II series.

It is a three-stage vehicle with a 110 tonne core liquid propellant stage and a strap-on stage with two solid propellant motors, each with 200 tonne propellant. The upper stage will be a cryogenic with a propellant loading of 25 tonne. It will have a lift off weight of about 629 tonnes and will be 42.4 m tall. The payload fairing will have a diameter of 5 metres and a payload volume of 100 cubic metres. GSLV Mark-III will make its maiden launch in 2009.

This vehicle will fulfill India's ambition to become a major player in the billion-dollar global satellite launch market.

The ISRO has completed preliminary design review of all sub-systems of the vehicle and has held the integrated technical review. Fabrication of S-200 motor cases and other vehicle structures have already commenced. The structural dynamic data of the vehicle has been generated and the vehicle configuration for the ground resonance testing finalised. Configuration of destruct systems for S-200 and L-110 stages and jettisoning motors for S-200 separation system has been finalised. Based on wind tunnel and computational fluid dynamic studies, the aerodynamic coefficients of the vehicle have been revised. A long duration engine qualification test for L-110 has been completed. The preliminary design review of the engine for C-25 cryogenic stage has been completed. Two series of cold flow test have been conducted on LOX proto type turbine using water. Further, progress has been made in the development of Cryogenic Upper

Stage (CUS) to replace the Russian procured cryogenic stage on GSLV.

24.4.3. Cryogenic Upper Stage Project (CUSP)

GSLV, in its present configuration (GSLV Mk I), uses the Russian supplied upper stage. For GSLV-Mk II, the ISRO has developed Cryogenic Upper Stage (CUS) that will increase the payload capability from the present 2000 kg to 2500 kg into the GTO. The CUSP envisages design and development of the indigenous cryogenic upper stage to replace the Russian-supplied cryogenic stage in GSLV.

The qualification hot tests of the integrated engine with steering engines have been successfully completed on the second engine with two steering engines. Endurance hot test for a duration of 1000 sec and test for simulating off-normal conditions of operation (120 sec) have been conducted. The third main engine with flight nozzle has been realised and tested successfully for 200 sec as part of acceptance testing. All major subsystems of fourth engine have also been realised. CUS main engine and steering engines have undergone tests for a cumulative duration of more than 5,700 secs and 4,400 secs respectively.

25.4.4. Polar Satellite Launch Vehicle (PSLV)

India has now acquired a significant capability in the launch vehicle area with the successful development of Polar Satellite Launch Vehicle (PSLV), capable of putting a 1,000-1200 kg class satellite into 820 km polar sun-synchronous orbit. PSLV is the workhorse launch vehicle of the Indian Space Research Organisation (ISRO) with nine consecutively successful flights so far. Since its first successful launch in 1994, PSLV has launched seven Indian remote sensing satellite, an amateur radio satellite, HAMSAT, and four small satellites for foreign customers into 550-800 km high polar SSOs. Besides, it has also launched India's exclusive meteorological satellite, Kalpana-1, into Geosynchronous Transfer Orbit (GTO), PSLV will also be used to launch India's first spacecraft mission to moon, Chandrayaan-1, during 2008.

Weight (t): 294

Payload (kg) : 1000-1200

Height (m) : 44.43

Orbit : Polar orbit

Table 25.7 : Design Features of Polar Satellite Launch Vehicle

	Stage-1	*Stage-2*	*Stage-3*	*Stage-4*
Nomenclature	Core PSI + Strap-on PSOM	PS2	PS3	PS4
Propellant	Solid HTPB Based	liquid UDMH +N204	Solid HTPB Based	Bi-Prop MMH + N204
Propellant Mass (tonnes)	138.0 + 6X9.0	40.6	7.2	2.0
Stage Mass (tonnes)	229	46	8.4	2.89
Max Thrust (kN)	4762 + 662 × 6	725	340	7.4 × 2
Burn time (sec)	107.4 45	163	76	415
Stage Dia (m)	2.8 1.0	2.8	2.0	1.3
Stage Length (m)	20 10	12.5	3.6	2.1
Control	SITVC for Pitch & Yaw, Reaction control Thrusters for roll SITVC, in 2 PSOMs for roll control augmentation	Engine Gimbal for Pitch & Yaw, Hot Gas Reaction Control Motor for	Flex Nozzle for Pitch & Yaw, PS4 RCS for Roll Control	Engine Gimbal for Pitch, Yaw and Roll, On-Off RCS for coast phase

25.4.5. PSLV Series

PSLV-C1. IRS-ID was launched on September, 29, 1997.

PSLV-C2. IRS-P4 (OCEANSAT) and two piggy back small satellites - Korean KITSAT and German TUBSAT - were launched on May 26, 1999 by this vehicle.

PSLV-C3. Technology Experiment Satellite (TES) of ISRO, BIRD of Germany and PROBA of Belgium were placed into their intended orbits by this vehicle on October 22, 2001.

PSLV-C4. It launched India's exclusive meteorological satellite, the 1060 kg KALPANA-1, into a GTO on September 12, 2002.

PSLV-C5. RESOURCESAT 1 (IRS P6) satellite was launched by PSLV C5 on October 17, 2003.

PSLV-C6. It placed India's 1535 kg CARTOSAT-1 and 42 kg HAMSAT satellite on May 5, 2005 into a 622 km sun-synchronous polar orbit.

PSLV-C7. PSLV-C7 successfully launched four satellites - India's remote sensing satellite 650 kg CARTOSAT-2, Space Capsule Recovery Experiment (SRE-1) and Indonesia's LAPANTUBSAT and Argentina's PEHUENSAT-1 into a 635 km high polar orbit with an inclination of 97.9 deg with respect to the equator on January 10, 2007.

PSLV-C7, it launched four payloads, in all weighing 1292 kg in addition to the DLA. Some of the modification incorporated in PSLV-C7 compared to the previous flight, PSLV-C6, are :

- Use of Dual Launch Adopter with the spacecraft mounted over the adaptor and the 600 kg SRE mounted inside to accommodate two primary satellites in tandem.
- Reduction of propellant from 2.5 tonnne to 2 tonne in the fourth liquid propellant stage, PS4.

After the final count down, PSLV-C7 lifted off from the first launch pad at SDSC SHAR, at 9.23 am with the ignition of the core first stage and four of the six strap-on motors. The remaining two strap-on motors were ignited at 25 sec after lift-off. The important flight events included the separation of the ground-lit strap-on motors, separation of air-lit strap-on motors and the first stage, ignition of the second stage, separation of the heatshield at about 121 km altitude after the vehicle had cleared the dense atmosphere, second stage separation, third stage ignition, third stage separation, fourth stage ignition and fourth stage cut-off.

The 680 kg main payload, CARTOSAT-2, mounted over DLA, was the first satellite to be injected into orbit at 981.3 sec after lift-off at an altitude of 639 km. About 45 sec later, DLA with the 6 kg PEHUENSAT-1 mounted on it, was separated. 120 sec later, the 550 kg Space capsule Recovery Experiment (SRE-1) mounted inside DLA was separated and finally, 190 sec later, the 56 kg LAPAN-TUBSAT, mounted on the equipment bay of PSLV fourth stage was separated.

LAPAN-TUBSAT and PEHUENSAT-1 : LAPAN-TUBSAT and PEHUENSAT-1 were launched under commercial argreements. LAPAN-TUBSAT is a cooperative venture between Indonesian Space Agency, LAPAN and Technical University of Berlin. It is an earth observation satellite besides a technical demonstrator in control systems. The 56 kg LAPAN-TUBSAT carrier two Charge Coupled Device (CCD) cameras with ground resolutions of 5 m and 200 m respectively. It also carries and experiment for message store and forward system.

PEHUENSAT-1 is a 6 kg Argentinean nano-satellite meant to serve educational, technological and scientific fields. PEHUENSAT-1, developed by University of Comahue of Argentina, AMSAT (Amateur Satellite Association of Argentina) and Argentina Association for Space Technology, is intended to provide an experiment platform ameteur radio experiments between colleges and universities of Argentina.

The 44 m tall PSLV has a lift-off mass of 295 tonne. It is a four-stage launch vehicle with the first and the third stages as well as the six strap-ons surrounding the first stage using HTPB based solid propellant. PSLV'S first stage is one of the largest solid propellant boosters in the world. Its second and fourth stages use liquid propellants. PSLV's bulbous payload fairing has a diameter of 3.2 metre. The vehicle has S-band telemetry and C-band transponder systems for monitoring its health and flight status. It also has sophisticated auxiliary systems like stage and payload fairing separation systems.

Space Capsule Recovery Experiment (SRE)

SRE in intended for demonstrating the capability to recover an orbiting space capsule. The experiment envisages the development of a 500 kg recoverable capsule and the associated technologies. SRE is intended to test reusable thermal protection system, navigation, guidance and control, hypersonic aero-thermodynamics, management of communication blackout, deceleration and floatation system, recovery operations, etc. The idea was to test some technologies towards eventually developing – and ambitious task – a reusable launch vehicle like the US Challenger spacecraft.

SRE comprises an aero-thermo structure, spacecraft platform, deceleration and floatation system and micro-gravity payloads. It has a sphere-cone-flare configuration with a spherical nose of about 0.5 m radius, base diameter of 2 metres and 1.6 metres height. The capsule is made of mild steel. The parachute, pyro devices, avionics package of triggering unit and sequencer, telemetry and tracking system, sensors for measurement of system performance parameters are placed inside SRE capsule.

After its launch by PSLV, SRE remained in orbit for a few days during which it was used to perform two experiments in micro-gravity environment — an Isothermal Heating Furnace [IHF] and Biomimetic (Biomineralisation of Inorganic materials) experiment. IHF was operated to perform metallurgical experiments while Biomimetic experiment was operated to perform Biomimetic synthesis.

Two days before de-orbiting, SRE-1 was placed in a Repetitive Elliptical Orbit. Subsequently, it will be reoriented and de boost rocket is fired to make it re-enter the earth's atmosphere. Close loop guidance system is employed during de-boost and coasting phases leading to its recovery. On re-entry, after initial aerodynamic braking, a parachute system will reduce the touch down velocity. SRE-1 will splashdown in the Bay of Bengal, east of Sriharikota coast. A floatation system will keep SRE afloat and enable its recovery.

PSLV-C8

PSLV-C8 mission launched the Italian astronomical satellite. AGILE under a commercial contract in April 2007. The 360 kg satellite was placed into a 550 km low earth orbit. Its configuration had only core vehicles and there were no six strap on motor as the weight of the satellite was very less and the thrust provided by the core vehicle would be enough to place the satellite in orbit.

PSLV-C9 is the thirteenth flight of ISRO's Polar Satellite Launch Vehicle (PSLV) and the third flight of its 'Core Alone' version as well. In this flight, PSLV launches ten payloads - India's 690 kg CARTOSAT-2A and 83 kg Indian Mini Satellite (IMS-1) as well as eight nanosatellites from abroad together weighing about 50 kg into a 635 km high polar Sun synchronous Orbit (SSO) inclined at an angle of 97.94 deg to the equator.

With much lighter payloads compared to the ones placed into orbit by its standard version, PSLV-C9 is configured without the six solid propellant strap-on motors of the first stage. The previous two launches of PSLV were also such 'Core Alone' versions. The Core-Alone PSLV-C9 will have a lift-off mass of 230 tonne.

PSLV has emerged as the workhorse launch vehicle of ISRO with eleven consecutively successful flights so far. Since its first successful launch in 1994, PSLV has launched eight Indian remote sensing satellites, HAMSAT - an amateur radio satellite, SRE-1 - a recoverable space capsule and six small satellites for foreign customers into 550-800 km high polar Sun Synchronous Orbits (SSO). Besides, it has launched two satellites from abroad into Low Earth Orbits (LEO) of low or medium inclination. PSLV has also launched KALPANA-1 - India's exclusive meteorological satellite into Geosynchronous Transfer Orbit (GTO). PSLV will be used to launch Chandrayaan - 1 - India's first spacecraft mission to moon, during 2008.

In its standard configuration, the 44m tall PSLV has a lift-off mass of 295 tonne. It is a four-stage launch vehicle with the first and the third stages as well as the six strap-ons surrounding the first stage using HTPB based solid propellant. PSLV's first stage is one of the largest solid propellant boosters in the world.

Its second and fourth stages use liquid propellants. PSLV's bulbous payload fairing has a diameter of 3.2 metre. The vehicle has

S-band telemetry and C-band transponder systems for monitoring its health and flight status respectively. It also has sophisticated auxiliary systems like stage and payload fairing separation systems.

PSLV was originally designed to place 1,000 kg class of India's remote sensing satellites into a 900 km polar SSO. The payload capability of PSLV has been successively enhanced and in its ninth flight, PSLV-C6, in May 2005 launched two payloads - 1,560 kg CARTOSAT-1 and 42 kg HAMSAT into a 620 km SSO. And, in its tenth flight, PSLV-C7 launched four payloads - 680 kg CARTOSAT-1, 550 kg Space capsule Recovery Experiment (SRE-1), 56 kg LAPAN-TUBSAT of Indonesia and 6 kg PEHUENSAT-1 of Argentina - into a 635 km high polar SSO with an inclination of 97.9 deg with respect to the equator.

PSLV-C9 is launched from the Second Launch Pad at Satish Dhawan Space Centre SHAR, Srhiharikota the Spaceport of India, situated at a distance of about 80 km North of Chennai in the Nellore District of Andhra Pradesh State. Compared to many space launch centers of the world, Sriharikota's proximity to Equator is advantageous for launching payloads into different orbits. It has facilities for solid propellant processing, static testing of solid motors, launch vehicle integration and launch operations, range operations comprising telemetry, tracking and command network and mission control centre. The second Launch Pad became operational in May 2005.

Table 25.8. PSLV-C9 stages at a glance

	Stage-1	*Stage-2*	*Stage-3*	*Stage-4*
Nomenclature	Core (PS1)	PS2	PS3	PS4
Propellant	Solid HTBP based	Liquid UH25 + N_2O_4	Solid HTPB based	Bi-prop MMH + MON-3
Mass (Tonne)	138.0+	41.5	7.6	1.6
Max Thrust (kN)	4762.0	800	246	7.3 × 2
Burn Time (sec)	106.9	147	122.5	318
Stage Dia (m)	2.8	2.8	2.0	2.8
Stage Length (m)	2.0	12.8	3.6	2.9
Control	SITVC for Pitch & Yaw, Reaction Control Thrusters for Roll	Engine Gimbal for Pitch & Yaw, Hot Gas Reaction Control Motor for Roll Control	Flex Nozzle for Pitch & Yaw, PS4 RCS for Roll	Engine Gimbal for Pitch, Yaw and Roll, on-off RCS for Coast Phase Control

PSLV-C10. The 230 tonne PSLV-C10, the 25th Satellite Launch Mission, launched TECSAR satellite on January 21, 2008 under a commercial contract with Antrix Corporation set up by the Department of Space. It had a 'core alone' configuration, only the second time such a configuration has been tried by ISRO. The first time it was used in PSLV-C8.

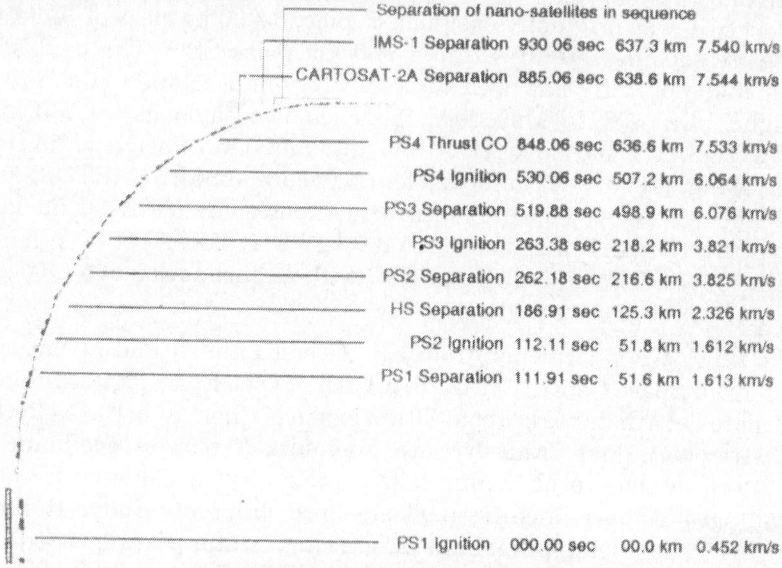

Fig. 25.1. PSLV-C9 Flight Profile (Typical)

The 300 kg TECSAR satellite was placed into its intended orbit with a perigee (nearest point to earth) of 450 km and apogee (farthest point to earth) of 580 km with an orbital inclination of 41 deg with respect to the equator. TESCAR is a Synthetic Aperture Radar (SAR) Technology satellite. The satellite is equipped with a SAR payload with the capability to see through the clouds and carry out day and night all weather imaging.

Developed by the Israeli aircraft industry, it will be Tel Aviv's first 260 kg satellite—with what is known as a synthetic aperture radar (SAR). This will allow the satellite to see objects below, which are extremely tiny. SAR is used by moving instruments like satellites over in mobile targets and has wide applications in the critical area of remote sensing. The Polaris is considered a spy satellite by many countries in the Gulf and Pakistan, who were opposed to India carrying out the launch.

PSLV-C11: The Launcher

PSLV-C11, chosen to launch Chandrayaan-1 spacecraft, is an uprated version of ISRO's Polar Satellite Launch Vehicle standard configuration. Weighing 316 tonnes at lift-off, the vehicle uses larger strap-on motors (PSOM-XL) to achieve higher payload capability.

PSLV is the trusted workhorse launch Vehicle of ISRO. During 1993-2008 period, PSLV had twelve consectively successful launches carrying satellites to Sun Synchronous, Low Earth and Geosynchronous Transfer Orbits. Now, its fourteenth flight is being used for launching Chandrayaan-1 to moon.

PSLV has repeatedly proved its reliability and versatility by launching 29 satellites into a variety of orbits. Of these, ten remote sensing satellites of India, an Indian satellite for amateur radio communications, a recoverable Space Capsule (SRF-1) and fourteen satellites from abroad were put into polar Sun Synchronous Orbits (SSO) of 550-820 km heights. Besides, PSLV has launched two satellites from abroad into Low Earth Orbits of low or medium inclinations. This apart, PSLV has launched KALPANA-1, a weather satellite of India, into Geosynchronous Transfer Orbit (GTO).

Table 25.9. PSLV C11 stages at a glance

	STAGE-1	*STAGE-2*	*STAGE-3*	*STAGE-4*
Nomenclature	Core (PSI) + Six Strap-ons (PSOM-XL)	PS2	PS3	PS4
Propellant	Solid HTBP Based	Liquid UH25 + N204	Solid HTPB based	Bi-prop MMH + MON-3
Mass (Tonne)	$138.0 + 6 \times 12$	41.5	7.6	2.5
Max Thrust	4910.0	800	246	7.31×2
	6×720			
Burn Time (sec)	$98 \neq 49$	147	107.6	525
Stage Dia (m)	$2.8 \neq 1.0$	2.8	2.0	2.8
Stage Length (m)	$20.2 \neq 12.4$	11.9	3.6	2.9
Control	SITVC for Pitch & Yaw, Reaction Control Thrusters for Roll, SITVC in two PSOMs for Roll Control	Engine Gimbal for Pitch & Yaw, Hot Gas Reaction Control Motor for Roll Control	Flex Nozzle for Pitch & Yaw, PS4 RCS for roll	Engine Gimbal for pitch, Yaw and Roll, on-off RCS for Coast Phase Control

PSLV was initially designed by ISRO to place 1,000 kg class Indian Remote Sensing (IRS) satellites into 900 km polar Sun Synchronous Orbits. Since the first successful flight in October 1994, the capability of PSLV was successively enhanced from 850 kg to 1,600 kg. In its ninth flight on May 5, 2005 from the Second Launch Pad (SLP), PSLV launched ISRO's remote sensing satellite, 1,560 kg CARTOSAT-1 and the 42 kg Amateur Radio satellite, HAMSAT, into a 620 km polar Sun Synchronous Orbit. The improvement in the capability over successive flights has been achieved through several means. They include increased propellant loading in the stage motors, employing composite material for the satellite mounting structure and changing the sequence of firing of the strap-on motors.

PSLV-C11 is 44.4 metre tall and has four stages using solid and liquid propulsion systems, alternately. The first stage, carrying 138 tonne of propellant, is one of the largest solid propellant boosters in the world. Six solid propellant strap-on motors (PSOM-XL), each carrying twelve tonne of solid propellant, are strapped on to the first stage. The second stage carries 41.5 tonne of liquid propellant. The third stage uses 7.6 tonne of solid propellant and the fourth has a twin engine configuration with 2.5 tonne of liquid propellant.

The 3.2 metre diameter metallic bulbous payload fairing protects the satellites and it is discarded after the vehicle has cleared dense atmosphere. PSLV employs a large number of auxilliary systems for stage separation, payload fairing separation and so on. It has sophisticated systems to control the vehicle and guide it through the predetermined trajectory. The vehicle performance is monitored through telemetry and tracking. The main modification in PSLV-C11 compared to its standard configuration is the use of larger strap-on motors (PSOM-XL) containing more propellants.

Vikram Sarabhai Space Centre (VSSC), Thiruvananthapuram, designed and developed PSLV-C11. ISRO Inertial Systems Unit (IISU) at Thiruvananthapuram developed the inertial systems for the vehicle. Liquid Propulsion Systems Centre (LPSC), also at Thiruvananthapuram, developed the liquid propulsion stages for the second and fourth stages of PSLV-C11 as well as reaction control systems. SDSC SHAR processes the solid motors and carries out launch operations. ISRO Telemetry, Tracking and Command Network (ISTRAC) provides telemetry, tracking and command support during PSLV-C11's flight.

Launch of Engineering Student's Satellites

A group of 30-40 students from the Indian Institute of Technology - Bombay (IIT-B) has designed a satellite that could be the first of its kind in the country to be launched into orbit. The ISRO will launch the 10 kg satellite into low Earth orbit (800 km-1000 km above the Earth's surface). A 10 kg micro-satellite project prepared by students of the Anna University in Chennai will also be launched by PSLV.

25.5. CHANDRAYAAN - 1: THE INDIAN LUNAR ORBITER MISSION

In its fourteenth flight conducted from Satish Dhawan Space Centre (SDSC) SHAR, Sriharikota this morning (***October 22, 2008***), the Indian Space Research Organisations's (ISRO's) Polar Satellite Launch Vehicle, PSLV-C11, successfully launched the 1380kg Chandrayaan-1 spacecraft into a transfer orbit with a perigee

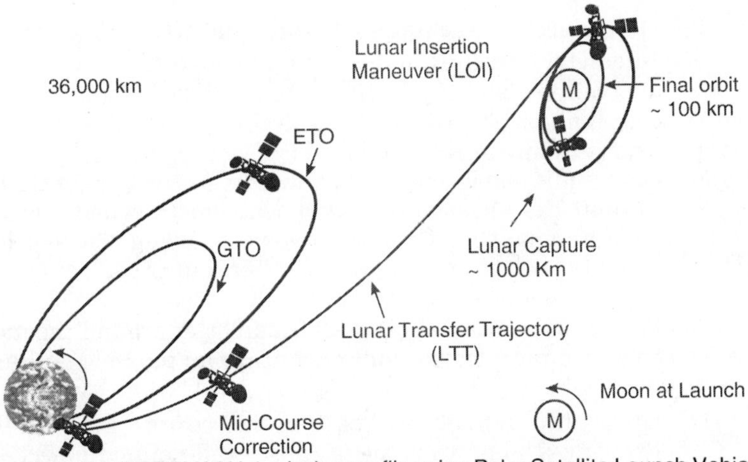

Fig. 25.2. CHANDRAYAAN-1 mission profile using Polar Satellite Launch Vehicle.

(nearest point to Earth) of 255 km and an apogee (farthest point to Earth) of 22,860 km, inclined at an angle of 17.9 deg to the equator.

After a 52 hour count down, PSLV-C11 lifted off from the Second Launch Pad at SDSC SHAR at 06.22 Hrs Indian Standard Time (IST) with the ignition of the core first stage. The important flight events included the separation of the first stage, ignition of the second stage, separation of the payload fairing at about 116 km altitude after the vehicle had cleared the dense atmosphere, second stage separation, third stage ignition, third stage separation, fourth stage ignition and fourth stage cut-off.

PSLV-C11 is the uprated version of ISRO'S Polar Satellite Lauch Vehicle in its standard configuration. Weighing 320 tonnes at lift-off, the vehicle uses larger strap-on motors (PSOM-XL) to achieve higher payload capability. PSOM-XL uses 12 tonnes of solid properllants instead of 9 tonnes used in the earlier configuration of PSLV. PSLV is a four stage launch vehicle employing both solid and liquid propulsions stages. PSLV is the trusted workhorse launch Vehicle of ISRO. During 1993-2008 period, PSLV had fourteen launches of which thirteen (including today's launch) are consecutively successful. PSLV has repeatedly proved its reliability and versatility by launching 30 spacecraft (14 Indian and 16 for international customers) into a variety of orbits so far.

Vikram Sarabhai Space Centre (VSSC), Thiruvananthapuram, designed and developed PSLV. ISRO Inertial Systems Unit (IISU) at Thiruvananthapuram developed the inertial systems. The Liquid Propulsion Systems Centre (LPSC), also at Thiruvananthapuram, developed the liquid propulsion stages for the second and the fourth stages of PSLV as well as reaction control systems. SDSC SHAR processed the solid propellant motors and carried out launch operation. ISRO Telemetry, Tracking and Command Network (ISTRAC) provided telemetry, tracking and command support.

Chandrayaan-1 is India's first spacecraft mission beyond Earth's orbit. It aims to further expand our knowledge about Earth's only natural satellite - the moon. With well-defined objectives, Chandrayaan-1 mission intends to put an unmanned spacecraft into an orbit around the moon and to perform remote sensing of our nearest celestial neighbour for about two years using eleven scientific instruments built in India and five other countries.

The primary objectives of Chandrayaan-1 are:

- To place an unmanned spacecraft, in an orbit around the moon
- To conduct mineralogical and chemical mapping of the lunar surface
- To upgrade the technological base in the country

Chandrayaan-1 aims to achieve these well-defined objectives through high-resolution remote sensing of moon in the visible, near infrared, microwave and X-ray regions of the electromagnetic spectrum. With this, preparation of a 3-dimensional atlas of the lunar surface and chemical and mineralogical mapping entire lunar surface is envisaged.

PSLV placed the Chandrayaan-1 spacecraft into a highly elliptical Transfer Orbit (TO) around the earth. Later, through a series of highly complex manoeuvres, the desired trajectories will be achieved. After circling the Earth in its Transfer Orbit, Chandrayaan-1 spacecraft will be taken into more elliptical 'Extended Transfer Orbits' by repeatedly firing its Liquid Apogee Motor (LAM) in a pre-determined sequence. Subsequently, the LAM is again fired to make the spacecraft to travel to the vicinity of the moon.

When it reaches the vicinity of the Moon and passes at a few hundred kilometers from it, its LAM is fired again so that the spacecraft slows down sufficiently to enable the gravity of the moon to capture it into an elliptical orbit.

Following this, the height of the spacecraft's orbit around the moon is reduced in steps. After a careful and detailed observation of the orbit pertubations there, the orbital height of Chandrayaan-1 will be finally lowered to its intended 100 km height from the lunar surface. Moon Impact Probe will be ejected from Chandrayaan-1 spacecraft at the earliest opportunity to hit the lunar surface in a chosen area.

Later, cameras and other scientific instruments are turned ON and thoroughly tested. This leads to the operational phase of the mission. The phase lasts for about two years during which Chandrayaan-1 spacecraft explores the lunar surface with its array of instruments that includes cameras, spectrometers and SAR.

25.5.1. The Spacecraft

Chandrayaan-1 spacecraft weighed about 1380 kg at the time of its launch and is a 1.5 m cuboid with a solar panel projecting from one of its sides. The spacecraft is powered by a single solar panel generating electrical power of 700 W. A Lithium ion battery supplies power when the solar panel is not illuminated by the sun. To make Chandrayaan-1 spacecraft to travel towards the Moon, its Liquid Apogee Motor (LAM) is used. Liquid propellants needed for LAM as well as thrusters are stored onboard the spacecraft. Chandrayaan-1 spacecraft's Dual Gimballed Antenna transmits the scientific data gathered by its eleven scientific instruments to Earth.

Features of Spacecraft for lunar mission:

- Accommodates eleven science payloads.
- 3-axis stabilized spacecraft using two star sensors, gyros and four-reaction wheels.
- The power generation would be through a canted single-sided solar array to provide required power during all phases of the mission. This deployable solar array consisting of a single panel generates 750W of peak power. Solar array along with yoke would be stowed on the south deck of the spacecraft in the launch phase. During eclipse, spacecraft will be powered by Lithium ion (Li-Ion) batteries.
- After deployment, the solar panel plane is canted by 30° to the spacecraft pitch axis.
- The spacecraft employs a X-band, 0.7 m diameter parabolic antenna for payload data transmission. The antenna employs a dual gimbal mechanism to track the earth station-when the spacecraft is in lunar orbit.
- The spacecraft uses a bipropellant integreated propulsion system to reach lunar orbit as well as orbit and attitude maintenance while orbiting the Moon.
- The propulsion system carries required propellant for a mission life of 2 years, with adequate margin.
- The Telemetry, Tracking & Command (TTC) communication is in S-band frequency.
- The scientific payload data transmission is in X-band frequency.
- The spacecraft has three Solid State Recorders (SSRs) onboard to record data from various payloads.
  - SSR-1 will store science payload data and has capability of storing 32Gb data.
  - SSR-2 will store science payload data along with spacecraft attitude information (gyro and star sensor), satellite house keeping and other auxillary data. The storing capacity of SSR-2 is 8Gb.

- M3 (Moon Mineralogy Mapper) payload has an independent SSR with 10Gb capacity.

25.5.2. The Ground Segment

The Ground facilites of Chandrayaan-1 perform the importnat task of receiving the health information as well as the scientific data from the spacecraft. It also transmits the radio commands to be sent to the spacecraft during all the phases of its mission. Besides, it processes and stores the scientific data sent by Chandrayaan-1 spacecraft.

ISRO Telemetry, Tracking and Command Network (ISTRAC) has a lead role in establishing the Ground Segment of Chandrayaan-1 with contribution from ISAC and SAC. The Ground Segment of Chandrayaan-1 consists of:

1. Indian Deep Space Network (IDSN)
2. Spacecraft Control Centre (SCC)
3. Indian Space Science Data Centre (ISSDC)

The Indian Deep Space Network receives the data sent by the Chandrayaan-1 spacecraft. Besides, it sends commands to the spacecraft at a power level of upto 20 kilowatts. IDSN consists of two large parabolic antennas - one with its 'seven mirror beam waveguide system', was indigenously designed, developed, built, installed, tested and qualified. The 18m antenna can support Chandrayaan-1 mission, but the 32m antenna can support spacecraft mission well beyond Moon.

The Spacecraft Control Centre, located near the ISTRAC campus at Peenya, North of Bangalore, is the focal point of all the operational activities of Chandrayaan-1 during all the phases of the mission.

The Indian Space Science Data Centre forms the third element of Charndrayaan-1 ground segment. Also located at Byalalu, ISSDC receives data from IDSN as well as other external stations that support Chandrayaan-1, and stores, processes, archives, retrieves and distributes scientific data sent by Chandrayaan-1 payloads to the user agencies.

25.5.3. Scientific Objectives

The Chandrayaan-1 mission is aimed at high-resolution remote sensing of the moon in visible, near infrared (NIR), low energy X-rays and high-energy X-ray regions. Specifically the objectives are;

- To prepare a three-dimensional atlas (with high spatial and altitude resolution of 5-10 m) of both near and far side of the moon.
- To conduct chemical and mineralogical mapping of the entire lunar surface for distribution of mineral and chemical elements

such as Magnesium, Aluminum, Silicon, Calcium, Iron and Titanium as well as high atomic number elements such as Radon, Uranium & Thorium with high spatial resolution.

The Simultaneous photogeological, mineralogical and chemical mapping through Chandrayaan-1 mission will enable identification of different geological units to infer the early evolutionary history of the Moon. The chemical mapping will enable to determine the stratigraphy and nature of the Moon's crust and thereby test certain aspects of magma ocean hypothesis. This may allow to determine the compositions of impactors that bombarded the Moon during its early evolution, which is also relevant to the formation of the Earth.

Radiation environment of the Moon produced by solar radiation and solar and galactic cosmic rays: The reflectance spectrum is useful for mineral identification, the fluorescent X-ray spectrum and solar and galactic cosmic-ray produced gamma radiation for chemical mapping and radiogenic gamma and alpha particle spectrum of mapping of radioactive nucleides (U, TH, K, etc.) and in understanding the leakage of radon from the lunar interior and its transport on the lunar surface. The uranium decay chain, which produces ^{222}Rn and its daughters, forming a thin 'paint' on the lunar surface, are shown on the right. The temperature regimes on the sunlit and night side of the Moon and the permanently shadowed cold Polar Regions are shown schematically. (Ref: Current Science, Bhandari 2004)

Mission Objectives

- To realise the mission goal of harnessing the science payloads, lunar craft and the launch vehicle with suitable ground support systems including Deep Space Network (DSN) station.
- To realise the integration and testing, launching and achieving lunar polar orbit of about 100 km, in orbit operation of experiemnts, communication/telecommand, telemetry data reception, quick look data and archival for scientific utilisation by scientists.

Prime Science Objectives and Wavelength range coverage are given below:

Prime Objective	Payload
• Search for water-ice	MiniSAR, HEX, SARA
• Chemical Mapping	CIXS, HEX
• Mineralogical Mapping	HySI, SIR-2, M3
• Topography Mapping	LLRI, TMC
• Radiation Environment	RADOM, HEX, CIXS
• Megnetic Field Mapping	SARA
• Volatile Transport	HEX
• Lunar Atmospheric constituent	MIP

Areas of special interest. Apart from a general study of the whole lunar surface, it is recognized that some areas are of special interest particularly on the far side of the Moon and the polar regions, which are under permanent shadows, where temperatures can be as low as – 230° C. Specially, the South Pole Aitken Basin (SPA), north and south poles. In addition, it will be useful to identify the end members of the highland rocks. The polar regions are of special interest because the volatiles are expected to be deposited there. Shackleton crater close to the south pole is expected to have water-ice on its walls and the bottom and would be a prime target for study.

CHANDRAYAAN-1, together with SMART-1, SELENE, LUNAR A, CHANG'E-1 and some other missions, which are being planned (*e.g.* by USA) will provide more than five years of continuous observation of the Moon. This may, constitute the longest continuous and overlapping period of study of the Moon and should help us resolve some of the outstanding questions regarding chemical, mineralogic and geological evolution of the lunar surface. Earth-Moon interactions in the remote past and size-dependent evolution of the planetary bodies.

25.5.4 The Payloads

There are 11 payloads (scientific instruments) through which Chandrayaan-1 intends to achieve its scientific objectives. They include five instruments designed and developed in India, three instruments from European Space Agency (one of which is developed jointly with India and the other with Indian contribution), one from Bulgaria and two from the United States.

The Indian payloads of Chandrayaan-1 are:

Terrain Mapping Camera (TMC), a CCD camera that maps the topography of the moon, which helps in better understanding of the lunar evolution process.

Hyperspectral Imager (HySI), another CCD camera, is designed for mapping of the minerals on the lunar surface as well as for understanding the mineralogical composition of Moon's interior.

Lunar Laser Ranging Instrument (LLRI) provides necessary data for accurately determining the height of lunar surface features.

High Energy X-ray Spectrometer (HEX) is designed to help explore the possibility of identifying Polar Regions covered by thick water-ice deposits as well as in identifying regions of high Uranium and Thorium concentrations.

Moon Impact Probe (MIP) demonstrates the technologies required for landing a probe at the desired location on the moon. It is also intended to qualify some of the technologies related to future soft landing missions.

The six international payloads of Chandrayaan-1 are:

Chandrayaan-1 Imaging X ray Spectrometer (C1XS), an ESA payload jointly developed by Rutherford Appleton Laboratory of England and ISRO Satellite Centre, Bangalore, intends to carry out high quality mapping of the moon using X-ray fluorescence technique for finding the presence of Magnesium, Aluminium, Silicon, Iron and Titanium distributed over the surface of the Moon.

Smart Near Infrared Spectrometer (SIR-2), another ESA payload, developed by Max Plank Institute of Germany, aims to study the lunar surface to explore the mineral resources and the formation of its surface features.

Sub Kiloelectronvolt Atom Reflecting Analyser (SAR), the third payload from ESA, is built by Swedish Institute of Space Physics and Space Physics Laboratory of Vikram Sarabhai Space Centre, Thiruvananthapuram. The aim of this instrument is to study the surface composition of the moon and the magnetic anomalies associated with the surface of the moon.

Radiation Dose Monitor (RADOM), a payload developed by Bulgarian Academy of Sciences, aims to characterise the radiation environment in a region of space surrounding the moon.

Mini Synthetic Aperture Radar (MiniSAR) is one of the two scientific instruments from the USA and is from Johns Hopkins University's Applied Physics Laboratory and Naval Air Warfare Centre, USA through NASA. MiniSAR is mainly intended for detecting water ice in the permanently shadowed regions of the lunar poles up to a depth of a few meters.

Moon Mineralogy Mapper (M3) is an imaging spectrometer from Brown University and Jet Propulsion Laboratory of the US through NASA, is intended to assess and map lunar mineral resources at high spatial and spectral resolution.

1. Terrain Mapping Camera (TMC)

Scientific Objective: The aim of TMC is to map topography of both near and far side of the Moon and prepare a 3- dimensional atlas with high spatial and elevation resolution of 5 m. Such high resolution mapping of complete lunar surface will help to understand the evolution processes and allow detailed study of regions of scientific interests. The digital elevation model available from TMC would improve upon the existing knowledge of Lunar Topography.

Payload Configuration Details: The TMC will image in the panchromatic spectral region of 0.5 to 0.85 μ m, with a spatial/ground resolution of 5 m and swath coverage of 20 km. The

Fig. 25.3

camera is configured for imaging in the pushbroom mode, with three linear 4k element detectors in the image plane for fore, nadir and aft views, along the ground track of the satellite. The fore and aft view angles are $\pm 25°$ respectively w.r.t. Nadir. TMC will measure the solar radiation reflected/scattered from the Moon's surface. The dynamic range of the reflected signal is quite large, represented by the two extreme targets - fresh crust rocks and mature mare soil.

TMC uses Linear Active Pixel Sensor (APS) detector with in-built digitizer. Single refractive optics will cover the total field of view for the three detectors. The output of the detector will be in digitized form. The optics is designed as a single unit catering to the wide field of view (FOV) requirement in the direction along the ground track. The incident beams from the fore $+25°$ and aft $-25°$ directions are directed on to the focusing optics, using mirrors. Modular camera electronics for each detector is custom designed for the system requirements using FPGA. The expected data rate is of the order of 50 Mbps. The dimension of TMC payload is 370 mm × 220 mm × 414 mm and mass is 6.3 kg.

2. Hyper Spectral Imager (HySI)

Scientific Objective: To obtain spectroscopic data for mineralogical mapping of the lunar surface. The data from this instrument will help in improving the available information on mineral composition of the surface of Moon. Also, the study of data in deep crater regions/central peaks, which represents lower crust or upper mantle material, will help in understanding the mineralogical composition of Moon's interior.

Payload Configuration Details: The uniqueness of the HySI is in its capability of mapping the lunar surface in 64 contiguous bands in the VNIR, the spectral range of 0.4 – 0.95μ m region with a

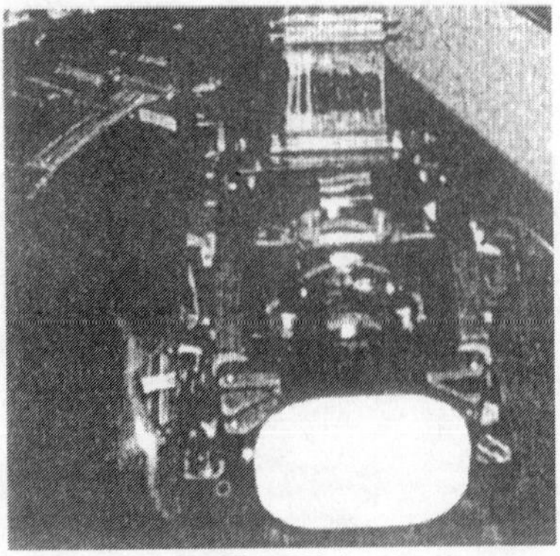

Fig. 25.4

spectral resolution of better than 15 nm and spatial resolution of 80 m, with swath coverage of 20 km. HySI will collect the Sun's reflected light from the Moon's surface through a tele-centric refractive optics and focus on to an APS area detector for this purpose.

The dispersion is achieved by using a wedge filter so as to reduce the weight and compactness of the system compared to using a prism/grating. The wedge filter is an interference filter with varying thickness along one dimension so that the transmitted spectral range varies in that direction. The wedge filter will be placed in close proximity to an area detector. Thus, different pixels in a row of the detector will be receiving irradiance from the same spectral region but different spatial regions in the across track direction. In the column direction of the detector, different rows will receive irradiance of different spectral as well as spatial regions in the along track direction. The full spectrum of a target is obtained by acquiring image data in push broom mode, as the satellite moves along the column direction of the detector. An Active Pixel Sensor (APS) area array detector with built-in digitizer would map the spectral bands. The payload mass is 2.5 kg and its size is 275 mm × 255mm × 205 mm.

3. Lunar Laser Ranging Instrument (LLRI)

The elevation map of the Moon prepared using the laser ranging instrument carried on board Chandrayaan-1 spacecraft will help in studying the morphology of large basins and other lunar features, study stress, strain and flexural properties of the lithosphere and when coupled with gravity studies, would be able to find the density distribution of the crust.

Scientific Objective:

To provide ranging data for determining the height difference between the spacecraft and the lunar surface.

Fig. 25.5

Payload Configuration Details:

LLRI works on the time-Of-Flight (TOF) principle. In this method, a coherent pulse of light from a high power laser is directed towards the target whose range is to be measured. A fraction of the light is scattered back in the direction of the laser source, where an optical receiver collects it and focuses it on to a photoelectric detector. By accurately measuring the roundtrip travel time of the laser pulse, highly accurate range/spot elevation measurements can be made.

LLRI consists of a 10 m J Nd:YAG laser with 1064 nm wave source operating at 10 Hz pulse repetition mode. The reflected laser pulse from the lunar surface is collected by a 200 mm Ritchey-Chretien Optical receiver and focused on to a Silicon Avalanche Photodetector. The output of the detector is amplified and threshold detected for generating range information to an accuracy <5m. Four constant fraction discriminators provide the slope information in addition to range information. The different modes of operation of LLRI and the range computations from the detector output are controlled and computed by a FPGA based electronics. The processed outputs of LLRI will be used for generating high accuracy lunar topography. The payload mass is 11.37 kg with base plate.

Fig. 25.6

4. High Energy X-ray Spectrometer (HEX)

The High-Energy X-ray spectrometer covers the hard X-ray region from 30 ke V to 270 Ke V. This is the first experiment to carry out spectral studies of planetary surface at hard X-ray energies using good energy resolution detectors. The High Energy X-ray (HEX) experiment is designed primarily to study the emission of low energy (30-270 ke V) natural gamma-rays from the lunar surface due to ^{238} U and ^{232} TH and their decay chain nucledes.

Scientific Objectives:

- To identify excess ^{210} Pb in lunar polar regions deposited there as a result of transport of gaseous ^{222}Rn, a decay product of ^{238}U from other regions of the Moon. This will enable us to understand transport of other volatiles such as water to the polar regions.
- To detect other radioactive emissions, to characterise various lunar terrains for their chemical and radioactive composition on the basis of specific/integrated signal in the 30-270 keV region.
- To explore the possibility of identifying polar regions covered by thick water-ice deposit from a study of the continuum back-ground.

Payload Configuration Details:

The geometric detector area of 144 cm^2 is realized by nine Cadmium Zinc Telluride (CZT) arrays, each 4 cm × 4 cm (5 mm thick), composed of 256 (16 × 16) pixels (size: 2.5 mm × 2.5 mm). Each CZT array is readout using two closely mounted Application Specific Integrated Circuits (ASICs), which provides self-triggering capability. The detector will be biased at the cathode with -550 V and the electronic charge signals are collected at the anode. A Cesium Iodide (CsI (TI)) scintillator crystal coupled to photomultiplier tubes (PMT), will be used as the anti-coincidence system (ACS). The ACS is used to reduce the detector background.

A specially designed collimator provides a field of view (FOV) of 33 km × 33 km at the lunar surface from a 100 km orbit. The spatial resolution of HEX is 33 km and the mass is 14.4 kg.

5. Moon Impact Probe (MIP)

The imapct probe of 35 kg mass will be attached at the top deck of the main orbiter and will be released during the final 100 km × 100 km orbit a predetermined time to impact at a pre-selected location. During the descent phase, it is spin-stabilized. The total flying time from release to impact on Moon is around 25 minutes.

The primary objective is to demonstrate the technologies re-quired for landing the probe at a desired location on the Moon and to qualify some of the technologies related to future soft landing missions.

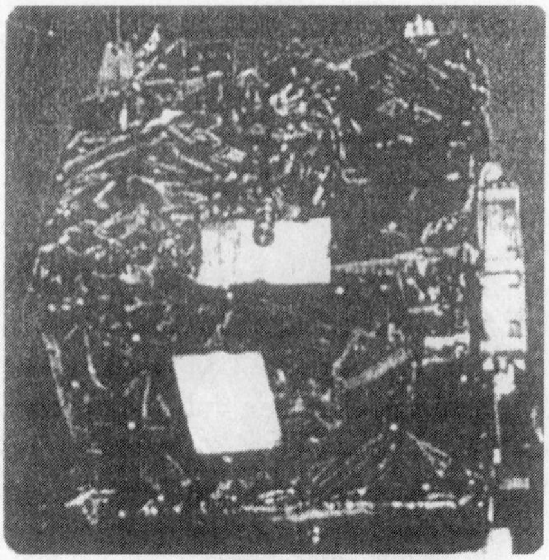

Fig. 25.7

Major Objectives:

- Design, development and demonstration of technologies required for impacting a probe at the desired location on the Moon.
- Qualify technologies required for future soft landing missions.
- Scientific exploration of the Moon from close range.

Payload Configuration Details:

- Radar Altimeter - for measurement of altitude of the Moon Impact Probe and for qualifying technologies for future landing missions. The operating frequency band is 4.3 GHz ± 100 MHz.
- Video Imaging System - for acquiring images of the surface of the Moon during the descent at a close range. The video imaging system consists of analog CCD camera.
- Mass spectrometer - for measuring the constituents of tenuous lunar atmosphere during descent. This instrument will be based on a state-of-the-art, commercially available Quadruple mass spectrometer with a mass resolution of 0.5 amu and sensitivities to partial pressure of the order of 10^{-14} torr.

The dimension of the impact probe is 375 mm × 375 mm × 470 mm.

The Moon Impact Probe (MIP) essentially consists of honeycomb structure, which houses all the subsystems and instruments. In addition to the instruments, the separation system, the de-boost spin and de-spin motors, it comprises of the avionics system and thermal control system. The avionics system supports the payloads and provides communication link between MIP and the main orbiter, from separation to impact and provides a database useful for future soft landing.

The mission envisages collection of all the instrument data during descent and transmission to main orbiter, which in turn will transmit them to the ground station during visible phases.

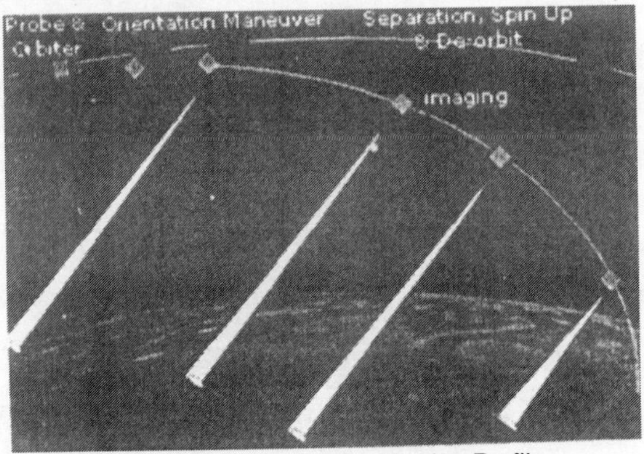

Fig. 25.8. Impact Probe Mission Profile

6. Chandrayaan-1-X-ray Spectrometer (C1XS)

Scientific Objective:

The primary goal of the C1XS instrument is to carry out high quality X-ray spectroscopic mapping of the Moon, in order to constrain solutions to key questions on the origin and evolution of the Moon. C1XS will use X-ray fluorescence spectrometry (1.0–10 keV) to measure the elemental abundance, and map the distribution, of the three main rock forming elements: Mg, Al and Si. During periods of enhanced solar activity (solar flares) events, it may be possible to determine the abundance of minor elements such as Ca, Ti and Fe on the surface of the Moon.

Payload Configuration Details :

The instrument utilises technologically innovative Swept Charge Device (SCD) X-ray sensors, which are mounted behind low profile gold/copper collimators and aluminium/polycarbonate thin film filters. The system has the virtue of providing superior X-ray detection, spectroscopic and spatial measurement capabilities, while also operating at near room temperature. A deployable proton shield protects the SCDs during passages through the Earth's radiation belts, and from major particle events in the lunar orbit. In order to record the incident solar X-ray flux at the Moon, which is needed to derive absolute lunar elemental surface abundances, C1XS also includes an X-ray Solar Monitor.

The X-ray Solar Monitor (XSM) is provided through collaboration between Rutherford Appleton Laboratory (RAL) and University

Fig. 25.9.

of Helsinki. With its wide field-of-view of ± 52 degrees, XSM provides observation of the solar X-ray spectrum from 1-20 keV with good energy resolution (250 keV @ 5.9 keV) and fast spectral sampling at 16 s intervals.

Throughout the normal solar conditions, C1XS will be able to detect abundance of Mg, Al and Si in the lunar surface. During solar flare events, it may additionally be possible to detect other elements such as Ca, Ti and Fe. The onboard solar monitor acting in real time will greatly enhance the capability of C1XS to determine absolute elemental abundances as well as their ratios. The total mass of C1XS and XSM is 5.2 kg.

7. Near-RI Spectrometer (SIR-2)

Scientific Objectives:

SIR-2 will address the surface-related aspects of lunar science in the following broad categories:

- Analyse the lunar surface in various geological/mineralogical and topographical units;
- Study the vertical variation in composition of crust;
- Investigate the process of basin, maria and crater formation on the Moon;
- Explore "Space Weathering" processes of the lunar surface;
- Survey mineral lunar resources for future landing sites and exploration.

The determination of the chemical composition of a planet's crust and mantle is one of the important goals of planetary research. Diagnostic absorption bands of various minerals and ices, which are

Fig. 25.10

expected to be found on the surfaces of planetary bodies, are located in the near-IR range, thus making near-infrared measurements of rocks, particularly, suitable for identifying minerals.

Payload Configuration Details:

SIR-2 is a grating NIR point spectrometer working in the 0.93-2.4 microns wavelength range with 6 nm spectral resolution. It collects the Sun's light reflected by the Moon with help of a main and a secondary mirror. This light is fed through an optical fibre to the instrument's sensor head, where it is reflected off a dispersion grating. The dispersed light reaches a detector, which consists of row of photosensitive pixels that measure the intensity as a function of wavelength and produces an electronic signal, which is read out and processed by the experiment's electronics.

The mass of the instrument is 3.3 kg and the instrument unit dimension is 260 mm × 171 mm × 143 mm.

8. Sub ke V Atom Reflecting Analyser (SARA)

Scientific Objectives:

SARA will image the Moon surface using low energy neutral atoms as diagnostics in the energy range 10 e V – 3.2 keV to address the following scientific objectives:

- Imaging the Moon's surface composition including the permanently shadowed areas and volatile rich areas
- Imaging the solar wind-surface interaction
- Imaging the lunar surface magnetic anomalies
- Studies of space weathering

The Moon does not possess a magnetosphere and atmosphere. Therefore, the solar wind ions directly impinge on the lunar surface, resulting in sputtering and backscattering. The kick-off and neutral-

Fig. 25.11

ized solar wind particles leave the surface mostly as neutral atoms. The notable part of the atoms has energy exceeding the escape energy and thus, such atoms propagate along ballistic trajectories. The SARA instrument is designed to detect such atoms with sufficient angular and mass resolution to address the above scientific objectives. SARA is the first ever energetic neutral atom imaging mass spectrometer.

Payload Configuration Details:

The SARA instrument consists of neutral atom sensor CENA (Chandrayaan -1 Energetic Neutrals Analyzer), solar wind monitor SWIM and DPU (Data Processing Unit). CENA and SWIM interface with DPU, which in turn interfaces with the spacecraft. The masses of CENA and SWIM interface with DPU, which in turn interfaces with the spacecraft. The masses of CENA, SWIM and DPU are 2 kg, 0.5 kg and 2 kg respectively, totaling the SARA mass as 4.5 kg.

9. Radiation Dose Monitor Experiment (RADOM)

Scientific Objective

RADOM will qualitatively and quantitatively characterise the radiation environment in near lunar space, in terms of particle flux, dose rate and deposited energy spectrum.

The specific objectives are

- Measure the particle flux, deposited energy spectrum, accumulated radiation dose rates in Lunar orbit;
- Provide an estimate of the radiation dose around the Moon at different altitudes and latitudes;
- Study the radiation hazards during the Moon exploration. Data obtained will be used for the evaluation of the radiation environment and the radiation shielding requirements of future manned Moon missions.

Radiation exposure of crew members on future manned space flight had been recognised as an important factor for the planning

Fig. 25.12

and designing of such missions. Indeed, the effects of ionising radiation on crew health, performance and life expectancy are a limitation to the duration of man's sojourn in space. Predicting the effects of radiation on humans during a long-duration space mission requires (*i*) accurate knowledge and modelling of the space radiation environment, (*ii*) calculation of primary and secondary particle transport through shielding materials and through the human body. and (*iii*) assessment of the biological effects of the dose.

The general purpose of RADOM is to study the radiation hazards during the Moon exploration. Data obtained will be used for the evaluation of radiation environment and radiation shielding requirements for future manned lunar missions.

Payload Configuration Details:

RADOM is a miniature spectrometer-dosimeter containing one semiconductor detector of 0.3 mm thickness, one charge-sensitive pre-amplifier and two micro controllers. The detector weighs 139.8 mg. Pulse analysis technique is used for obtaining the deposited energy spectrum, which is further converted to the deposited dose and flux in the silicon detector. The exposure time for one spectrum is fixed at 30 s. The RADOM spectrometer will measure the spectrum of the deposited energy from primary and secondary particles in 256 channels. RADOM mass is 160 g.

10. Miniature Synthetic Aperture Radar (Mini-SAR)

Scientific Objectives:

To detect water ice in the permanently shadowed regions on the Lunar poles, upto a depth of a few meters.

Although returned lunar samples show the Moon to be extremely dry, recent research suggest that water-ice may exist in the polar regions. Because its axis of rotation is perpendicular to the ecliptic plane, the poles of the Moon contain areas that never receive light and are permanently dark. This results in the creation of "cold trap", zones that, because they are never illuminated by the sun, may be very cold. Cometary debris and meteorites containing water-bearing minerals constantly bombard the Moon. Most of this water is lost to space, but, if a water molecule finds its way into a cold trap, it remains there forever - no physical process is known that can remove it. Over geological time, significant quantities of water could accumulate.

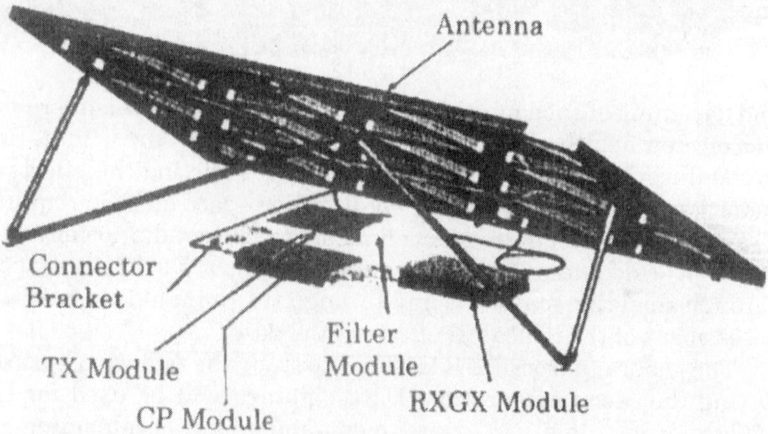

Fig. 25.13

An onboard SAR at suitable incidence would allow viewing of all permanently shadowed areas on the Moon, regardless of whether sunlight is available or the angle is not satisfactory. The radar would observe these areas at incidence angle near 45 degrees, recording echoes in both orthogonal senses of received polarization, allowing ice to be optimally distinguished from dry lunar surface.

The Mini-SAR radar system can operate as an altimeter/scatterometer, radiometer, and as a synthetic aperture radar imager.

Payload Configuration Details:

The Mini-SAR system will transmit Right Circular Polarization (RCP) and receive, both Left Circular polarization (LCP) and RCP. In scatterometer mode, the system will measure the RCP and LCP response in the altimetry footprint, along the nadir ground track. In radiometer mode, the system will measure the surface RF emissivity, allowing determination of the near normal incidence Fresnel reflectivity. Meter-scale surface roughness and circular polarization ratio (CPR) will also be determined for this footprint. This allows the characterization of the radar and physical properties of the lunar surface (*e.g.*, dielectric constant, porosity) for a network of points. When directed off nadir, the radar system will image a swath parallel to the orbital track by delay/Doppler methods (SAR mode) in both RCP and LCP.

The synthetic aperture radar system works at a frequency 2.38 GHz, with a resolution of 75 m per pixel from 100 km orbit and its mass is 8.77 kg.

11. Moon Mineralogy Mapper (M3)

M3 with high-resolution compositional maps will improve the understanding of the early evolution of a differentiated planetary body and provide a high-resolution assessment of lunar resources.

Scientific Objectives:

The primary Science goal of M3 is to characterize and map lunar surface mineralogy, in the context of lunar geologic evolution. This translates into several sub-topics relating to understanding the highland crust, basaltic volcanism, impact craters, and potential volatiles.

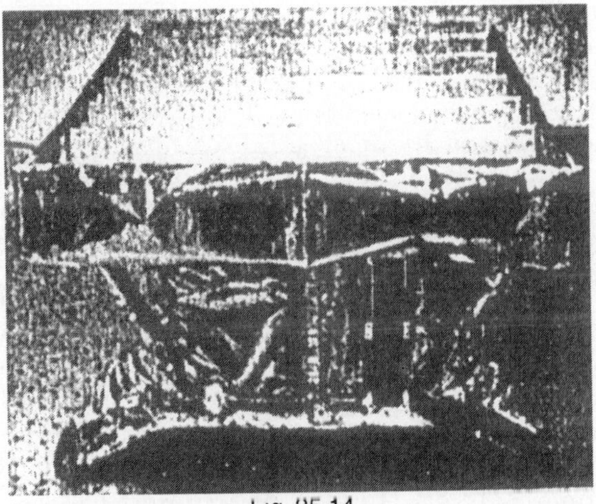

Fig. 25.11

The primary exploration goal is to assess and map lunar mineral resources at high spatial resolution to support planning for future, targeted missions.

These M3 goals translate directly into the following requirements:

- Accurate measurement of diagnostic absorption features of rocks and minerals;

- High spectral resolution for deconvolution into mineral components;
- High spatial resolution for assessment geologic context and active processes;

Payload Configuration Details:

The M3 scientific instrument is a high throughput pushbroom imaging spectrometer, operating in 0.7 to 3.0 μ m range. It measures solar reflected energy, using a two-dimensional HgCdTe detector array.

Sampling: 10 nanometers

Spatial resolution: 70 m/pixel [from 100 km orbit]

Field of View: 40 km [from 100 km orbit]

Mass: 8.2 kg

The spectral range 0.7 to 2.6 μm captures the absorption bands for the most important lunar minerals. In addition, the spectral range 2.5 to 3.0 μm is critical for detection of possible volatiles near the lunar poles. The presence of small amounts of OH or H_2O can be unambiguously identified from fundamental absorptions that occur near 3000 nm.

M3 measurements are obtained for 640 cross track spatial elements and 261 spectral elements. This translates to 70 m/pixel spatial resolution and 10 nm spectral resolution (continuous) from a nominal 100 km polar orbit for Chandrayaan-1. The M3 FOV is 40 km in order to allow contiguous orbit-to-orbit measurements at the equator that will minimize lighting condition variations.

25.6 SATELLITE INSTRUCTIONAL TELEVISION

Experimental (SITE) Program. SITE programme was conducted during Aug. 1975-Aug. 1976 using the ATS-6 satellite of NASA. This programme was very valuable in building indigenous expertise (hardware, TV software and research and evaluation and managerial) for the future satellite communications and broadcasting programmes of India. The main objective of SITE was to provide a systems test to the concept of satellite television and to gain experience in the development testing and management of a satellite based instructional TV system, particularly in rural areas to determine optimal systems parameters. In fact SITE helped to design and test uplink stations, testing of TV sets, receive only sets (TVROs) and the low power limited area rebroadcast TV transmitters. Thus, SITE was more than a technical demonstration cum experiment. It was a total satellite community reception TV system test in India and thus, had equally important social, TV software and organisational aspects, which were carefully studied and documented. It would be of importance to mention here that under SITE experiment that lasted over one year, 2400 villages in six states were able to receive specially made TV programmes related to agriculture and health care directly from ATS-6. Reception was accomplished with small community dishes often made from chicken fence wire.

25.7 SATELLITE TELECOMMUNICATIONS EXPERIMENTS

Project (STEP). STEP was carried out during 1977-79 for having a greater insight with regard to the telecommunication aspects of satellite technology. For STEP, use was made of Franco German Symphonie-1 satellite. This satellite was made available for STEP as a part of ISRO cooperation with CNES and DFVLR and was moved to 49° E longitude for the conduct of STEP. The project was mainly to experiment with digital satellite communications, single channels for carrier systems, radio networking and TV transmissions with several audio channels. A transportable Indian made terminal was built for use in experiment. Engineers said that the experiment effectively demonstrated the use of satellites for remote area and emergency communications. These STEP experiments were conducted jointly by ISRO and then P&T (now DOT). The vital experience gained in these experiments was instrumental for the inception of satellite communication technology in 1980 in the country, with the installation of 7 earth stations, the majority of which were installed in remote areas including islands, leasing transponders capacity from INTELSAT. All these experiments and experiences developed confidence among Indian planners for the launching of communications satellite in near future.

25.8 APPLE

APPLE was the first Indian experimental communications satellite launched on 19th June 1981 under an argreement with ESA, on board the third development flight of the European Ariane launcher. It was three axis stabilized and weighed 650 kg. The satellite was placed into a geostationary orbit, however, one of the two solar panels failed to deploy, although close systems management particularly thermal system meant that the satellite could be used for its intended purpose. The satellite was positioned at its assigned orbital position of 102° E longitude in early July 1981 and was decommissioned in September 1983 after completing its two year on-orbit life, which was constrained by on-board propellant loading.

Apple had a microwave C band (6/4 GHz band) transponders (plus a redundant transponders). It was totally designed and fabricated and largely tested in India and had a large number of indigenous components/assemblies/subsystems. These included the main structure, the 6/4 GHz payload (with improved TWTAs), a static horizon/earth sensor, a momentum wheel, a carbon fibre antenna reflector, a solid propellant apogee motor (derived from the fourth stage of Indian SLV-3 launcher) to boost the satellite from transfer orbit to a circular, equatorial, near geosynchronous orbit etc.

With APPLE a large number of communication experiments and service demonstrations were carried out using the indigenously developed equipment. These experiments included the testing of computer communication, TDMA (Time division multiple access) communications, spread spectrum multiple access (SSMA) communication, FAX transmission and TV broadcasting. Also, the social and educational experiments using the relayed TV signals were being conducted. APPLE, thus, gave a strong foundation to India for fixed satellite system (FSS) that led to the development of INSAT-II satellite.

25.9 THE INDIAN NATIONAL SATELLITE SYSTEM (INSATS)

INSAT system is the result of previous experiments such as those of SITE, STEP and APPLE. It is a multipurpose and multi-agency system. It transcends three vital national services such as long distance communications, TV and radio broadcastings and meteorology. It is a joint venture of Department of Space (DOS), Department of Telecommunications (DOT), Indian Meteorological Department (IMD), All India Radio (AIR) and Doordarshan. The overall coordination and management of the INSAT system rests with the secretaries level INSAT Coordination Committe (ICC). The Secretariat of this committee resides in the Department of Space. The Department of Space has the direct responsibility for establishment and operation of the INSAT space-segment facilities. Fig. 25.16 shows the INSAT SYSTEM MANAGEMENT.

The contract for developing the satellites for the first phase of the INSAT programme was awarded to Ford Aerospace in USA. The American Company also aided in the design and development of the Mission Control Center in Hassan (Karnataka) which has two 14 m diameter antennas for control of satellites.

The second phase of INSAT-2 systems was developed in India and launched by ISRO (INSAT-2A in 1992, INSAT-2B in 1993 and

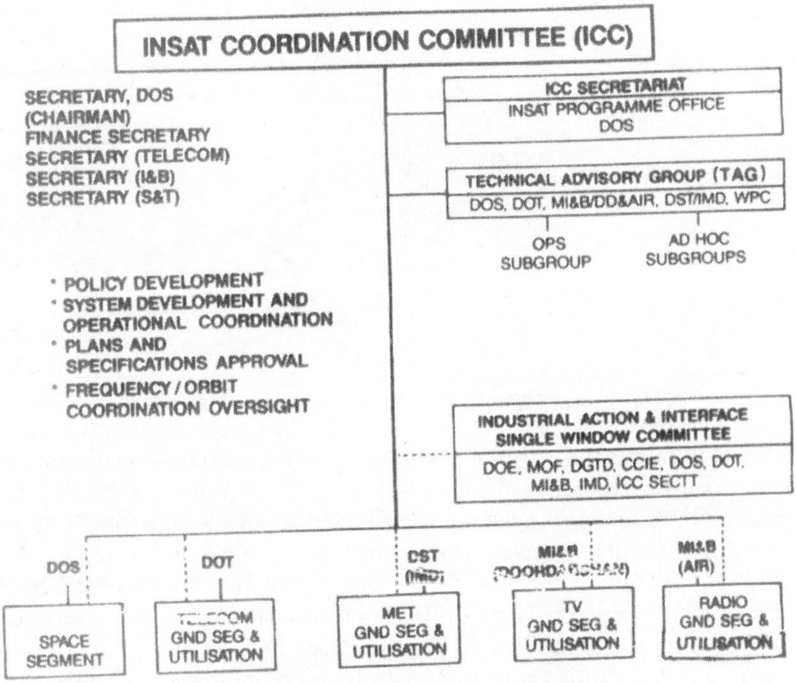

Fig. 25.15 INSAT System-Management

INSAT-2C in 1995). The INSAT-3 series (3B, 3C, 3A and 3E) reached the orbits in 2000, 2002 and 2003, all launched by ISRO.

25.9.1. INSAT-1 Systems

INSAT-1 system was envisaged as a space segment consisting of two multipurpose satellites, one as the primary satellite providing additional fixed as well as broadcast satellite services capacities and also certain on-orbit back up capability. Each INSAT-1 satellites weigh about 1200 kg at lift-off and about 650 kg in geostationary orbit. The satellites gave a five panel sun tracking solar array of roughly 11.5 sq.m. generating a power of 900 watts. These satellites are designed for a minimum of 7 years life. The transfer orbit configuration and the on orbit satellite configuration of INSAT-1 satellites are given in Fig. 25.16 and 25.17 respectively.

In geostationary orbit under fully deployed configuration the length of INSAT-1 satellite from the tip of solar sail to the extreme end of the solar array is about 19.4 m. The INSAT-1 satellites are biased momentrum three axis stabilized spacecraft with a stability required for the meteorological imaging mission. The satellites use an asymmetrical solar array in order to ensure an unobstructed clear

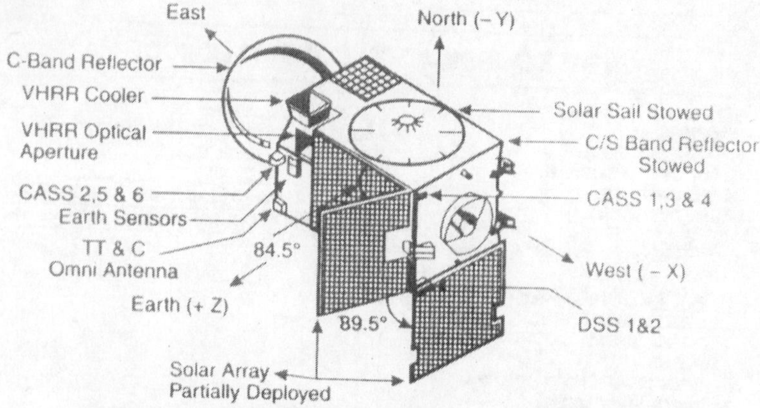

Fig. 25.16. TRANSFER Orbit Configuration of INSAT-1

field of view (FOV) into the cold space for the radiation cooler of the Very High Resolution Radiometer (VHRR) earth imaging instrument. There is a deployed solar sail used to offset solar pressure on account of the asymmetrical solar array. A magnetic torquer with a current coil placed around the periphery of the satellite body provides fine control. The satellite has a unified bipropellant propulsion system for transfer orbit to geostationary orbit ascent and for station and attitude maintenance. The transfer orbit to GSO ascent is also in three axis stabilized mode.

Each INSAT-1 satellite has the following 4 kind capabilities that are supposed to be in their individual 7 years life. These are (*i*) twelve national coverage telecommunication transponders of 36 MHz bandwidth each operating in *C* band with 32 dbw Effective Isotropic Radiated Power (EIRP) over the primary coverage area, (*ii*) two high power national coverage TV broadcast transponders operating in C-band uplink (earth to satellite) and S band downlink (satellite to earth), each capable of handling one direct broadcast (community reception) TV channel and several low level carriers for radio programme distribution with a 42 dbw EIRP over the primary coverage area, (*iii*) a very high resolution radiometer (VHRR) for meteorological earth imaging operating in visible and infrared channels with resolutions of 2.75 km and 11 km respectively, with half hourly full earth coverage and sector scan capability with a 402.75 MHz uplink for relay of meteorological, hydrological and oceanographic data from unattended land and ocean based automatic collection-cum transmission platforms.

The INSAT MCF is located at Hassan and it consists of 2 satellites control Earth Stations (one with a 14 m fully steerable antenna and the other with a 7.5 m limited steerability antenna). In

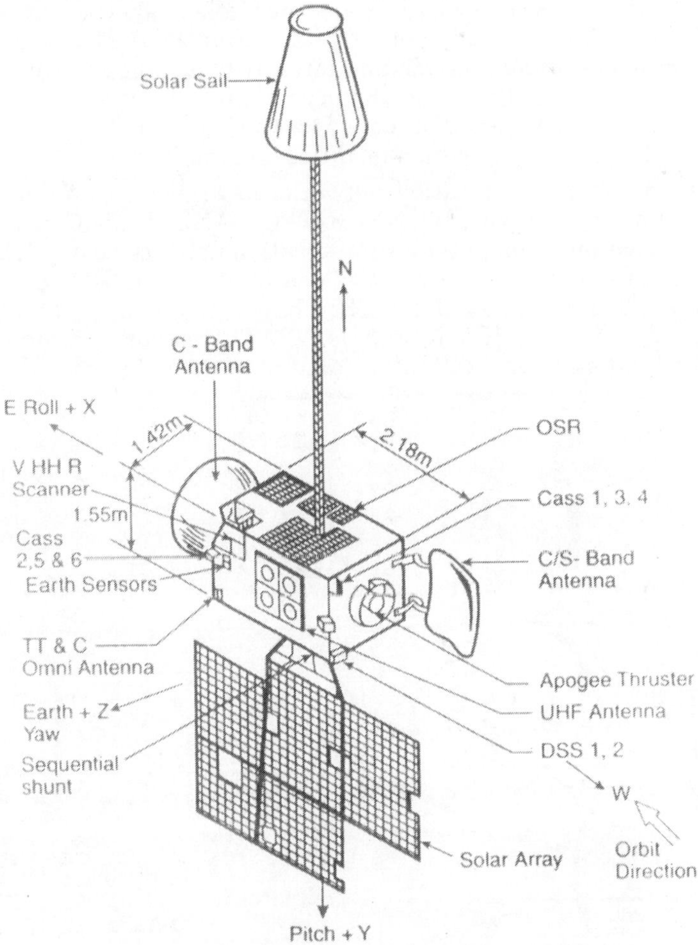

Fig. 25.17. ON-Orbit Satellite Configuration of INSAT-1

addition the MCF has an additional 14 m fully steerable antenna, INSAT-1 satellite control centre (SSC) with associated TT & C equipment, on-orbit checkout equipment, computer facilities and auxiliary power (including a no-break component). For further and expert monitoring of spacecraft health and formation of maneuver, satellite telemetry data are also available at INSAT-1 Space Segment Project Office (SSPO) and the ISRO Satellite Centre ISAC.

INSAT-1 Utilization

The INSAT-1 utilization as proposed and carried out by various national agencies are as per chart shown in Fig. 25.18. These services are proposed and carried out by the INSAT-1 systems arrangements given in Fig. 25.19. The telecommunications component of the two satellite INSAT-1 space-segment is designed to provide over 8000 two way long-distance telephone circuits potentially accessible from any part of India, even the remotest without regard to intervening terrain and terrestrial distance. According to a report based on 1988 some 48 telecommunications earth stations were working in telecommunication network using INSAT to provide long distance communication facilities on over 80 routes.

Business communication networks have also 51come up. Organizations like ONGC, ITI, NFL, NTPC, SAIL, CIL, IOC, DAE and TATA have their computer communication networks using INSAT. National Information Centre (NIC)'s satellites based NICNET using SSMA is being completed. NICNET have adopted a SSMA/CDMA type very small aperture terminals (VSATS) network working with a 13 mϕ antenna for the Master Earth Station (MES) located at the

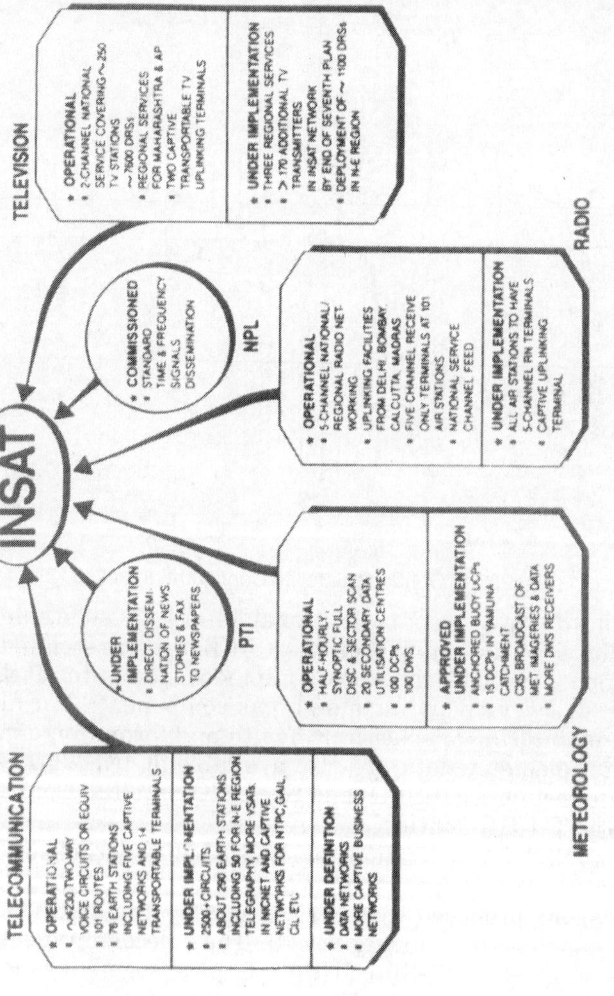

Fig. 25.18. INSAT-1 System Utilization.

NIC Headquarters in New Delhi. The micro earth stations or VSAT's in NICNET use a 1.8 mϕ parabolic antenna with a HPA of either IW (for 1200 bps) or 5W (for 9600 bps). In NICNET any micro earth

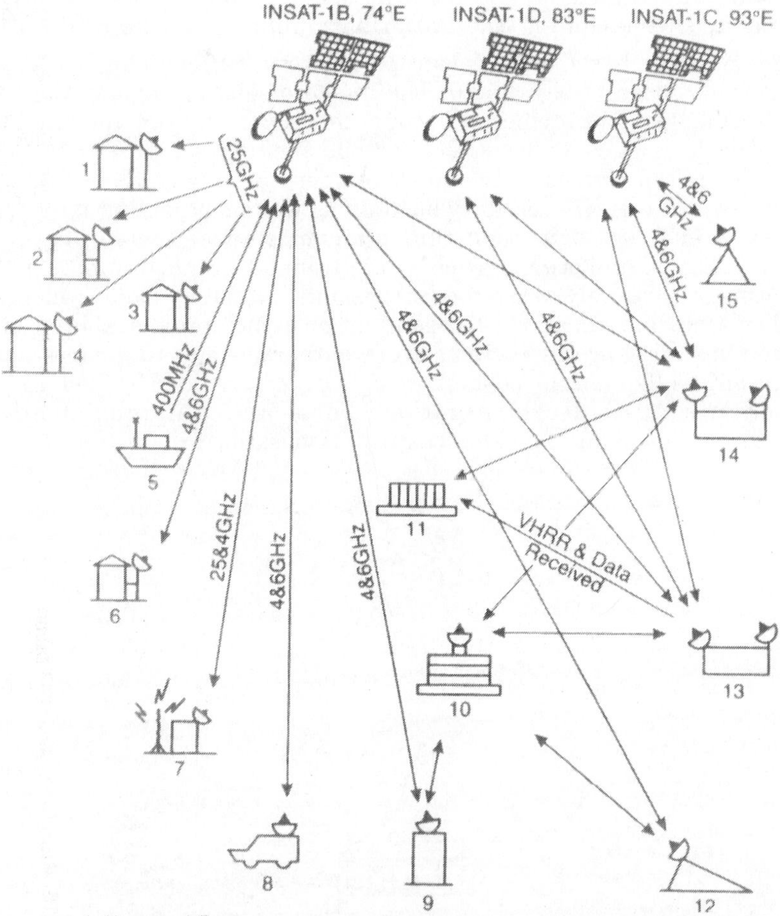

1. News and Fascimile Dissemination 2. Disaster Warning. 3. Meteorological Data, Fax and Imageries Dissemination. 4. Direct Broadcasting to Rural Commuities (TV). 5 Meteorological Data Collection and Relay Platforms. 6. Emergency Communication terminals Jeep Transportable and Airliftable for meeting Short notice Emergency disaster requirements. 7. Rediffusion of Satellite by Terrestrial Transmitters National Network (TV & Radio). 8. Transportable Terminals-for meeting emergent needs of Telephony and TV uplink Feed. 9. Remote area Terminals-Telephony and Telegraphy. 10. Network Operations Control Centre (Delhi). 11. Meteorological Data Utilization Centre (Delhi). 12. Medium Earth Stations-Trunk Telephony and TV Uplink Field. 13. Large Earth Stations-Intermain and Main Primary Trunk Telephony, Remote area communications, TV uplink for feeding TV channels, Reception of Meteorological Data from Satellite at New Delhi. 14. Master Control Facility (Hasan, Karnataka)-On Orbit control of Satellites, Health Monitoring os Satellites, Orbit Raising Control. 15 Computer Networking with VSAT'S Satellite based rural Telegraphy.

Fig. 25.19. INSAT-1 System Concept.

station can access any other micro earth station in the network by dialing the number of the earth station. Each of the microearth station has been assigned a unique code. By the time of INSAT-ID comes up NICNET is expected to have ninety microearth stations at remote sites including Kavarati, Dharmapuri, Ooty and Bhilwara.

Satellite based rural telegraph network (SBRTN) for INSAT is as that shown in Fig. 25.20. The meteorological component of the INSAT system provides (*i*) round the clock regular, half hourly synoptic images of weather systems including severe weather, cyclones, sea surface and cloud top temperatures, water bodies, snow etc. over the entire territory of India as well as adjoining land and sea areas, (*ii*) collection and transmission of meteorological, hydrological and oceanographic data from unattended remote platforms, (*iii*) timely warnings of possible disasters from cyclones, floods, storms etc. and (*iv*) dissemination of meteorological information including processed images of weather systems to the forecasting offices. The enhanced meteorological data provided by the INSAT benefits Agriculture, Aviation, Ports and Shipping, hydro-meteorological and flood forecasting services/sector.

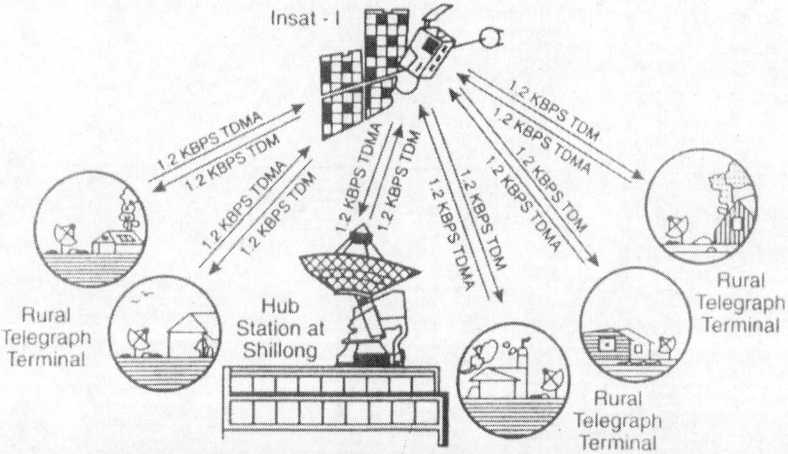

Fig. 25.20. Satellite Based Rural Telegraph Network (SBRTN)

The Imaging coverage and Data Relay Platform coverage of INSAT-1 system is shown in Fig. 25.21. Here the key facility is the Meteorological Data Utilization Centre (MDUC) located at Headquarters of IMD in New Delhi for processing and analyzing the meteorological data from INSAT satellites and disseminating the processed data to users. The meteorological data transmitted by INSAT-1B are first received at Delhi Earth Station (Sikandarabad of Bulandshahar District in U.P.) about 60 kms from Delhi from where they are transmitted to NDUC over a microwave link.

The INSAT Disaster Warning System (DWS) Concept is shown in Fig. 25.23. This scheme has been initially implemented on an

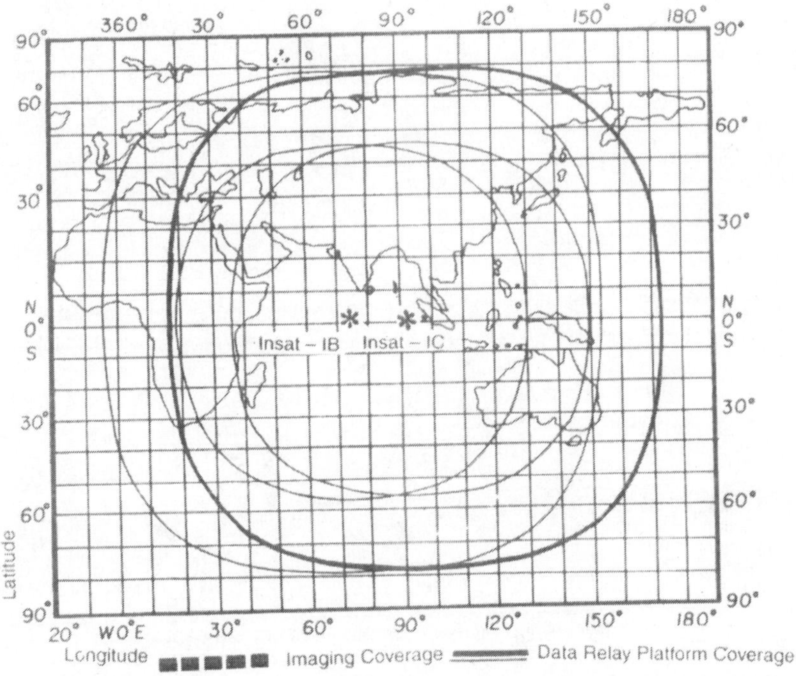

Fig. 25.21. Imaging and Data Relay Platform Coverage of INSAT-1 System

experimental basis in selected coastal areas of southern Andhra Pradesh and Northern Tamil Nadu. The warning messages originating from the Area Cyclone Warning Centre, Madras are transmitted to INSAT-1B from the Madras Earth Station of DOT. A *S* Band transponders on board INSAT-1B receives and relays back these signals for reception by Disaster Warning receivers deployed in southern Andhra Pradesh coast and northern Tamil Nadu coast. The signals selectively address specific DWS receivers. Receipt of timely warning helps the local authorities to take action on cyclones mitigation. The performance of initial phase of DWS scheme was satisfactory during the cyclonic storms of October and November 1987.

25.9.2. INSAT-II

With the successful launching and commissioning of INSAT-1 series of satellites (INSAT-1B, 1C and 1D), INSAT-1 series was gradually replaced by indigenously developed second generation INSAT-II series of satellites. Fig. 25.23 shows a basic comparison of INSAT-II and INSAT-I system, whereas Table 25.10 gives these differences in some detail.

The first phase of INSAT programme is also known as INSAT 1 series. Unifortunately, from the very beginning there were problems with INSAT-1 series satellites. The first INSAT-1 (INSAT-1A) when

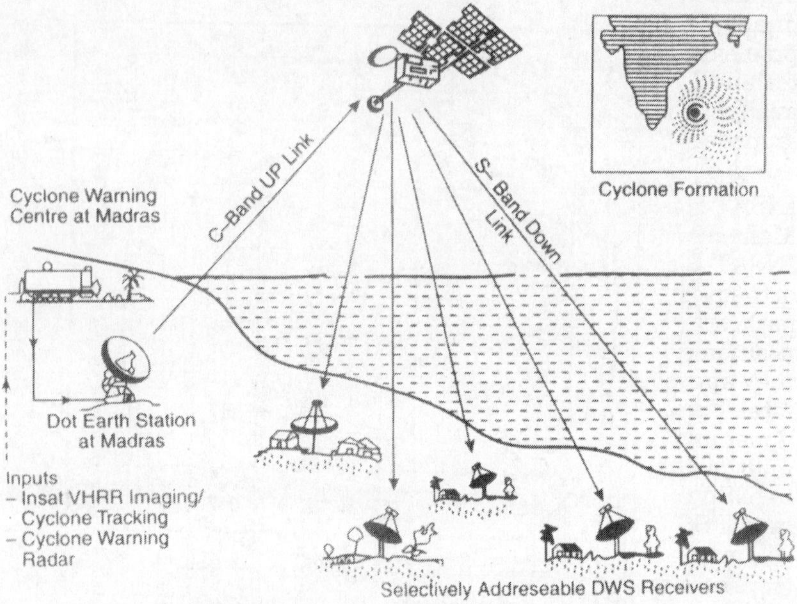

Fig. 25.22. Disaster Warning System Concept

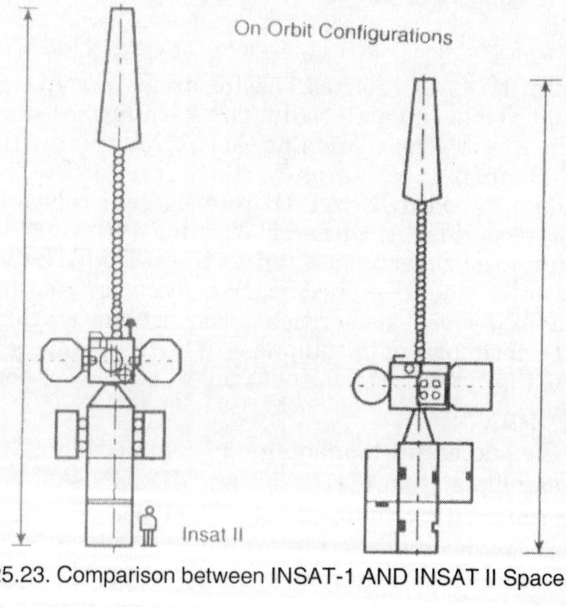

Fig. 25.23. Comparison between INSAT-1 AND INSAT II Space craft.

launched in 1982 could not get its solar sail opened and following a series of events, the satellite was ultimately abandoned 147 days after its launch. INSAT-1B, which was launched by the US Space shuttle in Aug. 1983 had problems with its solar arrays in the beginning. It required 11 days orbit maneuovers to deploy them finally, INSAT-1C, which was launched on July 22, 1988 had the problems of solar power. Its one of the two solar buses developed technical snag and is still unresolved. With this result the power availability for the spacecraft is nearly halved. INSAT-1D was launched in the end of June 1990 from USA.

The space segment concept of INSAT II is shown in Fig. 25.24. INSAT II is to be used by various agencies for a variety of services. Main users are DOT, IMD, AIR and Doordarshan. The initial all up INSAT-II space segment is to have three multipurpose satellites-two of them collected at the primary orbital positive and one at the major path orbital position. The two spacecraft at the primary orbital position are to be collected and station-kept in such a manner that they appear as in single large capacity spacecraft in terms of their total. Fixed Satellite Services (FSS) capacities in conventional *c*-and upper extended *C* band by use of orthogonal polarizations. Though multipurpose and somewhat similar in configuration polarizations to INSAT-1 spacecraft, each INSAT-II spacecraft has a considerably large FSS pay load complement and a higher resolution meteorological imaging (VHRR) instrument than an INSAT-1 spacecraft.

The overall capacity requirements for INSAT-II are as follows :

(*i*) *Fixed Satellite Services :* Transponders for telecommunications requiring 34 dbW EIRP in *C*-band and Extended *C*-band ; specialized telecommunications requirement for dedicated user networks using roof top terminal calling for higher EIRP (36 db W) in extended C-band with frequency allocations such that they are clear of interferences from and into terrestrial system ; transponders in the *C* band and extended C-band for nation wide distribution of TV programme for rebroadcast,

(*ii*) *Broadcast Satellite Services :* The requirement for broadcast satellite service for direct TV broadcast to community reception includes four operating S-band transponders with an EIRP of 42 dbW over the primary coverage area.

(*iii*) *Radio Networking and Other S-Band Point-to-multi-Point Services :* This requirement is to cater to at least 32 low level carriers for distribution of radio signals as disaster warning service, standard time and frequency synchronization, meteorological data distribution etc.

(*iv*) *Meteorological Services :* A very high resolution radiometer (VHRR) for coverage of the designed area (extended angle of 14 degree North to South and 20 degrees East to West) with a resolution of 2 km in visible and 8 km in infrared channels; facility for transmission of processed meteorological data *via* satellites ; a 400 MHz uplink and 4 GHz downlink data relay transponders for access by low cost unattended data collection platforms ; a disaster warning

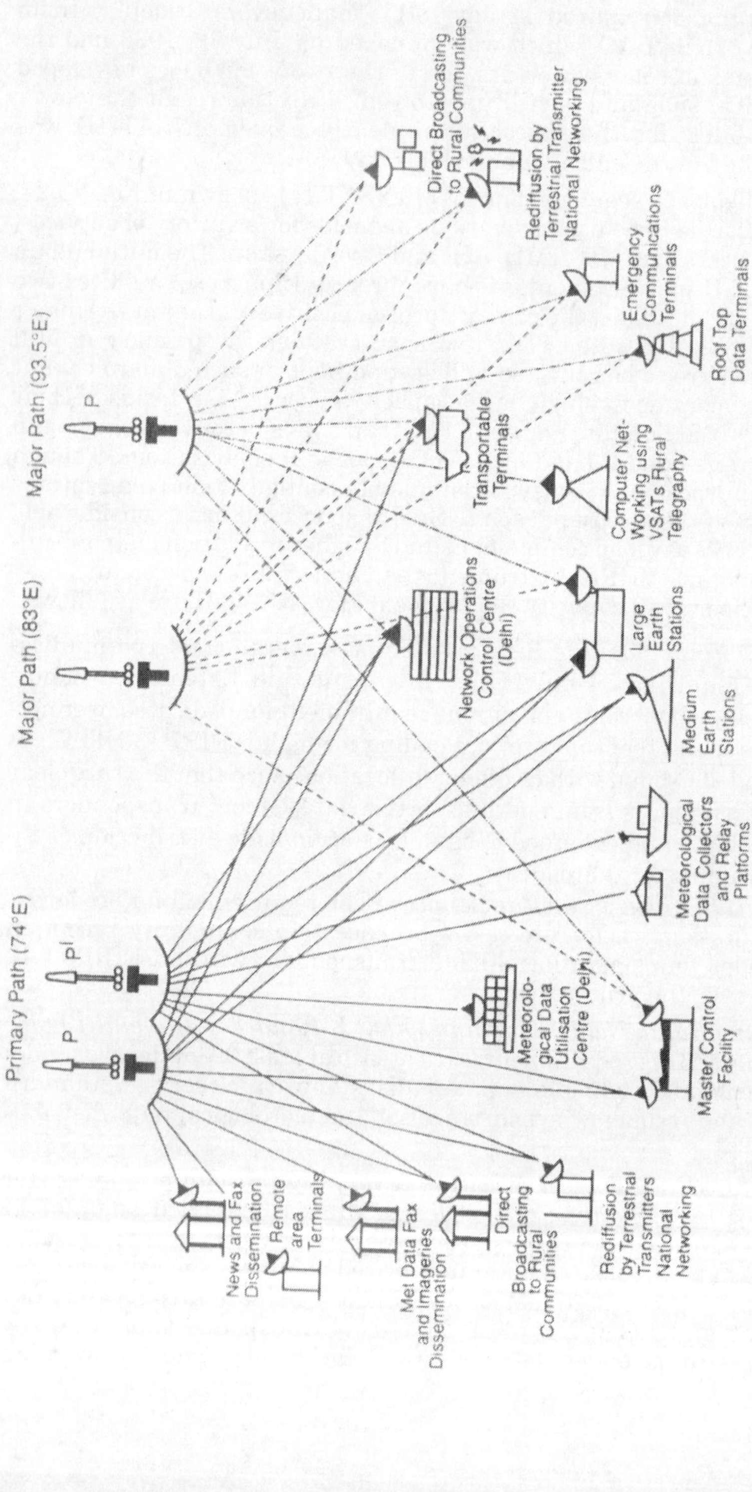

Fig. 25.24. INSAT-II Space Segment Concept.

service using low level RN type carriers to address selected individual receivers in disaster prone areas and

(*v*) *Satellite Aided Search and Rescue (SAS & R)*. This requires a provision of 406 MHz uplink and a 4 GHz downlink relay electronics to provide geostationary alert function in the overall Indian satellite aided search and resue programme and to form a part of International COSPAS-SARSAT system.

For the realisation of INSAT-II system, Govt. of India had approved in 1985 the INSAT-II test satellite project, which envisaged design, development and test to two INSAT-II satellites. First INSAT-II test satellites INSAT-IIA is scheduled for launch in the last quarter of 1991 and the second INSAT-IIB a year thereafter by Ariane. For the INSAT-II programme, the INSAT Master Control facility (MCF) at Hassan is being augmented. Two 11 m ϕ satellite control earth stations and as INSAT-II control centre (SSC) are being added together with VHRR on-orbit test and check out facilities etc.

Table 25.10 Comparison of INSAT-I and INSAT-II

	INSAT-I	*INSAT-II*
Length (m : fully deployed) Dry Mass (kg) EOL minimum power (W) Payload complement (in each spacecraft) C band FSS transponder channels	-19 m -550 kg -930 W 12 (32 db W EOC) Functional channel redundancy (10/12)	-23 m -860 kg -1180 W 18 total - 16 (32 db W EOC) and 2 (34 db W EOC) Functional reduncdancy in conventional C band (10/12) and 3:2 in output stages for 6 extended C band transponder channels
S band high power BSS channels VHRR and DRT	2 (42 db W EOC) 3/2 TWTA reundancy 2.75 Kms visible and 11 Kms IR resolution ; 2 : 1 redundancy in VHRR electronics x'mtr and DRT	2 (42 db W EOC) 3:2 TWTA redundancy VHRR (Improved resolution)-2 Kms visible and 8 Kms. IR resolution; S/C level VHRR and DRT redundancy as in INSAT-1.6 dB improvement in VHR x'mtr eirp included
406 MHz S & R transponder Eclipse operating capability for payload (in each s/c; equivalent at EOL) omni-TT & C	150 W (approx.) Yes, uses FSS transponder channel Nos. 4 and 5 TWTAs	340 W (approx.) An additional antenna added for improved coverage. Independent output stages, FSS channels not tied down.
Deployments: Solar array	Asymmetrical ; involves tiaxial deployments, partial deployment in transfer orbit	Asymmetrical, Accord on type ; simpler deployments, no partial deployment in transfer orbit

Antenna	Two deployables on East and West Faces. All 6 GHz receive functions on East face deployable antenna	Two deployables on East and West Faces but a third fixed antenna added for all 6 GHz receive and VHRR and DRT transmit functions. Greater mission functions saving in case of deployment anomalies.

25.9.3 INSAT Currently in Service

The following nine INSAT systems are currently in service providing a variety of country wide facilities:

1. INSAT-2E
2. INSAT-3A
3. INSAT-3B
4. INSAT-3C
5. INSAT-3E
6. INSAT-4A
7. INSAT-4C
8. INSAT-4B
9. INSAT-4CR

INSAT-2E

It is the last of the five satellites in INSAT-2 series that was launched by Ariane launcher in April 1999.

Payload : I. 17 *C-band* and lower extended C-band transponders providing zonal and global coverage with an Effective Isotropic Radiated Power (EIRP) of 36 dBW.

II. *Very High Resolution Radiometer* (VHRR) with imaging capacity in the visible (0.55 – 0.75 μm), thermal infrared (10.5 – 12.5 μ m) and water vapour (5.7 – 7.1 μm) channels and provides 2×2 km, 8×8 km and 8×8 km ground resolution, respectively.

III. *Charge Coupled Device (CCD) camera* providing 1×1 km ground resolution in the Visible (0.63 – 0.69 μm), Near Infrared (0.77 – 0.86 μm) and Shortwave Infrared (1.55 – 1.70 μm) bands.

INSAT-3 Series

INSAT-3A. The multipurpose satellite, INSAT-3A, was launched by *Ariane* in April, 2003. It is located at 93.5 degree East logitude. Its EIRP (C-band transponder) is 38 dbW. For Ku-band transponder, its EIRP has been increased from 46 db W in INSAT-2C to 48 db W.

Payload : I. 12 Normal C-band transponder (9 channels provide expanded coverage from Middle East to South East Asia with an

EIRP of 38 dBW, 3 channels provide India coverage with an EIRP of 36 dBW and 6 Extended C-band transponders provide India coverage with an EIRP of 36 dBW.

II. 6 Ku-band transponders provide India coverage with EIRP of 48 dBW.

III. Very High Resolution Radiometer (VHRR) with imaging capacity in the visible (0.55 – 0.75 μm), thermal infrared (10.5 – 12.5 μm) and Water Vapour (5.7 – 7.1 μm) channels, provide 2 × 2 km, 8 × 8 km ground resolutions, respectively.

IV. CCD camera provides 1 × 1 km ground resolution, in the visible (0.63 – 0.69 μm), near infrared (0.77 – 0.86 μm) and shortwave infrared (1.55 – 1.70 μm) bands.

V. Data Relay Transponder (DRT) having global receive coverage with a 400 MHz uplink and 4500 MHz downlink for relay of meteorological, hydrological and oceanographic data from unattended land and ocean-band automatic data collection-cum-transmission platforms.

VI. Satellite Aided Search and Rescue (SAS&R) *SARP* payload having global receive coverage with 406 MHz uplink and 4500 MHz downlink with India coverage, for relay of signals from distress beacons in sea, air or land.

INSAT-3B. It was launched in March 2000. It has a unique design, combining telecommunication, television/radio broadcasting and meteorological services upon a single platform. INSAT-3B is co-located with INSAT-2E at 83 degree East longitude.

Payload : I. 12 Extended C-band transponders and three Ku-band transponders that have coverage over the Indian region.

II. *Mobile Satellite Service* (MSS) payload with forward link between the hub and mobile station operating in C × S band and return link between the mobile station and the hub operating in S × C band.

INSAT-3C. Launched in January 2002 by Ariane, INSAT-3C is positioned at 74 degree East longitude.

Payload : I. Normal C-band transponder providing an EIRP of 37 dBW.

II. 6 Extended C-band transponders with EIRP of 37 dBW

III. 2 S-band transponders to provide BSS service with 42 dBW EIRP

IV. MSS payload similar to that on INSAT-3B

INSAT-3D

This meteorological satellite aims for a significant technological improvement in sensor capabilities as compared to earlier INSAT missions. It is an exclusive mission designed for enhanced meteorological observations and monitoring of land and ocean surfaces for weather forecasting and disaster warning. The three-axis stabilized geostationary satellite. INSAT-3D is configured around standard 2000 kg 12K spacecraft bus with 7-year life.

Payload : I. Six-channel Imager meteorological instrument with channels in Visible, Middle Infrared, Water Vapour and Thermal Infrared bands, and includes a SWIR channel for wider applications.

II. IR Sounder with 18 narrow spectral channels in 3 IR bands in addition to a channel in visible band.

III. On-the-fly correction of scan mirror pointing errors, biannual yaw rotation of the spacecraft, micro-stepping SADA, star sensors and integrated bus management unit to meet the stringent payload requirements like pointing accuracies, thermal management of IR detector and concurrent operation of both instruments.

INSAT-3E

This is the country's latest communication satellite launched by Ariane-5, on 28 September, 2003. It is positioned at 55 degree East longitude.

The satellite augmented the Insat satellite system's capacity for TV broadcast and communication in the country. Insat-3E is the fourth satellite in the Insat-3 series. The 162nd flight of Ariane (Ariane-5) also carried e-Bird of Eutelsat and Smart-1 of the European Space Agency. During the initial phase of Insat-3E operations, MCF utilised INMARSAT Organization's Telemetry, Tracking and Command (TTC) ground stations at Beijing (China), Fucino (Italy) and Lake Cowichan (Canada).

The Sun tracking solar energy of INSAT-3E has a total area of 29.6 sq.m and it is designed to generate 2.9 kW (BoL) of power in orbit. The satellite has two deployable antennas and one fixed antenna to carry out various transmit and receive functions. The three axis stabilisation made the spacecraft to be locked to Earth continuously through the optical sensors and it will maintain the correct altitude to look at the Earth in a stable manner. The Momentum Wheels onboard the satellite stabilised the nominal speed of 4500 revolutions per minute to provide gyroscopic stiffness and provide three axis stabilisation. The communication payloads were switched on after it reached the orbital slot.

It had 1595 kg propellant at the time of its injection into GTO by Ariane-5 launch vehicle on 28 September, 2003. After orbit raising operations, it had 510 kg of propellant remaining that is sufficient to arrest the drift and park it at its orbital slot, as well as, maintain the satellite in its orbit and controlling its orientation during its design life of more than 12 years.

440 Newton Liquid Apogee Motor on board was used to conduct the orbit raising manoeuvers and the satellite achieved an orbital period of 23 hours and 46 minutes and is continuously visible to MCF, Hassan. It reached its GTO slot of 55° east longitude of 649 km perigee and 36,000 km apogee with an orbital inclination of 7° with respect to the equatorial plane to its present near GSO orbit with zero degree inclination.

Payload : I. 24 Normal C-band transponders provide an edge of coverage EIRP of 37 dBW over India and 12 Extended C-band transponders provide an edge of coverage EIRP of 38 dBW over India. With its launch India now has 128 transponders in space. Insat-3E will replace Insat-2DT and leased transponders.

Table 25.11 Payloads on INSAT-3 Satellites

Payloads	*INSAT-3A*	*INSAT-3B*	*INSAT-3C*	*INSAT-3D*	*INSAT-3E*
C-band Transponder	12	—	24	—	24
Extended C-band Transponder	6	12	6	—	12
Ku-band Transponder	6	3	—	—	—
S-band Transponder	1	—	2	—	—
S-MSS Transponder	—	1	1	—	—
Very High Resolution Radiometer	1	—	—	—	—
CCD camera	1	—	—	—	—
DRT & SAR	—	—	—	1	—
Imager	—	—	—	6-Ch	—
Sounder	—	—	—	19-Ch	—

INSAT-4 Series

INSAT-4 series is planned to have seven satellites (see Table 25). The transponder capacity of this series has been worked out after evaluating the requirement projected by different uses/user departments.

Table 25.12 Distribution of Transponders in INSAT-4 Satellites

Satellite	*Transponders-band*
INSAT-4A	12 Ku, 12 C
INSAT-4B	12 Ku, 12 C
INSAT-4C	18 Ku
INSAT-4D (Spare)	12 C, 6 Ext C
INSAT-4E	12 C, 6 Ext C
INSAT-4F	12 C, 6 Ext C
INSAT-4G	18 Ku

INSAT-4A was tracked, monitored and controlled from the Master Control Facility (MCF) at Hassan in Karnataka. During the initial phase of INSAT-4A operations, MCF also utilised INMARSAT Organisation's Telemetry, Tracking and Command (TTC) ground stations at Beijing (China), Fucino (Italy) and lake Cowichan (Canada). The ISRO Telemetry, Tracking and Command Network (ISTRAC) ground station at Biak in Indonesia also monitored the satellite. The satellite's orbit was precisely determined by continuous ranging from the participating ground stations.

INSAT-4A was finally manoeuvered to its final geostationary orbit, which is about 36,000 km above the equator, by firing 440 Newton Liquid Apogee Motor (LAM). When the satellite reached near geosynchronous orbit, deployment of its solar panels and the two antennas carried out and the satellite put in its final 3-axis stabilised mode. This was followed by trim manoeuvers to take the satellite to its designated orbital slot. The payload was subsequently checked out before the commissioning of the satellite.

Launched in December, 2005 by the European *Ariane* launch vehicle, 3,080 kg INSAT-4A is the most advanced, heaviest and powerful satellite. It is positioned at 83 degree East longitude along with INSAT-2E and INSAT-3B. It has a design life of 12 years.

The satellite, which has two deployable antennas and one fixed antenna for various transmit and receive functions, is positioned at 83 degree East longitude as spacemates to INSAT-2E and INSAT-3B.

INSAT-4A was designed to give a major thrust to the fledgling Direct-to-Home (DTH) television broadcasting services. It is going to revolutionise the TV broadcasting directly to the homes and improve the entertaintment scenario in India.

Payload : I. 12 Ku-band 36 MHz bandwidth transponders employing 140 W TWTAs to provide an EIRP of 52 dBW at the edge of coverage polygon with footprint covering Indian main land to meet the requirement of DTH television services.

II. 12 C-band 36 MHz bandwidth transponders provide an EIRP of 39 dBW at the edge of coverage with expanded radiation patterns encompassing Indian geographical boundary, area beyond India in southeast and northwest regions. These transponders augmented the INSAT capacity for communication and TV services.

DTH service : The 12 Ku-band 36 MHz bandwidth high-powered transponders provide 140 to 150 DTH channels. Tata-Sky, the joint venture of the Tatas and the Rupert Murdoch-owned STAR group, has booked all th Ku-band transponders on the Rs 350 core satellite. At present, DD Direct and Dish TV of the Zee Telefilms are offering DTH service in India by using the NSS 6 satellite. Others who have planned to be in the DTH segment include Sun TV.

INSAT-4C

The launch of this satellite was unsuccessful as on *July 10, 2006* the *Geo-synchronous Satellite Launch Vehicle (GSLV-F02)* carrying the satellite veered from its projected path 60 seconds after the launch, and was self-destructed over the *Bay of Bengal*. The failure is being attributed to pressure of one of the strap-on motors dropping to zero pressure in the first stage of operation, thus causing it to deviate from its path by 10 degrees.

The heaviest satellite to be launched from the Indian soil, INSAT-4C weighed 2168 kg, and was designed to last for 10 years. It was an exclusive Ku-band spacecraft with 12 Ku-band transponders. The satellite would have given a boost to Direct-to-Home television services, video picture transmission and digital satellite news gathering, and would have also provided space for *National Informatics Centre's VSAT* connectivity.

ISRO also has plans to launch INSAT-4D and INSAT-4E from home soil, while the INSAT-4F and INSAT-4G projects, which complete the INSAT-4 series are awaiting Government approval.

INSAT-4B

It was launched in March 2007 by the European *Ariane* launch vehicle. It is co-located with INSAT-3A at 93.5 degree E longitude. INSAT-4B augments the high power transponder capacity over India in Ku-band and over a wider region in C-band.

Payload : It has payloads identical to that of INSAT-4A, INSAT-4B:

I. 12 Ku-band to provide EIRP of 52 dBW.

II. 12 C-band transponders to provide EIRP of 39 dBW.

Two Tx/Rx dual grid offset fed shaped beam reflector of 2.2 m diameter for Ku-band and 2 m diameter for C-band are used.

INSAT-4CR

It was lauched on *2 September, 2007* by GSLV-F04. It is a replacement satellite of INSAT-4C. It was stabilised in its intended orbital position of 74 degree E longitude. The satellite is designed for a mission life in excess of ten years.

Payload : 12 Ku-band, 36 MHz bandwidth transponders employing 140 W TWTAs to provide an Effective Isotropic Radiated Power of 51.5 dBW at Edge of Coverage with footprint covering Indian mainland. It also incorporates a Ku-band Beacon as an aid to tracking the satellite.

Table 25.13

INSAT-4A	12 Ku-band 36 MHz bandwidth transponders and 12 C-band 36 MHz bandwidth transponders	83 degree East	December 22, 2005 Ariane-5
INSAT-4B	I. 12 Ku-band to provide EIRP of 52 dBW. II. 12 C-band transponders to provide EIRP of 39 dBW.	GSO; 93.5 degree E	Ariane-5 on March 12, 2007.
INSAT-4C			*10 July 2006 ;* Not placed in orbit due to launch failure to GSLV-F02
INSAT-4CR	12 Ku-band 36 MHz bandwidth transponders	GS0 74° E	GSLV (GSLV-F04) on *2 September 2007*

25.9.4. GSAT Series

GSATs are technology experiment satellite to be launched on board the development test flights of India's Geosynchronous Satellite Launch Vehicle (GSLV). Four satellites, GSAT-1 to GSAT-4 constitute this series.

1. demonstrating digital audio broadcast
2. demonstrating internet services
3. demonstrating compressed digital TV experiments and
4. developmental communication.

Table 25.14. Features of GSAT-1 and GSAT-2

Launch	*Launch vehicle*	*Orbit*	*Weight*	*Payload*	*Stabilizations*	*Life Span*
GSAT-1 18 April, 2001 from Sriharikota Space Center (SHAR)	GSVL-D1	Failed to reach the intended orbit	1540 kg	3 C Band and 2 S Transponders	3-axis	3-5 years

GSAT-2 8 May, 2003 from Sriharikota Space Center (SHAR)	GSLV-D2	GEO 48° E	1800 kg	4 C-band and 2 Ku-band transponders, Mobile Satellite Service (MSS), Total Radiation Dose monitor (TRDM), Surface Charge Monitor (SCM), Solar X-ray Spectrometer (SOXS), Coherent Radio Beacon Experiment (CRABEX)		

Note : The GSAT-2 after going into the GTO was taken to its final geo-stationary orbit by firing the liquid apogee motor in phases.

After reaching the geo-stationary orbit, its antenna and solar panels were deployed and the satellite was finally placed in its allocated slot of 48° E longitude.

GSAT-1. It was launched on board GSAT-D1 in April 2001. The satellite was used to validate several technologies like Fast Recovery Star Sensor, a new earth sensor using pyro electric detectors, an orbit raising strategy using a combination of four 22 Newton thrusters, thermal control using heat pipes, new technique of power management, orbit raising using perigee firing strategy and validating 10 Newton reaction control thrusters.

GSAT-2. Launched by the second flight of *GSLV* in May 2003, GSAT-2 is located at 48 degree East longitude and carries four Normal C-band transponders to provide 36 dBW EIRP with India coverage, two Ku-band transponders with 42 dBW EIRP over India and an MSS payload similar to those on INSAT-3B and INSAT-3C, will carry four C-band, two Ku-band India beam transponders and one MSS payload.

GSAT-3 (EDUSAT). Configured for audio-visual medium employing digital interactive classroom lessons and multimedia content, GSAT-3 (EDUSAT) was launched by GSLV F-01 in September 2004. It is positioned at 74 degree East logitude and is co-located with KALPANA-1 and INSAT-3E. Its transponders and their ground coverage are specially configured to cater to the educational requirements.

Payload : One Ku-band transponder covering the Indian mainland region with 50 dBW EIRP, five Ku-band spot beam transponders for South, West, Central, North and North East regional coverage with 55 dBW EIRP and six Extended C-band transponder with India coverage with 37 dbW EIRP.

GSAT-4. It will include eight channels each in Ku-band regenerative and bent-pipe payload and navigation payloads using CXL & CXC links. Unfurlable antenna is also planned to be tested on this satellite.

25.11 METSAT

Indian forays into satellite meteorology started with the launch of the Indian National Satellite (INSAT) in the early 80s. The INSAT series consists of multi-purpose satellites with payloads for communication, broadcasting and meteorology services, orbiting in geostationary orbit. INSAT-1 series, consisted of four satellites and was followed by INSAT-2 series which was indigenously developed, with improved Very High Resolution Radiometer (VHRR). With the operational use of INSAT data and the growth of meteorological services and the emerging data requirements, the need for dedicated meteorological satellites has been projected by users. The Indian Space Research Organisation (ISRO) initiated work in this direction and the recent lauch of METSAT is the successful culmination of these effort.

It was launched on 12th September, 2002 from Sriharikota launch center from the PSLV-C4, launch vehicle into its orbit — GEO, initially positioned at 37° E then shifted to 74° E, weight 1055 kg, 3-axis stabilized and its life span being 7 years or more. The Payload consists of : Very High Resolution Radiometer (VHRR) operating in visible, thermal infrared, and water vapour infrared band each at a spatial resolution of 2 km × 2 km and Data Relay Transponder (DRT).

It is unique and a dedicated satellite for meteorology. With the heralding of the satellite era in the early 80s with the INSAT series, weather services received impetus in terms of operational meteorological data covering the Indian region. The operational products included could cover sea surface temperature, cloud motion vectors, outgoing longwave radiation, quantiative precipitaion estimation, etc. The satellite data also helped in improving the skills in forecasting using weather prediction models. The need for a dedicated satellite for meteorology spurred the Indian Space Research Organisation to take up developmental efforts. The METSAT payload included water-vapour channel, which is a key parameter for monsoon. The future missions with advanced payloads such as atmospheric sounders and radiation budget etc. auger well for the meteorological services in the country.

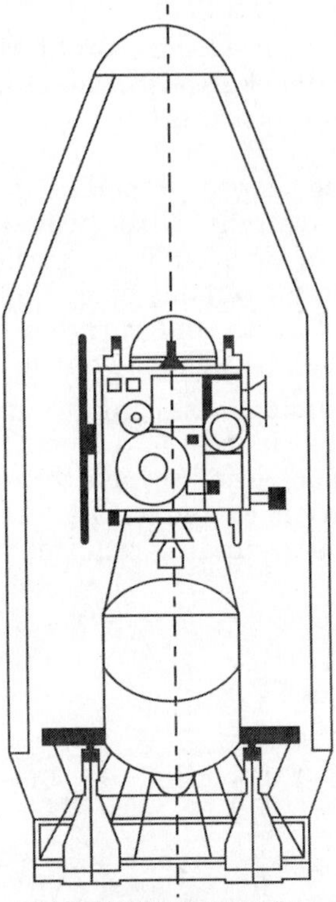

Fig. 25.25. METSAT in PSLV-C4 envelope.

Mission objectives. The METSAT mission objectives are :

- Round-the clock synoptic images of weather systems, including severe weather conditions, cyclones, etc. and to provide operational geophysical parameters such as cloud cover, sea surface temperature, snow cover, cloud motion vectors, outgoing longwave radiation and quantitative precipitation estimation.
- Collection and transmission of meteorological, hydrological and oceanographic data from remote areas through data collection platforms.

PSLV-C4 / METSAT mission

Polar Satellite Launch Vehicle (PSLV), the operational launcher developed by ISRO accomplished its sixth successful mission in the C4 flight which took off on 12 September, 2002 from Satish Dhawan Space Centre, Sriharikota. The significance of this flight was that it was a geosynchronous Transfer Orbit (GTO) mission performed for the first time by PSLV, which has proved itself as a reliable workhorse of ISRO through a string of six successful flights in a row. PSLV was essentially developed to carry out launch of Indian remote sensing satellites to polar orbit.

Unique aspects of METSAT

The developments and realization of METSAT spacecraft bus with a lift-off mass of 1055 kg and mission life by 7 years challenging task. This new 1000 kg class bus has been configured around a new Carbon Fibre Reinforced Plastic (CFRP) cylindrical structure with use of indigenously developed propellant tanks, optimized control thrusters, bus sub-systems with proven flight heritage and meteorological payload derived from earlier INSAT-mission, inclusive of modification for reliable operation. METSAT has several features implemented in its configuration due to the lift-off mass constraints imposed by PSLV lauch vehicle.

The spacecraft structure was configured with CFRP designed to achieve a structure that is light and meets various design requirements. Aluminium honeycombs have been used to a minimum extent. CFRP structure is coated with electrically conductive black paint to meet electrical grounding requirements.

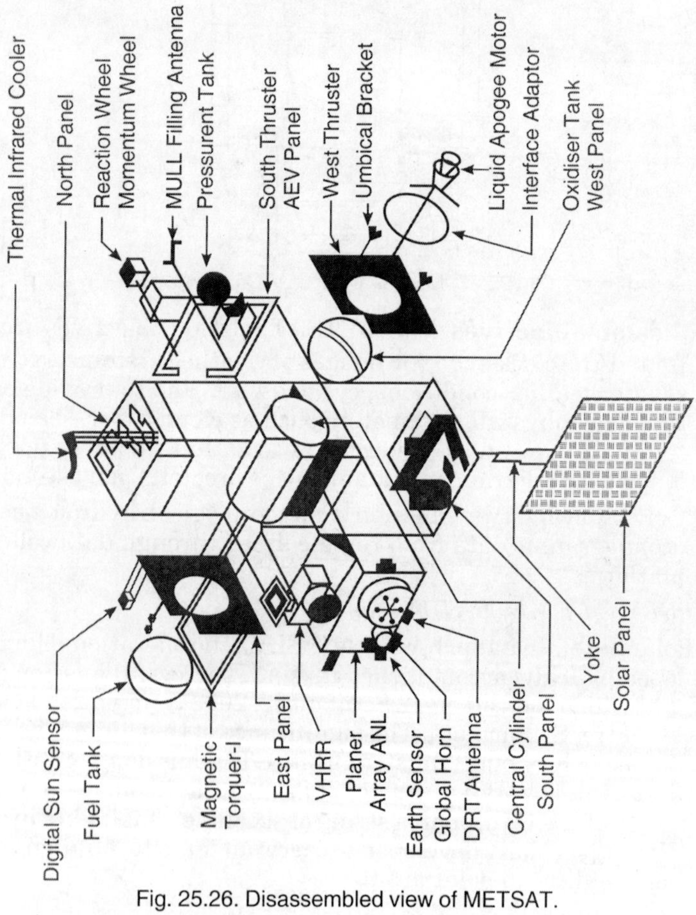

Fig. 25.26. Disassembled view of METSAT.

In order to de-couple the uncertainty in VHRR radiative cooler performance associated with the sail/boom configuration in earlier missions, METSAT configuration has been simplified with no sail/boom the north side of the spacecraft and with one solar carry deployed on other side of the spacecraft. METSAT uses linear, controlled, higher capacity-sized magnetic torques to take care of solar radiation pressure imbalances exerted on solar panel.

The solar panel is 2.15 m × 1.8 m in size using GaAs/Ge technology and generates 640 W of power at BOL equinox season. Power available at EOL summer solistice is about 500 W against a requirement of 460 W. The Solar Array Driven Assembly (SADA) slip rings and drive mechanism are modified to meet the power transfer and driven requirements, and it is mass-optimized (Fig. 25.26).

Some of the unique factors of the spacecraft are :

- A new element called planar array antenna is used to transmit VHRR and Data Relay Transponder (DRT) data.
- It has a 440 N apogee motor and only twelve RCS thrusters with a distribution of a set of four each on east, west and south faces, compared to earlier INSAT missions with 16 RCS thrusters.
- It has a single power bus and 18 AH battery for optimizing the weight.

Potential applications of METSAT data. The METSAT data are received and processed at the MDUC. Reception facility also exists at MCF, Hassan and Space Applications Centre, Ahmedabad

Fig. 25.27. First image from METSAT VHRR visible band.

for sensor health monitoring, satellite housekeeping and in-house R & D activites.

Figure. 25.27 shows the first image from METSAT VHRR in visible channel.

Operational applications of METSAT data. The foremost application of data from METSAT will be towards operational services in terms of the following :

(*i*) Watch and monitor the growth of weather phenomena like cumulonimbus cells, thunderstorm, fog, etc. and their decay.

(*ii*) Track movements of migrating systems such as tropical cyclones, monsoon depressions, western disturbance, etc.

(*iii*) Identify and locate primary synoptic systems like surface lows, trough/ridges, jet streams, regions of intensive convection, inter-tropical convergence zones, etc.

(*iv*) Monitor onset and progress of monsoon systems.

(*v*) Detect genesis and growth of tropical cyclones and monitor their intensification and movement till land-fall.

In this context, the capability of METSAT payload to provide data in three imaging modes is found to be of relevance. These special imaging modes permit scanning of intense weather systems frequently, to get insight into the dynamics of the atmosphere. The higher of 2 km in visible and 8 km in thermal IR, permits study of mesoscale events.

Besides the monitoring capability through imageries, the METSAT payloads are capable of providing several operational parameters for assimilation in weather presiction models and atmospheric research.

Monsoon studies using METSAT data. Considering the studies in the past using INSAT data, the data from METSAT are expected to contribute to several aspects of monsoon research. The addition of WV channel in the VHRR payload is useful in studying (*i*) intertropical covergence zone dynamics, (*ii*) large-scale moisture built-up prior to monsoon onset, (*iii*) low frequency modes such as the 40-day oscillations in monsoon circulation. The parameters such as cloud-motion vector, SST and OLR are used for initial fields in models with improved forecasts.

25.12 SMALL EARTH STATIONS IN INDIA

Alongwith the master earth stations for INTELSAT, INMARSAT, LANDSAT, INSAT, IRS-IA, there are several small earth stations in India and the number is increasing day by day. Fig. 25.28 indicates the growth of earth stations in India, since 1967 onwards. It is hoped that by the end of the present century, there will be several thousands of such small earth stations in India, which are used for a variety of purposes. Table 25.15 indicates the typical parameters of small earth stations used in India. Table 25.16 gives typical link budget of small earth stations working in compounded FM-SCPC-FDMA Mode. Table 25.17 shows the cost of these small earth stations alongwith the cost of testing equipments (there are 1987 quote). In India, initially these earth station equipment were imported mainly from USA. Now these are indigenously manufactured in India. Two R & D units-Telecommunications Research centre of the Dot and SAC of ISRO have been involved with the indigenous development of earth station equipment. A number of manufacturing units have been associated with the production and supply of equipment including antenna of various sizes, HPAs, LANs, CFM-SCPC equipment, echo-suppressers, multiplex equipment, and uniterrupted power supply (UPS) equipment.

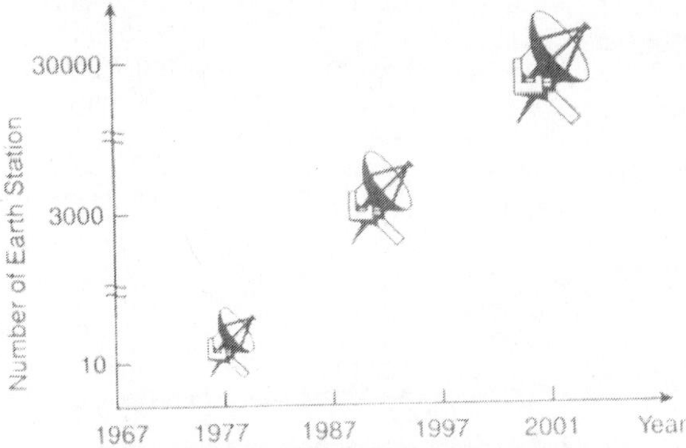

Fig. 25.28. Growth of Earth Stations in India.

Table 25.15 Typical Parameters of Small Earth Stations in India

Items	*Sub-items*	*Parameters*
System	G/T	19.7 db/K
Performance	S/N	50.0 dB
Antenna	Size	4.5 M Dia
	Category	Cassegrain feed
	Mount	X-Y
	Tracking at 6 GHz	Manual
	Receive gain at 4 GHz	42.5 dB
Transmitter	Amplifier type output power	FET Amplifier 20 Watts
Receiver	Amplifier type Noise Temperature	Uncooled FET Amplifier 90 K
Mode of Communication	Modulation	CFM-SCPC
	Access	FDMA
	Assignment	Preassigned and Demand Assignment

Indian Telephone Industries has now a days started manufacturing lowcost satellite communication equipment for transmission using a special technology called Spread Spectrum Mulitple Acess (SSMA). ITI Equatorial SatCom Ltd, a joint venture of ITI with Equatorial Pacific International Company of USA, are going to manufacture these low cost earth stations, which are supposed to revolutionize the data transmission. These microearth stations operating in a satellite based network of their own, offer a cost solution of thin route data communication between central host computers and a large number of remote sites. The equatorial network is expected to upgrade Government and private sector telecommunications infrastructure, at a low cost.

Table 25.16 Typical Link Budget of Small Earth Stations Working in Compounded FM-SCPC-FDMA MODE

Parameters	*Small Earth Station (19.7 db / K) to Master, Earth Station (31.7 dB / K)*	*Master Earth Station (31.7 dB / K) to Small Earth Station (19.7 dB / K)*	*Unit*
1. General			
(*a*) Type of carrier	CFM-SCPC	CFM-SCPC	
(*b*) Connectivity	4.5-11.0	11.0-4.5	m
(*c*) RF Spacing	45	45	KHz
(*d*) Noise Bandwidth	20	20	kHz
2. (*a*) Earth Station EIRP per channel.	36.8	45.8	db W
(*b*) Path loss	200.0	200.0	dB
(*c*) Satellite G/T	–6.0	-5.0	dB/K
(*d*) Earth Station	1.5	0.0	dB
Tracking Error			
(*e*) Noise Bandwidth	43.0	43.0	dB
(*f*) Boltzmann Constant	-228.0	-228.6	dbW/KHz
(*g*) C/N UPLINK	14.9	26.4	dB
(*h*) C/N/IM	18.0	18.0	dB
3. (*a*) Satellite EIRP per channel	0.8	9.8	dbW
(*b*) Path Loss	196.0	196.0	dB
(*c*) Earth Station G/T	31.7	19.7	dB/K
(*d*) Earth Station Tracking Error	Nil	-1.5	dB
(*e*) Contour Loss	-0.1	-4.0	dB
(*f*) Boltzmann Constant	-228.0	-228.0	dbW/kHz
(*g*) Noise Bandwidth	43.0	43.0	dB
(*h*) C/N/DN LINK	21.1	13.6	dB
4. (*a*) C/N/total	12.5	12.1	dB
(*b*) C/N/Threshold	8.0	8.0	dB
(*c*) Margin	4.5	4.1	dB

Table 25.17. Typical Equipment Cost of Small Earth Station (with Indian Equipment)

Equipment	*Quantity*	*Price in Indian Rupees*
1. 4.5 m dia cassegrain feed antenna	1	375,000
2. 20 WHPA in redundant configuration with auto switch over facility	1	900,000
3. 90° / *k* LNA in redundant configuration with auto switch facility	1	425,000
4. Up/Down converter in redundant configuration with common equipment for SCPC subsystem	1	1800,000
5. SCPC Modems (preassigned)	4	520,000
6. Power Plant	1	200,000
	Total =	4220,000
7. Testing Instruments (imported) : Dual Beam Oscilloscops RF Spectrum Analyzer, Transmission Test Set, Frequency Counter, Power Meter		250,000
	Grand Total =	4470,000
	=	US $ 350,000

25.13 INDIA'S PARTICIPATION IN OTHER INTERNATIONAL COMMUNICATIONS SATELLITE SYSTEMS

Before INSAT's India was already using INTELSAT services. India is also the founder member of INMARSAT. Mobile satellite communication services are also set up for use by both business and Government agencies including Indian Railways. Standard *C* ship

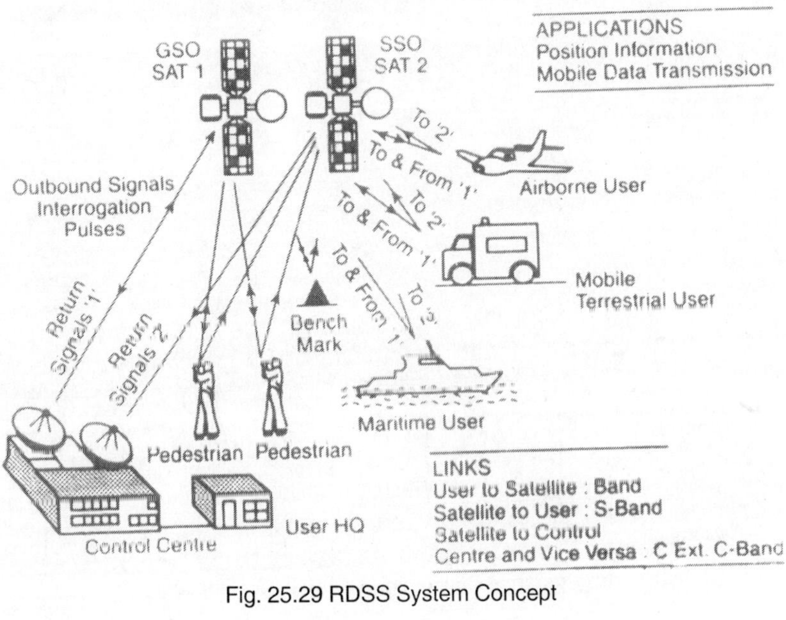

Fig. 25.29 RDSS System Concept

Earth station that has been introduced by INMARSAT for small ships, aircraft and land vehicle is being developed by ISRO. Development of Global positioning system (GPs) receiver is being taken up for introducing satellite navigation in India.

RDSS : In 1986, Department of Space (DOS) concluded a Memorandum of Under standing (MOU) with the GEOSTAR Corporation of USA for a joint feasibility study for implementing a Radio Determination Satellite Services (RDSS). Fig. 25.29 indicates this RDSS system concept in Indian Ocean region. ISRO has also been providing the principal technical support for the active Indian participation in International Civil Aviatation Organization (ICAO's) Future Air Navigation System (FANS) committee which is responsile for defining the basic functional specifications/characteristics for future satellite communication and navigation systems/services and allied matters for civil aviation purposes. India is getting involved in early demonstration/testing phase of aeronautical satellite communication.

SAS & R : Another area in which India is having International Cooperation in satellite communication is Satellite Based Search and Rescue Operations Service. The Govt. of India has launched a programme to promote, participate in and contribute to the development of international satellite-aided search and rescue system (SAS&R) for maritime, airborne and land distress alert detection

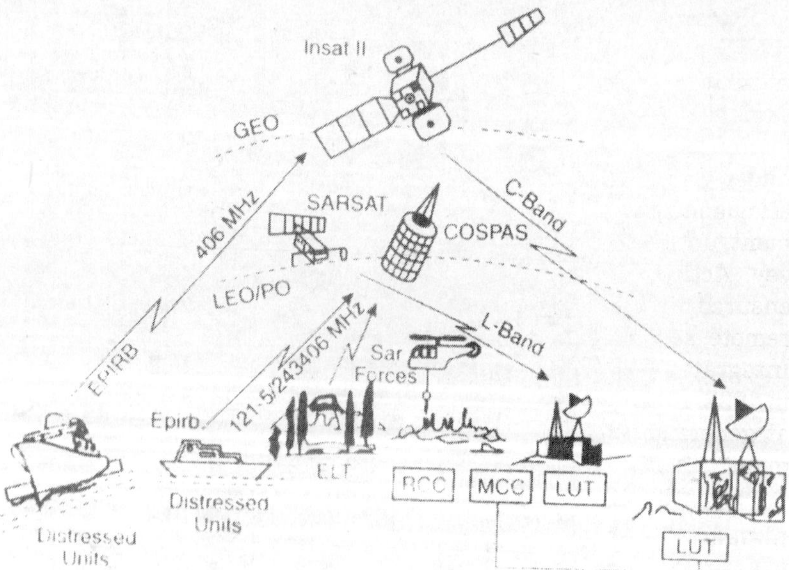

Fig. 25.30. Satellite-aided Search and Rescue.

and position location. The national (SAS & R) is a multi-pronged plan involving (*i*) use of the existing USA-USSR-France and Canada COSPAS-SARSAT Space Segment and establishment of a Local User Terminal (LUT) in India, (*ii*) indigenous development of 406 MHz emergency locator becons (ELBs), (*iii*) testing of a sample of existing 121.5 and 243 MHz ELBs in inventory and under indigenous production for COSPAS-SARSAT compatibility, (*iv*) contribution to the future international SAS & R space segment by carriage of SAS & R payloads on future Indian satellites; and (*v*) securing a first-level participation for India in the international SAS & R system. Fig. 25.30 indicates this SAS & R scheme.

25.14 Indian Remote Sensing Satellite Programme

India began development of an indigenous IRS (Indian Remote Sensing Satellite) programme to support the national economy in the areas of "agriculture, water resources, forestry and ecology, geology, water sheds, marine fisheries and coastal management". The Indian Remote Sensing satellites are the main-stay of National Natural Resources Management system (NNRMS), for which Department of Space (DOS) is the nodal agency, providing operational remote sensing data services. Data from the IRS satellites is received and disseminated by several countries all over the world. With the advent of high resolution satellites new applications in the areas of urban sprawl, infrastructure planning and other large scale applications for mapping have been initiated.

Remote sensing applications in the country, under the umbrella of NNRMS, now cover diverse fields, such as; crop acreage and yield estimation, drought warning and assessment, flood control and damage assessment, land use/land cover information, agro-climatic planning, wasteland management, water resources management, under-ground water exploration, prediction of snow-melt run-off management of water-sheds and command areas, fisheries development, under development mineral prospecting, forest resources survey. Active involvement of the user ministries/departments has ensured in an effective harnessing of the potential of space-based remote sensing. An important application of IRS data is in the Integrated Mission for Sustainable Development (IMSD) initiated in 1992. IMSD, under which 174 districts have been identified, aims at generating locale-specific action plans for sustainable development.

The primary source of remote sensing data for NNRMS is the Indian Remote Sensing. (IRS) Satellite system, which was established in March, 1998.

IRS-ID was launched in September 1997 by PSLV-C1, which was the first time that an IRS-series satellite was launched by an indigenous launch vehicle.

IRS-P3 was launched in March, 1996. It has been providing data from its wide field sensor besides data from its scientific payload *i.e.* X-ray monitor. Data from Modular Optoelectronics Scanner, which was flown on this satellite, is being regularly received and used for ocean colour monitoring applications.

These satellites have become the principal components in the National Natural Resource Management System and the data is being used in various applications, *viz.*, agriculture and soil, land form and land use studies, water resources, forestry, drought and flood monitoring, cartography, town planning and coastal zone monitoring. Especially IRS-IC/D data has been used for cartographic and town planning application up to 1:10,000 scale. These satellites also provide stereo pairs of imageries to get height information to an accuracy of approximately 10 meters.

Table 25.17 lists the satellites launched in the formative years of the Indian space programmes. Table 25.18 lists the seven satellites in the Rohini series.

Table 25.17. Initial satellite series.

Aryabhata	19.04.1975	First Indian satellite. Provided technological experience in building and operating a satellite system. Launched by Russian launch vechial-Intercosmos
Bhaskara-I	07.06.1979	First experimental remote sensing satellite. Carried TV and microwave cameras. Launched by Russian launch vehicle-Intercosmos.
Bhaskar-II	20.11.1981	Second experimental remote sensing satellite similar to Bhaskara-1. Provided experience in building and operating a remote sensing satellite system on an end-to-end basis. Launched by Russian launch vehicle- Intercosmos.
Arine Passenger Payload Experiment (APPLE)	19.06.1981	First experimental communication satellite. Provided experience in building and operating a three-axis stabilised communication satellite. Launched by the European Ariane.

Table 25.18. Rohini satellite series

Rohini (RS-1)	18.07.1980	Used for measuring in-flight performance of second experimental launch of SLV-3.
Rohini (RS-D1)	31.05.1981	Used for conducting some remote sensing technology studies using a landmark sensor payload. Launched by the first developmental launch of SLV-3.
Rohini (RS-D2)	17.04.1983	Identical to RS-D1. Launched by the second developmental launch of SLV-3.

Stretched Rohini Satellite Series (SROSS-1)	24.03.1987	Carried payload for launch vehicle performance monitoring and for Gamma Ray astronomy. Could not be placed in orbit.
Stretched Rohini Satellite Series (SROSS-2)	13.07.1988	Carried remote sensing payload of German space agency in addition to Gamma Ray astronomy payload. Could not be placed in orbit.
Stretched Rohini Satellite Series (SROSS-C)	20.05.1992	Launched by third developmental flight of ASLV. Carried Gamma Ray astronomy and aeronomy payload.
Stretched Rohini Satellite Series (SROSS-C2)	04.05.1994	Launched by fourth developmental flight of ASLV. Identical to SROSS-C. Still in service.

25.14.1. The IRS Series

IRS-IA. It was, first operational remote sensing satellite, launched by a Russian Vostok in March 1988.

IRS-1B. It was also launched by a Russian launch vehicle, Vostok in August 1991. It is still in service.

IRS-1C. It was launched by Russian Molniya launch vehicle in December 1995. It is still in service. With a unique combination of panchromatic camera with 5.8 metre resolution and stereo capability, a multi-spectral camera with 23 metre resolution and a wide field sensor with 188 metre resolution paved the way for India to enter the global commercial remoting sensing market. International ground stations were established at many places in the world to receive IRS data.

IRS-1E. It carried remote sensing payloads, but could not be placed in orbit during its launch in September 1993.

IRS-P2. Launched by second developmental flight of PSLV in October 1994. It carried remote sensing payload.

IRS-P3. It was orbited by PSLV-D3 on March 21, 1996. Its salient features are given in next table :

IRS-P4. The application potential of IRS-System was enhanced by successful launch of **IRS-P4** (OCEANSAT-1) on board PSLV-C2 in May, 1999. Areas related to oceanography were covered. The satellite payload included (*i*) Ocean Colour Monitor (OCM) and (*ii*) Multispectral Scanning Microwave Radiometer (MSMR). Operating in four frequencies to provide valuable Ocean-surface related observation capabilities.

Mission	Remote sensing of earth's resources, Study of X-ray Astronomy, Periodic calibration of PSLV tracking radar located at tracking stations
Mass	920 kg
Orbit	817 km polar sunsynchronous with equatorial crossing at 1030 am (descending node)
Payload	Wide Field Sensor (WiFS), Modular Opto-electronic Scanner (MOS), X-ray Astronomy Experiment
Onboard power	817 Watts
Stabilization	Three axis body stabilized
Inclination	98.69 deg.
Repetivity	WiFS : 5 days
Mission life	One year (nominal)

KALPANA-1 : Technology Experimental Satellite (TES). It is a meterological satellite launched by *PSLV* on September 12, 2002. It carries *VHRR* and DRT payloads to provide meteorological services. It is located at 74 degree East longitude. It is the first exclusive meteorological satellite built by ISRO. So far, meteorological services had been combined with telecommunication and television services in the INSAT system. It is a precursor to the future INSAT system, that will have separate satellites for meterology and telecommunications and broadcasting services, this will enable larger capacity to be built into INSAT satellites, both in terms of transponders and their radiated power, without the design constraints imposed by meteorological instruments.

The 1,060 kg KALPANA-1 was designed using a new spacecraft bus employing lightweight structural elements like Carbon Fibre Reinforced Plastic (CFRP). The satellite has a solar array generating 550 Watt of power.

Payloads. KALPANA-1 carries a Very High Resolution Radiometer (VHRR) capable of imaging the earth in the visible, thermal infrared and water vapour bands. It also carries a Data Relay Transponder (DRT) for collecting data from unattended meteorological platforms and relay the data to the Meteorological Data Utilisation Centre at New Delhi. Such platforms have been installed all over the country.

IRS-P5 (CARTOSAT-1). This satellite was launched by PSLV on May 05, 2005. It was envisaged as a mission to meet the stereo data requirements of the user community. The objectives of the mission are :

I. To design, develop, launch and operate an advanced space based mission with enhanced spatial resolution (2.5 m) with a long track stereo viewing capability for large scale mapping applications (up to 1:5000 scale)

II. To further stimulate newer areas of cartographic applications, urban management, disaster assessment, relief planning and management, environmental impact assessment and GIS applications.

Orbital features. The nominal life of IRS-P5 is five years. Its orbital features are:

Orbit	Polar, sun-synchronous
Orbital Altitude	618 km
Semi Major Axis	6996.14 km
Eccentricity	0.001
Inclination	97.87 degress
Local time	10:30 A.M
Revisit	5 days
Repetivity	126 days
Orbits/day	14
Period	97 minutes

Payload. The payload system of IRS-P5 consists of:

I. Two Panchromatic solid state cameras - Fore and Aft, mounted at +26 degrees and -5 degrees with respect to nadir to generate stereoscopic image of the area along the track. Both the cameras work on the 'pushbroom scanning' concept using linear arrays of Charge Coupled Devices (CCDs) as sensors. The spacecraft body is steerable to compensate the earth rotation effect and to force both Fore and Aft cameras to look at the same ground strip, when operated in stereo mode. It is also possible to operate the cameras in wide swath mode by suitably manoeuvering the spacecraft. The spacecraft has roll tilt capability, which can be utillized for faster global coverage. Major specifications of the sensors are :

Parameter	*Specification*
Swath Fore Aft	29.42 km 26.24 km
IGFOV Fore Aft	2.452 m (Across track) 2.187 m (Across track)
Ground sample distance	2.54 (Along track)
Spectral band	0.5 — 0.85 microns
Quantization	10 bits (1024)
Number of detectors	12 K
Pixel size	7 × 7 micron

Integration time	0.336 ms
Focal length	1945 mm
Data rate per Camera	336 Mbps
Data compression Ratio	3.2:1
Type of compression	JPEG like
Data rate transmitted to ground	105 Mbps

II. On-Board Solid State Recorder (OBSSR) for collecting data outside the vicinity of the ground stations. The OBSSR has a capacity of 120 Gb. It can record data of 9 minutes.

Spacecraft Technical Elements: The Spacecraft is configured with the Panchromatic cameras, which are mounted such that one camera is looking at +26 deg. w.r.t. nadir and the other at -5 deg w.r.t. nadir along the track. These two cameras when combined provide stereoscopic image pairs in the same pass. Also the whole spacecraft is steerable across track to provide wider coverage in a shorter period.

It was launched by PSLV-C5 in October 2003 to provide stereoscopic image pairs in the same pass. Also the whole spacecraft is steerable across track to provide wider coverage in a shorter period.

Remote Sensing Payloads: The payload performs the function of imaging an area along the track and transmits the data for ground processing. Each Panchromatic camera consists of three 3 mirror off-axis-all reflective telescope with primary, secondary and tertiary mirrors. These mirrors are made from special zerodur glass blanks and are light weighted to about 60%. These mirrors are polished to an accuracy of 1/80 and are coated with enhanced A1O2 coating. The mirrors are mounted to the Electro-optical module using iso-static mounts, so that the distortion on the light weighted mirrors is very minimum. In order to meet the high resolution and the swath requirement 12K, 7 micron linear array CCD is planned to be used as a detector. The CCD processing electronics will be using high speed devices to meet the high data rate requirements.

Orbit Considerations : A polar sun synchronous orbit of altitude 618 kms with an inclination of 97.87 deg. and an equatorial cross-over local time of 10:30 hours and the descending node has been selected based on various considerations. The sun-synchronous orbit provides the imagery collection under near-constant illumination conditions throughout the life and repetitive coverage of the same area at a specified interval. In order to revisit the same place at a more frequent interval than the repetitive cycle, an off-nadir viewing capability is provided. Using this facility, any area which could not be imaged on a given day due to cloud cover, etc. may be imaged on another day. The typical revisit cycle is 5 days with the off-nadir cross-track steering facility.

Spacecraft main frame systems: The spacecraft bus has to support the payload systems in terms of structure, thermal control, power supply, data compression, data formating, encryption and transmissions, data storage, TTC, etc. The spacecraft is equipped with precision Attitude and Orbit Control system along with attitude sensors and propulsion systems.

A brief description of various main frame systems is given below.

Cartosat-1-Platform Configuration: The spacecraft is a 3-axis body stabilised by using 4 high torque Reaction Wheels mounted in a tetrahedral arrangement. The power generation capacity will be about 1100 watts at the end of life, to meet the global operation of the payloads. The overall spacecraft size is about 24 m × 2.7 m and will weight about 1450 kg.

Attitude and Orbit Control System (AOCS): In order to meet the stringent requirements of the high resolution payloads, it is necessary to have a precision Attitude Control System to provide a stable platform. Also, in order to provide the required swath, overlap and to provide time invariant data and revisit requirements, the orbit control will be carried out periodically. Some of the important specifications of the AOCS are given below :

Attitude Pointing Accuracy (deg.) of all axes : 0.05
Attitude drift (deg/sec) : 5 × 10 – 5
Attitude determination accuracy (deg) : 0.01
Ground location accuracy (m) : < 220

The drift rate determines the image internal distortion figures, whereas, the jitter affects the resolution parameters. The AOCS will meet the stringent attitude pointing accuracy and the stability using a wide area star sensor in Attitude Control loop and better control algorithms and using dynamic friction compensation technique for the ball bearing Reaction Wheels. AOCS will be configured with MIL-STD 31750 processor and with ASIC and HMCs. Various sen sors like, earth sensors, ster stensors, precision yaw sensors and precision digital sun-sensors are used to control and determine the attitude of the spacecraft precisely. Hydrazine mono-propellant Reaction Control System with 4 Nos. of 11 Newton Thrusters and 8 Nos. of 1 Newton Thrusters will be used for backup control and for momentum dumping purposes. About 131 kg of RCS fuel will be planned to provide a minimum mission life of 5 years.

Earth Rotation Compensation : In the case of along track stereo data acquisition, same scene on the surface of earth is imaged with a time difference. The time difference is a function of the difference in forward and backward look angles chosen from other criteria and can be anywhere between 50-100 secs. Major change in imaging condition during this time period is due to rotation of earth. At the equator, the effect of earth rotation is to shift the imaged point to the East by a distance of approximately 463.3 m for every one second. Thus, during 50 seconds the shift is of the order of 23.2 km. At 25 degrees latitude, the shift is 20.09 km. If the separation in time between forward and backward imaging is more than 65 seconds then no overlap between them is present in case of zero yaw angle. In order to ensure stereo imaging it is necessary that the aft camera views the earth's surface in such a way as to image the shifted point. This condition can be achieved by a continuous yaw manoeuvering. For any given latitude, it can also be achieved by mounting the payloads at appropriate yaw angle with respect to each other. A combination of fixed Mounting, caterinty to stereo acquisition requirements for Indian latitudes and a yaw manoeuvered for other regions with minimum power consumption shall be adopted. Alternatively, the spacecraft is manouvered such that the image strips will fall side by side so that wider swath images are obtained by the two cameras.

Data Handling System: The realisation of high precision cameras calls for the development of very high speed precision electronic systems, and requires gain bandwidth of low noise analog system in the range of a few GHz. Due to small IFOV, the signal amplitudes are also expected to be very low. The detectors also require ultra low noise, biases and high frequency read out clocks. The data rate requirement for 2.5 m. resolution system is about 340 MBPS for a typical 10 bit quantisation. This high bit rate of Data is compressed by 3.2:1 by JPEG Compression technique to bring down the data rate to 105 m compatible for X-Band Data transmission system. The payload data is transmitted in two X-band carriers one for each PAN camera, after QPSK modulation to the Data Reception Station (DRS). A spherical Phased Array Antenna with steerable beam to the required DRS is used to transmit the payload data. A solid state recorder with 120 GB capacity to store about 9.5 min. of payload data and payback to the required ground station is also planned for the global operation payloads.

IRS-P5 Products. The various products offered from this mission can be categorized into :

I. Area of Interest (AOI) based products: One or more scenes covering the user's area of interest are provided as tiled products (not mosaiced). The different tiles are not radiometrically normalized. The maximum order area is 25 km × 25 km. The location accuracy of these products will be better than 250m. All AOI based products are provided as digital products (CD/DVD) only. These products can be supplied with different processing levels: Radiometrically corrected and Systematic corrections.

II. Scene based Ortho kit products: The ortho kit products are supplied with systematic corrections. A file consisting of the rational polynomial coefficients is also provided for further processing at user's end.

III. Ortho-rectified products: These are mosaiced and ortho rectified products. These products can be supplied with different area coverages - 7½ × 7½ (both Survey of India (SOI) map sheet based and floating), 5′ × 5′, 3.75′ × 3.75′ and 2.5′ × 2.5′. All of these products are supplied as a single product with seamless radiometry, in case the area is covered on two different dates. The location accuracy of these products will be better than 25m. The features of these products are given below :

Area coverage	*Level of processing*	*Photo print scale*	*Digital data format / media*
Geo-referenced mono scene (27.5 km × 27.5 km)	Standard	—	GeoTIFF/CDROM
Stereo Pairs (27.5 km × 27.5 km)	Radiometrically corrected	—	LGSOWG/CDROM
Map sheet based/Float 7.5′ × 7.5′ (14 km × 14 km)	Ortho	1:25,000	GeoTIFF/CDROM
Map sheet based/Float 5′ × 5′ (9 km × 9 km)	Ortho	1:12,000	GeoTIFF/CDROM
LSM Compatible (3.75′ × 3.75′)	Ortho	1:10,000	GeoTIFF/CDROM
2.25′ × 2.25′ (4 km × 4 km)	Ortho	1:5,000	GeoTIFF/CDROM

IRS-P6 would provide us an unique capability in remote sensing

CARTOSAT-2. It was launched by PSLV-C7 in January, 2007, with latest remote sensing payload. Twelfth in the Indian Remote Sensing (IRS) satellite series, CARTOSAT-2 is an advanced remote sensing satellite capable of providing scene-specific spot imagery. It will join the other six IRS satellites, which are in service -- IRS-IC, IRS-ID, OCEANSAT-1, Technology Experimental Satellite (TES), RESOURCESAT-1 and CARTOSAT-1.

Payload. CARTOSAT-2 carries a Panchromatic camera (PAN) to provide imageries with a spatial resolution of better than one metre and a swath of 9.6 km. The satellite can be steered up to 45

deg along as well as across the track. The data from the satellite will be used for cartographic applications at cadastral level, urban and rural infrastructure development and management, as well as applications in Land Information System (LIS) and Geographical Information System (GIS).

IRS-P6 also called RESOURCESAT-1 is meant for providing continuity of services being offered by IRS-1C and 1D, mainly for agricultural applications. RESOURCESAT, however, has enhanced capabilities like LISS-3 camera providing 23.6 m spatial resolution in all four spectral bands and LISS-4 camera providing better than 6 m resolution operating in three spectral bands of Green, Red and near IR. The third camera (Advanced Field Sensor) has spatial resolution of 70 m in three spectral bands and a swath of about 720 km.

These sensors provide data which is useful for vegetation related applications and will allow multiple crop discrimination and species level discrimination. Together with an advanced Wide Field Sensor (WiFS) with 80 m resolution and 1400 km swath, the payloads greatly aid crop/vegetation and integrated land and water resources related applications.

CARTOSAT-2A. It was launched by PSLV-C9 on April 28, 2008. The 690 kg CARTOSAT-2A is a state-of-the art remote sensing satellite with a spatial resolution of about one metre and swath of 9.6 km.

Some of the featues of CARTOSAT-2A include:

- Hexagonal-shaped, Lightweight and compact spacecraft structure
- CFRP-based large size and light weight two-mirror on-axis telescope
- Use of Bus Management Unit for integrated main spacecraft bus functions
- High bit rate telemetry, telecommand and data handling systems
- 64 GB Solid State Recorder
- Dual Gimballed (DG) Antenna
- Advanced triple junction solar cells
- Improved Inertial Reference Unit
- High performance Star Sensor

Payload. It carries a panchromatic camera (PAN) capable of taking black-and-white pictures in the visible region of electromagnetic spectrum. It is steerable along as well as across the direction of its movement to facilitate imaging of any area more frequently. The satellite will provide high-resolution data, which would be invaluable in urban and rural development applications calling for large scale mapping.

Indian Mini Satellite (IMS-1). 83 kg Indian Mini Satellite (IMS-1) was also launched by PSLV-C9 on April 28,2008. It was an auxiliary payload on board PSLV-C9 and weighing 83 kg at lift-off, and was developed by ISRO for remote sensing applications.

Payload. The IMS-1 carries two remote sensing payloads, which include a multi-spectral camera (Mx Payload) and a hyper-spectral camera (HySI Payload), operating in the visible and near infrared regions of the electromagnetic spectrum. The data from this mission will be made available to interested space agencies and student community from developing countries to provide necessary impetus to capacity building in using satellite data. This satellite has been specifically developed to carry different payloads in future without significant changes in it and has a design life time of two years.

IRS-1E	—	—	remote sensing payloads	—	Launch failure in September 1993
IRS-P2			remote sensing payload		second developmental flight of PSLV in October 1994
IRS-1D		In service	Advanced remote sensing cameras		PSLV-C1 on September 1997
Technology Experimental Satellite (TES)	3-axis	—	Very High Resolution Radiometer (VHRR) capable of imaging the earth in the visible, thermal infrared and water vapour bands. It also carries a Data Relay Transponder (DRT) for collecting data from unattended meteorological platforms and relay the data to the Meteorological Data Utilisation Centre at New Delhi.	Geosynchr-onous Transfer Orbit (GTO)	PSLV-C4 in September 12, 2002.

CARTO SAT-1			Two Panchromatic solid state cameras - Fore and Aft to generate stereoscopic image of the area along the track. The spacecraft has roll tilt capability, which can be utilized for faster global coverage; On-Board Solid State Recorder (OBSSR) for collecting data outside the vicinity of the ground stations. The OBSSR has a capacity of 120 Gb. It can record data of 9 minutes.		By PSLV on May 05, 2005.
CARTO SAT-2			Panchromatic camera (PAN) to provide imageries with a spatial resolution of better than one metre and a swath of 9.6 km.		PSLV-C7 in January 2007
CARTO SAT-2A			panchromatic camera (PAN) capable of taking black-and-white pictures in the visible region of electromagnetic spectrum.		PSLV-C9 on April 28, 2008.
Indian Mini Satellite (IMS-1)		2 years	two remote sensing payloads which include a multi-spectral camera (Mx Payload) and a hyper-spectral camera (HySI Payload), operating in the visible and near infrared regions of the electromagnetic spectrum.		PSLV-C9 on April 28, 2008.

The IRS-2 series (OCEANSAT-2/CLIMATSAT-1/ATMOS-1) is an integrated mission that caters to global observations of climate, ocean and atmosphere. Microwave instruments to cater for oceanographic applications are a Ku band Altimeter, Ku band Scattermeter, Microwave Radiometer and Thermal Infrared Radiometer for observing oceanorgraphic parameters like winds, sea surface temperature, waves, bathometry and internal waves. Instruments for atmospheric chemistry applications include spectrometers, sounders and radiometers for studying the atmospheric constituents, for monitoring pollution and ozone and green-house effect. Instruments to observe climate and meterological parameters include microwave sounders, radiometers and rain radars.

IRS-3 all weather capabilities with multi-frequency and multi polarisation microwave payloads and other passive instruments.

HAMSAT. HAMSAT is a micro-satellite designed to provide satellite based Radio Amateur Services to Indian as well as International HAM (Amateur Radio Operators) community.

HAMSAT weighing about 40 kg was launched by PSLV-C6 on May 5, 2005.

Payload: Linear Mode B (UHF/VHF) transponders—one transponder to be built by Indian amateurs and the other is to be provided by AMSAT -Italy/The Netherlands.

IMS-1. Indian Mini Satellite-1 (IMS-1) is a mini satellite developed by ISRO for remote sensing. Weighing 83 kg at lift-off, IMS-1 incorporates many new technologies and has miniaturised subsystems. IMS-1 carries two optical payloads - a Multispectral camera (Mx Payload) and a Hyperspectal camera (HySI Payload). Both Mx and HySI payloads operate in the visible and near infrared region of the electromagnetic spectrum. The resolution (the smallest ground feature that can be distinguished clearly) of Mx camera is 37 metre while that of HySI is about 506 metre. The imagery from Mx camera are provided to the developing countries while those from HySI are meant for usage in India. The versatile IMS-1 has been

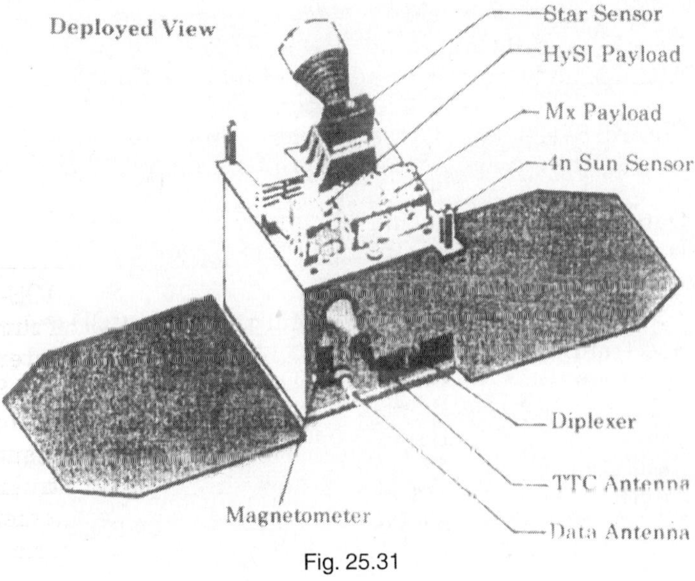

Fig. 25.31

specifically developed to carry different payloads in future without significant changes in it and has a design life time of two years. IMS-1 is flown as an auxiliary payload on board PSLV-C9 along with the main payload, CARTOSAT-2A.

The new technologies incorporated in IMS-1 are:

- Miniature magnetometers with MEMS based mag in one channel
- Minimature 4π Sun Sensors
- Minimature Micro Reaction Wheels and Gyro Cluster
- Minimature digital S-Band receiver and transmitter
- Miniature Satellite positioning system
- Miniature four band Multispectral Camera
- Innovative (mission specific) thermal subsystem
- Innovative integration and ground checkout procedures

IMS-1 at a glance

Mission

Orbit : Polar sun synchronous
Altitude : 635 km
Mission Life : 2 years
Physical dimensions : 0.604 × 0.980 × 1.29 m
Mass : 83 kg
Power : Two deployable sun pointing solar panels generating 220 W power, 10.5 Ah Lithium Ion battery

Telemetry,: S-band

Tracking and Command

Attitude and Orbit : Star Sensor, Miniature Sun Sensors, Magnetometers,
Control System Gyros, Miniature Micro Reaction Wheels, Magnetic Torquers, single 1 N Hydrazine Thruster
Data Handling : S-band
Data Storage : 16 Gb Solid State Recorder

Mx Payload

Type : Four Band Multispectural CCD camera
Spectral Bands : B1 (0.45 0.52 μ m)
B2 (0.52 0.59 μ m)
B3 (0.62 0.68 μ m)
B4 (0.77 0.86 μ m)
Resolution : 37 m
Swath : 151 km
Mass : 5.9 kg

HySI Payload

Type	: Hyper Spectral Camera
Spectral range	: 0.4 – 0.95 μm
No of bands	: 64 fixed
Spectral separation	: 8 Nanometre
Spatial resolution	: 505.6 m
Swath	: 129.5 km
Mass	: 3.4 kg

PAYLOADS FROM ABROAD

Eight nanosatellites from abroad are carried onboard PSLV-C9 as auxiliary payloads besides IMS-1 as well as CARTOSAT-2A, the main payload. The total weight of these nanosatellite payloads is about 50 kg.

Six of the eight nanosatellites are clustered together and have the collective name NLS-4. The other two nanosatellites are NLS-5 and RUBIN-8. NLS-4, developed by University of Toronto, Canada consists of six nanosatellites developed by various universities. Two of them CUTE 1.7 and SEEDS are built in Japan, while the other four CAN-X2, AAUSAT-II, COMPASS-1 and DELFI-C3 are built in Canada, Denmark, Germany and the Netherlands respectively. NLS-5 is also built by University of Toronto. RUBIN-8 is built by COSMOS International, Germany. These nanosatellites are primarily for scientific research purposes and for demonstration of miniaturized technologies.

The launch of these eight nanosatellite payloads was executed under a commercial contract between University of Toronto, COSMOS International and Antrix Corporation-the commerical arm of the Department of Space.

Name	*Weight (kg)*	*University / Country*	*Mission Objectives*
NLS-4 (cluster of six nanosatellites) consists of:		Spaceflight Laboratory, Univ of Toronto, Canada	
CAN-X2	7.0	Spaceflight Laboratory, University of Toronto, Canada	Flight-testing of nano cold gas propulsion system, innovative attitude sensors and commercial GPS receiver
CUTE-1.7	5.0	Tokyo Institute of Technology, Japan	Demonstration of Personal digital assistant based bus system and Avarenche Photo-diode

DELFI-C3	6.5	Technical University, Delfi, The Netherlands	Flight-testing of thin film solar cells, wireless sun sensor and advanced transceiver
AAUSAT-II	3.0	Aalborg University, Denmark	Gamma ray burst detecting, Flight testing of nano actuators and sensors for spacecraft 3 axis stabilaisation
COMPASS-I	3.0	University of Applied Science Aachen, Germany	Flight testing of miniaturized spacecraft bus
SEEDS	3.0	Nihon University, Japan	Demonstration of receiving spacecraft parameter data by SW signal, FM packet downlink and sound data by digi talker
NLS-5	16.0	Spaceflight Laboratory, University of Toronto, Canada	Perform survey of the maritime VHF band at 162 MHz. Payload is a VHF receiver.
RUBIN-8	8.0	COSMOS International, Germany	Testing of new space based receiver and data upload system for Automatic Maritime Identification System (AIS)

In its twelve consecutively successful flights so far, PSLV has repeatedly proved itself as a reliable and versatile workhorse launch vehicle. It has demonstrated multiple satellite launch capability having launched a total of sixteen satellites for international customers besides thirteen Indian payloads, which are for remote sensing, amateur radio communications and Space capsule Recovery Experiment (SRE-1). PSLV was used to launch ISRO's exclusive meteorological satellite, KALPANA-1, into a Geosynchronous Transfer Orbit (GTO) in September, 2002 and thus proved its versatility.

25.15 Technological Improvements in INSAT

25.15.1. Transponders

Transponder growth: The INSAT system (till 2007) consisting of 11 operational satellites has about 250 transponders in various bands (C, S, Extended C and Ku) catering to a demand of up to 11 Giga bits per second (GBPS) capacity. They serve the television and communication needs of the country. The satellites also incorporate transponder(s) for receiving distress alert signals for search and rescue missions in the South Asian and Indian Ocean Region, as ISRO is a member of the *Cospas-Sarsat* programme.

User-wise, All India Radio (AIR) accounts for 3.7 per cent of the total transponder capacity, Doordarshan 26.1 per cent, DoT 43.3 per cent, government including ISRO and TDCC 10.7 per cent, Indian private VSAT users 7.2 per cent, INTELSAT 3.5 per cent and spares 3.7 per cent.

Transponder capacity : The INSAT/GSAT capacity available in various bands has increased with launch of INSAT-4B. Higher order modulation techniques like 8-PSK, 16-QAM and higher compression techniques for transmission are now being used to maximize the satellite throughput.

Satellite grid computing protocol development DM SAR data handling, meteorology GAGAN and IRNSS Real time iono/tropo modelling, time sync/time transfer, atomic Aircraft landing and other accurate satellite-based clock, integrated receiver, encryption, navigation software, etc. navigation, standard time and frequency applications.

GSAT-4 Onboard processing, Ka-band propagation modelling, fade USAT mitigation techniques.

GSAT-6 Audio/video compression, handheld satellite terminals Satellite-based mobile multimedia services.

Disaster management Distress alert terminal Low cost alternative to PLB meant for fishermen.

Lift-off capacity: Th capacity of the INSAT satellites in terms of the lift-off mass is increasing. It increased from 1,905 kg in INSAT-2A to 2,958 kg in INSAT-3A. Fall in the percentage mass of structure vis-à-vis total spacecraft weight is a broad indicator of the technology growth and maturity. This figure was 15 for APPLE, 9.13 for INSAT-2A and it has fallen to 7.17 in INSAT-3A. The power at end of life (EoL) has increased from 1,160 W in INSAT-2A and 2B to 3,100 W in INSAT-3A.

EIRP. The minimum effective isotropic radiated power (eirp) which was 32 db W in C-band transponders of INSAT-2A and 2B increased to 36 db W in INSAT-2E and now to 51.5 db W in INST-4CR.

25.15.2. Technology of Payloads

The new breakthroughs in this field are :

Multiplexers : The multiplexers are now realized with dielectric loading, thereby improving the weight and real estate. INVAR (also called FeNi, is an alloy of iron (64%) and nickel (36%) with some carbon and chromium) based multiplexer have been realized to improve on thermal performance. Earlier, separate multiplexers were used for transmit and receive chains, that forced the designers to use separate transmit and receive antenna. Realization of contiguous multiplexer has helped payloads working with single antenna for both transmit and receive. Realization of SAW filters has improved the weight performance.

Amplifiers: High efficiency driver amplifiers, SSPA and linearized Travelling Wave Tube Amplifiers have been introduced. TWTAs have been realized that have helped in increasing the indigenous content in payload. Multi-collector TWTAs are used to improve upon the efficiency of power amplifiers. Indigenous high efficiency electronic power conditioners (EPC) for high power amplifiers were realized in all the bands.

Shaped and deployable reflectors : From the early days of single shell unshaped and fixed reflector, where simple eliptical coverage was used for India, the technology has been improved to shaped and deployable reflectors, where coverage was effectively controlled to required area within and outside India.

Dual-gridded reflectors: These were developed to improve the cross polarization performance so that satellites with different polarization could be co-located to enhance the capacity. More recently technology of multiple shaped beam coverage with good inter-beam cross-polarization has been realized to enhance the frequency reuse and hence, the system capacity.

Electronic power conditioner (EPC) which is an essential part of these subsystems to provide different current and voltage required by each subsystem, has been made efficient in terms of weight, size, power and performance.

MIC and MMIC receivers and converters: These have been realized for different communications bands. The earlier realized payload and noise figure of 3 dB has improved to 1.5 dB in later system.

25.15.3. Technology for Ground Systems

Major technological advances in this field are :

(*i*) The arrival of digital technology and availability of low cost,high-density memory and increase in processing power has resulted in development of smaller ground subsystems, with more user-friendly features like low power, increased capacity, etc.

(*ii*) Digital modulation techniques and error correction were introduced, which in turn reduced the transmit power requirement, both from satellite and ground.

(*iii*) Audio and video compression techniques reduced the bandwidth requirement per channel and helped in enhancing the capacity.

(*iv*) Use of GPS time and frequency in communications systems improved the local oscillator (LO) stability and enhanced access protocols like open loop Time Division Multiple Access (TDMA).

(*v*) Complex network protocol could be realized using relatively cheaper network managers.

(*vi*) In the radio frequency (RF) area, higher wattage and improved efficiency in solid state power amplifer (SSPA) became commercially available.

(*vii*) Use of advanced error coding and channel access techniques in almost all the old applications like Data Collection System (DCS) to Automatic Weather Station (AWS) leading to increase in the number of transmitters per carrier from 300 to 1800; and converting Disaster Warning System (DWS) to Digital Cyclone Warning and Disaster System (DCWDS).

25.16 Current Utilisation of INSAT System

Today, INSAT has become the largest domestic communication satellite system in the Asia-Pacific region with 11 satellites in service (including GSAT-2 and EDUSAT). Table 25.19 gives the mission status of INSAT satellites launched so far.

Table 25.19 Mission status of INSAT satellites

Sl.No.	*Satellite*	*Launch Date*	*Mission Status*
1	INSAT-1A	*10 April 1982*	Deactivated on *6 September 1982*
2	INSAT-1B	*30 August 1983*	Completed mission life
3	INSAT-1C	*22 July 1988*	Abandoned in November 1989
4	INSAT-1D	*12 June 1990*	Completed mission life
5	INSAT-2A	*10 July 1992*	India's First Indegenious communication Satellite. Completed mission life
6	INSAT-2B	*23 July 1993*	Completed mission life
7	INSAT-2C	*7 December 1997*	Completed mission life
8	INSAT-2D	*4 June 1997*	Became inoperable on *4 October 1997*
9	INSAT-2DT	In-orbit procurement	Completed mission life
10	INSAT-2E	*3 April 1999*	In service
11	INSAT-3A	*10 April 2003*	In service
12	INSAT-3B	*22 May 2000*	In service

13	INSAT-3C	*24 January 2002*	In service
14	*KALPANA-1*	*12 September 2002*	In service
15	*GSAT-2*	*8 May 2003*	In service
16	INSAT-3E	*28 September 2003*	In service
17	*EDUSAT*	*20 September 2004*	In service
18	INSAT-4A	*22 December 2005*	In service
19	*INSAT-4C*	*10 July 2006*	Not placed in orbit due to launch failure of GSLV-F02
20	INSAT-4B	*12 March 2007*	In service
21	INSAT-4CR	*2 September 2007*	in geo-synchronous orbit[1]

User-wise utilization of INSAT facility is described below.

Doordarshan

1. Doordarshan makes uses of the INSAT system to transmit the signals to its 1406 terrestrial transmitters respectively for local re-broadcast, providing access to 95% of India's population through national as well as regional services.
2. Use of transportable earth stations and satellite news gathering vehicles, now allow extensive real time coverage of important events anywhere in the country.
3. Doordarshan is providing about 60 channels for national, regional, **DSNG** and VSAT services through 11C band transponders in the INSAT system and 2C band transponders in PAS10 satellite.
4. In Ku-band, Direct to Home (DTH) service, 50 TV and 20 radio channels are being transmitted through INSAT, NSS-6 and PAS10 satellites. This service covers almost 100% landmass, except down range islands. More than 8 million households in India are now receiving the DTH satellite TV and radio transmissions from national and private broadcasters.

All India Radio (AIR)

1. AIR is operating 40 RN channels in S-band, 53 RN channels in C-band and 12 of DSNG using INSAT's and C-band transponders.
2. It uses satellite medium to transmit signals to its 213 terrestrial transmitters respectively for local re-broadcast.

The main benefits of satellite technology for AIR are improvements in the technical reception quality of programme relays from Delhi and state capitals, communication links to rural and remote areas, sky radio facility for people in other states via cable operator dish antenna, Satellite News Gathering (SNG) facility, and digital audio broadcast facility.

Telecommunications

1. In the INSAT system, currently 15 main, 68 primary and 6 remote earth stations totaling to 89 earth stations are operating in the BSNL network providing 3840 IDR channels, 1582 MCPC channels and 27 SCPC channels.
2. The number of two-way speech circuits is over 10,070, which cover about 492 routes and linking 704 earth stations of various sizes, the vast reach of the unique multipurpose INSAT and GSAT satellites has been advantageously used for providing nationwide radio networking, administrative, business and
3. Computer communication, VSAT networking and emergency communication services.
4. Portable terminals are used by BSNL mainly for disaster management and short duration functions in outlying areas. In Orissa cyclone and Bhuj earthquake, the portable terminals restored communication as soon as a helicopter could land in the disaster area. Maritime mobile terminals provide connectivity for coastal shipping and fishing vessels.

VSATs for closed user groups. More than 60,000 VSATs are operating with 90 hubs in the government and private sectors including those installed by the National informatics Centre (NIC-NET) are operating today to cater to the fast growing requirements of both public and private closed user groups. Satellite-based VSATs have advantages like wide geographical coverage, timely deployment and insatllation, economies of scale, reliability, multi-content distribution and capacity expansion at low incremental costs.

Internet: Internet generates many network externalities. Satellite based Internet is feasible with Ku-band. Community Information Centres in the North-Eastern Region based on VSATs is being planned. Internet-based community kiosks can improve efficiency of rural markets, raise productivity by creating access to opprtunities in input, credit, product and export markets and help integrating rural areas with the rest of the country.

Development TV. The National Television System (Doordarshan) is using the INSAT series of satellites. Doordarshan, at the national and regional level, produces and transmits many programmes meant for school and university students, women, children and youth.

Training and Development Communication Channels (TDCC). This programme of ISRO is being operated to feed over 6000 distant education/training classrooms spread across India to meet the training requirements of the field staff/functionaries of various departments like agriculture, health, women and child welfare, forest department etc. of the state governments. Besides, TDCC could also be utilized for imparting training under Panchayati Raj (self governance at village level) and more than 10 lakh participants/functionaries of more than 60 departments of various state governments have been trained in these centres.

A number of experiments have been conducted for imparting developmental education to target audiences of different types, both in the rural and urban areas.

Jhabua Development Communication Programme (JDCP): This experiment undertaken in Madhya Pradesh was implemented with more than 1500 receive terminals for imparting developmental education in the predominantly tribal areas. As a result, ISRO has helped several state governments like Karnataka, Gujarat, Madhya Pradesh and Orissa in setting up large networks.

Educational communication

In view of the increased rate of enrolment, inadequate infrastructure and lack of qualified and trained teachers in the primary and secondary education sector in the rural and far-flung areas across the country, the need for educational communication is as acute as that of developmental communication. The following institutions are involved in preparing and disseminating programmes in formal education sector:

1. Central Institute of Educational Technology (CIET) and several State Institutes of Educational Technology (SIETs) were set up for production of school-oriented TV programmes.
2. University Grants Commission (UGC) has set up a number of production centres in several universities, and started a one-hour transmission under the 'country-wide classroom'. The activity has grown substantially, since then and is now running as an independent channel called the Vyas Channel.
3. Indria Gandhi National Open University (IGNOU) has gradually built up the broadcasting activity to start an independent channel called Gyan Darshan. IGNOU in association with Indian Institute of Technology started transmitting programmes for engineering students and built this into an Eklavya Channel for a few hours, every day.

Edusat.

Edusat provides six Ext C-band national beam-one Ku band national beam and five Ku-band regional beams, facilating transmission of education in the regional languages. Depending on the requirement and location, the VSAT-networks operate in Ku or Ext C-band.

Under the Edusat utilization programme, two types of satellite-based programmes are provided : (*i*) Edusat-VSAT networks; and interactive networks consisting of Satellite Interactive Terminal (SITs) and receive-only networks Receive-Only-Terminals (ROTs). They are being used for imparting teacher's training and curriculum-based teaching to students of the arts and science colleges, polytechnics, and management and professional institutes. Similarly, the receive-only networks are being used for imparting curriculum-based education to primary and seconday schools students. At least one network connecting minimum 50 interactive terminals is being set up in most of the states. ISRO is providing one hub and 10 interactive terminals free of cost to every state under this phase.

More than 2500 interactive terminals have so far been set up as part of these networks. At present, under the Edusat implementation programme, two networks each in the North Eastern states, MP, Orissa and one each in Chhattisgarh, Maharashtra, Delhi and Andaman and Nicobar Islands are being set up and they will be established by October 2007.

Major achievements of the Edusat programme are:

1. Six primary schools-networks in the states of Kerala, Karnataka, Gujarat, AP, MP and Haryana have been set up and a total of around 27,000 ROTs are operating in various networks and this number is growing steadily.
2. Haryana school-network is currently under expansion and while more than 10,000 ROTs have already been setup, another 1000 terminals are proposed by the end of 2007.
3. About 40 interactive networks consisting of nine national networks and other regional networks in Tamil Nadu, Karnataka, Kerala, Haryana, West Bengal, Rajasthan, Punjab, J&K, Lakshadweep, Gujarat, Jharkhand, Tripura, Nagaland, Maharashtra and MP have been established.
4. One special network in Ext C band connecting about 50 engineering institutes across the country has been established to impart teaching by distinguished professors/faculty from top 21 universities in USA, who would visit India to conduct 8-week courses in various subjects in engineering.
5. One special network for blind schools has been set up in the state of Gujarat.

Gyan Darshan-2: The UGC-ISRO carried out, as a pilot project, one-way video, two-way audio for education with a ten-day special broadcast on the national network. Now, this programme is being operated by IGNOU.

Telemedicine Programme. The aim of this programme is to use Satcom and information technology to connect rural clinics to urban hospitals. The programme, which was started as a pilot exercise in five locations, has rapidly expanded to cover about 200 remote hospitals and 40 speciality hospitals. This has been able to provide connectivity to the remotest locations in the country like the Andaman and Nicobar Islands, the Lakshwadeep Islands, the North-eastern regions, and Jammu and Kashmir. Each super-speciality hospital is providing health care services to 5-6 remote hospitals.

Telemedicine network configuration: The telemedicine networks, set up by ISRO, consist of patient-end nodes, doctor-end nodes, servers and VSAT-based communication system. The software running in these systems interface the medical diagnostic instruments for acquiring medical images, for establising connectivity between patient-end and doctor-end computers for data exchange and facilitating the video-conferencing to enable the doctor and patient to interact in real time. Its functioning is as follows:

1. The patient diagnostic information is acquired and sent to doctor-end, along with his/her demographic data. At the doctor-end, a specialist views them and suggests the treatment. The doctor and the patient can interact in real time, through videoconferencing. A server is also located at the super-speciality hospital, which stores all the information of a patient. When a specialist is giving tele-consulation, the patient information is accessed from the server.

2. A patient-end terminal consists of a computer, videoconferencing camera, TV monitor, printer, one 1 kVA UPS, A3 size X-ray digitizer, 12 lead ECG. This terminal is connected to the VSAT terminal. The terminal at doctor-end also consists of a computer, videoconferencing camera, TV monitor and a 1 kVA UPS.

The telemedicine networks set up initially by ISRO used 3.8 m antenna and 2 W/5 W up link power in extended C-band working on SCPC-DAMA technology using INSAT 3A. The new telemedicine networks, however, are given connectivity through Edusat satellite in Ext C-band with the antenna size reduced to 1.8 m/2 W.

Mobile telemedicine vans have been deployed by ISRO for taking the telemedicine programme to the remote villages, where the permanent patient-end is not set up. These vans consist of one Ext C-band 1.8 m. motorized antenna, which is mounted onto the top of the van. The antenna can be folded/stowed to most stable position, while on the move and can be repositioned to look at the satellite after the van is stationed at the place, where the patient-end is to be set up. Stowing and deployment (folding and unfolding) of the antenna is motorised but can also be manualy operated. Two types of configuration are possible for antenna positioning :

(*i*) fully automated configuration takes care of the antenna positioning on its own, once put in autoposition mode, by calculating the look angles of the satellite using GPS-based controller and flux gate compass; and

(*ii*) manual configuration needs an operator for moving the antenna to the required look angles using the antenna-control-unit and associated servo electronics. The angle encoder, inclinometer, magnetic compass, etc. required for positioning of the antenna are the integral part of the system.

Village Resource Centers (VRC) Programme. This programme of ISRO provides space-based services directly related to the needs of rural development: weather information, land and water resources management, mitigation of impact of natural disasters, information on natural resources for planning and development at local level; interactive advisories on agriculture, fisheries, livestock management, interactive vocational training; e-governance; and tele-education; telemedicine. It is run in association with NGOs and trusts and state and central agencies.

Under this programme, more than 500 VRCs have been set up across the country. These are connected, through satellite-based VSAT networks, to the blocks, district headquarters and state capitals. Remote sensing data/imageries received from IRS satellites are used to provide useful inputs about other resources required for the development of the villages and its population.

Weather Forecast And Disaster Management. About 250 disaster warning receivers have been installed for this purpose along the cyclone-prone east and west coast of India. The cloud imageries collected by the satellites and over a hundred meteorological data-collection platforms installed all over the country that relay local weather parameters via the INSAT, have contributed greatly to improved meteorological services. Several thousand lives have been saved by INSAT disaster warning system through timely evacuation.

The INSAT system has become the primary backbone of round-the-clock, regular, half-hourly meterological imaging and continuous weather forecasting. The primary data from VHRR received by the Indian Meterological Department (IMD) at Delhi, is processed along with the data from automated unattended data collection platforms located in inaccessible areas to derive products like cloud motion vectors, sea surface temperature, precipitation estimation, etc.

The processed data along with cloud pictures are transmitted to about 40 Secondary Data Utilization Centres (SDUC) located in various parts of the country for further dissemination. The IMD is providing VHRR imagery through Kalpana-1 satellite on a regular basis. About 22 pictures are taken in a day.

Meteorological Data Distribution (MDD) service is uplinked from the Sikanderabad earth station on round-the-clock basis. The Data Relay Transponder (DRT) is being used by the India Meteorological Department, Central Water Commission, Narmada Control Authority, Snow and Avalanche Study Establishment and Andhra Pradesh Government for almost two decades now. Over 300 Area Cyclone Warning Centres (AWS) are using the Kalpana DRT for data collection from remote/unattended platforms.

During cyclones and other emergency situations, INSAT-VHRR is capable of imaging every 5 min in the sector scan mode.

Disaster management and search and rescue. ISRO has been a part of international satellite-based search and rescue system COSPAS-SARSAT, since the early 1990s. This system uses six LEO and four GEO satellites, of which, one GEO satellite is provided by India. ISRO, therefore, has a special status, among 40 member countries, as a geostationary space segment provider in this system.

Begining with the INSAT-2 series, a search and rescue payload was also added, which complements the efforts of COSPAS-SARSAT system and provide real time detection of 406 MHz distress alerts, within the Indian Ocean Region. At present INSAT-3A located at 93.5° E is providing the services with search and rescue payload on board. The payload picks up and relays alert signals originating from distress beacons of maritime, aviation and land users.

The 406 MHz automatic-activating position location beacons are mounted on commercial fishing vessels and all passenger ships, and are designed to transmit, to a rescue coordination centre, a vessel identification and an acurate location of the vessel from anywhere in the world. Currently, more than 3460 numbers of 406 MHz beacons are registered with Indian Mission Control Centre (INMCC) at Bangalore.

Newest designs incorporates GPS receivers to transmit highly accurate positions of distress in the form of precise GPS latitude—longitude location.

Two Local User Terminals (LUT), located at Bangalore and Lucknow are connected to the international search and rescue network and support 121.5, 243 and 406 MHz beacons. These LUTs are a part of the international maritime organization's Global Maritime Distress and Safety System (GDMSS) as also the International Civil Aviation Organisation (ICAO). DG (Shipping), Government of India has issued regulation for all Indian registered ships to carry 406 MHz.

A total of 224 numbers of 406 MHz alerts were received at INMCC during the year 2006 with a system availability of 99.5%. While 82% of these were undetermined, 16% were detected as non-distress and 2% as real calls. A total of 1611 lives have been saved in 53 incidents during 1991-2006 by Indian search and rescue system.

The IMD also uses satellite medium to transmit cyclone warnings in the local language of the coastal area that may get affected due to impending cyclone. These cyclone warning dissemination signals are transmitted from the Area Cyclone Warning Centres of IMD at Chennai, Mumbai and Kolkata earth stations.

Case Study : A detailed study of tropical cyclones and cylones management was attempted with focus on cyclones affecting Andhra Pradesh from 1971 to 1998. A comparative analysis of 2 super cyclones, which hit Andhra Pradesh in 1997 (before INSAT) and 1990 (after INSAT) is done. These 2 cyclones are similar in many respects. The number of districts affected was 8 in 1977 and 14 in 1990. In view of the successful tracking of the cyclone in 1990 and the success of the preparatory steps taken by the government, the loss of lives in 1990 was only 817 compared with 10,000 in 1997. The estimated damage to property in 1990 can be attributed to increase in population, increase in economic activity and inflation. It is also difficult to reduce the property losses in a few days.

Management of Natural Resources. The IRS-IC and IRS-ID are considered the best civilian remote sensing satellites in the world. IRS-P4 and IRS-P5 are also being used for cartographic applications, IRS-P6 for resources survey and OCEANSAT-1 for monitoring ocean resources and for understanding the atmosphere over the oceans.

Agriculture. The IRS data is being used for estimation of :

1. Average and yield of important crops, like wheat, rice, sorghum, oil seeds and sugarcane, forest survey,
2. Forecasting drought conditions,
3. Flood mapping and demarcation of flood risk zones,

4. Land use and land cover mapping for agro-climatic planning,
5. Waste land mapping and their classification for possible reclamation.

Advanced forecast of agricultural production helps the concerned government agencies, traders and farmers in planning decisions on exports and imports inventory, management, procurrent and other decisions. There are anecdotal evidences giving the impact of forecasts on raising farmers incomes or saving costs.

Crop Area and Production Estimation (CAPE) : This project is aimed at providing pre-harvest estimates of acreage and production at an accuracy of 90 percent with 90 per cent confidence for 6 major crops. The forecasts were gradually found reliable at the state level but not at the district level. The difficulties encountered were (*i*) inability of the visible and near infrared sensors to penetrate the persistent cloud cover during the kharif season, and (*ii*) identification of mixed, minor crops and varietal differences.

Forecasting Agricultural Output under Space, Agrometeorology and Land based Observation (FASAL) : This new project, initiated by the Ministry of Agriculture and ISRO addresses issues related to improvement of forecasts, provision of one more assessment during a crop season and provision for alternate forecast methodology, if the cloud cover hinders data collection.

Water sector. The IRS data is being used for preparation of hydro-geomorphological maps for locating sites for borewells, monitoring and development of irrigation command areas, snow-cover and snowmelt run-off estimation of the Himalayan rivers for optimal use of water.

In Rajiv Gandhi National Drinking Water Technology Mission, remote sensing technology has been useful in preparing geo-morphological maps on 1:250,000 scales showing areas suitable for targeting with the aid of ground geophysical methods, points for locating drinking water wells. Ground water prospect maps based on remote sensing technology enhanced the success rates of finding wells/borewells with water from 50 per cent to 80 per cent or more.

Biodiversity. The ISRO project on biodiversity mapping at landscape level using remote sensing is geared to quantify species richness, biodiversity valuation and phyto-sociological analysis and use these to characterize biodiversity in conjunction with other ecological paratmeters. This information base is useful for bio-prospecting for rare medical plants used in life-saving drugs and also for protecting environmental hotspots. Other programmes, which are leading to large social and environmental benefits are coastal zone mapping, environmental impact assessment, forecast of snow-melt run-off and disaster management.

Aviation : The aviation sector is also an important beneficiary of aviation meteorological services. Information about forecast of winds or temperature are useful for the flight planning. Analysis of information furnished by Jet Airways shows that the costs due to delayed departures, diversion and cancellation, all affected by weather, would be about Rs. 21.65 crores for one year.

25.17 ECONOMICS OF SPACE EXPENDITURE

The Indian space programme is one of the most successful and cost-effective endeavours, especially in terms of the wide range of benefits that have accrued to the nation and the society.

Space segment cost : The space segment cost at current prices (the capital cost attributable to the use of 686 transponder years) is estimated at Rs. 1,864 crores at current prices.

Transponder cost : The average unweighted cost of a transponder works out to Rs 2.72 crores. If the cost ratios for C-band/ext. C-band, Ku-band and S-band transponders is assumed as 1:2:2.5, the cost estimates are Rs. 2.35 crores per C-band/ext. C-band transponder, Rs. 4.70 crores for Ku-band transponder and Rs. 5.97 crores for S-band transponder.

Lease transponder charges : These are estimated to be US$ 0.876 million for low power transponders and US$ 0.985 million for high power transponders.

AIR : The cost of AIR transponders is estimated to be Rs. 5.87 crores per transponder. The overall space segment cost for AIR is estimated at Rs. 152.62 crores but AIR does not pay for the transponders. The ground segment investment expenditure attributable to use of the satellite technology is estimated at Rs 253.5 crores.

TV : The cost of ISRO for the transponder years at current prices is approximately Rs. 505 crores. Doordarshan does not pay for the transponders. In the early 2000s. The ground segment capital cost incurred by Doordarshan for use of the satellite technology is estimated around Rs. 1,500 crores. The Department of Space receives abour Rs. 45 crores per year from the lease of 8 transponders to private TV operators in India.

VSATS : The estimated space segment capital costs attributale to government and private VSATs, at current prices, are Rs. 244.55 crores and Rs. 138.58 crores respectively. The ground segment investment expenditures are :

1. Rs. 295 crores for government networks.
2. Rs. 90 crores for social networks.
3. Rs. 879 crores for commercial networks (corporate networks).
4. Rs. 43 crores for BSE and NSE.
5. Rs. 304 crores and Rs. 532 crores for VSAT providers.

The Department of Space receives about Rs. 50 crores per annum from private VSAT operators.

INTELSAT : The Department of Space is getting about Rs. 50 crores per year from the lease of eleven 36 MHz equivalent of transponders in INSAT-2E to INTELSAT.

Telecommunication: Revenue generation is approximately Rs. 75.6 crores per year.

Remote sensing : The National Remote Sensing Agency (NRSA), an autonomous organisation of DOS is the nodal agency for reception, archival, processing and dissemination of remote sensing data in India. It acquires data from Indian and foreign satellites (LANDSAT and NOAA of USA, SPOT of France and ERS). The total revenue earned by NRSA until 2002 was Rs. 160 crores.

Value addition of data products : Satellite data is to be presented in the form of thematic maps, tables, charts and reports suitable for application. The value of data products after the value addition is estimated at Rs. 560 crores. As the cost of preparing the product by conventional methods is about Rs. 1,680 crores, the cost savings resulting from the application of the satellite technology would be Rs. 1,120 crores.

Water sector : The cost savings due to avoidance of digging unsuccessful wells, by resorting to the use of ground water maps for the country, based on satellite imaging of underground water would be in the range Rs. 500 crores to Rs. 800 crores.

Urban planning : The satellite imaging-based urban planning as carried out for preparation of a perspective plan of Indore Metropolitan Region reveals savings in cost and time compared with the conventional methods. If such plans are perpared for all urban areas, the cost savings in comparison with conventional methods would be around Rs. 1,600 crores.

Wasteland development : The National Wasteland Inventory Project provides information on wastelends under 13 categories. By extrapolating the remote sensing data to the entire area of 2 million hectares under saline/alkaline soils in the country, an estimate of the gross income at Rs. 2,464 crores per annum can be generated. The net value added may be about one-fourth of the gross income.

Cost savings opportunities also do exist in preparation and use of Forest Working Plans and Potential Fishing Zone Advisories by trawler/boat owners.

ANTRIX Corporation. This company was set up by the Department of Space in 1992, for marketing harware and space services. Important commercial agreements include:

1. worldwide marketing of remote sensing data from Indian satellites,
2. lease of satellite capacity, launch of small satellites on board PSLV,
3. supply of satellite hardware,
4. tracking support for satellites using Indian ground stations and
5. training of personnel.

ANTRIX has an agreement with Space Imaging of USA for marketing IRS data outside the footprint of India's Ground Station at Hyderabad. The revenue earned by ANTRIX till 2002 was about Rs. 60 crores.

25.18 INDIA'S COMPARATIVE LAUNCH AND SATELLITE COST ADVANTAGE

India, now has the capability to launch satellites using the GSLV and PSLV rockets at about 80 per cent of international costs. The country also has comparative advantage in the manufacture of communication payloads.

Launch vehicles : The development cost of PSLV is US$ 612.06 million, while that of GSLV is US$ 733.45 million. These costs are lower than the development costs of comparable launch vehicles abroad (the average and median cost of US4 33,346 for the US launch vehicles, Atlas-2 AS and Delta-2 and US$ 26,213 for Ariane-44L and Ariane-5G, and Russian Proton).

Remote sensing satellites : A comparision of IRS-ID cost with the reported cost estimates of similar LANDSAT and SPOT satellites launched in 1997 and 1998 also shows that the cost of the foreign satellies is about 10 times as high as that of the Indian satellite.

Lease charges : The lease charge of IRS low-power transponder is only 75 per cent of the Thaicom transponder price. For high-power transponder cost with LMI-1 wide beam transponder (a low-priced transponder in the market), the estimated lease charge is only 64 per cent of the LMI-1 price after discount.

The major source of cost advantage of ISRO is its critical manpower. Comparison of the average compensation rate of the critical manpower in USA/Europe with that of Indian manpower and after an adjustment for productivity difference shows that the saving in annual cost to ISRO would be around Rs. 745 crores.

25.19 SPACE SCIENCE RESEARCH

The achievements of Indian space programmes in this field are:

1. Investigations in aeronomy as well as in astronomy by conducting space-based experiments.
2. Technologies for sounding rockets and ballon borne instrumentation.
3. Energy cosmic ray variability using neutron/meson/Cerenkov monitors.
4. Equatorial electrojet and spread-F ionization irregularities.
5. Ozone, aerosol and cloud phenomena.
6. Middle atmospheric radiation, dynamics and electrodynamics.
7. Solar physics.
8. IR astronomy.
9. Neutron star and black hole.
10. Astrophysics, planetary science and origin/evolution of life.
11. Scientific payloads to study celestial gamma ray bursts and X-rays sources and
12. Microgravity science.

Major space science research systems established in recent years are :

ASTROSAT : This is a multi-wavelength dedicated satellite mission for high-energy astronomy. The satellite carries soft and hard X-ray detectors and imaging payloads, all sky X-ray monitors and a UV/optical telescope system.

SOXS : The Solar X-ray Spectrometers payload development on board GSAT, for studying solar activity and flaring phenomena.

CRABEX : The Coherent Radio Beacon Experiment payload on board geo-stationary satellite and a ground-based chain of receivers located at various universities and research institutions for developing ionospheric tomography or 3-D models of ionisation and their structure.

Mesosphere, Stratosphere and Troposphere (MST) Radar: This facility has been set up at Gadanki near Tirupati, Andhra Pradesh, for conducting atmospheric research-with high resolution.

Planetary exploration : Development of sensors for planetary probes/missions to the moon or to asteroids or nearby plants.

40 RH-200 rocket flights have been conducted including 36 for the MIDAS campaign. An RH-300 Mk II was also launched for mesospheric turbulence and stratification studies. Two RH-200 Mk III flights were also conducted.

The ISRO has promoted participation of scientists in major international science campaigns, like monsoon experiment (MONEX), middle atmospheric programme (MAP), ISTEP, and INDOEX.

25.19 ISRO-INDUSTRY PARTNERSHIP

ISRO has nurtured a symbiotic partnership with more than 500 Indian firms. The nature of partnership varies from simple procurement contracts of standard items to supply of products needing significant enhancement/technical development and establishment of launch complex and processing facilities on turn-key basis. Some of the features of this partnership (as on March 31, 2002), are :

1. The annual flow of funds, as percent of the space budget, has grew from 20-25 in the late eithties and to 35-40 in recent years. The fund flow in 2001-02 was Rs. 853 crores.
2. 247 technologies have been transferred to industries.
3. ISRO transferred 247 technologies and licensed 172 firms.
4. ISRO has obtained 59 patents and 63 patent application are pending approval.

According to the ISRO's industrial partners, the space contracts have resulted in

1. improved product/service in non-space activities;
2. significant improvement in quality standard;
3. significant improvement in management practices;
4. development of critical manpower; and
5. access to new markets and exports markets.

2006 : 2nd operational flight of GSLV (Fo2) on July 10, carrying Inset - 4C.

2007 : Launch of CARTOSAT - 2, SRE-1, LAPAN - TUBSAT and PEHUENSAT-on PSLV C7, Jan 10.

2007 : SRE-1 splashed in Bay of Bengal on 22, Jan 2007 & recovered by the Indian Coast Gaurd and Ineloon Navy, mahing India one of the few countries to have re-entry technology.

2007 : INSAT-4B launched by Arianspace on March 12

2007 : PSLV-C8 places Italian sattelite AGILE in its orbit on April 23.

We giving 352 kgs sattelite meant to getter information about the origins of the universe m. It is country's first commercial space mission The PSLV on its 11th flight since 1993, put the Agile satellite into its intended orbit about 550 kms above the earth 20 minutes after the blest off. ISRO has changed US Dollars 11 million for the launch.

26

Satellites and Satellite Launch Vehicles

Introduction

This directory gives a brief description of all the major satellite systems and satellite launch vehicles. Amongst satellites, the directory includes the satellites currently in service as well as new ventures with a firm go ahead been included for the sake of continuity. The Satellites discussed here have been broadly categorised as :

1. Communications satellites including direct broadcast satellites 2. Satellites for earth observation 3. Satellites for scientific and technological experiments 4. Military satellites and 5. Weather satellites.

The Satellite launch vehicles have been grouped according to their manufacturers. The companies and organisations covered include :

1. Aerospatiale (France) 2. American Rocket Company (AMROC), U.S.A. 3. Arianespace (France) 4. ASI (Italy) 5. British Aerospace Space Systems (U.K.) 6. Cape York (Australia) 7. CIS (Russia) 8. CNES (France) 9. CNIE (Argentina) EER/SSI (U.S.A.) 10. E Prime (U.S.A.) 11. European Space Agency (France) 12. General Dynamics (U.S.A.) 13. Great Wall Industry (China) 14. General Technology Systems (U.K.) 15. ISRO (India) 16. ISAS (Japan) 17. IAE (Brazil) 18. Iraq (Iraq) 19. Israel Space Agency (Israel) 20. LTV (U.S.A.) 21. Martin Marietta (U.S.A.) 22. Mcdonnell Douglas (U.S.A.) 23. NASA (U.S.A.) 24. NASDA (Japan) 25. National Launch System (U.S.A.) 26. Orbital Sciences (U.S.A.) 27. Pacific American Launch Services (U.S.A) and 28. Strategic Defence Initiative Office (U.S.A.).

Important technical features and brief descriptions of different categories of satellites are given in Table-1 to Table-5. Similar in formation for the satellite launch vehicles is presented in Table-6.

Abbreviations used to describe propellants and orbits in Table-6 :

A50 ; Aerozine 50, **GEO** : Geostationary Orbit, **GTO** : Geostationary Transfer Orbit, **HTPB** : Hydroxyl Terminated Polybutadiene, **Kero** : Kerosine, **LEO** : Low Earth Orbit, **LOX** :

Fig. 26.1.

Fig. 26.2.

Liquid Oxygen, **MMH** : Mono Methy 1 Hydrazine, N_2O_4 : Nitrogen Tetroxide, **NMO3** : Nitric Acid, **PATP** : Polybutadiene Acrylic Acid Acrylonitrile Terpolymer, **RP-1** : Kerosene derivative, **Sun**

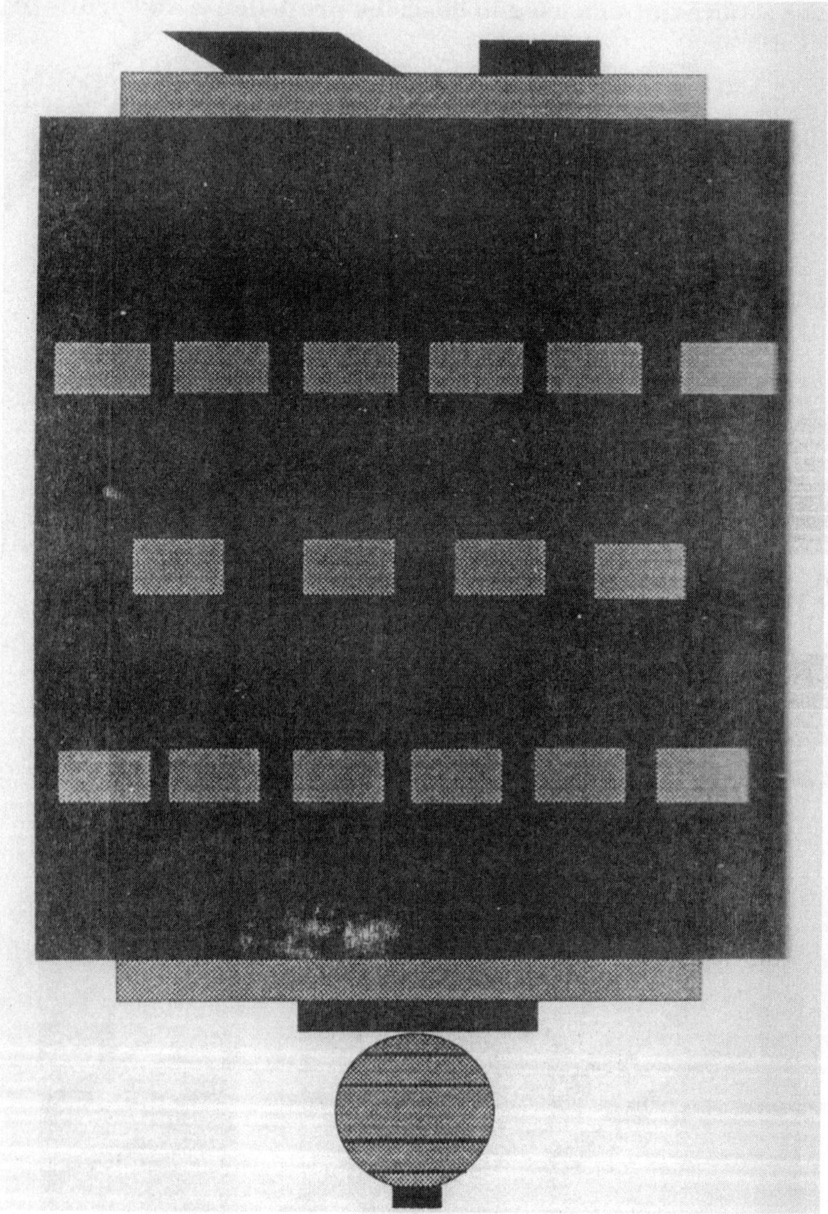

Fig. 26.3.

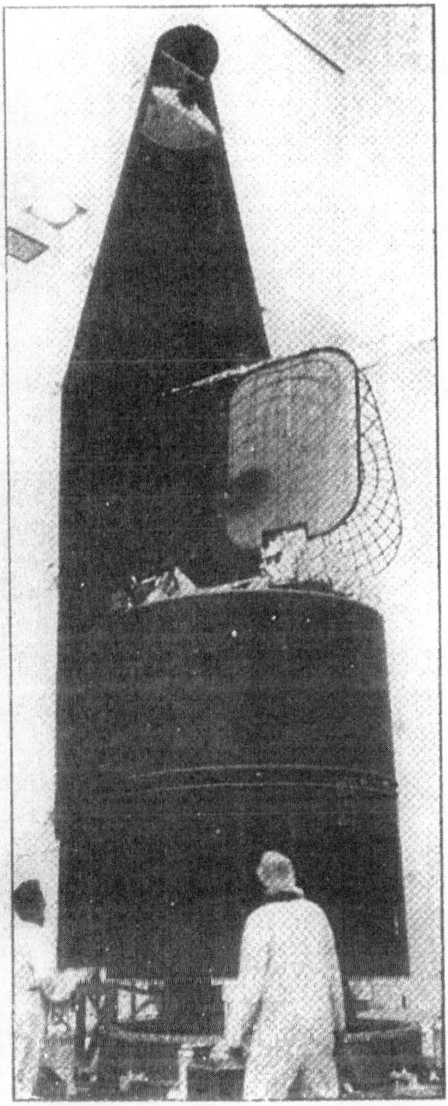

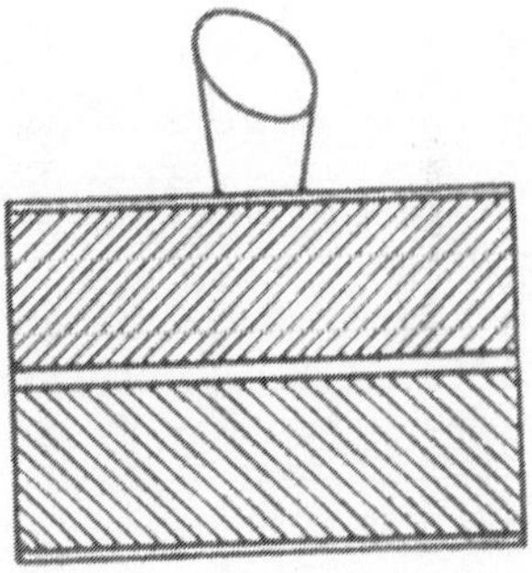

Fig. 26.6

Fig. 26.5.

Table 26.1. Communication Satellites (Contd.)

Satellite	*No.*	*Mfr.*	*Bus*	*Stabili-sation*	*Payload*	*Design Life, yrs*	*Location*	*Launch*	*Brief Description*
ASTRA (Fig. 26.2)	1	GE Astro	Satcom 4000	3-Axis	16 Ku-band	10	19°W	Dec 88, Ariane	Born from the abandoned LUXSAT project in 1983, the Direct Broadcasting satellite ASTRA is the product of Societe Europeene des satellites (SES) with primarily Luxembourg investment.
	2	Original Sat-com-K3	Satcom 4000	3-Axis	16-Ku-ba nd	10	19°W	Nov 90, Ariane	
AUSSAT (Fig. 26.3)	1A	Hughes	HS-376	Spin	15 Ku-band	8	160°E	Aug 85, STS	AUSSAT series satellites provide TV, Radio, Telephony, Telex, Fax, Data Mobile, Educational Video, Electronic funds transfer and other services to Australia and papua New Guinea, Australia's AUSSAT has proved to be one of the greatest successes in domestic commuication Satellite business.
	1B	Hughes	HS-376	Spin	15 Ku-band	8	164°E	Nov 85, STS	
	1C	Hughes	HS-376	Spin	15 Ku-band	8	164°E	Sep 87, Ariane	
	2A	Hughes	HS-601	3-Axis	15 Ku-band, 1 L-band 1 Ka-band	15	156°E	1991, Long March	
	2B	Hughes	HS-601	3-Axis	15 Ku-band 1 1-band 1 Ka-band	15	160°E	1992, Long March	
ARABSAT (Fig. 26.4)	1	Aerospatiale	Spacebus 200	3-Axis	25 C-band	7	19°E	Feb 85 Ariane	It is a 22-nation Arab project established in mid 1970's to provide TV and Telecommunication services to its member countries.
	2	Aerospatiale	Spacebus 200	3-Axis	25 C-band	7	26°E	Jun 85 STS	
	3	Aerospatiale	Spacebus 200	3-Axis	25 C-band	7	–	–	

Fig. 26.4

Table 26.1. Communication Satellites (Contd.)

Satellite	*No.*	*Mfr.*	*Bus*	*Stabili-sation*	*Payload*	*Design Life, Yrs*	Location	*Launch*	*Brief Description*
BRASILSAT	S1	Spar Aerospace	HS-376	Spin	24 C-Band	10	65°W	Feb 85, Ariane	BRASILSAT satellites provide national telephony, TV, military and high speed data links. EMBRATEL (the owner) is also offering transponders to other latin American countries.
	S2	Spar Aerospace	HS-376	Spin	24 C-Band	10	70°W	March 86, Ariane	
ASC	1	GE Astro	Satcom 3000	3-Axis	18 C-band, 6 Ku-band	10	128°W	Aug 85, STS	These satellites are operated by American satellite, a subsidiary of continental Telecom (Contel). The ASC satellites offer voice, data facsimile and video services, The option for the third satellite was not taken up and ASC-3 became panAm Sat (PAS) 1
	2	GE Astro	Satcom 3000	3-Axis	18 C-band, 6 Ku-band	10	70–40°W	March 91, Delta	
	3	Option sold to Aapha lyracom as PAS-1	–	–	–	–	–	–	

Table 26.1. Communication Satellites (Contd).

Satellite	*No.*	*Mfr*	*Bus*	*Stabili-sation*	*Payload*	*Design life, yrs*	*Location*	*Launch*	*Brief Description*
Comstar (Fig. 26.5)	D2	Hughes	INTELSAT -IV	Spin	24C-band	7	76°W	July 76, Atlas	Operated by COMSAT, the COMSTAR satellites were leased initially to AT & T and GTE for long distance telephone communication.
	D4	Hughes	INTELSAT -IV	Spin	24C-band	7	76°W	Feb 81, Atlas	
CS (Fig. 26.6)	2A	Mitsubishi	ford NATO-3	Spin	2 C-band 6-Ka-band	5	132°E	Feb 83, N-II	It is the domestic communications satellite system for Japan providing mainly telephony services. The satellites are operated by Japan's Telecommunications satellite. The CS-3 series includes Ka-band capacity.
	2B	Mitsubishi	Ford NATO-III	Spin	2 C-band 6 6 Ka-band	5	127°E	Aug 83, N-II	
	3A	Mitsubishi	Ford	Spin	2C-band 10 Ka-band	7	132°E	Feb 88, H-I	
	3B	Mitsubishi	Ford	Spin	2 C-band 10 Ka-band	7	135°E	Sep 88, H-I	
EUTELSAT	ECS-1	British Aerospace	ECS	3-Axis	12 Ku-band	7	17°E	June 83, Ariane	This thriving European telecommunications satellite organisation

Table 26.1. Communication Satellites (Contd.)

Satellite	*No.*	*Mfr.*	*Bus*	*Stabilisation*	*Payload*	*Design Life, yrs*	*Location*	*Launch*	*Brief Description*
	ECS-2	British Aerospace	ECS	3-axis	12 Ku-band	7	7°E	Aug 84, Ariane	offers a Ku-band regional satellite system for national postal and telecommunications monopolies to provide capacity for telephony, TV and business traffic.
	ECS-4	British Aerospace	ECS	3-axis	12 Ku-band	7	13°E	Sep 87, Ariane,	
	ECS-5	British Aerospace	ECS	3-axis	12 Ku-band	7	13°E	July 88, Ariane	The Eutelsat-1 (ECS) satellites are leased to Eutelsat European Space-Agency and have been now replaced by Eutelsat-II satellites system.
	Euutelsat-II	Aerospatiale	Spacebus 100 B	3-Axis	16 Ku-band	7	36°E	May 90, Ariane	
	II B	Aerospatiale	Spacebus 100 B	3-Axis	16 Ku-band	7	12°E	Nov 90, Ariane	
	II C	Aerospatiale	Spacebus 100 B	3-Axis	16 Ku-band	7	3°E	1991, Atlas	
	II D	Aerospatiale	Spacebus 100 B	3-Axis	16 Ku-band	7	—	—	—

Table 26.1. Communication Satellites (Contd.)

Satellite	*No.*	*Mfr*	*Bus*	*Stabilisation*	*Payload*	*Design Life, yrs*	*Location*	*Launch*	*Brief Description*
	II E	Aerospatiale	Spacebus 100 B	3-Axis	16 Ku-band	7	–	–	
BS	2 B	NEC	GE Astro SATCOM	3-Axis	2 Ku-band	4	110°E	Feb 86, N-II	This satellite system is operated by Japan Telecommunications satellite on behalf of the national TV network NHK. It was thwarted by the failure of BS-2A, the capacity of which was taken over by BS-2B to provide Japan's first DBS services to the mainland and outlying island. BS-3 series satellites are the latest in the series.
	2X	–	–	3-Axis	2 Ku-band	4	110°E	Feb 90, Ariane	
	3A	Nippon	GE Astro Satcom 3000	3-Axis	2 Ku-band	7	110°E	Sep 90, H-I	
DFS KOPERNIKUS	1	DFS Consortion	DFS	3-Axis	10 Ku-band, 1 Ku-band	10	24°E	May 29, Ariane	This Deutsche Bundepost Government funded project was ostensibly with an export with an export base for satellites. The capacity on these large satellites to provide telephony.

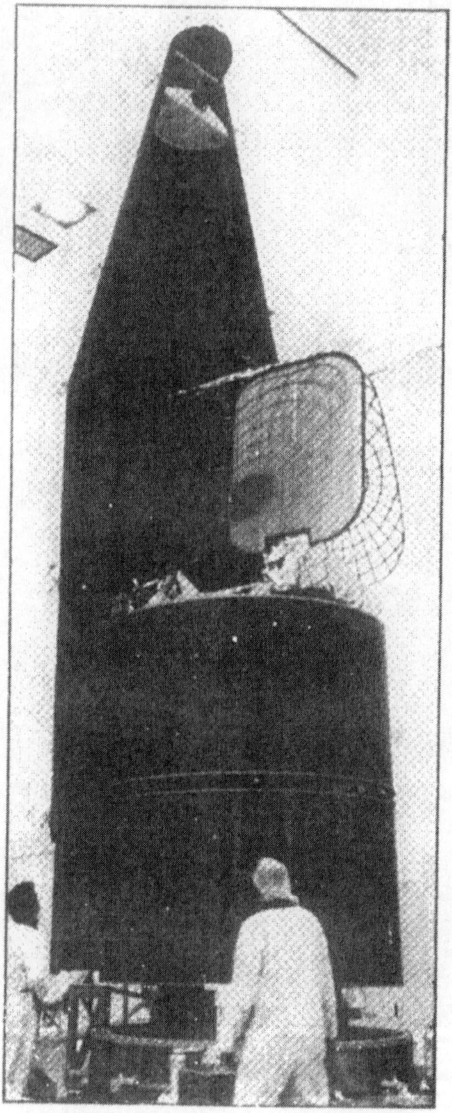

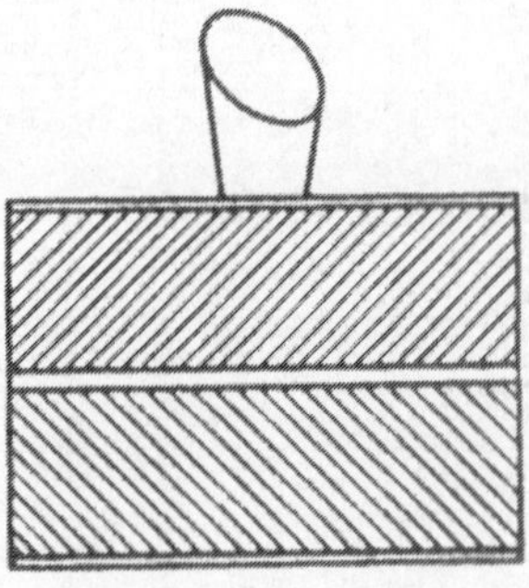

Fig. 26.6

Fig. 26.5

Table 26.1. Communication Satellites (Contd.)

Satellite	*No.*	*Mfr.*	*Bus*	*Stabilisation*	*Payload*	*Design Life, yrs*	*Location*	*Launch*	*Brief Description*
	2	DFS Consortium	DFS	3-Axis	10 Ku-band 1 Ka-band	–	28°E	–	business communications and cable television channel distribution is underused.
	3	DFS Consortium	DFS	3-Axis	10 Ku-band 1 Ka-band	–	–	–	
GALAXY	1	Hughes	HS-376	Spin	24 C-band	10	134°W	Jun 83, Data	Hughes Communications GLAXY provides C-band domestic voice, data and video traffic in U.S.A. using Galaxy 1-3 satellites followed by three Ku-band satellites (Galaxy 4-6) to provide corporate voice and data broadcasting and TV, financial information services and videoconferencing
	2	Hughes	HS-376	Spin	24 mC-band	10	74°W	Sep 83,	
	3	Hughes	HS-376	Spin	24 mC-band	10	93°W	Sep 84, Data	
	4	Hughes	HS-376	Spin	16 Ku-band	10	99°W	1991, Atlas	
	5	Hughes	HS-376	Spin	16 Ku-band	10	125°W	1992, Atlas	
	6	Hughes	HS-376	Spin	16 Ku-band	10	91°W	July 90, Ariane	

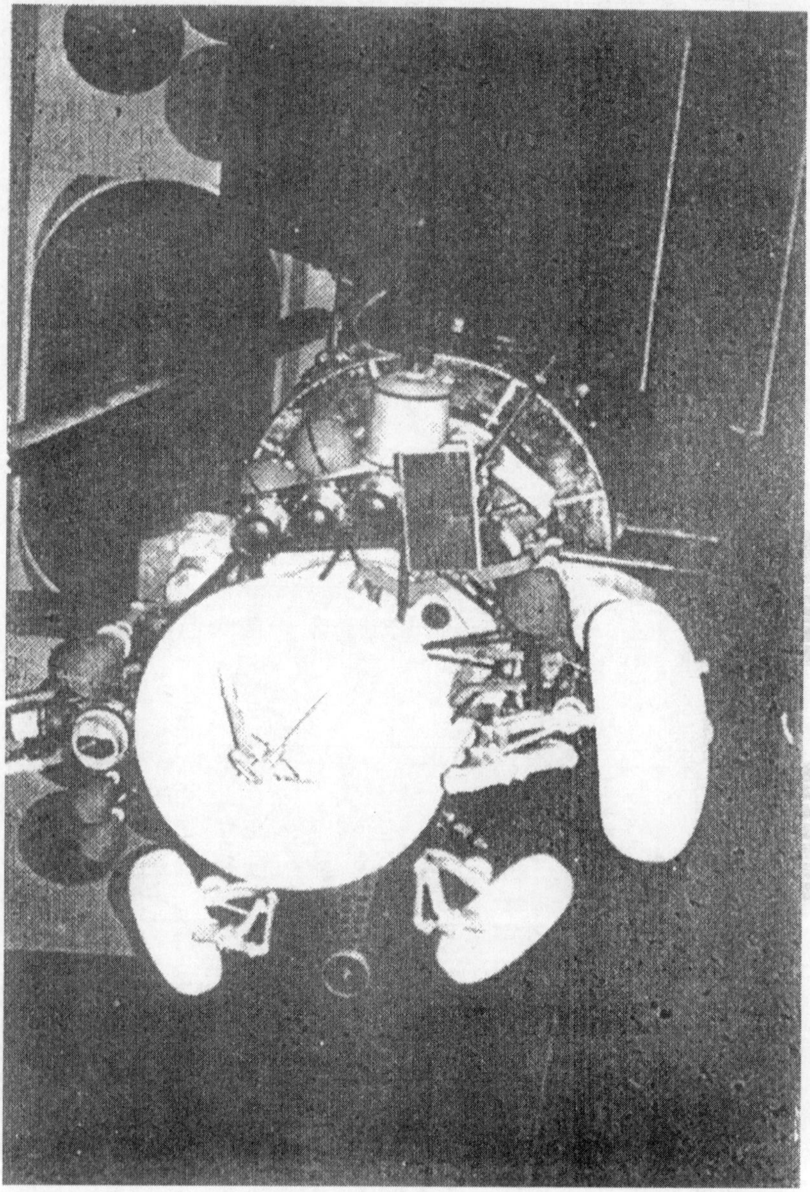

Fig. 26.7

Table 26.1. Communication Satellites (Contd.)

Satellite	No.	Mfr.	Bus	Stabilisation	Payload	Design Life, yrs	Location	Launch	Brief Description
GSTAR	1	GE-Astro	SATCOM 3000	3-Axis	16 Ku-band	10	103°W	May 85, Ariane	G-STAR satellites provide voice, and Data communications services offering further services to the U.S.A. and replacing those originally offered by the COMSAT Comstar satellites.
	2	GE-Astro	SATCOM 3000	3-Axis	16 Ku-band plus Geostar Link 1	10	105°W	March 86, Ariane	
	3	GE-Astro	SATCOM 30000	3-Axis	16 Ku-band plus Geostar Link-1	10	93°W	Sep 88, Ariane	
	4	GE-Astro	SATCOM 3000	3-Axis	16 Ku-band plus Geostar Link-2	10	136°W	Aug 90, Ariane	—

Table 26.1. Communication Satellites (Contd.)

Satellite	*No.*	*Mfr.*	*Bus*	*Stabili-sation*	*Payload*	*Design Life, yrs*	*Location*	*Launch*	*Brief Description*
GEOSTAR	1	GE-Astro	SATCOM 3000	3-Axis	L-band C-band S-band	10	70°W	1991	It is a US privately funded radio determination satellite service. Geostar is also a share holder in the Lockstar European RDSS system.
GORIZONT (Fig. 26.7)	12	-	Gorizont	3-Axis	6 C-band 1 Ku-band, 1 L-band	3	40°E	June 86 Proton	These Soviet Communications satellites have been offered for commercial use in the west.
	13	-	Gorizont	3-Axis	6 C-band 1 Ku-band, 1 L-band	3	90°E	Nov 86, Proton	
	14	-	Gorizont	3-Axis	6 C-band 1 Ku-band, 1 L-band	3	102°E	May 87, Proton	
	15	-	Gorizont	3-Axis	6 C-band 1 Ku-band 1L-band	3	14°E	March 88, Proton	

Table 26.1. Communication Satellites (Contd.)

Satellite	*No.*	*Mfr.*	*Bus*	*Stabilisation*	*Payload*	*Design Life, yrs*	*Location*	*Launch*	*Brief Description*
	16	–	Gorizont	3-Axis	6 C-band 1 Ku-band 1 L-band	3	80°E	Aug 88, Proton	–
	17	–	Gorizont	3-Axis	6 C-band 1 Ku-band 1 L-band	3	53°E	June 89, Proton	
HISPA-SAT	1	Matra	Eurostar	3-Axis	4 Ku-band 8 C-band 2 S-band	10	31°W	1992 Ariane	It was a Spanish government funded programme to support TV coverage of the olympic games in Barcelona in 1992 and to provide a wide range of national communications services.
	2	Matra	Eurostar	3-Axis	4 Ku-band 8 C-band 2 S-band	10	31°W	1992 Ariane	
	3	Matra	Eurostar	3-Axis	4 Ku-band 8 C-band 2 S-band	10	–	–	
INMAR-SAT	II-F1	British Aerospace	Eurostar	3-Axis	4 C-band 2 L-band	10	155°W		INMARSAT is the satellite system of the International Maritime communications organisation comprising 50 member countries. It provides a core market of over 5000 sea
	F2	British Aerospace	Eurostar	3-Axis	4 C-band 2 L-band	10	65°E	Feb 91, Ariane	

Table 26.1. Communication Satellites (Contd.)

Satellite	*No.*	*Mfr.*	*Bus*	*Stabilisation*	*Payload*	*Design Life, yrs.*	*Location*	*Launch*	*Brief Description*
	F3	British Aerospace	Eurostar	3-Axis	4 C-band 2 L-band	10	180°E	July 91, Ariane	going vessels with communication services. It is developing a much wider mobile communications market using future dedicated satellites. There are options for up to nine Inmarsat IIs and the plamed Inmarsat-3 fleat could also number 9.
	F4	British Aerospace	Eurostar	3-Axis	4 C-band 2 L-band	10	55°N	Nov 92, Ariane	
	F5	British Aerospace	Eurostar	3-Axis	–	–	–	–	
	F6-F9	British Aerospace	Eurostar	3-Axis					
INSAT (Fig. 26.8)	1B	Ford Aerospace	INSAT-I	3-Axis	2 S-band 1 C-band	7	74°E	Aug 83, STS	INSAT is a satellite project of the Goverment of India operated by ISRO, Department of space. It is a multipurpose communication and meteorological satellite system providing TV traffic, telephony, meteorology, radio and private network services.
	1C	Ford Aerospace	INSAT-I	3-Axis	2 S-band 1 C-band	7	94°E	July 88, Ariane	

Fig. 26.8

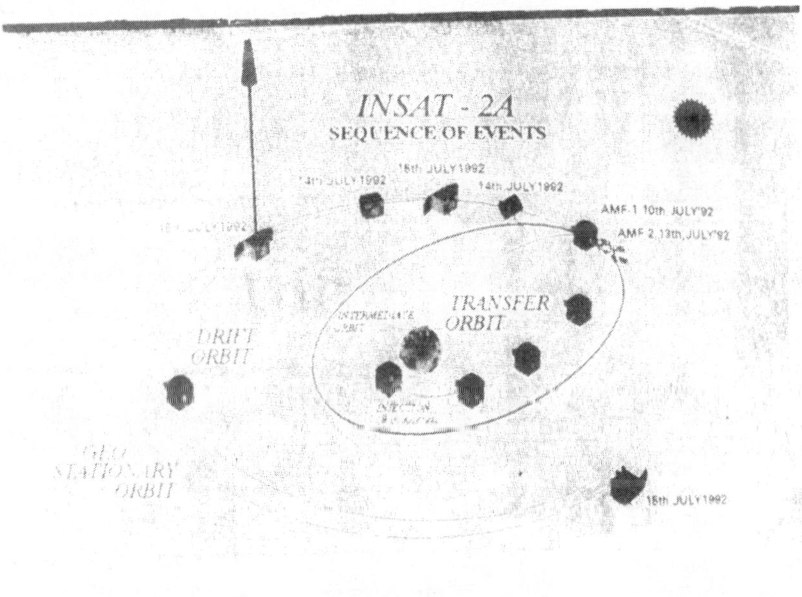

Fig. 26.9

Table 26.1. Communication Satellites (Contd.)

Satellite	*No.*	*Mfr.*	*Bus*	*Stabilisation*	*Payload*	*Design Life, yrs*	*Location*	*Launch*	*Brief Description*
	1D	Ford Aerospace	INSAT-I	3-Axis	2 S-band 1 C-band	7	83°E	22 June 90, Delta	
	2A	ISRO	INSAT-I	3-Axis	18 C-band 2 S-band	7	74°E	1992 Ariane	
	2B	ISRO	INSAT-I	3-Axis	18 C-band 2 S-band	7	–	1994 Ariane	
	2C	ISRO	INSAT-I	3-Axis	–	–	–	1995	
	2D	ISRO	INSAT-I	3-Axis	–	–	–	1996	
	2E	ISRO	INSAT-I	3-Axis	–	–	–	1997	
INSAT-3C	ISRO	INSAT-I	3-axis	24 C-band, 6 extended C-band, 2 S-band, 1 MSS transponders	–		74°E	Jan 2002, Ariane	
Intelsat (Fig. 26.9)	VF1	Ford Aerospace	Intelsat-V	3-Axis	21 C-band 6 Ku-band 2 L-band	9	177°E	May 81, Atlas	The International Telecommunications Satellite Organisation, INTELSAT with more than 100 members world-wide provides satellite capacity for member countries Post, Telegraph and Telecommunications (PTT) organisations and had a near monopoly until recently when competitive systems such as PanAm Sat (PAS) were given
	F2	Ford Aerospace	Intelsat-V	3-Axis	21 C-band 6Ku-band 2L-band	9	21°W	Dec 80, Atlas	
	F3	Ford Aerospace	Intelsat-V	3-Axis	21 C-band 6Ku-band 2L-band	9	174°W	Dec 81, Atlas	

Fig. 26.9A

Table 26.1. Communication Satellites (Contd.)

Satellite	*No.*	*Mfr.*	*Bus*	*Stabilisation*	*Payload*	*Design Life, yrs*	*Location*	*Launch*	*Brief Description*
	F4	Ford Aerospace			21 C-band 6 K2 L-band	9	35°W	March 82, Atlas	approval from the FCC. INTELSAT-VI is the most recent in the series. All INTELSAT-IV have retired. INTELSAT-V are to now replaced by INTELSAT-VII. A new satellite, Intelsat-K is a rapid response venture to competitive systems to provide dedicated Ku-band services using the second hand system Satcom K4
	F5	Ford Aerospace	Intelsat-V	3-Axis	21 C-band 6 Ku-band 2L-band	9	63°E	Sep 82, Atlas	
	F6	Ford Aerospace	Intelsat-V	3-Axis	21 C-band 6 Ku-band 2L-band	9	18°E	May 83, Atlas	
	F7	Ford Aerospace	Intelsat-V	3-Axis	21 C-band 6 Ku-band 2L-band	9	66°E	Oct 83, Atlas	–
	F8	Ford Aerospace	Intelsat-V	3-Axis	21 C-band 6 Ku-band 2L-band	9	180°E	May 84, Ariane	–
	V-A F10	Ford Aerospace	Intelsat-V	3-Axis	32 Ku-band 6 Ku-band	9	24°W	March 85, Atlas	–
	F11	Ford Aerospace	Intelsat-V	3-Axis	32 Ku-band 6 Ku-band	9	27°W	June 85, Atlas	–

Table 26.1. Communication Satellites (Contd.)

Satellite	*No.*	*Mfr.*	*Bus*	*Stabilisation*	*Payload*	*Design Life, yrs*	*Location*	*Launch*	*Brief Description*
INTELSAT	VA F12	Ford Aerospace	Intelsat-V	3-Axis	32 C-band 6 Ku-band	13	1°W	Sep 85, Ariane	–
	VB F13	Ford Aerospace	Intelsat-V	3-Axis	32 C-band 6 Ku-band	13	53°W	May 88, Ariane	–
	F15	Ford Aerospace	Intelsat-V	3-Axis	32 C-band 6 Ku-band	13	60°E	Jan 89, Ariane	–
	VI-F1	Hughes	Intelsat-VI	spin	36 C-band 10 Ku-band	13	37°W	Oct 89, Ariane	–
	F2	Hughes	Intelsat-VI	spin	36 C-band 6 Ku-band	13	Atlantic	1990, Titan	–
	F3	Hughes	Intelsat-VI	spin	36 C-band 6 Ku-band	13	Indian	1990, Titan	–
	F4	Hughes	Intelsat-VI	spin	36 C-band 6 Ku-band	13	Atlantic	1991, Ariane	–
	F5	Hughes	Intelsat-VI	spin	36 C-band 6 Ku-band	13	Indian	1991, Ariane	–
	VII-F1	Ford Aerospace	Intelsat-VII	3-Axis	26 C-band 10 Ku-band	15	Pacific	1992, Ariane	–

Table 26.1. Communication Satellites (Contd.)

Satellite	*No.*	*Mfr.*	*Bus*	*Stabilisation*	*Payload*	Design Life, yrs	*Location*	*Launch*	*Brief Description*
	F2	Ford Aerospace	Intelsat-VII	3-Axis	26 C-band 10 Ku-band	15	Pacific	1993, Ariane	
	F3	Ford Aerospace	Intelsat-VII	3-Axis	26 C-band 10 Ku-band	15	Atlantic	1993, Ariane	
	F4	Ford Aerospace	Intelsat-VII	3-Axis	26 C-band 10 Ku-band	15	Atlantic	1994, Ariane	
	F5	Ford Aerospace	Intelsat-VII	3-Axis	26 C-band 10 Ku-band	15	Atlantic	1994, Ariane	
	K	GE Astro originally	SATCOM 5000	3-Axis	16 Ku-band	10-15	130–158°W	1991, Atlas	
LOC STAR	1	Matra	Eurostar	3-Axis	3C/S Band 3L/C band	10-15	5°W	1992	This is an international consortium led by French space Agency CNES to provide an RDSS for Europe, Africa and the middle east. RDSS stands for Radio Determination Satellite Service.
	2	Matra	Eurostar	3-Axis	3C/S band 3 L/C band	10-15	20°E	1992	
JC SAT	1	Hughes	HS-376	spin	32 Ku-band	10	150°E	March 89, Ariane	It is a joint venture between Hughes communications and the Japanese companies, Itoh and Mitsu, to provide.

Table 26.1. Communication Satellites (Contd.)

Satellite	*No.*	*Mfr.*	*Bus*	*Stabilisation*	*Payload*	*Design Life, yrs*	*Location*	*Launch*	*Brief Description*
	2	Hughes	HS-376	Spin	32 Ku-band	10	154°E	June 90, Titan	Ku-band domestic services to overcome shortcomings of Government funded CS-2 and 3 projects and in competition with the Ford Aerospace backed Superbird satellites project
Marco-polo	1	Hughes	HS-376	Spin	3 Ku-band	10	31°E	Aug, 89, Delta	It is a British Satellite Broadcasting's (BSB) satellite system to operate UK's domestic broadcast service (DBS) TV system
	2	Hughes	HS-376	Spin	3 Ku-band	10	31°W	Aug 90, Delta	
Marisat (Fig. 26.10)	1	Hughes	–	Spin	1 L-band 1 C-band 1 UHF	5	15°W	Feb 76, Delta	These satellites, operated by COMSAT, are now inorbit spares for Inmarsat. These satellites were used initially for the U.S. Maritime Association.
	2	Hughes	–	Spin	1 L-band 1 C-band 1 UHF	5	72°E	June 76 Delta	
	3	Hughes	–	Spin	1 L-band 1 C-band 1 UHF	5	176°E	Oct 76, Delta	

Table 26.1. Communication Satellites (Contd.)

Satellite	*No.*	*Mfr.*	*Bus*	*Stabilisation*	*Payload*	*Design Life, yrs*	*Location*	*Launch*	*Brief Description*
ITALSAT	1	Selenia Spazio	ECS/Italsat	3-axis	16 Ku-band	10	13°E	Dec 90, Ariane	This national communications satellite, to be operated by teles pazio on behalf of Italian space Agency is ostensibly a preoperational experimental spacecraft but may be used commercially in some areas. It will provide PTT services and national TV.
MORELOS	A	Hughes	HS-376	Spin	18 C-band 4 Ku-band	9	113°W	June 85, STS	It is the Mexican satellites system. It uses Hughes satellites and provides telephony and television services. Mexico envisages its use for health, family planning and agricultural education.
	B	Hughes	HS-376	Spin	18 C-band 4 Ku-band	9	117°W	Nov 86, STS	
OLYMPUS Fig. 26.11	1	British Aerospace	Olympus	3-Axis	2 DBS 3 Ku-band 4 Ka-band	9	19°	July 89, Ariane	It is an ESA funded satellite. It is an experimental/R & D spacecraft but does have commercial applications such as educational and national TV.
ORION	1	British Aerospace	Eurostar	3-Axis	34 Ku-band	10	47°W	1992, Atlas	Originally established in 1983 to complete with INTELSAT in the Atlantic region, the

Fig. 26.10

Table 26.1. Communication Satellites (Contd.)

Satellite	*No.*	*Mfr.*	*Bus*	*Stabilisation*	*Payload*	*Design Life, yrs*	*Location*	*Launch*	*Brief Description*
	2	British Aerospace	Eurostar	3-Axis	34 Ku-band	10	37°W	1992, Atlas	Orion satellite venture finally ordered two Ku-band satellites from British Aerospace in 1989. BAe is a member of the Orion company and has formed a joint company, BAe-Tel with a Government license to provide domestic service in U.K.
PALAPA	B1	Hughes	HS-376	Spin	24 C-band	8	108°E	June 83, STS	Palapa is a C-band system providing PTT telephony TV, Radio and Government communications service to the Indonesian mainland. The system has been leased to philippines, Malaysia and Thailand.
	B2P	Hughes	HS-376	Spin	24 C-band	8	113°E	March 87, Delta	–
	B2R	Original Palopa B2	HS-376	Spin	24 C-band	8	118°E	March 90, Delta	–

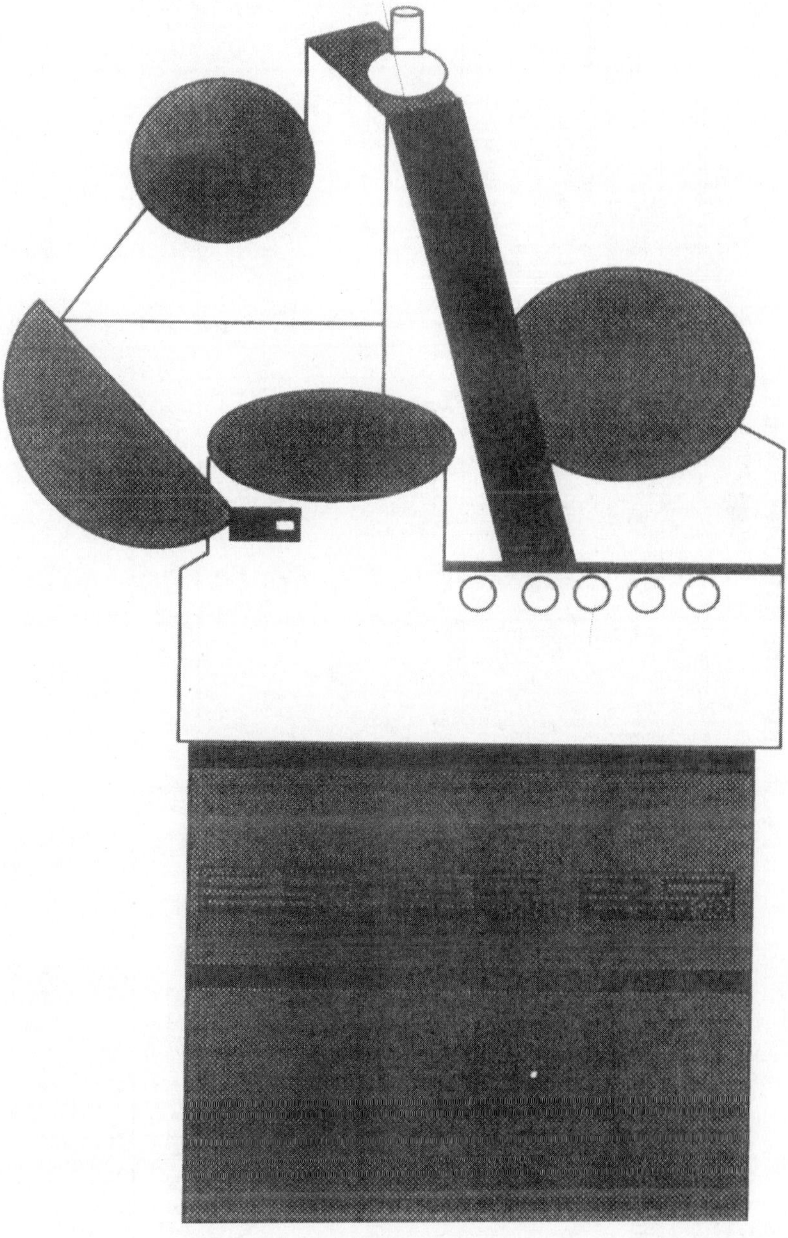

Fig. 26.11

Table 26.1. Communication Satellites (Contd.)

Satellite	*No.*	*Mfr.*	*Bus*	*Stabilisation*	*Payload*	*Design Life, yrs*	*Location*	*Launch*	*Brief Description*
SATCOM (Fig. 26.12)	III-R	GE Astro	Satcom 3000	3-Axis	24 C-band	8	131°W	Nov 81, Delta	Originally operated by RCA American communications, the SAT-COM fleet is now owned by GE Astro. SATCOM was the second U.S. domestic satellite communications system after Westar. It offers C-band and Ku band services for TV distribution in the U.S.A.
	IV	GE Astro	Satcom 3000	3-Axis	24 C-band	8	84°W	June 82, Delta	
	V	GE Astro	Satcom 3000	3-Axis	24 C-band	8	143°W	Oct 82, Delta	–
	VI-IR	GE Astro	Satcom 3000	3-Axis	24 C-band	8	139°W	April 83, Delta	–
	VII-IIR	GE Astro GE Astro	Satcom 3000	3-Axis	24 C-band	8	72°W	Sep 83, Delta	–
	VIII	GE Astro	Satcom 3000	3-Axis	24 C-band	8	136°W	1990, Ariane	–
	IX (C3)	GE Astro	Satcom 3000	3-Axis	24 C-band	8	131°W	1992, Ariane	–

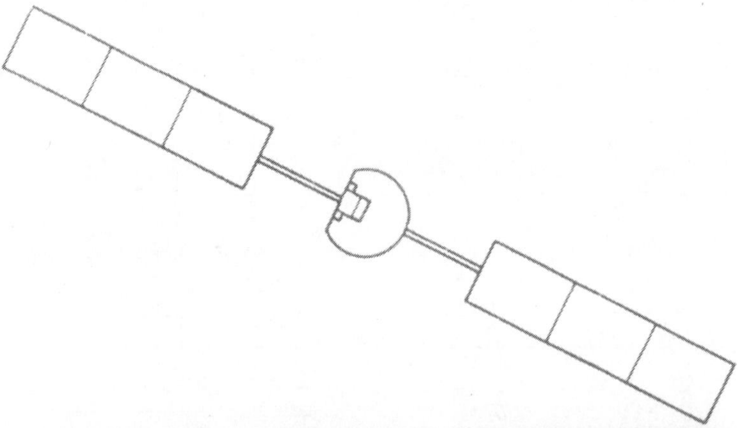

Fig. 26.12

Table 26.1. Communication Satellites (Contd.)

Satellite	*No.*	*Mfr.*	*Bus*	*Stabilisation*	*Payload*	*Design Life, yrs*	*Location*	*Launch*	*Brief Description*
	X (C4)	GE Astro	Satcom 3000	3-Axis	24 C-band	8	–	1993 Ariane	–
	K1	GE Astro	Satcom 3000	3-Axis	16 Ku-band	10	85°W	Jan 86 , STS	–
	K2	GE Astro	Satcom 3000	3-Axis	16 Ku-band	10	81°W	Nov 85, STS	–
	K3	GE Astro	Satcom 3000	3-Axis	16 Ku-band	10	–		–
	K4	GE Astro	Satcom 3000	3-Axis	16 Ku-band	10	130-158°W	1991 Atlas	–
PAS	1	GE Astro (original ASC-3 sold to Alpha lyracom)	Satcom 3000	3-Axis	18 C-band, 8 Ku-band	11	45°W	June 88, Ariane	Pan American Satellite (PAS), owned by Alpha Lyracom which is headed by a spanish entrepreneur, operates the first satellite to compete with the Intelsat monopoly providing low cost specialised services to north America, Europe and Latin America.

Table 26.1. Communication Satellites (Contd.)

Satellite	*No.*	*Mfr*	*Bus*	*Stabilisation*	*Payload*	*Design Life, yrs*	*Location*	*Launch*	*Brief Description*
SBS (Fig. 26.13)	1	Hughes	HS-376	Spin	10 Ku-band	7	99° W	Nov 80, Delta	Satellite Business Systems (SBS) was formed by IBM. Comsat and Aetna invested one billion dollars in a high speed digital data transmission- business service on SBS-1 to 5. SBS-1 and 2 are now owned by Comsat and SBS-3, 4 and 5 by MCI.
	2	Hughes	HS-376	Spin	10 Ku-band	7	99° W	Sep 81, Delta	
	3	Hughes	HS-376	Spin	10 Ku-band	7	91° W	Nov 82, STS	
	4	Hughes	HS-376	Spin	10 Ku-band	7	122° W	Aug 84, Delta	
	5	Hughes	HS-376	Spin	10 Ku-band	7	99° W	Sep 88, Ariane	–
	6	Hughes	HS-376	Spin	9 Ku-band Ku-band	15		June 90, Ariane	–
SPACENET	1	GE Astro	Satcom	3-Axis	12 C-band 12 Ku-band	10	120° W	May 84, Ariane	
	2	GE Astro	Satcom	3-Axis	12 C-band 12 Ku-band	10	69° W	Nov 84, Ariane	These satellites are the second in fleet operated by GTE spacenet and are used for video distribution and business traffic, primarily GTE's own sprint service.
	3R	GE Astro	Satcom	3-Axis	12 C-band 12 Ku-band plus Geostar Link 2 payload				

Table 26.1. Communication Satellites (Contd.)

Satellite	*No.*	*Mfr.*	*Bus*	*Stabilisation*	*Payload*	*Design Life, yrs*	*Location*	*Launch*	*Brief Description*
Superbird	A	Ford Aerospace	Supersat	3-Axis	12 Ku-band 23 Ka-band	10	158° W	June 89, Ariane	These satellites are operated by space communications of Japan, which is competing with JC SAT to provide cable TV, video conferencing, telephony, newspaper transmission, business applications, banking and other services. It was established with backing from Ford Aerospace which provides super satellite bus.
	B	Ford Aerospace	Supersat	3-Axis	12 Ku-band 23 Ka-band	10	–	Feb 90, Ariane	
TDF	1	Aerospatiale	Space bus 300	3-Axis	5 Ku-band	9	19° W	Oct 88, Ariane	This is the French equivalent of West German TV-SAT.
	2	Aerospatiale	Space bus 300	3-Axis	5 Ku-band	9	19° W	March 90, Ariane	
TELECOM	1A	Matra	ECS	3-Axis	6 Ku-band 4 C-band 2 X-band	7	8° W	Aug 84, Ariane	France's domestic telecommunications satellite system owned by the

Table 26.1. Communication Satellites (Contd.)

Satellite	*No.*	*Mfr.*	*Bus*	*Stabilisation*	*Payload*	*Design Life, yrs*	*Location*	*Launch*	*Brief Description*
	1B	Matra	ECS	3-Axis	6 Ku-band 4 C-band 2 X-band	7	140°E	May 85, Ariane	France PTT and French space agency CNES, provides TV, telephone, digital data communications and also a military channel called syracuse, covering home and overseas territories. The system is operated by France cables et Radio.
	1C	Matra	ECS	3-Axis	6 Ku-band 4 C-band, 2 X-band	7	5°W	March 88, Ariane	
	2A	Matra	Eusostar	3-Axis	11 Ku-band 10 C-band, 5 X-band	10	5°W	1992, Ariane	
	2B	Matra	Eusostar	3-Axis	11 Ku-band 10 C-band, 5 X-band	10	–	1993-94	–
	2C	Matra	Eusostar	3-Axis	11 Ku-band 10 C-band, 5 X-band	10	–	1993-94	–
TELSTAR (Fig. 26.14)	301	Hughes	HS-376	Spin	24 C-band	10	96°W	July 83, Delta	This is the AT & T commercial domestic C-band telephonic satellite system. It replaces the Comstar C-band capacity.
	302	Hughes	HS-376	Spin	24 C-band	10	97°W	Aug 84, STS	
	303	Hughes	HS-376	Spin	24 C-band	10	125°W	June 85, STS	

Fig. 26.13

Fig. 26.14

Table 26.1. Communication Satellites (Contd.)

Satellite	*No.*	*Mfr.*	*Bus*	*Stabilis-ation*	*Payload*	*Design Life, yrs*	*Location*	*Launch*	*Brief Description*
	401	GE Astro	Satcom 7000	3-Axis	24 C-band	12	101–85°W	1994	–
	402	GE Astro	Satcom 7000	3-Axis	24 C-band	12	101–85°W	1994	–
	403	GE Astro	Satcom 7000	3-Axis	24 C-band	12	101–85°W	1995	–
TELEX	1	Aerospatiale	Spacebus 100	3-Axis	3 Ku-band 4 C-band	7	5°E	April 89, Ariane	This is the Scandinavian version of TDF and TV-Sat DBS satellites. It is operated by Notelsat. Originally a Swedish project, has been joined by Norway, Finland, Iceland and Denmark.
TV-SAT (Fig. 26.15)	1	MBB	Aero-spatiale spacebus- 300	3-Axis	4 Ku-band	7	19°W	Nov 87, Ariane	This is the West German DBS satellite system operated by Deutsche Bundepost.

Table 26.1. Communication Satellites (Contd.)

Satellite	*No.*	*Mfr.*	*Bus*	*Stabilisation*	*Payload*	*Design Life, yrs*	*Location*	*Launch*	*Brief Description*
WESTAR	IV	Hughes	HS-376	Spin	24 C-band	10	99° W	Feb 82, Delta	Westars were the first domestic US communications satellites, launches starting in 1974, after the FCC decision to proceed with DOMSAT. The satellite provides domestic C-band capacity, which includes voice and data traffic as TV distribution services.
	V	Hughes	HS-376	Spin	24 C-band	10	122° W	June 82, Delta	
	VI	Hughes	HS-376	Spin	24 C-band	10	105–116° W	April 90, Long March	–
	VI-S	Hughes	HS-376	Spin	24 C-band	10	79° W		

Fig. 26.15

Fig. 26.16

Table 26.2. Satellites for Earth Observation

Satellite	*Stabilisation*	*Design Life, yrs*	*Payload*	*Orbit*	*Launch*	*Other Features*
Bhaskara-I (Fig. 26.16)	Spin	–	–	535 km inclined at 50.7°	June, 1979 Intercosmos Rocket	Also known as Satellite for Earth observation (SEO). Bhaskara-1 retired in Aug 1981 when its attitude control fuel was exhausted. The satellite resembles an octagonal section covered with solar cells. Bhaskaras were some of the first satellites built by India.
Bhaskara-II	Spin	–	A television camera operating in visible and infrared plus a microwave imaging system.		Nov., 1981 Inter cosmos Rocket	
ERS-I (Fig. 26.17)	3-Axis	Plus 2 years	Synthetic Aperture Radar (SAR) combined with wind scatterometer + radar altimeter	Sun Sync., 780 Km high	1987, Ariane 3	Manufactured by Dornier and owned by ESA, ERS-1 in Europe's first Earth Resources Satellite designed for ocean monitoring. Though a European space agency venture, Canada is involved to the tune of almost 10 per cent. It uses multimission bus developed by France for SPOT. Yaw steering for improved image quality and large fuel supply for orbit manoeuvring are other features.
IRS-1A (Fig. 26.18)	–	3-yrs	Cameras LISS-I and LISS-II	Polar Sun synchronous, 904 km high	March, 1988 VOSTOK	IRS-1A and 1B are the mainstay of the National Natural Resources Management system for providing remote sensing data services to various users.
IRS-1B	–	3-yrs	Cameras LISS-I and LISS-II	Sun synchronous, 904 km high	August, 1991	

Table 26.2 Satellites for Earth Observation (Contd.)

Satellite	*Stabilisation*	*Design Life, yrs*	*Payload*	*Orbit*	*Launch*	*Other Features*
IRS–IA (Fig. 26.18)	–	3–yrs	Cameras LISS–I and LISS–II	Polar Sun synchronous 904 km high	March, 1988 VOSTOK	IRS–IA and IB are the mainstay of the National Natural Resources Management system for providing remote sensing data services to various users.
IRS–IB	–	3–yrs	Cameras LISS–I and LISS–II	Sun synchronous 904 km high	August, 1991	
IRS–IC	–	–	Cameras with resolution better than that of LISS I and LISS–II and having stereo viewing	–	1994–95	
IRS–ID	–	–		–	1996–97	
IRS–IE	–	–	LISS–I Monocular	–	–	
IRS–2A/2B	–	–	–	–	1998–99	
IRS–P3	3–axis	–	Widefield sensor, X–raymonitor, Modular optoelectronics scanner (MOS)	817 km Polar Sun–synchronous or bit	March, 1996	
IRS–P4 (OCEAN-SAT)	3–axis	–	Ocean colour Monitor, Multi-spectral scanning Microwave Radiometer (MSMR)	720 km, Polar Sun synchronous orbit	May, 1999 PSLV–C2	
IRS–P5 (CAR-TOSAT–1)	3–axis	–	Panchromatic cameras with resolution of 2.3 m and swath of 30 km	617 km, Polar Sun synchronous orbit	During 2001–2002	
IRS–P6 (RESOUR-CESAT)	3–axis	–	Multispectral camera, LISS–III, LISS–IV, Advanced Wide Field Sensor	8m km, Polar Sun synchronous orbit	During 2001–2002	
CAR-TOSAT–2	3–axis	–	–	–	To be launched during Xth plan (2002–2007)	
MOS–1	3–axis	2	Multispectral electronic scanning radiometer + visible and	Sun Self Synchronous 910 km high	1986, N–2	MOS–1 is Japan's first earth observation satellite. It is an experimental satellite aimed at establishing the technology for an

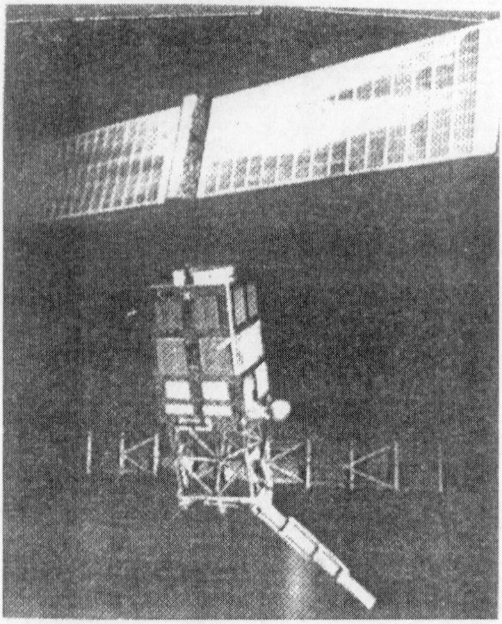

Fig. 26.17

Fig. 26.18

Fig. 26.18A

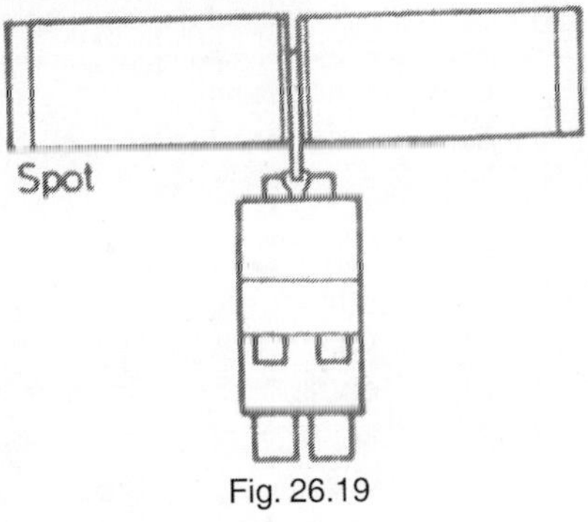

Fig. 26.19

Table 26.2. Satellites for Earth Observation (Contd.)

Satellite	*Stabilisation*	*Design Life, yrs*	*Payload*	*Orbit*	*Launch*	*Other Features*
			thermal infrared radiometer + microwave scanning radio meter + Data collection transponder	and inclined 99.1° Repeat cycle is 17 days		Operational system. Observing sea surface and atmosphere are the goals.
SPOT (Fig. 26.19)	3–Axis	2	Two identical high resolution visible imaging instruments. Each sees in visible or infrared in one of two modes–panchromatic or multispectral Resolution in panchromatic mode is 10m and in mullispectral mode is 20m.	Sun synchronous 832 Km high circular and inclined at 97.7°. Repeat cycle is 26 days	Jan 1985, Ariane	It is France's first earth observation satellite designed to monitor land resources such as crops, forests. Data obtained from SPOT is to be made available commercially through a new company called spot image.

Table 26.2. Satellites for Earth Observation (Contd.)

Satellite	*Stabilisation*	*Design Life, yrs*	*Payload*	*Orbit*	*Launch*	*Other Features*
Landsat–1	3–Axis	–	Multispectral Scanner	–		LANDSAT–series satellites are the earth observation satellites from U.S.A. LANDSAT–4 and LANDSAT–5 are the recent crafts in the series while LANDSAT–6 is in development stage. LANDSAT–4 and 5 have considerably improved the technology of remote sensing of earth thereby aiding resource management. The LANDSAT system is currently operated by EOSAT (Earth observation satellite company) which is an RCA–Hughes joint venture. GE Astrospace is under contact to EOSAT to develop an advanced LANDSAT–6 craft which will be based on the flight proven DMSP/Tiros weather satellite design.
Landsat–2	3–Axis	–	Multispectral Scanner	–		
Landsat–3 (Fig. 26.20)	3–Axis	–	Multispectral Scanner	–		
Landsat–4	3–Axis	3	Multispectral Scanner + Thematic Mapper	Sun Synchronous 706 Km high and inclined at 98°. Repeat cycle is 16 days	July 1982, Delta 3920	
Landsat–5	3–Axis	3	Multispectral Scarmer + Thematic Mapper	–	March 1984, Delta 3920	
Landsat–6	3–Axis	–	–	–	–	

Sync : Sun Synchronous Orbit, **UDMH** : Unsymmetrical demethy1 hydrazine, **UH 25** : Unsymmetrical hydrazine.

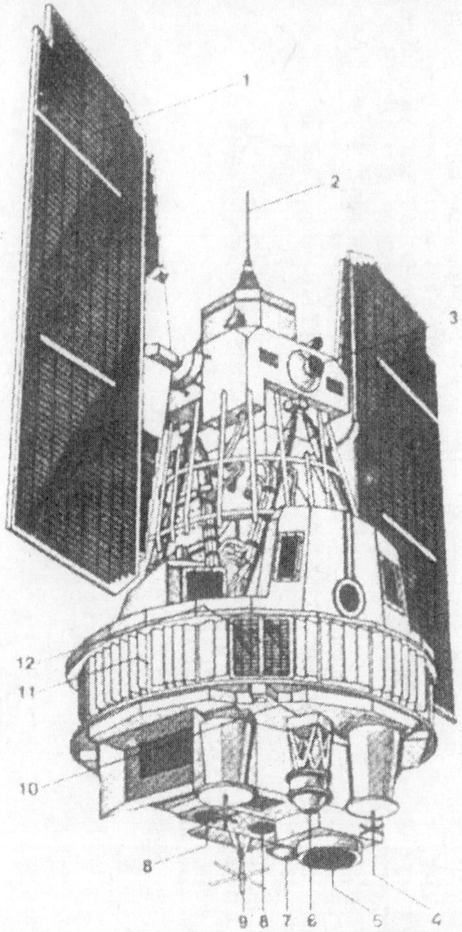

1. Solar Panel
2. Command antenna
3. Wide band antenna
4. Five band multi spectral scanner
5. Unified S band antenna
6. Attitude measurement sensor
7. Return beam vidicon cameras (2)
8. Data collection systems antenna
9. ERTS command auxillary memory (ECAM) subsystem
10. Sensory ring
11. Beacon antennas (4)

Fig. 26.20

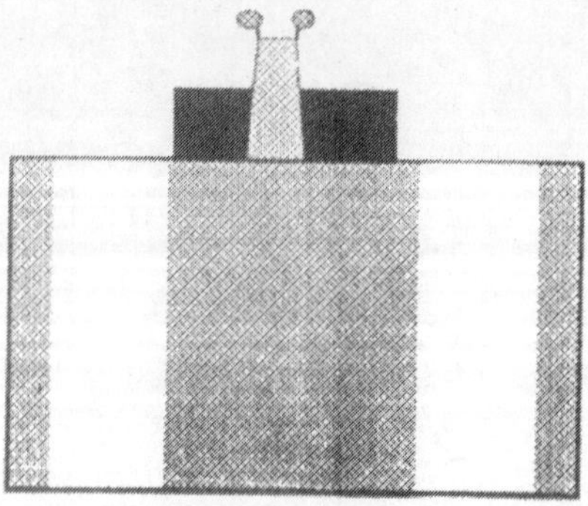

Fig. 26.21

Table 26.3. Weather Satellites

Satellite	*Stabilisation*	*Design Life, yrs*	*Payload*	*Orbit*	*Launch*	*Other Features*
GMS–1 (Fig. 26.21)	Spin	3	Visible / Infrared spin scan radiometer producing pictures of earth every 30 minutes + space environment	Geostationary 140°E	July, 1977 Delta	Geostationary Meteorological Satellite (GMS) is a series of meteorological satellites built by Hughes for Japan. GMS–1 GMS–2, GMS–3A and GMS–3B are the satellites in series. The GMS–series satellites have a shorter bus.
GMS–2	Spin	3	Visible / Infrared spin scan radiometer producing pictures of earth every 30 minutes + space environment	Geostationary 140°E	August, 1981 N–II	
GMS–3A	Spin	3	Visible / Infrared spin scan radiometer producing pictures of earth every 30 minutes + space environment	Geostationary	September 1984 N–II	
GMS–3B	Spin	3	Visible / Infrared spin scan radiometer producing pictures of earth every 30 minutes + space environment	Geostationary	1989 N–II	

Table 26.3. Weather Satellites (Contd.)

Satellite	*Stabilisation*	*Design Life, yrs*	*Payload*	*Orbit*	*Launch*	*Other Features*
GOES–1	Spin	7	Visible / Infrared spin / scan radiometric atmospheric sounder (RAS). Resolution of 0.9 km in visible light and 6.9 km in infrared. Other equipment includes data collection / relay system and a space environment monitor (GOES–1 to GOES–8)	Geostationary 135°W (GOES–4) and GOES–6) 75°W (GOES–5) 83°W (GOES–8)	Oct 1975 (GOES–1) June 1977 (GOES–2) June 1978 (GOES–3) Sep 1980 (GOES–4) May 1981 (GOES–5) April 1983 (GOES–5) 1986 (GOES–6) Feb 1987 (GOES–8) All launches from Delta	GOES (Geostationary Operational Environmental Satellite) is one of the two main elements in America's weather coverage. The other is polar orbiting TIROS–N– series. GOES–I to GOES–M are an advanced series of satellites ordered from Ford aerospace.
2	Spin	7				
3	Spin	7				
4	Spin	7				
5	Spin	7				
6	Spin	7				
7	Spin	7				
8	Spin	7				
GOES–I	Spin	–				
J	Spin	–				
K	Spin	–				
L	Spin	–				
M	Spin	–				

Table 26.3. Weather Satellites (Contd.)

Satellite	*Stabilisation*	*Design Life, yrs*	*Payload*	*Orbit*	*Launch*	*Other Features*
INSAT (Fig.23.22)	–	–	Very High Resolution Radiometer (Payload for weather role)	Geostationary	–	INSAT–series satellites are multipurpose satellites that combine direct broadcast, communications and weather roles.
METEO-SAT–1 (Fig. 26.23)	Spin	3	Radiometer operating in the visible, infrared and water vapour spectrum (A complete picture is produced every 30 minutes) + Data collection system (For METEOSAT–1 and METEOSAT–2)	Geostationary 0° longitude (METEOSAT –1) and Geostationary 10°E (METEOSAT –2)	Nov 1977, Thor–Delta	METEOSAT–series weather satellites are owned by European Space Agency and manufactured by Aerospatiale. Meteosat's main roles include production of weather pictures and relay of data from remote sites.
METEO-SAT–2	Spin	3			June, 1981 Ariane	
TIROSN / NOAA (Fig. 26.24)	3–Axis	–	Advanced very high resolution radiometer high resolution infrared	Sun synchronous and	All launches are by Atlas E/F. NOAA–6 in 1979	It is the polar-orbiting element of America's weather satellites. (GOES in geostationary orbit is the other).

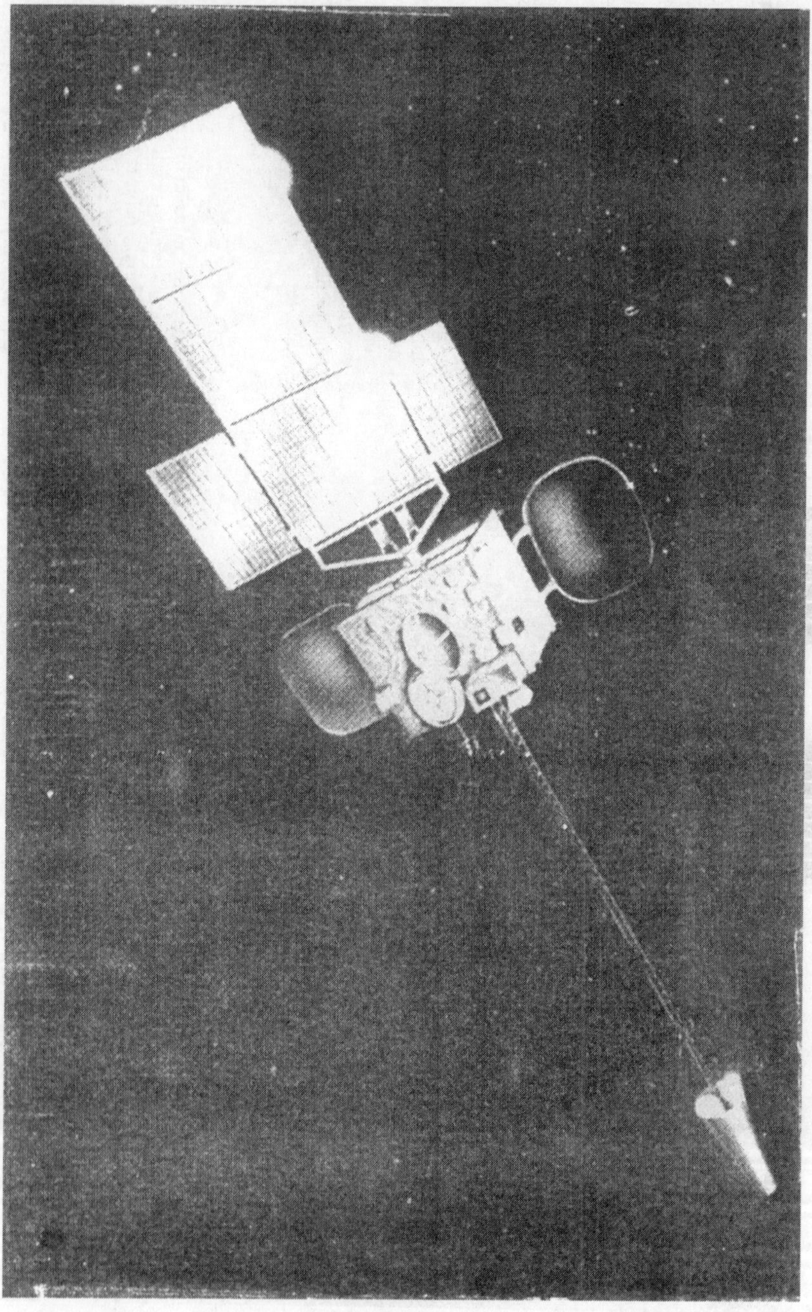

Fig. 26.22

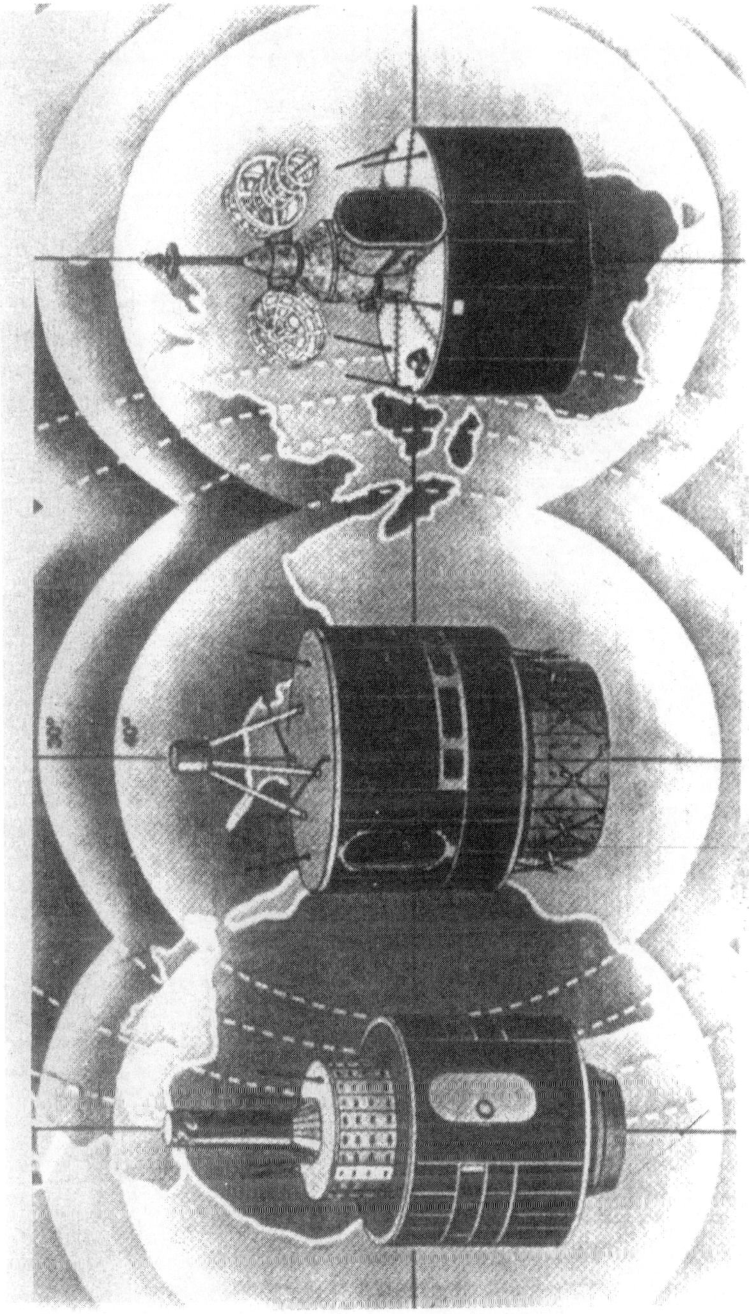

Fig. 26.23

Fig. 26.24

Table 26.3. Weather Satellites (Contd.)

Satellite	*Stabilisation*	*Design Life, yrs*	*Payload*	*Orbit*	*Launch*	*Other Features*
			sounder, stratospheric sounding unit, Microwave sounding unit and data collection system. Space Environment Meter (SEM) and Search and Rescue payload. Some advanced TIROS–N satellites carry solar Backscather Ultraviolet Instrument, Some satellites also carry Earth Radiation Budget Experiment payload.	inclined at 98.9°	NOAA–7 in 1980 and NOAA–8 in 1983	It Comprises of a series of eight satellites, the first of which was TIR–OSN launched in October 1978 and deactivated in Feb 1981. The next craft is called NOAA–6 and so on through to NOAA–12 NOAA–C through NOAA–1 before launch). The operational network comprises two craft in orthogonally intersecting orbits.
Nimbus (Nimbus–1 to Nimbus–7	3–Axis		Sensors including several pollutant sniffers and a coastal zone colour scanner	Sun Synchronous 995 km high (Nimbus–7 called Nimbus–G before launch) Repeat cycle' is 18 days	Nimbus–1 to Nimbus 7 were launched between 1964 and 1978 abroad Delta	This satellite series has served as an experimental platform for remote sensing equipment, rather than being an operational networks.

Table 26.4. Science and Technology Satellites

Satellite	*Stabilisation*	*Design Life, yrs*	*Payload*	*Orbit*	*Launch*	*Other Features*
AMPTE/ CCE / IRM	Spin	7 Months	–	CCE in a 300 × 50,000 km orbit with 28° inclination AMPTE keeps station on IRM at a distance of about 100 km	1984 (Thor Delta)	AMPTE (Active Magne–stospheric Particle Tracer and Explorer) is a sub satellite of a joint venture between USA and West Germany. The US craft called Charge Composition Explorer (CCE) and German Craft named Ion Release Module (IRM). All three crafts are released together.
EXOSAT (Fig. 26.25)	3–Axis	2	Two low energy imaging tele scopes + Medium energy proportional, Counter + Gas Scintillation Spectrometer	500 km × 200,000 km and inclined at 72.5°. Apogee is roughly above north pole	1983 (Thor Delta)	EXOSAT is Europe's first X– ray observer designed to measure the position, structural aspects and spectral and temporal characteristic of X–ray sources. Objectives also include detection of new sources and mapping of diffuse sources.
Galileo	Spin	—	Nine experiments on orbiter and six on the probe	—	1986 Space shuttle	It is US–West German joint effort to send an orbiter / Probe to an outer planet. The orbiter is designed to make 11 orbits of Jupiter over 20 months.

Fig. 26.25

Table 26.4. Science and Technology Satellite (Contd.)

Satellite	*Stabilisation*	*Design Life, yrs*	*Payload*	*Orbit*	*Launch*	*Other Features*
					places Galileo and its Centaur–G prime then puts the Orbiter / Probe in to interplanatory orbit	
Gamma Ray Observatory (GRO)	3–Axis	2	Transient event monitor + High energy gamma ray telescope + Imaging Compton telescope	400 km high circular and inclined at 28.5°	1988 (space shuttle)	America's science and technology satellite to observe the full range of gamma rays and to see sources upto ten times fainter than those previously observed. GRO follows work done by NASA's third high energy a astronomy observatory (HEAO).
HIPPARCOS	Slow Spin for scanning purpose	2.5	Baker–Schmidt reflecting telescope and detectors	Near geostationary with an inclination of less than 3°	1986 (Ariane)	Designed to measure accurately the positions, proper motions and parallaxes of more than 100,000 stars. It is Europe's first astro–metric satellite.

Table 26.4. Science and Technology Satellites (Contd.)

Satellite	*Stabilisation*	*Design Life, yrs*	*Payload*	*Orbit*	*Launch*	*Other Features*
Hubble–space Telescope (Fig. 26.26)	—	—	—		1990 (Challenger)	Hubble Space Telescope is equipped with 2.4 m diameter mirror which will allow observation of stars as faint as the 27th magnitude, fifty times fainter than those seen by 0.508m Mount Palomer telescope
IRAS (Fig. 26.27)	3–Axis	—	Cryogenically cooled Ritchey Chretion telescope with 0.57 m effective operature + Low resolution spectrometer short wavelength channel and chopped photometric channel	900km high circular	1983 (Delta 3910)	Infrared Astronomical Satellite (IRAS) is a joint venture by U.S.A., Britain and Netherlands. The objective was to perform all sky survey of infrared sources-free from the obscuring effect of earth's atmosphere.

Fig. 26.26

1. Gold-plated sunshade (to reffect solar and Earth IR radiation)
2. Coarse Sun Sensor (6)
3. Evacuated main shell
4. 125 gal (4751) superfluid helium tank (for telesocope cooling)

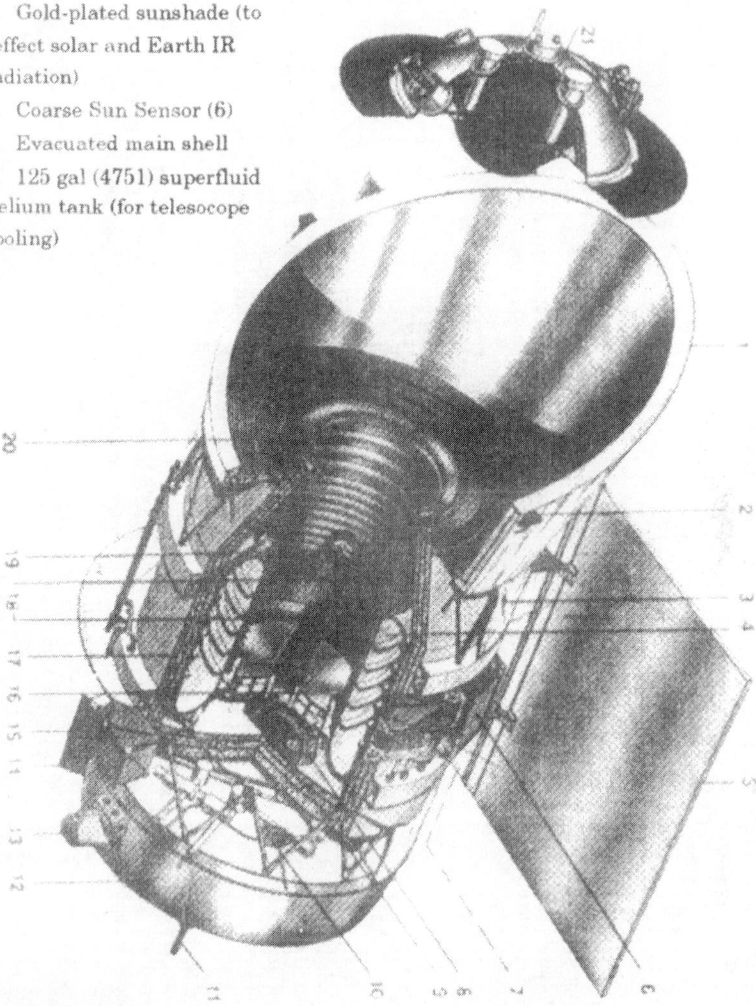

5. Deployable solar panel
6. Experiment electronics
7. Fine Sun Sensor (2) (behind solar panels)
8. Dutch Additional Experiment (DAX)
9. Focal plane assembly 62 rectangular detectors
10. Cryogenic valves and manifold
11. S band antenna
12. Spacecraft telemetry attitude control and command module
13. Horizon sensor (60° field of view)
14. Nickel-cadmium battery
15. DAX electronics
16. 22. 4in (57 cm)
17. Mylar and Dacron net insulation
18. Baffles
19. Secondary mirror
20. Baffle
21. Helium-cooled telescope aperture cover (ejected after IRAS check-out in orbit)

Fig. 26.27

Table 26.4. Science and Technology Satellites (Contd.)

Satellite	*Stabilisation*	*Design Life, yrs*	*Payload*	*Orbit*	*Launch*	*Other Features*
GIOTTO	Spin	1	Camera + Neutral Mass spectrometer + Ion Mass spectrometer + Dust Impact Mass spectrometer + Impact detector + Electron/Ion plasma analyser + Magnetometer + Ultraviolet spectrometer.	—	1985 (Ariane–1)	Mission to observe comet Halley. GIOTTO is a European venture. It uses Geos structure model and basic design Twin sheet bumper to protect Craft from particle impact at the encounter speed of 70 Km/s
ISO	—	—	0.6 m diameter telescope cooled by liquid helium and hydrogen + Infrared camera array + spectrometers + photo meter polarimeter	—		ISO (Infrared Science Observatory) is ESA's science project intended to complement space telescope's observation in visual range. Part of ISO's time will be spent in the sky survey and the rest in the detailed observations. It is more sensitive than even IRAS.
ISPM	3–Axis	—	Plasma spectrometer + solar wind ion composition spectrometer + Cosmic dust	—	1986 (Shuttle)	ISPM (International Solar Panel Mission) is an ESA–NASA joint venture. It involves sending a space craft out of ecliptic plane so that it can look down on

Table 26.4. Science and Technology Satellites (Contd.)

Satellite	*Stabilisation*	*Design Life, yrs*	*Payload*	*Orbit*	*Launch*	*Other Features*
			+ Magnetic field + Gamma and X–ray burst + low energy ion composition + cosmic ray and charged particle + Radio and plasma wave			sun's poles–from about the same distace as earth is now. It has sophisticated thermal control to cope with temperature extremes, autonomous operation to work around the long communications gap, radiation hardening to withstand Jupiter worst and high reliability to cope with the long mission.
ROSAT	3–Axis	1.5	Nother–class telescope + High resolution imager + Wide field camera	475 km high, circular and inclined at 57°	1987 (Shuttle)	ROSAT's objective was a survey of X–ray sources to be subsequently followed by detailed observation of interesting sources. The satellite was shaped like disc to minimise launch costs.
SMM (Fig. 26.28)	3–Axis	1	Gamma ray spectrometer + Hard X–ray burst spectrometer = ultraviolet spectrometer and polarimeter + X–ray polychromator + Coronagraph polarimeter + active cavity irradiance monitor	500 km high, Circular		SMM (Solar Maximum Mission) was intended to tell us more about solar flares. It was launched near the peak of sun's 2nd year sun spot cycle when disruptions are most frequent. A unique feature of this satellite was that it could be repaired in space.

Fig. 26.28

Fig. 26.29

Table 26.4. Science and Technology Satellites (Contd.)

Satellite	*Stabilisa-tion*	*Design Life, yrs*	*Payload*	*Orbit*	*Launch*	*Other Features*
Space Telescope (Fig. 26.29)	3–Axis	5	Optical telescope with 2.4 inch diameter reflecting cassegrain mirror. The four focal plane sensors are FOC, wide field planetary camera, high resolution spectro-graph, faint object spectrograph and high speed photometer.	500 km high, Circular and inclined at 28.5°	1985 (Space shuttle)	The space telescope had a resolution ten times better than ground based devices. Space telescope in a NASA venture with an ECA contribution in the form of faint object camera and solar arrays.
SROSS–C1	—	—	Gamma Ray Burst (GRB) Experiment and Retarding Potential Analyzer	—	May, 1992 by ASLV–D3	—
SROSS–C2	—	—	Same as above	—	May, 1994 by ASLV–D4	
VIKING (Fig. 26.30)	Spin	8 months	Electric field + Particle experiments + Wave experiment + Ultraviolet images	820 × 15000 km inclined at 98.7°	1985 (Ariane)	Viking owned by Swedish space corporation and manufactured by Saab Scania is a small scientific satellite design to investigate earth's magnetosphere. It should not be confused with NASA's Viking.

Fig. 26.30

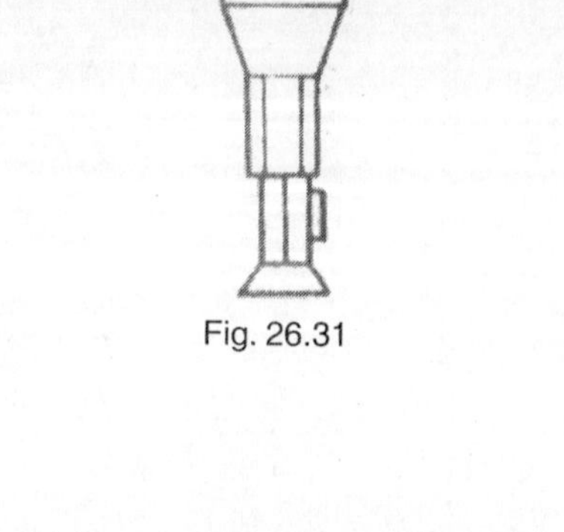

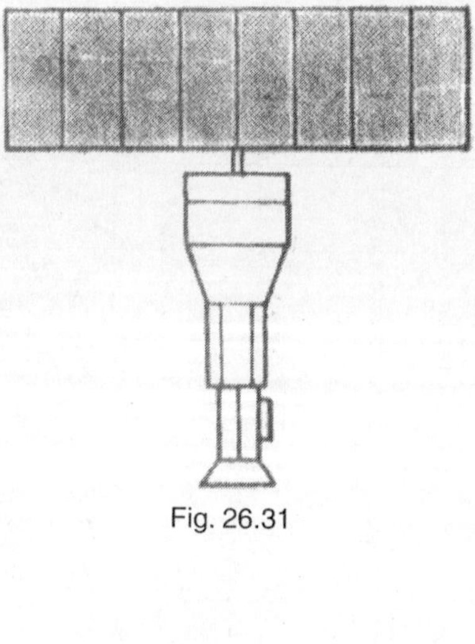

Fig. 26.31

Table 26.4. Science and Technology Satellites (Contd.)

Satellite	*Stabilisation*	*Design Life, yrs*	*Payload*	*Orbit*	*Launch*	*Other Features*
Voyager–1 and Voyager–2	3–Axis	—	Cosmic Ray + Low energy charged particle + Magnetic fields + Infrared + interferometer spectrometer and radiometer + Photo polarimeter +Planetary radio astronomy + plasma wave + Radio science + Two television cameras + Ultraviolet spectrometer	—	1977 Titan (centaurs)	These two probes provided some of the most spectacular discoveries of the century including volcanos on one of Jupiter's moons, several new moons of Jupiter and Saturn and spectacular pictures of planets and their moons. It was owned by NASA and manufactured by NASA's jet propulsion laboratory.

Table 26.5. Military Satellites

Satellite	*Stabilisation*	*Design Life, yrs*	*Payload*	*Orbit*	*Launch*	*Other features*
DMSP/ Block 5D (Fig. 26.31)	3–Axis	1.5	Line scanning radiometer operating in visual and infra red + Precipitating electron spectrometer	Sun–synchr-onous 830 km high inclined at 98.7°	Sep 1976 (DMSP–1) June 1977 (DMSP–2) May 1978 (DMSP–3) June 1979 (DMSP–4) all from Thor Burner (LV–2F)	DMSP–series (Defence Meteorological Satellite Programme) satellites are America's military weather satellites. The operational network typically comprises of two satellites in polar orbit. Data is made available to civilian users through NOAA.
DSCS–II (Fig. 26.32)	Spin	5	S–band transponders at 7/8 GHZ. Total of six channels	Geostationary	Launched in Pairs between Nov. 1971 and Oct. 1982 All abroad Titan–III	DSCS (Defence Satellite Communications system) pronounced as 'Discus' is owned by US department of Defence and manufactured by TRW defence space systems. There are a total of 16 DSCS–II satellites.
DSCS–III	3–Axis	10	S–band and SHF transponders at 7/8 GHZ. Total	Geostationary	first DSCS–III–series satellite launched in Oct 1982 abroad titan 34 d	Owned by US department of defence and manufactured by General Electric, DSCS–III is a replacement series for DSCS–II. The first two DSCS–III were considered Try–before–Buy prototypes.

Fig. 26.32

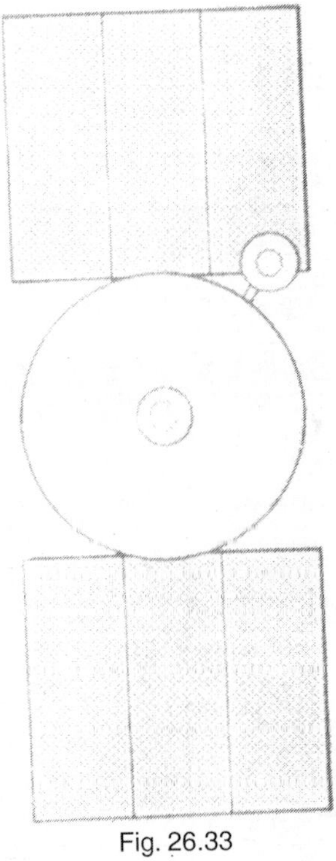

Fig. 26.33

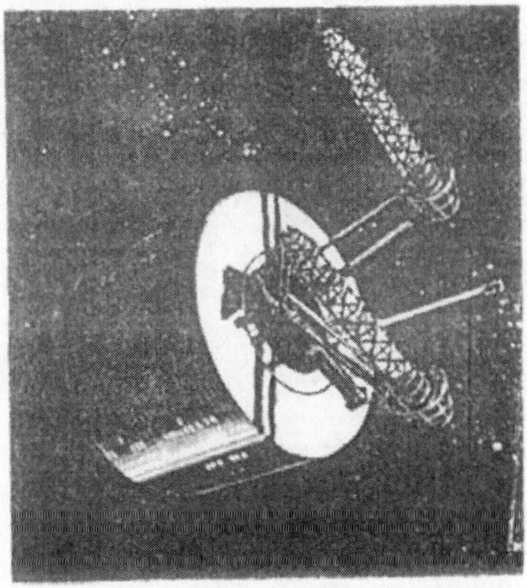

Fig. 26.34

Table 26.5. Military Satellites (Contd.)

Satellite	*Stabilisation*	*Design Life, yrs*	*Payload*	*Orbit*	*Launch*	*Other Features*
Fleetsatcom (Fig. 26.33)	3–Axis	5	23 transponders working at 244–400 MHZ. A fleet broad cast channel and nine relay transponders are dedicated to Navy, 12 narrowband channels to USAF and one wideband channel to USAF and DOD.	Geostationary	Fleetsatcom–1 (Feb 1978), Fleetsatcom–2 (May 1979), Fleetsat com–3 (Jan 1980), Fleetsatcom–4 (Oct–1980), Fleetsatcom–5 (Aug 1981), and Fleet satcom–6 (1985)	Fleetsatcom network owned by US department of defence and manufactured by TRW and Space systems provides global military coverage for the USAF and Navy. It provides UHF links among ships, submarines, Navy aircrafts and some land bases. It also provides a connection between USAF aircrafts and strategic air command centres.
LEASAT (Fig. 26.34)	Spin	7	Total of 13 transponders–six for relay, one wideband, five narrowband and one fleet–broadcast	Near Geostationary. 35740 km circular and incline at 3°	First flight in 1984 (Space shuttle). Subsequent flights at six months intervals.	The operational System comprises four satellites. LEASAT was a new concept in military communications satellites in which the US navy leased a network from the manufacturer. Hughes Aircraft.

Table 26.5. Military Satellites (Contd.)

Satellite	*Stabilisation*	*Design Life, yrs*	*Payload*	*Orbit*	*Launch*	*Other Features*
MILSTAR	—	—	Channels at EHF (a part of radio spectrum that recovers relatively fast from high altitude nuclear blasts.)	Some crafts in geostationary and some in polar orbits	.	MILSTAR is a successor to programmes like fleetsatcom. It provides strategic and tactical communications for USAF, Army and Navy. MILSTAR is highly jam resistant and is designed for high survivability against electronic warfare and physical attack.
NATO–III (Fig. 26.35)	Spin	7	Three transponders in 7/8 GHZ	Geostationary	NATO–III A (April 1976) NATO–III B (Jan. 1977) NATO–III C (Nov. 1978) NATO–III D (Oct. 1983) All abroad DELTA	Owned by NATO and manufactured by Ford aerospace, NATO–III series satellites provide rapid and secure communications among NATO members. The crafts are interoperable with DSCS
NATO–IV (Fig. 26.36)	3–Axis	—	—	Geostationary	—	Contract for building two satellites of NATO–IV series was awarded in 1987. It provides NATO members with secure military and diplomatic communications.

Table 26.5 Military Satellites (Contd.)

Satellite	*Stabilisation*	*Design Life, yrs*	*Payload*	*Orbit*	*Launch*	*Other Features*
NAVSTAR	3–Axis	5 for first 11 crafts and 7.5 for Block 2S	Three or four atomic clocks, Navstar–I to III each had three rubidium clocks. Navstar IV have these plus a caesium unit. Novstar addition (Possive sensors to monitor nuclear blasts	Satellite are distributed around each of three orbits providing global coverage. Each orbit is 20,200 km high, circular and inclined at 63°.	Block–1S (Atlas E/F) Block 2S (Delta- 2) Navstar–I (Feb 1978) Navstar–II (May 1978) Novstar–III (Oct 1978) Novstar–IV (Dec 1978) Navstar–V (Feb 1980), Navstar–VI (April 1980), Navstar–VII (Dec 1981) and Navstar–VIII (May 1983) Navstar–I (Block–2)(Feb 1989)	Navstar is a system for navigation via satellite. Navstar was designed to aid weapon aiming by telling users their position with a higher accuracy than other navigation systems. The USAF initially planned 24 satellites but subsequently their number was reduced to 18. This would provide users with a position accuracy of 15 m anywhere in the world, at least half of the time.
SKYNET IV Fig. 26.37	3–Axis	5	—	Geostationary	Dec 1988 from ariane 4 (Skynet–IVA), 1989 from Titan–III (skynet–IVB) and 1990 from Ariane–4 (Skynet–IV C)	Skynet–IV is Britain's military communication satellite. It provides links among ships, mobile terminals on land and control Centres. It has evolved from OTS/ECS technology.

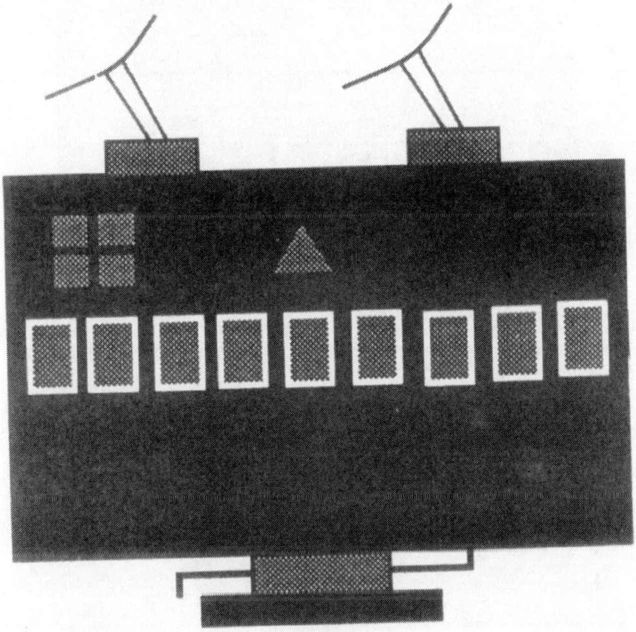

Fig. 26.35

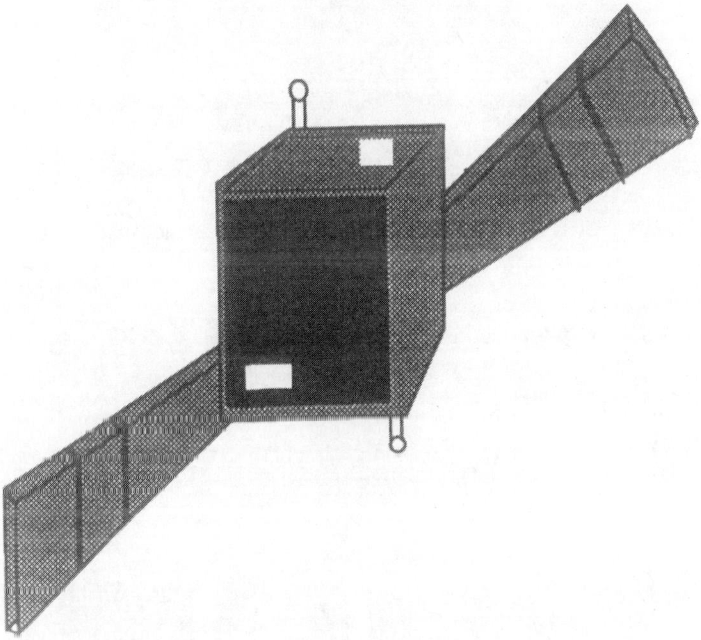

Fig. 26.36

Fig. 26.37

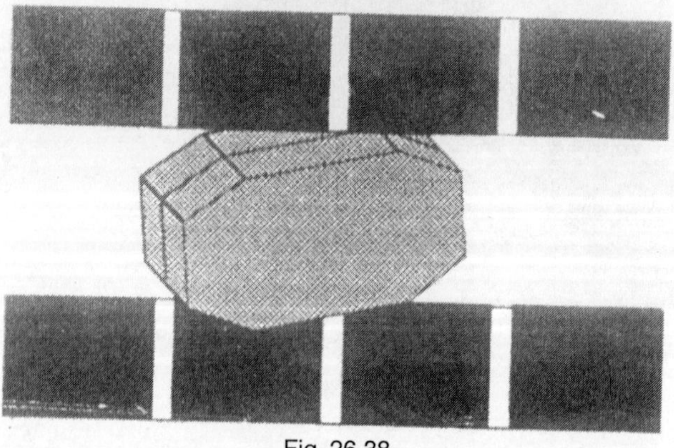

Fig. 26.38

Table 26.5. Military Satellites (Contd.)

Satellite	*Stabilisation*	*Design Life, yrs*	*Payload*	*Orbit*	*Launch*	*Other Features*
NOVA	Gravity Gradient	6	—	Polar, 1075 km high and Circular	May 1981	Nova is an improved version of US Navy's Transition satellite. It features on-board station-seeking and station–seeking which means that fewer updates are needed from ground stations.
TRANSIT / NAVSAT (Fig. 26.38)	Passive via Gravity Gradient	3	Beacons transmitting on 150 and 400 MHz.	Polar 1075 km high, circular)	—	TRANSIT is a series of navigation satellites operated by the US Navy and also used by civilians, particularly sailors. Position accuracy of about 100 m is possible in most of the world and intervals between fixes vary from 1/2 to 2 hrs. depending upon the latitude. It is owned by U.S. Navy (Department of Defence) and manufactured by RCA Astro Electronics

Table 26.6. Satellite Launch Vehicles

Mfr. / Vehicle	Stage	*Engine*	*Propellants*	*Thrust*	*Burn Time*	*Payload Fairing*	*Total Length, m*	*Payload Capability*
American Bocket	Ist	3 × H 1500	LOX + HTPB	2848 kN	75s	4.74 m long	30.78	1452 kg to polar (Note 2)
Company (USA)	2nd	1 × H1500 (Note–1)	LOX+HTPB	1052 kN	71s			—
Aquilla–31	3rd	UTC Orbus 21S	Solid	985 kN	148s			—
	4th	1 × Amroc U–75	N_2O_4 + HTPB	41 kN	85s			—
Ariane Space (Europe)	Ist	4 × SEP Viking 5	UH25 + N_2O_4	2700 kN	209s	short 8.6 m long	54	3290 kg to GTO
Ariane–44P		4 × SNIA–BPD (Note–8)	Solid	2600 kN	42s	Long (Note 5) 9.6m long	55	4100 kg to sun syn (Note–7)
	2nd	1 × SEP Viking 4	UHF + N_2O_4	798 kN	130s	Sylda (Note-9)	55	
	3rd	1 × SEP HM 7 B (Note–4)	LOX + LH	62 kN	750s	Short SPELDA (Note-10) ASAP (Note-7)	57	

Table 26.6. Satellite Launch Vehicles (Contd.)

Mfr./Vehicle	*Stage*	*Engine*	*Propellants*	*Thrust*	*Burn Time*	*Payload Fairing*	*Total Length, m*	*Payload Capability*
Ariane Space (Europe)	Ist	4 × SEP Viking 5	UH25 + N_2O_4	2700 kN	200s	Short 8.6m Long (Note–5)	54	2740 kg to GTO
Ariane–42 P		2 × SNIA–BDP (Note-8)	Solid	1300 kN	42s	Long (Note–5) 9.6m long	55	2740 kg to GTO
	2nd	1 × SEP Viking 4	UH25 + N_2O_4	798 kN	130s	Sylda (Note–9)	—	—
	3rd	1 × SDEP HM 7 B	LH + LOX	62 kN	750s	ASAP (Note–7)	—	—
Ariane Space (Europe)	Ist	4 × SEP Viking 5	UH25 + N_2O_4	2700 kN	154s	Short 8.6m long	54	2020 kg to GTO (Note–7)
Ariane 40P	2nd	1 × SEP Viking 4	UH25 + N_2O_4	798 kN	130s	Long (Note–5)	55	2700 kg to Sun syn. (Note–7)
	3rd	1 × SEP HM 7 B (Note–4)	LH + LOX	62 kN	750s	9.6 m long ASAP (Note–7)		
Ariane space (EUROPE)	Ist	4 × SEP Viking 5	UH25 + N_2O_4	2700 kN	205s	Short 8.6m long	54	3320 kg to GTO
Ariane–42 L		2 × SEP Viking (Note–8)	UH25 + N_2O_2	1500 kN	132s	Long 9.6 m (Note–5)	55	4500 kg to Sun Sync.

Table 26.6. Satellite Launch Vehicles (Contd.)

Mfr. / Vehicle	*Stage*	*Engine*	*Propellants*	*Thrust*	*Burn Time*	*Payload Fairing*	*Total Length, m*	*Payload Capability*
	2nd	1 × SEP HM 7 B	UH25 + $N_2 O_4$	798 kN	130s	SDS (Notes 9, 10)	55	—
	3rd	1 × SEP HM 7B (Note–4)	LH + LOX	62 kN	750s	—	—	—
Ariane space (EUROPE) Ariane 44 LP (Fig. 26.39)	Ist	4 × SEP Viking 5	UH25 + $N_2 O_4$	2700 kN	205s	Short 8.6 m long	54	4030 kg to GTO
		2 × SEP Viking 6 (Note–8)	UH25 + $N_2 O_4$	1500 kN	143s	Long 9.6m (Note–5)	55	5300 kg to Sun sync.
		2 × SNIA–BPD (Note–8)	Solid	1300 kN	42s	Short SPELDA (Note–10, 11)	57	—
	2nd	1 × SEP Viking 4	UH25 + $N_2 O_4$	798 kN	130s	Long SPELDA (Note–12)	58	—
	3rd	1 × SEP HM 7 B (Note–4)	LH + LOX	62 kN	750s	SDS (Notes 9, 13)	55	—

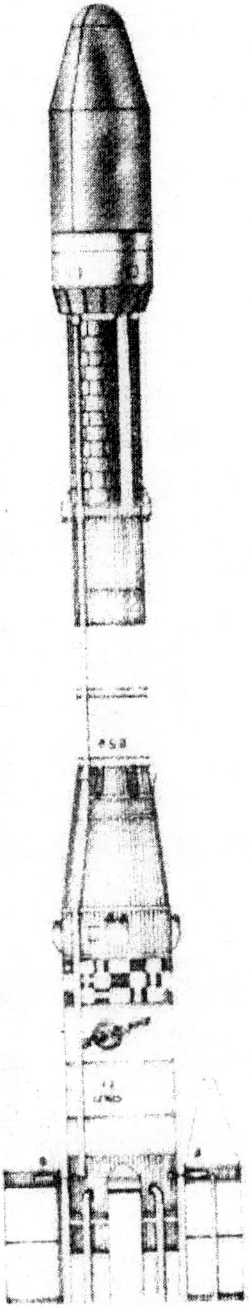

Fig. 26.39

Fig. 26.39

Fig. 26.40

Fig. 26.40

Table 26.6. Satellite Launch Vehicles (Contd.)

Mfr. / Vehicle	*Stage*	*Engine*	*Propellants*	*Thrust*	*Burn Time*	*Payload Fairing*	*Total Length, m*	*Payload Capability*
Ariane space (Europe) Arine 44 L	Ist	4 × SEP Viking 6 (Note-8)	UH25 + $N_2 O_4$	3000 kN	143s	Short 8.6m long	54	4460 kg to GTO
		4 × SEP Viking 5 (Note-8)	UH25 + $N_2 O_4$	2700 kN	209s	Long 9.6m Long (Note-5)	55	6150 kg to Sun Sync.
	2nd	1 × SEP Viking 4	UH25 + $N_2 O_4$	798 kN	130s	Short SPELDA (Notes-10, 11	57	—
	3rd	1 × SEP HM 7B (Note-4)	LH + LOX	62 kN	750s	SDS (Notes-9,10)	55	—
Common-wealth of Inde-pendent States (CIS) Proton SL-12 (Fig. 26.40)	Ist	6 × RD 253 (Note-14)	$N_2 O_4$ + UDMH	9438 kN	130s	7.6 m long	57.2	4600 kg to GTO (Note-16) and 2400 kg to GEO (Note-18)
	2nd	4 × RD-0210	$N_2 O_4$ + UDMH	2360 kN	300s			
	3rd	1 × RD 0210 + Verniers	$N_2 O_4$ + UDMH	620 kN	250s	—	—	—

Table 26.6. Satellite Launch Vehicles (Contd.)

Mfr. / Vehicle	*Stage*	*Engine*	*Propellants*	*Thrust*	*Burn Time*	*Payload Fairing*	*Total Length, m*	*Payload Capability*
	4th	Block DM (Note–15)	LOX + KERO	85 kN	600s			
Common wealth of Independent States (CIS) Proton SL–13	Ist	6 × RD – 253 (Note–14)	N_2O_4 + UDMH	9438 kN	130s	7.6 m long	51.7 (Note 17)	
	2nd	4 × RD – 0110	N_2O_4 + UDMH	2360 kN	300s			21000 kg to LEO (Note–18)
	3rd	1 × RD – 0210 + Verniers	N_2O_4 + UDMH	620 kN	250	—	—	
Common wealth of Independent States (CIS), Vostok SL–3 (Fig. 26.41)	Ist	1 × RD – 108 (Note–19)	LOX + KERO	745 kN	310s	7.7 m long	38.4	4730 kg to LEO 1840 kg to 650 km Sun Sync.
		4 × RD – 107 (Note–20)	LOX + KERO	3284 kN	120s	–	—	—
	2nd	1 × RD – 448 (Note–21)	LOX + KERO	298 kN	440s	–	—	1150 kg to 920 km Sun synchronous
Common-wealth of Independent States	Ist	1 × RD – 108 (Note–18)	LOX + KERO	745 kN	310s	10.14 m long	45.22	7500 kg to LEO

Table 26.6. Satellite Launch Vehicles (Contd.)

Mfr. / Vehicle	*Stage*	*Engine*	*Propellants*	*Thrust*	*Burn Time*	Payload Fairing	*Total Lenght, m*	*Payload Capability*
(CIS) Soyuz SL–4 (Fig. 26.42)		4 × RD – 107 (Note–19)	LOX + KERO	3284 kN	120s	Soyuz TM escape	49.52	
	2nd	1 × RD – 0110	LOX + KERO	298 kN	245s	Tower	–	
Common-wealth of Independent States (CIS)	Ist	1 × RD – 108 (Note–19)	LOX + KERO	745 kN	310s	–	45.2	1600 kg to 400 km × 40000 km orbit Molniya
Molniya SL–6		4 × RD – 107 (Note–20)	LOX + KERO	3284 kN	120s	–		
	2nd	1 × RD – 0110	LOX + KERO	298 kN	230s	–		900 kg to 400 km × 200,000 km orbit
	3rd	1 × Cl – 5400	LOX + KERO	67 kN	200s	–		
Common-wealth of Independent States (CIS) Cosmos SL–8	Ist	2 × RD – 216	N_2O_4 + UDMH	1470 kN	170s	–	32	1700kg to 180 Km LEO, 100 kg to 800 km × 1500 km orbit
(Fig. 26.43)	2nd	1 × (with Verniers)	N_2O_4 + UDMH	157 kN	375s	–	–	

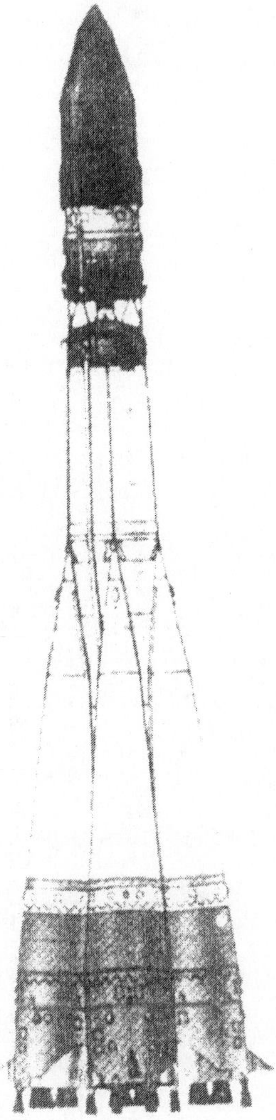

Fig. 26.41

Fig. 26.42

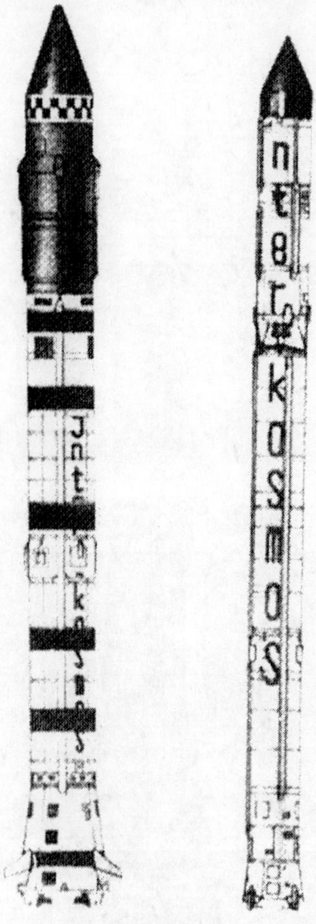

Fig. 26.43

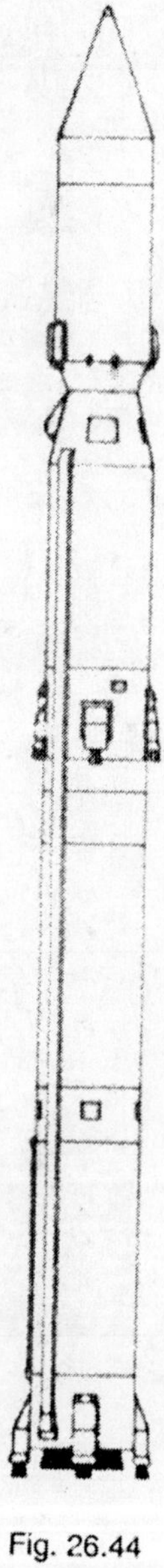

Fig. 26.44

Table 26.6. Satellite Launch Vehicles (Contd.)

Mfr./Vehicle	*Stage*	*Engine*	*Propellants*	*Thrust*	*Burn Time*	*Payload Fairing*	*Total Length, m*	*Payload Capability*
Common-wealth of Inde-pendent States (CIS)	Ist	1 × + 4 Verniers	N_2O_4 + UDMH	2747 kN	120s	11.3 m long	39.27	5500 kg to 65° LEO
Tsyklon SL–14 (Fig. 26.44)	2nd	1 × + 4 Verniers	N_2O_4 + UDMH	1012 kN	160s			
	3rd	1	N_2O_4 + UDMH	78 kN	118s			
Common-wealth of Inde-pendent States (CIS)	Ist	1 × + 4 Verniers	N_2O_4 + UDMH	2747 kN	120s	–	–	3000 kg to 65° LEO
Tsyklon SL–11	2nd	RD–219	HNO_3 + UDMH	883 kN	125s			
Common-wealth of Inde-pendent States (CIS)	Ist	1 × RD – 171	LOX + KERO	7259 kN	144s	13.65 m long	61.4	13740 kg to LEO
Zenit SL–16	2nd	1 × RD – 120 Verniers	LOX + KERO	912 kN	300s	11.15 m long	57	11380 kg to Sun synchronous

Table 26.6. Satellite Launch Vehicles (Contd.)

Mfr. / Vehicle	*Stage*	*Engine*	*Propellants*	*Thrust*	*Burn Time*	*Payload Fairing*	*Total Length, m*	*Payload Capability*
Common-wealth of Independent States (CIS), Energia SL–17	Ist	4 × RD – 0120 (Note–19)	LH + LOX	5804 kN	450s	42 m long (Note–22)	58.7	105,000 kg to LEO
		4 × RD – 170 (Note–20)	LOX + KERO	29028 kN	140s		58.7	85000 kg to sun sync.
	2nd	1 (Note–22)	LOX + KERO	85 kN		Buran (Note 23)–	58.7	
E Prime Aerospace (USA), Eagle S–2	Ist	1 × Thiokol ESM 9 (Note –28)	Solid	2234 kN	56s	8.99 m long	32.91	4535 kg to LEO
	2nd	1 × Thiokol ESM 9	Solid	2234 kN	56s			4989 kg to LEO (Note–26)
	3rd	1 × Thiokol ESM 3	Solid	383 kN	140s			4151 kg to GEO (Note 25 and 27)

Table 19.6. Satellite Launch Vehicles (Contd.)

Mfr./Vehicle	*Stage*	*Engine*	*Propellants*	*Thrust*	*Burn Time*	*Payload Fairing*	*Total Length, m*	*Payload Capability*
EER Systems / Space Services	Ist (Notes–29–31)	2 × Thiokol Castor 4 A	Solid	884 kN	54s	7.01 m long	15.82	816 kg to 480 km LEO (Note-32)
Inc. (U.S.A.) Conestoga 1620 (Note–28)		2 × Thiokol Castor 4B (Note–29)	Solid	735 kN	64s		—	
	2nd (Notes –29, 30)	2 × Thiokol Castor 4B	Solid	735 kN	64s	7.01 m long	15.82	
		1 × Thiokol Castor 4B	Solid	368 kN	64s	—	—	—
	3rd	1 × Thiokol Castor 4B	Solid	368 kN	64s	—	—	—
	4th	1 × Thiokol Star 48 V	Solid	70 kN	85s	—		—
European space Agency (ESA)	Ist	1 × SEP HM60 Vulcain	LH + LOX	1120 kN	590s	Short 12.7 m long	45.7	6900 kg to GTO (Single)

Table 26.6. Satellite Launch Vehicles (Contd.)

Mfr. / Vehicle	*Stage*	*Engine*	*Propellants*	*Thrust*	*Burn Time*	*Payload Fairing*	*Total Length, m*	*Payload Capability*
Ariane–5 (Fig. 26.45)		2 × BPD/SNPE (Note–33)	Solid	11800 kN	123s	Long 19.2 m long	51.4	5950 kg to GTO (Dual)
	2nd	1 × MBB L9 (Note 34,35)	N_2O_4 + MMH	28 kN	1150s	Short, SPELTRA (Note–36)	55.9	5115 kg to GTO (Triple) (Note–37)
						Long SPELTRA (Note–36)	52.2	1800 kg to 550 km 28°
						SPILMA (Note–37)	52.2	10000 kg to 800 km Sun Sync.
						HERMES (Note–39)	51.3	22600 kg to LEO Hermes (Note–38)
General Dynamics Commercial Launch	Ist	1 × Rocketdyne MA–5 (Note–39)	LOX + RP–1	195 kN	—	Medium 10.36 m long	42m	5900 kg to 85 km 28° LEO (Note–41)

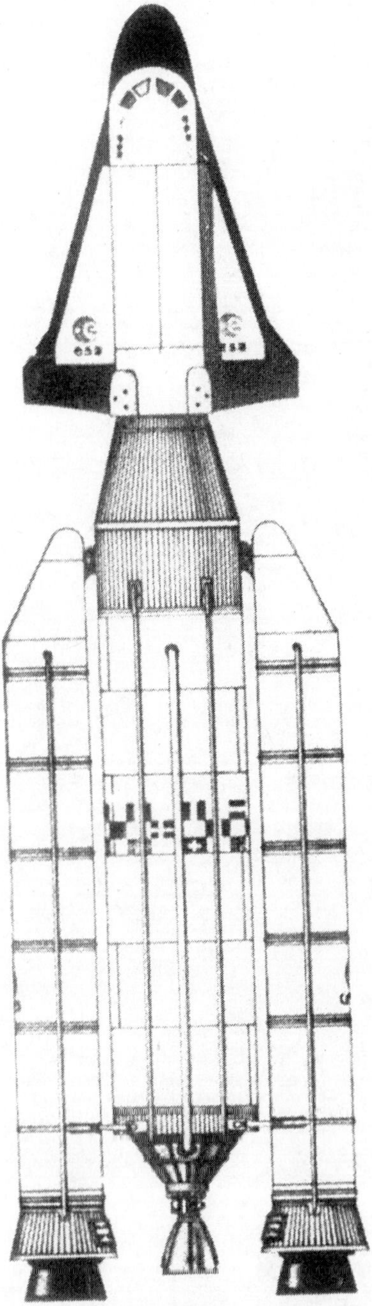

Fig. 26.45

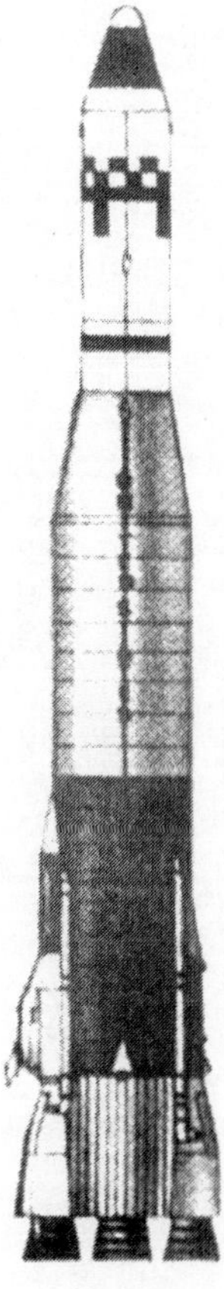

Fig. 26.46

Table 26.6. Satellite Launch Vehicles (Contd.)

Mfr. / Vehicle	*Stage*	*Engine*	*Propellants*	*Thrust*	*Burn Time*	*Payload Fairing*	*Total Length, m*	*Payload Capability*
Services (U.S.A.) Atlas–1		1 Sustainer			288s	–	–	2340 kg to GTO (Note-41)
		2 Booster Engines			169s	Long 12.22 m long	43.9	
	2nd	2 × P & W RL10 A–3–3A (Note–40)	LH/LOX	147 kN	473s	–	–	2250 kg to GTO (Notes 42,48)
General Dynamics Commercial Launch Services	Ist	Rocketdyne MA–5 (Note–39)	LOX + RP-1	2109 kN	–	Medium 10.36 m (Note 44)	45.6	6780 kg to 185 km 28° LEO (Note–41)
(U.S.A.) Atlas–2/MLV–2 (Note–43) (Fig. 26.46)		2 Booster Engines			169s	Long		28° LEO (Note–41)
		1–Sustainer			277s	Long 12.22 m long	47.6	6580 kg to 185 km 28° LEO (Note-42)

Table 26.6. Satellite Launch Vehicles (Contd.)

Mfr. / Vehicle	*Stage*	*Engine*	*Propellants*	*Thrust*	*Burn Time*	*Payload Fairing*	*Total Length, m*	*Payload Capability*
	2nd	2 × P & W RL 10A – 3 – 3–A (Note–40)	LH + LOX	147 kN	473s			2770 kg to GTO (Note–41)
								2580 kg to GTO (Note 42, 46)
General Dynamics Commercial	Ist	1 × Rocketdyne MS–5A	LOX+RP–1	2109 kN		Medium 10.36m long	45.6	7120 kg to 185 km
Launch Services		2 booster engines			169s	Long	47.6	28° LEO (Note–41)
(U.S.A.) Atlas 2A		1 Sustainer			277s	Long 12.22m		6920 kg to 185 km. 28E° (Note–42)
	2nd	2 × P & W RL – 10 – 4 (Note–40, 47)	LH + LOX	185 kN	473s			2900 kg to GTO (Note–41)
								2810 kg to GTO (Note–42)

Table 26.6. Satellite Launch Vehicles (Contd.)

Mfr. / Vehicle	*Stage*	*Engine*	*Propellants*	*Thrust*	*Burn Time*	*Payload Fairing*	*Total Length, m*	*Payload Capability*
General Dynamics Commercial Launch Services (U.S.A) Atlas 2 AS	Ist	1 × Rocket dyne MA–5A	LOX + RP–1	2109 kN				
		2 booster engines			169s	Medium 10.3 m long	45.6	8600 kg to 185 km 28° LEO (Note–42)
		1 Sustainer			277s	Long 12.22 m long	47.6	3630 kg to GTO (Note–41)
		4 × Thiokol Castor 4A	Solid	173 kN	56s			
	2nd	2 × P&W RL–10–4 (Note 40, 46)	LH + LOX	185 kN	473S			3490 kg to GTO (Note–42)
General Dynamics/US Air-force Atlas E/SVS (Note–49)		1 × Rocketdyne MA–3 (Note–50)	LOX + RP–1	1950 kN		7.62 m long	28	1814 kg to Sun Sync with Block–1 SVS

Table 26.6. Satellite Launch Vehicles (Contd.)

Mfr. / Vehicle	*Stage*	*Engine*	*Propellants*	*Thrust*	*Burn Time*	*Payload Fairing*	*Total Length, m*	*Payload Capability*
		2 boosters			172s			2041 kg to Sun Sync. with Block-2 SVS
		1 Sustainer			288s			
	2nd	Block 1 or 2 stage vehicles solid system (SVS)	Solid					750 kg to 900 km Sun Sync.
Greatwall Industry Corporation (China) Long March 2 CZ–2	Ist	4 × YF – 20	N_2O_4 + UDMH	2785 kN	132s	Medium 7.12m long	35.1	1200 kg to 200 km × 900 km
								2200 kg to 400 km × 185 km

Table 26.6. Satellite Launch Vehicles (Contd.)

Mfr. / Vehicle	*Stage*	*Engine*	*Propellants*	*Thrust*	*Burn Time*	*Payload Fairing*	*Total Length, m*	*Payload Capability*
	2nd	1 × YF–22 + Verniers	N_2O_4 + UDMH	762 kN	110s	Long 8.7 m long	38.4	1000 kg to GTO (Note–51)
								Piggiback Payloads LEO
Greatwall Industry Corporation (China) Long March 2E, CZ–2E	Ist	4 × YF – 20 (Note–59)	N_2O_4 + UDMH	2942 kN	158s	Medium 7.12 m long	35.1	9200 kg to 200 km 28° LEO (Note–53)
(Fig. 26.47)		4 × YF – 20 (Note-52)	N_2O_4 + UDMH	2942 kN	125s	Long 8.7 m long	38.4	7200 kg to 400 km 28° LEO (Note 53)
	2nd	1 × YF– 25/23	N_2O_4 + UDMH	832 kN	300s			2494 kg to GTO (Notes–54, 55)
								3370 kg to GTO (Notes–54, 56)

Table 26.6. Satellite Launch Vehicles (Contd.)

Mfr. /Vehicle	*Stage*	*Engine*	*Propellants*	*Thrust*	*Burn Time*	*Payload Fairing*	*Total Length, m*	*Payload Capability*
								4500 kg to GTO (Notes–54, 57)
Greatwall Industry Corporation (China)	Ist	4 ×– YF 20 (Notes–59)	N_2O_4 + UDMH	2942 kN	160s	2.9m long	41.89	4000 kg to LEO
Long March 3 A, CZ–3A (Fig. 26.48)	2nd	1 × YF–25	N_2O_4 + UDMH	766 kN	110s	8.4 m long	47.39	1000 kg to 1000 km orbit
	3rd	2 × YF–75 (Note–58)	N_2O_4 + UDMH	98 kN	410s	—		1500 kg to Sun Sync.
Greatwall Industry Corporation Long	Ist	4 × YF – 20 (Note–59)	N_2O_4 + UDMH	2942 kN	160s	2.9 m long	41.89	4000 kg to LEO
March, 4, CZ–4 (Fig. 26.49)	2nd	1 × YF – 25	N_2O_4 + UDMH	766 kN	110s	8.4 m long	47.39	1000 kg to 1000 km orbit
	3rd	2 × YF – 40 (Note-58)	N_2O_4 + UDMH	98 kN	410s			1500 kg to Sun Sync
Indian Space Research ISRO)	Ist	1 (Note–60)	Solid	503 kN	46s	—	23.5	150 kg to 400 km 45° Orbit

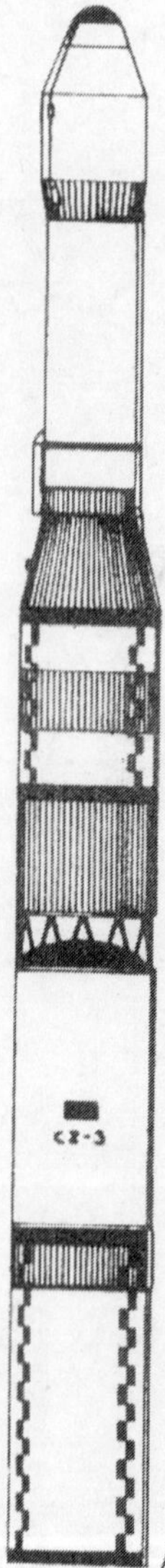

Fig. 26.47

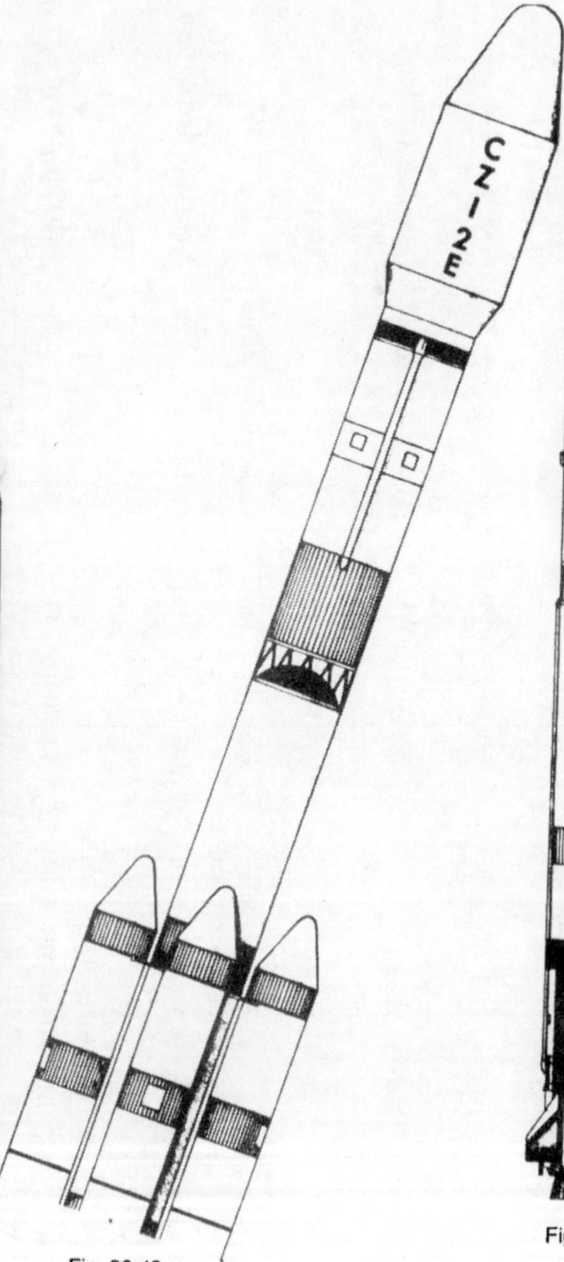

Fig. 26.48

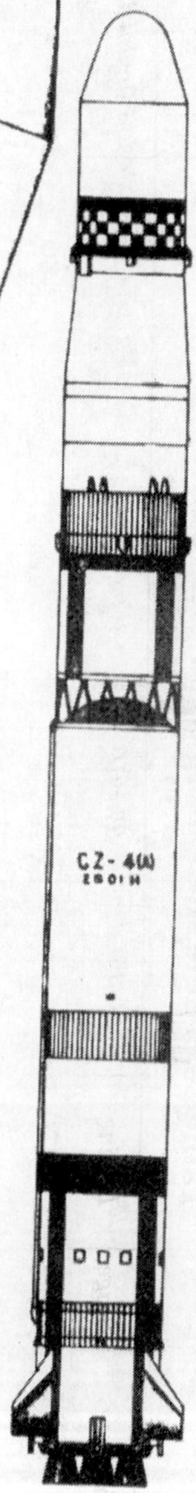

Fig. 26.49

Table 26.6. Satellite Launch Vehicles (Contd.)

Mfr./Vehicle	*Stage*	*Engine*	*Propellants*	*Thrust*	*Burn Time*	*Payload Fairing*	*Total Length, m*	*Payload Capability*
(INDIA) Augmented Satellite Launch Vehicle (ASLV)		2 (Note–61)	Solid	880 kN	50s	—		
	2nd	1	Solid	218 kN	36s	—		
(Fig. 26.50)	3rd	1	Solid	64 kN	44s	—		
	4th	1	Solid	26 kN	32s	—		
Indian Space Research Organisation ISRO	Ist	1	Solid	4600 kN	94s	8.3 m long	44.2	1000 kg to 904 km Sun Sync.
(INDIA) Polar Satellite Launch Vehicle (PSLV)		6 (Notes 61, 62)	Solid	2460 kN	54s			
	2nd	1 × Vikas	N_2O_4 + UDMH	735 kN	150s			3000 kg to LEO
(Fig. 26.51)	3rd	1	Solid	386 kN	74s			450 kg GTO
	4th	2	N_2O_4 + UDMH	14 kN	425s			
Institute of Space and Astronautical Sciences, ISAS (Japan) MS3 II	Ist	1 × Nissan	Solid	1275 kN	94s	6.86 m long	27.78	770 kg to 250 km LEO

Fig. 26.50

Fig. 26.51

Fig. 26.52.

Table 26.6. Satellite Launch Vehicles (Contd.)

Mfr./Vehicle	*Stage*	*Engine*	*Propellants*	*Thrust*	*Burn Time*	*Payload Fairing*	*Total Length, m*	*Payload Capability*
		2 × Nissan (Note–63)	Solid	327 kN	54s			460 kg to 500 km LEO
	2nd	1 × Nissan	Solid	524 kN	73s			
	3rd	1 × Nissan	Solid	132 kN	87s			
	4th	1 × Nissan	Solid	32 kN	44s			
Indian Space Research Organisation ISRO (INDIA)	—							
Geosynchronous Satellite launch Vehicles (GSLV)	Under Development : Five Launches Planned –1995–96 (First), 1996–97 (Second), 1997–98 (Third), 1999–2000 (Fourth and Fifth)							2500 kg to GTO
Institute of Space and Astronautical Sciences, ISAS (Japan) M5	1st	1 × M14	Solid	43000 kN	45s	5 m long (approx)	31.2	2000 kg to LEO
	2nd	1 × M24	Solid	1400 kN	63s			
	3rd	1 × M34	Solid	300 kN	101s			

Table 26.6. Satellite Launch Vehicles (Contd.)

Mfr. / Vehicle	*Stage*	*Engine*	*Propellants*	*Thrust*	*Burn Time*	*Payload Fairing*	*Total Length, m*	*Payload Capability*
Institute de Actividades Espaciais (Brazil) Veiculo Lancador de Satellites (VLS)	Ist	1 × S43 TM	Solid	303 kN	62s	1.18 m long	18.8	115 kg to 750 km
		4 × S43 (Note 64)	Solid	1172 kN	62s			160 kg to 650 km (Note–65)
	2nd	1 × S40 TM	Solid	191 kN	58s			
	3rd	1 × S44	Solid	31 kN	73s			
International Microspace (U.S.A.) Orbital Express	Ist	Thiokol Castor 4B	Solid	359 kN	64s	2.15m	21.33	180 kg LEO
	2nd	Thiokol Castor 1	Solid	240 kN	40s			
	3rd	Bristol Aerospace Nihka	Solid	51 kN	18s			
	4th	Thiokol Star 20	Solid	27 kN	30s			
International Microspace (U.S.A.)	Ist	5 × SS–1 Scud	Liquid	696 kN	–		24.4	150 kg to LEO
IRAQ (Tamouz)	2nd	1 × SS–1 Scud	Liquid	137 kN	–	–		

Table 26.6. Satellite Launch Vehicles (Contd.)

Mfr. / Vehicle	*Stage*	*Engine*	*Propellants*	*Thrust*	*Burn Time*	*Payload Fairing*	*Total length, m*	*Payload Capability*
Martin Marietta Space launch systems (U.S.A.) Titan 2G (Note–67)	Ist	2 × Aerojet LR–87–AJ 5	N_2O_4 + A 50	1913 kN	170s		37.5	2180 kg to 185 km polar
	2nd	1 × Aerojet LR9–AJ5	N_2O_4 + A 50	445 kN	183s			3082 kg 560 km Sun Sync (Note–68)
Martin Marietta Space launch Systems (U.S.A.) Titan 4 (NUS)	Ist	2 × Aerojet – LR–87–AJ 5	N_2O_4 + A 50	2434 kN	186s	17.06 m long	53.99	17770 kg LEO
		2 UTC SRM (Note–68)	Solid	14234 kN	127s			
	2nd	2 Aerojet–LR91 AJ–11A	N_2O_4 + A 50	467 kN	240s			
Martin Marietta Space Launch Systems (U.S.A.) Titan 4–(IUS)	Ist	2 Aerojet LR87–AJ 11–A	N_2O_4 + A 50	2434 kN	186s	17.06 long	53.99	2364 kg to GEO
		2 UTC SRM (Note–68)	Solid	14234 kN	127s			
	2nd	2 Aerriet–LR91 AJ–11A	N_2O_4 + A 50	467 kN	240s			

Table 26.6. Satellite Launch Vehicles (Contd.)

Mfr. / Vehicle	*Stage*	*Engine*	*Propellants*	*Thrust*	*Burn Time*	*Payload Fairing*	*Total Length, m*	*Payload Capability*
	3rd	1 × Boeing IUS Ist 2nd	solid	203 kN	152s			
		2nd	solid	82 kN	289s			
		–						
Martin Marietta Space Launch System (U.S.A.) Titan 4–Centaurs	Ist (Note–69)	2 × Aerojet LR 87 AJ–11A	N_2O_4 + A 50	2434 kN	186s	26.23 m long	63.14	4545 kg to GEO
	2nd	2 × Aerojet L R91 AJ-11A	N_2O_4 + A 50	467 kN	240s			
	3rd	2 × P & W RL–103–3–A (Note–71)	LH + LOX	147 kN	617s			
Martin Marietta Space Launch Systems (U.S.A.) Titan 4-IUS (SRMU) (Note–72)	Ist (Note–69)	2 × Aerojet LR87 AJ–11A	N_2O_4 + A 50	2434 kN	186s	17.06 m long	53.99	21900 kg to GEO
		2 × Hercules SRMU (Note–70)	Solid	15124 kN	145s			
	2nd	2 × Aerijet LR91 AJ–11A	N_2O_4 + A 50	467 kN	240s			

Table 26.6. Satellite Launch Vehicles (Contd.)

Mfr./Vehicle	*Stage*	*Engine*	*Propellants*	*Thrust*	*Burn Time*	*Payload Fairing*	*Total Length, m*	*Payload Capability*
	3rd		Liquid	—	—	—		
International Microspace	Ist	1	Solid	—	—	—	13 (Note–66)	150 kg to 250 km by 1150 km orbit
(U.S.A.) ISRAEL (Shavil)	2nd	1	Solid	—				
	3rd	1	Solid					
International Microspace	Ist	1 × UTC Algol 3A	Solid	465 kN	62s			
(U.S.A.) LTV USA	2nd	1 × Thiokol Castor 2A	Solid	268 kN	38s	—	22.9	205 kg to 555 km
(Scout G–1) (Fig. 26.52)	3rd	1 × Thiokol Antares 3A	Solid	81 kN	45s			37° orbit (Note-66)
	4th	1 × Thiokol Altair 3A	Solid	26 kN	29s			165 kg to 555 km Sun Sync (Note–67)
								220 kg to 555 km equatorial orbit (Note–68)

Table 26.6. Satellite Launch Vehicles (Contd.)

Mfr. / Vehicle	*Stage*	*Engine*	*Propellants*	*Thrust*	*Burn Time*	*Payload Fairing*	*Total Length, m*	*Payload Capability*
	3rd	1 × Being IUS Ist	Solid	203 kN	152s			
	2nd		Solid	82 kN	289s			
Martin Marietta Space Launch Systems (U.S.A.) Titan 4–NUS (SRMU) (Note–72)	Ist (Note–69)	2 × Aerojet LR 87 AJ–11A	N_2O_4 + A 50	2434 kN	186s	26.3 m long	63.14	5773 kg to GTO
		2 × Hercules SRMU (Note–70)	Solid	15124 kN	145s			
	2nd	2 × Aerojet LR91 AJ–11A	N_2O_4 + A 50	467 kN	240s			
Martin Marietta Commercial Titan (U.S.A.) Commercial Titan	Ist (Note-69)	2 × Aerojet LR 87–AJ–11	N_2O_4 + A 50	2438 kN	160s	10.4 m long	44.06	14742 kg to LEO
		2 × UTC (Note–70)	Solid	12454 kN	114s			1279 kg to GTO (Note–73)
	2nd	2 × Aerojet LR 91 AJ–11 A	N_2O_4 + A 50	467 kN	225s			4944 kg to GTO (Note–74)

Table 26.6. Satellite Launch Vehicles (Contd.)

Mfr./Vehicle	*Stage*	*Engine*	*Propellants*	*Thrust*	*Burn Time*	*Payload Fairing*	*Total Length, m*	*Payload Capability*
								49990 kg to GTO (Note–75)
Martin Marietta Space Launch Systems (U.S.A.) Titan 4–Centaru SRMU (Note–72)	Ist (Note–72)	2 × Aerojet LR87 AJ–11A	N_2O_4 + A 50	2434 kN	186s	2.6.3 m long	63.14	5773 kg to GTO
		2 × Hercules SRMU (Note–69)	Solid	15124 kN	145s			
	2nd	2 × Aerojet LR91 AJ–11A	N_2O_4 + A 50	467 kN	240s			
	3rd	2 × P&W RL–10–3–3–A	LH + LOX	147 kN	617s			
Mcdonnel Douglas U.S.A. Interim Delta–26920	Ist (Note–77)	1 × Rocketdyne RS–27	LOX + RP–1	920 kN	267s	8.5 m long	37.8	3983 kg to 185 km
	(Note–78)	9 × Thiokol Castor–A4	Solid	3829 kN	56s	9.7 m long	39	28° LEO (Note–80)

Table 26.6. Satellite Launch Vehicles (Contd.)

Mfr. / Vehicle	*Stage*	*Engine*	*Propellants*	*Thrust*	*Burn Time*	*Payload Fairing*	*Total Length, m*	*Payload Capability*
	2nd	1× Aerojet AJ–10/118 K (Note–79)	N_2O_4 + A 50	43 kN	440s			2413 kg to 833 km Sun Sync (Note–81)
Mcdonnel Douglas U.S.A. Interim Delta–26925	Ist (Note–77)	1 × Rocketdyne RS–27	LOX + RP – 1	920 kN	265s	8.5 m long	37.8	1447 kg to GTO (Note-80)
	Note–78	9 × Thiokol Castor–A4	Solid	3829 kN	56s	9.7 m long	39	
	2nd	1 × Aerojet AJ10–118 K (Note–79)	N_2O_4 + A 50	43 kN	440s			
	3rd	1 × MDC PAMD/Star 48 B	Solid	67 kN	88s			839 kg to GPS (Note–80)
Mcdonnel Douglas (U.S.A) Delta 2,7920	Ist	1 × Rocketdyne RS–27 (Note–82)	LOX + RP-1	894 kN	267s	8.5 m long	37.8	5039 kg to LEO (Note–80)

Table 26.6. Satellite Launch Vehicles (Contd.)

Mfr. / Vehicle	*Stage*	*Engine*	*Propellants*	*Thrust*	*Burn Time*	*Payload Fairing*	*Total Length, m*	*Payload Capability*
		9 × Hercules GEM (Note–78)	Solid	3957 kN	56s	9.7 m long	39	839 kg to GPS (Note–80)
	2nd	1 × Aerojet AJ10–118K (Note–79)	N_2O_4 + A 50	43 kN	440s			
Mcdonnel Douglas U.S.A. Delta–2,7925	Ist	1 × Rocketdyne RS–27 (Note–82)	LOX + RP–1	895 kN	265s	8.5 m long	37.8	1819 kg GTO (Note–80)
		9 × Hercules GEM (Note–78)	Solid	3957 kN	64s	9.7 m long	39	1134 kg to GPS (Note–80)
	2nd	1 × Aerojet Aj–10–118k (Note–79)	N_2O_4 + A 50	43 kN	413s			
	3rd	1 × MCDPAMD Star 48B	Solid	67 kN	88s			

Table 26.6. Satellite Launch Vehicles (Contd.)

Mfr. / Vehicle	*Stage*	*Engine*	*Propellants*	*Thrust*	*Burn Time*	*Payload Fairing*	*Total Length, m*	*Payload Capability*
NASDA / ISAS (Japan) J1	Ist	1 × Nissan (Note–83)	Solid	1569 kN	95s	3.85 m long	32.9	1000 kg to LEO
	2nd	1 × Nissan M 23 (Note–84)	Solid	524 kN	73s			200 kg to GTO
	3rd	1 × Nissan M 3B (Note–84)	Solid	132 kN	87s			
NASA (U.S.A.)	Ist	3 × Rocket dyne SSME (Note–86)	LH + LOX (Note–87)	5262 kN	520s	18.28 m long (Note–90)	56.14	24990 kg to 28° LEO
Space Shuttle Orbiters :		2 × Thiokol SRM	PATP (Note–88)	39360 kN	120s		37.24 (Note–91)	
Columbia, Atlantis, Discovery, Endeavour (Fig. 26.53)	2nd	3 × OMS Aerojet (Note–86)	N_2O_4 + UDMH	80 kN	15h			18600 kg to 57° LEO
NASA (U.S.A.) Space Shuttle ARSM (Note–92)	Ist	2 Rocket dyne SSME (Note–93)	LH + LOX (Note–87)	5262 kN	5D20s	18.28 m long (Note–90)	56.14	29483 kg to 28° LEO

Table 26.6. Satellite Launch Vehicles (Contd.)

Mfr. / Vehicle	*Stage*	*Engine*	*Propellants*	*Thrust*	*Burn Time*	*Payload Fairing*	*Total Length, m*	*Payload Capability*
		2 × Lockheed Aerojet ARSM	HTPB (Notes 85, 94)	31020 kN	130s		3.724 (Note-91)	
	2nd	3 × OMS Aerojet (Note–89)	N_2O_4 + UDMH	80 kN	15h			
National Space Development Agency Rocket Systems Corporation (Japan) H2 (Fig. 26.54)	Ist	1 × Mitsubishi LE–7	LH + LOX	912 kN	348s	12 m long	49	9400 kg to LEO
		2 × Nissan SRB (Note–95)	Solid	3138 kN	95s			3800 kg to LEO
	2nd	1 × Mitsubishi LE5 A (Note–96)	LH + LOX	122 kN	610s			2000 kg to GEO 4500 kg to Sun Sync.

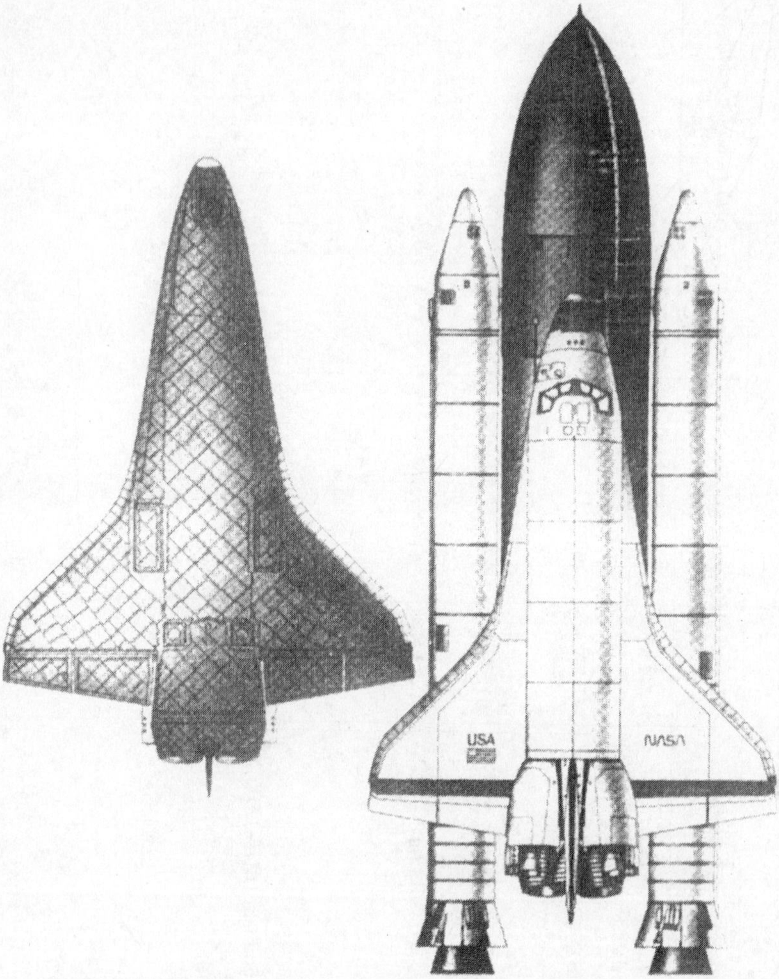

Fig. 26.53

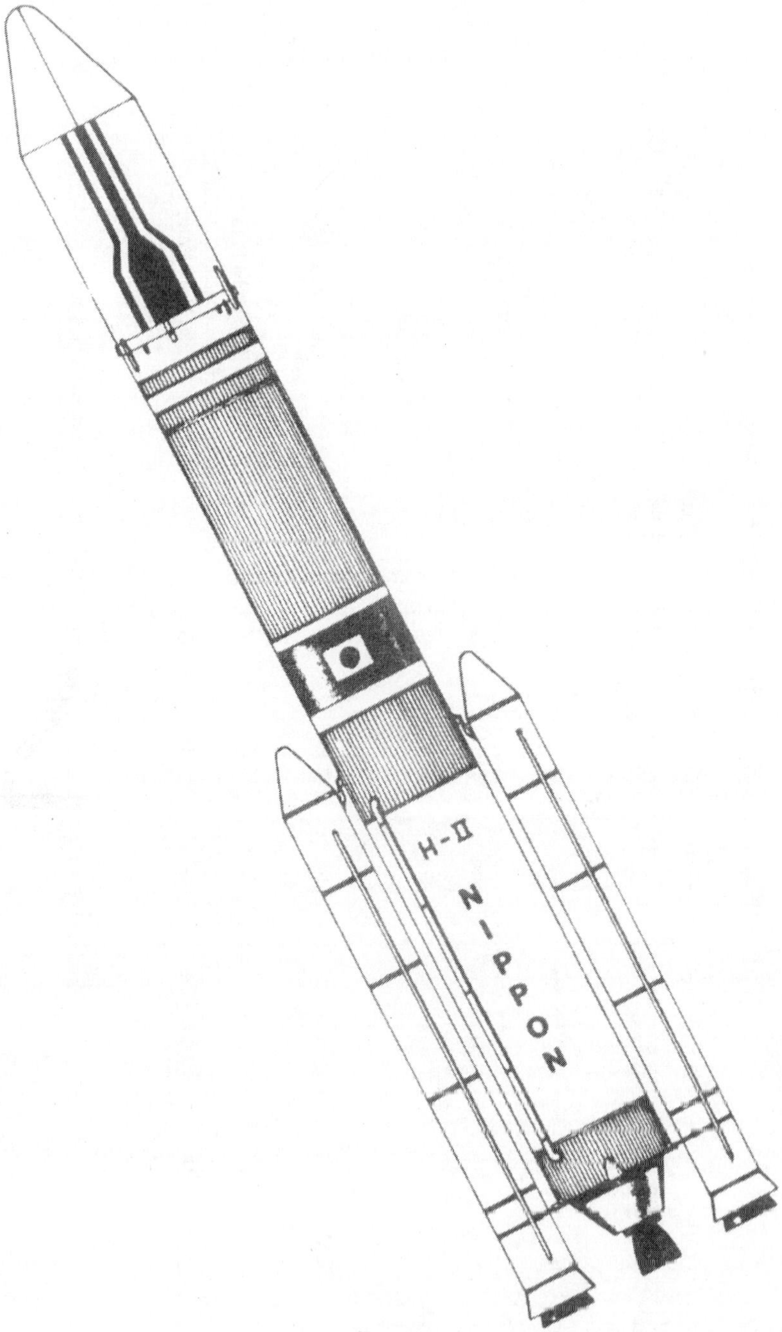

Fig. 26.54

Table 26.6. Satellite Launch Vehicles (Contd.)

Mfr. / Vehicle	*Stage*	*Engine*	*Propellants*	*Thrust*	*Burn Time*	Payload Fairing	*Total length, m*	*Payload Capability*
Orbital Sciences Corporation	Ist	1 × Hercules	Solid	487 kN	73s (Note–98)		15.51	260 kg to polar
OSC (U.S.A.) Pegasus (Note–97)	2nd	1 × Hercules	Solid	123 kN	72s			350 kg to equatorial, 185 kmorbits (Notes 99,100)
	3rd	1 × Hercules	Solid	35 kN	65s			
Orbital Sciences Corporation, OSC (U.S.A.)	Ist	1 × Thiokol (MX)	Solid	2200 kN	55s		27.51	1360 kg to LEO
Taurus / SSLV	2nd	1 × Hercules	Solid	487 kN	73s			330 kg to GTO
	3rd	1 × Hercules	Solid	123 kN	72s			930 kg to Polar
	4th	1 × Hercules	Solid	35 kN	65s			930 kg to Polar

Table-6)

1. Core stage ignites at 20,000
2. Acquilla 21 with 2 HI500s-, 134 kg to LEO
3. Target date depends on final funds.
4. New third stage H10 + intro Apr 92
5. 11.1 m Extra long fairing on request
6. Single payload only
7. Can carry microsats
8. Boosters
9. Used for dual launch, with long fairing
10. Used for dual launch with short fairing
11. Used with long or short fairing
12. Used with short fairing
13. ultra-short spelda for smaller payload flying with major satellite
14. Six UDMH modules around $N_2 O_4$ core
15. Restart capability / 2 hours
16. not used LEO
17. Depends on payload
18. Uprated Proton planned : 4500 kg to GEO and 23500 kg to LEO
19. Core called second stage
20. Strap-ons called first stage
21. Maximum
22. Piggiback
23. Piggiback + OMS engines
24. Ignites at 61 m after steam ejection canister launch
25. With aerojet USTM Motor
26. With post boast Motor
27. Variants of motor cluster combinations available.
28. Comet configuration
29. Strap-ons
30. Core stage
31. Four strap-ons burn as first stage, two strap-ons and core stage ignite at T + 60-61s
32. Variants of motor cluster combinations available
33. Boosters
34. Automatic launches / not Hermes
35. Restart capability
36. For dual launches
37. For triple launches with SPELTRA /not under development
38. Fully loaded, crewed needs MK2 Vulcain /not under development
39. + Verniers.
40. Restart capability

41. With medium fairing
42. With long fairing
43. Stretched Atlas and Centaur
44. MLV2 use medium only
45. MLV2
46. 8 percent performance increase optional with Block-1 enhancement package
47. Uprated Centaur
48. Boosters
49. Only Atlas flying
50. + two verniers
51. China CPK solid propellant stage available late 1992
52. Strap-ons
53. Jiuquan
54. Xichang
55. With PAM class perigee motor
56. China EPKM upper stage available 1993
57. China HO upper stage from CZ-3
58. Restart capability
59. Uprated CZ-3A available
60. Ignites at T + 49.5s
61. Strap-ons
62. Four strap-ons
63. Strap-ons
64. Strap ons
65. With small motor
66. Approx
67. Refurbished ICBM
68. With star-37 Kick stage
69. Ignites at (T + 116)s
70. Strap-ons
71. Restart capability
72. Under thread of cancellation
73. PAM D
74. IUS
75. TOS
76. Intelsat-6 stranded, no fault of Titan
77. Uprated Delta 3920
78. 6 ignite at launch, 3 at (T + 62)s
79. Restart
80. Canaveral
81. Vendenberg

82. Improved expansion ratio
83. H2SRB
84. M3S II stages
85. H1 pad
86. Throttled 65 percent -104 percent rated power
87. Fed from external tank
88. Strap-ons
89. Fired in pairs in 2s bursts. For final orbit and retro-fire.
90. Payload bay
91. Orbiter
92. NASA may cancel ARSM Sept 92
93. 104 percent continuous
94. Throttleable
95. Strap-ons
96. Restart capability
97. Winged booster, air launched by B-52/Tristar, Mach 0.8. 12000m
98. Incorporates 3rd stage
99. Optional 4th stage hydrazine HAPS engine provides 40kg+ to polar
100. East coast launch for equatorial.

27

Special Purpose Satellites

Countries use satellites in many areas. These areas include military, reconnaissance, agriculture, and oceanography. With the help of satellites in these areas, countries have strengthened their military power and have improved their economic systems. Although only certain countries have this technology, more and more are getting access due to the new developments of satellites which have reduced its cost.

This Chapter on *Special Purpose Satellites* gives details of major satellites launched by different organisations for – Space Exploration, Missions, Earth observation, Remote Sensing and Weather Forecasting Satellites alongwith various, Scientific, Defence and Navigational/Martime Satellites.

27.1. (a) Introduction

A part from the communication satellites described earlier, the global satellite technology scene is also populated by a series of special purpose satellite systems. These satellites are of the following types :

(*a*) Satellites dedicated to extended space exploration particularly, the planets in our solar system, asteroids and the missions of space sciences.

(*b*) Earth observation and remote sensing satellites which provide a range of scientific information on the various phenomena occuring on the earth, its lands, oceans and atmosphere.

(*c*) Weather forecasting satellites dedicated to the study of the processes of weather making in different regions of the globe and collecting meteorological data for weather forecasting.

(*d*) Maritime and search satellites like the IMARSAT which provide communication links with ships and aircrafts.

(*e*) Defence satellites which are set of big undivided nations to generate information related to defence and espionage.

27.1. Space Exploration Systems

These systems are launched to observe and carry out scientific investigations of various space phenomena, astronomical objects and planets. Using highly sophisticated sensors, instrumentation and camera-imaging system. They send extremely valuable information which helps space scientists to develop deep understanding of space. Important space missions have been sent to the Moon, Mars, Jupiter, Saturn and Asteroids. Some of the major systems are described below and it will highlight the readers with the type of payloads they carry on board for conducting the experiments and collecting data.

1. Cassini. It was developed by NASA's Jet Propulsion Laboratory in California, USA and launched on 15th October 1997 from Cape Canaveral in Florida, USA through Titan 4B, its launch vehicle. It reached Saturn in June 2004 and its Planetary orbit is around Saturn and was 3-axis stabilized.

The main aim of this launch was to conduct studies on structure, behaviour of the magnetosphere and rings of Saturn and its atmosphere at cloud level. Besides this its aim was also to conduct studies on composition of the satellite surfaces, their history with focus on Titan.

2. Chandra X-ray Observatory. It was launched on 23rd July 1999 from Kennedy Space Center in Cape Canaveral in Florida, USA through Space Shuttle Columbia, its launch vehicle into eccentric earth's orbit and was 3-axis stabilized.

Its on board payload consists of - AXAF Charged Couples Imaging Spectrometer, High Resolution Camera, High Energy Transmission Grating + ACIS-S and one Wolter Type, grazing incidence irridium- coated telescope.

It was the NASA's observatory which was designed to make observations on celestial objects and to know about the actual nature of processes which take place in astronomical objects physically, and to find out the history and evolution of the universe.

3. Hubble Space Telescope. It was launched on 24th April 1990 from Kennedy Space Center in Cape Canaveral, USA through Space Shuttle Discovery its launch vehicle. It's Orbit is LEO, Circular and was 3-axis stabilized.

Its on board payload consists of—Wide Field/Planetary Camera 2, Space Telescope Imaging Spectrograph, Near Infrared Camera, Multi-Object Spectrometer and Advanced Camera for Surveys.

It is a permanent space observatory, and joint program of the European Space Agency (ESA) and the National Aeronautics and Space Administration (NASA). The science instruments on-board the telescope provide high resolution images of astronomical objects (approx. 0.1 arc-secs.) as compared to the ground-based telescopes (approx. 1.0 arc-secs.) due to its location above the earth's atmosphere.

4. Jupiter Mission: Galileo Satellite was launched in 1989 from Space Shuttle Atlantis during the STS-34 mission and it took 5 years to reach Jupiter. It gave important data on the composition, speed, density, and temperature of the planet, and also detected evidence of underground salt water oceans and active valcanoes (Io moon) on Jupiter's moons. It was plunged into the dense layers of Jupiter's atmosphere on September 20, 2003 where it got burnt, after it went out of its fuel.

5. Mars Global Surveyor. It was launched on 7th November 1996, from Kennedy Space Center in Cape Canaveral, USA through Delta 7959A its launch vehicle in its planetary orbit around Mars.

It's main purpose was to get clear images of the surface, study the topography and gravity, the role of water and dust on the surface and in its atmosphere, its weather, its climate its and finally the existence and evolution of the Martian magnetic field.

After completion of its work its aim was to acquire new data and provide support for the 2001 Mars Odyssey mission.

6. Mars Odyssey. It was launched on 7th April, 2001 from Kennedy Space Center in Cape Canaveral, USA and through Delta 7925 its launch vehicle, in its Planetary orbit around Mars with 3-axis stabilization.

Its on board payload consists of — Gamma Ray Spectrometer, Thermal Emissions Imaging system and Martian Radiation Environment Experiment.

It's main objective is to study the Mars's surface and find out what the planet is made of and to trace out any ice or water. It mapped the planet's surface and took measurements about radiation and its composition. It is to be used as a relay for future missions and could become the first node in an interplanetary Internet as its mission ends.

7. Near Earth Asteroid Rendezous (NEAR). NEAR was NASA's space programme launched on 17th February 1996 from Vandenberg Air Force Base in Cape Canaveral, USA through Delta 7925, its launch vehicle into its orbit Heliocentric, and further around Asteroid 433 Eros.

Its on board payload consists of – Near Infrared Spectrograph, Multi-Spectral Imager, X-Ray/Gamma Ray Spectrometer and Near Laser Range Finder.

It main aim was to get information on asteroid's information on asteroid's volume, mass, shape, size, geology, texture, gravity magnetic field, morphology and its mineral composition.

8. New Horizons Mission for Pluto Exploration. It is the NASA's mission to Pluto and is launched on 20th January, 2006 from Kennedy Space Center in Cape Canaveral, Florida through Atlas V its launch vehicle.

As the first spacecraft to visit Pluto and its moon Charon, New Horizons looks to unlock one of the solar system's last, great planetary secrets. After launch abroad and Atlas V, the New Horizons spacecraft will cross the entire span of the solar system and conduct flyby studies of Pluto and its moon, Charon, in 2015. The seven science instruments on the piano-sized probe will shed light on the bodies surface properties, geology, interior makeup and atmospheres.

It can take upto 9 years to cross more than 3 billion miles of space, travelling at up to 30,000 mph, it will here to navigate with pin point accuracy to pass Pluto at its intended altitude of 6,000 miles. It will then have just 24 hours to bring its cameras and other instruments to bear before hurtling past and out of range.

The key tasks of the probe's instruments will be to find out what Pluto is made of, its compositions, and materials present on it.

9. Nozomi. It was launched on 4th July 1998 from Kagoshima Space Observation Center in Japan from M-5 its, launch vehicle. Its orbit being Heliocentric initially and later on to be further placed in highly eccentric Mars orbit, inclined at 170°. Its payload being Imaging camera, Neutral Mass Spectrometer, Dust Counter, Thermal Plasma Analyzer, Magnetometer, Electron and Ion Spectrum Analyzers, Ion Mass Spectrograph, High Energy Particles Experiment, VUV Imaging Spectometer, Sounder and Plasma Wave Detector, LF Wave Analyzer, Electron Temperature Probe and a UV Scanner.

It was a Japan's programme to Mars aimed at getting information about the upper atmosphere and its interaction with the solar wind and to develop technologies for use in future planetary missions. This mission gave the measurement of the structure, composition and dynamics of the ionosphere, aeronomical effects of the solar wind, the escape of atmospheric constituents, magnetic field, penetration of the solar-wind magnetic field, structure of the magnetosphere, and dust in the upper atmosphere and in orbit around Mars.

10. Odin. This satellite of Sweden was developed by Swedish corporation and launched on 20th February 2001 from Svobodny Space Center in Russia by launch vehicle — Start 1, with payload of Radiometer and Optical spectromter in LEO circular sun synchronous orbit and was 3-axis stabilized.

The objective of this satellite was to detect protostarts, comets, elements in the atmospheres of Jupiter and Saturn and to look into process of star formation activities in its near galaxies.

11. Unmanned Space Experiment Recovery System (USERS). It was developed by Mistsubishi Electric of Japan and Launched on 10th September, 2002 from Tanegashima Space Centre in Japan through H-2A, launch vehicle. Its orbit being LEO with payload of Super conductive materials processing equipment.

This was a satellite with Re-entry Module (REM) alongwith Service Module (SEM) to provide power and link to REM. The main aim was to conduct experiment on manufacturing of super conductive material – Gd-Ba-Cu-O.

12. Transition Region and Coronal Explorer (TRACE) or Small Explorer 6. It was launched on 2nd April, 1998 from Vandenberg Air Force Base in California, USA through Pegasus XL its launch vehicle. Its orbit being LEO, circular, polar sun synchronous and was 3-axis stabilized, alongwith payload of Two-axis gyros, Digital Sun Sensor, Six Coarse Sun Sensors, 3-axis magnetometer and Casse-grain telescope.

The main aim of this satellite of NASA's SMEX project was to watch the Sun for nearly 12 months and then find the relationship between the sun's magnetic fields and heating of its corona. Eventually help in under standing the events of sun which can pose danger to astronauts and have potential to interfere in activities of satellites in space. It will also give insight into dynamic solar events that have the potential to endanger astronauts, as well as disrupt the use of space-based satellites.

13. XMM-Newton Mission (X-ray Multi-Mirror Mission). This satellite of European Space agency, was developed by Dornier

Satellite Systems of Germany and launched on 10th December, 1999 from Kourou in French Guiana in France through Ariane 504, its launch vehicle. Its on board payload being European Photon Imaging Camera, Reflection Grating Spectrometer and Optical Monitor.

This satellite, a utmost and highly sensitive with main aim to assist scientists to understand the very origin of the universe, basics of black holes and other unsolved Cosmic mysteries.

27.2. Satellites for Scientific Missions

These satellite systems are dedicated to study various space phenomena such as solar radiation measurements, amount of sunlight falling on Earth, geomagnetic storms, atmospheric conditions, identification of matters in space, multi-spectral imaging of earth's condition from space, atmospheric events, especially changes in the ozone layers and predictions of long-term climate change among others. Some of major systems are described below, given also are the details of their tasks and payloads on board.

1. Active Cavity Radiometer Irradiance Monitor Satellite (ACRIMSAT). This satellite was launched in 1999 and its orbit being – LEO, near-circular near-polar sun-synchronous, with payload of Active Cavity Radiometer Irradiance Monitor III and it is spin stabilized.

The main aim of this satellite was to provide integrated data on environmental issues the global warming, depletion in ozone layer, shrinking glaciers, reasons of variations in solar radiation and measuring the amount of sunlight in earth's atmosphere.

2. Advanced Composition Explorer (ACE). This satellite was launched in 1997 by NASA L1 into Halo solar orbit and was spin stabilized with on board payload of Solar wind Ions Mass Spectrometer, Solar Wind Inscomposition Spectrometer, EPAM particle instrument (Electron, Proton and Alpha Monitor), Solar Isotope Spectrometer and Cosmic Ray Isotope Spectrometer.

Its main motive was to gain knowledge about the matter which comes close to earth from the sun, space and the Milky Way galaxy. It also works as the space weather station which gives advanced warning about the geomagnetic storms which can cause disturbance in communications, and can be hazardous to astronauts and cosmic Ray Isotope Spectrometer.

3. Advanced Land Observing Satellite. It was launched on 24th January, 2006 from Tanegashima Space Center in Japan. It was launched on Japan's domestically made H-2A rocket and was developed by the Japan Aerospace Exploration Agency (JAXA).

This satelllite will orbit 680 km above the Earth to collect topographic data to contribute to cartography and capture images of disaster-hit areas anywhere in the world and also to hunt for natural resources.

4. Citizen Explorer-1. This satellite was launched on 21st November, 2000 from Delta 7320, launch vehicle in the Orbit LEO, sun synchronous with on board a Spectrophotometer and a photometer. Its main aim was to study atmospheric events and to give information on the status of ozone layers in the atmosphere.

5. Data Relay Test Satellite (DRTS). The Japan's National Space Development Agencies this satellite was launched on 24th October, 1998 from Delta 7326, launch vehicle with its orbit being Planetary and 3-axis stabilized.

This satellite which is designed to lend operational support systems to some spacecrafts of the future. It had also been providing the infrastructure in space communications for two-way data relay between ground stations and the experimented spacecrafts.

6. Multispectral Thermal Imager Satellite (MTIS). This satellite was developed by Los Alamos National Laboratory, and was launched in 2000, through Taurus, launch vehicle. Its orbit being LEO, sun sunchronous with on board a High Energy X-ray Spectrometer. The main aim of this satellite was get information which could help to study the changes in climate, population in rivers, health of vegetations and environment degradations, using a sophisticated telescope that photographs the light and heat patterns on Earth.

7. Scientific Applications Satellite (SACI). This satellite was developed by INPE of Brazil and of was launched on 14th October, 1999 from Taiyuan Launching Centre in China through Long March CZ-4B, launch vehicle, its weight being just 60 kg. Its orbit being LEO Circular Sun-synchronous Near-Polar and was spin stabilized.

It consisted of SACI-I & SACI-2 series, of which SACI-2 was lost on launching. The main aim of this satellite was to conduct experiments on the physics of the atmosphere.

8. SNAP-1 Satellite. This was developed by Surrey Satellite Technology company of England and lauched on 28th June, 2000 from Plesetsk Cosmodrome in Russia through Kosmos 3 M, launch vehicle. It weighed 6 kg and was 3-axis stabilized with Machine Vision on board.

The main aim of this satellite was to exhibit the potentials of highly integrated, advanced nano satellites and its usage as autonomous robots for observing orbiting vehicles in the space.

27.3. Satellites for Forecasting of Weather

The field of meteorology entered the space age on April 1, 1960 with the launch of TIROS 1 (TIROS stands for Television and Infra-Red Observation Satellite). Since that time, numerous satellites with ever increasing capabilities and sophistication have been deployed.

Weather satellites provide valuable data and real-time cloud photographs. Most importantly, coverage includes the 70 percent of the earth's surface covered by water where few surface observations can be made. Before the deployment of weather satellites, many areas had no advance warning of impending severe storms. Today satellites can spot and accurately track hurricanes and typhoons while they are still far out in the ocean.

The advent of satellite-based observations, over the past two decades, has added new dimensions to the study of atmosphere and weather systems. The synoptic coverage on a repetitive basis as provided by satellites, is ideally suited to study weather-related atmospheric processes on different scales. The recent advances in satellite sensing and parameter retrieval in terms of high resolution, multispectral bands covering visible, infrared and microwave regions with enhanced radiometry have made space data an inevitable component in weather monitoring and dynamic modelling. The satellite data plays critical role in improved definition of initial and boundary conditions for weather-prediction models. The impact of satellite data is phenomenal in certain areas of meteorological applications such as short-range forecasts, cyclone monitoring, and aviation forecasts, especially in the tropics.

Modern satellites also carry many instruments used to measure various environmental variables, providing vital information to not only meteorologists, but farmers, geologists, fisherman, foresters and others.

27.3.1 Satellite Measurements

The following list details many of the uses of weather satellites:

- Radiation measurements from the earth's surface and atmosphere give information on the earth-atmosphere energy budget.
- Measurements from the ocean surface are translated into sea-surface temperatures - information valuable to the fishing industry as well as meteorologists.
- Satellites can monitor snow cover in winter, ice fields in the Arctic and Antarctic and the height of the ocean's surface.
- Infrared sensors on satellites can assess conditions of crops, areas of deforestation and regions of drought.
- Some satellites are equipped with a water vapor sensor that can profile the distribution of water vapor in the atmosphere.
- Volcanic eruptions and the motion of ash clouds can be detected.
- During the winter, satellites monitor the southward progress of freezing air in Florida and Texas, allowing forecasters to warn growers of impending low temperatures.
- Satellites can receive environmental information from remote data collection platforms on the surface. These include instrumented buoys, river gauges, automatic weather stations, siesmic and tsunami stations and ships. This information is then relayed to a central receiving station at Wallop's Island, Virginia, USA.

27.3.2 Satellite Types

There are two primary types of weather satellites in use:

1. Geostationary Satellites. Geostationary satellites (or *geosynchronous satellites*) orbit the equator at the same rate the earth spins, once per day. They orbit at a distance of 22,300 mi (36,000 km) above and constantly monitor a fixed spot on the earth's surface. This positioning allows continuous monitoring of a specific region. GOES 9 (*Geostationary Operational Environmental Satellite*) is the latest in a series of GOES satellites, launched on May 23rd, 1995.

Geostationary satellites measure in "real-time", meaning they transmit photographs to the receiving system on the ground as soon as the camera takes the picture. A succession of photographs from these satellites can be displayed in sequence to produce a movie showing cloud movement. This allows forecasters to monitor the progress of large weather systems such as floods, storms and hurricanes. Wind direction and speed can also be determined by monitoring cloud movement.

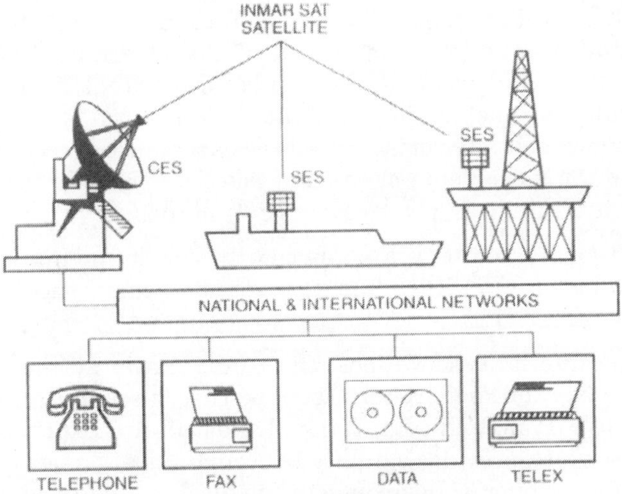

Fig. 27.1 The GOES Project.

2. Polar Orbiting Satellites. Polar orbiting satellites are closely parallel to the earth's meridian lines. They pass over the north and south poles on each revolution. As the earth rotates to the east beneath the satellite, each pass monitors an area to the west of the previous pass. These 'strips' can be pieced together to produce a picture of a larger area.

Polar satellites have the advantage of photographing clouds directly beneath them. Geostationary satellite images of the polar regions are distorted because of the low angle the satellite sees the region. Polar satellites also circle at a much lower altitude (about 530 mi., 850 km) providing more detailed information about violent storms and cloud systems.

1. Geostationary Operational Environmental Satellites (GOES). The GOES satellite system, USA's geostationary weather forecasting satellite system was launched by NASA and is in service of weather observations and forecasting since 25 years. It grew out of the successful use of geostationary weather satellites with the experimental –1 & –2 satellites. The first GOES 1 (A), was launched way back in the year 1974. Since then twelve GOES satellites have been launched, with GOES 12 launched in 2001, being the latest one. GOES satellites provide the kind of continuous monitoring over one position on the surface and therefore provide a constant vigil for the atmospheric "triggers" for severe weather conditions such as hurricanes, hail storms, flash floods, desert stroms, etc. are able to monitor and track their movements.

GOES satellite images also used to estimate rainfall during the thunderstorms and hurricanes for flash flood warnings, as well as estimates snowfall accumulations and overall extent of snow cover. Such data help meteorologists issue winter storm warnings and spring snow melt advisories. Satellite sensors also detect ice fields and map the movements of sea and lake ice. The GOES Program maintains 2 satellites which coveres 60% of the Earth.

The GOES satellites are equipped with Visible and Infrared Spin Scan Radiometer (VISSR), Imagers, Sounders and Space Environment Monitor.

In addition to observations, the GOES platform (the satellite stationed over the Pacific Ocean) has been used to create and operate PEACESAT (Pan-Pacific Educational and Cultural Experiments by Satellite) which provides satellite telecommunications to serve the educational, economic development, medical and cultural needs of many Pacific Countries.

The future plans for the GOES plan includes the launch of four more GOES satellites GOES N, GOES O, GOES P and GOES Q by the year 2012, and these satellites will provide more accurate location of severe storms and other weather phenomena, resulting in more precise warning to the public.

All the GOES satellites were launched from Kennedy Space Center in Cape Canaveral, USA with GOES 8, 9, 10 were launched by Atlas 1 and GOES 11 and 12 were launched by Atlas 2A and were 3-axis stabilized.

2. Feng Yun-2B. It was developed by Shanghai Institute of Space Technology launched on 25th June, 2000 from Xichang Satellite Launch Centre in Sichuan Province, China through Long March CZ-3A, launch vehicle and its orbit being GEO 106°E and was spin stabilized. It was equipped with Visible and Infrared Spin Scan Radiometer low resolution analog Wefax and a digital S-band for service.

3. Himawari series. *Himawari 5 (GMS 5)* is the 4th meteorological satellite of Japan in the Himawari Series with earlier 2, 3 and 4 having being launched. This satellite has an 5 years expected life of operation. It was developed by NEC, Japan and launched on 18th March, 1995 from Tanegashima Space Centre in Kagoshima, Japan rom H-2, its launch vehicle in GEO 140°E orbit and is spin stabilized.

4. Meteosat satellite. *Meteosat 7* is the seventh satellite for forecasting weather from European Space Agency in the Meteosat series with earlier Meteosat 2, 3, 4, 5 and 6 having being launched. This satellite has around 5 years of expected life of operation. It was developed by Alcatel Space Industries of France and launched on 2nd September, 1997 from Kourou in French Guiana, France through Ariane 44LP, its launch vehicle into GEO 10°W orbit and is spin stabilized.

5. Meteor 3M-1. It was developed by Elektromekaniki of Russia and launched on 10th December, 2001 from Baionour Cosmodrome in Kazakhstan through Zenit-2, its launch vehicle.

It is the meteorological satellite from Russia under Meteor 1, 2, 3 and 3M series, which is being launched since 1970's. Meteor 3M-1 with operational life span of over 3 years is the current one in the space and is 3-axis stabilized.

6. METSAT. It was launched on 12th September, 2002 from Sriharikota to meet India's meteorological requirements through PSLV-C4 into its orbit GEO at 74°E and is 3-axis stabilized with on board-Very High Resolution Radiometer (VHRR), Thermal Infrared and Water Infrared Band each at a spatial resolution of 2 × 2 kms and Data Relay Transponder (DRT).

METSAT is a unique and dedicated satellite for meterology. The satellite data will help in improving the skills in forecasting weather using weather prediction models.

7. MSG-1. This is first of the Meteosat second generation series satellites of Europe for meteorological purpose.

It was launched on 27th August, 2002 from Kourou in French Guiana, France through Ariane 5 G, its launch vehicle into GEO 10.5°W orbit and is spin stabilized with a 12 Channel VHRR on board.

8. National Oceanic and Atmospheric (NOAA series). NOAA series of satellites comprises of 10 satellites, namely NOAA 8, 9, 10, 11, 12, 13, 14, 15, 16, 17. NOAA N and N' are scheduled to be launched in the year 2004 and 2008 respectively.

It was developed by Lockheed Martin Missiles and Space company of USA and launched from Vandenberg Air Force Base in California, USA. NOAA-15 and 17 were launched on Titan 2 and NOAA-16 was launched on Titan 23G into the Orbit Leo, Sun-synchornous, Near circular, Near Polar, Mean radius of 800 km, and is 3-axis stabilized.

Payload on board Consists of :- Advanced Microwave Sounding Unit-A, B (AMSU-A, AMSU-B), Advanced Very High Resolution Radiometer (AVHRR/3), High Resolution Infrared Radiation Sounder (HIRS-3), Ocean Color Instrument (OCI), Search and Rescue Satellite aided Tracking (SARSAT), Advanced Picture Transmission (APT), High Resolution Picture Transmission (HRPT), Direct Sounder Broadcast (DSB), Space Environment Monitor (SEM), Solar Backscatter Ultravoilet radiometer (SBUV/2), ARGOS.

9. QuickSCAT. This satellite also known as Quick Scatterometer is NASA's satellite which gives daily report to meteorologists and climatologists with photos of the currents in seas, pattern of winds on the ocean's surface for weather forecasting.

27.4. Earth Observation and Remote Sensing Satellites

1. LANDSAT

LANDSAT-1 was first satellite launched in 1972 by NASA followed by LANDSAT-2, 3, 4, 5, 6 and 7 in its series.

Landsat is one of the earth exploration satelltie service (EESSS). This system involves observation of the earth for various purposes, *e.g.* meteorological (TIROS 1, Metostat), Geodesy (Transit), earth resources (LANDSAT, SPOT, SEASAT) ; data collection (ARGOS).

Landsat is a remote sensing satellite that is capable of sensing remotely the earth observation satellite provides valuable data on natural resources, meteorology and environment development. For scientists, it helps to understand and study various aspects of earth science such as hydrologic cycle, biochemical solid earth mysteries.

Remote sensing satellite's operation is based on sensors data processing, data analysis and data interpretation for different applications. Here physical measurements of reflected, emitted or radiated energy from various objects on the ground are made from distant platforms. Since different objects emits radiations in different bands so to recognise them correctly sending is done in discreate bands of the electromagnetic spectrum. Remote sensing is carried outin visible, infrared, thermal and microwave bands and each band has its only land observation but also ocean and atmospheric studies and many other new applications.

The sensors send the data back to earth stations from where it is collected and processed in the form of photographic prints of films, computer compatible floppies disks/CD (for analyzing on PC based systems) and stored. The photo-imageries can be visually interpreted while the tapes are anlysed on selected training samples. The final output are thermatic directly maps, histograms, statistical tables etc. which can be utilized directly by the decision makers for planning and execution of specific development projects.

LANDSATs provide world wide high resolution multispectral data of earth's surface. There are there kinds of sensor system in a number of satellites that have been launched in this series :

(*i*) three camera Return Beam Vidion (RBV)
(*ii*) four channel multispectral scanner (MSS) ; and
(*iii*) seven band thermatic mapper (TM).

Table 27.1 gives various kinds of processing, these sensors carry out.

Table 27.1. Data Product Capabilities of Various Landsats

Satellite / Sensor	*Type of Processing*	*Product Type*
Initial / capability		
LANDSAT-2 and 3 (MSS)	Radiometric and geometric corrections	70 mm QL film bulk corrected CCT. Bulk corrected film imageries
LANDSAT-3 (RBV)	Formatting	70 mm QL film
TIROS-N (NOAA)	Format conversation	Raw CCT 70 mm QL film
New capabilities Added		
LANDSAT-2 and 3 (MSS)	Radiometric and geometric corections	70 mm film
LANDSAT 4	Radiometric and geometric corrections	70 mm film, 240 mm film, CCT
LANDSAT-3 (RBV)	Geometric corrections	24 mm film CCT

The LANDSAT satellites are in circular sun synchronous near polar orbit at an altitude of approximately 705 km. They circle the earth every 103 minutes completing 14 orbits per day and view the entire earth in 16 days. The orbit is selected and trimmed so that each satellite ground trace repeates its earth coverage at the same time every day. There are many reception stations the world over which receive data from Landsat satellites. This is further processed and the data disseminated to the users.

Besides the Landsat series of satellites presently in operation are the Indian IRS-1 A, the French SPOT-1 satellites, European Remote Sensing Satellite ERS series and the Canadian Radarsat satellite and other vast earth observing systems world-wide, *e.g.* the NASA's upper atmosphere research satellite (UARS), TOPEX, the

Geopotential Research Mission (GRM) and the International Solar Terrestrial Project (ISTP). Some other latest measuring equipment are also be employed. These are moderate resolution imaging spectrometer (MODIS) high resolution imaging spectrometer (HIRIS), high resolution multi frequency microwave radiometer (HMMR), Liquid atmospheric sounder and altimeter (LASA), synthetic Aperture Radar, Radioaltimeter, Scatterometer, Doppler, Radar, upper atmospheric wind inferometers, tropospheric composition monitors, upper atmosphere composition monitors, energy and particle monitors.

2. Badr-B. It was developed by Pakistan's Space and Upper Atmosphere Research Centre, British Company SIL and launched on 10th December, 2001 from Baikonour in Kazakhstan through Zenit 2, launch vehicle in its orbit LEO Near Circular with Gravity Gradient single-axis stabilization and with its payload of CCD camera and Radiation Dosimeter.

3. Challenging Minisatellite Payload satellite (CHAMP). It was developed by European Space Company, Astrium and was launched on 15th July, 2000 from Plesetsk Cosmodrome in Russia through Cosmos-3M, launch vehicle with LEO Circular, Near-Polar, Non-sun synchronous being its orbit. It is 3-axis stabilized.

This is the Ist of three satellites of Germany under the European Scientific Mission which was launched for geoscientific and atmospheric research & applications. It is the first satellite to generate precise gravity and magnetic field measurements.

4. FM-6 (Samba). It was developed by Astrium company of Germany under programme of European Space Agency to help cosmology and get full image of the sky. It was launched on 16th July, 2000 from Baikonour cosmodrome in Kazakhstan through Soyuz 2, launch vehicle and is spin stabilized.

It is in series of Cluster-II satellties which consists of FM-5 (Rumba), FM-6 (Samba), FM-7 (Salsa) and FM-8 (Tongo) of European Space Agency. The mission was to map the Cosmic Microwave Background fluctuations and measure the clusters of several galaxies; to get image of the sky with angular resolution and sensitivity.

5. Formosat-1. It was developed by TRW Space and Electronics in California, USA under ROCSAT series of satellites of Taiwan's, Taiwanese National Space Program Office (NSPO).

It was launched on 24th January, 1999 from Cape Canaveral in Florida, USA through Athena 1, launch vehicle in its LEO, Sun-synchronous orbit with 3-axis stabilisation.

The main aim of this satellite is to monitor environment, ocean survillence and get data to be used in evaluating natural disasters, formulating urban planning and getting information to benefit the agriculture sector.

6. High Energy Transient Explorer (HETE). HETE-2 the latest in this series was launched on 9th October, 2000 from Kwajalein Missile Range facility in the Republic of the Marshall Islands through Pegasus XL, launch vehicle in its orbit (LEO, Circular and pointed in anti-solar direction) alongwith payload of Wide-Field X-ray Monitor, Soft X-ray Camera and French Gamma Ray Telescope.

HETE-2 is the second in HETE series, earlier being HETE-1 which was destroyed during its launch in 1996. It is a joint colaboration between France, Italy, Japan and the USA and it is aimed at conducting survey of sky to find Gamma Ray Bursts.

7. Imager for Magnetopause to Aurora Global Exploration (IMAGE). It was launched on 25th March, 2000 from Vandenberg Air Force Base in USA, through Delta 7326, launch vehicle. It is in the Elliptical Polar, (1000 × 45922 km, 90°) orbit and is spin stabilized, with payload of Neutral Atom Imager, Ultra Violet Imager and Radio Plasma Imager.

8. Thermosphere, Ionosphere, Mesosphere, Energetics and Dynamics satellite (TIMED). It was launched on 7th December, 2001 from Vandenberg Air Force Base, California through Delta 7920, launch vehicle in LEO Circular Orbit.

This satellite was launched to get the global image of ionosphere (lower thermosphere) and mesosphere to understand its corelation with activities in lower atmosphere.

9. Wilkinson Microwave Anisotropy Probe (WMAP). It was developed by NASA Goddard Space Flight Centre and Swales & Associates company of USA under NASA's scientific programme aiming to get insight in Cosmology.

It was launched on 30th June, 2001 from Cape Canaveral in USA through Delta, launch vehicle. It is in L2 Halo orbit and is spin stabilized.

27.5. Maritime and Search Satellites

1. INMARSAT.

It is an international organisation that controls satellite systems for communication between ships and coast so that emergency life saving services may be provided to the distressed people/ships. INMARSAT is accronym of International Maritime Satellite Organisation with headquarters at London. It came into being at midnight on 15th/16th July, 1979. The original member countries were 26 in number. It started to operate its global maritime satellite communication system in Feb. 1982. Initially it was using the systems offered by MARISAT joint venture of USA.

INMARSAT has now 85 member states. The USA maintains its lead in INMARSAT by holding maximum share in it. (Table 27.2) Signatories from member countries own INMARSAT, they contribute to the costs of the organisation and develop its policies. In fact maritime satellite communication via INMARSAT are available to all ships without discrimination on the basis of nationality.

Table 27.2. INMARSAT's Significant Share Holders

Country	*Share*	*Country*	*Share*	*Country*	*Share*
USA	28.6	Japan	8.7	USSR	2.3
U.K.	17.6	France	2.5	Netherlands	2.3
Norway	16.0	Singapore	2.4	Canada	2.2
		India (20th position)	0.44		

The importance of international maritime (shipping) communication is due to the fact that a large number of ships and lives are lost every year. The INMARSAT contributes in improving distress and safety of life at sea, communications, efficiency and management of ships, maritime public correspondence services and radio determination capabilities. It serves all needs for maritime communications and its services are for peaceful purposes with over 5000 ships, boats fitted with INMARSAT user equipment.

Finance of INMARSAT is met by the contributions of signatories. Signatories' contributions are repaid together with compensation for the use of capital after earning profits. Regarding mode of charges. INMARSAT levies space segment utilization charges on coast earth station (CES) accessing the system.

The areas of working of INMARSAT is shown in Fig. 27.1. This involves national and international networks covering telephone,

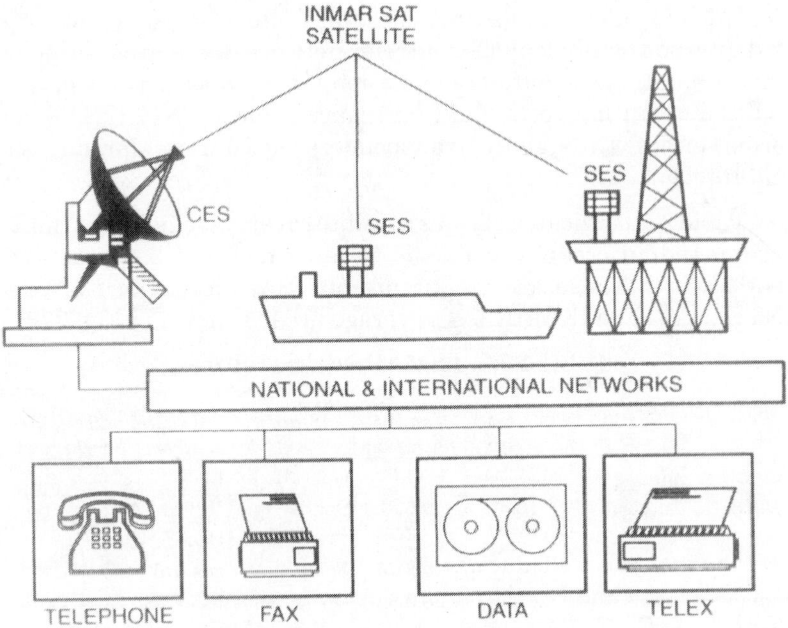

Fig. 27.1. Areas of working of INMARSAT.

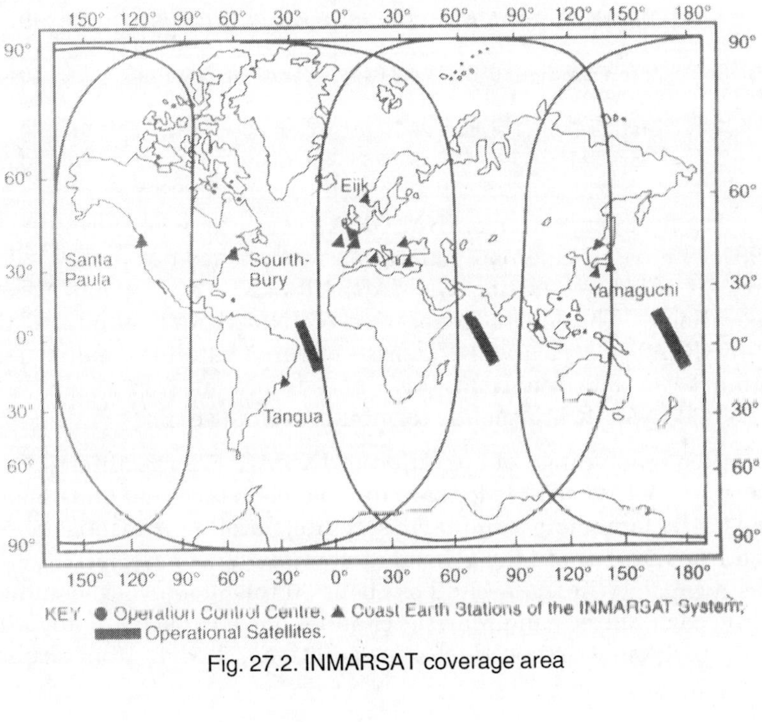

KEY. ● Operation Control Centre, ▲ Coast Earth Stations of the INMARSAT System; ▬ Operational Satellites.

Fig. 27.2. INMARSAT coverage area

fascimile, computer, telex etc. Use of the services available via INMARSAT offers (*a*) direct communication between vessels, rigs and international telephone and telex network, (*b*) reduced response time, (*c*) automatic data transmission, (*d*) increased efficiency, (*e*) reduced operating costs and (*f*) enhanced safety. INMARSAT performs services through the transponders leased from Marisat, ESA and Intelsat.

Table 27.3 indicates various satellite covering regions of Atlantic oceam, Indian ocean and Pacific Ocean which are being used by INMARSAT. These are : Marisats of USA, Marecs of ESA and INTELSAT. The INMARSAT coverage area is shown in Fig. 27.2.

Table 27.3. INMARSAT Satellites

Region	*Satellite*	*Orbit*	*Date of operation*	*Status*	*Leased from*	*Telephony channels*
Atlantic (AOR)	Marecs-B_2	26°W	9.11.84	Operational	ESA	80
	Intelsat V-MCSB	18.5° W	19.5.83	Spare	INTELSAT	50
					COMSAT	10
	Marisat-F_1	15°W	19.2.76	Spare	general	
Indian (IOR)	Intelsat V (MCS-A)	63°E	28.9.82	Operational	INTELSAT	50
	Intelsat V (MCB-C)	60°E	19.10.83	Spare	INTELSAT	50
	Marisat F_2	72.5°E	14.10.76	Spare	Comsat general	10
Pacific (POR)	Intelsat V (MCS-D)	180°E	4.3.84	Operational	Intelsat	50
	Marces-A	178°E	20.12.81	Spare	ESA	60
	Marisat-F_3	176.5°E	9.6.76	Spare	Comsat general	10

The first generation of INMARSAT satellites was phased out in 1991 whereas the second generation was phased out in 1995. The present third generation (INMARSAT 3 F1, 2, 3, 4 and 5) are operational. The fourth generation of INMARSAT satellites, the INMARSAT 4 series will comprise of three satellites namely the Inmarsat-4 F1, Inmarsat-4 F2 and Inmarsat-4 F3. Now over 1,25,000 INMARSAT mobile terminals are in use.

Frequency range of operation of INMARSAT satellites is in *L* band, 1535-1542.5 MHz for satellite to mobile terminal and 1636.5-1644 MHz for mobile terminal to satellite. Satellite transmissions to and from CES are in the *C* band at 4.6 GHz. East Intelsat Satellite has a capacity in the *L* band of about 30 telephone voice channels while each Marecs and Marisat channel has a capacity of about 50 and 10 channels respectively. An additional 1 MHz from ship-to-satellite has been allocated between 1645.5-1646.5 MHz and from satellite to ship, between 1544-1545 MHz exclusively for distress and safety purposes.

The Inmarsat satellite system comprises of :

(*a*) **The Space Segment :** This has four GEO satellites placed at one of the four ocean regions to provide a global coverage :

Two satellites are over the Atlantic Ocean Regions East and West, AORE-15.5°W and AORW-55.5°W respectively.

One over the Indian Ocean Region (IOR-64.5°E, one over the Pacific Ocean Region (POR-180°E).

The footprints of these satellites overlap so that two satellites are sufficient to provide various services in different parts around the world.

(*b*) **The Ground Segment :** This segment has :

(*i*) a large number of fixed earth stations (Gateways) and mobile earth stations (MES). (*ii*) Inmarsat Network Control Center (NCC) (*iii*) Three Satellite Control Centers (SCC) is for MES and the satellites for the physical management of Inmarsat satellites.

(*c*) The subscriber units including the satphones, fascimile, telex and the data terminals.

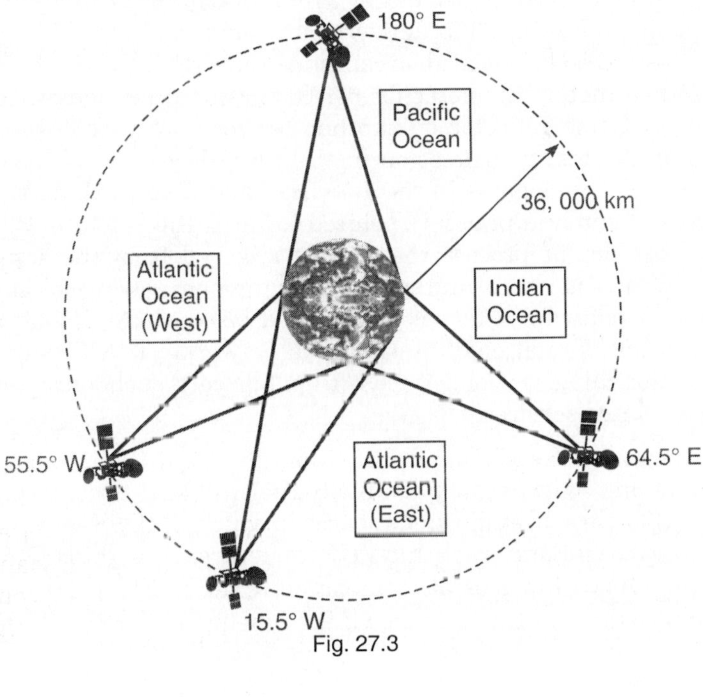

Fig. 27.3

As shown in Fig. 27.3, the calls can be made between two mobile users, and terrestrial phones. Standard Inmarsat satphones and telex terminals are used to make and receive calls using the Inmarsat satellite network. The calls to the terrestrial phones are routed via the satellite to the gateways from where they are sent directly to the terrestrial public switched networks. Satellite Gateway links; known as feeder links, employ 6 GHz band in the uplink direction and 4 GHz band in the downlink direction.

Table 27.4

Inmarsat D & D+ (1996-97)	(1) Low bit rate two way data communication using personal CD player sized terminals. (2) Data Broadcast e.g. financial data, vehicle tracking, personal messaging
Inmarsat mini-M (1996)	(1) Inmarsat's most popular service employing the smallest, lightest and the cheapest terminals to provide digital voice and data services. (2) Used by journalists, workers, business people, emergency services, rural telephony.
Inmarsat Aero-I 1998	(1) Telephone, data and fax services to short and medium-haul aircrafts. (2) Passenger voice telephone, facsimile, cockpit voice and data, air traffic control, secure voice access to major air traffic control centers.

As the coast earth station (CES) is an earth station alongwith a telephone exchange through which national, international telephone, telex and data networks are connected to the maritime user. Each CES has a parabolic antenna reflector of the size between 10 and 13 meters diameter for 6/4 GHz communications with the satellite. Same reflector or another between 1.5 and 3 diameter controls the test transmission in the 1.6 GHz band and monitors satellite to ship signals in the 1.5 GHz band. The tracking system keeps the antenna precisely pointed towards the satellite. RF and other equipment process the signals received from the satellite. Through access control and signalling equipment relying on complex computer software a link is established between the INMARSAT system and the national/international network. The CES provides two major categories of services: (*a*) public correspondence and (*b*) safety related services.

Alongwith the CES and ESS there is also a Global Maritime Distress and Safety system (GMDSS) that will be in operation since 1991. There are three divisions of area in which GMDSS works. Area A_1 covers coastal waters within VHF range, area A_2 within MF range and area A_3 within geostationary satellite range. The polar regions are not covered in this system, GMDSS helps in alerting the ships through distress signals. This distress signals is received by a shore-based Rescue Coordination Centre (RCC) cordinating rescue opertions which in turn alerts ships through Enhanced Group Call (EGC). This EGC using the standard *C* system provides two kinds of services the *safety net and fleenet* to ships round the clock. With safety net, a standard *C* terminal receives and record weather navigation distress and other emergency information relevant to vessels operating in, or approaching an area. Fleenet is intended for commercial information news, sports, commodity prices, currency notes, stock exchanges, reports, etc.

INMARSAT has also the system called *Distress Message Generator* that can be built in Standard *A* or *C* SES which is good for increasing the maritime safety. This device is capable of transmitting automatically distress messages including SES identity, position, nature of distress, course and speed of vessels, data/time of activation and the form of help required. In the worst case of ship sinking, the device will remain afloat and keep on transmitting data.

EPIRB (Emergency Position Indicating Radio Beacon) is another kind of safety device that thas also been used to work with INMARSAT. This device is used when the ship is sinking or in distress or the seamen are scattered in the sea. The device works automatically and infact when it floats emits radio signals telling its identity location which are picked up by the satellite and related to CES. Multichannel SES is also be used by very big ships having standard *A* antenna. These simultaneously work on four telephone or telex channels and will also provide a voice broadcast service allowing facsimile or voice to be broadcast.

Land based users : INMARSAT has opened its system for land-based users for long range communication is remote areas of the world. The organisation INMARSAT grants licenses for land based terminals on a case by basis, the chief criterion being a requirement for high quality communications where other facilities aren't available. Also, permission from the country in which the terminal is to be used must be obtained prior to INMARSAT commissioning.

Typical customers for land based satellite communications include disaster relief agencies, law enforcement, remote mining or construction sites, oil wells, land survey teams and newscasting. The INMARSAT system offers important advantages for land based users, including cost effectiveness, worldwide coverage, support of data/fax communications, ease of use and of deployment, and also security. With INMARSAT service is paid for only as it is used. There are no fixed charges other than the initial cost of buying the satellite terminal. The user doesn't have to pay for a leased satellite transponder or dedicated lines and there are there are no monthly minimums for system usage. This makes the system especially attractive to lower volume or those needing temporary communication satellites. The capital cost of buying and deploying the system are also minimal.

27.5.1. Navigational, Search and Rescue Satellite Systems

Navigational satellites are essentially radio transmetters of which the orbital positions are known. Through analysing the signals from three satellites, a navigator is not only able to determine his longitude and latitude but also, where appropriate, its altitudes.

The early navigational satellites in the Transi series used a radio-Doppler navigation method in which the ship's position was calculated from the observed change in the received frequency of the satellite radio transmission as the satellite passes across the sky. This technique is based on the principle that the orbit of a satellite can be accurately computed by the analysis of the Doppler shift of the radio transmissions by the satellite. The accuracy is, however, limited by the frequency stability of the satellite transmissions and the ability to predict the satellite's orbit between the time it is measured by a ground tracking station and the time the user observed the satellite.

Another method is based on time ranging. Here the user calculates his distance from a satellite by a measurement of the time that the radio signal of the satellite takes to cover the distance to the receiver. To achieve a reasonable accuracy, this method requires the three separate satellites and a very accurate clock. These systems have world wide satellite control networks and GPS reciever units that acquire the satellite's signals and translate them into position information and also provide navigation and timing information to military and civilians world wide.

The GPS system offers services ranging from drive assistance to avoid traffic jams, tracking dangerous cargos etc. to search-and-rescue help. It provides 3D model of the Earth specified to measure various aspects of the Earth's atmosphere, ocean, land, ice, etc.

Search and rescue satellites are designed to provide a way for vessels at sea and in the air to communicate from remote areas. These satellites can detect and locate emergency beacons carried by ships, aircrafts, or individuals in remote or dangerous places.

The first rescue aided by spacecraft was in September of 1982 when a Soviet satellite, Cosmos-1383, detected a distress beacon from a pair of small airplanes that had crushed. The satellite was able to give rescuers the location of the two downed planes; they were the airplanes of a young man and the young man's father who had set out looking for his son's plane crash site.

The idea of search and rescue satellites comes from weather satellite programmes. **Meteosat**, for example, monitors weather patterns by direct observation, but it also analyzes signals sent out from buoys floating in the ocean. Those buoys collect local weather information and transmit that to the satellite. The satellite then uses the *doppler effect* to find out where that particular buoy is. This mechanism is similar to the technology now used for search and rescue.

Satellites equipped with search and rescue equipment fly over a beacon that is releasing an emergency signal. Using mathematical calculations involving the *doppler effect*, scientists can translate that signal into coordinates, and determine the location of the distress signal within four kilometres.

In 1974, Canada made it law that all aircraft must carry a beacon an Emergency Locator Transmitter (ELT). After the ELT came the Emergency Position Indicating Radio Beacon (EPIRB). EPIRB's are automatic, self-powered, very portable, completely waterproof, and can float on water surface.

1. Cospas-Sarsat. The newest search and rescue system is the Cospas-Sarsat system. It is an international search and rescue system made up of a network of satellites in space, and control centres on Earth-ground stations, mission control centres, and rescue coordination centres. The Sarsat system was developed in a joint effort by the United States, Canada, and France. The Cospas system was developed by the Soviet Union. These four nations banded together in 1979 to form Cospas-Sarsat. In 1982, the first Cospas-Sarsat satellite was launched, and by 1984 the system was declared fully operational. From there, the Cospas-Sarsat organization continued to grow. The four original member nations have now been joined by 25 other nations that operate 28 ground stations and 15 mission control centres worldwide. In the eyes of the countries using this system, Cospas-Sarsat has very much helped the search and rescue efforts.

The satellites circle the globe at 1000 km altitudes in scanning a wide swath of the earth for distress signals and relaying them to specially built earth stations. It must be noted that this system is quite different to INMARSAT which is aimed mainly to commercial maritime industry. Cospas-Sarsat is useful to private and corporate fliers as well as airline crews, pleasure boaters and small scale commercial fishermen and merchant shippers. Whether a plane has gone down in a remote mountain range or ship is floundering in the subarctic Atlantic, satellites direct distress signals and alert rescue teams.

In Cospas-Sarsat system, a small industry powered transmitter on a ship or aircraft is activated-manually or automatically in an accident. Once activated, the transmitter of beacon emits a low power omnidirectional signal that is picked up by a satellite. The satellite then relays the distress signals to an earth station which in turn sends the message over conventional communication lines to a rescue center. These cospas-sarsat satellites are used with INMARSAT systems in a composite scheme as shown in Fig. 27.4. In such a system emergency alerts from aeronautical beacons would be relayed by Cospas-Sarsat satellites to an earth station and from there to a mission control center and the rescue coordination center nearest the downed aircraft. The duty of officer at the rescue coordination center then dispatches a search and rescue team.

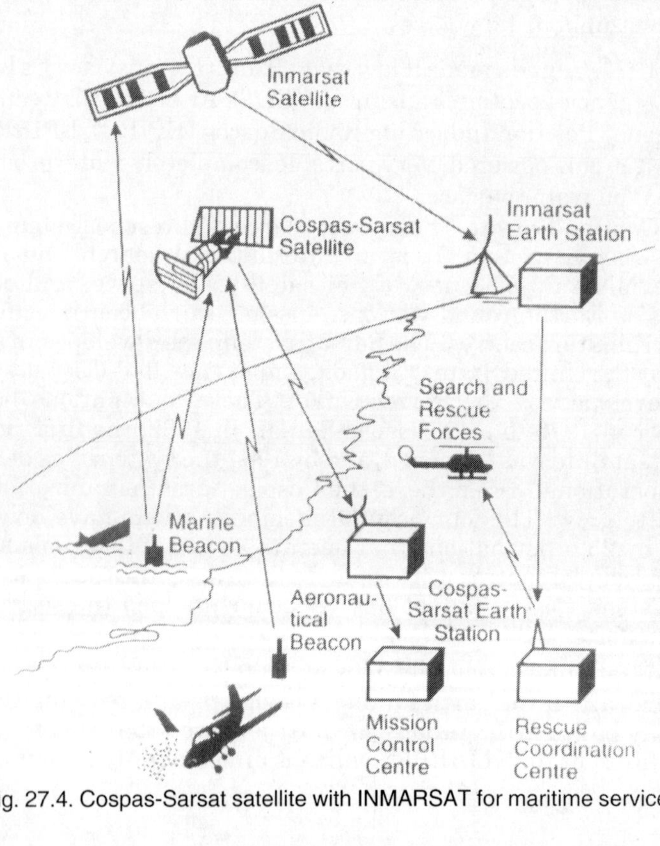

Fig. 27.4. Cospas-Sarsat satellite with INMARSAT for maritime services.

Marine distress signals picked up by the Cospas-Sarsat satellite follow a similar route. A marine signal received by an INMARSAT satellite on the other hand is relayed to one of Inmarsat's earth stations and from there transmitted directly to a rescue coordination center. For large ships the beacon would be integrated with the voice and telex satellite communication equipment.

As mentioned above the Sarsat system is a low polar orbit satellite which can be also termed as LEO satellite. Such satellites instead of remaining over one spot over the earth encircle it, passing over the Poles. The earth's rotation brings the satellite within view of every point on the ground several times a day. Such LEO satellites are also being used for communication services (*store and forward satellite communication*). Typical example of such a satellite is UOSAT-2 in which digital messages are transmitted to the LEO satellite when it is over one ground terminal. They are stored in computer memory on the satellite and then transmitted back to the earth when the satellite passes within range of the desination terminal. Such satellites have the advantages of being accessible even to polar regions.

Worldwide discussions are currently taking place regarding the discontinuation of COSPAS-SARSAT satellite coverage for 121.5 MHz and 243 MHz beacons. The 121.5 MHz frequency is used by older beacons which do not transmit any encoded information. The power output of these beacons is specified as 50, 75, or 100 mWatts. 121.5 MHz is also the transmission frequency of low power (25 mWatts) final homing transmitters included in many newer 406 MHz beacons. Presently there are approximately 590,000 beacons which operate on 121.5 MHz in use worldwide. The 243 MHz frequency is used in some older beacons deployed by the U.S. military and NATO forces. The 243 MHz frequency is not monitored by the Russian COSPAS satellites. Modern beacons which transmit digitally encoded information within the message use the 406.025 MHz frequency. Encoded information can include beacon ID to allow use of a user reference data base and beacon location determined by a sophisticated navigation device such as GPS. The RF power output 406 MHz beacons is specified as 5 watts. This higher output power allows these beacons to be received reliably by geostationary orbiting satellites. There are approximately 156,000 beacons presently in use worldwide which operate on 406.025 MHz.

COSPOS-SARSAT has been experimenting with 406 MHz receivers on geostationary earth orbiting (GEO) satellites. These experiments have proven the capability of GEOSAR to provide immediate alerting and identification of 406 MHz beacons. The GEO satellites are not able to use Doppler location processing since they have no relative motion between them and the emergency beacons. Therefore, they are not able to detemine a location for a beacon. They can, however, provide immediate alerts. This is valuable tool for SAR personnel since it allows them to begin their initial vertification of the alert using the NOAA beacon registration database. Often this detective work yields a general location of the vessel or aircraft in distress and SAR assets can be readied or dispatched to that general area. Ideally, a SARSAT or COSPAS polar orbiting satellite will overfly the beacon within the next hour and calculate a Doppler location which will be forwarded to the SAR personnel who may already be enroute.

2. Galileo. This is the Europe's navigation satellite system, providing a highly accurate, guaranteed global positioning service under civilian control. It will be inter-operable with GPS and GLONASS, the two other global satellite navigation systems.

A user will be able to take a position with the same receiver from any of the satellites in any combination. By offering dual frequencies as standard, however, Galileo will driver real-time positioning accuracy down to the metre range, which is unprecendented for a publicly available system.

It will guarantee availability of the service under all but the most extreme circumstances and will inform users within seconds of a failure of any satellite. This will make it suitable for applications where safety is crucial, such as running trains, guiding cars and landing aircraft.

The Galileo system consists of 30 satellites (27 operational + 3 active spares), positioned in three circular Medium Earth Orbit (MEO) planes in 23616 km altitude above the Earth, and at an inclination of the orbital planes of 56 degrees with reference to the equatorial plane. Once this is achieved, the Galileo navigation signals will provide a good coverage even at latitudes up to 75 degrees north, which corresponds to the North Cape, and beyond. The large number of satellites together with the optimisation of the constellation, and the availability of the three active spare satellites, will ensure that the loss of one satelline has no discernible effect on the user.

Two Galileo Control Centres (GCC) will be implemented on European ground to provide for the control of the satellites and to perform the navigation mission management. The data provided by a global network of twenty Galileo Sensor Stations (GSS) will be sent to the Galileo Control Centres through a redundant communications network. The GCC's will use the data of the Sensor Stations to compute the integrity information and to synchronize the time signal of all satellites and of the ground station clocks. The exchange of the data between the Control Centres and the satellites will be performed through so called up-link stations. Five S-band up-link stations and 10 C-band up-link stations will be installed around the globe for this purpose.

As a further feature, Galileo will provide a global Search and Recue (SAR) function, based on the operational Cospas-Sarsat system. To do so, each satellite will be equipped with a transponder, which is able to transfer the distress signals from the user transmitters to the Rescue Co-ordination Centre, which will then initiate the rescue operation. At the same time, the system will provide a signal to the user, informing him that his situation has been detected and that help is under way. This latter feature is new and is considered a major upgrade compared to the existing system, which does not provide a feedback to the user.

3. Navstar. The *Navstar series* of navigational satellite also known as Navigational Development Satellite (NDS) and the Global Positioning System (GPS). The satellites were developed for the US Navy by Rockwell and four satellites provided a positional fix with an accuracy of 30 m. It was also made available to civilian users. The 525 kg NS-7A Navstar satellite was fitted with three rubidium clocks and one caesium clock. It transmitted at 1575.42 MHz for civilian users and at 1227.6 MHz for military users.

The Navstar 2 system, designated as NS-7B, was also built by Rockwell. The operational system consisted of 21 satellites each 1665 kg satellite was equipped with an atomic clock with an accuracy of 1 second in 300,000 years. The transmissions were at 1575.42 MHz for civilian purposes and 1227.6 MHz for military purposes. Further improvements to the instrumentation was introduced with the Navstar 2R series, which was also designated as NS-7D. Whilst these satellites used the original Rockwell design, they were in fact built by Lockheed Martin.

The designation NS-7E refers to the Navstar 2F series of satellites. Boeing (which now owns Rockwell) has received an order to build six against a requirement of 33 by 2012. As it is recognised that over the years that the Navstar 2 F series will be launched, technology and needs will change, Boeing has adopted a modular approach which will allow them to meet those changes.

4. NNSS. The Navy Navigational Satellite System (NNSS), also called Oscar or Transit-O, was the first operational system. The principal objective was to provide positioning facilities with an accuracy of 150 m to submarines carrying Polaris missiles. At a later stage the system was also made available to civilian users. The satellites transmitted at 150 MHz and 400MHz. Whilst six satellites provide a useful coverage, additional satellites have been launched as in-orbit spares. The satellites had an initial mass of 32 kg and in total 32 were built by RCA. They have been identified by the third and fourth characters in the numeric designation whilst the meaning of the numeric '3' is not known.

5. Nova. The Nova military navigational satellite had a mass of 166 kg and tested new instruments and techniques. They also carried a tri-axis vector magnetometer, four solar detectors and internal mass displacement detector.

6. Transit series. The early navigational satellites of the United States were of an experimental nature. They were sponsored by the U.S. Navy and were built by RCA. The Transit-1A and -2 series carried two ultrastable oscillators, an electronic clock and four freqency transmitters which operated in the 162/216 MHz and 53/324 MHz bands. Transit-3 carried in addition a small magnetic memory. The Transit-4 series, which was of a different design, was unique in that they carried a Supplementary Nuclear Power (SNAP) source to generate the satellite's power requirements. Transmitters operated at 150/400 MHz. The Transit-5 series satellites were of an actogonal shape and carried dual frequency transmitters as well as a 30 m gravity gradient stabilisation boom. The 5A sub-series were powered by solar cells whilst the 5 B sub-series carried a SNAP-9A nuclear power source. The 5 C subseries reverted again to solar cells.

7. Timation/ NTS. The Timation or Navigation Technology Satellites (NTS) series tested new equipment to be used in the Global Positioning System (GPS). Timation-1 carried two high-precision quartz clocks for accurate measurements based on a three dimensional navigation technique. Timation-2 carried improved equipment and a dual frequency transmitter operating at 150/400 MHz. In addition Timation-3 or NTS-1 carried two rubidium vapor atomic clocks and operated at the 335 MHz and 1580 MHz frequencies whilst NTS-2 tested a ceasium clock. The satellite also carried an experimental solar array.

8. TIP. The satellites in the Transit Improvement Program (TIP) were considered as a precursor to the Nova series and incorporated the Disturbance Compensating System (Discos), hence Transit Improved And Discos (Triad), which was designed to maintain position in orbit by correcting disturbances caused by solar wind and atmospheric resistance. In addition TIP-1 carried a radio-isotope thermal generator.

27.6. Defence Satellites

27.6.1. Development of Military Satellites

Military satellites have developed through the years and have now a days became quite important for national security. In 1976, the first so called "*military satellite*" was let into space. It was known as the KH-11 and was equipped with large telescopes and video cameras to observe earth and to continuously transmit pictures to ground stations. Also, the KH-11 was one of the few satellites of the time with improved nightime observing ability. "It's rumored that KH-11's can pick out objects six inches long, and perhaps as little as two inches long; it may be possible to read automobile plates" (Waters, 63). Another major development of the military satellite was the development of the Cosmos 1426. This military satellite was developed and launched in 1982 by the Soviet Union in response to the United States' KH-11. The images obtained by this Satellite were in film form. Its quality was cheaper than that of the KH-11, but was produced and launched in more numbers. Also, in 1988, Israel and South Africa constructed and launched the Offea 1. France, Italy, and Spain have also collaboratively started their own network of military satellites.

27.6.2. Uses of Military Satellites

Countries use satellites in the military in various ways. Military satellites are used in the Air Force, Navy, and primarily in military detection. The United States is one of the leading countries involved in highly technologically advanced military satellites. Countries use military satellites for military detection. Military detection is primarily accomplished by Navigational Systems such as the NNSS (Navy Navigational Satellite System). However, there are also other examples of measurement and intelligence collection systems. These include the nuclear detonation detection systems of Global Positioning System Satellites; radar systems such as the missile tracking and detecting and detection radar.

These are capable of providing message, data and live telecasts across international boundaries (more loosely from any part of the world). Infact the present day balance of power depends on them and so techniques are also there to save them in case they are being attached by a killer satellite from enemy or so. Actually modern electronic warfare completely depends on satellite.

Military Satellites also serves meteorological, intelligence, navigation, and communications needs for the services. Civilians also are able to enjoy the benefits of the military technology however, as meteorologial and navigational systems are made available to civilian distribution authorities as well. For example DMSP data is available through National Oceanographic and Atmospheric Administration (NOAA) and Global Positioning System (GPS) data is available at a slightly less resolution to anyone with a commercial grade GPS receiver.

Intelligence satellites fall into several basic categories:

- SIGINT (electrical sensing, including COMINT, TELINT, RADINT, ELINT, LASINT, etc.)
- PHOTOINT (photo sensing...i.e. film)
- Electro-optical (television, infrared sensors, imaging radar, etc.)
- Aggressive (anti-satellite satellite).

In the early years of military satellites, the most common sensors were of the PHOTOINT variety, with infrared and SIGINT satellites following very quickly. Today the watchword for overhead recon is "real time". This literally means the gathering of data from the satellite and transmittal to the ground station and the "observers" on the ground, all as it happens. This being a much desired upgrade over the early versions of recon satellites which spit out film packages or recording packages on a parachute each of which had to be recovered in order to get the data you desired. Also of concern today and the *launch vehicles* for satellites especially since the Challenger explosion.

Satellites today serve one of three combinations of basic mission in terms of intelligence gathering :

1. *Dedicated :* Primary mission is to gather overhead reconaissance
2. *Collateral :* Military Satellite with a primary mission is other than space surveillance but either there is a second set of sensors on board or the primary sensor can be used for overhead reconaissance.
3. *Contributing :* Non-military satellites that contributes to military or intelligence quality overhead surveillance as a second or lower priority. Example: SPOT and its uses by the U.S. Military.

Military satellites may be both non-weapon or weapon satellites but it is the non-weapon ones that have been mostly used for a variety of purposes. SDI's have initiated the program of weapon satellites. The non-weapon military satellites are of roughly six primary categories, namely the reconnaisance satellites, early warning satellites, navigational satellites, communication satellites, meteorological satellites and geodetic satellite.

27.6.3 Reconnaissance satellites

These were the first which were deployed for military purposes. These are used to monitor objects and their movements on the ground. There are three kinds of such reconnaissance satellite, namely, the photo-reconnaissance, electronic reconnaissance and ocean reconnaissance satellites. Photo reconnaissance satellites are mostly used for monitoring conflict areas. Initially these were meant for area surveillance and were aimed at scanning large areas of strategic importance. Such satellites had short life of span of three to 5 weeks and were mission oriented. Such satellites could take photographs only when and were in orbit and were not in a position to transmit photographs back to earth.

Development of Spy/Reconnaissance Satellites

Spy and reconnaisance satellites have been developed throughout the years. This development was achieved through a series of steps. In the 1960's and 1970's, the U.S. developed satellites that could use their own rocket engines and navigational systems to move from one orbit to another, or swoop closer to Earth for especially detailed observations. The U.S. military continued to develop satellites that could relay information to Earth on radio waves. Film-dropping satellites remained essential for high-resolution pictures until 1976. The biggest step to reconnaissance satellites came as result of the Cold War." The Cold War was the development and deployment of increasingly sophisticated reconnaissance satellites, manned and unmanned spy planes, and land and sea-based listening posts" (High Flying 49). It was at this time that spy and reconnaissance satellites broke off from the other military satellites and formed their own category.

Today, spy satellites have differenciated into different types. There are four kinds of spy satellites; reconnaissance, ocean surveillance, early warning, and elint. The most important type of spy satellite is the reconnaissance. The reconnaissance satellites photograph missile bases and other places of military interest. They have to get close-up pictures, thus, they are placed in low orbits. The drag from the atmosphere slowly brings them down causing their life time to be only a few weeks.

Reconnaissance satellites have been used by countries in many ways and will be continued to be used in the future. It has been reported from the National Reconnaissance Office, which handles US intelligence satellite procurement, there has been the developing of an imaging satellite that would cover eight times more territory in a single image than the advanced KH-11. This wide-area capability, obtained at the cost of a reduced scale, makes it possible to cover far more territory with less effort. This will tremendously help countries in their spy and reconnaissance satellite technology. Also, due to the reduction of satellite cost, more countries will be able to enter the world of Reconnaisance satellites to reap its benefits and advantages.

27.6.4 Electronic reconnaissance satellites

Also called as Electronic intelligence (ELINT), these satellites are used to locate enemy's communications signals. Thus enemy's radars and other electronic equipment activities can be easily monitored by ELINT satellites and the electronic counter measure (ECM) equipment may be successfully used. *Ocean reconnaissance satellites* are used to locate targets of military importance at sea, say about naval force such as ships, submarines etc. Operation of such satellites is based on the use of sensors that measure the difference between the temperatures of sea cool water and water released by submarine.

Table 27.5. Types of Sensors on Board Satellite

Sensor	*Functions*	*Types of Satellite*
Photographic	Detection of ABM systems, ICBM and cruise missile deployment, military facilities and troop movements	US photographic reconnaissance satellites such as the KH services and many of the Soviet Cosmos satellites
Infrared	Detection of missiles, aircraft and cruise missiles (potentials)	US and Soviet warning satellites
Nuclear Radiation Detectors	Detection of nuclear explosions in the upper atmosphere and in outer space	US Vela satellites and IONDS-Integrating operational. Nuclear Detection System-carried on Board the GPS navigation satellites
Ultraviolet	Detection of fluorescence from gases surrounding booster or nose cones during ballistic flight.	US and Soviet early warning satellites

(Contd...)

Sensor	*Functions*	*Types of Satellite*
Electronic signal detectors	Radio and microwave telephonic transmission interception, radar signal detection, missile telemetry interception	Soviet Cosmos and US electronic reconnaissance satellites. US Rhyolite and Chalet satellites in geostationary orbit
Radar	Detection of Naval surface ships, many other ground based military objects	US Seasat-1 and Cosmos Ocean surveillance satellites
Thermal Infrared scanners or radiometers	Night time reconnaissance detection of targets such as burried structures of underground construction.	US Seasat-1

27.6.5 Early Warning Satellites

These are used to get information about and to detect, intercept and destroy an incoming enemy nuclear missile before it impacts on its targets. It is done by the use of infrared sensors of the satellite that are sensitive to infrared radiation emitted by the hot plume of rockets when the satellite is launched. To have better performance TV cameras are also placed on board such satellites to send pictures to ground stations. Such satellites are capable of sending information about the launch of missile to the ground station within 3 minutes and the trajectory and other characteristics of missiles can be established within 5 minutes.

Communication satellites of military are responsible for communication between various ground stations of military command located at different locations. C^3I (command, control, communications and intelligence) is transmitted *via* communication relays. Worldwide military command and control system (WWMCCS) is completely based on such military communications satellite. USA uses military communications satellites under different headlines such as Defence Satellite Communications Systems (DSCS) II, Air Force Satellite Communication System (AFSATCOM), the fleet satellite communications system (FLTSATCOM), satellite data system (SDS), military strategic tactial and relay satellite communications (MILSTAR), Airforce's Strategic Satellite System (SSS), Soviet Union also has several military communication satellites mostly under Molniya series.

Military Navigational satellites are used to determine the precise locations and velocity of mobile weapon systems such as aircraft, missile and submarines. These are mostly jam resistant like NAVSTAR GPS of USA and GLONASS of Russia. Meteorological satellites provide predictions about weather and atmospheric conditions such as information about temperature patterns at different altitudes, wind direction, water vapour, radiations, atmospheric density, electron and ion density etc. The data is stored at a central place.

Geodetic satellites give information about earth's gravitational field which is of high importance to nuclear and potentially nuclear weapon states. It helps in error-free computations of trajectories and computations in the inertial guidance systems of missile and aircraft. Also, it is being used for photomapping the earth's surface for precise ballistic missile launch and impact-point location functions.

Superpowers are trying to devise methods to destroy, kill and steal the enemy's satellites. They are developing ground based laser systems to do so. They have also developed rocket fired missiles systems capable of ramming into a satellite and destroying it. They have developed methods to retrieve launched satellites. Once such a situation arises (regarding killing of other country's satellite) then the individual country will have to have a space force just as it has army, navy and air force to protect its satellites.

In conclusion, countries use satellites in many areas and for different reasons. Whether its military reconnaissance, agriculture, or oceanography, satellites have improved a nations's military strength and/or economic strength. Satellites in these fields are still being advanced and will continue to play an important role in the future of all nations and the world.

27.6.6. America's Defense Satellite Program

When the Advent program was cancelled in 1962, a recommendation was made for another program that would be operational, not experimental. As a result, the Initial Defense Communication Satellite Program (IDCSP) was created. Its design principle was simplicity. Each IDCSP payload had a single repeater with a capacity of about 10 voice circuits or 1 megabit per second of data when communicating with large terminals on Earth.

Seven IDCSP satellites were launched in 1966 with additional groups of three to eight satellites on launched in 1967 and 1968. Twenty-eight satellites were placed into orbit, operating for periods ranging from one to ten years. The IDCSP satellites drifted in orbits slightly below geostationary altitude. In contrast, almost all subsequent DOD communication satellites operated in the geostationary orbit.

In the U.S., military satellites have a big impact on the Air Force and Navy. Just recently, the U.S. Air Force started building powerful electronic cameras to scan skies and calculate, automatically, motions of all satellites that enter their fields of view. These new systems of satellites, can detect fainter objects and analyze orbital maneuvers by satellites in minutes, whereas photographic techniques require a minimum of an hour and a half. Also, military satellites play a big role in the U.S. Navy. The U.S. Navy has just developed a Navigation Satellite System (NNSS). It has been developed initially for ballistic (Of or relating to projectiles, their motion, or their effects) missile submarines for use in their updating of the inertial navigational system. However, it has also been extended for ships. This was made assessable because now high accuracy fixes several times a day can be retrieved on every point on the Earth with the help of this new Nary Navigation Satellite System. NNSS is passive and uses low-orbit satellites to function.

1. Tactical Communication Satellite (TACSAT). The IDCSP satellites and the advanced satellites that followed them were for strategic communications between large-antenna, fixed or transportable ground stations and large shipborne equipment. The Tractical Communication Satellite (Tacsat), following the Lincoln satellites, was designed for a complementary function: operation with small land-mobile, airborne, or shipborne tactical terminals.

The Tacsat communication payload was designed with both UHF and X-band capabilities to permit operation with a wide variety

Fig. 27.5. The Tacsat satellite; the large cylinder was covered with solar cells, and the five helixes were the UHF antenna.

of terminals. The requirement to operate with small terminals called for the use of high-power transmitters, which necessitated a very large, cylindrical body to provide the required solar-cell area. The need for the large body in turn required the development of a new stabilization technique, which was refined and subsequently applied to many communication satellites.

Tascat was launched in 1969. On-orbit testing was done with a variety of terminals, including large ground stations, mobile ground stations, aircrafts, and ships. Tacsat was used for operational support of Apollo recovery operations; it connected the aircraft, the aircraft carrier, and the ground stations. Military use, especially of the UHF band, was extensive. Operations continued until an attitude-control failure in 1972.

2. Milsatcom Architecture. By the early 1970s, DOD had determined the need for a Milsatcom architecture to guide the development of technology and programs that would be responsive to military users' requirements and realizable within the DOD budget. In 1973 the Defense Communications Agency (DCA), now the Defense Information Systems Agency, was assigned responsibility for developing this architecture.

The first comprehensive milsatcom architecture, has three segments: wideband, mobile and tactical (or narrowband), and protected (or nuclear-capable). Within each segmnet is a mix of users similar enough to be supported by a common satellite system.

3. Defence Satellite Communication Systems Series (DSCS). The USA launched DSCS-1, 2 & 3 series to aid its Military Defense to provide high security data, voice communication services and to provide vital information during wars between its defense officials and commanders deployed in battlefields.

DSCS-1 gave Pentagon its communication systems, DSCS-2 provided voice and data communications for Defense and the DSCS-3 which is geostationary communication satellite aids US Military with anti-jam nuclear capability supporting its Defence Department and communications to White House.

Defense Satellite Communication System-II. The IDCSP satellites were the DSCS Phase I space segment. They demonstrated that satellite communications could satisfy certain DOD needs, so in 1968, DOD decided to proceed with the development of satellites for DSCS Phase II.

DSCS II satellites had a command subsystem, attitude control and stationkeeping capabilities (the ability, on command from Earth, to adjust satellite orientation or orbital position), and multiple communication channels with multiple-access capability. IDCSP had none of these features; however, the DSCS II design was compatible with modified Phase I ground terminals as well as new terminals specifically built for Phase II.

The DSCS II communication payload had four channels with various combinations of bandwidth and antennas. The combinations provided the flexibility to handle a wide variety of links and to communicate with many sizes of terminals. Initial terminals constructed at major nodes had 18.3-meter-diameter antennas.

The DSCS II program began with six satellites launched in pairs, the first in 1971. Major technical problems caused the satellites to fail in 1972 and 1973. Analyses of these problems, with significant Aerospace contributions, provided the basis for design modifications for the next satellites. By 1989 a total of 16 satellites were launched to establish and maintain an orbital constellation with at least four active and two spare satellites. All are now out of service and have been moved above the geosynchronous orbit to prevent interference with active satellites.

DSCS III. The DSCS program was planned for long-distance communications between major military locations. During the system's evolution, both the number and variety of terminals increased as more DOD units sought to benefit from satellite communications. By the 1990s, a majority of DSCS terminals fell into the categories of small, transportable, or shipboard. Phase III DSCS satellites were developed to operate in this diverse environment.

The primary DSCS III communication payload operates in the X-band and has eight antennas that can be connected in various ways to the six transponders ("transmitter/responders"). Each transponder can be configured to serve a specific type of user requirement. Besides Earth-coverage antennas, the satellite has one multibeam receiving antenna, which can form a beam of variable size, shape, and location, and two similar multibeam transmitting antennas.

DSCS III development started in 1977. The first satellite was launched in 1982, and 11 additional satellites have been launched since then. All are operational. Five occupy the prime operating locations of the DSCS constellation, which are spaced around Earth is geostationary orbit. The others, spares for the five primary satellites, augment the capacity and coverage of the constellation.

To satisfy increasing user needs, the last four DSCS II satellites were enhanced to improve their communications capacity by 200 percent, with up to a 700-percent increase in capacity to tactical users (those with small terminals) in certain scenarios. Aerospace played a key role in identifying and analyzing options for this enhancement program–and important activity, since the number of tactical users increased greatly over the past two decades. Many use truck- or trailer-mounted terminals with 2.4-meter-diameter antennas. Such terminals do not operate while in motion, but can be set up at an unprepared site by two or three people in less than 30 minutes.

4. Global Broadcast Service (GBS). This is another part of the milsatcom architecture's wideband segment. Its mission is to deliver high-rate intelligence, imagery, map and video data to tactical forces using small, portable terminals. Phase I of GBS used a commercial satellite and a limited number of commercial receive terminals. Phase II uses the GBS payload on UFO satellites 8 through 10. This payload uses 30-gigahertz uplink and 20-gigahertz downlink frequency, often called Ka-band. Phase III will be developed in the future.

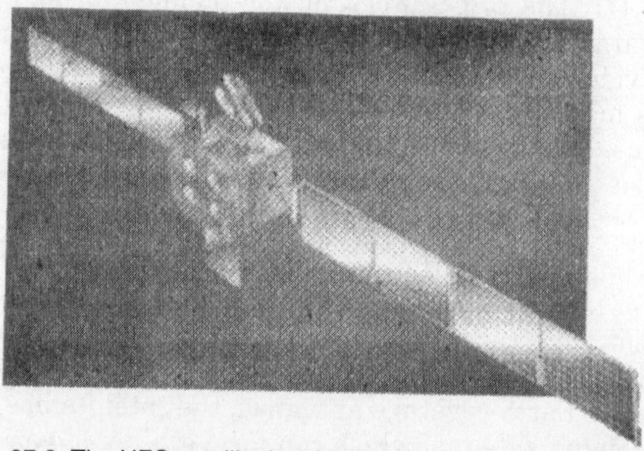

Fig. 27.6. The UFO satellite in orbit; the large structure on the front of the satellite body is the UHF transmit antenna, the small square toward the bottom of the body is the UHF receive antenna, and the equipment on the top is the GBS antenna apparatus

Information to be disseminated through GBS is assembled into a broadcast stream transmitted to the satellite and rebroadcast to a large number of users in one of several spot-beam coverage areas. (Spot-beam antennas focus on a limited area of Earth.) Each user, typically a small military unit, has an easily moverable set of receiving and display equipment.

5. Mobile and Tractical Systems. Users in the mobile-and-tactical segment of the architecture are characterized by small terminals with relatively low-gain antennas; they are located on ships, aircraft, and land vehicles. Data rates are low to moderate, and connectivity is typically in networks at distances ranging from in-theater to transoceanic. Systems in this segment are the Fleet Satellite Communication System, the Leasat program, and the UHF Follow-On (UFO) program.

6. Fleet Satellite Communications. Tascat and LES-5 and -6 were experimental satellites that demonstrated UHF (225- to 400-megahertz) links with mobile terminals. These satellites were used for numerous tests, and Tascat and LES-6 provided a limited operational capacity for DOD. The Fleet Satellite Communications (FLTSATCOM) system was DOD's first operational system (dedicated to supporting military operations) for tactical users.

Fig. 27.7 A ground mobile forces satellite terminal with the 2.4-meter antenna; communications electronics inside the truck.

FLTSATCOM served Navy surface ships, submarines, aircraft, and shore stations. The largest antenna, used for UHF transmissions, was a 5-meter-diameter paraboloid that had a solid center section and a deployable outer mesh section. The separate UHF receiving antenna was a single helix deployed to the side of the large paraboloid. Most links were in the UHF band.

The first FLTSATCOM was launched in 1978, and one satellite was damaged during ascent and could not be used. The others operated as expected and greatly exceeded their five-year design lives. They have been removed from service and replaced by UFO satellites.

7. LEASAT. The Leasat program, primarily served the Navy, plus Air Force and ground forces mobile users. FLTSATCOM terminals were used with Leasat. Leasat had four types of communication channels, with characteristics very similar to the FLTSATCOM channels, and four communications antennas: two X-band and two UHF; all were Earth-coverage.

The contract for Leasat development was awarded in 1978 and called for five years of communication service to be provided at each of four orbital locations. The first two launches took place in 1984, the last in 1990. Leases on satellites 2, 3, and 5 were extended into 1996. The Leasats have been removed from service and replaced by UFO satellites, with the exception of one now in use by the Australian Defence Forces.

8. UFO. The Navy replaced the older satellites with a constellation of eight UFOs, plus one spare. The UFO satellites have more channels than the earlier satellites and are designed to be comparatible with the more than 2000 UHF terminals used with FLTSATCOM and Leasat. Satellite capability increases have led to a reduction of terminal sizes. Some terminals can be carried, set up, and used by one person, thus minimizing the burden on military users and increasing the number of military units that can benefit from satellite communications.

Fig. 27.8. The Army's Enhanced Manpack UHF Terminal, which is capable of being carried, set up, and used by a single soldier, communicates via the UFO satellites.

The first UFO was lost as a result of a launch vehicle problem, but the next nine, successfully launched between 1993 and 1999, are still in use. Satellite 11 was launched in 2003. Besides performing its usual systems engineering tasks throughout the UFO program, Aerospace also developed a telemetry analysis workstation and installed it in a satellite control center.

Protected Systems. Mobility characterizes users of the protected segment of the milsatcom architecture, whether they are on ships, aircraft, or land vehicles. They accept very low to moderate data rates in exchange for considerable protection of their links against physical, nuclear, and electronic threats. Systems in the protected segment of the milsatcom architecture are the Milstar system and the Air Force Satellite Communications (AFSATCOM) and extremely high frequency (EHF) payloads.

9. AFSATCOM. It served Air Force strategic aircraft, airborne command posts, and ground terminals. AFSATCOM satellite payloads are on the FLTSATCOM satellites and on several satellites situated in high-inclination orbits to provide coverage of the north polar region, which is not visible from equatorial satellites. AFSATCOM also uses a single-channel transponder on DSCS III satellites.

AFSATCOM uses a mix of UHF and X-band frequencies with antijamming protection for most of its uplinks by frequency-hopping (rapid switching of frequencies during transmission). A portion of the Milstar communications payload continues the AFSATCOM mission.

10. FLTSATCOM (EHF). Fltsactom satellites 7 and 8 contained an EHF payload (44-gigahertz uplink and 20-gigahertz downlink) called the FEP (FLTSATCOM EHF Package). FEP was developed to demonstrate operational capabilities of EHF terminals and prove key functions of the Milstar system. This payload had both Earth-coverage and spot-beam antennas, and it processed received signals before their downlink transmission. Both links were frequency-hopped.

11. Milstar-Block I and II. The Milstar system is designed to emphasize flexibility and the ability to operate under adverse conditions, including jamming and nuclear attack. Aerospace played a key role in assessing Milstar system performance against a DOD-validated threat model. "Flexibility," in this context, is the ability to provide worldwide unscheduled access and worldwide connectivity to terminals on all types of platforms.

The Milstar program includes two Block I and four Block II satellites. These blocks are also known as LDR (low data rate) or

(TACSAT).

Milstar I, and MDR (medium data rate) or Milstar II. The block change resulted from a 1990 program restructure in response to global political changes.

Relaxation of survivability requirements and improvements in satellite electronics allows the MDR satellites to provide robustness and flexibility for 32 MDR channels, for single-user data rates up to 1.5 megabits per second, in addition to the 192 LDR channels, for single-user data rates up to 2.4 kilobits per seconds. Aerospace was a leader in the development of the standard for the LDR and MDR waveforms.

The Milstar system has three segments: mission control, terminal, and space. The mission control segment plans mission activities, allocates system resources, tests and controls the satellites, and resolves satellite anomalies. It includes a fixed site as well as mobile units. Intersatellite crosslinks enable monitoring and control of all Milstar satellites from a single location.

Fig. 27.9. The Milstar satellite in orbit with the two equipment wings and two longer solar-array wings deployed; various antennas are visible on the equipment wings. (Lockheed Martin Missiles and Space)

The terminal segment, developed by the Air Force, Navy, and Army, contains more than 1000 terminals of many types; some are vehicle-transportable or human-portable, while others are located at fixed sites or on airborne command posts or other aircraft, ships, or submarines. Antenna diameters vary from 14 centimeters for submarine terminals to 3 meters for fixed command-post terminals.

The space segment consists of the Milstar satellites. Each has a central bus, two payload wings, and two solar arrays. At the outer end of each wing is a crosslink antenna. Other antennas are mounted on the wings. Features that support the system's robustness include frequency-hopping, extensive onboard processing, and crosslinks. Features that support flexibility include multiple uplink and down link channels operating at various rates; multiple uplink and downlink beams, including agile beams; and routing of individual signals among uplinks, downlinks, and crosslinks.

The Block I satellites were launched in 1994 and 1995. Aerospace had a lead role in the analysis of one launch-vehicle failure and other anomaly just prior to the first launch, and provided launch-readiness verification for the Milstar 1 launch vehicle. The first Block II satellite was lost because of a launch problem. The second was launched in 2001; it and the Block I satellites are in operation. The third was launched in January, 2002.

12. UFO and Interim Polar EHF. Beginning with the fourth satellite in the UFO series, an EHF communications payload compatible with Milstar terminals was added to that satellite. An enhancement to the EHF payload beginning with UFO 7 doubled its communication capacity.

The EHF payload accommodates multiple uplinks distributed between the Earth-coverage antenna and the deployed steerable spot-beam antenna. Each uplink is time-shared by multiple users. The downlink (at 20 gigahertz) is a combination of all the uplinks (at 44 gigahertz). Both links are frequency-hopped.

The Interim Polar Program adapted the UFO/EHF payload for use on host satellite in high-inclination orbits. These payloads communicate with military forces operating above 65 degrees north latitude, where visibility to geostationary-orbit satellites is poor or impossible. The first launch with an interim polar payload was in 1997, and other two launches being in 2003 and 2005.

27.7. Multipurpose Satellites

1. Essaim 1, 2, 3, 4 Series. The Essaim demonstrator is a system of several micro-satellites (hence the name 'swarm' in French) for analysis of the electro-magnetic environment of the Earth's surface under development for the French Ministry of

Defence's procurement agency DGA. The system, is operational since 2004, also comprises a ground control segment and a ground station for data processing. It is called a 'demonstrator' as the mission's objective is to assess the operational capability of such a system, paving the way for the next generation.

The Essaim satellites are based on the *Myriade* micro-satellite multipurpose line developed jointly by Astrium and the French Space Agency CNES since 1998. In early 2000, the French Ministry of Defence (DGA) awarded Astrium the contract for the development, manufacturing of this turnkey system of micro-satellites and associated ground segment. Under the contract, Astrium is also responsible for launch services, personnel training and system operations during the three-year life duration of the programme.

The ESSAIM micro-satellites, launched at the end of 2004, have been operational since May, 2005. The French defence procurement agency DGA chose EADS Astrium as a joint prime contractor for the development of the ESSAIM system.

Fig. 27.10. The Essaim demonstrator is a system of several micro-satellites for electro-magnetic environment analysis of the Earth's surface for which EADS Astrium is prime contractor to the French Ministry of Defence.

The demonstrator, based on 4 micro-satellites flying in formation through space, will analyze the electromagnetic environment on the ground in a number of frequency bands used exclusively for military communications.

The ESSAIM program is a "turnkey" system, comprising the space segment, ground segment, satellite launch facilities and operations. The other partner in this program, Thales Airborne Systems, is contributing its electromagnetic system expertise.

Space segment. The space segment comprises four satellites, flying in controlled formation in two out-of-phase orbits. The four 120-kg micro-satellites are based on the Myriade platform, developed by French space agency CNES in partnership with EADS Astrium.

The program features the very latest space technologies to meet the payload weight and size restrictions imposed by micro-satellites. These technologies include triple junction gallium arsenide solar cells, lithium-ion batteries, highly-integrated electronic components and fiber-optic gyros.

Ground segment. Co-located X-band terminals at the mission center at the DGA's weapons electronics center (CELAR) in Bruz, near Rennes in western France will receive the data stored on the satellites, as they become visible.

The dedicated ESSAIM satellite control center is located at the CNES facility in Toulouse, near CNES's other Myriade micro-satellite control centers.

2. ROCSAT

In the early 1990's Taiwan adopted a long-range plan for acquiring technologies related to developing and operating spacecraft. The National Space Program Office was subsequently established to oversee a 15-year program which envisioned the launch of three LEO spacecraft with foreign assistance. The multidiscipline Rocsat program will include telecommunications payloads on at least the first two missions.

Rocsat 1, was launched on 16 January 1999 its orbit being: 600 km circular orbit, 35° inclination and was 3-axis stabilized. It was built by TRW and carried a Ka-band communications relay experiment. The communications payload was built and integrated by Taiwan's Microelectronics Technology. The 400-kg spacecraft was be placed into a low altitude, low inclination orbit (600 km, 35 degress) by a US LLV booster. Rocsat 2, with a more capable communications payload was launched in the year 2000. Integral Systems, Inc., of the US provides the satellite control facility for the Rocsat program.

Planning for the ROCSAT-I project began in 1992 and contracts were awarded starting in 1994. The project components include:

1. *Satellite bus* - A contract was signed with the American firm TRW in April 1994 for fabrication of the satellite bus. In order to achieve the goal of technology transfer, the Space Program Office sent 28 personnel to TRW to participate in planning, design, assembly and testing work over a two-year period.

2. *Ground system* - The ROCSAT ground system (RGS) consists of: a mission operation center, mission control center, science experiment control center and a flight dynamics facility located at the National Space Program Office; two telemetry, tracking and command stations located respectively at National Central University in Chungli and at the aerospace laboratory of National Cheng Kung University in Tainan; scientific data distribution centers located at National Taiwan Ocean University in Keelung, National Central University in Chungli, and the Space Program Office in Hsinchu; a ground communication network (GCN) linking all these facilities. Besides being used for the ROCSAT-1, the RGS will be used for future satellites.

3. *Payload instrumentation* - The three instrument packages includes Ocean Color Imager (OCI), Ionospheric Plasma and Electrodynamics Instrument (IPEI) and Experimental Communications Payload (ECP).

4. *Integrated testing facility* - The completed satellite integrated testing facility includes a large clean room, a highly-clean machine room, a machine shop, an electrical wiring shop and various laboratories and testing rooms.

5. *Launch services* - A contract was signed with America's Lockheed Martin Corporation to launch the ROCSAT-1 at Cape Canaveral using a LMLV-1 rocket.

Following its arrrival in Taiwan in May 1997, the ROCSAT-1 spacecraft and its three payloads were subjected to integrated testing by space program personnel. Scientific data collected by the satellite during the first four years after its launch was distributed to researchers throughout the world in order to make a contribution to science.

ROCSAT-1 is a member of the TRW lightsat family, a series of small, modular satellites whose flexible design is readily tailored to mission-specific requirements. Built in three modules to allow parallel development and test, the spacecraft is compatible with a wide range of launch vehicles. The ROCSAT-1 design easily accommodates larger payloads for future low-earth orbiting spacecraft; only minor modifications are needed for geosynchronous missions.

3. APMT

The Asia Pacific Mobile Telecommunications Satellite (APMT) consortium, in which Chinese participants initially held two-thirds equity, was formed in December 1995. APMT is a regional mobile satellite project providing seamless mobile telecommunications services, through National Service Providers in each country, in the

Asia Pacific region via a geostationary earth orbit satellite system and a network of ground gateway stations. The services include voice telephony, fascimile and data transmission. Communication is via handled, vehicular or fixed-site terminals. Frequent business travellers in the region are also expected to use APMT for roaming purposes. Coverage will be available from India in the west to Japan in the east, and from China in the north to Indonesia in the south.

APMT has a turnkey system from Hughes that includes one satellite, one spare satellite, five gateways, one network operations center, one satellite operations center, and an initial purchase of 70,000 user terminals. Each satellite will handle 16,000 simultaneous duplex circuits, from users in China, Singapore, Japan, Korea, Southeast Asia, India, Indonesia, Pakistan and the Phillippines. The satellites are high-power versions of Hughes' top-selling, body-stabilized spacecraft, the HS 601. Each will have two solar wings covered in gallium arsenide solar cells generating about 7 kilowatts of power to provide 6 kilowatts of payload power. The Hughes geomobile satellite system features an innovative, lightweight, 12.25-meter deployable antenna, and onboard digital signal processing and beamforming.

4. TDRSS (Tracking and Data Relay Satellite System)

This NASA communication relay system which provides links between low earth orbiting spacecraft and the ground. The system provides extended view times for LEO satellite communications links, and is capable of transmitting to and receiving data from any LEO spacecraft over at least 85% of its orbit. The TDRSS space segment currently consists of six first generation Tracking and Data Relay Satellites (TDRS) located in geosynchronous orbit, of which 3 are available for operational support at any given time. The remaining vehicles provide backup in the event of the failure of an operational spacecraft and, in some specialized cases, resources for target of opportunity activities. The TDRSS ground segment, the White Sands Ground Terminal located near Las Cruces, New Mexico, controls the TDRS satellites and receivers/transmits data from/to customers' LEO satellites through the TDRS satellites. The ground system, originally controlled and operated by the Contel Corporation, is now owned by NASA and operated by Allied Signal Technical Services Corp. In addition to its support of NASA communications links, the satellites also carry C- and Ku-band transponders for lease to private companies for commercial use. NASA missions supported by the system include the Hubble Telescope the Space Shuttle, GRO, Landsat, TOPEX, and EUVE and support is planned for the International Space Station.

27.8 New Technologies

27.8.1. Teleports

Teleports are the facilities or platforms which have at least 13 or more earth station which allow customers access to all domestic and international communication satellites. Customers are connected to the teleport throughout the metropolitan area *via* fibre optic network. It is essential for Teleport to sustain that it should be able to serve in an area at least 150,000 homes or more particularly in densest regions. Trend is therefore toward the development of miniteleports.

On analysing the reasons for the development and investment in teleport service, four basic reasons have been seen namely, enterpreneurial, nature, bypass purposes, economic development and real state development. Bypass means here to avoid existing communication networks of telephone companies such as those in USA, PTT, AT&T and Bell Canada etc.

There is a feeling among public as well as in Government that Teleports are necessary for economic development and therefore people would be encouraged to invest in Teleport. It is also hoped that Teleports will provide interface to business and other automation and technology users who will be making large capital investments in the ISDN environment. Teleports are also hoped to provide multinational services in future.

27.8.2 Geostationary Space Platforms

The word 'platform' for satellite communication means a very large spacecraft to be put in geostationary orbit. This is supposed to be an efficient means of increasing the capacity at a point in the geostationary orbital arc. Infact Geostationary Platform is considered to be a solution to the crowding of the orbital arc since it could provide the founction of many individual satellites of conventional design. It is also considered to carry very large antennas required for mobile communication or broadcast services, earth observation and other science payloads. Table 27.6 shows the milestones of the Geostationary platforms progress in USA.

Space platforms are considered to have several significant advantages such as (*i*) improved conservation of the geostationary arc by utilization of the radio frequency spectrum at a given point in the geostationary arc through the use of multiple payloads, giant antennas and on board signals routing and processing, (*ii*) increased data capacity per unit of arc, (*iii*) economics of scale due to shared bus, power systems, attitude large amounts dc power from a common source and (*iv*) synergism of collocating disperate payloads involving both communication and science. The disadvantages may be (*i*) high launch costs both earth to LEO and LEO to GEO, ARE : including the need to develop LEO to GEO transfer systems, (*ii*) service complexity associated with servicing during operations and (*iii*) difficulties in integrating disparate payloads.

Table 27.6. Conceptual Development of Geostationary Platform

* Genesis of concept, based on OAF (orbiting Antenna Farm)
* Shuttle assembly concepts introduced.
* Orbital arc efficiency drivers
* Industry studies by NASA
* Political problems in multiple ownership investigated.
* NASA/Comsmat/General Dynamics Study for single shuttle payload platform.
* NASA concept updates presented at various AIAA communications satellite systems Conferences.
* Mitsubushi and NASDA concepts developed ESA, Aeritalia, and MBB concepts/proposals.
* NASA started Space Station Development.
* NASA introduced staging base concept for space station
* Growing arc saturation at GEO at both C-band and Ku-band.
* Payload definition contracts to Ford and RCA for geostationary platforms by NASA.
* Bus definition contracts to Ford and Lockheed for geostationary platforms
* Completion of NASA payload/bus contracts.
* Science utilization proposals for geostationary platforms were introduced to the SESAC Task Force/Commitee at Standford Summer Study
* Proposals of geostationary platform for sound broadcasting.

Space stations alongwith the objectives mentioned above, have aims developing the capacity to assemble, service and repair satellites and other large structures in space. Space station is a complex family which at the initial operating capability (IOC) includes the LEO manned space station module, coorbiting platforms, tethered platforms or spacecrafts, free flyers, unmanned polar orbiting platforms and a staging base in the vicinity of the manner module.

27.9. Satellite Communication with Respect to Fibre Optic Communication

Fibre optic communication and the satellite communication arc being developed continuously on parallel courses for the last two decades. The capacity of these systems has greatly expanded over the last 20 years. Terrestrial wideband communication systems and communication satellite facilities are both on the order of 200 times larger than the initial satellite and fiber optic cable facilities of two decades ago. Infact very soon finding ways to fill these super large facilities quickly and efficiently will be a big challenge. The large investments they represent allow lower tolerance for errors. This 'increased risk' is an essential feature of the new telecommunication environment. It is therefore essential to study the coexistence of fibre optic cables and satellites and also the economic tradeoffs between the two technologies.

The first approach to study the two technologies would be to have a comparative study of their capabilities. Table 27.7 discusses the same. It is evident that neither of technology can replace each other though it is true to some extent that for many applications where satellites once looked atractive, fibre has come in and dried that up. It is true that fibre optics will impinge on the dominance of satellite in certain long distance communication routes between two points. The shift of fibre optics especially pronounced on point to point routes with heavy traffic such as North Atlantic paths between United States and Europe. But in communications between one point and many others, as in TV broadcasting satellites are to prevail. Satellites are also strong for sparesely populated regions where the relatively low volume of traffic does not justify the cost of installing fibre optic lines. Delays are capable of inroducing errors in data communication by satellite but delay compensators are already available from IBM, Western Union, American Satellite Corporation etc. Further latest developments in satellite coding techniques also bring the error to a down level.

Whereas there has been considerable advances in optical fibre communications such as those of dispersion shifted fibre which are capable of providing practical transmission rates exceeding 1 Gbits/sec over distances as great as 150 km satellite communication advancements are not lagging behind. Satellite communications technology is unchallengeable for point to multipoint communication. Satellites in 14/12 GHz band are already in use. Frequency reuse with on board processors have greatly increased satellite flexibility and capacity. Scanning spotbeams, channels switching particularly combined with companded single sideband modulation have increased satellite capacity to great extent. Teleports and Satellite Platforms in space are examples of latest advancements in technology.

Table 27.7. Comparative Capabilities : Fibre Optics Versus Satellite

Characteristics	*Fibre Optic System*	*Satellites*	*Comments*
Bandwidth	Limited only by electronics at terminals, theoretical bandwidth of fibre is 1 terahertz	Most transponders have bandwidths of 36, 54 or 72 MHz.	With fibre optic lines over 1.7 Gb/s. Satellite bandwidth depends on frequency reuse and number of spot beams
Immunity to interference	Immune to EM Interference	Transmission subject to interference from various sources including microwaves.	
Durability of links	Storms can knock down overhead lines	Storms can disable individual antennas but leave network intact.	
Security	Difficult to tap without detection	Signals must be encoded for security	
Multipoint capabilities	Primarily a point-to-point medium	point to multipoint communcations easily implemented	Large area of coverage makes satellites only cost effective means of reaching sparsely populated regions; multi-point to single point, communications also useful for data collection.
Flexibility	Difficult to reconfigure to meet changeing demand	Easy to reconfigure if hardware has been approximately designed.	
Connectivity to customer size	Local loops required	With antennas installed on customer premises, as with 14/12 GHz band, local loops not required.	

However, neither of these two of these technologies can compete each other but instead are being used as complimentary to each other. Such a joint venture of fibre optic and satellites are already performed in Teleports. Here high capacity fiber optic links are used to link satellite networks in teleports with customers or locations with high volumes of communication traffic. For such a case microwave transmission is not useful as it would cause interference particularly in cities already criss crossed with many microwave links.

It is believed that in future fibre optics submarine cable would be cost effective than the satellites communication. With the improvement in technology fibre optic submarine cable is going to have not only an improved life span but the number of circuits as well as the annual cost per circuit would also be improved. The argument in favour of satellite communication is that it is distance insensitive while the cost of submarine cable increases with the distance. It is seen that the cost analysis has indicated that the submarine cables are cost competitive upto a certain distance, called 'cross-one' distance. For the most advanced cable system the cross over distance is 3545 km, *e.g.* in PTAT-1. Therefore, on a long haul point to multipoint communications satellites have a definite edge over the submarine cable system. However, taking into account all the considerations it is seen that cost of a satellite circuit is almost double that of submarine cables and therefore most of the users are in favour of highly loaded submarine cable than satellite circuits. In future it seems that satellites will have achieveable lifetime compared to submarine cable fibre optics system which in turn would mean that satellites will have similar or greater capacity to fibre optics, similar lifetime and lower costs. Regarding ISDNs, satellites will play an improtant role in horizontal spread of ISDN by providing network connectivity to remote business subscriber where conventional ISDN link is uneconomic.

28

Amateur Radio Satellites

28.1 Introduction

Ham Radio also called Amateur Radio, is one of the oldest electronic hobby in which the members of ham radio clubs in different parts of the globe communicate with each other by sending signals on radio frequencies using their receivers. While till 1970s, ham radio was part of radio broadcasting system in which certain frequencies bands were allocated to this activity, by the end of the 1970s, more and more Amateur Radio operators were sharing the fun of talking via satellite links. The period witnessed rapid development of Amateur Radio satellite systems which are used to relay messages between amateur ham radio operators.

These satellites are typically small and simple in design and are often built by universities. Due to their small size and low budgets, these satellites are usually launched as secondary payloads alongwith much larger primary payload.

This chapter highlights early developments in the field of Amateur Radio satellite, major systems launched in the 1990s and in 2000s. Also described are future trends of this technology.

28.2 Early Developments

In the 1980s, a large number of hams built and sent sophisticated Amateur Radio satellites to orbit at a record pace. AMSAT, the world's foremost amateur radio satellite organisation, launched a new generation of Phase-3 satellites. The first Phase-3 spacecraft, nine years in planning and four years in construction, was built, integrated, and tested at Goddard. Hams in Canada, Hungary, Japan, West Germany and the United States built parts for the spacecraft. AMSAT then sent Phase-3B to space in 1983. With its second Phase-3 satellite safely in orbit in 1983, AMSAT started work on a third which was launched on an Ariane rocket June 15, 1988. Phase-3C was renamed AMSAT-OSCAR-13.

The amateurs in Russia have been at the forefront of ham radio satellite technology. The Amateur Radio club at the University of Moscow built a convey of new Amateur Radio satellites called Radiosputniks. After the launch of first satellitesRS-1 and RS-2, six Radiosputniks each weighing 88 lbs were launched, followed by Radiosputniks 10 and 11 in 1987.

Iskra series, another Russian systems built by the students and radio amateurs at Moscow's Ordzhjonikidze Aviation Institute had a transponder, telemetry beacon, ground-command radio, Codestore message bulletin board, and computer with memory. The satellite transponders received at 21 MHz and transmitted at 28 MHz. Their telemetry beacons were near 29 MHz.

Controlled by ground stations at Moscow and Kaluga, Iskras were intended for communication among Eastern Bloc hams in Bulgaria, Cuba, Czechoslovakia, East Germany, Hungary, Laos, Mongolia, Poland, Romania, USSR and Vietnam.

Great Britain was an early leader in spaceflight and satellite technology, launching its Black Knight satellite from Australia in 1971. Students at the University of Surrey were eager to get hands on experience. Those who were radio amateurs designed and built a Phase-2 hamsat known as UoSAT, short for University of Surrey Satellite. In space, the hamsat was called UoSAT-OSCAR-9, or simply UO-9. It transmitted data and had a television camera which sent pictures to Earth with 2 km or 1.24 mi. resolution. The satellite had one of the earliest two-dimensional charge-coupled device (CCD) arrays forming the first low-cost CCD television camera in orbit. The resulting images transmitted from space were spectacular, considering the freshness of its technology. UO-9 was not a stabilized Earth-pointing satellite so the areas covered by its photos were random. The hamsat had a magnetometer and detectors for radiation and particles. Two particle counters detected solar activity and auroras as they interfered with radio signals.

UO-9 also had a synthesized radio voice with 150-word vocabulary to read out spacecraft condition reports. Students around the world learned about space science by tuning receivers to OSCAR-9's so-called Digitalker.

The hamsat's radio beacons transmitted at 145 and 435 MHz. For propagation studies, there were additional beacons at shortwave frequencies near 7, 14, 21 and 28 MHz and microwave frequencies near 2 and 10 GHz.

UO-9 had Codestore for messages and a voice synthesizer for educational demonstrations. A computer control in the satellite could be reprogrammed from the ground. The satellite did not have a transponder for general chatting.

Japanese radio amateurs built their first Japan Amateur Satellite (JAS-1a) and sent it to a 932-mi.-high orbit August 12, 1986, from Japan's Tanegashima Radiosputnik-9.

28.3 Amateur Radio Satellites in 1990s

The widespread interest in building and sending hamsats to orbit flourished among Amateur Radio operators around the world in the 1990s. In fact, the very first year of the decade, 1990, was a record launch year. Eight hamsats were blasted to space that year. Close behind was 1991 with four Amateur Radio satellites and eight amateur-related satellites launched. Some more launches took place in the subsequent years. Given below are some of the systems launched during 1990's.

1. UoSAT-OSCAR-14 (1990). The space enthusiasts at England's University of Surrey had some complex new satellites ready to go to space. UoSAT-3, a.k.a. UoSAT-D, a radically smaller satellite built at the University of Surrey in the U.K., was launched January 22, 1990, on Ariane 4 rocket flight V35 from Kourou, French Guiana, to become UoSAT-OSCAR 14. Ariane flight V35 carried the commercial SPOT-2 satellite and six microsatellites - UO-14, UO-15, AO-16, DO-17, WO-18, and LO-19.

2. AMSAT-OSCAR-16 (1990). A radical design departure for Amateur Radio satellites was called for after the 1986 shuttle Challenger explosion made rides to space more expensive. The result was the startlingly small microsatellite introduced by AMSAT in 1991. The first from AMSAT, AO-16, also was launched January 22, 1990, on Ariane 4 rocket flight V35 from Kourou, French Guiana, to become AMSAT-OSCAR 16. Ariane flight V35 carried the commercial SPOT-2 satellite and six microsatellites - UO-14, UO-15, AO-16, DO-17, WO-18, and LO-19.

3. WEBERSAT-OSCAR-18 (1990). The Weber, Utah, state university hamsat WO-18 also was launched January 22, 1990, on Ariane 4 rocket flight V35 from Kourou, French Guiana, to become WEBERSAT-OSCAR 18. Ariane flight V35 carried the commercial

SPOT-2 satellite and six microsatellites - UO-14, UO-15, AO-16, DO-17, WO-18, and LO-19.

4. Fuji-OSCAR-20 (1990). Japanese hams readied a replacement hamsat to follow FO-12 (JAS-1a) that had been turned off in 1989 when its solar generator was unable to produce sufficient electricity for the battery. The new Japanese hamsat, JAS-1b, was launched to Earth orbit on February 7, 1990, to become Fuji-OSCAR 20.

5. Radiosputnik (14/AMSAT-OSCAR-21). RS-14/AO-21, launched January 29, 1991, was a joint venture between AMSAT-U (Russia) and AMSAT-DL (Germany). Like those popular Russian dolls inside dolls, an amateur Radiosputnik was inside a larger government spacecraft from the Ministry of Geology and Science. And, inside the Russian hamsat, was some German gear. The ham gear was mounted piggyback on the large government geology satellite INFORMATOR-1. Amateur Radio lost a valuable asset when the Russian government ran out of funds for the project and turned the entire satellite off on September 16, 1994. RS-14/AO-21 had been a popular satellite because it was easy to communicate through RS-14/AO-21. The hamsat was an FM repeater that also transmitted recorded messages commemorating events like the 25th anniversary of the first landing on the Moon when it rebroadcast the first words of Neil Armstrong as he had stepped on the Moon in 1969.

6. Gerswin-OSCAR-32. The Israeli hamsat TechSat-1b also was launched July 10, 1998, from Russia's Baikonur Cosmodrome. GO-32 was a microsat project of students and scientists at the Technion Institute of Technology in Haifa, Israel, along with the Israel Amateur Radio Club. GO-32 included a camera. Its first picture was of the French Riviera near Saint-Tropaz. The satellite was a replacement for TechSat-1a that was lost when its Russian Start-1 rocket failed after blastoff from the Plesetsk Cosmodrome in 1995.

7. Radiosputnik-18/Sputnik-41. The tiny hamsat was launched by hand November 10, 1998, by cosmonauts aboard the Mir space station. RS-18 was the same size as the earlier Sputnik 40 as it, too, was a one-third scale replica of Sputnik 1. It transmitted a "beep-beep" beacon to remind listeners of the 1957 Sputnik 1 signal.

RS-18 transmitted, on 145.8125 MHz, two pre-recorded voice greetings in English, Russian and French as well as a beacon tone. The messages said, "1998 was the International Year of Air and

Space" and "International Space School Sputnik Program." RS-18 was dubbed "A Satellite for Education."

28.4 Amateur Radio Satellites in 2000s

An unending interest among ham radio operators around the world in satellite communications and science continued in the 2000s. Some of the major systems launched in this period are described below.

1. ASUSat, OPAL, JAWSAT. A complex set of hamsats was launched January 27, 2000, from the Commercial Launch Facility at Vandenburg Air Force Base in California. The small satellites were blasted to orbit on a Minotaur rocket, also referred to as OSPSLV, which stands for Orbital Suborbital Program Space Launch Vehicle.

This rocket was built from parts recycled from retired nuclear missiles. A six-story launch vehicle, it combined the first and second stages of decommissioned Minuteman-2 missiles with third and fourth stages from Orbital Sciences' commercial air-launched Pegasus rocket. The launch proved that the combo was capable of ferrying satellites to space.

2. OPAL-OSCAR-38. Stanford University's OPAL also was launched by the Minotaur on January 27, 2000 from Vandenburg Air Force Base in California to Earth orbit where it was labelled as OPAL-OSCAR 38 (OO-38). Stanford University's Satellite Systems Development Laboratory (SSDL), Stanford Aeronautics and Astronautics, developed the spacecraft called OPAL which was an acronym for Orbiting Picosatellite Automated Launcher.

OPAL housed SQUIRT, the Satellite QUIck Research Testbed. SQUIRT held a cluster of six picosatellites that it ejected from the OPAL-OSCAR 38 (OO-38) platform.

3. StenSAT. StenSAT Amateur Radio Picosatellite also was launched by the Minotaur on to Earth orbit on January 27, 2000, from Vandenburg Air Force Base in California, as part of OPAL-OSCAR 38. In space, OPAL ejected StenSAT into its own orbit on February 10, 2000. StenSAT was built by Amateur Radio operators at Washington, D.C., as part of Stanford University's OPAL Orbiting Picosatellite Automated Launcher project. Stensat was one tiny spacecraft in a cluster of six picosatellites that were ejected from the OPAL-OSCAR 38 (OO-38) platform into their own orbits.

StenSAT was a mere 12 cubic inches in size and weighed only 8.2 ounces. It was a Mode J single-channel FM voice repeater with uplink at 145.84 MHz and downlink at 436.625 MHz. Periodically, StenSAT would transmit packets of telemetry.

4. JAWSAT-Weber-OSCAR. JAWSAT stood for Joint Air Force Academy - Weber State University Satellite. It was built at the Center for Aerospace Technology (CAST) at Weber State University, Utah. It also was launched by the Minotaur in 2000, from Vandenburg Air Force Base in California. JAWSAT was built by students working alongside aerospace professionals. Initially planned to be only a pulsed-plasma thruster to train U.S. Air Force Academy cadets, the project grew to include several universities, aerospace companies, the Air Force Research Laboratory and NASA.

JAWSAT carried a clutch of small satellites to be released in space. Once JAWSAT reached its target orbit of 466 miles above Earth, it deployed four independent amateur-radio and amateur-related satellites. In turn, one of those satellites deployed other satellites. In addition, JAWSAT had a permanently-mounted Multi-Payload Adaptor (MPA) built by students working with aerospace professionals. That framework held two other experiments - NASA's Plasma Experiment Satellite Test (PEST) and Weber's Attitude Controlled Platform (ACP).

JAWSAT's four little satellites were: ASUSat, OCSE, OPAL and FalconSat.

OPAL in turn had six satellites. The five picosatellites "squirted" out into space by OPAL-1 and OPAL-1 itself: DARPA Picosat-1A weighed about 1.5 lbs. and was designed by the The Aerospace Corp. to carry out technology research for the Defense Advanced Research Program Agency (DARPA),

DARPA Picosat-1B, Artemis Picosat built at Santa Clara University to carry out technology research while MASat-1, built by the Stanford Mentors Team for Amateur Radio use, StenSat designed and built for Amateur Radio use, and OPAL-1 was built at Stanford University.

OSPSLV is a relatively small rocket that can can lift 750 lbs. to a 400-nautical-mile sun-synchronous orbit. That is 1.5 times the capability of the commercial Pegasus XL rocket.

JAWSAT served as what is known in the satellite business as a "bus" for the several deployable payloads and the Plasma Experiment Satellite Test (PEST).

The telemetry stream from JAWSAT, including data from PEST, was transmitted on Amateur Radio frequencies. Amateur Radio operators (hams) contributed to the experimental program by recording the downlinked data transmitted at rates as high as 38.4 kb/s on 437.175 MHz or 2403.2 MHz.

5. AMSAT-OSCAR-40. Phase-3D was launched on an Ariane 5 rocket from Kourou, French Guiana, on November 16, 2000, to become AMSAT-OSCAR 40. The highly complex new Amateur Radio satellite was designed to serve at least ten years as an educational aid enabling students around the world to familiarize themselves with space techniques and communications. The designers also hoped the satellite would allow radio amateurs to use simple and inexpensive equipment to establish communications networks covering a large portion of the Earth for long periods of time.

AO-40 was intended to allow its amateur radio operators to assess the effectiveness of a highly eccentric orbit - known as a Molniya orbit - for long-distance point-to-point communications. AO-40 was built to carry two-way communications using transponders on numerous frequencies. It transmits telemetry data on radio beacons on several frequencies. When they were on, the U-band and L1-band uplinks were connected to the S-2 transmitter passband downlink. Today, the S-Band transmitter is active.

6. SCOPE. The satellite has two full-color CCD digital cameras. SCOPE is an acronym for "Spacecraft Camera experiment for Observation of Planets and the Earth". JAMSAT, the Japan AMSAT Association, designed and built the SCOPE module for AO-40. SCOPE takes full color pictures of Earth from the satellite's high-altitude orbit. Although there are several amateur satellites that have CCD cameras, most are monochrome and in low Earth orbits. SCOPE is capable of showing Earth floating in space like the Apollo astronauts saw our planet on their way to the Moon. As Earth sensors, the SCOPE cameras are alignment tools in the satellite's three-axis attitude control system, which includes three momentum wheels, an Earth sensor and a Sun sensor.

JAMSAT now has a plan for an amateur satellite that would fly away from Earth to another planet. Because the SCOPE cameras are capable of seeing relatively bright stars, a similar camera could be a star tracker for that future satellite's flight guidance system. SCOPE also could capture the image of a destination planet. Using up the ammonia. Ground controllers were able during spring and summer 2001 to change AO-40's orbit through successive cold firings of the onboard arcjet motor. Cold firings used only ammonia gas and did not actually energize the arcjet built into the satellite. The move apparently depleted the spacecraft's ammonia supply. That means

AO-40 probably will remain in its current orbit as long as it is in space. Controllers said an ammonia leak may have accounted for the loss of fuel, but they don't know for sure. Possibly a flow controller failed and allowed more ammonia gas to pass than it should have. Before the maneuver they had thought there would be ammonia fuel left.

AO-40 was expected to demonstrate use of GPS for managing and monitoring operation of an Amateur Radio satellite. Hams hoped to use the satellite to study technology and operating procedures for a multiple-access transponder using a technique known as Frequency Division Multiple Access (FDMA).

The digital RUDAK communications processor was activated. RUDAK was to provide digital store-and-forward message service, and serve as the primary communications path for interacting with various experiments on board the satellite known as CEDEX, GPS, MONITOR, and SCOPE.

7. Saudi-OSCAR-41. SaudiSat-1a was launched September 26, 2000, aboard a converted Soviet ICBM ballistic missile from the Baikonur Cosmodrome, along with two other Amateur Radio satellites on the same launch.

SO-41 and SO-42 were built in the Kingdom of Saudi Arabia by the Space Research Institute at the King Abdulaziz City for Science and Technology. The pair of hamsats have digital store-and-forward bulletin board systems (BBS) as well FM voice repeaters.

8. Malaysian-OSCAR-46. The Malaysian hamsat TiungSAT-1 was launched September 26, 2000, aboard a converted Soviet ICBM ballistic missile from the Baikonur Cosmodrome. It was one of three Amateur Radio satellites on the same flight.

This satellite is out of chronological order in this list. However, it is in OSCAR number order. While MO-46 was launched before the hamsats SO-43, NO-44, and NO-45, it received its OSCAR number after them.

Malaysia's first microsatellite, TiungSAT-1 was named after that nation's mynah bird. TiungSAT-1 was built at the University of Surrey in the U.K. for Astronautic Technology (M) Sdn. Bhd. (ATSB) and the Malaysian government.

MO-46 was a mixture of Amateur Radio satellite and amateur-related satellite. It carried commercial land and weather imaging payloads as well as Amateur Radio FM and FSK communication equipment.

9. Radiosputnik-21/Kolibri-2000. Students in Sydney, Australia, and Obninsk, Russia, moved into the world of Amateur Radio in space when the Russians wanted to demonstrate that space is of vital interest to mankind and that educating young people about space flight and research is very important. Russia's School Scientific-Research Micro-Satellite (SSRMS) program - the International School Space Program - wanted to involve elementary and secondary school children in designing research experiments for microsatellites. The tiny satellite was built by the Special Workshop of Space Research Institute (IKI) of the Russian Academy of Sciences, Tarusa, Kaluga. The Sydney and Obninsk students named it Kolibri-2000. Kolibri means hummingbird. The complete name of RS-21was Russian-Australian Scientific and Educational Microsatellite KOLIBRI-2000.

The satellite rode the Russian Progress M-17 cargo freighter up to the International Space Station in December 2001. The IKI engineers had attached a radio-controlled remote launching port to the Progress capsule that held Kolibri while docked at the ISS. Then, as the Progress rocket backed away and departed from the ISS, the 44-pound Kolibri was ejected into space March 20, 2002. Kolibri had no engine or thrusters of its own. After it popped off the cargo freighter, Kolibri dropped slowly, circled Earth 711 times, and burned up in Earth's atmosphere after about four months. While falling into the atmosphere during the late winter and spring months, it sent down telemetry data and digitally recorded voice messages on the downlink frequency of 145.825 MHz.

10. Echo (AMSAT-OSCAR-51). This satellite of the AMSAT North America was launched in 2004. Previously referred to as OSCAR-E, the satellite was the first in a new series of small user-friendly repeater satellites.

Echo is a microsatellite cube sporting electricity-generating solar panels on all six sides. It was ferried to space by Russia using an SS-18 intercontinental ballistic missile (ICBM) converted into a space rocket. Echo was one of eight spacecraft from France, Saudi Arabia, Italy and the United States on board the Dnepr rocket as it lifted off from a silo in the ground at Baikonur Cosmodrome in Kazakhstan. All of the payloads were inserted into sun-synchronous orbits at altitudes around 450 miles. Echo incorporates 21st century hamsat electronics and RF technology. The analog and digital VHF/UHF FM radios aboard Echo are similar to those aboard the UOSAT OSCAR 14 (UO 14) and AMRAD-OSCAR 27 (AO-27) hamsats.

Echo offers the following services:

1. Telemetry at 435+ MHz.
2. Analog FM voice communications.
3. Digital communications with APRS.
4. Two seven-watt high power UHF FM downlink transmitters for the downlink that can be operated simultaneously.
5. Four miniature VHF FM receivers weighing less than two ounces each for communications and command-and-control.
6. Two downlink transmitter channels.
7. Simultaneous voice and data.
8. Wide-coverage multi-mode receiver covering 100 KHz to 1.3 GHz.

11. India's HamSat. AMSAT-India sent its first satellite, HamSat, to orbit on May 5, 2005. Known on orbit as VUSat-OSCAR 52 (or VO-52 HamSat), the 94-lb. microsat was launched from Satish Dhawan Space Centre (SDSC) in Sriharikota, India, as an auxiliary payload on India's Polar Satellite Launch Vehicle (PSLV) rocket. The primary payload on this flight was the government's remote sensing satellite CARTOSAT-1. Both the satellites were ferried to a nearly-circular polar sun synchronous orbit at approximately 390 miles altitude with an inclination of 97.8 deg with respect to the equator.

VO-52 provides amateur radio UHF/VHF communications. One of its transponders was built by ham radio operators in India with the help of ISRO. The second transponder was built by a Dutch amateur radio operator William Gerard Leijenaar, a graduate student in engineering at the Higher Technical Institute, Venlo, The Netherlands.

The features of VO-52 are:

- Uplink transponder frequency: 435.250 MHz
- Downlink transponder frequency: 145.900 MHz
- Beacon frequencies: 145.860 MHz CW telemetry and 145.936 MHz unmodulated carrier.
- Transponder bandwidth: 60 kHz
- Transmitter output power: 1 watt
- Antennas: VHF and UHF turnstiles
- Communication modes: CW, SSB, FM

- Electrical power: Gallium Arsenide solar panels charging a Lithium Ion battery.
- Onboard computer: MAR 31750 processor in the spacecraft's electronic bus management unit for attitude control, telemetry, telecommand for ground control, sensor and actuator functions.

Each transponder is recognized by its beacon. The Indian transponder has an unmodulated carrier on 145.940 MHz. The Dutch transponder is modulated with telemetry information on 145.860 MHz. Both are linear transponders offering the CW, USB and FM modes of amateur radio communication. They operate Mode-B for U-V operation with UHF uplink and VHF downlink.

The satellite is spin stabilized. It spins at about 4 RPM.

12. PCsat-2. Midshipman at the U.S. Naval Academy Satellite Lab constructed the PCsat-2 amateur radio APRS equipment that is attached to the outside of the International Space Station (ISS) in Earth orbit by shuttle Discovery in 2005.

PCsat-2 is a small electronic communications station built in a suitcase, which was carried outside the space station on August 3, 2005, by astronaut Soichi Noguchi on a spacewalk. He attached the case to a truss.

Known as a Passive Experiment Container (PEC), the suitcase is left open to the dark vacuum of space. One side of the case has a solar panel to generate electricity for communications. Antennas stick out from the suitcase into space.

The PCSat-2 communications system operates like a hamsat in coordination with ARISS (Amateur Radio aboard the International Space Station). It has an FM repeater for use in voice communications with the ISS crew; a PSK-31 multi-user transponder; an AX.25 packet radio system for use as a UI digipeater; and for telemetry, command, control; an APRS packet digipeater; and a telemetry data transmitter. APRS is the Automatic Position Reporting System used to track vehicles and networks.

PCSAT-2 VHF uplink and UHF downlink are:

- Uplink frequency: 145.825 MHz
- Downlink frequency: 435.275 MHz

13. XO-53 SSETI Express. Students from twelve different European countries built the SSETI Express as the first pan-European student satellite. In 18 months, 15 teams of students at

10 universities in nine countries designed, built and tested SSETI Express. The spacecraft was launched October 27, 2005, on a Cosmos 3M rocket from the Plesetsk Cosmodrome in the Archangel region of Russia. It is flying in a low-Earth, Sun-synchronous orbit, 426 miles above Earth. After it arrived in space, AMSAT assigned the number XO-53 to SSETI.

SSETI Express ferried to orbit three educational CUBESAT pico-satellites developed by universities. SSETI, which stands for Student Space Exploration and Technology Initiative, was created by the European Space Agency (ESA) Education Department to involve European students in real space missions to give students hands-on experience and build their interest in working in space science to ensure a workforce for the future.

On board the SSETI Express spacecraft at launch were three very tiny pico-satellites. Each of those extremely small satellites weighed about 2 lbs.

The three CUBESATs dropped off in space by SSETI Express are:

1. XI-V from the University of Tokyo, Japan.
2. UWE-1 from the University of W zburg, Germany.
3. Ncube-2 from the Andoya Rocket Range in Norway.

The SSETI Express mission is educational intended to:

1. deploy the CUBESATs using a so-called T-Pod device built in Canada by the University of Toronto Institute for Aerospace Studies (UTIAS) Space Flight Laboratory.
2. take pictures of Earth.
3. act as a test-bed and technology demonstration for the future European Student Earth Orbiter.
4. function as a ham radio radio transponder for the duration of its flight.

28.5 Future Amateur Radio Satellites

Highly sophisticated and powerful hamsats with higher frequencies and on new modes are slanted to be launched in the near future facilitating radio amateurs around the world to communicate and conduct experiments. Below are described some of Amateur Radio satellites to be launched soon.

1. Phase-3E Express. AMSAT-Germany is constructing Phase-3E Express, a follow-on to the large Phase-3D satellite that became

OSCAR 40 when it was launched in 2000. Plans call for several frequency bands between 145 MHz and 10 GHz to be used for communication with the P3E hamsat. Referred to as Phase-3E during development, the spacecraft is planned for launch in 2006 or later.

2. Phase-5A. This AMSAT Germany's amateur radio satellite will fly to Mars and enter an orbit around the Red Planet. P5A would carry science experiments as well as a sub-payload to be dropped on the Martian surface. P5A would receive and relay to Earth signals from the sub-payload's experiments in the planet's atmosphere and on the Martian surface. AMSAT Germany is building on its experience with the Phase-3D hamsat (AMSAT-OSCAR 40), launched in 2000, which appeared to have sufficient bus and propulsion capabilities for a flight to Mars. There will be suitable Mars launch windows for the Phase-5A spacecraft in 2007 and 2009.

3. Eagle. This Phase-3F satellite of AMSAT North America will be placed in elliptical geosynchronous transfer orbit (GTO) orbit. It will be similar to AMSAT-OSCAR 40. Radio transponders are planned for the U, V, L and S bands, permitting high altitude Mode V/U communications. Eagle will have experimental gear. Development of Eagle is on the back burner pending completion of the German Phase-3E. Construction and launch of Eagle would be in the future.

4. KiwiSAT. KiwiSAT will be a microsatellite from AMSAT New Zealand (AMSAT-ZL) flying in a low Earth orbit (LEO). As an OSCAR, it would be used by amateur radio operators worldwide. KiwiSat will have 2M downlinks and 70cm and 23cm uplinks. KiwiSat will have both linear and FM transponders and a digipeater. It may carry a camera. The hamsat will transmit its telemetry and science experiment data as packet radio.

5. SATEDU. AMSAT France (AMSAT-F)'s SATEDU Project will be an Easy Sat offering easy access to ground stations. The satellite will operate on amateur radio frequencies at 146MHz, 435MHz, and 2.4GHz. It will offer:

1. FM transponder for one uplink and one downlink channel with uplink at 435MHz and downlink 146MHz or 2.4GHz.
2. Linear transponder with a 25 kHz passband and uplink at 435MHz and downlink 146MHz or 2.4GHz.
3. Short message mode, with digipeating of short messages using AFSK V23 or 9600Bd and downlink at 146MHz.

4. Telemetry on the main channel using AFSKv23 1200Bd.
5. Telemetry on the service channel, permanently using 400Bd in BPSK format.
6. Voice recorder with play-back of a taped message upon demand.
7. Electricity will be generated by four solar panels.

6. VOXSAT-1. VOXSAT-1 is being developed by AMSAT Argentina (AMSAT-LU), with the help of AMSAT RUSSIA. It is intended for education and research. It will offer an FM crossband repeater, with an uplink in the 70 cm amateur radio band and a downlink in 2 meter amateur radio band. It will have a beacon transmitter at 145.995 MHz and a repeater downlink and audio broadcast at 145.810 MHz. The repeater uplink frequency is at 435.990 MHz. The FM receiver for control is at 432 MHz. The satellite will be carried to space as part of MODULE M, a Russian experimental satellite, from which VOXSAT receives electrical power.

7. SPICE. The Satellite Project for Imaging and Communication Experiments (SPICE) is a hamsat from Germany's Arbeitskreis Amateurfunk und Telekommunikation in der Schule (AATiS), the Working Group Amateur Radio and Telecommunications in the School). It may be placed in its orbit in or after September 2004. SPICE will carry a camera and science instruments recording temperature and magnetic field. User uplink will be at 70cm and downlink at 2m. There will be 13 cm beacon.

8. EMERALD. This nanosatellite is a project of Stanford University SSDL and Santa Clara University, California, to demonstrate distributed space systems technology and applications. It is funded by the Air Force Office of Scientific Research and Defense Advanced Research Projects Agency to explore creative thinking in space systems design. The students working on the satellite plan to launch it from a space shuttle flight in 2005.

9. HAND. The Human Activated Nanosatellite Demonstration (HAND) project is being developed by Bristol University in the U.K. The stick-like HAND would be launched by space shuttle astronauts tossing it overboard during a spacewalk. The four-ft.-long HAND weighs 14 lbs. It houses batteries, sensors and a radio transmitter. To launch HAND, an astronaut would unfold it, which would would turn on its electrical power. The astronaut then would point it away, start the propulsion systems, and let it go rocketing off into space. HAND would fly away collecting data and radioing it down to hams on the ground tuned to an amateur radio band. The data telemetry would be decoded by hams' personal computers.

10. CubeSats. These CubeSats, are also referred to as nanosats and picosats because they are tiny, measuring just $4 \times 4 \times 4$ inches. To be exact, they are 10 ccm satellites weighing less than 1 kg.

CubeSat Project is a collaborative effort between California Polytechnic State University San Luis Obispo and Stanford University's Space Systems Development Laboratory to provide a standard design for picosatellites with a common deployer. This will have the advantages reduced costs and development time, while increasing accessibility to space with frequent launches. Dozens of high schools, colleges, and universities around the world are developing CubeSats.

Solved Problems

Example 1 : *Calculate the radius of a geostationary satellite.*

Solution : The orbit period of a geostationary satellite in second is given by

$$T^2 = \frac{4\,\pi^2\,a^3}{\mu} \quad \text{or} \quad a^3 = T^2\,\frac{\mu}{4\pi^2}$$

where μ = Kepler's constant = gravitational constant (G) $\times$ Mass of earth (M_E) $= 3.986 \times 10^5$ km^3/sec^2

Now the time period of earth rotations is once per sidereal day of 23 hours 56 min 4.09 sec. or $T = 86{,}164.09$ sec.

Hence $$a^3 = (86{,}164.1)^2 \times 3.986 \times 10^5\ (4\pi^2)$$

$$= 7.496 \times 10^{13}\ \text{km}^3 \text{ or } a = 42{,}164 \text{ km.}$$

Example 2 : *The space shuttle, a low earth orbit satellite often orbits at an altitude of 250 km above the earth's surface. If the mean earth's radius is approximately 6378.14 km., calculate the period of its orbit if it is circular. What happens if the altitude of the shuttle becomes less than 250 km. ?*

Solution : The radius of space shuttle orbit at the 250 km altitude is

$$a = (r_e + h) = 6378.14 + 250.0 = 6628.14 \text{ km}$$

Therefore, the period of the orbit will be

$$T^2 = \frac{4\pi^2\,a^3}{\mu} = 4\pi^2 \times \frac{6628.14^3}{3.986 \times 10^5}\ \text{sec}^2$$

$$= 2.88401145 \times 10^7\ \text{sec}^2$$

or $$T = 5370.30 \text{ sec} = 89 \text{ min } 30.3 \text{ sec.}$$

At a lower altitude, the shuttle will slow down due to friction with the earth's atmosphere and it will return to earth. Thus, the spacecraft will be in stable if its orbit period is more than 89 min 30 sec.

Example 3. *In the above question, estimate the linear velocity of the shuttle along its orbit.*

Solution : The circumference of the orbit is

$$2\pi a = 2\ \pi \times 6628.14 = 41{,}645.83 \text{ km}.$$

Therefore, the velocity of the shuttle in orbit will be

$$v_S = \frac{2\pi a}{T} = \frac{41{,}645.83}{5370.3} \text{ km/sec} = 7.755 \text{ km/sec}.$$

Example 4. *A satellite is rotating in an elliptical orbit with a perigee (point where satellite is closest to earth) of 1000 km and an apogee (point where satellite is farthest from earth) of 4000 km. Calculate its orbital period. Take mean earth radius = 6378.14 km.*

Solution : The major axis of the elliptical orbit is a straight line between the apogee and perigee, as seen in Fig. 29.1. Hence, for earth radius R_E, perigee height h_p, and apogee height h_a, the major axis will be given by

$$2a = 2R + h_p + h_a$$

$$= 2 \times 6378.14 + 1000 + 4000 = 17{,}756.28 \text{ km}$$

or $$a = 8878.14 \text{ km}.$$

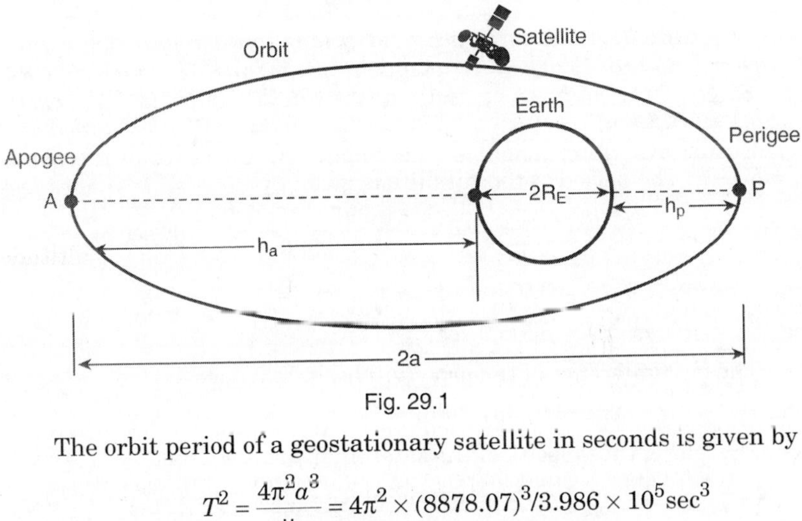

Fig. 29.1

The orbit period of a geostationary satellite in seconds is given by

$$T^2 = \frac{4\pi^2 a^3}{\mu} = 4\pi^2 \times (8878.07)^3/3.986 \times 10^5 \text{sec}^3$$

$$= 6.93 \times 10^7 \text{ sec}^2$$

or $$T = 8325.1864 \text{ sec} = 2 \text{ hours } 18 \text{ min } 45.19 \text{ sec.}$$

Example 5. *A satellite is in a circular equatorial orbit near the geosynchronous altitude. If the satellite does not have a period of one sidereal day one solar day, calculate the radius of the orbit.*

Solution : Here, the orbital period is one solar day, that is exactly 24 hours.

Therefore, $$T = 24 \text{ hours} = 86{,}400 \text{ sec.}$$

$$T^2 = \frac{4\pi^2 a^3}{\mu}$$

$$a^3 = \frac{T^2 \mu}{4\pi^2} = \frac{(86{,}400)^2 \times 3.986 \times 100^5}{4\pi^2}$$

$$= 7.537 \times 10^{13} \text{ km}^3 \text{ hence } a = 42{,}241 \text{ km.}$$

Example 6. *In the above question, estimate the rate of drift around the equator of the sub-satellite point in degree per (solar) day. Is the satellite moving towards the east or toward the west ?*

Solution : The orbit period of the satellite is one solar day which is longer than a sidereal day by 3 min 55.9 sec or 235.9 sec. Clearly, this will lead to the drift of the sub-satellite point at a rate of

$$\text{Draft rate} = 360° \times 235.9/86400 \text{ per day} = 0.983° \text{ per day.}$$

Since the earth moves towards the east at a faster rate than the satellite, the drift of the satellite from earth will appear to an observer on the earth to be towards the west.

Example 7. *A low-earth orbit satellite is in a circular polar orbit with an altitude of 1000 km. A transmitter on the satellite has a frequency of 2.65 GHz. Calculate the velocity of the satellite in orbit. Take earth radius = 6378 km.*

Solution : Here, height of the satellite from centre of the earth $a = R_e + h$. The period of the satellite is given by

$$T^2 = \frac{4\pi^2 a^3}{\mu} = 4\pi^2 \times \frac{(6378 + 1000)^3}{3.986} \times 10^5 \text{ sec}$$

$$= 3.978 \times 10^7 \text{sec}^2$$

or $$T = 6306.9 \text{ sec}$$

The circumference of the orbit will be

$$2\pi a = 46{,}357.3 \text{ km.}$$

Therefore, the velocity of the satellite in orbit will be

$$v_S = \frac{\text{Orbit circumference}}{\text{Orbital period}} = \frac{2\pi a}{T} = \frac{46{,}357.3}{6306.94}$$

$$= 7.350 \text{ km/sec.}$$

Example 8. *In the above problem, calculate the component of velocity towards an observer at an earth station as the satellite appears over the horizon, for an observer who is in the plane of the satellite orbit.*

Solution : The component of velocity an observer in the plane of the orbit as the satellite appears over the horizon as will be

$$V_{TR} = v_s \cos\theta$$

where θ is the angle between the satellite velocity vector and the direction of the observer at the satellite.

The angle θ will be

$$\cos\theta = \frac{R_e}{R_e + h} = \frac{6378}{7378} = 0.8645$$

Hence the component of satellite velocity toward the observer is

$$V_{TR} = v_s \cos\theta = \frac{7.350 \times 6378}{7378}$$

$$= 6.354 \text{ km/sec.}$$

Example 9. *In the same problem, the satellite carries a Ka-band transmitter at 20.0 GHz. Find the Doppler shift of the received signal at the earth station. The earth radius is 6378 km. Discuss the impact of this shift on signal bandwidth.*

Solution : The Doppler shift of the received signal is given by

$$\Delta f = \frac{V_{TR}}{\lambda}$$

where V_{TR} = component of the transmitter velocity towards the receiver.

and λ = wavelength of the transmitted frequency.

For Ka-band transmitter with frequency 20.0 GHz,

$$\lambda = 0.015 \text{ m}$$

Therefore, the Doppler shift at the receiver will be

$$\Delta f = V_T/\lambda = 6354/0.015 = 423.60 \text{ kHz}$$

Doppler shift at Ka band with a LEO satellite can be very large and requires a fast frequency tracking receiver. Ka-band LEO satellites are better suited to wideband signals than narrowband voice communications.

Example 10. *The continental Asia subtends an angle of approximately 6° × 2° when viewed from geostationary orbit. Calculate the dimension of a reflector antenna so as to cover half this area with a circular beam 3° in diameter at 11 GHz.*

Solution : We know that the bandwidth of an aperture antenna is given as

$$\theta_{3dB} = \frac{75\lambda}{D} \text{ degrees}$$

where, λ = wavelength

and D = dimension of the antenna in metres.

Here $\theta_{3dB} = 6° - 2° = 4°$ and $\lambda = 0.0272$ m

Therefore, $D = \dfrac{75\lambda}{\theta_{3dB}} = \dfrac{7.5 \times 0.0272}{4} = 0.51$ metres.

Example 11. *A satellite located at 40,000 km from earth operates at a frequency of 11 GHz and has EIRP of 21 dBW. If the receiving antenna has a gain of 50.5 dB, find the received power.*

Solution.

$$P_R = EIRP + G_R - \text{path loss}$$

Here $EIRP = 21.0$ dBW

$G_R = 50.5$ dB and $h = 40{,}000$ km

The path loss is given by

$$\text{Path loss} = (4\pi h/\lambda)^2 = 20 \log_{10} \frac{(4\pi \times 4 \times 10^7)}{(2.727 \times 10^{-2})} \text{ dB} = -205.3 \text{ dB}$$

Therefore, by substituting

$$P_R = 21.0 + 50.5 - 205.3$$

$$= -133.8 \text{ dBW.}$$

Example 12. *In a C-band GEO satellite, satellite transponder output power is 20W, transponder output backoff is –1.0 dB, satellite antenna gain on axis is 30.0 dB and earth station antenna gain is 59.2 dB. If free space path loss at 4 GHz is 195.0 dB, edge of beam loss for satellite antenna is 2.0 dB, clear air atmospheric loss is 0.2 dB and other losses are 0.4 dB, calculate the received power at earth station.*

Solution. The satellite transponder output power is

$P_T = 20W = 10 \log 20$ dBW $= 13.0$ dBW

B_{To} = Transponder output backoff = 1.0 dB

G_T = Satellite antenna gain, on axis = 30 dB

G_R = Earth station antenna gain = 59.2 dB

L_{fs} = Free space path loss at 4 GHz = 195.0 dB

L_a = Edge of beam loss for satellite antenna = – 2.0 dB

L_{air} = Clear air atmospheric loss = 0.2 dB

L_o = Other losses = 0.4 dB

The received power at earth station will be

$$P_R = P_T + G_T + G_R - B_{To} - \text{All losses}$$
$$= 13 + 30 + 59.2 - 1 - 195 - 2 - 0.2 - 0.4$$
$$= -96.4 \text{ dBW}.$$

Example 13. *In the above problem, find downlink noise power budget in clear air if the noise bandwidth is 27 MHz.*

Solution. Here, K = Boltzmann's constant = – 228.6 dBW/K/Hz

T_s = System noise temperature = 75 K = 10 log 75 = 18.8 dBK

B_N = Noise bandwidth, 27 MHz = 10 log 27×10^6 = 74.3 dBHz

The receiver noise power will be

$$N_R = kB_NT_s = (K + B_N + T_S) \text{ dBW}$$
$$= -228.6 + 18.8 + 74.3 = -135.5 \text{ dBW}.$$

Example 14. *In the above problem, find C/N ratio in receiver in clear air.*

$$\text{C/N ratio} = \frac{P_R}{N_R} = (P_R - N_R) \text{ dBW}$$
$$= -96.4 - (-135.5) = 39.1 \text{ dBW}$$
$$= 10 \text{ Antilog } 39.1 \text{ W} = 12.6 \text{ W}.$$

Example 15. *In a satellite link, the antenna of the earth station used to receive a signal at 4150 MHz, has diameter of 30 m and an overall efficiency of 68%. The system noise temperature is 79 K when the antenna points at the satellite at an elevation angle of 28°. Find the earth station G/T ratio.*

Solution. For an antenna with circular aperture, the gain is given by

$$G_a = \eta_a \left(\frac{\pi D}{\lambda}\right)^2$$

Here, $\eta_a = 0.68$, $D = 30$ m and $\lambda = \dfrac{2\pi}{4150 \times 10^6} = 0.072$ m

$$\text{Therefore, } G = \frac{0.68 \times (\pi \times 30)^2}{(0.072)^2} = 1.16 \times 10^6 = 60.6 \text{ dB}$$

T_s = 79 K in dB will be

T_s = 10 log 79 = 19 dB/k

Therefore, G/T ratio

$$= (G_a - T_s) \text{ dB/k} = 60.6 - 19 = 41.6 \text{ dB/k}$$

Example 16. *In the above problem, if heavy rain causes the sky temperature to increase, resulting the system noise temperature to rise to 88 K, calculate the new G/T value.*

Solution :

Here, $T_s = 10 \log 88 \text{ dBK} = 19.4 \text{ dBK}$

Therefore, $\frac{G}{T}$ ratio $= 60.6 - 19.4$ dBK

$= 41.2$ dBK.

Example 17. *In a satellite link, the bandwidth of satellite transponder is 36 MHz. If the earth stations use RRC filters with roll-off factor of 0.4, Calculate the maximum bit rate that can be sent through this transponder with BPSK.*

Solution : The maximum symbol rate for an RF link is given by

$$r_{SYM} = \frac{B}{1+\alpha} = \frac{36m}{1.4} = 25.7m \text{ Mbits/sec}$$

For BPSK, $m = 1$. Therefore, the bit rates will be

$r_{SYM} = 25.7$ M bits/sec.

Example 18. *In the above problem, calculate the maximum bit rate that can be sent through this transponder with QPSK.*

Solution : For QPSK, $m = 2$. Therefore, the bit rates will be

$r_{SYM} = 2 \times r_{SYM} = 51.4$ Mbits/sec.

Example 19. *In a satellite link, thermal noise in an earth station results in a ratio of 25.0 dB. A signal is received from a transponder with a carrier-to-noise ratio of 20.0 dB. Find the value of overall (C/N)0 at the earth station.*

The overall C-N ratio is given by

$$(C/N)_0 = \frac{1}{\frac{1}{(C/N)_{UP}} + \frac{1}{(C/N)_{DN}}}$$

$$= \frac{1}{1/25 + 1/20} = 45 = 10 \log 45 = 14.5.$$

Example 20. *In a Ku-band satellite, the transponder has a linear gain of 127 dB and a nominal output power at saturation of 5 W. If the gain of the satellite's 14-GHz receiving antenna is 26 dB on axis, calculate the power output of an uplink transmitter that gives an output power of 1 W rom the satellite transponder at a frequency of 14.45 GHz. Given :*

The earth station antenna has a gain of 50 dB and there is a 1.5-dB loss in the waveguide run between the transmitter and antenna.

The atmosphere loss is 0.5 dB under clear sky conditions.

The path loss is 207 dB.

The earth station is located on the – 2 dB contour of the satellite's receiving antenna.

Solution : Here, output of the transponder is

$$P_0 = 1\ W = 10 \log 1 = 0 \text{ dBW}$$

Therefore, the received power will be

$$P_R = 0 - 127 \text{ dBW} = -127 \text{ dBW}$$

Now uplink power budget is written as

$$P_R = P_T + G_r + G_t - \text{Losses dBW}$$

or

$$P_T = P_R - G_r - G_t + \text{Losses}$$

$$= -127 - 50 - 26 + 207 + 1.5 + 0.5 + 2.0 \text{ dBW}$$

$$= 7.2 \text{ dB/W} = 5.2 \text{ W}.$$

Example 21. *In the above question, if the rain attenuation is 7 dB for 0.01% of the year, find output power rating required for the transmitter to ensure that a 1W output can be obtained from the satellite transponder for 99.99% of the year if uplink power control.*

Solution.

With rain attenuation of 7dB, the transmitted power will be

$$P_T \text{ (rain)} = 7.2 + 7 = 14.2 \text{ dBW}.$$

Example 22. *A satellite TV distribution system employs a Ku-band geostationary satellite with bent pipe transponders for distribution of digital TV signals from an earth station to many receiving stations. The design requires that an overall C / N ratio of 9.5 dB be available in the TV receiver to ensure that the video signal on the TV screen is held to an acceptable level. The satellite is located at 73° W. The gain of the uplink antenna is 56.2 dB. The required C / N in Ku-band transponder is 30dB, the required overall C / N at earth station is 17 dB and satellite antenna gain is 25 dB.*

Calculate the uplink transmitter power required to achieve $(C/N)_{UP} =$ *30 dB in clear air atmospheric conditions. Assume free space losses = 207 dB and other losses = 3 dB. The signal bandwidth is 43.2 MHz.*

Solution : We first estimate the noise power in the transponder for 43.2 MHz bandwidth, Here,

k = Boltzmann's constant = –228.6 dBW/K/Hz

$T_0 = 500\ K = 10 \log 500 = 27$ dB

$B = 43.2 \text{ MHz} = 10 \log 43.2 \times 10^6 = 76.4$ dBHz

The transponder noise power is given by

$$N_{TR} = kT_s\,B = k + T_s + B \text{ dBW}$$
$$= -228.6 + 27 + 76.4 = -125.2 \text{ dBW}$$

The received power level at the transponder input must be 30 dB greater than the noise power. Therefore,

$$P_R = N_{TR} + 30 \text{ dBW} = -95.2 \text{ dBW}$$

Therefore, the required transmitted power for the transponder is

$$P_T = P_R + G_{St} + G_{ESt} - \text{Losses}$$

where G_{St} = Satellite antenna gain

G_{ESt} = Earth station antenna gain

Substituting, the values

$$P_T = 95.2 + 56.2 + 25 - 207 - 3$$
$$= -73.6 \text{ dBW.}$$

Example 23. *The bandwidth of an RF channel in a satellite link is 1.0 MHz. The transmitter and receiver have RRC filter with roll-off of 0.5. Calculate symbol rate for this link.*

Solution : The signal bandwidth expressed in terms of symbol rate is given by

$$B_s = r_{SYM}\,(1 + \alpha) \text{ Hz}$$

or
$$r_{SYM} = \frac{B_s}{1+\alpha} = \frac{10^6}{1+0.5}$$
$$= 666.7 \text{ Kbits/sec.}$$

Example 24. *In a Ku-band satellite uplink, the carrier frequency is 14.125 MHz and carries a symbol stream at rate of 16 Msps. If the transmitter and receiver have RRC filter with roll-off of 0.25. Estimate the bandwidth occupied by the RF signal and the frequency range of transmitted signal.*

Solution : Here the signal bandwidth is

$$B_s = r_{SYM}\,(1 + \alpha) \text{ Hz}$$
$$= 16 \times 10^6\,(1 + 0.25) = 20 \text{ MHz}$$

The frequency range occupied by the RF signal is given by

$$\left[f_c - \frac{r_{SYM}}{2}(1+\alpha)\right] \text{ to } \left[f_c + \frac{r_{SYM}}{2}(1+\alpha)\right]$$

Here, f_c = 14.125 MHz.

$$\therefore \quad \left[14.125 - \frac{16}{2}(1+0.25)\right] \text{ to } \left[14.125 + \frac{16}{2}(1+0.25)\right]$$

or $\qquad (14.125 - 0.01)$ to $(14.125 + 0.01)$

or $\qquad$ 14.115 MHz to 14.135 GHz.

Example 25. *In a satellite system, the downlink transmission rate is 60 Mbits / sec. If the required energy per bit to noise power density is 8 dB, Calculate the required carrier-to-noise ratio.*

Solution : Here, r_b = 60 Mbits/sec

$$= 10 \log 60 \times 10^6 \text{ dB bits/sec}$$

$$= 77.8 \text{ dB Hz}$$

and $\qquad E_b/N_0 = 8$ dB

The C/N ratio is given by

$$\left(\frac{C}{N_0}\right) = \left(\frac{E_b}{N_0}\right) + r_b = (8 + 77.8) = 85.8.$$

Example 26. *A 14-GHz uplink operates with transmission losses and margins totaling 210 dB and a satellite G / T = 8 dB / K. The required uplink E_b/N_0 is 9 dB. Assuming FDMA operation and an earth station uplink antenna gain of 42 dB, calculate the earth station transmitter power needed for transmission of a baseband signal which has bit rate of 1.544 Mbits / sec.*

Solution : Here the bit rate is r_b = 1.544 Mbits/sec

$$= 10 \log 1.544 \times 10^6 \text{ dB bits/sec}$$

$$= 62 \text{ dBbits/sec.}$$

And $$\frac{E_b}{N_0} = \frac{\text{Energy per bit}}{\text{noise power density}} = 9 \text{ dB}$$

Now $$\left(\frac{C}{N_0}\right) = \left(\frac{E_b}{N_0}\right) + r_b$$

Substituting above values

$$\frac{C}{N} = 9 + 62 = 671 \text{ dB}$$

Now EIRP is given by

$$\text{EIRP} = \left(\frac{C}{N_0}\right) + \left(\frac{G}{T}\right) + \text{Losses} - k$$

$$= 71 - 8 + 210 - 228.6 = 44.4 \text{ dBW}$$

Therefore, the required power of the transmitter will be

$$P_t = \text{EIRP} - G_{UPa} = 44.4 - 42 = 2.4 \text{ dBW}$$

$$= \text{Antilog}_{10}\ 2.4 = 251.2 \text{ dW.}$$

Example 27. *In the above problem, if the downlink transmission rate is fixed at 71 dBbits/sec, calculate the uplink power increase required for TDMA operation.*

Solution : Here, bit rate ≅ 62 dBbits/sec. When TDMA is employed, the uplink bit rate increase will be

$$\Delta r_{bUP} = 71 - 62 = 9 \text{ dB}$$

The EIRP must be increased by 9 dB. Therefore, the earth station transmitted power will be

$$P_{UP} = (2.4 + 9) \text{ dBW} = 11.4 \text{ dBW}.$$

Example 28. *Calculate the EIRP of a satellite downlink which at 12 GHz operates with a transmit power of 6 W and an antenna gain of 50.2 dB.*

Solution : The EIRP is given by

$$\text{EIRP} = \log P_S + G_a \text{ dBW} = \log 6 + 50.2$$

$$= 7.8 + 50.2 = 58.0 \text{ dBW}.$$

Example 29. *Calculate the gain of a 3-m paraboloidal antenna with an aperture efficiency of 0.55 operating at a frequency of 12 GHz.*

Solution : For a paraboloidal antenna, the isotropic gain is given by

$$G_i = \eta(10.472\, f D)$$

where, η = aperture efficiency

f = frequency

D = diameter of the antenna in metres.

Therefore, $G_i = 0.55 \times (10.472 \times 12 \times 3)^2 = 78{,}168$

Hence $G_i = 10 \log 78{,}168 = 48.9$ dB.

Example 30. *For the system shown in Fig. 29.2. below, if the receiver noise figure is 12 dB, the cable loss is 5 dB, the LNA gain is 50 dB, its noise temperature 150 K and the antenna noise temperature is 35 K. Calculate the overall noise temperature of the system.*

Solution : Here, the antenna noise temperature $(T_a) = 35\ K$. The receiver noise figure is

$$F = 12 \text{ dB}$$

or $10 \log_{10} F = 12$

$\log_{10} F = 1.2$ dB

or $F = 10^{1.2} = 15.85.$

Similarly, the cable loss $(L_c) = 10^{0.5} = 3.16$ and LNA gain $(G_{LNA}) = 10^5$.

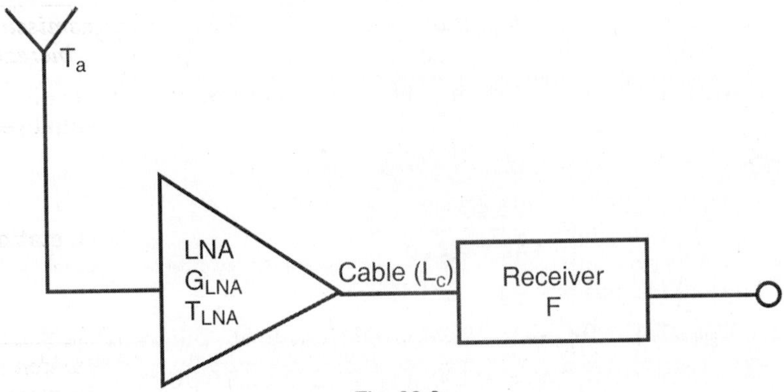

Fig. 29.2

Now, the overall noise temperature of this system is given by

$$T_s = T_a + T_{LNA} + \frac{(L_c - 1) \times T_0}{G_{LNA}} + \frac{L_c (F - 1)\, T_0}{G_{LNA}}$$

$$= 35 + 150 + \frac{(3.16 - 1) \times 290}{10^5}$$

$$+ \frac{3.16\,(15.85 - 1) \times 290}{10^5} = 185 \text{ K.}$$

Example 31. *In the link budget of a satellite, the free-space loss at 12 GHz is 210 dB, the antenna pointing loss is 2 dB, and the atmospheric absorption is 2 dB. If the receiver G/T ratio is 19 dB/K, receiver feeder losses are 1 dB and the EIRP is 50 dBW, calculate the carrier-to-noise spectral density ratio.*

Solution :

Here $k = -228.6$ dB

EIRP = 50 dBW

$G/T = 19.5$ dB/K

Losses = Free-space less + atmospheric absorption loss + antenna pointing loss + receiver feedback losses

= 210 + 2 + 2 + 1 = 215 dB

Now the C/N spectral density ratio is given by

$$(C/N_0) = \text{EIRP} + \frac{G}{T} - \text{Losses} - k$$

$$= 50 + 19 - 215 - (-286) = 140 \text{ dBW.}$$

Example 32. *An uplink of a satellite system operates at 14 GHz, and the flux density required to saturate the transponder is – 100 dB W/m^2. The free-space loss is 200 dB, and the other propagation losses amount* *to 3 dB. Calculate the earth-station EIRP required for saturation, assuming clear-sky conditions.*

Solution : The effective area of an isotropic antenna (A_0) is given by

$$A_0 = -(21.45 + 20 \log f)$$
$$= -(21.45 + 20 \log 14)$$
$$\cong -44.4 \text{ dB}$$

The $(EIRP)_{Sat} = \Psi_{STR} + A_0 + \text{Losses}$

where Ψ_{STR} is the flux density required to saturate the transponder.

Therefore, $(\text{EIRP})_{\text{Sat}} = -100 - 44.4 + 200 = 55.6$ dBW.

Example 33. *The EIRP of the Astra 1A satellite is 52 dBW in the main central service area, and that the transponder power is 45 W, calculate the effective isotropic radiated power in watts as seen by the antenna.*

$$EIRP = 10 \log P_S$$

or $$P_S = 10^{(\text{EIRP}/10)} = 10^{(52/10)}$$
$$= 158.5 \text{ kW.}$$

Example 34. *An antenna has a noise temperature of 40 K and is matched into a receiver which has a noise temperature of 100 K. Calculate the noise power for a bandwidth of 36 MHz.*

Solution : Here $T_a = 40$ K and $T_R = 100$ K.

Therefore, total noise of thus explain (antenna + receiver) $= T_N = 40 + 100 = 140$ K

Now the noise power for a bandwidth of B_N is

$$P_N = kT_NB_N$$

where $k = 1.38 \times 10^{-23}$ J/K.

Therefore, for $B_N = 36$ MHz

$$P_N = 1.38 \times 10^{-23} \times 140 \times 36 \times 10^6$$
$$= 0.0696 \text{ pW.}$$

Example 35. *A satellite link operating at 14 GHz has receiver feeder losses of 2 dB and a free-space loss of 202 dB. The atmospheric absorption loss is 0.5 dB, and the antenna pointing loss is 1 dB. Calculate the total link loss.*

Solution : The total link loss is the sum of all the losses. Therefore

Losses = (free-space loss + receiver feeder loss + atmospheric absorption loss + antenna pointing loss)

$= 202 + 2 + 0.5 + 1$ dB $= 205.5$ dB.

Example 36. *Determine the clear-sky carrier-to-noise ratio for a satellite TV system having worst case EIRP of 51 dBW at the receiver site. The free space loss is 205.34 dB, the nominal usable figure of merit is 13.12 dB, and the gaseous attenuation due to atmospheric absorption is 0.17 dB. The highest video frequency is 5 MHz and peak-to-peak video signal frequency deviation is 16 MHz.*

Solution :

Here $EIRP = 51$ dBW, $L_{fs} = 205.34$ dB

$$G/T = 13.12 \text{ dB}, \quad L_{atm} = 0.17 \text{ dB}$$

$$B = \Delta f + 2 f_v = 16 + 10 = 26 \text{ MHz}$$

$$k = 1.38 \times 10^{-23}$$

$$C/N = EIRP - L_{fs} + G/T - L_{atm} - 10 \log (kB)$$

$$= 51 - 205.34 + 13.12 - 10 \log (1.38 \times 10^{-23} \times 26 \times 10^{6}) - 0.17$$

$$= 51 - 205.34 + 13.12 - (-154.45) - 0.17 = 13.16.$$

Example 37. *A satellite link is carrying data at rates of 24 Kbits / sec when a block length of 127 bits is used and the one-way path delay is 240 msec. A double error detecting code (127, 120) ARQ scheme is used. If 1 in every 79 received blocks has an error, calculate the transmission bit rate for Stop and Wait system.*

Solution : The data rate is 24 Kbits/sec. Therefore, time taken for transmitting one bit is $t_{bit} = \dfrac{1}{24 \times 10^3}$ sec = 0005 sec.

In Stop-and-Wait method, we transmit the block of 127 bits and wait for acknowledgement. Since the one-way path delay is 240 msec or 0.240 sec, the two way path delay will be 2 × 0.240 = 0.480 sec.

Therefore, sending 127 bits and waiting for acknowledgement takes (0.480 + 0.005) sec or 0.485 sec.

Now after 79 blocks one error is detected, that is, after 79/2 = 39.5 sec.

Therefore, bit transmission rate will be

$$r_b = \frac{\text{No. of blocks transmitted without error and ACK} \times \text{No. of bits/block}}{\text{Time taken for transmission}}$$

$$= \frac{79 \times 127}{39.5} \text{ bits/sec}$$

$$= 254 \text{ bits/sec.}$$

Example 38. *Repeat the above calculation for Go-back N ARQ scheme. What should be the capacity of the transmit buffer?*

Solution : The time required to transmit 79 blocks each of 127 bits at 24 kbits/sec will be

$$= \frac{79 \times 127}{24 \times 10^3} = 0.418 \text{ sec.}$$

Now in Go-back-N method, when error is detected in the 79th block, the NAK system is sent to request retransmission of block 79. However, sending of NAK and retransmission takes two-path delay time *i.e.* 2 × 24 msec or 0.48 sec. During this period, the number of blocks which arrive at the receiver will be

$$= \frac{0.48 \text{ sec}}{\text{Transmission time per block}} = \frac{0.48}{0.418/79} = 91.$$

These 91 blocks are discarded when the retransmission of 79 blocks starts. The transmission time decreases by 0.48/0.898 = 0.54. Therefore, the bit rate falls by 54% of the original value of 24 Kbits/sec, that is, 11.2 Kbits/sec.

The required capacity of transmit buffer should be to hold 91 blocks or 91 × 127 bits or 11,557 ≅ 11,600 bits.

Example 39. *Repeat the same calculation for Selective Repeat ARQ system.*

Solution : In this system, time is lost only in the retransmission of 79 blocks which show an error. Clearly, 78 blocks are without error. Therefore, the rate efficiency of the system will be 78/79 = 0.987. As a result, the bit transmission rate will be

$$r_b = 24 \times 0.987 \text{ Kbits/sec}$$
$$= 23.70 \text{ Kbits/sec.}$$

Example 40. *In a typical VSAT system, each VSAT station sends and receives a 64-Kbits / sec data stream to and from the hub. Digital data are sent to the hub from the VSATs by the inbound link via one transponder at a message bit rate of 64 Kbits / sec using binary phase shift keying (BPSK) and half rate forward error correction (FEC) coding, giving a transmitted bit rate of 128 Kbits / hr.*

The occupied RF bandwidth of each VSAT channel is 160 KHz, corresponding to ideal RRC filters with a = 0.25. Multiple access for the inbound link is by SCPC-FDMA with RF channels spaced 200 kHz apart to allow a 40-KHz guard band between channels.

Data from the hub station to the VSATs (the outbound link) are sent as a continuous TDM stream of packets using a second transponder and BPSK with half rate FEC.

The VSAT antenna has a diameter of 1m and saturated out power of 2 W. The transponder noise temperature is 500 K and that of receiver at hub station is 150 K.

Calculate the noise power in transponder-1 or in the inbound SCPC–FDMA channels.

Solution: The inbound VSAT links that pass through transponder-1 have a message data rate of 64 Kbits/sec with half rate FEC encoding. Therefore, with BPSK modulation ($m = 2$), the transmitted bit rate will be 64×2 or 128 Kbits/sec. The noise bandwidth will be 128 KHz, since but rate in BPSK is one bit per symbol.

The noise power, N_p, is given by

$$N = kT_S B_N \text{ Watts}$$

Now $$k = -228.6 \text{ dBW/K/Hz},$$

$$B_N = 10 \log 128 \times 10^6 \text{ dBHz}$$

$$= 51.1 \text{ dBHz}$$

and $T_S = 500\ K = 10 \log 500$ dBK $= 27$ dBK.

$$\therefore \quad N_{TR1} = k + T_S + B_N = -228.6 + 27 + 51.1 = -150.5 \text{ dBW}.$$

Example 41. *In the above question, calculate the noise power in the hub station receiver or in inbound SCPC – FDMA Channel.*

The inbound VSAT signals reach the hub station after they are retransmitted through transponder by the satellite. The noise bandwidth again will be 128 kHz, because at the hub station, each VSAT channel is received by a separate IF receiver.

Here, $T_S = 150\ K = 21.8$ dBK, $B_N = 128$ kHz

$$\therefore \quad N_H = -228.6 + 21.8 + 51.1 = -155.7 \text{ dBW}.$$

Example 42. *In the same question, calculate the Noise Power in transponder-2 i.e. in outbound TDM channels, assume a starting value of noise bandwidth of 1 MHz in the VSAT receiver.*

Solution : The outbound TDM bit stream from the hub station to the VSATs passes through transponder-2. Since not all of the VSATs will be transmitting and receiving simultaneously, we assume that the TDM stream on an average has starting value noise bandwidth of 1 MHz in the VSAT receiver. This corresponds to a BPSK signal with a baseband data rate of 500 kbits/sec and half-rate FEC encoding.

Therefore $B_N = 1$ MHz $= 10 \log 10^6$ dBHz $= 60$ dBHz

For transponder-2, $T_S = 500$ K $= 27$ dBK.

Therefore, $$N_{TR2} = -228.6 + 27 + 60$$

$$= -141.6 \text{ dBW}.$$

Example 43. *In the same question, calculate the noise power in the VSAT receivers, i.e. in outbound TDM Channel.*

Solution : As already seen, each VSAT in the network receives the outbound TDM stream from the hub station in a noise bandwidth of 1 MHz. Here $T_S = 150\ K = 21.8$ dBK and $B_N = 1$ MHz = 60 MHz.

$$\therefore \qquad N_{VR} = -228.6 + 21.8 + 60 = -146.8 \text{ dBW}.$$

Example 44. *In the same question, calculate the power received at the satellite transmitted from the VSAT uplink. Assume as the worst case that the VSAT is located at the satellite beam's edge-of-coverage, the –2 dB contour of the satellite's uplink (receiving) antenna pattern. The gain of the VSAT transmit antenna is 42 dB and that of satellite receive antenna 30 dB. Assume free path loss of 207 dB.*

Solution : The power received at the satellite from a single VSAT, in dB, is given by

$$P_R = P_T + G_T + G_R - L_p - \text{other losses}$$

Here P_T = transmit power = 2W = 10 log 2 = 3 dBW

G_T = gain of the VSAT transmit antenna = 42 dB

G_R = gain of the satellite receive antenna = 30 dB

L_p = free space path loss at 14 HGz = 207 dB

other losses = satellite antenna edge of beam loss (2 dB) + clear air uplink atmospheric loss due to gases (0.5 dB) + miscellaneous losses of 0.5 dB to account for antenna mispointing feed loss.

Therefore, power received by the transponder is

$$P_R = 3 + 42 + 30 - 207 - 2 - 0.5 - 0.5$$
$$= -135 \text{ dB}.$$

Example 45. *In the same question, calculate the uplink inbound C/N ratio is transponder-1.*

Solution : Each VSAT has a separate receiver in the hub station of noise bandwidth of 28 kHz. Since the received power at the transponder input as calculated in preceding example is – 135 dB, and noise power in transponder-1 (in Example 40) is – 150.5 dBW, the required C/N ratio will be

$$(C/N)_{TRI} = \frac{P_{TRI}}{N_{TRI}}$$
$$= -135 - (-150.5) \text{ dB} = 15.5 \text{ dB}.$$

Example 46. *In a VSAT link, the saturated output power of the satellite transponder is 20 W. The VSAT channels are accessing this transponder by SCPC-FDMA method. If the amplifier in the transponder has a backoff of 2 dB, calculate the maximum number of VSAT channels that can be handled by the system. Assume each VSAT channel uses 1W of power on the downlink.*

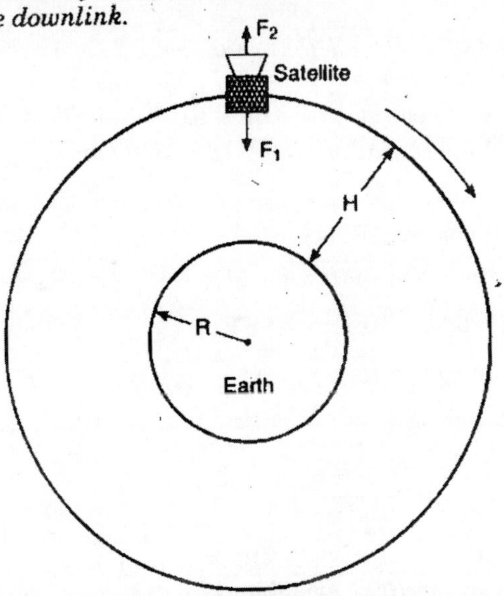

Fig. 29.3

Solution : The saturated transponder output power

$$= 20 \text{ W} = 10 \log 20 = 13 \text{ dBW}.$$

With 2 dB backoff, this power becomes (13–2) = 11 dBW = 10 log 11 = 12.6 W. Since the power for VSAT channel is 1W, the number of channels that can be handled is 12.6/1 ≡ 12 channels.

Example 47. *Refer to Fig. 29.3. The basis of a satellite orbitting around earth is the centripetal force (F_1) due to earth's gravitation acting towards the center of the earth balancing the centrifugal force (F_2) acting away from the center. Calculate the centrifugal force for a satellite of mass 100 kg orbitting with a velocity of 8 km/s at a height of 200 km above the surface of earth. Assume mean radius of earth to be 6370 km.*

Solution :

$$\text{Centripetal force} = \frac{mV^2}{(R + H)}$$

where m = mass of satellite
V = orbital velocity
R = mean radius of earth

H = height of satellite above surface of earth

The centripetal force balances the centrifugal force.

$$\text{Therefore, Centrifugal force} = \frac{mV^2}{(R+H)} = \frac{100 \times (8000)^2}{(6370 + 200) \times 10^3}$$

$$= \frac{64 \times 10^8}{6570 \times 10^3} = 974 \text{ Newtons}$$

Example 48. *Determine the orbital velocity of a satellite moving in a circular orbit at a height of 150 km above the surface of earth given that gravitation constant, $G = 6.67 \times 10^{-11}$ N–m²/kg², mass of earth, $M = 5.98 \times 10^{24}$ kg, radius of earth, Re = 6370 km.*

Solution :

The orbital velocity (V) is given by

$$V = \sqrt{\mu/(R+H)}$$

where $\mu = GM = 6.67 \times 10^{-11} \times 5.98 \times 10^{24}$

$= 39.8 \times 10^{13}$ Nm²/kg

R = 6370 km

H = 150 km

$V = \sqrt{39.8 \times 10^{13}/(6370 + 150) \times 10^3}$ = 7.813 km/s.

Example 49. *A satellite in an elliptical orbit has an apogee of 30,000 km and a perigee of 1000 km. Determine the semi-major axis of the elliptical orbit.*

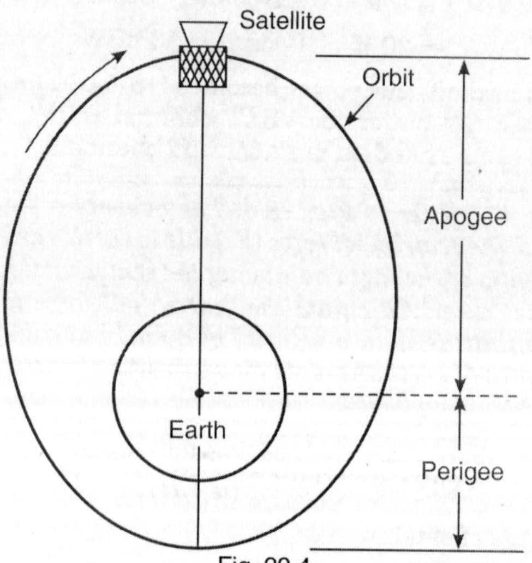

Fig. 29.4

Solution :

$$\text{Semi-major axis} = \frac{\text{Apogee} + \text{Perigee}}{2}$$

$$= \frac{30000 + 1000}{2} = 15500 \text{ km}$$

Fig. 29.4 illustrates the point further.

Example 50. *A satellite moving in an elliptical eccentric orbit has the semi-major axis of the orbit equal to 16000 km (Fig. 29.5). If the difference between the apogee and the perigee is 30000 km, determine the orbit eccentricity.*

Solution :

$$\text{Apogee} = a\ (1 + e)$$

$$\text{Perigee} = a\ (1 - e)$$

where a = semi–major axis of the ellipse

e = orbit eccentricity

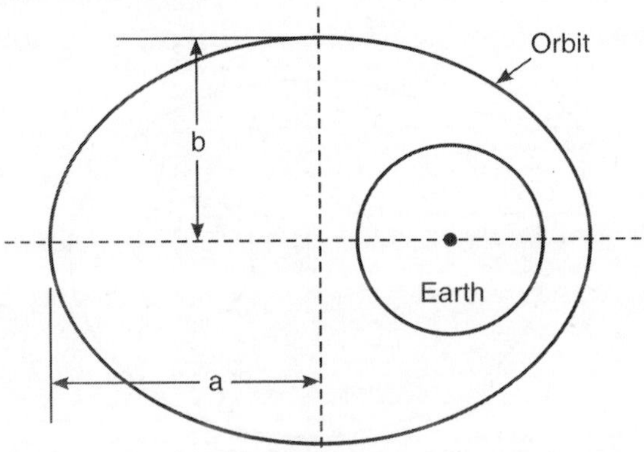

Fig. 29.5

$$\text{Apogee} - \text{Perigee} = a\ (1 + e) - a\ (1 - e) = 2ae$$

or Eccentricity, $$e = \frac{\text{Apogee} - \text{Perigee}}{2a}$$

$$= \frac{30000}{2 \times 16000}$$

$$= \frac{30000}{3200} = 0.93.$$

Example 51 : *The furthest and the closest points in a satellite's elliptical eccentric orbit from earth's surface are 30,000 km and 200 km respectively. Determine the apogee, the perigee and the orbit eccentricity. Assume radius of earth to be 6370 km.*

Solution :

$$\text{Apogee} = 30000 + 6370 = 36370 \text{ km}$$

$$\text{Perigee} = 200 + 6370 = 6570 \text{ km}$$

$$\text{Eccentricity} = \frac{\text{Apogee} - \text{Perigee}}{2a}$$

where a = semi–major axis of the elliptical orbit

Also, $$a = \frac{\text{Apogee} + \text{Perigee}}{2}$$

or $$2a = \text{Apogee} + \text{Perigee}$$

Therefore, orbit eccentricity $$= \frac{\text{Apogee} - \text{Perigee}}{\text{Apogee} + \text{Perigee}}$$

$$= \frac{36370 - 6570}{36370 + 6570} = \frac{29800}{42940} = 0.693.$$

Example 52 : *Refer to Fig. 29.6 showing a satellite moving in an elliptical, eccentric orbit. Determine the apogee and perigee distances if the orbit eccentricity is 0.5.*

Solution :

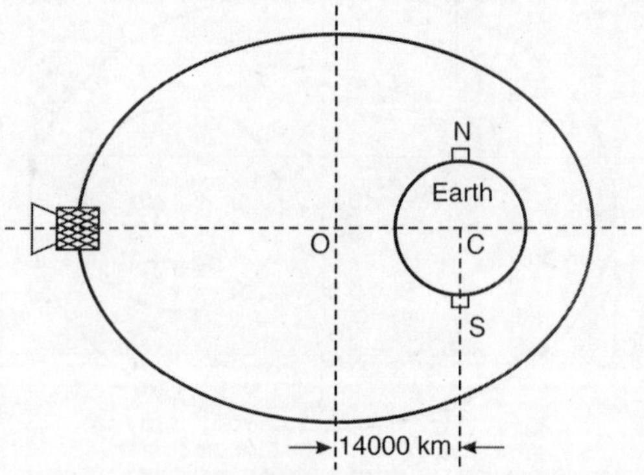

Fig. 29.6

The distance from center of ellipse (o) to the centre of earth (c) is given by ($a \times e$) where (a) is the semi-major axis and (e) is the eccentricity.

Therefore, $a \times e = 14000$

$$a = \frac{14000}{0.5} = 28000 \text{ km}$$

Now apogee $= a(1 + e) = 28000(1 + 0.5) = 42000$ km

Perigee $= a(1 - e) = 28000(1 - 0.5)$

$= 28000 \times 0.5 = 14000$ km.

Example 53 : *Satellite-1 in an elliptical orbit has the orbit semi-major axis equal to 18000 km and Satellite-2 in an elliptical orbit has semi-major axis equal to 24000 km (Fig. 29.7). Determine the relationship between their orbital periods.*

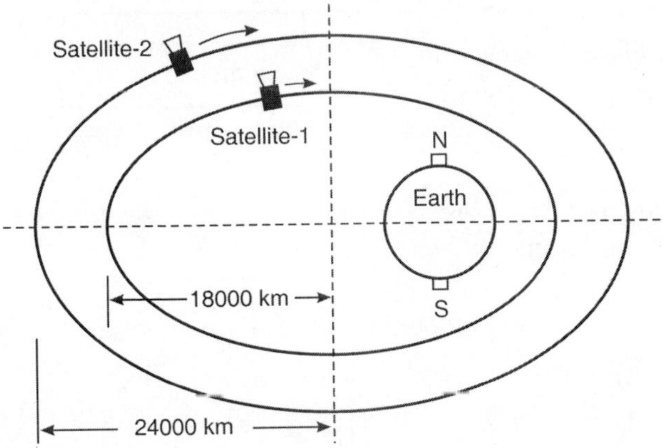

Fig. 29.7

Solution :

The orbital time period (T) is given by

$$T = 2\pi \sqrt{a^3/\mu}$$

where $\mu = GM$

G = Earth's gravitational constant

M = mass of earth

a = semimajor axis of ellipse

If (a_1) and (a_2) are the values of the semi-major axis of the elliptical orbits of the satellites-1 and 2, (T_1) and (T_2) are the corresponding orbital periods, then

$$T_1 = 2\pi \sqrt{a_1^3/\mu} \quad \text{and} \quad T_2 = 2\pi \sqrt{a_2^3/\mu}$$

$$T_2/T_1 = (a_2/a_1)^{3/2} = \left(\frac{24000}{18000}\right)^{3/2} = (4/3)^{3/2} = 1.54.$$

Thus orbital period of satellite-2 is 1.54 times the orbital period of satellite-1.

Example 54 : *Determine the escape velocity for an object to be launched from surface of earth from a point where earth's radius is 6360 km. ($G = 6.67 \times 10^{-11}$ Nm^2/kg^2 and $M = 5.98 \times 10^{24}$ kg).*

Solution :

Escape velocity = $\sqrt{2\mu/r}$

Here $r = 6360$ km $= 6360 \times 10^3$m

$$\mu = GM = 6.67 \times 10^{-11} \times 5.98 \times 10^{24}$$

$$= 39.8 \times 10^{13} \text{ Nm}^2/\text{kg}$$

$$\text{Therefore, Escape Velocity } = \sqrt{\frac{2 \times 39.8 \times 10^{13}}{6360 \times 10^3}}$$

$$= \sqrt{\frac{79.6 \times 10^{10}}{6360}} = 11.2 \text{ km/s.}$$

Example 55. *Calculate the orbital period of a satellite in an eccentric elliptical orbit shown in Fig. 29.8.*

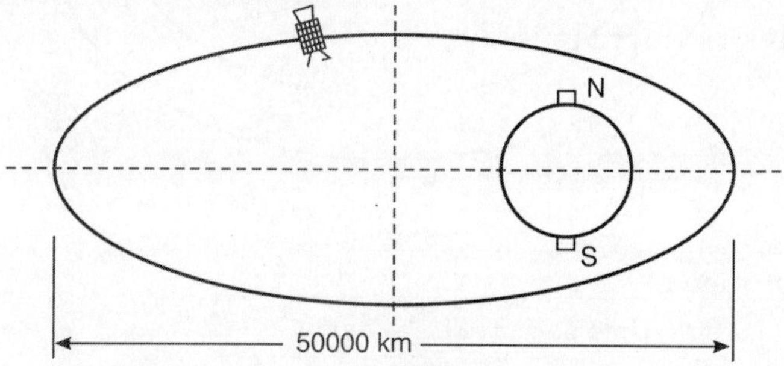

Fig. 29.8

Solution. Semi major axis, $a = \dfrac{50000}{2} = 25000$ km

Orbital time period, $T = 2\pi\sqrt{a^3/\mu}$

and (r_p) are the apogee and perigee distances, then

$$\mu = GM = 6.67 \times 10^{-11} \times 5.98 \times 10^{24}$$

$$= 39.8 \times 10^{13} \text{ Nm}^2/\text{kg}$$

$$T = 2 \times 3.14 \sqrt{\frac{(25000 \times 10^3)^3}{39.8 \times 10^{13}}}$$

$$= 6.28 \sqrt{\frac{15625 \times 10^{18}}{39.8 \times 10^{13}}}$$

$$= 6.28 \times 6.25 \times 10^3 = 39250 \text{ seconds}$$

$$= 10 \text{ hours } 54 \text{ minutes.}$$

Example 56 : *A satellite moving in a highly eccentric Molniya orbit having the farthest and the closest points as 35000 km and 500 km respectively from the surface of the earth. Determine the orbital time period and the velocity at the apogee and perigee point. (Assume earth's radius = 6360 km.)*

Solution.

Apogee distance $= 35000 + 6360 = 41360$ km

Perigee distance $= 500 + 6360 = 6860$ km

Semi-major axis of elliptical orbit,

$$a = \frac{41360 + 6860}{2} = 24110 \text{ km}$$

Orbital time period, $T = 2\pi \sqrt{a^3/\mu}$

$$= 6.28\sqrt{\frac{(24110 \times 10^3)^3}{6.67 \times 10^{-11} \times 5.98 \times 10^{24}}}$$

$= 10$ hrs 20 minutes

Velocity at any point on the orbit is given by:

$$V = \sqrt{\mu\,[(2/r) - (1/a)]}$$

$$V = GM = 6.67 \times 10^{-11} \times 5.98 \times 10^{24}$$

$$= 39.8 \times 10^{13} \text{ Nm}^2/\text{kg}$$

At apogee point, $r = 41360$ km. Therefore,

$$V = \sqrt{39.8 \times 10^{13}\left[\frac{2}{41360 \times 10^3} - \frac{1}{24110 \times 10^3}\right]}$$

$$= \sqrt{39.8 \times 10^{13}\left[\frac{48220 - 41360}{41360 \times 24110 \times 10^3}\right]}$$

$$= \sqrt{\frac{39.8 \times 10^{13} \times 6860}{41360 \times 24110 \times 10^3}} = 523 \text{ m/s}$$

At perigee point, $r = 6860$ km. Therefore,

$$\vartheta = \sqrt{39.8 \times 10^{13}\left[\frac{2}{6860 \times 10^3} - \frac{1}{24110 \times 10^3}\right]}$$

$$= \sqrt{39.8 \times 10^{13}\left[\frac{48220 - 6860}{6860 \times 24110 \times 10^3}\right]}$$

$$= \sqrt{\frac{39.8 \times 10^{13} \times 41360}{6860 \times 24110 \times 10^3}} = 9.976 \text{ km/s.}$$

Example 57 : *The sum of apogee and perigee distance of a certain elliptical satellite orbit is 50000 km and the difference of apogee and perigee distance is 30000 kms. Determine the target eccentricity (e).*

Solution :

If (r_a) and (r_p) are the apogee and perigee distances, then

$$e = \left(\frac{r_a - r_p}{r_a + r_p}\right) = \frac{30000}{50000} = 0.6.$$

Example 58 : *The semi-major axis and the semi-minor axis of an elliptical satellite orbit are 20,000 km and 16000 km respectively. Determine the apogee and perigee distances.*

Solution :

If (r_a) and (r_p) are apogee and perigee distances respectively, then

$$\text{semi-major axis} = \frac{r_a + r_p}{2}$$

$$\text{Semi-minor axis} = \sqrt{r_a\, r_p}$$

$$\frac{r_a + r_p}{2} = 20000 \text{ km}$$

Therefore, $r_a + r_p = 40000$ km

$$\sqrt{r_a \times r_p} = 16000$$

Therefore, $r_a\, r_p = 256000000$

Now $\quad r_a + r_p = 40000 \quad$ ...(1)

$r_a \times r_p = 256000000 \quad$ ...(2)

Substituting the value of (r_p) from (2) in (1)

$$r_a\,(40000 - r_a) = 256000000$$

or $r_a^2 - 40000\, r_a + 256000000 = 0$

$$r_a = \frac{40000 \pm \sqrt{16 \times 10^8 - 10.24 \times 10^8}}{2}$$

$$= \frac{40000 \pm \sqrt{5.76 \times 10^8}}{2} = \frac{40000 \pm 2.4 \times 10^4}{2}$$

$$= 3.2 \times 10^4,\ 1.6 \times 10^4 = 32000 \text{ km},\ 16000 \text{ km}$$

$r_a = 32000$ km as it cannot be 16000 km if the semi-major axis is 20,000 km.

$$r_p = 40000 - 32000 = 8000 \text{ km}.$$

Example 59 : *A satellite is moving in a near earth circular orbit at a distance of 640 km. Determine its orbital period. (Assume R = 6360 km.)*

Solution :

$$\text{Orbital velocity} = \sqrt{\frac{GM}{(R+H)}} = \sqrt{\frac{6.67 \times 10^{-11} \times 5.98 \times 10^{24}}{7000 \times 10^3}}$$

$$= \sqrt{\frac{39.8 \times 10^{13}}{7 \times 10^6}} = 7.54 \text{ km/s}.$$

$$\text{Orbital period} = \frac{2\pi (R + H)}{V} = \frac{6.28 \times 7000}{7.54}$$

$$= 5830 \text{ sec} = 1 \text{ hour } 37 \text{ minutes.}$$

Example 60 : *A satellite moving in an eccentric elliptical orbit has semi-major axis and semi-minor axis of (a) and (b) respectively and an eccentricity of 0.6. The satellite takes 3 hrs 10 minutes in moving from B to A in the direction shown. What will be the time taken by the satellite to move from A to B in the direction shown in Fig. 29.9.*

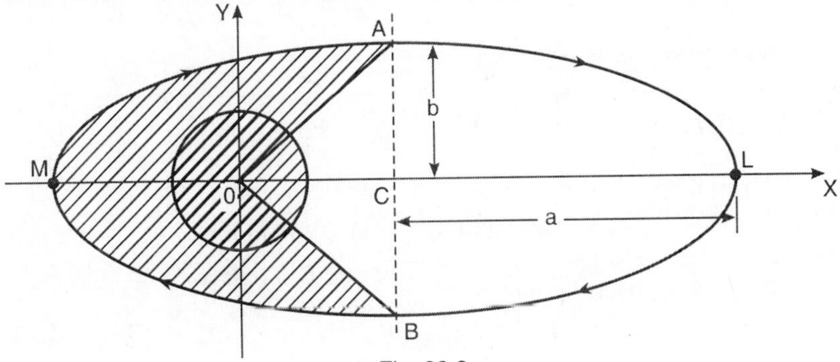

Fig. 29.9

Solution :

According to Kepler's law for elliptical satellite orbits, the line joining the satellite and the center of the earth spans equal ellipse area in equal time.

As a first step, we shall determine the area spanned while moving from B to A. It is given by shaded region and is given by

Area of half of ellipse - Area of ΔAOB

$$= \frac{\pi\, ab}{2} - b \times OC = \frac{\pi\, ab}{2} - bae$$

$$= ab\,(\pi/2 - e) = ab\left(\frac{3.14}{2} - 0.6\right)$$

$$= 0.97\, ab \cong ab$$

The area spanned in moving from A to B.

$$= \frac{\pi\, ab}{2} + 0.6\, ab = ab\,(\pi/2 + 0.6) = 2.2\, ab.$$

The ratio of the two areas is $\frac{2.2\, ab}{ab} = 2.2.$

Therefore, the time taken by satellite to move from A to B should be 2.2 times the time taken by the satellite to move from B to A in the direction shown. Therefore,

Time taken $= 2.2 \times 3$ hrs 10 min $= 7$ hrs.

Example 61 : *For an eccentric elliptical satellite orbit with an apogee and perigee points at a distance of 50,000 km and 8000 km respectively from the centre of earth. Determine the semi-major axis, semi-minor axis and the orbit eccentricity.*

Solution :

Apogee distance, $r_a = 50000$ km

Perigee distance, $r_p = 8000$ km

Semi-major axis, $a = \dfrac{r_a + r_p}{2}$

$= \dfrac{50000 + 8000}{2} = 29000$ km

Semi-minor axis, $b = \sqrt{r_a \times r_p}$

$= \sqrt{50000 \times 8000} = 20000$ km

Orbit eccentricity, $e = \left(\dfrac{r_a - r_p}{r_a + r_p}\right) = \left(\dfrac{50000 - 8000}{50000 + 8000}\right)$

$= \dfrac{42000}{58000} = 0.724.$

Example 62. *Satellite-1 and Satellite-2 are orbitting in different elliptical orbits with same perigee but different apogee distances as shown in Fig. 29.10. The semi-major axes of the two orbits are 16000 km and 24000 km. If the orbital period of satellite-1 is 10 hours, determine the orbital period of satellite-2.*

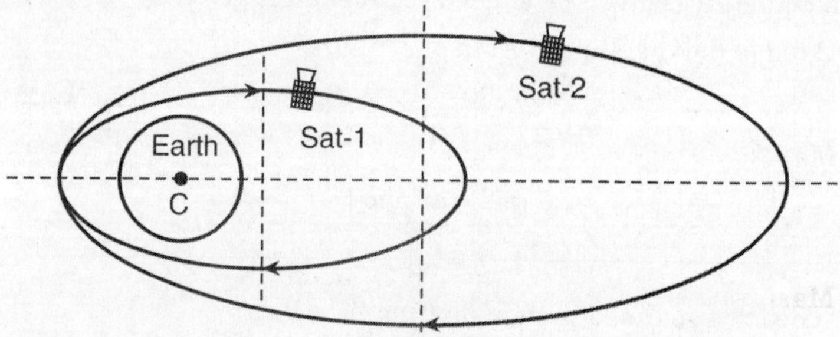

Fig. 29.10

Solution :

Orbital period (T) is given by, $T = 2\pi \sqrt{a^3/\mu}$

where a = semi–major axis

$\mu = GM$

If (T_1) and (T_2) are the orbital periods of satellite-1 and satellite-2 respectively, then

$$\left(\frac{T_2}{T_1}\right) = \frac{2\pi\sqrt{a_2^3/\mu}}{2\pi\sqrt{a_1^3/\mu}} = \left(\frac{a_2}{a_1}\right)^{3/2}$$

$$T_2 = T_1\left(\frac{a_2}{a_1}\right)^{3/2} = 10\left(\frac{24000}{16000}\right)^{3/2}$$

$$= 10(1.5)^{3/2} = 18.37 \text{ hours.}$$

Example 63 : *A geosynchronous satellite moving in an equatorial circular orbit at a height of 35800 km above the surface of earth gets inclined at an angle of 2° due to some reasons. Calculate the maximum deviation in latitude, if the maximum deviation in longitude (with reference to longitude of ascending node) is 0.0175°, determine maximum displacements in kms caused by latitude and longitude displacements. (Assume earth's radius = 6364 km).*

Solution :

Height of orbit = 35800 km

Earth's radius = 6364 km

Therefore, Orbit radius, r = 35800 + 6364 = 42164 km

Angle of inclination = 2°

Maximum latitude deviation from equator due to inclination (i) is given by :

$$\lambda_{max} = i = 2°$$

Maximum displacement (in km) due to λ_{max} is given by:

$$D_\lambda\,(\text{max}) = ai\left(\frac{\pi}{180}\right) \quad \text{where } (i) \text{ is in deg}$$

$$= \frac{42164 \times 2 \times \pi}{180} = 1471 \text{ km.}$$

Maximum longitude deviation from ascending node,

$$\psi_{max} = \frac{i^2}{228} = \frac{2^2}{228} = \frac{4}{228} = 0.0175°$$

Maximum displacement (D_ψ) due to (ψ_{max}) is given by:

$$D_\psi = D_\lambda\left(\frac{\psi_{max}}{\lambda_{max}}\right) = 1471 \times \frac{0.0175}{2} = 12.9 \text{ km.}$$

Example 64 : *Determine the magnitude of velocity impulse needed to correct the inclination of 2° in the satellite orbit of example 63.*

Solution : The magnitude of velocity impulse is given by:

$$\sqrt{\frac{\mu}{r}}\tan i = \sqrt{\frac{39.8 \times 10^{13}}{42164 \times 10^3}}\tan 2° = 107 \text{ m/s.}$$

Example 65 : *A geosynchronous satellite orbitting at 42164 km from earth's center has a circular and equatorial orbit. The orbit gets inclined due to some reason and it is observed that the maximum displacement due to latitude deviation in 500 km. Determine angle of inclination (i) between the new orbital plane and the equatorial plane.*

Solution :

Maximum displacement $D\lambda$ (max) due to latitude deviation is given by

$$D\lambda\ (\text{max}) = r\ \lambda_{\max}$$

where $\lambda_{\max}$ = maximum latitude deviation = i (angle of inclination)

or $$D\lambda\ (\text{max}) = r \times i$$

Therefore, $$i = D\lambda\ (\text{max})/r = \frac{500}{42164} = 0.012 \text{ rad} = 0.68 \text{ deg.}$$

Example 66 : *A geostationary satellite moving in an equatorial circular orbit is at a height of 35786 km from earth's surface. If the earth's radius is taken as 6378 km, determine the theoretical maximum coverage angle. Also determine the maximum slant range.*

Solution :

For theoretical maximum coverage angle, elevation angle, $E = 0$.

Maximum coverage angle, $2\alpha_{\max} = 2 \sin^{-1}\left(\frac{\text{Re}}{\text{Re} + H} \cos E_{\min}\right)$

where R_e = earth's radius

H = height of satellite above earth's surface

$$2\ \alpha_{\max} = 2 \sin\left(\frac{6378}{35786 + 6378} \cos 0°\right) = 17.4°$$

or $$\alpha_{\max} = 8.7°$$

If D is the maximum slant range, then

$$D^2 = R_e^2 + (R_e + H)^2 - 2R_e\ (R_e + H) \times \sin\left[E + \sin^{-1}\left(\frac{R_e}{R_e + H} \cos E\right)\right]$$

$$= (6378)^2 + (42164)^2 - 2 \times 6378 \times 42164 \times \sin 8.7°$$

$$= 40678884 + 1777802896 - 537843984 \times 0.1512$$

$$= 1737139041$$

or $$D = 41679 \text{ km.}$$

Example 67. *What would be the new maximum coverage angle and the slant range if the minimum possible elevation angle is 5° and not zero as in Example-66 (Refer to Fig. 29.11).*

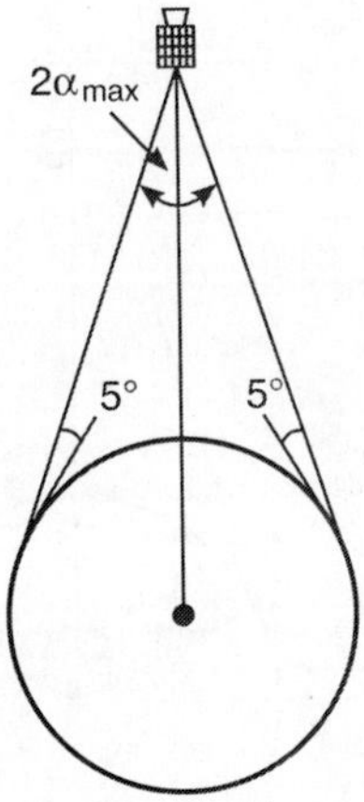

Fig. 29.11

Solution :

The maximum coverage angle, $(2\alpha_{max})$ is given by

$$2\alpha_{max} = 2\sin^{-1}\left[\left(\frac{Re}{Re+H}\right)\cos E_{min}\right]$$

where E_{min} = Minimum elevation angle

$$2\,\alpha_{max} = 2\sin^{-1}\left[\left(\frac{6378}{6378+35786}\right)\cos 5°\right]$$

$$= 2\sin^{-1}[0.1512 \times 0.996]$$

$$= 2\sin^{-1} 0.1506$$

$$= 2 \times 8.66 = 17.32°.$$

Example 68 : *Refer to Fig. 29.12 showing a geostationary satellite orbitting earth. Calculate the angle (θ) subtended by the arc of the satellite's footprint at the center of earth.*

Solution : $\theta = \theta_1 + \theta_2$

$\theta_1 = 90° - \alpha_1 - E_1$ $(E_1 = 5°)$

$\theta_2 = 90° - \alpha_2 - E_2$ $(E_2 = 0°)$

Therefore $\theta = (90 - \alpha_1 - E_1) + (90 - \alpha_2 - E_2)$

$$= 180 - (\alpha_1 + \alpha_2) - (E_1 + E_2)$$

$$= 175° - (\alpha_1 + \alpha_2)$$

$$\alpha_1 = \sin^{-1}\frac{6378}{6378+35786}\cos 5°$$

$$= \sin^{-1}\frac{6378\cos 5°}{42164} = 8.66°$$

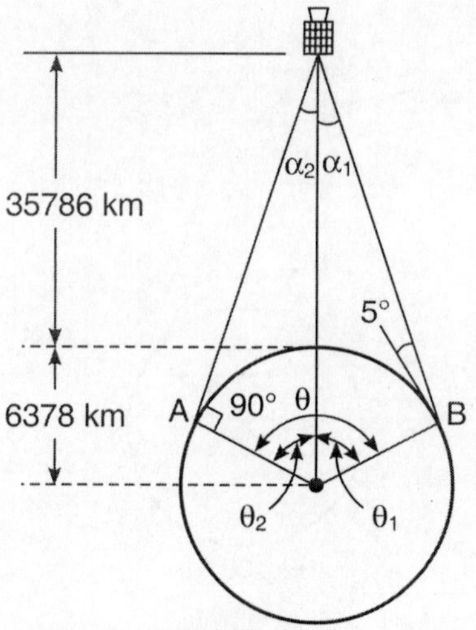

Fig. 29.12

$$\alpha_2 = \sin^{-1} \frac{6378}{6378 + 35786} \cos 0° = 8.69°$$

Therefore, $\theta = 175° - (8.66 + 8.69) = 157.65°.$

Example 69 : *Determine the round trip delay for an earth station located at point B in Example 68.*

Solution :

As a first step, we need to determine the slant range for the earth station located at point B. The slant range (d) is given by :

$$d^2 = (6378)^2 + (6378 + 35786)^2 - 2 \times 6378 \times 35786 \times \sin\left[5° + \sin^{-1}\left(\frac{6378}{6378 + 35786} \cos 5°\right)\right]$$

$$= 40678884 + 1777802896 - 126984965$$

$$= 1691496815$$

Therefore, $d = \sqrt{1691496815} = 41127.8$ km

Round trip time, $\tau = \frac{2d}{c}$

where $c = 3 \times 10^8$ m/s $= 3 \times 10^5$ km/s

$$\tau = \frac{2 \times 41127.8}{3 \times 10^5} \text{ secs} = 0.274 \text{ sec} = 274 \text{ ms.}$$

Example 70 : *Determine the maximum shadow angle that occurs at equinoxes for a satellite orbitting in a circular equatorial orbit at a height of 13622 km above the surface of earth. Assume earth's radius to be 6378 km. Also determine the maximum daily eclipse duration.*

Solution : Refer to Fig. 29.13.

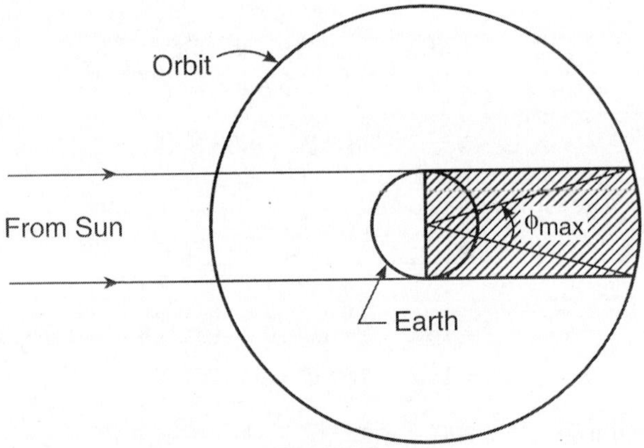

Fig. 29.13

The radius of circular orbit = 13622 + 6378 = 20,000 km

$$\text{Maximum shadow angle, } \phi_{max} = 180° - 2\cos^{-1}\left(\frac{6378}{20{,}000}\right)$$

$$\phi_{max} = 180° - 2\cos^{-1} 0.3189$$
$$= 180° - 2 \times 71.4$$
$$= 180° - 142.8 = 37.2°$$

$$\text{Maximum daily eclipse duration} = \frac{37.2}{360} \times 24 \text{ hours}$$
$$= 2.48 \text{ hours.}$$

Example 71 : *We know that the first day of eclipse before an equinox and last day of the eclipse after an equinox correspond to the relative position of the sun so that the sun rays tangent to the earth pass through the satellite orbit. Determine the total time from the first day of eclipse to the last day of the eclipse for the satellite orbit of Example 70. Also determine the same for a geostationary orbit at a height of 35786 km above earth's surface.*

Solution : The angle of inclination $i_e(t)$ between the equatorial plane and the direction of sun as a function of time during the time period of earth's one rotation around sun is given by

$$i_e(t) = 23.4 \sin\frac{2\pi t}{T}, \qquad \text{where } T = 365 \text{ days}$$

23.4° is the maximum inclination that occurs on summer and winter solstices.

For a circular orbit of 20,000 km radius, $\phi = 37.4°$. Therefore, the time from first day of eclipse to the equinox is given by substituting $i_e(t) = 18.7°(= 37.4°/2)$

i.e. $$18.7 = 23.4 \sin \frac{2\pi t}{365}$$

or $$t = \frac{365}{2\pi} \sin^{-1}\left(\frac{18.7}{23.4}\right) = \frac{365}{2\pi}(53°)$$

$$= \frac{365}{2\pi} \times 53 \times \frac{\pi}{180} = 53.8 \text{ days}$$

For the geostationary orbit,

$$\phi_{max} = 180° - 2\cos^{-1}\left(\frac{6378}{6378 + 35786}\right)$$

$$= 180° - 2\cos^{-1}0.1512 = 180° - 2 \times 81.3°$$

$$= 180° - 162.6° = 17.4°$$

Therefore, $$t = \frac{365}{\pi} \sin^{-1}\left(\frac{8.7}{23.4}\right) = \frac{365}{\pi}(21°)$$

$$= \frac{365}{\pi} \times 21 \times \frac{\pi}{180} \text{ days} = 22.13 \text{ days.}$$

Example 72: *A satellite is currently in its elliptical transfer orbit (Fig. 29.14) with apogee and perigee being at distances of 35786 km and 300 km respectively above the surface of earth. If the transfer orbit inclination to the equatorial plane is 0°, calculate the incremental velocity to be given to the satellite at the apogee point by the apogee kick motor to circularize the orbit (Assume earth's radius = 6378 km).*

Solution: The velocity (V) at any point along an elliptical orbit is given by:

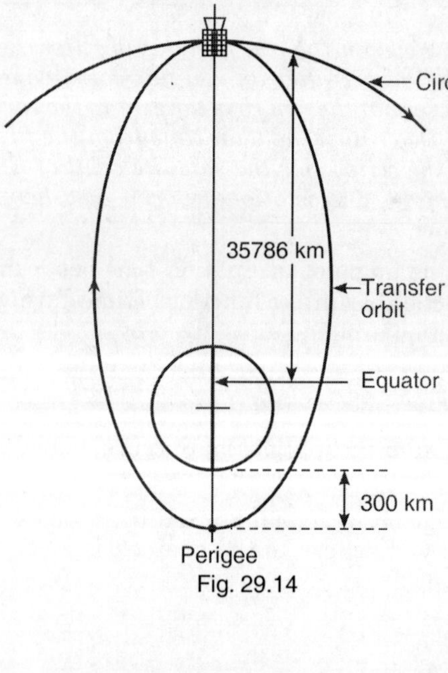

Fig. 29.14

$$V = \sqrt{\mu\left(\frac{2}{r} - \frac{1}{a}\right)}$$

where $\mu = GM$

r = apogee distance from centre of earth

a = semi–major axis of ellipse

Now $$r = 35786 + 6378 = 42164 \text{ km}$$

$$a = \frac{35786 + 6378 + 6378 + 300}{2} = 24421 \text{ km}$$

The velocity (V_a) at the apogee point can then be computed from

$$V_a = \sqrt{\mu\left(\frac{2}{r} - \frac{1}{a}\right)}$$

$$V_a^2 = 39.8 \times 10^{13}\left(\frac{2}{42164} \times 10^{13} - \frac{1}{24421} \times 10^{3}\right)$$

$$= \frac{39.8 \times 10^{13} \times 6678}{42164 \times 24421 \times 10^3}$$

$$= 2.58 \times 10^6$$

$$V_a = \sqrt{2.58 \times 10^6} = 1.61 \text{ km/s}$$

For a circular orbit with a radius of 42164 km,

$$V_c = \sqrt{\frac{\mu}{r}} = \sqrt{\frac{39.8 \times 10^{13}}{42164 \times 10^3}} = 3.07 \text{ km/s}$$

The velocity change (ΔV) required to circularize is given by

$$\Delta V = \sqrt{V_a^2 + V_c^2 - 2V_a V_c \cos i}$$

Here $$i = 0°$$

Therefore, $$\Delta V = \sqrt{V_a^2 + V_c^2 - 2\, V_a V_c}$$

$$= (V_a - V_c) \text{ or } (V_c - V_a)$$

$$= \sqrt{(V_a - V_c)^2}$$

$$= 3.07 - 1.61 = 1.46 \text{ km/s.}$$

Example 73 : *If the satellite in Example 72 was launched from Cape Kennedy having a latitude of 28° N and if the injection of the satellite at perigee point was horizontal, determine the velocity change required to circularize the orbit and correct the inclination.*

Solution : The elliptical transfer orbit has an inclination that is equal to or greater than the launch point latitude. If the satellite injection is horizontal at the perigee, it equals the launch point latitude.

Here $i = 28°$

Therefore, $\Delta V = \sqrt{(1.61)^2 + (3.07)^2 - 2 \times 1.61 \times 3.07 \times \cos 28°}$

$= \sqrt{2.59 + 9.42 - 8.73} = \sqrt{3.276} = 1.81$ km/s

Example 74 : *Determine the maximum line of sight distance between two communication satellites moving in a circular orbit at a height (H) above the surface of earth.*

Solution : Maximum line of sight distance between the two satellites would occur when the satellites are so placed that the line joining the two becomes tangent to the earth's surface as shown in Fig. 29.15.

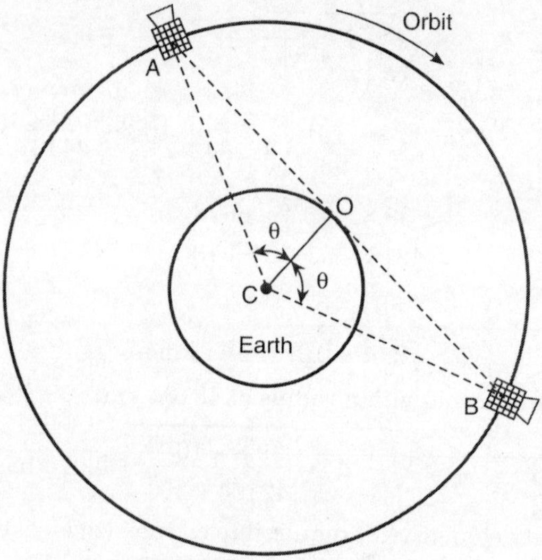

Fig. 29.15

The maximum line of sight distance = $AB = OA + OB = 2 \times OA$ or $2 \times OB$ as $OA = OB$. If (R) is the radius of earth and (H) the height of the orbit, then

$$OA = AC \sin \theta = (R + H) \sin \theta$$

Now $\theta = \cos^{-1}\left(\frac{R}{R+H}\right)$

Therefore, $OA = (R + H) \sin\left(\cos^{-1} \cdot \frac{R}{R+H}\right)$

Maximum line of distance $= 2(R + H) \sin\left[\cos^{-1}\left(\frac{R}{R+H}\right)\right]$

Example 75 : *If the two satellites in Example 74 have an orbital radius that is twice the radius of earth, determine the maximum line of sight distance. Repeat the example for geostationary satellites having an orbital radius of 42164 km. (Assume earth's radius, R = 6370 km).*

Solution :

Maximum line of sight distance = $2(R + H) \sin\left[\cos^{-1}\left(\frac{R}{R+H}\right)\right]$

It is given that $(R + H) = 2R$. Therefore, maximum line of sight distance,

$$= 2 \times 2R \sin[\cos^{-1} 0.5] = 4 R \sin 60°$$

$$= \frac{4\sqrt{3}}{2} R = 2\sqrt{3}\, R = 2\sqrt{3} \times 6370 = 22066 \text{ km}$$

For geostationary satellites, $(R + H) = 42164$ km

Therefore, maximum line of sight distance

$$= 2 \times 42164 \sin\left(\cos^{-1}\frac{6370}{42164}\right)$$

$$= 84328 \sin(\cos^{-1} 81.3) = 84328 \times 0.998$$

$$= 83361 \text{ km.}$$

Example 76 : *Two communication satellites in the same circular orbit but located at 130° W and 70° W longitudes communicate via an inter-satellite link. Find the round trip propagation delay.*

Solution :

The angular difference in the longitudes of the two satellites

$$= 130°\text{W} - 70°\text{W} = 60°$$

Also, a longitudinal difference of 180° corresponds to the two satellites located diametrically opposite to each other. The current situation is depicted in Fig. 29.16.

The line-of-sight distance between the two satellites can be computed from triangle ABC where

$$AB = \sqrt{AC^2 + BC^2 - 2AC \times BC \cos 60°}$$

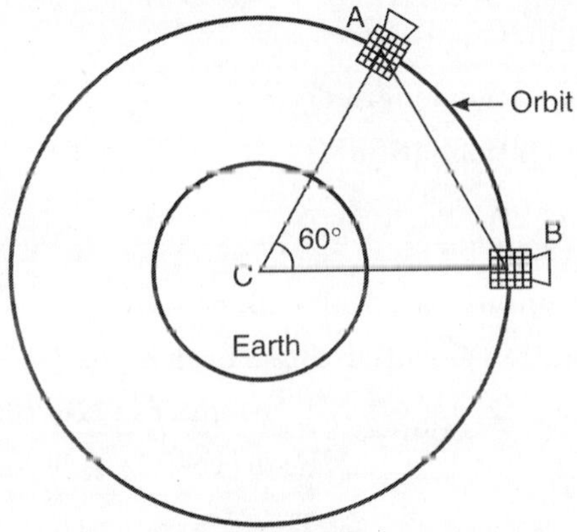

Fig. 29.16

Here $AC = BC = R$ .... (orbital radius)

Therefore $AB = \sqrt{R^2 + R^2 - 2R^2 \times 0.5} = R$

Round trip time $= \dfrac{2R}{3 \times 10^8}$, where ($R$) is in metres.

Example 77: *If the location of the two satellites in Example-76 was 30°W and 15°E and if the orbital radius was 10000 km, determine the round trip propagation delay.*

Solution:

The angular difference = 30° + 15° = 45°

The two figures have been added as one satellite is towards west of the reference while the other is towards east.

Line-of-sight distance

$$= \sqrt{(10000)^2 + (10000)^2 - 2 \times (10000)^2 \cos 45^\circ}$$

$$= \sqrt{10^8 + 10^8 - 1.41 \times 10^8}$$

$$= 0.765 \times 10^4 \text{ km} = 7650 \text{ km}.$$

Round trip propagation delay $= \dfrac{2 \times 7650}{3 \times 10^5}$ sec = 51 ms.

Example 78: *An earth station is located at 30°W longitude and 60°N latitude. Determine the earth station azimuth and elevation angles with respect to geostationary satellite located at 50°W longitude. (Assume orbital radius = 42164 km and earth's radius = 6378 km).*

Solution:

Earth station azimuth angle, $A = 180° - A'$ if the earth station is in the northern hemisphere and is towards the west of the satellite.

$$A' = \tan^{-1}\left[\frac{\tan|\theta_S - \theta_L|}{\sin \theta_l}\right]$$

where θ_s = satellite longitude

θ_L = earth station longitude

θ_l = earth station latitude

$$A' = \tan^{-1}\left[\frac{\tan 20^\circ}{\sin 60^\circ}\right] = 22.8^\circ$$

Therefore, azimuth, $A = 180° - 22.8° = 157.2°$

The earth station elevation angle is given by

$$E = \tan^{-1}\left[\frac{r - R_e \cos\theta_l \cos|\theta_s - \theta_L|}{R_e \sin\left(\cos^{-1} \cos\theta_l \cos|\theta_s - \theta_L|\right)}\right] - \cos^{-1}[\cos\theta_l \cos|\theta_s - \theta_L|]$$

where r = orbital radius

R_e = earth's radius

$$E = \tan^{-1}\left[\frac{42164 - 6378 \cos 60° \cos 20°}{6378 \sin\left[\cos^{-1} \cos 20° (\cos 60° \cos 20°\right]}\right]$$

$$- \cos^{-1}(\cos 60° \cos 20°)$$

$$= \tan^{-1}\left(\frac{42164 - 2998}{6378 \sin (\cos^{-1} 0.47)}\right) - \cos^{-1} 0.47$$

$$= \tan^{-1}\left(\frac{39166}{5631}\right) - 62° = 81.8° - 62° = 19.8°$$

Azimuth = 157.2°,

Elevation = 19.8°.

Example 79: *A satellite is in a circular equatorial orbit at an altitude of 10000 km form earth's surface. Determine the maximum eclipse time in a day during the full eclipse period (Assume earth's radius = 6378 km).*

Solution: The maximum shadow angle and consequently the maximum daily eclipse duration occurs at equinoxes *i.e.* when the earth's equatorial plane's inclination to the direction of the sun is 0° (Fig. 29.17).

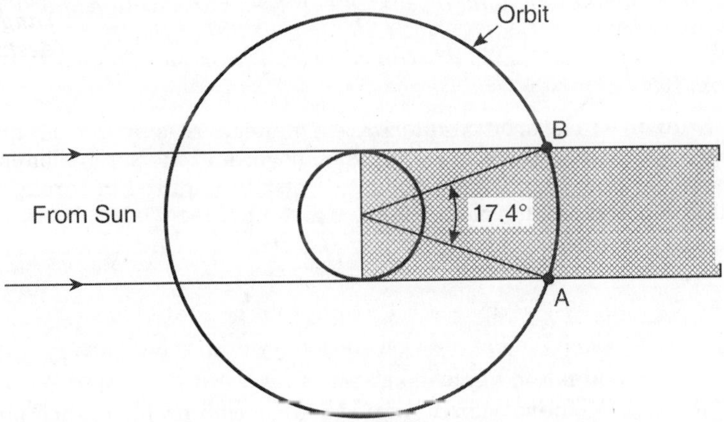

Fig. 29.17

The shadow angle in this case is given by

$$\phi_{max} = 180° - 2 \cos^{-1}\left(\frac{R_e}{R_e + H}\right)$$

where R_e = earth's radius

H = height of satellite orbit

Substituting the values of (*Re*) and (*H*)

$$\phi_{max} = 180° - 2\cos^{-1}\left(\frac{6378}{6378 + 10000}\right)$$

$$= 180° - 2\cos^{-1} 0.389 = 180° - 2 \times 67° = 46°$$

The eclipse duration is the time taken by the satellite to move from point A to B (Fig. 29.17)

Therefore eclipse duration $= \frac{46}{360} \times$ orbital period

Now orbital period $= 2\pi\sqrt{a^3/\mu}$

where (a) here is the orbital radius

Orbital period $= 2\pi\sqrt{\frac{(16378 \times 10^3)^3}{39.8 \times 10^{13}}} = 5.8$ hours

Therefore, eclipse duration $= \frac{46}{360} \times 5.8 = 0.74$ hours

$= 44.5$ minutes.

Example 80 : *A geostationary satellite launched by ESA's Ariane rocket from Kourou in French Guiana has the perigee of its elliptical transfer orbit at 450 km. Find the incremental velocity required to correct the orbit inclination and to achieve orbit circularization given that Kourou is located at 5.3° N latitude and also that the line joining the apogee and perigee is the node line (line joining ascending and descending nodes).*

Solution : The orbit circularization manoeuvre is carried out at the apogee point and if the line joining the apogee and the perigee happens to be nodal line, then the incremental velocity required to correct the inclination and circularize the orbit is given by

$$\Delta V = \sqrt{V_a^2 + V_c^2 - 2V_aV_c\cos i}$$

where V_a = velocity at apogee = 1.61 km/s for geostationary orbit

V_c = velocity of circular geostationary orbit = 3.07 km/s

i = inclination angle = 5.3°

(V_a) and (V_c) have been computed in an earlier problem. Inclination angle being equal to the latitude of the launch point has also been explained.

$$\Delta V = \sqrt{(1.61)^2 + (3.07)^2 - 2 \times 1.61 \times 3.07\cos 5.3°}$$

$$= \sqrt{2.59 + 9.42 - 9.88 \times 0.995}$$

$$= \sqrt{2.59 + 9.42 - 9.837} = \sqrt{2.173}$$

$$= 1.474 \text{ km/s.}$$

Example 81 : *Consider two earth stations A and B with longitudes at 60°W and 90°W respectively and latitudes at 30°N and 45°N respectively. They are communicating with each other via a geostationary satellite located at 105°W. Find the total delay in sending 500 kilobits of information from one station to the other if the transmission speed is 10 Mbps. (Assume satellite orbital radius = 42164 km and earth's radius = 6378 km.)*

Solution: Earth station A latitude, $Q_{lA} = 30°$

Earth station A longitude, $Q_{LA} = 60°$

Satellite longitude, $\theta_s = 105°$

The elevation angle of earth station A, E_A

$$\tan^{-1}\left[\frac{42164 \times 10^3 - 6378 \times 10^3 \cos 30° \cos 45°}{6378 \times 10^3 \sin\{\cos^{-1}(\cos 30° \cos 45°)\}}\right] - \cos^{-1}(\cos 30° \cos 45°)$$

$$= \tan^{-1}\left[\frac{42164 - 6378 \times 0.612}{6378 \times \sin 52.2°}\right] - \cos^{-1} 0.612$$

$$= \tan^{-1}\left[\frac{38260}{5039}\right] - 52.2° = 82.5° - 52.2° = 30.3°$$

Earth station B latitude, $\theta_{lB} = 45°N$

Earth station B longitude, $\theta_{LB} = 90°W$

The elevation angle of earth station B,

$$E_B = \tan^{-1}\left[\frac{42164 \times 10^3 - 6378 \times 10^3 \cos 45° \cos 15°}{6378 \times 10^3 \sin\{\cos^{-1}(\cos 45° \cos 15°)\}}\right] - \cos^{-1}(\cos 45° \cos 15°)$$

$$= \tan^{-1}\left[\frac{42164 - 6378 \times 0.682}{6378 \sin(\cos^{-1} 0.682)}\right] - \cos^{-1}(0.682)$$

$$= \tan^{-1}\left[\frac{37814}{4656}\right] - 47° = 83° - 47° = 36°$$

In the next step, we shall determine the slant range of the earth stations.

Refer to Fig. 29.18. The slant range (d_A) of the earth station A can be computed from:

$$d_A^2 = (42164 \times 10^3)^2 + (6378 \times 10^3)^2 - 2 \times 6378 \times 42164 \times 10^6 \times \sin\left[30.3° + \sin^{-1}\left\{\frac{6378}{42164} \cos 30.3°\right\}\right]$$

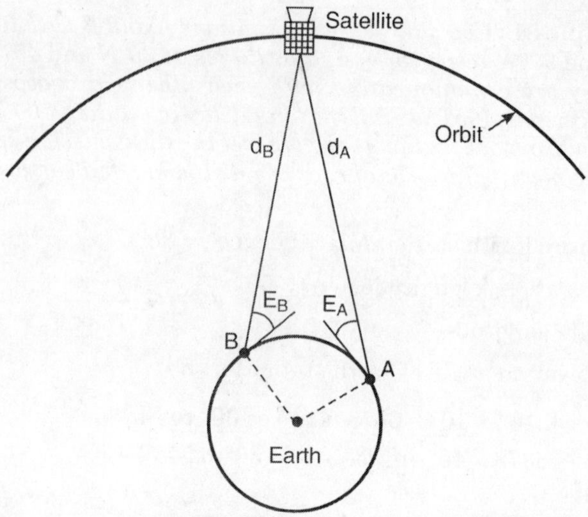

Fig. 29.18

$$= 1777802896 \times 10^6 + 40678884 \times 10^6 - 537843984 \times 10^6 \times \sin 37.8°$$

$$= 1488833409 \times 10^6$$

or $$d_A = \sqrt{1488883409 \times 10^6} = 38585 \text{ km}$$

The slant range (d_B) of the earth station B can be computed from:

$$d_B^2 = (42164 \times 10^3)^2 + (6378 \times 10^3)^2 - 2 \times 6378 \times 42164 \times 10^6 \times \sin\left[36° + \sin^{-1}\left\{\frac{6378}{42164}\cos 36°\right\}\right]$$

$$= 1777802896 \times 10^6 + 40678884 \times 10^6 - 537843984 \times 10^6 \sin 43°$$

or $$d_B = \sqrt{1451673065 \times 10^6} = 38101 \text{ km}$$

Total range to be covered = 38585 + 38101 = 76686 km

$$\text{Propagation delay} = \frac{76686}{3 \times 10^5} = 255.6 \text{ ms}$$

The time required to transmit 500 Kbps at a transmission speed of 10 Mbps is given by

$$\frac{500000}{10^7} \text{ sec} = 50 \text{ ms}$$

Therefore, total propagation delay = 255.6 + 50 = 305.6 ms.

Example 82 : *Calculate the power gain of a paraboloid reflector antenna with a mouth diameter of 10 m at 6 GHz. Assume antenna aperture efficiency to be 80%.*

Solution : Mouth diameter, $D = 10$ m

Frequency, $f = 6$ GHz

Aperture efficiency, $\eta = 0.8$

Antenna gain (G) is given by

$$G = \eta \frac{4 \pi A}{\lambda^2}$$

where A = aperture area $= \frac{\pi D^2}{4} = \frac{\pi \times (10)^2}{4} = 78.5 \text{ m}^2$

$$\lambda = \text{wavelength} = \frac{c}{f} = \frac{3 \times 10^8}{6 \times 10^9} = 0.05 \text{ m}$$

Therefore, $$G = \frac{0.8 \times 4 \times 3.14 \times 78.5}{0.05 \times 0.05} = 315507$$

Gain in decibels $= 10 \log 315507 = 10 \times 5.5 = 55$ dB.

Example 83 : *If the radiated beam in case of the antenna of Example 82 has a beamwidth of 1° in the azimuth direction, determine its width in degrees in the elevation direction.*

Solution : The power gain (G) if the antenna is also given by :

$$G = \frac{4\pi}{\Delta\theta \, \Delta\phi}$$

where, $\Delta\theta$ = azimuth beamwidth in radians

$\Delta\phi$ = elevation beamwidth in radians

In the present case, $G = 315507$

$$\Delta\theta = 1^\circ = \frac{\pi}{180} \text{ rad}$$

Therefore, $$\Delta\phi = \frac{4 \pi}{G \, \Delta \theta} = \frac{4 \pi \times 180}{315507 \times \pi}$$

$$= \frac{720}{315507} \text{ rad} = \frac{720 \times 180}{315507 \times \pi} \text{ deg} = 0.13 \text{ deg.}$$

Example 84 : *A paraboloid dish antenna having a mouth diameter of 20 m and an aperture efficiency of 90% produces a radiated beam with a solid angle of 3×10^{-4} steradians. Determine the antenna's power gain in decibels and also the operational frequency.*

Solution : Solid angle of the antenna beam

$$= 3 \times 10^{-4} \text{ steradians}$$

Power gain $\quad G = \dfrac{4\,\pi}{\Omega}$

where, Ω = beam solid angle in steradians

Therefore, $\quad G = \dfrac{4\,\pi}{3 \times 10^{-4}} = 41904$

Power gain in decibels = 10 log 41904

$$= 10 \times 4.622 = 46.22 \text{ dB}$$

Power gain is also expressed by

$$G = \eta\,\frac{4\,\pi\,A}{\lambda^2}$$

where A = Antenna's area of crossection

λ = operational wavelength

η = aperture efficiency

Therefore $\quad G = \dfrac{0.90 \times 4 \times \pi \times \pi \times (20)^2}{4\,\lambda^2} = 41904$

or $\quad \lambda^2 = \dfrac{0.9 \times 4\pi^2 \times 400}{4 \times 41904} = 0.0847$

$$\lambda = \sqrt{0.0847} = 0.291 \text{ m}$$

Operational frequency, $f = \dfrac{c}{\lambda} = \dfrac{3 \times 10^8}{0.291} = 1030.92$ MHz.

Example 85. *A Ku-band 20 m Cassegrain antenna designed for a satellite earth station has the following specifications for the antenna efficiency :*

Parameter	*Operational*	*Frequency*
	11.95 GHz	14.25 GHz
Illumination efficiency	0.98	0.96
Spillover efficiency		
Main reflector	0.99	0.99
Sub reflector	0.97	0.97
Blocking efficiency	0.85	0.85
Feed system efficiency	0.90	0.90
Surface tolerance efficiency	0.92	0.92

Determine antenna's power gain at 11.95 GHz and 14.25 GHz.

Solution : Power gain (G) is given by:

$$G = \eta \frac{4 \pi A}{\lambda^2}$$

$$A = \frac{\pi D^2}{4} = \frac{\pi \times 400}{4} = 314 \text{ m}^2$$

(*i*) For f = 11.95 GHz

$$\lambda = \frac{c}{f} = \frac{3 \times 10^8}{11.95 \times 10^9} = 0.0251 \text{ m}$$

$$\eta = 0.98 \times 0.99 \times 0.97 \times 0.85 \times 0.90 \times 0.92 = 0.66$$

Therefore, G (at f = 11.95 GHz) $= \dfrac{0.66 \times 4 \times 3.14 \times 314}{(0.0251)^2}$

$= 4131576$

Gain in decibels = 10 log 4131576 = 66.16 dB

(*ii*) For f = 14.25 GHz

$$\lambda = \frac{c}{f} = \frac{3 \times 10^8}{14.25 \times 10^9} = 0.021 \text{ m} \ \eta = 0.648$$

Therefore, G (at f = 14.25 GHz) $= \dfrac{0.648 \times 4 \times 3.14 \times 314}{(0.021)^2}$

$= 5795030$

Gain in decibels = 10 log 5795030 = 67.63 dB

Example 86 : *A satellite earth station antenna having a maximum gain of 60 dB at the operational frequency is fed from a power amplifier generating 10 KW. If the feed system has a loss of 2 dB, determine earth station EIRP (Effective Isotropic Radiated Power).*

Solution :

Power at the output of amplifier = 10 kW = 40 dBW

Antenna gain = 60 dBW

Power loss in feed system = 2 dBW

Therefore, $EIRP$ = 40 + 60 – 2 = 98 dWB

Example 87 : *Fig. 29.19 shows a cascaded arrangement of three gain blocks. It is given that $G_1 = 10^6$ and its associated equivalent noise temperature $T_{e1} = 100$ deg Kelvin, $G_2 = 10^4$ and $T_{e2} = 60$ deg K, $G_3 = 1000$ and $T_{e3} = 20$ deg K. Determine the equivalent noise temperature of the cascaded arrangement*

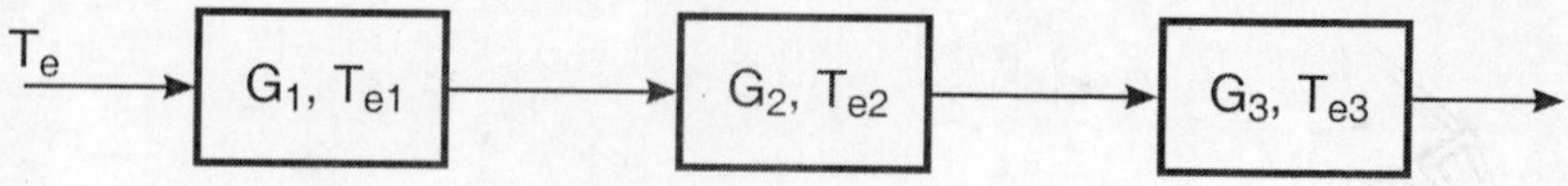

Fig. 29.19

Solution : If (T_e) is the equivalent noise temperature of the cascaded arrangement,

Then $$T_e = T_{e1} + \frac{T_{e2}}{G_1} + \frac{T_{e3}}{G_1 G_2}$$

$$= 100 + \frac{60}{10^6} + \frac{20}{10^6 \times 10^4}$$

$$= 100 + 60 \times 10^{-6} + 20 \times 10^{-10} \cong 100\text{K}$$

Example 88 : *Fig. 29.20 shows the cascaded arrangement of four gain blocks with their gain and noise figures as* $G_1 = 100, F_1 = 2, G_2 = 10, \quad F_2 = 10, G_3 = 10, F_3 = 15, G_4 = 10, \quad F_4 = 20.$ *Determine the noise figure of the cascaded arrangement.*

Fig. 29.20

Solution : The overall noise figure (F) is given by

$$F = F_1 + \frac{F_2 - 1}{G_1} + \frac{F_3 - 1}{G_1 G_2} + \frac{F_4 - 1}{G_1 G_2 G_3}$$

$$= 2 + \frac{10 - 1}{100} + \frac{15 - 1}{100 \times 10} + \frac{20 - 1}{100 \times 10 \times 10}$$

$$= 2 + 0.9 + 0.014 + 0.0019 = 2.1059 = 3.2 \text{ dB}.$$

Example 89 : *Fig. 29.21 shows the receive side of satellite earth station comprising of earth station antenna followed by waveguide that connects the antenna feed point to the low noise amplifier input with the output of the low noise amplifier feeding the down-converter. Assume that the receive antenna has a gain of 66 dB at the received down link frequency of 11.9 GHz. The other parameters characterising the receive chain are :*

Antenna noise temperature, $T_A = 60$ *K*

Loss in the waveguide, $L_1 = 1.075$ (0.3 *dB*)

Equivalent noise temperature of low noise amplifier, $T_{e2} = 160$ *K*

Low noise amplifier gain, $G_2 = 10^6$

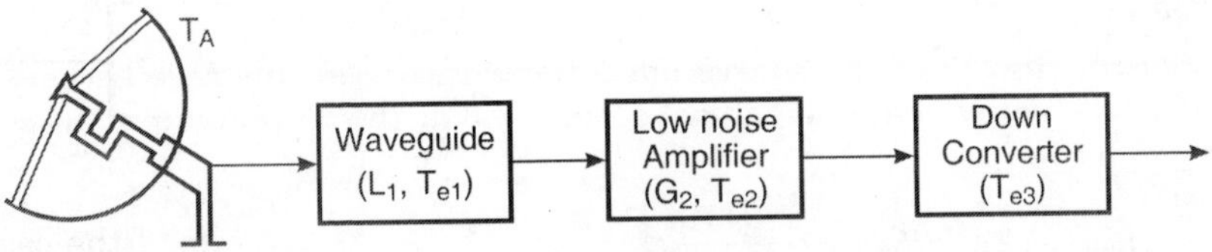

Fig. 29.21

Down converter equivalent noise temperature, $T_{e3} = 10000\ K$

Ambient temperature, $T_0 = 290\ K$

Determine the earth station system noise temperature and (G/T) referred to the input of the low noise amplifier.

Solution : Earth station system noise temperature referred to the input of the low noise amplifier is given by :

$$T = T_s + T_e$$

where T_s = Noise temperature measured at the output of the waveguide
T_e = Equivalent noise temperature at the input of low noise amplifier

Now
$$T_s = \frac{T_A}{L_1} + \frac{(L_1 - 1)\, T_0}{L_1}$$

$$= \frac{60}{1.075} + \left(\frac{1.075 - 1}{1.075}\right) 290$$

$$= 55.81 + 20.23 = 76.04 \text{ K}$$

$$T_e = T_{e2} + \frac{T_{e3}}{G_2} = 160 + \frac{10000}{10^6}$$

$$= 160 + 0.01 = 160.01$$

Therefore, $T = 76.04 + 160.01 = 236.05$ K

The antenna gain referred to the input of the low noise amplifier is given by

$$G = 66 - 0.3 = 65.7 \text{ dB}$$

The antenna gain to noise temperature ratio in dB per kelvin is given by

$$\frac{G}{T} = G \text{ (in dB)} - 10 \log T = 65.7 - 10 \log 236.05$$

$$= 65.7 - 23.73 = 41.97 \text{ dB/K.}$$

Example 90 : *For the data given in Example - 89, determine the earth station system noise temperature and (G/T) referred to the (a) input* *of waveguide (b) input of down converter. What do you deduce from the results ?*

Solution : (*a*) The source noise temperature in this case become (T_A). The equivalent noise temperature (T_e) at the waveguide input is given by :

$$(L_1 - 1)\,T_0 + T_{e2}\,L_1 + \frac{T_{e3}\,L_1}{G_2} \quad \ldots\ldots\ldots\ldots\ldots \left(G_1 = \frac{1}{L_1}\right)$$

$$= (1.075 - 1)\,290 + 160 \times 10.75 + \frac{10000 \times 1.075}{10^6}$$

$$= 290 \times 0.075 + 172 + 0.01 = 193.76 \text{ K}$$

Therefore, $T_s = 60 + 193.76 = 253.76$ K

In this case, $G = 66\ dB$

Therefore $\frac{G}{T} = 66 - 10 \log 253.76$

$$= 66 - 24.03 = 41.97 \text{ dB/K}$$

(*b*) The source noise temperature is given by

$$\frac{T_A\,G_2}{L_1} + \left(\frac{L_1 - 1}{L_1}\right) T_0\,G_2 + T_{e2}\,G_2 + T_{e3}$$

$$\frac{60 \times 10^6}{1.075} + \frac{0.075}{1.075} \times 290 \times 10^6 + 160 \times 10^6 + 10^4$$

$$= 55.81 \times 10^6 + 20.23 \times 10^6 + 160 \times 10^6 + 10^4$$

$$= 236.05 \times 10^6 \text{ K}$$

Gain, $G = 66 - 0.3 + 60 = 125.7$ dB

$$\frac{G}{T} = 125.7 - 10 \log 236.05 \times 10^6$$

$$= 125.7 - 83.73 = 41.97 \text{ dB/K}$$

The results obtained in Example - 89 and in this problem prove that value of (*G*/*T*) is invariant regardless of the chosen reference point. For the given example, (*G*/*T*) turns out to be 41.97 dB/K irrespective of whether the reference point is input of waveguide or input of low noise amplifier or input of down converter.

Example 91 : *Consider a dual up-converter (Fig. 29.22) with the following parameters :*

Uplink frequency spectrum = 5.9 to 6.4 GHz

First intermediate frequency = 70 MHz

Carrier bandwidth = 36 MHz

BPF-1 center frequency = 1 GHz

Find (a) First local oscillator frequency (b) range of second local oscillator frequency (c) frequency spectrum of the unwanted sideband. Fig. 31.22.

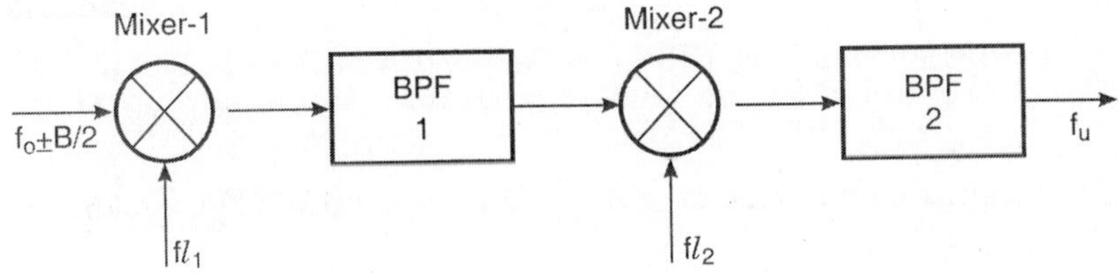

Fig. 29.22

Solution: (*a*) First local oscillator frequency, fl_1 = 1 GHz – 70 MHz = 930 MHz

(*b*) Minimum second local oscillator frequency, fl_2 (min) is given by

$$fl_2 \text{ (min)} = 5.9 - 1 = 4.9 \text{ GHz}$$

Maximum second local oscillator frequency, fl_2 (max) is given by:

$$fl_2 \text{ (max)} = 6.4 - 1 = 5.4 \text{ GHz}$$

Second local oscillator range = 4.9 GHz to 5.4 GHz

(*c*) Frequency spectrum of the unwanted sideband is from :

$$\{fu \text{ (min)} - 2 (fl_1 + fo)\} \text{ to } \{fu \text{ (max)} - 2 (fl_1 + fo)\}$$

$$= \{5.9 - 2 (0.930 + 0.070)\} \text{ to } \{6.4 - 2 (0.930 + 0.070)\}$$

$$= 3.9 \text{ GHz to } 4.4 \text{ GHz}$$

Example 92 : *Consider a dual up-converter as in Fig. 29.22 above with the following specifications:*

(*i*) *Uplink frequency spectrum = 14 to 14.5 GHz*

(*ii*) *First intermediate frequency = 140 MHz*

(*iii*) *Carrier bandwidth = 72 MHz*

(*iv*) *BPF-1 center frequency = 1.19 GHz*

Determine (a) first local oscillator frequency (b) range of second local oscillator frequency (c) frequency spectrum of unwanted sideband (d) bandwidths of BPF-1 and BPF-2.

Solution:

(*a*) First local oscillator frequency = 1190 – 140 = 1050 MHz

(*b*) Minimum second local oscillator frequency, $fl2$ (min) is given by:

$$fl2 \text{ (min)} = 14 - 1.19 = 12.81 \text{ GHz}$$

Maximum second local oscillator frequency, $fl2$ (max) is given by:

$$fl2 \text{ (min)} = 14.5 - 1.19 = 13.31 \text{ GHz}$$

Second local oscillator range is therefore 12.81 to 13.31 GHz

(c) Frequency spectrum of the unwanted sideband is from:

$$\{f_u(\min) - 2(f_{l1} + f_0)\} \text{ to } \{f_u(\max) - 2(f_{l1} + f_0)\}$$

$$= \{14 - 2(1050 + 140)\} \text{ to } \{14.5 - 2(1050 + 140)\}$$

$$= 11.62 \text{ to } 12.12 \text{ GHz}$$

(d) Bandwidth of BPF–1 = Bandwidth of first IF = 140 MHz
Bandwidth of BPF–2 = uplink frequency spectrum bandwidth = 500 MHz.

Example 93 : *Consider a dual Down-Converter (Fig. 29.23) with following specifications:*

(i) *Downlink frequency,* $f_d = 4$ *GHz*

(ii) *Intermediate frequency,* $f_0 = 70$*MHz*

(iii) *Downlink frequency spectrum = 3.7 to 4.2 GHz*

(iv) *Carrier bandwidth = 36 MHz*

Determine (a) first local oscillator frequency (b) second local oscillator frequency (c) center frequency of BPF-1 and its bandwidth.

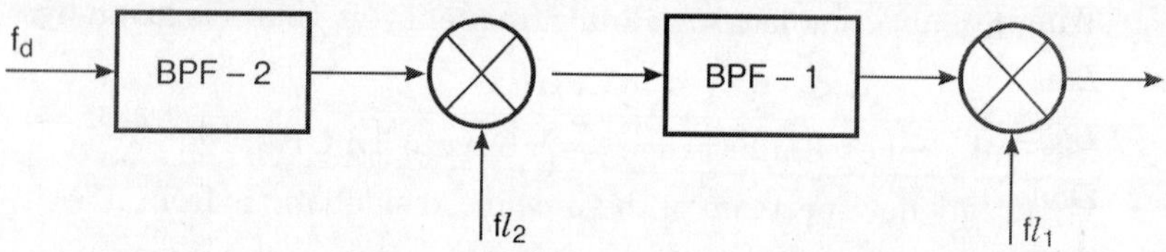

Fig. 29.23

Solution :

With reference to Fig. 29.23, the sum of first and second local oscillator frequencies is given by :

$$f_{l1} + f_{l2} = f_d - f_0$$

Also $(f_d - f_{l2})$ should be greater than f_d frequency spectrum bandwidth, 500 MHz in the present case.

Choose $(f_d - f_{l2}) = 1$ GHz

which gives $f_{l2} = f_d - 1 \text{ GHz} = 4 - 1 = 3 \text{ GHz}$

$$f_{l1} = f_d - f_0 - f_{l2} = 4 - 0.07 - 3 = 930 \text{ MHz}$$

Center frequency of BPF–1 = 1 GHz

Bandwidth = 36 MHz.

Example 94: *Consider a dual Down-Converter with the following parameters*

(i) *Down link frequency spectrum = 10.7 to 11.7 GHz*

(ii) *First local oscillator frequency = 2.1 GHz*

(iii) *Carrier bandwidth = 72 MHz*

(iv) *First intermediate frequency = 140 MHz*

Determine (a) center frequency and bandwidth of BPF-1 (Fig. 29.23 above) (b) second local oscillator frequency range.

Solution : (*a*) Center frequency of BPF–1 = $f_{l1} + f_0$

$$= 2.1 + 0.140 = 2.24 \text{ GHz}$$

Bandwidth of BPF - 1 = 140 MHz

(*b*) Minimum second local oscillator frequency ($f_{l2}(min)$) is given by:

$$f_{l2}(\text{min}) = 10.7 - 2.24 = 8.46 \text{ GHz}$$

$$f_{l2}(\text{max}) = 11.7 - 2.24 = 9.46 \text{ GHz}$$

Second local oscillator frequency range is from 8.46 to 9.46 GHz.

Example 95: *Consider the earth station receive chain as shown in Fig. 29.21. Find the system noise temperature and (G/T) as referred to the input of low noise amplifier for the specifications listed below.*

Antenna gain = 55 dB

Waveguide loss = 0.1 dB

Low noise amplifier gain = 55 dB

Low noise amplifier equivalent noise temperature 45° K

Down converter equivalent noise temperature = 215000°K

Ambient temperature = 300°K

Antenna noise temperature contributors: Main beam = 25°K,

Subreflector spill–over = 3.3° K, *Main reflector spillover = 1°K,*

Blockage = 10° K and *Feed loss = 15°K.*

Solution :

Earth station system noise temperature referred to the input of the low noise amplifier is given by:

$$T = T_S + T_e$$

where T_S = noise temperature measured at the output of the waveguide

T_e = equivalent noise temperature at the input of low noise amplifier

Antenna noise temperature is given by:

$$T_A = 25 + 3.3 + 1 + 10 + 15 = 54.3°\text{K}$$

Equivalent noise temperature of waveguide = $(L - 1) \times T_0$

where L = waveguide loss = 0.1 dB = 1.023

Therefore, $(L - 1)\, T_0 = (1.023 - 1) \times 300 = 6.9°\text{K}$

$$T_S = 54.3 + \frac{6.9}{1.023} = 54.3 + 6.74 = 61.04°\text{K}$$

Low noise amplifier gain = 55 dB = 316227.7

Therefore, $$T_e = 45 + \frac{315000}{316227.7}$$

$$= 45 + 0.68 = 45.68°K$$

Therefore, $$T = T_s + T_e = 61.04 + 45.68 = 106.72°K$$

Gain (G) as referred to low noise amplifier input

$$= 55 - 0.1 = 54.9 \text{ dB}$$

Therefore, $$(G/T) = 54.9 - 10 \log 106.72$$

$$= 54.9 - 20.28 = 34.62 \text{ dB/K.}$$

Example 96. *Consider the receive side of the earth station as shown in Fig. 31.21. The antenna gain is 65 dB and its noise contribution is 60°K. The waveguide loss is 0.5 dB. Determine the equivalent noise temperature of the low noise amplifier assuming that the noise contribution by the down converter is negligible and earth station (G/T) is 40 dB/K (T_0 = 300°K).*

Solution :

System gain with respect to low noise amplifier input = 65 – 0.5 = 64.5 dB.

System noise with respect to low noise amplifier input,

$$T = T_s + T_e$$

where T_s = noise contribution of antenna and waveguide

T_e = equivalent noise temperature of low noise amplifier

$$T_s = \frac{60}{L} + \left(\frac{L-1}{L}\right) \times 300$$

where $L = \text{Antilog } \frac{0.5}{10} = 1.122$

$$T_s = \frac{60}{1.122} + \frac{0.122}{1.122} \times 300 = 53.47 + 32.62 = 86.09°K$$

Now $$\frac{G}{T} = 40 \text{ dB/K}$$

or G (in dB) – 10 log T = 40

or $$\log T = \frac{64.5 - 40}{10} = 2.45 \qquad T = 281.83°K$$

Therefore, $$T_e = 281.83 - 86.09 = 195.74°K.$$

Example 97: *Fig. 29.24 shows a cascaded arrangement of two 3 dB couplers used to combine three carriers at frequencies f_1, f_2 and f_3. Determine the output powers of the three carriers if the input powers for the three carriers are 50 dB (at f_1), 40 dB (at f_2) and 25 dB (at f_3).*

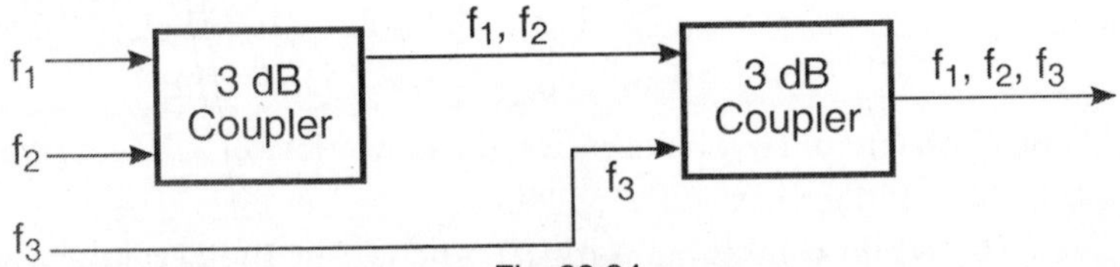

Fig. 29.24

Solution : In the first 3 dB coupler, both (f_1) and (f_2) suffer 3 dB carrier power loss.

Therefore, the carrier powers at (f_1) and (f_2) at the input of second 3 dB coupler are respectively 47dB and 37dB.

Carrier power at (f_3) at the input of second 3 dB coupler = 25 dB

Therefore, carrier power at (f_1) at the output = 47 – 3 = 44 dB

carrier power at (f_2) at the output = 37 – 3 = 34 dB

and carrier power at (f_3) at the output = 25 – 3 = 225 dB.

Example 98. *Refer to the coupler arrangement of Fig. 29.25. Determine the power loss suffered by each one of the five carriers after all have combined and appeared at the output.*

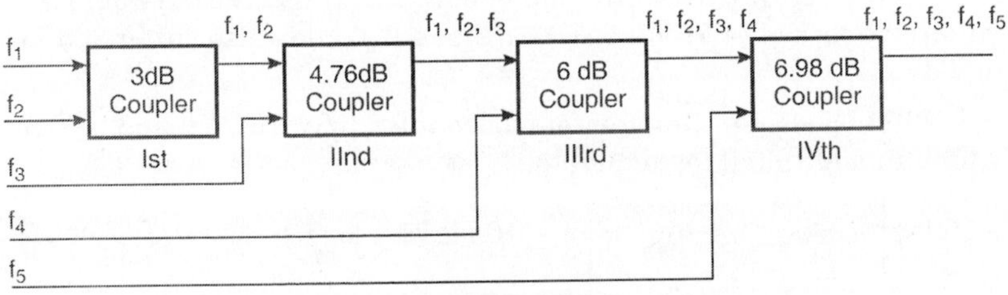

Fig. 29.25

Solution : In these directional couplers, one of the inputs suffers a power loss equal to the designated figure, 3 dB, 4.77 dB, 6 dB or 6.97 dB as the case may be. The other input or inputs suffer a power loss that is given by:

$$-10 \log \beta^2, \text{ where, } \beta^2 = (1 - \alpha^2)$$

and
$$\alpha^2 = \log^{-1}\left[\frac{-\text{designed figure}}{10}\right]$$

We will now analyse different couplers one at a time.

First directional coupler (3 dB coupler): Let us say (f_2) suffers a 3 dB loss, then the loss suffered by (f_1) will be:

$$= -10 \log\left[1 - \log^{-1}\left\{\frac{-\text{designated figure}}{10}\right\}\right]$$

$$= -\log[1 - \log^{-1}(-0.3)] = -10 \log (1 - 0.5)$$

$$= -10 \log (0.5) = -10(-0.3) = 3 \text{ dB}$$

Thus, both (f_1) and (f_2) have suffered a power loss of 3 dB each when they reach the input of second coupler.

Now (f_3) while combining with (f_1) and (f_2) in the second coupler suffers a 4.76 dB loss. (f_1) and (f_2) will suffer a further loss of

$$-10 \log\left[1 - \log^{-1}\left\{\frac{-4.76}{10}\right\}\right] = -10 \log\left[1 - \log^{-1}(-0.476)\right]$$

$$= -10 \log (1 - 0.333) = -10 \log 0.666$$

$$= 1.76 \text{ dB}$$

Thus, at the output of second coupler, (f_1) and (f_2) have suffered a loss of (3 + 1.76) = 4.76 dB each. (f_3) has also suffered a loss of 4.76 dB.

Now, (f_2) (f_1) and (f_3) will suffer a loss in the third coupler equal to

$$-10 \log\left[1 - \log^{-1}\left\{\frac{-6}{10}\right\}\right] = -10 \log^{-1} [1 - \log^{-1} (-0.6)]$$

$$= -10 \log (1 - 0.25) = -10 \log 0.75$$

$$= 1.24 \text{ dB}$$

Therefore, upto the third coupler output, (f_1), (f_2) and (f_3) would have suffered a loss of (4.76 + 1.24) = 6 *dB* each. (f_4) has also suffered a loss of 6 dB.

While passing through fourth coupler, (f_1), (f_2), (f_3) and (f_4) will suffer an additional loss equal to:

$$-10 \log\left[1 - \log^{-1}\left\{\frac{-6.97}{10}\right\}\right] = -10 \log\left[1 - \log^{-1}(-0.697)\right]$$

$$= -10 \log (1 - 0.2)$$

$$= -10 \log 0.8 = 0.98 \text{ dB}$$

At the final output, therefore, (f_1), (f_2), (f_3), (f_4) have suffered a loss of (6+0.98) = 6.98 dB each. Also, (f_5) in fourth coupler suffers a loss of 6.97 dB. Thus, at the end, all carriers have suffered a loss of 6.98 dB in the process of combining.

Example 99. *In a certain satellite communication link, the uplink carrier-to-noise ratio $(C/N)_u$ is 25 dB whereas the downlink carrier-to-noise ratio $(C/N)_d$ is 20 dB. Find the link carrier-to-noise ratio (C/N).*

Solution : The link carrier-to-noise ratio (C/N) is given by

$$\frac{C}{N} = \left[\left(\frac{C}{N}\right)_u^{-1} + \left(\frac{C}{N}\right)_d^{-1}\right]^{-1}$$

$$\left(\frac{C}{N}\right)_u = 25\ dB = \log^{-1}\left(\frac{25}{10}\right) = 316.22$$

$$\left(\frac{C}{N}\right)_d = 20\ dB = \log^{-1}\left(\frac{20}{10}\right) = 100$$

Therefore, $\frac{C}{N} = \left(\frac{1}{316.22} + \frac{1}{100}\right)^{-1} = \left(\frac{416.22}{31622}\right)^{-1}$

$= 76 = 18.8$ dB.

Example 100 : *The system parameters of Ku-band (14/12 GHz) satellite link are as follows :*

(I) Satellite Parameters :

Antenna gain-to-noise temperature ratio = 1.6 dB / K

Satellite saturation EIRP = 44 dBW

TWTA input back-off = 0 dB

TWTA output back-off = 0 dB

(II) Earth station parameters :

Tracking Loss = 1.5 dB (uplink) and 1 dB (downlink)

Transmit antenna gain = 57.6 dB

Receive antenna gain = 56.3 dB

Maximum uplink and downlink slant range = 37000 km

System noise temperature = 160°K

Carrier Power into antenna = 200 W

(III) Noise bandwidth = 36 MHz, Boltzmann's constant,

$$K = 1.38 \times 10^{-23} J/K$$

Determine $\left(\frac{C}{N}\right)_u$, $\left(\frac{C}{N}\right)_d$ and $\left(\frac{C}{N}\right)$

Solution : $\left(\frac{C}{N}\right)_u$ is given by :

$$\left(\frac{C}{N}\right)_u = (EIRP)_{sat} \times \left(\frac{c}{4\pi f_u d_u}\right)^2 \times \left(\frac{G_u}{T_u}\right) \times \left(\frac{1}{KB}\right) BO_i^{-1} \times L^{-1}$$

$$= (EIRP)_{sat}\ (\text{in dBW}) - 20\log\left(\frac{4\pi f_u d_u}{c}\right) + \left(\frac{G_u}{T_u}\right) \text{in } (dB/K)$$

$$- 10\log K - 10\log B - BO_i\ (\text{in dB}) - L\ (\text{in dB})$$

where

$(EIRP)_{sat}$ = Carrier EIRP required to saturate satellite TWTA

f_u = uplink frequency

d_u = uplink slant range

(G_u/T_u) = Satellite antenna gain to noise temperature ratio

K = Boltzmann's constant

B = Noise bandwidth

BO_i = Input backoff TWTA

L = Sum of antenna tracking loss and atmospheric attenuation

$$(EIRP)_{sat} = EIRP \times BO_i$$

$$= EIRP(\text{in dB}) + BO_i \text{ (in } dB)$$

$$= \text{Carrier power (in dB)} + \text{Transmit antenna gain (in dB)} + BO_i \text{ (in dB)}$$

$$= 10 \log 200 + 57.6 + 0 = 23 + 57.6 = 80.6 \text{ dBW}$$

$$K = 1.38 \times 10^{-23} J/K = 10(\log 1.38 - 23 \log 10)$$

$$= -228.6 \text{ dBW/K} - \text{Hz}$$

$$B = 36 \text{ MHz} = 10 \log 36 \times 10^6 = 75.6\ dB - Hz$$

$$L = 1.5 \text{ dB}$$

Substituting the values,

$$\left(\frac{C}{N}\right)_u = 80.6 - 20 \log\left(\frac{4 \times 3.14 \times 14 \times 10^9 \times 37000 \times 10^3}{3 \times 10^8}\right) + 1.6 - (-228.6) - 75.6 - 0 - 1.5$$

$$= 80.6 - 206.7 + 1.6 + 228.6 - 75.6 - 1.5 = 27 \text{ dB}$$

$\left(\frac{C}{N}\right)_d$ is given by :

$$EIRP_s\ (sat) \text{ (in } dBW) - 20 \log\left(\frac{4\pi f_d d_d}{c}\right) + \frac{G}{T} \text{ (in dB/K)} - 10 \log K - 10 \log B - BO_0 \text{(in dB)} - L'\text{(dB)}$$

where $EIRP_s\ (sat)$ = Satellite saturation EIRP

f_d = downlink frequency

d_d = downlink slant range

$\left(\frac{G}{T}\right)$ = Earth station antenna gain to noise temperature ratio

BO_0 = Satellite TWTA output backoff

L' = Downlink antenna tracking loss + Atmospheric attenuation

Now $(G/T) = G \text{ (in dB)} - 10 \log T = 56.3 - 10 \log 160$

$$= 56.3 - 22 = 34.3 \text{ dB/K}$$

Substituting the values,

$$\left(\frac{C}{N}\right)_d = 44 - 20 \log \left(\frac{4\pi \times 12 \times 10^9 \times 37000 \times 10^3}{3 \times 10^8}\right) + 34.3 - (-228.6) - 75.6 - 0 - 1$$

$$= 44 - 205.4 + 34.3 + 228.6 - 75.6 - 1$$

$$= 24.9 \text{ dB}$$

Now $\left(\frac{C}{N}\right)_u = 27 \text{ dB} = 501.2$

$$\left(\frac{C}{N}\right)_d = 24.9 \text{ dB} = 309$$

Therefore $\left(\frac{C}{N}\right) = \frac{501.2 \times 309}{501.2 + 309} = 191.15 = 22.8 \text{ dB}$

Example 101 : *The carrier power to the earth station transmit antenna is 500 watts. If the satellite TWTA's input back-off is 1 dB, determine the carrier EIRP required to saturate the satellite TWTA if the transmit antenna gain is 60 dB.*

Solution : The input back off (BO_i) is given by:

$$BO_i = \frac{EIRP\ (sat)}{EIRP}$$

or $BO_i \text{ (in dB)} = EIRP(sat) \text{ (in dBW)} - EIRP \text{ (in dBW)}$

Now $EIRP = P_T G_T = 10 \log 500 + 60 = 87\ dBW$

Therefore, $EIRP\text{(sat)} = EIRP \text{ (in dBW)} + BO_i \text{ (in dB)}$

$$= 87 + 1 = 88 \text{ dBW}.$$

Example 102 : *In a satellite link, the satellite saturation EIRP is 50 dBW. If the satellite TWTA output back off is 2, determine the satellite EIRP for the retransmitted carrier.*

Solution : Satellite TWTA output back-off, $BO_0 = \frac{EIRP_s\ (sat)}{EIRP_s}$

where $EIRP_s\ (sat)$ = satellite saturation EIRP

and $EIRP_s$ = satellite EIRP for retransmitted carrier

$EIRP_s$ (in dB) = $EIRP_s$ (sat) in dB − BO_0 (in dB)

$$BO_0 = 2 = 10 \log 2 = 3 \text{ dB}$$

Therefore $EIRP_s$ (in dB)= 50 − 3 = 47 dBW

Example 103 : *Two geostationary satellites A and B in the same orbit of 42164 km radius are stationed at 85°W and 25°W longitudes. The two satellites have a slant range of 38000 km and 36000 km from a common earth station respectively. Determine the angular separation of the two satellites as viewed by the earth station. Also determine the separation distance between the two satellites in the orbit.*

Solution : Refer to Fig. 29.26

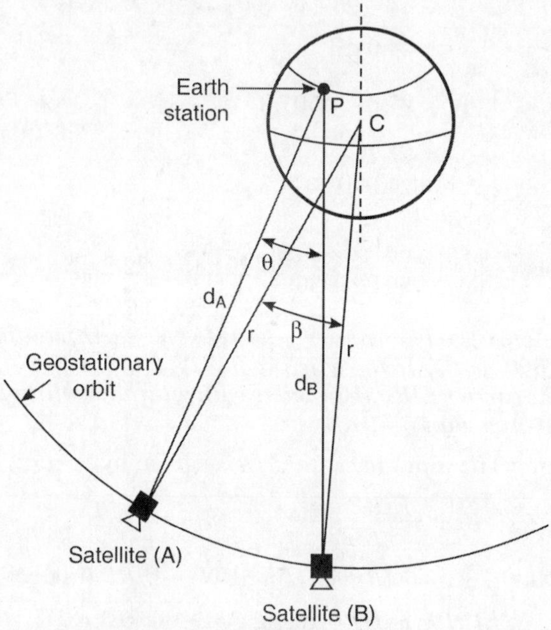

Fig. 29.26

If (d) is the separation distance between the satellites A and B, then

$$d^2 = d_A^2 + d_B^2 - 2d_A\, d_B \cos\theta$$

Also
$$d^2 = r^2 + r^2 - 2r^2 \cos\beta$$

Therefore, $d_A^2 + d_B^2 - 2d_A\, d_B \cos\theta = 2\,r^2\,(1 - \cos\beta)$

or
$$\theta = \cos^{-1}\left[\frac{d_A^2 + d_B^2 - 2r^2(1-\cos\beta)}{2d_A d_B}\right]$$

θ = angular separation between satellites A and B as viewed from earth station

β = angular separation between two satellites

$$= 85° - 25° = 60°$$

r = geostationary orbit radius = 42164 km

$$\theta = \cos^{-1}\left[\frac{(38000)^2 + (36000)^2 - 2 \times (42164)^2(1 - \cos 60°)}{2 \times 38000 \times 36000}\right]$$

$$= \cos^{-1}\left[\frac{1444 \times 10^6 + 1296 \times 10^6 - 1777.8 \times 10^6}{2736 \times 10^6}\right]$$

$$= \cos^{-1}\left[\frac{962.2}{2736}\right] = \cos^{-1} 0.3516 = 69.4°$$

The separation distance (d) can be computed from

$$d = \sqrt{2\, r^2\, (1 - \cos \beta)} = 1.414\, r\, \sqrt{(1 - \cos \beta)}$$

$$= 1.414 \times 42164\sqrt{1 - \cos 60°} = 42164 \text{ km.}$$

Example 104 : *For the situation depicted in Example 103, if the satellites A and B were located at 25°W and 30°W respectively, determine angular separation (θ) and separation distance (d).*

Solution: The angular separation (θ) is given by:

$$\theta = \cos^{-1}\left[\frac{(38000)^2 + (36000)^2 - 2(42164)^2(1 - \cos 5°)}{2 \times 38000 \times 36000}\right] \quad ...\beta = 5°$$

$$= \cos^{-1}\left[\frac{1444 \times 10^6 + 1296 \times 10^6 - 1777.8 \times 10^6 \times 7.6 \times 10^{-3}}{2736 \times 10^6}\right]$$

$$= \cos^{-1}\left(\frac{1444 + 1296 - 13.5}{2736}\right) = \cos^{-1}(0.9965) = 4.77°$$

The separation distance (d) is given by:

$$d = 1.414\, r\, \sqrt{1 - \cos \beta} = 1.414 \times 42164\sqrt{1 - \cos 5°}$$

$$= 1.414 \times 42164\sqrt{1 - 0.996}$$

$$= 1.414 \times 42164 \times 0.063$$

$$= 3756 \text{ km.}$$

Example 105 : *A geostationary satellite is located at 100°W longitude. Calculate the power flux density at the satellite for an earth station located at 90°W longitude and 40°N latitude given that*

Earth station antenna diameter = 5 m

Antenna efficiency = 0.55

Carrier frequency = 14 GHz

Earth station power amplifier saturation power = 500 W

Power amplifier output back-off = 3 dB

Waveguide loss between amplifier output and antenna input = 0.5 dB

Orbital radius = 42164 km and Earth's radius = 6378 km.

Solution:

Antenna gain, $G = \eta \dfrac{4\,\pi\, A\, f^2}{c^2} = \eta \left(\dfrac{\pi f D}{c}\right)^2$

$$= 0.55 \left(\frac{\pi \times 14 \times 10^9 \times 5}{3 \times 10^8}\right)^2 = 295240 = 54.7 \text{ dB}$$

Earth station power amplifier saturation power

$$= 500 \text{ watts} = 26.98 \text{ dB}$$

Power amplifier output back-off = 3 dB

Therefore, operating power = 26.98 – 3 = 23.98 dB

Waveguide loss = 0.5 dB

Therefore, power fed to antenna input = 23.98 – 0.5 = 23.48 dB

$$EIRP = 23.48 + 54.7 = 78.18 \text{ dB} = 65765784$$

The power flux density at the satellite is given by

$$\left(\frac{EIRP}{4\,\pi\, d^2}\right)$$

where d = slant range from satellite to earth station

$$d^2 = R^2 + r^2 - 2\,Rr \sin\left[E + \sin^{-1}\left(\frac{r}{R}\cos E\right)\right]$$

where R = orbital radius

r = earth's radius

E = angle of elevation

Also, $E = \tan^{-1}\left[\dfrac{R - r\cos\theta_l \cos|\theta_s - \theta_L|}{r \sin\{\cos^{-1}\cos\theta_l \cos|\theta_s - \theta_L|\}}\right]$

$$- \cos^{-1}(\cos\theta_l \cos|\theta_s - \theta_L|)$$

$$= \tan^{-1}\left[\frac{42164 - 6378 \cos 40° \cos 10°}{6378 \sin\{\cos^{-1}(\cos 40° \cos 10°)\}}\right] - \cos^{-1}(\cos 40\,° \cos 10°)$$

$$= \tan^{-1}\left[\frac{42164 - 6378 \times 0.754}{6378 \sin(\cos^{-1} 0.754)}\right] - \cos^{-1} 0.754$$

$$= \tan^{-1}\left(\frac{37355}{4184}\right) - 41° = 83.6° - 41° = 42.6°$$

Therefore, $d^2 = (42164)^2 + (6378)^2 - 2 \times 42164 \times 6378$

$$\times \sin\left[41° + \sin^{-1}\frac{6378}{42164}\cos 41°\right]$$

$= 1777802896 + 40678884 - 537843984 \sin [41° + 6.55°]$

$= 1777802896 + 40678884 - 537843984 \times 0.7378$

$= 1777802896 + 40678884 - 396821291 = 1421660489$

or $d = \sqrt{1421660489} = 37705$ km

The power flux density at the satellite

$$= \frac{EIRP}{4\pi\,(37705 \times 10^3)^2} = \frac{65765784}{12.56 \times 1421667025 \times 10^6}$$

$$= 3.68 \times 10^{-9}\ \text{W/m}^2 = -84.34\ \text{dBW/m}^2$$

Example 106 : *Determine the theoretical maximum area of the earth's surface that would be in view from a geostationary satellite at a height of 35786 km from earth's surface. Also determine the area in view for a minimum elevation angle of 10°. (Assume earth's radius = 6378 km)*

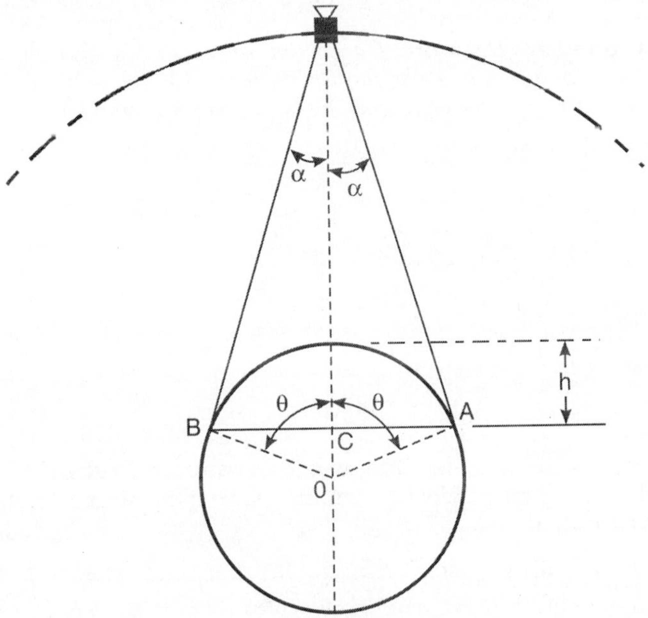

Fig. 29.27

Solution : Refer to Fig. 29.27. For theoretical maximum coverage, elevation angle, $E = 0°$

Therefore, $\alpha = \sin^{-1}\left(\frac{R_e}{R_e + H}\right)$

where R_e = earth's radius; H = height of satellite above earth's surface

$$\alpha = \sin^{-1}\left(\frac{6378}{6378 + 35786}\right) = 8.7°$$

$$\theta = 90° - \alpha - E = 90° - 8.7° = 81.3°$$

In the right angle triangle AOC,

$$OC = OA \sin 8.7° \ldots \angle OAC = 8.7°$$

$$= 6378 \sin 8.7° = 964.74 \text{ km}$$

Therefore, distance $(h) = 6378 - 964.74 = 5413.26$ km from geometry, surface area of the shaded region is given by:

$$2\pi R_e h = 2\pi \times 6378 \times 5413.26 = 216821850 \text{ km}^2$$

For $\quad E = 10°, \alpha = \sin^{-1}\left(\frac{6378}{6378 + 42164}\cos 10°\right) = 8.56°$

$$\theta = 90 - \alpha - E = 90 - 8.56 - 10 = 71.44°$$

The new value of $OC = 6378 \sin 18.56° = 2030$ km

The new value of $(h) = 6378 - 2030 = 4348$ km

Therefore covered area $= 2\pi \times 6378 \times 4348 = 174154096 \text{ km}^2$.

Example 107 : *Determine the percentage of earth's area covered for the two cases of angle of elevation in Example-106. How many geostationary satellites, you think, would be required for global coverage?*

Solution : Percentage of earth's surface area covered

$$= \frac{2\pi R_e h}{4\pi R_e^2} \times 100 = \frac{h}{2R_e} \times 100$$

For $E = 0°$, $h = 5413.26$ km

Percentage of area covered $= \dfrac{5413.26}{2 \times 6378} \times 100 = 42.4\%$

For $E = 10°$, $h = 4348$ km

Percentage of earth's surface area covered $= \dfrac{4348}{2 \times 6378} \times 100 = 34\%$

Three geostationary satellites would be required for global coverage provided that minimum elevation angle required for the earth stations does not exceed 10°.

Example 108. *A geostationary satellite is equipped with both a spot beam antenna with a covering angle of 4.5° and a global coverage antenna with a beam angle of 17.34°. Determine the gain of spot beam antenna if the global coverage antenna has a gain of 50 dB.*

Solution : The surface of the beam angle is roughly inversely proportional to the gain of the antenna.

Gain of global coverage antenna = 50 dB = 100000

Therefore, gain of spot beam antenna

$$= 100000 \times \left(\frac{17.34}{4.5}\right)^2 = 14.85 \times 10^5 = 61.7 \text{ dB.}$$

30

Self Assessment Questions

Below are given objective type questions in the form of multichoice questions, incomplete statements and True/False statements. Each of the multichoice questions is followed by some possible answers with only one of the answers being correct. The incomplete statements are also provided with two or three possible choices with only one of them being the right one. You have to pick the right answer or the correct choice for the first two types of questions and identify true and false statements in the third category of questions.

Part—I
Multichoice Questions

1. One of the following laws governs the movement of artificial satellites in earth orbits.

(*a*) Newtonian laws of mechanics
(*b*) Laws of quantum mechanics
(*c*) Galilean laws
(*d*) Kepler's laws

2. If (G) is the earth's gravitational constant and (M) the mass of earth, then for a circular orbit of radius (R), the satellite's orbital velocity (V) is given by :

(*a*) $V = \sqrt{GM/R}$ (*b*) $V = \sqrt{2GM/R}$
(*c*) $V = \sqrt{R/GM}$ (*d*) $V = \sqrt{2}\ G/R$

3. In a satellite orbit around earth, the force acting outwards from the center of earth is the

(*a*) force of gravitation (*b*) centripetal force
(*c*) centrifugal force (*d*) none of these

4. One of the following satellite systems is used for intercontinental communications.

(*a*) DOMSAT (*b*) TIROS-N
(*c*) INTELSAT (*d*) MARISAT

5. One of the following satellite systems is used for weather forecast applications.

(*a*) GORIZONT (*b*) TIROS-N
(*c*) COMSAT (*d*) SPOT

6. One of the following satellite systems is used for earth's resources survey.

(*a*) INTELSAT (*b*) SPOT
(*c*) EUTELSAT (*d*) TIROS-N

7. One of the following satellites is not used for communication services.

(*a*) GORIZONT (*b*) EKRAN
(*c*) INSAT (*d*) LANDSAT

8. One of the following communication satellites is in a highly eccentric, inclined orbit.

(*a*) Molniya series (*b*) Raduga
(*c*) Ekran (*d*) Gorizont

9. With reference to satellite communication systems, doppler frequency shift is absent in one of the following satellite systems

(*a*) Geostationary satellite
(*b*) Near earth orbit satellites
(*c*) Domestic satellite systems
(*d*) Geosynchronous satellites

10. One of the following expressions can be used to compute the eccentricity (e) of an eccentric elliptical orbit with apogee and perigee distances of (r_a) and (r_p) respectively.

(*a*) $e = \frac{r_p}{r_a}$ (*b*) $e = \left(\frac{r_a - r_p}{r_a + r_p}\right)$
(*c*) $e = \left(\frac{r_a + r_p}{r_a - r_p}\right)$ (*d*) $e = \frac{r_a}{r_p}$

11. Satellite transponders

(*a*) use a single frequency for reception and retransmission of information to and from earth
(*b*) use a lower frequency for reception and a higher frequency for retransmission
(*c*) use a higher frequency for reception and a lower frequency for retransmission
(*d*) none of these

12. In the C-band transponders, the uplink frequency is about

(*a*) 6 GHz (*b*) 4 GHz
(*c*) 14 GHz (*d*) 11 GHz

13. The down-link frequency in a C-band transponder is about

(*a*) 6 GHz (*b*) 4 GHz
(*c*) 14 GHz (*d*) 11 GHz

14. A geosynchronous orbit is the one when the
- (*a*) satellite is placed in an orbit 15,000 miles above earth's surface in a north to south orbital path
- (*b*) the satellite is placed 22,000 miles above earth's surface in an orbit that matches one of the longitudinal lines of earth
- (*c*) the satellite is placed 35,000 miles above earth's surface in equatorial orbit
- (*d*) the satellite is placed 22,000 miles above earth's surface in an orbit in equatorial plane
- (*e*) the satellite's orbital velocity is in synchronism with the earth's rotation

15. Satellites allow earth stations to share the satellite equipment through
- (*a*) Time Division Multiplexing (TDM)
- (*b*) Frequency Division Multiplexing (FDM)
- (*c*) Multiple Frequency UP and DOWN links
- (*d*) focussed spot beams and zone beams
- (*e*) all of above

16. Higher the frequency of satellite or earth station transmitter,
- (*a*) higher is the potential bandwidth that can be used for communications
- (*b*) closer the satellites can be spaced without interfering with each other
- (*c*) narrower is the radiation beamwidth for a given earth station and satellite antenna diameter
- (*d*) all of above
- (*e*) none of these

17. Satellite capacity depends on
- (*a*) weight that can be placed in orbit
- (*b*) panel area available for energy dissipation
- (*c*) transmitter power
- (*d*) all of above

18. A spin stabilised satellite
- (*a*) uses solar panels whose cells are continually oriented towards the sun
- (*b*) uses solar cells mounted on a cylindrical body that is continually rotated so that about 40 percent of the cells receive solar radiation at a given time
- (*c*) uses gyroscopic action of a spinning satellite
- (*d*) both (*a*) and (*b*) (*e*) both (*b*) and (*c*)
- (*f*) both (*a*) and (*c*)

19. A body stabilised satellite
- (*a*) users solar panels whose cells are continually oriented towards the sun

(*b*) users solar cells mounted on a cylindrical body that continually rotates so that about 40 percent of the cells receive solar radiation at a given time
(*c*) uses a spinning satellite to maintain orientation in space
(*d*) uses a spinning momentum wheel to maintain orientation in space
(*e*) both (*a*) and (*c*) (*f*) both (*b*) and (*d*)
(*g*) both (*a*) and (*d*)

20. For the earth station antennas to be 6 feet in diameter, the satellite frequency bands must be in
(*a*) 4/6 GHz range (*b*) 12/14 GHz range
(*c*) 20/30 GHz range (*d*) both (*a*) and (*b*)

21. Satellites may re-use the same frequency in the same area by
(*a*) having many small antennas
(*b*) overlapping radiation zones
(*c*) TDMA (*d*) FDMA
(*e*) any of above (*f*) (*c*) and (*d*)

22. The satellite orbit almost invariably used with remote sensing satellite is the
(*a*) geostationary orbit (*b*) geosynchronous orbit
(*c*) sun synchronous orbit (*d*) Molniya orbit

23. With reference to geosynchronous and geostationary satellite orbits,
(*a*) the two are identical
(*b*) the geosynchronous satellite orbit is in the plane of the equator
(*c*) while geosynchronous orbits are mainly used for meteorological applications, geostationary satellite orbits are mainly used for communication applications
(*d*) while a geostationary orbit is in the equatorial plane, the orbital plane of a geosynchronous satellite is inclined to the equatorial plane.

24. One of the following satements is wrong
(*a*) The Molniya orbit is a highly eccentric, near polar orbit.
(*b*) The true geostationary orbit is circular and is in the plane of the equator.
(*c*) The inclined elliptical orbit can never be used for communication purposes.
(*d*) The orbital plane of a satellite in sun synchronous orbit rotates in synchronism with earth around Sun.

25. The location of a geostationary satellite is always given in terms of
(*a*) a certain longitude (*b*) a certain latitude

(*c*) longitude and latitude (*d*) distance from earth's surface

26. The orbital velocity of the satellite

(*a*) is directly proportional to its distance from earth's surface

(*b*) is inversely proportional to square root of its distance from earth's center

(*c*) depends upon the thrust with which it is launched

(*d*) is continuously changing as the satellite revolves

27. With reference to satellites, the first orbital velocity (v_1) which is the minimum horizontal launch velocity required to put a satellite into a circular orbit around earth and second orbital velocity (v_2) which is the horizontal launch velocity which makes the satellite escape earth's gravitational attraction are interrelated by

(*a*) $v_2 = 2\,v_1$ (*b*) $v_2 = \dfrac{v_1}{\sqrt{2}}$

(*c*) $v_2 = \sqrt{2}\,v_1$ (*d*) $v_2 = 2\sqrt{v_1}$

28. For orbital velocity between the first orbital velocity (v_1) and the second orbital velocity (v_2), the satellite orbit would

(*a*) be circular (*b*) bc clliptical

(*c*) have zero eccentricity (*d*) be eccentric

(*e*) both (*a*) and (*c*) (*f*) both (*b*) and (*d*)

29. The first orbital velocity for launching a satellite at a given height above the surface of earth turns out to be 6 km/s. If the said satellite is launching with a horizontal velocity of 8 km/s, the satellite orbit would be

(*a*) circular and eccentric (*b*) elliptical and eccentric

(*c*) circular (*d*) elliptical

30. The satellite orbit that is highly inclined, elliptical and eccentric is the

(*a*) Molniya orbit (*b*) geostationary orbit

(*c*) geosynchronous orbit (*d*) sub synchronous orbit

(*e*) both (*a*) and (*b*) (*f*) both (*b*) and (*c*)

31. One of the following is a standard payload of any meteorological satellite

(*a*) Very High Resolution Radiometer (VHRR)

(*b*) Return Beam Vidicon (RBV)

(*c*) C-band transponder

(*d*) Optical telescope

(*e*) Retarding Potential Analyser (RPA)

32. A payload that is invariably found on all communication satellites is the

(*a*) optical telescope (*b*) VHRR

(*c*) transponder (*d*) vidocon camera

33. The multiple satellite access technique suitable only for digital transmission is the

(*a*) Time Division Multiple Access (TDMA)
(*b*) Frequency Division Multiple Access (FDMA)
(*c*) Code Division Multiple Acess (CDMA)
(*d*) Both (*a*) and (*b*)

34. The commonly used multiple access technique that suffers from the disadvantage of likelihood of intermodulation distortion is
(*a*) Time Division Multiple Access (TDMA)
(*b*) Frequency Division Multiple Access (FDMA)
(*c*) Code Division Multiple Access (CDMA)
(*d*) Packet Access

35. The commonly used multiple access technique that has very stringent timing and synchronising requirements for the earth station is the
(*a*) Code Division Multiple Access (CDMA)
(*b*) Frequency Division Multiple Access (FDMA)
(*c*) Time Division Multiple Acess (TDMA)
(*d*) Both (*a*) and (*b*)

36. The minimum number of geostationary satellite needed for uninterrupted global coverage is
(*a*) 3 (*b*) 4
(*c*) 1 (*d*) 2

37. With reference to satellite orbit, Apogee is the
(*a*) highest point in the orbit
(*b*) lowest point in the orbit
(*c*) point in the parking orbit
(*d*) name given to the boost motor that puts the satellite in the right parking slot

38. With reference to satellite orbit, Perigee is the
(*a*) point in an intermediate orbit
(*b*) highest point in the orbit
(*c*) lowest point in the orbit
(*d*) none of these

39. In a circular geostationary orbit in the equatorial plane,
(*a*) the apogee equals the perigee
(*b*) the apogee is twice the perigee
(*c*) the perigee is twice the apogee
(*d*) none of these

40. The satellite series from ISRO (India) meant for earth observation applications is the
(*a*) SROSS-C series (*b*) INSAT-2 series
(*c*) IRS-series (*d*) INSAT-1 series

41. The satellite series developed by ISRO (India) for carrying out scientific studies is the
(*a*) SROSS-C satellite series

(*b*) IRS series
(*c*) INSAT-2 series (*d*) LANDSAT series

42. The value of 'g' in the microgravity environment typically available in space stations is of order of

(*a*) $10^{-6}\,g$ (*b*) $10^{-4}\,g$
(*c*) $10^{-12}\,g$ (*d*) zero

43. When a satellite of mass (m) is orbiting earth at a high (h) from the surface of earth with a veocity (v), then the centrifugal force acting on the satellite away from the center of the earth having a mean radius of (R) is given by

(*a*) mv^2/h (*b*) $mv^2/(R + H)$
(*c*) $mv/(R + h)$ (*d*) mv^2/R

44. When a satellite of mass (m) is orbiting earth at a height (h) from earth's surface with a velocity (v), then the centripetal force due to gravitational attraction of the earth is given by (Assume 'G' as the gravitation constant and 'M' as the mass of earth earth)

(*a*) $\dfrac{GMm}{(R+h)^2}$ (*b*) $\dfrac{GM}{(R+h)}$
(*c*) $\dfrac{GMm}{R^2}$ (*d*) $\dfrac{GMm}{4\pi\,(R+h)^2}$

45. For an eccentric elliptical orbit with eccentricity (e) and semimajor axis (a), the apogee point distance from the center of earth having a radius of (R) is given by

(*a*) $r_a = a\,(1 + e)$ (*b*) $r_a = a\,(1 - e)$
(*c*) $r_a = a\,(1 + e)/R$ (*d*) $r_a = aR/(1 + e)$

46. For an eccentric elliptical orbit with semi-major axis (a) and eccentricity (e), the perigee point distance from the center of earth having a radius of (R) is given by

(*a*) $r_p = a\,(1 - e)\,/R$ (*b*) $r_p = a\,(1 - e)$
(*c*) $r_p = a\,(1 + e)$ (*d*) $r_p = a\,R/(1 - e)$

47. If the apogee distance from earth's center is eight times the perigee distance from earth's center, the orbit eccentricity is approximately

(*a*) 0.12 (*b*) 0.78
(*c*) 0.4 (*d*) 0.6

48. If the escape velocity at a height of (h) above earth surface is 10 km/s then the escape velocity at a height ($4h$) above the earth's surface would be

(*a*) 5 km/s (*b*) 20 km/s
(*c*) 2.5 km/s (*d*) 40 km/s

49. The most commonly employed analog modulation technique in satellite communication is the

(*a*) Amplitude Modulation (AM)
(*b*) Frequency Modulation (FM)

(c) Pulse Amplitude Modulation (PAM)
(d) Pulse Width Modulation (PWM)

50. PCM system is used in satellite communication for transmission of
(a) television signals (b) speech signals
(c) telegraph signals (d) none of these

51. Earth station figure-of-merit is defined as
(a) $10 \log \left(\frac{G}{T}\right)$ (b) $10 \log \left(\frac{G}{T}\right)$
(c) $10 \log GT$ (d) $20 \log \left(\frac{G}{T}\right)$

52. An empirical relationship that gives an idea as regards free space attenuation of RF signals as a function of frequency (f) and distance (d) is
(a) $20 \log_{10} f + 20 \log_{10} d$ (b) $20 \log_{10} (d/t)$
(c) $32.5 + 20 \log_{10} f + 10 \log_{10} d$
(d) $32.5 + 20 \text{ Ln } f + 20 \text{ Ln } d$

53. When the orbit eccentricity (e) equals zero, the orbit is
(a) a parabola (b) a hyperbola
(c) elliptical (d) circular

54. When the orbit eccentricity (e) is greater than zero but less than 1, the orbit is
(a) an ellipse (b) a circle
(c) a parabola (d) a hyperbola

55. When the orbit eccentricity equals 1, the orbit takes the shape of
(a) an ellipse (b) a parabola
(c) a hyperbola (d) circle

56. An eccentricity figure of greater than unity would imply that
(a) the satellite orbit becomes elliptical
(b) the satellite orbit becomes parabolic
(c) the satellite escapes from the orbit
(d) none of these

57. The angular velocity (v) of a satellite at a height (H) from the surface of earth with a mean radius of (R) is given by
(a) $v = R\sqrt{\frac{g}{(R+H)}}$ (b) $v = \sqrt{\frac{g}{(R+H)}}$
(c) $v = \frac{Rg}{\sqrt{(R+H)}}$ (d) $v = \sqrt{\frac{GMm}{(R+H)}}$

58. The orbit of a geostationary satellite with an orbital velocity of approximately 3 km/s is slightly inclined at 2° to equatorial plane. The magnitude of the velocity impulse required to be given perpendicular to orbital plane to correct the orbit inclination is equal to (Given that sin 2° = 0.035, cos 2° = 0.999)

(*a*) 105 m/s (*b*) 3 km/s
(*c*) indeterminate (*d*) none of these

59. The earth coverage angle for a geostationary satellite at an altitude of 42000 km from center of earth for a 0° earth station elevation would be (assume earth's radius = 6370 km)

(*a*) $2 \tan^{-1} 0.15$ (*b*) $\cos^{-1} 0.15$
(*c*) $2 \sin^{-1} 0.15$ (*d*) $\sin^{-1} 0.15$

60. The spread spectrum communication techniques are used in one of the following multiple access methods in satellite communication
(*a*) Time Division Multiple Access (TDMA)
(*b*) Frequency Division Multiple Access (CDMA)
(*c*) Code Division Multiple Access (CDMA)
(*d*) Random Access

61. The multiple access technique that is particularly suitable for communication satellites with military applications is
(*a*) TDMA (*b*) FDMA
(*c*) CDMA (*d*) Random access

62. Mark the wrong statement :
(*a*) An inclined polar orbit can never be a geosynchronous orbit
(*b*) All geostationary orbits are geosynchronous orbits whereas all geosynchronous orbits are not geostationary orbits
(*c*) Molniya orbit is popular with Russian communication satellites
(*d*) A spin stabilised satellite uses a simple technique for stabilisation or attitude control but large number of solar cells whereas a body stabilised satellite uses a very complex stabilisation mechanism but a fewer solar cells.

63. When a geostationary satellite is launched, it is first launched into a low earth orbit from where the orbit is boosted to another transfer orbit which is usually elliptical and eccentric. With another manoeuvre, the elliptical orbit is transformed to a geostationary circular orbit. If the apogee point in the elliptical transfer orbit is the same as the apogee point in the final circular geostationary orbit, then the velocity of the satellite at the apogee point in the circular orbit is
(*a*) equal to the velocity at the apogee point in the elliptical orbit.
(*b*) less than the velocity at the apogee point in the elliptical orbit
(*c*) greater than the velocity at the apogee point in the elliptical orbit
(*d*) at least four times the velocity at the apogee point in the elliptical transfer orbit.

64. With reference to Q-63, if (a) is the semi-major axis of elliptical transfer orbit and (r) is the distance of a given point on the orbit from the centre of earth, then the orbital velocity of the satellite at that point is given by ($\mu = GM$)

(*a*) $v = \sqrt{\left(\frac{2\,\mu}{r} - \frac{\mu}{a}\right)}$ (*b*) $v = \left[\frac{2\,\mu}{r} - \frac{\mu}{a}\right]$

(*c*) $v^2 = \left[\frac{\mu}{r} - \frac{1}{a}\right]$ (*d*) $\sqrt{\frac{\mu}{r + a}}$

65. The orbital velocity at the apogee point in an eccentric elliptical orbit when the elliptical orbit is transformed into a circular orbit with apogee point remaining the same. This increment in velocity is the minimum when

(*a*) elliptical orbit plane is inclined at 45° to the circular orbit plane
(*b*) elliptical orbit plane is at right angles to the circular orbit plane
(*c*) elliptical orbit and circular orbit are in the same plane
(*d*) none of these

66. Molniya orbit serves the purposes of a geosynchronous orbit for high latitude regions. The number of satellites usually required at different phases of the same Molniya orbit to provide uninterrupted service to a given area is

(*a*) 3 (*b*) 6
(*c*) 1 (*d*) 4

67. Highly inclined, highly eccentric elliptical Molniya orbit has a perigee of 500 km and an apogee of 40,000 km above the surface of earth, then the orbital velocity at the apogee would approximately be (Assume earth's radius = 6578 km).

(*a*) 1.5 km/s (*b*) 150 m/s
(*c*) 15 km/s (*d*) 3 km/s

68. For the orbit in Q-67, the semi-major axis of the elliptical orbit is (Assume radius of earth = 6578 km)

(*a*) 26828 km
(*b*) 20,000 km
(*c*) 22500 km
(*d*) indeterminate from given data

69. For the orbit in Q-67, the semi-major axis of the elliptical orbit is (Assume radius of earth = 6578 km)

(*a*) 250 km (*b*) 20,000 km
(*c*) 500 km (*d*) 18,125 km

70. The eccentricity of an elliptical orbit with the apogee point at 43,000 km and the perigee point at 7000 km from centre of earth is

(*a*) 0.72 (*b*) 0.16

(c) 0.45 (d) indeterminate from given data

71. In an eccentric elliptical orbit, the distance between centre of ellipse and centre of earth is 15,000 km. If the orbit eccentricity is 0.6, the semi-major axis of the orbit equals

(a) 9000 km (b) 25,000 km
(c) 6000 km (d) 37,500 km

72. For the orbit in Q-71, the distance of apogee point from earth's centre is

(a) 50,000 km (b) 25,000 km
(c) 40,000 km (d) 10,000 km

73. For the orbit in Q-71, the distance of perigee point from the centre of earth is

(a) 10,000 km (b) 500 km
(c) 7500 km (d) 15,000 km

74. The satellite in which the antennas are mounted on a de-spun platform is the

(a) geostationary satellite
(b) sun synchronous satellite
(c) spin stabilised satellite
(d) 3-axis body stabilised satellite

75. In a spin stabilised geostationary satellite, the spin axis is

(a) perpendicular to the orbital plane
(b) in the plane of the orbit
(c) inclined at 45° to the orbital plane
(d) none of these

76. The satellite in which the solar cells are mounted on panels external to the space craft body, allowing them to be oriented towards the sun, is the

(a) communication satellite
(b) direct broadcast satellite
(c) 3-axis body stabilised satellite
(d) spin stabilised satellite

77. Satellite (S_1) and (S_2) are orbiting in two different equatorial circular orbits. The radius of S1-orbit is four times the radius of S2-orbit. The orbital period of S-1 orbit will therefore be

(a) 4 times the orbital period of satellite S2
(b) 8 times the orbital period of satellite S2
(c) twice the orbital period of satellite S2
(d) same as the orbital period of satellite S2

78. The satellite orbit is termed as a retrograde orbit when its angle of inclination

(a) becomes 45° (b) exceeds 90°
(c) zero (d) becomes 90°

79. With reference to the solar eclipses caused to a communication satellite by the earth and the moon,

(*a*) the eclipse due to earth is of a smaller duration
(*b*) the eclipse due to earth affects the satellite much more than the eclipse due to moon
(*c*) while the eclipse due to earth is harmful, the one due to moon is useful
(*d*) while the eclipse due to earth is useful, the one due to moon is harmful

80. With reference to transponder capacity utilisation in case of TDMA and FDMA techniques,

(*a*) the capacity utilisation is almost 100% irrespective of number of accesses in TDMA
(*b*) the capacity utilisation can never be 100% in FDMA
(*c*) the capacity utilisation is 100% in TDMA for a single access only
(*d*) none of these

81. The earth station antenna is fed from a power amplifier producing 2 KW at its output. If the waveguide joining the amplifier output and the antenna input has a loss of 2 dB and the antenna has a gain of 51 dB at the operating uplink frequency, the EIRP of the antenna is

(*a*) 82 dB
(*b*) 49 dB
(*c*) 86 dB
(*d*) indeterminate from given data

82. For an antenna with a circular aperture, if the operating frequency is doubled, then for the same antenna gain, the antenna diameter

(*a*) can be reduced to one-fourth
(*b*) can be reduced to half
(*c*) can be increased to four times
(*d*) can be reduced to one-third

83. A satellite earth station antenna has a gain of 10^6 and a noise temperature of 100°K. The earth station (G/T) in dB per Kelvin is

(*a*) 40 dB/K (*b*) 80 dB/K
(*c*) indeterminate (*d*) none of these

84. A typical satellite earth station has, on its receive side, the antenna followed by a low noise amplifier and a down converter in the same order. The earth station (G/T) ratio in dB/K as referred to the input of low noise amplifier is 50 dB/K. If the down converter equivalent noise temperature is 10000 K, the system (G/T) ratio as referred to input of down converter would be

(*a*) 10 dB/K (*b*) 60 dB/K
(*c*) 50 dB/K (*d*) none of these

85. A satellite earth station has dual down converter. If the down link frequency is 46 Hz and the IF is 70 MHz, then sum of first and second local oscillator frequencies would be

(*a*) 3.93 GHz (*b*) 4.07 GHz
(*c*) 8.14 GHz (*d*) none of these

86. For nearly distortion-less received signal in pulse modulation, it is required that the speed should be

(*a*) less than the signal frequency.
(*b*) less than twice the signal frequency.
(*c*) more than twice the signal frequency.
(*d*) equal to the signal frequency

87. A communication channel has a bandwidth of 5 KHz and if signal-to-noise ratio is 5, the corresponding channel capacity will be

(*a*) 18000 bits/sec. (*b*) 4000 bits/sec.
(*c*) 1500 bits/sec. (*d*) 1000 bits/sec.

88. According to Shanon's theorem, the output from any source of rate R can be coded and transmitted over a channel of capacity C with the condition that

(*a*) $C < R$ (*b*) $C < R^2$
(*c*) $C > R$ (*d*) $C > R^2$

89. The capacity of a channel is

(*a*) the maximum rate of information transmission
(*b*) the bandwidth required for information
(*c*) volume of information it can take
(*d*) the number of digits used in coding.

90. According to sampling theorem,

(*a*) the signal should be sampled at least twice each cycle of its lowest frequency
(*b*) twice each cycle of its highest frequency
(*c*) guard time should be as large as possible
(*d*) Nyquist rate should be as slow as possible

91. If sampling time is less than the Nyquist interval,

(*a*) simpler filters can be used to obtain original signal
(*b*) band-width increases
(*c*) channel capacity increases
(*d*) guard time become less

92. In communications, the sampling technique leads to

(*a*) better efficiency
(*b*) highest speed of communication
(*c*) less costly equipment
(*d*) All of these

93. A signal of maximum frequency of 8 KHz is sampled at Nyquist rate. The time intervals between the two successive samples will be

(*a*) 62.5 μsec (*b*) 125 μsec
(*c*) 1250 μsec (*d*) zero

94. The effect of noise in a communication system is most adverse with reference to

(*a*) source (*b*) encoder
(*c*) channel (*d*) receiver

95. Which of the following requirements is necessary for fast communication?

(*a*) high transmitter power
(*b*) large bandwidth
(*c*) higher channel capacity
(*d*) high S/N ratio

96. Which of the following techniques is different from others?

(*a*) PDM (*b*) PWM
(*c*) PCM (*d*) PPM

97. In PCM, the number of pulses '*p*' in a code-group for '*q*' quantising levels is given by

(*a*) $\log_2 q$ (*b*) $\log_{10} q$
(*c*) $\log_{10} q$ (*d*) $\ln p$

98. In PCM, the number of quantising level is 16. The number of pulses in code group will be

(*a*) 16 (*b*) 8
(*c*) 4 (*d*) 3

99. In the above question, the number of code-groups is

(*a*) 7 (*b*) 8
(*c*) 15 (*d*) 16

100. In PCM, if the signal is sampled at a rate of f_s and the number of pulses in one-group is p, then the number of pulses per second is

(*a*) f_s (*b*) pf_s
(*c*) $\frac{1}{pf_s}$ (*d*) $\frac{f_s}{p}$

101. The bandwidth required for transmitting 4 KHz signal using PCM with 128 quantising levels is

(*a*) 8 KHz (*b*) 16 KHz
(*c*) 28 KHz (*d*) 128 Khz

102. In a PCM system there are 256 quantising levels, and pulse allocation width of 0.625. Many messages each of bandwidth 4 KHz are simultaneously transmitted on a single channel. The number of pulses per code-groups is

(*a*) 3 (*b*) 4
(*c*) 8 (*d*) 16

103. In the above question, the time period of each code-group is
(*a*) 0.625 μsec (*b*) 2.5 μsec
(*c*) 5 μsec (*d*) 10 μsec

104. In the same question, the time period between two samples is
(*a*) 5 μsec (*b*) 2.5 μsec
(*c*) 5 μsec (*d*) 10 μsec

105. In the same question, the number of messages that be transmitted is
(*a*) 10 (*b*) 15
(*c*) 25 (*d*) 50

106. The standard value of sampling rate is
(*a*) 4000 samples per sec
(*b*) 8000 samples per sec
(*c*) 10000 samples per sec
(*d*) 16000 samples per sec

107. As compared to PCM, which of the following is *not* an advantage of other pulse modulation system ?
(*a*) PCM circuitry is complex
(*b*) PCM requires large bandwidth
(*c*) PCM is not noise immune
(*d*) None of these

108. Which of the following statements is *not* true for compounding process?
(*a*) The signal is compressed at the transmitter and expanded at the receiver
(*b*) Small amplitude signals are expanded by an amplifier
(*c*) It can be used in PCM, PDM and PAM
(*d*) It reduces quantising noise

109. Which of the following events will *not* happen when quantising noise is decreased in PCM?
(*a*) Increase in the number of standard levels
(*b*) Increase in bandwidth
(*c*) Decrease in channel noise
(*d*) Decrease in randomness due to difference in digits sent and actual signal at an instant

110. To generate PCM, the signal is sampled and converted into
(*a*) PWM (*b*) PPM
(*c*) PAM (*d*) PDM

111. In PCM, for 128 standard quantising levels, the maximum error will be

(a) 1/28 of the total amplitude range
(b) 1/256 of the total amplitude range
(c) 1/64 of the total amplitude range
(d) 1/4 of the total amplitude range

112. For transmission of normal speech signal, the PCM channel needs a bandwidth of
(a) 64 KHz (b) 8 KHz
(c) 4 KHz (d) None of these

113. The main advantage of PCM system is lower
(a) band-width (b) power
(c) noise (d) None of these

114. A signal of 4 KHz is to be transmitted using sampling techniques. The time between two samples should be
(a) 62.5 μsec (b) 125 μsec
(c) 250 μsec (d) 400 μsec

115. A TDM system
(a) needs lower bandwidth
(b) gives lower signal-to-noise ratio
(c) uses simple circuits as compared to FDM
(d) All of these

116. In TDM, if number of signals being multiplexed are band- limited in f_m the band-width requirement is
(a) $\leq nf_m$ (b) $\geq. nf_m$
(c) $\leq 2nf_m$ (d) $\geq 2nf_m$

117. Which of the following statements is *not* true for TDM ?
(a) Pulse modulated signals can be sent wide spaces of narrow pulses
(b) The transmitter and receiver are to be synchronized
(c) Analog signals can also be combined
(d) None of these

118. In high speed TDM, the channels are separated in the receiver employing
(a) OR gate (b) AND gate
(c) NAND gate (d) NOR gate

119. Which of the following statements is *not true* for a decoder?
(a) It selects the desired signal from other signals
(b) It demodulates the signal
(c) It transforms the signal into a form suitable for decoding process
(d) It amplifies the signal

120. Which of the following is *not* uniformly distributed over all frequencies ?

(*a*) White Noise (*b*) Flicker Noise
(*c*) Shot Noise (*d*) Thermal-Noise

121. At high frequencies, which of the following type of noise becomes most important?

(*a*) Flicker noise (*b*) Short noise
(*c*) Thermal noise (*d*) Transit time noise

122. In a circuit, the value of a resistor is halved. The thermal noise power generated would become

(*a*) doubled (*b*) halved
(*c*) unchanged (*d*) one-fourth

123. As far as the effect of thermal-agitational noise is concerned, a noisy resistor can be considered as a noise-free resistor

(*a*) in series with a constant current generator
(*b*) in parallel with a constant current generator
(*c*) in parallel with a constant voltage generator
(*d*) None of these

124. Which of the following measures can *not* be used to reduce noise?

(*a*) By increasing the channel bandwidth
(*b*) By increasing the transmitted powder
(*c*) By reducing the signaling rate
(*d*) By using redundancy

125. The advantage of guard time between pulses is that

(*a*) it increases the efficiency of transmission
(*b*) it suppresses the cross talk
(*c*) message can be reconstructed with practical filters
(*d*) None of these

126. The term noise temperature is used for

(*a*) white-noise source only
(*b*) thermal-noise source only
(*c*) non-thermal-noise source only
(*d*) All of these

127. The noise figure of a receiver connected to an antenna whose resistance is 50 ohms and has an equivalent noise of 30 ohms is

(*a*) 1.6 dB (*b*) 2.04 dB
(*c*) 4.2 dB (*d*) 6.03 dB

128. In the above question, the equivalent noise temperature is

(*a*) 102 K (*b*) 155 K
(*c*) 174 K (*d*) 300 K

129. If the bandwidth in a PCM system is B, the ratio of S/N ratio at the output and input of the receiver is proportional to

(*a*) B (*b*) B^2

(c) $(2)^{2B}$ (d) $1/B$

130. Which of the following statements is *not* true for PCM?
(a) The noise is removed by regenerating pulses at each repeater station
(b) The noise accumulates throughout the transmission path
(c) Noise-free signal is transmitted at each repeater station
(d) Only noise on the link between repeater stations is to be considered

131. Quantising noise is produced in
(a) all pulse modulation system
(b) PCM
(c) all modulation system
(d) FDM

132. Quantising noise can be reduced by increasing
(a) bandwidth
(b) sampling rate
(c) number of standard quantum levels
(d) All of these

133. Noise temperature is
(a) the same as physical temperature of the body
(b) a measure of the available noise power for non-thermal sources
(c) a measure of noise figure of a receiver
(d) None of these

134. Satellite tracking stations are located in remote areas in order to minimise the effect of
(a) solar noise (b) man-made noise
(c) cosmic noise (d) thermal noise

135. Geo-stationary satellites are placed in equatorial orbits at a height of approximately
(a) 900 km (b) 1600 km
(c) 22 000 km (d) 36 000 km

136. In how much time, a geo-stationary satellite makes one revolution around the earth?
(a) 12 hours 40 minutes
(b) 23 hours 56 minutes
(c) 36 hours 30 minutes
(d) The satellite is stationary and thus no revolution

137. The source of primary power for a satellite is
(a) nickel cadmium cells
(b) solar cells
(c) inverters
(d) load batteries

138. The purpose of a satellite repeater is
(*a*) to repeat the satellite signals many times
(*b*) to translate signal to new frequency band
(*c*) to receive signal from the satellite
(*d*) None of these

139. Before transmitting to the satellite, the wideband satellite signal is amplified by
(*a*) klystron
(*b*) travelling wave tube
(*c*) tunnel-diode amplifier
(*d*) waveguide

140. The carrier-to-noise ratio for a satellite depends upon
(*a*) effective isotropically radiated power
(*b*) band-width
(*c*) free-space path losses
(*d*) All of these

141. The signal is sent back to Earth by satellite by mean of
(*a*) chicken-mesh antenna
(*b*) horn antenna
(*c*) yagi antenna
(*d*) duplexer

142. The purpose of steerable spot-beam paraboloid aerials is
(*a*) to increase *EIRP*
(*b*) to reduce band-width
(*c*) to increase receiver gain to noise temperative ratio
(*d*) None of these

143. Which of the following statement is *not* correct for multiple access system in a satellite earth station?
(*a*) Access to same repeater sub-systems and same RF channel is possible
(*b*) Frequency division multiple access is used
(*c*) Several carriers are not amplified by same TWT
(*d*) All of these

144. In multiple access system, for digital signals
(*a*) TDMA is employed
(*b*) FDMA is employed
(*c*) both TDMA and FDMA are amplified
(*d*) None of these

145. Which of the following operations is to be carried out by INSAT?
(*a*) Telecasting (*b*) Telecommunicating
(*c*) Metecology (*d*) All of these

146. The Satellite Instructional Television Experiment (SITE) conducted in India employed

(*a*) INSAT (*b*) ATS-6 satellite
(*c*) APPLE (*d*) Bhaskara

147. Which of the following systems in an international system?

(*a*) INSAT (*b*) INTELSAT
(*c*) ATS-6 (*d*) All of these

148. Which of the following is India's first operational satellite?

(*a*) SITE (*b*) INSAT
(*c*) APPLE (*d*) Aryabhatta

149. To telecast programmes directly to TV receivers, the additional circuit required with the receiver is

(*a*) modulation converter
(*b*) front-end converter
(*c*) frequency converter
(*d*) All of these

150. The INSAT operates in

(*a*) *S* band (*b*) *C* band
(*c*) *Q* band (*d*) None of these

151. The number of microprocessor typical 10000-line digital telephone exchange would require is about

(*a*) 500 (*b*) 1000
(*c*) 2000 (*d*) 4000

152. The range of K band is

(*a*) 16-24 GHz (*b*) 24-36 GHz
(*c*) 1-2 GHz (*d*) None of these

153. The range of Ka band is

(*a*) 8-16 GHz (*b*) 24-36 GHz
(*c*) 16-24 GHz (*d*) None of these

154. The range of Ku band is

(*a*) 24-36 (*b*) 8-16 GHz
(*c*) 16-24 (*d*) None of these

155. The range of L band is

(*a*) 1-2 GHz (*b*) 4-8 GHz
(*c*) 8-16 GHz (*d*) None of these

156. The range of Q band is

(*a*) 8-16 GHz (*b*) 16-24 GHz
(*c*) 24-36 GHz (*d*) 36-46 GHz

157. MODEM is a combination of

(*a*) Modulator/Demodulator
(*b*) Mux/Demux
(*c*) AD/DA converter
(*d*) All of there

158. The function of Mux is
(*a*) To combine signals into a single bit stream
(*b*) To multiply signals into a single signal
(*c*) To separate signals from bit stream
(*d*) None of these

159. Codec is a unit which carries only
(*a*) Encoding (*b*) Decoding
(*c*) Both of these (*d*) None of these

160. QAM stands for
(*a*) Quadrature Amplitude Modulation
(*b*) Quality Amplitude Modulation
(*c*) Quantised Amplitude Modulation
(*d*) None of these

161. QAM is
(*a*) QPSK and M combined
(*b*) QPSK and multiple access combined
(*c*) QPSK and ASK combined
(*d*) Nonc of these

162. ADPCM stand for
(*a*) Adaptive Differential Pulse Code Modulation
(*b*) Advanced Digital Pulse Code Modulation
(*c*) Advanced Differential Packet Channel Modulation
(*d*) None of these

163. The world's first commercial satellite was
(*a*) Early Bird (*b*) Telestar
(*c*) ATS (*d*) Apple

164. The first commercial satellite was launched in
(*a*) 1962 (*b*) 1965
(*c*) 1967 (*d*) 1977

165. The Telestar was placed in
(*a*) Medium height orbit
(*b*) elliptical orbit
(*c*) geo-stationary orbit
(*d*) None of these

166. Early Bird was placed in
(*a*) Low-earth orbit (*b*) elliptical orbit
(*c*) geo stationary orbit
(*d*) None of these

167. The duration of orbit of a satellite increases as the height of the satellite above the earth
(*a*) increases (*b*) decreases
(*c*) is not affected (*d*) first increases, then decreases

168. The apogee motor changes the orbit from

(*a*) elliptical to circular
(*b*) circular to elliptical
(*c*) elliptical to another elliptical
(*d*) None of these

169. Weather satellites employ
(*a*) Polar orbit satellites
(*b*) Geo-stationary satellites
(*c*) Both of these
(*d*) Either of these

170. INMARSAT consists of
(*a*) Single satellites (*b*) Two satellites
(*c*) Three satellites (*d*) Four satellites

171. In telecommunication set-up via satellite, the satellite receives the signal from
(*a*) the appropriate earth station
(*b*) the main broadcast station where the signal originates
(*c*) some microwave repeater station
(*d*) None of these

172. Satellites used for intercontinental communications are known as
(*a*) COMSAT (*b*) MARISAT
(*c*) DOMSAT (*d*) INTELSAT

173. Which of the following satellite systems is a regional system ?
(*a*) INSAT (*b*) ASASAT
(*c*) INTELSAT

174. Weather satellites employ
(*a*) Polar orbit satellite
(*b*) Geo-stationary satellites
(*c*) Both of these
(*d*) Either of these

175. In broadcast satellites, the high power transmitters are based on
(*a*) TWT (*b*) Lasers
(*c*) Masers (*d*) None of these

176. For maximum gain, the transmit antenna on-board a broadcasting satellites is of the type :
(*a*) Horn (*c*) Yagi
(*b*) off-set fed parabolic
(*d*) Mesh antenna

177. A telephone communication link between two countries which do not face a common satellite is established preferrably with
(*a*) a double-hop satellite system
(*b*) a composite system using a submarine cable and a satellite
(*c*) submarine cable only
(*d*) None of these

178. As compared to submarine cables, satellite communication set-ups have
(*a*) High reliability
(*b*) Low reliability
(*c*) both have almost same reliability
(*d*) None of these

179. The geo-stationary satellites need echo suppressers or not?
(*a*) Yes (*b*) No
(*c*) Depends upon the height of the satellite
(*d*) Depends upon the transponder capacity of the satellite

180. EIRP is the abbreviation of
(*a*) Equivalent Inter-Transmit Receive Pulse
(*b*) Error Integrated Radiated Power
(*c*) Equivalent Isotropically Radiated Power
(*d*) None of these

181. Which statement is true for EIRP ?
(*a*) It combines power and antenna gain
(*b*) It is S/N ratio
(*c*) It is error detection efficiency of a code
(*d*) None of these

182. CDM is
(*a*) form of digital modulation technique
(*b*) form of multiple access technique
(*c*) form of spread spectrum multiplexing
(*d*) frequency multiplexing

183. CDMA stands for
(*a*) Code Division Multiple Access
(*b*) Carrier Differentiation Modulation Access
(*c*) Command Division Multiple Access
(*d*) None of these

184. DAMA stands for
(*a*) Differential Amplitude Modulation Access
(*b*) Demand Assigned Multiple Access
(*c*) Digital Assembled Multiple Access
(*d*) None of these

185. FDM is a method of
(*a*) combining signals at different frequencies into a single signal
(*b*) differentiating frequencies into a single signal
(*c*) frequency differentrated modulation
(*d*) frame differentrated modulation

186. SCPC stands for
(*a*) Single Correcting Pulse Code
(*b*) Single-Channel Pulse Command
(*c*) Single Carrier Per Channel
(*d*) Single Channel Per Carrier

187. SCPC essentially is a
(*a*) non-multiplexed low capacity TDMA
(*b*) non-multiplexed, low capacity FDMA
(*c*) Multiplexed, low capacity FDMA
(*d*) None of these

188. When a modem is ready to send data, it turns on its
(*a*) RTS (*b*) CTS
(*c*) DCD (*d*) None of these

189. TDMA is the same as
(*a*) TDM (*b*) PCM
(*c*) CDMA (*d*) None of these

190. Time division multiplexing is a
(*a*) multiple access technique
(*b*) bandwidth expansion technique
(*c*) signal digitising technique
(*d*) All of these

191. In TDMA, several sources, such as earth stations, transmit in sequence so that a sequence of RF signals is assembled at
(*a*) satellite
(*b*) earth stations in others locations
(*c*) transmitting antenna
(*d*) All of these

192. Which of the following is a random access technique ?
(*a*) ALOHA (b) TDMA
(*c*) CDMA (*d*) FDMA

193. ALOHA is a
(*a*) form of FDMA (*b*) form of TDMA
(*c*) shared random packet access channel
(*d*) shared packet access in a sequence

194. The satellite link BER typically is around
(*a*) 10^{-2} (*b*) 10^{-4}
(*c*) 10^{-6} (*d*) 10^{-8}

195. Burst errors can be reduced by
(*a*) Special burst error correction codes
(*b*) Scrambling of data bits
(*c*) interleaving of data bits
(*d*) All of these

196. Forword error correction (FEC) provides correction of errors at the receiving terminal
(*a*) with retransmission of data
(*b*) without retransmission of data
(*c*) Either of these
(*d*) None of these

197. The FEC is used in
(*a*) satellite telephone enter
(*b*) VSAT terminals
(*c*) DBS satellites
(*d*) All of these

198. FEC is used on satellite links where the C/N ratio at the receiver is
(*a*) very low
(*b*) very high
(*c*) always constant
(*d*) None of these

199. When error detector schemes are employed, it is necessary to have
(*a*) retransmission scheme
(*b*) error correcting codes
(*c*) Either of these
(*d*) Both of these

200. Retransmission schemes use
(*a*) FEC
(*b*) ARQ
(*c*) decoding
(*d*) None of these

201. Coding of data is used in
(*a*) correcting errors at the receiving terminal
(*b*) making S/N ratio constant at the receiver terminal
(*c*) detecting errors at the receiving terminal
(*d*) None of these

202. For transmission of digital speech signals, the acceptable bit rate is up to
(*a*) 10^{-10}
(*b*) 10^{-8}
(*c*) 10^{-6}
(*d*) 10^{-4}

203. For transmission of data signals, the errors are detected and corrected by
(*a*) adding redundancy bits to the transmitted data
(*b*) increasing C/N ratio
(*c*) using ARQ
(*d*) All of these

204. Encoding is the process of
(*a*) sending an additional error control data stream
(*b*) adding coding bits to encoded data stream
(*c*) modulating data stream
(*d*) None of these

205. In a block code, if each block contains k binary bits, then a data word is defined as
(*a*) $k/2$ bits
(*b*) k bits
(*c*) k–1 bits
(*d*) $2k$ bits

206. In the above question, the number of datawords will be
(*a*) $2k$
(*b*) k^2
(*c*) 2^k
(*d*) $k/2$

207. If k datawords are encoded into code words of n bit size by using additional r bits, then

(*a*) $n = k \times r$ (*b*) $n = k/r$

(*c*) $n = k - r$ (*d*) $n = k + r$

208. If a dataword has k bits and the encoded message of n bits, the code ratio r_c is equal to

(*a*) $\frac{k}{n}$ (*b*) $k \times n$

(*c*) $k - n$ (*d*) $k + n$

209. A coding technique is highly efficient if

(*a*) number of errors detected is high

(*b*) number of errors corrected is high

(*c*) Both of these

(*d*) Neither of these

210. Cyclic codes are

(*a*) linear codes (*b*) non-linear codes

(*c*) weighted codes (*d*) FEC codes

211. The Reed-Solomon code is a

(*a*) block error detecting code

(*b*) block error correcting code

(*c*) Cyclic code

(*d*) All of these

212. In a message, errors occuring in bursts (due to impluse-type noise or interference) are corrected by using

(*a*) BCH codes

(*b*) Cyclic codes

(*c*) Reed-Solomon codes

(*d*) Convoluted codes

213. ARQ stands for

(*a*) Amplitude Rated Quality

(*b*) Antenna Rated Quality

(*c*) Automatic Repeat Request

(*d*) None of these

214. ARQ is a

(*a*) modulation method

(*b*) digitising method

(*c*) frame retransmission procedure

(*d*) None of these

215. ASCII stands for

(*a*) Asian Standard Computer Interchange of Information

(*b*) American Standard for the Computer Interchange of Information

(c) Australian Standard Interchange of Information
(d) None of these

216. BER (Bit Error Rate) in digital circuits is equivalent to
(a) Error in modulation of analog modulated signal
(b) Error caused by noise in analog communication systems
(c) Modulate increase in an analog circuit
(d) SNR is an analog circuit

217. VSAT stands in
(a) V-band Satellite
(b) Very Small Antenna Terminal
(c) Video Signal Access Terminal
(d) None of these

218. Hub is
(a) part of satellite configuration
(b) central earth station of a VSAT STAR network
(c) link between two adjacent satellites
(d) None of these

219. In the layered structure for inter connecting data terminals in VSAT systems, which two layers are shown in wrong place ?

User

A	Physical
B	Presentation
C	Session
D	Transport
E	Network
F	Link
G	Application

(a) F & C (b) D & E
(c) A & G (d) B & C

220. The function of protocol emulation in a VSAT network is to operate seamlessly with
(a) VSAT antenna (b) terrestial network
(c) space link (d) satellite

221. Typical binary digital rates for digitised speech signal is
(a) 4800 bps (b) 64 kbps
(c) 3 Mbps (d) 6 MBps

222. Typical binary digital rates in digitised video signal is
(a) 32 kbps (b) 64 kbps

(c) 1–2 Mbps (d) 3–6 Mbps

223. In digital signaling, if the time separation between signaling bit is 750 μsec, the signal rate will be
(a) 0.62 kbps (b) 1.33 kbps
(c) 2.66 kbps (d) 3.32 kbps

224. If f_s is the sampling frequency in a digitised signal and n is the number of bits per sample, the the but rate will be equal to
(a) f_s/n (b) $f_s \times n$
(c) n/f_s (d) $n - f_s$

225. For a stereo CD recording, the sampling frequency is 44.1 kHz and the number of bits per sample is 16. The bit rate will be
(a) 705.6 kbps (b) 1411.2 kbps
(c) 2822.4 kbps (d) 3644.8 kbps

226. In the above question, if the CD recording is not stereo, then the bit rate will be
(a) 705.6 kbps (b) 1411.2 kbps
(c) 2822.4 kbps (d) 36644.8 kbps

227. Digital DBS-TV transmission takes place in
(a) L band (b) S band
(c) Ka band (d) Ku band

228. Which of the following is *not* associated with DBS-TV system?
(a) QPSK demodulation
(b) MPEG decoding
(c) decryption (d) C-band satellite

229. Digital TV signals are transmitted as
(a) QPSK signal occupying 27 MHz of transponder bandwidth
(b) PSK signal occupying 20 MHz transponder bandwidth
(c) TDM signal occupying 15 MHz transponder bandwidth
(d) Either of these

230. Digital DBS-TV signals are transmitted as
(a) 20-Mbps PSK (b) 10-Mbps PSK
(c) 20-Mbps QPSK (d) 10-Mbps QSK

231. DBS satellite can also be used to serve Internet users for down loading large blocks of data. This statement is
(a) True (b) False
(c) True but only within the beam coverage area.

232. DBS-TV system employs
(a) Small antennas and low-cost receiving systems
(b) Big antennas and low-cost receiving systems
(c) antennas mounted on high towers
(d) None of these

233. The link margin of a typhoid DBS-TV signal is in the range of
(a) 0–2 dB (b) 1–2 dB
(c) 2–4 dB (d) 4 – 8 dB

234. In a DBS-TV receiver, low-noise block converter is mounted
(*a*) inside TV set (*b*) on antenna feed
(*c*) on roof top (*d*) Either of these

235. In a DBS-TV system, the bit rate of an MPEG-2 coded signal in the case of live program with a lot of motion increases above this average value of
(*a*) 3.1 Mbits/sec (*b*) 6.2 Mbits/sec.
(*c*) 12.4 Mbits/sec (*d*) 24.8 Mbits/sec.

236. With the help of MPEG-2 encoding, for a 23 M bits/sec signal, the number of live compressed digital video signals that data can counting is
(*a*) 1 (*b*) 2
(*c*) 3 (*d*) 4

237. Digital DBS-TV transmission use a transmitted symbol rate of
(*a*) 10 Mbits/sec using QPSK
(*b*) 20 Mbits/sec using QPSK
(*c*) 10 Mbits/sec using PSK
(*d*) 20 Mbits/sec using PSK

238. A feature film to be telecast on DBS TV system is digitised and processed through MPEG-2 compression. As a result, the data rate is reduced to
(*a*) 1.6 Mbits/sec (*b*) 3.2 Mbits/sec
(*c*) 6.4 Mbits/sec (*d*) 20 Mbits/sec

239. Decoding operation in a DBS-TV signal involves
(*a*) encoding by Reed-Solomon code and decoding by Convolutional code
(*b*) encoding by Convolutional code and decoding by Reed-Solomon code
(*c*) encoding by Reed-Solomon code, interleaving and encoding by Convolutional code
(*d*) None of these

240. As compared to CD recording, error control in digital signals is
(*a*) highly efficient (*b*) less efficient
(*c*) same (*d*) None of these

241. The double layer of error control encoding is done by using
(*a*) Reed-Solomon code
(*b*) Cyclic code
(*c*) Golay code
(*d*) Reed-Solomon and Convolutional codes

242. The double layer of error control coding in a digital video signal bit stream is called
(*a*) Reed-Solomon code
(*b*) Convoluted code
(*c*) Concatenated code
(*d*) Golay code

243. The uplink RF signal in a DBS-TV earth station is
(*a*) PSK modulated *Ka* band concern
(*b*) QPSK modulated *Ku* band carrier
(*c*) PSK modulated K_a band carrier
(*d*) QPSK modulated K_a band carrier

244. In uplink signal from DBS–TV earth station, the intermediate frequency in QPSK modulation typically is
(*a*) 15 MHz (*b*) 27 MHz
(*c*) 70 MHz (*d*) 17 GHz

245. The line margin in a typical DBS–TV system is
(*a*) 4 to 8 dB (*b*) 8 – 16 dB
(*c*) 16 – 32 dB (*d*) 32 – 64 dB

246. In a DBS-TV receiving terminal, the electronically controlled polariser behind the antenna feed can be set to receive
(*a*) Left-hand circular polarisation
(*b*) Right-hand circular polarisation
(*c*) Either of these
(*d*) None of these

247. In a DBS-TV system, the dual polarisation is required when
(*a*) two channels are to be received
(*b*) main programme channel and encoding channel are to be received
(*c*) more than than one channel is to be received
(*d*) None of these

248. Typical diameter of a DBS-TV antenna is
(*a*) 0.45 m (*b*) 1 m
(*c*) 1.25 m (*d*) 2.65 m

249. An uplink operates at 14 GHz, and the flux density required to saturate the transponder is – 120 dBW/m^2. The free-space loss is 207 dB, and the other propagation losses amount to 2 dB. If the effective area of an isotropic antenna is – 44.37 dBW/m^2, then the earth-station [*EIRP*] required for saturation will be about
(*a*) 44.6 dBW (*b*) 85.2 dBW
(*c*) 116.4 dBW (*d*) 232.8 dBW

250. The space segment of a global positioning system has
(*a*) 1 satellite (*b*) 3 satellites
(*c*) 12 satellites (*d*) 24 satellites

251. In a GPS system, the method used in locating the position of a receiver is
(*a*) cross-sectional (*b*) trilateration
(*c*) bilateration (*d*) quadilation

252. The GPS satellites transit frequency known as

(a) L_1 frequency (b) L_2 frequency
(c) Both of these (d) Either of these

253. In a GPS system psendo-random bit sequence called P code is used to modulate
(a) L_1 signal (b) L_2 signal
(c) Both L_1 and L_2 (d) Either L_1 and L_2

254. In a GPS system, C/A code is used to modulate
(a) L_1 signal (b) L_2 signal
(c) Both L_1 and L_2 (d) Either L_1 and L_2

255. To track a receiver, a GPS system uses
(a) P-code (b) C/A code
(c) Either of these (d) Both of these

256. To find the locate of a receiver, a GPS system uses
(a) 1 satellite (b) 2 satellites
(c) 3 satellites (d) 4 satellites

257. The satellite signal acquisition by a receiver is governed by
(a) Doppler shift (b) Code synchronisation
(c) Both of these (d) Either of these

258. In a GPS system, typical value within which the Doppler shift must be accommodated is
(a) ± 1 KHz (b) ± 2 KHz
(c) ± 3 KHz (d) ± 4 KHz

259. HTTP stand for
(a) High Technical Text Protocol
(b) Hyper Text Transfer Protocol
(c) Hyper Text Transport Protocol
(d) None of these

260. HTML stands for
(a) High Terminal Modulation Link
(b) Hyper Text Makeup Lauguage
(c) High Tracking Mid-pills Link
(d) None of these

261. WWW stands for
(a) Web World Wide (b) Wide World Web
(c) World Wide Web (d) None of these

262. ISP stands for
(a) Internet Satellite Protocol
(b) Internet Service Provider
(c) Internet Specific Programme
(d) None of these

263. Browser is a
(a) software (b) hardware

(*c*) Either of these (*d*) Both of these

264. Internet Explorer is a
(*a*) brewser (*b*) ISP
(*c*) doman (*d*) URL

265. TCP stands for
(*a*) Transfer Code Protocol
(*b*) Transform Code Protocol
(*c*) Transmission Control Protocol
(*d*) None of these

266. Which of the following is *not* a domain?
(*a*) com (*b*) Internet Explorer
(*c*) org (*d*) net

267. IP stands for
(*a*) Indian Protocol
(*b*) Internet Protocol
(*c*) International Protocol
(*d*) Internet Protocol

268. Windows is a
(*a*) Satellite opening for internet hardware
(*b*) TCP
(*c*) Browser
(*d*) IP

269. Which of the following Statements is *not* true for Internet?
(*a*) Internet provides linking together globally unique address space
(*b*) It supports communication by using TCP/IP.
(*c*) It has its own physical structure in terms of satellite and terrestial links
(*d*) All of these

270. NSP stands for
(*a*) Network for Space Providers
(*b*) Network for Satellite Providers
(*c*) Network Service Providers
(*d*) None of these

271. In the internet system, users first connect to
(*a*) NSPs (*b*) ISPs
(*c*) TCPs (*d*) IPs

272. Internet service providers connect users to
(*a*) Servers (*b*) NSPs
(*c*) VoIPs (*d*) All of these

273. Network service providers connect users to
(*a*) ISPs (*b*) servers
(*c*) VoIPs (*d*) All of these

274. Servers are

(*a*) Computers specially dedicated to provide information to the Internet
(*b*) Satellites decidated to internet services
(*c*) Software for different Internet applications
(*d*) None of these

275. Servers run specialised software for
(*a*) file transfers
(*b*) long-distance computing
(*c*) e-mail
(*d*) All of these

276. Routers are
(*a*) part of TCP/IPs (*b*) computers
(*c*) servers (*d*) None of these

277. The internet groups do not represent
(*a*) Internet Engineering Task Force
(*b*) WWW groups
(*c*) Internet Architecture Board
(*d*) Internet Research Task Force

278. In the network layers of the Internet, physical layers represent
(*a*) IP layer (*b*) digital data blocks
(*c*) satellite and earth states links
(*d*) None of these

279. Data-link represent
(*a*) IP layer (*b*) digital data blocks
(*c*) satellite and earth states links
(*d*) None of these

280. The Transport layer in the Internet layered structure represents
(*a*) TCP (*b*) IP
(*c*) Either of these (*d*) None of these

281. In the terrestrial Internet, the data link connects data upto
(*a*) blocks (*b*) cells
(*c*) frames (*d*) None of these

282. UDP stands for
(*a*) Ultimate Duration Protocol
(*b*) Universal Data Protocol
(*c*) User Datagram Protocol
(*d*) None of these

283. UDP is used to send
(*a*) stand-alone messages
(*b*) data packets
(*c*) error detecting bits
(*d*) None of these

284. In the Internet system, data are transmitted as
(*a*) packets (*b*) stand-alone signals
(*c*) frames (*d*) None of these

285. ATM technology stands for
(*a*) Automatic Transfer Mode
(*b*) Asychronous Transfer Mode
(*c*) Automatic Transfer Money
(*d*) None of these

286. Byte is a unit of
(*a*) 8 bits (*b*) 6 bits
(*c*) 4 bits (*d*) 2 bits

287. Kilobyte is equal to
(*a*) 1000 bytes (*b*) 1024 bytes
(*c*) 986 bytes- (*d*) 4048 bytes

288. The TCP link of the Internet is a
(*a*) physical link (*b*) buffer link
(*c*) virtual link (*d*) None of these

289. The satellite links with TCP layers
(*a*) affects the veritical link between TCP layers
(*b*) do not affect TCP link between TCP layers
(*c*) modify the virtual link suitably
(*d*) None of these

290. The Round-trip time (RTT) is the time interval that elapses between sending a TCP signal and receiving its
(*a*) BDP (*b*) ACK
(*c*) its NACK (*d*) Either of these

291. Path MTU-Discovery is a method that allows a sender to find
(*a*) largest packet (*b*) largest TCP signal
(*c*) Both of these (*d*) Neither of these

292. MTU stands for
(*a*) Master Telecommunicate Union
(*b*) Maximum Transmission Unit
(*c*) Minimum Transfer Unit
(*d*) None of these

293. In the Internet, PAWS and RTTM are the extensions used with
(*a*) low windows (*b*) medium windows
(*c*) large windows (*d*) Either of these

294. Splitting of TCP connection in the Internet Protocol is called
(*a*) Spoofing (*b*) time division multiplexing
(*c*) URL (*d*) None of these

295. In an Internet connection, aymmetric channels exist because of
- (*a*) different sizes of data flow
- (*b*) different physical capacity of links
- (*c*) Both of these
- (*d*) Either of these

296. A customer URL request goes out though a modem to
- (*a*) URL (*b*) NSP
- (*c*) ISP (*d*) None of these

297. The term URL stands for
- (*a*) Universal Resource Locator
- (*b*) Upper Range Limit
- (*c*) Universal Range Locator
- (*d*) Upper Resource Limit

298. RFC is the way to improve the performance of over
- (*a*) satellite links (*b*) TCP
- (*c*) IP (*d*) None of these

299. The low bit rate error on terrestrial links leads to
- (*a*) packet losses due to congestion
- (*b*) Low S/N ratio
- (*c*) High S/N ratio
- (*d*) None of these

300. ACK indicates
- (*a*) establishing link between satellite and user
- (*b*) Sequence number indicating correct reception in a protocol
- (*c*) Communicate network is working fine
- (*d*) None of these

301. NACK is Negative ACK in a protocol representing
- (*a*) retransmission request.
- (*b*) reception request
- (*c*) Stop transmission request
- (*d*) restart request

302. Packet Assembler/Disassembler (PAD) is an interface between
- (*a*) mux and demux
- (*b*) packet and non-packet networks
- (*c*) two packet frames
- (*d*) None of these

303. ATM means
- (*a*) Asynchronous Transfer Mode
- (*b*) Amplitude Transform Method
- (*c*) Antenna Transmit Mode
- (*d*) Aerial Transmit Mode

304. Match the following:
- (*a*) DBSTV system (*x*) employs three Satellites

(*b*) VSAT system (*y*) uses DTH receives
(*c*) GPS system (*z*) very small receiving antenna
(*d*) Telecommunication Satellite system (*w*) employs gateways

305. Match the following:

(*a*)	INSAT	(*x*)	Global telecommunication satellite
(*b*)	IRS Satellite	(*y*)	DTH TV satellite
(*c*)	INTELSAT	(*z*)	Polar satellite
(*d*)	Ecostar	(*w*)	Metrology

Part—II
Incomplete Statements

1. "An artificial satellite at the correct distance from earth would make one revolution every 24 hours and thus would remain stationary above the same spot." This statement was made by a famous British science fiction writer in 1945 in the journal Wireless World. His name was ___________.
(Arthur C. Clarke, Johannes Kepler, Issac Newton)

2. "The line joining the centre of earth and the satellite sweeps over equal areas in equal intervals of line." This is one of the famous ___________.
(Kepler's laws, Newtonian laws, Galilean laws)

3. The earth observation satellites are placed in ___________ orbits.
(sun synchronous, geosynchronous, geostationary)

4. The orbital inclination correlation manoeuvre is carried out at ___________.
(midnight, nodal points, regular intervals)

5. The manoeuvre to circularize the orbit and make it geostationary while it is in the intermediate transfer orbit is always carried out at the___________.
(apogee point, perigee point, nodal point)

6. The maximum daily eclipse duration experienced by a satellite is at ___________.
(spring and autumn equinoxes, summer and winter solstices)

7. The angle of inclination between the earth's equatorial plane and the direction of sun at equinoxes is ___________.
(0°, 45°, 90°)

8. The angle of inclination between the earth's equatorial plane and the direction of sun at summer solstice is ___________.
(0°, 90°, 23.4°)

9. The duration of a sidereal day is __________.
(24 days, 23 days 46 minutes, 23 days 56 minutes 9 seconds)

10. In a satellite communication link, if the allowable minimum angle of elevation of the earth station antenna increases, the satellite's coverage area __________. (increases too, decreases, remains unchanged)

11. A larger diameter dish antenna, operational frequency remaining same, produces a __________ beamwidth.
(narrow, wider)

12. The dish antenna that has a higher pointing accuracy, lower noise temperature and flexibility in feed design is the __________.
(paraboloid antenna, cassegrain antenna)

13. In a cassegrain antenna, the hyperboloid subreflector is so placed as to have the feed phase center located at __________ of the subreflector.
(real focal point, virtual focal point)

14. In a given earth station antenna, the antenna aperture efficiency has two predominant components; main reflector illumination efficiency of 0.9 and spill-over efficiency of 0.8. The overall efficiency would be __________.
(0.72, 0.85)

15. The semi-major axis of a certain elliptical satellite orbit is 20,000 km. The apogee and perigee distances from earth's center of another elliptical satellite orbit are both twice their counterparts in the first elliptical orbit. In that case, the semi-major axis of the second orbit would be __________.
(10,000 km, 40,000 km)

16. If the perigee and apogee distances from earth's center in an elliptical eccentric orbit are both changed by factor (K), the orbit eccentricity would __________.
(remain unaffected, change by the same factor K, change by a factor 2 K)

17. In an elliptical satellite orbit, the center of earth lies __________.
(at one of foci of ellipse, at a point on its semi-minor axis)

18. The semi-major axis of the ellipse of an elliptical satellite orbit is given by __________.
(average of the apogee and perigee distances, geometric mean of the apogee and perigee distances)

19. The semi-major axis of the ellipse of an elliptical orbit is given by __________.
(geometric mean of apogee and perigee distances, arithmetic mean of apogee and perigee distances)

20. The semi-major axis and the perigee distance from earth's center of an elliptical orbit are respectively 16000 km and 8000 km. The apogee distance from earth's center would be ____________.
(32000 km, 24000 km, 64000 km)

21. In a satellite link, the carrier saturation EIRP at the satellite is 1000 watts. If the input and output back-offs of the satellite TWTA are 6 dB and 4 dB respectively, the carrier EIRP would be ____________.
(24 dBW, 26 dBW, 20 dBW)

22. If for the data given in the above statement, the satellite EIRP for the retransmitted carrier is 40 dBW, the satellite saturation EIRP for the retransmitted carrier would be ________.
(36 dBW, 44 dBW, 50 dBW)

23. In a satellite link, the uplink and downlink carrier to noise ratios are 30 dB and 20 dB respectively. The overall link carrier to noise ratio would be ____________.
(50 dB, 10 dB, 12 dB, 19.6 dB)

24. The multiple satellite access system that suffers from presence of intermodulation products is ______________.
(FDMA, TDMA)

25. The multiple access system in which each earth station has the entire transponder bandwidth available to it is ______________.
(FDMA, TDMA)

Part—III
Identify TRUE and FALSE Statements

1. All geostationary satellites are geosynchronous while the reverse is not true.
2. The velocity of the satellite at a certain point in the orbit is the same for elliptical and circular orbits as long as the point in question is at the same distance from center of earth.
3. The velocity of the satellite at its apogee point is always greater than the velocity at its perigee point.
4. The spin stabilised satellites have a despun platform on which antennas are mounted.
5. The geostationary satellite location is specified in terms of its longitude.
6. The earth observation satellites are put in sun synchronous orbits so as to ensure that they receive uninterrupted solar radiation throughout the year.
7. Molniya orbit is the Russian name for a geostationary orbit.
8. The communication satellites with extensible solar sails are three-axis stabilised.

9. The communication satellites with body mounted solar cells are spin stabilised.

10. India's INSAT series satellites are multipurpose satellites combining communication, TV broadcast, weather forecast and earth observation roles.

11. The idea of geostationary satellite was first expressed by Johannas Kepler.

12. The satellite velocity depends upon the thrust with which it is launched and is constant for a given orbit.

13. Transponder is the essential instrumentation payload of all satellites.

14. The escape velocity at a height (H) above earth's surface would be higher than the escape relocity at a height (2 H).

15. Only geostationary satellites can be used for international communication and TV broadcast purposes.

16. A 6 GHz/4 GHz satellite communication link needs a C-band transponder.

17. The up-link frequency is always higher than the down link frequency.

18. A radiometer would be found on a meteorological satellite.

19. The satellite velocity is minimum at the perigee point.

20. The spot beam satellite antennas produce a circular cross-section on the ground.

21. The earth station antennas accessing geostationary satellites needs to continuously track the satellites at a rate equal to earth's rotation.

22. Three geostationary satellites spaced 120° apart can provide full global coverage including polar regions.

23. A rocket carrying a geostationary satellite is fired from a station with a latitude of 4°N. The satellite's orbital plane would be inclined at least 4° to equatorial plane in the absence of any inclination correction manoeuvre.

24. In a spin stabilised geostationary satellite, the spin axis is perpendicular to the geographical polar axis.

25. In a two-way satellite communication link such as an international telephone communication link, the total round trip propagation delay is about 480 ms.

ANSWERS

Part—I Multichoice Questions

1. (*d*)	2. (*a*)	3. (*c*)	4. (*c*)	5. (*b*)
6. (*b*)	7. (*d*)	8. (*a*)	9. (*a*)	10. (*b*)
11. (*c*)	12. (*a*)	13. (*b*)	14. (*e*)	15. (*e*)
16. (*c*)	17. (*d*)	18. (*e*)	19. (*g*)	20. (*b*)
21. (*e*)	22. (*c*)	23. (*d*)	24. (*c*)	25. (*a*)
26. (*b*)	27. (*c*)	28. (*f*)	29. (*b*)	30. (*a*)
31. (*a*)	32. (*c*)	33. (*a*)	34. (*b*)	35. (*c*)
36. (*a*)	37. (*a*)	38. (*c*)	39. (*a*)	40. (*c*)
41. (*a*)	42. (*b*)	43. (*b*)	44. (*a*)	45. (*a*)
46. (*b*)	47. (*b*)	48. (*a*)	49. (*b*)	50. (*b*)
51. (*a*)	52. (*c*)	53. (*d*)	54. (*a*)	55. (*b*)
56. (*c*)	57. (*a*)	58. (*a*)	59. (*c*)	60. (*c*)
61. (*c*)	62. (*a*)	63. (*c*)	64. (*a*)	65. (*c*)
66. (*a*)	67. (*a*)	68. (*a*)	69. (*d*)	70. (*a*)
71. (*b*)	72. (*c*)	73. (*c*)	74. (*c*)	75. (*a*)
76. (*c*)	77. (*b*)	78. (*b*)	79. (*b*)	80. (*a*)
81. (*a*)	82. (*b*)	83. (*a*)	84. (*c*)	85. (*a*)
86. (*c*)	87. (*a*)	88. (*c*)	89. (*a*)	90. (*b*)
91. (*a*)	92. (*b*)	93. (*a*)	94. (*c*)	95. (*b*)
96. (*c*)	97. (*a*)	98. (*c*)	99. (*d*)	100. (*b*)
101. (*c*)	102. (*c*)	103. (*c*)	104. (*d*)	105. (*c*)
106. (*b*)	107. (*c*)	108. (*c*)	109. (*c*)	110. (*c*)
111. (*b*)	112. (*a*)	113. (*c*)	114. (*b*)	115. (*c*)
116. (*b*)	117. (*c*)	118. (*b*)	119. (*d*)	120. (*b*)
121. (*d*)	122. (*c*)	123. (*b*)	124. (*b*)	125. (*c*)
126. (*d*)	127. (*b*)	128. (*c*)	129. (*c*)	130. (*b*)
131. (*b*)	132. (*c*)	133. (*c*)	134. (*b*)	135. (*d*)
136. (*b*)	137. (*a*)	138. (*b*)	139. (*b*)	140. (*d*)
141. (*b*)	142. (*a*)	143. (*c*)	144. (*a*)	145. (*d*)
146. (*b*)	147. (*b*)	148. (*b*)	149. (*b*)	150. (*b*)
151. ()	152. (*a*)	153. (*b*)	154. (*b*)	155. (*a*)
156. (*d*)	157. (*a*)	158. (*b*)	159. (*c*)	160. (*a*)
161. (*c*)	162. (*a*)	163. (*a*)	164. (*b*)	165. (*b*)
166. (*c*)	167. (*a*)	168. (*a*)	169. (*c*)	170. (*c*)
171. (*a*)	172. (*d*)	173. (*b*)	174. (*a*)	175. (*a*)
176. (*b*)	177. (*c*)	178. (*a*)	179. (*a*)	180. (*c*)
181. (*a*)	182. (*c*)	183. (*a*)	184. (*b*)	185. (*a*)
186. (*d*)	187. (*b*)	188. (*c*)	189. (*d*)	190. (*b*)
191. (*a*)	192. (*a*)	193. (*c*)	194. (*c*)	195. (*d*)
196. (*b*)	197. (*d*)	198. (*a*)	199. (*a*)	200. (*b*)
201. (*c*)	202. (*d*)	203. (*a*)	204. (*b*)	205. (*b*)
206. (*c*)	207. (*d*)	208. (*a*)	209. (*c*)	210. (*a*)
211. (*d*)	212. (*c*)	213. (*c*)	214. (*c*)	215. (*b*)
216. (*d*)	217. (*b*)	218. (*b*)	219. (*c*)	220. (*c*)
221. (*b*)	222. (*d*)	223. (*b*)	224. (*b*)	225. (*b*)

226. (*a*) 227. (*d*) 228. (*d*) 229. (*a*) 230. (*c*)
231. (*c*) 232. (*b*) 233. (*d*) 234. (*b*) 235. (*b*)
236. (*c*) 237. (*b*) 238. (*a*) 239. (*c*) 240. (*c*)
241. (*d*) 242. (*c*) 243. (*b*) 244. (*c*) 245. (*a*)
246. (*c*) 247. (*b*) 248. (*a*) 249. (*a*) 250. (*d*)
251. (*c*) 252. (*c*) 253. (*b*) 254. (*a*) 255. (*d*)
256. (*c*) 257. (*c*) 258. (*d*) 259. (*c*) 260. (*b*)
261. (*c*) 262. (*b*) 263. (*a*) 264. (*a*) 265. (*c*)
266. (*b*) 267. (*b*) 268. (*d*) 269. (*d*) 270. (*c*)
271. (*b*) 272. (*b*) 273. (*b*) 274. (*a*) 275. (*d*)
276. (*b*) 277. (*b*) 278. (*c*) 279. (*b*) 280. (*a*)
281. (*c*) 282. (*c*) 283. (*a*) 284. (*a*) 285. (*b*)
286. (*a*) 287. (*b*) 288. (*c*) 289. (*b*) 290. (*b*)
291. (*c*) 292. (*b*) 293. (*c*) 294. (*a*) 295. (*c*)
296. (*c*) 297. (*a*) 298. (*a*) 299. (*a*) 300. (*b*)
301. (*a*) 302. (*b*) 303. (*a*)
304. *a-y*, *b-z*, *c-x*, *d-w* 305. *a-w*, *b-z*, *c-x*, *d-y*

ANSWERS

PART—II Incomplete Statements

1. Arthur C. Clarke
2. Kepler's laws
3. Sun synchronous
4. nodal points
5. apogee point
6. spring and autumn equinoxes
7. 0°
8 . 23.4°
9. 23 days, 56 minutes, 9 seconds
10. decreases
11. narrower
12. cassegrain antenna
13. real focal point
14. 0.72
15. 40000 Km
16. remain unaffected
17. at one of foci of ellipse
18. geometric mean of perigee and apogee distances
19. arithmetic mean of perigee and apogee distances
20. 32000 Km
21. 24 dBW
22. 44 dBW
23. 19.6 dB
24. FDMA
25. TDMA

ANSWERS

PART—III TRUE and FALSE Statements

1. True 2. False 3. False 4. True 5. True
6. False 7. False 8. True 9. True 10. False
11. False 12. False 13. False 14. True 15. False
16. True 17. True 18. True 19. False 20. False
21. False 22. False 23. True 24. False 25. True.

31

Illustrated Glossary of Satellite Relevant Terms and Definitions

Access Control Protocol for Data Communication: The ISO/OSI Model: It is very useful as a conceptual model which identifies functions that must be performed somewhere in every data communication network. Here user one and user two are conducting a two-way communications session with each other. Each user interacts with their local device (e.g., a computer keyboard/visual display unit) at the application layer of the ISO-OSI stack. Their transaction is then routed via the various layers, with suitable conversions, etc., until the content is ready to be transmitted via the physical layer.

Advanced Mobile Phone Service (AMPS): This mobile system has been set up in the USA and has the following features:

1. There are two separate frequency bands, adjacent to each other, designated as B and A and B and B. Each band provides 416 channel frequency pairs, having 30-kHz channel separation. Each frequency pair is isolated by 45 MHz, which permits duplex operation.
2. Out of 416 channels, 21 channels are designated *control channels*. Control channels are used for call setup. The remaining channels are used as voice channels. In a cellular base station, a single transceiver is used per channel.
3. Each voice channel pair supports a single conversation at a time. Four different types of signals are transmitted over the voice channel during the course of a cellular call: voice signals; supervisory audio tone; signaling tone; and data.

On the transmitting side, the voice signals are first compressed by a 2 :1 syllabic compressor and then modulated by an FM modulator. On the receiving side, the incoming signal is demodulated and decompressed as 1:2 to recover the voice. This process improves the performance of FM transmission.

Data transmission over the RECC is based on encoding 36 control bits into a (48, 36, 5) BCH code. This code has a word length of 48 bits, 36 control bits, (48 - 36) = 12 parity bits, and a Hamming distance of 5. The number of errors that can be detected by means of this encoded word is (5 - 1)/2 = 2. This means that if the decoded word encounters more than two errors due to noise, interference, and fading, an alarm will be generated and the word will be declared invalid, thus reducing the RECC capacity. Both FOCC and RECC channels are full duplex and operate in a coordinated manner.

AMPS: This is the first-generation mobile system which is based on frequency-division multiple access (FDMA). In the 1990s, new communication standards came into effect, such as time-division multiple access (TDMA) and code-division multiple access (CDMA). In the TDMA (IS-54) standard, each AMPS channel is time shared by six mobiles (see Fig. 24.11). When one mobile has access to the channel, the other two are idle. This is accomplished by a special frame structure. TDMA channel capacity is therefore 3x FDMA or 6 x FDMA.

Analog Interpolation: In digital communication systems, interleavers use the same principle as described in the above example (but using binary data). They are used to break up burst errors and make possible correction of the received data. This method is used very successfully on audio compact discs and in digital video broadcast transmissions. Compact discs store audio data bits as changes in the reflectivity of the disc. Since the bits are about a micron long, a scratch or a speak of dust on the surface of the CD will cause a lengthy burst error. A long interleaver is used to spread out the burst error and this makes reconstruction of the analog waveform possible for burst errors as long as several thousand bits. The interleavers used in satellite transmission of digital video signals are generally shorter than those used on a CD, typically 12 × 7.

Antenna Gain (Fig. 31.1.) : It is a measure of the directionality of the antenna or its capability to concentrate power in a preferred direction. It is directly proportional to the aperture area of the antenna and the square of the transmission frequency. A given antenna transmits and receives with the same gain. Also, the antenna beam angle when squared is roughly inversely proprtional to the aperture which enables a comprison of the gains of the antennas on the basis of the beam angles. For instance, a spot beam antenna with a covering angle of 4.5° would have a gain that would be

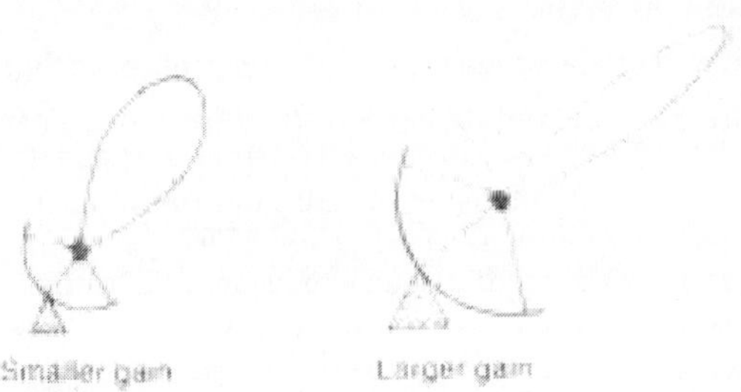

Fig. 31.1.

$(17.34/4/5)^2$ = 14.85 times the gain of a global coverage antenna with a 17.34° beam angle.

$$G = \frac{4\pi A}{\lambda^2}$$

Apogee (31.2) : Apogee is that ponit in the satellite orbit that is the farthest from the center of the earth. It would be relevant only in case of an elliptical orbit. With reference to the elliptical orbit shown in Fig. 31.2, if (*a*) is the semi major axis of the ellipse, then the apogee distance (distance of apogee point from center of earht) is given by $a \times (1 + e)$ where e is the orbit eccentricity. Also, the satellite velocity is the lowest at the apogee point.

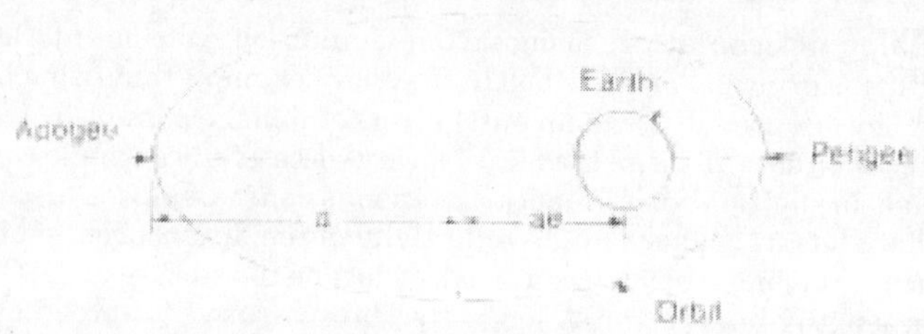

Fig. 31.2.

Arianespace: Arianespace is the name of the company established for the purpose of producing, financing and marketing European Space Agency's (ESA) launch vehicle.

Artificial Gravity: Use of centrifugal force to simulate weight reaction in a condition of free fall. It may be achieved by spinning the vehicle to kae the centrifugal force of outer periphery, or bodies within the vehicle to replace the weight reaction experienced at the surface of earth.

ARQ throughput: This is defined at the ratio of the average number of data bits accepted at the receiver in a given time to the number of data bits that could have been accepted if ARQ had not been used.

ASAT: It is an anti-satellite, satellite meant for the purpose of intercepting another satellite.

Astronautics: The science and technology of space flight.

Asymmetric channel-based Satellite Internet Network: Fig. 23.6 shows DirecPC turbo Webcast developed by Hughes Network Systems, which employs asymmetric channels to provide satellite transfer of Internet data to the individual consumer and homeowner. The system can be used for all TCP/IP-based software applications such as email, Telnet, and the World Wide Web (WWW). Clearly the advantage of the system is that the large data files are returned over a high-speed link rather than back through the low-speed modem.

Asynchronous Transport Mode (ATM): This digital packet-switching technique is used to handle bursts of high-speed data as well as the ebb and flow of the slower phone calls. It is now a popular high-speed switching technology, which integrates voice, data and video, besides connecting local and wide area networks and services into a seamless link. It is based on the so-called statistical multiplexing technique. It takes advantage of the statistical nature of the need to transfer information. Accordingly, it suppresses the silent periods and carries other voices or data in the gaps. The basic unit of transmission is called a cell, a short, fixed length packet. Each cell is 53 bytes long (48 bytes of information and a 5-byte header for path and channel identifiers, cell loss priority and generic flow control, etc.). No speed rates are specified. It can move data at varying speeds (e.g. 100 Mbit/s or 155 Mbit/s or higher).

Asynchronous Transfer Mode (ATM): In such systems, the satellite part of the network may carry the Internet Protocol (IP) over what is known as Asynchronous Transfer Mode (ATM). With ATM, the data are partitioned into fixed-length packets, called *cells*, of length 53 bytes total: five bytes form the header for the cell, and the remaining 48 bytes are the payload.

Attitude : Attitude of a space vehicle is its orientation as determined by relationship between its axes and some reference plane.

Attitude Control System : It is the system that achieves and maintain the required attitude. The main functions of attitude control system include maintaining accurate satellite position throughout the life span of the satellite, controlling satellite manoeuvres while in the transfer orbit and also during station keeping. The requirements of attitude control system mainly depend on whether the satellite is spin stablished or three-axis stablished.

Audio Compression: In DBS systems, MPEG-1 is used for audio compression. MPEG-1 and MPEG-2 cover audio and video, but MPEG-1 video is not designed for DBS transmissions. MPEG-1 audio supports mono and two-channel stereo only, which is considered adequate for DBS systems currently in use.

Automatic Repeat Request (ARQ): It is an automatic procedure, by which the receiver to request a retransmission when an error has been detected. Its advantages are: Error detection can be performed without correction which is more efficient than forward error correction in terms of code utilization. It is less complicated to implement.More errors can be detected. ARQ is mostly used with block encoding. We now make an estimate of the probability of an error remaining undetected can be made.

AWGN : AWGN stands for Additive White Gaussian Noise.

Azimuth Angle : It is defined as the angle produced by intersection of local horizontal plane and the plane passing through the earth station the satellite and center of earth. Depending upon thye location of the earth station and the subsatellite point (point of intersection of line joining satellite and center of earth and equator), the azimuth angle (A) can be computed as follows :

For earth station in northern hemisphere,

$A = 180° - A'$ ... Earth station west of satellite

$A = 180° + A'$ ... Earth station east of satellite

For earth station in sourthern hemisphere,

$A = A'$ ... Earth station west of satellite

$A = 360° - A'$ ... Earth station east of satellite

$$A' = \tan^{-1}\left[\frac{\tan|\theta_S - \theta_L|}{\sin\theta_l}\right]$$

where θ_S = satellite longitude

θ_L = earth station longitude

θ_l = earth station latitude

Backout (Radio) : A temporary loss of radio communication between a sapcecraft re-entering the atmosphere and the ground stations due to an ionised sheath of plasma that develops around the vehicle.

Bandwidth-delay product (BDP): The RTT is also used in determining an important factor known as the *bandwidth delay product* (BDP). The delay part of this refers to the RTT, since a sender has to wait this amount of time for the ACK before sending more data. The bandwidth refers to the channel bandwidth.

Big LEOs: These are equivalent of cellular telephone service and offer global voice, facsimile and possibly broadband services. and computer (Internet) networking which may be offered by optical fibres in many countries. The applications are grouped into three categories, based on bandwidth requirements. These are:

1. Narrowband (upto 64 Kbit/s) for voice transmission, e-mail, facsimile, etc.,
2. Wideband (from 64 Kbit/s to 1.544/2.048 Mbit/s) for voice/data networking, e-mail, business, TV, etc.;
3. Broadband (above 1.544/2.048 Mbit/s) for voice/data turnking; high-definition TV, etc.

Bit error rate (BER): Satellite links have a higher bit error rate (BER) than the terrestrial links forming the Internet. Typically, the satellite link BER without error control coding is around 10^{-6}, whereas a level of 10^{-8} or lower in needed for successful TCP transfer.

Bit Rates for Digital Television: The bit rate for digital television depends very much on the picture format. It varies from 118 Mb/s for standard television at the lowest pixel resolution to 995 Mb/s for high-definition TV at the highest resolution. According to the international CCIR-601 television standard, for studio-quality television pictures when digitized, the required bit rate is 216 Mb/sec. For commercial viability reasons, a single DBS transponder needs to carry somewhere between four and eight TV programmes. The programmes may originate from a variety of sources, film, analog TV, CDs and videocassette. Before transmission, these are all converted to digital, compressed, and then time-division multiplexed (TDM). This TDM baseband signal is applied as QPSK modulation to the uplink carrier reaching a given transponder. The compressed bit rate, and hence the number of channels that are carried, depends on the type of programme material. For programmes like talk shows since there is little movement lowest bit rate is required. But sports channel with lots of movement require comparative large bit rates. Typical values for various programmes are: 4 Mb/s for a movie channel, 5 Mb/s for a variety channel, and 6 Mb/s for a sports channel.

Booster : The first stage of a missile or a rocket.

Browser: This is a software used for viewing different sites on the Internet as well as sending and receiving your e-mails. The most well-known browsers are Internet Explorer and Netscape.

Byte: Common usage has established the byre (symbol B) as a unit of 8 bits, and this practice will be followed here. It should be noted, however, that in computer terminology, a byte can mean a unit other than 8 bits, and the 8-bit unit may be called an octel.

Cable TV (CTV) systems: These are used for distribution of satellite TV signals. In such a system, one transponder on a GEO satellite can send a video signal to thousands of independent cable systems distributed throughout the country. Satellites are a very effective way to distribute wideband signals, and there was rapid growth in the use of C-band transponders for video signals, using FM and one rapid growth in the use of C-band transponders for video signals, using FM and one transponder for each video signal.

CCITT H.261 algorithm image processing: Current videoconferencing systems use a codec based on the H.261 algorithm image processing to squeeze a video signal into the limited band space of a telephone line and they are basically designed to run at Integrated Services Digital Network (ISDN) data rates. CCIT Committee has laid an international standard for world-wide application which permits users to converse without having to concern themselves over the existence of the two different television scanning standards, namely 625/50 and 525/60.

CDMA-based WLL: This is based on cellular telephony with applications in macro-cells. In this technique, CDMA is used whereby multiple transmitters occupy the same frequency and time space. Transmitted data are spread over the space and each all is assigned a unique sequence code. The data rate of 32 Kbit/sec claimed for the DECT technology is not really necessary for carrying voice because the actual information content of the human voice is very low and sophisticated coding techniques can support it at a lower data rate. A mix of data rates is possible in a packet format in line with the varying requirements instead of a fixed data rate of 32 Kbit/sec. CDMA-based WLL (IS-95 standard) achieves maximum efficiency in using frequencies through a common frequency (as in CDMA), signal processing and power control. Using CDMA, one can derive 80-90 per cent of the theoretical limit predicted by Shannon as against 5-10 per cent in other systems.

CDMA Standard: It is based on the spread-spectrum (SS) technique in which multiple users have access to the same band. This is done by assigning a unique orthogonal code (Walsh code) to each user. The spreading is also accomplished by means of the same code. This code is generated from a *pseudonise* (PN) sequence whose chip rate (switching rate) is many times that of the input binary data. As shown in Fig. 24.12, the chip rate of the PN sequence is typically 1.25 MHz which derives 10 different frequency bands from the existing 12.5 MHz cellular carrier (*A* or *B*). Each of these bands can support 64 Walsh codes.

Cellular Communication System: This is an integrated network comprising a land-based wireline telephone network and a composite wired-wireless network. The composite wires-wireless system is the basis of the cellular network. The heart of this system is also a digital multiplex switch, which has been derived from the PSTN used in line telephony by adding several functions required by the mobile phone system. It is called *mobile switching center* (MSC). *Cellular base stations* are located at different convenient locations within the service area. The coverage of a base station varies from less than a kilometer to then to kilometers, depending on the propagation environment and traffic density. For example, in a dense urban environment, typical cell radii would be less than a kilometer to a few kilometers (km), whereas in a flat rural environment, the cell radii would be tens of kilometers. The mobile and portable units are generally known as *subscriber units.* The cell site (base station) includes the needed cell equipment, towers, and antennas, and the supporting base station's equipment.

Cellular Digital Packet Data (CDPD): Data transmission over the analog cellular channel can be carried out by cellular digital packet data (CDPD). It is based on the existing cellular networks and uses an unused AMPS channel from a given frequency set in a cell site. Many services can be provided over the CDPD channel, including fax transmission, computer data transmission, stock exchange portfolio access, news wire service access, commodity price list access, travel information and many more services that current rely on e-mail. The CDPD channel is composed of a forward CDPD (FOCDPD) channel and a reverse CDPD (RECDPD) channel over which data transmission takes place between the base station and the mobile.

Centrifugal Force (Fig. 31.3.) : A force that is directed away from the center of rotation. A satellite orbiting around earth with center of earth as its center of rotation is always acted upon by a centrifugal force (= $mV2/R$) acting in a direction away from the center of earth as shown in Fig. 31.3. Here (m) is mass of satellite, (R) is its orbital radius and (V) is the orbital velocity.

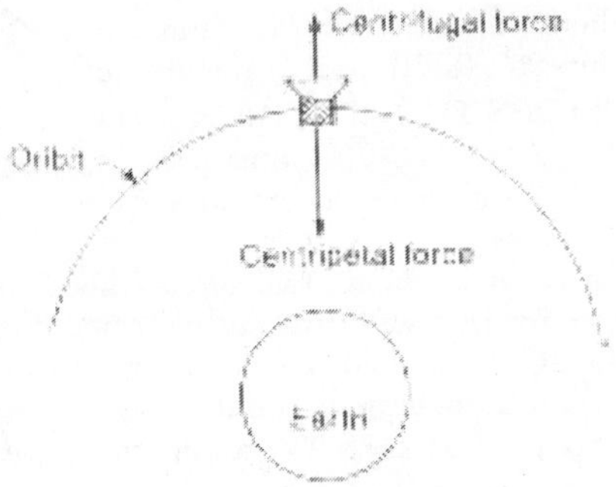

Fig. 31.3.

Centripetal Force (Fig. 3.13.) : A force that is directed towards the center of rotation. A satellite orbiting earth is always acted upon by a centripetal force directed towards the center of earth due to gravitational attraction. The magnitude of this centripetal force is given by :

$$\frac{G \times Mm}{R^2}$$

Here (G) is earth's gravitation constant, (M) is mass of satellite and (R) is orbital radius. The centrifugal force acting outwards counterbalances the centripetal force acting inwards as shown in Fig. 31.3 and this keeps the satellite in orbit. Infact, a satellite would move in a circular orbit around earth at given height only with a velocity that makes the centrifugal force counterbalance the centripetal force.

Channel capacity in a mobile system: This is expressed as the available voice channels per cell, translated into Erlangs. Assuming 10 square miles/cell in an area, a cluster of seven cells will be able to serve 7,350 subscribers/7,000 square miles in the NES and 9,660 subscribers/7,000 square miles in the ES.

Channel Coding and Decoding: The C/N requirement in VSATs are significantly reduced by channel coding. There are two types of channel coding: Block code or a convolutional coding in which the encoding and decoding process is applied to a group of bits in sequence rather than a bit at a time; and Block FEC code, which is applied to the channel prior to transmission. Convolutional and block codes can be used together on a channel.

Circular Polarisation: The satellites at each orbit location transmit in opposite hands of circular polarization (CP). Signals with opposite hands of circular polarization are orthogonal, and a suitably designed earth station antenna can separate two signals with opposite hands of circular polarization. In the simplest DBS-TV receiving terminal, an electronically controlled polarizer is used immediately behind the antenna feed. The polarizer can be set to receive LHCP (left-hand circular polarization) of RHCP (right-hand circular polarization) by changing the voltage supplied to the low noise block converter (LNB) unit at the antenna.

C/N margin in DBS-TV System Design: The most important requirement for a DBS-TV system is that it must provide a received signal power at the small receiving antenna that provides an adequate C/N margin in clear air. However, there are two difficulties. First is that the C/N margins used in DBS-TV systems are small, to avoid the need for a large receiving antenna. Second, heavy rain will cause attenuation that exceeds the link margin, so occasional outages will be experienced, especially during the summer months when thunderstorms and heavy rain more frequent. The selection of a C/N margin for a DBS-TV system, therefore, is a design tradeoff between:

1. the outage level that customers can be expected to tolerate,
2. the maximum allowable diameter of the receiving dish antenna, and
3. the power output from the satellite transponders.

Code Rate: This is defined as the ratio of dataword bits to codeword bits (note that although it is called a rate, it is not a rate in bits per second). For a give level of performance (i.e., number of errors detected or corrected), the greater the code rate, the more efficient is the code. In practice, codes that are more efficient than repetitive encoding are used.

Code Rate: This is defined as the ratio of dataword bits to codeword bits (note that although it is called a rate, it is not a rate in bits per second). For a give level of performance (i.e., number of errors detected or corrected), the greater the code rate, the more efficient is the code. In practice, codes that are more efficient than repetitive encoding are used.

Common Antenna TV System: The common or community antenna TV system is used to receive the DBS signal from the satellite which after processing is sent to various TV units in the homes in a locality. There is no separate receiver for each user.

Common Channel Signalling: In this signaling, a separate channel - a high-speed 64 Kbit/sec-link is provided to carry out for signaling functions. It is actually computer-to-computer communication, as all the switches used are under stored program control. Networks are used more efficiently because no trunks are committed to a call until the path between stations and the destination become available. Signalling rates are also faster.

Concatenated Codes: Concatenation is the process of combining codes designed to correct for burst errors with codes designed to correct for random errors. The term outer refers to the outermost encoding/decoding units in the equipment chain, and the term inner refers to the innermost encoding/decoding unit. In digital satellite television, the outer code is a Reed-

Solomon code, and the inner code is a convolutional code. The inner decoder utilises Viterbi decoding.

Concatenated coding: This is used extensively in many communications systems (for example in direct broadcast satellite television systems described in Chapter 16), since the interleaved coding will counter burst errors while the convolutional FEC coding will counter individual bit errors. It is also used in the recording of music on CDs.

Convolution Codes: These are another form of linear codes. A convolution encoder consists of a shift register which provides temporary storage and a shifting operation for the input bits and exclusive-OR logic circuits which generate the coded output from the bits currently held in the shift register.

Countdown : A count in inverse numerical order in hours, minutes and finally in seconds, of the time remaining before the launch of a rocket. The final preparations, such as checking various systems and subsystems, are donw during this period. In general, countdown refers to a series of events leading to a climatic finish, each even in the series being in accordance with a schedule in which time is counted backwards twoards zero, the finishing point.

Cycle Codes: These are a subclass of linear block codes. They possess the property that a cycle shift of a codeword is also a codeword. The advantage of cycle codes is that they are easily implemented in practice through the use of shift registers and modulo-2 address. Cyclic codes are widely used in satellite transmission, and the properties of the most important of these are summarized in the following sections. Only certain combinations of k and n are permitted in these codes.

2-DRMS error: This is the accuracy measurement for a low-cost GPS receiver using the GPS C/A code is called 2-DRMS error, where DRMS is the distance root mean square error of the measured position relative to the true position of the receiver. Its typical value is 30 metres.

Data-link layer: The function of this layer is to organize the digital data into blocks as required by the physical layer. For example, if the physical layer uses Asynchronous Transfer Mode (ATM) technology, the data are organized into cells. Digital transmission by satellite frequently uses TDMA, and satellite systems are being developed which transmit Internet data over ATM. Thus the data-link layer has to organize the data into a suitable format to suite the physical layer technology. In the terrestrial Internet, the data link converts the data into frames. The data-link layer and the physical layer are closely interrelated, and it can be difficult sometimes to identify the interface between these two layers

Dedicated Internet Access: This access needs dedicated a phone line connecting a LAN or PC to the Internet 24 Hours a day. A dedicated Internet access requires substantial initial investment in equipment and a high monthly fee for the user of the line. It varies with line capacity, and line capacity determines how many users can connect to the Internet simultaneously.

Demand Assignment Multiple Access (DAMA) : While the conventional Frequency Division Multiple Access FDMA, Time Division Multiple Access (TDMA) and Single Channel Per Carrier (SCPC) multiple access techniques, in their basic form, allocate fixed amounts of capacity to users, the use of DAMA technique enables the allocated capacities to be varied dynamically according to individual demands. Demand assignment is used in conjunction with SCPC and TDMA systems.

Digital DBS-TV: The television signal from the studio is relayed over a terrestrial link to the uplink station. This transmits a very narrowbeam signal to the satellite in the 14-GHz band. The satellite retransmits the television signal in a wide beam in the 12-GHz frequency band. Individual TV receivers within the beam coverage area are able to receive the satellite signal. Digital DBS-TV signals are transmitted as a 20-Msps QPSK signal occupying about 27 MHz of transponder bandwidth. The 40-Mbps signal has a data rate between 23 and 27 Mbps with the remaining bits used for error control and system operation. DBS-TV digital signals make extensive use of error correction and error detection techniques in the form of a double layer of error control coding with interleaving. The recovery of a good quality analog signal from a bit stream with bit errors relies on deinterleaving to spread out bursty errors, correction of some errors by the inner layer of convolutional coding, and detection of remaining, uncorrected, errors by the outer layer of Reed-Solomon linear block coding. Detected errors that remain after the decoding of the digital signal typically result in single word effors.

DBS-satellites have a higher (EIRP) than for the other categories of satellites. Typically value of EIRP is in the range 51 to 60 dBW. According to the standards laid by the Regional Administrative Radio Conference (RARC), this value is 57 dBW. Transponders are rated by the power output of their high-power amplifiers. Typically, a satellite may carry 32 transponders. If all 32 are in use, each will operate at the lower power rating of 120 W. If the high-power amplifiers are doubles, the number of transponders is reduced will be 16. But each transponder now has to operate at the higher power rating of 240 W.

Digital enhanced cordless telecommunications (DECT): It is a standard proposed by the European Telecommunications Standards Institute, is a variation of the cellular system. It defines the air interface to the user. Known as CorDECT wireless in local loop, a technique has been jointly developed by the Indian Institute of Technology, Chennai, and five Chennai-based companies. It has a portable handset or a wallset, with an antenna built in or placed on the roof-top and will have a line-of-sight wireless link with a compact base station through a DECT interface unit (DIU) by radio, cable or fibre. Apart from the wireless link, the wallset is connected to the existing land line. The subscriber can simultaneously use the telephone and the Internet, though the speed of the phone link comes down to 35 Kbit/sec, when both channels are used. If only the Internet is used, the speed is

70 Kbit/sec. One base station can serve 1,000 subscribers with 120 channels. The system can handle a million subscribers in a city using dynamic channel selection. In rural areas the CorDECT system consists of a two-hop link, one from the wallset to a relay base station which is connected to a compact base station which is connected to a compact base station (both mounted on towers) some 25 km away.

Diplexer. Diplexer is a three port filter device that allows two receivers or transmitters to be connected to a single antenna without undesired interaction. It should not be confused with a Duplexer which is a device that allows to use the same antenna for both transmission as well as reception.

Direction frequency reuse plan: This method enhances cellular performance and capacity. It provides an additional carrier-to-interference ratio (C/I), determined by the antenna front-to-back ratio. As shown in Fig. In this method, a group of channels is reused in the same direction in which the antenna is pointing, thus fully exploiting the antenna front-to-back ratio. Because a typical directional antenna has more than a 210 dB front-to-back ratio, a frequency can be reused more often as long as it repeats in the same direction, leading to enhanced AMPS-TDMA capacity.

Direct Connectivity: This highest and most expensive type of connectivity is achieved by high speed lines to go on-line on the Internet. Internet is available round the clock. It is usually opted with heavy load and a number of users using a mainframe computer.

Direct-sequence modulation systems: CDMA channel establishment: In this, spread spectrum communication system, the source data is first "exclusive ORed" with a relatively long digital codeword. The "exclusive OR" operation replaces a 1 of the source data with the given codeword while a 0 of the source data is replaced with the bit-wise complement of the codeword. If a codeword contains n bits, the occupied spectrum of the transmitted signal is n times as wide as if the source data were directly transmitted. Signals of other CDMA channels occupy the same band of frequencies but do so with different spectrum-spreading codes, which allows separation of the signals in the signal processing circuitry of a receiver. The separating of CDMA channels in a receiver is carried out by correlating a received signal with each of the various codewords (i.e., channels) assigned to the cell.

DMS-MTX: Digital multiplex switch-mobile telephone exchange (DMS-MTX), also called mobile telephone switching office (MTSO), mobile switching centre (MSC) (depending on the manufacturer) which supporting 800-MHz cellular communication systems. It is a part of the PSTN family provides the following cellular functions:

1. Manage and control cell site equipment and connections.
2. Support multiple-access technologies such as AMPS, TDMA, CPDP and CDMA.

3. Provide the PSTN interface.
4. Provide a visitor location register (VLR)
5. Provide a home location register (HLR).
6. Support intersystem connectivity (IS-41)
7. Support call processing functions.
8. Provide billing and operation and measurement (O&M).
9. Provide trunking facilities (T1 link) between the cell site and the DMS-MTX and between the DMS-MTX and the PSTN.

Each of these blocks is further divided into several unique functional elements, supporting the end-to-end communication protocol specified by several FCC and CCITT standards.

Domain: It is a sub-section of the Internet. It is a space anyone can purchase and book on the Internet under a specific name to display information of his/her particular choice. The main domain are COM,INT,NET, MIL, and ORG, which refer to commercial, International, Network Military, and Organisation.

Doppler Effect : Doppler effect is the apparent change in frequency due to relative motion of the source and the observer. The change in frequency due to Doppler effect is given by :

$$\pm\left(\frac{2v_r}{\lambda}\right)$$

where (θ_r) is the relative velocity and (λ) is the wavelength. The frequency increases when the two are moving towards each other and decreases when they are moving away from each other.

Down Converter. The Down-Converter receives the modulated RF carrier and translates the RF in the down-link frequency spectrum of the satellite to the IF. Down conversion is usually accomplished in a dual conversion process.

Drag. The resistance offered by a gas or a liquid to a body moving through it.

DTH Home Receiver: It consists of two units, an outdoor unit and an indoor unit togther called complete receiver as an integrated receiver decoder (IRD). Its operation is as follows:

Dumb terminal packages: These, like ProComm Plus for DOS/Windows use a computer as a keyboard and display attached to the remote machine.

Earth centered earth fixed (ECEF) coordinate system: This system is used for calculating position location in GPS systems. In position location, first, the coordinates of the GPS receiver and the GPS satellites are defined in a rectangular coordinate system with its origin at the center of the earth. The ECEF coordinate system is part of the WGS-84 description of the earth. WGS-84 is an internationally agreed description of the earth's shape and parameters, derived from observations in many countries.

Eclipse (Fig. 31.4) : During equinox periods, the earth, the sun and the satellite are in alignment with the result that earth's shadow eclipses the satellite and the sun light fails to reach the satellite solar cells. This interrupts the battery recharging process. This does not significantly affect the performance of low power satellites which can usually continue their operation using back-up power but high power satellites shut down for all but essential services. The eclipse effect is noticeable for periods of about four weeks and the maximum daily eclipse duration is about 1.20 hours.

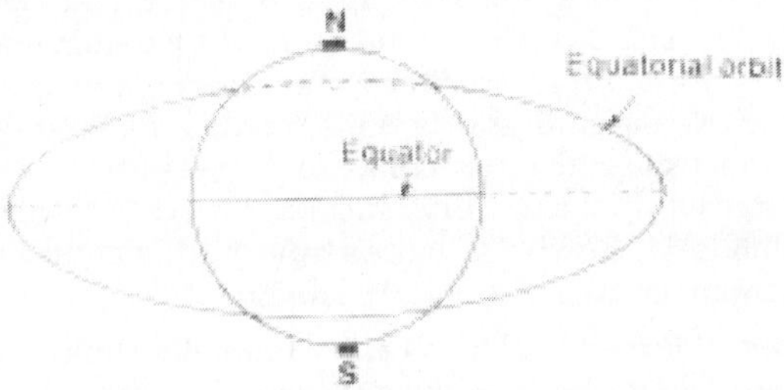

Fig. 31.4.

Encoding and Decoding: This refers to the process of adding coding bits to the uncoded bit stream, and decoding refers to the process of recovering the original (uncoded) bit stream from the coded bit stream. Both processes are usually combined in one unit termed a codec. The principle of error detection coding is based on *adding redundant bits to a data stream in such a way that one or more errors in the data stream can be detected.* One redundant bit is added for every N data bits which allows a single error within that block of N bits to be detected, whatever the number of bits in the block.

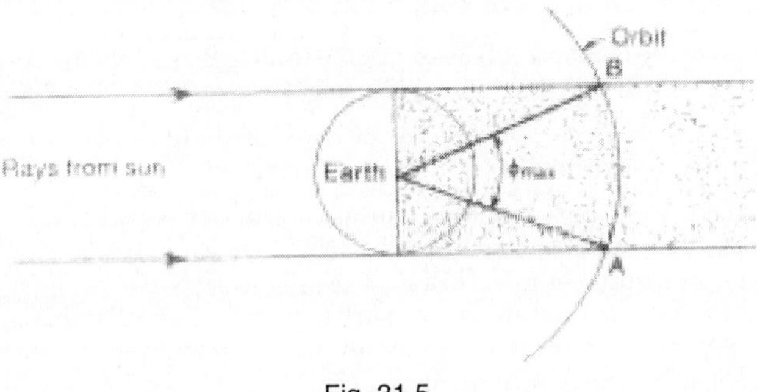

Fig. 31.5.

Equatorial Orbit (Fig. 31.5.) : An orbit in the plane of equator.

Equinox (Fig. 31.4.) : It is the point of time when the sun crosses the equator making the lengths of day and night equal. We have the autumn equinox occurring on September 21 and spring equinox according to March 21. Equinoxes are relevant to communication satellites and the eclipse duration is the maximum at the equinoxes. Fig. 28.4. shows the shadow angle at an equinox. The eclipse duration here is the time taken by the satellite to move from point A to B. For a geostationary satellite, the eclipse duration at equinox is about 1.20 hours.

Equivalent Isotropic Radiated Power (EIRP) : It is a measure of radiated or transmitted power of an antenna. It can be computed from the antenna gain and the power fed to the antenna input. That is, $EIRP = PtGt$ or $EIRP$ (in dBW) = Pt (in dBW) + G_t (in dB). In simple words, *EIRP* is the transmitter power which would be required to be fed to an isotropic antenna to give the same result as the transmitter and the antenna under consideration. Although, the *EIRP* is defined and measured at the transmitter antenna, its practical significance is at the receiving end of the link. *EIRP* of the earth station transmitting antenna can for instance be used to compute the power received by the satellite under a variety of transmission path conditions. Similarly, *EIRP* of satellite's transmitting antenna can be used to compute power received at the earth station.

Error Detection on Satellite Links: In satellite links, error detection is a process of facilitating sending and reception of data with a greatly reduced probability of error with a very high probability that uncorrected errors are identified and located within a block of data, so that the existence of an error is known. Error correction is applied in a communication system by use of error detection and retransmission which requires the use of protocols. A protocol is an agreed-upon set of actions that define how each end of the data link proceeds so that data are transmitted in an accurate and ordered fashion through the link.

Escape Velocity : Escape velocity is the minimum velocity away from a parent body that a particle or another body must acquire to escape permanently from the gravitational attraction of the parent. In case of launching of satellites or rockets, the vehicle has to escape from the gravitational attraction of the earth. It can be computed from $\sqrt{2\mu / R}$ where $\mu = G.M.$ (G being earth's gravitation constant and M being its mass) and (R) is the distance of the vehicle from center of earth. This figure is 11.6 km/s for bodies trying escape from the surface of earth.

EUTELSAT: This provides digital international links with Europe, closely the TDMA system operated by INTELSAT and using satellite and earth station equipment (EUTELSAT) configuration also arise in some of the North America satellite networks. Recent satellite designs, like EUTELSAT to have transponders with higher output power, and saturation rating of 50 watts if often found now.

Exhaust Velocity : The velocityof the exhaust leaving the nozzle of a rocket motor.

FAX : A fax modem converts a documents into a low resolution digital bit mapped image by the scanner and the edited by the computer using editor software. The digital stream is then transmitted over the phone line as an analog signal and sent to the exchanges from where it is sent to the destination. At the receiving end, the text is extracted from the fax image through processing by Optical Character Recognition (OCR) software. The OCR outputs either plain text or formatted text in a word processor format.

File Transfer Protocol (FTP): This allows transfer of files between computers on the Internet. It serves two purposes: providing to a user access to computing facilities at another institution; and the Internet is a vast repository of publicly available files of very conceivable type: electronic scholarly journals; text files containing literary texts, bibliographies or episode guides to cult TV series; graphics files of great works of art; fonts for various operating systems; large amounts of free of shareware software. All of these can be downloaded to a local system.

Foot Print (Fig. 31.6) : It is earth's surface area illuminated by the satellite antenna. Its shape and size depend upon a number of factors including antenna design and angle of a elevation.

Technically speaking, footprint is used to describe equipower flux contours provided by a satellite transmitting antenna. Footprints are usually drawn for either equal power flux density (dBW/m^2) or EIRP (dB). The size and shape of territory the transponder is to serve. For instance, a circular beam would not serve any useful purpose while illuminating territories such as that of Japan. Fig. 31.6. shows the use of multiple feeds to shape the beam and hence the footprint.

Formation of Blocks of Data: In general, typically n bits are transmitted in a block, made up of k message bits plus r parity bits. There are two ways in which the blocks of data can be formed: In a packet transmission system, the block is usually long, typically 64 to 2048 bits, and checksum or *cyclic redundancy check* (CRC) bits are added to the block that generate an error condition at the receiver if there are errors in the block. The blocks are made members of a set of n-bit *codewords*. Coding schemes in which the message bits appear at the beginning of the codeword, followed by the parity bits, are called *systematic block codes*.

Forward Error Correction (FEC): This technique is employed both detecting and correcting errors at the receiving terminal without retransmission of data. FEC codes add redundant parity check bits to the data bits in a way that allows errors to be located within a codeword. In general, twice as many errors can be detected by a FEC code as can be corrected. The advantage of FEC over error detection is that a single unit at each end of the link (a codec) can insert and remove the FEC code and make corrections as required. It also allows errors to be corrected without the need for retransmission, but this is more difficult and costly to implement than ARQ. FEC is used on all satellite links where the C/N ratio at the receiver is likely to be low such as satellite telephones, VSAT terminals, and direct broadcast satellite television. These systems make use of the coding gain from rate one-half or rate three-quarters FEC to achieve low BER.

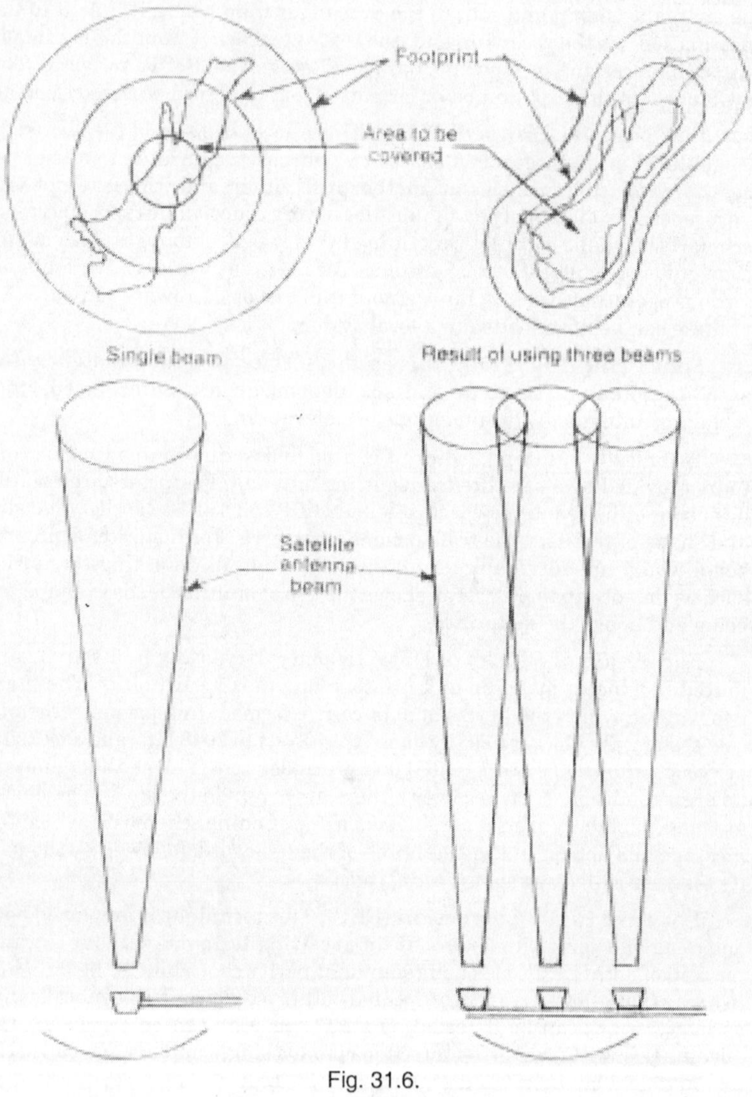

Fig. 31.6.

Frame Relay: The grouping of data into packets of digital data and transferring them as discrete units of information. In frame relay (middle), frames of data are transmitted by means of addresses contained within the packets of data. The cells have a variable length of information (64 to over 1,500 bytes, besides a 2-byte header). The Frame Relay Protocol allots bandwidth dynamically. Note that unlike time division multiplexing (TDM) where sound as well as silence are transmitted, frame relay does not allocate a path until data have to be sent. The packets or frames can vary in length (e.g. 64 to over 1,500 bytes). It is a standard method of connecting data communication devices for bit rates ranging from 56 thousand bits to 2 million bits per second, although it can support lower or higher speeds.

Free Fall : Free falls is the ideal falling motion of a body acted upon by the pull of earth's gravitational field.

Frequency Division Multiple Access (FDMA) (Fig. 31.7) : It is the earliest and still the commonest form of all the multiple access techniques of satellite communications. Each of the earth stations within the satellite's footprint transmits one or more carriers at different center frequencies. Each carrier is assigned a frequency band with a center frequencies. Each carrier is assigned a frequency band with a small guard band to avoid overlapping between adjacent carrier. The satellite transponder receives all the carriers within its bandwidth, does the necessary translation and amplification and retransmits them back to earth. The different earth stations are capable of selecting the carriers containing messages of their interest. Two FDMA techniques are in operation today. One is multi-channel per carrier where the earth station frequency division multiplexes several channels into one carrier base band assembly which then frequency modulates and RF carrier and is transmitted to FDMA satellite transponder. This technique is called FDM-FM-FDMA. In the other technique called Single Channel Per Carrier (SCPC), each channel modulates a separate RF carrier and is transmitted to FDMA transponder.

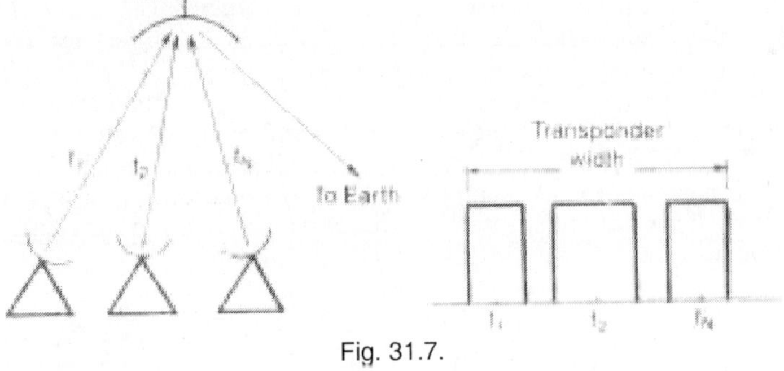

Fig. 31.7.

Frequency-hopping systems: These are spread spectrum communication systems in which transmission at any particular instant is confined to a relatively narrow band of frequencies commensurate with the inherent bandwidth of the message. Instead of staying within one particular band as a conventional communications system does, a frequency- hopping system jumps between narrow bands of frequencies within a large block of spectrum in some prescribed manner. As said earlier, a GSM cellular system has the ability to operate with frequency hopping (specifically, slow frequency hopping).

Gateway connectivity: In this connection, when one of the computers on a small network or BBS gets the Internet access, all the remaining computers on the network get hooked up to it. Thus this intersection point computer provides a gateway to Internet access for the rest of the network.

General packet-switching radio services (GPRS): This technology offers a low-cost access to the Internet. It will be linked to the GSM, which has already been adopted in India. Existing GSM networks can be upgraded in a cost-effective manner. Mobile wireless phone operators around the world have decided to market GPRS phones. The technique will facilitate access to the Internet. Several applications of GPRS are: e-mail, e-commerce, file transfer and weather/sports/stocks/travel updates. GPRS is making the Internet mobile, just as GSM has made voice mobile.

Geodesy : The science of earth's shape.

GEO Satellites for Mobile Services: Hand-held phones can work with satellites in the geostationary orbit also. The Asia cellular satellite (ACS) system is designed to cover a large region from India to Indonesia and Australia. The satellite has onboard processor and unfurlable antenna. The satellite located at 1180E over Borneo, can form a maximum of 150 spot beams in its coverage area. The ACS will link not only with hand-held devices but also with mobile and fixed terminals.

Global Positioning Satellite Systems (GPSs): These are used as means of navigation for ships and aircraft and in surveying and many other applications.

Geostationary Orbit (Fig. 31.8). : It is an equatorial circular orbit at such a height from earth's surface that a satellite moving from west to east has a velocity so as to orbit the earth once in a time equal to the time taken by earth to complete one rotation around its axis. This time is about 24 hours. In such a case, the satellite appears stationary to an observer on earth. The orbital radius of a geostationary satellite tunes out to be 42164.2 km. The movement of the satellite is thus in synchronism with earth's rotation. All geostationary satellites are geosynchronous but the reverse is not true. It is known as a Clarke's orbit.

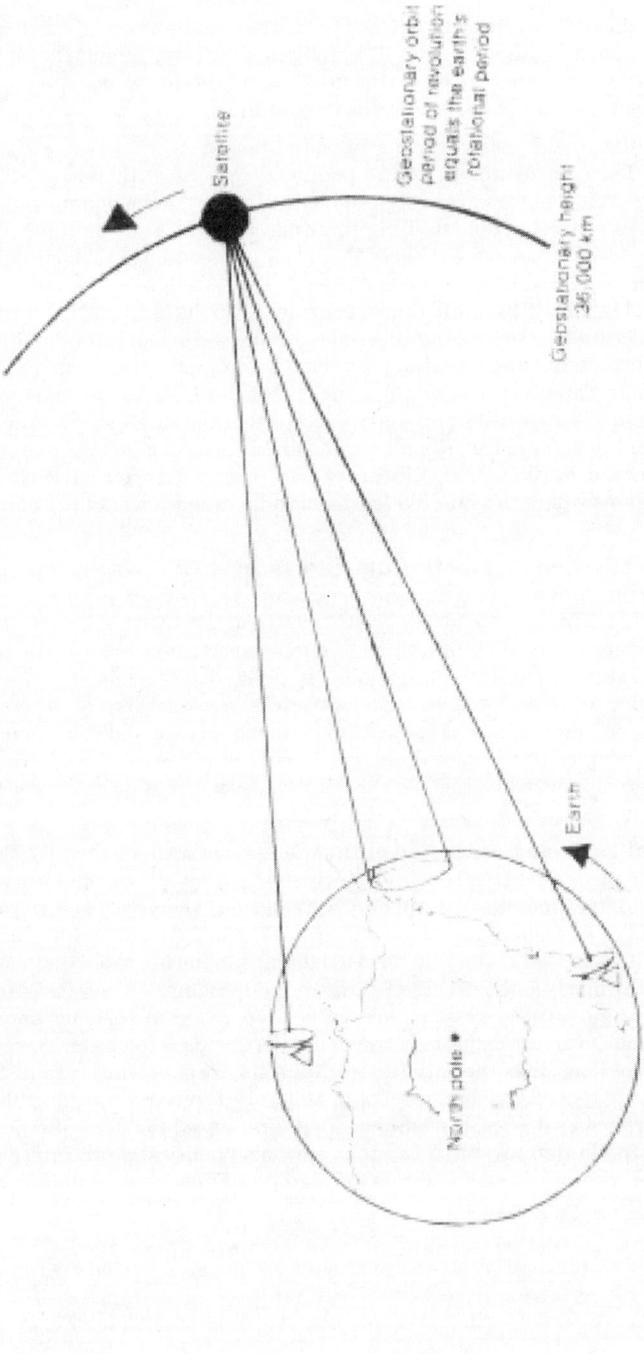
Satellite
Geostationary orbit
period of revolution
equals the earth's
rotational period
Geostationary height
36 000 km
Earth
North pole

Fig. 31.3.

Global Position System (GPS) : GPS is a positioning and navigation system designed to use some 18 to 24 satellites, each carry atomic clocks, to provide a receiver anywhere on earth with extremly accurate measurement of its three dimensional position, velocity and time.

Globalstar: It is a low Earth orbit satellite system with 52 satellites, including four spares aimed at the populous regions of the earth. The Globalstar orbital planes are therefore inclined at 50° to the equator, thus ignoring the sparsely populated high-latitude regions. The satellites are simpler in design than some others. The satellite functions as a 'bent pipe' transponder inclined at 52° to the equator. The satellites go in circular orbits at 1,414 km altitude and concentrate on the areas between 70° North and South latitudes. There is neither onboard processing nor inter-satellite links. All processing and switching are done by ground stations each with three or four antennas, track and work with the satellites. No onboard processing or ISLs are used; the signals received at the satellite are simply transponded down and the 78 gateway earth stations process the signals for the onward routing. Like Ellipso, service over water is restricted to coastal regions where the satellite is within radio range of a gateway earth station.

Global System for Mobile Communications: GSM is a cellular mobile communications system that has been adopted worldwide as the international digital mobile standard. For this system, the International Telecommunication Union (ITU) allocated frequency spectrum at: 935-960 MHz for the downlink (base station to mobile); and 890-915 MHz for the established analog systems. GSM is a circuit-switched system, like most wireless networks. Nowadays, packet-switching is favoured to provide high bandwidth and operate packet-based microcells instead of today's broad areas of wireless coverage, using high power. Microcells facilitate spectrum reuse and address the problem of spectrum shortage.

Global Telecommunications Links: The global trunk network links fixed points at national centers and provincial centers all over the world, carrying massive amounts of telephone, data and video channels and all the other kinds of telecommunication facilities that can be conveyed by such channels. It is routed mainly by terrestrial and submarine cable (increasingly optical fibre) and terrestrial radio relay systems. As compared to satellite systems, these systems are very competitive in cost, for short distances. However, the distance between link terminals is sometimes large, and for these long links the satellite medium, the costs of which are little affected by distance, may be lower than those of terrestrial media. n the satellite systems, some of the transponders are leased for domestic networks but the larger part of the system provides facilities for an international network linking earth stations owned by national telecommunications operating organizations.

Go back-N ARQ: This ARQ allows continuous transmission of blocks incorporating the retransmission of corrupted blocks when these are detected. It carries this out by having the blocks and the acknowledgement signals numbered. The advantages are: A delay will only be encountered when an NAK signal is received.Since there is a delay in transmission only when a NAK is received, the throutghput on this system is much greater than with the stop-and-wait method. The disadvantage Goback N is that there is the additional time loss resulting from the retransmission of the good blocks following the corrupted block.

GPS Satellite Clock: This is an atomic clock, which is calibrated against time standards in the GPS control stations around the world. This is called *GPS time*, a time standard that is available in every GPS satellite. The accuracy of an atomic clock is typically 1 part in 10^{11}.

GSM Frequency Hopping: The mobile station can move between a transmit, receive, and monitor time slot within one TDMA frame, all of which are normally on different frequencies. For this, it uses *slow frequency hopping.* In this, the mobile and BTS transmit each TDMA frame on a different carrier frequency. The frequency-hopping algorithm is broadcast on the broadcast control channel. Since multi-path fading is dependent on carrier frequency, slow frequency hopping helps alleviate the problem. Moreover, co-channel interference is more random than in fixed-frequency allocations.

GSM Mobile Station: This consists of (i) Mobile equipment (the terminal) and (ii) A smart card called the Subscriber Identity Module (SIM).

GSM Network: A GSM network divides the service area into a number of cells, each of which is serviced by a base station. A switching center processes the calls (between GSM and the public-switched telephone network) and handles billing. Each cell is divided into several sectors, each of which is given radio frequency carriers. Each carrier has eight timeslots for voice/data, allowed on a TDMA basis. One carrier is reserved for paging mobile units. There is provision to track the location of the mobile units, check their identity and monitor and control the network.

GSM Short Message Service (SMS): This is a bi-directional messaging service that allows GSM cellular subscribers to send and receive data, Individual messages (with GSM) can be up to 160 bits in length. Because the SACCH is used for SMS data transmission, messages can be received or transmitted during a voice call. Initial applications of SMS focused on alphanumeric paging services with fundamental differences: SMS is bi-directional and message delivery is guaranteed. Subsequent applications served by SMS are voice mail notification, e-mail delivery, stock quotes, and downloading/updating of SIM cards.

GTO : Geostationary Transfer Orbit.

Handy-21: Combination of Cellular, Wireless Internet, Digital Radio, TV and Pager: This system developed by M.I.T. Laboratory consists of a powerful hand-held computer that combines the functions of a cellular phone, a wireless link to the Internet, a radio, a TV and a pager. Various functions can be selected by changing the software. It has an antenna to transmit and receive signals, which are handled by a general-purpose microprocessor. A number of new features are being introduced, for instance, if a mobile unit experiences high data transmission, Handy-21 may transfer the link to a dedicated, more powerful link.

Host/Terminal Connection (Shell Accounts): In a host/terminal connection, a given computer acts as if it were a terminal directly connected to some Internet host. The programme signals its modem to dial and handles the transfer of characters from your terminal to the host computer and back. It means that the host computer is one that is "on the Internet", and therefore, when it transfers files, the files are transferred to the host. The user now can download the files to his/her computer using your communications programmes.

HTML (Hyper Text Markup Language): HTML is the native language for HTTP. It is the format used for writing the hypertext web documents It a code used to make documents readable across a variety of platform and software. It operates through a series of codes placed within an ASCII (that is, text) document. These codes are translated by a World Wide Web client, such as Netscape, Internet Explorer, NetCruiser, or Mac Web, into specific kinds of formats to be displayed on the screen.These items include links, lists, headings, titles, images, forms, and maps.

HTTP (Hyper Text Transport Protocol): The Web document prepared by CERN (http:// info.cern.ch/hypertext/www/Protocols/HTTP/HTTP2.HTML) tells us, the transaction takes place in four basic HTTP phases: connection, request, response and close.

Hybrid fibre coaxial (HEC): It provides integrated services including telephone and the Internet through a single access line. The system combines optical fibre and coaxial cable. Traditional cable TV is a one-way transmission. As the Internet is bi-directional, one-way amplifiers have to be replaced by two-way units. It is not quite easy to manage. One of the TV channels could be reserved for data. HEC can bring data at 30-40 Mbit/s on the TV and 10 Mbit/s on the PC, which is about 100 times faster than the dial-up mode. The system can provide for interactive facility, as it can transmit upto 2 Mbit/s in the uplink. HFC is cost-effective when existing coaxial cables are used and not when new networks are needed. A new generation of modems is emerging for use in the system, based on voice and image compression.

In-band Signalling: It is used between crossbar exchanges. It is a multi-frequency signaling in which instead of using 3,825 Hz, which is outside the speech band, two out of six frequencies inside the voice band are selected to establish the digits. The combination of one lower and one higher frequency identifies the digit dialed. For example, the digit 0 in a push button dial is a combination of 941 Hz and 1,336 Hz. Multi-frequency signaling is used only for conveying the dialed digit information and its acknowledgement. Out-of-band signaling is used in addition, for supervision of calls during and after speech.

Inclination (Fig. 31.9). the angle between the orbital plane and equatorial plane.

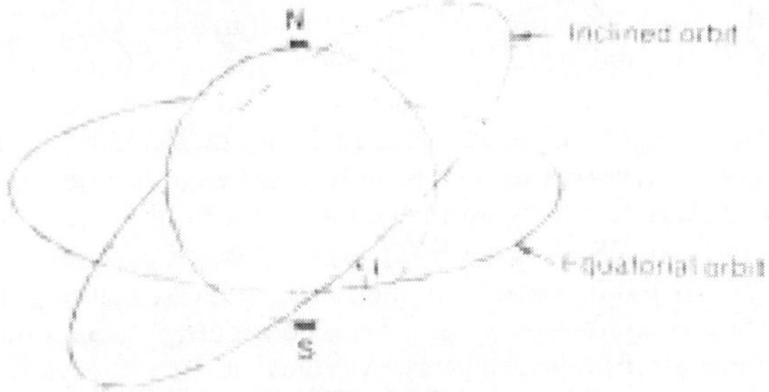

Fig. 31.9.

Indian National Internet: The Internet was formally introduced in India in 1995. International gateways to worldwide Internet are available at six nodes (as of 1999) at Calcutta, Chennai, Bangalore, Mumbai, New Delhi and Pune, provided by the Videsh Sanchar Nigam Ltd. (VSNL). The Department of Telecommunications and VSNL maintain 54 Internet nodes, most of which are connected to the international gateway nodes through digital trunk lines (operating at 2 Mbit/s). All the Internet nodes provide customers dial-up access. Leased line and ISDN access are provided on a limited scale. Internet customers of the Department of Telecommunications will have access through the public-switched telephone network. The dial-up access could be at 56 Kbit/s, or through the packet-switched public data network (X.25 called Inet).

Individual Computer TCP/IP Link: An individual computer TCP/IP link allows a computer to function as an Internet host. It is the user as host running whatever software he elects to run, providing only the service he has chosen to provide. These links are called either *SLIP* (*serial link Internet protocol*) or *PPP* (*point to point protocol*) links. Both types of links can handle dialup. Both take advantage of new software techniques that condense or compress the data being transmitted so that transferring information takes less time.

Inertial Guidance : Inertial guidance is an on-board system for launch vehicles and spacecraft where the gyros, accelerometers and other devices meet the guidance requirement. More precisely, it is a self contained navigation system which basically comprises of accelerаters mounted on a gyrostablished platform. An accelerometer is required for each direction of possible motion. The accelerometer output can be integrated twice to determine position. The gyros can be used to provide information about the orientation of the vehicle.

INTELSAT Global Telecommunication System: All current INTELSAT satellite series have transponders operating in both the 6GHz and 4GHz and the 14GHz and 111-12GHz bands. High gain spot beam dish antennas, steerable from the ground, are used for the transponders operating in the higher frequency band. Earth station antennas having access to INTELSAT satellite for the global network are required to have high performance, to ensure that bandwidth and satellite power can be used efficiently. Until recently the standard receiving Figure of Merit (G/T) was 40.7 dB/K at 4GHz and 39dB/K at 11GHz, requiring antennas with primary reflectors about 32 metres and 17 metres in diameter respectively. Most antennas now in service meet these requirements, but the minimum G/T requirements for new all purpose antenna has been reduced to 37dB/K (1GHz) and 35dB/K (11GHz). Both time division and frequency division multiple methods are used in the INTELSAT global network for the transmission of narrow band channels which are designed priority telephony. The earth stations combine the telephone channels is transmits to many onto one or a few multiplexed carriers. A typical station, therefore, receives multiplex carriers from many other earth extracting.

Internet: It is a collection of computer networks connected to each other through telephone cables satellites and various other modes, which have a common way of passing material between them, in effect creating a single world-wide network. Thus, the Internet is the global network of networks, which use certain protocols to interact with other networks via gateway.

Internet account: An Internet account is a user's gateway to the Internet. It is bought an ISP such as VSNL , MTNL, Satyan Online, Dishnet, Mantra Online, and BPL Net. The ISP a your signs up with will give the local telephone number(s), which you will dial to access the Internet through a modem. Once connected, the user will have to type in his name and password to gain access to the Internet.

Interleaving: This is the process of changing the order in which the bits are encoded so that a burst of errors gets dispersed across a number of codewords rather than being concentrated in one codeword.

Internet Protocol (IP): This takes care of addressing, or making sure that the routers know what to do with the data when it arrives. Some addressing information goes at the beginning of a message sent, giving enough information to the network deliver the packet of data.

Internet Telephony: This technology is based on packet switching in which as we know, the analogue signal of the caller's voice is digitized, formed into digital packets, time-stamped and transmitted in a compressed format, to be decoded and converted back to analogue form at the other end. Packet switching in the Internet employs out-of-band signaling which enables the separation and processing of signaling information. The service will have general-purpose computing facilities without the need of the switching system.

Internet Traffic Centers: These are:

1. London	(18 terabits/s)	9. Washington, DC	(4.0 terabits/s)
2. New York	(13.2 terabits/s)	10. San Francisco	(3.9 terabits/s)
3. Amsterdam	(10.9 terabits/s)	11. Toronto	(3.5 terabits/s)
4. Frankfurt	(10.5 terabits/s)	12. Chicago	(2.7 terabits/s)
5. Paris	(9.7 terabits/s)	13. Seattle	(2.6 terabits/s)
6. Brussels	(6.2 terabits/s)	14. Vancouver	(2.5 terabits/s)
7. Geneva	(5.9 terabits/s)	15. Tokyo	(2.4 terabits/s)
8. Stockholm	(4.4 terabits/s)		

Iridium: This system, which became operational in 1998, facilitates communication from anywhere to anywhere in the world, even where there is no telecommunications infrastructure from low power handset. It consists of 72 polar orbitating LEO satellites at 780 km above the Earth and are linked via ISLs. Each of the satellites in the constellation acts as a switching mode. Uplink signals are received and demodulated at the satellite using onboard processing to recover individual data packets at baseband so that the header information can be read. This information and links to the network control stations are used to find out the next mode for each packet and the packet is reformatted with the next address. The baseband data packet is now processed and up-converted for transmission either to the ground at L-band directly to another Iridium user or at 20 GHz to a gateway earth station, or over one of the four ISL links (at 23 GHz) to the next satellite in the chain. Onboard processing carries out the entire message routing and formatting functions.Each satellite can process 1,100 simultaneous calls and can directly link with hand-held, pocket-size satellite phones. The global coverage through 48 spot beams includes the higher latitudes and polar areas.

IP Address: An IP address is a unique, numeric identifier used to specify a particular host on a particular network, and is part of a global, standardized scheme for identifying machines that are connected to the Internet.

ISDN: The subscriber lines that could be used for both speech and data is called ISDN. It is provided on ordinary telephone lines of subscribers. ISDN is not a separate network, as it is based on PSTN with some changes. By using ISDN, it is possible to have two simultaneous calls on the existing pair to wires of the telephone. The two calls can be of any type: data, image, video or speech. The basis for ISDN is CCS-7, approved by ITU, and introduced in India in 1996. CCS-7 enables processors to exchange information needed for providing the desired services. It is essential for operating the so-called intelligent network which involves access to different databases (e.g. an 800 toll-free number for calling business firms) and working personal communication systems.

Kilobyte: The kilobyte (symbol kB) is 1024 bytes. Transmission rates may be stated in kilobytes per second, or kB/s.

L2 frequency carrier: This signal in GPS satellites is modulated with 10.23 Mbps <MI>pseudorandom<D> (<MI>PN<D>) *bit sequence* called the P code. This is used by military positioning systems. The P code is transmitted in an encrypted from known as the Y code, which restrict the use of the P code to authorized users.

L2 frequency carrier: This signal in GPS satellites is modulated by a 1.023 Mbps PN sequence called the <MI>*coarse acquisition*(*C/A*) *code* that is available for public use, and also carries the P code as a quadrature modulation. The higher bit rate of the P code provides better measurement accuracy than the 1.023 Mbps C/A code.

Launch Complex : The complex of site facilities and equipment used to launch a missile or a space vehicle.

Launch Pad : Launch pad is the load bearing base from where a rocket or a spacecraft positioned on its launcher is fired.

Launch Window : Launch window is the time interval during which a space vehicle can be launched to accomplish a given mission.

Lift-off. Lift-off marks the start of a rocket's flight from its launch pad.

Linear Block Codes: For a block code, it is necessary that the message stream be partitioned into blocks of bits. Considering only binary messages, suppose each block contains k bits, and let these k bits define a dataword. Therefore, the number of datawords is 2^k. Clrealy there is no redundancy in the system, which means that even a single bit error in transmission will convert one dataword into another, leading to an error.

Little LEOs: These satellites provide low-speed text and data services and are comparable to paging systems. The word 'little' indicates both the small size of the satellite and the low cost of implementation. They would be useful in a wide range of applications; limited Internet access, two-way paging, emergency services, tracking transportation, environmental monitoring, remote monitoring, weather monitoring, educational information, and medical advice to remote areas. Little LEOs do not replace existing services but would enhance them.

Mach Number. The ratio of the speed of a vehicle (or of a liquid or gas) to the speed of sound.

Magnetic Storm : A disturbance of the earth's magnetic field initiated by a solar flare or sun spot.

Magnetosphere : The region of space surrounding earth which is dominated by magnetic field.

Mass Memory: The SPC system has a 'mass memory' with very short access time. The memory relates to programme store, translation store and data on subscribers and route information. The translation store contains data like the charging information, status of the calling lines called and their calling codes. Purely transient data like busy or idle state of a line are also held in memory. It is arranged in words containing 16, 18 or 32 bits. Each word has a unique address for location: 1 mean 'busy' and 0 is for 'idle'. A word stores the address and the operation to be carried out.

Megabyte: The megabyte (symbol MB) is 1024 kilobytes. Transmission rates may be stated in megabytes per second or MB/s.

Mesh VSAT network: In this architecture, each of the VSATs has the ability to communicate directly with any of the other VSATs. Since the traffic can go to or from any VSAT, this architecture is referred to as a Mesh network. It will still be necessary to have network control and the duties of the hub can either be handled by one of the VSATs or the master control station functions can be shared among the VSATs.

Mobile equipment: It is uniquely identified by the International Mobile Equipment Identity (IMEI). The SIM card contains the International Mobile Subscriber Identity (IMSI) used to identify the subscriber to the system, a secret key for authentication, and other information. The IMEI and the IMSI are independent, thereby allowing personal mobility. The SIM card may be protected against unauthorized use by a password or personal identity number.

Mobile telephony: In a mobile telephone, each cell is a radio communication centre where a mobile subscriber establishes a cell with a land telephone through the mobile telephone exchange (MTX) and the public switching telephone network (PSTN). This composite platform enables to communicate with anyone at any time from anywhere within the service area. Note that MTX and PSTN are essentially multiple access points serving as system intelligence. Here the wireless segment of the communication system is shown as a cluster of seven hexagonal cells. This is a widely used cell plan, also known as the *N=7 frequency plan* in which all the available channels are evenly distributed among seven cells.

Modem: The transmission medium such as the telephone cable is meant for carrying analogue signals. So long as the telephone network is used to transmit digital information, a device is necessary to condition the digital output to suit the transmission medium. Such a device is called modem, short for modulator and demodulator. It is an interface that transforms a digital signal into an analogue for transmission by cable or radio waves. For this purpose, a modem modulates a transmission frequency by a digital input. Either two amplitudes of the transmission frequency or two frequencies of the transmission path can convey the two stages of the digital inputs. A modem at the receivend demodulates the transmitted signal and helps recover the original digital output. Different bit rates can be sent. Upto 300 bit/s, they are called subvoice speed, while medium speed ranges from 600-9,600 bit/s. Rates at 64,000 bit/s are in the high-speed category. Data transmission nowadays has reached the range of millions of bits per second.

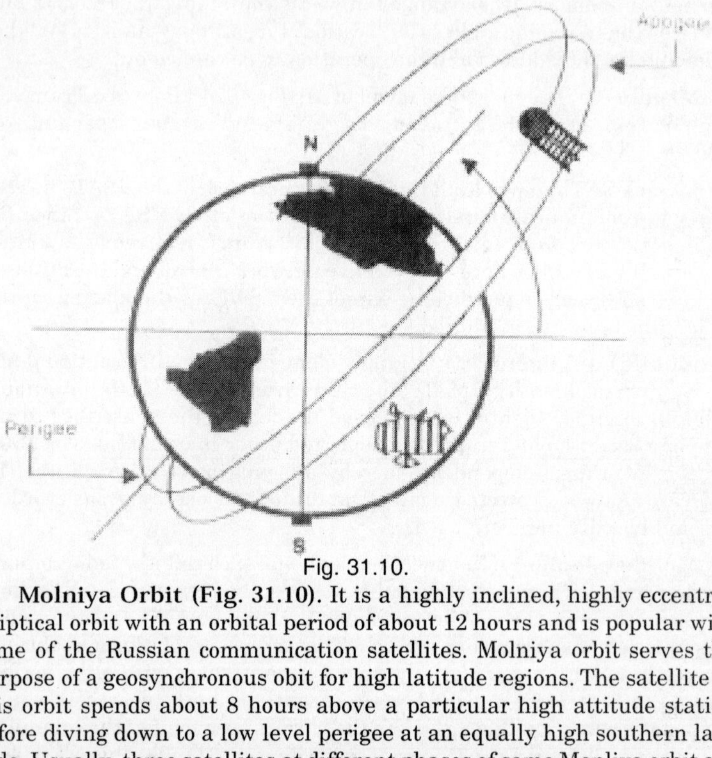

Fig. 31.10.

Molniya Orbit (Fig. 31.10). It is a highly inclined, highly eccentric, elliptical orbit with an orbital period of about 12 hours and is popular with some of the Russian communication satellites. Molniya orbit serves the purpose of a geosynchronous obit for high latitude regions. The satellite in this orbit spends about 8 hours above a particular high attitude station before diving down to a low level perigee at an equally high southern latitude. Usually, three satellites at different phases of same Monliya orbit are capable of providing uninterrupted servies.

MPEG (Moving Pictures Expert Group) standards: These are used for compression of bit rate is carried out to. MPEG is a group within the International Standards Organization and the International Electrochemical Commission (ISO/IEC), which has defined standards for the transmission and storage of moving pictures and sound. Note that the standards are concerned only with the bit-stream syntax and the decoding process and not with the encoding and decoding processes. Syntax covers such matters as bit rate, picture resolution, time frames for audio, and the packet details for transmission. The MPEG currently in use are: MPEG-1, MPEG-2, MPEG-4 and MPEG-7.

N=7 frequency plan: This is the most widely used frequency planning technique. In this plan, all the available channels are divided into 21 frequency groups, numbered 1 to 21. These frequency groups are then evenly distributed among seven cells, three groups per cell. This group (cluster) of 7 cells is then reused along with the associated frequency groups A 7-cell cluster is further surrounded by 12 cluster (not shown). In this manner, a given service area can be covered by cluster of cells with frequency reuse, thus providing mobility and capacity.

Network layer: This is strictly an Internet Protocol (IP) layer. The packets are passed along the Internet from router to router and to the host stations. No exact path is laid out beforehand, and the IP layers in the routers must provide the destination address for the next leg of the journey so to speak. This destination address is part of the IP header attached to the packet. The source address is also included as part of the IP header. The problems of lost packets or packets arriving out of sequence are not a concern of the IP layer, and for this reason, the IP layer is called *connectionless* (i.e., it does not require a connection to be established before sending a packet on). These problems are taken care of by the transport layer.

New ICO: This satellite system is primarily aimed at the LMS market (Land Mobile Services), also needed to provide capacity for maritime links. New ICO elected not to include ISLs in their system architecture nor any significant onboard processing. Since a LEO constellation would not provide maritime coverage without ISLs, a higher orbit was necessary. If little onboard processing is used, traffic routing from mobile to mobile would have to be carried out at the gateway earth stations (as it is for Ellipso and Globalstar) necessitating a double-hop link. A double-hop link involves two uplinks and two downlinks. (A the connection.) A double-hop configuration is not feasible for a GEO constellation since the overall delay would be completely unacceptable at about 1 s. New ICO therefore adopted a MEO constellation. An inclunation of 450 is used, but since the orbit altitude is so high, full global coverage is possible. Towards the end of 2000, it was learned that New ICO was modifying the payload and service offerings to provide two-way Internet-like connections in a joint venture with Teledesic.

One-Way Implementation: This is the mode of a satellite used in the broadcast satellite service (BSS). The introduction of digital technology allows the provider and user much greater flexibility in the operation of a broadcast network. By means of proprietary software in the user terminals, different parts of the downlink can be accessed by different subscribers according to the programs ordered from the supplier (and paid for by the user). This from of channel selection is called *narrowcasting*. There can be many narrowcasting groups within a large broadcasting area.

Orbit : The path of a body acted upon by the force of gravity. The word orbit is usually associated with the continuous path of a body which does not impact with its primary.

Orbit Period : The time taken to complete one orbit. The orbital period of a circular satellite orbit with a radius (R) is given by

$$\frac{2\pi R^{3/2}}{\sqrt{GM}}$$

The orbital period of an elliptical satellite orbit with its semi-major axis equal to (a) is given by

$$2\pi\sqrt{a^3 / GM}$$

Orbital Velocity : The velocity necessary to overcome the gravitational attraction of earth so as to keep the satellite in orbit. The orbital velocity in a circular orbit of radius (R) is given by :

$$\sqrt{GM/R}$$

The orbital velocity at any point distance (r) from the center of earth in an elliptical orbit with a semi-major axis equal to (a) given by:

$$\sqrt{GM\left[\left(\frac{2}{r}\right)-\left(\frac{1}{a}\right)\right]}$$

Orthogonal Mode Transducer: More complex receivers use an orthogonal mode transducer (OMT) with two LNBs so that both hands of circular polarization can be received at the same time by using two LNBs and two receivers. The dual-polarization receiving system is needed when more than one channel must be received at a time. A dual-channel DBS-TV receiver with a dual-polarized antenna allows two TV channels to be viewed by different people in the same household at the same time.

Out-to-band Signalling: In this widely used signaling method, the signaling frequency (3,825 Hz) is within the 4 KHz voice frequency channel, though it is outside the normal voice frequency range of 300-3400 Hz. This method is economical as voice transmission contains very little speech energy at the upper end of the voice band. Some filtering is also done by the telephone handset itself and the balance by the multiplex equipment. Higher signal levels can be used. However, it needs coordination between voice and signaling channels.The frequency of 3,825 Hz is added on to the telephone band of 4 KHz. With the help of filters, the signaling information conveyed through 3,825 Hz is identified. This will actuate a relay for ringing the particular telephone. The out-of-band signal frequency is used for point-to-point STD calls also.

Packet networks through polling: The VSAT interface/kernel sections also carry out polling activity from the terrestrial packet networks. The packet networks poll users to see if there are packets to be sent. The interface/kernel sections in the VSAT network respond to the polling signals of the terrestrial network immediately, thus avoiding the long delay that would occur if the polling signal had to be passed over the satellite link. Negative acknowledgements are made to the polling signals until a request to send data is received over the satellite link.

Packet Switching: Data were broken up into numerous packets and sent to the network with individual address to each packet. Since no single user needs the entire channel all the time, customers' messages are chopped up as packets of data (mixed with other users' data) and sent over a shared communications line and reassembled at the other end. The packets may not take the same route. The packets are handled by shifting them from one router to another and reassembled at the destination. A router en route stores the packets in memory and selects a suitable output link. The silent periods of a link (voice or its data equivalent and other data) are used to transmit other data. Silent periods are detected by a device called voice activity detector (VAD).

Parking Orbit (Fig. 31.11) : Parking orbit is a temporary earth orbit during which the space vehicle is checked out and its trajectory carefully measured to determine the amount and time of increasing velocity required to send it into a final orbit or into space in the desired direction.

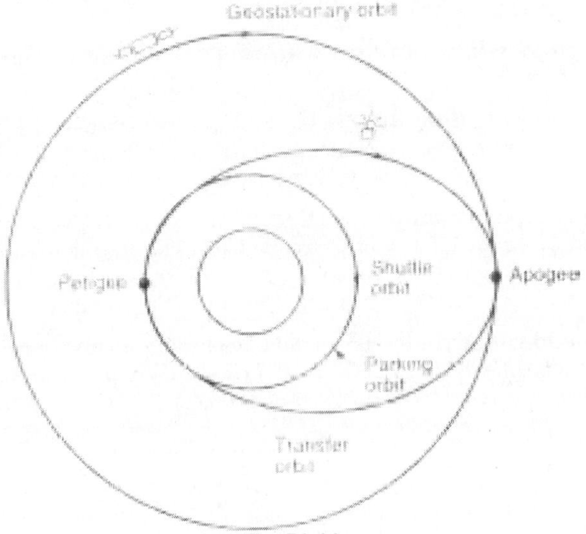

Fig. 31.11.

Payload : Payload is the useful cargo of a space vehicle. A rocket's payload may be a communications satellite and a satellite's payload may be a transponder.

Pay-up Services: The DBS-satellites are also used to address individual receivers and to load another lookup table that specifies which channels the user is authorized to receive. If the user fails to pay his or her bills to the service provider, the receiver will eventually be instructed to show only a message that it has been disconnected for failure to make timely payment for the service. This process involves a smart card, which identifies each receiving system, and enables decryption of the satellite signals.

P code for GPS satellites: This code is typically of long sequences because the long length of the P code sequene makes the distance measurements unambiguous. It repeats after 266.4 days, but is changed every 7 days for security reasons. Therefore, the P code sequences cannot be acquired easily because they do not repeat, and thus their unauthorized use is prevented.

Perigee : Perigee is the point in the orbit that is nearest to the earth. (Fig. 31.2). It would be relevant only in case of an elliptical orbit. With reference to the elliptical orbit shown in Fig. 31.2., if (a) is the semi-major axis of the ellipse. Then the perigee distance (distance of perigee point from center of earth) is given by a $(1 - e)$ where (e) is the orbit eccentricity.

Physical layer: This covers such items as the physical connectors, signal format, modulation, and the uplink and downlink in a satellite communications system.

Pitch. Movement of a spacecraft about an axis which is perpendicular to its longitudinal axis. It is the degree of elevation or depression.

Polar Orbit (Fig. 31.12) : An orbit which passes over the poloes. Polar orbits are relevant for those countries which are located near the poles.

Precise positioning service (PPS): Here the receivers track both P code and C/A code on L_1 and L_2 frequencies. The PPS is used mainly by military users, since the P code is encrypted into the Y code before transmission and requires decryption equipment in the receiver.

Psuedo-range: In a GPS system, this range is measured from the propagation time delay Ti between the satellite i and the GPS receiver.

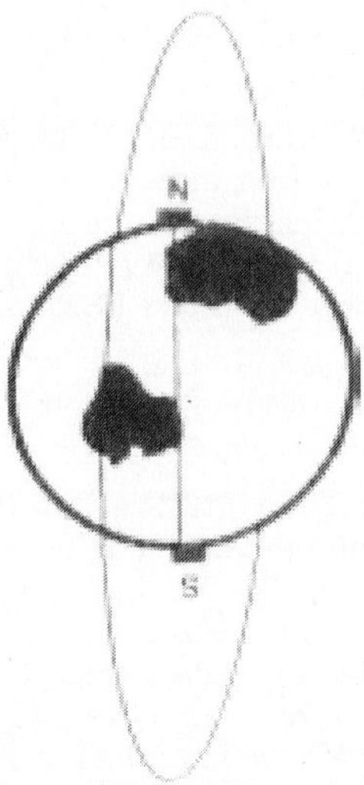

Fig. 31.12.

Primary : The body around which a satellite orbits. Earth is the primary for artificial satellites.

Project Irridium (Fig. 31.13) : Project Irridium is a global communication system conceived by Motorola that will make use of satellites placed in lower earth orbits. A total of 77 satellites are arranged in a distributed architecture with each satellite carrying (1/77) of the total system capacity. The system is intended to provide a variety of telecom services on the global leve

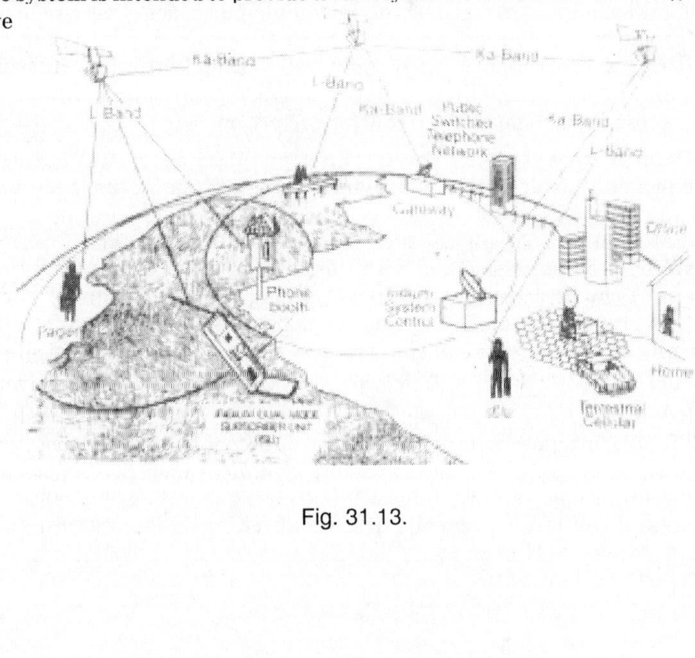

Fig. 31.13.

Propellent : A solid or liquid substance burnt in a rocket for the purpose of producing thrust.

Public switching telephone network (PSTN): It is a digitally controlled switching matrix that provides connectivity between two or more terminals. Depending on the population density, a PSTN may have well over 100,000 terminals connected to it. As a result, a major metropolitan area may have more than one PSTN switch connected to each other.

Radio Telescope : A receiving station for detecting radio waves emitted by celestial bodies or space vehicles.

Rain fade margins: There are two rain fade margins for the outbound link: (*i*) from the hub to the satellite (uplink); and (*ii*) from the satellite to the VSAT (downlink). The entire two-way system *drops below the performance minimum when any one of the low margin links becomes below threshold.* The link fade margin can be estimated by using the reciprocal formula (C/N) ratio with the $(C/N)^0$ value set to its threshold value. Consider a VSAT system which has linear, bent pipe transponders and networks that are connected via a satellite and which uses onboard processing (OBP).

Reed-Solomon codes: These codes are designed to correct errors that occur in bursts; that is, a number of bits that are close together may experience errors as a result of impulse-type noise or impulse-type interference. Here, instead of encoding directly in bits, the bits are grouped into symbols, and the dataword and codewords are encoded in these symbols. Errors affecting a group of bits are most likely to affect only one symbol that can be corrected by the Reed-Solomon codes. These codes do not provide efficient error correction where the errors are randomly distributed as distinct from occurring in bursts. To deal with this situation, codes may be joined together or concatenated, one providing for random error correction and one for burst error correction.

Remote Access Connectivity: This type of connectivity is achieved through a dial-up terminal connection. The mainframe on the Internet is used as a host using a dial up connection. The host carries out commands typed at terminal. This is the most widely used tpe of Internet connectivity. The problem associated with this level is that only the programs present at the host can be executed. Loading a new program or client does not provide the ability to execute it. Similarly downloading a file from any site becomes a two step process. Downloading from the site to host and then transferring from host to local terminal.

Roaming: A mobile moving out of its own territory and establishing a call from a foreign territory is known as a roamer and the process itself is known as roaming. Clearly, roaming enhances mobility. There are many cellular operators within the same city, using different switches, radios, and cell site equipment. But a subscriber is registered to one operator only. As a result, an agreement between these operators is needed to provide services to any subscriber irrespective of a call's origin. This is accomplished by means of a separate link between various switches, which is established by the IS-41 link protocol.

Round-trip time (RTT): The round-trip time (RTT) is the time interval that elapses between sending a TCP segment and receiving its ACK. With geostationary (GEO) satellites, the round-trip propagation path is ground station to satellite to ground station and back again.

Routers: These are computers that form part of the communications net and that route or direct the data along the best available paths in the network.

Satellite Signal Acquisition by GPS Receiver: This is carried out by the GPS receiver by two correlation processes: (*a*) code synchronisation with the satellites; and (*b*) Doppler frequency offset measurements.

Selective repeat ARQ: This method is an improvement over the above method. Here, only a correct version of the corrupted block is retransmitted, and not the subsequent blocks. However, it is necessary in this case to have a storage arrangement in the receiver because it must be able to store the subsequent blocks as it waits for the corrected version of the corrupted block.Selective repeat ARQ is used in the Internet protocol TCP/IP (transmission control protocol/internet protocol) because of relatively short delays on terrestrial paths used for Internet traffic. However, the TCP/IP protocol cannot be used over a geostationary link without modification because it is designed for terrestrial links with short delays. The protocol times out before repeat retransmissions and relies are received when a GEO satellite link is used.

Servers: These are computers dedicated to the purpose of providing information to the Internet. They run specialized software for each type of Internet application. These include email, discussion groups, long-distance computing, and file transfers.

Sidereal Day : A sidereal day is defined as the time taken by the earth to rotate on its axis relative to distant starts rather than the sun. A sidereal day is measured as 23 hours, 56 minutes, 4.09 seconds.

Signalling: It is the means and the process by which the various elements of a telephone connection communicate to establish and maintain that connections.

SIM: Its function is to provide personal mobility, so that the user can have access to subscribed services irrespective of a specific terminal. When a user inserts the SIM card into another GSM terminal, he is able to receive calls at the terminal, make calls from that terminal, and receive other subscribed services.

Sites and Hosts: All the information available on the Internet is located on specific computers (called "hosts") at particular sites. Each host had a unique number - the "IP number", which the average user doesn't need to bother with (IP stands for "Internet Protocol") - and a unique name, which functions as its address. That name (often called the "domain name") is made up of a number of components (typically 4) separated by periods

Skybridge: This satellite system is intended to carry wideband traffic and therefore use frequencies above 10 GHz. They chose to employ the same Ku-band frequencies as the FSS service in GEO uses : 12.75 - 14.5 GHz on the uplink 10-7-12.75 GHz on the downlink. To allow successful coordination with existing GSS GEO systems, they elected to prevent any operations (up or down) whenever a satellite look angle is within 10° of the GEO orbital plane. This requirement led to a relatively large number of satellites (80 vs 48) for the constellation. The decision not to use ISLs also required a very large number of gateway earth stations (on the order of 200). Skybridge also uses the concept of a fixed earth cell.

Spin-Stabilised Satellites (Fig. 31.14) : In a spin stabilized satellite, the body of the satellite spins at about 30 to 100 rpm about the axis perpendicular to the orbital plane. Spin stabilized satellite has gyroscopic stiffness as a result of rotating or spinning about its axis of maximum moment of maximum moment of inertia. Spin stabilized satellites are normally dual spin satellites with a spinning section and a despun section on which antennas are mounted. The despun section and hence the antennas are kept stationary with respect to earth by counter rotating the despun section. Spin stabilized satellites have body mounted solar cells.

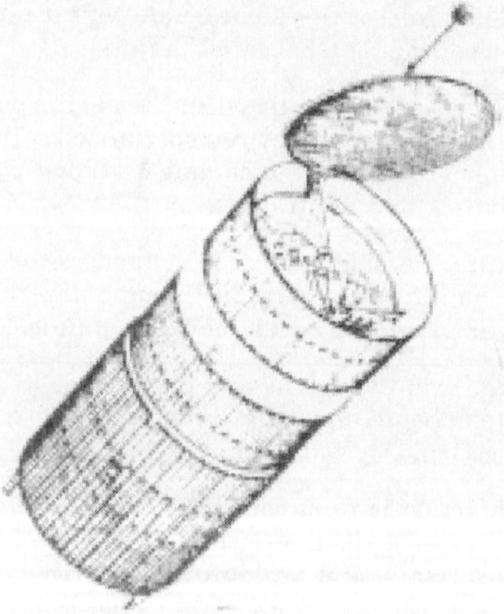

Fig. 31.14.

Split-Two-Way (Split IP) Implementation: This system is used when there is no normal return channel. For example, with Ku-band boradcast satellite service (BSS) systems that carry Internet traffic. The relatively high capacity downlink stream is not complemented by an uplink capability from the user terminal. If the BSS downlink is used as the download channel from an Internet service provider, the only option the user has for a return link is via another telecommunications channel, such as standard telephone line. The Internet protocol (IP) is therefore split between a satellite downlink (outbound) channel and a terrestrial telephone (inbound, or return) channel; hence the term split IP for this implementation. Its advantage is that the VSAT terminal does not require a transmit capability, which significantly reduces its cost and complexity. Its disadvantage is that the telephone line connection must usually be through a modem, with a bit rate generally restricted to 56 kbps or less.

Spoofing: In this process, a satellite terminal receives data using a terrestrial protocol and generates the acknowledgements, then transmits the data over the satellite link using a different protocol.

Spot Beam : A beam generated by a communication satellite antenna of sufficient size that the angular spread of the energy in the beam is very small with the result that a region that is only a few hundred kilometers in diameter is illuminated on earth.

Spread Spectrum Techniques : Spread spectrum techniques are used in military communications using satellites to give them an anti-jamming capability by forcing the jammer to deploy the transmitted jamming power over a much wider bandwidth than would be necessary for a conventional system. The spread spectrum approach expands or spreads the carrier spectrum relative to the information rate. Another important feature of a spread spectrum signal is the pseudorandomness which makes the signal appear similar to random noise and makes interception by the enemy very difficult. Direct sequence (DS) spreading and frequency hopping are the two commonly used techniques for spreading the carrier spectrum relative to the information rate.

Standard positioning services (SPS): Here the receivers track the C/A code on L1. This is the service that is used by the general public. The P(Y) and C/A codes transmitted by each satellite create direct sequence spread spectrum signals which occupy the same frequency bands. Both the C/A codes and the P code are publicly available, but the P code cannot be recovered in a GPS receiver without the knowledge of the Y code decryption algorithm.

Star VSAT network: In this network architecture, all of the traffic is routed via the master control station, or hub. If a VSAT wishes to communicate with another VSAT, they have to go via the hub, thus necessitating a "double hop" link via the satellite. Since all of the traffic radiates at one time or another from the hub, this architecture is referred to as a Star network.

Station Keeping : It is the process of maintenance of satellite's attitude against different factors that can cause drift with time. Satellites need to have their orbits adjusted from time to time because the satellite even though initially placed in the correct orbit, natural forces induce a progressive drift. The factors that cause drift include minor gravitational perturbations due to sun and moon, solar radiation pressure, the earth being an imperfect sphere and so on. The orbital adjustments are normally carried out by releasing jets of gas or by firing small rockets tied around the body of the satellite.

Stop-and-Wait ARQ: Now as the data are sent in coded blocks, the receiver acknowledges receipt of each block by sending back a positive acknowledgement or ACK signal if no errors are detected in the block and a negative acknowledgement or NAK signal if errors are detected. Here the transmitter stores copy of the block just transmitted and waits for the acknowledgement signal. If a NAK signal is received, it retransmits the block, and if an ACK signals is received, it transmits the next block. In this ARQ, the delay between transmissions is about half a second, the round-trip time to and from a geostationary satellite, which are unacceptable in many applications.

Stored Program Control (SPC): This system is similar to the manual exchange, except that just one unit performs the function of digit storage, path selection and translation for the entire exchange. The SPC electronic exchange has fully centralised common control. This common control is basically a switching processor, which masterminds the call set-up. It is a digital computer specially designed for handling telephone-switching functions in real time.

Synchronous transfer mode (STM): This is a common carrier system which carries voice over dedicated physical path connected by a dialed call or on a leased line, and is not routed by address. The cells have no address and are identified by their time slots. No other user can access the path for the duration of the call. The Ethernet protocol which uses 'connection-less' transmission techniques do not set up any path whatsoever for the various packets of data from their source to destination. Each packet takes a different route and gets reassembled at the end. There could be some delay in the arrival of the packets in this manner. While delayed data reception may be acceptable, it would not be tolerated if a voice link is affected by delays.

TCP/IP-based packages: These let a computer become a host on the Internet. They establish a computer as a workstation on a network

TCP Link: It is a *virtual communications* link exists between corresponding layers in a network. The header in the TCP segment carries instructions that enable communication between the send and receive TCP layers.

Of course, the communication has to pass through the other layers and along the physical link, but only the TCP layers act on the Transmission control Protocol (TCPs) contained in the segment header. There is no direct physical link between the TCP layers, and for this reason, it is called a *virtual link*.

Teledesic: This system is designed for Internet-like data traffic rather than voice communication. Any user can access any other user or ISP (Internet Service Provider) independent of location and the existing telecommunications infrastructure.

Terminal emulation software: This is communication software that enables a computer to communicate with another computer. Communications software is used in combination with modem. The software is used to give commands to the modem, to dial the other computer's modem, and then to issue commands and receive responses from the remote computer. The purpose of the modem (modulator demodulator) is to translate the digital signals that computers use to store and transmit information into the analog signals that telephone lines (or radio data systems) use to transmit information. A network that allows dial-in access provides one modem at its end, while a user who dials in provides the other.

Terminal packages: These are used for accessing most host/shell account systems.

Threshold $(C/N)^0$ value: This value is the minimum allowed carrier to noise ratio $(C/N)^0$. For a typical inbound VSAT link its value is 6.0 dB, with BPSK modulation and half rate FEC encoding, giving a BER of 10-6. This value varies depending on the modulation and FEC methods used on the link. Ignoring system errors, such as wrong pointing the antennas or satellite problems, the clear sky C/N ratio on a given inbound link can be reduced to the threshold $(C/N)^0$ by either a rain fade on the uplink or a rain fade on the downlink.

Three Axis Stabilised Satellite : In three-axis body stabilization, there is an internal momentum wheel with its axis perpendicular to the orbital plane. Control about pitch axis is through wheel's drive motor electronics while control about yaw and roll axes may be by gimballing the wheel or by use of hydrazine monopropellent thrusters to correct axis direction. Three axis stabilized satellites using extendible arrays are rotated so as to always face the sun. A disadvantage of any extendible array for synchronous orbit missions is the inability to provide power during transfer orbit when the array is stored. That is why geosynchronous satellites with 3-axis stabilization are also spin stabilized during the time they spend in transfer orbit.

Time Division Multiple Access (TDMA) (Fig. 31.15) : Time Division Multiple Access (TDMA) is a technique in which different earth stations in the satellite's footprint making use of satellite transponder use a single carrier on a time division basis. Different earth stations transmit traffic bursts in a periodic time frame called the TDMA frame. Over the

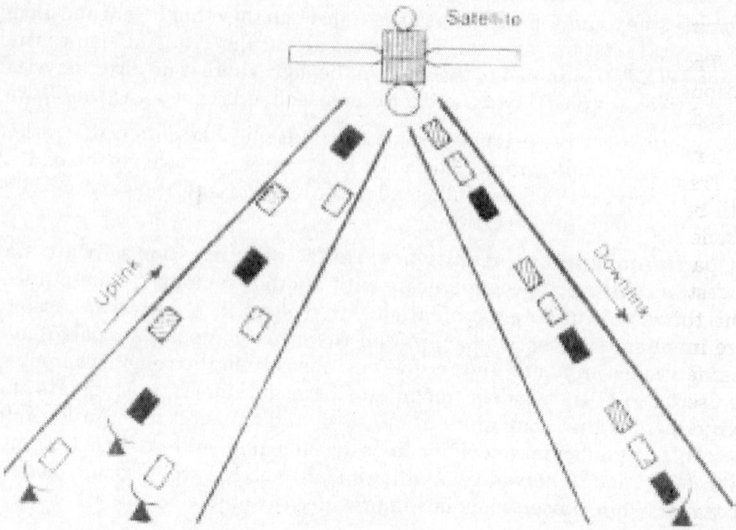

Fig. 31.15.

length of a burst, each earth station has the entire transponder bandwidth at its disposal. The traffic burst from different earth stations are synchronized so that all bursts arriving at the transponder are closely spaced but do not overlap. The transponder works on a burst at a time and retransmits back to the earth the sequence of bursts. All earth stations can receive the entire sequence and extract the signal of their interest.

Trajectgory : The flight path of a projectile, missile, rocket or satellite.

Transponder : The equipment that receives a signal, processes it and then retransmits at a different frequency.

Trellis Codes: The trellis code is a combination of Convolutional or linear block coding and digital modulation It uses a high level modulation such as 8-PSK or 16-PSK and allows only certain sequences of modulation states to be transmitted. The receiver detects errors in the received data strings if an invalid sequence of modulation states is received. Coding gain can be achieved with a smaller increase in bit rate than with conventional convolution encoding. However, trellis coding does not seem to have been adopted very widely.

Tracking Doppler frequency offset: Apart from locking to the C/A code of one satellite, the GPS receiver simutanously estimates the Doppler frequency offset for at least one satellite before final correlation can occur. The maximum Doppler shift in the L1 signal is 4.872 kHz. Therefore, allowing the satellite to reach an elevation angle of 5° before it is used for a position measurement limits the value of Doppler shift which must be accommodated by the receiver will be upto ± 4 kHz.

Transmission Control Protocol (TCP): This or its subsequent extensions/follow-ons, and/or other IP-compatible protocols which support the desired communication links.

Transport layer: Two sets of protocol are provided in this layer. With the Transmission Control Protocol (TCP), information is passed back and forth between transport layers, which controls the information flow. This include such functions as the correct sequencing of packets, replacement of lost packets, and adjusting the transmission rate of packets to prevent congestion. In the early days of the Internet when traffic was comparatively light, these problems could be handled even where satellite transmissions were involved. With the enoromous increase in traffic on the present-day Internet, these problems require special solutions where satellite systems are used, which are discussed in later sections. The TCP layer is termed *connection-oriented* (compared with the connectionless service mentioned above) because sender and receiver must be in communication with each other to implement the protocol. There are situations where a simle standalone message may need to be send which does not require the more complex TCP. For these types of message, another transport layer protocol called the *User Datagram Protocol* (UDP) is used. The UDP provides a connectionless service, similar to IP. The UDP header adds the port numbers for the source and destination applications.

Trilateration Method: This method is used Finding the Position of GPS Receiver. In this method, *the distance of the unknown point from three known points is measured.* The intersection of the arcs corresponding to three distances defines the unknown point relative to the known points, since three measurements can be used to solve three equations to give the latitude, longitude, and elevation for the receiver.

Two-Way Implementation: This system has a return link so that two-way communications can be set up over the same satellite, from the hub to the user and from the user back to the hub. Fig 15. 3 shows a two-way service between the hub (in this case the satellite gateway) and any VSAT terminal. The architecture selected is the key to the economics of two-way connections. It is of two types: Mesh or Star netwoks.

Universal Mobile Telephone System (UMTS): These are the third generation devices (abbreviated as 3G and 3Gt) are designed to offer a whole range of new services, such as Web browsing and multimedia access, personal location transfer of information and data, e-business, video conferencing and entertainment. The key requirements for UMTS are: small, low-cost pocket terminals, worldwide roaming and a single system for cellular and satellite as well as local calls capacity to handle high-speed data. The new system would use more spectrum and have advanced networking capabilities not only with the public-switched telephone networks but also with packet-based networks, including the Internet.

The US and Japan were developing their own standards for the third generation system (likely to be known as 363x). The European Telecommunications Standards Institute was developing its standard known as the universal mobile telephone system (UMTS). Since 1990, the International Telecommunications Union (ITU) had been reviewing several standards proposed for specifying a common but flexible standard (a family of systems) to be known as the International Mobile Telecommunications - 2000 (IMT-2000). IMT-2000, approved in May 2000 by ITU, is interoperable throughout the world, for e-commerce, multimedia Web access and data transfer. The standard would serve both fixed and mobile users through public and private networks.

UMTS is designed on the basis of a different network architecture and radio access method. It uses wideband CDMA, instead of a narrowband TDMA as in the GSM. The GSM is switch-centric, as all calls would pass through a mobile switching center. UMTS would be data-centric in line with the expected increase in Internet growth. It will resemble the Internet, with no single central switch, but a collection of broadband networks interconnected by packet switches. This arrangement would result in greater flexibility in providing new services and in better use of the switching functions by service providers. Users will be able to access different channels depending on the data rate chosen by them.

Up-Convertor : The up-converter accepts the modulated IF carrier and translates its IF frequency to the up-link RF frequency in the up-link frequency spectrum of the satellite. The up-converter in a satellite link is usually accomplished in a dual conversion process.

Uplink Master Control Station: The large number signals that are sent by the satellites are collected at a master control station and uplinked to the satellites by a group of large antennas with fade margins sufficient to overcome any expected rain fade. The video and audio signals that are uplinked to the satellites are available in prerecorded from on video tape or disc, or are collected from other satellites or fiber-optic lines. The uplink stations have hundreds of tape and video disc players, all under computer control, which supply the video and audio signals for each channel.

URL (Uniform Resources Locator): This is a more elaborate form of address, specifying not only the Internet site name, but also the directory and file in which a resource is located as well as which method to use when retrieving it. Currently, only the World-wide Web uses URLs.

Variable round-trip time: Where lower earth orbiting satellites are used such as those in low earth orbits (LEOs) and medium earth orbits (MEOs), the propagation delays will be much less than that for the GEO. The slant range to LEOs is typically on the order of a few thousand kilometers at most, and for MEOs, a few tens of thousand kilometers. The problems with these orbits is not so much the absolute value of delay as the variability. Because these satellites are not geo-stationary, the slant range varies, and for continuous communications there is the need for intersatellite links, which also adds to the delay and the variability. For example, for LEOs, the delay can vary from a few to about 80 ms.

Videoconferencing: A videoconference is a meeting between two or more groups of people in different locations any where in the world, which is organized via a two-way sound and vision link. The locations can be in very different parts of the world, in which case, satellites can play a vital role in the provision of the link. The effectiveness of these services lies in the reduction of travel for personnel and the speed with which international videoconferences can be organized. Typically, upto six persons can be comfortably catered for at each end terminal or studio. The space links for videoconference services are provided by such organizations as Eutelsat and Intelsat, with the large earth stations and back-haul links being provided by the PTTs and other national telecommunication organizations over wideband land lines. Face-to-face vision sub-system is the main information channel for the system. Here, each camera often provides a full frame view of up to three persons, sitting side by side.The middle strip of each frame from each camera output is selected and then electronically stacked, to provide a three-over-three, full frame view for transmission. This split screen approach avoids the corners of the camera images, where resolution and distortion is not of the best. The decoder receives this stacked image and generates two half-size images. These are now centrally positioned in each video frame, with the top and bottom sections blanked to black level. These are then displayed on two adjacent monitors to give a wide screen image of the distant studio.

VSAT System Design Considerations: These are:

(*a*) The VSAT system needs to be optimized carefully, balancing the transmission requirements of the inbound and outbound links so that the space segment capacity is used efficiently.

(*b*) Since Ku-band satellite transponders are to be used in a VSAT system, the steps are to be taken to develop a link budget, determine capacity information, and carry out trade-off calculations to optimize the links for a Star VSAT network.

(*c*) The design of a VSAT network is dominated by the low gain and small transmitter power of the VSAT station.

(*d*) The links must operate with low C/N ratios at the VSAT receivers and with low fade margins.

V-SAT System : VSAT systems are usually considered to be those designed to operate with antennas that are the equivalent of 1.8 m diameter or less. The relatively low gain of VSAT has to be countered by a careful design.

V-SAT/ Wireless Local Loop (WLL) Networks: In these systems, wireless local loop is coupled with VSAT distribution architectures. As shown in Fig. 15.1 the geostationary satellite links a large number of VSATs with the main switching center in a large city. Each VSAT acts as the link to the local switching center in the village or rural community, with the final mile of the telephony link being carried over a wireless local loop.

Wireless Application Protocol (WAP): This is a set of communication protocols adopted to standardise the way hand-held wireless devices access e-mail or the Web. WAP supports most wireless technologies (GSM, TDMA and CDMA). It also works with operating systems designed for hand-held devices. WAP is designed for applications including wireless, e-commerce, on-line banking and information access. The facilities include interactive news, data retrieval and online services. The mobile multimedia mode (WWW:MMM) initiative by three leading communications companies has simplified the identification of Internet sites and smart phones that can be connected by the mobile wireless terminal. The concept of WAP is the equivalent of the hypertext mark-up language (HTML) used for writing Web pages. In the way HTML serves as a common basic language that can be understood by any computer, WAP-enabled phones and other hand-held wireless devices permit interaction across different infrastructures. The WAP model also specifies also a client-server architecture but with an additional gateway in the communication path between client and server. Between the client and the gateway encoded communication by means of the WAP protocol stack is accomplished.

Wireless Internet: Web-enabled mobile devices have been introduced by which a Website can be accessed on a cell phone to get information. The wireless system delivering multimedia services (voice, data, video, etc.) to a global base of mobile terminals locate roaming terminals and transfer the call, if need be, from cell to cell (called handoff management).

Wireless Local Loop: This refers to the use of wireless technologies in the local loop between a subscriber and a based station instead of copper wire to access the public switched network. Since a part of the link (between the exchange and a base station) is wired, the technology is better termed wireless in local loop (WILL) and not WLL.

World Wide Web (WWW): It is the most widely used application on the Internet. The evolution and growth of the WWW has been rather similar to that of the Internet itself. It represents a convergence of computational concepts for presenting and linking information dispersed across the Internet in an easily accessible way.

Yaw : Yaw is the rotation of a vehicle about its vertical axis.

Zero 'g' : Zero 'g' is a state when the gravitational attraction is opposed by equal and opposite inertial forces and the body experiences no mechanical stress.

Launch Sites

ESMC. Eastern Space and Missile Center. Previously called Eastern Test Range (ETR), this US launch site is located at Cape Canaveral on the east coast of Florida at 28.5 deg N, 80.6 deg W. This site is primarily used for low inclination orbits (including geostationary) and for all manned missions.

Hammaguir. Located at a military base in the Sahara desert, Hammaguir was used by France to orbit 4 satellites during the mis '60s. However, the establishment of Algerian independence in 1967 forced France to abandon the facility.

Kagoshima Space Center. The Japanese launch center, Kagoshima, is located at 31.3 deg N, 131 deg E on the east coast of the Ohsumi peninsula. This launch site is dedicated to missions for Japan's ISAS space agency. Launches from this site are restricted to January/February and August/September due to range safety procedures established as a result of pressure from Japanese fisherman.

Kaputsin Yar. The Russian launch complex, Kaputsin Yar, is located at 48.4 N, 45.8 deg E. Although used fairly often during the 60's, the number of launches performed by this site fell dramatically during the 70's and 80's, during which the site averaged about 1 orbital launch per year. The most recent launch occurred in 1987.

Kourou. Kourou, in French Guiana (South America), is owned by ESA and operated by Arianespace. It is also called the Guiana Space Center (CSG) and is ideal for launching geosynchronous spacecraft due to its low latitude. The site also supports polar orbiting missions. Kourou is located at 5.2 deg N, 52.8 deg W.

Plesetsk. The Russian launch complex, Plesetsk, is located at 62.8 deg N, 40.4 deg E, and has launched the most satellites since the beginning of the Space Age.

San Marco. Italy's San Marco launch site consists of two offshore platforms located in the Indian Ocean just off of the coast of Kenya (2.9 deg. S, 40.3 deg. E). The platforms' near equatorial location makes it ideal for low inclination launches.

Shuang Cheng Tzu. The Chinese launch center Shuang Cheng Tzu, also called JSLC (Jiquan Satellite Launch Center), is located at approximately 40.6 deg N, 99.9 deg E in the Gobi desert. The facility is used for LEO launches into inclinations between 57 and 70 degrees.

Sriharikota Range. The Sriharikota Range Center (SHAR) is located on Sriharikota Island in India at 13.9 deg N, 80.3 deg E. Severe range safety restrictions on launch azimuth make it inefficient to launch into polar orbits.

Taiyuan. The Chinese launch center Taiyuan (TSLC), also known as Wazhai, supports missions with highly inclined (polar) orbits. The site is located at 37.5 deg N, 112.6 deg E in the Shanxi province.

Tanegashima Space Center. The Japanese launch center, Tanegashima, is located at 30.2 deg N, 130.9 deg E on the island of Tanegashima. This is the largest launch site in Japan, and is used for missions for Japan's NASDA space agency. Launches from this site are restricted to January/February and August/Spetember due to range safety procedures established as a result of pressure from Japanese fisherman.

Tyuratam. The Russian launch complex, Tyuratam (a.k.a. Baikonur Cosmodrome), is located in Kazakhstan at 45.6 deg N, 63.3 deg E. Although typically not quite as active as Plesetsk, this site is used for all Russian planetary and manned missions.

Wallops. The US's Wallops Island is located on the east coast of Virginia, and is an older launch site only used for small launch vehicles and suborbital launches. The site is located at 36.9 deg N, 75.5 deg W.

Woomera. The Australian launch complex, Woomera, is located at 31.1 deg S, 136.8 deg. E. Although used twice in the late 60's-early 70's to launch orbital payloads (with 2 other launch failures), facility was shut down due to funding cuts. No more orbital missions are currently planned from this site, although it is still occasionally used for sub-orbital launches.

WSMC. Western Space and Missile Center. Previously called Western Test Range (WTR), this US launch facility is located within Vandenberg Air Force Base (VAFB) on the west coast of California. The site is located at 34.7 deg N, 120.6 deg W, and is primarily used for polar orbiting missions.

Xichang. The chinese launch center Xichang (XSLC) is used to launch GEO spacecraft. It is located approximately 28.3 deg N, 102.0 deg E in the Sichuan province.

Yavne. The classified Israeli launch complex, Yavne, is located at 31.5 deg N, 34.5 deg E in or near Palmachim AFB. Launches are restricted to retrograde orbits due to range safety restrictions.

Orbit Categories

GEO. *Geosynchronous orbit.* A satellite is circular orbit around the Earth's equator at 23000 miles altitude (36000 km) will remain stationary over the same location on Earth (*i.e.,* the spacecraft goes around once in its orbit for every revolution of the Earth). This feature is very useful for communications satellites (allowing one satellite to provide continual coverage to a given area of the Earth's surface). As a result, the majority of satellites in geostationary orbit are comsats. Some satellites have orbits slightly higher or lower than GEO, but for simplicity sake, all satellites with apogees and perigees between 30000 and 40000 km are termed GEO.

HEO. *Highly Elliptical Orbit.* This class covers orbits which have large eccentricities (are highly elliptical). Molnyia orbits are a common example of this type of orbit. Although definitions of HEO vary from source to source, MSL defines HEO as orbits having perigees below 3000 km with apogees above 30000 km.

Jupiter. The Jupiter orbit class includes all missions which went into orbit around Jupiter or entered the Jovian atmosphere.

LEO. *Low Earth Orbit.* Although definitions of LEO vary from source to source, MSL defines LEO as orbits having apogees and perigees below 3000 km. The large majority of all satellites are in Low Earth Orbit.

Lunar. The Lunar orbit class includes all missions which went into orbit around Venus or impacted the planet's surface.

Mars. The Mars orbit class includes all missions which went into orbit around Mars or impacted the planet's surface.

MEO. *Medium Earth Orbit.* Although definitions of MEO vary from source to source, MSL degines MEO as orbits having apogees greater than 3000 km but less that 30000 km. These are sometimes used by navigation (*e.g.*, GPS) and communications (*e.g.*, Odyssey) missions.

Solar System Escape Trajectory. The Solar System Escape Trajectory class includes all missions have achieved Solar escape velocity and will thus (eventually) depart the Solar system.

Solar. The Solar Orbit class includes all missions where the spacecraft has achieved Earth escape velocity and goes in orbit about the Sun. This class includes missions designed to observe the Sun, as well as planetary flyby missions which entered solar orbit following rendezvous with their targets.

VHO. Very High Orbit. This type of orbit includes all orbits which have perigees at or above GEO and apogees above GEO, yet remain in orbit around the Earth (or Earth-Moon system). Orbits in this class are often highly elliptical, with apogees several hundred thousand kilometers in altitude.

Venus. The Venus orbit class includes all missions which went into orbit around Venus or impacted the planet's surface.

Mission Categories

Amateur Radio. Amateur radio satellites are used to relay messages between amateur ham radio operators. These satellites are typically small and simple in design, and are often built by universities. Due to their small size and typically low budgets, these satellites are usually launched as secondary payloads along with much larger primary payloads.

ASAT (Anti-Satellite). ASAT missions are related to the development of vehicles used to destroy orbiting satellites. This category includes the ASAT interceptors themselves, as well as vehicles placed into orbit as test targets.

Astronomy. Astronomy satellites are dedicated to the study of stellar objects, ranging from extremely distant galaxies, nebulae etc. our own nearby Sun.

DBS. Direct Broadcast Satellite (DBS) are a subset of the domestic communications class. These missions broadcast television or radio signals to subscriber's ground based satellite dishes.

Domestic Communications. Domestic communication missions relay domestic transmissions, such as telephone, radio, and TV signals, from one point on the Earth's surface to another.

Earth Resources. The mission class refers to missions which collect information about the Earth's atmosphere, land and oceans for scientific research and resource management.

ELINT (Elect. Intelligence). ELINT satellites are military spacecraft used to monitor (spy) on the military and domestic electronic communications of other nations. These types of satellites are also known as ferrets.

EW (Early Warning). Military spacecraft used to detect the launch of missiles and rockets from the Earth's surface are called early warning satellites. Information from these satellites is used to quickly detect the launch of offensive missiles, as well as track the long-term patterns of foreign countries' space programs.

Geodesy. Geodetic spacecraft are used to measure the location of points on the Earth's surface with great accuracy. These measurements are used to determine the exact size and shape of the Earth, act as references for mapping, and track movements of the Earth's crust.

Lunar. Lunar missions are designed to gather information about the Earth's Moon or the purpose of scientific research. The class includes arbiters, flybys, hard lenders, and soft lenders (including manned missions).

Military Communications. Military communications satellites are dedicated to relaying signals between elements of a nation's armed forces.

Military (Unknown/Unique). This category includes all military satellites whose purpose is either unknown (such as still-secret surveillance, ELINT and EW spacecraft) or unique in nature.

Navigation. Navigation systems are designed to assist in air, land and oceanic navigation. These include such missions as Transit, GPS and Glonass.

Nuclear Detection. Nuclear detection satellite are used to detect nuclear explosions on the Earth's surface. Although primarily used to observe nuclear treaty compliance, nuclear detection spacecraft have also been used to detect/observe galactic events, such as supernova.

Planetary. Planetary missions leave the Earth's gravitational field to perform up close observations of other planets, asteroids, and comets. These types of missions can range from quick flybys to long term observations from orbits around the body. Planetary missions have also dropped probes into planets' atmospheres, soft and hard landed (*i.e.*, crashed) on planets' surfaces, and flown in formation with comets and asteroids.

Research. This general class of missions includes the many space science disciplines not falling into any or the other mission categories. A few examples include zero-g materials processing tests, biological studies, and space physics experiments.

Space Stations. Space stations are large orbiting structures designed to support manned operations for extended periods of time (months to years). Space stations have performed both military and civilian objectives.

Surveillance. Surveillance spacecraft are military vehicles which provide imagery reconnaissance data. These missions include visible, infrared, and radar imaging. Information about these satellites (as well as most other military missions) is very often secret. As a result, the information on these vehicles is often sketchy, and is often derived from indirect observations.

Technology. This general class of missions includes all missions designed as technical tests of satellite or ground based systems. Examples include tests of new satellite components, investigations of launch vehicle performance, calibration of ground based systems (such as radar), and demonstration of new sensor technonolies.

Transport. Transport missions include all spacecraft that are used to ferry people are materials from the Earth to orbit without performing significant research. Missions in this class include space station resupply vehicles and Shuttle missions whose primary purpose is to carry satellites into orbit for deployment.

Weather. Weather satellites monitor the Earth's atmospheric conditions and provide data to help predict/understand the Earth's weather patterns

Space Agencies and Organizations

AT&T. Americal Telephone and Telegraph Corporation.

COMSAT. Communication Satellite Corporation

DARPA. Defense Advanced Research Projects Agency. (U.S. government agency.)

ELDO. European Launcher Development Organization (Precursor to ESA)

EOSAT. Earth Observation Satellite Company

ESA. European Space Agency

ESRO. European Space Research Organization (Precursor to ESA)

ESSA. Environmental Sciences Services Administration (U.S. government agency. Precursor to NOAA)

NASA. National Aeronautics and Space Administration

NATO. North Atlantic Treaty Organization

NOAA. National Oceanic and Atmospheric Organization (U.S. government agency)

Spacecraft Systems (Hardware and Stuff)

ACS. *Attitude Control System.* This is the spacecraft subsystem which sis responsible for pointing the spacecraft in the desired direction and knowing where the spacecraft is pointed at all times.

CDMA. *Code Division Multiple Access.* A multiple access scheme for digital communications which uses spectrum modulation and orthogonal codes to avoid interference and permit many users to occupy all of the transponder bandwidth all of the time.

CPV. *Common Pressure Vessel.* This refers to a particular packaging technique in batteries where more than one battery cell is housed within a single pressure vessel. This increases the specific energy of the battery assembly.

GaAs. *Gallium Arsenide.* GaAs solar cells have an efficiency in the range of 17-19 percent. In addition to having a higher efficiency than silicon cells, they are more resistant to radiation effects, however, they have a higher density and higher cost compared to silicon cells.

GFRP. *Graphite Fiber Reinforced Plastic.* GFRP is a generic term for advanced graphite epoxy composite materials. While more expensive than aluminium construction, composites offer high stiffness- to-weight ratio and low thermal expansion/ contraction properties. These are constructed by bonding together layers of composite fabric using various fiber orientations. Other fibers in these composites include boron, Kevlar, and glass.

HGA. *High Gain Antenna.* These are frequently parabolic dishes and serve to provide high amplification of RF signals (either transmitting or receiving). These antennas much be pointing accurately toe useful.

Hydrazine. Hydrazine is the name for the most commonly used monopropellant fuel. The composition of monopropellant hydrazine is N2H4. The hydrazine is ignited by passing it over a heated catalyst to decompose the fuel. This produces exhaust gasses of NH3, N 2, and H2. The catalyst consists of alumina pellets impregnated with iridium, and the most common brand name is Shell 405. The specific impulse of hydrazine systems is typically in the range of 200 to 220 seconds.

LGA. *Low Gain Antenna.* These are small antennas which provide low amplification of RF signals and have very wide antenna patterns-not requiring precise antenna pointing.

MLI. *Multi-Layer Insulation.* It is commonly used to provide thermal insulation. MLI usually consists of 25 μm thick polyester or polyamide layers or films that are metalliized wit aluminum or gold on one both side by vacuum deposition to achieve low emittance. Glass-fiber paper, plastic and silk netting, thin sheets of foam, and embossed plastic film might be used to separate these sheets and minimize the conductance between layers. Some MLI has no discrete spacer material and instead the material is crinkled so the conductance between layers is minimized.

NiCd. Nickel Cadmium is the most popular battery type used in spacecraft. These batteries are rechargeable and can withstands of thousands of charge/discharge cycles. The electrolyte is a diluted potassium hydroxide solution.

QPSK. *Quadrature Phase Shift Keying.* QPSK is the most popular modulation technique for digital satellite communications. Basically, a digital data stream is taken two bits at a time to generate one of four possible phase states of the transmitted carrier. In *greek-speak:* QPSK is the superposition of two biphase PSK signals in time quadrature.

RCS. *Reaction Control System.* This is type of attitude control system which uses reaction jets (small thrusters) to control the orientation of the spacecraft. These systems usually use a cold gas such as nitrogen, however, some have used hydrazine. Typical pointing accuracies achieved are 0.5 to 0.1 degrees.

RTG. *Radioisotope Thermoelectric Generator.* These power sources are ideal for planetary missions because of their long life and steady power in sunlight or darkness. RTGs use banks of thermoelectrics elements (typically Si-Ge unicouples) to convert the heat generated by radioisotope decay (typically plutonium 238) into electric power. They are heavy and produce radiation which can interfare with electronics and science instruments. They are typically mounted at some distance from the spacecraft to reduce the effects of both nuclear and thermal radiation. RTGs are also very expensive.

Index

A

B

C

D

E

F

G

J

K

L

M

T

U

V

W